your Thill/Bovée?

Balanced Presentation of Fundamentals

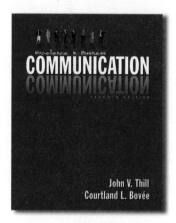

ISBN: 0-13-187076-9

Excellence in Business Communication Custom One-Color Option

The Core

Optional Chapters

W9-CFH-084

Contact your local PH Rep for more information on the custom/core option.

Excellence in Business Communication

SEVENTH EDITION

Excellence in Business Communication

SEVENTH EDITION

JOHN V. THILL
Chief Executive Officer
Communication Specialists of America

COURTLAND L. BOVÉE
Professor of Business Communication
C. Allen Paul Distinguished Chair
Grossmont College

PEARSON

Prentice
Hall

Upper Saddle River, New Jersey 07458

Library of Congress Cataloging-in-Publication Data

Thill, John V.

  Excellence in business communication / John V. Thill & Courtland L. Bovée.-- 7th ed.

    p. cm.

  Includes bibliographical references and index.

  Various other multi-media instructional materials are available to supplement the text.

  ISBN 0-13-187076-9

  1. Business communication--United States--Case studies.   I. Thill, John V. II.

Title.

  HF5718.2.U6T45 2007

  658.4'5--dc22   2006003357

Senior Acquisitions Editor: David Parker
VP/Editorial Director: Jeff Shelstad
Product Development Manager: Ashley Santora
Editorial Assistant: Stephanie Kamens
Product Development Manager, Media: Nancy Welcher
Marketing Manager: Anne Howard
Associate Director, Production Editorial: Judy Leale
Managing Editor, Production: Renata Butera
Production Editor: Marcela Boos
Permissions Coordinator: Charles Morris
Associate Director, Manufacturing: Vinnie Scelta
Manufacturing Buyer: Diane Peirano
Design/Composition Manager: Christy Mahon
Composition Liaison: Suzanne Duda
Designer: Steve Frim
Interior Design: Heather Peres
Cover Design: John Christiana
Manager, Visual Research: Beth Brenzel
Image Permissions Coordinator: Joanne Dippel
Photo Researcher: Melinda Alexander
Composition: Carlisle Publishing Services
Full-Service Project Management: Lynn Steines, Carlisle Editorial Services
Printer/Binder: Quebecor
Typeface: 10/12 Times

Credits and acknowledgments for material borrowed from other sources and reproduced, with permission, in this textbook appear on page AC-1.

Microsoft® and Windows® are registered trademarks of the Microsoft Corporation in the U.S.A. and other countries. Screen shots and icons reprinted with permission from the Microsoft Corporation. This book is not sponsored or endorsed by or affiliated with the Microsoft Corporation.

Pearson Prentice Hall™ is a trademark of Pearson Education, Inc.
Pearson® is a registered trademark of Pearson plc
Prentice Hall® is a registered trademark of Pearson Education, Inc.

Pearson Education LTD.
Pearson Education Singapore, Pte. Ltd
Pearson Education, Canada, Ltd
Pearson Education–Japan

Pearson Education Australia PTY, Limited
Pearson Education North Asia Ltd
Pearson Educación de Mexico, S.A. de C.V.
Pearson Education Malaysia, Pte. Ltd.

1 0 9 8 7 6 5 4 3 2 1
ISBN: 0-13-187076-9

Contents in Brief

Contents

Thill/Bovée, Excellence in Business Communication, 7th Edition, delivers an abundance of the most realistic model documents so your students can learn by example.

SUCCESSFUL COMMUNICATION MODELS FOR REFERENCE, ANALYSIS, AND PRACTICAL LEARNING

Years of positive feedback from instructors and students confirm the importance of the many model documents offered in *Excellence in Business Communication*. This tradition of success continues with the seventh edition, with both updated documents in the text and new computer-gradable documents online.

Model Documents with Concise Annotations

Students can examine numerous sample documents, many collected by the authors in their consulting work at well-known companies. Many documents are accompanied by a customized graphic of the three-step writing process, and all documents include marginal annotations to help students understand how to apply the principles being discussed. For the seventh edition, the model documents and annotations have been extensively revised and improved in response to reviewer input.

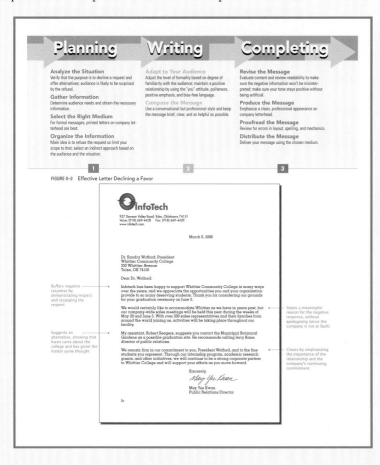

FIGURE 8–2 Effective Letter Declining a Favor

Document Makeovers: Online, Interactive Documents for Analysis

Students have the opportunity in every chapter to critique and revise a wide selection of documents, including e-mail messages, letters, memos, report sections, and résumés. By experiencing firsthand the elements that make a document successful, students gain the insights they need to analyze and improve their own business messages.

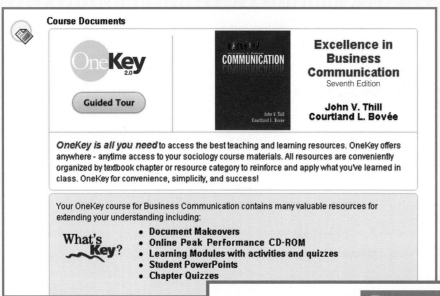

Course Documents

OneKey 2.0

Guided Tour

Excellence in Business Communication
Seventh Edition

John V. Thill
Courtland L. Bovée

OneKey is all you need to access the best teaching and learning resources. OneKey offers anywhere - anytime access to your sociology course materials. All resources are conveniently organized by textbook chapter or resource category to reinforce and apply what you've learned in class. OneKey for convenience, simplicity, and success!

Your OneKey course for Business Communication contains many valuable resources for extending your understanding including:

What's Key?

- Document Makeovers
- Online Peak Performance CD-ROM
- Learning Modules with activities and quizzes
- Student PowerPoints
- Chapter Quizzes

Document Makeover

IMPROVE THIS MEMO

To practice correcting drafts of actual documents, visit your online course or the access-code protected portion of the Companion Website. Click "Document Makeovers," then click Chapter 8. You will find a memo that contains problems and errors relating to what you've learned in this chapter about handling negative messages. Use the "Final Draft" decision tool to create an improved version of this memo. Check the message for the use of buffers, apologies, explanations, subordination, embedding, positive action, conditional phrases, and upbeat perspectives.

NEW AND IMPORTANT COVERAGE OF CRITICAL TOPICS

Even as technology continues to revolutionize business communication, business leaders are placing renewed emphasis on the human factor—teamwork, listening, etiquette, ethics, and other key topics. The seventh edition provides comprehensive, up-to-date coverage of all these vital subjects.

Integrated Approach to Communication Technology

Technology and communication skills are interwoven throughout the text, reflecting the expectations and opportunities in today's workplace:

- computer animation
- corporate blogs
- digital rights
- electronic documents
- electronic forms
- electronic presentations
- electronic résumé production
- e-mail
- e-portfolios
- extranets
- graphic design software
- groupware and shared online workspaces
- idea-generation and document-planning software
- image processing tools
- instant messaging and online chat systems
- interactive media
- Internet telephony (VoIP)
- interview simulators
- intranets
- latest online research techniques
- linked and embedded documents
- multimedia documents
- multimedia presentations
- online survey tools
- podcasting
- résumé scanning systems
- RSS newsfeeds
- search and metasearch engines
- security and privacy concerns in electronic media (including e-mail hygiene)
- social networking applications
- streaming media
- text messaging
- templates and stylesheets
- translation software
- videoconferencing and telepresence
- virtual agents and bots
- virtual private networks (VPNs)
- web directories
- web publishing systems
- web-based virtual meetings
- webcasts
- website accessibility
- wireless networks

Enhanced Coverage of Listening and Teams

To help students strengthen their communication skills, material on listening and on effectively working in teams has been expanded and updated. Improved coverage provides students with skills they'll need to gain a competitive edge in today's workplace, including overcoming the tendency to prejudge, listening across cultural and language barriers, and using short-term memorization techniques that boost retention and reduce misinterpretation.

Extensive Coverage of Business Etiquette

Feedback from employers continues to stress the need for new hires to learn proper business etiquette. *Excellence in Business Communication* advises students in such areas as personal appearance, face-to-face interactions, written correspondence (including maintaining etiquette in both negative and persuasive messages), research (such as respecting the privacy of interview subjects), IM and e-mail, telephone interactions (including reducing cell phone disruptions and using voice mail), intercultural interactions, and job searches and interviewing. Moreover, the seventh edition incorporates the latest thinking on the controversial subject of corporate apologies.

Peak Performance Grammar and Mechanics

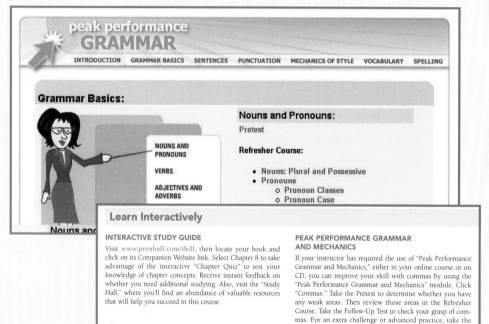

This feature, available in both online and CD formats, helps students improve their skills with mechanics and specific parts of speech. Each chapter module has a pretest that lets students determine whether they have any weak areas. Students can then review those areas in the module's refresher course and verify learning with the follow-up test. An advanced test offers an extra challenge or additional practice.

Learn Interactively

INTERACTIVE STUDY GUIDE
Visit www.prenhall.com/thill, then locate your book and click on its Companion Website link. Select Chapter 8 to take advantage of the interactive "Chapter Quiz" to test your knowledge of chapter concepts. Receive instant feedback on whether you need additional studying. Also, visit the "Study Hall," where you'll find an abundance of valuable resources that will help you succeed in this course.

PEAK PERFORMANCE GRAMMAR AND MECHANICS
If your instructor has required the use of "Peak Performance Grammar and Mechanics," either in your online course or on CD, you can improve your skill with commas by using the "Peak Performance Grammar and Mechanics" module. Click "Commas." Take the Pretest to determine whether you have any weak areas. Then review those areas in the Refresher Course. Take the Follow-Up Test to check your grasp of commas. For an extra challenge or advanced practice, take the Advanced Test. Finally, for additional reinforcement, go to the "Improve Your Grammar, Mechanics, and Usage" section that follows, and complete those exercises.

THOROUGH UPDATES TO CONTENT, FEATURES, AND ACTIVITIES

No matter how successful it may be, no business text can stand still in today's dynamic environment. The seventh edition is thoroughly updated, from the learning objectives that launch each chapter to the exercises, activities, and cases that help students apply what they've learned. (A complete list of chapter-by-chapter changes and improvements is available in the Instructor's Manual.)

Real-Company Vignettes, Simulations, and Cases

Every chapter starts with an "On-the-Job" vignette highlighting a recent communication dilemma that a business professional solved by applying the very same concepts the student is about to learn. The chapter-ending simulation then places students in a professional role in that company and challenges them to resolve four intriguing communication dilemmas. All 15 of these vignette/simulation pairs are new in the seventh edition and feature such firms as blogging innovator Six Apart, Mark Burnett Productions (creators of *Survivor* and *The Apprentice*), Scion (Toyota's youth-oriented brand), and *Rolling Stone* magazine.

The broad selection of cases has also been extensively updated, with a wider variety of short, medium, and long cases and activities involving the latest communication technologies. In addition to creating more-traditional memos, letters, and reports, students can practice drafting blog postings, scripting podcasts, and writing instant messages.

Refinements to the Proven Three-Step Writing Process

The three-step writing process at the heart of *Excellence in Business Communication* has been further refined to present substeps in a more logical order. As before, the process is customized and illustrated throughout the text to show students how to apply it to a wide range of writing tasks.

VERSATILE RESOURCES FOR INSTRUCTORS AND STUDENTS

The total *Excellence in Business Communication* package helps instructors and students take full advantage of new advances in technology that can have a highly positive effect on learning. The blending of print and online materials makes this text the most effective teaching and learning tool you'll find for a business communication course.

Instructor's Resource Center

At www.prenhall.com/irc, instructors can access a variety of print, digital media, and presentation resources available with this text in downloadable, digital format. Registration is simple and gives you immediate access to new titles and new editions. As a registered faculty member, you can download resource files and receive immediate access and instructions for installing course management content on your campus server.

If you ever need assistance, our dedicated technical support team is ready to help with the media supplements that accompany this text. Visit www.247.prenhall.com for answers to frequently asked questions and toll-free user support phone numbers.

The following supplements are available to adopting instructors (for detailed descriptions, please visit www.prenhall.com/irc):

- **Instructor's Resource Center (IRC) on CD-ROM**—ISBN: 0-13-187082-3
- **Printed Instructor's Manual**—ISBN: 0-13-187083-1
- **Printed Test Item File**—ISBN: 0-13-187085-8
- **TestGen Test Generating Software**—Available at the IRC (online or on CD-ROM).
- **PowerPoint Slides**—Both basic and enhanced versions are available at the IRC (online or on CD-ROM).
- **Classroom Response Systems (CRS)**—Available at the IRC (both online and on CD-ROM). Learn more at www.prenhall.com/crs.
- **Image Bank**—Visit the IRC on CD-ROM for this resource.
- **Custom Videos on DVD**—ISBN: 0-13-187088-2
- **Custom Videos on VHS**—ISBN: 0-13-187087-4
- **Transparency Package**—ISBN: 0-13-187086-6

OneKey Online Courses: OneKey for Convenience, Simplicity, and Success.

OneKey offers complete teaching and learning online resources all in one place. OneKey is all that instructors need to plan and administer courses, and OneKey is all that students need for anytime, anywhere access to online course material. Conveniently organized by textbook chapter, these resources save time and help students reinforce and apply what they have learned. OneKey is available in three course management platforms: Blackboard, CourseCompass, and WebCT.

OneKey resources include

- **Learning modules** (Each section within each chapter offers a 5-question pretest, a summary for review, an online learning activity, and a 10-question posttest.)
- **Peak Performance Grammar and Mechanics**
- **Two versions of Document Makeovers** (One version feeds your gradebook, and one provides student practice.)
- **Access to Mydropbox.com**
- **Peer review software**
- **E-Lecture Student PowerPoints**

OneKey requires an access code, which can be shrink-wrapped with new copies of this text. Please contact your local sales representative for the correct ISBN. Codes may also be purchased separately at www.prenhall.com/management.

Password-Protected Interactive Media

A new access-code protected website has been developed to accompany the seventh edition. This website houses the Peak Performance Grammar and Mechanics and Document Makeover features. This site has been designed for professors who wish to use this material but do not want the rest of the OneKey content and who do not need this information to feed the gradebook.

   The Prentice Hall Business Communication Website requires an access code, which professors can ask to have shrink-wrapped with new copies of this text. Please contact your local sales representative for the correct ISBN. Codes may also be purchased separately at www.prenhall.com/management.

Study Guide

This handy guide (ISBN: 0-13-187081-5) helps students assess, explore, and improve each of the skills they're expected to master throughout the course.

Companion Website

This text's Companion Website at www.prenhall.com/thill contains valuable resources for both students and professors, including access to a student version of the PowerPoint package, an online Study Guide, the English-Spanish Audio Glossary of Business Terms, the Handbook of Grammar, Mechanics, and Usage, and the Business Communication Study Hall, which allows students to brush up on several aspects of business communication—grammar, writing skills, critical thinking, report writing, résumés, and PowerPoint development.

SafariX eTextbooks Online

SafariX eTextbooks Online were developed for students looking to save money on required or recommended textbooks. Students simply select their eText by title or author and purchase immediate access to the content for the duration of the course using any major credit card. With a SafariX eText, students can search for specific keywords or page numbers, make notes online, print out reading assignments that incorporate lecture notes, and bookmark important passages for later review. For more information, or to purchase a SafariX eTextbook, visit www.safarix.com.

VangoNotes in MP3 Format

Study on the go with VangoNotes—chapter reviews from your text in downloadable MP3 format. Now wherever you are—whatever you're doing— you can study by listening to the following for each chapter of your textbook:

- Big Ideas: Your "need to know" for each chapter
- Practice Test: A gut check for the Big Ideas—tells you if you need to keep studying
- Key Terms: Audio "flashcards" to help you review key concepts and terms
- Rapid Review: A quick drill session—use it right before your test

VangoNotes are **flexible**; download all the material directly to your player, or only the chapters you need. And they're **efficient**. Use them in your car, at the gym, walking to class, wherever. So get yours today. And get studying. Visit www.VangoNotes.com.

AUTHORS' E-MAIL HOTLINE FOR FACULTY

Integrity, excellence, and responsiveness are the authors' hallmarks. That means providing you with textbooks that are academically sound, creative, timely, and sensitive to instructor and student needs. As an adopter of *Excellence in Business Communication*, you are invited to use the authors' E-mail Hotline (hotline@leadingtexts.com) if you ever have a question or concern related to the text or its supplements. You can also access the hotline at the authors' website: www.leadingtexts.com.

FEEDBACK

The authors and the product team would appreciate hearing from you! Let us know what you think about this textbook by writing to college_marketing@prenhall.com. Please include "Feedback about Thill/Bovee 7e" in the subject line.

If you have questions related to this product, please contact our customer service department online at www.247.prenhall.com.

REVIEWERS

Our thanks to the many individuals whose valuable suggestions and constructive comments contributed to the success of this book. The authors are deeply grateful to Janet Adams, Minnesota State University–Mankato; Gus Amaya, Florida International University; Anita S. Bednar, Central State University; Donna Cox, Monroe Community College; Sauny Dills, California

Polytechnic State University–San Luis Obispo; Ruthann Dirks, Emporia State University; Cynthia Drexel, Western State College; Mary DuBoise, DeVry Institute of Technology–Dallas; J. Thomas Dukes, University of Akron; Karen Eickhoff, University of Tennessee; Lindsay S. English, Ursuline College; Mike Flores, Wichita State University; Charlene A. Gierkey, Northwestern Michigan College; Sue Granger, Jacksonville State University; Bradley S. Hayden, Western Michigan University; Joyce Hicks, Valparaiso University; Michael Hignite, Southwest Missouri State; Mark Hilton, Lyndon State College; Cynthia Hofacker, University of Wisconsin–Eau Claire; Louise C. Holcomb, Gainesville College; Larry Honl, University of Wisconsin–Eau Claire; Kenneth Hunsaker, Utah State University; Sandie Idziak, University of Texas; Robert O. Joy, Central Michigan University; Paula R. Kaiser, University of North Carolina–Greensboro; Paul Killorin, Portland Community College; Linda M. LaDuc, University of Massachusetts–Amherst; Jennifer Loney, Portland State University; Al Lucero, East Tennessee State University; Rachel Mather, Adelphi University; Linda McAdams, Westark Community College; Melinda McCannon, Gordon College; Bronna McNeely, Midwestern State University; William McPherson, Indiana University of Pennsylvania; Russ Meade, Tidewater Community College; Betty Mealor, Abraham Baldwin College; Mary Miller, Ashland University; Joe Newman, Faulkner University; Barbara Oates, Texas A&M University; Richard Profozich, Prince George's Community College; Brian Railsback, Western Carolina University; John Rehfuss, California State University–Sacramento; Joan C. Roderick, Southwest Texas State University; Salvatore Safina, University of Wisconsin; Jean Anna Sellers, Fort Hays State University; Andrea Smith–Hunter, Siena College; Carol Smith White, Georgia State University; Karen Sneary, Northwestern Oklahoma State University; Jeanne Stannard, Johnson County Community College; Terisa Tennison, Florida International University; Michael Thompson, Brigham Young University; Robert von der Osten, Ferris State University; Betsy Vardaman, Baylor University; Karl V. Winton, Marshall University; Billy Walters, Troy State University; George Walters, Emporia State University; John L. Waltman, Eastern Michigan University; F. Stanford Wayne, Southwest Missouri State; Robert Wheatley, Troy State University; Rosemary B. Wilson, Washtenaw Community College; Beverly C. Wise, SUNY–Morrisville; Aline Wolff, New York University; Bonnie Yarbrough, University of North Carolina–Greensboro.

We also appreciate the notable talents and distinguished contributions of Deborah Valentine, Emory University; Anne Bliss, University of Colorado–Boulder; Carolyn A. Embree, University of Akron; Carla L. Sloan, Liberty University; Doris A. Van Horn Christopher, California State University–Los Angeles; and Susan S. Rehwaldt, Southern Illinois University.

REVIEWERS OF "DOCUMENT MAKEOVER" FEATURE

We sincerely thank the following reviewers for their assistance with the Document Makeover feature: Lisa Barley, Eastern Michigan University; Marcia Bordman, Gallaudet University; Jean Bush-Bacelis, Eastern Michigan University; Bobbye Davis, Southern Louisiana University; Cynthia Drexel, Western State College; Kenneth Gibbs, Worcester State College; Ellen Leathers, Bradley University; Diana McKowen, Indiana University; Bobbie Nicholson, Mars Hill College; Andrew Smith, Holyoke Community College; Jay Stubblefield, North Carolina Wesleyan College; Dawn Wallace, South Eastern Louisiana University.

REVIEWERS OF MODEL DOCUMENTS

The many model documents in the text and their accompanying annotations received invaluable review from Dacia Charlesworth, Robert Morris University; Diane Todd Bucci, Robert Morris University; Estelle Kochis, Suffolk County Community College; Sherry Robertson, Arizona State University; Nancy Goehring, Monterey Peninsula College; James Hatfield, Florida Community College at Jacksonville; Avon Crismore, Indiana University.

PERSONAL ACKNOWLEDGMENTS

Excellence in Business Communication, Seventh Edition, is the product of the concerted efforts of a number of people. A heartfelt thanks to our many friends, acquaintances, and business associates who provided materials or agreed to be interviewed so that we could bring the real world into the classroom.

A very special acknowledgment goes to George Dovel, whose superb editorial skills, distinguished background, and wealth of business experience assured this project of clarity and completeness. Also, recognition and thanks to Jackie Estrada for her outstanding skills and excellent attention to details. Her creation of the Peak Performance Grammar and Mechanics material is especially noteworthy.

We also feel it is important to acknowledge and thank the Association for Business Communication, an organization whose meetings and publications provide a valuable forum for the exchange of ideas and for professional growth.

The supplements package for *Excellence in Business Communication* has benefited from the able contributions of several individuals. We would like to express our thanks to them for creating the finest set of instructional supplements in the field. The supplement authors include Rolanda Pollard of San Jose State University, who wrote the Study Guide; William Peirce of Prince Georges Community College, who developed material for the Internet Study Guide and OneKey Learning Modules; Myles Hassell of University of New Orleans, who created the PowerPoint package; Jay Stubblefield, North Carolina Wesleyan College, who wrote the test bank; Dacia Charlesworth of Robert Morris University, who created the gradable Document Makeovers in the online course material; and Steve Soucy, Santa Monica College, who wrote and recorded the new E-Lecture Audio PowerPoint Series.

We want to extend our warmest appreciation to the devoted professionals at Prentice Hall. They include Jerome Grant, president; Jeff Shelstad, vice-president and editorial director; David Parker, senior acquisitions editor; Anne Howard, executive marketing manager; Ashley Santora, product development manager, Stephanie Kamens, editorial assistant; all of Prentice Hall Business Publishing; and the outstanding Prentice Hall sales representatives. Finally, we thank Renata Butera, managing editor of production, and Marcela Boos, production editor, for their dedication; and we are grateful to Lynn Steines, project manager at Carlisle Publishing Services; Melinda Alexander, photo researcher; and Steve Frim, designer, for their superb work.

John V. Thill
Courtland L. Bovée

Part I
Understanding the Foundations of Business Communication

CHAPTER 1

Achieving Success Through Effective Business Communication

CHAPTER 2

Communicating in Teams and Mastering Listening and Nonverbal Communication

CHAPTER 3

Communicating Interculturally

Achieving Success Through Effective Business Communication

Learning Objectives

AFTER STUDYING THIS CHAPTER, YOU WILL BE ABLE TO

1 Explain why effective communication is important to your success in today's business environment

2 Identify seven communication skills that successful employers expect from their employees

3 Describe the five characteristics of effective business communication

4 List six factors that make business communication unique

5 Describe five strategies for communicating more effectively on the job

6 Explain three strategies for using communication technology successfully

7 Discuss the importance of ethics in business communication and differentiate between ethical dilemmas and ethical lapses

On the Job

COMMUNICATING AT SIX APART

MENA TROTT REDEFINES THE NATURE OF COMMUNICATION

Many people transform personal interests into successful business enterprises, using their hobbies to start a wide variety of businesses. Mena Trott used her hobby to help start a revolution.

In 2001, Trott was among the first wave of World Wide Web users to keep a *web log,* or *blog,* an online journal that can cover any topic from politics to pets. As the popularity of her blog continued to grow, she found that the rudimentary blogging tools available at the time couldn't keep up. Trott and her husband, Ben, decided to create their own software that would handle high-volume blogging—and make it easy for anyone to blog.

The Trotts' first product, Movable Type, caught on quickly as web users around the world welcomed the opportunity to become instant online publishers. Before long, Ben and Mena became first-name celebrities in the "blogosphere," and an effort that had started as an extension of a hobby soon grew into a multinational business. (The Trotts named their new company Six Apart in honor of the fact that the two of them were born just six days apart.)

Thousands of companies have great product ideas, of course, but Six Apart is one of those select few that help change the way people live. In Six Apart's case, that change is all about communication, and in particular, fulfilling the web's promise to create a global village in which "neighbors" can live on opposite sides of the

Through both the company she co-founded with husband Ben and her own widely read blog, Six Apart's Mena Trott is an influential figure in the world of blogging.

ocean. With software or online services such as those offered by Six Apart, bloggers began to influence the worlds of politics, journalism—and business. For instance, the lockmaker Kryptonite discovered the power of blogging the hard way, when a blog devoted to bicycling displayed a video showing how to pick the popular bike lock with a ballpoint pen. Within days, bicyclists from around the world learned about the vulnerability, and Kryptonite had a public relations nightmare and a $10 million product-replacement problem on its hands.

On the positive side, businesspeople began to use blogs themselves to communicate with current and potential customers. The best of these business blogs tear down the barriers that can make companies seem impersonal or unresponsive. Companies ranging from Boeing to General Motors to Microsoft now use blogs to put a human face on giant organizations, and millions of people read these blogs to keep up on the latest news about the products and companies that interest them.

Blogging is changing so rapidly that it's hard to predict what the future holds for Six Apart, but Trott summed up the impact of blogging when she said, "I can't imagine where we'll be in a year, let alone five years, but I'm certain weblogging is here to stay."[1]

www.sixapart.com

ACHIEVING SUCCESS IN TODAY'S COMPETITIVE ENVIRONMENT

Your career success depends on effective communication.

Successful professionals such as Mena Trott will tell you that to succeed in business today, you need the ability to communicate with people both inside and outside your organization. Whether you are competing to get the job you want or to win the customers your company needs, your success or failure depends to a large degree on your ability to communicate. In fact, if you're looking for a surefire way to stand out from your competition in the job market, improving your communication skills might be the single most important step you can take. Employers often express frustration at the poor communication skills of many employees—particularly recent college graduates who haven't yet learned how to adapt their casual communication style to the professional business environment. If you learn to write well, speak well, listen well, and recognize the appropriate way to communicate in various business situations, you'll gain a major advantage that will serve you throughout your career.[2]

Whether you are exchanging e-mail, giving a formal presentation, or chatting with co-workers around the espresso machine, you are engaging in **communication,** the process of sending and receiving messages. However, communication is considered *effective* only when others understand your message correctly and respond to it the way you want them to. Effective communication helps you manage your work flow, improves business relationships, enhances your professional image, and provides a variety of other important benefits (see Figure 1–1). In all these activities, the essence of successful communication is sharing—providing data, information, and insights in an exchange that benefits both you and the people with whom you are communicating.[3]

Communication is vital to every company's success.

Effective communication is at the center of virtually every aspect of business because it connects the company with all its **stakeholders,** groups affected in some way by the company's actions: customers, employees, shareholders, suppliers, neighbors, the community, and the nation.[4] If you want to improve efficiency, quality, responsiveness, or innovation, you'll need to do so with the help of strong communication skills. Conversely, when communication breaks down, the results can be anything from time-wasting to tragic (see "Practicing Ethical Communication: The High

FIGURE 1–1
The Benefits of Effective Communication

PRACTICING ETHICAL COMMUNICATION

The High Cost of Failure

"No warning. Nothing. The train came and tried to kill us." That's how Ana Rosa Cabrera described the shock when 11 runaway cars from a Union Pacific freight train jumped the tracks and tore through her neighborhood east of Los Angeles in the summer of 2003.

After a series of errors and miscommunications, a string of 31 freight cars broke free in a switching yard in the town of Montclair on the morning of June 20. As the cars picked up speed on the downhill track, eventually traveling as fast as 86 miles per hour, railroad managers faced a tough decision. With no locomotive engine attached to the cars, they had no way to control or brake the runaways. Ahead on the track: other trains and downtown Los Angeles. Around noon, Union Pacific decided to switch the cars onto a siding track that led to another switching yard, hoping they'd make it that far and at least crash in a safer area. Unfortunately, the cars barreled over the switching device at more than three times the speed it was designed for. Eleven of them derailed and smashed into a residential neighborhood in the city of Commerce, demolishing several homes and damaging others. To everyone's amaze-

ment, no one was killed, but more than a dozen people received minor injuries.

Shock turned to anger when residents learned the cars had been diverted through Commerce on purpose and that Union Pacific had failed to warn local police, who might have had time to start evacuating homes in the cars path. The railroad defended the decision to derail, saying it was the safest alternative in a tough situation, and government investigators reached the same conclusion.

The failure to warn anyone is another matter, of course, and Union Pacific's chief of railroad operations, Ted Lewis, acknowledges that: "We thought we had a system to notify in case we had an emergency, but we didn't."

CAREER APPLICATIONS

1. Are the residents of Commerce, California, stakeholders in Union Pacific? Please explain.

2. Can a complex business such as a railroad realistically plan a communication system that covers every possible situation like the one in Commerce? Please explain your answer.

Cost of Failure"). At every stage of your career, communication is the way you'll succeed, and the higher you rise in your organization, the more important it becomes. In fact, top managers spend as much as 85 percent of their time communicating with others.[5]

What Employers Expect from You

No matter how good you are at accounting, law, science, or whatever professional specialty you pursue, most companies expect you to be competent at a wide range of communication tasks. Employers spend millions of dollars on communication training every year, but they expect you to come prepared with basic skills so that you can take full advantage of the learning opportunities they make available to you.

In fact, employers start judging your ability to communicate before you even show up for your first interview, and the process of evaluation never really stops. Improving your communication skills helps ensure that others will recognize and reward your talents and contributions. Fortunately, the specific skills that employers expect from you are the very skills that will help you advance in your career:

Employers are constantly evaluating your communication skills.

- **Organizing ideas and information logically and completely.** You'll often be required to find, process, and organize substantial amounts of raw data and random information so that others can easily grasp its significance.

Employers expect you to maintain an acceptable level of basic communication skills.

- **Expressing and presenting ideas and information coherently and persuasively.** Whenever you're called on to offer an opinion or recommendation, you'll be expected to back it up with solid evidence. However, organizing your evidence well is only half the battle; you'll also need to convince your audience with compelling arguments.

- **Listening to others effectively.** Effective listening is not as easy as you might think. Amidst all the distractions on the job, you'll need to use specific skills to find out what people are really trying to tell you. (For a more extensive discussion of listening, see Chapter 2.)

- **Communicating effectively with people from diverse backgrounds and experiences.** You'll often be called on to communicate with people who differ from you in gender, ethnic background, age, profession, and so on.

- **Using communication technologies effectively and efficiently.** Chances are, you're already familiar with e-mail, **instant messaging** (an alternative to e-mail that allows two or more people to transmit text messages instantaneously), and online research. Increasingly, employers will also expect you to use web conferencing, electronic presentations, and a variety of other technological tools.

- **Following accepted standards of grammar, spelling, and other aspects of high-quality writing and speaking.** You and your friends are probably comfortable with informal communication that doesn't put a high value on precision and correctness. However, to be successful in business, you will need to focus on the quality of your communication efforts. Particularly with audiences who don't know you well, careless writing and disregard for accepted standards reflects poorly on both you and your company. Rather than giving you the benefit of the doubt, many people will assume you either don't know how to communicate or don't care enough to communicate well.

- **Communicating in a civilized manner that reflects contemporary expectations of business etiquette.** Even when the pressure is on, you'll be expected to communicate with courtesy and respect in a manner that is appropriate to the situation.

- **Communicating ethically, even when choices aren't crystal clear.** Whether you're simply reporting on the status of a project or responding to a complicated, large-scale crisis, you're certain to encounter situations that call for you to make sound ethical choices.

You'll have the opportunity to practice all these skills throughout this course—but don't stop there. Successful professionals continue to hone communication skills throughout their careers.

Characteristics of Effective Communication

You can have the greatest ideas in the world, but they're no good to your company or your career if you can't express them clearly and persuasively. As one project manager at NASA's Marshall Space Flight Center put it, "Knowledge may be power, but communication skills are the primary raw materials of good client relationships." Every job description for a new position on this manager's staff includes the following line: "Required—effective organization skills and mastery of the English language in written and oral forms."[6]

Effective business documents share five key attributes.

To make your messages effective, make them practical, factual, concise, clear about expectations, and persuasive:[7]

- **Provide practical information.** Give recipients useful information, whether it's to help them perform a desired action or understand a new company policy. For instance, if you review Mena Trott's blog (www.sixapart.com/corner), you'll see that every posting helps advance the cause of bloggers in some way.

- **Give facts rather than impressions.** Use concrete language, specific detail, and information that is clear, convincing, accurate, and ethical. Even when an opinion is called for, present compelling evidence to support your conclusion.

- **Clarify and condense information.** Highlight the most important information, rather than dumping everything on the reader. Most business professionals find themselves wading in a flood of data and information. Messages that clarify and summarize are more effective than those that do not.

- **State precise responsibilities.** Write messages to generate a specific response from a specific audience. Clearly state what you expect from audience members or what you can do for them.

- **Persuade others and offer recommendations.** Show your readers precisely how they will benefit from responding to your message the way you want them to. Including reader benefits is the key to persuading employers, colleagues, customers, or clients to adopt a plan of action or purchase a product.

Keep these five important characteristics in mind as you review Figures 1–2 and 1–3. Both e-mails appear to be well-constructed at first glance, but Figure 1–2 is far less effective, as explained in the margin comments. It shows the negative impact that poorly conceived messages can have on an audience. In contrast, Figure 1–3 shows how an effective message can help everyone work more efficiently (in this case, by helping them prepare effectively for an important meeting).

FIGURE 1–2
Ineffective Communication

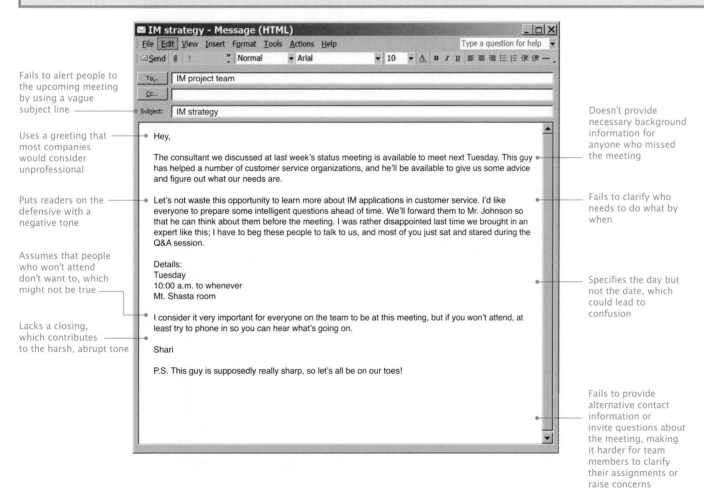

Fails to alert people to the upcoming meeting by using a vague subject line

Uses a greeting that most companies would consider unprofessional

Puts readers on the defensive with a negative tone

Assumes that people who won't attend don't want to, which might not be true

Lacks a closing, which contributes to the harsh, abrupt tone

Doesn't provide necessary background information for anyone who missed the meeting

Fails to clarify who needs to do what by when

Specifies the day but not the date, which could lead to confusion

Fails to provide alternative contact information or invite questions about the meeting, making it harder for team members to clarify their assignments or raise concerns

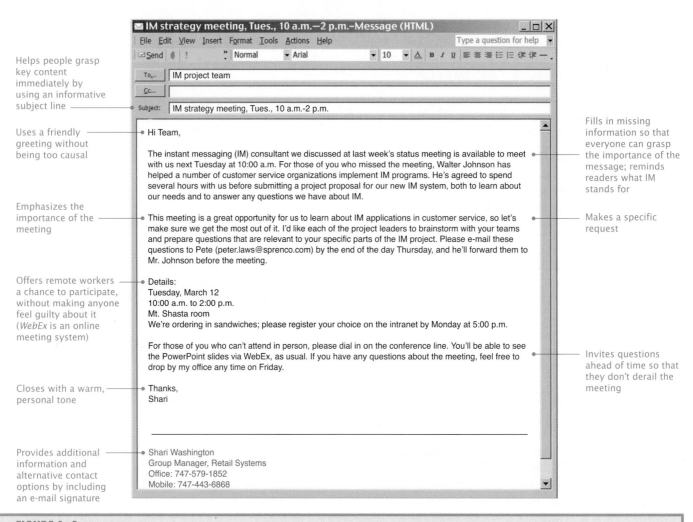

Helps people grasp key content immediately by using an informative subject line

Uses a friendly greeting without being too casual

Emphasizes the importance of the meeting

Offers remote workers a chance to participate, without making anyone feel guilty about it (*WebEx* is an online meeting system)

Closes with a warm, personal tone

Provides additional information and alternative contact options by including an e-mail signature

Fills in missing information so that everyone can grasp the importance of the message; reminds readers what IM stands for

Makes a specific request

Invites questions ahead of time so that they don't derail the meeting

FIGURE 1–3
Effective Communication

Communication in Organizational Settings

No matter what your level in the organization, you have an important communication role.

In every part of the business organization, communication provides the vital link between people and information. Whether you're a top manager or an entry-level employee, you have information that others need in order to perform their jobs, and others have information that is crucial to you. You exchange information with people inside your organization, called **internal communication,** and you exchange information and ideas with others outside your organization, called **external communication.** This information travels over both *formal* and *informal* channels (see Figure 1–4).

Formal and Informal Communication   Every organization has a **formal communication network,** in which ideas and information flow along the lines of command (the hierarchical levels) in your company's organization structure (see Figure 1–5). Throughout the internal formal network, information flows in three directions:

Formal communication flows in three directions.

- **Downward flow.** Downward communication flows from executives to employees, sharing executive decisions and providing information that helps employees do their jobs.

- **Upward flow.** Upward communication flows from employees to executives, providing accurate, timely reports on problems, trends, opportunities, grievances, and performance—thus allowing executives to solve problems and make intelligent decisions.

	Internal	External
Formal	Planned communication among insiders (letters, reports, memos, e-mail, and instant messages) that follows the company's chain of command	Planned communication with outsiders (letters, reports, memos, speeches, websites, instant messages, and news releases)
Informal	Casual communication among employees (e-mail, instant messages, face-to-face conversations, phone calls, and blogs) that does not follow the company's chain of command	Casual communication with suppliers, customers, investors, and other outsiders (face-to-face conversations, e-mail, instant messages, phone calls, and blogs)

FIGURE 1–4
Forms of Communication

- **Horizontal flow.** Lateral or diagonal communication flows between departments to help employees share information and coordinate tasks. Such communication is especially useful for solving complex and difficult problems.[8]

Every organization also has an **informal communication network**—a *grapevine*—that operates anywhere two or more employees are in contact, from the lunchroom to the golf course to the company's e-mail and instant-messaging systems. Some executives are wary of the informal network, but savvy managers tap into it to spread and receive informal messages.[9] Grapevines tend to be most active when employees believe the formal network is not providing the information they want or need.

External communication flows into and out of the organization along formal lines (carefully prepared letters, announcements, e-mail messages, face-to-face meetings, and so on). It can also take place by informal means, such as discussing work with your friends, meeting potential sales contacts at industry gatherings, networking at social events, talking with customers, and so on. Although these interactions are informal, they can still be vital to the company's success, so they require the same care and skill as formal communication.

Grapevines flourish when employees don't receive information they want or need.

FIGURE 1–5
Formal Communication Network

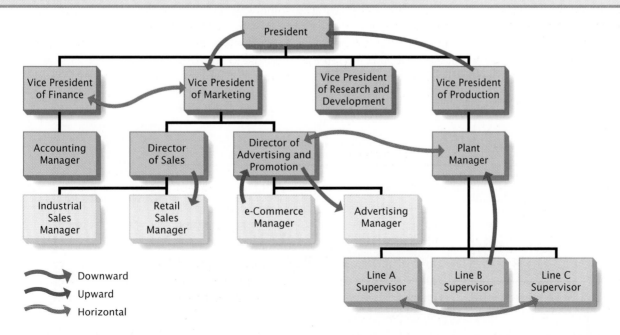

In fact, these informal exchanges are considered so important that a new class of technology is springing up to enable them. *Social networking* software, such as Spoke Connect, and websites, such as LinkedIn.com and Ryze.com, help companies take advantage of all the connections their employees may have. These solutions typically work by indexing e-mail and instant messaging address books, calendars, and message archives, then looking for connections between names. For instance, you might find that the sales lead you've been struggling to contact at a large customer might be a golf buddy of someone who works just down the hall from you.[10]

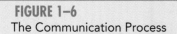

Senders and receivers connect through a six-step process.

The Communication Process   No matter what form of communication is taking place, the communication process connects sender and receiver through a series of six phases (see Figure 1–6):

1. **The sender has an idea.** You conceive an idea and want to share it.

2. **The sender encodes the idea.** When you put your idea into a message that your receiver will understand, you are **encoding** it. You decide on the message's form (words, facial expressions, gestures, illustrations, and so on), length, organization, tone, and style—all of which depend on your idea, your audience, and your personal style or mood.

3. **The sender transmits the message.** To transmit your message to your receiver, you select a **communication channel** such as the telephone, a letter, a memo, an e-mail—even a facial gesture. This choice of channel depends on your message, your audience's location, the media available to you, your need for speed, and the formality required.

4. **The receiver gets the message.** You have no guarantee that your message will actually get through. The receiver may not hear you, or your e-mail might get caught in an anti-spam filter. In fact, one of the biggest challenges you'll face as a communicator in today's crowded business environment is cutting through the clutter and noise in whatever medium you choose.

5. **The receiver decodes the message.** Your receiver tries to extract your idea from the message in a form that he or she can understand, a step known as **decoding.** If all goes well, the receiver interprets your message correctly, assigning the same meaning to your words as you intended and then responding in the way you desire.

6. **The receiver sends feedback.** After decoding your message, the receiver has the option of responding in some way. This **feedback** enables you to evaluate the

FIGURE 1–6
The Communication Process

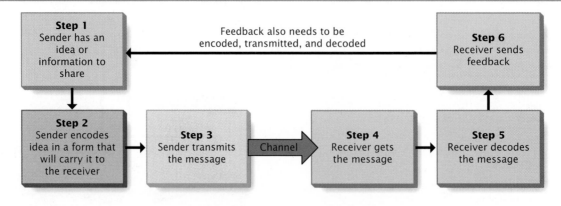

effectiveness of your message: Feedback often initiates another cycle through the process, which can continue until both parties are satisfied with the result. Successful communicators place considerable value on feedback, not only as a way to measure effectiveness but also as a way to learn.

Be aware that this is a simplified model; real-life communication is usually more complicated. Both sender and receiver might be talking at the same time, or the receiver might be trying to talk on the phone with one person while instant messaging with another, or the receiver may ignore the sender's request for feedback, and so on.

UNDERSTANDING WHY BUSINESS COMMUNICATION IS UNIQUE

Business communication is far more demanding than the communication you typically engage in with family, friends, and school associates. Expectations are higher on the job, and the business environment is so complex that your messages can fail for reasons you've never even heard of before. Business communication is affected by factors such as the globalization of business and the increase in workforce diversity, the increasing value of information, the pervasiveness of technology, the growing reliance on teamwork, the evolution of organizational structures, and numerous barriers to successful communication.

The complexity of business communication makes it vulnerable to factors such as
- Globalization and diversity
- Growing value of information
- Technology
- Teamwork
- Organizational structures
- Communication barriers

The Globalization of Business and the Increase in Workforce Diversity

Today's businesses increasingly reach across international borders to market their products, partner with other businesses, and employ workers and executives—an effort known as **globalization.** A number of companies and brands that you may think of as American (including Ben & Jerry's, Dr. Pepper, Pillsbury, Carnation, and Shell Oil) are in fact owned by organizations based in other countries.[11] Moreover, many U.S. companies rely on exports for a significant portion of their sales, often more than 50 percent. Companies such as Boeing, Microsoft, Coca-Cola, and Ford, among many others, frequently communicate with customers and colleagues in other countries.

As people and products cross borders, businesses of all shapes and sizes are paying more attention to **workforce diversity**—all those differences among the people you come into contact with on the job, including differences in age, gender, sexual orientation, education, cultural background, religion, life experience, and so on. Consider a 20-year-old man from a small town in the West and a 60-year-old woman from a large city on the East Coast. Even if they share the same ethnic background, they might have more trouble communicating than two next door neighbors of different ethnic background who grew up immersed in the same culture. As Chapter 3 discusses in more detail, successful companies realize two important facts: (1) the more diverse their workforce, the more attention they need to pay to communication, and

Successful companies know that diverse workforces can create powerful competitive advantages, but such workforces require closer attention to communication in order to eliminate barriers between groups with different communication styles.

People with different cultural backgrounds and life experiences may have different communication styles.

(2) a diverse workforce can yield a significant competitive advantage by bringing more ideas and broader perspectives to bear on business challenges.

The Increasing Value of Business Information

Information has become one of the most important resources in business today.

As competition for jobs, customers, and resources continues to grow, the importance of information continues to escalate as well. An organization's information is now every bit as important as its people, money, raw materials, and other resources. Even companies not usually associated with the so-called Information Age, such as manufacturers, often rely on **knowledge workers**: employees at all levels of the organization who specialize in acquiring, processing, and communicating information.

The valuable information you'll be expected to communicate on the job addresses such key areas as competitive insights, customer needs, and regulations and guidelines:

- **Competitive insights.** Successful companies work hard to understand their competitors' strengths and weaknesses. The more you know about your competitors and their plans, the more able you will be to adjust your own business plans.

- **Customer needs.** Most companies invest significant time and money in the effort to understand the needs of their customers. This information is collected from a variety of sources and needs to be analyzed and summarized so that your company can develop goods and services that better satisfy customer needs.

- **Regulations and guidelines.** Today's businesses must understand and follow a wide range of government regulations and guidelines covering such areas as employment, environment, taxes, and accounting. Your job may include the responsibility of researching and understanding these issues and then communicating them throughout the organization.

The Pervasiveness of Technology

Technology can help or hinder communication, depending on how it's designed and used.

The blogging innovations from Mena Trott and her colleagues at Six Apart represent another important theme in contemporary business, which is the influence that technology now has in virtually every aspect of business communication. However, even those technological developments intended to enhance communication can actually impede it if they are not used intelligently. Moreover, staying on top of technology requires time, energy, and constant improvement of skills. If your level of technical expertise doesn't keep up with that of your colleagues and co-workers, the imbalance can put you at a disadvantage and complicate the communication process. For example, if instant messaging becomes popular in your organization but you resist or avoid it, you'll be excluded from an important communication channel.

For a concise overview of the technologies you're most likely to encounter, see "Using Technology to Improve Business Communication," later in this chapter. Throughout this course, you'll learn about numerous technological tools and systems, and it's important to have a general understanding of the Internet and its uses. If you'd like a brief introduction to the Internet and related technologies, click on "Internet Basics" at www.prenhall.com/thill.

The Evolution of Organizational Structures

Organizations with tall structures may unintentionally restrict the flow of information.

As Figure 1–5 illustrates, every business has a particular structure that defines the relationships between the various people and departments within the organization. These relationships, in turn, affect the nature and quality of communication throughout the organization. Tall structures have many layers of management between the lowest and highest positions, so they can suffer communication breakdowns and delays as messages are passed up and down through multiple layers.

To overcome such problems, many business are now adopting flatter structures that reduce the number of layers. With fewer layers, communication generally flows faster and with fewer disruptions and distortions. On the other hand, with fewer formal lines of control and communication in these organizations, individual employees are expected to assume more responsibility for communication. For instance, you may be expected to communicate across department boundaries with colleagues and team members across the company.

Flatter organizational structures usually make it easier to communicate effectively.

In the pursuit of speed and agility, some businesses have adopted flexible organizations that pool the talents of employees and external partners. For instance, when launching a new product, a company might supplement the efforts of internal departments with help from a public relations firm, an ad agency, a marketing consultant, a web developer, and a product distributor. With so many individuals and organizations involved in the project, everyone must share the responsibility for giving and getting necessary information, or communication will break down.

Corporate cultures with an open climate benefit from free-flowing information and employee input.

Regardless of the particular structure a company uses, your communication efforts will also be influenced by the organization's **corporate culture,** the mixture of values, traditions, and habits that give a company its atmosphere and personality. Successful companies encourage employee contributions by ensuring that communication flows freely down, up, and across the organization chart. Open climates encourage candor and honesty, helping employees feel free enough to admit their mistakes, disagree with the boss, and express their opinions. Of course, as with any honest relationship, sending or receiving negative news is not always easy. In Chapter 8, you'll learn effective strategies for crafting messages that convey bad news in a professional and respectful manner.

Open cultures promote the flow of information. In fact, some modern office buildings are even designed to encourage casual interaction and impromptu meetings.

The Growing Reliance on Teamwork

Roughly half of all North American companies now rely on teams extensively, and many others plan to do so in the future. Consequently, you'll probably find yourself on a number of teams throughout your career. When teams replace or complement the formal channels in the organization chart, information may no longer be conveyed automatically, so every team member becomes more responsible for communication. This responsibility includes both sending and receiving messages; for example, you might seek out the information you need rather than waiting for someone to deliver it to you. In fact, you and your fellow team members may have to invent your own communication processes to make sure that everyone gets the right information at the right time. This extra attention to communication can pay off dramatically in higher performance and a more satisfying work experience.

Working in a team makes you even more responsible for communicating effectively.

The Barriers to Effective Communication

Throughout your career, you'll find that perfectly effective messages can fail for a variety of reasons. Your attempts to transmit and receive messages can be disrupted, distorted, even blocked by **communication barriers** such as these:

Communication is blocked by various types of barriers.

FIGURE 1–7
How Shared Experience
Affects Understanding

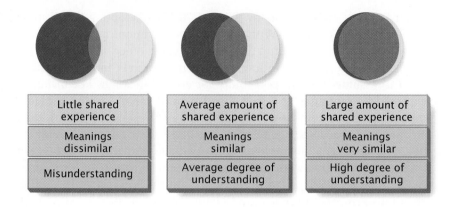

Little shared experience	Average amount of shared experience	Large amount of shared experience
Meanings dissimilar	Meanings similar	Meanings very similar
Misunderstanding	Average degree of understanding	High degree of understanding

- **Distractions.** Business messages can be interrupted or distorted by a wide variety of distractions. Physical distractions range from bad connections and poor acoustics to illegible printing and uncomfortable meeting rooms. Emotional distractions on the part of either sender or receiver can affect the way you prepare and deliver messages and the way your audience interprets those messages.

- **Information overload.** The sheer number of messages that people receive on the job can be distracting. Too many messages can result in **information overload,** which not only makes it difficult to discriminate between useful and useless information but also amplifies workplace stress.[12]

- **Perceptual differences.** Our minds organize incoming sensations into a mental map that represents our individual **perception** of reality. As a sender, you choose the details that seem important to you. As a receiver, you try to fit new details into your existing pattern; however, if a detail doesn't quite fit, you are inclined to distort the information rather than rearrange your pattern—a process known as **selective perception.**[13] The more experiences you share with another person, the more likely you are to share perception and thus share meaning (see Figure 1–7).

- **Language differences.** The very language we use to communicate can turn into a barrier if two people define a given word or phrase differently. When a boss asks for something "as soon as possible," does that mean within 10 seconds, 10 minutes, 10 days?

- **Restrictive environments.** Companies that restrict the flow of information, either intentionally or unintentionally, limit their competitive potential. With their many levels between top and bottom, tall hierarchies often result in significant loss of message quality in both directions.[14]

- **Deceptive tactics.** Given the difficulty of communication in the best of circumstances, deceptive communication is regrettably easy. Unscrupulous communicators can present opinions as facts, omit crucial information, exaggerate benefits, or downplay risks.

COMMUNICATING MORE EFFECTIVELY ON THE JOB

No single solution will overcome all communication barriers. However, a careful combination of strategies can improve your ability to communicate effectively. For example, you can minimize distractions, adopt an audience-centered approach, improve your basic communication skills, make your feedback constructive, and be sensitive to business etiquette.

Minimizing Distractions

Everyone in the organization can help overcome distractions. Start by reducing as much noise, visual clutter, and interruption as possible. A small dose of common sense and courtesy goes a long way. Turn off that cell phone before you step into a meeting. Don't talk across the tops of cubicles when people inside them are trying to work. Be sensitive to personal differences, too; for instance, some people may be able to work with music blaring, but many others can't.

Don't let e-mail, instant messaging, or telephones interrupt you every minute of the day. Set aside time to attend to messages all at once so that you can think and focus the rest of the time. In fact, one of the most important steps you can take is simply sending fewer messages.

Writer Richard Saul Wurman summed up the great irony of the Information Age nicely: Information used to be a precious commodity, but now it's "like crabgrass; something to be kept at bay."[15] You never want to undercommunicate, but sending unnecessary messages or sending the right message to the wrong people is almost as bad. E-mail is compounding this problem, making it so easy to send and forward messages to dozens or hundreds of people at once. Think before you click that "send" button.

In addition, if you must send a message that isn't urgent or crucial, let people know so that they can prioritize. If a long report requires no action from recipients, tell them up front so that they don't have to search through it looking for action items. Most e-mail and voicemail systems let you mark messages as urgent; however, use this feature only when it's truly needed. Too many so-called urgent messages that aren't particularly urgent will lead to annoyance and anxiety, not action.

Try to overcome emotional distractions by recognizing your own feelings and by anticipating emotional reactions from others.[16] When a situation might cause tempers to flare, choose your words carefully. As a receiver, avoid placing blame and reacting subjectively.

Overcome distraction by
- *Using common sense and courtesy*
- *Sending fewer messages*
- *Informing receivers of your message's priority*

Emotionally charged situations require extra care when communicating.

Adopting an Audience-Centered Approach

An **audience-centered approach** means focusing on and caring about the members of your audience, making every effort to get your message across in a way that is meaningful to them. Learn as much as possible about the biases, education, age, status, style, and personal and professional concerns of your receivers. If you're addressing strangers and unable to find out more about them, try to project yourself into their position by using your common sense and imagination.

The more you know about the people you're communicating with, the easier it will be to concentrate on their needs—which, in turn, will make it easier for them to hear your message, understand it, and respond positively. For instance, the presentation slide in Figure 1–8 takes an audience-centered approach. Rather than trying to cover all the technical and legal details that are often discussed in insurance plans, this slide addresses the common fears and worries that employees might have as their company moves to a new health insurance plan.

If you haven't had the opportunity to communicate with a diverse range of people in your academic career so far, you might be surprised by the different communication styles you will surely encounter on the job. Recognizing and adapting to your audience's style will improve not only the effectiveness of your communication but the quality of your working relationship as well.[17] The audience-centered approach is emphasized throughout this book, so you'll have plenty of opportunity to practice this approach to communicating more effectively.

Keeping your audience's needs in mind helps you ensure successful messages.

FIGURE 1–8
PowerPoint Slide Showing Audience-Centered Communication

Fine-Tuning Your Business Communication Skills

Work on your communication skills before you start your business career.

Your own skills as a communicator will be as much a factor in your business success as anything else. No matter what your skill level, opportunities to improve are numerous and usually easy to find. As mentioned earlier, many employers provide communication training in both general skills and specific scenarios, but don't wait. Use this course to begin mastering your skills now.

Lack of experience may be the only obstacle between you and effective communication. Perhaps you're worried about a limited vocabulary or uncertain about questions of grammar, punctuation, and style. If you're intimidated by the idea of writing an important document or appearing before a group, you're not alone. Everyone gets nervous about communicating from time to time, even people you might think of as "naturals." People aren't born writing and speaking well; they master these skills through study and practice. Someone who has written 10 reports or given 10 speeches is usually better at it than someone who has produced only 2, so seek out opportunities to practice. Even simple techniques, such as keeping a reading log and writing practice essays, will improve not only your writing skills but also your scholastic performance.[18]

This course lets you practice in an environment that provides honest and constructive feedback. You'll have ample opportunity to plan and produce documents, collaborate in teams, listen effectively, improve nonverbal communication, and communicate across cultures—all skills that will serve your career well.

Giving—and Responding to—Constructive Feedback

Constructive feedback focuses on improvement, not personal criticism.

Feedback doesn't end when you leave school. While searching for employment and once on the job, you will encounter numerous situations in which you are expected to give and receive feedback. Whether giving or receiving criticism, be sure you do so in a constructive way. **Constructive feedback,** sometimes called *constructive criticism,* focuses on the process and outcomes of communication, not on the people involved (see Table 1–1). In contrast, **destructive feedback** delivers criticism with no effort to stimulate improvement.[19] For example, "This proposal is a confusing mess, and you failed to convince me of anything" is destructive feedback. Your goal is to be more constructive: "Your proposal could be more effective with a clearer description of the construction process and a well-organized explanation of why the positives outweigh the negatives." When giving feedback, avoid personal attacks and give the person clear guidelines for improvement.

GIVING CONSTRUCTIVE FEEDBACK		Table 1–1

How to Be Constructive	*Explanation*
Evaluate effectiveness	Does the document accomplish its intended purpose with accurate information and clear language?
Think through your suggested changes carefully	Isolated or superficial edits can do more harm than good.
Discuss improvements rather than flaws	Instead of saying "this illustration is confusing," explain how it can be improved to make it clearer.
Focus on controllable behavior	Since the writer may not have control over every variable that affected the quality of the message, focus on those things that the writer can control.
Be specific	Comments such as "I don't get this" or "Make this clearer" don't identify what the writer needs to fix.
Keep feedback impersonal	Focus comments on the message, not the person who created it.
Verify understanding	Ask for confirmation from the recipient to make sure that the person understood your feedback.
Time your feedback carefully	Make sure the writer will have sufficient time to implement the changes you suggested.
Highlight any limitations your back may have	If you didn't have time to give the document a feed-thorough edit, or if you're not an expert in some aspect of the content, let the writer know so that he or she can handle your comments appropriately.

When you receive constructive feedback, resist the all-too-human impulse to defend your work or deny the validity of the feedback. Remaining open to criticism isn't always easy when you've poured your heart and soul into a project, but feedback is a valuable opportunity to learn and improve. Try to disconnect your emotions from the work and view it simply as something you can make better. Many writers also find it helpful to step back, think about the feedback for a while, and let their emotions settle down before diving in to make corrections. For all that, don't automatically assume that even well-intentioned feedback is necessarily correct. You have the responsibility for the final quality of the message, so make sure that any suggested changes are valid ones.

Try to react unemotionally when you receive constructive feedback.

Being Sensitive to Business Etiquette

In today's hectic, competitive world, the notion of **etiquette** (the expected norms of behavior in a particular situation) can seem outdated and unimportant. However, the way you conduct yourself can have a profound influence on your company's success and your career. When executives hire and promote you, they expect your behavior to protect the company's reputation. The more you understand such expectations, the better chance you have of avoiding career-damaging mistakes.

Understanding communication etiquette can help you avoid needless blunders.

Throughout this book, you'll encounter advice for a variety of business situations, but even if you don't know the specific expectations in a given situation, some general guidelines will get you through any rough spots. Start by being sensitive to the fact that people can have different expectations about the same situation. Something you find appalling or embarrassing might be business as usual for a colleague, and vice versa. Moreover, etiquette expectations don't always make sense, nor are they always fair in the eyes of everyone concerned. For example, some high-ranking women executives say some male colleagues who aren't bothered when men use coarse language (particularly words and phrases with sexual undertones) often view such language as unacceptable for women to use. These women acknowledge that the situation isn't fair, but they've learned to work within the prevailing behavior norms in order to avoid hindering their careers.[20]

Respect, courtesy, and common sense will get you through most etiquette challenges on the job.

In any setting, long lists of etiquette "rules" can be overwhelming. You'll never memorize all of them or remember to follow all of them in the heat of the moment. Just remember three principles that will get you through just about any situation: respect, courtesy, and common sense. Moreover, these principles will encourage forgiveness if you do happen to make a mistake. As you encounter new situations, take a few minutes to learn the expectations of the other people involved. Travel guidebooks are a great source of information about norms and customs in other countries, as are such commercial products as CultureGrams (see if your library has online access to the CultureGram database). Don't be afraid to ask questions, either. People will respect your concern and curiosity. You'll gradually accumulate considerable knowledge, which will help you feel comfortable and be effective in a wide range of business situations.

USING TECHNOLOGY TO IMPROVE BUSINESS COMMUNICATION

Communicating in today's business environment nearly always requires some level of technical competence.

Today's businesses rely heavily on technology to improve the communication process. Companies and employees who use technology wisely can communicate more effectively and therefore compete more successfully.

You will find that technology is discussed extensively throughout this book, with specific advice on using common tools to meet communication challenges. The four-page photo essay "Powerful Tools For Communicating Efficiently" (pp. 20–23) offers an overview of the technologies that connect people in offices, factories, and other business settings. In addition, some aspects of communication technology are undergoing exciting changes almost daily. Technologies such as the following have the potential to dramatically enhance business communication:

- **Voice technologies.** The human voice will always be central to business communication, and it's being supplemented by a variety of new technologies. *Voice synthesis* regenerates a human speaking voice from computer files that represent words or parts of words. *Voice recognition* converts human speech to computer-compatible data. Both technologies continue to improve every year, gaining richer vocabularies and more human-sounding voices.

- **Virtual agents.** The dream of replicating or even surpassing human capabilities with computers has been driving artificial intelligence research for years. **Virtual agents** are a limited form of machine intelligence, also known as *bots* (derived from *robot*), *verbots,* and *V-reps.* These virtual operators are used in customer service departments and other areas where people tend to ask similar questions over and over. Through a combination of voice recognition, voice synthesis, and basic problem-solving skills, these virtual operators are some 40 percent faster than menu-based touch-tone calls, and they cost about half as much as a call handled by a human.[21] A variation on virtual phone communication is the virtual meeting, in which technology creates the illusion of sitting next to someone who might actually be thousands of miles away.

- **Mobile communication.** If you're accustomed to studying on the go, moving from dorm room to coffee shop to library, you'll fit right in with today's untethered work environments. In many cases, mobile workers don't even have traditional offices, using temporary cubicles at work, home offices, cars, airports, and even new Internet-equipped airplanes for office space. Location data from the **Global Postitioning System (GPS)** is also creating new forms of mobile communication, such as remote monitoring of medical patients and trucking fleets.

- **Networking advances.** You might already be using four new networking technologies that are just now making serious inroads into the corporate world. As noted earlier, instant messaging lets two or more people exchange text instantaneously, without the delays of going through central e-mail servers. **Peer-to-peer (P2P) computing** extends this concept by letting multiple PCs communicate directly so that they can share files or work on large problems simultaneously. **Wireless networking,** commonly known as *Wi-Fi,* extends the reach of the Internet with wireless access points that connect to PCs and handheld devices via radio signals. **Short messaging service (SMS)** is a text communication feature that has been common on mobile phones in other parts of the world for several years and has recently gained a presence in North America. The First National Bank in South Africa uses SMS to improve Internet banking security for its customers. Whenever an account is accessed online, the bank immediately sends a text message to the customer so he or she can verify that the access is legitimate.[22] (Note that while *instant messaging* and *text messaging* perform a similar function, instant messaging is generally considered a computer-to-computer activity and text messaging is a phone-to-phone or computer-to-phone function.)

Even though such impressive enhancements are available, anyone who has used a computer knows that the benefits of technology are not automatic. When poorly designed or inappropriately used, technology can hinder communication more than it helps. To communicate effectively, you need to keep technology in perspective, use technological tools productively, spend time and money on technology wisely, and disengage from the computer frequently to communicate in person.

Keeping Technology in Perspective

Technology is an aid to interpersonal communication, not a replacement for it. Technology can't think for you or communicate for you, and if you lack some essential skills, technology probably can't fill in the gaps.

Don't let technology overwhelm the communication process.

The spellchecker in your word processor is a great example. It's happy to run all your words through the dictionary, but it doesn't know whether you're using the correct words or the best words possible. Similarly, presentation software such as Microsoft PowerPoint can decorate your slide show with color, animation, sound bites, dancing text, and even video clips, but you have to provide the well-thought-out content.

Technology is not always the answer to your communication needs. The sheer number of possibilities in many technological tools can get in the way of successful communication. For example, both senders and receivers may be distracted if they're having trouble configuring their computers to participate in an online meeting. Or the content of a message may be obscured if an electronic presentation is overloaded with visual effects. Moreover, if technological systems aren't adapted to a user's (or an organization's) needs, people won't adapt to the technology—they won't use it effectively, or worse, they won't use it at all.

Using Technological Tools Productively

You don't have to become an expert to use most communication technologies effectively, but you will need to be familiar with the basic features and functions of the tools your employer expects you to use. This includes using everyday tools such as word processing and e-mail efficiently and adapting to new tools such as blogging, podcasting, and virtual meetings as they become available.

Employees who are comfortable using communication technologies have a competitive advantage in today's marketplace.

Powerful Tools for Communicating Efficiently

The tools of business communication evolve with every new generation of digital technology. Selecting the right tool for each situation can enhance your business communication in many ways. In today's flexible office settings, communication technology helps people keep in touch and stay productive. When co-workers in different cities need to collaborate, they can meet and share ideas without costly travel. Manufacturers use communication technology to keep track of parts, orders, and shipments—and to keep customers well-informed. Those same customers can also communicate with companies in many ways at any time of day or night.

Flexible Workstations

Many professionals have abandoned desktop PCs for laptops they can carry home, on travel, and to meetings. Back at their desks, a docking station transforms the laptop into a full-featured PC with network connection. Workers without permanent desks sometimes share PCs that automatically reconfigure themselves to access each user's e-mail and files.

Wireless Networks

Laptop PCs with wireless and handheld capability let workers stay connected to the network from practically anywhere within the office—any desk, any conference room. This technology offers high-speed Internet access within range of a wireless access point. New smart phones will continue this trend of connectivity on the go.

Follow-Me Phone Service

Rather than juggling multiple numbers for home, one or more office locations, and mobile phones, workers can use *follow-me phone service*. Callers dial one number to reach the person anywhere—at the office, a remote site, a home office, or anywhere with cell phone service. The system automatically forwards calls to a list of preprogrammed numbers and transfers unanswered calls to voice mail.

Redefining the Office

Technology makes it easier for people to retrieve information and stay connected with colleagues, suppliers, and customers—wherever they are. To simplify life for employees and reduce office expenses, many companies now enable their staffs to work from home or from special satellite offices that are closer to residential areas than their main office complexes. For example, Sun Microsystems lets staff members choose to work either at the main office or at remote offices called "drop-in centers." Many Sun facilities have specially equipped "iWork" areas that can quickly reconfigure phone and computer connections to meet individual requirements.

Electronic Presentations

Combining a color projector with a laptop or personal digital assistant (PDA) running the right software lets people give informative business presentations that are enhanced with sound, video animation, and live web links. Having everything in electronic form also makes it easy to customize a presentation or to make last-minute changes.

Communicating in the Office

Intranets

Businesses use Internet technologies to create an intranet, a private computer network that simplifies information sharing within the company. Intranets can handle a variety of communication needs and become "virtual office spaces" for geographically dispersed teams. To ensure the security of company communication and information, intranets are shielded from the public Internet.

Wall Displays

Teams commonly solve problems by brainstorming at a whiteboard. Wall displays take this concept one step further, letting participants transmit words and diagrams to distant colleagues via the corporate intranet. Users can even share the virtual pen to make changes and additions from more than one location.

Web-Based Meetings

Workers can actively participate in web-based meetings by logging on from a desktop PC, laptop, or cell phone. Websites such as WebEx help users integrate voice, text, and video and let them share applications such as Microsoft PowerPoint and Microsoft Word in a single browser window.

Collaborating

Working in teams is essential in almost every business. Teamwork can become complicated, however, when team members work in different parts of the company, in different time zones, or even for different companies. Technology helps bridge the distance by making it possible to brainstorm, attend virtual meetings, and share files, and even modify websites and software using *wiki* technology, all from widely separated locations. Communication technology also helps companies save money on costly business travel without losing most of the benefits of face-to-face collaboration.

Internet Videophone

Person-to-person video calling has long been possible through popular instant messaging programs. Internet videophone services do even more, letting multiple users participate in a videoconference without the expense and complexity of a full-fledged videoconferencing system. Some services are flexible enough to include telecommuters who have broadband Internet connections.

Shared Workspace

Online workspaces such as Documentum's eRoom and Microsoft's SharePoint make it easy for far-flung team members to access shared files anywhere, anytime. Accessible through a web browser, the workspace contains a collection of folders and has built-in intelligence to control which team members can read, edit, and save specific files.

Communicating Remotely

Videoconferencing and Telepresence

Less costly than travel, videoconferencing provides many of the same benefits as an in-person meeting. Advanced systems include telepresence and robot surrogates, which use computers to "place" participants in the room virtually, letting them see and hear everyone while being seen and heard themselves. Such realistic interaction makes meetings more productive.

Warehouse RFID

In an effort to reduce the costs and delays associated with manual inventory reports, Wal-Mart requires its top suppliers to put radio-frequency identification (RFID) tags on all their shipping cases and pallets. These tags automatically provide information that was previously collected by hand via barcode scanners.

Extranet

Extranets are secure, private computer networks that use Internet technology to share business information with suppliers, vendors, partners, and customers. Think of an extranet as an extension of the company intranet that is available to people outside the organization by invitation only.

Wireless Warehouse

Communication technology is a key source of competitive advantage for shipping companies such as FedEx and UPS. Hand-worn scanners use wireless links to help warehouse personnel access instant information that lets them process more packages in less time at transit hubs. Currently, 300 package loaders at four UPS hub facilities are testing the new wireless application called UPScan. A pager-size cordless scanner worn on the loader's hand captures data from a package bar code and transmits the data via Bluetooth® wireless technology to a Symbol Technologies wireless terminal worn on the loader's waist.

Sharing the Latest Information

Companies use a variety of communication technologies to create products and services and deliver them to customers. The ability to easily access and share the latest information improves the flow and timing of supplies, lowers operating costs, and boosts financial performance. Easy information access also helps companies respond to customer needs by providing them timely, accurate information and service and by delivering the right products to them at the right time.

Package Tracking

Senders and receivers often want frequent updates when packages are in transit. Handheld devices such as the FedEx PowerPad enhance customer service by letting delivery personnel instantly upload package data to the FedEx network. The wireless PowerPad also aids drivers by automatically receiving weather advisories.

Communicating About Products and Services

Supply Chain Management

Advanced software lets suppliers, manufacturers, and retailers share information—even when they have incompatible computer systems. Improved information flow increases report accuracy and helps each company in the supply chain manage stock levels efficiently.

Over-the-Shoulder Support

For online shoppers who need instant help, many retail websites make it easy to connect with a live sales rep via phone or instant messaging. The rep can provide quick answers to questions and, with permission, can even control a shopper's browser to help locate particular items.

Help Lines

Some people prefer the personal touch of contact by phone. Moreover, some companies assign preferred customers special ID numbers that let them jump to the front of the calling queue. Many companies are addressing the needs of foreign-language speakers by connecting them with external service providers who offer multilingual support.

Corporate Blogs

Web-based journals let companies offer advice, answer questions, and promote the benefits of their products and services in a fast, personal style. Elements of a successful blog include frequent updates and the participation of knowledgeable contributors. Adding a subtle mix of useful commentary and marketing messages helps get customers to visit blogs frequently or sign up for automatic updates through really simple syndication (RSS).

Interacting

Maintaining an open dialog with customers is a great way to gain a better understanding of their likes and dislikes. Today's communication technologies make it easier for customers to interact with a company whenever, wherever, and however they wish. A well-coordinated approach to phone, web, and in-store communication helps a company build stronger relationships with its existing customers, which increases the chances of doing more business with each one.

Retail RFID

Customers can't buy what they can't find, and manual reporting is often too slow for fast-paced retailing. To keep enough goods on the shelves, some retailers use RFID tags to monitor products on display. Clerks use wireless readers to scan tagged products and report stock data to a computerized inventory system that responds with an up-to-the-minute restocking order.

Communicating with Customers

In-Store Kiosks

Staples is among the retailers that let shoppers buy from the web while they're still in the store. Web-connected kiosks were originally used to let shoppers custom-configure their PCs, but the kiosks also give customers access to roughly 8,000 in-store items as well as to the 50,000 products available online.

Recent advances in technology make it possible for all business communicators to create presentations that once required expensive professional equipment and specialized skills. For example, with Visual Communicator from Serious Magic, you can easily combine audio, video, and PowerPoint slides to create multimedia presentations.

People who are proficient at using their technological tools can produce impressive results, but the expectations of production quality seem to increase with every new capability. Only a few years ago, the norm for presentations was typed content on overhead transparencies. Today's standard is computer-based, full-color presentations on liquid crystal displays (LCDs). The presentations are certainly more attractive and sometimes more effective, but the technology has forced millions of businesspeople to learn a new set of skills. At some point in the future, you might have to learn how to program your virtual identity robot to attend meetings for you. Technology will always require some new skill to be learned. Whatever the tool, if you learn the basics, your work will be less frustrating and far more productive.

Reconnecting with People Frequently

In spite of technology's efficiency and speed, it may not be the best choice for every communication situation. For one thing, even in the best circumstances, technology can't match the rich experience of person-to-person contact. Let's say you e-mail a colleague asking how she did with her sales presentation to an important client, and her answer comes back simply as "Fine." What does *fine* mean? Is an order expected soon? Did she lose the sale? Was the client rude and she doesn't want to talk about it? If you reconnect with her, perhaps visit her in person, she might provide additional information, or you might be able to offer advice or support during a difficult time.

For another thing, most human beings need to connect with other people. You can create amazing documents and presentations without ever leaving your desk or meeting anyone in person. But if you stay hidden behind technology, people won't get to know you nearly as well. You might be funny, bright, and helpful, but you're just a voice on the phone or a name on a document until people can interact with you in person. As technological options increase, people seem to need the human touch even more.

No matter how much technology is involved, communication is still about people connecting with people.

MAKING ETHICAL COMMUNICATION CHOICES

Ethics are the accepted principles of conduct that govern behavior within a society. Put another way, ethical principles define the boundary between right and wrong. Former Supreme Court Justice Potter Stewart defined ethics as "knowing the difference between what you have a right to do and what is the right thing to do."[23] To make the right choices as a business communicator you have a responsibility to think through not only what you say but also the consequences of saying it.

Of course, people in a society don't always agree on what constitutes ethical behavior. For instance, the emergence of *stealth marketing,* in which customers don't know they're being marketed to, has raised a new set of concerns about ethics. Two common stealth marketing techniques are sending people into public places to use particular products in a conspicuous manner and then discuss them with strangers—as though they were just regular people on the street, when in fact they are employed by a marketing firm—and paying consumers (or plying them with insider information and other benefits) to promote products to their friends without telling them it's a form of advertising. Critics complain that such techniques are deceptive because they don't give their targets the opportunity to raise their instinctive defenses against the persuasive powers of marketing messages.[24]

Ethical behavior is a companywide concern, of course, but because communication efforts are the public face of a company, they are subjected to particularly rigorous scrutiny from regulators, legislators, investors, consumer groups, environmental groups, labor organizations, and anyone else affected by business activities. **Ethical communication** includes all relevant information, is true in every sense, and is not deceptive in any way. In contrast, unethical communication can include falsehoods and misleading information (or withhold important information). Some examples of unethical communication include:[25]

Any time you try to mislead your audience, the result is unethical communication.

- **Plagiarism.** Stealing someone else's words or other creative product and claiming it as your own

- **Selective misquoting.** Deliberately omitting damaging or unflattering comments to paint a better (but untruthful) picture of you or your company

- **Misrepresenting numbers.** Increasing or decreasing numbers, exaggerating, altering statistics, or omitting numerical data

- **Distorting visuals.** Making a product look bigger or changing the scale of graphs and charts to exaggerate or conceal differences

An ethical message is accurate and sincere. It avoids language and images that manipulate, discriminate, or exaggerate. On the surface, such ethical practices appear fairly easy to recognize, but deciding what is ethical can be a considerable challenge in complex business situations.

Distinguishing Ethical Dilemmas from Ethical Lapses

Every company has responsibilities to its stakeholders, and those various groups often have competing interests. For instance, employees generally want higher wages and more benefits, but investors who have risked their money in the company want management to keep cost low so profits are strong enough to drive up the stock price. Both sides have a valid position; neither one is "right" or "wrong."

An **ethical dilemma** involves choosing among alternatives that aren't clear-cut. Perhaps two conflicting alternatives are both ethical and valid, or perhaps the alternatives lie somewhere in the gray area between clearly right and clearly wrong. Suppose you are president of a company that's losing money. You have a duty to your shareholders to try to reduce your losses and a duty to your employees to be fair and honest. After looking at various options, you conclude that you'll have to lay off 500 people immediately. You suspect you may have to lay off another 100 people later on, but right now you need those 100 workers to finish a project. What do you tell them? If you confess that their jobs are shaky, many of them may quit just when you need them most. However, if you tell them that the future is rosy, you'll be stretching the truth.

An ethical dilemma is a choice between alternatives that may all be ethical and valid.

Unlike a dilemma, an **ethical lapse** is a clearly unethical (and frequently illegal) choice. In 2004, several insurance companies were accused of misleading military personnel at Fort Benning in Georgia, Camp Pendleton in California, and other bases around the country. Many of these young men and women thought they were signing up for savings programs when in fact they were buying extremely expensive and frequently unnecessary life insurance policies. The policies were often sold during mandatory financial training sessions for the soldiers, who were given no time to read the documents they signed. After the situation was brought to national attention by the *New York Times* and other news media, at least two of the companies involved, Madison National Life Insurance Company and American Amicable Life Insurance, began issuing full refunds.[26]

An ethical lapse is knowing that something is wrong and doing it anyway.

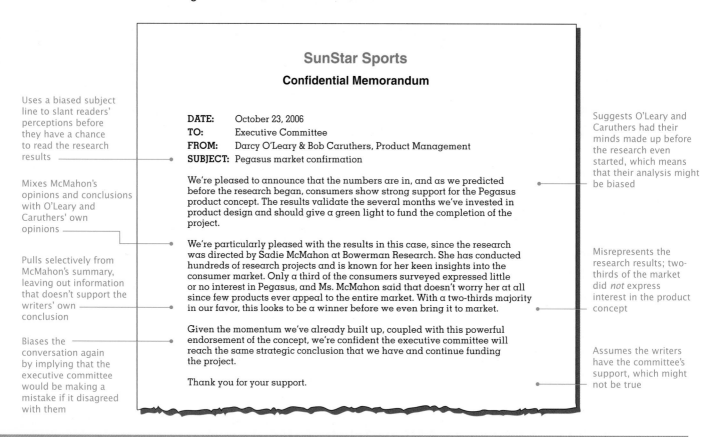

Uses a biased subject line to slant readers' perceptions before they have a chance to read the research results

Mixes McMahon's opinions and conclusions with O'Leary and Caruthers' own opinions

Pulls selectively from McMahon's summary, leaving out information that doesn't support the writers' own conclusion

Biases the conversation again by implying that the executive committee would be making a mistake if it disagreed with them

SunStar Sports

Confidential Memorandum

DATE: October 23, 2006
TO: Executive Committee
FROM: Darcy O'Leary & Bob Caruthers, Product Management
SUBJECT: Pegasus market confirmation

We're pleased to announce that the numbers are in, and as we predicted before the research began, consumers show strong support for the Pegasus product concept. The results validate the several months we've invested in product design and should give a green light to fund the completion of the project.

We're particularly pleased with the results in this case, since the research was directed by Sadie McMahon at Bowerman Research. She has conducted hundreds of research projects and is known for her keen insights into the consumer market. Only a third of the consumers surveyed expressed little or no interest in Pegasus, and Ms. McMahon said that doesn't worry her at all since few products ever appeal to the entire market. With a two-thirds majority in our favor, this looks to be a winner before we even bring it to market.

Given the momentum we've already built up, coupled with this powerful endorsement of the concept, we're confident the executive committee will reach the same strategic conclusion that we have and continue funding the project.

Thank you for your support.

Suggests O'Leary and Caruthers had their minds made up before the research even started, which means that their analysis might be biased

Misrepresents the research results; two-thirds of the market did *not* express interest in the product concept

Assumes the writers have the committee's support, which might not be true

FIGURE 1–9
Unethical Communication

With both internal and external communication efforts, the pressure to produce results or justify decisions can make unethical communication a tempting choice. Compare the messages in Figures 1–9 and 1–10, in which the results of a marketing research project are presented to company executives. In Figure 1–9, the memo writers clearly want the company to continue funding their pet project, even though the marketing research doesn't support such a decision. By comparing the two memos, you can see how the writers twisted the truth and omitted evidence in order to put a positive "spin" on the research. Figure 1–10 presents the evidence in a more honest and ethical manner.

Ensuring Ethical Communication

Ensuring ethical business communications requires three elements: ethical individuals, ethical company leadership, and the appropriate policies and structures to support employees' efforts to make ethical choices.[27] Moreover, these three elements need to work together in harmony. If employees see company executives making unethical decisions and flouting company guidelines, they might conclude that the guidelines are meaningless and emulate their bosses' unethical behavior.

Responsible employers establish clear ethical guidelines for their employees to follow.

Employers have a responsibility to establish clear guidelines for ethical behavior, including business communication. Many companies establish an explicit ethics policy by using a written **code of ethics** to help employees determine what is acceptable. A code is often part of a larger program of employee training and communication channels that allow employees to ask questions and report instances of questionable ethics. For example, United Technologies, a large aerospace and defense company based in Hartford, Connecticut, offers employees, customers, and suppliers a confi-

Tries not to "sell" the conclusion ahead of time, using an even-handed subject line

Offers full disclosure of all the background information

Provides the complete text of the researcher's summary

Separates the researcher's observations and opinions from the writers' own

Invites further discussion of the situation

SunStar Sports
Confidential Memorandum

DATE: October 23, 2006
TO: Executive Committee
FROM: Darcy O'Leary & Bob Caruthers, Product Management
SUBJECT: Market research summary for Pegasus project

The market research for the Pegasus Project concluded last week with phone interviews of 236 sporting goods buyers in 18 states. As in the past, we used Bowerman Research to conduct the interviews, under the guidance of Bowerman's survey supervisor, Sadie McMahon. Ms. McMahon has directed surveys on more than two hundred consumer products, and we've learned to place a great deal of confidence in her market insights.

A complete report, including all raw data and verbatim quotes, will be available for downloading on the Engineering Department intranet by the end of next week. However, in light of the project-funding discussions going on this week, we believe the conclusions from the research warrant your immediate attention.

Sadie McMahon's research summary

Consumer interest in the new product code-named Pegasus is decidedly mixed, with 34% expressing little or no interest in the product but 37% expressing moderate to strong interest. The remaining 29% expressed confusion about the basic product concept and were therefore unable to specify their level of interest. The segment expressing little or no interest is not a cause for concern in most cases; few products appeal to the entire consumer market.

However, the portion of the market expressing confusion about the fundamental design of the product is definitely cause for concern. We rarely see more than 10 or 15% confusion at this stage of the design process. A 29% confusion figure suggests that the product design does not fit many consumers' expectations and that it might be difficult to sell if SunStar goes ahead with production.

Our recommendations

At $7.6 million, the development costs for Pegasus are too high to proceed with this much uncertainty. The business case we prepared at the beginning of the project indicated that at least 50% consumer acceptance would be needed in order to generate enough sales to produce an acceptable return on the engineering investment. We would need to convince nearly half of the "confused" segment in order to reach that threshold. We recommend that further development be put on hold until the design can be clarified and validated with another round of consumer testing.

Please contact Darcy at ext. 2354 or Bob at ext. 2360 if you have any questions or concerns.

Emphasizes the skills of the researcher without biasing the readers regarding her conclusions

Alerts the executive committee to a situation that is relevant to another set of decisions occurring simultaneously

Illustrates clearly that the market expert is concerned about the project

States clearly and honestly that the project will not live up to original hopes

FIGURE 1–10
Ethical Communication

dential way to report suspected fraud and other ethical concerns. The people who share their concerns through the program then receive a written response that explains how the situation was resolved.[28] To ensure ongoing compliance with their codes of ethics, many companies also conduct **ethics audits** to monitor ethical progress and to point out any weaknesses that need to be addressed.

Whether or not formal guidelines are in place, every employee has the responsibility to communicate in an ethical manner. Although ethics can be a murky place to navigate, a good place to start is with the law. If something is illegal, you don't do it. No questions asked. Many companies have lawyers on staff or outside attorneys that you can call on for advice when necessary.

However, the law doesn't cover every situation that you'll encounter in your career. Moreover, you may find yourself with a choice that is legal but still unethical. For example,

Document Makeover

IMPROVE THIS MEMO

To practice correcting drafts of actual documents, visit your online course or the access-code protected portion of the Companion Website. Click "Document Makeovers," then click Chapter 1. You will find a memo that contains problems and errors relating to what you've learned in this chapter about overcoming communication barriers in business messages. Use the Final Draft decision tool to create an improved version of the memo. Check the message for an audience-centered approach, ethical communication, efficient communication, and facilitation of feedback.

a debate has been raging for years regarding the labels on dietary supplements. Current laws treat supplements more like food products than drugs and consequently don't require the same degree of disclosure regarding potential safety issues. In one analysis, 89 out of 100 supplement labels failed to provide any information about adverse reactions or side effects, and 85 out of 100 failed to provide clear information about maximum doses. Even though the manufacturers may be following current laws, are they practicing sound ethics?[29]

In the absence of clear legal boundaries or ethical guidelines, ask yourself the following questions about your business communications:[30]

- Have you defined the situation fairly and accurately?

- What is your intention in communicating this message?

- What impact will this message have on the people who receive it, or who might be affected by it?

- Will the message achieve the greatest possible good while doing the least possible harm?

- Will the assumptions you've made change over time? That is, will a decision that seems ethical now seem unethical in the future?

- Are you comfortable with your decision? Would you be embarrassed if it were printed in tomorrow's newspaper or spread across the Internet?

If you can't decide whether a choice is ethical, picture yourself explaining it to someone whose opinion you value.

If all else fails, think about a person whom you admire and ask yourself what he or she would think of your decision. If you wouldn't be proud to describe your choice to someone you admire and respect—someone whose opinion of you matters—that's a strong signal that you might be making a poor ethical choice.

APPLYING WHAT YOU'VE LEARNED

At the beginning of this chapter, you met Six Apart's Mena Trott in "On the Job: Communicating at Six Apart." Trott is just one of the many real business professionals you'll meet throughout this book—people who successfully handle the same communication challenges you'll face on the job. Each chapter opens with one of these slice-of-life vignettes, and as you read through each chapter, think about the person and the company highlighted in the vignette. Become familiar with the various concepts presented in the chapter, and imagine how they might apply to the featured scenario.

At the end of each chapter, you'll take part in an innovative simulation called "On the Job: Solving Communication Dilemmas." You'll play the role of a person working in the highlighted organization, and you'll face situations you'd encounter on the job. You will be presented with several communication scenarios, each with several possible courses of action. It's up to you to recommend one course of action from each scenario as homework, as teamwork, as material for in-class discussion, or in a host of other ways. These scenarios let you explore various communication ideas and apply the concepts and techniques from the chapter.

Now you're ready for the first simulation. As you tackle each problem, think about the material you covered in this chapter and consider your own experience as a communicator. You'll probably be surprised to discover how much you already know about business communication.

On the Job

SOLVING COMMUNICATION DILEMMAS AT SIX APART

As president of Six Apart, Mena Trott plays a vital role in keeping communication flowing and making sure that everyone receives necessary information by helping employees overcome potential barriers to effective communication. To assist her with a growing workload of internal and external communication tasks, she has recently hired you as an assistant with special responsibilities for communication. Use your knowledge of communication to choose the best response for each of the following situations. Be prepared to explain why your choice is best.

1. One of the reasons for Six Apart's success is its friendly, open style of communication with its customers, even those occasional customers who make unrealistic demands or expect special treatment. Unfortunately, you've learned that some of the customer service representatives have been letting their emotions get in the way when dealing with these difficult customers. Several customers have complained about rude treatment. You're sensitive to the situation because you know that customer service can be a difficult job. However, a reputation for hostile customer service could spell doom for the company, so you need to communicate your concerns immediately. Which of the following sentences would be the best way to begin an e-mail message to the customer service staff?

    a. We must all work harder at serving customers in an efficient, timely manner.
    b. The growing problem of abusive customer communications must stop immediately—after all, without customers, we have no revenue; without revenue, you have no jobs.
    c. Positive customer support is one of our most important competitive advantages, but it has come to management's attention that some of you are ruining the company's reputation by mistreating customers.
    d. Thank you for your continued efforts at supporting our customers; I know this can be a challenging task at times.

2. Six Apart has developed a corporate culture that reflects both the engaging personalities of Ben and Mena Trott and the generally informal "vibe" of the blogosphere. However, as the company continues to grow, new employees bring a variety of communication styles and expectations. In particular, the new accounting manager tends to communicate in a formal, distant style that some company old-timers find off-putting and impersonal. Several of these people have expressed concerns that the new manager "doesn't fit in" even though she's doing a great job otherwise. How should you respond?

    a. Tell these people to stop complaining; the finance manager is doing her job well, and that's what counts.
    b. In a private conversation with the manager, explain the importance of fitting into the corporate culture and give her a four-week deadline to change her style.
    c. In a private conversation with the manager, explain the reasoning behind the company's informal culture and its contribution to the company's success; suggest that she might find her work here more enjoyable if she modifies her approach somewhat.
    d. Allow the manager to continue communicating in the same style; after all, that's her personal style, and it's not up to the company to change it.

3. A false rumor has begun circulating online that Six Apart plans to sell one of its product lines to a competitor and lay off most of the employees who currently work on those products. Trott asks your advice in handling the situation; which of the following would you recommend?

    a. Try to plant a counter-rumor on the online grapevine so that the employees who are worried about their jobs will get the right message the same way they got the wrong one.
    b. Immediately schedule a companywide, in-person meeting to set the record straight, emphasizing to everyone in the firm that Six Apart has no plans to shed that product line.
    c. Post a message on Mena's Corner (her blog on the Six Apart website), setting the record straight and assuring the workforce that all jobs are safe; employees and customers alike are accustomed to getting information from her blog, so it's the right way to communicate this message.
    d. Ignore the rumor. Like all false rumors, it will eventually die out.

4. As Microsoft, Google, and other major companies join the market for blogging software and services, Six Apart is forced to lower its prices to remain competitive. Unfortunately, lower prices mean the company will have to lower its operating costs if it is to remain profitable, and employee salaries are the single biggest cost. The management team has decided to enact a 10 percent salary reduction for the next six months and then reevaluate the company's financial health at that point. However, some of the executives are convinced that the salary reductions will have to continue for a year at least—and perhaps even be permanent. In light of this knowledge, which of the following communication strategies would best balance the needs of the company and the needs of the employees?

    a. Tell employees that the 10 percent pay cut will last six months, without implying that it could last longer or even be permanent—if employees worry that their income could be reduced permanently,

they'll start looking for other jobs now, which will be a big drain on worker productivity and make the financial situation even worse.
b. Tell employees that the 10 percent pay cut is *scheduled* to last six months, leaving open the possibility that it could last longer without stating so.
c. Explain that the pay reduction is likely to be permanent, even if you're not sure that will be the case; it's better to give employees the worst possible news, then offer a pleasant surprise if the situation works out more favorably than expected.
d. Tell employees that the pay cut will last for six months, at which point the management team will evaluate the situation and decide if the cut needs to be extended beyond that. Explain that you'd like to be able to provide more solid information, but the uncertainties in the market make that unrealistic. The best that you can do is to tell employees everything you know—and don't know.

Learning Objectives Checkup

Assess your understanding of the principles in this chapter by reading each learning objective and studying the accompanying exercises. For fill-in items, write the missing text in the blank provided; for multiple choice items, circle the letter of the correct answer. You can check your responses against the answer key on page AK-1.

Objective 1.1: Explain why effective communication is important to your success in today's business environment.
1. Your ability to communicate can help your company
   a. Become more efficient
   b. Increase quality
   c. Improve responsiveness
   d. Become more innovative
   e. Do all of the above
2. As your career advances and you achieve positions of greater responsibility with an organization, your communication skills will
   a. Become less important because you will delegate these tasks
   b. Become more important because you will communicate about increasingly important matters to larger and larger audiences
   c. Remain as important as they were during the early stages of your career

Objective 1.2: Identify seven communication skills that successful employers expect from their employees.
3. Which of the following skills did the chapter identify as those that employers are likely to expect?
   a. Organizing ideas and information
   b. Programming HTML webpages
   c. Designing graphics for reports and websites
   d. Expressing and presenting ideas coherently and persuasively
   e. Training other employees
   f. Using communication technologies
   g. Communicating in at least three languages
   h. Communicating in an ethical manner

Objective 1.3: Describe the five characteristics of effective business communication.
4. Effective business messages are
   a. Entertaining, blunt, and persuasive
   b. Practical, objective, concise, clear, and persuasive
   c. Personal, clear, and challenging
5. Why is it important for business messages to clearly state expectations regarding who is responsible for doing what in response to the message?
   a. To make sure other employees don't avoid their responsibilities
   b. To make sure that the person who sent the message isn't criticized if important tasks don't get completed
   c. To eliminate confusion by letting each affected person know what his or her specific responsibilities are

Objective 1.4: List six factors that make business communication unique.
6. How has teamwork affected business communication in recent years?
   a. Businesses have decided that team-based communication is inefficient, and most companies have stopped using teams.
   b. Businesses increasingly rely on teams, but most companies have communication specialists who are responsible for communication within each team.
   c. Businesses increasingly rely on teams, and they expect every member of a team to be able to communicate effectively in a team setting.
   d. Innovative businesses use blogs as the primary means of communicating in teams.
7. The evolution toward flatter organizational structures is affecting communication by
   a. Reducing the workload of upper managers by reducing the number of messages they receive
   b. Reducing the number of layers of management
   c. Giving employees more responsibility for communication
   d. Slowing down business decisions and processes

8. Which of the following is a common barrier to successful communication?
   a. Distractions
   b. Information overload
   c. Perceptual differences
   d. All of the above
9. Successful companies tend to view workforce diversity as
   a. A legally mandated requirement
   b. An opportunity to learn more about markets and communicate more effectively with various market segments
   c. An unavoidable cost of doing business
   d. A reason to outsource more business functions in order to reduce the confusion created by diversity
10. Which of the following is the most accurate characterization of current business use of communication technology?
    a. Companies can't afford to waste money on new technology, so few have adopted e-mail, instant messaging, blogs, and other tools that many consumers use.
    b. Only large companies use technologies such as e-mail and websites.
    c. Technology affects virtually every aspect of business communication today.
    d. The use of technology always improves the effectiveness of communication.

Objective 1.5: Describe five strategies for communicating more effectively on the job.

11. An audience-centered approach to communication
    a. Starts with the assumption that the audience is always right
    b. Improves the effectiveness of communication by focusing on the information needs of the audience
    c. Is generally a waste of time because it doesn't accommodate the needs of the sender
    d. Always simplifies the tasks involved in planning and creating messages
12. Constructive feedback focuses on _____ rather than criticism.
13. Sensitivity to business etiquette
    a. Reduces the chance of interpersonal blunders that might negatively affect communication

b. Is considered by most companies to be a waste of time in today's fast-paced markets
c. Is now legally required in all 50 states
d. Always increases the cost of business communication

Objective 1.6: Explain three strategies for using communication technology successfully.

14. Successful users of business communication technology make sure that it _____ the communication effort, rather than overwhelming or disrupting it.
15. Learning how to use communication technologies effectively
    a. Helps you focus on communicating rather than on the tool being used
    b. Forces you to focus on the tool, rather than on the communication process
    c. Is a waste of time for anyone with top-management aspirations
    d. Is no longer necessary
16. Reconnecting frequently with colleagues and customers in person
    a. Is widely considered an inappropriate use of time, given all the electronic options now available
    b. Is frowned on by successful managers
    c. Is critical because it helps ensure that technology doesn't hinder human interaction

Objective 1.7: Discuss the importance of ethics in business communication, and differentiate between ethical dilemmas and ethical lapses.

17. Ethical communication
    a. Is the same thing as legal communication
    b. Costs more because there are so many rules to consider
    c. Is important only for companies that sell to consumers, rather than to other businesses
    d. Is important because communication is the public face of a company
18. An ethical _____ exists when a person is faced with two conflicting but ethical choices; an ethical _____ occurs when a person makes an unethical choice.

Apply Your Knowledge

1. Why do you think good communication in an organization improves employee attitudes and performance? Explain briefly.
2. Is it possible for companies to be too dependent on communication technology? Explain briefly.
3. Would written or spoken messages be more susceptible to noise? Why?
4. As a manager, how can you impress on your employees the importance of strong business ethics when dealing with colleagues, customers, and the general public?

5. **Ethical Choices** Because of your excellent communication skills, your boss always asks you to write his reports for him. When you overhear the CEO complimenting him on his logical organization and clear writing style, he responds as if he'd written all those reports himself. What kind of ethical choice does this response represent? What can you do in this situation? Briefly explain your solution and your reasoning.

Practice Your Knowledge

DOCUMENT FOR ANALYSIS

Read the following document, then (1) analyze whether the document is effective or ineffective communication (be sure to explain why); and (2) revise the document so that it follows this chapter's guidelines.

It has come to my attention that many of you are lying on your time cards. If you come in late, you should not put 8:00 on your card. If you take a long lunch, you should not put 1:00 on your time card. I will not stand for this type of cheating. I simply have no choice but to institute an employee monitoring system. Beginning next Monday, video cameras will be installed at all entrances to the building, and your entry and exit times will be logged each time you use electronic key cards to enter or leave.

Anyone who is late for work or late coming back from lunch more than three times will have to answer to me. I don't care if you had to take a nap or if you girls had to shop. This is a place of business, and we do not want to be taken advantage of by slackers who are cheaters to boot.

It is too bad that a few bad apples always have to spoil things for everyone.

Exercises

For active links to all web sites discussed in this chapter, visit this text's website at **www.prenhall.com/thill**. Locate your book and click on its Companion Website link. Then select Chapter 1, and click on "Featured Websites." Locate the name of the page or the URL related to the material in the text. Please note that links to sites that have been removed from the web after publication of the book will be removed from the Featured Websites section.

1.1 **Effective Business Communication: Understanding the Difference** Bring to class a sales letter that you received in the mail or via e-mail. Comment on how well the communication
   a. provides practical information
   b. gives facts rather than impressions
   c. clarifies and condenses information
   d. states precise responsibilities
   e. persuades others and offers recommendations

1.2 **Internal Communication: Planning the Flow** For the following tasks, identify the necessary direction of communication (downward, upward, horizontal), suggest an appropriate type of communication (casual conversation, formal interview, meeting, workshop, web conference, instant message, newsletter, memo, bulletin board notice, and so on), and briefly explain your suggestion.
   a. As personnel manager, you want to announce details about this year's company picnic.
   b. As director of internal communication, you want to convince top management of the need for a company newsletter.
   c. As production manager, you want to make sure that both the sales manager and the finance manager receive your scheduling estimates.
   d. As marketing manager, you want to help employees understand the company's goals and its attitudes toward workers.

1.3 **Communication Networks: Formal or Informal?** An old college friend phoned you out of the blue to say, "Truth is, I had to call you. You'd better keep this under your hat, but when I heard my company was buying you guys out, I was dumbfounded. I had no idea that a company as large as yours could sink so fast. Your group must be in pretty bad shape over there!" Your stomach suddenly turned queasy, and you felt a chill go up your spine. You'd heard nothing about any buyout, and before you could even get your college friend off the phone, you were wondering what you should do. Of the following, choose one course of action and briefly explain your choice.
   a. Contact your CEO directly and relate what you've heard.
   b. Ask co-workers whether they've heard anything about a buyout.

   c. Discuss the phone call confidentially with your immediate supervisor.

   d. Keep quiet about the whole thing (there's nothing you can do about the situation anyway).

1.4 **Ethical Choices** In less than a page, explain why you think each of the following is or is not ethical.

   a. Keeping quiet about a possible environmental hazard you've just discovered in your company's processing plant

   b. Overselling the benefits of instant messaging to your company's management; they never seem to understand the benefits of technology, so you believe that stretching the truth just a bit is the only way to convince them to make the right choice

   c. Telling an associate and close friend that she'd better pay more attention to her work responsibilities or management will fire her

   d. Recommending the purchase of unnecessary equipment to use up your allocated funds before the end of the fiscal year so that your budget won't be cut next year

1.5 **The Changing Workplace: Personal Expression at Work** Blogging has become a popular way for employees to communicate with customers and other parties outside the company. In some cases, employee blogs have been quite beneficial for both companies and their customers by providing helpful information and "putting a human face" on other formal and imposing corporations. However, in some other cases, employees have been fired for posting information that their employers said was inappropriate. One particular area of concern is criticism of the company or individual managers. Should employees be allowed to criticize their employers in a public form such as a blog? In a brief e-mail message, argue for or against company policies that prohibit any critical information in employee blogs.

1.6 **Internet** Cisco is a leading manufacturer of equipment for the Internet and corporate networks and has developed a code of ethics that it expects employees to abide by. Visit the company's website at www.cisco.com and find the Code of Conduct. In a brief paragraph, describe three specific examples of things you could do that would violate these provisions; then list at least three opportunities that Cisco provides its employees to report ethics violations or ask questions regarding ethical dilemmas.

1.7 **Communication Etiquette** Potential customers frequently visit your production facility before making purchase decisions. You and the people who report to you in the sales department have received extensive training in etiquette issues because you deal with high-profile clients so frequently. However, the rest of the workforce has not received such training, and you worry that someone might inadvertently say or do something that would offend one of these potential customers. In a two-paragraph e-mail, explain to the general manager why you think anyone who might come in contact with customers should receive basic etiquette training.

1.8 **Ethical Choices** Knowing that you have numerous friends throughout the company, your boss relies on you for feedback concerning employee morale and other issues affecting the staff. She recently approached you and asked you to start reporting any behavior that might violate company polices, from taking office supplies home to making personal long-distance calls. List the issues you'd like to discuss with her before you respond to her request.

1.9 **Formal Communication: Self-Introduction** Write a memo or prepare an oral presentation introducing yourself to your instructor and your class. Include such things as your background, interests, achievements, and goals. If you write a memo, keep it under one page, and use Figure 1–3 as a model for the format. If you prepare an oral presentation, plan to speak for no more than 2 minutes.

1.10 **Teamwork** Your boss has asked your work group to research and report on corporate child-care facilities. Of course, you'll want to know who (besides your boss) will be reading your report. Working with two team members, list four or five other things you'll want to know about the situation and about your audience before starting your research. Briefly explain why each of the items on your list is important.

1.11 **Communication Process: Analyzing Miscommunication** Use the six phases of the communication process to analyze a miscommunication you've recently had with a co-worker, supervisor, classmate, teacher, friend, or family member. What idea were you trying to share? How did you encode and transmit it? Did the receiver get the message? Did the receiver correctly decode the message? How do you know? Based on your analysis, identify and explain the barriers that prevented your successful communication in this instance.

1.12 **Ethical Choices** You've been given the critical assignment of selecting the site for your company's new plant. After months of negotiations with landowners, numerous cost calculations, and investments in ecological, social, and community impact studies, you are about to recommend building the new plant on the Lansing River site. Now, just 15 minutes before your big presentation to top management, you discover a possible mistake in your calculations: Site-purchase costs appear to be $500,000 more than you calculated, nearly 10 percent over budget. You don't have time to recheck all your figures, so you're tempted to just go ahead with your recommendation and ignore any discrepancies. You're worried that management won't approve this purchase if you can't present a clean, unqualified solution. You also know that many projects run over their original estimates, so you can probably work the extra cost into the budget later. On your way to the meeting room, you make your final decision. In a few paragraphs, explain the decision you made.

1.13 **Communication Etiquette** In group meetings, some of your colleagues have a habit of interrupting and arguing with the speaker, taking credit for ideas that aren't theirs, and criticizing ideas they don't agree with.

You're the newest person in the group and not sure if this is accepted behavior in this company, but it concerns you both personally and professionally. Should you adopt their behavior or stick with your own communication style, even though your quiet, respectful approach might limit your career potential? In two paragraphs, explain the pros and cons of both approaches.

Expand Your Knowledge

LEARNING MORE ON THE WEB

CHECK OUT THESE RESOURCES AT THE BUSINESS WRITER'S FREE LIBRARY
www.mapnp.org/library/commskls/cmm_writ.htm

The Business Writer's Free Library is a terrific resource for business communication material. Categories of information include basic composition skills, basic writing skills, correspondence, reference material, and general resources and advice. Log on and read about the most common errors in English, become a word detective, ask Miss Grammar, review samples of common forms of correspondence, fine-tune your interpersonal skills, join a newsgroup, and more. Follow the links and improve your effectiveness as a business communicator.

ACTIVITIES

It takes plenty of practice and hard work to become an effective communicator. Start now by logging on to the Business Writer's Free Library and expand your knowledge of the topics discussed in this chapter.

1. How do the objectives of professional writing differ from the objectives of composition and literature?

2. What is the purpose of feedback?
3. What are some basic guidelines for giving feedback?

EXPLORING THE WEB ON YOUR OWN

Review these chapter-related websites on your own to learn more about achieving communication success in the workplace.

1. Netiquette Home Page, www.albion.com/netiquette/index.html. Learn the dos and don'ts of online communication at this site, then take the Netiquette Quiz.

2. The Information and Communication Technology tutorial provided by Resource Discovery Network in Great Britain, www.vts.rdn.ac.uk, offers a free tutorial to improve your Internet skills (look under "Internet for Further Education"). Learn helpful techniques for searching the Internet, figure out what you can trust and what you can't, and find out how to use the Internet in your work.

3. 101 Best Web Sites for Writers, at www.writersdigest.com, points the way to great search engines and general reference sites. While aimed primarily at professional writers, the list has something to offer all business communicators. The site list is updated every year, so be sure to select the current year's list.

Learn Interactively

INTERACTIVE STUDY GUIDE

Visit www.prenhall.com/thill, then locate your book and click on its Companion Website link. Select Chapter 1 to take advantage of the interactive "Chapter Quiz" to test your knowledge of chapter concepts. Receive instant feedback on whether you need additional studying. Also, visit the "Study Hall" where you'll find an abundance of valuable resources that will help you succeed in this course.

PEAK PERFORMANCE GRAMMAR AND MECHANICS

If your instructor has required the use of "Peak Performance Grammar and Mechanics," either in your online course or on CD, you can improve your skill with nouns by using the "Peak Performance Grammar and Mechanics" module. (Mechanics are basic style issues such as capitalization, spelling, and numbers.) Click "Nouns and Pronouns." Take the Pretest to determine whether you have any weak areas. Then review those areas in the Refresher Course. Take the Follow-Up Test to check your grasp of nouns and pronouns. For an extra challenge or advanced practice, take the Advanced Test. Finally, for additional reinforcement, go to the "Improve Your Grammar, Mechanics, and Usage" section that follows, and complete those exercises.

Improve Your Grammar, Mechanics, and Usage

The following exercises help you improve your knowledge of and power over English grammar, mechanics, and usage. Turn to the Handbook of Grammar, Mechanics, and Usage at the end of this textbook and review all of Section 1.1 (Nouns). Then look at the following 10 items. Underline the preferred choice within each set of parentheses. (Answers to these exercises appear on page AK-3.)

1. She remembered placing that report on her (bosses, boss's) desk.
2. We mustn't follow their investment advice like a lot of (sheep, sheeps).
3. Jones founded the company back in the early (1990's, 1990s).
4. Please send the (Joneses, Jones') a dozen of the following: (stopwatchs, stopwatches), canteens, and headbands.
5. Our (attorneys, attornies) will talk to the group about incorporation.
6. Make sure that all (copys, copies) include the new addresses.
7. Ask Jennings to collect all (employee's, employees') donations for the Red Cross drive.
8. Charlie now has two (sons-in-law, son-in-laws) to help him with his two online (business's, businesses).
9. Avoid using too many (parentheses, parenthesises) when writing your reports.
10. Follow President (Nesses, Ness's) rules about what constitutes a (weeks, week's) work.

For additional exercises focusing on nouns, go to www.prenhall.com/thill, then locate your text and click on its Companion Website link. Click on Chapter 1, click on "Additional Exercises to Improve Grammar, Mechanics and Usage," then click on "1. Possessive nouns" or "2. Antecedents."

Chapter 2

Communicating in Teams and Mastering Listening and Nonverbal Communication

Learning Objectives

AFTER STUDYING THIS CHAPTER, YOU WILL BE ABLE TO

1 Highlight the advantages and disadvantages of working in teams

2 Outline an effective approach to team communication

3 Explain how group dynamics can affect team effectiveness

4 Discuss the role of etiquette in team settings, both in the workplace and in social settings

5 Describe how meeting technologies can help participants communicate more successfully

6 Describe the listening process and explain how good listeners overcome barriers at each stage of the process

7 Clarify the importance of nonverbal communication and briefly describe six categories of nonverbal expression

On the Job

COMMUNICATING AT THE CONTAINER STORE

SOLID TEAMWORK + EFFECTIVE COMMUNICATION = A GREAT SHOPPING EXPERIENCE

Let's face it: frontline jobs in retail don't have the greatest reputation. For employees, these positions often combine low pay with high stress, leading to rapid burnout and frequent turnover. From a customer's perspective, retail employees seem to fall into two categories: poorly trained and poorly motivated rookies or aggressive sellers who seem more intent on getting their commissions than helping customers.

What if you wanted to shatter expectations by creating a shopping environment that is a pleasant, welcome experience for both employees and customers?

This is the challenge Garrett Boone and Kip Tindell set for themselves when they opened their first retail operation, The Container Store in Dallas, Texas, with the ambition to be the "best retail store in the United States." The chain carries a staggering array of containers, filing systems, hooks, hangers, baskets, and other items that help customers organize their lives, and store employees are expected to help customers assemble storage solutions for everything from tax records to DVDs.

As millions of frustrated consumers know all too well, though, delivering great customer service isn't easy. The Container Store manages to do so through respect for employees, open communication, and a structure that promotes teamwork over individual competition.

When selecting new employees, for instance, the company engages in a comprehensive interviewing and selection process to find the perfect person for each position, driven by the belief that one great employee equals three good ones. At The Container

Daily "huddles" at The Container Store, informal meetings among team members, reinforce company values and let people exchange important information.

Store, a great employee is self-motivated, team-oriented, and passionate about customer service.

That emphasis on teamwork is reinforced twice a day, before opening and after closing, through a meeting called "the huddle." Similar to a huddle in football, it helps to give everyone a common purpose: set goals, share information, boost morale, and bond as a team. Morning sessions feature spirited discussions of sales goals and product applications and may include a chorus of "Happy Birthday" for celebrating team members. Evening huddles include more team building and friendly competitions, such as guessing the daily sales figures. Team-building efforts are further encouraged by participation in community outreach activities, such as school supply drives, and through purely recreational activities dreamed up by the employees on the Fun Committee.

Through a commitment to teamwork and effective communication, The Container Store paves the way for its employees to deliver great customer service. People outside the company are starting to notice, too. The Container Store has become a consistent winner in such nationwide forums as the annual Performance Through People Award, presented by Northwestern University, and *Fortune* magazine's annual list of The 100 Best Companies to Work For. Tindell believes that full, open communication with employees takes courage but says, "The only way that people feel really, really a part of something is if they know everything."[1]

www.containerstore.com

37

IMPROVING YOUR PERFORMANCE IN TEAMS

Team members have a shared mission and are collectively responsible for their work.

You may never work in a retail operation such as The Container Store, but chances are quite good that your career will involve working in teams and other group situations that will put your communication skills to the test. A **team** is a unit of two or more people who share a mission and the responsibility for working to achieve their goal. However, not all groups in an organization qualify as teams. For example, if the various employees in your department were working on separate projects with individual goals, they would not be considered a team.[2]

Organizations establish several types of teams, and each type may communicate a little differently. Companies can create *formal teams* that become part of the organization's structure, or they can establish *informal teams,* which aren't part of the formal organization but are created to solve a problem, work on a specific activity, or encourage employee participation. Some teams stay together for years; others may meet their goals in just a few days and then disband.

Two popular types of informal teams are problem-solving teams and task forces.

Problem-solving teams and **task forces** are informal teams that assemble to resolve specific issues and then disband once their goal has been accomplished. Such teams are often *cross-functional,* pulling together people from a variety of departments with different areas of expertise and responsibility. The resulting diversity of opinions and interests can lead to tensions that highlight the need for effective communication. For instance, in a team charged with making a product more competitive in the marketplace, a representative from the sales department might advocate lowering the price, but someone from accounting might resist such a move because doing so would lower the profit margin. In turn, both of these team members might pressure the manufacturing department to lower the production cost so that the product could be sold at a lower price without sacrificing profits. The manufacturing specialist might then counter that the product is already being built as inexpensively as possible and suggest that the sales department isn't doing an adequate job of selling it. Balancing these competing interests without letting them boil over into personal animosity requires skill at listening, speaking, and writing.

Committees are formal teams that usually have a long life span and can become a permanent part of the organizational structure. Committees typically deal with regularly recurring tasks. For example, an executive committee may meet monthly to plan strategy and review results, and a grievance committee may be formed as a permanent resource for handling employee complaints and concerns.

Effective communication is essential to every aspect of team performance.

Whether the task is to write reports, give oral presentations, produce a product, solve a problem, or investigate an opportunity, you and your fellow team members must be able to communicate effectively with each other and with people outside your team. As Chapter 1 points out, this ability often requires taking on additional responsibility for communication: sharing information with team members, listening carefully to their inputs, and crafting messages that reflect the team's collective ideas and opinions.

Advantages and Disadvantages of Teams

Teams are a popular form of organization in business today and when they are successful, they improve productivity, creativity, employee involvement, and even job security.[3] Teams are often at the core of **participative management,** the effort to involve employees in the company's decision making. Some companies even base pay raises and promotions on an employee's effectiveness as a team player.

To be an effective collaborator in a team setting, you and your colleagues should recognize that each individual brings valuable assets, knowledge, and skills to the team. Strong collaborators are willing to exchange information, examine issues, and work through conflicts that arise. They trust each other, working toward the greater good of the team and organization rather than focusing on personal agendas.[4] The most effective teams have a clear sense of purpose, communicate openly and honestly, reach decisions by consensus, think creatively, and know how to resolve conflict.[5] Learning these team skills takes time and practice, so U.S. companies now teach teamwork more frequently than any other aspect of business.[6]

In contrast, unsuccessful teamwork can waste time and money, generate lower-quality work, and frustrate both managers and employees alike. One of the most common reasons for failure is poor communication, particularly when teams have to operate across cultures, countries, and time zones.[7]

Teams can play a vital role in helping an organization reach its goals, but they are not appropriate for every situation—and even when they are appropriate, companies need to weigh both the advantages and disadvantages of a team-based approach. A successful team can provide a number of advantages:[8]

Companies in fast-moving industries rely on teams to work closely and quickly to solve problems and capitalize on market opportunities.

- **Increased information and knowledge.** By pooling the resources of several individuals, teams have access to more information in the decision-making process.

- **Increased diversity of views.** Team members bring a variety of perspectives to the decision-making process.

- **Increased acceptance of a solution.** Those who participate in making a decision are more likely to support the decision enthusiastically and encourage others to accept it.

> Effective teams can pool knowledge, take advantage of diverse viewpoints, and increase acceptance of solutions the team proposes.

- **Higher performance levels.** Working in teams can unleash new amounts of creativity and energy in workers who share a sense of purpose and mutual accountability. Furthermore, teams fill the individual worker's need to belong to a group, reduce employee boredom, increase feelings of dignity and self-worth, and reduce stress and tension between workers.

Although teamwork has many advantages, it also has a number of potential disadvantages. At their worst, teams are unproductive and frustrating, and they waste everyone's time. This outcome is particularly a risk with standing committees that have outlived their original purpose but continue to meet anyway. Teams need to be aware of and work to counter the following disadvantages:

> Teams need to avoid the negative impact of groupthink, hidden agendas, free riders, and excessive costs.

- **Groupthink.** Like all social structures, business teams can generate tremendous pressures to conform with accepted norms of behavior. **Groupthink** occurs when these peer pressures cause individual team members to withhold contrary or unpopular opinions. The result can be decisions that are worse than ones the team members might have made individually.

- **Hidden agendas.** Some team members may have a **hidden agenda**—private motives that affect the group's interaction. Sam might want to prove that he's more powerful than you, you might be trying to share the risk of making a decision, and Laura might be looking for a chance to postpone doing "real" work. Each person's hidden agenda can detract from the team's effectiveness.

- **Free riders.** Some team members may be **free riders**—those who don't contribute their fair share to the group's activities. Perhaps these members aren't being held individually accountable for their work. Or perhaps they don't believe they'll receive adequate recognition for their individual efforts.

- **Cost.** Still another drawback to teamwork is the high cost of coordinating group activities. Aligning schedules, arranging meetings, and coordinating individual parts of a project can eat up a lot of time and money.

Collaborative Communication

Team presentations and reports can give an organization the opportunity to show off its brightest talent while capitalizing on each person's unique presentation and communication skills. In other words, you can take the collective energy and expertise of the team and create something that transcends what you could do otherwise.[9] However, collaborating on team messages requires special effort.

To begin with, team members coming from different backgrounds may have different work habits or concerns: A technical expert may focus on accuracy and scientific standards, whereas an editor might be more concerned about organization and coherence, and a manager might focus on schedules, cost, and corporate goals. In addition, team members will differ in writing styles and personality traits—two factors that can complicate the creative nature of communication.

To collaborate effectively, everyone involved must be flexible and open to other opinions, focusing on team objectives rather than on individual priorities.[10] Successful writers know that most ideas can be expressed in many ways, so they avoid the "my way is best" attitude. The following guidelines will help you collaborate more successfully on team messages:[11]

Successful collaboration requires a number of steps, from selecting the right partners and agreeing on project goals to establishing clear processes and avoiding writing as a group.

- **Select collaborators carefully.** Choose a combination of people who have the experience, information, and talent needed for each project.

- **Agree on project goals before you start.** Starting without a clear idea of where you hope to finish inevitably leads to frustration and wasted time. Chapter 4 shows you how to plan messages successfully.

- **Give your team time to bond before diving in.** Even if a virtual team doesn't have the opportunity to meet in person, spend at least some of your time online socializing so that people are more comfortable working together.

- **Clarify individual responsibilities.** Since members will be depending on each other, make sure individual responsibilities are clear, including who is supposed to do what and by when.

- **Establish clear processes.** Make sure everyone knows how the work will be done, including checkpoints and decisions to be made along the way. For instance, if the team members will report their progress once a week, make this expectation obvious at the beginning so that everyone will be prepared.

- **Make sure tools and techniques are ready and compatible across the team.** Even minor details such as different versions of software can delay projects. If you plan to use technology for sharing or presenting materials, test the system before work begins.

- **Avoid writing as a group.** The actual composition is the only part of developing team messages that usually does not benefit from group participation. Group writing is often a slow, painful process that delivers bland results. Plan, research, and outline together, but assign the actual writing to one person. If you must divide and share the writing for scheduling reasons, try to have one person do a final pass to ensure a consistent style.

- **Check to see how things are going along the way.** Don't assume everything is working just because you don't hear anything negative. Periodically ask team members how they think the project is going, then fix any problems quickly so they don't derail the team's efforts.

Perhaps more than any other single attribute, effective teams engage in open and honest communication. The culture on such teams encourages discussion and debate. Team members speak openly and honestly, without the threat of anger, resentment, or retribution. They listen to and value feedback from others. As a result, all team members participate. Conversely, members who either don't share valuable information because they don't understand that it's valuable—or worse, withhold information as a way to maintain personal power—can undermine a team's efforts.[12]

Group Dynamics

To accomplish their goals successfully, team members constantly connect with one another. The interactions and processes that take place between the members of a team are called **group dynamics.** Some teams are more effective than others simply because the dynamics of the group facilitate member input and the resolution of differences. To keep things moving forward, productive teams also tend to develop rules that are conducive to business. Often unstated, these rules become group **norms**—informal standards of conduct that members share and that guide member behavior. For example, some teams may develop a casual approach to schedules, with members routinely showing up 10 or 15 minutes late for meetings, while other teams may expect strict adherence to time commitments.

Teams with a strong sense of identity and cohesiveness can develop overly strong expectations for group behavior with little tolerance for deviations from those norms. Such strong identity can lead to higher levels of commitment and performance. Unfortunately, it can also lead to groupthink or make it difficult for new members to fit in. Group dynamics are affected by several factors: the roles that team members assume, the current phase of team development, the team's success in resolving conflict, and its success in overcoming resistance.

> Group dynamics are the interactions and processes that take place in a team.

Assuming Team Roles   Members of a team can play various roles, which fall into three categories (see Table 2–1). Members who assume **self-oriented roles** are motivated mainly to fulfill personal needs, so they tend to be less productive than other members. Far more likely to contribute to team goals are those members who assume **team-maintenance roles** to help everyone work well together, and those who assume **task-facilitating roles** to help solve problems or make decisions.

To a great extent, the roles that you assume in a team depend on whether you joined the group voluntarily or involuntarily and on your status in that group. Your status is determined by many variables, some substantive (expertise, past successes, education) and some superficial (personal attractiveness, age, social background, organizational position). Your status can also change over time, particularly when a team is just starting to form. In most teams, as people try to establish their relative status, an undercurrent of tension can get in the way of the real work. Until roles and status have stabilized, a team may have trouble accomplishing its goals.

> Each member of a group plays a role that affects the outcome of the group's activities.

Allowing for Team Evolution   Teams can rarely jump right to work and start making decisions; you and your fellow team members need time to establish rapport and let natural leadership roles emerge. Experts suggest that teams evolve through a number of phases on their way to becoming productive (see Figure 2–1). One common model identifies five phases:[13]

> Teams typically evolve through five phases: orientation, conflict, brainstorming, emergence, and reinforcement.

1. **Orientation.** Team members socialize, establish their roles, and begin to define their task or purpose.

2. **Conflict.** Team members begin to discuss their positions and become more assertive in establishing their roles. If you and the other members have been carefully selected to represent a variety of viewpoints and expertise, disagreements are a natural part of this phase.

Table 2–1	**TEAM ROLES PEOPLE PLAY**	
Dysfunctional	**Functional**	
Self-Oriented Roles	**Team-Maintenance Roles**	**Task-Facilitating Roles**
Controlling: Dominating others by exhibiting superiority or authority	**Encouraging:** Drawing out other members by showing verbal and nonverbal support, praise, or agreement	**Initiating:** Getting the team started on a line of inquiry
Withdrawing: Retiring from the team either by becoming silent or by refusing to deal with a particular aspect of the team's work	**Harmonizing:** Reconciling differences among team members through mediation or by using humor to relieve tension	**Information giving or seeking:** Offering (or seeking) information relevant to questions facing the team
Attention seeking: Calling attention to oneself and demanding recognition from others	**Compromising:** Offering to yield on a point in the interest of reaching a mutually acceptable decision	**Coordinating:** Showing relationships among ideas, clarifying issues, summarizing what the team has done
Diverting: Focusing the team's discussion on topics of interest to the individual rather than on those relevant to the task		**Procedure setting:** Suggesting decision-making procedures that will move the team toward a goal

3. **Brainstorming.** Team members air all the options and discuss the pros and cons fully. At the end of this phase, members begin to settle on a single solution to the problem.

4. **Emergence.** Team members reach a decision. Consensus is reached when the team finds a solution that is acceptable enough for all members to support (even if they have reservations). This consensus happens only after all members have had an opportunity to communicate their positions and feel that they have been listened to.

5. **Reinforcement.** Group feeling is rebuilt, and the solution is summarized. Members receive their assignments for carrying out the group's decision, and they make arrangements for following up on those assignments.

These phases almost always occur regardless of what task or what type of decision is being considered. (You might also hear the process defined as *forming, storming, norming, performing,* and *adjourning;* this was one of the earliest models of group development.[14]) Moreover, team members naturally use this process, even when they lack experience or training in teamwork.

Resolving Conflict   Conflict is a natural part of any team experience, but conflict isn't necessarily bad. When handled poorly, conflict can lead to complete failure of a group's efforts. However, the right approach to conflict can push the team to better performance.

Conflict can arise for any number of reasons. Team members may believe that they need to compete for money, information, or other resources. Or members may disagree about who is responsible for a specific task (usually the result of poorly defined responsibilities and job boundaries). Various members can also bring ideas that are equally good but incompatible, such as two different solutions to a given problem.

FIGURE 2–1
Phases of Group Development

1. Orientation	**2. Conflict**	**3. Brainstorming**	**4. Emergence**	**5. Reinforcement**
Team members get to know each other and establish roles	Different opinions and perspectives begin to emerge	Team members explore their options and evaluate alternatives	The team reaches a consensus on the chosen decision	Team harmony is reestablished and plans are made to put the decision into action

Also, poor communication can lead to misunderstandings about other team members, and intentionally withholding information can undermine trust. Basic differences in values, attitudes, and personalities may lead to arguments. Power struggles may result when one member questions the authority of another or when people or teams with limited authority attempt to increase their power or exert more influence. Conflict can also arise because individuals or teams are pursuing different goals.[15]

Conflict can be both constructive and destructive to a team's effectiveness. Conflict is constructive if it forces important issues into the open, increases the involvement of team members, and generates creative ideas for the solution to a prob-

Conflict in teams can be either constructive or destructive

lem. Conflict is destructive if it diverts energy from more important issues, destroys the morale of teams or individual team members, or polarizes or divides the team.[16]

Destructive conflict can lead to win-lose or lose-lose outcomes, in which one or both sides lose, to the detriment of the entire team. If you approach conflict with the idea that both sides can satisfy their goals to at least some extent (*win-win strategy*), no one loses. However, for the win-win strategy to work, everybody must believe that (1) it's possible to find a solution that both parties can accept, (2) cooperation is better for the organization than competition, (3) the other party can be trusted, and (4) greater power or status doesn't entitle one party to impose a solution.

One of the first steps to finding a win-win solution is to consider the other party's needs. Find out what is acceptable to the other people on the team. Keep your eyes and ears open; ask questions that will help you understand their needs. Search for mutually satisfactory solutions or compromises whose results are better for the team overall.[17] And remember that both sides can usually get what they want if both are willing to work together. In many cases, the resolution process is chiefly an exchange of opinions and information that gradually leads to a mutually acceptable solution.[18]

Conflict is an inevitable part of working in teams, but effective teams know how to keep destructive conflict from distracting the team from its objectives.

Here are seven measures that can help team members successfully resolve conflict:

- **Proaction.** Deal with minor conflict before it becomes major conflict.
- **Communication.** Get those directly involved in the conflict to participate in resolving it.
- **Openness.** Get feelings out in the open before dealing with the main issues.
- **Research.** Seek factual reasons for the problem before seeking solutions.
- **Flexibility.** Don't let anyone lock into a position before considering other solutions.
- **Fair play.** Don't let anyone avoid a fair solution by hiding behind the rules.
- **Alliance.** Get opponents to fight together against an "outside force" instead of against each other.

Overcoming Resistance   Resistance to change is a particular type of conflict that can affect work in teams. Some of this resistance is clearly irrational, such as when people resist any kind of change, whether it makes sense or not. Sometimes, however, the resistance is perfectly logical. A change might require someone to relinquish authority or give up comfortable ways of doing things. In any event, you can help overcome resistance with calm, reasonable give-and-take:

When you encounter resistance or hostility, try to maintain your composure and address the other person's emotional needs.

- **Express understanding.** Show that you sympathize. You might say, "I can understand that this change might be difficult, and if I were in your position, I might be reluctant myself." Help the other person relax and talk about his or her anxiety so that you have a chance to offer reassurance.[19]

- **Bring resistance out into the open.** When people are noncommittal and silent, they may be tuning you out without even knowing why. Continuing with your argument is futile. Deal directly with the resistance, without being accusing. You might say, "You seem cool to this idea. Have I made some faulty assumptions?" Such questions force people to face and define their resistance.[20]

- **Evaluate others' objections fairly.** Don't simply repeat yourself. Focus on what the other person is expressing, both the words and the feelings. Get the person to open up so that you can understand the basis for the resistance. Others' objections may raise legitimate points that you'll need to discuss, or they may reveal problems that you'll need to minimize.[21]

- **Hold your arguments until the other person is ready for them.** Getting your point across depends as much on the other person's frame of mind as it does on your arguments. You can't assume that a strong argument will speak for itself. By becoming more audience-centered, you will learn to address the other person's emotional needs first.

Etiquette in Team Settings

Etiquette is particularly important in team settings because the ability to get along with teammates is vital to everyone's success. Nobody wants to spend weeks or months working with someone who is rude to colleagues or an embarrassment to the company. Here are some key etiquette points to remember when you're in the workplace and out in public. None of the following material is unique to team settings, of course; it's good advice for all your business efforts.

Attention to basic business etiquette will help your career at every stage.

In the Workplace   Knowing how to behave and how to interact with people in business will help you appear polished, professional, and confident.[22] Understanding business etiquette also helps you put others at ease so that they are comfortable enough to do business with you.[23] Both of these factors—the impression you make on others and your ability to help others feel comfortable—will be major contributors to your career success.

Personal appearance can have considerable impact on your success in business.

For instance, rightly or wrongly, your personal appearance often has considerable impact on your career success. Pay attention to the style of dress where you work and adjust your style to match, particularly if you work with people from diverse backgrounds and age groups. If you're not sure, dress moderately and simply—earn a reputation for what you can *do,* not for what you can wear. Table 2–2 offers some general guidelines on assembling a business wardrobe that's both cost-effective and flexible enough for a wide variety of work situations. Naturally, you'll need to adapt any wardrobe advice for the specific job, company, and industry because expectations vary widely. The financial industries tend to be more formal than high technology, for instance, and sales and executive positions usually come with more formal expectations than staff positions in engineering or manufacturing. Observe others carefully, and don't be afraid to ask for advice if you're not sure.

In addition to your clothing, grooming affects the impression you give others in the workplace. Pay close attention to cleanliness and avoid using products with powerful scents, such as perfumed soaps, colognes, shampoos, and after-shave lotions (many people are bothered by these products, and some are allergic to them). Shampoo frequently, keep hands and nails neatly manicured, use mouthwash and deodorant, and make regular trips to a hair stylist.[24] Some companies have specific policies regarding hairstyles, which you may be expected to follow.[25]

ASSEMBLING A BUSINESS WARDROBE			Table 2–2
1 ***Smooth and Finished (Start with this)***	**2** ***Elegant and Refined (To column 1, add this)***	**3** ***Crisp and Starchy (To column 2, add this)***	**4** ***Up-to-the-Minute Trendy (To column 3, add this)***
1. Wear well-tailored clothing that fits well. 2. Keep buttons, zippers, and hemlines in good repair. 3. Keep shoes shined and in good condition. 4. Make sure the fabrics you wear are clean, are carefully pressed, and do not wrinkle easily. 5. Choose colors that flatter your height, weight, skin tone, and style.	1. Choose form-fitting (but not skin-tight) clothing—not swinging or flowing fabrics, frills, or fussy trimmings. 2. Choose muted tones and soft colors or classics, such as the dark blue suit or the basic black dress. 3. If possible, select a few classic pieces of jewelry (such as a string of pearls or diamond cuff links) for formal occasions.	1. Wear blouses or shirts that are or appear starched. 2. Choose closed top-button shirts or button-down shirt collars, higher-neckline blouses, long sleeves with French cuffs and cuff links. 3. Wear creased trousers or longer skirt hemline. 4. Wear jackets that complement an outfit and lend an air of formality to your appearance. Avoid jackets with more than two tones—one color should dominate.	1. Add trendy clothing items to your wardrobe often. 2. Choose bold colors (but sparingly so that you won't appear garish). 3. Embellish your look with trendy jewelry and hairstyles.

Something as simple as your smile also affects the way people do business with you. When you smile, do so genuinely. A fake smile is obvious because the timing is frequently off and the expression fails to involve all the facial muscles that a genuine smile would.[26] Repeated false smiling may earn you the reputation of being a phony. However, certain occasions require smiling, such as when you're introduced to someone, when you give or receive a compliment, and when you applaud someone's efforts.[27]

Phone skills have a definite impact on your success. Phone calls lack the visual richness of face-to-face conversations, so you have to rely on your attitude and tone of voice to convey confidence and professionalism. When you place phone calls, plan them as carefully as you would plan a meeting. Be ready with relevant questions or information, and schedule calls for times that are convenient for the other party. For example, you usually want to avoid calling first thing in the morning, when many people like to answer e-mail and plan the day. Likewise, avoid calling near the end of the day, when most people are trying to wrap up business and leave the office. Table 2–3 summarizes helpful tips for placing and receiving phone calls in a confident, professional manner.

If you're accustomed to using your cell phone anywhere and everywhere, get ready to change your habits; many companies are putting restrictions on their use. Cell phones are causing so much disruption in the workplace that some senior executives now ban their use in meetings, even going so far as to fine employees whose phones ring during meetings. (The fines are typically donated to charity or used to buy team lunches.) As Ian Campbell of Nucleus Research puts it, "A cell phone has gone from a symbol of status to a device of scorn." Moreover, this problem of wireless interruptions is only going to get worse, with the proliferation of personal digital assistants (PDAs), laptop computers, and other devices with wireless access.[28]

Table 2–3 — QUICK TIPS FOR IMPROVING YOUR PHONE SKILLS

General Tips	Placing Calls	Receiving Calls	Using Voicemail
Use frequent verbal responses that show you're listening ("Oh yes," "I see," "That's right").	Be ready before you call so that you don't waste the other person's time.	Answer promptly and with a smile so that you sound friendly and positive.	When recording your own outgoing message, make it brief and professional.
Increase your volume just slightly to convey your confidence.	Minimize distractions and avoid making noise that could annoy the other party.	Identify yourself and your company (some companies have specific instructions for what to say when you answer).	If you can, record temporary greetings on days when you are unavailable all day so that callers will know you're gone for the day.
Don't speak in a monotone; vary your pitch and inflections so people know you're interested.	Identify yourself and your organization, briefly describe why you're calling, and verify that you've called at a good time.	Establish the needs of your caller by asking, "How may I help you?" If you know the caller's name, use it.	Check your voice mail messages regularly and return all necessary calls within 24 hours.
Slow down when conversing with people whose native language isn't the same as yours.	Don't take up too much time. Speak quickly and clearly, and get right to the point of the call.	If you can, answer questions promptly and efficiently; if you can't help, tell them what you can do for them.	Leave simple, clear messages with your name, number, purpose for calling, and times when you can be reached.
Stay focused on the call throughout; others can easily tell when you're not paying attention.	Close in a friendly, positive manner and double-check all vital information such as meeting times and dates.	If you must forward a call or put someone on hold, explain what you are doing first.	State your name and telephone number slowly so that the other person can easily write them down; repeat both if the other person doesn't know you.
		If you forward a call to someone else, try to speak with that person first to verify that he or she is available and to introduce the caller.	Be careful what you say; most voicemail systems allow users to forward messages to anyone else in the system.
		If you take a message for someone else, be complete and accurate, including the caller's name, number, and organization.	Replay your message before leaving the system to make sure it is clear and complete.

Plan phone calls as carefully as you plan meetings.

In Social Settings From business lunches to industry conferences, you represent your company when you're out in public, so make sure your appearance and actions are appropriate to the situation. First impressions last a long time, so get to know the customs of the culture when you meet new people. In North America, a firm handshake is expected when two people meet, whereas a respectful bow of the head is more appropriate in Japan. If you are expected to shake hands, be aware that the passive "dead fish" handshake creates an extremely negative impression. Also, women and men should shake hands on equal terms; the days of a woman offering just her fingertips are long gone in the business world. If you are physically able, always stand when shaking someone's hand.

When introducing yourself, include a brief description of your role in the company. When introducing two other people, speak both their first and last names clearly, then try to offer some information (perhaps a shared professional interest) to help these two people ease into a conversation.[29] Generally speaking, the lower-ranking person is introduced to the senior-ranking person, without regard to gender.[30] When you're introduced to someone, repeat the person's name as soon as possible. Doing so is both a compliment and a good way to remember it.[31]

Business is often conducted over meals, and knowing the basics of dining etiquette will make you more effective in these situations.[32] Choose foods that are easy to eat; you don't want to wrestle with a lobster while trying to carry on a conversation. If a drink is appropriate, save it for the end of the meal so that you can stay clear and composed. Leave business papers under your chair until entrée plates have been removed; the business aspect of the meal doesn't usually begin until then.

Misuse of mobile phones in restaurants and other public places is a common etiquette blunder. When you use your cell phone in public, you send the message that people around you aren't as important as your call and that you don't respect your caller's privacy.[33] Older colleagues who grew up without cell phones may find them particularly offensive in social settings. If it's not a matter of life and death—literally—wait until you're back in the office.

You represent your company when you're out in public, so etiquette continues to be important.

Business meals are a forum for business, period. Don't get on your soapbox about politics, religion, or any other topic likely to stir up emotions. Some light chatter and questions about personal interests is fine, but don't get too personal. Don't complain about work, avoid profanity, and be careful with humor—a joke that might entertain some people could offend others. In general, learn from co-workers who are respected by customers and colleagues. You'll find that they choose topics carefully, listen with respect, and leave a positive impression with everyone they meet.

Document Makeover

IMPROVE THIS E-MAIL MESSAGE

To practice correcting drafts of actual documents, visit your online course or the access-code protected portion of the Companion Website. Click "Document Makeovers," then click Chapter 2. You will find an e-mail message that contains problems and errors relating to what you've learned in this chapter about communicating in teams. Use the Final Draft decision tool to create an improved version of the e-mail. Check the message for clarity, relevance of topics to meeting participants, proper approach to group collaboration, and communication of meeting etiquette.

MAKING YOUR MEETINGS MORE PRODUCTIVE

Meetings are a primary communication venue for today's businesses, whether held in formal conference rooms, an informal setting such as The Container Store's daily huddles, or on the Internet as *virtual meetings*. Well-run meetings can help you solve problems, develop ideas, and identify opportunities. Much of your workplace communication will occur in small-group meetings; therefore, your ability to contribute to the company and to be recognized for those contributions will depend on your meeting participation skills.

Much of the communication you'll participate in will take place in meetings.

Unfortunately, many meetings are unproductive. In one study, senior and middle managers reported that only 56 percent of their meetings were actually productive and that 25 percent of them could have been replaced by a phone call or a memo.[34] The three most frequently reported problems with meetings are getting off the subject, not having an agenda, and running too long.[35] Given such demoralizing statistics and the high cost of meetings—which can run hundreds or thousands of dollars an hour in lost work time and travel expenses—it's no wonder that companies are focusing on making their meetings more productive. You'll help your company make better use of meetings by preparing carefully, conducting meetings efficiently, and using meeting technologies wisely.

A single poorly run meeting can waste thousands of dollars.

Preparing for Meetings

Careful preparation helps you avoid the two biggest meeting mistakes: (1) holding a meeting when a memo or other message would do the job or (2) holding a meeting without a specific goal in mind. Before you even begin preparing for a meeting, make sure it's truly necessary. Once you're sure, proceed with four preparation tasks:

- **Identify your purpose.** Although many meetings combine purposes, most focus on one of two types: *Informational meetings* involve sharing information and perhaps coordinating action. *Decision-making meetings* involve persuasion, analysis, and problem solving. They often include a brainstorming session, followed by a debate on the alternatives. Moreover, decision-making meetings require that each participant be aware of the nature of the problem and the criteria for its solution. Whatever your purpose, make sure it is clear and clearly communicated to all participants.

To ensure a successful meeting, decide on your purpose ahead of time, select the right participants, choose the time and facility carefully, and set a clear agenda.

- **Select participants for the meeting.** With a clear purpose in mind, it's easier to identify the right participants. If the session is purely informational and one person will do most of the talking, you can invite a large group. *Webcasts* (Chapter 13) are an increasingly popular way to reach large or geographically widespread audiences used for such meetings. For problem-solving and decision-making meetings, invite only those people who are in a direct position to help the meeting reach its objective. The more participants, the more comments and confusion you're likely to get, and the longer the meeting will take. However, make sure you invite all the key decision-makers, or your meeting will fail to satisfy its purpose.

- **Choose the time and the facility.** For working sessions, morning meetings are usually more productive than afternoon sessions. Also, consider the seating arrangements: Are rows of chairs suitable, or do you need a conference table or some other setting? Plus, give some attention to details such as room temperature, lighting, ventilation, acoustics, and refreshments; any of these seemingly minor details can make or break a meeting.

- **Set the agenda.** The success of any meeting depends on the preparation of the participants. Distribute a carefully written agenda to participants, giving them enough time to prepare as needed. A typical agenda format (see Figure 2–2) may seem overly formal, but it will help you start on time and stay on track. A productive agenda answers three key questions: (1) What do we need to do in this meeting to accomplish our goals? (2) What issues will be of greatest importance to all participants? (3) What information must be available in order to discuss these issues?[36] In addition to improving productivity, this level of agenda detail shows respect for participants and the other demands on their time.

Leading and Participating in Meetings

Everyone shares the responsibility for successful meetings.

Everyone in a meeting shares the responsibility for keeping the meeting productive and making it successful. If you're the designated leader of a meeting, however, you have an extra degree of responsibility and accountability. To ensure productive meetings, be sure to do the following:

- **Keep the meeting on track.** A good meeting draws out the best ideas and information the group has to offer. Good leaders occasionally guide, mediate, probe, stimulate, and summarize, but mostly they encourage participants to share. Experience will help you recognize when to push the group forward, and when to step back and let people talk. If the meeting lags, you'll need to ask questions to encourage participation. Conversely, there will be times when you have no choice but to cut off discussion in order to stay on schedule.

- **Follow agreed-upon rules.** Business meetings run the gamut from informal to extremely formal, complete with detailed rules for speaking, proposing new items to discuss, voting on proposals, and so on. The larger the meeting, the more formal you'll need to be to maintain order. Formal meetings use **parliamentary pro-**

AGENDA

PLANNING COMMITTEE MEETING

Monday, October 23, 2006
10:00 A.M. to 11:00 A.M.

Executive Conference Room

		Person	Proposed Time
I.	Call to Order		
II.	Roll Call		
III.	Approval of Agenda		
IV.	Approval of Minutes from Previous Meeting		
V.	Chairperson's Report on Site Selection Progress		
VI.	Subcommittee Reports		
	a. New Markets	Alan	5 minutes
	b. New Products	Jennifer	5 minutes
	c. Finance	Craig	5 minutes
VII.	Old Business—Pricing Policy for New Products	Terry	10 minutes
VIII.	New Business		
	a. Carson and Canfield Data on New Product Sales	Sarah	10 minutes
	b. Restructuring of Product Territories Due to New Product Introductions	Edith	10 minutes
IX.	Announcements		
X.	Adjournment		

FIGURE 2–2
Typical Meeting Agenda

cedure, a time-tested method for planning and running effective meetings. The best-known guide to this procedure is *Roberts Rules of Order.* Whatever system of rules you employ, make sure everyone is clear about the expectations.

- **Encourage participation.** As the meeting gets under way, you'll discover that some participants are too quiet and others are too talkative. The quiet participants might be shy, they might be expressing disagreement or resistance, or they might be answering e-mail or instant messages on their laptop computers. Draw them out by asking for their input on issues that particularly pertain to them. For the overly talkative, simply say that time is limited and others need to be heard from.

- **Participate actively.** If you're a meeting participant, try to contribute to both the subject of the meeting and the smooth interaction of the participants. Use your listening skills and powers of observation to size up the interpersonal dynamics of the people; then adapt your behavior to help the group achieve its goals. Speak up if you have something useful to say, but don't monopolize the discussion.

- **Close effectively.** At the conclusion of the meeting, verify that the objectives have been met; if not, arrange for follow-up work as needed. Either summarize

✓ CHECKLIST: Improving Meeting Productivity

A. Prepare carefully

✓ Make sure the meeting is necessary.
✓ Decide on your purpose.
✓ Select participants carefully.
✓ Choose the time and facility.
✓ Set the agenda.

B. Lead effectively and participate fully

✓ Keep the meeting on track.
✓ Follow agreed-upon rules.
✓ Encourage participation.
✓ Participate actively.
✓ Close effectively.

the general conclusion of the discussion or list the actions to be taken. Make sure all participants agree on the outcome and give people a chance to clear up any misunderstandings.

To review the tasks that contribute to productive meetings, refer to "Checklist: Improving Meeting Productivity."

For formal meetings, it's good practice to appoint one person to record the *minutes,* a summary of the important information presented and the decisions made during a meeting. In smaller or informal meetings, attendees often make their own notes on their copies of the agenda. In either case, a clear record of the decisions made and the people responsible for follow-up action is essential.

If your company doesn't have a specific format for minutes, follow the generic format shown in Figure 2–3. Key elements include a list of those present and a list of those who were invited but didn't attend, followed by the times the meeting started and ended, all major decisions reached at the meeting, all assignments of tasks to meeting participants, and all subjects that were deferred to a later meeting. In addition, the minutes objectively summarize important discussions, noting the names of those who contributed major points. Outlines, subheadings, and lists help organize the minutes, and additional documentation (such as tables or charts submitted by meeting participants) are noted in the minutes and attached. Many companies now post meeting minutes on an intranet site for easy reference. Whichever method you use, make sure that responsibilities are clear so that all issues raised at the meeting will be addressed.

Using Meeting Technologies

Virtual meeting technologies connect people spread around the country or around the world.

Not all teams have the luxury of meeting face to face, as employees at The Container Store do. Fortunately, geographically dispersed teams have plenty of options for staying in close contact. In recent years, the high cost of travel, loss of valuable work time, increased security concerns, and growing reliance on global workforces and partnerships have all stimulated a number of advances in meeting technologies. Instead of hopping on a plane and spending a couple of days and a couple of thousand dollars for a meeting, you can now hop on the Internet and have that meeting for a fraction of the cost and time commitment. The rise of these technologies has spurred the emergence of **virtual teams,** whose members work in different locations and interact electronically through **virtual meetings.** People may work together for months or years and never meet face to face. At times, technology replaces meetings entirely, such as when team members use e-mail or instant messaging to interact over the course of several hours or days, rather than meet online or over the phone at a specific time. One of the newest virtual tools is *online brainstorming,* in which companies conduct "idea campaigns" to generate new ideas from people across the organization. For example, the chemical manufacturing division of W. R. Grace has generated more than 70 new product ideas and more than 60 process improvements through online brainstorming.[37] Another new twist is *wiki* (the Hawaiian word for "quick"), a website technology

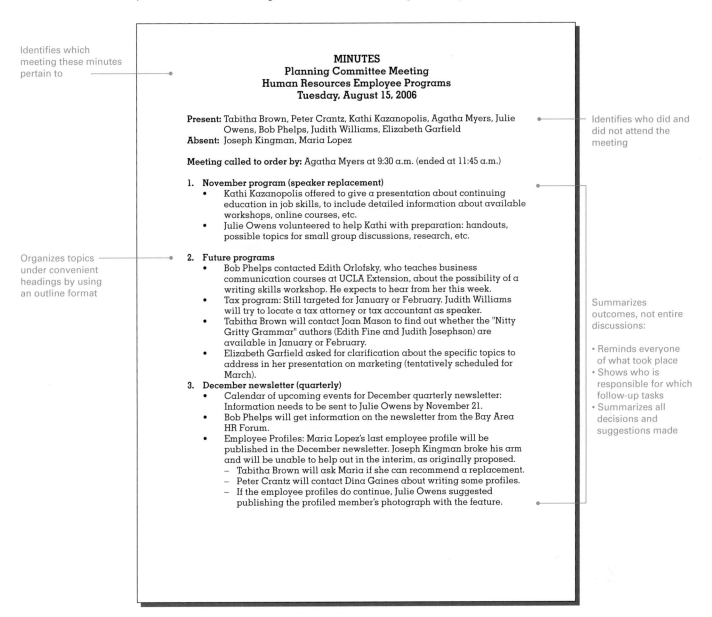

Identifies which meeting these minutes pertain to

Identifies who did and did not attend the meeting

Organizes topics under convenient headings by using an outline format

Summarizes outcomes, not entire discussions:

• Reminds everyone of what took place
• Shows who is responsible for which follow-up tasks
• Summarizes all decisions and suggestions made

MINUTES
Planning Committee Meeting
Human Resources Employee Programs
Tuesday, August 15, 2006

Present: Tabitha Brown, Peter Crantz, Kathi Kazanopolis, Agatha Myers, Julie Owens, Bob Phelps, Judith Williams, Elizabeth Garfield
Absent: Joseph Kingman, Maria Lopez

Meeting called to order by: Agatha Myers at 9:30 a.m. (ended at 11:45 a.m.)

1. **November program (speaker replacement)**
   • Kathi Kazanopolis offered to give a presentation about continuing education in job skills, to include detailed information about available workshops, online courses, etc.
   • Julie Owens volunteered to help Kathi with preparation: handouts, possible topics for small group discussions, research, etc.

2. **Future programs**
   • Bob Phelps contacted Edith Orlofsky, who teaches business communication courses at UCLA Extension, about the possibility of a writing skills workshop. He expects to hear from her this week.
   • Tax program: Still targeted for January or February. Judith Williams will try to locate a tax attorney or tax accountant as speaker.
   • Tabitha Brown will contact Joan Mason to find out whether the "Nitty Gritty Grammar" authors (Edith Fine and Judith Josephson) are available in January or February.
   • Elizabeth Garfield asked for clarification about the specific topics to address in her presentation on marketing (tentatively scheduled for March).

3. **December newsletter (quarterly)**
   • Calendar of upcoming events for December quarterly newsletter: Information needs to be sent to Julie Owens by November 21.
   • Bob Phelps will get information on the newsletter from the Bay Area HR Forum.
   • Employee Profiles: Maria Lopez's last employee profile will be published in the December newsletter. Joseph Kingman broke his arm and will be unable to help out in the interim, as originally proposed.
     – Tabitha Brown will ask Maria if she can recommend a replacement.
     – Peter Crantz will contact Dina Gaines about writing some profiles.
     – If the employee profiles do continue, Julie Owens suggested publishing the profiled member's photograph with the feature.

FIGURE 2–3
Typical Minutes of a Meeting

that allows team members to revise the content of a website as they get new ideas. The community-written online encyclopedia Wikipedia (www.wikipedia.org) is a good example of such collaborative writing on a global scale.

As with most new technologies, electronic meeting tools are evolving rapidly, and the lines separating these tools have become blurred. For example, instant messaging and videoconferencing are both stand-alone capabilities; both are also common features in **groupware,** an umbrella term for systems that let people communicate, share files, present materials, and work on documents simultaneously.

Naturally, before you and your colleagues can interact electronically, you need some way to connect. Expect to encounter some combination of wired and wireless networking that uses both the public Internet and private corporate networks. Your company might have you connect via a *virtual private network (VPN)*, a secure "tunnel" through the public Internet. VPNs let you connect from the office, from home, and from the road—costing much less than an actual private network and providing greater security than regular Internet access. Clothing maker Bernard Chaus replaced its private network and extensive use of postal mail with a VPN; its New York office now communicates with its offices in Hong Kong, South Korea, and Taiwan more effectively than before and at one-sixth the cost.[38] Whatever the network, you'll connect with colleagues and customers using such technologies as e-mail and instant messaging, shared workspaces, and virtual meetings.

E-Mail and Instant Messaging In addition to their everyday communication uses, e-mail and instant messaging (IM) are also used extensively to both supplement and replace meetings. With the cost, hassles, and even risks of travel, more and more companies look to these tools to help teams interact without being in the same room together. By giving employees a fast, inexpensive way to communicate, e-mail and IM enhance information sharing and project collaboration.

Of the two technologies, e-mail is less effective for real-time communication because it forces you to check for incoming messages, which can be delayed for several seconds or even longer as they pass through the e-mail system. However, e-mail is still used to set up and supplement meetings. For example, the group scheduling capabilities in e-mail programs such as Microsoft Outlook make it easy for you to verify everyone's schedules and send out invitation messages. You can also use e-mail during teleconferences and videoconferences to share files. In a pinch, e-mail can even substitute for IM and face-to-face meetings, although it becomes unwieldy when more than two or three people are involved.

Instant messaging is a recent entry into the corporate communication scene, but it is catching on rapidly. Indeed, IM may soon surpass e-mail as the more commonly used tool for communicating with business associates and customers. Some businesses use the same consumer-oriented IM systems that you might already be familiar with, such as AOL Instant Messenger, Yahoo!, and MSN Messenger from Microsoft. However, many companies use business-oriented versions of these systems, or they choose systems designed specifically for business or even for a particular industry. For example, a custom-built IM network now connects thousands of users in the financial services industry, which is required by law to archive all written communication with customers (something a typical IM system can't do).

Various business IM systems offer a range of capabilities, including basic chat, *presence awareness* (the ability to quickly see which people are at their desks and available to IM), remote display of documents, video capabilities, remote control of other computers, automated newsfeeds from blogs and websites, and the bot capability you read about in Chapter 1.[39] All these capabilities can supplement both one-on-one conversations and group meetings, and can even replace meetings in many cases.

The benefits of IM for meetings (and in the workplace in general) include its rapid response to urgent messages, lower cost than both phone calls and e-mail, ability to mimic conversation more closely than e-mail, and availability on a wide range of devices from PCs to phones to PDAs.[40]

The drawbacks include both technical and behavioral issues. The primary technical issues are security (one quarter of all U.S. corporations have blocked employee access to consumer IM systems because of worries that sensitive communications might be intercepted by outsiders), user authentication (making sure that online correspondents are really who they appear to be), the inability to log messages for later review and archiving, and incompatibility between competing IM systems. Although developers will eventually solve all these problems, the human side of IM will be an ongoing concern. To use IM effectively for meetings, all users need to pay attention to some important behavioral issues: the potential for constant interruptions, the ease of accidentally mixing personal and business messages, the risk of being out of the loop (if a hot discussion or impromptu meeting flares up when you're away from your PC

Instant messaging (IM) has become an important business technology, frequently replacing or supplementing meetings.

or other IM device), and the "vast potential for wasted time" (in the words of MIT labor economist David Autor). On top of all that, you're at the mercy of other people's typing abilities, which can make IM agonizingly slow.[41]

Regardless of the system you're using, you can make IM more efficient and effective for both meetings and general communication by following these tips:[42]

- Unless a meeting is scheduled, make yourself unavailable when you need to focus on other work.

- If you're not on a secure system, don't send confidential information.

- Be extremely careful about sending personal messages—they have a tendency to pop up on other people's computers at embarrassing moments.

- Don't use IM for important but impromptu meetings if you can't verify that everyone concerned will be available.

- Unless your system is set up for it, don't use IM for lengthy, complex messages; e-mail is better for those.

- If IM has become the primary communication channel in your company, particularly for important meetings, make sure everyone is comfortable with the technology and both capable and willing to use it.

- Try to avoid carrying on multiple IM conversations at once to minimize the chance of sending messages to the wrong people.

- Don't assume that whatever IM slang you might use in personal communications is appropriate for business messages; your colleagues may not be familiar or comfortable with it.

- If your IM system has filters for *spim,* the IM version of e-mail spam, make sure they're active and up to date.[43]

Shared Workspaces   **Shared workspaces** are "virtual offices" that give everyone on a team access to the same set of resources and information: databases, calendars, project plans, pertinent IM and e-mail exchanges, shared reference materials, and team-created documents (see Figure 2–4). Workspaces such as Documentum eRoom, Microsoft SharePoint, and IBM Lotus Team Workspace create a seamless, comprehensive environment for collaboration. Such workspaces make it easy for geographically dispersed team members to access shared files anytime, anywhere. Typically accessible through a web browser, the workspace lets you and your team organize its files into a collection of electronic folders.

> Shared workspaces give team members instant access to shared resources and information.

Most systems also have built-in intelligence to control which team members can read, edit, and save specific files. *Revision control* goes one step further: It allows only one person at a time to check on a given file or document and records all the changes that person makes. This feature prevents two people from independently editing the same report at the same time, thus avoiding the messy situation in which a team would end up with two versions of the same document. Many systems also include the presence awareness offered by IM systems so that you can tell instantly which team members are online and available to chat or to attend an impromptu meeting.[44]

Virtual Meetings   Virtual meeting technologies cover a wide range of tools that let team members in different locations interact at the same time without the hassle, risk, and cost of travel.[45] IM chat sessions and telephone conference calls are the simplest forms of virtual meetings. **Videoconferencing** combines audio communication with live video, letting team members see each other, demonstrate products,

> Virtual meetings range from videoconferencing to web-based systems.

FIGURE 2–4
Shared Workspaces

and transmit other visual information. Videoconferencing is available in two systems. *Room systems* require specialized conference room facilities but offer large-screen displays and the ability to accommodate more participants. *Desktop systems* typically use a webcam attached to each participant's PC, with the video displayed on the computer monitor and audio provided either over the Internet or a standard phone connection.

The most sophisticated **web-based meeting systems** combine the best of IM, shared workspaces, and videoconferencing with other tools such as virtual whiteboards that let teams collaborate in real time (see Figure 2–5). Attendees can log on from a desktop or laptop PC, a PDA, or even a web-enabled cell phone from almost anywhere in the world.

Through web-based collaboration, far-flung teams can work together on documents, designs, and other materials as though they were in the same room. For instance, you and your team might have the task of laying out the floor plan of the company's new offices. Rather than trying to verbally describe visual ideas to one another, you can all make changes to the same graphic design file. One person has control of the cursor at a time, and he or she can add walls, move tables, and so on. If you then see a better way to arrange the walls, you can ask for control of the cursor and then move the walls yourself. Not only does this level of interaction help the team work together more closely, but the document or drawing is ready to go immediately. You don't have to wait for one person to incorporate everyone's inputs and produce a new version of the drawing.

The latest twist in online meetings are *darknets,* small, invitation-only networks that are typically more secure than other networks. Although they are popular with people sharing pirated music files, darknets have legitimate business uses as well, primarily to exchange highly confidential information.

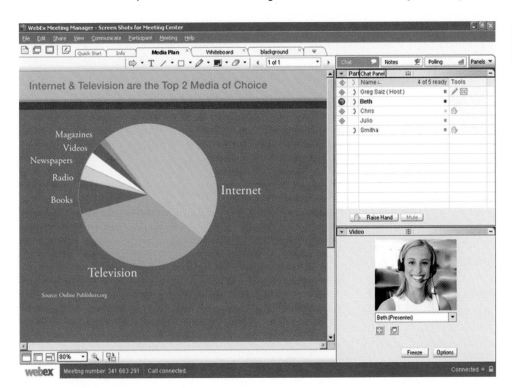

FIGURE 2-5
Web-Based Meetings

IMPROVING YOUR LISTENING SKILLS

The importance of listening, whether in meetings and other business contexts or in your personal life, is self-evident: If a receiver won't or can't listen, the speaker's message simply won't get through. Some 80 percent of top executives say that listening is the most important skill needed to get things done in the workplace.[46]

Effective listening strengthens organizational relationships, enhances product delivery, alerts the organization to opportunities for innovation, and allows the organization to manage growing diversity both in the workforce and in the customers it serves.[47] Companies whose employees and managers listen effectively stay informed, up to date, and out of trouble. Conversely, poor listening skills can cost companies millions of dollars a year as a result of lost opportunities, legal mistakes, and other errors. Effective listening is vital to the process of building trust not only between organizations but also between individuals.[48] Throughout your own career, effective listening will give you a competitive edge, enhancing your performance and thus the influence you have within your company. Learn from the example of Carol Kobuke Nelson, whose "quietly effective" leadership skills helped her become president and CEO of Seattle-based Cascade Bank. Says one of her peers, "She's a good listener. A lot of times people just want someone to listen to them. By understanding what that person's real concern is and doing something about it—that's how you win people over."[49]

> Listening is one of the most important skills in the workplace.

Recognizing Various Types of Listening

Understanding the nature of listening is the first step toward improving your listening skills. People listen in a variety of ways, and although how they listen is often an unconscious choice, it influences both what they hear and the meaning they extract. For instance, an employee who values teamwork and relationships will naturally be inclined to look for ways to bond with a speaker. In contrast, an action-oriented listener will listen more for information related to tasks that need to be completed.

In either case, relying on a single approach to listening limits your effectiveness. A people-oriented listener might miss important information about an upcoming deadline, whereas an action-oriented listener might miss an important clue that there's a personal problem brewing between two team members.[50] As you read the following paragraphs about the three types of listening, reflect on your own inclination as a listener, and consider how learning to use several methods could make your listening more effective.

To be a good listener, adapt the way you listen to suit the situation.

The primary goal of **content listening** is to understand and retain the speaker's message. For instance, Henry Nordhoff, CEO of the San Diego–based pharmaceutical company Gen-Probe, has a business background and relies on content listening to gather technical information from the scientists whose work he oversees.[51] When you're listening for content, the emphasis is on information and understanding. Ask questions to clarify the material and probe for details. Since you're not evaluating at this point, it doesn't matter whether you agree or disagree, approve or disapprove— only that you understand. Try to overlook the speaker's style and any limitations in the presentation; just focus on the information.[52]

The goal of **critical listening** is to understand and evaluate the meaning of the speaker's message on several levels: the logic of the argument, the strength of the evidence, the validity of the conclusions, the implications of the message for you and your organization, the speaker's intentions and motives, and the omission of any important or relevant points. If you're skeptical, ask questions to explore the speaker's point of view and credibility. Be on the lookout for bias that might color the way the information is presented, and be careful to separate opinions from facts.[53]

When you engage in empathic listening, you pay attention to feelings, needs, and wants—not just the spoken words.

The goal of **empathic listening** is to understand the speaker's feelings, needs, and wants so that you can appreciate his or her point of view, regardless of whether you share that perspective. By listening in an empathic way, you help the individual vent the emotions that prevent a calm, clear-headed approach to the subject. Sometimes the only thing an upset colleague is looking for is somebody to listen, so avoid the temptation to jump in with advice unless the person specifically asks for it. Also, don't judge the speaker's feelings and don't try to tell people they shouldn't feel this or that emotion. Instead, let the speaker know that you appreciate his or her feelings and understand the situation. Once you establish that connection, you can then help the speaker move on to search for a solution.[54]

Understanding the Listening Process

No matter which mode of listening you use in a given conversation, it's important to recognize that listening is a far more complex process than most people think. As a consequence, most of us aren't very good at it. Given such complexity, it's no wonder most of us listen at or below a 25 percent efficiency rate, remember only about half of what's said during a 10-minute conversation, and forget half of that within 48 hours.[55] Furthermore, when questioned about material we've just heard, we are likely to get the facts mixed up.[56]

Why is such a seemingly simple activity so difficult? The answer lies in the complexity of the process. To listen effectively, you need to successfully complete five separate steps:[57]

- **Receiving:** You start by physically hearing the message and acknowledging it. Physical reception can be blocked by noise, impaired hearing, or inattention. Some experts also include nonverbal messages as part of this stage, since these factors influence the listening process as well.

- **Interpreting:** Your next step is to assign meaning to sounds, which you do according to your own values, beliefs, ideas, expectations, roles, needs, and personal history.

- **Remembering:** Before you can act on the information, you need to store it for future processing. First you need to capture it in *short-term memory,* which is your brain's temporary note pad. Information disappears from short-term memory quickly, though, so you need to transfer it to *long-term memory* for safekeeping.

- **Evaluating:** With the speaker's message captured, you next step is to evaluate it by applying critical thinking skills. Separate fact from opinion and evaluate the quality of the evidence.

- **Responding:** After you've evaluated the speaker's message, you now react. If you're communicating one-on-one or in a small group, the initial response generally takes the form of verbal feedback. If you're one of many in an audience, your initial response may take the form of applause, laughter, or silence. Later on, you may act on what you have heard.

If any one of these steps breaks down, the listening process becomes less effective or even fails entirely. For example, if you work in a noisy environment, you may never hear a message intended for you. If you do receive the message, a lack of shared meaning or shared language between you and the speaker might lead to a different interpretation than the speaker intended. Or you might've looked away when the person was speaking and thereby missed an important nonverbal clue that would've helped you decipher the intended meaning. And even if you did interpret the meaning as the speaker hoped, you might forget it before you get around to acting on the information.

As both a sender and receiver, you can reduce the failure rate by recognizing and overcoming a variety of physical and mental barriers to effective listening.

Listening involves five steps: receiving, interpreting, remembering, evaluating, and responding.

Overcoming Barriers to Effective Listening

Good listeners look for ways to overcome potential barriers throughout the listening process (see Table 2–4). You are unlikely to have control over some barriers to physical reception, such as conference room acoustics, poor cell phone reception, background music, and so on. However, you can certainly control other barriers, such as interrupting speakers or creating distractions that make it hard for others to pay attention. If you have questions for a speaker, wait until he or she has finished speaking. And don't think that you're not interrupting just because you're not talking. Rustling papers, tapping on your PDA, checking your watch, making eye contact with someone over the speaker's shoulder—these are just a few of the many nonverbal behaviors that can interrupt a speaker and degrade physical reception.

Selective listening is one of the most common barriers to effective listening. If your mind wanders, you often stay tuned out until you hear a word or phrase that gets your

Good listeners actively try to overcome the barriers to successful listening.

Table 2–4	DISTINGUISHING EFFECTIVE LISTENERS FROM INEFFECTIVE LISTENERS	
	Effective Listeners	*Ineffective Listeners*
	• Listen actively	• Listen passively
	• Take careful and complete notes	• Take no notes or ineffective notes
	• Make frequent eye contact with the speaker (depends on culture to some extent)	• Make little or no eye contact
	• Stay focused on the speaker and the content	• Allow their minds to wander; are easily distracted
	• Mentally paraphrase key points to maintain attention level and ensure comprehension	• Fail to paraphrase
	• Adjust listening style to the situation	• Listen with the same style, regardless of the situation
	• Give the speaker nonverbal cues (such as nodding to show agreement or raising eyebrows to show surprise or skepticism)	• Fail to give the speaker nonverbal feedback
	• Save questions or points of disagreement until an appropriate time	• Interrupt whenever they disagree or don't understand
	• Overlook stylistic differences and focus on the speaker's message	• Are distracted by or unduly influenced by stylistic differences; are judgmental
	• Make distinctions between main points and supporting details	• Unable to distinguish main points from details
	• Look for opportunities to learn	• Assume they already know everything that's important to know

attention once more. But by that time, you're unable to recall what the speaker *actually* said; instead, you remember what you *think* the speaker probably said.[58]

One reason listeners' minds tend to wander is that people think faster than they speak. Most people speak at about 120 to 150 words per minute. However, studies indicate that, depending on the subject and the individual, humans can process audio information at around 500 words per minute.[59] In other words, your brain has a lot of free time whenever you're listening, and if left unsupervised, it will find a thousand other things to think about. Rather than listening part time, make a conscious effort to focus on the speaker, and use the extra time to analyze what you hear, prepare questions you might need to ask, and engage in other relevant thinking.

Your mind can process information much faster than most speakers talk.

A common barrier to successful interpretation is prejudgment—making up your mind before truly hearing what another person has to say. Remember, assumptions that work in one situation or in one area of your life might be inappropriate for other situations. Similarly, some people listen defensively, always on the lookout for perceived personal attacks. To protect their self-esteem, they distort messages by tuning out anything that doesn't confirm their view of themselves.

Overcoming such interpretation barriers can be difficult because you might not even be aware of them. As Chapter 1 noted, selective perception leads listeners to mold a message to fit their own conceptual framework. The speaker's frame of reference may be quite different from yours, so work hard to determine what the speaker

✓ CHECKLIST: Overcoming Barriers to Effective Listening

✓ Control whatever barriers to physical reception you can (especially interrupting speakers by asking questions or by exhibiting disruptive nonverbal behaviors).

✓ Avoid selective listening by trying to focus on the speaker and analyzing what you hear.

✓ Keep an open mind by avoiding any prejudgment and by not listening defensively.

✓ Try to paraphrase the speaker's ideas, giving that person a chance to confirm or correct your interpretation.

✓ Don't count on your memory, but record, write down, or capture information in some other physical way.

✓ Improve your short-term memory by repeating information, organizing it into patterns, or breaking it into shorter lists.

✓ Improve your long-term memory by association, categorization, visualization, and mnemonics.

really means. Listening with an open mind will help you overcome many interpretation barriers.

Even when your intentions are the best, you can still misinterpret incoming messages if you and the speaker don't share enough language or experience. Lack of common ground is why misinterpretation is so frequent between speakers of different native languages, even when they're trying to speak the same language. When listening to a speaker whose native language or life experience is different from yours, try to paraphrase that person's ideas. Give the speaker a chance to confirm what you think you heard or to correct any misinterpretation.

Overcoming memory barriers is a slightly easier problem to solve, but it takes some work. One simple rule: Don't count on your memory. If the information is crucial, record it, write it down, or capture it in some other physical way. However, if you do need to memorize something, you can capture information in short-term memory for a few seconds or a few minutes by repeating it to yourself (silently, if need be), organizing it into patterns (perhaps in alphabetical order or as steps in a process), and breaking a long list of items into several shorter lists. To store information in long-term memory, four techniques can help: (1) associate new information with something closely related (such as the restaurant in which you met a new client), (2) categorize the new information into logical groups (such as alphabetizing the names of products you're trying to remember), (3) visualize words and ideas as pictures, and (4) create mnemonics such as acronyms or rhymes. Note that all four techniques have an important factor in common: You have to *do* something to make the information stick.

If you can overcome all these barriers to effective listening, you're finally ready to evaluate what you hear and respond as needed. Your response might be simple, even automatic, such as laughing or thanking the speaker and following her directions to the office building around the corner. However, your response might require a far more rigorous process of analysis, such as interpreting the results of a series of in-depth market research interviews before making recommendations about future product development. For a reminder of the steps you can take to overcome listening barriers, see "Checklist: Overcoming Barriers to Effective Listening."

> When information is crucial, don't count on your memory.

IMPROVING YOUR NONVERBAL COMMUNICATION SKILLS

The boss walks out of the conference room after explaining that your department needs to double its sales next year. You're skeptical, though. You turn to a colleague on your right and raise your eyebrows. She smiles and nods, sitting upright on the edge of her seat—she seems to relish the challenge. You turn to the left, but that colleague seems to dread what lies ahead, rolling his eyes and sighing. He is slumped so far down in his chair you wonder how he keeps from sliding off.

A complex conversation has just taken place without a single word being spoken. **Nonverbal communication** is the interpersonal process of sending and receiving information, both intentionally and unintentionally, without using written or spoken language. Nonverbal signals play three important roles in communication. The first is complementing verbal language. Nonverbal signals can strengthen a verbal message (when nonverbal signals match words), weaken a verbal message (when nonverbal signals don't match words), or replace words entirely.

The second role for nonverbal signals is revealing truth. People find it much harder to deceive with nonverbal signals. You might tell a client that the project is coming along nicely, but your forced smile and nervous glances send a different message. In fact, nonverbal communication often conveys more to listeners than the words you speak—particularly when they're trying to decide how you really feel about a situation or when they're trying to judge your credibility and aptitude for leadership.[60] However, even the power of nonverbal cues is not infallible when it comes to detecting truth. In one recent study, most people failed to detect dishonest speech roughly half the time; only a tiny fraction of the population are able to consistently detect when people are lying to them.[61]

The third role for nonverbal signals is conveying information efficiently. Nonverbal signals can convey both nuance and rich amounts of information in a single instant, as the previous conference room example suggests.

Recognizing Nonverbal Communication

Although you've been tuned into nonverbal communication since your first contact with other human beings, paying special attention to these signals in the workplace will enhance your ability to communicate successfully. Moreover, as you interact with business associates from other backgrounds, you'll discover that some nonverbal signals don't necessarily translate across cultures. You'll learn more about cultural influences on nonverbal communication in Chapter 3. The range and variety of nonverbal signals is almost endless, but you can grasp the basics by studying five general categories:

- **Facial expression.** Your face is the primary site for expressing your emotions; it reveals both the type and the intensity of your feelings.[62] Your eyes are especially effective for indicating attention and interest, influencing others, regulating interaction, and establishing dominance.[63]

- **Gesture and posture.** By moving or not moving your body, you express both specific and general messages, some voluntary and some involuntary. Many gestures—a wave of the hand, for example—have a specific and intentional meaning. Other types of body movement are unintentional and express a more general message. Slouching, leaning forward, fidgeting, and walking briskly are all unconscious signals that reveal whether you feel confident or nervous, friendly or hostile, assertive or passive, powerful or powerless.

- **Vocal characteristics.** Your voice also carries both intentional and unintentional messages. Consider the sentence "What have you been up to?" If you repeat that question, changing your tone of voice and stressing various words, you can consciously convey quite different messages. However, your voice can also reveal things of which you are unaware. Your tone and volume, your accent and speaking pace, and all the little *um*'s and *ah*'s that creep into your speech say a lot about who you are, your relationship with the audience, and the emotions underlying your words.

Nonverbal communication supplements spoken language.

Nonverbal clues help you ascertain the truth of spoken information.

Nonverbal signals include facial expression, gesture and posture, vocal characteristics, personal appearance, touch, and time and space.

- **Personal appearance.** People respond to others on the basis of their physical appearance, sometimes fairly and other times unfairly. Although an individual's body type and facial features impose limitations, most people are able to control their appearance to some degree. Grooming, clothing, accessories, style—you can control all of these. If your goal is to make a good impression, adopt the style of the people you want to impress.

- **Touch.** Touch is an important way to convey warmth, comfort, and reassurance. Touch is so powerful, in fact, that it is governed by cultural customs that establish who can touch whom and how in various circumstances. In the United States and Great Britain, for instance, people usually touch less frequently than people in France or Costa Rica. Even within each culture's norms, however, individual attitudes toward touch can vary widely. A manager might be comfortable using hugs to express support or congratulations, but his or her subordinates might interpret those hugs as either a show of dominance or sexual interest.[64] Touch is a complex subject. The best advice: When in doubt, don't touch.

Dressing too casually or too formally for a given business setting can send a signal that you don't understand or don't respect the situation.

- **Time and space.** Like touch, time and space can be used to assert authority, imply intimacy, and send other nonverbal messages. For instance, some people try to demonstrate their own importance or disregard for others by making other people wait; others show respect by being on time. The manipulation of space works in a similar way. When top executives gather for lunch in a private dining room, they send a strong signal to all the employees crowding into the cafeteria downstairs. The decision to respect or violate someone's "private space" is another powerful nonverbal signal. Again, attitudes toward time and space vary from culture to culture (see Chapter 3).

Using Nonverbal Communication Effectively

Paying attention to nonverbal cues will make you both a better speaker and a better listener. When you're talking, be more conscious of the nonverbal cues you might be sending (see "Sharpening Your Career Skills: Sending the Right Signals"). Are they effective without being manipulative? Consider a situation in which an employee has come to you to talk about a raise. This situation is a stressful one for the employee, so don't say you're interested in what she has to tell you and then spend your time glancing at your computer or checking your watch. Conversely, if you already know you won't be able to give her the raise, be honest in expressing your emotions. Don't overcompensate for your own stress by smiling too broadly or shaking her hand too vigorously. Both nonverbal signals would raise her hopes without justification. In either case, match your nonverbal cues to the tone of the situation.

> Work to make sure your nonverbal signals match the tone and content of your spoken communication.

Also consider the nonverbal signals you send when you're not talking—the clothes you wear, the way you sit, the way you walk. Are you talking like a serious business professional but dressing like you belong in a dance club or a frat house? The way you look and act sends signals too; make sure you're sending the right ones.

> What signals does your personal appearance send?

When you listen, be sure to pay attention to the speaker's nonverbal clues. Do they amplify the spoken words or contradict them? Is the speaker intentionally using

SHARPENING YOUR CAREER SKILLS

Sending the Right Signals

The nonverbal signals you send can enhance—or undermine—your verbal message, so make sure to use nonverbal cues to your advantage. In U.S. business culture, the following signals are key to building and maintaining professional credibility:

- **Eye behavior.** Maintain direct, but not continuous, eye contact. Don't look down before responding to a question, and be careful not to shift your eyes around. Don't look away from the other person for extended periods, and try not to blink excessively.

- **Gestures.** When using gestures to emphasize points or convey the intensity of your feelings, keep them spontaneous, unrehearsed, and relaxed. Keep your hands and elbows away from your body, and avoid hand-to-face gestures, throat clearing, fidgeting, and tugging at clothing. Work to minimize visible perspiration on your face and body. Don't lick your lips, wring your hands, tap your fingers, or smile out of context.

- **Posture.** Assume an open and relaxed posture. Walk confidently, with grace and ease. Stand straight, with both feet on the floor, and sit straight in your chair without slouching. Hold your head level, and keep your chin up. Shift your posture while communicating, leaning forward and smiling as you begin to answer a question. Avoid keeping your body rigid or otherwise conveying a sense of tension.

- **Voice.** Strive for a conversational style, while speaking at a moderately fast rate. Use appropriate variation in pitch, rate, and volume. Avoid speaking in a monotone. Avoid sounding flat, tense, or nasal. Try not to speak at an excessive rate, and avoid frequent, lengthy pauses. Do your best to avoid *ah*'s or *um*'s, repeating words, interrupting or pausing mid-sentence, omitting parts of words, and stuttering.

CAREER APPLICATIONS

1. What message might you get if your boss smiles but looks away when you ask if you'll be getting a raise this year? Explain your interpretation of these nonverbal signals.

2. Would you be reluctant to hire a job candidate who stares intently at you through an entire job interview? Why or why not?

nonverbal signals to send you a message that he or she can't put into words? Be observant, but don't assume that you can "read someone like a book." Nonverbal signals are powerful, but they aren't infallible. Just because someone doesn't look you square in the eye doesn't mean he or she is lying, contrary to popular belief.[65] If something doesn't feel right, ask the speaker an honest and respectful question—doing so might clear everything up, or it might uncover issues you need to explore further. See "Checklist: Improving Nonverbal Communication Skills" for a summary of key ideas regarding nonverbal skills.

✓ CHECKLIST: Improving Nonverbal Communication Skills

A. Understand the roles that nonverbal signals play in communication

- ✓ Nonverbal signals complement verbal language by strengthening, weakening, or replacing words.
- ✓ Nonverbal signals reveal the truth, often conveying more to listeners than spoken words.

B. Recognize nonverbal communication signals

- ✓ Note that facial expressions (especially eye contact) reveal the type and intensity of a speaker's feelings.
- ✓ Watch for clues from gesture and posture.
- ✓ Listen for vocal characteristics that signal who the speaker is, the speaker's relationship with the audience, and the emotions underlying the speaker's words.
- ✓ Recognize that listeners are influenced by physical appearance.
- ✓ Be careful with physical contact; touch can convey positive attributes but can also be interpreted as dominance or sexual interest.
- ✓ Pay attention to the use of time and space.

On the Job

SOLVING COMMUNICATION DILEMMAS AT THE CONTAINER STORE

After joining The Container Store, you quickly demonstrated your skills on the sales floor and soon earned an invitation to enter the company's management training program. With that training completed, you couldn't be more excited to take over your first store and begin the managerial phase of your career. That's the good news. The bad news is that the store you've been assigned to developed some morale problems under the previous manager, and you have some challenges ahead to restore a sense of teamwork and positive communication. Apply the concepts you learned in this chapter to the following challenges.

1. The eight employees who now report to you once had a reputation for being a tight-knit, supportive team, but you quickly figure out that this team is in danger of becoming dysfunctional. For example, minor issues that functional teams routinely handle, from cleaning up the lunch area to helping each other on the sales floor, frequently generate conflict within this group. What steps should you take to help your crew return to positive behavior?

   a. Give the team the task of healing itself, without getting directly involved. Explain the steps necessary in forming an effective team, then let them figure out how to make it happen.

   b. Lead the "team restoration" project yourself so that you can mediate whatever conflicts arise, at least until the team is able to function on its own in a more positive manner.

   c. Don't try to interfere; the negative behaviors were probably caused by an ineffective manager in the past, but now that you're in charge, the team will return to positive behavior under your enlightened guidance.

   d. Your professional reputation and the store's sales are on the line, so you don't have time for the niceties of team building. Sit down with the group and demand that the negative, unprofessional behavior stop immediately.

2. While you're trying to figure out how to handle the overall team situation, you notice that the morning and evening huddles often degenerate into little more than complaint sessions. Workers seem to gripe about everything from difficult customers to the temperature in the store. Some of these sound like valid business issues that might require additional training or other employee support efforts; others are superficial issues that you suspect are simply byproducts of the negative atmosphere. How should you handle complaints during the huddles?

   a. Try to defuse each complaint with humor; after awhile, employees will begin to lighten up and stop complaining so much.

   b. Ask employees to refrain from complaining during the huddles; after all, these are important business meetings, not random social gatherings.

   c. Set up a whiteboard and write down each issue that is raised. After you've compiled a list over the course of a week or so, add a problem-solving segment to each huddle, in which you and the team tackle one issue per meeting to determine the scope of each problem and identify possible solutions.

   d. Whenever a complaint is raised, stop the huddle and confront the person who raised the issue. Challenge him or her to prove that the problem is a real business issue and not just a personal complaint. By doing this, you will not only identify the real problems that need to be fixed, but also discourage people from raising petty complaints that shouldn't be aired in the workplace.

3. After observing the staff in action for a couple of weeks and interviewing several dozen shoppers, you conclude that some employees are more effective than others when it comes to listening to customers and helping them find the right solutions to their individual needs. For instance, a few customers complained that the store employees who waited on them "didn't seem to hear what I was saying," and several others said that "they expected me to know the names of every product in the store before they could help me." You recognize these as classic listening challenges, and you want to work with the corporation's training specialists to design a short course in effective listening. Which of the following strategies will you emphasize in the course?

   a. Content listening is the best strategy, since that is the only way to find out exactly what customers need. Train employees to filter out small talk and listen carefully for the precise terms customers use to describe the products they need, then work to match those needs with the store's vast inventory of products.

   b. Since research shows that customers who enjoy the shopping experience in a store tend to stay longer and buy more, you should encourage employees to focus on empathic listening. By creating emotional bonds with shoppers, rather than jumping right in to talk about products, the sales staff will make shoppers more comfortable, which will eventually lead to increased sales.

   c. One of the issues your interviews uncovered is that customers often don't know exactly what they're looking for, either because they don't know what some products are called or because they simply don't know what's available in the marketplace. Consequently, critical listening—looking beyond the words and phrases customers use to identify the true needs they are trying to express—should be the primary focus.

d. No single listening strategy is appropriate for all customers in all situations, so the best approach is to train employees to quickly assess each customer encounter in order to determine the best listening style to use. Design the training to help employees identify the clues they can use to decide how to proceed with each customer. For instance, if a couple walks in arguing about whether they should even be spending money on organizational products, the best approach might be empathic listening: Diffuse the negative emotions and encourage the shoppers to focus on their storage needs. In contrast, straightforward content listening is best for a customer who walks in with a printout from The Container Store website and asks to see a specific product.

4. First impressions can make or break the sale in retailing, and those impressions are created by everything from the cleanliness of the parking lot to the personal appearance of the store employees. Four job candidates are waiting outside your office, and you have a few moments to observe them before inviting them in for an initial interview (you can see them through the glass wall but can't hear them). Based on the following descriptions, which of these people seems like the best fit for The Container Store? Why?

a. Candidate A: A woman who is dressed perfectly for an interview at The Container Store. Her appearance is contemporary "business casual," but a notch or two more formal than the store

employees, which suggests that she appreciates and shows respect for the business situation she finds herself in. However, you are slightly troubled by the fact that she's listening to her iPod and has kicked off her shoes and tucked her feet under her while she waits in the chair.

b. Candidate B: A man who has also dressed the part, although this candidate's behavior is nothing like the relaxed, carefree attitude that Candidate A is showing. He seems to be juggling multiple tasks at once: checking notes on a PDA, organizing a collection of papers he pulled from his briefcase, reattaching several sticky notes that keep falling loose, and fiddling with a cell phone that he has answered at least twice in the few minutes you've been watching.

c. Candidate C: A woman who closed the notebook she was scanning in order to help Candidate B with some problem he was having with his cell phone (if you had to guess, he was having trouble figuring out how to silence the ringer). After their interaction, they shake hands and appear to be introducing themselves with cordial smiles. Unfortunately, although the city is suffering through record high temperatures, her sun dress and sandals strike you as a bit too casual for a job interview.

d. Candidate D: A man wearing what appears to be a finely tailored, conservative suit. His appearance is more dignified and businesslike than the other three, and he knows how to dress for success—carefully knotted tie, starched shirt, perfect posture, the works. He keeps to himself and avoids bothering the other candidates, although his facial expressions make it clear that he disapproves of the noise Candidate B is making with his cell phone.

Learning Objectives Checkup

Assess your understanding of the principles in this chapter by reading each learning objective and studying the accompanying exercises. For fill-in items, write the missing text in the blank provided; for multiple choice items, circle the letter of the correct answer. You can check your responses against the answer key on page AK-1.

Objective 2.1: Highlight the advantages and disadvantages of working in teams.

1. Teams can achieve a higher level of performance because
   a. They combine the intelligence and energy of multiple individuals
   b. Motivation and creativity flourish in team settings
   c. They bring more input and a greater diversity of views, which tends to result in better decisions
   d. They do all of the above

2. Which of the following is a potential disadvantage of working in teams:
   a. Teams always stamp out creativity by forcing people to conform to existing ideas and practices.
   b. Teams increase a company's clerical workload because of the additional government paperwork required for administering workplace insurance.
   c. Team members are never held accountable for their individual performance.
   d. Social pressure within the group can lead to groupthink, in which people go along with a bad idea or poor decision even though they may not really believe in it.

Objective 2.2: Outline an effective approach to team communication.

3. Which of the following is the best way for a team of people to write a report?
   a. Each member should plan, research, and write his or her individual version, then the group can select the strongest report.
   b. The team should divide and conquer—one person doing the planning, one doing the research, one doing the writing, and so on.
   c. To ensure a true group effort, every task from planning through final production should be done as a team, preferably with everyone in the same room at the same time.
   d. Research and plan as a group, but assign the actual writing to one person, or at least assign separate sections to individual writers and have one person edit them all to achieve a consistent style.

4. Which of the following steps should be completed before anyone from the team does any planning, researching, or writing?
   a. The team should agree on the project's goals.
   b. The team should agree on the report's title.
   c. To avoid compatibility problems, the team should agree on which word processor or other software will be used.
   d. Team should always step away from the work environment and enjoy some social time in order to bond effectively before starting work.

Objective 2.3: Explain how group dynamics can affect team communication.

5. Self-oriented roles are a type of _____ behavior in group settings.

6. Which of the following is the most accurate description of groupthink?
   a. The ability of teams to generate more new ideas than a single employee can
   b. A situation in which team members value harmony more than effective decision making
   c. The ability of teams to uncover hidden agendas and ensure open, constructive communication
   d. The existence of peer pressure in group settings

7. Conflict in team settings can be beneficial when it is _____ but harmful when it is _____.

Objective 2.4: Discuss the role of etiquette in team settings, both in the workplace and in social settings.

8. Which of the following is the best characterization of etiquette in today's business environment?
   a. Business etiquette is impossible to generalize because every company has its own culture; you have to make it up as you go along.
   b. With ferocious international competition and constant financial pressure, etiquette is an old-fashioned luxury that businesses simply can't afford today.
   c. Ethical businesspeople don't need to worry directly about etiquette because ethical behavior automatically leads to good etiquette.

d. Etiquette plays an important part in the process of forming and maintaining successful business relationships.

9. If you forgot to shut off your cell phone before stepping into a business meeting, then receive a call during the meeting, the most appropriate thing to do is to
   a. Lower your voice to protect the privacy of your phone conversation
   b. Answer the phone then quickly hang it up to minimize the disruption to the meeting
   c. Excuse yourself from the meeting and find a quiet place to talk
   d. Continue to participate in the meeting while taking the call; this shows everyone that you're an effective multitasker

10. Your company has established a designated "quiet time" from 1:00 to 3:00 every afternoon, during which office phones, instant messaging (IM), and e-mail are disabled so that people can concentrate on planning, researching, writing, and other intensive tasks without being interrupted. However, a number of people continue to flout the guidelines by leaving their cell phones on, saying their families and friends need to be able to reach them. With all the various ring tones going off at random, the office is just as noisy as it was before. What is the best response?
    a. Agree to reactivate the office phone system if everyone will shut off their cell phones, but have all incoming calls routed through a receptionist who will take messages for all routine calls and deliver a note if an employee truly is needed in an emergency.
    b. Give up on quiet time; with so many electronic gadgets in the workplace today, you'll never achieve peace and quiet.
    c. Get tough on the offenders by confiscating cell phones whenever they ring during quiet time.
    d. Without telling anyone, simply install one of the available cell phone jamming products that block incoming and outgoing cell phone calls.

11. Constantly testing the limits of your company's dress and grooming standards sends a strong signal that you
    a. Don't understand or don't respect your company's culture
    b. Are a strong advocate for worker's rights
    c. Are a creative and independent thinker who is likely to generate lots of successful business ideas
    d. Represent the leading edge of a new generation of enlightened workers who will redefine the workplace according to contemporary standards

Objective 2.5: Describe how meeting technologies can help participants communicate more successfully.

12. The "presence awareness" feature in an instant messaging system is a handy way to
    a. Monitor employees' computer usage to make sure they're not playing games at work
    b. See who is at their desks and available to IM
    c. See if your team is staying on schedule
    d. Plan meetings

13. Online meeting technologies allow geographically dispersed teams to conduct _____ meetings over the Internet.

Objective 2.6: Describe the listening process, and explain how good listeners overcome barriers at each stage of the process.

14. After receiving messages, listeners _____ what they've heard by assigning meaning to the sounds.
15. If you're giving an important presentation and notice that many of the audience members look away when you try to make momentary eye contact, which of the following is most likely going on?
    a. These audience members don't want to challenge your authority by making direct eye contact.
    b. You work with a lot of shy people.
    c. The information you're presenting is making your audience uncomfortable in some way.
    d. The audience is taking time to carefully think about the information you're presenting.
16. If you don't agree with something the speaker says in a large, formal meeting, the best response is to
    a. Signal your disagreement by folding your arms across your chest and staring defiantly back at the speaker
    b. Use your cell phone or wireless PDA to begin sending text messages to other people in the room, explaining why the speaker is wrong
    c. Immediately challenge the speaker so that the misinformation is caught and corrected
    d. Quietly make a note of your objections, then wait until a question and answer period to raise your hand

Objective 2.7: Clarify the importance of nonverbal communication, and briefly describe six categories of nonverbal expression.

17. Nonverbal signals can be more influential than spoken language because
    a. Body language is difficult to control and therefore more difficult to fake, so listeners often put more trust in such cues than in the words a speaker uses
    b. Nonverbal signals communicate faster than spoken language, and most people are impatient
    c. Body language saves listeners from the trouble of paying attention to what a speaker is saying
18. Which of the following is true about nonverbal signals?
    a. They can strengthen a spoken message.
    b. They can weaken a spoken message.
    c. They can replace spoken messages.
    d. All of the above.

Apply Your Knowledge

1. How can nonverbal communication help you run a meeting? How can it help you call a meeting to order, emphasize important topics, show approval, express reservations, regulate the flow of conversation, and invite a colleague to continue with a comment?
2. Your boss frequently asks for feedback from you and her other subordinates, but she blasts anyone who offers criticism, which causes people to agree with everything she says. You want to talk to her about it, but what should you say? List some of the points you want to make when you discuss this issue with her.
3. Is conflict in a team good or bad? Explain your answer.
4. At your last department meeting, three people monopolized the entire discussion. What might you do at the next meeting to encourage other department members to voluntarily participate?
5. **Ethical Choices** Strange instant messages occasionally pop up on your computer screen during your team's virtual meetings, followed quickly by embarrassed apologies from one of your colleagues in another city. You eventually figure out that this person is working from home, even though he says he's in the office; moreover, the messages suggest that he's running a sideline business from his home. Instant messaging is crucial to your team's communication, and you're concerned about the frequent disruptions, not to mention your colleague's potential ethical violations. What should you do? Explain your choice.

Practice Your Knowledge

DOCUMENT FOR ANALYSIS

A project leader has made notes about covering the following items at the quarterly budget meeting. Prepare a formal agenda by putting these items into a logical order and rewriting, where necessary, to give phrases a more consistent sound.

- Budget Committee Meeting to be held on December 12, 2006, at 9:30 A.M.
- I will call the meeting to order.
- Real estate director's report: A closer look at cost overruns on Greentree site.
- The group will review and approve the minutes from last quarter's meeting.
- I will ask the finance director to report on actual versus projected quarterly revenues and expenses.
- I will distribute copies of the overall divisional budget and announce the date of the next budget meeting.
- Discussion: How can we do a better job of anticipating and preventing cost overruns?
- Meeting will take place in Conference Room 3, with WebEx active for remote employees
- What additional budget issues must be considered during this quarter?

Exercises

For active links to all websites discussed in this chapter, visit this text's website at www.prenhall.com/thill. Locate your book and click on its Companion Website link. Then select Chapter 2, and click on "Featured Websites." Locate the name of the page or the URL related to the material in the text. Please note that links to sites that become inactive after publication of the book will be removed from the Featured Websites section.

2.1 Teamwork With a classmate, attend a local community or campus meeting where you can observe a group discussion, vote, or other group action. During the meeting, take notes individually and, afterwards, work together to answer the following questions.

   a. What is your evaluation of this meeting? In your answer, consider (1) the leader's ability to articulate the meeting's goals clearly, (2) the leader's ability to engage members in a meaningful discussion, (3) the group's dynamics, and (4) the group's listening skills.

   b. How did group members make decisions? Did they vote? Did they reach decisions by consensus? Did those with dissenting opinions get an opportunity to voice their objections?

   c. How well did the individual participants listen? How could you tell?

   d. Did any participants change their expressed views or their votes during the meeting? Why might that have happened?

   e. Did you observe any of the communication barriers discussed in Chapter 1? Identify them.

   f. Compare the notes you took during the meeting with those of your classmate. What differences do you notice? How do you account for these differences?

2.2 Team Communication: Overcoming Barriers Every month, each employee in your department is expected to give a brief oral presentation on the status of his or her project. However, your department has recently hired an employee with a severe speech impediment that prevents people from understanding most of what he has to say. As department manager, how will you resolve this dilemma? Please explain.

2.3 Team Development: Resolving Conflict Describe a recent conflict you had with a team member at work or at school, and explain how you resolved it. Did you find a solution that was acceptable to both of you and to the team?

2.4 Ethical Choices During team meetings, one member constantly calls for votes before all the members have voiced their views. As the leader, you asked this member privately about his behavior. He replied that he was trying to move the team toward its goals, but you are concerned that he is really trying to take control. How can you deal with this situation without removing the member from the group?

2.5 Online Communication: Staying on Track with Blog Replies As the leader of a product-development team, you write a daily blog to inform team members of questions, concerns, and other developments related to your project. Team members are always encouraged to reply to your online posts, but lately a number of people have been wandering off track with their replies, raising new issues in the middle of a discussion thread or posting on matters unrelated to the item to which their replying. As a result, the blog is becoming less useful for everyone because individual message threads no longer stick to a single topic. Write a brief blog posting, three or four sentences at most, courteously reminding everyone why it's important to stick to the subject at hand when replying to blog items.

2.6 Internet Visit the PolyVision website at www.websterboards.com and read about electronic whiteboards. What advantages do you see in using this kind of whiteboard during a meeting? Draft a short internal memo to your boss outlining the product's advantages, using the memo format in Figure 1.10 on page 27.

2.7 Listening Skills: Overcoming Barriers Identify some of your bad listening habits and make a list of some ways you could correct them. For the next 30 days, review your list and jot down any improvements you've noticed as a result of your effort.

2.8 Nonverbal Communication: Analyzing Written Messages Select a business letter and envelope that you have received at work or home. Analyze their appearance. What nonverbal messages do they send? Are these messages consistent with the content of the letter? If not, what could the sender have done to make the nonverbal communication consistent with the verbal communication?

2.9 Nonverbal Communication: Analyzing Body Language Describe what the following body movements suggest when someone exhibits them during a conversation. How do such movements influence your interpretation of spoken words?

   a. Shifting one's body continuously while seated

   b. Twirling and playing with one's hair

   c. Sitting in a sprawled position

   d. Rolling one's eyes

   e. Extending a weak handshake

2.10 Listening Skills: Self-Assessment How good are your listening skills? Use the following chart to rate yourself on each element of listening. Then examine your ratings to identify where you are strongest and where you can improve, using the tips in this chapter.

Element of Listening	Always	Frequently	Occasionally	Never
1. I look for areas of interest when people speak.	_____	_____	_____	_____
2. I focus on content rather than delivery.	_____	_____	_____	_____
3. I wait to respond until I understand the content.	_____	_____	_____	_____
4. I listen for ideas and themes, not isolated facts.	_____	_____	_____	_____
5. I take notes only when needed.	_____	_____	_____	_____
6. I really concentrate on what speakers are saying.	_____	_____	_____	_____
7. I stay focused even when the ideas are complex.	_____	_____	_____	_____
8. I keep an open mind despite emotionally charged language.	_____	_____	_____	_____

Expand Your Knowledge

LEARNING MORE ON THE WEB
MAKING MEETINGS WORK

www.3m.com/meetingnetwork

Meetings are an essential part of business, but meetings that are poorly planned waste time and money. Fortunately, you can learn from the experts how to avoid such problems. The 3M Meeting Network contains a wide selection of articles on planning effective meetings, designing activities to build teamwork, and making better presentations.

ACTIVITIES

Log onto the 3M Meeting Network, click on "Articles and Advice" to find the appropriate articles, and then answer the following questions:
1. How can you know if a meeting should be held or not?
2. How can good leaders show they trust the group's ability to perform successfully?
3. What are the advantages and disadvantages of "open space" meetings, which take place without formal agendas or facilitation?

EXPLORING THE WEB ON YOUR OWN

Review these chapter-related websites on your own to learn more about achieving communication success in the workplace.
1. CRInfo, www.crinfo.org, is a website dedicated to providing support for conflict resolution.
2. The Business of Touch website, www.businessoftouch.com, lets you explore cultural standards and expectations for touching, physical distance, and other elements of nonverbal communication between business colleagues in more than 15 countries.
3. Symbols.com, www.symbols.com, offers a graphical search engine that explains the meaning of 2,500 graphical symbols. Find out what that unusual symbol on a foreign-language website means, or verify that the symbols you plan to use don't convey some inappropriate nonverbal meaning. The Word Index feature lets you see the graphical symbols associated with thousands of words and ideas.

Learn Interactively

INTERACTIVE STUDY GUIDE

Visit www.prenhall.com/thill, then locate your book and click on its Companion Website link. Select Chapter 2 to take advantage of the interactive "Chapter Quiz" to test your knowledge of chapter concepts. Receive instant feedback on whether you need additional studying. Also, visit the "Study Hall," where you'll find an abundance of valuable resources that will help you succeed in this course.

PEAK PERFORMANCE GRAMMAR AND MECHANICS

If your instructor has required the use of "Peak Performance Grammar and Mechanics," either in your online course or on

CD, you can improve your skill with pronouns, by using the "Peak Performance Grammar and Mechanics" module. Click first on "Nouns and Pronouns," then on "Vocabulary II." In both sections, take the Pretest to determine whether you have any weak areas. Then review those areas in the Refresher Course. Take the Follow-Up Test to check your grasp of pronouns. For an extra challenge or advanced practice, take the Advanced Test. Finally, for additional reinforcement, go to the "Improve Your Grammar, Mechanics, and Usage" section that follows, and complete those exercises.

Improve Your Grammar, Mechanics, and Usage

The following exercises help you improve your knowledge of and power over English grammar, mechanics, and usage. Turn to the Handbook of Grammar, Mechanics, and Usage at the end of this textbook and review all of Section 1.2 (Pronouns). Then look at the following 10 items. Underline the preferred choice within each set of parentheses. (Answers to these exercises appear on page AK-3.)

1. The sales staff is preparing guidelines for (*their, its*) clients.
2. Few of the sales representatives turn in (*their, its*) reports on time.
3. The board of directors has chosen (*their, its*) officers.
4. Gomez and Archer have told (*his, their*) clients about the new program.
5. Each manager plans to expand (*his, their, his or her*) sphere of control next year.

6. Has everyone supplied (*his, their, his or her*) Social Security number?
7. After giving every employee (*his, their, a*) raise, George told (*them, they, all*) about the increased work load.
8. Bob and Tim have opposite ideas about how to achieve company goals. (*Who, Whom*) do you think will win the debate?
9. City Securities has just announced (*who, whom*) it will hire as CEO.
10. Either of the new products would readily find (*their, its*) niche in the marketplace.

For additional exercises focusing on pronouns, go to www.prenhall.com/thill, then locate your text and click on its Companion Website link. Click on Chapter 2, click on "Additional Exercises to Improve Your Grammar, Mechanics, and Usage," then click on Chapter "3. Case of pronouns" or "4. Possessive pronouns."

Chapter 3

Communicating Interculturally

Learning Objectives

AFTER STUDYING THIS CHAPTER, YOU WILL BE ABLE TO

1 Discuss the opportunities and challenges of intercultural communication

2 Define culture and explain how culture is learned

3 Define ethnocentrism and stereotyping, then give three suggestions for overcoming these limiting mindsets

4 Explain the importance of recognizing cultural variations and list six categories of cultural differences

5 Outline strategies for studying other cultures

6 List seven recommendations for writing clearly in multilanguage business environments

On the Job

COMMUNICATING AT IBM

ENSURING SUCCESS BY EMBRACING DIVERSITY

The "I" in IBM stands for "International," but it could just as easily stand for "Intercultural" as a testament to the computer giant's longstanding commitment to embracing diversity. Ted Childs, IBM's vice president of global workforce diversity, knows from years of experience that communicating successfully across cultures is no simple task, however—particularly in a company that employs more than 325,000 people and sells to customers in roughly 175 countries around the world.

Language alone presents a formidable barrier to communication, when you consider that IBM's workforce speaks more than 165 languages, but language is just one of many elements that play a role in communication between cultures. Differences in age, ethnic background, gender, sexual orientation, physical ability, and economic status can all affect the communication process. Childs recognizes that these differences represent both a challenge and an opportunity, and a key part of his job is helping IBM executives and employees work together in a way that transforms their cultural differences into a critical business strength. As he puts it, workforce diversity has "moved from being a moral imperative to being a strategic imperative."

IBM's diversity efforts help the company in virtually every aspect of its operations, starting with attracting the most talented people it can find and then helping those employees communicate effectively, regardless of cultural background. Employees are supported through more than 100 networking groups that unite IBM staffers with a variety of back-

Ted Childs oversees IBM's efforts to build competitive advantage by capitalizing on the benefits of a diverse workforce.

grounds and personal and professional interests. Diversity efforts extend outside the corporation, too, reaching out to both suppliers and customers. In fact, one of the key advantages that Childs sees in IBM's diverse workforce is the ability to communicate more effectively with an increasingly diverse marketplace.

While workforce diversity has become a hot topic in recent years, respect for the individual has long been a core value in the IBM corporate culture. For instance, the company decreed in 1935 that women would receive equal opportunities and the same pay for the same work—28 years before pay equity was written into U.S. law. IBM was also the first corporation in the United States to establish a policy ensuring equal employment opportunities for people of all races and religions—more than a decade before the Civil Rights Act made such principles the law of the land.

Throughout its long history of employing and working with people from different cultures, IBM has learned some powerful lessons. Perhaps the most significant is the recognition that successfully managing a diverse workforce and competing in a diverse marketplace starts with embracing those differences, not trying to ignore them or pretend they don't affect interpersonal communication. And it's a lesson that every aspiring business professional can take to heart. As Ted Childs puts it, "No matter who you are, you're going to have to work with people who are different from you . . . and manage people who are different from you."[1]

www.ibm.com

UNDERSTANDING THE OPPORTUNITIES AND CHALLENGES OF INTERCULTURAL COMMUNICATION

Effective intercultural communication
- Opens up business opportunities around the world
- Improves the contributions of employees in a diverse workforce

IBM's experience illustrates both the challenges of intercultural communication and the opportunities available for business professionals who know how to communicate across cultures. **Intercultural communication** is the process of sending and receiving messages between people whose cultural background could lead them to interpret verbal and nonverbal signs differently. Every attempt to send and receive messages is influenced by culture, so to communicate successfully, you'll need a basic grasp of the cultural differences you may encounter and how you might overcome them. Your efforts to recognize and surmount cultural differences will open up business opportunities throughout the world and maximize the contribution of all the employees in a diverse workforce.

The Opportunities in a Global Marketplace

You will communicate with people from other cultures throughout your career.

You might be a business manager looking for new customers or new sources of labor. Or you might be an employee looking for new work opportunities. Either way, chances are good that you'll be looking across international borders sometime in your career.

Thousands of U.S. businesses depend on exports for significant portions of their revenues. Every year, these companies export roughly $700 billion in materials and merchandise, along with billions more in personal and professional services. If you work in one of these companies, you may well be called on to visit or at least communicate with a wide variety of people who speak languages other than English and who live in cultures quite different from what you're used to. Of the top 10 export markets for U.S. goods, only 2 (Canada and Great Britain) speak English as an official language, and Canada has two official languages, English and French.

In the global marketplace, most natural boundaries and national borders are no longer the impassible barriers they once were. Domestic markets are opening to worldwide competition as businesses of all sizes look for new growth opportunities outside their own countries. Automotive giant Ford markets to customers in some 130 countries with websites that offer local information, usually in the local language.[2]

Even small companies in remote locations can sell and support their products on a global scale, thanks to e-mail, the Internet, and worldwide delivery services. Pygmy Boats is a small manufacturer of kayak kits in the equally small town of Port Townsend, Washington, and yet it reaches customers all over the world via its website.[3] Giardino Italiano, an Italian retailer of fountain pens, watches, walking sticks, and other items, sells its products globally through a multilingual website.[4] Large or small, companies know that in the global marketplace, they face cultural and language barriers among customers and employees.

Advantages of a Multicultural Workforce

The diversity of today's workforce brings distinct advantages to businesses:
- A broader range of views and ideas
- A better understanding of diverse markets
- A broader pool of talent from which to recruit

Even if you never visit another country or transact business on a global scale, you will interact with colleagues from a variety of cultures and with a wide range of life experiences. Smart business leaders such as IBM's Ted Childs recognize the competitive advantages of a diverse workforce made up of men and women from a broad mix of national, religious, and ethnic backgrounds. Such workforces offer a broader spectrum of viewpoints and ideas, help companies understand and identify with diverse markets, and enable companies to tap into the broadest possible pool of talent. As Reneé Wingo of Virgin Mobile USA, a cell phone operator based in Warren, New Jersey, puts it, "You're not going to create any magic as a manager unless you bring together people with diverse perspectives who aren't miniversions of you."[5]

Diversity is simply a fact of life for all companies. The United States has been a nation of immigrants from the beginning, and that trend continues today. The Western and Northern Europeans who made up the bulk of immigrants during the nation's early years now share space with people from across Asia, Africa, Eastern Europe, and other parts of the world. By 2010 recent immigrants will account for half of all new U.S. workers.[6] Even the term "minority," as it applies to nonwhite residents, makes less and less sense every year: In two states (California and New Mexico) and several dozen large cities, Caucasian Americans no longer constitute a clear majority.[7] Nor is this pattern of immigration unique to the United States: Workers from Africa, Asia, and the Middle East are moving to Europe in search of new opportunities, while workers from India, the Philippines, and Southeast Asia contribute to the employment base of the Middle East.[8]

Communication among people of diverse cultural backgrounds and life experiences is not always easy, but doing it successfully can create tremendous strategic advantages.

However, you and your colleagues don't need to be recent immigrants to constitute a diverse workforce. Differences in everything from age and gender to religion and ethnic heritage to geography and military experience enrich the workplace. Both immigration and workforce diversity create advantages—and challenges—for business communicators throughout the world.

A company's cultural diversity affects how its business messages are conceived, composed, delivered, received, and interpreted.

The Challenges of Intercultural Communication

Cultural diversity affects how business messages are conceived, planned, sent, received, and interpreted in the workplace. Today's increasingly diverse workforce encompasses a wide range of skills, traditions, backgrounds, experiences, outlooks, and attitudes toward work—all of which can affect employee behavior on the job. Supervisors face the challenge of communicating with these diverse employees, motivating them, and fostering cooperation and harmony among them. Teams face the challenge of working together closely, and companies are challenged to coexist peacefully with business partners and with the community as a whole.

Culture influences everything about communication, including
- Language
- Nonverbal signals
- Word meaning
- Time and space issues
- Rules of human relationships

The interaction of culture and communication is so pervasive that separating the two is virtually impossible. The way you communicate—from the language you speak and the nonverbal signals you send to the way you perceive other people—is influenced by the culture in which you were raised. The meaning of words, the significance of gestures, the importance of time and space, the rules of human relationships—these and many other aspects of communication are defined by culture. To a large degree, your culture influences the way you think, which naturally affects the way you communicate as both a sender and a receiver.[9] So you can see how intercultural communication is much more complicated than simply matching language between sender and receiver. It goes beyond mere words to beliefs, values, and emotions.

Throughout this chapter, you'll see numerous examples of how communication styles and habits vary from one culture to another. These examples are intended to illustrate the major themes of intercultural communication, not to give an exhaustive list of styles and habits of any particular culture. With an understanding of these major themes, you'll then be prepared to explore the specifics of any culture.

ENHANCING YOUR INTERCULTURAL SENSITIVITY

The good news is that you're already an expert in culture, at least in the culture you grew up with. You understand how your society works, how people are expected to communicate, what common gestures and facial expressions mean, and so on. The bad news is that because you're such an expert in your own culture, your communication is largely automatic; that is, you rarely stop to think about the communication rules you're following. An important step toward successful intercultural communication is becoming more aware of these rules and of the way they influence your communication. A good place to start is to understand what culture is.

Understanding the Concept of Culture

Culture is a shared system of symbols, beliefs, attitudes, values, expectations, and behavior norms.

For the purposes of communication, **culture** can be defined as a shared system of symbols, beliefs, attitudes, values, expectations, and norms for behavior. In other words, your cultural background influences the way you prioritize what is important in life, helps define your attitude toward what is appropriate in any given situation, and establishes rules of behavior.[10]

You belong to several cultures, each of which affects the way you communicate.

Actually, you belong to several cultures. The most obvious is the culture you share with all the people who live in your own country. In addition, you belong to other cultural groups, including an ethnic group, possibly a religious group, and perhaps a profession that has its own special language and customs. With its large population and long history of immigration, the United States is home to a vast array of cultures. In contrast, Japan is much more homogeneous, having only a few separate cultural groups.[11]

All members of a culture have similar assumptions about how people should think, behave, and communicate, and they all tend to act on those assumptions in much the same way. However, cultures differ widely and may vary in their rate of change, their degree of complexity, and their tolerance toward outsiders. These differences affect the level of trust and openness that you can achieve when communicating with people of other cultures.

People learn culture directly and indirectly from other members of their group. As you grow up in a culture, you are taught who you are and how best to function in that culture by the group's members. Sometimes you are explicitly told which behaviors are acceptable; at other times you learn by observing which values work best in a particular group. In these ways, culture is passed on from person to person and from generation to generation.[12]

Cultures tend to be both coherent and complete views of life.

In addition to being automatic, established cultures tend to be coherent; that is, they are fairly logical and consistent throughout. For instance, the notion of progress is deeply embedded in the culture of the United States. Those who achieve are admired and rewarded, and those who don't are sometimes viewed negatively, even if they live perfectly happy and contented lives. Such coherence generally helps a culture function more smoothly internally, although it can create disharmony between cultures that don't view the world in the same way.

Cultures also tend to be complete; that is, they provide most of their members with most of the answers to life's big questions. This idea of completeness dulls or even suppresses curiosity about life in other cultures. Therefore, such completeness can complicate communication with other cultures.[13]

Participation in group activities is an important method of learning about a culture's rules and expectations.

Overcoming Ethnocentrism and Stereotyping

Ethnocentrism is the tendency to judge all other groups according to the standards, behaviors, and customs of one's own group.

The very nature of culture being automatic, coherent, and complete can lead the members of one culture to form negative attitudes about—and rigid, oversimplified views of—other cultures. **Ethnocentrism** is the tendency to judge all other groups according to the standards, behaviors, and customs of one's own group. When making such comparisons, people too often decide that their own group is superior.[14] An even more extreme reaction is **xenophobia,** a fear of strangers and foreigners. Clearly, businesspeople who take these views will not interpret messages from other cultures correctly, nor are they likely to send successful messages.

Xenophobia is a fear of strangers.

As you recall from Chapter 1, selective perception leads people to rearrange incoming information to fit their existing beliefs. Thus, someone with a negative view of another culture is likely to continue holding that view, even if he or she sees evidence to the contrary.

Distorted views of other cultures or groups also result from **stereotyping,** assigning a wide range of generalized attributes to an individual on the basis of membership in a particular culture or social group, without considering the individual's unique characteristics. Whereas ethnocentrism and xenophobia represent negative views of everyone in a particular group, stereotyping is more a matter of oversimplifying and of failing to acknowledge individuality. For instance, assuming that an older colleague will be out of touch with the youth market or that a younger colleague can't be an inspiring leader is an example of stereotyping age groups. Many people in the United States have stereotypical views both of co-cultures within the United States and of cultures in other countries. Likewise, the people in these other countries sometimes exhibit stereotypical views of U.S. residents.

Stereotyping is assigning generalized attributes to an individual on the basis of membership in a particular group.

Those who want to show respect for other people and to communicate effectively in business need to adopt a more positive viewpoint, in the form of **cultural pluralism**— the practice of accepting multiple cultures on their own terms. When crossing cultural boundaries, you'll be even more effective if you move beyond simple acceptance and adapt your own communication style to that of the new cultures you encounter—even integrating aspects of those cultures into your own.[15] A few simple habits can help you avoid both the negativity of ethnocentrism and the oversimplification of stereotyping:

Cultural pluralism is the acceptance of multiple cultures on their own terms.

- **Avoid assumptions.** Don't assume that others will act the same way you do, that they will operate from the same values and beliefs, or that they will use language and symbols the same way you do.

- **Avoid judgments.** When people act differently, don't conclude that they are in error, that their way is invalid, or that their customs are inferior to your own.

- **Acknowledge distinctions.** Don't ignore the differences between another person's culture and your own.

You can avoid ethnocentrism and stereotyping by avoiding assumptions and judgments and by accepting differences.

Unfortunately, overcoming ethnocentrism and stereotyping is no simple task, even for people who are highly motivated to do so. You may need to change patterns of beliefs that you've had your entire life and even change the way you view yourself and your culture. Moreover, recent research suggests that people often have beliefs and biases that they're not even consciously aware of—and that may even conflict with the beliefs they *think* they have. (To see if you might have some of these *implicit beliefs,* visit the Project Implicit website at **https:/implicit.harvard.edu/implicit** and take some of the simple online tests.)[16]

Recognizing Cultural Variations

When you communicate with someone from another culture, you encode your message using the assumptions of your own culture. However, members of your audience decode your message according to the assumptions of their culture, so your meaning may be misunderstood. The greater the difference between cultures, the greater the chance for misunderstanding.[17] Consider the differences in communication styles, personal values, and nonverbal symbols that led to the following cultural mishaps:

- When Hewlett-Packard (HP) brought its U.S. engineers together with its French engineers to design software, the U.S. engineers sent long, detailed e-mails to their

Cultural differences can lead to miscommunication in the workplace.

counterparts in France. But the engineers in France viewed the lengthy messages as patronizing and replied with quick, concise e-mails. That response made the U.S. engineers believe that French engineers were withholding information. The situation spiraled out of control until HP hired a consulting firm to provide cultural training so that both sides could learn to work through their differences.[18]

- A Canadian employer rewarded a Polish-born engineer for his excellent job performance over the years with every possible award it could give him and a salary on the same level as many senior managers. However, in the engineer's view, the company should have rewarded him by putting him in charge of a large number of subordinates—as top performers are typically rewarded in his native Poland. Even though the company thought it was communicating its gratitude with pay and awards, the talented engineer left the company.[19]

- Exhibitors at a trade show could not understand why Chinese visitors were not stopping by their booth. The exhibitors were wearing green hats and giving them away as promotional items. They soon discovered that for many Chinese people, green hats are associated with infidelity: The Chinese expression "He wears a green hat" indicates that a man's wife has been cheating on him. As soon as the exhibitors discarded the green hats and started giving out T-shirts instead, the Chinese attendees began visiting the booth.[20]

Communication breakdowns such as these arise when we assume, wrongly, that other people's attitudes and lives are like ours. Part of the problem stems from treating others the way *you* want to be treated. The best approach when communicating with people from other cultures is to treat them the way *they* want to be treated.

You can begin to learn how people in other cultures want to be treated by recognizing and accommodating six main types of cultural differences: contextual, legal and ethical, social, nonverbal, age, and gender.

Contextual Differences

Every attempt at communication occurs within a **cultural context,** the pattern of physical cues, environmental stimuli, and implicit understanding that convey meaning between two members of the same culture. However, cultures around the world vary widely in the role that context plays in communication (see Figure 3–1).

In a **high-context culture** such as South Korea or Taiwan, people rely less on verbal communication and more on the context of nonverbal actions and environmental setting to convey meaning. For instance, a Chinese speaker expects the receiver to discover the essence of a message and uses indirectness and metaphor to provide a web of meaning.[21] In high-context cultures, the rules of everyday life are rarely explicit; instead, as individuals grow up, they learn how to recognize situational cues (such as gestures and tone of voice) and how to respond as expected.[22] Also, in a high-context culture, the primary role of communication is building relationships, not exchanging information.[23]

In a **low-context culture** such as the United States or Germany, people rely more on verbal communication and less on circumstances and cues to convey meaning. An English speaker feels responsible for transmitting the meaning of the message and often places sentences in chronological sequence to establish a cause-and-effect pattern.[24] In a low-context culture, rules and expectations are usually spelled out through explicit statements such as "Please wait until I'm finished" or "You're welcome to browse."[25] Exchanging information is the primary task of communication in low-context cultures.[26]

Contextual differences are apparent in the way cultures approach situations such as decision making, problem solving, and negotiating: For instance, in lower-context cultures, businesspeople tend to focus on the results of the decisions they face, a reflection of the cultural emphasis on logic and progress. Will this be good for our company? For my career? In comparison, higher-context cultures emphasize the means or the method by which the decision will be made. Building or protecting rela-

---

Treat people the way they expect to be treated, not the way you expect to be treated.

Cultural context is the pattern of physical cues, environmental stimuli, and implicit understanding that conveys meaning between members of the same culture.

High-context cultures rely heavily on nonverbal actions and environmental setting to convey meaning; low-context cultures rely more on explicit verbal communication.

FIGURE 3–1
How Cultural Context Affects Business

IN LOW-CONTEXT CULTURES	IN HIGH-CONTEXT CULTURES
Executive offices are separate with controlled access.	Executive offices are shared and open to all.
Workers rely on detailed background information.	Workers do not expect or want detailed information.
Information is highly centralized and controlled.	Information is shared with everyone.
Objective data are valued over subjective relationships.	Subjective relationships are valued over objective data.
Business and social relationships are discrete.	Business and social relationships overlap.
Competence is valued as much as position and status.	Position and status are valued much more than competence.
Meetings have fixed agendas and plenty of advance notice.	Meetings are often called on short notice, and key people always accept.

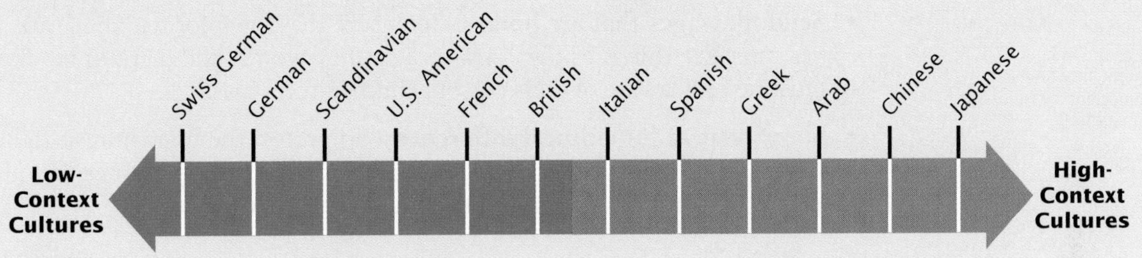

Low-Context Cultures → High-Context Cultures

Swiss German · German · Scandinavian · U.S. American · French · British · Italian · Spanish · Greek · Arab · Chinese · Japanese

tionships can be as important as the facts and information used in making the decisions.[27] Consequently, negotiators working on business deals in such cultures may spend most of their time together building relationships, rather than hammering out contractual details.

Whether you're making a decision, solving a problem, or negotiating a business deal, the communication tactics that work well in a high-context culture may backfire in a low-context culture, and vice versa. The key to success is understanding why the other party is saying and doing particular things and then adapting your approach accordingly.

> Negotiations in low-context cultures are usually viewed impersonally as a series of problems to be overcome; high-context cultures emphasize harmony and agreement.

Legal and Ethical Differences   Cultural context also influences legal and ethical behavior. For example, because low-context cultures value the written word, they consider written agreements binding. But high-context cultures put less emphasis on the written word and consider personal pledges more important than contracts. They also tend to take a more flexible approach regarding adherence to the law, whereas low-context cultures would adhere to the law strictly.[28]

> Low-context cultures tend to value written agreements and interpret laws strictly, whereas high-context cultures view adherence to laws as being more flexible.

As you conduct business around the world, you'll find that legal systems differ from culture to culture. In the United Kingdom and the United States, someone is presumed innocent until proved guilty, a principle rooted in English common law. However, in Mexico and Turkey, someone is presumed guilty until proved innocent, a principle rooted in the Napoleonic code.[29]

As discussed in Chapter 1, making ethical choices can be difficult, even within your own culture. When communicating across cultures, ethics can be even more complicated. What does it mean for a business to do the right thing in Thailand? In Nigeria? In Norway? What happens when a certain behavior is unethical in the United States but an accepted practice in another culture?

> Cultural differences can complicate ethical choices.

For example, in the United States, bribing officials is illegal, but many Kenyans consider paying such bribes a part of life. To get something done right, they pay *kitu kidogo* (or "something small"). In China businesses pay *huilu*, in Russia they pay *vzyatka*, in the Middle East it's *baksheesh*, and in Mexico it's *una mordida* ("a small bite").[30]

The United States enacted the Foreign Corrupt Practices Act in 1977, making it illegal for U.S. companies to pay bribes, even in countries where the practice is accepted (or expected). To help level the playing field for U.S. businesses around the world, the U.S. government has successfully lobbied many other nations to also outlaw bribery as well.[31]

Making ethical choices across cultures can seem incredibly complicated, but doing so actually differs little from the way you choose the most ethical path in your own culture (see Chapter 1). When communicating across cultures, keep your messages ethical by applying four basic principles:[32]

Honesty and respect are cornerstones of ethical communication, regardless of culture.

- **Actively seek mutual ground.** To allow the clearest possible exchange of information, both parties must be flexible and avoid insisting that an interaction take place strictly in terms of one culture or another.

- **Send and receive messages without judgment.** To allow information to flow freely, both parties must recognize that values vary from culture to culture, and they must trust each other.

- **Send messages that are honest.** To ensure that the information is true, both parties must see things as they are—not as they would like them to be. Both parties must be fully aware of their personal and cultural biases.

- **Show respect for cultural differences.** To protect the basic human rights of both parties, each must understand and acknowledge the other's needs and preserve each other's dignity by communicating without deception.

Social Differences The nature of social behavior varies among cultures, sometimes dramatically. These behaviors are guided by rules. Some rules are formal and specifically articulated (table manners are a good example), and some are informal, learned over time (such as the comfortable standing distance between two speakers in an office or whether it's acceptable for male and female employees to socialize outside of work). The combination of both types of rules influences the overall behavior of everyone in a society, or at least most of the people most of the time. In addition to the factors already discussed, social rules can vary from culture to culture in the following areas:

Formal rules of etiquette are explicit and well defined, but informal rules are learned through observation and imitation.

- **Attitudes toward work and success.** Although the United States is home to millions of people having different religions and values, the major social influence is still the Puritan work ethic. Many U.S. citizens hold the view that material comfort earned by individual effort is a sign of superiority, and that people who work hard are better than those who don't. This view is reflected in the number of hours that U.S. employees work every year (see Figure 3–2). Workers in Australia, Japan, and Spain also average at least 1,800 hours of work per year, significantly more than workers in France, Germany, and Norway.

Respect and rank are reflected differently from culture to culture in the way people are addressed and in their working environment.

- **Roles and status.** Culture dictates, or at least tries to dictate, the roles that people play, including who communicates with whom, what they communicate, and in what way. For example, in many countries women still don't play a prominent role in business, so women executives who visit these countries may find that they're not taken seriously as businesspeople.[33] Culture also dictates how people show respect and signify rank. For example, people in the United States show respect by addressing top managers as "Mr. Roberts" or "Ms. Gutierrez." However, people in China are addressed according to their official titles, such as "President" or "Manager."[34]

The rules of polite behavior vary from country to country.

- **Use of manners.** What is polite in one culture may be considered rude in another. For instance, asking a colleague "How was your weekend?" is a common way of making small talk in the United States, but the question sounds intrusive to people in cultures where business and private lives are seen as totally separate. In Arab countries it's impolite to take gifts to a man's wife, but it's acceptable to take gifts to

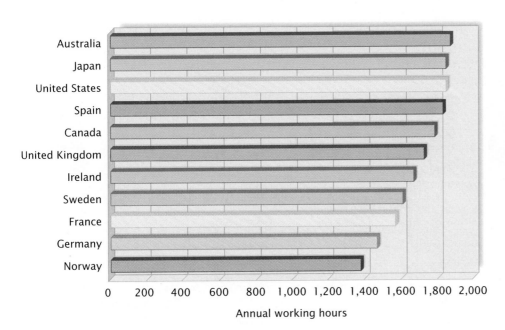

FIGURE 3–2
Working Hours Vary from
Culture to Culture

his children. In India, if you're invited to visit someone's home "any time," you should make an unexpected visit without waiting for a definite invitation. Failure to take the "any time" invitation literally would be an insult, a sign that you don't care to develop the friendship. Research a country's expectations before you visit, then watch carefully and learn after you arrive.

- **Concepts of time.** Business runs on schedules, deadlines, and appointments, but these matters are regarded differently from culture to culture. People in high-context cultures see time as a way to plan the business day efficiently, often focusing on only one task during each scheduled period and viewing time as a limited resource. However, executives from low-context cultures often see time as more flexible. Meeting a deadline is less important than building a business relationship. So the workday isn't expected to follow a rigid, preset schedule.[35] Trying to coax a team into staying on a strict schedule would be an attractive attribute in U.S. companies but could be viewed as pushy and overbearing in other cultures.

> Attitudes toward time, such as strict adherence to meeting schedules, can vary throughout the world.

Nonverbal Differences   As discussed in Chapter 2, nonverbal communication can be a reliable guide to determining the meaning of a message. However, this notion of reliability is valid only when the communicators belong to the same culture. For instance, the simplest hand gestures change meaning from culture to culture. A gesture that communicates good luck in Brazil is the equivalent of giving someone "the finger" in Colombia.[36] In fact, the area of gestures is so complicated that entire books have been written about it. Don't assume that the gestures you grew up with will translate to another culture; doing so could lead to embarrassing mistakes (see Figure 3–3).

From colors to facial expression, nonverbal elements add yet another layer of richness and complexity to intercultural communication. When you have the opportunity to interact with people in another culture, the best advice is to study the culture in advance, then observe the way people behave in the following areas:

- **Greetings.** Do people shake hands, bow, or kiss lightly (on one side of the face or both)?

> Nonverbal differences can vary widely from culture to culture.

- **Personal space.** When people are conversing, do they stand closer together or farther away than you are accustomed to?

- **Touching.** Do people touch each other on the arm to emphasize a point or slap each other the back to show congratulation? Or do they refrain from touching altogether?

FIGURE 3–3
Avoiding Nonverbal Mishaps

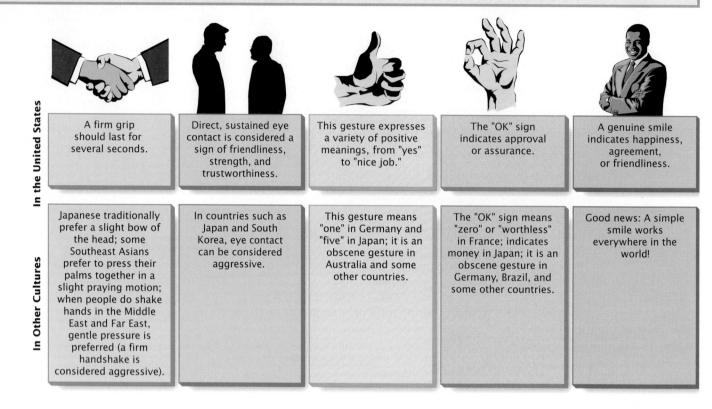

In the United States	A firm grip should last for several seconds.	Direct, sustained eye contact is considered a sign of friendliness, strength, and trustworthiness.	This gesture expresses a variety of positive meanings, from "yes" to "nice job."	The "OK" sign indicates approval or assurance.	A genuine smile indicates happiness, agreement, or friendliness.
In Other Cultures	Japanese traditionally prefer a slight bow of the head; some Southeast Asians prefer to press their palms together in a slight praying motion; when people do shake hands in the Middle East and Far East, gentle pressure is preferred (a firm handshake is considered aggressive).	In countries such as Japan and South Korea, eye contact can be considered aggressive.	This gesture means "one" in Germany and "five" in Japan; it is an obscene gesture in Australia and some other countries.	The "OK" sign means "zero" or "worthless" in France; indicates money in Japan; it is an obscene gesture in Germany, Brazil, and some other countries.	Good news: A simple smile works everywhere in the world!

- **Facial expressions.** Do people shake their heads to indicate "no" and nod them to indicate "yes"? This is what people are accustomed to in the United States, but it is not universal.

- **Eye contact.** Do people make frequent eye contact or avoid it? Frequent eye contact is often taken as a sign of honesty and openness in the United States, but in other cultures it can be a sign of aggressiveness or lack of respect.

- **Posture.** Do people slouch and relax in the office and in public, or do they sit up straight?

- **Formality.** In general, does the culture seem more or less formal than yours?

Following the lead of people who grew up in the culture is not only a great way to learn but a good way to show respect as well.

A culture's views on youth and aging affect how people communicate with one another.

Age Differences   The United States celebrates youth in general and successful young businesspeople in particular. The emphasis on youth is so strong that millions of older people spend millions of dollars every year trying to look or feel younger, whether it's dying that gray hair back to its original color or surgically reversing the effects of aging. Business publications frequently publish lists of successful young executives who are making their mark before age 30 or 40. Youth is associated with strength, energy, possibilities, and freedom, whereas age is too often associated with declining powers and a loss of respect and authority.[37] As a result, younger employees in U.S. companies often communicate with older colleagues as equals, even to the point of openly disagreeing with them.

However, in cultures that value age and seniority, longevity earns respect and increasing power and freedom. For instance, in many Asian societies, the oldest employees hold the most powerful jobs, the most impressive titles, and the greatest degree of freedom and decision-making authority. If a younger employee disagrees with one of these senior executives, the discussion is never conducted in public. The notion of "saving face," of avoiding public embarrassment, is too strong. Instead, if a senior person seems to be in error about something, other employees will find a quiet, private way to communicate whatever information they feel is necessary.[38]

As with all diversity issues, the solution to age-related conflicts can be found in respecting one another and working toward common goals. As Virginia Byrd, a veteran career counselor from Encinitas, California, put it, "It's a real blessing to have different generations in our workplaces. There is so much we can share, if we make the effort."[39]

Communication styles and expectations can vary widely between age groups, putting extra demands on teams that include workers of varying ages.

Gender Differences   The perception of men and women in business also varies from culture to culture. In the United States today, women find a much wider range of business opportunities than existed just a few decades ago. For instance, women now hold top positions or are in line for the top job at a number of leading corporations, including eBay, Avon, MTV, Lucent Technologies, and Xerox.[40] However, such opportunity is not the case in more tradition-oriented societies, where men tend to hold most or all of the positions of authority and women are expected to play a more subservient role. Female executives who visit other cultures may not be taken seriously until they successfully handle challenges to their knowledge, capabilities, and patience.[41]

As more women enter the workforce and take on positions of increasing responsibility, it's important for company leaders to revisit assumptions and practices.[42] For instance, company cultures that have been dominated by men for years may have adopted communication habits that some women have difficulty relating to—such as the constant use of sports metaphors or the acceptance of coarse language.

Whatever the culture, evidence suggests that men and women tend to have slightly different communication styles. Broadly speaking, men tend to emphasize content in their communication efforts whereas women place a higher premium on relationship maintenance.[43] Again, these are broad generalizations that do not apply to every person in every situation, but keeping them in mind can help men and women overcome communication hurdles in the workplace.

Generally speaking, the communication styles of men and women can differ on several points.

IMPROVING INTERCULTURAL COMMUNICATION SKILLS

The better you are at intercultural communication, the more successful you'll be in today's business environment. However, communicating successfully from one culture to another requires a variety of skills (see Figure 3–4). You can improve your intercultural skills throughout your entire career. Begin now by studying other cultures and languages, respecting preferences for communication styles, learning to write and speak clearly, listening carefully, knowing when to use interpreters and translators, and helping others adapt to your culture.

Improving intercultural skills is a career-long effort.

Studying Other Cultures

Effectively adapting your communication efforts to another culture requires not only knowledge about the culture but also both the ability and the motivation to change your personal habits as needed.[44] In other words, it's not a simple task. Unfortunately,

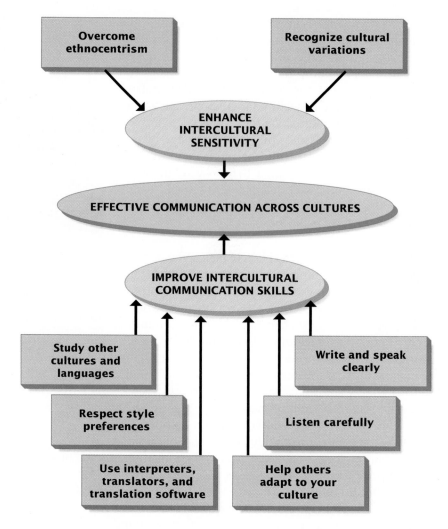

a thorough knowledge of another culture and its communication patterns (both verbal and nonverbal) can take years to acquire. Fortunately, you don't need to learn about the whole world all at once. Many companies appoint specialists for specific countries or regions, giving you a chance to focus on fewer cultures at a time.

Nor do you need to learn everything about a culture to ensure some level of communication success. Even a small amount of research and practice will help you get through many business situations. In addition, most people respond positively to honest effort and good intentions, and many business associates will help you along if you show an interest in learning more about their cultures.

Try to approach situations with an open mind and a healthy sense of humor. Recognize that everybody who tries to communicate across cultures makes mistakes. When it happens, simply apologize if appropriate, ask the other person to explain the accepted way, and then move on. As business becomes ever more global, even the most tradition-bound cultures are learning to deal with outsiders more patiently and overlook the occasional cultural blunder.[45]

Numerous websites and books offer advice on traveling to and working in specific cultures; they're a great place to start. Also try to sample newspapers, magazines, and even the music and movies of another country. For instance, a movie can demonstrate nonverbal customs even if you don't grasp the language. (However, be careful not to rely solely on entertainment products. If people in other countries based their opinions of U.S. culture only on the silly teen flicks and violent action movies that the United States exports around the globe, what sort of impression do you imagine they'd get?) For some of the key issues to research before doing business in another country, refer to Table 3–1.

Mistakes will happen, and when they do, apologize (if appropriate), ask about the accepted way, and move on.

DOING BUSINESS ABROAD   Table 3–1

Action	Details to Consider
Understand social customs	• Is the society homogeneous or heterogeneous? • How do people react to strangers? Are they friendly? Hostile? Reserved? • How do people greet each other? Should you bow? Nod? Shake hands? • How do you express appreciation for an invitation to lunch, dinner, or someone's home? Should you bring a gift? Send flowers? Write a thank-you note? • Are any phrases, facial expressions, or hand gestures considered rude? • How do you attract the attention of a waiter? Do you tip the waiter? • When is it rude to refuse an invitation? How do you refuse politely? • What topics may or may not be discussed in a social setting? In a business setting?
Learn about clothing and food preferences	• What occasions require special clothing? • What colors are associated with mourning? Love? Joy? • Are some types of clothing considered taboo for one gender or the other? • How many times a day do people eat? • How are hands or utensils used when eating? • Where is the seat of honor at a table?
Assess political patterns	• How stable is the political situation? • Does the political situation affect businesses in and out of the country? • What are the traditional government institutions? • Is it appropriate to talk politics in social or business situations?
Understand religious and folk beliefs	• To which religious groups do people belong? • Which places, objects, actions, and events are sacred? • Is there a tolerance for minority religions? • How do religious holidays affect business and government activities? • Does religion require or prohibit eating specific foods? At specific times?
Learn about economic and business Institutions	• Is the society homogeneous or heterogeneous? • What languages are spoken? • What are the primary resources and principal products? • Are businesses generally large? Family controlled? Government controlled? • Is it appropriate to do business by telephone? By fax? By e-mail? • What are the generally accepted working hours? • How do people view scheduled appointments? • Are people expected to socialize before conducting business?
Appraise the nature of ethics, values, and laws	• Is money or a gift expected in exchange for arranging business transactions? • Do people value competitiveness or cooperation? • What are the attitudes toward work? Toward money? • Is politeness more important than factual honesty?

Studying Other Languages

Consider what it must be like to work at IBM, where the global workforce speaks more than 165 languages. Without the ability to communicate in more than one language, how could this diverse group of people ever conduct business? As commerce continues to become more globalized, the demand for multilingual communicators continues to grow as well. Some countries have emphasized language diversity more than others over the years. For instance, in the Netherlands, with its long history of international trade, fluency in multiple languages is considered an essential business skill.[46] Shifts in business patterns can dramatically affect language learning, too. As U.S. companies continue to outsource a variety of business functions to facilities in

English is the most prevalent language in international business, but it's a mistake to assume that everyone understands it.

India, many Indians now view English skills as an important career asset. Conversely, the growing international status of China as a manufacturing powerhouse is prompting many professionals in the United Sates and other countries to learn Mandarin, the official language in China.[47]

To simplify matters, some multinational companies ask all their employees to use English when communicating with employees in other countries, wherever they're located. Employees of Nissan, Japan's third-largest automaker, use English for internal e-mail and memos to colleagues around the world. When the company formed a strategic relationship with Renault, a French carmaker, the situation at Nissan headquarters became even more interesting since English is not the native language of either Japanese or French employees.[48]

Similarly, a number of U.S. companies are teaching their English-speaking employees a second language to facilitate communication with their co-workers. For instance, the Target retail chain is among those sponsoring basic Spanish classes for English-speaking supervisors of immigrant employees. Elsewhere around the country, enrollment is growing in specialized classes such as health-care Spanish and Spanish for professionals.[49]

Even if your colleagues or customers in another country do speak your language, it's worth the time and energy to learn common phrases in theirs. Learning the basics not only helps you get through everyday business and social situations but also demonstrates your commitment to the business relationship. After all, the other person probably spent years learning your language.

Lastly, don't assume that two countries speaking the same language speak it the same way. The French spoken in Quebec and other parts of Canada is often noticeably different from the French spoken in France. Similarly, it's often said that the United States and the United Kingdom are two countries divided by a common language. For instance, *apartment*, *elevator*, and *gasoline* in the United States are *flat*, *lift*, and *petrol* in the United Kingdom.

Respecting Preferences for Communication Style

Communication style—including the level of directness, the degree of formality, preferences for written versus spoken communication, and other factors—varies widely from culture to culture. Knowing what your communication partners expect can help you adapt to their particular style. Once again, watching and learning is the best way to improve your skills; however, you can infer some generalities from what you already know about a culture. For instance, U.S. workers typically prefer an open and direct communication style; they find other styles frustrating or suspect. Directness is also valued in Sweden as a sign of efficiency, but unlike discussions in the United States, heated debates and confrontations are unusual. Italian, German, and French executives don't soften up colleagues with praise before they criticize—doing so seems manipulative to them. However, professionals from high-context cultures, such as Japan or China, tend to be less direct.[50]

In international correspondence, U.S. businesspeople will generally want to be somewhat more formal than they would be when writing to people in their own country. The letter in Figure 3–5 was written by a supplier in Germany to a nearby retailer; you can see how the tone is more formal than would be used in the United States. In Germany, business letters usually open with a reference to the business relationship and close with a compliment to the recipient. Of course, if you carry formality to extremes, you'll sound unnatural.

Writing and Speaking Clearly

In addition to learning the preferred style of your communication partners, you can help ensure successful messages by taking extra care with your writing. When send-

Many companies find that they must be able to conduct business in languages other than English.

If you have a long-term business relationship with people of another culture, it is helpful to learn at least some basic words and phrases of their language.

Business correspondence is often more formal in other countries than it is in the United States.

FIGURE 3–5
Effective German Business Letter (Translated)

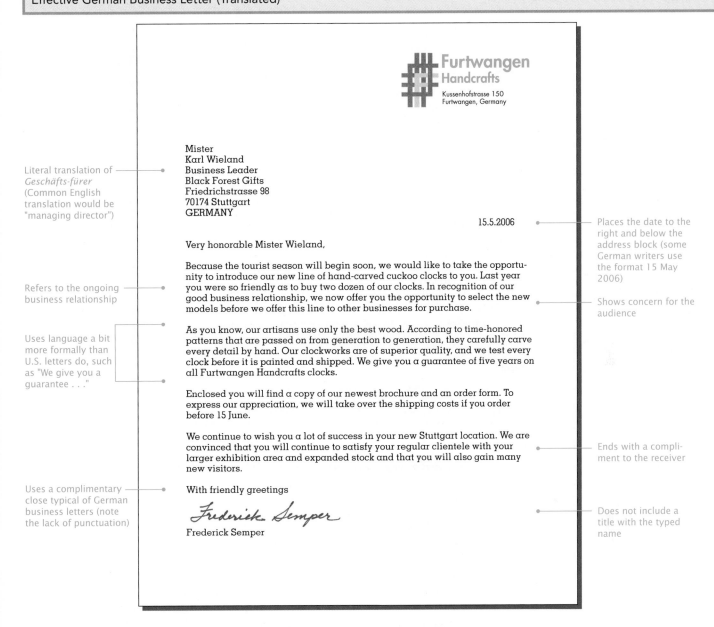

Literal translation of *Geschäfts-fürer* (Common English translation would be "managing director")

Refers to the ongoing business relationship

Uses language a bit more formally than U.S. letters do, such as "We give you a guarantee . . ."

Uses a complimentary close typical of German business letters (note the lack of punctuation)

Places the date to the right and below the address block (some German writers use the format 15 May 2006)

Shows concern for the audience

Ends with a compliment to the receiver

Does not include a title with the typed name

Furtwangen Handcrafts
Kussenhofstrasse 150
Furtwangen, Germany

Mister
Karl Wieland
Business Leader
Black Forest Gifts
Friedrichstrasse 98
70174 Stuttgart
GERMANY

15.5.2006

Very honorable Mister Wieland,

Because the tourist season will begin soon, we would like to take the opportunity to introduce our new line of hand-carved cuckoo clocks to you. Last year you were so friendly as to buy two dozen of our clocks. In recognition of our good business relationship, we now offer you the opportunity to select the new models before we offer this line to other businesses for purchase.

As you know, our artisans use only the best wood. According to time-honored patterns that are passed on from generation to generation, they carefully carve every detail by hand. Our clockworks are of superior quality, and we test every clock before it is painted and shipped. We give you a guarantee of five years on all Furtwangen Handcrafts clocks.

Enclosed you will find a copy of our newest brochure and an order form. To express our appreciation, we will take over the shipping costs if you order before 15 June.

We continue to wish you a lot of success in your new Stuttgart location. We are convinced that you will continue to satisfy your regular clientele with your larger exhibition area and expanded stock and that you will also gain many new visitors.

With friendly greetings

Frederick Semper

Frederick Semper

---

ing written communication to businesspeople from another culture, familiarize yourself with their written communication preferences and adapt your approach, style, and tone to meet their expectations. To help you prepare effective written communications for multicultural audiences, follow these recommendations:[51]

- **Use simple, clear language.** Use precise words that don't have the potential to confuse with multiple meanings. For instance, the word *rich* has at least half a dozen different meanings, whereas *wealthy* has exactly one, leaving no room for ambiguity.

- **Be brief.** Use simple sentences and short paragraphs, breaking information into smaller chunks that are easier for your reader to capture and translate.

- **Use transitional elements.** Help readers follow your train of thought by using transitional words and phrases. Precede related points with expressions such as *in addition* and *first, second,* and *third.*

FIGURE 3–6
Ineffective Intercultural Letter

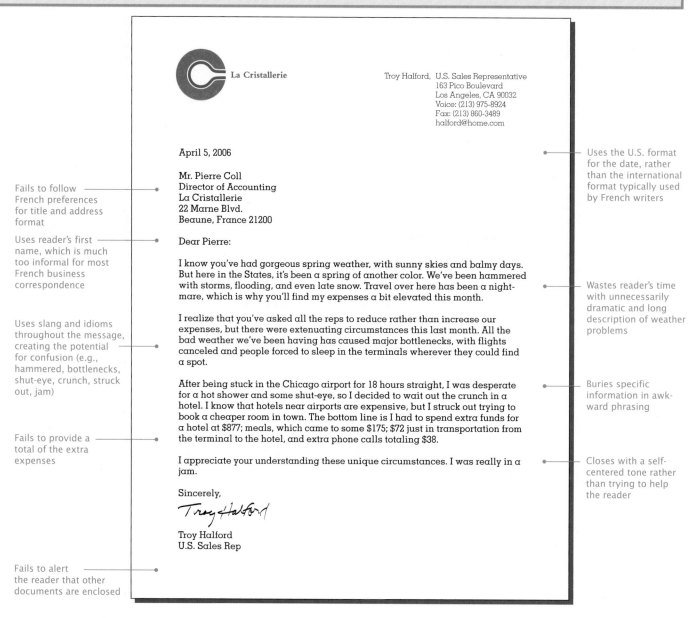

Fails to follow French preferences for title and address format

Uses reader's first name, which is much too informal for most French business correspondence

Uses slang and idioms throughout the message, creating the potential for confusion (e.g., hammered, bottlenecks, shut-eye, crunch, struck out, jam)

Fails to provide a total of the extra expenses

Fails to alert the reader that other documents are enclosed

Uses the U.S. format for the date, rather than the international format typically used by French writers

Wastes reader's time with unnecessarily dramatic and long description of weather problems

Buries specific information in awkward phrasing

Closes with a self-centered tone rather than trying to help the reader

La Cristallerie

Troy Halford, U.S. Sales Representative
163 Pico Boulevard
Los Angeles, CA 90032
Voice: (213) 975-8924
Fax: (213) 860-3489
halford@home.com

April 5, 2006

Mr. Pierre Coll
Director of Accounting
La Cristallerie
22 Marne Blvd.
Beaune, France 21200

Dear Pierre:

I know you've had gorgeous spring weather, with sunny skies and balmy days. But here in the States, it's been a spring of another color. We've been hammered with storms, flooding, and even late snow. Travel over here has been a nightmare, which is why you'll find my expenses a bit elevated this month.

I realize that you've asked all the reps to reduce rather than increase our expenses, but there were extenuating circumstances this last month. All the bad weather we've been having has caused major bottlenecks, with flights canceled and people forced to sleep in the terminals wherever they could find a spot.

After being stuck in the Chicago airport for 18 hours straight, I was desperate for a hot shower and some shut-eye, so I decided to wait out the crunch in a hotel. I know that hotels near airports are expensive, but I struck out trying to book a cheaper room in town. The bottom line is I had to spend extra funds for a hotel at $877; meals, which came to some $175; $72 just in transportation from the terminal to the hotel, and extra phone calls totaling $38.

I appreciate your understanding these unique circumstances. I was really in a jam.

Sincerely,

Troy Halford

Troy Halford
U.S. Sales Rep

- **Address international correspondence properly.** Refer to Table 1–2 in Appendix A for an explanation of different address elements and salutations commonly used in certain foreign countries.

- **Cite numbers and dates carefully.** In the United States, 12–05–06 means December 5, 2006, but in many other countries, it means May 12, 2006. Dates in Japan and China are usually expressed with the year first, followed by the month and then the day; therefore, to write December 5, 2006 in Japan, write it as 2006–12–05. Similarly, 1.000 means one with three decimal places in the United States and Great Britain, but it means one thousand in many European countries.

- **Avoid slang, idiomatic phrases, and business jargon.** Everyday speech and writing is full of slang and **idiomatic phrases,** phrases that mean more than the sum of their literal parts. Many of these informal usages are so deeply ingrained, in fact, that

FIGURE 3–7
Effective Intercultural Letter

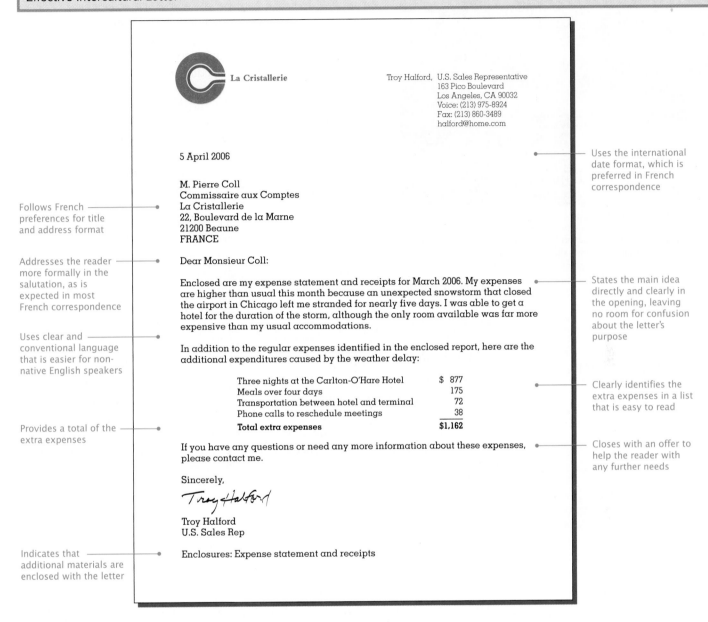

La Cristallerie

Troy Halford, U.S. Sales Representative
163 Pico Boulevard
Los Angeles, CA 90032
Voice: (213) 975-8924
Fax: (213) 860-3489
halford@home.com

Uses the international date format, which is preferred in French correspondence

5 April 2006

M. Pierre Coll
Commissaire aux Comptes
La Cristallerie
22, Boulevard de la Marne
21200 Beaune
FRANCE

Follows French preferences for title and address format

Dear Monsieur Coll:

Addresses the reader more formally in the salutation, as is expected in most French correspondence

Enclosed are my expense statement and receipts for March 2006. My expenses are higher than usual this month because an unexpected snowstorm that closed the airport in Chicago left me stranded for nearly five days. I was able to get a hotel for the duration of the storm, although the only room available was far more expensive than my usual accommodations.

States the main idea directly and clearly in the opening, leaving no room for confusion about the letter's purpose

Uses clear and conventional language that is easier for non-native English speakers

In addition to the regular expenses identified in the enclosed report, here are the additional expenditures caused by the weather delay:

Three nights at the Carlton-O'Hare Hotel	$ 877
Meals over four days	175
Transportation between hotel and terminal	72
Phone calls to reschedule meetings	38
Total extra expenses	**$1,162**

Clearly identifies the extra expenses in a list that is easy to read

Provides a total of the extra expenses

If you have any questions or need any more information about these expenses, please contact me.

Closes with an offer to help the reader with any further needs

Sincerely,

Troy Halford

Troy Halford
U.S. Sales Rep

Enclosures: Expense statement and receipts

Indicates that additional materials are enclosed with the letter

you may not even be aware that you're using them. Examples from U.S. English include phrases like "Off the top of my head," "Crossing the finish line," "More bang for the buck," and "Face the music." Your foreign correspondent may have no idea what you're talking about when you use such phrases.

- **Avoid humor and other references to popular culture.** Jokes and references to popular entertainment usually rely on subtle cultural issues that your audience may be completely unaware of.

Compare the letters shown in Figures 3–6 and 3–7, in which someone from the United States is writing to a French business partner to explain why his expenses were unusually high for the previous month. Although some of these differences may seem trivial, meeting the expectations of an international audience illustrates both knowledge of and respect for the other cultures.

Experienced international speakers, such as Dell founder Michael Dell, are careful to incorporate culture and language variations into their communication efforts.

Whether you're traveling to another country or teaming up with someone who is visiting or immigrating to your country, you're likely to speak with people whose native language is different from yours. Even when you know the vocabulary and grammar of the other person's language, the processing of everyday conversations can be difficult. For instance, speakers from the United States are notorious for stringing together multiple words into a single pseudo-word that mystifies non-native English speakers. "Did you eat yet?" becomes "Jeetyet?" and "Can I help you?" becomes "Cannahepya?" Similarly, the French language frequently uses a concept known as *liaison,* in which one word is intentionally joined with the next. Without a lot of practice, new French speakers have a hard time telling when one word ends and the next one begins.

To be more effective in intercultural conversations, remember to (1) speak slowly and clearly; (2) don't rephrase until it's obviously necessary (immediately rephrasing something you've just said doubles the translation workload for the listener); (3) look for and ask for feedback to make sure your message is getting through; (4) don't talk down to the other person by overenunciating words or oversimplifying sentences; and (5) at the end of the conversation, doublecheck to make sure you and the listener agree on what has been said and decided.

Speaking clearly and getting plenty of feedback are two of the keys to successful intercultural conversations.

Listening Carefully

Languages vary considerably in the significance of tone, pitch, speed, and volume. The English word *progress* can be a noun or a verb, depending on which syllable you accent. In Chinese, the meaning of the word *mà* changes depending on the speaker's tone; it can mean *mother, pileup, horse,* or *scold.* Regular Arabic speech can sound excited or angry to an English-speaking U.S. listener.[52] Conversely, businesspeople from Japan tend to speak more softly than Westerners.

To listen more effectively in intercultural situations, accept what you hear without judgment and let people finish what they have to say.

With some practice, you can start to get a sense of vocal patterns. The key is simply to accept what you hear first, without jumping to conclusions about meaning or motivation. Let other people finish what they have to say. If you interrupt, you may miss something important. You'll also show a lack of respect. If you do not understand a comment, ask the person to repeat it. Any momentary awkwardness you might feel in asking for extra help is less important than the risk of unsuccessful communication.

Using Interpreters, Translators, and Translation Software

You may encounter business situations that require using an interpreter (for spoken communication) or a translator (for written communications). In addition, most customers expect to be addressed in their native language, particularly concerning advertising, warranties, repair and maintenance manuals, and product labels. These documents certainly require the services of a translator. Microsoft spends several hundred million dollars a year to make virtually all of its software products, websites, and help documents available in dozens of languages; the company is believed by some to be the world's largest purchaser of translation services.[53]

Document Makeover

IMPROVE THIS LETTER

To practice correcting drafts of actual documents, visit your online course or the access-code protected portion of the Companion Website. Click "Document Makeovers," then click Chapter 3. You will find a letter that contains problems and errors relating to what you've learned in this chapter about developing effective intercultural communication skills. Use the "Final Draft" decision tool to create an improved version of this letter. Check the message for a communication style that keeps the message brief, does not become too familiar or informal, uses transitional elements appropriately, and avoids slang, idioms, jargon, and technical language.

USING THE POWER OF TECHNOLOGY

The Gist of Machine Translation

What is the writer trying to say in the following sentence?

We have the need to balance for the barriers on this one or the market could draw well after us.

Can you figure it out? Here's the original sentence, which uses a tone that is overly casual and colloquial—a common problem in U.S. business documents:

We need to swing for the fences on this one or the market could shoot right past us.

When this sentence was run through a simple computerized translation service, from English to French and back to English, the software clearly had trouble with the "swing for the fences" and "shoot right past us" figures of speech.

Without hands-on intervention from experienced human translators, machine translation systems can produce results that are anywhere from amusing to nonsensical to downright dangerous. Whether you're using one of the automatic website translation services available from such sites as Alta Vista and Google or a text translator such as the one available at WorldLingo (www.worldlingo.com), keep in mind that you won't get the same quality that you'd get from a human translator.

However, you won't always have the luxury of waiting for, or paying for, a human translator. For example, your sales department might receive an unexpected e-mail message from somebody who appears to be a potential customer in another country. You don't want the expense of hiring a translator this early in the relationship, but you don't want to let a big deal slip away either. By running the message through a basic machine translator, chances are you can get a basic idea of the message almost instantly. At the very least, you'll probably be able to tell whether

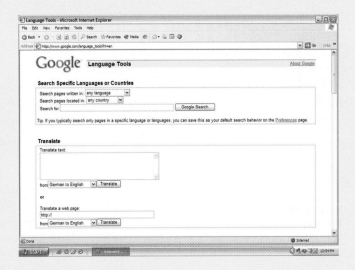

the message is important enough to warrant the time and expense of a translator. And if you get results that make you scratch your head or laugh out loud, do call in a translator to make sure that you and the sender understand one another correctly.

CAREER APPLICATIONS

1. Why do you think a computer might have trouble translating "swing for the fences" (a baseball phrase for trying as hard as one can to hit the ball out of the park)?

2. What are some examples of business documents that would probably be safe to read via machine translation? What are some that would be dangerous to trust to software?

Interpreters and translators can be expensive, but skilled professionals provide invaluable assistance for communicating in other cultural contexts.[54] Keeping up with current language usage in a given country or culture is also critical in order to avoid embarrassing blunders. Landor Associates, a leading marketing agency, usually engages three native-language speakers to review translated materials to make sure the sense of the message is compatible with current usage and slang in a given country.[55] Some companies use *back-translation* to ensure accuracy. Once a translator encodes a message into another language, a different translator retranslates the same message into the original language. This back-translation is then compared with the original message to discover any errors or discrepancies.

The time and cost required for professional translation has encouraged the development of **machine translation,** any form of computerized intelligence used to translate one language to another. Dedicated software tools and online services such as WorldLingo (www.worldlingo.com) and Alis Technologies (www.alis.com) offer some form of automated translation. Major search engines such as Alta Vista and Google let you request a translated version of the websites you find. Although none of these tools promises translation quality on a par with human translators, they can be quite useful with individual words and short phrases, and they can give you the overall gist of a message (see "Using the Power of Technology: The Gist of Machine Translation").[56]

Machine translation uses computerized intelligence (such as software on websites) to translate material from one language to another.

✓ CHECKLIST: Improving Intercultural Communication Skills

✓ Study other cultures so that you can appreciate cultural variations.

✓ Study other languages, even if you can learn only a few basic words and phrases.

✓ Help nonnative English speakers learn English.

✓ Respect cultural preferences for communication style.

✓ Write clearly, using brief messages, simple language, generous transitions, and appropriate international conventions.

✓ Avoid slang, humor, and references to popular culture.

✓ Speak clearly and slowly, giving listeners time to translate your words.

✓ Ask for feedback to ensure successful communication.

✓ Listen carefully and ask speakers to repeat anything you don't understand.

✓ Use interpreters and translators for important messages.

Helping Others Adapt to Your Culture

Now that you have a good appreciation for the complexity of getting your message across to someone in another culture, you can also appreciate the challenge faced by people from other cultures when they try to communicate with you. Whether a younger person is unaccustomed to the formalities of a large corporation or a colleague from another country is working on a team with you, look for opportunities to help people fit in and adapt their communication style. For more ideas on how to improve communication in the workplace, see "Checklist: Improving Intercultural Communication Skills."

Remember that speaking and listening are usually much harder in a second language than writing and reading. Oral communication requires participants to process sound in addition to meaning, and it doesn't provide any time to go back and reread or rewrite. So instead of asking a foreign colleague to provide information in a conference call, you could set up an intranet site where the person can file a written report. Similarly, using instant messaging and e-mail is often easier for colleagues with different native languages than participating in live conversations. An added plus with many of these technologies is overcoming the barrier of time zones. You can simply carry on a written conversation online, rather than participating in phone calls early in the morning or late at night.

Whatever assistance you can provide will be greatly appreciated. Smart businesspeople recognize the value of intercultural communication skills. Moreover, chances are that while you're helping others, you'll learn something about other cultures, too.

On the Job

SOLVING COMMUNICATION DILEMMAS AT IBM

Ted Childs is responsible for overall diversity planning and strategy at IBM, but every manager throughout the company is expected to foster a climate of inclusion and support for employees of every cultural background. As a team leader in one of IBM's software development labs, you're learning to exercise sound business judgment and use good listening skills to help resolve situations that arise within your diverse group of employees. How would you address each of these challenges?

1. Joo Mi Kang, a recent immigrant from South Korea, is a brilliant programmer who continues to impress everyone with her technical innovations. Unfortunately, she usually doesn't do a good job of documenting her code, an admittedly tedious process in which programmers are supposed to write descriptions of what they've created and explain how it works so that other people can come in later and fix it if needed. You suspect from seeing some of her e-mails that she has trouble writing in English. What should your first step be?

   a. Send her an e-mail reminding her of the need to document her code; attach a copy of her job description.

   b. Suggest she find a tutor to help her develop her English skills.

c. Visit her in her office and discuss the situation; ask if she understands the importance of documenting her code and whether she has encountered any difficulty in doing so.

d. Assign several other programmers the task of pitching in to take care of her documentation chores.

2. Your employees are breaking into ethnically based cliques. Members of ethnic groups eat together, socialize together, and often chat in their native languages while they work. You appreciate how these groups give their members a sense of community, but you worry that these informal communication channels are alienating nonmembers and fragmenting the flow of information. How do you encourage a stronger sense of community and teamwork across your department?

a. Ban the use of languages other than English at work.

b. Do nothing. This is normal behavior, and any attempt to disrupt it will only generate resentment.

c. Structure work assignments and other activities (such as volunteer projects) in ways that bring people from the various cultural groups into regular contact with one another and make them more dependant on one another as well.

d. Send all of your employees to diversity training classes.

3. Vasily Pevsner, a Russian immigrant, has worked in the department for five years. He works well alone, but he resists working with other employees, even in team settings where collaboration is expected. How do you handle the situation?

a. Stay out of the way and let the situation resolve itself. Pevsner has to learn how to get along with the other team members.

b. Tell the rest of the team to work harder at getting along with Pevsner.

c. Tell Pevsner he must work with others or he will not progress in the company.

d. Talk privately with Pevsner and help him understand the importance of working together as a team. During the conversation, try to uncover why he doesn't participate more in team efforts.

4. IBM boasts one of the most highly educated workforces in the world, and your department is no exception. However, you've been surprised at the confusion that some of your memos and other written messages have generated lately. You suspect your casual and often humorous writing style might be the culprit and decide to "test drive" a different writing style. You've drafted four versions of a blog posting that explains a new policy aimed at keeping software projects on schedule as they near completion. Which of these do you choose and why?

a. "As each new project nears completion, I recognize how hard you all try to keep projects on schedule, even with the last-minute problems that are always part of software projects. To lighten your workload during the hectic final phase, you'll no longer be expected to attend routine department meetings or tend to other nonessential tasks during the final four weeks of each project."

b. "As each new project races toward the finish line, I appreciate that all of you work like dogs to keep projects on schedule, even with the inevitable glitches and gremlins that always seem to attack software projects at the last minute. Good news: During the last four weeks of every project, you'll be excused from nonessential tasks such as routine department meetings so that you can focus on your programming work (admit it—I know you hate coming to these meetings anyway!)."

c. "As usual, the solution to all of life's problems can be found on television! While watching the Raiders-Chiefs game yesterday, I realized that we need to have our own version of the two-minute drill. To help avoid schedule slippage during the crazy final few weeks of each project, team members will be excused from routine meetings and other nonessential tasks not directly related to their project responsibilities."

d. "As you should all be aware, numerous entities both internal and external to the corporation rely on us for timely project completion. While the inherent nature of software development presents unexpected difficulties during the final stages of a project, it is incumbent upon us to employ every tactic possible to avoid significant completion delays. Henceforth, team members will be excused from nonessential tasks during the final four weeks of every development project."

Learning Objectives Checkup

Assess your understanding of the principles in this chapter by reading each learning objective and studying the accompanying exercises. For fill-in items, write the missing text in the blank provided; for multiple choice items, circle the letter of the correct answer. You can check your responses against the answer key on page AK-1.

Objective 3.1: Discuss the opportunities and challenges of intercultural communication.

1. Which of the following factors is a significant reason why U.S. business professionals often need to understand the cultures of other countries?

a. Recent changes to government regulations require cultural education before companies are granted export licenses.

b. The U.S. economy has been shrinking for the past 20 years, forcing companies to look overseas.

c. Many countries require business executives to be fluent in at least two languages.

d. Thousands of U.S. companies, including many of the largest corporations in the country, rely on markets in other countries for a significant portion of their sales.

2. Which of the following is a benefit of a multicultural workforce?

a. Providing a broader range of viewpoints and ideas

b. Giving companies a better understanding of diverse markets

c. Enabling companies to recruit workers from the broadest possible pool of talent

d. All of the above

3. A culturally rich workforce, composed of employees representing a wide range of ethnicities, religions, ages, physical abilities, languages, and other factors

a. Always slows down the decision-making process

b. Can be more challenging to manage but can pay off in a variety of important ways

c. Is easier to manage because so many new ideas are present

d. Is a concern only for companies that do business outside the United States

Objective 3.2: Define culture, and explain how culture is learned.

4. Culture is defined as

a. A distinct group that exists within a country

b. A shared system of symbols, beliefs, attitudes, values, expectations, and norms for behavior

c. The pattern of cues and stimuli that convey meaning between two or more people

d. Serious art forms such as classical music, painting, sculpture, drama, and poetry

5. Which of the following is *not* an example of a cultural group?

a. Hindus

b. Wrestling fans

c. Television viewers

d. Members of a fraternity

6. Culture is learned from

a. Family members

b. Explicit teaching by others in the culture

c. Observations of the behavior of others in the culture

d. All of the above

Objective 3.3: Define ethnocentrism and stereotyping, then give three suggestions for overcoming these limiting mindsets.

7. _____ is the tendency to judge all other groups according to the standards, behaviors, and customs of one's own group.

8. _____ is the mistake of assigning a wide range of generalized attributes to individuals on the basis of their membership in a particular culture or social group, without considering an individual's unique characteristics.

9. Which of the following is one of several techniques you can use to make sure you don't fall into the traps of ethnocentrism and stereotyping?

a. Minimize interactions with people whose cultures you don't understand.

b. Make sure that the people you work with clearly understand your culture.

c. Insist that every employee who works for you strictly follows the company's guidelines for intercultural communication.

d. Avoiding making assumptions about people in other cultures.

Objective 3.4: Explain the importance of recognizing cultural variations, and list six categories of cultural differences.

10. In business, recognizing cultural differences is important because

a. Doing so helps reduce the chances for misunderstanding

b. Someone from another culture may try to take advantage of your ignorance

c. If you don't, you'll be accused of being politically incorrect

d. Doing so helps you become more ethnocentric

11. An example of low-context cultural communication would be

a. Someone from China using metaphors to convey meaning

b. Someone from Greece insisting on reaching agreement on every detail of a deal

c. Someone from Canada vigorously arguing his point of view in a problem-solving situation

d. Someone from Japan encouraging socializing before entering into official negotiations

12. Which of the following is generally true about high-context cultures?

a. Employees work shorter hours in such cultures because context allows them to communicate less often.

b. People rely less on verbal communication and more on the context of nonverbal actions and environmental setting to convey meaning.

c. People rely more on verbal communication and less on the context of nonverbal actions and environmental setting to convey meaning.

d. The rules of everyday life are explicitly taught to all people within the culture.

13. Contextual differences between cultures refer to

a. The degree to which various cultures rely on verbal or nonverbal actions to convey meaning

b. Whether cultures emphasize written or spoken communication

c. The role of the Internet (including e-mail and instant messaging) in international communication

d. Attitudes toward work and success

14. Differing attitudes toward greetings, personal space, touching, facial expression, eye contact, posture, and formality are common examples of _____ differences between cultures.

Objective 3.5: Discuss what you can do to improve your intercultural communication skills.

15. When communicating orally to those who speak English as a second language, you should make a habit to always

a. Immediately rephrase every important point you make in order to the give your listeners two options to choose from

b. Speak louder if listeners don't seem to understand you

c. Ignore the other person's body language

d. Rephrase your key points if you observe body language that suggests a lack of understanding

Objective 3.6: Outline strategies for studying other cultures.

16. Understanding the nuances of a culture can take years to learn, so your best approach when preparing to communicate with people in a culture that you don't know well is to

a. Learn as much as you can from websites, travel guides, and other resources, then don't be afraid to ask for help while you are communicating in that new culture

b. Learn as much as you can from websites, travel guides, and other resources, but never ask for help because doing so will only show everyone how ignorant you are

c. Learn as much as you can from TV shows and movies that feature the other culture; the combination of spoken words, visuals, and music is the best way to learn a culture

d. Don't worry about cultural variations; you'll never have time to understand them all, so your energy is better spent on other business issues

Objective 3.7: List seven recommendations for writing clearly in multilanguage business environments.

17. When writing for audiences who don't speak the same native language as you speak, you can improve communication by

a. Spelling out numbers rather than writing them as figures

b. Using simple sentences and careful word choices

c. Using long paragraphs to reduce the number of visual breaks on the page

d. All of the above

18. When you are writing for multilanguage audiences, humor

a. Should be used often because it makes your audience feel welcome on a personal level

b. Should rarely, if ever, be used because humor is one of the most difficult elements of communication to encode or decode in a second language

c. Should never be used because movies and other entertainment products rarely cross over national boundaries

d. Should be used at least once per letter to show that you appreciate your audience as human beings

Apply Your Knowledge

1. What are some of the intercultural differences that managers of a U.S.-based firm might encounter during a series of business meetings with a China-based company whose managers speak English fairly well?

2. What are some of the intercultural communication issues to consider when deciding whether to accept an overseas job with a firm whose headquarters are in the United States? A job in the United States with a local branch of a foreign-owned firm? Explain.

3. How do you think company managers from a country that has a relatively homogeneous culture might react when they do business with the culturally diverse staff of a company based in a less homogeneous country? Explain your answer.

4. Your company has relocated to a U.S. city where Vietnamese culture is strongly established. Many of your employees will be from this culture. What can you do to improve communication between your management and the Vietnamese Americans you are currently hiring?

5. **Ethical Choices** Your office in Turkey desperately needs the supplies that have been stuck in Turkish customs for a month. Should you bribe a customs official to speed up delivery? Explain your decision.

Practice Your Knowledge

DOCUMENT FOR ANALYSIS

Your boss wants to write a brief blog posting to welcome employees recently transferred to your department from your Hong Kong branch. They all speak English, but your boss asks you to review her message for clarity. What would you do to improve this message, given the intended audience—and why? Would you consider this message to be audience centered? Why or why not?

> *I wanted to welcome you ASAP to our little family here in the States. It's high time we shook hands in person and not just across the sea. I'm pleased as punch about getting to know you all, and I for one will do my level best to sell you on America.*

Exercises

For active links to all websites discussed in this chapter, visit this text's website at **www.prenhall.com/thill**. Locate your book and click on its Companion Website link. Then select Chapter 3, and click on "Featured Websites." Locate the name of the page or the URL related to the material in the text. Please note that links to sites that become inactive after publication of the book will be removed from the Featured Websites section.

3.1 **Intercultural Sensitivity: Recognizing Variations** You represent a Canadian toy company that's negotiating to buy miniature truck wheels from a manufacturer in Osaka, Japan. In your first meeting, you explain that your company expects to control the design of the wheels as well as the materials that are used to make them. The manufacturer's representative looks down and says softly, "Perhaps that will be difficult." You press for agreement, and to emphasize your willingness to buy, you show the prepared contract you've brought with you. However, the manufacturer seems increasingly vague and uninterested. What cultural differences may be interfering with effective communication in this situation? Explain.

3.2 **Ethical Choices** A U.S. manager wants to export machine parts to a West African country, but an official there expects a special payment before allowing the shipment into his country. How can the two sides resolve their different approaches without violating U.S. rules against bribing foreign officials? On the basis of the information presented in Chapter 1, would you consider this situation an ethical dilemma or an ethical lapse? Please explain.

3.3 **Teamwork** Working with two other students, prepare a list of 10 examples of slang (in your own language) that might be misinterpreted or misunderstood during a business conversation with someone from another culture. Next to each example, suggest other words you might use to convey the same message. Do the alternatives mean *exactly* the same as the original slang or idiom?

3.4 **Intercultural Communication: Studying Cultures** Choose a specific country, such as India, Portugal, Bolivia, Thailand, or Nigeria, with which you are not familiar. Research the culture and write a brief summary of what a U.S. manager would need to know about concepts of personal space and rules of social behavior in order to conduct business successfully in that country.

3.5 **Multicultural Workforce: Bridging Differences** Differences in gender, age, and physical abilities contribute to the diversity of today's workforce. Working with a classmate, role-play a conversation in which
   a. A woman is being interviewed for a job by a male personnel manager
   b. An older person is being interviewed for a job by a younger personnel manager
   c. An employee who is a native speaker of English is being interviewed for a job by a hiring manager who is a recent immigrant with relatively poor English skills
   How did differences between the applicant and the interviewer shape the communication? What can you do to improve communication in such situations?

3.6 **Intercultural Sensitivity: Understanding Attitudes** As the director of marketing for a telecommunications firm based in Germany, you're negotiating with an official in Guangzhou, China, who's in charge of selecting a new telephone system for the city. You insist that the specifications be spelled out in the contract. However, your Chinese counterpart seems to have little interest in technical and financial details. What can you do or say to break this intercultural deadlock and obtain the contract so that both parties are comfortable?

3.7 **Cultural Variations: Ability Differences** You are a new manager at K & J Brick, a masonry products company that is now run by the two sons of the man who founded it 50 years ago. For years, the co-owners have invited the management team to a wilderness lodge for a combination of outdoor sports and annual business planning meetings. You don't want to miss the event, but you know that the outdoor activities weren't designed for someone with your physical impairments. Draft a short memo to the rest of the management team, suggesting changes to the annual event that will allow all managers to participate.

3.8   Culture and Time: Dealing with Variations When a company knows that a scheduled delivery time given by an overseas firm is likely to be flexible, managers may buy in larger quantities or may order more often to avoid running out of product before the next delivery. Identify three other management decisions that may be influenced by differing cultural concepts of time, and make notes for a short (two-minute) presentation to your class.

3.9   Intercultural Communication: Using Interpreters Imagine that you're the lead negotiator for a company that's trying to buy a factory in Prague, capital of the Czech Republic. Although you haven't spent much time in the country in the past decade, your parents grew up near Prague, so you understand and speak the language fairly well. However, you wonder about the advantages and disadvantages of using an interpreter anyway. For example, you may have more time to think if you wait for an intermediary to translate the other side's position. Decide whether to hire an interpreter, and then write a brief (two- or three-paragraph) explanation of your decision.

3.10   Internet: Translation Software Explore the powers and limitations of computer translation at AltaVista, www.altavista.com. Click on "translate" and enter a sentence such as "We are enclosing a purchase order for four dozen computer monitors." Select "English to Spanish" and click to complete the translation. Once you've read the Spanish version, cut and paste it into the "text for translation" box, select "Spanish to English," and click to translate. Try translating the same English sentence into German, French, or Italian and then back into English. How do the results of each translation differ? What are the implications for the use of automated translation services and back-translation? How could you use this website to sharpen your intercultural communication skills?

3.11   Intercultural Communication: Improving Skills You've been assigned to host a group of Swedish college students who are visiting your college for the next two weeks. They've all studied English but this is their first trip to your area. Make a list of at least eight slang terms and idioms they are likely to hear on campus. How will you explain each phrase? When speaking with the Swedish students, what word or words might you substitute for each slang term or idiom?

3.12   Intercultural Communication: Podcasting Your company was one of the first to use the Apple iPod and other digital music players as business communication tools. Executives often record messages (such as monthly sales reports) as digital audio files and post them on the company's intranet site, a technique known as *podcasting*. Employees from the 14 offices in Europe, Asia, and North America then download the files to their music players and listen to the messages while riding the train to work, eating lunch at their desks, and so on. Your boss asks you to draft the opening statement for a podcast that will announce a revenue drop caused by intensive competitive pressure. She reviews your script then hands it back with a gentle explanation that it needs to be revised for international listeners. Improve the following statement in as many ways as you can:

Howdy, comrades. Shouldn't surprise anyone that we took a beating this year, given the insane pricing moves our knucklehead competitors have been making. I mean, how those clowns can keep turning a profit is beyond me, what with steel costs still going through the roof and labor costs heating up—even in countries where everybody goes to find cheap labor—and hazardous waste disposal regs adding to operating costs, too.

Expand Your Knowledge

LEARNING MORE ON THE WEB

CULTURAL SAVVY FOR COMPETITIVE ADVANTAGE

www.executiveplanet.com

Want to improve your cultural sensitivity? Log on to ExecutivePlanet.com, where you'll find country reports, business and cultural tips, and links to interviews, profiles, articles, books, and more learning resources. Avoid culture shock by developing your ability to understand the traditions, assumptions, etiquette, and values of other cultures as well as your own. This site is your business and cultural guide to the world.

ACTIVITIES

Visit ExecutivePlanet.com and read the country reports and cultural tips. Follow the site's links to interviews, profiles, articles, books, and more. Then answer the following questions.

1. Why should you understand negotiating practices of people from a different culture?
2. Every culture has its own business protocol. What should you know about a culture's business protocol before you transact business with that culture?
3. What are some examples of cultural gift-giving taboos?

EXPLORING THE WEB ON YOUR OWN

Review these chapter-related websites on your own to learn more about intercultural communication.

1. Country Background Notes, www.state.gov, provides helpful background information on every country with which the United States has an official relationship. This site is published by the U.S. State Department. Just click on Country Background Notes in the Travel and Living Abroad section.

2. Get insights into how countries differ in the personal and social values that affect business visit; Geert Hofstede Analysis, www.cyborlink.com/besite/hofstede.htm.

3. Travlang, www.travlang.com, can help you learn a foreign language. Check out the site's translating dictionaries and learn a new word in a foreign language every day.

Learn Interactively

INTERACTIVE STUDY GUIDE

Visit www.prenhall.com/thill, then locate your book and click on its Companion Website link. Select Chapter 3 to take advantage of the interactive "Chapter Quiz" to test your knowledge of chapter concepts. Receive instant feedback on whether you need additional studying. Also, visit the "Study Hall," where you'll find an abundance of valuable resources that will help you succeed in this course.

PEAK PERFORMANCE GRAMMAR AND MECHANICS

If your instructor has required the use of "Peak Performance Grammar and Mechanics," either in your online course or on CD, you can improve your skill with verbs by using the "Peak Performance Grammar and Mechanics" module. Click "Verbs." Take the Pretest to determine whether you have any weak areas. Then review those areas in the Refresher Course. Take the Follow-Up Test to check your grasp of verbs. For an extra challenge or advanced practice, take the Advanced Test. Finally, for additional reinforcement, go to the "Improve Your Grammar, Mechanics, and Usage" section that follows, and complete those exercises.

Improve Your Grammar, Mechanics, and Usage

The following exercises help you improve your knowledge of and power over English grammar, mechanics, and usage. Turn to the Handbook of Grammar, Mechanics, and Usage at the end of this textbook and review all of Section 1.3 (Verbs). Then look at the following 10 items. Circle the letter of the preferred choice in the following groups of sentences. (Answers to these exercises appear on page AK-3.)

1. Which sentence contains a verb in the present perfect form?
   a. I became the resident expert on repairing the copy machine.
   b. I have become the resident expert on repairing the copy machine.
2. Which sentence contains a verb in the simple past form?
   a. She knows how to conduct an audit when she came to work for us.
   b. She knew how to conduct an audit when she came to work for us.
3. Which sentence contains a verb in the simple future form?
   a. Next week, call John to tell him what you will do to help him set up the seminar.
   b. Next week, call John to tell him what you will be doing to help him set up the seminar.
4. Which sentence is in the active voice?
   a. The report will be written by Leslie Cartwright.
   b. Leslie Cartwright will write the report.

5. Which sentence is in the passive voice?
   a. The failure to record the transaction was mine.
   b. I failed to record the transaction.
6. Which sentence contains the correct verb form?
   a. Everyone upstairs receives mail before we do.
   b. Everyone upstairs receive mail before we do.
7. Which sentence contains the correct verb form?
   a. Neither the main office nor the branches is blameless.
   b. Neither the main office nor the branches are blameless.
8. Which sentence contains the correct verb form?
   a. C&B Sales are listed in the directory.
   b. C&B Sales is listed in the directory.
9. Which sentence contains the correct verb form?
   a. When measuring shelves, 7 inches is significant.
   b. When measuring shelves, 7 inches are significant.
10. Which sentence contains the correct verb form?
   a. About 90 percent of the employees plans to come to the company picnic.
   b. About 90 percent of the employees plan to come to the company picnic.

For additional exercises focusing on verbs, go to www.prenhall.com/thill, then locate your text and click on its Companion Website link. Click on Chapter 3, click on "Additional Exercises to Improve Grammar, Mechanics and Usage," then click on "5. Verb tenses," "6. Transitive and intransitive verbs," or "7. Voice of verbs."

Part II
Applying the Three-Step Writing Process

Chapter 4

Planning Business Messages

Learning Objectives

AFTER STUDYING THIS CHAPTER, YOU WILL BE ABLE TO

1 Describe the three-step writing process

2 Explain why it's important to define your purpose carefully and list five questions that can help you test that purpose

3 Describe the importance of analyzing your audience and identify the six factors you should consider when developing an audience profile

4 Discuss gathering information for simple messages and identify three attributes of quality information

5 List factors to consider when choosing the most appropriate medium for your message

6 Explain why good organization is important to both you and your audience

7 Summarize the process for organizing business messages effectively

On the Job

COMMUNICATING AT THE COMPLETE IDIOT'S GUIDES

BUILDING A PUBLISHING EMPIRE BY PUTTING THE READER FIRST

You can't wait to use that new computer—or digital camera, or mobile phone, or other innovative gadget—you've just purchased. It will simplify your life and give you amazing new capabilities. But will it just end up gathering dust in your closet? That scenario happens all too often, because many modern devices are difficult to use, and the manuals that come with them are sometimes of little or no help.

Joe Kraynak is on your side. A successful writer who sympathizes with consumers, Kraynak wrote *The Complete Idiot's Guide to PCs*, *The Complete Idiot's Guide to Microsoft Office 2000*, and *The Complete Idiot's Guide to Upgrading Your PC*. He thinks people are right to criticize the manuals that come with PCs, phones, and other complex products. Many high-tech products make intelligent people feel, well, like idiots. That frustration with complex topics and ineffective attempts at explaining them has fueled the rapid growth of the Complete Idiot's series, which now covers hundreds of subjects. Kraynak and other experts know that the problem is often the user manual, not the user. Of course, Kraynak and other authors in the Complete Idiot's series don't think their readers are idiots at all—quite the contrary. In fact, the first words on the publisher's website illustrate that respect for their audience: "You're no idiot! Like most of our visitors, you're smart, curious, at ease with yourself, and interested in learning."

Its tongue-in-cheek name aside, the Idiot's Guide series has grown to hundreds of volumes on the strength of its clear, audience-focused writing.

In Kraynak's mind, the problem is that too many product manuals are written without enough attention to the reader's real needs. The engineers or technicians who typically do the writing are intimately familiar with their products and technologies, and they sometimes mistakenly assume that readers are, too. This disregard for what readers need can lead not only to inadequate explanations of new topics but also to overuse of befuddling jargon and acronyms. Moreover, too many manuals focus on descriptions of products when what readers really want are explanations of how to use them. Such problems aren't limited to technology, either; people writing about finances, government regulations, business processes, and other complex topics frequently fail to understand and accommodate their readers' needs.

"I try to put myself in the shoes of a new user, to think like somebody I know," says Kraynak. He advises all writers to do the same. What essential information do your readers need first? Which less-important details can wait until later? What style of writing will be most effective? In addition to explaining complex ideas, Kraynak tries to entertain and educate. Follow his example and focus on your readers—it will keep your business messages from gathering dust like all those forgotten high-tech products in your closet.[1]

www.idiotsguides.com

UNDERSTANDING THE THREE-STEP WRITING PROCESS

Like Joe Kraynak, you'll face a variety of communication assignments in your career, both oral and written. Some of your tasks will be routine, requiring little more than jotting down a few sentences on paper or keyboarding a brief e-mail message; others will be more complex, involving weeks of reflection, research, and careful document preparation.

As soon as the need to create a message appears, inexperienced communicators are often tempted to dive directly into writing. However, spending even a few minutes analyzing, organizing, adapting, and revising can often save you hours of reworking later on—and help you generate much more effective messages. Successful communicators such as Kraynak follow a writing process that can be divided into three major steps (see Figure 4–1):

The three-step writing process consists of planning, writing, and completing your messages.

- **Planning business messages.** To plan any message, first *analyze the situation* by defining your purpose and developing a profile of your audience. Once you're sure what you need to accomplish with your message, *gather information* that will meet your audience's needs. Next, *select the right medium* (oral, written, or electronic) to deliver your message. With those three factors in place, you're ready to *organize the information* by defining your main idea, limiting your scope, selecting a direct or an indirect approach, and outlining your content. Planning messages is the focus of this chapter.

- **Writing business messages.** Once you've planned your message, *adapt to your audience* with sensitivity, relationship skills, and style. Be sensitive to your audience's needs by adopting the "you" attitude, being polite, emphasizing the positive, and using bias-free language. Build strong relationships with your audience by establishing your credibility and projecting your company's image. Be sure to con-

FIGURE 4–1
The Three-Step Writing Process

Planning

Analyze the Situation
Define your purpose and develop an audience profile.

Gather Information
Determine audience needs and obtain the information necessary to satisfy those needs.

Select the Right Medium
Choose the best medium for delivering your message.

Organize the Information
Define your main idea, limit your scope, select a direct or an indirect approach, and outline your content.

Writing

Adapt to Your Audience
Be sensitive to audience needs with a "you" attitude, politeness, positive emphasis, and bias-free language. Build a strong relationship with your audience by establishing your credibility and projecting your company's image. Control your style with a conversational tone, plain English, and appropriate voice.

Compose the Message
Choose strong words that will help you create effective sentences and coherent paragraphs.

Completing

Revise the Message
Evaluate content and review readability, then edit and rewrite for conciseness and clarity.

Produce the Message
Use effective design elements and suitable layout for a clean, professional appearance.

Proofread the Message
Review for errors in layout, spelling, and mechanics.

Distribute the Message
Deliver your message using the chosen medium; make sure all documents and all relevant files are distributed successfully.

1   2   3

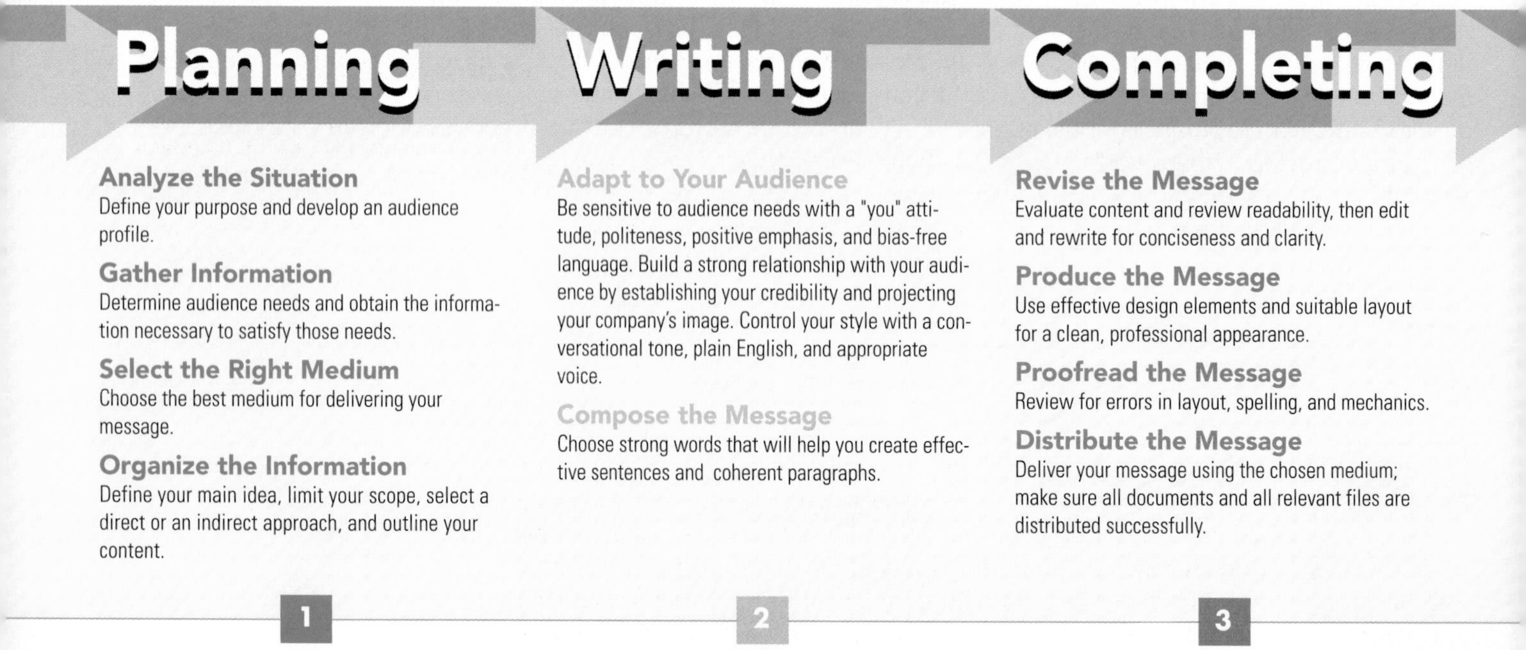

trol your style by using a conversational tone, plain English, and the correct voice. Then you're ready to *compose your message* by choosing strong words, creating effective sentences, and developing coherent paragraphs. Writing business messages is discussed in Chapter 5.

- **Completing business messages.** After writing your first draft, *revise your message* by evaluating the content, reviewing readability, and then editing and rewriting until your message comes across concisely and clearly, with correct grammar, proper punctuation, and effective format. Next *produce your message.* Put it into the form that your audience will receive, and review all design and layout decisions for an attractive, professional appearance. *Proofread* the final draft for typos, spelling errors, and other mechanical problems. Finally, *distribute your message,* using the best combination of personal and technological tools. Completing business messages is discussed in Chapter 6.

Throughout this book, you'll see the three steps in this process applied to a wide variety of business messages: basic tasks for short messages (Chapters 7 through 9), additional tasks for longer messages (Chapters 10 through 12), special tasks for oral presentations (Chapter 13), and distinct tasks for employment messages (Chapters 14 and 15).

Optimizing Your Writing Time

The more you use the three-step writing process, the more intuitive and automatic it will become. As you become familiar with the process, you will develop messages faster and easier. You'll also get better at allotting your time for each task during a writing project.

As a starting point, try to use half your time for planning, one quarter for writing, and one quarter for completing your messages.

As a general rule, try using roughly half your time for planning—defining your purpose, getting to know your audience, immersing yourself in your subject matter, and working out media selection and organization. Try to use no more than about a quarter of your time for writing your document. Reserve the remaining quarter of your time for completing the project, so that you don't shortchange important completion steps such as revising, producing, proofreading, and distributing.[2]

Of course, these time allotments will change significantly, depending on the project; for example, if you already know your material intimately, the planning step might take less than half your time. Then again, if you're delivering your message via complex multimedia such as CD-ROM or DVD, the completion step could take far longer than a quarter of your time. Simple efforts such as instant messages and interoffice memos take far less time and energy than long reports, websites, and other sophisticated projects.

Seasoned professionals understand that there is no right or best way to write all business messages. As you work through the writing process presented in this chapter and Chapters 5 and 6, try not to view it as a list of how-to directives but as a way to understand the various tasks involved in effective business writing.[3]

Home Depot, the world's largest home improvement retailer, keeps its operations running smoothly by carefully planning communication efforts and designing messages that meet the needs of its customers, suppliers, and employees.

Planning Effectively

When deadlines loom and assignments pile up, it's tempting to rush through the planning phase and jump directly into writing. However, more often than not, trying to save time up front costs you more time as you struggle to complete a message that wasn't well thought out. Even if you have only 20 or 30 minutes to prepare and send a message, work through all three steps quickly to ensure that your time is well used. Analyzing your audience helps you to find and assemble the facts they're looking for and to deliver that information in a concise and compelling way.

Trying to save time by skimping on planning usually costs you more time in the long run.

Planning your message reduces indecision as you write and helps eliminate work as you review and revise.

ANALYZING YOUR SITUATION

A successful message starts with a clear purpose that connects the sender's needs with the audience's needs. Identifying your purpose and your audience is usually a straightforward task for simple, routine messages; however, this task can be more demanding in more intricate situations. For instance, if you need to communicate about a shipping problem between your Beijing and Los Angeles factories, your purpose might be simply to alert upper management to the situation, or it might involve asking the two factory managers to explore and solve the problem. These two scenarios have different purposes and different audiences; therefore, they yield dramatically different messages. If you launch directly into writing without clarifying both your purpose and your audience, you'll waste time and energy, and you'll probably generate a less-effective message.

Defining Your Purpose

Your general purpose may be to inform, to persuade, or to collaborate.

All business messages have a **general purpose**: to inform, to persuade, or to collaborate with your audience. This purpose helps define the overall approach you'll need to take, including the information you need to gather, your choice of media, and even the way you organize your message. The general purpose also determines both the appropriate degree of audience participation and the amount of control you have over your message.

Informing your audience requires little interaction (see Figure 4–2). Audience members absorb the information and accept or reject it, but they don't contribute to message content; you control the message. To persuade your audience, you require a moderate amount of participation, such as giving people the chance to ask questions so that you can answer any doubts; nevertheless, you need to retain a moderate amount of message control. Finally, to collaborate with audience members, you need maximum participation. Your control of the message is reduced because you must adjust to new, unexpected input and reactions.

To determine the specific purpose, think of how the audience's ideas or behavior should be affected by the message.

Within the scope of its general purpose, each message also has a **specific purpose**, which identifies what you hope to accomplish with your message and what your audience should do or think after receiving your message. For instance, is your goal simply to update your audience on an event, or do you want them to take immediate action? State your specific purpose as precisely as possible, even identifying which audience members should respond, how they should respond, and when.

FIGURE 4–2
The Relation Between the General Purpose of a Business Message and Communicator Control

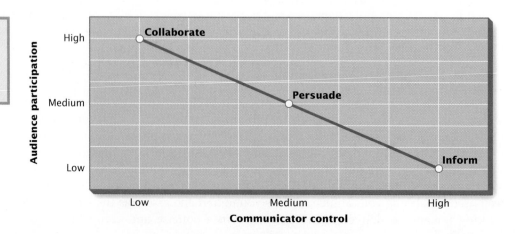

Once you have defined your specific purpose, you can decide whether that purpose merits the time and effort required for you to prepare and send the message. Test your purpose by asking five questions:

- **Will anything change as a result of your message?** Make sure you don't contribute to information overload by sending messages that won't change anything. For instance, if you don't like your company's latest advertising campaign, but you're not in a position to influence it, sending a critical message to your colleagues won't change anything and won't benefit anyone.

- **Is your purpose realistic?** If your purpose involves a radical shift in action or attitude, go slowly. Consider proposing a first step so that your message acts as the beginning of a learning process.

- **Is the time right?** Think through the potential impact of your message—both intentional and unintentional—to see whether this is a good time to send it. Many professions and departments have recurring cycles in their workloads, so messages sent during peak times might be ignored. Similarly, employees in departments that are in the midst of a reorganization, series of layoffs, or other changes won't be able to give your message their full attention.

- **Is the right person delivering your message?** Even though you may have done all the work, achieving your objective is usually more important than taking the credit. For instance, if a respected senior colleague might be a more convincing messenger, consider asking this person to deliver your message.

- **Is your purpose acceptable to your organization?** Your company's business objectives may dictate whether a purpose is acceptable. For instance, you may be tempted to fire off a stern reply to a particularly unpleasant customer, suggesting the person take his or her business elsewhere, but this might go against your company's priorities of retaining all current customers.

Once you are satisfied that (1) you have a clear and meaningful purpose and (2) now is a smart time to proceed, your next step is to understand the members of your audience and their needs.

> Defer a message, or do not send it at all, if
> - Nothing will change as a result of sending
> - The purpose is not realistic
> - The timing is not right
> - You are not the right person to deliver the message
> - The purpose is not acceptable to your organization

Developing an Audience Profile

Before your own audiences will take the time to read or hear your messages, they need to be interested in what you're saying. They need to see what's in it for them—which of their problems will be solved by listening to your advice or doing what you ask. The more you know about your audience, their needs, and their expectations, the more effectively you'll be able to communicate with them.

If you're communicating with someone you know well, audience analysis is relatively easy. You can identify the person's needs and predict his or her reaction to any given message without a lot of research. On the other hand, your audience could be made up of strangers—potential customers or suppliers you've never met, a new boss, or new employees. In these situations, you'll need to learn more in order to adjust your message to meet the needs of your audience. For an example of the kind of information you need to compile in an audience analysis, see the planning sheet in Figure 4–3. To conduct an audience analysis:

- **Identify your primary audience.** For some messages, certain audience members might be more important than others. Don't ignore the needs of less influential members, but make sure you address the concerns of the key decision makers.

- **Determine audience size and geographic distribution.** A message aimed at 10,000 people spread around the globe might require a different approach than one aimed at a dozen people down the hall.

> Ask yourself some key questions about your audience:
> - Who are they?
> - How many people do you need to reach?
> - How much do they already know about the subject?
> - What is their probable reaction to your message?

Audience Analysis Notes

Project: A report recommending that we close down the on-site exercise facility and subsidize private memberships at local health clubs.

- **Primary audience:** Nicole Perazzo, vice president of operations, and her supervisory team.

- **Size and geographic distribution:** Nine managers total; Nicole and five of her staff are here on site; three other supervisors are based in Hong Kong.

- **Composition:** All have experience in operations management, but several are new to the company.

- **Level of understanding:** All will no doubt understand the financial considerations, but the newer managers might not understand the importance of the on-site exercise facility to many of our employees.

- **Expectations and preferences.** They're expecting a firm recommendation, backed up with well-thought-out financial rationale and suggestions for communicating the bad news to employees. For a decision of this magnitude, a formal report is appropriate; e-mail distribution is expected.

- **Probable reaction.** From one-on-one discussions, I know that several of the managers receiving this report are active users of the on-site facility and won't welcome the suggestion that we should shut it down. However, some nonexercisers generally think it's a luxury the company can't afford. Audience reactions will range from highly positive to highly negative; the report should focus on overcoming the highly negative reactions since they're the ones I need to convince.

- **Determine audience composition.** Look for both similarities and differences in culture, language, age, education, organizational rank and status, attitudes, experience, motivations, and any other factors that might affect the success of your message. For example, if you're reporting the results of a market research project, the vice president of sales will probably want to know what's happening right now, whereas the vice president of engineering might be more interested in how the market will look a year or two from now, when that department's new products will be ready to sell.

If audience members have different levels of understanding of the topic, aim your message at the most influential decision makers.

- **Gauge audience members' level of understanding.** If audience members share your general background, they'll probably understand your material without difficulty. If not, your message will need an element of education, and deciding how much information to include can be a challenge. Try to include only enough information to accomplish the specific purpose of your message. If the members of your audience have various levels of understanding, gear your coverage to your primary audience (the key decision makers).

- **Understand audience expectations and preferences.** Will members of your audience expect complete details or just a summary of the main points? Do they want an e-mail or will they expect a formal memo? In general, the higher up the organization your message goes, the fewer details people want to see, simply because they have less time to read them.

A gradual approach and plenty of evidence are required to win over a skeptical audience.

- **Forecast probable audience reaction.** As you'll read later in the chapter, audience reaction affects message organization. If you expect a favorable response, you can state conclusions and recommendations up front and offer minimal supporting evidence. If you expect skepticism, you can introduce conclusions gradually, with more proof. By anticipating the primary audience's response to certain points, you can vary the amount of evidence you'll need to address those issues.

GATHERING INFORMATION

With a clear picture of your audience and their needs, your next step is to assemble the information that you will include in your message. For simple messages, you may already have all the information at hand, but more complex messages can require considerable research and analysis before you're ready to begin writing. Chapter 10 explores formal techniques for finding, evaluating, and processing information, but you can often use a variety of informal techniques to gather insights and focus your research efforts:

- **Considering other viewpoints.** Putting yourself in someone else's position helps you consider what that person might be thinking, feeling, or planning.

- **Reading reports and other company documents.** Your company's files may be a rich source of the information you need for a particular memo or e-mail message. Consider annual reports, financial statements, news releases, memos, marketing reports, and customer surveys for helpful information. Find out whether your company has a *knowledge management system,* a centralized database that collects the experiences and insights of employees throughout the organization.

- **Talking with supervisors, colleagues, or customers.** Fellow workers and customers may have information you need, or they may know what your audience will be interested in. Conducting telephone or personal interviews is a convenient way to gather information.

- **Asking your audience for input.** If you're unsure of what audience members need from your message, ask them—whether through casual conversation (face-to-face or over the phone), informal surveys, or unofficial interviews. Admitting you don't know but want to meet their needs will impress an audience more than guessing and getting it wrong.

Gathering information from co-workers in conversations or informal interviews helps Levi Strauss editors determine how much detail about a project their audience expects in the company newsletter.

Uncovering Audience Needs

In many situations your audience's information needs are readily apparent, such as when a consumer sends an e-mail asking a specific question. In other cases, your audience might be unable to articulate exactly what is needed. If someone makes a vague or broad request, ask questions to narrow the focus. If your boss says, "Find out everything you can about Interscope Records," ask which aspect of the company and its business is most important. Asking a question or two often forces the person to think through the request and define more precisely what is required.

If you're given a vague request, ask questions to clarify it before you plan a response.

Also, try to think of information needs that your audience may not even be aware of. Suppose your company has just hired a new employee from out of town, and you've been assigned to coordinate this person's relocation. At a minimum, you would write a welcoming letter describing your company's procedures for relocating employees. With a little extra thought, however, you might include some information about the city: perhaps a guide to residential areas, a map or two, brochures about cultural activities, or information on schools and transportation. In some cases, you may be able to tell your audience something they consider important but wouldn't have thought to ask. Although adding information of this sort lengthens your message, it can also create goodwill.

Include any additional information that might be helpful, even though the requester didn't specifically ask for it.

Providing Required Information

Test the completeness of your document by making sure it answers all the important questions: who, what, when, where, why, and how.

Once you've defined your audience's information needs, be sure you satisfy those needs completely. One good way to test the thoroughness of your message is to use the **journalistic approach**: Check to see whether your message answers *who, what, when, where, why,* and *how.* Using this test, you can quickly tell whether a message fails to deliver—such as this letter requesting information from a large hotel:

Dear Ms. Hill:

I just got back from a great vacation in Hawaii. However, this morning I discovered that my favorite black leather shoes are missing. Since I wore them in Hawaii, I assume I left them at your hotel. Please check the items in your "lost and found" and let me know whether you have the missing shoes.

The letter fails to tell Hill everything she needs to know. The *what* could be improved by including a detailed description of the missing shoes (size, brand, distinguishable style or trim). Hill doesn't know *when* the writer stayed at the hotel, *where* (in which room) the writer stayed, or *how* to return the shoes. Hill will have to write or call the writer to get the missing details, and the inconvenience may be just enough to prevent her from complying with the request.

Be certain that the information you provide is accurate and that the commitments you make can be kept.

Be Sure the Information Is Accurate   Inaccurate information communicated in business messages can cause a host of problems, from embarrassment and lost productivity to serious safety and legal issues. Inaccurate information might persist for months or years after you distribute it, or you might commit the organization to promises it isn't prepared or able to keep.

You can minimize mistakes by double-checking every piece of information you collect. If you are consulting sources outside the organization, ask yourself whether they are current and reliable. Be particularly careful when using sources you find on the Internet. As you'll see in Chapter 10, the simplicity of online publishing and frequent lack of editorial oversight call for extra care in using online information. Be sure to review any mathematical or financial calculations. Check all dates and schedules, and examine your own assumptions and conclusions to be certain they are valid.

Ethics should guide your decisions when determining how much detail to include in your message.

Be Sure the Information Is Ethical   By working hard to ensure the accuracy of the information you gather, you'll also avoid many ethical problems in your messages. If you do make an honest mistake, such as delivering information you initially thought to be true but later found to be false, contact the recipients of the message immediately and correct the error. No one can reasonably fault you in such circumstances, and most people will respect your honesty.

Messages can also be unethical if important information is omitted. Of course, as a business professional, you may have legal or other sound business reasons for not including every detail about every matter. So just how much detail should you include? Make sure you include enough detail to avoid misleading your audience. If you're unsure how much information your audience needs, offer as much as you believe best fits your definition of complete, and then offer to provide more upon request.

Try to figure out what points will especially interest your audience, then give those points the most attention.

Be Sure the Information Is Pertinent   When gathering information for your message, remember that some points will be more important to your audience than others. They will appreciate your efforts to prioritize the information they need and filter out the information they don't. Moreover, by focusing on the information that concerns your audience the most, you increase your chances of sending an effective message.

If you don't know your audience, or if you're communicating with a large group of people with diverse interests, use common sense to identify points of interest. Audience factors such as age, job, location, income, and education can give you a clue. If you're trying to sell memberships in a health club, you might adjust your message for athletes, busy professionals, families, and people in different locations or in different income brackets. The comprehensive facilities and professional trainers would appeal to athletes, whereas the low monthly rates would appeal to college students on tight budgets.

Some messages necessarily reach audiences with a diverse mix of educational levels, subject awareness, and other variables. In these cases, your only choice is to try to accommodate the likely range of audience members. For instance, Figure 4–4 (on the following page) shows two pages from a local water district's annual water quality report, which does a good job of presenting a technical subject to the general public (all of the households in this particular city). Notice how the report presents scientific information accurately but supplements that with clear explanations of what the information means and how it pertains to water users.

> Rely on common sense if you don't know enough about your audience to know exactly what will interest them.

SELECTING THE RIGHT MEDIUM

Selecting the best medium for your message can make the difference between effective and ineffective communication.[4] A **medium** is the form through which you choose to communicate your message. You may choose to talk with someone face to face, write a letter, send e-mail, or leave a voice-mail message—and there are many other media to choose from.

In fact, categorizing media has become increasingly blurred in recent years with the advent of so many options that include multimedia formats. For the sake of discussion, you can think of media as traditionally being either oral or written. Nowadays, electronic media extend the reach of both oral and written media, and even combine all three forms. Each type of medium has advantages and disadvantages.

Oral Media

Primary oral media include face-to-face conversations, interviews, speeches, in-person presentations, and meetings. Being able to see, hear, and react to each other can benefit communicators, giving oral media several advantages:

> Oral communication is best when you need to encourage interaction, express emotions, or monitor emotional responses.

- They provide immediate feedback.

- They allow a certain ease of interaction.

- They involve rich nonverbal cues (both physical gesture and vocal inflection).

- They allow you to express the emotion behind your message.

Traditional oral media are useful for getting people to ask questions, make comments, and work together to reach a consensus or decision. However, if you don't want or need all that interaction, then oral media can have several disadvantages:

> Oral media limit participation to those who are present, reduce your control over the message, and make it difficult to revise or edit your message.

- They restrict participation to those physically present.

- Unless recorded, they provide no permanent, verifiable record of the communication.

- They reduce the communicator's control over the message.

- They often rule out the chance to revise or edit your spoken words.

Written Media

Written messages take many forms, from traditional memos to glossy reports that rival magazines in production quality. Most letters and memos are relatively brief documents, generally one or two pages, although some run much longer. Memos are

FIGURE 4–4
Audience Focused Report (selected pages)

Helps readers understand the scientific terms used to describe water quality

Provides helpful contact information

Answers a question that many concerned customers are likely to have

Helps readers grasp significance of very small numbers by providing a selection of analogous measurements

Shows test results in appropriate scientific format, but helps nontechnical readers by explaining what the various substances are and whether the water complies with government standards

---

ANNUAL WATER QUALITY REPORT

Important Terms Used In This Report

Maximum Contaminant Level Goal (MCLG) - The maximum goal level of a contaminant in drinking water below which there is no known or expected risk to health. MCLG's allow for a margin of safety.

Maximum Contaminant Level (MCL) - The level of a contaminant allowed in drinking water.

Treatment Technique (TT) - A required process intended to reduce the level of contaminant in drinking water.

Action Level (AL) - The concentration of a contaminant which, if exceeded, triggers treatment or other requirements that a water system must follow.

Parts per Million (ppm) Parts per Billion (ppb) - A part per million means that one part of a particular contaminant is present for every million parts of water. Similarly, parts per billion indicate the amount of contaminant per billion parts of water.

Not Applicable (NA) – Means that EPA has not established MCLG's for these substances.

Disinfection By-Products (DBP's) - Organic compounds resulting from the interaction of chlorine with natural organic matter in water supplies.

Who Can I Contact For More Information?

To obtain more information on water quality issues contact any of the following agencies:

Alderwood Water & Wastewater District
Water Quality Division
Telephone: 425-787-0250
www.alderwoodwater.com

U.S. Environmental Protection Agency
Safe Drinking Water Hotline
Telephone: 800-426-4791

Washington State Department of Health
Regional DOH Office
Telephone: 253-395-6750
www.doh.wa.gov/ehp/dw

How can I get involved in water quality decisions?

The Alderwood Water & Wastewater District regular Board of Commissioners meetings are scheduled at the District Administration Building at 3626 156th Street SW, Lynnwood WA. each first and third Monday of the month.

Terms Simply Stated

Parts per million (ppm)	Parts per billion (ppb)
3 drops in 42 gallons	1 drop in 14,000 gallons
1 second in 12 days	1 second in 32 years
1 penny in $10,000	1 penny in $10,000,000
1 inch in 16 miles	1 inch in 16,000 miles

ANNUAL WATER QUALITY REPORT

Water Quality Results

Last year, your drinking water was tested for hundreds of possible contaminants. The contaminants that were detected are listed in the following tables. In reading this data, it is important to note that all of these contaminants were present in amounts below the United States Environmental Protection Agency's (USEPA) allowable levels. To ensure tap water is safe to drink USEPA prescribes regulations that limit the amount of certain contaminants in the water provided by public water systems.

SUBSTANCE	UNITS	IDEAL LEVEL/ GOAL (MCLG)	MAXIMUM ALLOWABLE (MCL)	Range or Other	Average Value or Highest Result	Comply?
Nitrate	ppm	10	10	0.05 - 0.12	0.09	YES
The small amount of Nitrate comes from natural sources in the water source						
Total Coliform Bacteria	% Positive	0	Not More Than 5% Positive Per Month	0%	0%	YES
Total coliform bacteria testing is used to monitor microbial quality in the water distribution system. In Alderwood, a minimum of 100 samples must be collected each month. Not more than 5% of the monthly total can be positive for total coliforms.						
Fluoride	ppm	2	4	0.7 - 1.1	1.0	YES
Fluoride is added to your water in carefully controlled levels for dental health.						
Haloacetic Acids (5)	ppb	NA	60	16.6 - 45.1	35.5	YES
Total Trihalomethanes	ppb	NA	80	30.2 - 58.7	47.3	YES
Haloacetic acids and trihalomethanes form as by-products of the chlorination process that is used to kill or inactivate disease-causing microbes.						
Turbidity	NTU	NA	TT	100%	0.08	YES

Turbidity is a measurement of the amount of particulates in water measured in Nephelometric Turbidity Units (NTU). Particulates in water can include bacteria, viruses and protozoans that can cause disease. Turbidity measurements are used to determine the effectiveness of the treatment processes used to remove these particulates. Values reported are the lowest monthly percentage of samples that met the turbidity limit (0.3 NTU for EPA and 0.1 NTU for the State) and the highest filtered water turbidity measurement obtained in 2004.

Cryptosporidium Reporting

Cryptosporidium is a microscopic organism that, when ingested, may cause diarrhea, fever, and other gastrointestinal distress. It can be found in all of Washington's rivers and streams and comes from animal wastes in the watershed. Cryptosporidium is eliminated by effective treatment including filtration, sedimentation and disinfection. Your water is tested regularly for the presence of Cryptosporidium.

Cryptosporidium	Units	Ideal Level/ Goal (MCLG)	Range	Average
Cryptosporidium parvum oocysts	oocysts/L	N/A	0 - 1	0
One monthly sample of the raw, source water showed the presence of Cryptosporidium.				

In 2004, one of the 12 monthly samples of the raw, source water showed the presence of Cryptosporidium. However, no Cryptosporidium was detected in the finished/treated water you receive.

used for the routine, day-to-day exchange of information within an organization. Because of their open construction and informal method of delivery (e-mail or interoffice mail), memos are less private than letters.

Letters are written messages sent to recipients outside the organization, so in addition to conveying a particular message, they perform an important public relations function in fostering good working relationships with customers, suppliers, and others. Many organizations rely on form letters to save time and money on routine communication. Form letters are particularly handy for such one-time mass mailings as sales messages about products, information about organizational activities, and goodwill messages such as seasonal greetings. Chapters 7 through 9 discuss memos, letters, instant messages, and other short-message forms, and Appendix A explains how to format these business documents.

Reports and proposals are usually longer than letters and memos. These factual, objective documents may be distributed to insiders or outsiders, depending on their purpose and subject. They come in many formats, including preprinted forms, letters, memos, and manuscripts. In length, they range from a few pages to several hundred, and they are generally more formal in tone than a typical business letter or memo. Chapters 12 through 14 discuss reports and proposals in detail.

Written media have a number of advantages over oral media:

> Written media increase your control, help you reach dispersed audiences, and minimize distortion.

- They allow you to plan and control your message.

- They offer a permanent, verifiable record.

- They help you reach an audience that is geographically dispersed.

- They minimize the distortion that can accompany oral messages.

- They can be used to avoid immediate interactions.

- They de-emphasize any inappropriate emotional components.

Disadvantages of written media include the following:

> The disadvantages of written media include difficulty of feedback, lack of nonverbal cues, and the time and skill sometimes required to prepare written messages.

- Many are not conducive to speedy feedback.

- They lack the rich nonverbal cues provided by oral media.

- They often take more time and more resources to create and distribute.

- Elaborate printed documents can require special skills in preparation and production.

Electronic Media

Electronic media include choices such as e-mail, telephones, CD-ROM, faxes, voice mail, instant messaging, websites, blogs, and many more. When you want to make a powerful impression on supervisors, customers, investors, or other key audiences, using electronic media can increase the excitement and visual appeal with computer animation, video, even music. The growth of electronic communication options is both a blessing and a curse. You have more tools than ever to choose from, but the choice itself can complicate the communication process. The secret is to pick the tool that does the best overall job in each situation. Although no hard rules dictate which tool to use in each case, here are a few pointers that will help you determine when to select electronic over more traditional forms:[5]

- **Telephone calls** are still the lifeblood of many organizations, for both internal and external communication. But even the humble telephone has joined the Internet age, thanks to the emerging capability to place phone calls over the Internet. Known by the technical term VoIP (which stands for *Voice over IP*, the Internet Protocol), Internet-based phone service promises to offer cheaper long-distance service for businesses worldwide.[6]

- **Voice mail** can replace short memos and phone calls when an immediate response isn't crucial. However, voice mail is a poor choice for lengthy, complex messages, since the information is difficult to retrieve.

- **Teleconferencing and videoconferencing** are best for informational meetings and less effective for highly interactive meetings such as negotiation. New online meetings are less expensive than traditional videoconferencing.

- **Videotapes and DVDs** are often effective for sending a motivational message to a large number of people. By communicating nonverbal cues, they can strengthen the sender's image of sincerity and trustworthiness; however, they offer no opportunity for immediate feedback.

- **Electronic documents** let you send written materials over e-mail and instant messaging networks or on CD-ROM. Other than simple word processor files, Adobe's Portable Document Format (PDF) is the most popular type of electronic document. Computer users can view PDFs on screen with free reader software, and PDFs are more secure and less vulnerable to viruses than word processor files.

- **Faxes** can overcome time-zone barriers when a hard copy is required. They have all the characteristics of a written message, except (1) they lack the privacy of a letter, and (2) they may appear less crisp, even less professional, depending on the quality of the audience's machine. Internet-based fax services, such as eFax, lower the cost by eliminating the need for a dedicated fax line and fax machine.

- **E-mail** offers speed, low cost, portability, and convenience. It's best for brief, noncomplex information that is time sensitive. With such a quick turnaround time, e-mail tends to be more conversational than traditional media. (Chapter 5 presents more advice on writing effective e-mail messages.)

- **Instant messaging** (IM) allows real-time, one-on-one and small-group text conversations via personal computer. At computer giant IBM, for instance, employees send more than 5 million instant messages a month.[7] IM is more versatile than a phone call and quicker than e-mail. You can type a text message that is immediately displayed on your receiver's computer screen, and you get a response within seconds. Similarly, you can use IM to exchange documents or hold a virtual meeting online in a private chat area. Newer IM systems offer file attachments, streaming audio and video, and other enhancements. *Text messaging*, a phone-based medium that has long been popular with consumers in Asia and Europe, is finally catching on in the United States.[8] Although it lacks many of the capabilities of IM, text messaging does give businesses an easy way to transmit simple messages.

- **Websites and blogs** have become vital communication platforms for many businesses. A well-designed website can tailor the same information for numerous readers by steering each audience group to specific sections on a website. Blogs have become common in business in recent years as communicators search for fast, informal ways to reach customers and other audiences. *Video blogs (vlogs)* and *mobile blogs (moblogs)* are the latest developments in this exciting new medium.[9] You can learn more about writing for the web at www.prenhall.com/thill.

In general, use electronic media to deliver messages quickly, to reach widely dispersed audiences, and to take advantage of rich multimedia formats.

As you can see, electronic messages offer considerable advantages:

- They deliver messages with great speed.

- They reach audiences physically separated from you.

- They reach a dispersed audience personally.

- They offer the persuasive power of multimedia formats.

- They can increase accessibility and openness in an organization.

Industries that rely on up-to-the-minute information quickly adopted blogging as a communication medium. For example, fashion industry insiders count on the *Daily Fashion Report* for the latest news on top designers, photographers, fashion shows, buying trends, and other important business issues.

For all their good points, electronic media are not problem-free. Consider some of these disadvantages:

- **They can inadvertently create tension and conflict.** Electronic messages can give the illusion of anonymity, so people sometimes say things in e-mail or IM that they would never say in person or in a traditional document.

- **They are easy to overuse.** The ability to send or forward messages to multiple recipients has become a major cause of information overload.

- **They expose companies to data security threats and malicious software.** Connecting computers to the Internet exposes companies to a host of potential security problems, including computer viruses, information theft, and *spyware* (malicious software that sneaks onto personal computers to capture credit card numbers and other confidential information).

- **They often lack privacy.** Some people are careless about screening their distribution lists; plus, any recipient can easily forward your message to someone else. In addition, employers can legally monitor e-mail, instant messaging, and voice mail, and all of them can be subpoenaed for court cases.

Electronic media have several potential disadvantages, including a lack of privacy and the loss of productivity that occurs when people send unnecessary messages.

- **They can seriously drain employee productivity.** Employees can be easily distracted either by constant streams of e-mail, IM, voice mail, conference calls, and faxes or by surfing the web and visiting non-business-related websites during working hours. Companies are responding to the productivity problem by such means as limiting web surfing and even shutting off e-mail during certain times of the week.

Factors to Consider When Choosing Media

When choosing a medium for your message, balance your needs with your audience's needs. You certainly want to select the medium whose advantages offer you the best fit with the situation and your audience (see Figure 4–5). Just as critical, however, is considering how your message is affected by important factors such as the following:

Complicated messages often require richer media.

- **Media richness.** Richness is a medium's ability to (1) convey a message through more than one *informational cue* (visual, verbal, vocal), (2) facilitate feedback, and (3) establish personal focus. The richest medium is face-to-face communication; it's personal, it provides immediate feedback (verbal and nonverbal), and it conveys the emotion behind a message.[10] Multimedia presentations and multimedia webpages are also quite rich, with the ability to presents images, animation, text, music, sound effects, and other elements, plus many can be personalized to a degree. At the other end of the richness continuum are the leanest media—those that communicate in the simplest ways, provide no opportunity for audience feedback, and aren't personalized (see Figure 4–6). Use the richest media to send nonroutine, complex messages, to humanize your presence throughout the organization, to communicate caring to employees, and to gain employee commitment to company goals. Use leaner media to send simple, routine messages.

FIGURE 4–5
Choosing the Most
Appropriate Medium

Use Written Media When
• You don't need or want immediate feedback
• You don't want or need immediate interaction with the audience
• Your message is complex
• You need a permanent, verifiable record
• Your audience is large and geographically dispersed
• You need to ensure that the message cannot be altered after you send it
• Your message has limited emotional content
• The situation calls for more formality

Use Oral Media When
• You want immediate feedback from the audience
• Your message is straightforward and easy to accept
• You don't need a permanent record
• You can gather your audience conveniently and economically
• You want to encourage interaction to solve a problem or reach a group decision
• You want to read the audience's body language or hear the tone of their response
• Your message has an emotional content

Use Electronic Media When
• You need to deliver a message quickly
• You're physically separated from your audience
• You want to give the audience an opportunity to edit the message (such as editing a word processing document)
• Your message can benefit from multiple media, such as audio and video
• You want to take advantage of electronic media

FIGURE 4-6
Media Richness

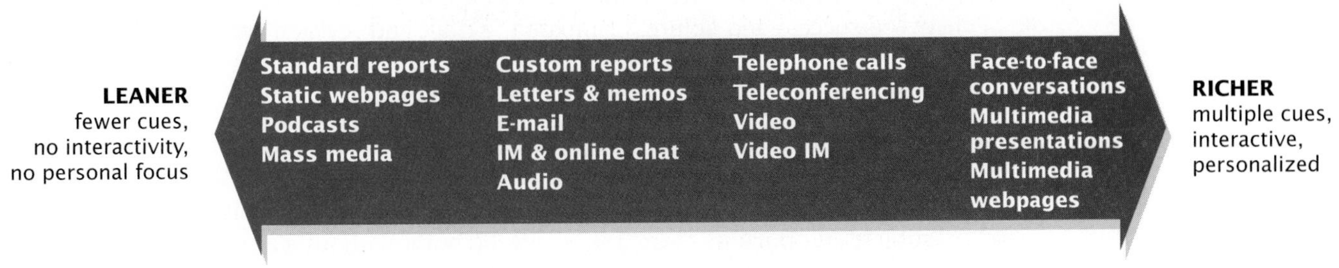

LEANER
fewer cues,
no interactivity,
no personal focus

Standard reports	Custom reports	Telephone calls	Face-to-face
Static webpages	Letters & memos	Teleconferencing	conversations
Podcasts	E-mail	Video	Multimedia
Mass media	IM & online chat	Video IM	presentations
	Audio		Multimedia
			webpages

RICHER
multiple cues,
interactive,
personalized

- **Message formality.** Your media choice governs the style and tone of your message. For instance, you wouldn't write an e-mail message with the same level of formality that you would use in a letter. Thus, if your purpose were to share simple information with employees, such as changes in the cafeteria hours, you would probably send an e-mail message rather than write a formal letter or make a lengthy face-to-face presentation. Similarly, drafting a few notes for a conversation with an employee would be less formal than drafting a letter of reprimand.

- **Media limitations.** Every medium has limitations. Although face-to-face communication is the richest medium, it's one of the most restrictive because you and your audience must be in the same place at the same time.[11] Or consider instant messaging; it's perfect for communicating simple, straightforward messages, but it is ineffective for sending complex ones.

- **Sender intentions.** Your choice of medium influences your audience's perception of your intentions. If you want to emphasize the formality of your message, use a more formal medium, such as a memo or a letter. To emphasize the confidentiality of your message, use voice mail rather than a fax, send a letter rather than a memo, or address the matter in a private conversation rather than during a meeting. To instill an emotional commitment to corporate values, consider a visual medium such as a personal speech or a video conference. For immediate feedback meet face-to-face, make a phone call, or use IM.[12] However, if you need a written record, use one of the written media or an electronic equivalent such as an intranet posting.

  Your intentions heavily influence your choice of medium.

- **Urgency and cost.** If your message is urgent, you'll probably use the phone or IM. But don't forget to weigh cost against speed. For instance, you wouldn't think twice about telephoning an important customer in Australia if you just discovered that your company had erroneously sent the wrong shipment, but you'd probably choose to fax or e-mail a routine order acknowledgment to that same customer.

  Time and cost also affect medium selection.

- **Audience preferences.** Make sure to consider which media your audience expects or prefers.[13] What would you think if your college tried to deliver your diploma by fax? You'd expect the college to hand it to you at graduation or mail it to you. In addition, some cultures tend to favor one channel over another. For example, the United States, Canada, and Germany emphasize written messages, whereas Japan emphasizes oral messages—perhaps because its high-context culture carries so much of the message in nonverbal cues and "between the lines" interpretation.[14]

  When choosing the appropriate medium, don't forget to consider your audience's expectations.

Once you select the best medium for your purpose, situation, and audience, you are ready to start thinking about the organization of your message.

ORGANIZING YOUR INFORMATION

For anything beyond the simplest messages, organization can make the difference between success and failure. Compare the draft and revision versions of the letter in Figure 4–7, in which the writer is requesting the replacement of a faulty DVD drive. The draft version exhibits four of the most common organization mistakes:

Most disorganized communication suffers from problems with clarity, relevance, grouping, and completeness.

- **Taking too long to get to the point.** The writer, Jill Saunders, didn't introduce her topic, the faulty DVD drive, until the third paragraph. Then she waited until the final paragraph to state her purpose: requesting a replacement. *Solution:* Make the subject and purpose clear, and get to the point without wasting the reader's time.

- **Including irrelevant material.** The first draft is full of irrelevant information: that ComputerTime used to be smaller, that it used to be in a different location, that Saunders's department now has 15 employees, and so on. *Solution:* Include only information that is related to the subject and purpose.

- **Getting ideas mixed up.** Saunders tries to make several points: (1) Her company has been customer for a long time, (2) it has purchased numerous items at ComputerTime, (3) the DVD drive doesn't work, and (4) Saunders wants a replacement. However, the ideas are mixed up and located in the wrong places. *Solution:* Group similar ideas and present them in a logical way, where one idea leads to the next.

- **Leaving out necessary information.** ComputerTime may want to know the make, model, and price of the DVD drive; the date of purchase; and the specific problems the device has had. Saunders also failed to say what she wants the store to do: send her a new DVD drive of the same type, send her a different model, or simply refund her money. *Solution:* Include all the information necessary for the audience to respond as the writer wishes.

The revised version corrects all four mistakes, and the result is a much stronger letter.

To organize a message,
- Define your main idea
- Limit the scope
- Choose the direct or indirect approach
- Group your points

As you'll see in the following chapters, various types of messages may require different organizational schemes. Nevertheless, in every case, you can organize your message in a logical and compelling way by recognizing the importance of good organization, defining your main idea, limiting your scope, choosing either a direct or an indirect approach, and outlining your content.

Recognizing the Importance of Good Organization

Poor organization can waste time, reduce efficiency, and damage relationships.

At best, poor organization creates unnecessary work for your readers, forcing them to piece your message together in a sensible way. At worst, poor organization leads readers to form inaccurate conclusions or tempts them to stop reading or listening. If you gain the reputation as a disorganized communicator, people will find ways to ignore your messages. In other words, poorly organized messages are bad for business and bad for your career.

Effective organizing also saves you time and consumes less of your creative energy. Your draft goes more quickly because you don't waste time putting ideas in the wrong places or composing material that you don't need. You might also use your organizational plan to get advance input from your audience. That way, you can be sure you're on the right track *before* you spend hours working on your draft. Furthermore, if you're working on a large, complex project, you can use your organization plan to divide the writing job among co-workers.

Good organization helps audience members understand your message, accept your message, and save time.

In addition to helping you, good organization helps the members of your audience in three key ways. First, it helps your audience understand your message. By making your main point clear at the outset and by presenting information logically, a well-organized message satisfies your audience's need for information.

FIGURE 4–7
Improving the Organization of a Letter

Draft

General Nutrition Corporation has been doing business with ComputerTime since I was hired six years ago. Your building was smaller then, and it was located on the corner of Federal Avenue and 2nd N.W. Jared Mallory, our controller, was one of your first customers. I still remember the day. It was the biggest check I'd ever written. Of course, over the years, I've gotten used to larger purchases.

Our department now has 15 employees. As accountants, we need to have our computers working so that we can do our jobs. The DVD recorder we bought for my assistant, Suzanne, has been a problem. We've taken it in for repairs three times in three months to the authorized service center, and Suzanne is very careful with the machine and hasn't abused it. After all those repairs, it still doesn't work right, and she's tired of hauling it back and forth. We're all putting in longer hours because it is our busy season, and none of us has a lot of spare time.

This is the first time we've returned anything to your store, and I hope you'll agree that we deserve a better deal.

- Fails to explain the purpose of the letter and immediately gets bogged down in irrelevant details
- Waits until the second paragraph to even introduce the main idea
- Fails to provide specific information about the problem
- Fails to specify what she wants the reader to do

GNC LiveWell.

Revision

September 13, 2006

Customer Service
ComputerTime
247 Allison Avenue
Pittsburgh, PA 15202

Dear Customer Service Representative:

Can you please exchange the faulty DVD record/play drive (Olympic Systems, Model PRS-2) that GNC purchased on November 15, 2004? The drive began malfunctioning soon after my assistant installed it on her computer (an HP Compaq dc5100), and we've had trouble with it ever since.

We took the drive to the authorized service center and were assured that the problem was merely a loose connection. The service representative fixed the drive, but in April we had to have it fixed again—another loose connection. For the next three months, the drive worked reasonably well, although the recording time was occasionally slow. Two months ago, the drive stopped working again. Once more, the service representative blamed a loose connection and made the repair. Although the drive is again operational, it occasionally makes odd noises and takes an inordinate amount of time to record a disc.

Although all the repairs have been relatively minor and have been covered by the one-year warranty, we are not satisfied with the drive. We would like to exchange it for a similar model from another manufacturer.

GNC has done business with your store for six years, and we look forward to purchasing from you in the future after this matter is resolved successfully. Please let us know your answer by September 20.

Sincerely,

Jill Saunders

Jill Saunders
Accounting Supervisor

st

- Provides details in the body so that the reader can understand why Saunders thinks a problem exists
- Requests a specific action from the reader
- Opens with her request and immediately follows that with relevant details
- Provides a detailed history of the problem so that the reader clearly understands her frustration
- Emphasizes (in a calm, respectful way) that GNC won't be buying anything else until this problem is resolved

Second, it helps your audience accept your message. Effective messages often require a bit more than simple, clear logic. A diplomatic approach helps receivers accept your message, even if it's not exactly what they want to hear. In the case of ComputerTime's response to Jill Saunders's request for a replacement product from a different manufacturer, ComputerTime isn't able to do exactly what Saunders requested (they've arranged a replacement from the same manufacturer instead). Consequently, the response letter from Linda Davis has a negative aspect to it, but the style of the letter is tactful and positive (see Figure 4–8).

Third, good organization saves your audience time. Well-organized messages are efficient. They contain only relevant ideas, and they are brief. Moreover, all the information in a well-organized message is in a logical place. Audience members receive only the information they need, and because that information is presented as accessibly and succinctly as possible, audience members can follow the thought pattern without a struggle. Before you can even begin arranging the information in your message, take a moment to define your main idea.

FIGURE 4–8
Letter Demonstrating a Tactful Organization Plan

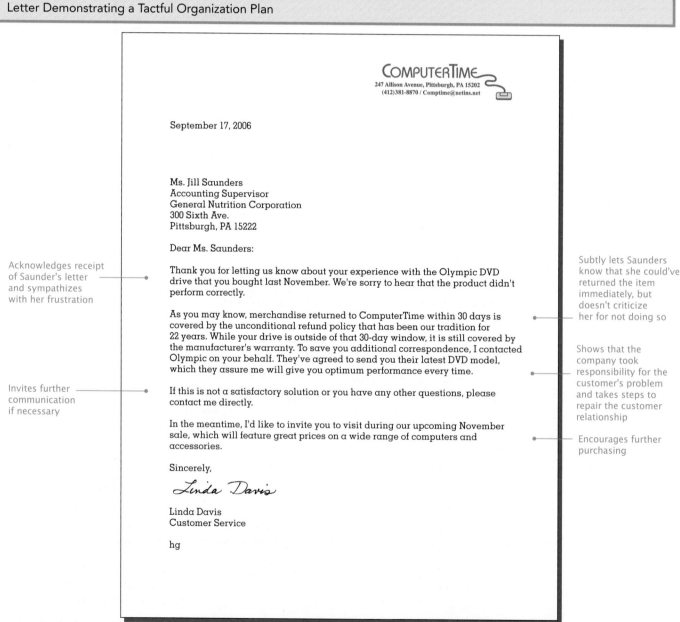

Defining Your Main Idea

The broad subject, or **topic**, of every business message is condensed to one idea, whether it's soliciting the executive committee for a larger budget or apologizing to a client for an incident of poor customer service. Your entire message supports, explains, or demonstrates your **main idea**—a specific statement about the topic of your message (see Table 4–1).

The topic is the broad subject; the main idea makes a statement about the topic.

Your main idea may be obvious when you're preparing a brief message with simple facts that have little emotional impact on your audience. If you're responding to a request for information, your main idea may be simply, "Here is what you wanted." However, defining your main idea is more complicated when you're trying to persuade someone or when you have disappointing information to convey. In these situations, try to define a main idea that will establish a good relationship between you and your audience. For example, you may choose a main idea that highlights a common interest you share with your audience or one that emphasizes a point you can both agree on.

Defining your main idea is more difficult when you're trying to persuade someone or convey disappointing information.

In longer documents and presentations, you often need to unify a mass of material, so you'll need to define a main idea that encompasses all the individual points you want to make. Finding a common thread through all these points can be a challenge. Sometimes you won't even be sure what your main idea is until you sort through the information. For tough assignments like these, consider a variety of techniques to generate creative ideas:

- **Brainstorming.** Working alone or with others, generate as many ideas and questions as you can, without stopping to criticize or organize. After you capture all these pieces, look for patterns and connections to help identify the main idea and the groups of supporting ideas. For example, if your main idea concerns whether or not to open a new restaurant in Denver, you'll probably find a group of ideas related to financial return, another related to competition, and so on. Identifying such groups helps you see the major issues that will lead you to a conclusion you can feel confident about.

- **Journalistic approach.** Introduced earlier in the chapter, the journalistic approach asks *who, what, when, where, why,* and *how* questions to distill major ideas from piles of unorganized information.

- **Question-and-answer chain.** Start with a key question, from the audience's perspective, and work back toward your message. In most cases, you'll find that each answer generates new questions, until you identify the information that needs to be in your message.

- **Storyteller's tour.** Some writers find it easier to talk through a communication challenge before they try to write. Pretend you're giving a colleague a guided tour of your message and capture it on a tape recorder. Then listen to your talk, identify ways to

DEFINING TOPIC AND MAIN IDEA			Table 4–1
General Purpose	**Specific Purpose**	**Topic**	**Main Idea**
To inform	Teach customer service representatives how to file insurance claims	Insurance claims	Proper filing saves the company time and money.
To persuade	Convince top managers to increase spending on research and development	Funding for research and development	Competitors spend more than we do on research and development.
To collaborate	Solicit ideas for a companywide incentive system that ties wages to profits	Incentive pay	Tying wages to profits motivates employees and reduces compensation costs in tough years.

FIGURE 4-9
Using the Mind-Mapping Technique to Plan a Writing Project

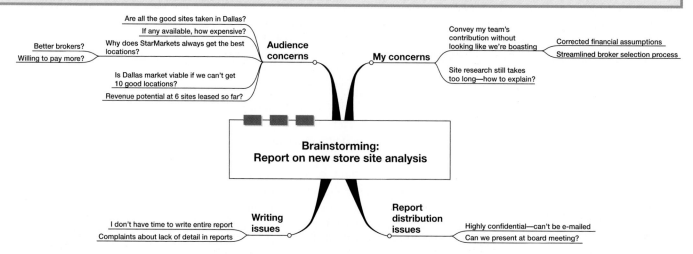

tighten and clarify the message, and repeat the process. Working through this recording several times will help you distill the main idea down to a single, concise message.

- **Mind mapping.** You can also generate and organize ideas using a graphic method called mind mapping. Start with a main idea, and then branch out to connect every other related idea that comes to mind. For instance, the map in Figure 4–9 outlines the writer's own concerns about a report, her insights into the audience's concerns, and several issues related to writing and distributing the report.

Limiting Your Scope

The **scope** of your message is the range of information you present, the overall length, and the level of detail—all of which need to correspond to your main idea. For a report outlining your advice on whether to open a new restaurant in Denver, your message, including all supporting evidence, needs to focus on that question alone. Your plan for new menu selections and your idea for a new source of financing both would be outside the scope of your message.

Whether your audience expects a one-page memo or a one-hour speech, work within that framework to develop your main idea with major points and supporting evidence. Once you have a tentative statement of your main idea, test it against the length limitations that have been imposed on your message. If you don't have enough time or space to develop your main idea fully, or if your main idea won't fill up the time and space allotted, you'll need to redefine it accordingly. If you don't have a fixed limit to work against, plan to make the document or presentation only as long as it needs to be to convey your main idea and critical support points.

Whatever the length of your message, limit the number of major support points to half a dozen or so—and if you can get your idea across with fewer points, all the better. Listing 20 or 30 support points might feel as if you're being thorough, but your audience will view such detail as disorganized and rambling. Instead, look for ways to group supporting points under major headings, such as finance, customers, competitors, employees, or whatever is appropriate for your subject. Just as you might need to refine your main idea, you may also need to refine your major support points so that you have a smaller number with greater impact.

If your message is brief (say, four minutes or one page), plan on only one minute or one paragraph each for the introduction, conclusion, and major points. Because the amount of evidence you can present is limited, your main idea will have to be both easy to understand and easy to accept. However, if your message is long (say, 60 minutes or

Limit the number of support points; having fewer, stronger points is a better approach than using many, weaker points.

20 pages), you can develop the major points in considerable detail. You can spend about 10 minutes or 10 paragraphs (more than three pages of double-spaced, typewritten text) on each of your key points, and you'll still have room for your introduction and conclusion.

How much you can communicate in a given number of words depends on the nature of your subject, your audience members' familiarity with the topic, their receptivity to your conclusions, and your credibility. You'll need fewer words to present routine information to a knowledgeable audience that already knows and respects you. You'll need more time to build a consensus about a complex and controversial subject, especially if the members of your audience are skeptical or hostile strangers.

Choosing Between Direct and Indirect Approaches

After you've defined your ideas, you're ready to decide on the sequence you will use to present your points. You have two basic options:

- **Direct approach (deductive).** When you know your audience will be receptive to your message, start with the main idea (such as a recommendation, a conclusion, or a request), and follow that with your supporting evidence.

- **Indirect approach (inductive).** When your audience will be skeptical about or even resistant to your message, start with the evidence first and build your case before presenting the main idea.

Use a direct approach if the audience's reaction is likely to be positive and the indirect approach if it is likely to be negative.

To choose between these two alternatives, analyze your audience's likely reaction to your purpose and message. Bear in mind, however, that each message is unique. No simple formula will solve all your communication problems. For example, although an indirect approach may be best when you're sending bad news to outsiders, if you're writing a memo to an associate, you may want to get directly to the point, even if your message is unpleasant. The direct approach might also be a good choice for long messages, regardless of your audience's attitude—because delaying the main idea could cause confusion and frustration. Figure 4–10 summarizes how

Audience reaction can range from eager to unwilling.

FIGURE 4–10
Choosing Between the Direct and Indirect Approaches

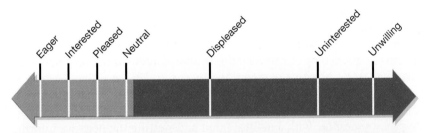

	Direct approach		
Audience Reaction	Eager/interested/ pleased/neutral	Displeased	Uninterested/unwilling
Message Opening	Start with the main idea, the request, or the good news.	Start with a neutral statement that acts as a transition to the reasons for the bad news.	Start with a statement or question that captures attention.
Message Body	Provide necessary details.	Give reasons to justify a negative answer. State or imply the bad news, and make a positive suggestion.	Arouse the audience's interest in the subject. Build the audience's desire to comply.
Message Close	Close with a cordial comment, a reference to the good news, or a statement about the specific action desired.	Close cordially.	Request action.

your approach may differ depending on the likely audience reaction. The type of message also influences the choice of a direct or indirect approach.

Routine and Positive Messages   The most straightforward business messages are routine and positive ones. If you're inquiring about products or placing an order, your audience will usually want to comply. If you're announcing a price cut, granting an adjustment, accepting an invitation, or congratulating a colleague, your audience will most likely be pleased to hear from you. If you're providing routine information as part of your regular business, your audience will probably be neutral, neither pleased nor displeased.

Aside from being easy to understand, routine messages are easy to prepare. In most cases you use the direct approach. In the opening, you state your main idea directly, without searching for some creative introduction. By starting off with your positive idea, you emphasize the pleasing aspect of your message. You put your audience in a good frame of mind and encourage them to be receptive to whatever else you have to say. The body of your message can then provide all necessary details. The close is cordial and emphasizes your good news or makes a statement about the specific action desired. Routine and positive messages are discussed in greater detail in Chapter 7.

Negative Messages   If you're refusing credit, denying a request for an adjustment, or otherwise delivering bad news, your audience will be disappointed. In such cases, it may be best to use the indirect approach—putting the evidence first and building up to the main idea. This approach strengthens your case as you go along, not only making the receiver more receptive to the eventual conclusion but also treating the receiver in a more sensitive manner, which helps you retain as much goodwill as possible. Astute businesspeople know that every person they encounter could be a potential customer, supplier, or contributor or could influence someone who is a customer, supplier, or contributor.

If you have bad news, try to put it somewhere in the middle, cushioned by other, more positive ideas.

Successful communicators take extra care with their negative messages. They often open with a neutral statement that acts as a transition to the reasons for the bad news. In the body, they give the reasons that justify the negative answer, announcement, or information before they state or imply the bad news. And they are always careful to close cordially.

The challenge of negative messages lies in being honest but kind. You don't want to sacrifice ethics and mislead your audience; nor do you want to be overly blunt. To achieve a good mix of candor and kindness, focus on some aspect of the situation that makes the negative news a little easier to take.

Using the indirect approach gives you an opportunity to get your message across to an uninterested or skeptical audience.

Keep in mind that the indirect approach is neither manipulative nor unethical. As long as you can be honest and reasonably brief, you're often better off opening a bad-news message with a neutral point and putting the negative information after the explanation. Then if you can close with something fairly positive, you're likely to leave the audience feeling at least okay—not great, but not hostile either (which is often about all you can hope for when you must deliver bad news). Negative messages are discussed further in Chapter 8.

Persuasive Messages   Persuasive messages present a special communication challenge because you're asking your audience to give, do, or change something, whether it's contributing to a charity, buying a product, or changing a belief or an attitude. Professionals who specialize in persuasive messages such as sales letters and other advertising spend years perfecting their craft, and the best practitioners command salaries on a par with some high-ranking executives. You might not have the opportunity to take your skills to that level, but you can learn some basic techniques to improve your own persuasive messages.

Before you try to persuade people to do something, capture their attention and get them to consider your message with an open mind. Make an interesting point, and provide supporting facts that encourage your audience to continue paying attention. In most persuasive messages, the opening mentions a reader benefit, refers to a problem that the recipient might have, poses a question, or mentions an interesting statistic. Then the body builds interest in the subject and arouses audience members' desire to comply. Once you have them thinking, you can introduce your main idea. The close is cordial and requests the desired action. Persuasive messages are discussed at greater length in Chapter 9.

Document Makeover

IMPROVE THIS LETTER

To practice correcting drafts of actual documents, visit your online course or the access-code protected portion of the Companion Website. Click "Document Makeovers," then click Chapter 4. You will find a letter that contains problems and errors relating to what you've learned in this chapter about planning and organizing business messages. Use the Final Draft decision tool to create an improved version of this letter. Check the document for audience focus, the right choice of medium, and the proper choice of direct or indirect approach.

Outlining Your Content

Once you have chosen the right approach, it's time to figure out the most logical and effective way to provide your supporting details. Even if you've resisted creating outlines in your school assignments over the years, try to get into the habit when you're preparing business documents and presentations. You'll save time, get better results, and do a better job of navigating through complicated business situations. Whether you use the outlining features provided with word-processing software or simply jot down three or four points on the back of an envelope, making a plan and sticking to

USING THE POWER OF TECHNOLOGY

Create and Collaborate with Powerful Outlining Tools

Experienced business communicators recognize the power of a well-planned outline. However, outlining doesn't have to be the dull exercise you might remember from book reports and other school projects. Today's outlining tools, such as Microsoft Word's outline mode, make it easy to organize and reorganize ideas quickly, and some can even help ignite your creativity and generate new ideas.

For example, by following a consistent scheme of headings and subheadings, you can quickly add, delete, and rearrange sections to make sure your overall structure is logical and coherent. Also, if you ever feel like you've gotten lost in a long document after you've started writing, you can find your way again by shifting to outline mode. Collapse the outline down to just the first-level headings, then expand one level at a time—it's a great way to rediscover the shape of the forest when you're lost in the trees. Outline software is also a powerful way to study the layout of a website because you can see the entire structure underneath the home page and make sure that your visitors won't get lost in or frustrated by confusing navigation.

For complex reports, you'll often need to collaborate on the outline with one or more colleagues, who might be in different locations around the world. Groupware collaboration tools let multiple people work on an outline at the same time, often with integrated IM so that you can brainstorm and evaluate ideas on the fly. Rather then sending the outline around via e-mail and letting each person modify it individually—which can create endless rounds of revision and compromise—using a groupware outliner lets everyone contribute, argue, and collaborate all at once.

CAREER APPLICATIONS

1. Assume your boss has asked you to deliver a presentation on a report you've just completed. She says you don't need to start from scratch, though. Figure out the steps needed to transfer your report structure from Microsoft Word to Microsoft PowerPoint.

2. Product designers use a process called *reverse engineering* to find out how a finished product is put together. You can do the same thing with finished articles and reports to see how they're organized. Cut and paste the text of a substantial online news article into your word processor, then distill it down to an outline. Do you see any ways to improve the organization of the article?

FIGURE 4–11
Two Common Outline Forms

ALPHANUMERIC OUTLINE

I. First Major Point
  A. First subpoint
  B. Second subpoint
    1. Evidence
    2. Evidence
      a. Detail
      b. Detail
    3. Evidence
  C. Third subpoint
II. Second Major Point
  A. First subpoint
    1. Evidence
    2. Evidence
  B. Second subpoint

DECIMAL OUTLINE

1.0 First Major Point
  1.1 First subpoint
  1.2 Second subpoint
    1.2.1 Evidence
    1.2.2 Evidence
      1.2.2.1 Detail
      1.2.2.2 Detail
    1.2.3 Evidence
  1.3 Third subpoint
2.0 Second Major Point
  2.1 First subpoint
    2.1.1 Evidence
    2.1.2 Evidence
  2.2 Second subpoint

A good way to visualize how all the points will fit together is to construct an outline.

it will help you cover the important details. For a look at some of the most powerful outlining tools available today, see "Using the Power of Technology: Create and Collaborate with Powerful Outlining Tools."

When you're preparing a longer, more complex message, an outline is indispensable, because it helps you visualize the relationships among the various parts. Without an outline, you may be inclined to ramble. As you're describing one point, another point may occur to you, so you describe it. One detour leads to another, and before you know it, you've forgotten the original point and wasted precious time and energy. With an outline to guide you, however, you can communicate in a more systematic way. Following an outline also helps you insert transitions so that your message is coherent and your audience can understand the relationships among your ideas.

You're no doubt familiar with the basic outline formats that identify each point with a number or letter and that indent certain points to show which ones are of equal status. A good outline divides a topic into at least two parts, restricts each subdivision to one category, and ensures that each subdivision is separate and distinct (see Figure 4–11).

You may want to experiment with other organizational schemes in addition to traditional outlines.

Another way to visualize the outline of your message is to create an "organization chart" similar to the charts used to show a company's management structure (see Figure 4–12). The main idea is shown in the highest-level box and, like a top executive, establishes the big picture. The lower-level ideas, like lower-level employees, provide the details. All the ideas are logically organized into divisions of thought, just as a company is organized into divisions and departments.[15] Using a visual chart instead of a traditional outline has many benefits. Charts help you (1) see the various levels of ideas and how the parts fit together, (2) develop new ideas, and (3) restructure your information flow. The mind-mapping technique used to generate ideas works in a similar way.

FIGURE 4–12
Organization Chart Method for Outlining

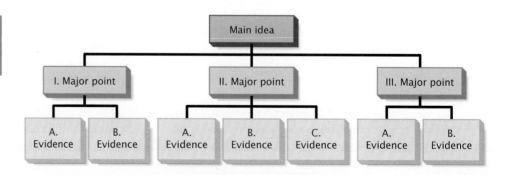

Whichever outlining or organizing scheme you use, start your message with the main idea, follow that with major supporting points, and then illustrate these points with evidence.

Start with the Main Idea   The main idea helps you establish the goals and general strategy of the message, and it summarizes two things: (1) what you want your audience to do or think and (2) why they should do so. Everything in your message either supports the main idea or explains its implications. As discussed earlier in this chapter, some messages state the main idea quickly and directly, whereas other messages delay the main idea until after the evidence is presented.

State the Major Points   Now it's time to support your main idea with the major points that clarify and explain your ideas in more concrete terms. If your purpose is to inform and the material is factual, your major points might be based on something physical or financial—something you can visualize or measure, such as activities to be performed, functional units, spatial or chronological relationships, or parts of a whole. When you're describing a process, the major points are almost inevitably steps in the process. When you're describing an object, the major points correspond to the components of the object. When you're giving a historical account, major points represent events in the chronological chain. If your purpose is to persuade or to collaborate, select major points that develop a line of reasoning or a logical argument that proves your central message and motivates your audience to act.

> Major supporting points clarify your main idea.
>
> You can divide major points according to physical relationships, the description of a process, the components of an object, or a historical chronology.

Illustrate with Evidence   After you've defined the main idea and identified supporting points, you're ready to illustrate each point with specific evidence that helps audience members understand and remember the more abstract concepts you're presenting. For example, if you're advocating that your company increase its advertising budget, you can support your major point by providing evidence that your most successful competitors spend more on advertising than you do. You can also describe a case in which a particular competitor increased its ad budget and achieved an impressive sales gain. Then you can show that over the past five years, your firm's sales have gone up and down in response to the amount spent on advertising.

If you're developing a long, complex message, you may need to carry the outline down several levels. Remember that every level is a step along the chain from the abstract to the concrete, from the general to the specific. The lowest level contains the evidence, the individual facts and figures that tie the generalizations to the observable, measurable world. The higher levels are the concepts that reveal why those facts are significant.

Up to a point, the more evidence you provide, the more conclusive your case will be. If your subject is complex and unfamiliar, or if your audience is skeptical, you'll need a lot of facts and figures to demonstrate your points. On the other hand, if your subject is routine and your audience is positively inclined, you can be more sparing with the evidence. You want to provide enough support to be convincing but not so much that your message becomes boring or inefficient.

> Each major point must be supported with enough specific evidence to be convincing, but not so much that your message becomes long and boring.

Another way to keep your audience interested is to vary the type of detail you include. As you draft your message, try to incorporate the methods described in Table 4–2. Switch from facts and figures to narration, add a dash of description, throw in some examples or a reference to authority. If it makes sense, you can reinforce all these details with visual aids. Think of your message as a stew: a mixture of ingredients seasoned with a blend of spices. Each separate flavor adds to the richness of the whole.

If your schedule permits, try to put aside your outline for a day or two before you begin composing your first draft. Then review it with a fresh eye, looking for opportunities to improve the flow of ideas. For a reminder of the planning tasks involved in preparing your messages, see "Checklist: Planning Business Messages."

Table 4–2   SIX TYPES OF DETAIL

Type of Detail	Example	Comment
Facts and figures	Sales are strong this month. We have two new contracts worth $5 million and a good chance of winning another worth $2.5 million.	Adds more credibility than any other type. Can become boring if used excessively. Most common type used in business.
Example or illustration	We've spent four months trying to hire recent accounting graduates, but so far, only one person has joined our firm. One candidate told me that she would love to work for us, but she can get $5,000 more a year elsewhere.	Adds life to a message, but one example does not prove a point. Idea must be supported by other evidence as well.
Description	Upscale hamburger restaurants target burger lovers who want more than the convenience and low prices of a McDonald's. These places feature wine and beer, half-pound burgers, and generous side dishes (nachos, potato skins). "Atmosphere" is key.	Helps audience visualize the subject by creating a sensory impression. Does not prove a point, but clarifies it and makes it memorable. Begins with overview of function; defines its purpose, lists major parts, and explains how it operates.
Narration	Under former management, executives worked in blue jeans, meetings rarely started on time, and lunches ran long. When Jim Wilson became CEO, he completely overhauled the operation. A Harvard MBA who favors Brooks Brothers suits, Wilson has cut the product line in half and chopped $12 million off expenses.	Works well for attracting attention and explaining ideas, but lacks statistical validity.
Reference to authority	I discussed this idea with Jackie Loman in the Chicago plant, and she was very supportive. As you know, Jackie has been in charge of that plant for the past six years. She is confident that we can speed up the number 2 line by 150 units an hour if we add another worker.	Bolsters a case while adding variety and credibility. Works only if "authority" is recognized and respected by audience.
Visual aids	Graphs, charts, tables	Helps audience grasp specific data. Used more in memos and reports than in letters.

✓ CHECKLIST: Planning Business Messages

A. Analyze your situation

✓ Determine whether the purpose of your message is to inform, persuade, or collaborate.
✓ Identify what you want your audience to think or do.
✓ Make sure your purpose is worthwhile and realistic.
✓ Make sure the time is right for your message.
✓ Make sure the right person is delivering your message.
✓ Make sure your purpose is acceptable to your organization.
✓ Identify the primary audience.
✓ Determine audience size and composition.
✓ Estimate your audience's level of understanding and probable reaction to your message.

B. Gather information

✓ Decide whether to use formal or informal techniques for gathering information.

✓ Find out what your audience wants to know.
✓ Provide all required information and make sure it's accurate, ethical, and pertinent.

C. Select the best medium for your message

✓ Understand the advantages and disadvantages of oral, written, and electronic media.
✓ Consider media richness, formality, media limitations, sender intentions, urgency, cost, and audience preference.

D. Organize your information

✓ Define your main idea.
✓ Limit your scope.
✓ Choose a direct or indirect approach.
✓ Outline content by starting with the main idea, adding major points, and illustrating with evidence.

On the Job

SOLVING COMMUNICATION DILEMMAS AT THE COMPLETE IDIOT'S GUIDES

Joe Kraynak's audience-centered approach to writing books has been so successful that he's hired you as a research assistant to help with a variety of new projects. He has also offered to mentor you as you begin your own career as a business writer, and you'll have the opportunity to write sections for several of his books as well. Use what you've learned in this chapter to solve these planning dilemmas.

1. Kraynak's next project is writing a how-to book for the enormously popular Motorola Razr phone, a stylish model that includes everything from video playback to Bluetooth wireless capability for adding wireless headsets and other accessories. The writer's challenge is balancing the needs of several types of users, including people who've never used a cell phone before, people who have used phones before but don't care about advanced features, and "power users" who want to use every feature possible in every way imaginable. You've sketched out several outlines and need to select the one you'll recommend to Kraynak.

    a. Organize the book in five sections: (1) an introduction to cell phones (which readers can skip if they choose), (2) a quick graphical overview of the phone that identifies all the buttons and other features, (3) a guide to basic operation of the phone, (4) a guide to advanced capabilities, and (5) a short glossary/index that defines the various features and functions and refers readers to more information in sections 1 to 4.

    b. Organize the entire book like an encyclopedia, describing the phone's individual features and functions in detail and in alphabetical order. This way people can quickly find information about the phone, no matter how much experience they have.

    c. Write three books in one: (1) an introductory guide that explains the basic concepts of using a cell phone, along with instructions on basic operation; (2) an experienced user's guide that covers just the instructions on basic operation; and (3) a power user's guide that covers the basic operation as well as all the advanced features. This book will be considerably longer, but it'll give each audience exactly what it needs.

    d. Advise Kraynak to turn down the project; there's no way anybody can write a single book that addresses the needs of so many different audiences.

2. One of the keys to Kraynak's success is identifying areas in which inexperienced product users are likely to need extra information and explanation. For the Razr book, he has asked for your help in pinpointing those issues. Unfortunately, the publisher has him on a tight schedule, and you have only one day to conduct this research. Which of the following should you do?

    a. Study the manual that Motorola provides with the Razr; that document is likely to have all the information you need.

    b. Visit as many online blogs, customer support websites, and discussion groups (such as Google Groups) as you can, scanning for questions that people seem to have about using the Razr phone.

    c. Interview every cell phone owner you know, asking them to recall the questions they had when they first started using their current phones. Although many of them won't be Razr owners, the questions might be similar enough to help.

    d. Use the Razr yourself for a day, trying to approach it the same way a new user would: what questions do you have when you first open the box, can you figure out how to charge the battery and get the phone ready for use, is it easy to add new names to the phone book, and so on. By putting yourself in the readers' shoes, you can identify all the questions they're likely to have.

3. Books aren't the only documents that authors such as Joe Kraynak have to write, of course. The business of being a writer involves a wide range of business communication efforts, including memos, letters, e-mails, progress reports, and proposals, to name a few. While you're working on the Razr book, Kraynak comes up with the idea of a website that would provide helpful information for all popular cell phones. The site would take advantage of the strong consumer awareness of the Complete Idiot's brand name, but have the advantage of being much easier to update than a printed book. However, he has heard from another author that the editors of the Complete Idiot's series aren't interested in online publishing at this point, since they're busy and successful with printed books. However, you think the new website idea could be a winner for everyone (the publisher, Kraynak, and you), so you offer to draft a proposal on the issue. Which of these organizing approaches should you take? Why?

    a. Launching a big, commercial website is a serious business decision. Come right out and say what you propose, then back that up with details in the body of the message. The audience will study the supporting details, then evaluate your idea on its merits alone.

    b. They don't want to publish online? Everybody wants to publish online—and virtually everybody is. Your proposal needs to be not only direct but also blunt: If the Idiot's Guide series doesn't create such a website, somebody else surely will. Without exactly saying so, you need to convey the message that only an idiot would ignore an opportunity like this for the Idiot's Guide series.

c. Your proposal should take an indirect approach, since the readers will initially be resistant to the idea. Moreover, it would be bad form to dictate precisely what the solution should be, so write only in general terms (such as "the opportunity for online publishing is significant") and let the readers reach a conclusion on their own (as in, deciding specifically to create a Complete Idiot's website for popular phones).

d. If the proposal doesn't quickly address the audience's reservations regarding web publishing, they won't bother to read the details or to consider the proposal. Consequently, an indirect approach is best. Start by announcing that you've identified a business opportunity that is ideal for Idiot's Guides but needs to be acted upon soon or a competitor will get there first. After you've captured the audience's attention with that intriguing opening, continue with your persuasive argument in favor of the website (including, for instance, the possibility that the website will increase the demand for books).

4. Kraynak emphasizes that the website proposal needs to provide enough evidence to be convincing, but not so much that it becomes long and tiresome to read. Which of the following support points does *not* belong in the proposal? Why not?

a. A list of companies that would possibly be interested in advertising on the website, along with an estimate of the advertising revenue the site might be able to generate

b. A brief history on online publishing, from the days before the World Wide Web to the latest in blogging

c. A plan for updating the website content as new phone models are released

d. An estimate of the number of cell phone owners who are likely to use such a website

Learning Objectives Checkup

Assess your understanding of the principles in this chapter by reading each learning objective and studying the accompanying exercises. For fill-in items, write the missing text in the blank provided; for multiple choice items, circle the letter of the correct answer. You can check your responses against the answer key on page AK-1.

Objective 4.1: Describe the three-step writing process.

1. The three major steps in the three-step writing process are
   a. Writing, editing, and producing
   b. Planning, writing, and completing
   c. Writing, editing, and distributing
   d. Organizing, defining your purpose, and writing

2. The first step of the three-step writing process is
   a. Writing the first draft
   b. Organizing your information
   c. Planning your message
   d. Preparing an outline

3. The purpose of limiting your scope when planning a writing project is to
   a. Make your job easier
   b. Reduce the number of things you need to think about
   c. Make sure your memos are never longer than one page
   d. Make sure that your message stays focused on the main idea and any necessary supporting details

4. Which of the following tasks should you do when you're planning a writing project?
   a. Defining your purpose
   b. Revising carefully to make sure you haven't made any embarrassing mistakes
   c. Choosing words and sentences carefully to make sure the audience understands your main idea
   d. All of the above

5. The _____ of a message indicates whether you intend to use the message to inform, to persuade, or to collaborate.

Objective 4.2: Explain why it's important to define your purpose carefully, and list five questions that can help you test that purpose.

6. After you've defined the purpose of your message, which of the following questions should you ask yourself before continuing the writing process?
   a. Will anything change as a result of my delivering this message?
   b. Is this message realistic?
   c. Is this message acceptable to my organization?
   d. Am I the right person to deliver this message?
   e. All of the above

7. If you were to write a letter to a manufacturer complaining about a defective product and asking for a refund, your general purpose would be
   a. To inform
   b. To persuade
   c. To collaborate
   d. To entertain

Objective 4.3: Describe the importance of analyzing your audience, and identify the six factors you should consider when developing an audience profile.

8. Which of the following audience analysis steps should always be taken, no matter what the message is or the audience you want to reach?
   a. The information your audience needs in order to grasp your main idea
   b. The names of everyone in the target audience

c. The percentage of audience members who are likely to agree with your message

d. A complete demographic profile of your audience

9. If audience members will vary in the amount of information they already know about your topic, your best approach is to

a. Provide as much extra information as possible to make sure everyone gets every detail

b. Provide just the basic information; if your audience needs to know more, they can find out for themselves

c. Gear your coverage to your primary audience and provide the information most relevant to them

d. Include lots of graphics

Objective 4.4: Discuss gathering information for simple messages, and identify three attributes of quality information.

10. To make sure you have provided all the necessary information, use the journalistic approach, which is to

a. Interview your audience about its needs

b. Check the accuracy of your information

c. Verify that whether your message answers the questions of *who, what, when, where, why,* and *how*

d. Make sure your information is ethical

11. To determine whether the information you've gathered is good enough, verify that it is

a. Accurate

b. Ethical

c. Pertinent to the audience's needs

d. All of the above

12. If you realize you have given your audience incorrect information, the most ethical action would be to

a. Say nothing and hope no one notices

b. Wait until someone points out the error, then acknowledge the mistake

c. Post a correction on your website

d. Contact the audience immediately and correct the error

Objective 4.5: List factors to consider when choosing the most appropriate medium for your message.

13. A medium's ability to convey a message using more than one informational cue, to facilitate feedback, and to establish personal focus is a measure of its _____.

14. Which of the following choices would be best for communicating a complex policy change to employees in a company with offices all over the world?

a. A teleconference followed by an e-mail message

b. Instant messaging (IM)

c. A traditional typed memo sent via regular postal mail

d. A website posting with an e-mail message alerting employees to the change and directing them to the website for more information

Objective 4.6: Explain why good organization is important to both you and your audience.

15. Which of the following is an important benefit of taking time to organize your business messages?

a. You can delay the actual writing.

b. You save time and conserve creative energy because the writing process is quicker.

c. Organizing your thoughts and information saves you the trouble of asking colleagues for input.

d. In many cases, you can simply send a detailed outline and save the trouble of writing the document.

Objective 4.7: Summarize the process for organizing business messages effectively.

16. Starting with the main idea then offering supporting evidence is known as the _____ approach.

17. Starting with evidence first and building toward your main idea is known as the _____ approach.

18. When your audience is likely to have a skeptical or even hostile reaction to your main idea, you should generally use

a. An indirect approach

b. A direct approach

c. An open-ended approach

d. A closed approach

Apply Your Knowledge

1. Some writers argue that planning messages wastes time because they inevitably change their plans as they go along. How would you respond to this argument? Briefly explain.

2. As a member of the public relations department, what medium would you recommend using to inform the local community that your toxic-waste cleanup program has been successful? Why?

3. Would you use a direct or an indirect approach to ask employees to work overtime to meet an important deadline? Please explain.

4. Which approach would you use to let your boss know that you'll be out half a day this week to attend your father's funeral—direct or indirect? Why?

5. **Ethical Choices** The company president has asked you to draft a memo to the board of directors informing them that sales in a line of gourmet fruit jams the company recently acquired have far exceeded anyone's expectations. However, you happen to know that this increase reflects a trend across the industry, with many consumers switching from moderately priced jams to gourmet products. In fact, sales of your company's traditional products have slipped in recent months. You were not asked to add this information, but you think it's important for the board to be able to put the new sales data in proper context. What should you do?

Practice Your Knowledge

DOCUMENT FOR ANALYSIS

A writer is working on an insurance information brochure and is having trouble grouping the ideas logically into an outline. Prepare the outline, paying attention to appropriate subordination of ideas. If necessary, rewrite phrases to give them a more consistent sound.

ACCIDENT PROTECTION INSURANCE PLAN

- Coverage is only pennies a day
- Benefit is $100,000 for accidental death on common carriers
- Benefit is $100 a day for hospitalization as result of motor vehicle or common carrier accident
- Benefit is $20,000 for accidental death in motor vehicle accident
- Individual coverage is only $17.85 per quarter; family coverage is just $26.85 per quarter
- No physical exam or health questions
- Convenient payment—billed quarterly
- Guaranteed acceptance for all applicants
- No individual rate increases
- Free, no-obligation examination period
- Cash paid in addition to any other insurance carried
- Covers accidental death when riding as fare-paying passenger on public transportation, including buses, trains, jets, ships, trolleys, subways, or any other common carrier
- Covers accidental death in motor vehicle accidents occurring while driving or riding in or on automobile, truck, camper, motor home, or nonmotorized bicycle

Exercises

For active links to all websites discussed in this chapter, visit this text's website at www.prenhall.com/thill. Locate your book and click on its Companion Website link. Then select Chapter 4, and click on "Featured Websites." Locate the name of the page or the URL related to the material in the text. Please note that links to sites that become inactive after publication of the book will be removed from the Featured Websites section.

4.1 **Message Planning Skills: Self-Assessment** How good are you at planning business messages? Use the following chart to rate yourself on each element of planning an audience-centered business message. Then examine your ratings to identify where you are strongest and where you can improve, using the tips in this chapter.

Element of Planning	Always	Frequently	Occasionally	Never
1. I start by defining my purpose.	_____	_____	_____	_____
2. I analyze my audience before writing a message.	_____	_____	_____	_____
3. I investigate what my audience wants to know.	_____	_____	_____	_____
4. I check that my information is accurate, ethical, and pertinent.	_____	_____	_____	_____
5. I consider my audience and purpose when selecting media.	_____	_____	_____	_____

4.2 **Planning Messages: General and Specific Purpose** Make a list of communication tasks you'll need to accomplish in the next week or so (for example, a job application, a letter of complaint, a speech to a class, an order for some merchandise). For each, determine a general and a specific purpose.

4.3 **Planning Messages: Specific Purpose** For each of the following communication tasks, state a specific purpose (if you have trouble, try beginning with "I want to . . . ").

a. A report to your boss, the store manager, about the outdated items in the warehouse
b. A memo to clients about your booth at the upcoming trade show
c. A letter to a customer who hasn't made a payment for three months
d. A memo to employees about the department's high cell phone bills
e. A phone call to a supplier checking on an overdue parts shipment

f. A report to future users of the computer program you have chosen to handle the company's mailing list

4.4 Planning Messages: Audience Profile For each communication task below, write brief answers to three questions: Who is my audience? What is my audience's general attitude toward my subject? What does my audience need to know?

a. A final-notice collection letter from an appliance manufacturer to an appliance dealer, sent 10 days before initiating legal collection procedures

b. An unsolicited sales letter asking readers to purchase computer disks at near-wholesale prices

c. An advertisement for peanut butter

d. Fliers to be attached to doorknobs in the neighborhood, announcing reduced rates for chimney lining or repairs

e. A cover letter sent along with your résumé to a potential employer

f. A request (to the seller) for a price adjustment on a piano that incurred $150 in damage during delivery to a banquet room in the hotel you manage

4.5 Meeting Audience Needs: Necessary Information Choose a product (such as a digital music player, camera, or cell phone) that you know how to operate well. Write two sets of instructions for operating the device: one set for a reader who has never used that type of device and one set for someone who is generally familiar with that type of device but has never operated the specific model. Briefly explain how your two audiences affect your instructions. (Limit your instructions to the basic functions, such as placing and receiving calls on a cell phone.)

4.6 Selecting Media: Defining the Purpose List three messages you have received lately, such as direct-mail promotions, letters, e-mail messages, telephone calls, and class lectures. For each, determine the general and the specific purpose; then answer the following questions: (a) Was the message well timed? (b) Did the sender choose an appropriate medium for the message? (c) Did the appropriate person deliver the message? (d) Was the sender's purpose realistic?

4.7 Selecting Media: Identifying an Audience Barbara Marquardt is in charge of public relations for a cruise line that operates out of Miami. She is shocked to read a letter in a local newspaper from a disgruntled passenger, complaining about the service and entertainment on a recent cruise. Marquardt will have to respond to these publicized criticisms in some way. What audiences will she need to consider in her response? What medium should she choose? If the letter had been published in a travel publication widely read by travel agents and cruise travelers, how might her course of action differ?

4.8 Teamwork: Audience Analysis Your team has developed a new method for testing the durability of your company's power tools. The test will be performed by assembly line workers, but it also affects

two other groups: the engineers who design the tools (because the tests may lead to design changes) and the manufacturing manager (who needs to be convinced the test is necessary and who will need to find money in the budget to buy some special equipment needed to perform the test). Now the team needs to prepare three separate reports on the findings: one for the manufacturing manager, another for the engineers, and a third for the training manager, whose department will need to train the workers on the new method. To determine the audience's needs for each of these reports, the team has listed the following questions: (1) Who are the readers? (2) Why will they read my report? (3) Do they need introductory or background material? (4) Do they need definitions of terms? (5) What level or type of language is needed? (6) What level of detail is needed? (7) What result does my report aim for? Working with two other students, answer the questions for each of these audiences:

a. The manufacturing manager

b. The engineers

c. The training manager

4.9 Internet: Planning Your Message Go to the PepsiCo website at www.pepsico.com and follow the link to the latest annual report (if you don't see a link on the home page, look under investor information). Locate and read the chairman's letter within the report. Who is the audience for this message? What is the general purpose of the message? What do you think this audience wants to know from the chairman of PepsiCo? Summarize your answers in a brief (one-page) memo or oral presentation.

4.10 Message Organization: Outlining Your Content Using the GNC letter in this chapter (Figure 4–7), draw an organizational chart similar to the one shown in Figure 4–12. Fill in the main idea, the major points, and the evidence provided in this letter. (Note: Your diagram may be smaller than the one provided in Figure 4–12.)

4.11 Message Organization: Limiting Scope Suppose you are preparing to recommend that top management install a new heating system that uses a process called cogeneration, in which production waste is used to generate heat. The following information is in your files. Eliminate topics that aren't essential; then arrange the other topics so that your report will give top managers a clear understanding of the heating system and a balanced, concise justification for installing it.

- History of the development of the cogeneration heating process
- Scientific credentials of the developers of the process
- Risks assumed in using this process
- Your plan for installing the equipment in your building
- Stories about its successful use in comparable facilities

- Specifications of the equipment that would be installed
- Plans for disposing of the old heating equipment
- Costs of installing and running the new equipment
- Advantages and disadvantages of using the new process
- Detailed 10-year cost projections
- Estimates of the time needed to phase in the new system
- Alternative systems that management might wish to consider

4.12 Message Organization: Choosing an Approach Indicate whether a direct or an indirect approach would be best in each of the following situations; then briefly explain why. Would any of these messages be inappropriate for e-mail? Explain.

   a. A letter asking when next year's automobiles will be put on sale locally

   b. A letter from a recent college graduate requesting a letter of recommendation from a former instructor

   c. A letter turning down a job applicant

   d. An announcement that because of high air-conditioning costs, the plant temperature will be held at 78 degrees during the summer

   e. A final request to settle a delinquent debt

4.13 Message Organization: Audience Focus If you were trying to persuade people to take the following actions, how would you organize your argument?

   a. You want your boss to approve your plan for hiring two additional people.

   b. You want to be hired for a job.

   c. You want to be granted a business loan.

   d. You want to collect a small amount from a regular customer whose account is slightly past due.

   e. You want to collect a large amount from a customer whose account is seriously past due.

4.14 Ethical Choices: Providing Information Your supervisor, whom you respect, has asked you to withhold important information that you think should be included in a report you are preparing. Disobeying him could be disastrous for your relationship with him and possibly your career. Obeying him could violate your personal code of ethics. What should you do? On the basis of the discussion in Chapter 1, would you consider this situation to be an ethical dilemma or an ethical lapse? Please explain.

4.15 Three-Step Process: Other Applications How can the material discussed in this chapter also apply to meetings as discussed in Chapter 2? (Hint: Review the section headings in this chapter and think about making your meetings more productive.)

Expand Your Knowledge

LEARNING MORE ON THE WEB

CORPORATE BLOGGING WITH A EUROPEAN FLAVOR

www.corporateblogging.info/basics

See how blogging is changing the business of business communication and learn the basic steps needed to set up your own company blog. Plus, you can explore a variety of blogs hosted by European companies to get a feel for the international nature of blogging.

ACTIVITIES

Browse the Business Blogging Basics section and sample a few of the European blogs (the blogs from the United Kingdom are in English, as are selected blogs from other countries), then answer the following questions

1. What are the key advantages of creating a company blog?
2. What are the various methods of reading content from other blogs?

3. Do the European blogs differ in style from one another or from blogs you've seen from U.S. companies?

EXPLORING THE WEB ON YOUR OWN

Review these chapter-related websites on your own to learn more about achieving communication success in the workplace:

1. Get hundreds of free tips on improving your business writing at Bull's Eye Business Writing Tips, www.businesswritingtips.com.
2. See how to put phone text messaging to work in business applications at Text.It, www.text.it (click on Text for Business).
3. Discover how e-mail works and how to improve your e-mail communications by following the steps at About Internet for Beginners—Harness E-Mail, www.learnthenet.com/english/section/email.html.

Learn Interactively

INTERACTIVE STUDY GUIDE

Visit www.prenhall.com/thill, then locate your book and click on its Companion Website link. Select Chapter 4 to take advantage of the interactive "Chapter Quiz" to test your knowledge of chapter concepts. Receive instant feedback on whether you need additional studying. Also, visit the "Study Hall," where you'll find an abundance of valuable resources that will help you succeed in this course.

PEAK PERFORMANCE GRAMMAR AND MECHANICS

If your instructor has required the use of "Peak Performance Grammar and Mechanics," either in your online course or on CD, you can improve your skill with adjectives by using the "Peak Performance Grammar and Mechanics" module. Click "Adjectives." Take the Pretest to determine whether you have any weak areas. Then review those areas in the Refresher Course. Take the Follow-Up Test to check your grasp of adjectives. For an extra challenge or advanced practice, take the Advanced Test. Finally, for additional reinforcement, go to the "Improve Your Grammar, Mechanics, and Usage" section that follows, and complete those exercises.

Improve Your Grammar, Mechanics, and Usage

The following exercises help you improve your knowledge of and power over English grammar, mechanics, and usage. Turn to the Handbook of Grammar, Mechanics, and Usage at the end of this textbook and review all of Section 1.4 (Adjectives). Then look at the following 10 items. Underline the preferred choice within each set of parentheses. (Answers to these exercises appear on page AK-3.)

1. Of the two products, this one has the (*greater, greatest*) potential.
2. The (*most perfect, perfect*) solution is *d*.
3. Here is the (*interesting, most interesting*) of all the ideas I have heard so far.
4. The (*hardest, harder*) part of my job is firing people.
5. A (*highly placed, highly-placed*) source revealed Dotson's (*last ditch, last-ditch*) efforts to cover up the mistake.
6. A (*top secret, top-secret*) document was taken from the president's office last night.
7. A (*30 year old, 30-year-old*) person should know better.
8. The two companies are engaged in an (*all-out no-holds-barred; all-out, no-holds-barred*) struggle for dominance.
9. A (*tiny metal; tiny, metal*) shaving is responsible for the problem.
10. You'll receive our (*usual cheerful prompt; usual, cheerful, prompt; usual cheerful, prompt*) service.

For additional exercises focusing on adjectives, go to www.prenhall. com/thill, then locate your text and click on its Companion Website link. Click on Chapter 4, click on "Additional Exercises to Improve Your Grammar, Mechanics and Usage," then click on "8. Adjectives."

Chapter 5

Writing Business Messages

Learning Objectives

AFTER STUDYING THIS CHAPTER, YOU WILL BE ABLE TO

1 Explain the importance of adapting your messages to the needs and expectations of your audience

2 Discuss four ways of achieving a businesslike tone with a style that is clear and concise

3 Briefly describe how to select words that are not only correct but also effective

4 Explain how sentence style affects emphasis within your message

5 List five ways to develop coherent paragraphs

6 Discuss the importance of effective e-mail subject lines and explain how to write them

On the Job

COMMUNICATING AT CREATIVE COMMONS

REDEFINING TWO CENTURIES OF COPYRIGHT LAW FOR THE DIGITAL AGE

That tiny © symbol printed on books, DVDs, music CDs, and other media products might seem like a small character indeed, but it is at the heart of a multibillion-dollar dilemma that affects everything from downloaded music to digital movies to scientific discovery. The © means that the person who created the item is granted *copyright* protection, the exclusive legal right to produce, distribute, and sell that creation. Anyone who wants to resell, redistribute, or adapt such works usually needs to secure permission from the current copyright holder, and this protection currently lasts for 70 years past the creator's death.

Lawrence Lessig, co-founder of Creative Commons, uses a variety of communication vehicles to convince copyright owners to explore new ways of sharing and protecting their creative works.

For more than 200 years, this "all rights reserved" model generally made sense and fulfilled the U.S. Constitution's intent of using copyright law to promote the collective well-being by encouraging individual creative work in the arts and sciences. However, suppose you *want* people to remix the song you just recorded or rewrite the ending to your short story? Or what if someone just needs a few of your photos for a website or a piece of background music for a student film? Other than for limited personal and educational use, a conventional copyright requires every person to negotiate a contract with you for every application or adaptation of every piece of work he or she wants to use.

The search for some middle ground between all rights reserved and simply giving your work away led Stanford University law professor Lawrence Lessig to co-found Creative Commons. This nonprofit organiza-

tion's goal is to provide a simple, free, and legal way for musicians, artists, writers, teachers, scientists, and others to collaborate and benefit through the sharing of art and ideas. Instead of the everything-or-nothing approach of traditional copyright, Creative Commons offers "some rights reserved" options such as *attribution* (others can use your work if they give you credit), *noncommercial use* (others can use or modify your work as long as they don't profit from it), and *no derivative works* (others can copy, distribute, and perform your work but can't derive new works from it).

Persuading people to rethink two centuries of legal precedent is no simple task, particularly when years of creative effort and potential income might be at stake. Through books, articles, and speeches, Lessig has been a tireless promoter of the Creative Commons concept, working to convince people that society benefits from the free exchange of art and ideas and that overuse of the copyright law is endangering not only creative expression but important scientific research. The message is clearly getting through: Within the first year, more than a million license agreements were initiated for musical works, short films, educational materials, novels, and more through Creative Commons. This approach can't solve the entire dilemma of copyrights in the digital age, but it has already created a better way for creative people to communicate and collaborate.[1]

FIGURE 5–1
Step Two in the Three-Step Writing Process: Write Your Messages

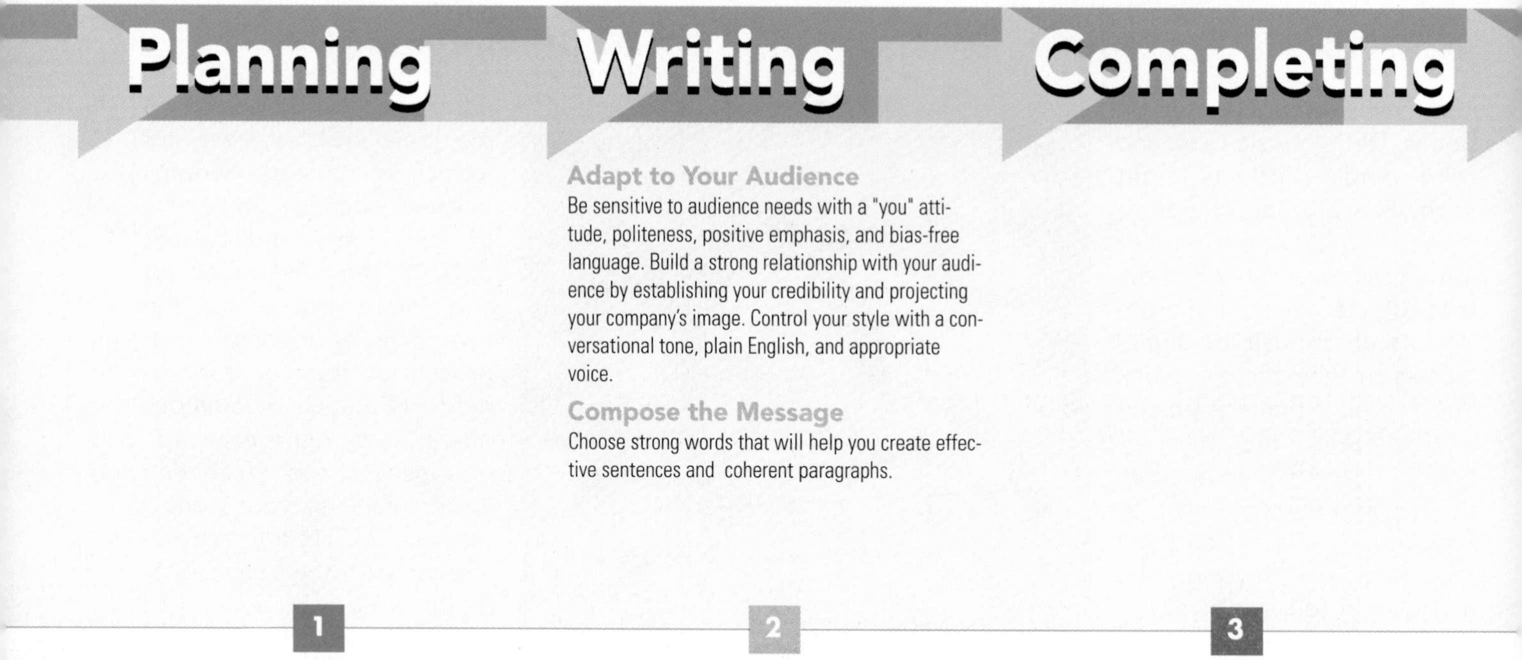

Planning   Writing   Completing

Adapt to Your Audience
Be sensitive to audience needs with a "you" attitude, politeness, positive emphasis, and bias-free language. Build a strong relationship with your audience by establishing your credibility and projecting your company's image. Control your style with a conversational tone, plain English, and appropriate voice.

Compose the Message
Choose strong words that will help you create effective sentences and coherent paragraphs.

1   2   3

BRINGING YOUR IDEAS TO LIFE

With a solid plan in place (see Chapter 4), you're ready to choose the words and craft the sentences and paragraphs that will carry your ideas to their intended audiences. Figure 5–1 lists the tasks involved in adapting to your audience and composing your message.

ADAPTING TO YOUR AUDIENCE

Audiences want to know how your messages will benefit them.

Whether consciously or not, audiences greet most incoming messages with a question: "What's in this for me?" If your intended audience thinks a message does not apply to them or doesn't meet their needs, they'll be far less inclined to pay attention to it. Follow the example set by Lawrence Lessig and his colleagues on the Creative Commons website, which addresses an extremely diverse audience of artists, lawyers, and business professionals, but fine-tunes specific messages for each group of people. By adapting your communication to the needs and expectations of your audiences, you'll provide a more compelling answer to the "What's in this for me?" question and improve the chances of your message being successful.

However, as Lessig can also attest, adapting your message is not always a simple task. Some situations will require you to balance competing or conflicting needs—for example, when you're trying to convince people to change their minds or when you're delivering bad news. Other situations may tempt you to adapt your personal style, but be careful. Although adjusting your style is a positive move, don't go so far that you come across as someone you're not. You won't be comfortable with this approach, and your audience will probably see through it.

A good relationship with your audience is essential to effective communication.

To adapt your message to your audience, try to be sensitive to your audience's needs, build a strong relationship with your audience, and control your style to maintain a professional tone.

Being Sensitive to Your Audience's Needs

Even in simple messages intended merely to share information, it's possible to use all the right words and still not be sensitive to your audience and their needs. You can improve your audience sensitivity by adopting the "you" attitude, maintaining good standards of etiquette, emphasizing the positive, and using bias-free language.

Using the "You" Attitude   You are already becoming familiar with the audience-centered approach, trying to see a subject through your audience's eyes. Now you want to project this approach in your messages by adopting a **"you" attitude**—that is, by speaking and writing in terms of your audience's wishes, interests, hopes, and preferences.

On the simplest level, you can adopt the "you" attitude by replacing terms that refer to yourself and your company with terms that refer to your audience. In other words, use *you* and *yours* instead of *I, me, mine, we, us,* and *ours:*

The "you" attitude is best implemented by expressing your message in terms of the audience's interests and needs.

Instead of This	Use This
To help us process this order, we must ask for another copy of the requisition.	So that your order can be filled promptly, please send another copy of the requisition.
We are pleased to announce our new flight schedule from Atlanta to New York, which is any hour on the hour.	Now you can take a plane from Atlanta to New York any hour on the hour.
We offer MP3 players with 10, 15, or 20 gigabytes of storage capacity.	Select your MP3 player from three models with 10, 15, or 20 gigabytes of storage capacity.

When business messages use an "I" or "we" attitude, they risk sounding selfish and uninterested in the audience. The message tells what the sender wants, and the audience is expected to go along with it. Even so, using *you* and *yours* requires finesse. If you overdo it, you're likely to create some rather awkward sentences, and you run the risk of sounding overly enthusiastic and artificial.[2]

The "you" attitude is not intended to be manipulative or insincere. It's an extension of the audience-centered approach. In fact, the best way to implement the "you" attitude is to sincerely think about your audience when composing your message.

Nor is the "you" attitude simply a matter of using one pronoun rather than another; it's a matter of genuine empathy. You can use *you* 25 times in a single page and still ignore your audience's true concerns. In other words, it's the thought and sincerity that count, not the pronoun *you.* If you're talking to a retailer, try to think like a retailer; if you're dealing with a production supervisor, put yourself in that position; if you're writing to a dissatisfied customer, imagine how you would feel at the other end of the transaction. The important thing is your attitude toward audience members and your appreciation of their position.

Be aware that on some occasions it's better to avoid using *you,* particularly if doing so will sound overly authoritative or accusing. For instance, instead of saying, "You failed to deliver the customer's order on time," you could minimize ill will by saying, "The customer didn't receive the order on time," or "Let's figure out a system that will ensure on-time deliveries."

Jenny J. Ming, president of Old Navy, combines her passion for fashion with the ability to communicate effectively with others. Ming recognizes that people's needs change as quickly as the latest fashion trends, so she takes extra care to focus on every audience's changing needs.

Avoid using *you* and *yours* when doing so
- Makes you sound dictatorial
- Makes someone else feel guilty
- Goes against your organization's style

Instead of This	Use This
You should never use that type of paper in the copy machine.	That type of paper doesn't work very well in the copy machine.
You must correct all five copies by noon.	All five copies must be corrected by noon.

As you practice using the "you" attitude, be sure to consider the attitudes of other cultures and the policies of your organization. In some cultures, it is improper to single out one person's achievements because the whole team is responsible for the outcome; in that case, using the pronoun *we* or *our* (when you and your audience are part of the same team) would be more appropriate. Similarly, some companies have a tradition of avoiding references to *you* and *I* in their memos and formal reports. If you work for a company that expects a formal, impersonal style, confine your use of personal pronouns to informal letters and memos.

Maintaining Standards of Etiquette   Another good way to demonstrate interest in your audience and to earn their respect is to demonstrate etiquette in your messages. You know how it feels to be treated inconsiderately; when that happens, you probably react emotionally and then pay less attention to the offending message. By being courteous to members of your audience, you show consideration for them and foster a more successful environment for communication.

> Although you may be tempted now and then to be brutally frank, try to express the facts in a kind and thoughtful manner.

On those occasions when you experience frustration with co-workers, customers, or others you deal with, you might be tempted to say what you think in blunt terms. But venting your emotions rarely improves the situation and can jeopardize your audience's goodwill. Demonstrate your diplomatic skills by controlling your emotions and communicating calmly and politely:

Instead of This	Use This
Once again, you've managed to bring down the website through your incompetent programming	Let's go over what went wrong with the last site update so that we can find out how to improve the process.
You've been sitting on our order for two weeks, and we need it now!	Our production schedules depend on timely delivery of parts and supplies, but we have not yet received the order you promised to deliver two weeks ago. Please respond today with a firm delivery commitment.

> Use extra tact when communicating with people higher up the organization chart or outside the company.

Of course, some situations require more diplomacy than others. If you know your audience well, a less formal approach might be more appropriate. However, when you are communicating with people who outrank you or with people outside your organization, an added measure of courtesy is usually needed.

Written communication generally requires more tact than oral communication. When you're speaking, your words are softened by your tone of voice and facial expression. Plus, you can adjust your approach according to the feedback you get. If you inadvertently offend someone in writing, you usually won't get the immediate feedback you would need to resolve the situation. In fact, you may never know that you offended your audience.

Keep these points in mind as you review the draft and revised versions of the letter in Figure 5–2. Because of a death in the family, a restaurant owner closed his business for three days over Labor Day weekend. Unfortunately, someone left the freezer door ajar, and over the course of three days, the motor burned out and all the food spoiled. The total cost to replace the motor and replace the food was over $2,000. The customer wrote a letter explaining the situation and requesting that Eppler Appliances cover these costs, but Eppler had to refuse. Notice how much more diplomatic the revised version is, communicating the necessary information without offending the reader.

Another simple but effective courtesy is to be prompt in your correspondence. If possible, answer voice mail, instant messages, and e-mail within 24 hours and answer regular mail within two or three days. If you need more time to prepare a

FIGURE 5–2
Revising a Customer Letter to Improve Diplomacy

Dear Mr. Carpaccio:

Draft

Subject: Burned-out motor

We have received your request for reimbursement. Although your Crown Freezer is under warranty for two more months, you can't honestly expect us to be liable for the cost of a new motor and of your spoiled food when the problem clearly resulted from your own negligence. These freezers were not designed to operate at full capacity with the door ajar for any length of time, let alone for three days over Labor Day weekend in some of the hottest weather we've had in a decade.

Crown products were designed to endure everyday use in a typical commercial kitchen. They are constructed of top-quality materials, insulated with non-CFC in-place polyurethane foam, and are "performance rated" using environmentally safe refrigerants. Your top-mounted freezer model includes casters, heavy-duty lift-off hinges, durable looking stainless steel doors, and exterior dial thermometer.

However, we would like to offer to pay for the service call, in the spirit of good customer relations. I'm sorry, but that's the best we can do for you at this time.

Sincerely,

Uses "you" inappropriately, emphasizing negatives and blaming the reader

Reacts to the request in an emotional, unprofessional manner

Clutters the letter with irrelevant information

Ends on a negative note, without offering any information that could benefit the reader

Revision

EPPLER APPLIANCES
7142 Conrad Avenue, Lima, OH 45801
Voice: (419) 768-1927   Fax: (419) 768-1928

September 9, 2006

Mr. Joseph Carpaccio
Carpaccio's Ristoranti
847 Broadway
Lima, OH 45806

Dear Mr. Carpaccio:

Subject: Burned-out freezer motor, Invoice # 3770 46 010122

Thank you for your letter about your freezer repairs. Please accept our condolences regarding your family's recent loss.

Although your freezer is under warranty until November 15, the situation you've described is unfortunately not covered under the terms of your warranty (I've included a copy of the warranty for your convenience). With their top-quality materials and high performance ratings, Crown Freezers are built to endure years of normal use in commercial kitchens. However, as is the case with all commercial refrigeration manufacturers, Crown's warranty does not cover accidents attributed to improper use. In appreciation for your past business, though, we would like to help by refunding the $75 you paid for the service call.

To avoid unexpected costs in the future, you may be interested in a new business insurance service that we've recently started offering in conjunction with Crown. For just $135 a year, the insurance covers parts, labor, and damages, regardless of the cause. The enclosed brochure gives all the details, or you can visit our website at www.eppler.com.

Sincerely,

Kjiersten Lejunhud

Kjiersten Lejunhud
Customer Relations

Enclosures (3)

Provides complete identifying information to simplify future references to this situation

Communicates the denial of the request without blaming the reader or bluntly saying "we refuse to fulfill your request"

Expresses thanks for the customer's past business

Acknowledges receipt of the letter and expresses sympathy for the customer's personal loss

Provides some reassuring information about the quality of the product

Closes on a friendly note, with detailed information about actions the reader might take to avoid such expenses in the future reply, call or write a brief note to say that you're working on an answer. Your audience will appreciate the courtesy.

Emphasizing the Positive   During your career, you will face situations in which you need to communicate bad news—maybe dozens or hundreds of times. However, there is a big difference between delivering negative news and being negative. When the tone of your message is negative, you put unnecessary strain on business relationships, which can cause people to distance themselves from you and your ideas.

> You can communicate negative news without being negative.

If you're facing a potentially negative situation, look for ways to soften the blow or emphasize positive aspects of a situation. For example, when Alaska Airlines instituted surcharges for heavy luggage in an attempt to reduce injuries to baggage handlers, the company presented the change to passengers with posters that said, "Pack Light & Save."[3] By presenting the situation as an opportunity to save money, rather than as an added cost of travel, Alaska worked to maintain a positive relationship with its customers. Never try to hide the negative news, but always be on the lookout for positive points that will foster a good relationship with your audience:[4]

Instead of This	Use This
It is impossible to repair your car today.	Your car can be ready by Tuesday. Would you like a loaner until then?
We apologize for inconveniencing you during our remodeling.	The renovations now under way will help us serve you better.
We wasted $300,000 advertising in that magazine.	Our $300,000 advertising investment did not pay off; let's analyze the experience and apply the insights to future campaigns.

> When you are offering criticism or advice, focus on what the person can do to improve.

When you find it necessary to criticize or correct, don't dwell on the other person's mistakes. Avoid referring to failures, problems, or shortcomings. Focus instead on what the person can do to improve:

Instead of This	Use This
The problem with this department is a failure to control costs.	The performance of this department can be improved by tightening cost controls.
You filled out the order form wrong.	Please check your color preferences on the enclosed card so that we can process your order.

> Show your audience how they will benefit from complying with your message.

If you're trying to persuade the audience to buy a product, pay a bill, or perform a service for you, emphasize what's in it for them. Don't focus on why *you* want them to do something. An individual who sees the possibility for personal benefit is more likely to respond positively to your appeal:

Instead of This	Use This
We will communicate a late payment notice to all three credit reporting agencies if you do not pay your overdue bill within 10 days.	Paying your overdue bill within 10 days will prevent a negative entry on your credit record.
We need your contribution to the Boys and Girls Club.	You can help a child make friends and build self-confidence through your donation to the Boys and Girls Club.

In general, try to state your message without using words that might hurt or offend your audience. Substitute *euphemisms* (mild terms) for those that have unpleasant connotations. You can be honest without being harsh. Gentle language won't change the facts, but it will make them more acceptable:

Try to avoid words with negative connotations; use meaningful euphemisms instead.

Instead of This	Use This
cheap merchandise	economy merchandise
used cars	preowned cars
failing	underperforming
elderly	senior citizen
fake	imitation or faux

On the other hand, don't carry euphemisms to extremes. If you're too subtle, people won't know what you're talking about. "Derecruiting" workers to the "mobility pool" instead of telling them that they have six weeks to find another job isn't really very helpful. When using euphemisms, you walk a fine line between softening the blow and hiding the facts. It would be unethical to speak to your community about "relocating refuse" when you're really talking about your plans for disposing of toxic waste. Such an attempt to hide the facts would likely backfire, damaging your business image and reputation. In the end, people respond better to an honest message delivered with integrity than they do to a sugar-coated message filled with empty talk.

Using Bias-Free Language   Chapter 3 points out that you are often unaware of the influence of your own culture on your behavior, and this circumstance extends to the language you use. Any bias present in your culture is likely to show up in your language, often in subtle ways that you might not even recognize. However, chances are that your audience will. **Bias-free language** avoids words and phrases that unfairly and even unethically categorize or stigmatize people in ways related to gender, race, ethnicity, age, or disability. Contrary to what some might think, biased language is not simply about "labels." To a significant degree, language reflects the way we think and what we believe, and biased language may well perpetuate the underlying stereotypes and prejudices that it represents.[5] Moreover, since communication is all about perception, being fair and objective isn't enough; to establish a good relationship with your audience, you must also *appear* to be fair.[6] Good communicators make every effort to change biased language (see Table 5–1).Bias can come in a variety of forms:

Avoid biased language that might offend your audience.

- **Gender bias.** Avoid sexist language by using the same label for everyone (don't call a woman *chairperson* and then call a man *chairman*). Reword sentences to use *they* or to use no pronoun at all. Vary traditional patterns by sometimes putting women first (*women and men, she and he, her and his*). Note that the preferred title for women in business is *Ms.*, unless the individual asks to be addressed as *Miss* or *Mrs.* or has some other title, such as *Dr.*

- **Racial and ethnic bias.** Avoid language suggesting that members of a racial or an ethnic group have stereotypical characteristics. The best solution is to avoid identifying people by race or ethnic origin unless such a label is relevant to the matter at hand—and it rarely is.

- **Age bias.** As with gender, race, and ethnic background, mention the age of a person only when it is relevant. Moreover, be careful of the context in which you use words that refer to age. Such words carry a variety of positive and negative connotations—and not only when referring to people beyond a certain age. For example, *young* can imply youthfulness, inexperience, or even immaturity, depending on how it's used.

Table 5–1   OVERCOMING BIAS IN LANGUAGE

Examples	Unacceptable	Preferable
Gender Bias		
Using words containing "man"	Man-made	Humanity, human beings, human race, people
	Mankind	Artificial, synthetic, manufactured, constructed
	Manpower	Workers, workforce
	Businessman	Executive, manager, businessperson
	Salesman	Sales representative, salesperson, clerk
	Foreman	Supervisor
Using female-gender words	Actress, stewardess	Actor, flight attendant
Using special designations	Woman doctor, male nurse	Doctor, nurse
Using "he" to refer to "everyone"	The average worker . . . he	The average worker . . . he or she
Identifying roles with gender	The typical executive spends four hours of his day in meetings.	Most executives spend four hours a day in meetings.
	the consumer . . . she	consumers . . . they
	the nurse/teacher . . . she	nurses/teachers . . . they
Identifying women by marital status	Norm Lindstrom and Maria	Norm Lindstrom and Maria Drake
	Norm Lindstrom and Ms. Lindstrom	Mr. Lindstrom and Ms. Drake
Racial/Ethnic Bias		
Assigning stereotypes	My African-American assistant speaks more articulately than I do.	My assistant speaks more articulately than I do.
	Jim Wong is an unusually tall Asian.	Jim Wong is tall.
Identifying people by race or ethnicity	Mario M. Cuomo, Italian American politician and ex-governor of New York	Mario M. Cuomo, politician and ex-governor of New York
Age Bias		
Including age when irrelevant	Mary Kirazy, 58, has just joined our trust department.	Mary Kirazy has just joined our trust department.
Disability Bias		
Putting the disability before the person	Crippled workers face many barriers on the job.	Workers with physical disabilities face many barriers on the job.
	An epileptic, Tracy has no trouble doing her job.	Tracy's epilepsy has no effect on her job performance.

• **Disability bias.** No painless label exists for people with a physical, mental, sensory, or emotional impairment. Avoid mentioning a disability unless it is pertinent. However, if you must refer to someone's disability, avoid terms such as *handicapped, crippled,* or *retarded.* Put the person first and the disability second.[7] Present the whole person, not just the disability, by showing the limitation in an unobtrusive manner.

Building Strong Relationships with Your Audience

Focusing on your audience's needs is vital to effective communication, but you also have your own priorities as a communicator. Sometimes these needs are obvious and direct, such as when you're appealing for a budget increase for your department. At other times, the need may be more subtle. For instance, you might want to demonstrate your understanding of the marketplace or your company's concern for the natural environment. Two key efforts help you address your own needs while building positive relationships with your audience: establishing your credibility and projecting your company's image.

Establishing Your Credibility   Your audience's response to every message you send depends heavily on their perception of your **credibility**, a measure of your believability based on how reliable you are and how much trust you evoke in others. With colleagues and long-term customers, you've already established some degree of credibility based on past communication efforts, and these people automatically lean toward accepting each new message from you because you haven't let them down in the past. With audiences who don't know you, however, you need to establish credibility before they'll listen fully to your message. Whether you're working to build credibility with a new audience, to maintain credibility with an existing audience, or even to restore credibility after a mistake, consider emphasizing the following characteristics:

> People are more likely to react positively to your message when they have confidence in you.

- **Honesty.** Honesty is the cornerstone of credibility. No matter how famous, important, charming, or attractive you are, if you don't tell the truth most people will eventually lose faith in you. On the other hand, demonstrating honesty and integrity will earn you the respect of your colleagues and the trust of everyone you communicate with, even if they don't always agree with or welcome the messages you have to deliver.

> To enhance your credibility, emphasize such factors as honesty, objectivity, and awareness of audience needs.

- **Objectivity.** Audiences appreciate the ability to distance yourself from emotional situations and to look at all sides of an issue. They want to believe that you have their interests in mind, not just your own.

- **Awareness of audience needs**. Let your audience know that you understand what's important to them. If you've done a thorough audience analysis, you'll know what your audience cares about and their specific issues and concerns in a particular situation.

- **Credentials, knowledge, and expertise.** Every audience wants to be assured that the messages they receive come from people who know what they're talking about—that's why doctors hang their medical school diplomas on their office walls and why public speakers often arrange to be introduced with brief summaries of their experience and qualifications. When you need to establish credibility with a new audience, put yourself in their shoes and try to identify the credentials that would be most important to them. Is it your education, a professional certification, special training, success on the job? Express these qualifications clearly and objectively, without overshadowing the message. Sometimes it's as simple as using the right technical terms or mentioning your role in a successful project.

- **Endorsements.** If your audience doesn't know anything about you, you might be able to get assistance from someone they do know and trust. Once the audience learns that someone they trust in turn trusts you, they'll be more receptive to your messages.

- **Performance.** Who impresses you more, the person who always says, "If you ever need me, all you have to do is call," or the one who actually shows up when you need to move or when you need a ride to the airport? It's easy to say you can do something, but following through can be much harder. That's why demonstrating impressive communication skills is not enough; people need to know they can count on you to get the job done.

Document Makeover

IMPROVE THIS LETTER

To practice correcting drafts of actual documents, visit your online course or the access-code protected portion of the Companion Website. Click "Document Makeovers," then click Chapter 5. You will find a letter that contains problems and errors relating to what you've learned in this chapter about establishing a good relationship with your audience. Use the Final Draft decision tool to create an improved version of this letter. Check the document for "you" attitude, positive language, communication etiquette, bias-free language, and phrases that establish credibility.

• **Communication style.** If you support your points with evidence that can be confirmed through observation, research, experimentation, or measurement, audience members will recognize that you have the facts, and they'll respect you. On the other hand, trying to spice up your messages with terms such as *amazing, incredible, extraordinary, sensational,* and *revolutionary* strains your credibility unless you can support these terms with some sort of proof.

You also risk losing credibility if you seem to be currying favor with insincere compliments. Try to support compliments with specific points that show you are aware of a person's contributions and not just spouting off a generic thanks:

Instead of This	Use This
My deepest heartfelt thanks for the excellent job you did. It's hard these days to find workers like you. You are just fantastic! I can't stress enough how happy you have made us with your outstanding performance.	Thanks for the great job you did filling in for Sean at the convention on such short notice. Despite the difficult circumstances, you managed to attract several new orders with your demonstration of the new line of coffeemakers. Your dedication and sales ability are truly appreciated.

Even though arrogance turns listeners off, displaying too much modesty or too little confidence can hurt your credibility. If you lack faith in yourself, you're likely to communicate an uncertain attitude that undermines your credibility. The key to being believable is to believe in yourself. If you are convinced that your message is sound, you can state your case with authority so that your audience has no doubts. Avoid vague sentiments and confidence-draining words such as *if, hope,* and *trust:*

Instead of This	Use This
We hope this recommendation will be helpful.	We're glad to make this recommendation.
If you'd like to order, mail us the reply card.	To order, mail the reply card.
We trust that you'll extend your service contract.	By extending your service contract, you can continue to enjoy top-notch performance from your equipment.

Finally, keep in mind that credibility can take days, months, even years to establish—and it can be wiped out in an instant. An occasional mistake or letdown is usually forgiven, but major lapses in honesty or integrity can destroy your reputation. On the other hand, when you do establish credibility, communication becomes much easier because you no longer have to spend time and energy convincing people that you are a trustworthy source of information and ideas.

Projecting the Company's Image When you communicate with outsiders, on even the most routine matter, you serve as the spokesperson for your organization. The impression you make can enhance or damage the reputation of the entire company. Thus, your own views and personality must be subordinated, at least to some extent, to the interests and style of your company.

Many organizations have specific communication guidelines that show everything from the correct use of the company name to preferred abbreviations and other grammatical details. Specifying a desired style of communication is more difficult, however. Observe more experienced colleagues to see how they communicate, and never hesitate to ask for editorial help to make sure you're conveying the appropriate tone. For instance, with clients entrusting thousands or millions of dollars to it, an investment firm communicates in a style quite different from that of a clothing retailer. And a clothing retailer specializing in high-quality business attire communicates in a style different from that of a store catering to the latest trends in casual wear.

Controlling Your Style and Tone

Style is the way you use words to achieve a certain **tone**, or overall impression. You can vary your style—your sentence structure and vocabulary—to sound forceful or objective, personal or formal, colorful or dry. The right choice depends on the nature of your message and your relationship with the reader. Although style can be refined during the revision phase (see Chapter 6), you'll save time and a lot of rewriting if you use a style that allows you to achieve the desired tone from the start.

Using a Conversational Tone The tone of your business messages can range from informal to conversational to formal. If you're in a large organization and you're communicating with your superiors or with customers, your tone would tend to be more formal and respectful.[8] However, that formal tone might sound distant and cold if used with close colleagues.

Compare the three versions of the letter in Table 5–2. The first is too formal and stuffy for today's audiences, whereas the third is too casual for any audience other than close associates or friends. The second message demonstrates the conversational tone used in most business communication—using plain language that sounds businesslike without being stuffy or full of jargon. You can achieve a conversational tone in your messages by following these guidelines:

- **Avoid obsolete and pompous language.** Business language used to be much more formal than it is today, and some out-of-date phrases still remain. You can avoid using such language if you ask yourself, "Would I say this if I were talking with someone face to face?" Similarly, avoid using big words, trite expressions, and overly complicated sentences to impress others. Such pompous language sounds self-important (see Table 5–3).

- **Avoid preaching and bragging.** Few things are more irritating than people who think that they know everything and that others know nothing. If you do need to remind your audience of something obvious, try to work the information casually, perhaps in the middle of a paragraph, where it will sound like a secondary comment rather than a major revelation. Also, avoid bragging about your accomplishments or those of your organization (unless your audience is a part of your organization).

- **Be careful with intimacy.** Most business messages should avoid intimacy, such as sharing personal details or adopting a casual, unprofessional tone. However, when you do have a close relationship with your audience, such as among the members of a close-knit team, a more intimate tone is sometimes appropriate and even expected.

Table 5–2	THREE LEVELS OF TONE: FORMAL, CONVERSATIONAL, AND INFORMAL		
Formal Tone	**Conversational Tone**	**Informal Tone**	
Reserved for the most formal occasions	Preferred for most business communication	Reserved for communication with friends and close associates	

Formal Tone

Reserved for the most formal occasions

Dear Ms. Navarro:

Enclosed please find the information that was requested during our telephone communication of May 14. As was mentioned at that time, Midville Hospital has significantly more doctors of exceptional quality than any other health facility in the state.

As you were also informed, our organization has quite an impressive network of doctors and other health-care professionals with offices located throughout the state. In the event that you should need a specialist, our professionals will be able to make an appropriate recommendation.

In the event that you have questions or would like additional information, you may certainly contact me during regular business hours.

Most sincerely yours,

Samuel G. Berenz

Conversational Tone

Preferred for most business communication

Dear Ms. Navarro:

Here's the information you requested during our phone conversation on Friday. As I mentioned, Midville Hospital has the best doctors and more of them than any other hospital in the state.

In addition, we have a vast network of doctors and other health professionals with offices throughout the state. If you need a specialist, they can refer you to the right one.

If you would like more information, please call any time between 9:00 and 5:00, Monday through Friday.

Sincerely,

Samuel G. Berenz

Informal Tone

Reserved for communication with friends and close associates

Hi Gabriella:

Hope all is well. Just sending along the information you asked for. As I said on Friday, Midville Hospital has more and better doctors than any other hospital in the state.

We also have a large group of doctors and other health professionals with offices close to you at work or at home. Need a specialist? They'll refer you to the right one.

Just give me a ring if you want to know more. Any time from 9:00 to 5:00 should be fine.

Take care,

Sam

- **Be careful with humor.** Humor can be an effective tool to inject interest into dry subjects or take the sting out of negative news. However, use it with great care: the humor must be connected to the point you're trying to make. Business messages are not a forum for sharing jokes. Never use humor in formal messages or when you're communicating across cultural boundaries. Humor can easily backfire and divert attention from your message. If you don't know your audience well or you're not skilled at using humor in a business setting, don't use it at all. When in doubt, leave it out.

Using Plain English   What do you think this sentence is trying to say?

> We continually exist to synergistically supply value-added deliverables such that we may continue to proactively maintain enterprise-wide data to stay competitive in tomorrow's world.[9]

If you don't have any idea what it means, you're not alone. However, this is a real sentence from a real company, written in an attempt to explain what the company does and why. This sort of incomprehensible, buzzword-filled writing is driving a widespread call to use *plain English*.

Plain English is a way of presenting information in a simple, unadorned style so that your audience can easily grasp your meaning, without struggling through specialized, technical, or convoluted language. Because it's close to the way people normally

STAYING UP TO DATE AND DOWN TO EARTH		Table 5–3

Obsolete	*Up to Date*
in due course	today, tomorrow (or a specific time)
permit me to say that	(permission is not necessary)
we are in receipt of	we have received
pursuant to	(omit)
in closing, I'd like to say	(omit)
the undersigned	I; me
kindly advise	please let us know
we wish to inform you	(just say it)
attached please find	enclosed is
it has come to my attention	I have just learned; Ms. Garza has just told me
our Mr. Lydell	Mr. Lydell, our credit manager
please be advised that	(omit)

Pompous	*Down to Earth*
Upon procurement of additional supplies, I will initiate fulfillment of your order.	I will fill your order when I receive more supplies.
Perusal of the records indicates a substantial deficit for the preceding annum due to the continued utilization of obsolete equipment.	The records show a company loss last year due to the use of old equipment.

speak, plain English is easily understood by anyone with an eighth- or ninth-grade education. The Plain English Campaign (a nonprofit group in England campaigning for clear language) defines plain English as language "that the intended audience can read, understand and act upon the first time they read it."[10] You can see how this definition supports using the "you" attitude and shows respect for your audience.

> Audiences can understand and act on plain English without reading it over and over.

On the Creative Commons website, for instance, the licenses are available in three versions, labeled "human-readable," "lawyer-readable," and "machine-readable." The first explains the licensing terms in nontechnical language that anyone can understand, the second spells out the contractual details in specific legal terms, and the third is a snippet of software that people can copy to their websites in order to display the Creative Commons "Some Rights Restricted" logo.

Even though few people argue with the value of plain English, the fact is that murky, pompous, and unnecessarily complex writing is still more common than it should be. One reason is that writers are unsure about their own writing skills and about the impact their messages will have. They mistakenly believe that packaging simple ideas in complex writing makes their messages seem more impressive. Another reason is inadequate planning, which results in messages that meander in search of a conclusion. A third reason is that some writers intentionally try to create distance between themselves and their audiences. Whatever the cause, the result of unnecessarily complex writing is always the same: ineffective communication that wastes time, wastes money, and annoys everyone who comes in contact with it.

As frustration builds over confusing, grandiose writing, groups such as the Plain English Campaign are raising awareness of the costs of poor communication. A number of government agencies and businesses are also working to improve matters. To help financial managers write more clearly, the U.S. Securities and Exchange Commission (SEC; the agency in charge of monitoring financial markets) produced *A Plain English Handbook: How to Create Clear SEC Disclosure Documents*. Deloitte Consulting (a large management consulting firm) went so far as to create Bullfighter software, a tool that runs in Microsoft Word and PowerPoint to catch jargon, buzzwords, and other instances of poor writing.[11]

Even though plain English is intended for audiences who speak English as their primary language, plain English can also help you simplify the messages you prepare for audiences who speak English only as a second or even third language. For example, by choosing words that have only one interpretation, you will communicate more clearly with your intercultural audience (see Achieving Intercultural Communication: Communicating with a Global Audience on the Web).[12]

For all its advantages, plain English does have some limitations. It sometimes lacks the precision or subtlety necessary for scientific research, engineering documents, intense feeling, and personal insight. Moreover, it doesn't embrace all cultures and dialects equally.

Selecting Active or Passive Voice   Your choice of active or passive voice also affects the tone of your message. You are using **active voice** when the subject performs the action, and the object receives the action: "John rented the office." You're using **passive voice** when the subject receives the action: "The office was rented by John." As you can see, the passive voice combines the helping verb *to be* with a form of the

ACHIEVING INTERCULTURAL COMMUNICATION

Communicating with a Global Audience on the Web

Reaching an international audience on the web involves more than simply offering translations of the English language. Successful global sites address the needs of international customers in five ways:

1. **Consider the reader's perspective.** Many communication elements that you might take for granted may be interpreted differently by audiences in different countries. Should you use the metric system, different notations for times or dates, or even different names for countries? For example, German citizens don't refer to their country as *Germany*; it's *Deutschland* to them. Review the entire online experience and look for ways to improve communication, including such helpful tools as interactive currency converters and translation dictionaries.

2. **Take cultural differences into account.** For instance, since humor is rooted in cultural norms, U.S. humor may not be so funny to Asian or European readers. Avoid idioms and references that aren't universally recognized, such as "putting all your eggs in one basket" or "jumping out of the frying pan into the fire."

3. **Keep the message clear.** Use simple words and sentences and write in the active voice. Define abbreviations, acronyms, and words an international audience might not be familiar with.

4. **Complement language with visuals.** Use drawings, photos, and other visuals to help communicate when words can't.

5. **Consult local experts.** Seek the advice of local experts about phrases and references that might be expected. Even terms as simple as *homepage* differ from country to country. Spanish readers refer to the "first page," or *pagina inicial*, whereas the French term is "welcome page," or *page d'accuei*.

CAREER APPLICATIONS

1. Visit Sony's Global Headquarters website at www. sony.net and examine Sony's music-oriented websites for Argentina, France, and Germany. How does Sony "localize" each country's site?

2. Compare Sony Music's international sites to IBM's global webpages at www.ibm.com. How does Sony's approach differ from IBM's? Do both corporations successfully address the needs of a global audience? Write a two-paragraph summary that compares the international sites of both companies.

CHOOSING ACTIVE OR PASSIVE VOICE — Table 5–4

In general, avoid passive voice in order to make your writing lively and direct

Dull and Indirect in Passive Voice	Lively and Direct in Active Voice
The new procedure was developed by the operations team.	The operations team developed the new procedure.
Legal problems are created by this contract.	This contract creates legal problems.
Reception preparations have been undertaken by our PR people for the new CEO's arrival.	Our PR people have begun planning a reception for the new CEO.

However, passive voice is helpful when you need to be diplomatic or want to focus attention on problems or solutions rather than on people

Accusatory or Self-congratulatory in Active Voice	More Diplomatic in Passive Voice
You lost the shipment.	The shipment was lost.
I recruited seven engineers last month.	Seven engineers were recruited last month.
We are investigating the high rate of failures on the final assembly line.	The high rate of failures on the final assembly line is being investigated.

verb that is usually similar to the past tense. When you use active sentences, your messages generally sound less formal and make it easier for readers to figure out who performed the action (see Table 5–4). In contrast, using passive voice de-emphasizes the subject and implies that the action was done by something or someone.

Using the active voice help makes your writing more direct, livelier, and easier to read. In contrast, the passive voice is not wrong grammatically, but it is often cumbersome, can be unnecessarily vague, and can make sentences longer. In most cases, the active voice is your best choice.[13] Nevertheless, using the passive voice can help you demonstrate the "you" attitude in some situations:

Active sentences are usually stronger than passive ones.

- When you want to be diplomatic about pointing out a problem or error of some kind (the passive version seems less like an accusation)
- When you want to point out what's being done without taking or attributing either the credit or the blame (the passive version leaves the actor completely out of the sentence)

Use passive sentences to soften bad news, to put yourself in the background, or to create an impersonal tone.

- When you want to avoid personal pronouns in order to create an objective tone (the passive version may be used in a formal report, for example)

The second half of Table 5–4 illustrates several situations in which the passive voice helps you focus your message on your audience.

COMPOSING YOUR MESSAGE

With these insights into how you can adapt to your audience, you're ready to begin composing your message. Composition is easiest if you've already figured out what to say and in what order (refer to the outlining advice in Chapter 4), although you may need to pause now and then to find the right word. You may also discover as you go along that you can improve on your outline. Feel free to rearrange, delete, and add ideas, as long as you don't lose sight of your purpose.

As you compose your first draft, try to let your creativity flow. Don't try to draft and edit at the same time or worry about getting everything perfect. Make up words if you can't think of the right word, draw pictures, talk out loud—do whatever it takes to get the ideas out of your head and onto your computer screen or a piece of paper. You'll have time to revise and refine the material later.

If you get stuck and feel unable to write, try to overcome writer's block by jogging your brain in creative ways: skip to another part of the document (the opening paragraph is often the hardest to write, but you don't need to write it first), work on non-text elements such as graphics or your cover page, revisit your purpose and confirm your intent in writing the message, or give yourself a mental break by switching to a different project. Sometimes all you need to do is start writing without worrying about what you're writing or how it sounds. Words will start flowing, your mind will engage, and the writing will come easier.

The most successful messages have three important elements: strong words, effective sentences, and coherent paragraphs.

Choosing Strong Words

Correctness is the first consideration when choosing words.

Effective messages depend on carefully chosen words, whether you select them during your first draft or edit them in later.[14] First, pay close attention to correctness. The "rules" of grammar and usage are constantly changing to reflect changes in the way people speak. Even editors and grammarians occasionally have questions about correct usage, and they sometimes disagree about the answers. For example, the word *data* is the plural form of *datum,* yet some experts now prefer to treat *data* as a singular noun when it's used in nonscientific material to refer to a body of information. You be the judge: Which of the following sentences sounds better?

Our market share data is consistent from region to region.

Our market share data are consistent from region to region.

Correct grammar enhances your image.

Although debating the finer points of usage may seem like nitpicking, using words correctly is important. If you make grammatical or usage errors, you lose credibility with your audience—even if your message is otherwise correct. Poor grammar implies that you're uninformed, and audiences put less faith in an uninformed source. Worse still, poor grammar can imply that you don't respect your audience enough to get things right. Even if an audience is broad-minded enough to withhold such a judgment, grammatical errors are distracting.

If you have doubts about what is correct, look up the answer, and use the proper form of expression. Check the "Handbook of Grammar, Mechanics, and Usage" at the end of this book, or consult the many special reference books and resources available in libraries, in bookstores, and on the Internet. Most authorities agree on the basic conventions.

Effectiveness is the second consideration when choosing words.

Just as important as selecting the correct word is selecting the most suitable word for the job at hand. Naturally, using the right words is important in life-and-death situations. But even when you're dealing with less perilous circumstances, the right words can make all the difference in the success of your communication efforts. Word effectiveness is generally more difficult to achieve than correctness, particularly in written communication. Even professional writers with decades of experience continue to work at their craft to use functional and content words correctly and to find the words that communicate.

Functional words (conjunctions, prepositions, articles, and pronouns) express the relationships among content words (nouns, verbs, adjectives, and adverbs).

Using Functional and Content Words Correctly   Words can be divided into two main categories. **Functional words** express relationships and have only one unchanging meaning in any given context. They include conjunctions, prepositions, articles, and pronouns. Your main concern with functional words is to use them correctly. **Content words** are multidimensional and therefore subject to various interpretations. They include nouns, verbs, adjectives, and adverbs. These words carry the meaning of a sentence. In your sentences, content words are the building blocks, and functional words are the mortar that holds them together. In the following sentence, all the content words are underlined:

Some objective observers of the cookie market give Nabisco the edge in quality, but praise Frito-Lay for superior distribution.

Both functional words and content words are necessary, but your effectiveness as a communicator depends largely on your ability to choose the right content words for your message.

Denotation and Connotation   Content words have both a denotative and a connotative meaning. The **denotative meaning** is the literal, or dictionary, meaning. The **connotative meaning** includes all the associations and feelings evoked by the word.

> Content words have both a denotative (explicit, specific) meaning and a connotative (implicit, associative) meaning.

The denotative meaning of *desk* is "a table used for writing." Some desks may have drawers or compartments, and others may have a flat top or a sloping top, but the literal meaning is generally well understood. The connotative meaning of *desk* may include thoughts associated with work or study, but the word *desk* has fairly neutral connotations—neither strong nor emotional. However, some words have much stronger connotations than others. For example, the connotations of the word *fail* are negative and can carry strong emotional meaning. So if you say that a student *failed* to pass a test, the connotative meaning suggests that the person is inferior, incompetent, below some standard of performance.

In business communication, be careful with words that have multiple interpretations and are high in connotative meaning. By saying that a student achieved a score of 65 percent, you communicate the facts and avoid a heavy load of negative connotations. If you use words that have relatively few possible interpretations, you are less likely to be misunderstood. In addition, because you are trying to communicate in an objective, rational manner, you want to avoid emotion-laden comments.

Abstraction and Concreteness   Words vary dramatically in the degree of abstraction or concreteness they convey. An **abstract word** expresses a concept, quality, or characteristic. Abstractions are usually broad, encompassing a category of ideas, and they are often intellectual, academic, or philosophical. *Love, honor, progress, tradition,* and *beauty* are abstractions. In contrast, a **concrete word** stands for something you can touch or see. Concrete terms are anchored in the tangible, material world. *Chair, table, horse, rose, kick, kiss, red, green,* and *two* are concrete words; they are direct, clear, and exact.

> The more abstract a word is, the more it is removed from the tangible, objective world of things that can be perceived with the senses.

You might assume that concrete words are better than abstract words because they are more precise, but this isn't always the case. For example, try to rewrite this sentence without using the underlined abstract words:

> In business communication, use concrete, specific terms whenever possible; use abstractions only when necessary.

We hold these truths to be self-evident, that all men are created equal, that they are endowed by their Creator with certain unalienable Rights, that among these are Life, Liberty, and the Pursuit of Happiness.

As you can see, the Declaration of Independence needs abstractions, and so do most business messages. Abstractions let you rise above the common and tangible. They allow you to refer to concepts such as *morale, productivity, profits, quality, motivation,* and *guarantees.*

Even though they're indispensable, abstractions can be troublesome. They tend to be fuzzy and subject to many interpretations. Moreover, it isn't always easy to get excited about ideas, especially if they're unrelated to concrete experience. The best way to minimize such problems is to blend abstract terms with concrete ones, the general with the specific. State the concept, then pin it down with details expressed in more concrete terms. Save the abstractions for ideas that cannot be expressed any other way.

Because words such as *small, numerous, sizable, near, soon, good,* and *fine* are imprecise, try to replace them with terms that are more accurate. Instead of referring to a *sizable loss,* talk about a *loss of $32 million.*

Finding Words That Communicate   By practicing your writing, learning from experienced writers and editors, and reading extensively, you'll find it easier to choose words that communicate exactly what you want to say. When you compose your business messages, think carefully to find the most powerful words for each situation (see Table 5–5).

Try to use words that are powerful and familiar.

- **Choose powerful words.** Choose words that express your thoughts most clearly, specifically, and dynamically. Nouns and verbs are the most concrete and should do most of the communication work in your messages. Verbs are especially powerful because they tell what's happening in the sentence, so make them dynamic and specific. For instance, you might replace *rise* or *fall* with *soar* or *plummet* if appropriate. Adjectives and adverbs have obvious roles, but if you find yourself using them often, you're probably trying to compensate for weak nouns and verbs.

- **Choose familiar words.** You'll communicate best with words that are familiar to both you and your readers. Moreover, trying to use an unfamiliar word for the first time in an important document can lead to embarrassing mistakes.

Table 5–5	FINDING THE WORDS THAT COMMUNICATE WITH POWER
Avoid Weak Phrases	***Use Strong Terms***
Wealthy businessperson	Tycoon
Business prosperity	Economic boom
Hard times	Slump
Avoid Unfamiliar Words	***Use Familiar Words***
Ascertain	Find out, learn
Consummate	Close, bring about
Peruse	Read, study
Circumvent	Avoid
Increment	Growth, increase
Unequivocal	Certain
Avoid Clichés and Buzzwords	***Use Plain Language***
An uphill battle	A challenge
Writing on the wall	Prediction
Call the shots	Be in charge
Take by storm	Attack
Cost an arm and a leg	Expensive
A new ballgame	Fresh start
Fall through the cracks	Be overlooked
Think outside the box	Be creative

- **Avoid clichés.** Although familiar words are generally the best choice, beware of terms and phrases so common that they have lost some of their power to communicate. Because clichés are used so often, readers tend to slide right by them to whatever is coming next. Most people use these phrases not because they think it makes their message more vivid and inviting but because they don't know how to express themselves otherwise and don't invest the energy required for original writing.[15]

- **Use jargon carefully.** Handle technical or professional terms with care. Although jargon has a bad reputation in general, it's usually an efficient way to communicate within specific groups that understand their own special terms. After all, that's how jargon develops in the first place, as people with similar interests develop ways to communicate complex ideas quickly. For instance, when a recording engineer wants to communicate that a particular piece of music is devoid of reverberation and other sound effects, it's a lot easier to simply describe the track as "dry." Of course, to people who aren't familiar with such insider terms, jargon is meaningless and intimidating—one more reason it's so important to understand your audience before you start writing.

> Avoid clichés and trendy buzzwords in your writing and use jargon only when your audience is completely familiar with it.

Remember, you improve your business writing skills through imitation and practice. As you read business journals, newspapers, and even novels, make a note of the words you think are effective and keep them in a file. Look through your file before drafting your next letter or report, and try using some of these words in your document. You may be surprised how they can strengthen your writing.

Creating Effective Sentences

Making every sentence count is a key step in creating effective messages. Start by selecting the optimum type of sentence, then arrange words to emphasize the most important point in each sentence.

Choosing from the Four Types of Sentences   Sentences come in four basic varieties: simple, compound, complex, and compound-complex. A **simple sentence** has one main clause (a single subject and a single predicate), although it may be expanded by nouns and pronouns serving as objects of the action and by modifying phrases. Here's a typical example (with the subject underlined once and the predicate verb underlined twice):

> A simple sentence has one main clause.

<u>Profits</u> <u>increased</u> in the past year.

A **compound sentence** has two main clauses that express two or more independent but related thoughts of equal importance, usually joined by *and, but,* or *or.* In effect, a compound sentence is a merger of two or more simple sentences (independent clauses) that are related. For example:

> A compound sentence has two main clauses.

Wage <u>rates</u> <u>have declined</u> by 5 percent, and employee <u>turnover</u> <u>has been</u> high.

The independent clauses in a compound sentence are always separated by a comma or by a semicolon (in which case the conjunction—*and, but, or*—is dropped).

A **complex sentence** expresses one main thought (the independent clause) and one or more subordinate thoughts (dependent clauses) related to it, often separated by a comma. The subordinate thought, which comes first in the following sentence, could not stand alone:

> A complex sentence has one main clause and one subordinate clause.

Although you may question Gerald's conclusions, <u>you</u> <u>must admit</u> that his research is thorough.

A compound-complex sentence has two main clauses and at least one dependent clause.

A **compound-complex sentence** has two main clauses, at least one of which contains a subordinate clause:

> <u>Profits</u> <u>have increased</u> in the past year, and although you may question Gerald's conclusions, <u>you</u> <u>must admit</u> that his research is thorough.

When constructing a sentence, choose the form that matches the relationship of the ideas you want to express. If you have two ideas of equal importance, express them as two simple sentences or as one compound sentence. However, if one of the ideas is less important than the other, place it in a dependent clause to form a complex sentence. For example, although the following compound sentence uses a conjunction to join two ideas, they aren't truly equal:

> The chemical products division is the strongest in the company, and its management techniques should be adopted by the other divisions.

By making the first thought subordinate to the second, you establish a cause-and-effect relationship. So the following complex sentence is much more effective:

> Because the chemical products division is the strongest in the company, its management techniques should be adopted by the other divisions.

Writing is more effective if it balances all four sentence types.

To make your writing as effective as possible, strive for variety and balance using all four sentence types. If you use too many simple sentences, you won't be able to properly express the relationships among your ideas, and your writing will sound choppy and abrupt. If you use too many long, compound sentences, your writing will sound monotonous. On the other hand, an uninterrupted series of complex or compound-complex sentences is hard to follow.

Using Sentence Style to Emphasize Key Thoughts The English language offers tremendous flexibility in saying what you want to say and in developing your own style. For business communication, however, clarity and efficiency take precedence over literary style, so strive for straightforward simplicity.

In every message, some ideas are more important than others. You can emphasize these key ideas through your sentence style. One obvious technique is to give important points the most space. When you want to call attention to a thought, use extra words to describe it. Consider this sentence:

Emphasize parts of a sentence by
- Devoting more words to them
- Putting them at the beginning or at the end of the sentence
- Making them the subject of the sentence

> The chairperson of the board called for a vote of the shareholders.

To emphasize the importance of the chairperson, you might describe her more fully:

> Having considerable experience in corporate takeover battles, the chairperson of the board called for a vote of the shareholders.

You can increase the emphasis even more by adding a separate, short sentence to augment the first:

> The chairperson of the board called for a vote of the shareholders. She has considerable experience in corporate takeover battles.

You can also call attention to a thought by making it the subject of the sentence. In the following example, the emphasis is on the person:

> *I* can write letters much more quickly using a computer.

However, by changing the subject, the computer takes center stage:

> The *computer* enables me to write letters much more quickly.

Another way to emphasize an idea is to place it either at the beginning or at the end of a sentence:

Less Emphatic: We are cutting the *price* to stimulate demand.

More Emphatic: To stimulate demand, we are cutting the *price*.

In complex sentences, the placement of the dependent clause hinges on the relationship between the ideas expressed. If you want to emphasize the idea, put the dependent clause at the end of the sentence (the most emphatic position) or at the beginning (the second most emphatic position). If you want to downplay the idea, bury the dependent clause within the sentence.

Dependent clauses can determine emphasis.

Most Emphatic: The electronic parts are manufactured in Mexico, *which has lower wage rates than the United States.*

Emphatic: *Because wage rates are lower there,* the electronic parts are manufactured in Mexico.

Least Emphatic: Mexico, *which has lower wage rates,* was selected as the production point for the electronic parts.

Techniques such as these give you a great deal of control over the way your audience interprets what you have to say.

Crafting Coherent Paragraphs

Paragraphs organize sentences related to the same general topic. Readers expect each paragraph to focus on a single unit of thought and to be a logical link in an organized sequence of the thoughts that make up a complete message. As with sentences, you can control the elements of each paragraph. Doing so helps your readers grasp the main idea of your document and understand how the specific pieces of support material back up that idea.

Even when reading online, readers expect each paragraph to address one main idea and all the paragraphs in a document to link together logically.

Elements of the Paragraph   Paragraphs vary widely in length and form. You can communicate effectively in one short paragraph or in pages of lengthy paragraphs, depending on your purpose, your audience, and your message. The typical paragraph contains three basic elements: a topic sentence, support sentences that develop the topic, and transitional words and phrases.

Topic Sentence   Every properly constructed paragraph is *unified*; it deals with a single topic. The sentence that introduces that topic is called the **topic sentence**. In informal and creative writing, the topic sentence may be implied rather than stated. In business writing, the topic sentence is generally explicit and is often the first sentence in the paragraph. The topic sentence gives readers a summary of the general idea that will be covered in the rest of the paragraph. The following examples show how a topic sentence can introduce the subject and suggest the way that subject will be developed:

Most paragraphs consist of
- A topic sentence that reveals the subject of the paragraph
- Related sentences that support and expand the topic
- Transitional elements that help readers move between sentences and paragraphs

The medical products division has been troubled for many years by public relations problems. [In the rest of the paragraph, readers will learn the details of the problems.]

> Relocating the plant in New York has two main disadvantages. [The disadvantages will be explained in subsequent sentences.]
>
> To get a refund, you must supply us with some additional information. [The details of the necessary information will be described in the rest of the paragraph.]

Support Sentences In most paragraphs, the topic sentence needs to be explained, justified, or extended with one or more support sentences. These related sentences must all have a bearing on the general subject and must provide enough specific details to make the topic clear:

> The medical products division has been troubled for many years by public relations problems. Since 2002 the local newspaper has published 15 articles that portray the division in a negative light. We have been accused of everything from mistreating laboratory animals to polluting the local groundwater. Our facility has been described as a health hazard. Our scientists are referred to as "Frankensteins," and our profits are considered "obscene."

The support sentences are all more specific than the topic sentence. Each one provides another piece of evidence to demonstrate the general truth of the main thought. Also, each sentence is clearly related to the general idea being developed, which gives the paragraph its unity. A paragraph is well developed when (1) it contains enough information to make the topic sentence convincing and interesting and (2) it contains no extraneous, unrelated sentences.

Transitional Elements In addition to being unified and well supported, effective paragraphs are *coherent;* that is, they are arranged in a logical order so that the audience can understand the train of thought. You achieve coherence by using transitions that show the relationship between paragraphs and among sentences within paragraphs. Transitions are words or phrases that tie ideas together by showing how one thought is related to another. They not only help readers understand the connections you're trying to make but also smooth your writing. Ideally, you begin planning these transitions while you're outlining, as you decide how the various ideas and blocks of information will be arranged and connected.[16]

You can establish transitions in a variety of ways:

Transitional elements include
- Connecting words (conjunctions)
- Repeated words or phrases
- Pronouns
- Words that are frequently paired

- **Use connecting words:** *and, but, or, nevertheless, however, in addition,* and so on.
- **Echo a word or phrase from a previous paragraph or sentence:** "A system should be established for monitoring inventory levels. *This system* will provide . . ."
- **Use a pronoun that refers to a noun used previously:** "Ms. Arthur is the leading candidate for the president's position. *She* has excellent qualifications."
- **Use words that are frequently paired:** "The machine has a *minimum* output of . . . Its *maximum* output is . . ."

Some transitional elements serve as mood changers; that is, they alert the reader to a change in mood from the previous paragraph. Some announce a total contrast with what's gone on before, some announce a causal relationship, and some signal a change in time. Transitional elements prepare your reader for what is coming. Here is a list of transitions frequently used to move readers smoothly between sentences and paragraphs:

Additional detail:	moreover, furthermore, in addition, besides, first, second, third, finally
Causal relationship:	therefore, because, accordingly, thus, consequently, hence, as a result, so
Comparison:	similarly, here again, likewise, in comparison, still

Contrast:	yet, conversely, whereas, nevertheless, on the other hand, however, but, nonetheless
Condition:	although, if
Illustration:	for example, in particular, in this case, for instance
Time sequence:	formerly, after, when, meanwhile, sometimes
Intensification:	indeed, in fact, in any event
Summary:	in brief, in short, to sum up
Repetition:	that is, in other words, as I mentioned earlier

Although transitional words and phrases are useful, they're not sufficient in themselves to overcome poor organization. Put your ideas into a strong framework first, and then use transitions to link them together even more strongly.

Consider using a transition whenever it might help the reader understand your ideas and follow you from point to point. You can use transitions inside paragraphs to tie related points together and between paragraphs to ease the shift from one distinct thought to another. In longer reports, transitions that link major sections or chapters are often complete paragraphs that serve as mini-introductions to the next section or as summaries of the ideas presented in the section just ending. Here's an example:

> Given the nature of this product, the alternatives are limited. As the previous section indicates, we can stop making it altogether, improve it, or continue with the current model. Each of these alternatives has advantages and disadvantages, which are discussed in the following section.

This paragraph makes it clear to the reader that the analysis of the problem (offered in the previous section) is now over, and that the document is making a transition to an analysis of alternatives (to be offered in the next section).

Five Ways to Develop a Paragraph   The coherence in your paragraph strongly depends on how you develop it, and the best way to do that is to use a structure that is familiar to your readers, appropriate to the idea you're trying to portray, and suited to your purpose. Five of the most common development techniques are illustration, comparison or contrast, cause and effect, classification, and problem and solution (see Table 5–6).

Five ways to develop paragraphs:
- Illustration
- Comparison or contrast
- Cause and effect
- Classification
- Problem and solution

In practice, you'll occasionally combine two or more methods of development in a single paragraph. To add interest, you might begin by using illustration, shift to comparison or contrast, and then shift to problem and solution. However, when combining approaches, do so carefully so that you don't lose readers partway through the paragraph. In addition, before settling for the first approach that comes to mind, consider the alternatives. Think through various methods before committing yourself. By avoiding the easy habit of repeating the same old paragraph pattern time after time, you can keep your writing fresh and interesting.

USING TECHNOLOGY TO COMPOSE AND SHAPE YOUR MESSAGES

As with every phase of business communication, careful use of technology can help you compose and shape better messages in less time. You're likely to use a variety of electronic tools to compose messages: software for creating regular web content that constitutes the bulk of most websites, *web logs* or *blogs* for frequently updated web postings, instant messaging (IM) for brief exchanges and support for online meetings, and e-mail and word processing for lengthier messages. You read about effective IM in Chapter 2; Chapter 6 highlights some of the ways blogs are being used to distribute business messages, and

Table 5–6   FIVE TECHNIQUES FOR DEVELOPING PARAGRAPHS

Technique	Description	Example
Illustration	Giving examples that demonstrate the general idea	Some of our most popular products are available through local distributors. For example, Everett & Lemmings carries our frozen soups and entrees. The J. B. Green Company carries our complete line of seasonings, as well as the frozen soups. Wilmont Foods, also a major distributor, now carries our new line of frozen desserts.
Comparison or Contrast	Using similarities or differences to develop the topic	When the company was small, the recruiting function could be handled informally. The need for new employees was limited, and each manager could comfortably screen and hire her or his own staff. However, our successful bid on the Owens contract means that we will be doubling our labor force over the next six months. To hire that many people without disrupting our ongoing activities, we will create a separate recruiting group within the human resources department.
Cause and Effect	Focusing on the reasons for something	The heavy-duty fabric of your Wanderer tent probably broke down for one of two reasons: (1) a sharp object punctured the fabric, and without reinforcement, the hole was enlarged by the stress of pitching the tent daily for a week or (2) the fibers gradually rotted because the tent was folded and stored while still wet.
Classification	Showing how a general idea is broken into specific categories	Successful candidates for our supervisor trainee program generally come from one of several groups. The largest group, by far, consists of recent graduates of accredited business management programs. The next largest group comes from within our own company, as we try to promote promising staff workers to positions of greater responsibility. Finally, we do occasionally accept candidates with outstanding supervisory experience in related industries.
Problem and Solution	Presenting a problem and then discussing the solution	Selling handmade toys online is a challenge because consumers are accustomed to buying heavily advertised toys from major chain stores or well-known websites such as Amazon.com. However, if we develop an appealing website, we can compete on the basis of product novelty and quality. In addition, we can provide unusual crafts at a competitive price: a rocking horse of birch, with a hand-knit tail and mane; a music box with the child's name painted on the top; a real teepee, made by Native American artisans.

you can read about effective blog and web content development at www.prenhall.com/thill. The following sections offer advice on crafting effective e-mail messages and using your word processor's formatting features to full advantage.

Composing Effective E-Mail Messages

E-mail messages need as much care and attention as other business messages.

Even though e-mail messages may seem transitory, attention to detail is just as important for these documents as for any other type of business writing. Too many people, particularly younger professionals accustomed to using e-mail, IM, and text messaging for personal communication, assume that business e-mail is automatically less formal. Some seasoned business professionals even advocate a general disregard of punctuation, grammar, spelling, and other conventions in e-mail writing because paying attention to details takes too much time.

However, this approach fails to consider a number of important factors, all of which can hurt your career. First, sloppy writing may require less time for writers, but it usually demands *more* time from readers who are forced to dig the meaning out of misspelled words and confusing sentences. Second, people who care about effective communication often judge the quality of your work by the quality of your writing. Since this group includes the vast majority of senior executives (as in, the people who decide whether or not you get promoted) think carefully about the reputation you're creating with your e-mail. Third, at the click of a mouse, e-mail messages can travel to places you never imagined, including the CEO's computer screen, a newspaper, a lawyer's office, or a thousand websites and blogs on the Internet. A careless or angry colleague might forward your message to a senior manager, or an executive recruiter who has pegged you as a budding superstar might run across your shabby e-mail and decide you're not so hot after all. You don't need to compose perfect works of art to tell people that lunch will be served in the conference room, but as a general rule, the time you might save with sloppy e-mail writing won't make up for the damage it can do to your career.[17]

In addition to the principles and techniques already discussed in this chapter, remember to consider a few additional points when writing e-mail messages. First and foremost, as an employee, you have a responsibility to follow your company's e-mail guidelines. Organizations expect their employees to use e-mail in a responsible, businesslike manner. Thus, many companies actually train their employees in e-mail use. At the very least, most organizations develop e-mail guidelines to help you reduce unnecessary communication and confusion. Typical e-mail guidelines include the following:

> Follow your company's e-mail guidelines, but use common sense, too.

- **Restrict e-mail usage to appropriate content.** In most organizations, e-mail is used for sharing information such as goals, schedules, research, company news, and the like. An electronic message is not the medium for delivering tragic news or for disciplining people. Such messages should be reserved for face-to-face interactions.

- **Avoid sending personal messages at work.** In countless incidents, employees have been dismissed for sending personal e-mail, including messages that criticize their company, discuss starting a new business, or mention a new position with another company. Moreover, many companies now archive all e-mail; therefore, that ill-considered message you zap out in a careless moment might live for a long time—whether personal or business related.

- **Respect the chain of command.** In many companies, any employee can e-mail anyone else, including the president and CEO. However, take care that you don't abuse this freedom. For instance, when corresponding with superiors, don't send an e-mail complaint straight to the top just because it's easy to do so. Your e-mail will usually be more effective if you follow the organizational hierarchy and give each person a chance to address the situation in turn.

- **Pay attention to e-mail hygiene.** *E-mail hygiene* refers to all the efforts that companies are making to keep e-mail clean and safe—from spam blocking and virus protection to content filtering.[18] Make sure you understand what your employer expects from you, and follow those guidelines. For example, to reduce the chances that spammers can find company e-mail addresses, some companies no longer put employee e-mail addresses on their websites.

Of course, company policies can't cover every aspect of e-mail or every situation. The extraordinary ease of e-mail is also its greatest shortcoming: It's far too easy to send too many needless messages. How many people would send jokes and photos around the company if they had to walk to the photocopier every time? Think twice before you create new messages, and think three times before you forward any. The things that annoy your recipients are the same things you find annoying—unfunny jokes, vacation photos, messages that have been forwarded so many times they have multiple screens full of useless header information, messages you've already read five times, angry complaints full of inappropriate language—so don't contribute to the problem. Let common sense be your guide.

The subject line in an e-mail might seem like a minor detail, but it's actually one of the most important parts of every e-mail message because it helps recipients decide which messages to read and when. Missing or poorly written subject lines often result in messages being deleted without even being opened. To capture your

Table 5–7	TIPS FOR EFFECTIVE E-MAIL MESSAGES

Tip	**Why It's Important**
When you request information or action, make it clear what you're asking for, why it's important, and how soon you need it; don't make your reader write back for details.	People will be tempted to ignore your messages if they're not clear about what you want or how soon you want it.
When responding to a request, either paraphrase the request or include enough of the original message to remind the reader what you're replying to.	Some businesspeople get hundreds of e-mail messages a day and may need reminding what your specific response is about.
If possible, avoid sending long, complex messages via e-mail.	Long messages are easier to read as printed reports or web content.
Adjust the level of formality to the message and the audience.	Overly formal messages to colleagues are perceived as stuffy and distant; overly informal messages to customers or top executives are perceived as disrespectful.
Activate a signature file, which automatically pastes your contact information into every message you create.	Saves you the trouble of retyping vital information and ensures that recipients know how to reach you through other means.
Don't let unread messages pile up in your in-basket.	You'll miss important information and create the impression that you're ignoring other people.
Never type in all caps.	ALL CAPS ARE INTERPRETED AS SCREAMING.
Don't overformat your messages with background colors, colored type, unusual fonts, and so on.	Such messages can be difficult and annoying to read on screen.
Remember that messages can be forwarded anywhere and saved forever.	Don't let a moment of anger or poor judgment haunt you for the rest of your career.
Use the "return receipt requested" feature only for the most critical messages.	This feature triggers a message back to you whenever someone receives or opens your message; many consider this an invasion of privacy.
Make sure your computer has up-to-date virus protection.	One of the worst breaches of "netiquette" is unknowingly infecting other computers because you haven't bothered to protect your own system.
Pay attention to grammar, spelling, and capitalization.	Some people don't think e-mail needs formal rules, but careless messages make you look unprofessional and can annoy readers.
Use acronyms sparingly.	Shorthand such as IMHO (in my humble opinion) and LOL (laughing out loud) can be useful in informal correspondence with colleagues, but don't use them in other messages.

audience's attention, make sure your subject line is both informative and compelling. Do more than just describe or classify message content. Use the opportunity to build interest with key words, quotations, directions, or questions:[19]

Ineffective Subject Line	**Effective Subject Line**
July sales figures	Send figures for July sales
Tomorrow's meeting	Bring consultant's report to Friday's meeting
Marketing report	Need budget for marketing report
Employee parking	Revised resurfacing schedule for parking lot
Status report	Warehouse remodeling is on schedule

If you are exchanging multiple e-mails with someone on the same topic, be sure to periodically modify the subject line of your message to reflect the revised message content. Most e-mail programs will copy the subject line when you click on Reply, so you need only revise it. When numerous messages have identical subject lines, trying

FIGURE 5–3
Draft E-Mail Message

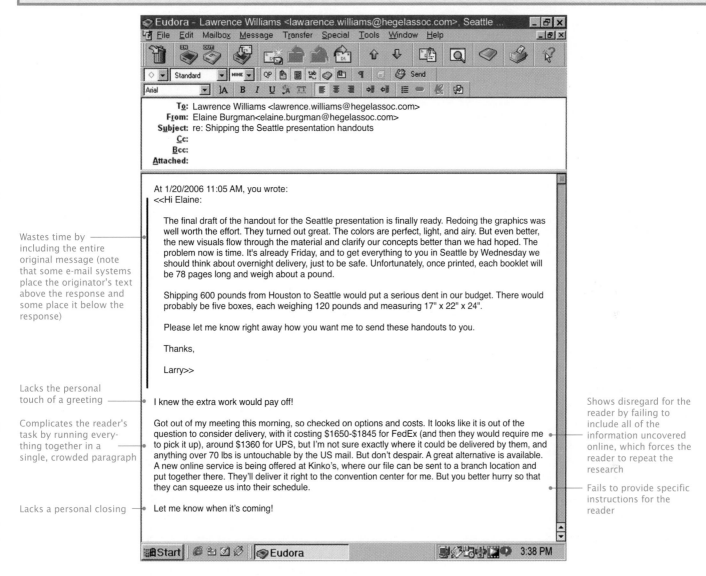

Wastes time by including the entire original message (note that some e-mail systems place the originator's text above the response and some place it below the response)

Lacks the personal touch of a greeting

Complicates the reader's task by running everything together in a single, crowded paragraph

Lacks a personal closing

Shows disregard for the reader by failing to include all of the information uncovered online, which forces the reader to repeat the research

Fails to provide specific instructions for the reader

to find a particular one can be confusing and frustrating. Moreover, some messages sharing the same subject line may actually have absolutely nothing to do with the original topic. Modifying the subject line with each new response will save you time and make it easier to locate a message at a later date.

Finally, never let your emotions get the best of you when you're composing e-mail. A message that contains insensitive, insulting, or critical comments is called a *flame*. If you're upset about something or angry with someone, compose yourself before composing your e-mail. If you're fuming, cool off before writing your e-mail message. If you do write an emotionally charged message, let it sit for at least a day. Ask yourself, "Would I say this to my audience face to face?" Remember that a live person is on the receiving end of your communication—and that your message can be forwarded easily and stored forever.

Table 5–7 lists a number of other helpful tips that will help ensure that your e-mail messages are both effective at their purpose and at establishing you as a knowledgeable professional when it comes to using this vital business tool.

To see these principles in action, review the draft and revised e-mails in Figures 5–3 and 5–4. Pay close attention to the subject line, organization, word choice, tone, and sentence structure used in each e-mail message.

Keep your emotions under control when creating and responding to e-mail.

FIGURE 5–4
Revised E-Mail Message

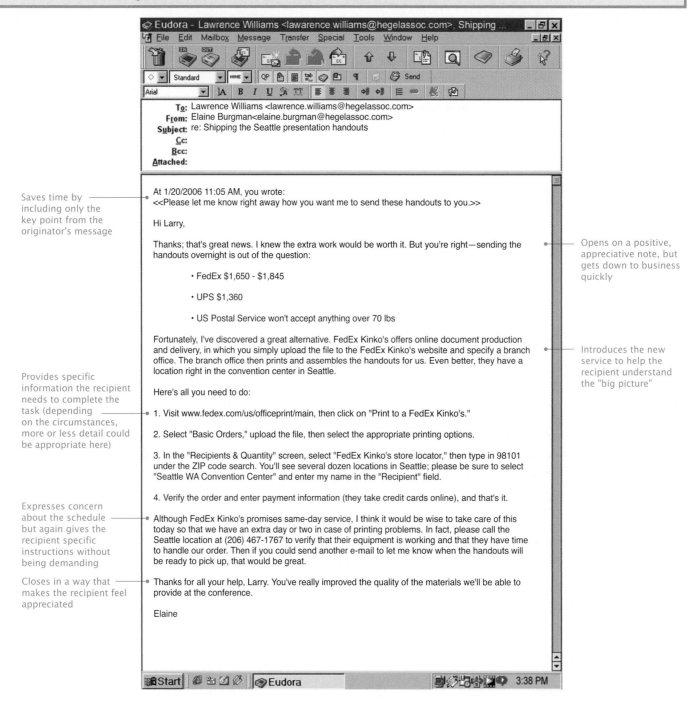

Saves time by including only the key point from the originator's message

Provides specific information the recipient needs to complete the task (depending on the circumstances, more or less detail could be appropriate here)

Expresses concern about the schedule but again gives the recipient specific instructions without being demanding

Closes in a way that makes the recipient feel appreciated

Opens on a positive, appreciative note, but gets down to business quickly

Introduces the new service to help the recipient understand the "big picture"

Shaping Your Documents with Word Processing Tools

Take full advantage of your word processor's formatting capabilities to help you produce effective, professional documents in less time.

As you probably know, today's word processing software provides a wide range of tools to help writers compose documents. Most of these tools take care of the "housekeeping chores" often associated with business document preparation, allowing you to focus on the creative aspects of writing. If you're not aware of all these capabilities in your word processing software, spend a few minutes with them to see how they can help:

- **Style sheets.** Most word processors offer some form of style sheets, which are master lists of predefined styles for headlines, paragraph text, and so on. These styles specify font, type size, paragraph indents, and so on. Many organizations provide employees with approved style sheets to ensure a consistent look for all company documents. Style sheets can eliminate hours of design time by making many of your choices for you.

- **Templates.** A template provides standardization on a larger scale, defining such factors as page design, available fonts, and other features. Templates can include *boilerplate,* or sections of text that are reused from document to document. For example, the last paragraph of a press release is commonly boilerplate, providing a standard message regarding the company's background. Like style sheets, templates save you time by making choices for you in advance.

- **Autocompletion.** Software called *autocompletion* (or something similar) inserts a ready-made block of text when you type the first few characters. For example, instead of typing your company's name, address, phone number, fax number, e-mail address, and website URL, you can set the software to enter all this information as soon as you type the first three letters of the company name. This feature also reduces the chance of typos.

- **Autocorrection.** Another automatic feature in some programs instantly corrects spelling and typing errors and converts text to symbols, such as converting (c) to the © copyright symbol. However, autocorrection may make changes that you *don't* want made, such as converting "nd," "st," or "th" to superscript characters when paired with numbers, as in "21st century." (Although the use of such superscripts is common in word processing, many design professionals consider it poor typesetting.) Check the settings in your word processor to specify which autocorrections you want to use. In addition, depending on autocorrection to take care of your spelling errors can be risky, since this feature catches only the most common typing mistakes.

- **File merge, mail merge.** Today's software makes it easy to combine files, an especially handy feature when several members of a team write different sections of a report. For particularly complex reports, you can set up a master document that merges a number of subdocuments automatically when it's time to print. *Mail merge* lets you personalize form letters by inserting names and addresses from a database.

- **Endnotes, footnotes, indexes, and tables of contents.** Your computer can also help you track footnotes and endnotes, renumbering them every time you add or delete references. For a report's indexes and table of contents, you can simply flag the items you want to include, and the software assembles the lists for you.

- **Wizards.** Programs such as Microsoft Word offer *wizards* that step you through the process of creating letters, résumés, and other common documents. You still need to provide the content and perform the writing, of course, but the wizards can be helpful reminders of the various elements you need to include in the document.

As with every other communication technology, using these tools efficiently and effectively requires some balance. You need to learn enough about the features to be handy with them, without spending so much time that the tools distract the writing process. Chances are somebody in your organization has already figured out the feature you're trying to use and can offer advice.

For a reminder of the tasks involved in writing your messages, see "Checklist: Writing Business Messages."

✓ CHECKLIST: Writing Business Messages

A. Adapt to your audience

✓ Use the "you" attitude.
✓ Maintain good etiquette through polite communication.
✓ Emphasize the positive whenever possible.
✓ Use bias-free language.
✓ Establish your credibility in the eyes of your audience.
✓ Project your company's preferred image.
✓ Use a conversational but still professional and respectful tone.
✓ Use plain English for clarity.

B. Compose your message

✓ Choose strong words that communicate efficiently.
✓ Make sure you use functional and content words correctly.
✓ Pay attention to the connotative meaning of your words.
✓ Balance abstract and concrete terms to convey your meaning accurately.
✓ Avoid clichés and trendy buzzwords.
✓ Use jargon only when your audience understands it and prefers it.
✓ Vary your sentence structure for impact and interest.
✓ Develop coherent, unified paragraphs.
✓ Use transitional elements generously to help your audience follow your message.

On the Job

SOLVING COMMUNICATION DILEMMAS AT CREATIVE COMMONS

To achieve their mission of popularizing a new approach to copyrighting songs, artwork, literature, and other creative works, Lawrence Lessig and his staff at Creative Commons need to convince people that the traditional approach to copyright doesn't meet the needs of today's digital society. This is no small challenge: Not only do they need to convince people to reconsider more than 200 years of legal precedent and habit, they also need to communicate with an extremely diverse audience—everyone from lawyers and business managers to artists, writers, musicians, and scientists. After graduating with a business degree, you've joined Creative Commons as a communication intern for a year before entering law school. Apply your knowledge of effective writing to these four scenarios.

1. Creative Commons offers several varieties of its "Sampling" license, which makes it easier for artists to give other people the opportunity to use snippets of their work in new creative works. Digitally sampling pieces of existing songs for use in new songs is common today, but sampling also applies to photographs, graphic designs, and any other work that people might want to borrow from. Which of the following

does the best job of describing the Sampling and Sampling Plus licenses and the key difference between the two?

a. Both the Sampling and Sample Plus licenses allow people to take pieces of your work and reuse them in new creative works for any purpose other than advertising. Sample Plus also allows people to copy and distribute your entire work for non-commercial purposes only.

b. Sampling is more restrictive than Sampling Plus because it forbids the copying and distribution of your entire work. Both licenses allow people to use pieces of your work for any purpose other than advertising.

c. Unlike the Sampling license, Sampling Plus allows people to copy and distribute your entire work, although for noncommercial purposes only (e.g., they can't resell it or use it in advertising).

d. The Sampling Plus license also gives people the right to copy and distribute your entire work, although for noncommercial purposes only (e.g., they can't resell it or use it in advertising).

2. A key part of the communication challenge for Creative Commons is translating legal documents

into language that musicians, artists, and other with no legal training can easily understand. Which of these does the best job of adapting the following legal phrase (which is part of the licensing contracts) into language for a general audience?

The above rights may be exercised in all media and formats whether now known or hereafter devised. The above rights include the right to make such modifications as are technically necessary to exercise the rights in other media and formats.

a. The rights granted by this licensing contract extend to any current or future media, and you also have the right to modify the material as needed to meet the technical needs of any media.
b. You may use this material in any present or future media and modify it as needed to work with any media.
c. Be advised that your rights within the scope of this contract include the right to use this material in any media that either exists now or might be devised in the future. Moreover, you are also granted the right to modify the material as any current or future media might technically demand.
d. You are hereby granted the right to use this material in any media, including modifications required by that media.

3. The single most important concept in the Creative Commons approach is the idea of a spectrum of possibilities between *all rights reserved* (a conventional copyright) and *no rights reserved* (being in the public domain, where anybody is free to use material in any way they please). Review the structure of these four sentences and choose the one that does the best job of emphasizing the importance of the "spectrum of possibilities."

a. Conventional copyrights, in which the creator reserves all rights to a work, and the public domain, in which the creator gives up all rights, represent two black-and-white extremes.
b. Between the all-or-nothing extremes of a conventional copyright and being in the public domain, Creative Commons sees a need for other possibilities.
c. The primary contribution of Creative Commons is developing a range of possibilities between the extremes of *all rights reserved* (conventional copyright) and *no rights reserved* (public domain).
d. The black-and-white choice of *all rights reserved* (conventional copyright) and *no rights reserved* (public domain) does not meet everyone's needs, so Creative Commons is developing a range of possibilities between these two extremes.

4. Like many organizations these days, Creative Commons must occasionally deal with online rumors spread by bloggers who aren't always sure of their facts. You've been asked to reply to an e-mail query from a *Wall Street Journal* reporter who read a blog rumor that Creative Common's real objective is to destroy ownership of all copyrights. Which of the following has the right style and tone for your response?

a. That blog posting is an absolute crock. The person who wrote it is either a liar or a fool.
b. As our website and other materials strive to make clear, the objective of Creative Commons is to work within the framework of existing copyright law but to establish a range of possibilities for people whose needs aren't met by conventional copyright choices.
c. You wouldn't believe how much time and energy we have to spend defending ourselves against idiotic rumors like this.
d. Creative Commons has never expressed, in print or in online materials, nor in any speeches or presentations given by any of our current or former staff or board members, any plans or strategies that would allow anyone to reach a valid conclusion that our intent is to weaken existing copyright protections.

Learning Objectives Checkup

Assess your understanding of the principles in this chapter by reading each learning objective and studying the accompanying exercises. For fill-in items, write the missing text in the blank provided; for multiple choice items, circle the letter of the correct answer. You can check your responses against the answer key on page AK-1.

Objective 5.1: Explain the importance of adapting your messages to the needs and expectations of your audience.

1. Why should you take the time to adapt your messages to your audience?
   a. People are more inclined to read and respond to messages that they believe apply to them and their concerns.

b. Adapting messages to audiences is corporate policy in nearly all large companies.

c. Adapting your message saves time during planning and writing.

d. You can manipulate audience responses more easily by adapting your messages.

2. How is your audience likely to respond to a message that doesn't seem to be about their concerns or written in language they don't understand?

a. They will ignore the message.

b. If they do read the message, they will be less inclined to respond in a positive way.

c. They will assume the writer doesn't respect them enough to adapt the message.

d. All of the above could occur.

Objective 5.2: Discuss four ways of achieving a businesslike style that is clear and concise.

3. A good way to achieve a businesslike tone in your messages is to

a. Use formal business terminology, such as "In re your letter of the 18th"

b. Brag about your company

c. Use a conversational style that is not intimate or chatty

d. Use plenty of humor

4. Plain English is

a. Never recommended when speaking with people for whom English is a second language

b. A movement toward using "English only" in American businesses

c. A way of writing and arranging technical materials to make them more understandable

d. An attempt to keep writing at a fourth- or fifth-grade level

5. If you want to avoid attributing blame or otherwise calling attention to a specific person, the _____ voice is a more diplomatic approach.

6. The _____ voice usually makes sentences shorter, more direct, and livelier.

Objective 5.3: Briefly describe how to select words that are not only correct but also effective.

7. Which of the following defines the connotative meaning of the word *flag?*

a. A flag is a piece of material with a symbol of some kind sewn on it.

b. A flag is a symbol of everything that a nation stands for.

c. A flag is fabric on a pole used to mark a geographic spot.

d. A flag is an object used to draw attention.

8. Which of the following is a concrete word?

a. Little

b. Mouse

c. Species

d. Kingdom

9. If you're not sure about the meaning of a word you'd like to use, which of the following is the most appropriate way to handle the situation?

a. Your readers probably have instant access to online dictionaries these days, so go ahead and use the word.

b. Use the word but include a humorous comment in parentheses saying that you're not really sure what this big, important word means.

c. Either verify the meaning of the word or rewrite the sentence so that you don't need to use it.

d. Find a synonym in a thesaurus and use that word instead.

10. Using jargon is

a. Often a good idea when discussing complex subjects with people who are intimately familiar with both the subject and common jargon relating to it

b. Never a good idea

c. A good way to build credibility, no matter what the purpose of the message is

d. A sign of being an "insider"

Objective 5.4: Explain how sentence style affects emphasis within your message.

11. What is the most emphatic place to put a dependent clause?

a. At the end of the sentence

b. At the beginning of the sentence

c. In the middle of the sentence

d. It doesn't really matter

12. Devoting more words to a particular idea shows your audience that

a. The idea is complicated

b. The idea is the topic sentence

c. The idea is important

d. The idea is new and therefore requires more explanation

Objective 5.5: List five ways to develop coherent paragraphs.

13. When developing a paragraph, keep in mind

a. That you should stick to one method of development within a single paragraph

b. That once you use one method of development, you should use that same method for all the paragraphs in a section

c. That your choice of technique should take into account your subject, your intended audience, and your purpose

d. All of the above

14. To develop a paragraph by illustration, give your audience enough _____ to help them grasp the main idea.

15. Paragraphs organized by comparison and contrast point out the _____ or _____ between two or more items.

16. To explain the reasons why something happened, which of these paragraph designs should you use?

a. Cause and effect

b. Opposition and argument

c. Classification

d. Prioritization

Objective 5.6: Discuss the importance of effective e-mail subject lines and explain how to write them.

17. Which of the following is true of e-mail subject lines?

a. Only "newbies" bother to use them anymore.

b. Subject lines should never give away the content of the message because no one will bother to read them if they already know what the messages are about.

c. They can make the difference between a message being read right away, skipped over for later attention, or ignored entirely.

d. They should always be in "all caps" to get the audience's attention.

18. To capture attention in your e-mail messages, be sure to
    a. Make your subject line longer than you would in a memo
    b. Avoid key words, quotations, directions, and questions
    c. Make your subject line informative
    d. Retain the same subject line in multiple e-mails on the same topic no matter how the content changes

Apply Your Knowledge

1. How can you apply the "you" approach when you don't know your audience personally?
2. When composing business messages, how can you be yourself and project your company's image at the same time?
3. What steps can you take to make abstract concepts such as *opportunity* feel more concrete in your messages?
4. Considering how fast and easy it is, should instant messaging completely replace meetings and other face-to-face communication in your company? Why or why not?

5. **Ethical Choices** Seven million people in the United States are allergic to one or more food ingredients. Every year 30,000 of these people end up in the emergency room after suffering an allergic reaction, and every year 200 of them die. Many of these tragic events are tied to poorly written food labels that either fail to identify dangerous allergens or use scientific terms that most consumers don't recognize. Do food manufacturers have a responsibility to ensure that consumers read, understand, and follow warnings on food products? Explain your answer.

Practice Your Knowledge

DOCUMENT FOR ANALYSIS

Read the following document; then (1) analyze the strengths and weaknesses of each sentence and (2) revise the document so that it follows this chapter's guidelines.

I am a new publisher with some really great books to sell. I saw your announcement in Publishers Weekly *about the bookseller's show you're having this summer, and I think it's a great idea. Count me in, folks! I would like to get some space to show my books. I thought it would be a neat thing if I could do some airbrushing on T-shirts live to help promote my hot new title, T-Shirt Art. Before I got into publishing, I was an airbrush artist, and I*

could demonstrate my techniques. I've done hundreds of advertising illustrations and have been a sign painter all my life, so I'll also be promoting my other book, hot off the presses, How to Make Money in the Sign Painting Business.

I will be starting my PR campaign about May 2007 with ads in PW and some art trade papers, so my books should be well known by the time the show comes around in August. In case you would like to use my appearance there as part of your publicity, I have enclosed a biography and photo of myself.

P.S. Please let me know what it costs for booth space as soon as possible so that I can figure out whether I can afford to attend. Being a new publisher is mighty expensive!

Exercises

For active links to all websites discussed in this chapter, visit this text's website at www.prenhall.com/thill. Locate your book and click on its Companion Website link. Then select Chapter 5, and click on "Featured Websites." Locate the name of the page or the URL related to the material in the text. Please note that links to sites that become inactive after publication of the book will be removed from the Featured Websites section.

5.1 Audience Relationship: Courteous Communication Substitute a better phrase for each of the following:
  a. You claim that
  b. It is not our policy to

c. You neglected to
d. In which you assert
e. We are sorry you are dissatisfied
f. You failed to enclose
g. We request that you send us
h. Apparently you overlooked our terms
i. We have been very patient
j. We are at a loss to understand

5.2 Audience Relationship: The "You" Attitude Rewrite these sentences to reflect your audience's viewpoint.
  a. Your e-mail order cannot be processed; we request that you use the order form on our website instead.

b. We insist that you always bring your credit card to the store.

c. We want to get rid of all our CRT monitors to make room in our warehouse for the new LCD flat screen monitors. Thus we are offering a 25 percent discount on all sales this week.

d. I am applying for the position of bookkeeper in your office. I feel my grades prove that I am bright and capable, and I think I can do a good job for you.

e. As requested, we are sending the refund for $25.

5.3 Audience Relationship: Emphasize the Positive Revise these sentences to be positive rather than negative.

a. To avoid the loss of your credit rating, please remit payment within 10 days.

b. We don't make refunds on returned merchandise that is soiled.

c. Because we are temporarily out of Baby Cry dolls, we won't be able to ship your order for 10 days.

d. You failed to specify the color of the blouse that you ordered.

e. You should have realized that waterbeds will freeze in unheated houses during winter. Therefore, our guarantee does not cover the valve damage, and you must pay the $9.50 valve-replacement fee (plus postage).

5.4 Audience Relationship: Emphasize the Positive Provide euphemisms for the following words and phrases:

a. Stubborn
b. Wrong
c. Stupid
d. Incompetent
e. Loudmouth

5.5 Audience Relationship: Bias-Free Language Rewrite each of the following to eliminate bias:

a. For an Indian, Maggie certainly is outgoing.
b. He needs a wheelchair, but he doesn't let his handicap affect his job performance.
c. A pilot must have the ability to stay calm under pressure, and then he must be trained to cope with any problem that arises.
d. Candidate Renata Parsons, married and the mother of a teenager, will attend the debate.
e. Senior citizen Sam Nugent is still an active salesman.

5.6 Ethical Choices Your company has been a major employer in the local community for years, but shifts in the global marketplace have forced some changes in the company's long-term direction. In fact, the company plans to reduce local staffing by as much as 50 percent over the next 5 to 10 years, starting with a small layoff next month. The size and timing of future layoffs has not been decided, although there is little doubt more layoffs will happen at some point. In the first draft of a letter aimed at community leaders, you write that "this first layoff is part of a continuing series of staff reductions anticipated over the next several years." However, your boss is concerned about the vagueness and nega-

tive tone of the language and asks you to rewrite that sentence to read "this layoff is part of the company's ongoing efforts to continually align its resources with global market conditions." Do you think this suggested wording is ethical, given the company's economic influence in the community? Please explain your answer.

5.7 Message Composition: Controlling Style Rewrite the following letter to Mrs. Betty Crandall (1597 Church St., Grants Pass, OR 97526) so that it conveys a helpful, personal, and interested tone:

We have your letter of recent date to our Ms. Dobson. Owing to the fact that you neglected to include the size of the dress you ordered, please be advised that no shipment of your order was made, but the aforementioned shipment will occur at such time as we are in receipt of the aforementioned information.

5.8 Message Composition: Selecting Words Write a concrete phrase for each of these vague phrases (make up any information you need):

a. Sometime this spring
b. A substantial saving
c. A large number attended
d. Increased efficiency
e. Expanded the work area
f. Flatten the website structure

5.9 Message Composition: Selecting Words List terms that are stronger than the following:

a. Ran after
b. Seasonal ups and downs
c. Bright
d. Suddenly rises
e. Moves forward

5.10 Message Composition: Selecting Words As you rewrite these sentences, replace the clichés with fresh, personal expressions:

a. Being a jack-of-all-trades, Dave worked well in his new general manager job.
b. Moving Leslie into the accounting department, where she was literally a fish out of water, was like putting a square peg into a round hole, if you get my drift.
c. I knew she was at death's door, but I thought the doctor would pull her through.
d. Movies aren't really my cup of tea; as far as I am concerned, they can't hold a candle to a good book.
e. It's a dog-eat-dog world out there in the rat race of the asphalt jungle.

5.11 Message Composition: Selecting Words Suggest short, simple words to replace each of the following:

a. Inaugurate
b. Terminate
c. Utilize
d. Anticipate
e. Assistance
f. Endeavor
g. Ascertain
h. Procure
i. Consummate
j. Advise
k. Alteration
l. Forwarded
m. Fabricate
n. Nevertheless
o. Substantial

5.12 Message Composition: Selecting Words Write up-to-date, less-stuffy versions of these phrases; write *none* if you think there is no appropriate substitute:
  a. As per your instructions
  b. Attached herewith
  c. In lieu of
  d. In reply I wish to state
  e. Please be advised that

5.13 Message Composition: Creating Sentences Suppose that end-of-term frustrations have produced this e-mail message to Professor Anne Brewer from a student who believes he should have received a B in his accounting class. If this message were recast into three or four clear sentences, the teacher might be more receptive to the student's argument. Rewrite the message to show how you would improve it:

> *I think that I was unfairly awarded a C in your accounting class this term, and I am asking you to change the grade to a B. It was a difficult term. I don't get any money from home, and I have to work mornings at the Pancake House (as a cook), so I had to rush to make your class, and those two times that I missed class were because they wouldn't let me off work because of special events at the Pancake House (unlike some other students who just take off when they choose). On the midterm examination, I originally got a 75 percent, but you said in class that there were two different ways to answer the third question and that you would change the grades of students who used the "optimal cost" method and had been counted off 6 points for doing this. I don't think that you took this into account, because I got 80 percent on the final, which is clearly a B. Anyway, whatever you decide, I just want to tell you that I really enjoyed this class, and I thank you for making accounting so interesting.*

5.14 Message Composition: Creating Sentences Rewrite each sentence so that it is active rather than passive:
  a. The raw data are entered into the customer relationship management system by the sales representative each Friday.
  b. High profits are publicized by management.
  c. The policies announced in the directive were implemented by the staff.
  d. Our computers are serviced by the Santee Company.
  e. The employees were represented by Janet Hogan.

5.15 Message Composition: Writing Paragraphs In the following paragraph, identify the topic sentence and the related sentences (those that support the idea of the topic sentence):

> *The style of business writing is also changing. The rise of e-mail and other electronic channels has coincided with a growing need for executives to ensure that their communication is more direct, more personal. Flatter management structures mean that executives can no longer rely on hierarchical power to get things done. Issuing edicts is less often an option. Instead, managers must increasingly rely on persuasion—and inspiration.*

> *This requires a more sophisticated style of communication, one that is directed at the individual and imbued with emotional context as well as content. One survey of 60 executives found that the messages that get attention are those in which the message is personalized, evokes an emotional response, comes from a trustworthy or respected sender, and is concise.[20]*

Now add a topic sentence to this paragraph:

> *Our analysis of the customer experience should start before golfers even drive through the front gate here at Glencoe Meadows; it should start when they phone in or log onto our website to reserve tee times. When they do arrive, the first few stages in the process are also vital: the condition of the grounds leading up to the club house, the reception they receive when they drop off their clubs, and the ease of parking. From that point, how well are we doing with check-in at the pro shop, openings at the driving range, and timely scheduling at the first tee? Then there's everything associated with playing the course itself and returning to the club house at the end of the round.*

5.16 Teamwork Working with four other students, divide the following five topics among yourselves and each write one paragraph on his or her selected topic. Be sure each student uses a different technique when writing his or her paragraph: One student should use the illustration technique, one the comparison or contrast technique, one a discussion of cause and effect, one the classification technique, and one a discussion of problem and solution. Then exchange paragraphs within the team and pick out the main idea and general purpose of the paragraph one of your teammates wrote. Was everyone able to correctly identify the main idea and purpose? If not, suggest how the paragraph might be rewritten for clarity.
  a. Types of digital cameras (or dogs or automobiles) available for sale
  b. Advantages and disadvantages of eating at fast-food restaurants
  c. Finding that first full-time job
  d. Good qualities of my car (or house, or apartment, or neighborhood)
  e. How to make a dessert recipe (or barbecue a steak or make coffee)

5.17 Internet Visit the Security Exchange Commission's (SEC) plain English website at www.sec.gov, click on "Online Publications," and review the online handbook. In one or two sentences, summarize what the SEC means by the phrase "plain English." Now read the SEC's online advice about how to invest in mutual funds. Does this document follow the SEC's plain-English guidelines? Can you suggest any improvements to organization, words, sentences, or paragraphs?

5.18 Message Organization: Transitional Elements Add transitional elements to the following sentences to improve the flow of ideas. (Note: You may need to eliminate or add some words to smooth out your sentences.)

a. Steve Case saw infinite possibilities in online business. Steve Case was determined to turn his vision into reality. The techies scoffed at his strategy of building a simple Internet service for ordinary people. Case doggedly pursued his dream. He analyzed other online services. He assessed the needs of his customers. He responded to their desires for an easier way to access information over the Internet. In 1992, Steve Case named his company America Online (AOL). Critics predicted the company's demise. By the end of the century, AOL was a profitable powerhouse. An ill-fated merger with Time Warner was a financial disaster and led to Case's ouster from the company.

b. Facing some of the toughest competitors in the world, Harley-Davidson had to make some changes. The company introduced new products. Harley's management team set out to rebuild the company's production process. New products were coming to market and the company was turning a profit. Harley's quality standards were not on par with those of its foreign competitors. Harley's costs were still among the highest in the industry. Harley made a U-turn and restructured the company's organizational structure. Harley's efforts have paid off.

c. Whether you're indulging in a doughnut in New York or California, Krispy Kreme wants you to enjoy the same delicious taste with every bite. The company maintains consistent product quality by carefully controlling every step of the production process. Krispy Kreme tests all raw ingredients against established quality standards. Every delivery of wheat flour is sampled and measured for its moisture content and protein levels. Krispy Kreme blends the ingredients. Krispy Kreme tests the doughnut mix for quality. Krispy Kreme delivers the mix to its stores. Financial critics are not as kind to the company as food critics have been. Allegations of improper financial reporting have left the company's future in doubt.

5.19 **Ethical Choices** Under what circumstances would you consider the use of terms that are high in connotative meaning to be ethical? When would you consider it to be unethical? Explain your reasoning.

Expand Your Knowledge

LEARNING MORE ON THE WEB

COMPOSE A BETTER BUSINESS MESSAGE
http://owl.english.purdue.edu/

At Purdue University's Online Writing Lab (OWL), you'll find tools to help you improve your business messages. For advice on composing written messages, for help with grammar, and for referrals to other information sources, you'd be wise to visit this site. Purdue's OWL offers online services and an introduction to Internet search tools. You can also download a variety of handouts on writing skills.

ACTIVITIES

Check out the resources at the OWL homepage, then answer the following questions:

1. Explain why positive wording in a message is more effective than negative wording. Why should you be concerned about the position of good news or bad news in your written message?

2. What six factors of tone should you consider when conveying your message to your audience?

3. What points should you include in the close of your business message? Why?

EXPLORING THE WEB ON YOUR OWN

Review these chapter-related websites on your own to learn more about writing business messages.

1. Write it right by paying attention to these writing tips, grammar pointers, style suggestions, and reference sources at www.webgrammar.com.

2. Can't find the right word to use when writing about specialized topics? Check out one of the hundreds of subject-area glossaries available at www.glossarist.com.

3. Maximize your e-mail effectiveness by visiting A Beginner's Guide to Effective E-Mail, www.webfoot.com/advice/email.top.html.

Learn Interactively

INTERACTIVE STUDY GUIDE

Visit www.prenhall.com/thill, then locate your book and click on its Companion Website link. Select Chapter 5 to take advantage of the interactive "Chapter Quiz" to test your knowledge of chapter concepts. Receive instant feedback on whether you need additional studying. Also, visit the "Study Hall," where you'll find an abundance of valuable resources that will help you succeed in this course.

**PEAK PERFORMANCE GRAMMAR
AND MECHANICS**

If your instructor has required the use of "Peak Performance Grammar and Mechanics," either in your online course or on CD, you can improve your skill with adverbs by using the "Peak Performance Grammar and Mechanics" module. Click "Adverbs." Take the Pretest to determine whether you have any weak areas. Then review those areas in the Refresher Course. Take the Follow-Up Test to check your grasp of adverbs. For an extra challenge or advanced practice, take the Advanced Test. Finally, for additional reinforcement, go to the "Improve Your Grammar, Mechanics, and Usage" section that follows, and complete those exercises.

Improve Your Grammar, Mechanics, and Usage

The following exercises help you improve your knowledge of and power over English grammar, mechanics, and usage. Turn to the Handbook of Grammar, Mechanics, and Usage at the end of this textbook and review all of Section 1.5 (Adverbs). Then look at the following 10 items. Underline the preferred choice within each set of parentheses. (Answers to these exercises appear on page AK-3.)

1. Their performance has been (*good/well*).
2. I (*sure/surely*) do not know how to help you.
3. He feels (*sick/sickly*) again today.
4. Customs dogs are chosen because they smell (*good/well*).
5. The redecorated offices look (*good/well*).
6. Which of the two programs computes (*more fast, faster*)?
7. Of the two we have in stock, this model is the (*best, better*) designed.
8. He doesn't seem to have (*any, none*).
9. That machine is scarcely (*never, ever*) used.
10. They (*can, can't*) hardly get replacement parts for this equipment (*any, no*) more.

For additional exercises focusing on adverbs, go to www.prenhall.com/thill, then locate your text and click on its Companion Website link. Click on Chapter 5, click on "Additional Exercises to Improve Your Grammar, Mechanics and Usage," then click on "9. Adverbs."

Chapter 6

Completing Business Messages

Learning Objectives

1 Discuss the value of careful revision and list the main tasks involved in completing a business message

2 List four writing techniques you can use to improve the readability of your messages

3 Describe the steps you can take to improve the clarity of your writing

4 Discuss why it's important to make your message more concise and give four tips on how to do so

5 Explain how design elements help determine the effectiveness of your documents

6 Highlight the types of errors to look for when proofreading

7 Discuss the most important issues to consider when distributing your messages

On the Job

COMMUNICATING AT *ROLLING STONE*

PUTTING DESIGNS ON A NEW GENERATION OF READERS

The next time you pick up your favorite magazine, don't read it. Instead, flip through the pages and look at the design and presentation. What kinds of fonts are used for headlines and text? How many photos or illustrations appear with each article? How is color used? Is the publication easy to read? Editors and designers use such design elements to connect with their readers and create the overall style of a magazine. *Rolling Stone* magazine is a classic example. Born in the 1960s in San Francisco, *Rolling Stone* has remained relevant for decades because publisher and founder Jann Wenner has made dozens of changes over the years.

One of the most dramatic changes was initiated when the magazine began to lose sales to both new music publications such as *Blender* and *Spin* and the new wave of "laddie magazines," including *FHM* and *Maxim*. Wenner responded to the competitive threat with a plan to make his magazine more relevant to contemporary demands and more appealing to its target audience—without losing its core focus on music and culture. He started by hiring an editor from *FHM* and asking him to update the magazine's look, tone, and personality. "We're responding to an overall change in the media landscape and an overall change in the way people use and consume media," explained Wenner.

The result of this effort was a major redesign that touched every aspect. The in-depth articles that *Rolling Stone* had built its reputation on were de-emphasized in favor of shorter pieces, flashier graphics, and provocative photography. In short, *Rolling Stone*

Founder Jann Wenner continues to keep Rolling Stone on the cutting edge of culture with topical content and contemporary design.

started to look a lot more like its younger competitors.

Some critics were less than kind, accusing Wenner of dumbing down the magazine to cater to an attention-challenged new generation. University of Mississippi journalism professor Samir Husni compared the makeover to a midlife crisis, in which someone who feels youth slipping away "buys a convertible and starts acting like a teenager."

Wenner responded to the criticism by emphasizing that the culturally relevant messages would still be there, just packaged differently. And he clearly made the right moves in the opinion of the marketplace. Within a few months, sales were on the rise again as *Rolling Stone* showed it could handle the competitive heat.

True to form, however, Wenner didn't rest on that success. Less than three years into the new format, he sensed that the "laddie magazine" phenomenon of simpler and flashier journalism was reaching its peak and readers were ready for more depth. Out went the editor from *FHM* and back came the focus on in-depth journalism. And once again, the market responded, and sales increased.

Chances are, your business writing won't endeavor to become the voice of a generation as *Rolling Stone* started out to be, but even with everyday memos you can learn from Wenner's skill at adapting to an audience. By applying the same attention to audience needs and design details, you too can keep your business messages more relevant and appealing year after year.[1]

www.rollingstone.com

MOVING BEYOND YOUR FIRST DRAFT

First drafts are rarely as effective as they could be.

Once you've completed the first draft of your message, you may be tempted to breathe a sigh of relief and go on to the next project. Resist the temptation. Professional communicators such as Jann Wenner recognize that the first draft is rarely as tight, clear, and compelling as it needs to be. Careful revision can mean the difference between a rambling, unfocused message and a lively, direct message that gets noticed. Figure 6–1 lists the tasks in the third step of the three-step writing process: revising your message to achieve optimum quality, then producing, proofreading, and distributing it.

REVISING YOUR MESSAGE

If you have time, put your draft aside for a day or two before you begin the revision process.

Even though you've generally done some revising as you write the first draft, be sure to set aside time for a thorough, top-to-bottom revision after completing the writing. With important messages, the best approach is to put your draft aside for a day or two before you begin the revision process so that you can approach the material with a fresh eye. Then start with the "big picture," making sure that the document accomplishes your overall goals before moving to finer points such as readability, clarity, and conciseness.

Look closely at Figure 6–2, the draft of a letter responding to Louise Wilson's request for information about the frequent-guest program at the Commerce Hotel. (In this case, the draft document was edited on paper. It was printed double-spaced to allow room for the *proofreading marks* shown in red. You can see descriptions of the basic proofreading marks below the letter, and a full set of marks is shown in Appendix C on page A-27. However, in many instances you'll use the electronic markup features in your word processor, as shown later in this chapter on page 183.)

Now review the letter in Figure 6–3, which incorporates all the revisions. As you can see, Figure 6–3 provides the requested information more clearly, in a more organized fashion, with a friendlier style, and with precise mechanics.

FIGURE 6–1
Step Three in the Three-Step Writing Process: Complete Your Messages

Planning

Analyze the Situation
Define your purpose and develop an audience profile.

Gather Information
Determine audience needs and obtain the information necessary to satisfy those needs.

Select the Right Medium
Choose the best medium for delivering your message.

Organize the Information
Define your main idea, limit your scope, select a direct or an indirect approach, and outline your content.

Writing

Adapt to Your Audience
Be sensitive to audience needs with a "you" attitude, politeness, positive emphasis, and bias-free language. Build a strong relationship with your audience by establishing your credibility and projecting your company's image. Control your style with a conversational tone, plain English, and appropriate voice.

Compose the Message
Choose strong words that will help you create effective sentences and coherent paragraphs.

Completing

Revise the Message
Evaluate content and review readability, then edit and rewrite for conciseness and clarity.

Produce the Message
Use effective design elements and suitable layout for a clean, professional appearance.

Proofread the Message
Review for errors in layout, spelling, and mechanics.

Distribute the Message
Deliver your message using the chosen medium; make sure all documents and all relevant files are distributed successfully.

1   2   3

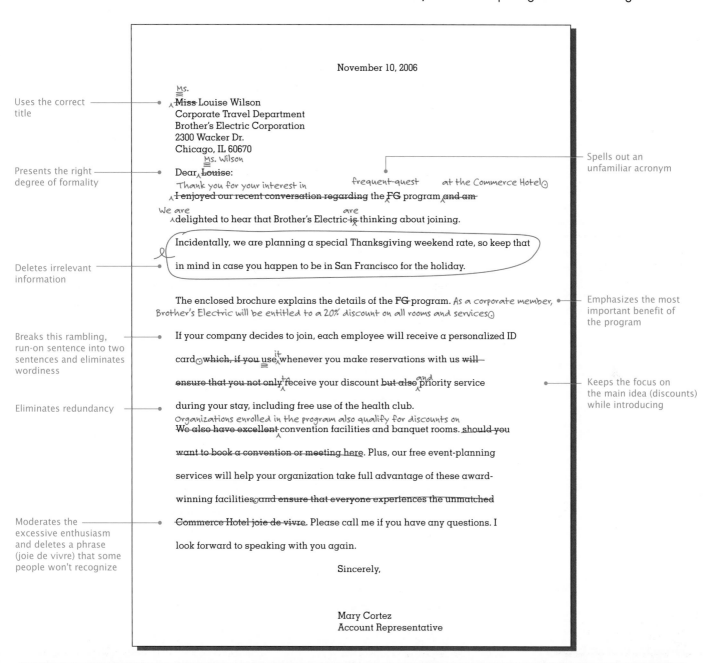

November 10, 2006

Uses the correct title ————•

Ms.
~~Miss~~ Louise Wilson
Corporate Travel Department
Brother's Electric Corporation
2300 Wacker Dr.
Chicago, IL 60670

Presents the right degree of formality ————•

Ms. Wilson
Dear ~~Louise~~:

Thank you for your interest in
~~I enjoyed our recent conversation regarding~~ the FG program ~~and am~~

Spells out an unfamiliar acronym •————

frequent-guest   at the Commerce Hotel.

We are
~~delighted~~ to hear that Brother's Electric ~~is~~ thinking about joining.
                                     are

Deletes irrelevant information ————•

(Incidentally, we are planning a special Thanksgiving weekend rate, so keep that

in mind in case you happen to be in San Francisco for the holiday.)

The enclosed brochure explains the details of the ~~FG~~ program. As a corporate member,
Brother's Electric will be entitled to a 20% discount on all rooms and services.

Emphasizes the most important benefit of the program •————

Breaks this rambling, run-on sentence into two sentences and eliminates wordiness ————•

If your company decides to join, each employee will receive a personalized ID

                                                       it
card. ~~which, if you use~~ whenever you make reservations with us ~~will~~

~~ensure that you not only~~ receive your discount ~~but also~~ priority service
                                                and

during your stay, including free use of the health club.

Keeps the focus on the main idea (discounts) while introducing •————

Eliminates redundancy ————•

Organizations enrolled in the program also qualify for discounts on
~~We also have excellent~~ convention facilities and banquet rooms. ~~should you~~

~~want to book a convention or meeting here~~. Plus, our free event-planning

services will help your organization take full advantage of these award-

winning facilities. ~~and ensure that everyone experiences the unmatched~~

Moderates the excessive enthusiasm and deletes a phrase (joie de vivre) that some people won't recognize ————•

~~Commerce Hotel joie de vivre~~. Please call me if you have any questions. I

look forward to speaking with you again.

Sincerely,

Mary Cortez
Account Representative

Common Proofreading Symbols (see page A-29 for more)

~~strikethrough~~	Delete text
ℓ	Delete individual character or a circled block of text
∧	Insert text (text to insert is written above)
⊙	Insert period
∧	Insert comma
⌐	Start new line
¶	Start new paragraph
≡	Capitalize

FIGURE 6–2
Improving a Customer Letter Through Careful Revision

Addresses the reader appropriately

Opens with an upbeat "you" orientation

Highlights the benefits of the program and maintains focus on the main idea of discounts

Introduces additional benefits while staying focused on discounts

Commerce Hotel
333 Sansome Street · San Francisco, CA 94104
(800) 323-7347 · (415) 854-2447 · Fax (415) 854-7669
www.CommerceHotel.com

November 10, 2006

Ms. Louise Wilson
Corporate Travel Department
Brother's Electric Corporation
2300 Wacker Dr.
Chicago, IL 60670

Dear Ms. Wilson:

Thank you for your interest in the frequent-guest program at the Commerce Hotel. We are delighted to hear that Brother's Electric is thinking about joining.

The enclosed brochure explains the details of the program. As a corporate member, Brother's Electric will be entitled to a 20% discount on all rooms and services. If your company decides to join, each employee will receive a personalized ID card. Use it whenever you make reservations with us to obtain your discount and priority service during your stay, including free use of the health club.

Organizations enrolled in the program also qualify for discounts on convention facilities and banquet rooms. Plus, our free event-planning services will help your organization take full advantage of these award-winning facilities. Please call me if you have any questions. I look forward to speaking with you again.

Sincerely,

Mary Cortez

Mary Cortez
Account Representative

Enclosure

FIGURE 6–3
Revised Customer Letter

Evaluating Your Content, Organization, Style, and Tone

When you begin the revision process, focus your attention on content, organization, style, and tone. To evaluate the content of your message, ask yourself these questions:

- Is the information accurate?

- Is the information relevant to your audience?

- Is there enough information to satisfy your reader's needs?

- Is there a good balance between the general and the specific?

Once you are satisfied with the content of your message, you can review its organization. Ask yourself another set of questions:

- Are all your points covered in the most logical order?

- Do the most important ideas receive the most space, and are they placed in the most prominent positions?

- Would the message be more convincing if it were arranged in another sequence?

- Are any points repeated unnecessarily?

- Are details grouped together logically, or are some still scattered through the document?

With the content in place and effectively organized, next consider whether you have achieved the right style and tone for your audience. Is your writing formal enough to meet the audience's expectations without being too formal or academic? Is it too casual for a serious subject? Does your message emphasize the audience's needs over your own?

Spend a few extra moments on the beginning and ending of your message; these sections have the greatest impact on the audience. Be sure that the opening of your document is relevant, interesting, and geared to the reader's probable reaction. In longer documents, check to see that the first few paragraphs establish the subject, purpose, and organization of the material. Review the conclusion to be sure that it summarizes the main idea and leaves the audience with a positive impression.

The beginning and end of a message have the greatest impact on your readers.

Reviewing for Readability

Once you're satisfied with the content, organization, style, and tone of your message, make a second pass to look at its readability. Most professionals are inundated with more reading material than they can ever hope to consume, and they'll appreciate your efforts to make your documents easier to read. You'll benefit from this effort, too: If you earn a reputation for well-crafted documents that respect the audience's time, people will pay more attention to your work.

You might be familiar with one of the many indexes that have been developed over the years in an attempt to measure readability. For example, the Flesch-Kincaid Grade Level score computes reading difficulty relative to grade-level achievement. Thus, a score of 10 suggests that a document can be read and understood by the average tenth-grader. Most business documents score in the 8–11 range. Technical documents often score in the 12–14 range. A similar scoring system, the Flesch Reading Ease score, ranks documents on a 100-point scale; the higher the score, the easier the document is to read. Both of these measurements are built into Microsoft Word, making them easy to use for most business communicators.

Readability indexes offer a useful reference point, but they are all limited by what they are able to measure: word length, number of syllables, sentence length, and paragraph length. They can't measure any of the other factors that affect readability, such as audience analysis, writing clarity, and document design. Compare these two paragraphs:

Readability formulas can give you a helpful indication, but they can't measure everything that affects readability.

> Readability indexes offer a useful reference point, but they are all limited by what they are able to measure: word length, number of syllables, sentence length, and paragraph length. They can't measure any of the other factors that affect readability, from "you" orientation to writing clarity to document design.

> Readability indexes can help. But they don't measure everything. They don't measure whether your writing clarity is good. They don't measure whether your document design is good or not. Reading indexes are based on word length, syllables, sentences, and paragraphs.

The first paragraph scores 12.0 on grade level and 27.4 on reading ease. The second paragraph scores much better on both grade level (8.9) and reading ease (45.8). However, the second example is choppy, unsophisticated, and poorly organized. As a general rule, then, don't assume that a piece of text is readable if it scores well on a readability index. It may still suffer from other problems. Conversely, if a piece of text scores poorly (with a high grade level or a low reading ease score), examine it carefully to see whether you can use simpler words or shorter sentences. Chances are you can make the piece easier to read without making it sound choppy or amateurish.

Beyond shortening words and sentences for readability measurements, you can improve the readability of a message by making the document interesting and easy to skim. Most business audiences—particularly influential senior managers—skim most documents looking for key ideas, conclusions, and recommendations. Skimming also helps readers assess the worthiness of the document. If they determine that the document contains valuable information or requires a response, they will read it more carefully when time permits. You can adopt a number of techniques to make your message easier to skim: varying sentence length, using shorter paragraphs, using lists and bullets instead of narrative, and adding effective headings and subheadings.

> The effort to make your documents more readable will pay for itself in greater career success.

Varying Your Sentence Length

Variety is a creative way to make your messages interesting and readable. By choosing words and sentence structure with care, you can create a rhythm that emphasizes important points, enlivens your writing style, and makes your information appealing to your reader. For example, a short sentence that highlights a conclusion at the end of a substantial paragraph of evidence makes your key message stand out. Effective documents, therefore, usually use a mixture of sentences that are short (up to 15 words or so), medium (15–25 words), and long (more than 25 words).

> To keep readers' interest, use both long and short sentences.

Each sentence length has its advantages. Short sentences can be processed quickly and are easier for nonnative speakers and translators to interpret. Medium-length sentences are useful for showing the relationships among ideas. Long sentences are often the best way to convey complex ideas, list multiple related points, or summarize or preview information.

Of course, each sentence length also has disadvantages. Too many short sentences in a row can make your writing choppy. Medium sentences lack the punch of short sentences and the informative power of longer sentences. Meanwhile, long sentences are usually harder to understand than short sentences because they are packed with information that must all be absorbed at once. Because readers can absorb only a few words per glance, longer sentences are also more difficult to skim. Thus, the longer your sentence, the greater the possibility that the reader who skims it will not read enough words to process its full meaning.

By choosing the best sentence length for each communication need and remembering to mix sentence lengths for variety, you'll get your message across while keeping your documents lively and interesting.

Keeping Your Paragraphs Short

Unlike the variety needed in sentence length, the optimum paragraph length is short to medium in most cases. Large blocks of text can be intimidating. Unless you break up your thoughts somehow, you'll end up with a three-page paragraph that's guaranteed to intimidate even the most dedicated reader. Short paragraphs (of 100 words or fewer; this paragraph has 95 words) are easier to read than long ones, and they make your writing look inviting. They also help audiences read more carefully. You can also emphasize an idea by isolating it in a short, forceful paragraph.

> Short paragraphs are easier to read than long ones.

However, don't go overboard with short paragraphs. Be careful to use one-sentence paragraphs only occasionally and only for emphasis. Also, if you need to divide a subject into several pieces in order to keep paragraphs short, be sure to help your readers keep the ideas connected by guiding them with plenty of transitional elements.

Using Lists and Bullets to Clarify and Emphasize

An effective alternative to using conventional sentences is to set off important ideas in a **list**—a series of words, names, or other items. Lists can show the sequence of your ideas, heighten their

> Lists are effective tools for highlighting and simplifying material.

impact visually, and increase the likelihood that a reader will find your key points. In addition, lists provide readers with clues, simplify complex subjects, highlight the main point, break up the page visually, ease the skimming process for busy readers, and give the reader a breather. Consider the difference between the following two approaches to the same information:

Narrative	**List**
Owning your own business has many advantages. One is the ease of establishment. Another advantage is the satisfaction of working for yourself. As a sole proprietor, you also have the advantage of privacy because you do not have to reveal your information or plans to anyone.	Owning your own business has three advantages: • Ease of establishment • Satisfaction of working for yourself • Privacy of information

When creating a list, you can separate items with numbers, letters, or bullets (a general term for any kind of graphical element that precedes each item). Bullets are generally preferred over numbers, unless the list is in some logical sequence or ranking, or specific list items will be referred to later on. The following three steps need to be performed in the order indicated, and the numbers make that clear:

1. Find out how many employees would like on-site day-care facilities.

2. Determine how much space the day-care center would require.

3. Estimate the cost of converting a conference room for the on-site facility.

Lists are easier to locate and read if the entire numbered or bulleted section is set off by a blank line before and after, as the preceding examples demonstrate. Furthermore, when using lists, make sure to introduce them clearly so that people know what they're about to read. One way to introduce lists is to make them a part of the introductory sentence:

The board of directors met to discuss the revised annual budget. To keep expenses in line with declining sales, the directors voted to
• Cut everyone's salary by 10 percent
• Close the employee cafeteria
• Reduce travel expenses

If necessary, add further discussion after the lists to complete your thought. Another way to introduce a list is to precede it with a complete introductory sentence, followed by a colon:

The decline in company profit is attributable to four factors:
• Slower holiday sales
• Increased transportation and fuel costs
• Higher employee wages
• Slower inventory turnover

Regardless of the format you choose, the items in a list should be parallel; that is, they should all use the same grammatical pattern. For example, if one list item begins with a verb, all list items should begin with a verb. If one item is a noun phrase, all should be noun phrases.

Nonparallel List Items	Parallel List Items
• Improve our bottom line	• Improving our bottom line
• Identification of new foreign markets for our products	• Identifying new foreign markets for our products
• Global market strategies	• Developing our global market strategies
• Issues regarding pricing and packaging size	• Resolving pricing and packaging issues

John Hutchison *(far right)* knows that his success depends on clarity in all his business communication. For instance, his sales contracts for Golden State Insurance break out specific clauses in bulleted lists that are easy to locate, read, and understand.

Parallel forms are easier to read and skim. You can create parallelism by repeating the pattern in words, phrases, clauses, or entire sentences (see Table 6–1).

Adding Headings and Subheadings A **heading** is a brief title that tells readers about the content of the section that follows. Headings are similar to the subject line in memos and e-mail correspondence. However, subject lines merely identify the purpose of the memo or e-mail, whereas headings and subheadings also advise the reader about the material included in the section to follow. **Subheadings** are subordinate to headings, indicating subsections with a major section. Headings and subheadings serve these important functions:

- **Organization.** Headings show your reader at a glance how the document is organized. They act as labels to group related paragraphs together and effectively organize your material into short sections.

- **Attention.** Informative, inviting, and in some cases intriguing headings grab the reader's attention, make the text easier to read, and help the reader find the parts he or she needs to read—or skip.

- **Connection.** Using headings and subheadings together helps readers see the relationship between main ideas and subordinate ones so that they can understand your message more easily. Moreover, headings and subheadings visually indicate shifts from one idea to the next.

Informative headings are generally more helpful than descriptive ones.

Headings fall into two categories. **Descriptive headings,** such as "Cost Considerations," identify a topic but do little more. **Informative headings,** such as "A New Way to Cut Costs," put your reader right into the context of your message.

Table 6–1	**ACHIEVING PARALLELISM**	
Method	*Example*
Parallel words	The letter was approved by Clausen, Whittaker, Merlin, and Carlucci.
Parallel phrases	We are gaining market share in supermarkets, in department stores, and in specialty stores.
Parallel clauses	I'd like to discuss the issue after Vicki gives her presentation but before Marvin shows his slides.
Parallel sentences	In 2004 we exported 30 percent of our production. In 2005 we exported 50 percent.

Informative headings guide readers to think in a certain way about the topic. They are also helpful in guiding your work as a writer, especially if written in terms of questions you plan to address in your document. Well-written informative headings are self-contained, which means that readers can read just the headings and subheadings and understand them without reading the rest of the document. For example, "Introduction" conveys little information, whereas the heading "Staffing Shortages in Finance and Accounting Cost the Company $150,000 Last Year" provides a key piece of information and captures the reader's attention. Whatever types of headings you choose, keep them brief, and use parallel construction as you would for an outline, lists, or a series of words.

> Use the same grammatical form for each heading.

Editing for Clarity and Conciseness

Once you've reviewed and revised your message for readability, you'll want to make sure that your message is clear. Perhaps a sentence is so cluttered that readers can't unravel it. Its wording may be so vague that readers can interpret it in several ways. Perhaps pronouns or tenses switch midsentence so that readers lose track of who is talking or when an event took place. Sentence B may not be a logical sequel to sentence A, or an important word may be used incorrectly.[2]

> Clarity is essential to getting your message across accurately and efficiently.

Ask yourself whether your sentences are easy to decipher. Do your paragraphs have clear topic sentences? Are the transitions between ideas obvious? Are your statements simple and direct? A clear sentence is no accident. Few sentences come out exactly right the first time. See Table 6–2 for examples of the following tips:

- **Break up overly long sentences.** Don't connect too many clauses with *and* or *or*. If you find yourself stuck in a long sentence, you're probably trying to make the sentence do more than it can reasonably do, such as expressing two dissimilar thoughts or peppering the reader with too many pieces of supporting evidence at once (did you notice how difficult this long sentence was to read?). You can often clarify your writing style by separating a string of items into individual sentences.

- **Rewrite hedging sentences.** Sometimes you have to write *may* or *seems* to avoid stating a judgment as a fact. However, when you have too many such hedges, you risk coming across as unsure of what you're saying.

> Don't be afraid to present your opinions without qualification.

- **Impose parallelism.** When you have two or more similar ideas to express, make them parallel. Repeating the same grammatical construction shows that the ideas are related, of similar importance, and on the same level of generality. Parallelism is discussed earlier in this chapter, in the section on lists and bullets.

> When you use the same grammatical pattern to express two or more ideas, you show that they are comparable thoughts.

- **Correct dangling modifiers.** Sometimes a modifier is not just an adjective or an adverb but an entire phrase modifying a noun or a verb. Be careful not to leave this type of modifier dangling, with no connection to the subject of the sentence. The first unacceptable example under "Dangling Modifiers" in Table 6–2 implies that the red sports car has both an office and the legs to walk there. The second example shows one frequent cause of dangling modifiers: passive construction.

- **Reword long noun sequences.** When multiple nouns are strung together as modifiers, the resulting sentence can be hard to read. You might be trying too hard to create the desired effect; first see if a single well-chosen word will do the job. If the nouns are all necessary, consider moving one or more to a modifying phrase as shown in Table 6–1. Although you add a few more words, your audience won't have to work as hard to understand the sentence.

- **Replace camouflaged verbs.** Watch for words that end in *-ion, -tion, -ing, -ment, -ant, -ent, -ence, -ance,* and *-ency*. These endings often change verbs into nouns and adjectives, requiring you to add a verb just to get your point across. To prune and enliven your messages, use verbs instead of noun phrases.

- **Clarify sentence structure.** Keep the subject and predicate of a sentence as close together as possible. When the subject and predicate are far apart, readers may

> Subject and predicate should be placed as close together as possible, as should modifiers and the words they modify.

Table 6–2	REVISING FOR CLARITY	
Issues to Review	**Unacceptable**	**Preferable**
OVERLY LONG SENTENCES Taking compound sentences too far	The magazine will be published January 1, and I'd better meet the deadline if I want my article included.	The magazine will be published January 1. I'd better meet the deadline if I want my article included.
HEDGING SENTENCES Overqualifying sentences	I believe that Mr. Johnson's employment record seems to show that he may be capable of handling the position.	Mr. Johnson's employment record shows that he is capable of handling the position.
UNPARALLEL SENTENCES Using dissimilar construction for similar ideas	Mr. Simms had been drenched with rain, bombarded with telephone calls, and his boss shouted at him.	Mr. Sims had been drenched with rain, bombarded with telephone calls, and shouted at by his boss.
	Ms. Reynolds dictated the letter, and next she signed it and left the office.	Ms. Reynolds dictated the letter, signed it, and left the office.
	To waste time and missing deadlines are bad habits.	Wasting time and missing deadlines are bad habits.
	Interviews are a matter of acting confident and to stay relaxed.	Interviews are a matter of acting confident and staying relaxed.
DANGLING MODIFIERS Placing modifiers close to the wrong nouns and verbs	Walking to the office, a red sports car passed her.	A red sports car passed her while she was walking to the office.
	After a three-week slump, we increased sales.	After a three-week slump, sales increased.
LONG NOUN SEQUENCES Stringing too many nouns together	The window sash installation company will give us an estimate on Friday.	The company that installs window sashes will give us an estimate on Friday.
CAMOUFLAGED VERBS Changing verbs and nouns into adjectives	The manager undertook implementation of the rules.	The manager implemented the rules.
	Verification of the shipments occurs weekly.	Shipments are verified weekly.
Changing verbs into nouns	reach a conclusion about	conclude
	make a discovery of	discover
	give consideration to	consider
SENTENCE STRUCTURE Separating subject and predicate	A 10% decline in market share, which resulted from quality problems and an aggressive sales campaign by Armitage, the market leader in the Northeast, was the major problem in 2005.	The major problem in 2005 was a 10% loss of market share, which resulted from both quality problems and an aggressive sales campaign by Armitage, the market leader in the Northeast.
Separating adjectives, adverbs, or prepositional phrases from the words they modify	Our antique desk lends an air of strength and substance with thick legs and large drawers.	With its thick legs and large drawers, our antique desk lends an air of strength and substance.
AWKWARD REFERENCES	The Law Office and the Accounting Office distribute computer supplies for legal secretaries and beginning accountants, respectively.	The Law Office distributes computer supplies for legal secretaries; the Accounting Office distributes those for beginning accountants.
TOO MUCH ENTHUSIASM	We are extremely pleased to offer you a position on our staff of exceptionally skilled and highly educated employees. The work offers extraordinary challenges and a very large salary.	We are pleased to offer you a position on our staff of skilled and well-educated employees. The work offers challenges and an attractive salary.

need to read the sentence twice to figure out who did what. Similarly, adjectives, adverbs, and prepositional phrases usually make the most sense when they're placed as close as possible to the words they modify.

- **Clarify awkward references.** In an effort to save words, business writers sometimes use expressions such as *the above-mentioned, as mentioned above, the aforementioned, the former, the latter,* and *respectively.* These words cause readers to jump from point to point, which hinders effective communication. You'll often be more successful using specific references, even if that means adding a few more words.

- **Moderate your enthusiasm.** An occasional adjective or adverb intensifies and emphasizes your meaning, but too many can degrade your writing and damage your credibility.

Showing enthusiasm for ideas is fine, but be careful not to go so far that you sound unprofessional.

In addition to clarity, readers appreciate conciseness in business messages. The good news is that most first drafts can be cut by as much as 50 percent.[3] By reorganizing your content, improving the readability of your document, and correcting your sentence structure for clarity, you will have already eliminated most of the excess. Now it is time to examine every word you put on paper. As you begin your editing task, simplify, prune, and strive for order. See Table 6–3 for examples of the following tips:

- **Delete unnecessary words and phrases.** To test whether a word or phrase is essential, try the sentence without it. If the meaning doesn't change, leave it out. For instance, *very* can be a useful word to achieve emphasis, but more often it's simply clutter. There's no need to call someone "very methodical." The person is either methodical or not. In addition, avoid the clutter of too many or poorly placed relative pronouns (*who, that, which*). Even articles can be excessive (mostly too many *the*'s). However, well-placed relative pronouns and articles prevent confusion, so make sure you don't obscure the meaning of the sentence by removing these.

Make your documents tighter by removing unnecessary words.

- **Shorten long words and phrases.** Short words are generally more vivid and easier to read than long ones. The idea is to use short, simple words, *not* simple concepts.[4] Plus, by using infinitives in place of some phrases, you not only shorten your sentences but also make them clearer.

- **Eliminate redundancies.** In some word combinations, the words tend to say the same thing. For instance, "visible to the eye" is redundant because *visible* is enough without further clarification; "to the eye" adds nothing.

- **Recast "It is/There are" starters.** If you start a sentence with an indefinite pronoun such as *it* or *there,* odds are the sentence could be shorter.

As you rewrite, concentrate on how each word contributes to an effective sentence and on how that sentence develops a coherent paragraph. Be sure to consider the effect your words will have on readers. Look for opportunities to make the material more interesting through the use of strong, lively words and phrases (as discussed in Chapter 5). For a reminder of the tasks involved in revision, see "Checklist: Revising Business Messages."

Sometimes you'll find that the most difficult problem in a sentence can be solved by simply removing the problem itself. When you come upon a troublesome element, ask yourself, "Do I need it at all?" Possibly not. In fact, you may find that it was giving you so much grief precisely because it was trying to do an unnecessary job.[5] Once you remove the troublesome element, the afflicted sentence will spring to life and breathe normally. Of course, before you delete anything, you'll probably want to keep copies of your current version. Using a word processor, you can

Document Makeover

IMPROVE THIS LETTER
To practice correcting drafts of actual documents, visit your online course or the access-code protected portion of the Companion Website. Click "Document Makeovers," then click Chapter 6. You will find a letter that contains problems and errors relating to what you've learned in this chapter about revising messages. Use the "Final Draft" decision tool to create an improved version of this routine letter. Check the message for organization, readability, clarity, and conciseness.

Table 6–3 REVISING FOR CONCISENESS

Issues to Review	Unacceptable	Preferable
UNNECESSARY WORDS AND PHRASES		
Using wordy phrases	for the sum of	for
	in the event that	if
	prior to the start of	before
	in the near future	soon
	at this point in time	now
	due to the fact that	because
	in view of the fact that	because
	until such time as	when
	with reference to	about
Using too many relative pronouns	Cars that are sold after January will not have a six-month warranty.	Cars sold after January will not have a six-month warranty.
	Employees who are driving to work should park in the underground garage.	Employees driving to work should park in the underground garage.
Using too few relative pronouns	The project manager told the engineers last week the specifications were changed.	The project manager told the engineers last week that the specifications were changed.
		The project manager told the engineers that last week the specifications were changed.
LONG WORDS AND PHRASES		
Using overly long words	During the preceding year, the company accelerated productive operations.	Last year the company sped up operations.
	The action was predicated on the assumption that the company was operating at a financial deficit.	The action was based on the belief that the company was losing money.
Using wordy phrases rather than infinitives	If you want success as a writer, you must work hard.	To be a successful writer, you must work hard.
	He went to the library for the purpose of studying.	He went to the library to study.
	The employer increased salaries so that she could improve morale.	The employer increased salaries to improve morale.
REDUNDANCIES		
Repeating meanings	absolutely complete	complete
	basic fundamentals	fundamentals
	follows after	follows
	free and clear	free
	refer back	refer
	repeat again	repeat
	collect together	collect
	future plans	plans
	return back	return
	important essentials	essentials
	end result	result
	actual truth	truth
	final outcome	outcome
	uniquely unusual	unique
	surrounded on all sides	surrounded
Using double modifiers	modern, up-to-date equipment	modern equipment
IT IS/THERE ARE STARTERS Starting sentences with *it* or *there*	It would be appreciated if you would sign the lease today.	Please sign the lease today.
	There are five employees in this division who were late to work today.	Five employees in this division were late to work today.

✓ CHECKLIST: Revising Business Messages

A. Evaluate content, organization, style, and tone

✓ Make sure the information is accurate, relevant, and sufficient.
✓ Check that all necessary points appear in logical order.
✓ Verify that you present enough support to make the main idea convincing and interesting.
✓ Be sure the beginning and ending are effective.
✓ Make sure you've achieved the right tone.

B. Review for readability

✓ Consider using a readability index, being sure to interpret the answer carefully.
✓ Use a mix of short and long sentences.
✓ Keep paragraphs short.
✓ Use bulleted and numbered lists to emphasize key points.
✓ Make the document easy to scan with headings and subheadings.

C. Edit for clarity

✓ Break up overly long sentences and rewrite hedging sentences.
✓ Impose parallelism to simplify reading.
✓ Correct dangling modifiers.
✓ Reword long noun sequences and replace camouflaged verbs.
✓ Clarify sentence structure and awkward references.
✓ Moderate your enthusiasm to maintain a professional tone.

D. Edit for conciseness

✓ Delete unnecessary words and phrases.
✓ Shorten long words and phrases.
✓ Eliminate redundancies.
✓ Rewrite sentences that start with "It is" or "There are."

save the original and all revisions of your documents either for long-term reference or to rely on the "undo" function while you're editing.

Using Technology to Revise Your Message

When it's time to revise and polish your message, your word processor can help you add, delete, and move text with functions such as *cut and paste* (taking a block of text out of one section of a document and pasting it in somewhere else) and *search and replace* (tracking down words or phrases and changing them if you need to). Be careful using this feature though; choosing the "replace all" option can result in some unintended errors. For example, finding *power* and replacing all occurrences with *strength* will also change the word *powerful* to *strengthful*.

Software tools such as *revision marks* and *commenting* keep track of proposed editing changes electronically and provide a history of a document's revisions. In Microsoft Word, the revisions appear in a different font color than the original text (see Figure 6–4), giving you a chance to review changes before accepting or rejecting them. Adobe Acrobat lets you attach notes to PDF files (see Figure 6–5). Revision marks and commenting features are also a great way to keep track of editing changes made by team members. Programs such as Microsoft Word let you choose different colors for different reviewers as well, so you can keep everyone's comments separate.

In addition to the many revision tools, four software functions can help bring out the best in your documents. First, a *spell checker* compares your document with an electronic dictionary, highlights unrecognized words, and suggests correct spellings. Spell checkers are a wonderful way to weed major typos out of your documents, but they are no substitute for good spelling skills. For example, if you use *their* when you mean to use *there*, your spell checker won't notice, because *their* is spelled correctly. If you're in a hurry and accidentally omit the *p* at the end of *top*, your spell checker will read *to* as correct. Or if you mistakenly type a semicolon instead of *p*, your spell checker will read *to;* as a correctly spelled word. Plus, some of the "errors" that the spell checker indicates may actually be proper names, technical words, words that you misspelled on purpose, or simply words that weren't included in the spell checker's

Spell checkers, grammar checkers, and computerized thesauruses can all help with the revision process, but they can't take the place of good writing and editing skills.

FIGURE 6–4
Revision Marks

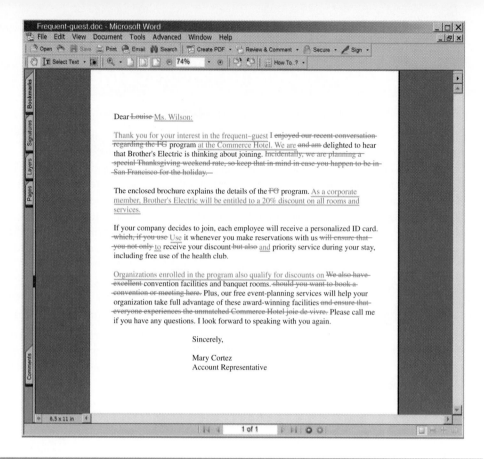

FIGURE 6–5
PDF File with Comments

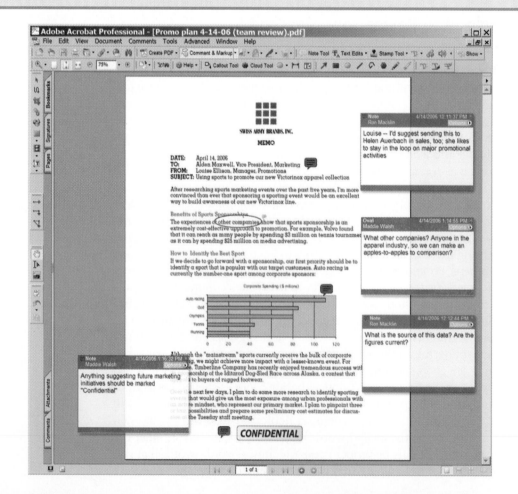

dictionary. It's up to you to decide whether each flagged word should be corrected or left alone, and it's up to you to find the errors that your spell checker has overlooked.

Second, a computer *thesaurus* gives you alternative words, just as a printed thesaurus does. A computer thesaurus is much faster and lets you try multiple alternatives in just a few seconds to see which works best. The best uses of any thesaurus, printed or computerized, are to find fresh, interesting words when you've been using the same word too many times and to find the word that most accurately conveys your intended meaning. In contrast, don't fall into the temptation of using your thesaurus to find impressive words to spice up your writing; if you're not comfortable using the word, it won't sound natural in your documents.

Third, the *grammar checker* tries to do for your grammar what a spell checker does for your spelling. Because the program doesn't have a clue about what you're trying to say, it can't tell whether you've said it correctly. Moreover, even if you've used all the rules correctly, a grammar checker still can't tell whether your document communicates clearly. However, grammar checkers can perform some helpful review tasks (such as pointing out noun-verb agreement problems) and highlighting items you should consider changing, such as passive voice, long sentences, and words that tend to be misused or overused.

Fourth, a *style checker* can also monitor your word and sentence choices and suggest alternatives that might produce more effective writing. For instance, the style checking options in Microsoft Word range from basic issues, such as spelling out numbers and using contractions, to more subjective matters, such as sentence structure and the use of technical terminology.

By all means, use any software that you find helpful when revising your documents. Just remember that it's unwise to rely on them to do all your revision work, and you're responsible for the final product.

PRODUCING YOUR MESSAGE

Now it's time to put your hard work on display. The *production quality* of your message—the total effect of page design, graphical elements, typography, paper, and so on—plays an important role in its effectiveness. A polished, inviting design not only makes your document easier to read but also conveys a sense of professionalism and importance.[6] When producing your message, look for effective ways to enhance your message with carefully chosen graphics as well as sound, video, and hypertext links for electronic documents and online material.

> The quality of your document design affects both readability and audience perceptions.

Adding Graphics, Sound, Video, and Hypertext

Fortunately, today's word processors and other software tools make it easy to produce impressive documents that enliven your text with full-color pictures, sound and video recordings, and hypertext links. The software for creating business visuals falls into two basic groups: *Presentation software,* which helps you create overhead transparencies and computerized slide shows (electronic presentations are discussed in Chapter 13), and *graphics software,* which ranges from basic tools that help you create simple business diagrams to the comprehensive tools preferred by artists and graphic designers. You can create graphics yourself, use *clip art* (collections of uncopyrighted images), or scan in drawings or photographs.

> Take advantage of your word processor's ability to incorporate other communication elements.

Adding sound bites or video clips to electronic documents is an exciting new way to get your message across. Several systems let you record brief messages and attach them to particular places in a document. The reader then clicks on a speaker icon to play each comment, such as "Please convert this paragraph to a bulleted list."

You can also use hypertext markup language (HTML) to insert hyperlinks into your message. Readers can easily jump from one document to another by clicking on such a link. They can go directly to a website, jump to another section of your document, or go to a different document altogether. Suppose you're preparing a report on this year's budget. Rather than include pages and pages of budget details from prior years, you can connect to them using hyperlinks. If readers need to access details from prior years, they simply click on the appropriate links. By using hyperlinks, you can customize your documents to meet the individual information needs of your readers—just as you can on a webpage. Of course, you'll have to make sure that the file (or the software program used to open that file) is included with your electronic document, installed on the recipient's computer, or accessible via a network connection.

Designing for Readability

Design affects the impression your message makes.

The design of your document affects readability in two important ways. First, if done carefully, the various elements of visual design can improve the effectiveness of your message. If done poorly, design elements can act as barriers, blocking your communi-

FIGURE 6–6
Ineffective Document Design

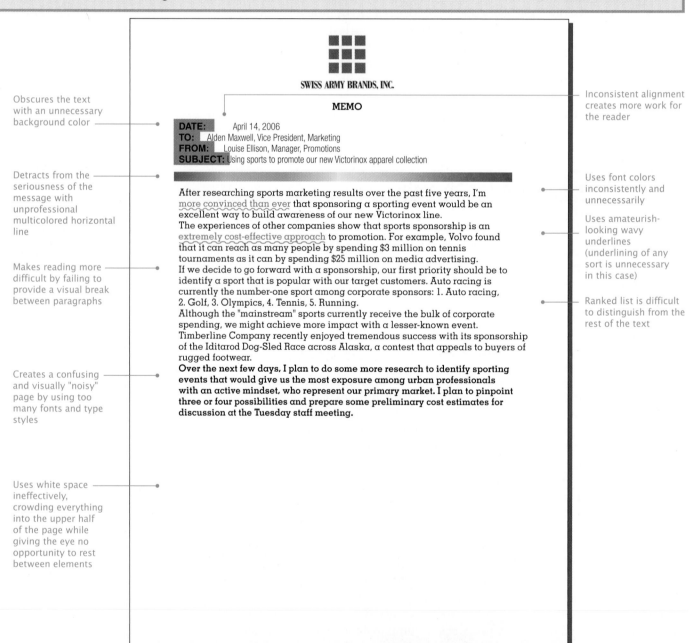

SWISS ARMY BRANDS, INC.

MEMO

DATE: April 14, 2006
TO: Alden Maxwell, Vice President, Marketing
FROM: Louise Ellison, Manager, Promotions
SUBJECT: Using sports to promote our new Victorinox apparel collection

After researching sports marketing results over the past five years, I'm more convinced than ever that sponsoring a sporting event would be an excellent way to build awareness of our new Victorinox line.
The experiences of other companies show that sports sponsorship is an extremely cost-effective approach to promotion. For example, Volvo found that it can reach as many people by spending $3 million on tennis tournaments as it can by spending $25 million on media advertising.
If we decide to go forward with a sponsorship, our first priority should be to identify a sport that is popular with our target customers. Auto racing is currently the number-one sport among corporate sponsors: 1. Auto racing, 2. Golf, 3. Olympics, 4. Tennis, 5. Running.
Although the "mainstream" sports currently receive the bulk of corporate spending, we might achieve more impact with a lesser-known event. Timberline Company recently enjoyed tremendous success with its sponsorship of the Iditarod Dog-Sled Race across Alaska, a contest that appeals to buyers of rugged footwear.
Over the next few days, I plan to do some more research to identify sporting events that would give us the most exposure among urban professionals with an active mindset, who represent our primary market. I plan to pinpoint three or four possibilities and prepare some preliminary cost estimates for discussion at the Tuesday staff meeting.

Obscures the text with an unnecessary background color

Detracts from the seriousness of the message with unprofessional multicolored horizontal line

Makes reading more difficult by failing to provide a visual break between paragraphs

Creates a confusing and visually "noisy" page by using too many fonts and type styles

Uses white space ineffectively, crowding everything into the upper half of the page while giving the eye no opportunity to rest between elements

Inconsistent alignment creates more work for the reader

Uses font colors inconsistently and unnecessarily

Uses amateurish-looking wavy underlines (underlining of any sort is unnecessary in this case)

Ranked list is difficult to distinguish from the rest of the text cation. For example, people age 65 and over are the fastest-growing segment of online consumers in the United States, but many websites don't take into account the natural changes that occur in eyesight as people age. Many older people find it difficult to read the small type that is common on websites—and many websites make the even greater mistake of preventing viewers from enlarging type size in their browsers.[7] Second, the visual design itself sends a nonverbal message to the audience, influencing their perceptions of the communication before they read a single word. When the editors of *Rolling Stone* wanted to attract an audience that was less interested in in-depth journalism, for instance, they changed the appearance of the magazine to make it look less serious and intimidating.

Compare the two memos shown in Figures 6–6 and 6–7. They contain virtually the same information but send dramatically different messages to the reader. Figure 6–6 is

FIGURE 6–7
Effective Document Design

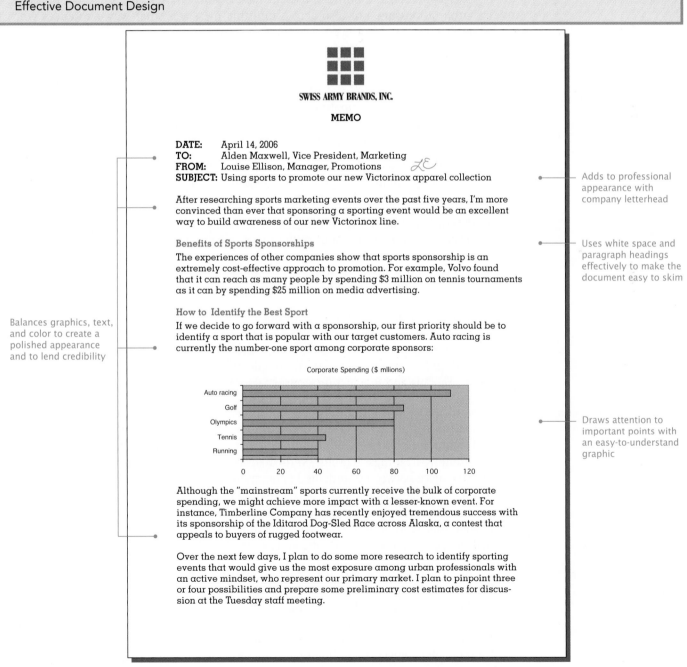

Adds to professional appearance with company letterhead

Uses white space and paragraph headings effectively to make the document easy to skim

Balances graphics, text, and color to create a polished appearance and to lend credibility

Draws attention to important points with an easy-to-understand graphic crowded, uninviting, and difficult to read. The amateurish use of color is distracting. In contrast, Figure 6–7 is open, inviting, and easy to either read entirely or scan quickly. This section explains why the two designs produce such different results and how you can improve the design of your documents.

Effective design helps you establish the tone of your document and helps guide your readers through your message. To achieve an effective design, pay careful attention to the following design elements:

For effective design, pay attention to
- Consistency
- Balance
- Restraint
- Detail

- **Consistency.** Throughout each message, be consistent in your use of margins, typeface, type size, and spacing (such as in paragraph indents, between columns, and around photographs). Figure 6–6 violates this rule in several ways, starting with too many fonts (three in the heading alone, all different from the font used for the text). It also uses too many type styles (screens, wavy underlines, different colors, regular and bold) and uses them inconsistently as well. Also be consistent when using recurring design elements, such as vertical lines, columns, and borders. In many cases, you'll want to be consistent not only within a message but also across multiple messages; that way, audiences who receive messages from you recognize your documents and know what to expect.

- **Balance.** To create a pleasing design, balance the space devoted to text, artwork, and white space. Balance is a subjective issue. One document may have a formal, rigid design in which the various elements are placed in a grid pattern, while another has a less formal design in which elements flow more freely across the page—and both could be in balance. However, the design in Figure 6–6 is out of balance and much less effective than the formal design used in Figure 6–7.

- **Restraint.** Strive for simplicity in design. Don't clutter your message with too many design elements, too much highlighting, too many colors, or too many decorative touches. Let "simpler" and "fewer" be your guiding concepts.

- **Detail.** Pay attention to details that affect your design and thus your message. For instance, headings and subheadings that appear at the bottom of a column or a page can annoy readers when the promised information doesn't appear until the next column or page. Also, narrow columns with too much space between words can be distracting.

If you will be designing a lot of documents that go beyond simple memos and reports, consider taking a course in page layout or graphic design to make the most of your creative efforts. However, even without special training, you can make your printed and electronic messages more effective by understanding the use of white space, margins and line justification, typefaces, and type styles.

White space separates elements in a document and helps guide the reader's eye.

White Space   Any space free of text or artwork is considered **white space** (note that "white space" isn't necessarily white). These unused areas provide visual contrast and important resting points for your readers. White space includes the open area surrounding headings, margins, vertical space between columns, paragraph indents or extra space between unindented paragraphs, and horizontal space between lines of text. One of the reasons Figure 6–6 is so hard to read is the lack of white space; readers have to work to separate the various pieces of the document. To increase the chance that readers will read your documents, be generous with white space; it makes pages feel less intimidating and easier to read.[8]

Most business documents use a flush left margin and a ragged right margin.

Margins and Justification   Margins define the space around your text and between text columns. They're influenced by the way you place lines of type, which can be set (1) justified (flush on the left and flush on the right), (2) flush left with a ragged right margin, (3) flush right with a ragged left margin, or (4) centered. Justified type "darkens" your message's appearance, because the uniform line lengths lack the white space created by ragged margins. It also tends to make your message look more formal and less like a personalized message. Justified type is often considered more difficult to read, because large gaps can appear between words and because more words are hyphenated (excessive hyphenation is distracting and hard to follow). Even so, many magazines, newspapers, and books use justified type because it can accommodate more text in a given space. Moreover, in most professionally published documents such as these, character spacing and word spacing are adjusted to eliminate problems caused by justification.

Flush-left, ragged-right type "lightens" your message's appearance. It gives a document an informal, contemporary feeling of openness. Spacing between words is the same, and only long words that fall at the ends of lines are hyphenated.

Centered type is rarely used for text paragraphs but is commonly used for headings and subheadings. Flush-right, ragged-left type is rarely used in business documents.

Typefaces   **Typeface** refers to the physical design of letters, numbers, and other text characters. Most computers offer innumerable choices of fonts or typefaces. Each typeface influences the tone of your message, making it look authoritative or friendly, businesslike or casual, classic or modern, and so on (see Table 6–4). Be sure to choose fonts that are appropriate for your message.

Serif typefaces have small crosslines (called serifs) at the ends of each letter stroke. Serif faces such as Times Roman are commonly used for text; they can look busy and cluttered when set in large sizes for headings or other display treatments. Typefaces with rounded serifs can look friendly; those with squared serifs can look official.

Sans serif typefaces have no serifs. Faces such as Helvetica and Arial are ideal for display treatments that use larger type. Sans serif faces can be difficult to read in long blocks of text. They look best when surrounded by plenty of white space—as in headings or in widely spaced lines of text.

> Serif typefaces are commonly used for text; sans serif typefaces are commonly used for headings.

For most documents, you shouldn't need to use more than two typefaces, although if you want to make captions or other text elements stand out, you can use another font.[9] You can't go too far wrong with a sans serif typeface (such as Arial) for heads and subheads, and a serif typeface (such as Times New Roman) for text and captions. Using too many typefaces clutters the document and can produce an amateurish look (as seen in Figure 6–6).

Type Styles   *Type style* refers to any modification that lends contrast or emphasis to type, including boldface, italic, underlining, and other highlighting and decorative styles. Using boldface type for subheads breaks up long expanses of text. You can also boldface isolated words in the middle of a text block to draw more attention to them. However, if you set too many words in boldface, you might create a "checkerboard" appearance within a paragraph, and you will darken the appearance of your entire message, making it look heavy and uninviting.

TYPEFACE PERSONALITIES: SERIOUS TO CASUAL TO PLAYFUL — Table 6–4

Serif Typefaces (Best for text)	Sans Serif Typefaces (Best for headlines; some work well for text)	Specialty Typefaces (For decorative purposes only)
Bookman Old Style	Arial	ANNA
Century Schoolbook	Eras Bold	Bauhaus
Courier	Franklin Gothic Book	Edwardian
Garamond	Frutiger	Lucida Handwriting
Rockwell	Gill Sans	Old English
Times Roman	Tekton	STENCIL

Use italic type for emphasis. Although italics are sometimes used when irony or humor is intended, quotation marks are usually best for that purpose. Italics can also be used to set off a quote and are often used in captions. Boldfaced type and italics are most effective when reserved for key words—those that help readers understand the main point of the text. A good example of using boldface type effectively is found in the document-revision tips listed under the heading "Editing for Clarity and Conciseness" on pages 179–182 of this chapter. Here the boldfaced type draws attention to the key tips, followed by a short, regular-typeface explanation of each tip.

As a general rule, avoid using any style in a way that slows your audience's progress through the message. For instance, underlining or using all uppercase letters can interfere with your reader's ability to recognize the shapes of words, improperly placed boldface or italicized type can slow down your reader, and shadowed or outlined type can seriously hinder legibility.

Make sure the size of your type is proportionate to the importance of your message and the space allotted. For most business messages, use a type size of 10 to 12 points for regular text, and 12 to 18 points for headings and subheadings (a point is approximately 1/72 of an inch). Resist the temptation to reduce your type size to squeeze in text or to enlarge it to fill up space. Type that is too small is hard to read, whereas extra-large type looks unprofessional.

> Avoid using any type style that inhibits your audience's ability to read your messages.

Using Technology to Produce Your Message

The production tools you'll have at your disposal might vary widely, depending on the software and systems you're using. Some IM and e-mail systems offer limited formatting and production capabilities, whereas most word processors now offer some capabilities that rival professional publishing software for many day-to-day business needs. Desktop publishing software such as Quark XPress, Adobe InDesign, and Microsoft Publisher go beyond word processing with more advanced layout capabilities that are designed to accommodate photos, technical drawings, and other elements. (Quark and InDesign are used mainly by design professionals.) Microsoft PowerPoint is the most widely used software for electronic presentations, and it offers a wide range of tools for formatting and displaying your message. Companies with large websites frequently have web publishing systems that make it easy to produce web pages with graphics, animation, and other eye-catching features. Multimedia production tools such as Microsoft Producer let you combine slides, audio commentary, video clips, and other features into computer-based presentations that once cost thousands of dollars to create.

> Your word processor will be your primary communication tool; learn to use it effectively.

However, most of your message production work is likely to be done with a word processor such as Microsoft Word. If you're not already familiar with the ins and outs of your software, a few hours of exploration on your own or an introductory training course can dramatically improve the production quality of your documents. At a minimum, you'll benefit from being proficient with the following features:

- **Templates and stylesheets.** As Chapter 5 noted, you can save a tremendous amount of time by using templates (which preset various aspects of page design such as margins) and stylesheets (which standardize formatting decisions for various headings, subheadings, paragraphs, captions, and so forth). Many companies provide templates and stylesheets to ensure a consistent look and feel for all company documents, thus relieving employees from making many of the organizational and formatting decisions discussed throughout this text.

- **Page setup.** Use page setup to control margins, orientation (*portrait* is vertical; *landscape* is horizontal), and the location of *headers* (text and graphics that repeat at the top of every page) and *footers* (similar to headers but at the bottom of the page). Use these controls to ensure adequate white space in your documents.

- **Column formatting.** Most business documents use a single column of text per page, but multiple columns can be an attractive format for documents such as newsletters. Columns are also a handy way to format long lists.

- **Paragraph formatting.** Take advantage of the various paragraph formatting controls to enhance the look of your documents. You can offset quotations by increasing margin width around a single paragraph, subtly compress line spacing to fit a document on a single page, or use hanging indents to offset the first line of a paragraph. If you use your word processor only as a glorified typewriter—simply hitting the Enter key at the end of each line or hitting Enter multiple times to put space between lines or paragraphs—you miss out on some of the most powerful features a word processor has to offer.

Paragraph formatting gives you greater control over the look of your documents.

- **Font formatting.** In addition to typeface selection and the basics of bold, italics, and underlining, your word processor probably offers a way to expand or compress text horizontally. This feature can be a lifesaver, for instance, when you need to fit a headline on a single line. However, use this expand/compress feature carefully, or it can produce amateurish results. As a general rule, avoid the "special font effects" your word processor might offer, such as blinking, sparkling, or shimmering text. They might be entertaining but they're out of place in any business document.

- **Numbered and bulleted lists.** Let your word processor do the busywork of formatting numbered and bulleted lists, too. It can also automatically renumber lists when you add or remove items, saving you the embarrassment of misnumbered lists.

- **Tables.** Tables are a great way to display any information that lends itself to rows and columns: calendars, numerical data, comparisons, and so on. Use paragraph and font formatting thoughtfully within tables for the best look.

- **Pictures, text boxes, and objects.** Your word processor probably lets you insert a wide variety of *pictures* (using one of the industry-standard formats such as JPEG or GIF). *Text boxes* are small blocks of text that stand apart from the main text (great for captions, callouts, margin notes, and so on). *Objects* can be anything from a spreadsheet to a sound clip to an engineering drawing. Used carefully, all these elements can enhance your documents.

Even though you may need a few hours and some practice to become proficient at using all these features, your time will be well spent. By improving the appearance of your documents, you improve your readers' impressions of you.

PROOFREADING YOUR MESSAGE

Imagine that you're a quality inspector for a car company. As each car rolls off the assembly line, you make sure the engine runs properly, the doors close tightly, the paint shines to glossy perfection, and so on. All the work is supposedly final, but you look closely just in case. Your company's reputation is at stake, and you don't want to let a faulty product out the door. Think of proofreading as the quality inspection stage for your documents, as your last chance to make sure that your document is ready to carry your message—and your reputation—to the intended audience. (Strictly speaking, *proofreading* is the process of inspecting a printed piece to make sure that all necessary corrections have been made, but you can benefit by approaching proofreading as an overall quality-assurance review.)

Your credibility is affected by your attention to the details of mechanics and form.

Look for two types of problems: (1) undetected mistakes from the writing, design, and layout stages and (2) mistakes that crept in during production. For the first category, you can review format and layout guidelines in Appendix A on page A-1 and brush up on writing basics with "Handbook of Grammar, Mechanics, and Usage" on page H-1. The second category can include anything from computer glitches such as missing fonts or misaligned page elements to problems with the ink used in printing. Be particularly vigilant with complex documents and complex production processes that involve teams of people and multiple computers; strange things can happen as

The types of details to look for when proofreading include language errors, missing material, design errors, and typographical errors.

✓ CHECKLIST: Proofing Business Messages

A. Look for writing errors

✓ Typographical mistakes
✓ Misspelled words
✓ Grammatical errors
✓ Punctuation mistakes

B. Look for missing elements

✓ Missing text sections
✓ Missing exhibits (drawings, tables, photographs, charts, graphs, and so on)
✓ Missing source notes, copyright notices, or other reference items

C. Look for design and formatting mistakes

✓ Incorrect or inconsistent font selections
✓ Column sizing, spacing, and alignment
✓ Margins
✓ Special characters
✓ Clumsy line and page breaks
✓ Page numbers
✓ Page headers and footers
✓ Adherence to company standards

files move from computer to computer, especially when lots of graphics and different fonts are involved. See "Checklist: Proofing Business Messages" for a handy list of items to review during proofing.

Far from being a casual scan up and down the page (or screen, for online material), proofreading should be a methodical procedure in which you look for specific problems that might occur. Start by reviewing the advice in "Sharpening Your Career Skills: Proofread Like a Pro to Create Perfect Documents." You might also find it helpful to create a checklist of items to review; this can be a handy tool whenever you need to review one of your own documents or you're asked to review someone else's work.

Plan to spend more time proofing documents that are long, complex, and important.

The amount of time you need to spend on proofing depends on both the length and complexity of the document and the situation. A typo in a memo to your team might not be a big deal, but a typo in a financial report or a medical file certainly could be serious. As with every task in the writing process, practice helps—you become not only more familiar with what errors to look for but also more skilled in identifying those errors.

DISTRIBUTING YOUR MESSAGE

With the production finished, you're ready to distribute the message. As with every other aspect of business communication, your options for distribution multiply with every advance in technology. In some cases, the choice is obvious: just hit the Send button in your e-mail program, and your message is on its way. In other cases, such as when you have a 100-page report with full-color graphics or a multimedia presentation that is too big to e-mail, you'll need to plan the distribution carefully so that your message is received by everyone who needs it and only those who need it. When planning your distribution, consider the following factors:

Consider cost, convenience, time, security, and privacy when choosing a distribution method.

- **Cost.** Cost won't be a concern for most messages, but for lengthy reports or multimedia production, it might well be. Printing, binding, and delivering reports can be an expensive proposition, so weigh the cost versus the benefits before you decide. If you're trying to land a million-dollar client, spending $1,000 on presentation materials could be a wise investment.

- **Convenience.** How much work is involved for you and your audience? Although it's easy to attach a document to an e-mail message, things might not be so simple for the people on the other end. They may not have access to a printer, might be accessing your message from a slow dial-up connection in a hotel, or might not have the software needed to open your file. If you're sending large files as IM or e-mail attachments, consider a file compression utility such as WinZip or StuffIt to shrink the file first. For extremely large files, see whether your audience would prefer a CD-ROM instead.

SHARPENING YOUR CAREER SKILLS

Proofread Like a Pro to Create Perfect Documents

Before you click on "Send" or tote that stack of reports off to the shipping department, make sure the document represents the best possible work you can do. Your colleagues will usually overlook errors in everyday e-mails, but higher-profile mistakes in messages to outside audiences can damage your company and hinder your career.

Use these techniques from professional proofreaders to help ensure high-quality output:

- **Multiple passes.** Go through the document several times, focusing on a different aspect each time. The first pass might be to look for omissions and errors in content; the second pass might be to check for typographical, grammatical, and spelling errors; and a final pass could be for layout, spacing, alignment, colors, page numbers, margins, and other design features.

- **Perceptual tricks.** You've probably experienced the frustration of reading over something a dozen times and still missing an obvious error that was staring you right in the face. This happens because your brain has developed a wonderful skill of subconsciously supplying missing pieces and correcting mistakes when it "knows" what is supposed to be on the page. To keep your brain from tricking you, you need to trick it by changing the way you process the visual information. Try (1) reading each page backward, from the bottom to the top; (2) placing your finger under each word and reading it silently; (3) making a slit in a sheet of paper that reveals only one line of type at a time; and (4) reading the document aloud and pronouncing each word carefully.

- **High-priority items.** Double-check the spelling of names and the accuracy of dates, addresses, and any number that could cause grief if incorrect (such as telling a potential employer that you'd be happy to work for $5,000 a year when you meant to say $50,000).

- **Distance.** If possible, don't proofread immediately after finishing the document; let your brain wander off to new topics, then come back fresh later on.

- **Vigilance.** Avoid reading large amounts of material in one sitting, and try not to proofread when you're tired.

- **Focus.** Concentrate on what you're doing. Try to block out distractions, and focus as completely as possible on your proofreading task.

- **Caution.** Take your time. Quick proofreading is not careful proofreading.

CAREER APPLICATIONS

1. Why is it so valuable to have other people proofread your documents?

2. Proofread the following sentence:

   aplication of thse methods in stores in San Deigo nd Cinncinati have resultted in a 30 drop in roberies an a 50 precent decling in violnce there, acording ot thedevelpers if the securty sytem, Hanover brothrs, Inc.

- **Time.** How soon does the message need to reach the audience? Don't waste money on overnight delivery if the recipient won't read the report for a week.

- **Security and privacy.** The convenience offered by IM, e-mail, blogs, and other technologies needs to be weighed against security and privacy concerns. For the most sensitive documents, your company will probably restrict both the people who can receive the documents as well as the means you can use to distribute them. In addition, most computer users are wary of opening attachments these days. Instead of sending Word files (which might be vulnerable to macro viruses and other risks), consider using Adobe Acrobat to convert your documents to PDF files.

Distribution technologies continue to advance, so be on the lookout for new ways to put your messages in the hands of your audience. For example, blogs (see Chapter 5) offer an easy way to publish running commentaries on virtually any subject. *Fast Company* magazine features a blog on its website that gives company staff a forum for sharing ideas and information that either don't make it into the magazine itself or appear in between the monthly publication schedule. (Go to **www.fastcompany.com**, and click on "blog" in the top navigation bar.) Editor-in-Chief John A. Byrne says the blog lets *Fast Company* respond to fast-breaking news and help involve readers in an ongoing discussion of important issues.

Many websites and blogs now offer *really simple syndication (RSS)*, a means to automatically retrieve new content via a software program known as a news aggregator. RSS-enabled websites make it easy for audiences to collect information they want without repeatedly visiting favorite blogs or subscribing to multiple e-mail newsletters and thus encountering the rampant spam problem associated with e-mail.[10] Technologies such as these can help you deliver the information your audiences want in ways that are most convenient and appealing to them. To learn more about the possibilities of blogging and RSS feeds, explore the following sites:

- Blogdex (http://blogdex.media.mit.edu)
- Blogdigger (www.blogdigger.com)
- BlogStreet (www.blogstreet.com)
- Feedster (www.feedster.com)
- Blogger (www.blogger.com)

On the Job

SOLVING COMMUNICATION DILEMMAS AT ROLLING STONE

In addition to *Rolling Stone*, Wenner Media also publishes *Men's Journal* and (through a joint venture with Disney) *US Weekly*. After several years on the staff of *Rolling Stone*, your hard work has been rewarded by a promotion to director of new projects. Jann Wenner has asked you to investigate and pursue new publishing opportunities in both print and electronic media. Use the skills you've developed so far to resolve these communication situations.

1. The popularity of extreme sports such as skysurfing, mountain biking, and free diving continues to grow. Not surprisingly, advertisers have jumped on the opportunity to reach enthusiastic fans, which in turn creates demand for publications that cater to this audience. Which of the following sentences is the best way to summarize this opportunity?

   a. In just a few short years, "extreme sports" has developed into an extremely broad category, encompassing several dozen outdoor activities, all of which center around feats of agility in the face of danger.
   b. The "extreme sports" category now encompasses several dozen events with a total fan base of at least 20 million people worldwide.
   c. The "extreme sports" category now encompasses several dozen events with a total fan base of at least 20 million people worldwide, and advertisers are clamoring for more media vehicles to reach this audience.
   d. We're going to be extremely sorry if we don't get into extreme sports.

2. Like all executives, Jann Wenner is extremely busy, with limited time to devote to reading reports and other business documents. You've learned that effective headings and subheadings are a great way to get your points across, even if Wenner or other readers do nothing more than skim through one of your reports. Which of the following is the most effective subheading that goes into detail about the extreme sports fan base?

   a. Growing to Extremes: the Explosion of Extreme Sports
   b. The Extreme Sports Fan Base: 20 Million and Growing
   c. Traditional Sports Lack Appeal for Many Younger Sports Fans
   d. The Extreme Opportunity in Extreme Sports Publishing

3. You've been discussing the extreme sports magazine concept with media buyers (the people who purchase advertising space on behalf of their clients) in several advertising agencies. Their feedback is encouraging, but they pepper you with questions. One person asked whether the new magazine would have the style and tone of a conventional sports magazine or the hipper, less-formal style of *Rolling Stone*. For your reply by e-mail, which of the following sentences provides the clearest answer?

   a. *Rolling Stone* became a cultural icon precisely because Jann Wenner rejected conventional publishing ideology in the pursuit of his own iconoclastic vision of being the voice of a new generation and this same attitude would drive the personality of the new publication devoted to extreme sports.
   b. Extreme sports = extreme attitude.
   c. An extreme sports magazine published by Wenner Media would reflect the same unconventional attitude and no-holds-barred journalism that made *Rolling Stone* the voice of a new generation.
   d. Launching a magazine devoted to extreme sports would reflect the same out-of-the-box visionary thinking that made *Rolling Stone* the voice of its generation.

4. On your recommendation, Wenner has decided to launch the extreme sports magazine. As soon as word of this gets out, several editors and writers from *Rolling Stone*, *Men's Journal*, and *Us Weekly* send you e-mails

inquiring about working on the new publication. Although you won't be in charge of hiring, you do have definite ideas about the qualifications that should be established for writers and editors when hiring begins in several months. You decide to post a short message on the company's intranet to let people know what sort of talent the new magazine should look for. Which of these sentences is the best way to summarize what you consider to be the two most important criteria—experience in extreme sports and the ability to convey that excitement to readers?

a. Experience in a variety of extreme sports, along with the ability to generate excitement about them through superior writing and editing skills—these are the qualities that should be considered paramount when the time comes to begin hiring

the writing and editing staff for the new magazine, which will focus on extreme sports.

b. The new magazine, which is intended to focus on extreme sports, will need writers and editors who have participated in a variety of extreme sports themselves and who have the journalistic skills needed to convey the excitement of extreme sports from an insider's perspective.

c. The new extreme sports magazine will need writers and editors who have participated in a variety of these sports and have the journalistic skills needed to convey the excitement of these sports from an insider's perspective.

d. The new extreme sports magazine will need writers and editors with hands-on experience and exciting writing skills.

Learning Objectives Checkup

Assess your understanding of the principles in this chapter by reading each learning objective and studying the accompanying exercises. For fill-in items, write the missing text in the blank provided; for multiple choice items, circle the letter of the correct answer. You can check your responses against the answer key on page AK-1.

Objective 6.1: Discuss the value of careful revision, and list the main tasks involved in completing a business message.

1. Which of these is the most important reason why you should take care to revise messages before sending them?
   a. Revising shows your audience how hard you work.
   b. Revising lowers the word count.
   c. Revising makes it cheaper to e-mail messages.
   d. Revising can usually make your messages more successful.

2. Which of the following is *not* one of the main tasks involved in completing a business message?
   a. Drafting the message
   b. Revising the message
   c. Producing the message
   d. Proofreading the message

Objective 6.2: List four writing techniques you can use to improve the readability of your messages.

3. Regarding sentence length, the best approach for business messages is to
   a. Keep all sentences as short as possible
   b. Make most of your sentences long, since you will usually have complex information to impart
   c. Vary the length of your sentences
   d. Aim for an average sentence length of 35 words

4. Regarding paragraph length, the best approach for business messages is to
   a. Keep paragraphs short
   b. Make most of your paragraphs long, since that is standard practice in business writing
   c. Make most of your paragraphs one sentence in length

d. Aim for an average paragraph length of 200 words

5. Regarding the use of lists, the best approach for business messages is to
   a. Avoid using lists except where absolutely necessary
   b. Make sure listed items are in parallel form
   c. Use numbered lists rather than bulleted ones
   d. Do all of the above

6. Which of the following is *not* an informative heading?
   a. Why We Need a New Distributor
   b. Five Challenges Facing Today's Distributors
   c. Distributors Are a Better Choice for Us Than Wholesalers
   d. Distributor Choices

Objective 6.3: Describe the steps you can take to improve the clarity of your writing.

7. Which of the following sentences contains hedging words?
   a. It appears that we may have a problem completing the project by May 20.
   b. There is a possibility that the project might be done by May 20.
   c. It seems that the project could possibly miss its completion date of May 20.
   d. All of the above contain hedging words.

8. Which of the following sentences lacks parallelism?
   a. Consumers can download stock research, electronically file their tax returns, create a portfolio, or choose from an array of recommended mutual funds.
   b. Consumers can download stock research, can electronically file their tax returns, create a portfolio, or they can choose from an array of recommended mutual funds.
   c. Consumers can download stock research, can electronically file their tax returns, can create a portfolio, or can choose from an array of recommended mutual funds.
   d. Consumers can download stock research, they can electronically file their tax returns, they can create a portfolio, or they can choose from an array of recommended mutual funds.

9. Which of the following sentences does *not* have a dangling modifier?
   a. Lacking brand recognition, some consumers are wary of using Internet-only banks.
   b. Because Internet-only banks lack brand recognition, some consumers are wary of using them.
   c. Because of a lack of brand recognition, some consumers are wary of using Internet-only banks.
   d. All have dangling modifiers.

Objective 6.4: Discuss why it's important to make your message more concise, and give four tips on how to do so.

10. When editing for conciseness you should look for
    a. Unnecessary words and phrases
    b. Dangling modifiers
    c. Lack of parallelism
    d. Awkward references

11. Which of the following is *not* an example of a redundancy?
    a. Visible to the eye
    b. Free gift
    c. Very useful
    d. Repeat again

Objective 6.5: Explain how design elements help determine the effectiveness of your documents.

12. A well-designed document
    a. Includes a wide variety of typefaces
    b. Balances the space devoted to text, artwork, and white space
    c. Fills as much of the available space as possible with text and art
    d. Does all of the above

13. Any blank areas in a document are referred to as _____ _____.

14. Type that is "justified" is
    a. Flush on the left and ragged on the right
    b. Flush on the right and ragged on the left
    c. Flush on both the left and the right
    d. Centered

15. A sans serif typeface would be best for
    a. The headings in a report
    b. The text of a report
    c. Both the headings and the text of a report
    d. Elements such as footnotes and endnotes

Objective 6.6: Highlight the types of errors to look for when proofreading.

16. When proofreading, you should look for errors in
    a. Spelling and punctuation
    b. Grammar and usage
    c. Typography and format
    d. All of the above

Objective 6.7: Discuss the most important issues to consider when distributing your messages.

17. As a general rule, the cost of distributing a business message should be balanced against
    a. The importance and urgency of the message
    b. The length of the message
    c. Your career goals, as they relate to the message
    d. The number of recipients

18. Which of the following concerns is the *most* important to consider when distributing messages through electronic media such as e-mail?
    a. The difficulty of reading on-screen
    b. Privacy and security
    c. Differences between flat screen and CRT monitors
    d. The difficulty of keeping e-mail addresses current

Apply Your Knowledge

1. Why is it helpful to let a first draft "age" for a while before you begin the editing process?
2. Given the choice of only one, would you prefer to use a grammar checker or a spell checker? Why?
3. When you are designing a formal business letter, which design elements do you have to consider and which are optional?
4. Which distribution method would you choose for a highly confidential strategic planning report that needs to be sent to top executives at six locations in North America, Asia, and Europe? Explain your choice.
5. **Ethical Choices** What are the ethical implications of murky, complex writing in a document explaining how customers can appeal the result of a decision made in the company's favor during a dispute?

Practice Your Knowledge

DOCUMENTS FOR ANALYSIS

Read the following documents, then (1) analyze the strengths and weaknesses of each sentence and (2) revise each document so that it follows the guidelines in Chapters 4 through 6.

DOCUMENT 6.A

The move to our new offices will take place over this coming weekend. For everything to run smooth, everyone will have to clean out their own desk and pack up the contents in boxes that will be provided. You will need to take everything off the walls too, and please pack it along with the boxes.

If you have a lot of personal belongings, you should bring them home with you. Likewise with anything valuable. I do not mean to infer that items will be stolen, irregardless it is better to be safe than sorry.

On Monday, we will be unpacking, putting things away, and then get back to work. The least amount of disruption is anticipated by us, if everyone does their part. Hopefully, there will be no negative affects on production schedules, and current deadlines will be met.

DOCUMENT 6.B

Dear Ms. Giraud:

Enclosed herewith please find the manuscript for your book, Careers in Woolgathering. After perusing the first two chapters of your 1,500-page manuscript, I was forced to conclude that the subject matter, handicrafts and artwork using wool fibers, is not coincident with the publishing program of Framingham Press, which to this date has issued only works on business endeavors, avoiding all other topics completely.

Although our firm is unable to consider your impressive work at the present time, I have taken the liberty of recording some comments on some of the pages. I am of the opinion that any feedback that a writer can obtain from those well versed in the publishing realm can only serve to improve the writer's authorial skills.

In view of the fact that your residence is in the Boston area, might I suggest that you secure an appointment with someone of high editorial stature at the Cambridge Heritage Press, which I believe might have something of an interest in works of the nature you have produced.

Wishing you the best of luck in your literary endeavors, I remain

Arthur J. Cogswell

Editor

DOCUMENT 6.C

For delicious, air-popped popcorn, please read the following instructions: The popper is designed to pop 1/2 cup of popcorn kernels at one time. Never add more than 1/2 cup. A half cup of corn will produce three to four quarts of popcorn. More batches may be made separately after completion of the first batch. Popcorn is popped by hot air. Oil or shortening is not needed for popping corn. Add only popcorn kernels to the popping chamber. Standard grades of popcorn are recommended for use. Premium or gourmet type popping corns may be used. Ingredients such as oil, shortening, butter, margarine, or salt should never be added to the popping chamber. The popper, with popping chute in position, may be preheated for two minutes before adding the corn. Turn the popper off before adding the corn. Use electricity safely and wisely. Observe safety precautions when using the popper. Do not touch the popper when it is hot. The popper should not be left unattended when it is plugged into an outlet. Do not use the popper if it or its cord has been damaged. Do not use the popper if it is not working properly. Before using the first time, wash the chute and butter/measuring cup in hot soapy water. Use a dishcloth or sponge. Wipe the outside of the popper base. Use a damp cloth. Dry the base. Do not immerse the popper base in water or other liquid. Replace the chute and butter/measuring cup. The popper is ready to use.

Exercises

For active links to all websites discussed in this chapter, visit this text's website at www.prenhall.com/thill. Locate your book and click on its Companion Wesite link. Then select Chapter 6, and click on "Featured Websites." Locate the name of the page or the URL related to the material in the text. Please note that links to sites that become inactive after publication of the book will be removed from the Featured Websites section.

6.1 **Message Readability: Writing Paragraphs** Rewrite the following paragraph to vary the length of the sentences and to shorten the paragraph so it looks more inviting to readers.

Although major league baseball remains popular, more people are attending minor league baseball games because they can spend less on admission, snacks, and parking and still enjoy the excitement of America's pastime. Connecticut, for example, has three AA minor league teams, including the New Haven Ravens, who are affiliated with the St. Louis Cardinals; the Norwich Navigators, who are affiliated with the New York Yankees; and the New Britain Rock Cats, who are affiliated with the Minnesota Twins. These teams play in relatively small stadiums, so fans are close enough to see and hear everything, from the swing of the bat connecting with the ball to the thud of the ball landing in the outfielder's glove. Best of all, the cost of a family outing to see rising stars play in a local minor league game is just a fraction of what the family would spend to attend a major league game in a much larger, more crowded stadium.

6.2 **Message Readability: Using Bullets** Rewrite the following paragraph using a bulleted list:

With our alarm system, you'll have a 24-hour security guard who signals the police at the suggestion of an intruder. You'll also appreciate the computerized scanning device that

determines exactly where and when the intrusion occurred. No need to worry about electrical failure, either, thanks to our backup response unit.[11]

6.3 **Revising Messages: Clarity** Break these sentences into shorter ones by adding more periods:

a. The next time you write something, check your average sentence length in a 100-word passage, and if your sentences average more than 16 to 20 words, see whether you can break up some of the sentences.

b. Don't do what the village blacksmith did when he instructed his apprentice as follows: "When I take the shoe out of the fire, I'll lay it on the anvil, and when I nod my head, you hit it with the hammer." The apprentice did just as he was told, and now he's the village blacksmith.

c. Unfortunately, no gadget will produce excellent writing, but using a yardstick like the Fog Index gives us some guideposts to follow for making writing easier to read because its two factors remind us to use short sentences and simple words.

d. Know the flexibility of the written word and its power to convey an idea, and know how to make your words behave so that your readers will understand.

e. Words mean different things to different people, and a word such as *block* may mean city block, butcher block, engine block, auction block, or several other things.

6.4 **Revising Messages: Conciseness** Cross out unnecessary words in the following phrases:

a. Consensus of opinion

b. New innovations

c. Long period of time

d. At a price of $50

e. Still remains

6.5 **Revising Messages: Conciseness** Revise the following sentences, using shorter, simpler words:

a. The antiquated calculator is ineffectual for solving sophisticated problems.

b. It is imperative that the pay increments be terminated before an inordinate deficit is accumulated.

c. There was unanimity among the executives that Ms. Jackson's idiosyncrasies were cause for a mandatory meeting with the company's personnel director.

d. The impending liquidation of the company's assets was cause for jubilation among the company's competitors.

e. The expectations of the president for a stock dividend were accentuated by the preponderance of evidence that the company was in good financial condition.

6.6 **Revising Messages: Conciseness** Use infinitives as substitutes for the overly long phrases in these sentences:

a. For living, I require money.

b. They did not find sufficient evidence for believing in the future.

c. Bringing about the destruction of a dream is tragic.

6.7 **Revising Messages: Conciseness** Rephrase the following in fewer words:

a. In the near future

b. In the event that

c. In order that

d. For the purpose of

e. With regard to

f. It may be that

g. In very few cases

h. With reference to

i. At the present time

j. There is no doubt that

6.8 **Revising Messages: Conciseness** Condense these sentences to as few words as possible:

a. We are of the conviction that writing is important.

b. In all probability, we're likely to have a price increase.

c. Our goals include making a determination about that in the near future.

d. When all is said and done at the conclusion of this experiment, I'd like to summarize the final windup.

e. After a trial period of three weeks, during which time she worked for a total of 15 full working days, we found her work was sufficiently satisfactory so that we offered her full-time work.

6.9 **Revising Messages: Modifiers** Remove all the unnecessary modifiers from these sentences:

a. Tremendously high pay increases were given to the extraordinarily skilled and extremely conscientious employees.

b. The union's proposals were highly inflationary, extremely demanding, and exceptionally bold.

6.10 **Revising Messages: Hedging** Rewrite these sentences so that they no longer contain any hedging:

a. It would appear that someone apparently entered illegally.

b. It may be possible that sometime in the near future the situation is likely to improve.

c. Your report seems to suggest that we might be losing money.

d. I believe Nancy apparently has somewhat greater influence over employees in the accounting department.

e. It seems as if this letter of resignation means you might be leaving us.

6.11 **Revising Messages: Indefinite Starters** Rewrite these sentences to eliminate the indefinite starters:

a. There are several examples here to show that Elaine can't hold a position very long.

b. It would be greatly appreciated if every employee would make a generous contribution to Mildred Cook's retirement party.

c. It has been learned in Washington today from generally reliable sources that an important announcement will be made shortly by the White House.

d. There is a rule that states that we cannot work overtime without permission.

e. There are at least three ways in which a wireless network would improve productivity in the sales department.

6.12 **Revising Messages: Parallelism** Present the ideas in these sentences in parallel form:

a. Mr. Hill is expected to lecture three days a week, to counsel two days a week, and must write for publication in his spare time.

b. She knows not only accounting, but she also reads Latin.

c. Both applicants had families, college degrees, and were in their thirties, with considerable accounting experience but few social connections.

d. This book was exciting, well written, and held my interest.

e. Don is both a hard worker and he knows bookkeeping.

6.13 **Revising Messages: Awkward References** Revise the following sentences to delete the awkward references:

a. The vice president in charge of sales and the production manager are responsible for the keys to 34A and 35A, respectively.

b. The keys to 34A and 35A are in executive hands, with the former belonging to the vice president in charge of sales and the latter belonging to the production manager.

c. The keys to 34A and 35A have been given to the production manager, with the aforementioned keys being gold embossed.

d. A laser printer and an inkjet printer were delivered to John and Megan, respectively.

e. The walnut desk is more expensive than the oak desk, the former costing $300 more than the latter.

6.14 **Revising Messages: Dangling Modifiers** Rewrite these sentences to clarify the dangling modifiers:

a. Running down the railroad tracks in a cloud of smoke, we watched the countryside glide by.

b. Lying on the shelf, Ruby saw the seashell.

c. Based on the information, I think we should buy the property.

d. Being cluttered and filthy, Sandy took the whole afternoon to clean up her desk.

e. After proofreading every word, the memo was ready to be signed.

6.15 Revising Messages: Noun Sequences Rewrite the following sentences to eliminate the long strings of nouns:

a. The focus of the meeting was a discussion of the bank interest rate deregulation issue.

b. Following the government task force report recommendations, we are revising our job applicant evaluation procedures.

c. The production department quality assurance program components include employee training, supplier cooperation, and computerized detection equipment.

d. The supermarket warehouse inventory reduction plan will be implemented next month.

e. The State University business school graduate placement program is one of the best in the country.

6.16 Revising Messages: Sentence Structure Rearrange the following sentences to bring the subjects closer to their verbs:

a. Trudy, when she first saw the bull pawing the ground, ran.

b. It was Terri who, according to Ted, who is probably the worst gossip in the office (Tom excepted), mailed the wrong order.

c. William Oberstreet, in his book *Investment Capital Reconsidered*, writes of the mistakes that bankers through the decades have made.

d. Judy Schimmel, after passing up several sensible investment opportunities, despite the warnings of her friends and family, invested her inheritance in a jojoba plantation.

e. The president of U-Stor-It, which was on the brink of bankruptcy after the warehouse fire, the worst tragedy in the history of the company, prepared a press announcement.

6.17 Revising Messages: Camouflaged Verbs Rewrite each sentence so that the verbs are no longer camouflaged:

a. Adaptation to the new rules was performed easily by the employees.

b. The assessor will make a determination of the tax due.

c. Verification of the identity of the employees must be made daily.

d. The board of directors made a recommendation that Mr. Ronson be assigned to a new division.

e. The auditing procedure on the books was performed by the vice president.

6.18 Producing Messages: Design Elements Look back at your revised version of Document 6.C (see exercise under "Documents for Analysis"). Which design elements could you use to make this document more readable? Produce your revision of Document 6.C using your selected design elements. Then experiment by changing one of the design elements. How does the change affect readability? Exchange documents with another student and critique each other's work.

6.19 Web Design Visit the stock market page of Bloomberg's website at www.bloomberg.com and evaluate the use of design in presenting the latest news. What design improvements can you suggest to enhance readability of the information posted on this page?

6.20 Teamwork Team up with another student and exchange your revised versions of Document 6.A, 6.B, or 6.C (see exercises under "Documents for Analysis"). Review the assignment to be sure the instructions are clear. Then read and critique your teammate's revision to see whether it can be improved. After you have critiqued each other's work, take a moment to examine the way you expressed your comments and the way you felt listening to the other student's comments. Can you identify ways to improve the critiquing process in situations such as this?

6.21 Proofreading Messages: E-Mail Proofread the following e-mail message and revise it to correct any problems you find:

Our final company orrientation of the year will be held on Dec. 20. In preparation for this sesssion, please order 20 copies of the Policy handbook, the confidentiality agreenemt, the employee benefits Manual, please let me know if you anticipate any delays in obtaining these materials.

6.22 Ethical Choices Three of your company's five plants exceeded their expense budgets last month. You want all the plants to operate within their budgets from now on. You were thinking of using e-mail to let all five managers see the memo you are sending to the managers of the three overbudget plants. Is this a good idea? Why or why not?

Expand Your Knowledge

LEARNING MORE ON THE WEB

WRITE IT RIGHT: TIPS TO HELP YOU RETHINK AND REVISE

www.powa.org

Are you sure that readers perceive your written message as you intended? If you want help revising a message that you're completing, use the Paradigm Online Writing Assistant (POWA). With this interactive writer's guide, you can select topics to get tips on how to edit your work, reshape your thoughts, and rewrite for clarity. Read discussions about perfecting your writing skills, and for practice, complete one of the many online activities provided to reinforce what you've learned. Or select the Forum to talk about writing.

ACTIVITIES

Explore POWA's advice then answer the following questions:

1. Why is it better to write out ideas in a rough format and later reread your message to revise its content? When revising your message, what questions can you ask about your writing?
2. Name the four elements of the "writing context." Imagine that you're the reader of your message. What questions might you ask?
3. When you revise a written message, what is the purpose of "tightening"? What is one way to tighten your writing as you complete a message?

EXPLORING THE WEB ON YOUR OWN

Review these chapter-related websites on your own to learn more about writing business messages.

1. Learn the ins and outs of document design at About.com's Desktop Publishing section. Use the great tips on graphic design and typography to produce professional-quality business documents. Visit http://desktoppub.about.com then look in the Essentials menu for "DTP, Graphic Design, Typography Info."
2. Troubled by those tricky word choices that bother every writer? Not sure if "alternate" or "alternative" is the right choice? Visit the Grammar Slammer at http://englishplus.com/grammar and click on "Common Mistakes and Choices" for advice on dozens of common word choice dilemmas.
3. Learn the basics of page layout in Microsoft Word to make sure your documents are designed effectively. Visit http://office.microsoft.com, click on Assistance, find the link to browse assistance for Word, then click through the pages of advice on document formatting.

Learn Interactively

INTERACTIVE STUDY GUIDE

Visit www.prenhall.com/thill, then locate your book and click on its Companion Website link. Select Chapter 6 to take advantage of the interactive "Chapter Quiz" to test your knowledge of chapter concepts. Receive instant feedback on whether you need additional studying. Also, visit the "Study Hall," where you'll find an abundance of valuable resources that will help you succeed in this course.

PEAK PERFORMANCE GRAMMAR AND MECHANICS

If your instructor has required the use of "Peak Performance Grammar and Mechanics," either in your online course or on CD, you can improve your skill with prepositions, conjunctions, and articles by using the "Peak Performance Grammar and Mechanics" module. Click "Prepositions, Conjunctions, and Articles." Take the Pretest to determine whether you have any weak areas. Then review those areas in the Refresher Course. Take the Follow-Up Test to check your grasp of prepositions, conjunctions, and articles. For an extra challenge or advanced practice, take the Advanced Test. Finally, for additional reinforcement, go to the "Improve Your Grammar, Mechanics, and Usage" section that follows, and complete those exercises.

Improve Your Grammar, Mechanics, and Usage

The following exercises help you improve your knowledge of and power over English grammar, mechanics, and usage. Turn to the Handbook of Grammar, Mechanics, and Usage at the end of this textbook and review all of Sections 1.6 (Other Parts of Speech). Then look at the following 10 items. Underline the preferred choice within each set of parentheses. (Answers to these exercises appear on page AK-3.)

1. Where was your argument (*leading to, leading*)?
2. I wish he would get (*off, off of*) the phone.
3. U.S. Mercantile must become (*aware, aware of*) and sensitive to its customers' concerns.
4. Dr. Namaguchi will be talking (*with, to*) the marketing class, but she has no time for questions.
5. Matters like this are decided after thorough discussion (*among, between*) all seven department managers.
6. We can't wait (*on, for*) their decision much longer.
7. Their computer is similar (*to, with*) ours.
8. This model is different (*than, from*) the one we ordered.
9. She is active (*in not only, not only in*) a civic group but also in an athletic organization.
10. She had neither the preferred educational background, nor (*did she have suitable experience, the suitable experience*).

For additional exercises focusing on prepositions, go to www.prenhall.com/thill, then locate your text and click on its Companion Website link. Click on Chapter 6, click on "Additional Exercises to Improve Your Grammar, Mechanics, and Usage," then click on "10. Prepositions."

Part III

Writing Letters, Memos, E-Mail, and Instant Messages

Chapter 7

Writing Routine and Positive Messages

Learning Objectives

On the Job

COMMUNICATING AT CONE, INC.

USING POSITIVE MESSAGES TO POSITIVELY AFFECT THE LIVES OF HUNGRY CHILDREN

Considering the number of corporate scandals in recent years, it's tempting to assume that all businesses are up to no good. Although a few companies fill headlines with bad news, thousands of other companies continue to conduct business ethically, and even more than that, they work to make significant contributions in their communities. Ready to help them in their efforts to help others is Cone, Inc., a Boston-based agency that specializes in *cause marketing.* CEO Carol Cone explains: "Consumers no longer have trust in anything, so they look to companies for a lot more. They look to see what companies stand for."

ConAgra's Feeding Children Better program supports thousands of children every year, and the company's public relations agency uses these successes to focus nationwide attention on the problems of childhood hunger.

One of Cone's clients, ConAgra Foods, took up the cause of child hunger in the United States through its Feeding Children Better program. By writing positive messages and news releases, Cone helps ConAgra spread the message about its efforts. A centerpiece of those efforts is the Kids Cafés, an after-school program that serves free, hot, nutritious meals to kids in need. Since it became the national sponsor of Kids Cafés, ConAgra has contributed funds for over 160 new Kids Cafés, each one providing more than 10,000 meals a year. ConAgra also helps in the battle against childhood hunger by partnering in the Rapid Food Distribution System, which is using modern distribution and tracking technologies to make sure that donated food is transported swiftly to points of need. The system not only helps ensure that highly perishable foods don't spoil while waiting to be delivered, it also tracks donations from various food companies to ensure they are given appropriate tax credits—which encourage even more donations.

Cone focuses her news releases on the three main goals of ConAgra's Feeding Children Better program: (1) getting food to children who need it, (2) repairing the breakdowns in food distribution, and (3) raising national awareness about child hunger. ConAgra and Cone have received numerous awards for their good work and effective communication, such as the Corporate Citizenship Award from the U.S. Chamber of Commerce and the Cause Marketing Halo Award.

What makes Cone's messages so effective? Simply calling attention to ConAgra's good deeds would be a positive business result, but doing so would primarily benefit ConAgra, not the various hunger relief programs. Cone puts her news releases to work by highlighting ConAgra's progress toward each goal. She focuses attention on ConAgra's activities to highlight the problems of childhood hunger, thereby helping her client accomplish even more positive outcomes through the use of positive messages.

Regardless of the subject matter of your business messages, you can make them more effective by following Cone's advice to stay focused on your overall business goals and to emphasize the audience's concerns whenever you write.[1]

www.coneinc.com

203

USING THE THREE-STEP WRITING PROCESS FOR ROUTINE AND POSITIVE MESSAGES

Like Carol Cone, you'll be composing numerous routine and positive messages during the typical business day. In fact, most business communication is about routine matters: orders, information, company policies, claims, credit, employees, products, operations, and so on. Such messages are rarely long or complex, but the three-step writing process still gives you a great way to produce effective messages efficiently.

Step 1: Plan Your Message

Even simple messages can benefit from thoughtful planning.

Even though planning routine and positive messages may take only a few minutes, the four tasks of planning still apply. First, analyze the situation, making sure that your purpose is clear and that you know enough about your audience to craft a successful message. Second, gather whatever information your audience needs to know. Even something as simple as a team meeting can involve dozens of details, from presentation setups to lunch arrangements to parking. Including all necessary information the first time saves you and your audience the time and trouble of additional messages to fill in the gaps. Third, select the right medium for the message and the audience. Both routine and positive messages are often sent via e-mail and instant messaging, but printed memos and letters are still common. Fourth, organize your information effectively. This task includes defining your main idea, limiting your scope, selecting a direct or an indirect approach, and outlining your content. Throughout this chapter, you'll learn more about performing all four of these tasks for a variety of routine and positive message types.

Step 2: Write Your Message

Start by adapting your approach to your audience. Be sensitive to your audience's needs by maintaining a "you" attitude, being polite, emphasizing the positive, and using bias-free language. To strengthen your relationship with your audience, establish your credibility and project your company's image. Also, even though your tone is usually conversational, some messages may need to be more formal than others. You'll want to use plain English and make your writing as active as possible.

With some practice, you'll be able to compose most routine messages quickly. In fact, the ability to generate such messages quickly is a key skill for most business executives. Your main idea is probably well defined already; just be sure you stick to it by limiting the scope of your message.

For routine requests and positive messages
- *State the request or main idea*
- *Give necessary details*
- *Close with a cordial request for specific action*

Also, your readers in most cases will be interested or at least neutral, so you can usually adopt the direct approach for routine and positive messages: Open with a clear statement of the main idea, include all necessary details in the body, and then close cordially. However, even though these messages are the least complicated to write, communicating across cultural boundaries can be a challenge, especially if you're not familiar with the cultural differences involved.

Step 3: Complete Your Message

No matter how brief or straightforward your message, maximize its impact by giving yourself plenty of time to revise, produce, proofread, and distribute it. First, revise your message by evaluating content and organization to make sure you've said what you want to in the order you want to say it. Review your message's readability. Edit and rewrite to make it concise and clear. Second, design your document to suit your purpose and your audience. Even simple e-mails and instant messages can benefit from careful font selection, the use of white space, and other design choices. Next, proofread the final version of your message, looking for typos, errors in spelling and mechanics, alignment problems, poor print quality, and so on. Finally, choose a distribution method that balances cost, convenience, time, security, and privacy. Increasingly, routine and positive messages are delivered electronically, on intranets (for internal audiences), extranets (for restricted external audiences), or websites and blogs (for general external audiences), or via e-mail and instant messaging.

MAKING ROUTINE REQUESTS

Making requests—for information, action, products, adjustments, or other matters—is a routine part of business. In most cases, your audience will be prepared to comply, as long as you're not being unreasonable or asking someone to do something they would expect you to do yourself. By applying a clear strategy and tailoring your approach to each situation, you'll be able to generate effective requests quickly.

Strategy for Routine Requests

Like all business messages, routine requests have three parts: an opening, a body, and a close. Using the direct approach, open with your main idea, which is a clear statement of your request. Use the body to give details and justify your request. Then close by requesting specific action (see Figure 7–1).

Take care that your direct approach doesn't come across as abrupt or tactless.

State Your Request Up Front   Begin routine requests by placing your request first—up front is where it stands out and gets the most attention. Of course, getting right to the point should not be interpreted as a license to be abrupt or tactless:

- **Pay attention to tone.** Even though you expect a favorable response, the tone of your initial request is important. Instead of demanding action ("Send me your latest catalog"), soften your request with words such as *please* and *I would appreciate.*

- **Assume your audience will comply.** An impatient demand for rapid service isn't necessary. You can generally make the assumption that your audience will comply with your request once the reason for it is clearly understood.

- **Punctuate questions and polite requests differently.** A polite request in question form requires no question mark: "Would you please help us determine whether Kate Kingsley is a suitable applicant for this position." A direct question within your message does require a question mark: "Did Kate Kingsley demonstrate an ability to work smoothly with clients?"

- **Be specific.** State precisely what you want. For example, if you request the latest market data from your research department, be sure to say whether you want a one-page summary or a hundred pages of raw data.

Perry Klebahn's firm, Atlas Snow-Shoe Company, sells high-end showshoes in more than 1,000 stores across the United States, ringing up annual sales of more than $10 million. Klebahn tells his employees to establish a good relationship with their audience by learning what they need to know and by using language that is positive and polite.

FIGURE 7–1
Organizing Routine and
Positive Messages

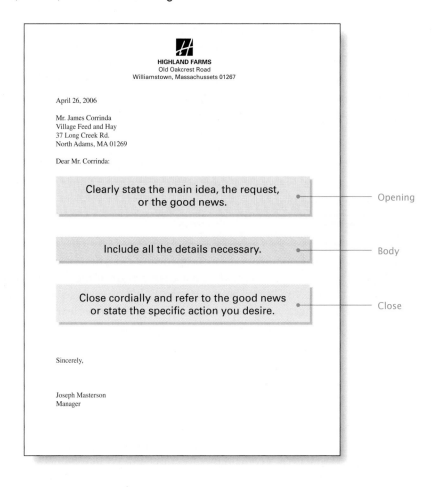

HIGHLAND FARMS
Old Oakcrest Road
Williamstown, Massachussets 01267

April 26, 2006

Mr. James Corrinda
Village Feed and Hay
37 Long Creek Rd.
North Adams, MA 01269

Dear Mr. Corrinda:

Clearly state the main idea, the request, or the good news. — Opening

Include all the details necessary. — Body

Close cordially and refer to the good news or state the specific action you desire. — Close

Sincerely,

Joseph Masterson
Manager

Explain and Justify Your Request   Use the body of your message to explain your initial request. Make the explanation a smooth and logical outgrowth of your opening remarks. If possible, point out how complying with the request could benefit the reader. For instance, if you would like some assistance interpreting complex quality-control data, point out how a better understanding of quality-control issues would improve customer satisfaction and ultimately lead to higher profits for the entire company.

Using lists help readers sort through multiple related items or multiple requests.

Whether you're writing a formal letter or a simple instant message, you can use the body of your request to list a series of questions. This list of questions helps organize your message and helps your audience identify the information you need. Just keep in mind a few basics:

- **Ask the most important questions first.** If cost is your main concern, you might begin with a question such as "What is the cost for shipping the merchandise by air versus truck?" Then you may want to ask more specific but related questions about, say, discounts for paying early.

- **Ask only relevant questions.** To help expedite the response to your request, ask only those questions that are central to your main request. Doing so will generate an answer sooner and make better use of the other person's time.

- **Deal with only one topic per question.** If you have an unusual or complex request, break it down into specific, individual questions so that the reader can address each one separately. Don't put the burden of untangling a complicated request on your reader. This consideration not only shows respect for your audience's time but also gets you a more accurate answer in less time.

Close request messages with
- A request for some specific action
- Information about how you can be reached
- An expression of appreciation

Request Specific Action in a Courteous Close   Close your message with three important elements: (1) a specific request, (2) information about how you can be reached (if it isn't obvious), and (3) an expression of appreciation or goodwill. When you ask

✓ CHECKLIST: Writing Routine Requests

A. State your request up front

✓ Write in a polite, undemanding, personal tone.
✓ Use the direct approach, since your audience will probably respond favorably to your request.
✓ Be specific and precise in your request.

B. Explain and justify your request

✓ Justify the request or explain its importance.
✓ Explain any potential benefits of responding.

✓ Ask the most important questions first.
✓ Break complex requests into individual questions that are limited to only one topic each.

C. Request specific action in a courteous close

✓ Make it easy to comply by including appropriate contact information.
✓ Express your gratitude.
✓ Clearly state any important deadlines for the request.

readers to perform a specific action, ask that they respond by a specific time, if appropriate ("Please send the figures by April 5 so that I can return first-quarter results to you before the May 20 conference"). Plus, by including your phone number, e-mail address, office hours, and other contact information, you help your readers respond easily.

Conclude your message by sincerely expressing your goodwill and appreciation. However, don't thank the reader "in advance" for cooperating. If the reader's reply warrants a word of thanks, send it after you've received the reply. To review, see "Checklist: Writing Routine Requests."

Common Examples of Routine Requests

The various types of routine requests are innumerable, from asking favors to requesting credit. However, many of the routine messages that you'll be writing will likely fall into a few main categories: asking for information and action, asking for recommendations, and making claims and requesting adjustments.

Asking for Information and Action   When you need to know about something, to elicit an opinion from someone, or to request a simple action, you usually need only ask. In essence, simple requests say

• What you want to know or what you want readers to do

• Why you're making the request

• Why it may be in your readers' interest to help you

If your reader is able to do what you want, such a straightforward request gets the job done with a minimum of fuss. Follow the direct approach by opening with a clear statement of your reason for writing. In the body, provide whatever explanation is needed to justify your request. Then close with a specific account of what you expect, and include a deadline if appropriate. In more complex situations, readers might be unwilling to respond unless they understand how the request benefits them, so be sure to include this information in your explanation.

Naturally, you'll adapt your request to your audience and the situation. For instance, requests to fellow employees are usually casual and get straight to the point. The memo in Figure 7–2 was sent to all employees of Ace Hardware seeking their input about a new wellness and benefits program. The tone is matter-of-fact, and the memo assumes some shared background, which is appropriate when communicating about a routine matter to someone in the same company. (For more information on formatting memos and other business messages, see Appendix A.)

In contrast to requests sent internally, those sent to people outside the organization usually adopt a more formal tone. You'll most likely be in a position to ask businesses,

Analyze the Situation

Verify that the purpose is to request feedback from fellow employees.

Gather Information

Gather accurate, complete information on program benefits and local gyms.

Select the Right Medium

Office memo is appropriate for this message; printed format makes it easy for readers to sign and return the form.

Organize the Information

The main idea is saving money while staying healthy. Save time and meet audience expectations by using a direct approach.

Adapt to Your Audience

Show sensitivity to audience needs with a "you" attitude, politeness, positive emphasis, and bias-free language. Writer already has credibility as manager of the department.

Compose the Message

Style is conversational but still businesslike, using plain English and appropriate voice.

Revise the Message

Evaluate content and review readability; avoid unnecessary details.

Produce the Message

Simple memo format is all the design this message needs.

Proofread the Message

Review for errors in layout, spelling, and mechanics.

Distribute the Message

Deliver the message via the company's interoffice mail delivery system.

1   2   3

FIGURE 7–2   Effective Memo Requesting Action from Company Insiders

ACE   *Ace Hardware Corporation*

INTERNAL MEMORANDUM

Routes message efficiently, with all needed information

DATE: October 10, 2006
TO: All Employees
FROM: Tony Ramirez, Human Resources
SUBJ: New Wellness Program Opportunity

The benefits package committee has asked me to contact everyone about an opportunity to save money and stay healthier. As you know, the Benefits Committee has been meeting to decide on changes in our benefits package. Last week, we sent you a memo detailing the Synergy Wellness Program.

States purpose in opening to avoid wasting busy readers' time

Presents the situation that makes the inquiry necessary

In addition to the package as described in last week's memo (life, medical, and dental insurance), Synergy has made the offer even more attractive by offering us a 10% discount. However, to qualify for the discount, we have to show proof that at least 25% of our employees participate in aerobic exercise at least three times a week for at least 20 minutes.

After looking around, we discovered a gymnasium just a few blocks south on Haley Boulevard. Sports Midwest will give our employees unlimited daytime access to their indoor track, gym, and pool for a group fee that comes to approximately $4.50 per month per employee if at least half of us sign up.

Lists reader benefits and requests action

In addition to using the track and pools, we can play volleyball, participate in Jazzercise, form our own intramural basketball teams, and much more. Our spouses and children can also participate at a deeply discounted monthly fee. If you have questions, please e-mail or call me (or any member of the committee). Let us know your wishes on the following form.

Gives clear instructions and a deadline for response

Please mark your choice(s) on the form below, then sign and return it to your immediate supervisor no later than Friday, October 27.
= =

Provides an easy-to-use response form

_____ Yes, I will participate in the Synergy Wellness program and pay $4.50 a month.
_____ Yes, I am interested in a discounted family membership.
_____ No, I prefer not to participate.

Signature _____

Employee ID Number _____

customers, or others outside your organization to provide information or to take some simple action (attend a meeting, return an information card, endorse a document, confirm an address, and so on). Such requests are often in letter form, although some are sent via e-mail. These messages are usually short and simple, but still formal and professional, like the following request for information:

Would you please supply me with information about the lawn services you provide. Pralle Realty owns 27 pieces of rental property in College Station, and we're looking for a lawn service to handle all of them. We are making a commitment to provide quality housing in this college town, and we are looking for an outstanding firm to work with us.

Makes overall request in polite question form (no question mark)

Keeps reader's interest by hinting at possibility of future business

1. **Lawn care:** What is your annual charge for each location for lawn maintenance, including mowing, fertilizing, and weed control?

Avoids making an overly broad request by using a series of specific questions

2. **Shrubbery:** What is your annual charge for each location for the care of deciduous and evergreen bushes, including pruning, fertilizing, and replacing as necessary?

Itemizes questions in a logical sequence

3. **Contract:** How does Agri-Lawn Service structure such large contracts? What additional information do you need from us?

Avoids useless yes-or-no answers by including open-ended questions

Please let us hear from you by February 15. We want to have a lawn-care firm in place by March 15.

Specifies a time limit in the courteous close

A more complex request might require not only greater detail but information on how responding will benefit the reader.

Sometimes you may need to reestablish a relationship with former customers or suppliers. In many cases, when customers are unhappy about some purchase or about the way they were treated, they don't complain; they simply stay away from the offending business. Thus, a letter of inquiry might encourage customers to use idle credit accounts, offering them an opportunity to register their displeasure and then move on to a good relationship. In addition, a customer's response to such an inquiry may give you insights into ways to improve your products and customer service. Even if they have no complaint, customers still welcome the personal attention.

The purpose of some routine requests to customers is simply to reestablish communication.

Asking for Recommendations   The need to inquire about people arises often in business. For example, before awarding credit, contracts, jobs, promotions, scholarships, and so on, some companies ask applicants to supply references. If you're applying for a job and your potential employer asks for references, you may want to ask a close personal or professional associate to write a letter of recommendation. Or, if you're an employer considering whether to hire an applicant, you may want to write directly to the person the applicant named as a reference.

Companies ask applicants to supply references who can vouch for their ability, skills, integrity, character, and fitness for the job. Before you volunteer someone's name as a reference, ask permission do to so. Some people won't let you use their names, perhaps because they don't know enough about you to feel comfortable writing a letter or because they have a policy of not providing recommendations. In any event, you are likely to receive the best recommendation from people who agree to write about you, so check first.

Always ask for permission before using someone as a reference.

Because requests for recommendations and references are routine, you can assume your reader will honor your request, and you can organize your inquiry using the direct approach. Open your message by clearly stating that you're applying for a position and that you would like your reader to write a letter of recommendation. If you haven't had contact with the person for some time, use the opening to recall the nature of the relationship you had, the dates of association, and any

Refresh the memory of any potential reference you haven't been in touch with for a while.

Analyze the Situation
Verify that the purpose is to request a recommendation letter from a college professor.

Gather Information
Gather information on classes and dates to help the reader recall you and to clarify the position you seek.

Select the Right Medium
The letter format gives this message an appropriate level of formality, although many professors prefer to be contacted by e-mail.

Organize the Information
Messages like this are common and expected, so a direct approach is fine.

Adapt to Your Audience
Show sensitivity to audience needs with a "you" attitude, politeness, positive emphasis, and bias-free language.

Compose the Message
Style is respectful and businesslike, while still using plain English and appropriate voice.

Revise the Message
Evaluate content and review readability; avoid unnecessary details.

Produce the Message
Simple memo format is all the design this message needs.

Proofread the Message
Review for errors in layout, spelling, and mechanics.

Distribute the Message
Deliver the message via postal mail or e-mail if you have the professor's e-mail address.

1   **2**   **3**

FIGURE 7–3   Effective Letter Requesting a Recommendation

1181 Ashport Drive
Tate Springs, TN 38101
March 14, 2006

Professor Lyndon Kenton
School of Business
University of Tennessee, Knoxville
Knoxville, TN 37916

Dear Professor Kenton:

I recently interviewed with Strategic Investments and have been called for a second interview for their Analyst Training Program (ATP). They have requested at least one recommendation from a professor, and I immediately thought of you. May I have a letter of recommendation from you?

As you may recall, I took BUS 485, Financial Analysis, from you in the fall of 2005. I enjoyed the class and finished the term with an "A." Professor Kenton, your comments on assertiveness and cold-calling impressed me beyond the scope of the actual course material. In fact, taking your course helped me decide on a future as a financial analyst.

My enclosed résumé includes all my relevant work experience and volunteer activities. I would also like to add that I've handled the financial planning for our family since my father passed away several years ago. Although I initially learned by trial and error, I have increasingly applied my business training in deciding what stocks or bonds to trade. This, I believe, has given me a practical edge over others who may be applying for the same job.

If possible, Ms. Blackmon in Human Resources needs to receive your letter by March 30. For your convenience, I've enclosed a preaddressed, stamped envelope.

I appreciate your time and effort in writing this letter of recommendation for me. It will be great to put my education to work, and I'll keep you informed of my progress. Thank you for your consideration in this matter.

Sincerely,

Joanne Tucker

Joanne Tucker

Enclosure

Opens by stating the purpose of the letter and making the request, assuming the reader will want to comply with the request

Includes information near the opening to refresh the reader's memory about this former student

Refers to résumé in the body and mentions experience that could set applicant apart from other candidates

Gives a deadline for response and includes information about the person expecting the recommendation

Mentions the preaddressed, stamped envelope to encourage a timely response

special events that might bring a clear, favorable picture of you to mind. Consider including an updated résumé if you've had significant career advancement since your last contact.

Close your letter with an expression of appreciation and the full name and address of the person to whom the letter should be sent. When asking for an immediate recommendation, you should also mention the deadline. You'll make a response more likely if you enclose a stamped, preaddressed envelope, which is a considerate step in any event. The letter from Joanne Tucker in Figure 7–3 covers all these points and adds important information about some qualifications that might be of special interest to her potential employer:

Making Claims and Requesting Adjustments   If you're dissatisfied with a company's product or service, you can opt to make a **claim** (a formal complaint) or request an **adjustment** (a claim settlement). In either case, it's important to maintain a professional tone in all your communication, no matter how angry or frustrated you might be. Keeping your cool will help you get the situation resolved sooner. In addition, be sure to document your initial complaint and every correspondence after that.

In most cases, and especially in your first letter, assume that a fair adjustment will be made, and follow the plan for direct requests. Open with a straightforward statement of the problem. In the body, give a complete, specific explanation of the details. Provide any information an adjuster would need to verify your complaint. In your close, politely request specific action or convey a sincere desire to find a solution. And if appropriate, suggest that the business relationship will continue if the problem is solved satisfactorily.

Companies usually accept the customer's explanation of what's wrong, so ethically it's important to be entirely honest when filing claims. Also, be prepared to back up your claim with invoices, sales receipts, canceled checks, dated correspondence, and any other relevant documents. Send copies and keep the originals for your files.

If the remedy is obvious, tell your reader exactly what you expect from the company, such as exchanging incorrectly shipped merchandise for the right item or issuing a refund if the item is out of stock. In some cases you might ask the reader to resolve a problem. However, if you're uncertain about the precise nature of the trouble, you could ask the company to make an assessment then advise you on how the situation could be fixed. Supply your contact information so that the company can discuss the situation with you if necessary.

Compare the tone of the draft version in Figure 7–4 with the revised version. If you were the person receiving the complaint, which version would you respond to more favorably?

A rational, clear, and courteous approach is best for any routine request. To review the tasks involved in making claims and requesting adjustments, see "Checklist: Making Claims and Requesting Adjustments."

In your claim letter
- Explain the problem and give details
- Provide backup information
- Request specific action

Be prepared to document your claim. Send copies and keep the original documents.

SENDING ROUTINE REPLIES AND POSITIVE MESSAGES

Just as you'll make numerous requests for information and action throughout your career, you'll also respond to similar requests from other people. When responding positively to a request, sending routine announcements, or sending a positive or goodwill message, you have several goals: to communicate the information or the good news, answer all questions, provide all required details, and leave your reader with a good impression of you and your firm.

Draft

We have been at our present location only three months, and we don't understand why our December utility bill is $815.00 and our January bill is $817.50. Businesses on both sides of us, in offices just like ours, are paying only $543.50 and $545.67 for the same months. We all have similar computer and office equipment, so something must be wrong.

Opens with emotion and details

Small businesses are helpless against big utility companies. How can we prove that you read the meter wrong or that the November bill from before we even moved in here got added to our December bill? We want someone to check this meter right away. We can't afford to pay these big bills.

Uses a defensive tone and blames the meter reader

This is the first time we've complained to you about anything, and I hope you'll agree that we deserve a better deal.

Closes with irrelevant information and a weak defense

Sincerely,

Laura Covington

Laura Covington
Proprietor

Revision

The European Connection
Specialist Purveyors of European Antiques
for over 30 years

P.O. Box 804 • Cayucos, California 93430
Telephone: (805) 979-7727 Fax: (805) 979-2828
EuroConnect@nemesis.net

February 23, 2006

Customer Service Representative
City of San Luis Obispo Utilities
955 Morro St.
San Luis Obispo, CA 93401

Dear Customer Service Representative:

A comparison of our utility bills with those of our neighboring businesses suggests that the utility meter in our store may not be accurate. Please send a technician to check it.

Opens by clearly and calmly stating the problem

Provides details in the body so that the reader can understand why Covington thinks a problem exists

The European Connection has been at our current location since December 1, almost three months. Our monthly bill is nearly triple those of neighboring businesses in this building, yet we all have similar storefronts and equipment. We paid $815.00 in December and $817.50 in January. In contrast, the highest bills that neighboring businesses paid were $543.50 and $545.67 for those two months.

Presents details clearly, concisely, and completely

If your representative would visit our store, he or she could do an analysis of how much energy we are using. We understand that you regularly provide this helpful service to customers.

Requests specific action in the closing and provides contact information to make responding easy

We would appreciate hearing from you this week. You can reach me by calling (805) 979-7727 during business hours. I look forward to hearing from you.

Sincerely,

Laura Covington

Laura Covington
Proprietor

FIGURE 7–4
Poor and Improved Versions of Claim Letter

✓ CHECKLIST: Making Claims and Requesting Adjustments

✓ Maintain a professional tone, even if you're extremely frustrated.
✓ Open with a straightforward statement of the problem.
✓ Provide specific details in the body.
✓ Present facts honestly and clearly.

✓ Politely summarize desired action in the closing.
✓ Clearly state what you expect as a fair settlement, or ask the reader to propose a fair adjustment.
✓ Explain the benefits of complying with the request, such as your continued patronage.

Strategy for Routine Replies and Positive Messages

Like requests, routine replies and positive messages have an opening, a body, and a close. Since readers receiving these messages will generally be interested in what you have to say, you'll usually use the direct approach. Place your main idea (the positive reply or the good news) in the opening. Use the body to explain all the relevant details, and close cordially, perhaps highlighting a benefit to your reader.

Use a direct approach for positive messages.

Start with the Main Idea   By opening your routine and positive messages with the main idea or good news, you're preparing your audience for the detail that follows. Try to make your opening clear and concise. Although the following introductory statements make the same point, one is cluttered with unnecessary information that buries the purpose, whereas the other is brief and to the point:

Instead of This	Write This
I am pleased to inform you that after deliberating the matter carefully, our human resources committee has recommended you for appointment as a staff accountant.	Congratulations. You've been selected to join our firm as a staff accountant, beginning March 20.

The best way to write a clear opening is to have a clear idea of what you want to say. Before you put one word on paper, ask yourself, "What is the single most important message I have for the audience?"

Provide Necessary Details and Explanation   The body of routine and positive messages is typically the longest. You need the space to explain your point completely so that your audience will experience no confusion or lingering doubt. In addition to providing details in the body, maintain the supportive tone established in the opening. This tone is easy to continue when your message is entirely positive, as in this example:

Through the training programs offered by Homeboy Industries in Los Angeles, former gang members such as Abel Munoz learn valuable business skills—including techniques for communicating in a professional manner.

Your educational background and internship have impressed us, and we believe you would be a valuable addition to Green Valley Properties. As discussed during your interview, your salary will be $4,300 per month, plus benefits. In that regard, you will meet with our benefits manager, Paula Sanchez, at 8 a.m. on Monday, March 21. She will assist you with all the paperwork necessary to tailor our benefit package to your family situation. She will also arrange various orientation activities to help you acclimate to our company.

Try to embed any negative information in a positive context.

However, if your routine message is mixed and must convey mildly disappointing information, put the negative portion of your message into as favorable a context as possible:

Instead of This	Write This
No, we no longer carry the Sportsgirl line of sweaters.	The new Olympic line has replaced the Sportsgirl sweaters that you asked about. Olympic features a wider range of colors and sizes and more contemporary styling.

The more complete description is less negative and emphasizes how the audience can benefit from the change. Be careful, though: You can use negative information in this type of message *only* if you're reasonably sure the audience will respond positively. Otherwise, use the indirect approach (discussed in Chapter 8).

If you are communicating to customers, you might also want to use the body of your message to assure the customer of the wisdom of his or her purchase selection (without being condescending or self-congratulatory). Talking favorably about something the customer has bought even though it may not have been delivered yet is a good way to build customer relationships. Such favorable comments are commonly included in acknowledgments of orders and other routine announcements to customers, and they are most effective when they are relatively short and specific:

The zipper on the carrying case you purchased is double-stitched and guaranteed for the life of the product.

The Kitchen Aid mixer you ordered is our best-selling model. It should meet your cooking needs for many years.

Make sure the audience understands what to do next and how that action will benefit them.

End with a Courteous Close Your message is most likely to succeed if your readers are left feeling that you have their best interests in mind. You can accomplish this task either by highlighting a benefit to the audience or by expressing appreciation or goodwill. If follow-up action is required, clearly state who will do what next. See "Checklist: Writing Routine Replies and Positive Messages" to review the primary tasks involved in this type of business message.

Common Examples of Routine Replies and Positive Messages

As with routine requests, you'll encounter the need for a wide variety of routine replies and positive messages. You can expect to write letters for most routine messages directed

✓ CHECKLIST: Writing Routine Replies and Positive Messages

A. Start with the main idea

✓ Be clear and concise.
✓ Identify the single most important message before you start writing.

B. Provide necessary details and explanation

✓ Explain your point completely to eliminate any confusion or lingering doubts.
✓ Maintain a supportive tone throughout.

✓ Embed negative statements in positive contexts or balance them with positive alternatives.
✓ Talk favorably about the choices the customer has made.

C. End with a courteous close

✓ Let your readers know that you have their personal well-being in mind.
✓ If further action is required, tell readers how to proceed and encourage them to act promptly.

to people outside the company, although e-mail and instant messaging (with live operators or automated bots) are gaining in popularity in customer-service applications. Most routine and positive messages fall into six main categories: answers to requests for information and action, grants of claims and requests for adjustment, recommendations, informative messages, good-news announcements, and goodwill messages.

Answering Requests for Information and Action   Every professional answers requests for information and action from time to time, and some business functions answer such requests many times a day. If the response to a request is a simple yes or some other straight-forward information, the direct plan is appropriate. A prompt, gracious, and thorough response will positively influence how people think about you and the organization you represent. Depending on the resources your company offers, you might use letters, memos, e-mail, or instant messaging to answer these requests (see Figure 7–5).

Many requests can be similar. For example, a human resources department gets numerous routine inquiries about job openings. To handle repetitive queries like these quickly and consistently, companies usually develop form responses. With a form message as the starting point, you can personalize it for each recipient by using the mail merge capability in your word processor. For example, instead of addressing a form reply to "Dear Applicant," you can have the computer insert the recipient's name. If you have time and the message is important, go beyond this and revise the content of each letter with unique information about each recipient.

E-mail messages may be standardized as well. For example, when Julian Zamakis sent an e-mail to Herman Miller asking for information about employment opportunities, he received the encouraging e-mail reply in Figure 7–6.

When you're answering requests and a potential sale is involved, you have three main goals: (1) to respond to the inquiry and answer all questions, (2) to leave your reader with a good impression of you and your firm, and (3) to encourage the future sale. The following letter meets all three objectives:

Document Makeover

IMPROVE THIS E-MAIL MESSAGE

To practice correcting drafts of actual documents, visit your online course or the access-code protected portion of the Companion Website. Click "Document Makeovers," then click Chapter 7. You will find an e-mail message that contains problems and errors relating to what you've learned in this chapter about routine, good news, and goodwill messages. Use the "Final Draft" decision tool to create an improved version of this routine e-mail. Check the message for skilled presentation of the main idea, clarity of detail, proper handling of negative information, appropriate use of resale, and the inclusion of a courteous close.

Here is the brochure "Entertainment Unlimited" that you requested. This booklet describes the vast array of entertainment options available to you with an Ocean Satellite Device (OSD).
(Starts with a clear, statement of the main point)

On page 12 of "Entertainment Unlimited" you'll find a list of the 338 channels that the OSD brings into your home. You'll have access to movie, sport, and music channels; 24-hour news channels; local channels; and all the major television networks. OSD gives you a clearer picture and more precise sound than those old-fashioned dishes that took up most of your yard—and OSD uses only a small dish that mounts easily on your roof.
(Presents key information immediately, along with resale and sales promotion)

More music, more cartoons, more experts, more news, and more sports are available to you with OSD than with any other cable or satellite connection in this region. Yes, it's all there, right at your fingertips.
(Encourages readers to take one more step toward a purchase by highlighting product benefits)

Just call us at 1-800-786-4331, and an OSD representative will come to your home to answer your questions. You'll love the programming and the low monthly cost. Call us today!
(Points toward the sale confidently)

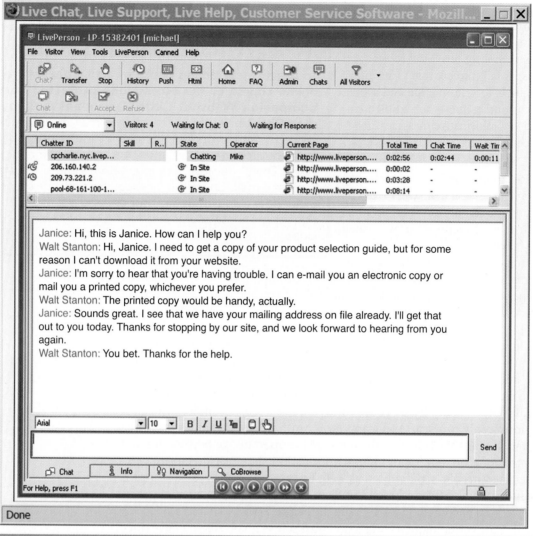

FIGURE 7–5
Effective Instant Messaging Response to Information Request

Granting Claims and Requests for Adjustment   Even the best-run companies make mistakes, from shipping the wrong order to billing the customer's credit card inaccurately. In other cases, the customer or a third party might be responsible for the mistake, such as misusing a product or damaging it in shipment. Each of these events represents a turning point in your relationship with your customer. If you handle the situation well, your customer will likely be even more loyal than before because you've proven that you're serious about customer satisfaction. However, if a customer believes that you mishandled a complaint, you'll make the situation even worse. Dissatisfied customers often take their business elsewhere without notice and tell numerous friends and colleagues about the negative experience. A transaction that might be worth only a few dollars by itself could cost you many times that amount in lost business. In other words, every mistake is an opportunity to improve a relationship.

Few people go to the trouble of requesting an adjustment unless they actually have a problem, so most businesses start from the assumption that the customer is correct. From there, your response to the complaint depends on both your company's policies for resolving such issues and your assessment of whether the company, the customer, or some third party is at fault.

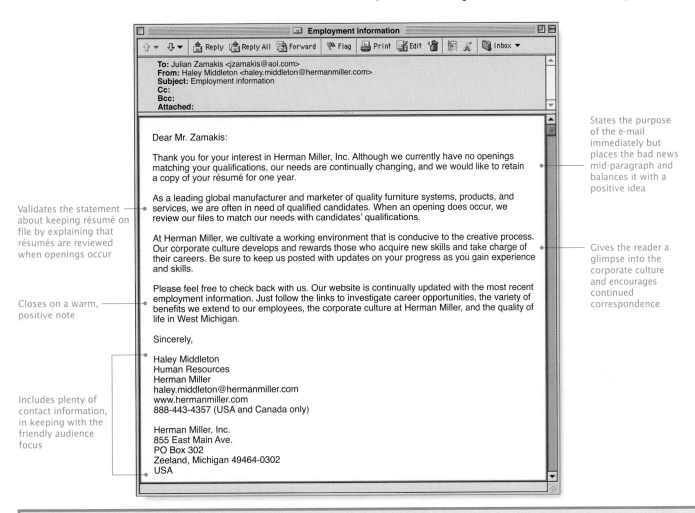

States the purpose of the e-mail immediately but places the bad news mid-paragraph and balances it with a positive idea

Validates the statement about keeping résumé on file by explaining that résumés are reviewed when openings occur

Gives the reader a glimpse into the corporate culture and encourages continued correspondence

Closes on a warm, positive note

Includes plenty of contact information, in keeping with the friendly audience focus

---

Employment information

⬆ ⬇ | 📥 Reply 📨 Reply All 📤 Forward | 🚩 Flag | 🖨 Print ✏ Edit 🗑 | ▦ A⁺ | 📥 Inbox ▾

To: Julian Zamakis <jzamakis@aol.com>
From: Haley Middleton <haley.middleton@hermanmiller.com>
Subject: Employment information
Cc:
Bcc:
Attached:

Dear Mr. Zamakis:

Thank you for your interest in Herman Miller, Inc. Although we currently have no openings matching your qualifications, our needs are continually changing, and we would like to retain a copy of your résumé for one year.

As a leading global manufacturer and marketer of quality furniture systems, products, and services, we are often in need of qualified candidates. When an opening does occur, we review our files to match our needs with candidates' qualifications.

At Herman Miller, we cultivate a working environment that is conducive to the creative process. Our corporate culture develops and rewards those who acquire new skills and take charge of their careers. Be sure to keep us posted with updates on your progress as you gain experience and skills.

Please feel free to check back with us. Our website is continually updated with the most recent employment information. Just follow the links to investigate career opportunities, the variety of benefits we extend to our employees, the corporate culture at Herman Miller, and the quality of life in West Michigan.

Sincerely,

Haley Middleton
Human Resources
Herman Miller
haley.middleton@hermanmiller.com
www.hermanmiller.com
888-443-4357 (USA and Canada only)

Herman Miller, Inc.
855 East Main Ave.
PO Box 302
Zeeland, Michigan 49464-0302
USA

FIGURE 7–6
Effective E-mail Replying to Request for Information

When Your Company Is at Fault Whenever you communicate about a mistake your company has made, do so carefully. Before you respond, make sure you know your company's policies in such cases, which might even dictate specific legal and financial steps to be taken. For serious problems that go beyond routine errors, your company should have a *crisis management plan* that outlines communication steps both inside and outside the organization (see Chapter 8).

Most routine responses should take your company's specific policies into account and address the following points:

- **Acknowledge receipt of the customer's claim or complaint.** Even if you can't solve the problem immediately, at least let the other party know that somebody is listening.

- **Take (or assign) personal responsibility for setting matters straight.** Customers don't want their complaints to fall into a bureaucratic black hole.

- **Sympathize with the customer's inconvenience or frustration.** Letting the customer see that you're on his or her side helps defuse the emotional element of the situation.

- **Explain precisely how you have resolved, or plan to resolve, the situation.** If you can respond exactly as the customer requested, be sure to communicate that. If you can't, explain why.

- **Take steps to repair the relationship.** Keeping your existing customers is almost always less expensive than acquiring new customers, so look for ways to go beyond simply granting the claim or fixing the problem, such as offering coupons to encourage future business.

- **Follow up to verify your response was correct.** Follow-up not only helps improve customer service but also gives you another opportunity to show how much you care about your customer.

In addition to these positive steps, maintain professional demeanor by avoiding some key negative steps as well: Don't blame anyone in your organization by name, don't make exaggerated apologies that sound insincere, don't imply that the customer is at fault, and don't promise more than you can deliver.

As with requests for information or action, some claims are likely to occur again and again, such as claims made against insurance policies or requests to correct orders. A form letter is an efficient way to begin the communication process. In the following example, a large mail-order clothing company created a form letter to respond to customers who complain that they haven't received exactly what was ordered. The form letter can easily be customized through word processing (perhaps to state the good news in the opening) and then individually signed:

Acknowledges receipt of the customer's communication

Explains what will happen next and when, without making promises the writer can't keep

Your letter concerning your recent Klondike order has been forwarded to our director of order fulfillment. Your complete satisfaction is our goal, and a customer service representative will contact you within 48 hours to assist with the issues raised in your letter.

Takes steps to repair the relationship and ensure continued business

In the meantime, please accept the enclosed $5 gift certificate as a token of our appreciation for your business. Whether you're skiing or driving a snowmobile, Klondike Gear offers you the best protection from wind, snow, and cold—and Klondike has been taking care of customers' outdoor needs for over 27 years.

Closes with statement of company's concern for all its customers

Thank you for taking the time to write to us. Your input helps us better serve you and all our customers.

In contrast, a response letter written as a personal answer to a unique claim would open with a clear statement of the good news: the settling of the claim according to the customer's request. The following is a more personal response from Klondike Gear:

Here is your heather-blue wool-and-mohair sweater (size large) to replace the one returned to us with a defect in the knitting. Thanks for giving us the opportunity to correct this situation. Customers' needs have come first at Klondike Gear for 27 years.

I've enclosed our newest catalog and a $5 gift certificate that's good toward any purchase from it. Whether you are skiing or driving a snowmobile, Klondike Gear offers you the best protection available from wind, snow, and cold. Please let us know how we may continue to serve you and your sporting needs.

When the Customer Is at Fault   Communication about a claim is a delicate matter when the customer is clearly at fault. You can (1) refuse the claim and attempt to justify your refusal or (2) simply do what the customer asks. If you refuse the claim, you may lose your customer—as well as many of the customer's friends and colleagues, who will hear only one side of the dispute. You must weigh the cost of making the adjustment against the cost of losing future business from one or more customers.

If you choose to grant the claim, you can open with the good news: You're replacing the merchandise or refunding the purchase price. However, the body needs more attention. Your job is to make the customer realize that the merchandise was mistreated, but you want to avoid being condescending ("Perhaps you failed to read the instructions carefully") or preachy ("You should know that wool shrinks in hot water"). The dilemma is this: If the customer fails to realize what went wrong, you may commit your firm to an endless procession of returned merchandise; but if you insult the customer, your cash refund will have been wasted because you'll lose your customer anyway. Close in a courteous manner that expresses your appreciation for the customer's business. Without being offensive, the letter in Figure 7–7 educates a customer about how to treat his in-line skates.

When a Third Party Is at Fault Sometimes neither your company nor your customer is at fault. for example, ordering a music CD from Amazon.com involves not only Amazon.com but also a distribution service such as Federal Express or the U.S. Postal Service, the manufacturer of the CD, a credit card issuer, and a company that processes credit card transactions. Any one of these other partners might be at fault, but the customer is likely to blame Amazon.com, since that is the entity that receives the customer's payment. In some transactions, the customer might not even be aware that third parties were involved.

No general scheme applies to every case involving a third party, so evaluate the situation carefully and know your company's policies before responding. For instance, an online retailer and the companies that manufacture its merchandise might have an agreement specifying that the manufacturers automatically handle all complaints about product quality. However, regardless of who eventually resolves the problem, if customers contact you, you need to respond with messages that explain how the problem will be solved. Pointing fingers is both unproductive and unprofessional; resolving the situation is the only issue customers care about. See "Checklist: Granting Claims and Adjustment Requests" to review the tasks involved in these kinds of business messages.

Providing Recommendations When writing a letter of recommendation, your goal is to convince readers that the person being recommended has the characteristics necessary for the job, project assignment, or other objective the person is seeking. A successful recommendation letter contains a number of relevant details:

- The candidate's full name

- The position or other objective the candidate is seeking

- The nature of your relationship with the candidate

- An indication of whether you're answering a request from the person or taking the initiative to write

- Facts and evidence relevant to the candidate and the opportunity

- A comparison of this candidate's potential with that of peers, if available (for example, "Ms. Jonasson consistently ranked in the top 10 percent of her class")

- Your overall evaluation of the candidate's suitability for the opportunity

As surprising as this might sound, the most difficult recommendation letters to write are often those for truly outstanding candidates. Your audience will have trouble believing uninterrupted praise for someone's talents and accomplishments. To enhance your credibility—and the candidate's—illustrate your general points with specific examples that point out the candidate's abilities and fitness for the job opening.

When granting an unjustified claim, maintain a respectful and positive tone while informing the customer that the claim was a result of misuse or mistreatment of the product.

Handling routine banking communication in a friendly, audience-focused way is one of the many reasons that Alexandria, Virginia-based Burke & Hebert enjoys almost fanatical customer loyalty. President Hunt Burke helps ensure that customer inquiries are handled promptly and courteously.

Planning

Analyze the Situation
Verify that the purpose is to grant the customer's claim, tactfully educate him, and encourage further business.

Gather Information
Gather information on product care, warranties, and resale information.

Select the Right Medium
The letter format gives this message an appropriate level of formality, which shows respect for the reader.

Organize the Information
You're responding with a positive answer, so a direct approach is fine.

Writing

Adapt to Your Audience
Show sensitivity to audience needs with a "you" attitude, politeness, positive emphasis, and bias-free language.

Compose the Message
Style is respectful while still managing to educate the customer on product usage and maintenance.

Completing

Revise the Message
Evaluate content and review readability, avoid unnecessary details.

Produce the Message
Emphasize a clean, professional appearance appropriate for a letter on company stationery.

Proofread the Message
Review for errors in layout, spelling, and mechanics.

Distribute the Message
Deliver the message via postal mail.

1   **2**   **3**

FIGURE 7–7   Effective Letter Responding to a Claim When the Buyer is at Fault

Skates Alive!

20901 El Dorado Hills
Laguna Niguel, CA 92677
(714) 332-7474 • Fax: (714) 336-5297
skates@speed.net

February 7, 2006

Mr. Steven Cox
1172 Amber Court
Jacksonville, FL 32211

Dear Mr. Cox:

Thank you for contacting Skates Alive! about your in-line skates. Even though your six-month warranty has expired, Skates Alive! is mailing you a complete wheel assembly replacement free of charge. The enclosed instructions make removing the damaged wheel line and installing the new one relatively easy.

[Acknowledges reader communication, keeps opening positive by avoiding words such as "problem," and conveys the good news right away]

The "Fastrax" (model NL 562) you purchased is our best-selling and most reliable skate. However, wheel jams may occur when fine particles of sand block the smooth rotating action of the wheels. These skates perform best when used on roadways and tracks that are relatively free of sand. We suggest that you remove and clean the wheel assemblies (see enclosed directions) once a month and have them checked by your dealer about every six months.

[Explains the problem without blaming the customer by avoiding the pronoun "you" and by suggesting ways to avoid future problems]

Because of your Florida location, you may want to consider our more advanced "Glisto" (model NL 988) when you decide to purchase new skates. Although this model is more expensive than the Fastrax, the Glisto design helps shed sand and dirt quite efficiently and should provide years of carefree skating.

[Includes sales promotion in the body, encouraging the customer to "trade up"]

Enjoy the enclosed copy of "Rock & Roll," with our compliments. Inside, you'll read about new products, hear from other skaters, and have an opportunity to respond to our customer questionnaire.

[Gives the reader a glimpse into the corporate culture and encourages continued correspondence]

We love hearing from our skaters, so keep in touch. All of us at Skates Alive! wish you good times and miles of healthy skating.

[Closes on an enthusiastic, positive note that conveys an attitude of excellent customer service]

Sincerely,

Candace Parker

Candace Parker
Customer Service Representative

Enclosure

✓ CHECKLIST: Granting Claims and Adjustment Requests

A. Responding when your company is at fault

✓ Be aware of your company's policies in such cases before you respond.
✓ For serious situations, refer to the company's crisis management plan.
✓ Start by acknowledging receipt of the claim or complaint.
✓ Take or assign personal responsibility for resolving the situation.
✓ Sympathize with the customer's frustration.
✓ Explain how you have resolved the situation (or plan to).
✓ Take steps to repair the customer relationship.
✓ Verify your response with the customer and keep the lines of communication open.

B. Responding when the customer is at fault

✓ Weigh the cost of complying with or refusing the request.
✓ If you choose to comply, open with the good news.
✓ Use the body of the message to respectfully educate the customer about steps needed to avoid a similar outcome in the future.
✓ Close with an appreciation for the customer's business.

C. Responding when a third party is at fault

✓ Evaluate the situation and review your company's policies before responding.
✓ Avoid placing blame; focus on the solution.
✓ Regardless of who is responsible for resolving the situation, let the customer know what will happen to resolve the problem.

Most candidates aren't perfect, however, and you'll need to decide how to handle each situation that comes your way. Omitting a reference to someone's shortcomings may be tempting, especially if the shortcomings are irrelevant to the demands of the job in question. Even so, you have an obligation to refer to any serious shortcoming that could be related to job performance. You owe it to your audience, to your own conscience, and even to better-qualified candidates. You don't have to present the shortcomings as simple criticisms, however. A good option is to list them as areas for improvement, even as areas the person might be working on now.

The danger in writing a critical letter is that you might inadvertently engage in libel, publishing a false and malicious written statement that injures the candidate's reputation. On the other hand, if that negative information is truthful and relevant, it may be unethical and even illegal to omit it from your recommendation. If you must refer to a shortcoming, you can best protect yourself by sticking to the facts, avoiding value judgments, and placing your criticism in the context of a generally favorable recommendation, as in Figure 7–8. In this letter, the writer supports all statements and judgments with evidence.

You can also avoid trouble by asking yourself the following questions before mailing a recommendation letter:

A serious shortcoming cannot be ignored, but beware of being libelous:
- Include only relevant, factual information
- Avoid value judgments
- Balance criticisms with favorable points

- Does the party receiving this personal information have a legitimate right to it?

- Does all the information I've presented relate directly to the job or benefit being sought?

- Have I put the candidate's case as strongly and as honestly as I can?

- Have I avoided overstating the candidate's abilities or otherwise misleading the reader?

- Have I based all my statements on firsthand knowledge and provable facts?

Before you dash off any recommendation letter, even for someone you know closely and respect without reservation, keep in mind that every time you write a recommendation, you're putting your own reputation on the line (see "Practicing Ethical Communications: What's Right to Write in a Recommendation Letter?"). If the person's shortcomings are so pronounced that you don't think he or she is a good fit for

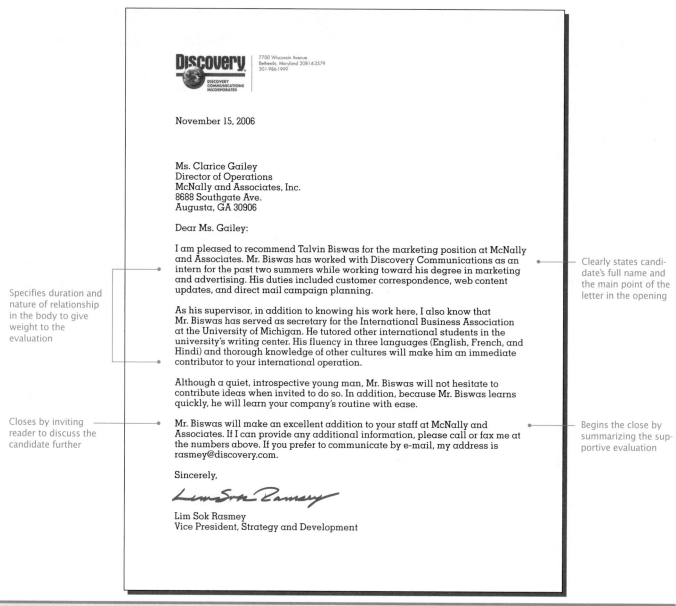

FIGURE 7–8
Effective Recommendation Letter

the job, the only choice is to not write the letter at all. Unless your relationship with the person warrants an explanation, simply suggest that someone else might be in a better position to provide a recommendation.

Creating Informative Messages All companies send routine informative messages such as reminder notices and policy statements. For instance, you may need to inform employees of organizational changes or tell customers about new shipping and return policies. Use the opening of informative messages to state the purpose (to inform) and briefly mention the nature of the information you are providing. Unlike the replies discussed earlier, informative messages are not solicited by your reader, so make it clear up front why the reader is receiving this particular message. In the body, provide the necessary details and end your message with a courteous close.

Most informative communications are neutral. That is, they stimulate neither a positive nor a negative response from readers. For example, when you send depart-

When writing informative messages:
- State the purpose at the beginning and briefly mention the nature of the information you are providing
- Provide the necessary details
- End with a courteous close

PRACTICING ETHICAL COMMUNICATION

What's Right to Write in a Recommendation Letter?

You were Frank Walker's supervisor for four years. When he left the company recently, he asked you to write a letter of recommendation for him. However, your company's legal experts said no.

WHY NOT GIVE RECOMMENDATIONS?

Thousands of lawsuits have been filed (and won) by employees, charging former employers with making slanderous (oral) and libelous (written) statements in job recommendations. During one seven-year period in California, employees won 72 percent of the libel and related suits they brought against employers, and their average award was $582,000. One employer lost for saying an employee had "suddenly resigned," which implied that the employee had resigned under "a veil of suspicion," said the court. Another employer lost for saying an employee was fired "for causes." Plus, when employees prove actual malice, damage awards skyrocket. To complicate matters, one court ruling held an employer liable for omitting information about a former employee.

So what sort of information should or should not be included in a recommendation? Even though some states have passed laws protecting companies against lawsuits when the employer acts in good faith, legal and human resources experts often advise companies to control what's being said by centralizing all recommendations. The cautious approach is to supply only dates of employment and titles of positions held—and to give that information only to people who have written authorization from former employees.

BUT WHAT IF YOU WANT TO GIVE A RECOMMENDATION?

Even so, Frank Walker was a terrific employee—a good friend—and you believe he really deserves a recommendation. You have two options. First, you can write the letter with Walker so that the contents satisfy you both and then discuss the letter with your human resources department before releasing it. The second option is to ask Walker to list you as a personal reference, which removes your company from any responsibility for statements you make. But be careful—you can still be held personally responsible for your comments.

Of course, if it had been Sharon Brown who asked for your recommendation, you'd be facing a different dilemma. Brown wasn't the greatest employee. So would you owe her potential employer the whole story? Including negative information could get you sued by Brown, and omitting negative information could get you sued by the hiring company for "failure to disclose" or "negligent referral."

Regardless of the circumstances, consult your human resources or legal department, and be sure to (1) comment only on your own experience working with a former employee, (2) make all comments in writing, and (3) limit your remarks to provable facts (don't exaggerate).

CAREER APPLICATIONS

1. A former employee was often late for work but was an excellent and fast worker who got along well with everyone. Do you think it's important to mention the tardiness to potential employers? If so, how will you handle it?

2. Step outside yourself for a moment and write a letter of recommendation about you from a former employer's perspective. Practice honesty, integrity, and prudence.

---

mental meeting announcements and reminder notices, you'll generally receive a neutral response from your readers (unless the purpose of the meeting is unwelcome). Simply present the factual information in the body of the message and don't worry too much about the reader's attitude toward the information.

Some informative messages may require additional care. For instance, policy statements or procedural changes may be good news for a company (perhaps by saving money). However, it may not be obvious to employees that such savings may make available additional employee resources or even pay raises. In instances where the reader may not initially view the information positively, use the body of the message to highlight the potential benefits from the reader's perspective.

Announcing Good News   To develop and maintain good relationships, smart companies recognize that it's good business to spread the word about positive developments. These can include opening new facilities, appointing a new executive, introducing new products or services, or sponsoring community events—such as the announcements that Carol Cone and her staff write for ConAgra and other clients. Because good news is always welcome, use the direct approach.

Writing to a successful job applicant is one of the most pleasant good-news messages you might have the opportunity to write. The following example uses the direct approach and provides information that the recipient needs:

Announces news in a friendly, welcoming tone →

> Welcome to Lake Valley Rehabilitation Center. A number of excellent candidates were interviewed, but your educational background and recent experience at Memorial Hospital make you the best person for the position of medical records coordinator.

Explains all necessary details →

> As we discussed, your salary is $29,200 a year. We would like you to begin on Monday, February 1. Please come to my office at 9 a.m. I will give you an in-depth orientation to Lake Valley and discuss the various company benefits available to you. You can also sign all the necessary employment documents.

Explains first day's routine to ease new employee's uncertainty →

> After lunch, Vanessa Jackson will take you to the medical records department and help you settle into your new responsibilities at Lake Valley Rehabilitation Center. I look forward to seeing you first thing on February 1.

Job-offer letters should be reviewed by legal experts familiar with employment law because they can be viewed as legally binding contracts.

Although letters like these are pleasant to write, they require careful planning and evaluation in order to avoid legal troubles. For instance, letters that imply lifetime employment or otherwise make promises about the length or conditions of employment can be interpreted as legally binding contracts, even if you never intended to make such promises. Similarly, downplaying potentially negative news (such as rumors of a takeover) that turns out to affect the hired person in a negative way can be judged as fraud. Consequently, experts advise that a company's legal staff either scrutinize each offer letter or create standardized content to use in such letters.[2]

Good-news announcements are usually communicated via a letter or a **news release**, also known as a *press release,* a specialized document used to share relevant information with the local or national news media. In most companies, news releases are usually prepared (or at least supervised) by specially trained writers in the public relations department (see Figure 7–9). The content follows the customary pattern for a positive message: good news, followed by details and a positive close. However, news releases have a critical difference: You're not writing directly to the ultimate audience (such as the readers of a newspaper); you're trying to interest an editor or reporter in a story, and that person will then write the material that is eventually read by the larger audience. To write a successful news release, keep the following points in mind:[3]

- Make sure your information is newsworthy and relevant. Most editors are overwhelmed with news releases, so those with little or no news content quickly find their way into the recycling bin—and damage the writer's credibility, too.

- Focus on one subject; don't try to pack a single news release with multiple, unrelated news items.

- Put your most important idea first. Don't force editors to hunt for the news.

- Be brief: Break up long sentences and keep paragraphs short.

- Eliminate clutter such as redundancy and extraneous facts.

- Be as specific as possible.

- Minimize self-congratulatory adjectives and adverbs; if the content of your message is newsworthy, the media professionals will be interested in the news on its own merits.

- Follow established industry conventions for style, punctuation, and format.

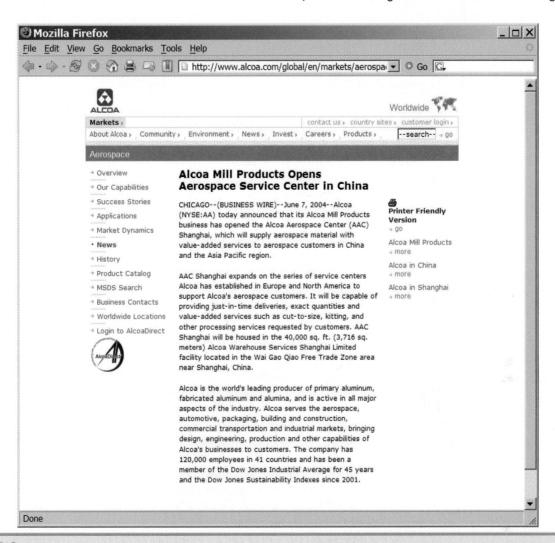

FIGURE 7–9
Online News Release

As with many aspects of business communication, the process of creating and distributing news releases and other media materials is continually improved by technological advances. Online distribution systems such as PR Newswire and BusinessWire make it easy for even the smallest companies to reach editors and reporters at the most prominent publications around the world. **Webcasting**, an online alternative to press conferences, lets you reach stock market analysts, reporters, and potential customers with a combination of *streaming audio* and *streaming video* presentations that bring voice and video to anyone with Internet access. Many companies also create special media pages on their websites that contain their latest news releases, background information on the company, and archives of past news releases.

Fostering Goodwill   All business messages should be written with an eye toward fostering goodwill among business contacts, but some messages are written primarily and specifically to build goodwill. You can use these messages to enhance your relationships with customers, colleagues, and other businesspeople by sending friendly, even unexpected notes with no direct business purpose.

Effective goodwill messages must be sincere and honest. Otherwise, you'll appear to be interested in personal gain rather than in benefiting customers, fellow workers, or your organization. To come across as sincere, avoid exaggerating, and back up any

Goodwill is the positive feeling that encourages people to maintain a business relationship.

Make sure your compliments are both sincere and honest.

compliments with specific points. In addition, readers often regard more restrained praise as being more sincere:

Instead of This	Write This
Words cannot express my appreciation for the great job you did. Thanks. No one could have done it better. You're terrific! You've made the whole firm sit up and take notice, and we are ecstatic to have you working here.	Thanks again for taking charge of the meeting in my absence and doing such an excellent job. With just an hour's notice, you managed to pull the legal and public relations departments together so that we could present a united front in the negotiations. Your dedication and communication abilities have been noted and are truly appreciated.

Taking note of significant events in someone's personal life helps cement the business relationship.

Sending Congratulations One prime opportunity for sending goodwill messages is to congratulate someone for a significant business achievement—perhaps for being promoted or for attaining an important civic position. Compare the congratulatory notes in Figure 7–10, in which a manager at Office Depot corporate headquarters congratulates an advertising agency that was awarded a prestigious national contract. The draft version sounds vague and insincere, and it doesn't bother to actually offer congratulations until the final sentence. In contrast, the revised version moves swiftly to the subject: the good news. It gives reasons for expecting success and avoids extravagant and essentially meaningless praise such as "Only you can do the job!"

Other reasons for sending congratulations include the highlights in people's personal lives—weddings, births, graduations, success in nonbusiness competitions. You may congratulate business acquaintances on their own achievements or on the accomplishments of a spouse or child. You may also take note of personal events, even if you don't know the reader well. If you're already friendly with the reader, a more personal tone is appropriate.

Some companies even develop a mailing list of potential customers by assigning an employee to clip newspaper announcements of births, engagements, weddings, and graduations or to obtain information on real estate transactions in the local community. Then they introduce themselves by sending out a form letter that might read like this:

Congratulations on your new home! All of us at Klemper Security Solutions hope it brings you and your family many years of security and happiness.

Please accept the enclosed *Homeowner's Guide to Home Security* with our compliments. It lists a number of simple steps you can take to keep your home, your family, and your possessions safe.

This simple message has a natural, friendly tone, even though the sender has never met the recipient.

An effective message of appreciation documents a person's contributions.

Sending Messages of Appreciation An important business quality is the ability to recognize the contributions of employees, colleagues, suppliers, and other associates. Your praise does more than just make the person feel good; it encourages further excellence. Moreover, a message of appreciation may become an important part of someone's personnel file. So when you write a message of appreciation, try to specifically mention the

FIGURE 7–10
Poor and Improved Versions of a Letter Congratulating a Business Acquaintance

We are so pleased when companies that we admire do well. When we attended our convention in Atlanta last month, we heard about your firm's recent selection to design and print media advertisements for the National Association of Business Suppliers (ABS).

We have long believed that high-visibility projects such as these should be awarded to only the top-tier companies in the industry, and Lambert, Cutchen & Browt is clearly the only company for the job.

We wish you the best of luck with your new ad campaign. Congratulations on a job well done!

Sincerely,

Janice McCarthy

Jaince McCarthy
Director, Media Relations

Draft

Sounds condescending and self-centered—expressing the reason but failing to actually congratulate the reader

Seems insincere because of the lack of supporting reasons and the exaggeration

Congratulating the reader in the close makes it seem like an afterthought

---

Office DEPOT, Inc.
2200 Old Germantown Road, Delray Beach, FL 33445   407/278-4800

March 2, 2006

Revision

Mr. Ralph Lambert, President
Lambert, Cutchen & Browt, Inc.
14355 Pasadena Parkway
Pasadena, TX 74229

Dear Mr. Lambert:

Congratulations on your firm's recent selection to design and print media advertisements for the National Association of Business Suppliers (ABS). Your appointment was announced at the national convention in Atlanta last month, and here at Office Depot we can think of no better firm to help our industry achieve wide recognition.

Over the course of many years, your firm's work for Office Depot has been nothing short of excellent. Both our corporate advertising staff here in Florida and regional promotional managers around the country continue to offer compliments on the quality of LCB's efforts. The campaign you will design for ABS is sure to yield similar positive responses.

You can be sure we will follow your media campaign with great interest.

Sincerely,

Janice McCarthy

Janice McCarthy
Director, Media Relations

tw

Opens by immediately expressing the reason for congratulating the reader

Uses body to make compliment more effective by showing knowledge of the reader's work— without exaggeration

Closes by expressing interest in following the future success of the firm person or people you want to praise. The brief message that follows expresses gratitude and reveals the happy result:

> Thank you for sending the air-conditioning components by overnight delivery. You allowed us to satisfy the needs of two customers who were getting very impatient with the heat.
>
> Special thanks to Susan Brown, who answered our call for help and never said, "It can't be done." Her initiative on our behalf is greatly appreciated.

The primary purpose of condolence messages is to let the audience know that you and the organization you represent care about the person's loss.

Offering Condolences   In times of serious trouble and deep sadness, well-written condolences and expressions of sympathy can mean a great deal to people who've experienced loss. Granted, this type of message is difficult to write, but don't let the difficulty of the task keep you from responding promptly. Those who have experienced a health problem, the death of a loved one, or a business misfortune appreciate knowing that others care.

Open condolences with a brief statement of sympathy, such as "I was deeply sorry to hear of your loss." In the body, mention the good qualities or the positive contributions made by the deceased. State what the person or business meant to you. In closing, you can offer your condolences and your best wishes. One considerate way to end this type of message is to say something that will give the reader a little lift, such as a reference to a brighter future. Here are a few general suggestions for writing condolence messages:

- **Keep reminiscences brief.** Recount a memory or an anecdote (even a humorous one), but don't dwell on the details of the loss, lest you add to the reader's anguish.

- **Write in your own words.** Write as if you were speaking privately to the person. Don't quote "poetic" passages or use stilted or formal phrases. If the loss is a death, refer to it as such rather than as "passing away" or "departing."

- **Be tactful.** Mention your shock and dismay, but remember that bereaved and distressed loved ones take little comfort in lines such as "Richard was too young to die" or "Starting all over again will be so difficult." Try to strike a balance between superficial expressions of sympathy and painful references to a happier past or the likelihood of a bleak future.

- **Take special care.** Be sure to spell names correctly and to be accurate in your review of facts. Try to be prompt.

- **Write about special qualities of the deceased.** You may have to rely on reputation to do this, but let the grieving person know you valued his or her loved one.

- **Write about special qualities of the bereaved person.** A pat on the back helps a bereaved family member feel more confident about handling things during such a traumatic time.[4]

Supervisor George Bigalow sent the following condolence letter to his administrative assistant, Janice Case, after learning of the death of Janice's husband:

> My sympathy to you and your children. All your friends at Carter Electric were so very sorry to learn of John's death. Although I never had the opportunity to meet him, I do know how very special he was to you. Your tales of your family's camping trips and his rafting expeditions were always memorable.

To review the tasks involved in writing goodwill messages, see "Checklist: Sending Goodwill Messages."

✓ CHECKLIST: Sending Goodwill Messages

✓ Be sincere and honest.

✓ Don't exaggerate or use vague, grandiose language; support positive statements with specific evidence.

✓ Use congratulatory messages to build goodwill with clients and colleagues.

✓ Send messages of appreciation to emphasize how much you value the work of others.

✓ When sending condolence messages, open with a brief statement of sympathy, followed by an expression of how much the deceased person meant to you or your firm (as appropriate), then close by offering your best wishes for the future.

On the Job

SOLVING COMMUNICATION DILEMMAS AT CONE, INC.

In addition to serving hot meals, the Kids Café program also provides a safe, nurturing environment that keeps kids out of trouble during the risky afternoon hours from 3:00 to 6:00. To make that time more valuable, many Kids Cafés have started offering sports, crafts, mentoring, and tutoring. These activities require qualified volunteers who are willing to spend a few hours each week working with the kids. To staff the tutoring program, ConAgra has asked Cone to create a recruiting campaign that will attract volunteers qualified to help with math, English, and science homework. As part of your job supervising the recruiting campaign, how would you handle these challenges?

1. One of the most important recruiting tools will be a letter addressed to current monetary donors, asking them to give as little as three hours a month. Donors in such situations are often asked to volunteer their time, so you can safely assume that the request will be received as a routine matter. Which of the following sounds like the best way to begin this letter?

   a. Money may make the world go 'round, but time is what our kids really need. Just a few hours a week is all we're asking for.

   b. Everyone involved with the Kids Café program sincerely appreciates your generous financial support, and I thank you personally as well. Since you've already demonstrated your commitment to the children, could we ask you to consider donating a few hours of your time every week as a tutor?

   c. Think of how easily we all waste three or four hours every week—whether it's watching pointless television shows or gabbing on the telephone. Wouldn't you welcome the opportunity to make something wonderful happen with a few of those wasted hours?

   d. As a successful adult, you've no doubt experienced one of those moments when you ask yourself, "Could I make a difference in a child's life by teach-

ing?" Just think of the sense of satisfaction that such a wonderful experience could bring to your life.

2. You've finished writing your opening and the body of the letter, which includes information about the volunteering program and the experience of being a tutor. Which of these closes would be the best way to conclude your letter?

   a. If you can lend a hand to our volunteer efforts by tutoring children in these subjects, please contact me by July 20 (my e-mail address and phone number are shown below). Thank you once again for your kind financial support, and I hope we'll be able to add you to our list of volunteer tutors as well.

   b. Please let me know if you'd be interested in helping out with the tutoring program. After all, anybody can write a check. Real heroes give of themselves—their time, their energy, and their skills.

   c. If you can lend a hand to our volunteer efforts by tutoring children in these subjects for two to four hours a week, or if you might be interested but want to know more about the program, please contact me by July 20 (my e-mail address and phone number are shown below). Thank you once again for your kind financial support, and I hope we'll be able to add you to our list of volunteer tutors as well.

   d. Thank you once again for your kind financial support, and I hope we'll be able to add you to our list of volunteer tutors as well. I look forward to hearing from you.

3. It's nine months later and the recruiting program has been a success. Most Kids Cafés have filled their volunteer openings, and some are expanding the tutoring program to other subjects because so many people volunteered. Now it's time write a letter to thank everyone who helps the children by volunteering their time every week. Each letter will include two free movie passes as a gesture of appreciation, and each will be personally signed by the CEO of

ConAgra. Which of these openings is the best way to start this letter of appreciation?

a. Executives such as myself are constantly asked to volunteer for a variety of community organizations, so I know how challenging it can be to find those free hours in your schedule every week—even if you're not busy running a multibillion-dollar corporation.

b. You are a miracle worker! Not many people are equipped with the skills, dedication, and commitment to the children that it takes to be a volunteer tutor, but you are definitely in that select company.

c. Helping people is what it's all about, isn't it? And now it's time for the good folks at ConAgra to help you in return with these FREE movie passes. Enjoy!

d. On behalf of everyone at ConAgra and everyone involved in the Kids Café program, please accept my sincere thanks for the time you've taken out of your busy schedule to help tutor the children at Kids Cafe. It's a small token, to be sure, but please accept these movie passes—I hope you'll find time to relax for a few hours with someone special.

4. One of the volunteer tutors from the Kids Café near your office has e-mailed you with a request to write a letter of recommendation for him. He says you have inspired him so much that not only does he want to work in the public relations field, but he wants to apply for a writing position at Cone. You're pleased to be an inspiration, but he just hasn't worked out as an English tutor because his own writing skills are too limited. In fact, you've been searching for other volunteer opportunities for him so that you can transfer him out of the tutoring program. How should you handle his request?

a. Ignore the request. The volunteer will get the message that you don't think his skills are sufficient to work at Cone.

b. Write the letter but steer clear of endorsing the volunteer's writing skills. Instead, focus on his ability to work with others, his commitment to helping the community, and his record of dependability.

c. Telephone the volunteer and explain that PR agencies have extremely high expectations for writers, and that his chances of being hired could be improved through some formal training and additional writing experience.

d. Reply by e-mail with an explanation that you don't really have time to write the letter now, but you'll try to get to it when things calm down.

Learning Objectives Checkup

Assess your understanding of the principles in this chapter by reading each learning objective and studying the accompanying exercises. For fill-in items, write the missing text in the blank provided; for multiple choice items, circle the letter of the correct answer. You can check your responses against the answer key on page AK-2.

Objective 7.1: Apply the three-step writing process to routine and positive messages.

1. When it comes to routine messages, you can
   a. Skip the planning stage
   b. Keep the planning stage brief
   c. Begin by gathering all the information you'll need
   d. Begin by choosing the channel and medium

2. When writing routine messages, you
   a. Can assume that your readers will be interested or neutral
   b. Should open with an "attention getter"
   c. Should use the indirect approach with most audiences
   d. Need not allow much time for revision, production, or proofreading

Objective 7.2: Illustrate an effective strategy for writing routine requests.

3. When writing a routine request, you begin
   a. With a personal introduction, such as "My name is Lee Marrs, and I am . . ."

   b. With a vague reference to what you are writing about, such as "I have something to ask you."
   c. With a strong demand for action
   d. By politely stating your request

4. What should you do when asking questions in a routine request?
   a. Begin with the least important question and work your way up to the most important question.
   b. Include all possible questions about the topic, even if the list gets long.
   c. Deal with only one topic per question.
   d. Do all of the above.

5. Which of the following should you do when closing a routine request?
   a. Be sure to thank the reader "in advance" for complying with the request.
   b. Ask the reader to respond by a specific and appropriate time.
   c. Ask any remaining questions you may have.
   d. Do all of the above.

Objective 7.3: Explain how to ask for specific action in a courteous manner.

6. A courteous close contains
   a. A specific request

b. Information about how you can be reached (if it isn't obvious)

c. An expression of appreciation or goodwill

d. All of the above

Objective 7.4: Illustrate a strategy for writing routine replies and positive messages.

7. If you are making a routine reply to a customer, it's a good idea to

a. Leave out any negative information

b. Include resale information to assure the customer of the wisdom of his or her purchase

c. Leave out sales promotion material, which would be tacky to include

d. Do all of the above

8. A positive message should open with a clear and concise statement of _____.

9. If a message has both positive and negative elements, you should

a. Always start with the bad news to get it out of the way first

b. Write two separate messages; never mix good and bad news

c. Put the bad news in a postscript (p.s.) at the bottom of the letter

d. Try to put the negative news in a positive context

Objective 7.5: Discuss the importance of knowing who is responsible when granting claims and requests for adjustment.

10. Which of the following is not among the recommended elements to include in your message if you are responding to a claim or complaint when your company is at fault?

a. An acknowledgement that you received the customer's claim or complaint

b. An expression of sympathy for the inconvenience or loss the customer has experienced

c. An explanation of how you will resolve the situation

d. Complete contact information for your corporate legal staff

11. If a customer who is clearly at fault requests an adjustment, you should

a. Ignore the request; the customer is clearly wasting your time

b. Carefully weigh the cost of complying with the request against the cost of denying it, then decide how to respond based on the overall impact on your company

c. Always agree to such requests, since unhappy customers spread bad publicity about your company

d. Suggest in a firm but professional tone that the customer take his or her business elsewhere in the future

12. If a third party (such as a shipping company) is at fault when one of your customers makes a claim or requests an adjustment, the best response is to

a. Follow the terms of whatever customer service agreement your company has with the third party

b. Explain to the customer that your company is not at fault

c. Always grant the request; after all, it's your customer, and the customer holds you responsible

d. Forward the message to the third party as quickly as possible

Objective 7.6: Explain how creating informative messages differs from responding to information requests.

13. Which of the following is generally true about informative messages?

a. Audiences always request informative messages.

b. Your audience may or may not be expecting them and may or may not be motivated to read them.

c. Audiences don't request informative messages, so they always reject them when they arrive.

d. Informative messages are always positive.

Objective 7.7: Describe the importance of goodwill messages, and explain how to make them effective.

14. The purpose of goodwill messages is to

a. Generate sales

b. Impress others

c. Make yourself feel better

d. Enhance relationships with customers, colleagues, and other businesspeople

15. The most effective goodwill messages

a. Always try to find an "angle" that benefits the sender in addition to the receiver

b. Avoid details and focus on the emotions of the situation

c. Are sincere and honest

d. Do all of the above

Apply Your Knowledge

1. When organizing request messages, why is it important to know whether any cultural differences exist between you and your audience? Explain.

2. Your company's error cost an important business customer a new client; you know it and your customer knows it. Do you apologize, or do you refer to the incident in a positive light without admitting any responsibility? Briefly explain.

3. You've been asked to write a letter of recommendation for an employee who worked for you some years ago. You recall that the employee did an admirable job, but you can't remember any specific information at this point. Should you write the letter anyway? Explain.

4. Every time you send a direct-request memo to Ted Jackson, who works in another department in your company, he delays or refuses to comply. You're beginning to

get impatient. Should you send Jackson a memo to ask what's wrong? Complain to your supervisor about Jackson's uncooperative attitude? Arrange a face-to-face meeting with Jackson? Bring up the problem at the next staff meeting? Explain.

5. **Ethical Choices** You have a complaint against one of your suppliers, but you have no documentation to back it up. Should you request an adjustment anyway? Why or why not?

Practice Your Knowledge

DOCUMENTS FOR ANALYSIS

Read the following documents; then (1) analyze the strengths and weaknesses of each sentence and (2) revise each document so that it follows this chapter's guidelines.

DOCUMENT 7.A: REQUESTING ROUTINE INFORMATION FROM A BUSINESS

Our college is closing its dining hall for financial reasons, so we want to do something to help the students prepare their own food in their dorm rooms if they so choose. Your colorful ad in Collegiate Magazine *caught our eye. We need the following information before we make our decision.*

- *Would you be able to ship the microwaves by August 15th? I realize this is short notice, but our board of trustees just made the decision to close the dining hall last week and we're scrambling around trying to figure out what to do.*
- *Do they have any kind of a warranty? College students can be pretty hard on things, as you know, so we will need a good warranty.*
- *How much does it cost? Do you give a discount for a big order?*
- *Do we have to provide a special outlet?*
- *Will students know how to use them, or will we need to provide instructions?*

As I said before, we're on a tight time frame and need good information from you as soon as possible to help us make our decision about ordering. You never know what the board might come up with next. I'm looking at several other companies, also, so please let us know ASAP.

DOCUMENT 7.B: MAKING CLAIMS AND REQUESTS FOR ADJUSTMENT

At a local business-supply store, I recently purchased your Negotiator Pro *for my computer. I bought the CD because I saw your ad for it in* MacWorld *magazine, and it looked as if it might be an effective tool for use in my corporate seminar on negotiation.*

Unfortunately, when I inserted it in my office computer, it wouldn't work. I returned it to the store, but since I had already opened it, they refused to exchange it for a CD that would work or give me a refund. They told me to contact you and that you might be able to send me a version that would work with my computer.

You can send the information to me at the letterhead address. If you cannot send me the correct disk, please refund my $79.95. Thanks in advance for any help you can give me in this matter.

DOCUMENT 7.C: RESPONDING TO CLAIMS AND ADJUSTMENT REQUESTS WHEN THE CUSTOMER IS AT FAULT

We read your letter requesting your deposit refund. We couldn't figure out why you hadn't received it, so we talked to our maintenance engineer as you suggested. He said you had left one of the doors off the hinges in your apartment in order to get a large sofa through the door. He also confirmed that you had paid him $5.00 to replace the door since you had to turn in the U-Haul trailer and were in a big hurry.

This entire situation really was caused by a lack of communication between our housekeeping inspector and the maintenance engineer. All we knew was that the door was off the hinges when it was inspected by Sally Tarnley. You know that our policy states that if anything is wrong with the apartment, we keep the deposit. We had no way of knowing that George just hadn't gotten around to replacing the door.

But we have good news. We approved the deposit refund, which will be mailed to you from our home office in Teaneck, New Jersey. I'm not sure how long that will take, however. If you don't receive the check by the end of next month, give me a call.

Next time, it's really a good idea to stay with your apartment until it's inspected as stipulated in your lease agreement. That way, you'll be sure to receive your refund when you expect it. Hope you have a good summer.

DOCUMENT 7.D: LETTER OF RECOMMENDATION

Your letter to Kunitake Ando, President of Sony, was forwarded to me because I am the human resources director. In my job as head of HR, I have access to performance reviews for all of the Sony employees in the United States. This means, of course, that I would be the person best qualified to answer your request for information on Nick Oshinski.

In your letter of the 15th, you asked about Nick Oshinski's employment record with us because he has applied to work for your company. Mr. Oshinski was employed with us from January 5, 1995, until March 1, 2005. During that time, Mr. Oshinski received ratings ranging from 2.5 up to 9.6, with 10 being the top score. As you can see, he must have done better reporting to some managers than to others. In addition, he took all vacation days, which is a bit unusual. Although I did not know Mr. Oshinski personally, I know that our best workers seldom use all the vacation time they earn. I do not know if that applies in this case.

In summary, Nick Oshinski performed his tasks well depending on who managed him.

Exercises

For active links to all websites discussed in this chapter, visit this text's website at **www.prenhall.com/thill**. Locate your book and click on its Companion Website link. Then select Chapter 7, and click on "Featured Websites." Locate the name of the page or the URL related to the material in the text. Please note that links to sites that become inactive after publication of the book will be removed from the Featured Websites section.

7.1 Revising Messages: Directness and Conciseness Revise the following short e-mail messages so that they are more direct and concise; develop a subject line for each revised message.

   a. I'm contacting you about your recent order for a High Country backpack. You didn't tell us which backpack you wanted, and you know we make a lot of different ones. We have the canvas models with the plastic frames and vinyl trim and we have the canvas models with leather trim, and we have the ones that have more pockets than the other ones. Plus they come in lots of different colors. Also they make the ones that are large for a big-boned person and the smaller versions for little women or kids.

   b. Thank you for contacting us about the difficulty you had collecting your luggage at Denver International Airport. We are very sorry for the inconvenience this has caused you. As you know, traveling can create problems of this sort regardless of how careful the airline personnel might be. To receive compensation, please send us a detailed list of the items that you lost and complete the following questionnaire. You can e-mail it back to us.

   c. Sorry it took us so long to get back to you. We were flooded with résumés. Anyway, your résumé made the final ten, and after meeting three hours yesterday, we've decided we'd like to meet with you. What is your schedule like for next week? Can you come in for an interview on June 15 at 3:00 P.M.? Please get back to us by the end of this work week and let us know if you will be able to attend. As you can imagine, this is our busy season.

   d. We're letting you know that because we use over a ton of paper a year and because so much of that paper goes into the wastebasket to become so much more environmental waste, starting Monday, we're placing white plastic bins outside the elevators on every floor to recycle that paper and in the process, minimize pollution.

7.2 Revising Messages: Directness and Conciseness Rewrite the following sentences so that they are direct and concise.

   a. We wanted to invite you to our special 40% off by-invitation-only sale. The sale is taking place on November 9.

   b. We wanted to let you know that we are giving a tote bag and a voucher for five iTunes downloads with every $50 donation you make to our radio station.

   c. The director planned to go to the meeting that will be held on Monday at a little before 11 A.M.

   d. In today's meeting, we were happy to have the opportunity to welcome Paul Eccelson. He reviewed some of the newest types of order forms. If you have any questions about these new forms, feel free to call him at his office.

7.3 Internet Visit the Career eCards section of the Blue Mountain site at **www.bluemountain.com** and analyze one of the electronic greeting cards bearing a goodwill message of appreciation for good performance. Under what circumstances would you send this electronic message? How could you personalize it for the recipient and the occasion? What would be an appropriate close for this message?

7.4 Teamwork With another student, identify the purpose and select the most appropriate format for communicating these written messages. Next, consider how the audience is likely to respond to each message. Based on this audience analysis, determine whether the direct or indirect approach would be effective for each message, and explain your reasoning.

   a. A notice to all employees about the placement of recycling bins by the elevator doors

   b. The first late-payment notice to a good customer who usually pays his bills on time

7.5 Revising Messages: Conciseness, Courteousness, and Specificity Critique the following closing paragraphs. How would you rewrite each to be concise, courteous, and specific?

   a. I need your response sometime soon so I can order the parts in time for your service appointment. Otherwise your air-conditioning system may not be in tip-top condition for the start of the summer season.

   b. Thank you in advance for sending me as much information as you can about your products. I look forward to receiving your package in the very near future.

   c. To schedule an appointment with one of our knowledgeable mortgage specialists in your area, you can always call our hotline at 1-800-555-8765. This is also the number to call if you have more questions about mortgage rates, closing procedures, or any other aspect of the mortgage process. Remember, we're here to make the home-buying experience as painless as possible.

7.6 Ethical Choices Your company markets a line of automotive accessories for people who like to "tune" their cars for maximum performance. A customer has just written a furious e-mail, claiming that a supercharger he purchased from your website didn't deliver the extra engine power he expected. Your company has a standard refund process to handle situations such as this, and you have the information you need to inform the customer about that. You also have information that could help the customer find a more compatible supercharger from one of your competitors, but the customer's e-mail message is so abusive that you don't feel obligated to help. Is this an appropriate response? Why or why not?

Expand Your Knowledge

LEARNING MORE ON THE WEB

RECOMMENDED ADVICE FOR RECOMMENDATION LETTERS
http://businessmajors.about.com

Whether you're continuing on to graduate school or entering the workforce with your undergraduate degree, recommendation letters could play an important role in the next few steps of your career. From selecting the people to ask for recommendation letters to knowing what makes an effective letter, About.com extends the advice offered in this chapter with real-life examples and suggestions.

ACTIVITIES

Visit About.com's Business Majors website and click on "Recommendation letters." Read the advice you find, then answer the following questions:

1. What's a good process for identifying the best people to ask for recommendation letters?
2. What information should you provide to letter writers to help them produce a credible and compelling letter on your behalf?
3. What are the most common mistakes you need to avoid with recommendation letters?

EXPLORING THE WEB ON YOUR OWN

1. Get answers to just about any grammar question at GrammarStation, www.grammarstation.com. Check your writing using the online grammar checker, review the basic parts of speech, and get intensive practice from the basics up to advanced writing concepts.
2. Need to write a news release but don't have time to become an expert? Learn from an expert at www.stetson.edu/~rhansen/prguide.html.
3. Get advice on writing sensitive condolence letters at www.ABusinessResource.com (search for "condolence letter").

Learn Interactively

INTERACTIVE STUDY GUIDE

Visit www.prenhall.com/thill, then locate your book and click on its Companion Website link. Select Chapter 7 to take advantage of the interactive "Chapter Quiz" to test your knowledge of chapter concepts. Receive instant feedback on whether you need additional studying. Also, visit the "Study Hall," where you'll find an abundance of valuable resources that will help you succeed in this course.

PEAK PERFORMANCE GRAMMAR AND MECHANICS

If your instructor has required the use of "Peak Performance Grammar and Mechanics," either in your online course or on CD, you can improve your skill with sentences by using the "Peak Performance Grammar and Mechanics" module. Click "Sentences." Take the Pretest to determine whether you have any weak areas. Then review those areas in the Refresher Course. Take the Follow-Up Test to check your grasp of sentences. For an extra challenge or advanced practice, take the Advanced Test. Finally, for additional reinforcement, go to the "Improve Your Grammar, Mechanics, and Usage" section that follows, and complete those exercises.

Improve Your Grammar, Mechanics, and Usage

The following exercises help you improve your knowledge of and power over English grammar, mechanics, and usage. Turn to the Handbook of Grammar, Mechanics, and Usage at the end of this textbook and review all of Section 1.7 (Sentences). Then look at the following 10 items. Circle the letter of the preferred choice within each group of sentences. (Answers to these exercises appear on page AK-3.)

1. a. Joan Ellingsworth attends every stockholder meeting. Because she is one of the few board members eligible to vote.
   b. Joan Ellingsworth attends every stockholder meeting. She is one of the few board members eligible to vote.
2. a. The executive director, along with his team members, is working quickly to determine the cause of the problem.
   b. The executive director, along with his team members, are working quickly to determine the cause of the problem.
3. a. Listening on the extension, details of the embezzlement plot were overheard by the security chief.

b. Listening on the extension, the chief overheard details of the embezzlement plot.

4. a. First the human resources department interviewed dozens of people. Then they hired a placement service.

 b. First the human resources department interviewed dozens of people then they hired a placement service.

5. a. Andrews won the sales contest, however he was able to sign up only two new accounts.

 b. Andrews won the sales contest; however, he was able to sign up only two new accounts.

6. a. To find the missing file, the whole office was turned inside out.

 b. The whole office was turned inside out to find the missing file.

7. a. Having finally gotten his transfer, he is taking his assistant right along with him.

 b. Having finally gotten his transfer, his assistant is going right along with him.

8. a. Irving was recruiting team members for her project, she promised supporters unprecedented bonuses.

 b. Because Irving was recruiting team members for her project, she promised supporters unprecedented bonuses.

9. a. He left the office unlocked overnight. This was an unconscionable act, considering the high crime rate in this area lately.

 b. He left the office unlocked overnight. An unconscionable act, considering the high crime rate in this area lately.

10. a. When it comes to safety issues, the abandoned mine, with its collapsing tunnels, are cause for great concern.

 b. When it comes to safety issues, the abandoned mine, with its collapsing tunnels, is cause for great concern.

For additional exercises focusing on sentences, go to www.prenhall. com/thill, then locate your text and click on its Companion Website link. Click on Chapter 7, click on "Additional Exercises to Improve Your Grammar, Mechanics and Usage," then click on "12. Longer sentences," "13. Sentence fragments," "15. Misplaced modifiers," or "24. Transitional words and phrases."

Cases

Applying the Three-Step Writing Process to Cases

Apply each step to the following cases, as assigned by your instructor

Planning

Writing

Completing

Analyze the Situation

Identify both your general purpose and your specific purpose. Clarify exactly what you want your audience to think, feel, or believe after receiving your message. Profile your primary audience, including their backgrounds, differences, similarities, and likely reactions to your message.

Gather Information

Identify the information your audience will need to receive, as well as other information you may need in order to craft an effective message.

Select the Right Medium

Make sure your medium is both acceptable to the audience and appropriate for the message.

Organize the Information

Choose a direct or indirect approach based on the audience and the message; most routine requests and routine and positive messages should employ a direct approach. Identify your main idea, limit your scope, then outline necessary support points and other evidence.

Adapt to Your Audience

Show sensitivity to audience needs with a "you" attitude, politeness, positive emphasis, and bias-free language. Understand how much credibility you already have—and how much you may need to establish. Project your company's image by maintaining an appropriate style and tone.

Compose the Message

Draft your message using powerful words, effective sentences, and coherent paragraphs.

Revise the Message

Evaluate content and review readability, then edit and rewrite for conciseness and clarity.

Produce the Message

Use effective design elements and suitable layout for a clean, professional appearance.

Proofread the Message

Review for errors in layout, spelling, and mechanics; verify overall document quality.

Distribute the Message

Deliver your message using the chosen medium; make sure all documents and all relevant files are distributed successfully.

1

2

3

ROUTINE REQUESTS

1. Step on it: Letter to Floorgraphics requesting information about underfoot advertising You work for Alberta Greenwood, owner of Better Bike and Ski Shop. Yesterday, Alberta met with the Schwinn sales representative, Tom Beeker, who urged her to sign a contract with Floorgraphics. That company leases floor space from retail stores, then creates and sells floor ads to manufacturers such as Schwinn. Floorgraphics will pay Alberta a fee for leasing the floor space, as well as a percentage for every ad it sells. Alberta was definitely interested, and turned to you after Beeker left.

"Tom says that advertising decals on the floor in front of the product reach consumers right where they're standing when making a decision," explained Alberta. "He says the ads increase sales from 25 to 75 percent."

You both look down at the dusty floor, and Alberta laughs. "It seems funny that manufacturers will pay hard cash to put their names where customers are going to track dirt all over them! But if Tom's telling the truth, we could profit three ways: from the leasing fee, the increased sales of products being advertised, and the share in ad revenues. That's not so funny."

Your task: Alberta Greenwood asks you to write a letter for her signature to CEO Richard Rebh at Floorgraphics, Inc. (5 Vaughn Dr., Princeton, NJ 08540) asking for financial details and practical information about the ads. For example, how will you clean your floors? Who installs and removes the ads? Can you terminate the lease if you don't like the ads?[5]

2. Breathing life back into your biotech career: E-mail requesting a recommendation After five years of work in the human resources department at Cell Genesys (a company that is developing cancer treatment drugs), you were laid off in a round of cost-cutting moves that rippled through the biotech industry in recent years. The good news is that you found stable employment in the grocery distribution industry. The bad news is that in the three years since you left Cell Genesys, you truly miss working in the exciting biotechnology field and having the opportunity to be a part of something as important as helping people recover from life-threatening diseases. You know that careers in biotech are uncertain, but you have a few dollars in the bank now, and you're willing to ride that rollercoaster again.

Your task: Draft an e-mail to Calvin Morris, your old boss at Cell Genesys, reminding him of the time you worked together and asking him to write a letter of recommendation for you.[6]

3. Trans-global exchange: Instant message request for information from Chinese manufacturer Thank goodness your company, Diagonal Imports, chose the enterprise instant messaging software produced by IBM Lotus, called Sametime. Other products might allow you to carry on real-time exchanges with colleagues on the other side of the planet, but Sametime supports bidirectional machine translation, and you're going to need it.

The problem is that production on a popular line of decorative lighting appliances produced at your Chinese manufacturing plant inexplicably came to a halt last month. As the product manager in the United States, you have many resources you could call on to help, such as new sources for faulty parts. But you can't do anything if you don't know the details. You've tried telephoning top managers in China, but they're evasive, telling you only what they think you want to hear.

Finally, your friend Kuei-chen Tsao has returned from a business trip. You met her during your trip to China last year. She doesn't speak English, but she's the line engineer responsible for this particular product: a fiber-optic lighting display, featuring a plastic base with a rotating color-wheel. As the wheel turns, light emitted from the spray of fiber-optic threads changes color in soothing patterns. Product #3347XM is one of Diagonal's most popular items and you've got orders from novelty stores around the United States waiting to be filled. Kuei-chen should be able to explain the problem, determine whether you can help, and tell you how long before regular shipping resumes.

Your task: Write the first of what you hope will be a productive instant message exchange with Kuei-Chen. Remember your words will be machine-translated.[7]

4. Tracking the new product buzz: Text message to colleagues at a trade show The vast Consumer Electronics Show (CES) is the premier promotional event in the industry. More than 130,000 industry insiders from all over the world come to see the exciting new products on display from nearly 1,500 companies—everything from videogame gadgets to Internet-enabled refrigerators with built-in computer screens. You've just stumbled on a videogame controller that has a built-in webcam to allow networked gamers to see and hear each other while they play. Your company also makes game controllers, and you're worried that your customers will flock to this new controller-cam. You need to know how much "buzz" is circulating around the show: Have people seen it? What are they saying about it? Are they excited about it?

Your task: Compose a text message to your colleagues at the show, alerting them to the new controller-cam and asking them to listen for any "buzz" that it might be generating among the attendees at the Las Vegas Convention Center and the several surrounding hotels where the show takes place. Here's the catch: Your text messaging service limits messages to 160 characters, including spaces and punctuation, so your message can't be any longer than this.[8]

ROUTINE MESSAGES

5. Temper, temper: E-mail to Metro Power employees about technology failures This is the third time in two months that your company, Metro Power, has had to escort an employee from the building after a violent episode. Frankly, everyone is a little frightened by this development, and as a human resources administrator, you have the unhappy task of trying to quell the storm.

Metro Power rarely fires employees, preferring to transfer them to new responsibilities, which may either draw out their finer points (and prove better for everyone in the long run) or help them decide to seek greener pastures. But in three cases, you had no choice. In one incident, a man punched out his computer screen after the system failed. In another, a man threw his keyboard across the room when he couldn't get access to the company's intranet. And in a third incident, a woman kicked a printer while screaming obscenities.

In all three cases, co-workers were terrified by these sudden outbursts. Too many disgruntled workers have committed too many violent acts against others in recent years, and whenever workers lose their temper on the job these days, it causes great fear—not to mention financial losses from the destruction of property and the disruption of work flow.

People are on edge at Metro Power right now. Rising energy costs, public and government scrutiny, and cries of price gouging are causing additional work and stress for all your employees. Plus, too much overtime, unrealistic expectations for overworked departments, and high demands on sensitive equipment are contributing to the problem. Tempers are frayed and nerves strained. You're concerned that these three incidents are just the tip of the iceberg.

Your department head suggests that you write a reminder to all employees about controlling tempers in the workplace. "Tell them that technology glitches are commonplace and not some unholy disaster. And remind them to report routine computer failures to Bart Stone. He'll get to them in due course."

You say nothing to contradict her idea, but you wonder how to do what she asks without sounding trite or condescending? You don't want to sound like some nagging parent—no one will pay attention to your message. You sigh deeply as your boss strolls calmly back to her office. You're fairly certain that every employee already knows about reporting computer failures to Bart Stone, assistant director of information services.

Even so, you can think of a few suggestions that might be helpful, such as taking a walk to cool down, or recognizing that machines, like humans, are not infallible. You want cooler heads to prevail, and that's just the sort of cliché you'd like to avoid in your message.

Your task: Write the e-mail message to all employees. Instead of uttering platitudes or wagging your finger, include preventive maintenance tips for office equipment, such as turning systems off at night, keeping food and liquids away from keyboards, making use of dusting sprays and special cloths, and so on. Your boss also asked you to make it clear that abusive behavior will be reprimanded, so include that point in a tactful way.[9]

6. Listening to business: Using the iPod to train employees As a training specialist in Winnebago Industry's human resources department, you're always on the lookout for new ways to help employees learn vital job skills. While watching a production worker page through a training manual while learning how to assemble a new recreational vehicle, you get what seems to be a great idea: record the assembly instructions as audio files that workers can listen to while performing the necessary steps. With audio instructions, they wouldn't need to keep shifting their eyes between the product and the manual—and constantly losing their place. They could focus on the product and listen for each instruction. Plus, the new system wouldn't cost much at all; any computer can record the audio files, and you'd simply make them available on an Intranet site for download into iPods or other digital music players.

Your task: You immediately run your new idea past your boss, who has heard about podcasting but doesn't think it has any place in business. He asks you to prove the viability of the idea by recording a demonstration. Choose a process that you engage in yourself—anything from replacing the strings on a guitar to sewing a quilt to changing the oil in a car—and write a brief (one page or less) description of the process that could be recorded as an audio file. Think carefully about the limitations of the audio format as a replacement for printed text (for instance, do you need to tell people to pause the audio while they perform a time-consuming task?).

7. Got it covered? Letter from American Express about SUV rentals You can always tell when fall arrives at American Express—you are deluged with complaints from customers who've just received their summer vacation bills. Often these angry calls are about a shock-inducing damage repair bill from a car rental agency. Vacation car rentals can be a lot more complicated than most people think. Here's what happens.

Your credit card customers are standing at the Hertz or Avis counter, ready to drive away, when the agent suggests an upgrade to, say, a Ford Expedition or another large SUV. Feeling happy-go-lucky on vacation, your customers say, "Why not?" and hand over their American Express card.

As they drive off in large vehicles that many are unaccustomed to handling, 9 out of 10 are unaware that the most common accidents among rental cars take place at low speeds in parking lots. Plus, the upgraded vehicle they're driving is no longer fully covered either by their regular auto insurance or by the secondary car rental insurance they expect from American

Express. If they've agreed to pay the additional $10 to $25 a day for the car rental agency's "collision and liability damage wavier fee," they will be able to walk away from any accident with no liability. Otherwise, they're running a costly risk.

Soon they pull into a shopping mall with the kids to pick up the forgotten sunscreen and sodas, where they discover that luxury road-warrior mobile is not so easy to park in stalls designed in the 1970s and 1980s when compact cars were all the rage. *Thwack*—there goes the door panel. *Crunch*—a rear bumper into a light post. *Wham!* There goes the family bank account, but they don't realize it yet—not until they receive the bill from the rental agency, the one that comes *after* their auto insurance and credit card companies have already paid as much as they're going to pay for damages.

Auto insurers typically provide the same coverage for rentals as you carry on your own car. When customers use their credit card to pay for car rentals, American Express offers secondary protection that generally covers any remaining, unpaid damages. But there are important exceptions.

Neither insurance nor credit card companies will pay the "loss of vehicle use fees" that car rental agencies always tack on. These fees can run into thousands of dollars, based on the agency's revenue losses while their car is in the repair shop. When your customers are billed for this fee, they invariably call you, angrily demanding to know why American Express won't pay it. And if they've rented an SUV, they're even angrier.

American Express Green and Gold cards provide secondary coverage up to $55,000, and the Platinum card extends that to $75,000. But large SUVs such as the Ford Expedition, GMC Yukon, and Chevrolet Suburban are not covered at all. Such exclusions are common. For instance, Diners Club specifically excludes "high-value, special interest or exotic cars"—such as the Ferraris, Maseratis, and even Rolls Royces that are urged on customers by rental agencies.

Your task: As assistant vice president of customer service, you'd like to keep the phone lines cooler this summer and fall. It's April, so there's still time. Write a form letter to be sent to all American Express customers, urging them to check their rental car coverages, advising them against renting vehicles that are larger than they really require, and encouraging them to consider paying the rental agency's daily loss waiver fees.[10]

8. Stargazing: News release announcing new life for Mount Wilson Observatory Today, gazing at spectacular, four-color images of star clusters, nebulae, and galaxies requires only a click on the Internet, thanks to the Hubble Space Telescope and websites like the Hawaiian Astronomical Society's (www.hawastsoc.org/deepsky/index.html). But in 1929, Edwin P. Hubble searched the stars night after night, climbing up to a chilly wooden platform high in the dome that houses the 100-inch Hooker telescope at the Mount Wilson Observatory on the outskirts of Los Angeles. His computer-bereft studies of light from distant galaxies required endless analysis of crude photographic plates taken with the help of his assistant, a former mule skinner named Milton Humason. Their hard work paid off, however, and Hubble is credited with discovering the redshift that is the basis for the Big Bang theory of an expanding universe.

With the famous new space-based telescope named in his honor, we won't forget Hubble. But Mount Wilson and the Hooker telescope faded from importance as scientists rushed to larger scopes on bigger, darker mountains. In the 1980s, the Hooker was closed for eight years. Its 4.5-ton, green-glass mirror (built by a French wine-bottle manufacturer) became no more than a relic to curious visitors to the site in the San Gabriel Mountains, outside Pasadena.

Now the organization you work for, the Mount Wilson Institute, administers a reborn observatory, playing host to scientists from all over the map. And the Hooker telescope is once again making history.

For example, a team led by Dr. Laird Thompson of the University of Illinois is using the Hooker to test a computerized system of "laser adaptive optics." Adaptive optics have long been used to cancel the blur caused by atmospheric distortions, relying on natural guide stars to give computers a standard for making optical adjustments. But certain areas of space lack sufficient guide stars. Dr. Thompson's team is testing a 12-mile-high ultraviolet laser beam, sent into space at 333 pulses a second, as an artificial guide for adjustments. The resulting views are clearer than anything Hubble ever saw.

Mount Wilson also features an older, 60-inch telescope, a 60-foot solar tower operated by the University of Southern California for NASA, and a 150-foot solar tower run by the University of California at Los Angeles. A group headed by Dr. Harold A. McAlister (from Georgia State University) and another led by Nobel Prize–winning physicist Dr. Charles Townes (from the University of California at Berkeley) are both at the observatory conducting tests with "interferometry," using arrays of small telescopes to collect starlight simultaneously.

McAlister's team combines six small telescopes to mimic the effect of a single scope with an 1,100-foot mirror—impossible to build, but capable of detecting stellar details 200 times finer than the Hubble Space Telescope. Townes' group is using an array to make star surfaces visible beneath dust clouds.

Your task: Targeting science journalists, write a news release from the Mount Wilson Institute, a nonprofit, tax-exempt consortium of astronomers, educators, and private donors, which is directed by Dr. Robert Jastrow, former NASA scientist and author of astronomy books. You're hoping for news coverage of the observatory's new activities, which may attract donors. At the close of your release, invite journalists to sign up for a night tour with Dr. Jastrow and the scientists mentioned. Journalists can request a detailed science data sheet now or at the tour.[11]

ROUTINE REPLIES

9. Auto-talk: E-mail messages for Highway Bytes computers to send automatically You are director of customer services at Highway Bytes, which markets a series of small, handlebar-mounted computers for bicyclists. These Cycle Computers do everything, from computing speed and distance traveled to displaying street maps. Serious cyclists love them, but your company is growing so fast that you can't keep up with all the customer service requests you receive every day. Your boss wants not only to speed up response time but also to reduce staffing costs and allow your technical experts the time they need to focus on the most difficult and important questions.

You've just been reading about automated response systems, and you quickly review a few articles before discussing the options with your boss. Artificial intelligence researchers have been working for decades to design systems that can actually converse with customers, ask questions, and respond to requests. Some of today's systems have vocabularies of thousands of words and the ability to understand simple sentences. For example, *chatterbots* are automated bots that can actually mimic human conversation. (You can see what it's like to carry on a conversation with some of these bots by visiting www.botspot.com, clicking on Artificial Life Bots, and then selecting Chatterbots.)

Unfortunately, even though chatterbots hold a lot of promise, human communication is so complex that a truly automated customer service agent could take years to perfect (and may even prove to be impossible). However, the simplest automated systems are called *autoresponders* or *e-mail–on-demand*. They are fast and extremely inexpensive. They have no built-in intelligence, so they do nothing more than send back the same reply to every message they receive.

You explain to your boss that although some of the messages you receive require the attention of your product specialists, many are simply requests for straightforward information. In fact, the customer service staff already answers some 70 percent of e-mail queries with three ready-made attachments:

- *Installing Your Cycle Computer.* Gives customers advice on installing the cycle computer the first time or reinstalling it on a new bike. In most cases, the computer and wheel sensor bolt directly to the bike without modification, but certain bikes do require extra work.

- *Troubleshooting Your Cycle Computer.* Provides a step-by-step guide to figuring out what might be wrong with a malfunctioning cycle computer. Most problems are simple, such as dead batteries or loose wires, but others are beyond the capabilities of your typical customer.

- *Upgrading the Software in Your Cycle Computer.* Tells customers how to attach the cycle computer to their home or office PC and download new software from Highway Bytes.

Your boss is enthusiastic when you explain that you can program your current e-mail system to look for specific words in incoming messages and then respond, based on what it finds. For example, if a customer message contains the word "installation," you can program the system to reply with the "Installing Your Cycle Computer" attachment. This reconfigured system should be able to handle a sizeable portion of the hundreds of e-mails your customer service group gets every week.

Your task: First, draft a list of key words that you'll want your e-mail system to look for. You'll need to be creative and spend some time with a thesaurus. Identify all the words and word combinations that could identify a message as pertaining to one of the three subject areas. For instance, the word *attach* would probably indicate a need for the installation material, whereas *new software* would most likely suggest a need for the upgrade attachment.

Second, draft three short e-mail messages to accompany each ready-made attachment, explaining that the attached document answers the most common questions on a particular subject (installation, troubleshooting, or upgrading). Your messages should invite recipients to write back if the attached document doesn't solve the problem, and don't forget to provide the e-mail address: support2@highwaybytes.com.

Third, draft a fourth message to be sent out whenever your new system is unable to figure out what the customer is asking for. Simply thank the customer for writing and explain that the query will be passed on to a customer service specialist who will respond shortly.

10. The special courier: Letter of recommendation for an old friend In today's mail you get a letter from Non-Stop Messenger Service, 899 Sparks St., Ottawa, Ontario K1A 0G9, Canada. It concerns a friend of yours who has applied for a job. Here is the letter:

> Kathryn Norquist has applied for the position of special courier with our firm, and she has given us your name as a reference. Our special couriers convey materials of considerable value or confidentiality to their recipients. It is not an easy job. Special couriers must sometimes remain alert for periods of up to 20 hours, and they cannot expect to follow the usual "three square meals and eight hours' sleep" routine because they often travel long distances on short notice. On occasion, a special courier must react quickly and decisively to threatening situations.
>
> For this type of work, we hire only people of unquestioned integrity, as demonstrated both by their public records and by references from people, like you, who have known them personally or professionally.
>
> We would appreciate a letter from you, supplying detailed answers to the following questions: (1) How long and in what circumstances have you known the applicant? (2) What qualities does she possess that would qualify her for the position of special courier? (3) What qualities might be improved before she is put on permanent assignment in this job?

As vice president of human resources at DHL, you know how much weight a strong personal reference can carry, and you don't really mind that Kathryn never contacted you for permission to list your name—that's Kathryn. You met her during your sophomore year at San Diego State University—that would have been 1994—and you two were roommates for several years after. Her undergraduate degree was in journalism, and her investigative reporting was relentless. You have never known anyone who could match Kathryn's stamina when she was on a story. Of course, when she was between stories, she could sleep longer and do less than anyone else you have ever known.

After a few years reporting, Kathryn went back to school and earned her MBA from the University of San Diego, and after that you lost track of her for awhile. Somebody said that she had joined the FBI—or was it the CIA?—you never really knew. You received a couple of postcards from Paris and one from Madrid.

Two years ago, you met Kathryn for dinner. Only in town for the evening, she was on her way to Borneo to "do the text" for a photographer friend of hers who worked for National Geographic. You read the article last year on the shrinking habitat for orangutans. It was powerful.

Although you're in no position to say much about Kathryn's career accomplishments, you can certainly recommend her energy and enthusiasm, her ability to focus on a task or assignment, her devotion to ethics, and her style. She always seems unshakable—organized, thorough, and honorable, whether digging into political corruption or trudging the jungles of Borneo. You're not sure that her free spirit would flourish in a courier's position, and you wonder if she wouldn't be a bit overqualified for the job. But knowing Kathryn, you're confident she wouldn't apply for a position unless she truly wanted it.

Your task: Supplying any details you can think of, write as supportive a letter as possible about your friend Kathryn to Roscoe de la Penda, Human Resources Specialist, Non-Stop Messenger.

11. Shopping for talent: Memo at Clovine's recommending a promotion You enjoy your duties as manager of the women's sportswear at Clovine's—a growing chain of moderate to upscale department stores in South Florida. You especially enjoy being able to recommend someone for a promotion. Today, you received a memo from Rachel Cohen, head buyer for women's apparel. She is looking for a smart, aggressive employee to become assistant buyer for Clovine's women's sportswear division. Clovine's likes to promote from within, and Rachel is asking all managers and supervisors for likely candidates. You have just the person she's looking for.

Jennifer Ramirez is a salesclerk in the designer sportswear boutique of your main store in Miami, and she has caught your attention. She's quick, friendly, and good at sizing up a customer's preferences. Moreover, at recent department meetings, she's made some intelligent remarks about new trends in South Florida.

Your task: Write a memo to Rachel Cohen, head buyer, women's sportswear, recommending Jennifer Ramirez, and evaluating her qualifications for the promotion. Rachel can check with the human resources department about Jennifer's educational and employment history; you're mainly interested in conveying your positive impression of Jennifer's potential for advancement.

12. Lighten up: E-mail reply to a website designer at Organizers Unlimited When Kendra Williams, owner of Organizers Unlimited, wanted to create a website to sell her Superclean Organizer, she asked you, her assistant, to find a designer. After some research, you found three promising individuals. Williams chose Pete Womack, whose résumé impressed both of you. Now he's e-mailed his first design proposal and Williams is not happy.

"I detest cluttered websites!" she explodes. "This homepage has too many graphics and animations, too much 'dancing baloney.' He must have included at least a megabyte of bouncing cotton balls and jogging soap bars! Clever, maybe, but we don't want it! If the homepage takes too long to load, our customers won't wait for it and we'll lose sales."

Williams' dislike of clutter is what inspired her to invent the Superclean Organizer in the first place, a neat device for organizing bathroom items.

Your task: "You found him," says Williams, "now you can answer and tell him what's wrong with this design." Before you write the e-mail reply to Womack explaining the need for a simpler homepage, read some of the articles offering tips at www. sitepoint.com. On the homepage, under "Before You Code," select "Site Planning" and under "Design and Layout" select "Design Principles." Use these ideas to support your message.[12]

13. Yes, we do purple: Instant message from Lands' End When clothing retailer Lands' End offered its 2,500 telephone service representatives the chance to train on its new instant messaging system, "Lands' End Live," you jumped at the opportunity. As it turned out, so many volunteered for the new training that the company had to give preference to a few hundred who'd been on the job longest. You were one of the lucky ones.

Now you've had months of practice answering messages like the one you just received from a customer named Alicia. She wants to know if she can have a red Polartec Aircore-200 Scarf custom monogrammed—not in the standard, contrasting wheat-colored thread, but in radiant purple as a gift for her husband, whose favorite colors are red and purple.

On its website, Lands' End promises to fulfill nonstandard monogram requests "if technical limitations allow." You've done a quick check and yes, her husband can have his initials in bright purple on the red background.

Your task: Write the instant message reply to Alicia, telling her the good news.[13]

POSITIVE MESSAGES

14. Leveraging the good news: Blog announcement of a prestigious professional award You and your staff in the public relations (PR) department at Epson of America were delighted when the communication campaign you created for the new PictureMate Personal Photo Lab (www.epson.com/picturemate) was awarded the prestigious Silver Anvil award by the Public Relations Society of America. Now you'd like to give your team a pat on the back by sharing the news with the rest of the company.

Your task: Write a one-paragraph message for the PR department blog (which is read by people throughout the company but is not accessible outside the company), announcing the award. Take care not to "toot your own horn" as the manager of the PR department and use the opportunity to compliment the rest of the company for designing and producing such an innovative product.[14]

15. Our sympathy: Condolence letter to an Aetna underwriter As chief administrator for the underwriting department of Aetna Health Plans in Walnut Creek, California, you're facing a difficult task. One of your best underwriters, Hector Almeida, recently lost his wife in an automobile accident (he and his teenaged daughter weren't with her at the time). Since you're the boss, everyone in the close-knit department is looking to you to communicate the group's sympathy and concern.

Someone suggested a simple greeting card that everyone could sign, but that seems so impersonal for someone you've worked with every day for nearly five years. So you decided to write a personal note on behalf of the whole department. You met Hector's wife, Rosalia, at a few company functions although you knew her mostly through Hector's frequent references to her. Although you didn't know her well, you do know important things about her life, which you can celebrate in the letter.

Right now he's devastated by the loss. But if anyone can overcome this tragedy, Hector can. He's always determined to get a job done no matter what obstacles present themselves, and he does it with an upbeat attitude. That's why everyone in the office likes him so much.

You also plan to suggest that when he returns to work, he might like to move his schedule up an hour so that he'll have more time to spend with his daughter, Lisa, after school. It's your way of helping make things a little easier for them during this period of adjustment.

Your task: Write the letter to Hector Almeida, who lives at 47 West Ave., #10, Walnut Creek, CA 94596. (Feel free to make up any details you need.)[15]

Chapter 8

Writing Negative Messages

Learning Objectives

AFTER STUDYING THIS CHAPTER, YOU WILL BE ABLE TO

1 Apply the three-step writing process to negative messages

2 Explain the differences between the direct and the indirect approaches to negative messages, including when it's appropriate to use each one

3 Identify the risks of using the indirect approach, and explain how to avoid such problems

4 Adapt negative messages for internal and external audiences

5 Define defamation and explain how to avoid it in negative messages

6 Explain the role of communication in crisis management

7 List three guidelines for delivering negative news to job applicants and give a brief explanation of each one

On the Job

DOES AN APOLOGY MAKE GOOD BUSINESS SENSE?

Apologies can be a complex communication challenge, as you know from your own personal life. When someone offers you an apology, do you accept it? Reject it? Analyze why it was offered? And when you offer someone else an apology, what are your motives? Are you truly sorry when you say "I'm sorry," or is some small part of you just hoping to get out of trouble? Have you ever apologized for something and gotten in even more trouble as a result?

When businesses make mistakes, they face the same dilemmas and the same skepticism from their audiences. One school of thought says that in our litigious society, companies can't afford to apologize because doing so is an admission of guilt that can be used against them in lawsuits. However, an emerging school says that the risks associated with apologizing are actually lower than previously believed, and that courts tend to show leniency toward companies that have expressed remorse.

The large accounting firm KPMG faced this dilemma in 2005, when the U.S. Internal Revenue Service ruled that *tax shelters* the company had been advising for some of its wealthy clients were illegal. (A tax shelter is an investment opportunity created primarily to reduce the investor's overall tax burden.) In KPMG's case, the stakes were enormous. It faced a

When the accounting firm KPMG publicly apologized for the illegal actions of some of its partners (one of whom, Jeffrey Eischeid, is shown here leaving the courthouse), the admission of guilt helped save the firm from potentially devastating criminal charges but could work against it in numerous client lawsuits.

criminal investigation from the Justice Department and multiple lawsuits from individual clients, accusing the company of encouraging them to break the law. Just a few years earlier, former KPMG competitor Arthur Andersen had been convicted in criminal matters relating to accounting work it had done for clients—and it collapsed as a result, putting 85,000 people out of work.

KPMG faced a double dilemma, in fact. If it apologized in an effort to avoid criminal prosecution, that admission of guilt could be used against it in all those individual civil suits.

Apparently deciding that a criminal charge would be more dangerous, KPMG issued the following statement in a press release: "KPMG takes full responsibility for the unlawful conduct by former KPMG partners . . . and we deeply regret that it occurred." The apology seemed to help, as the firm avoided a criminal indictment by agreeing to pay a fine of nearly a half billion dollars and to get out of the tax shelter business. However, the admission of guilt was welcomed by lawyers representing individual clients. "It's stunning. Obviously, it's very helpful," said one. With those lawsuits likely to drag on for years, only time will tell how well that admission served the company.[1]

www.us.kpmg.com

USING THE THREE-STEP WRITING PROCESS FOR NEGATIVE MESSAGES

Five goals of negative messages:
- Give the bad news
- Ensure its acceptance
- Maintain reader's goodwill
- Maintain organization's good image
- Reduce future correspondence on the matter

Chances are slim that you'll ever need to issue messages like KPMG's, but communicating other kinds of negative news is a fact of life for all business professionals, from rejecting job applicants to telling customers that shipments will be late to turning down speaking invitations.

When you need to deliver bad news, you have five goals: (1) to convey the bad news, (2) to gain acceptance for it, (3) to maintain as much goodwill as possible with your audience, (4) to maintain a good image for your organization, and (5) if appropriate, to reduce or eliminate the need for future correspondence on the matter (in a few cases, you want to encourage discussion). Five goals are clearly a lot to accomplish in one message. However, by learning some simple techniques and following the three-step process, you can develop negative messages that reduce the stress for everyone involved and improve the effectiveness of your communication efforts.

When Bausch & Lomb, maker of optics and healthcare products, was forced to reduce staff in recent years, President and CEO William Carpenter chose in-person communication to deliver the bad news because it gave employees the opportunity to ask questions and raise concerns.

Choose the medium with care when preparing negative messages.

The appropriate organization helps readers accept your negative news.

Step 1: Plan Your Message

When planning negative messages, you can't avoid the fact that your audience does not want to hear what you have to say. To minimize the damage to business relationships and to encourage the acceptance of your message, analyze the situation carefully to better understand the context in which the recipient will process your message.

Be sure to consider your purpose thoroughly—whether it's straightforward (such as rejecting a job application) or more complicated (such as drafting a negative performance review, in which you not only give the employee feedback on past performance but also help the person develop a plan to improve future performance). Similarly, your audience profile can be simple and obvious in some situations (such as rejecting a credit request) and far more complex in others (such as telling a business partner that you've decided to terminate the partnership).

With a clear purpose and your audience's needs in mind, identify and gather the information your audience will need in order to understand and accept your message. Negative messages can be intensely personal to the recipient, and in many cases recipients have a right to expect a thorough explanation of your answer (although this isn't always the case). For instance, if one of your hardest-working employees has asked for a raise but you don't think her performance warrants it, you can carefully explain the difference between hard work and productive results to help her accept your message.

Selecting the right medium is critical when delivering negative messages. For example, you might badly damage a working relationship if you use voice mail to reject a long-time employee's request for a promotion. Since the employee would surely have some important questions to ask, and you would certainly want to soothe hurt feelings, a face-to-face meeting would be the best choice for this situation. However, if your company receives 10,000 credit applications a month, you can't afford to engage every rejected applicant in a one-on-one conversation. A form letter that limits response options would be a better choice. Review the media selection guidelines in Chapter 4 if you're unsure of the best way to deliver your message.

Defining your main idea in a negative message is often more complicated than simply saying *no*. For instance, in the case of the hardworking employee who requested a raise, your message would go beyond saying no to explain how she can improve her performance by working smarter, not just harder. On the other hand, be sure to limit your scope and include only the information your audience needs. For example, a credit denial is not the place to lecture customers on better financial habits.

Step 2: Write Your Message

When adapting a negative message to your audience, every aspect of effective, diplomatic writing is amplified; after all, your audience does not want to hear a negative message and might disagree strongly with you. Be sure to maintain a "you" attitude, strive for polite language that emphasizes the positive whenever appropriate, and make sure your word choice is without bias. For more advice, see "Adapting to Your Audience" later in this chapter.

If your credibility hasn't already been established with an audience, lay out your qualifications for making the decision in question. Recipients of negative messages who don't think you are credible are more likely to challenge your decision. And as always, projecting and protecting your company's image is a prime concern; if you're not careful, a negative answer could spin out of control into negative feelings about your company.

When you use language that conveys respect and avoids an accusing tone, you protect your audience's pride. This kind of communication etiquette is always important, but it demands special care with negative messages. Moreover, you can ease the sense of disappointment by using positive words rather than negative, counterproductive ones (see Table 8–1).

Chances are you'll spend more time on word, sentence, and paragraph choices for negative messages than for any other type of business writing. People who receive negative messages often look for subtle shades of meaning, seeking flaws in your reasoning or other ways to challenge the decision. By writing clearly and sensitively, you can take some of the sting out of bad news and help your reader accept the decision and move on.

Step 3: Complete Your Message

Your need for careful attention to detail continues as you complete your message. Revise your content to make sure everything is clear, complete, and concise—bearing in mind that even small flaws are magnified as readers react to your negative news.

CHOOSING POSITIVE WORDS   **Table 8–1**

Examples of Negative Phrasings	**Positive Alternatives**
Your request *doesn't make any sense.*	Please clarify your request.
The *damage* won't be fixed for a week.	The item will be repaired next week.
Although it wasn't our *fault*, there will be an *unavoidable delay* in your order.	We will process your order as soon as we receive an aluminum shipment from our supplier, which we expect to happen within 10 days.
You are clearly *dissatisfied.*	We are doing what we can to make things right.
I *regret* the misunderstanding.	I'll try my best to be more clear from now on.
I was *shocked* to learn that you're unhappy.	Thank you for sharing your concerns about the service you received while shopping with us.
Unfortunately, we haven't received it.	It hasn't arrived yet.
The enclosed statement is *wrong*.	Please recheck the enclosed statement.

Produce clean, professional documents, and proofread carefully to eliminate mistakes. Finally, be especially sure that your negative messages are delivered promptly and successfully; waiting for bad news is hard enough without wondering whether a message was lost.

DEVELOPING NEGATIVE MESSAGES

As you apply the three-step writing process to develop negative messages, keeping several points in mind will help you craft effective messages quickly: First, before organizing the main points of a message, it is vital to choose a direct or an indirect approach. Second, before actually composing your message, be sensitive to variations across cultures or between internal and external audiences. And third, to fulfill the spirit of audience focus, be sure you maintain high ethical standards.

Choosing the Best Approach

You probably already have an instinctive feel for when to use direct or indirect approaches.

Without even thinking about it, you've probably been using both the direct and indirect approaches to deliver negative messages your entire life. When you come right out and tell somebody some bad news, you're using a direct approach. When you try to soften the impact by easing your way into the conversation before delivering the bad news, you're using an indirect approach. Chances are, you've already developed an instinctive feel for which approach to use in many situations. In your business writing, you'll need to make a similar choice whenever you deliver bad news; however, there are no clear guidelines to help you choose in every case. Some researchers even suggest that the way you organize the message is less important than achieving a personal tone.[2] Even so, you have to choose one approach or the other, so ask yourself the following questions:

- **Will the bad news come as a shock?** The direct approach is fine for business situations in which people readily acknowledge the possibility of receiving bad news. You know you won't get every job you apply for or close every sales opportunity, and consumers realize that orders are sometimes delayed or mishandled. However, if the bad news might come as a shock to readers, use the indirect approach to help them prepare for it.

- **Does the reader prefer short messages that get right to the point?** If you know that your boss always wants brief messages that get right to the point, even when they deliver bad news, the direct approach is your best choice. If you don't know a reader's preferences, let the other questions in this list guide your choice.

- **How important is this news to the reader?** For minor or routine scenarios, the direct approach is nearly always best. When Amazon.com can't find an out-of-print book for a customer, the company sends a brief e-mail stating that fact directly. However, if the reader has an emotional investment in the situation or the consequences to the reader are considerable, the indirect approach is often best because it gives you a chance to prepare that reader to accept your news.

- **Do you need to maintain a close working relationship with the reader?** Pay attention to the relationship as you deliver your bad news. The indirect approach makes it easier to soften the blow of bad news and can therefore be the better choice when you need to preserve a good relationship.

- **Do you need to get the reader's attention?** If someone has ignored repeated messages from you or is buried under hundreds of e-mails, instant messages, and memos, the direct approach can help you get his or her attention. In fact, a poorly written indirect message that obscures the bad news might be the reason the person has been ignoring you in the first place.

- **What is your organization's preferred style?** Some companies have a distinct communication style, ranging from blunt and direct to gentle and indirect. In most cases, people in the organization expect everyone to follow that general style. However, going against expectations can be an effective way to get people's attention in a dramatic way. When Coca-Cola CEO E. Neville Isdell wanted to let both insiders and outsiders know that the company's continuing sales slump was due to more than just temporary market factors, he issued uncharacteristically blunt statements such as saying that the company suffers from both "a people deficit and a skills deficit."[3]

- **How much follow-up communication do you want?** If you want to discourage a response from your reader, the direct approach signals the finality of your message more effectively. However, if you use the indirect approach to list your reasons before announcing a decision, you leave the door open for a follow-up response from your reader—which might actually be the best strategy at times. For example, if you're rejecting a project team's request for funding, based on the information you currently have at hand, you might be wise to invite the team to provide any new information that could encourage you to reconsider your decision.

Using the Direct Approach Effectively   A negative message using the direct approach opens with the bad news, proceeds to the reasons for the situation or the decision, and ends with a positive statement aimed at maintaining a good relationship with the audience (see Figure 8–1). Depending on the circumstances, the message may also offer alternatives or a plan of action to fix the situation under discussion. Stating the bad news at the beginning can have two advantages: (1) It makes a shorter message possible, and (2) it requires less time for the audience to reach the main idea of the message.

> Use the direct approach when your negative answer or information will have minimal personal impact.

Open with a Clear Statement of the Bad News   Whether it's something relatively minor, such as telling a supplier that you're planning to reduce the size of your orders in the future, or something major, such as telling employees that revenues dropped the previous quarter, come right out and say it. Even if the news is devastating, maintain a

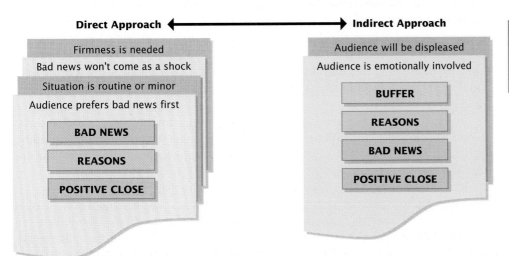

FIGURE 8–1
Choosing the Indirect or Direct Approach for Negative Messages

calm, professional tone that keeps the focus on the news and not on individual failures. Also, if necessary, remind the reader why you're writing:

Reminds the reader that your company has a standing order, and announces the change immediately

> Please modify our standing order for the FL-205 shipping cases from 3,000 per month to 2,500 per month.

Reminds the reader that he or she applied for life insurance with your firm, and announces your decision

> Transnation Life is unable to grant your application for SafetyNet term life insurance.

Eases into the bad news with a personal acknowledgment to the staff, even though it delivers the news directly and immediately

> In spite of everyone's best efforts to close more sales this past quarter, revenue fell 14 percent compared to the third quarter last year.

Notice how the third example still manages to ease into the bad news, even though it delivers the bad news directly and quickly. In all three instances, the recipient gets the news immediately, without reading the reasons why the news is bad.

Provide Reasons and Additional Information In most cases, you'll follow the direct opening with an explanation of why the news is negative:

Reassures the reader that the product in question is still satisfactory but is no longer needed in the same quantity

> Please modify our standing order for the FL-205 shipping cases from 3,000 per month to 2,500 per month. The FL-205 continues to meet our needs for medical packaging, but our sales of that product line have leveled off.

Offers a general explanation as the reason the application was denied and discourages further communication on the matter

> Transnation Life is unable to grant your application for SafetyNet term life insurance. The SafetyNet program has specific health history requirements that your application does not meet.

Lets readers know why the news is negative and reassures them that job performance is not the reason

> In spite of everyone's best efforts to close more sales this past quarter, revenue fell 14 percent compared to the third quarter last year. Reports from the field offices indicate that the economic downturn in Asia has reduced demand for our products.

The amount of detail you provide depends on your relationship with the audience.

The extent of your explanation depends on the nature of your news and your relationship with the reader. In the first example, for instance, a company wants to assure its long-time supplier that the product is still satisfactory. It's in the best interest of both parties to maintain a positive relationship even when circumstances between them are sometimes negative.

In the second example, the insurance company provides a general reason for the denial because listing a specific health issue (such as diabetes) might encourage additional communication from the reader to negotiate or to explain the situation ("My father had diabetes and lived to be 84"). The company's decision is final, and any further communication on the issue would be counterproductive for both parties.

In the third example, the explanation points out why the news is bad and also reassures employees that no one in the firm is personally responsible for the failure. Of course, if the bad news *were* a result of poor performance, this message would need to be revised appropriately.

In some situations, it's a good idea to follow the explanation with a statement of how you plan to correct or respond to the negative news. For instance, in the case of the sales decline, you might follow by telling the staff you plan to increase advertising to help stimulate sales. Alternatively, you might invite ideas from the staff. In any event, your readers will want to know how they should respond to the news, so additional information would be helpful.

You will encounter some situations in which explaining negative news is neither appropriate nor helpful, for example, when the reasons are confidential, excessively complicated, or irrelevant to the reader. To maintain a cordial working relationship with the reader, you might want to explain why you can't provide the information.

Sometimes detailed reasons should not be provided.

Should you apologize when delivering bad news? As the KPMG vignette at the beginning of the chapter illustrated, the answer isn't quite as simple as one might think. The notion of *apology* is hard to pin down. To some people, it simply means an expression of sympathy that something negative has happened to another person. At the other extreme, it means admitting fault and taking responsibility for specific compensations or corrections to atone for the mistake.

The decision about whether to apologize depends on a number of factors.

Some experts have advised that a company should never apologize, even when it knows it has made a mistake, as the apology might be taken as a confession of guilt that could be used against the company in a lawsuit. This is the dilemma that KPMG faced when deciding how to respond to illegal actions taken by a few of its employees. However, several states have laws that specifically prevent expressions of sympathy from being used as evidence of legal liability. In fact, judges, juries, and plaintiffs tend to be more forgiving of companies that express sympathy for wronged parties; moreover, the apology can help repair the company's reputation. Recently, some prosecutors have begun pressing executives to publicly admit guilt and apologize as part of the settlement of criminal cases—unlike the common tactic of paying fines but refusing to admit any wrongdoing.[4]

The best general advice in the event of a serious mistake or accident is to immediately and sincerely express sympathy and offer help, if appropriate, without admitting guilt; then seek the advice of your company's lawyers before elaborating. As one recent survey concluded, "The risks of making an apology are low, and the potential reward is high."[5]

Close on a Positive Note After you've explained the negative news, close the message in a positive, but still honest and respectful, manner:

Close your message in a positive but respectful tone.

Please modify our standing order for the FL-205 shipping cases from 3,000 per month to 2,500 per month. The FL-205 continues to meet our needs for medical packaging, but our sales of that product line have leveled off. We appreciate the great service you continue to provide and look forward to doing business with you.

Reinforces the relationship you have with the reader and provides a positive view toward the future without unduly promising a return to the old level of business

Transnation Life is unable to grant your application for SafetyNet term life insurance. The SafetyNet program has specific health history requirements that your application does not meet. We wish you success in finding coverage through another provider.

Ends on a respectful note, knowing that life insurance is an important subject for the reader, but also makes it clear that the company's decision is final

In spite of everyone's best efforts to close more sales this past quarter, revenue fell 14 percent compared to the third quarter last year. Reports from the field offices indicate that the economic downturn in Asia has reduced demand for our products. However, I continue to believe that we have the best product for these customers, and we'll continue to explore ways to boost sales in these key markets.

Helps readers respond to the news by letting them know that the company plans to fix the situation, even if the plan for doing so isn't clear yet

Notice how all three examples deliver bad news quickly and efficiently, without being unduly disrespectful or overly apologetic. Consider offering your readers an alternative solution, if you can. For instance, if you know that another insurance company has a program for higher-risk policies, you can alert your reader to that opportunity.

Use the indirect approach when some preparation will help your audience accept your bad news.

Using the Indirect Approach Effectively The indirect approach helps readers prepare for the bad news by presenting the reasons for it first. However, don't assume that the indirect approach is meant to obscure bad news, delay it, or limit your responsibility. Rather, the purpose of this approach is to ease the blow and help readers accept the situation. When done poorly, the indirect approach can be disrespectful and even unethical. But when done well, it is a good example of "you" oriented communication crafted with attention to both ethics and etiquette.

A buffer establishes common ground with the reader.

Open with a Buffer The first step in using the indirect approach is to write a **buffer**, a neutral, noncontroversial statement that is closely related to the point of the message (look back at Figure 8–1). A buffer establishes common ground with your reader; moreover, if you're responding to a request, a buffer validates that request. Some critics believe that using a buffer is manipulative and unethical, even dishonest. However, buffers are unethical only if they're insincere or deceptive. Showing consideration for the feelings of others is never dishonest.

Poorly written buffers mislead or insult the reader.

A poorly written buffer might trivialize the reader's concerns, divert attention from the problem with insincere flattery or irrelevant material, or mislead the reader into thinking your message actually contains good news. A good buffer, on the other hand, can express your appreciation for being considered (if you're responding to a request), assure your reader of your attention to the request, or indicate your understanding of the reader's needs. A good buffer also needs to be relevant and sincere.

The following examples were all written in response to a manager of the order fulfillment department, who requested some temporary staffing help from your department (a request you won't be able to fulfill):

Establishes common ground with the reader and validates the concerns that prompted the original request without promising a positive answer → Our department shares your goal of processing orders quickly and efficiently.

Establishes common ground, but in a negative way that downplays the recipient's concerns → As a result of the last downsizing, every department in the company is running shorthanded.

Potentially misleads the reader into concluding that you will comply with the request → You folks are doing a great job over there, and I'd love to be able to help out.

Trivializes the reader's concerns by opening with an irrelevant issue → Those new state labor regulations are driving me crazy over here; how about in your department?

Only the first of these buffers can be considered effective; the other three are likely to damage your relationship with the other manager—and to lower his or her opinion of you. Table 8–2 shows several types of effective buffers you could use to tactfully open a negative message.

Given the damage that a poorly composed buffer can do, consider each one carefully before you send it. Is it respectful? Is it relevant? Is it neutral, implying neither yes nor no? Does it provide a smooth transition to the reasons that follow? If you can answer yes to every question, you can proceed confidently to the next section of your message. However, if that little voice inside your head tells you that your buffer sounds insincere or misleading, it probably is, in which case you'll need to rewrite it.

Provide Reasons and Additional Information An effective buffer serves as a stepping stone to the next part of your message, in which you build up the explanations and information that will culminate in your negative news. The nature of the information you provide is similar to that of the direct approach—it depends on the audience and the situation—but the way you portray this information differs from any portrayal in a direct message because your reader doesn't know your conclusion yet.

TYPES OF BUFFERS

Table 8–2

Buffer Type	Strategy	Example
Agreement	Find a point on which you and the reader share similar views.	We both know how hard it is to make a profit in this industry.
Appreciation	Express sincere thanks for receiving something.	Your check for $127.17 arrived yesterday. Thank you.
Cooperation	Convey your willingness to help in any way you realistically can.	Employee Services is here to smooth the way for all of you who work to achieve company goals.
Fairness	Assure the reader that you've closely examined and carefully considered the problem, or mention an appropriate action that has already been taken.	For the past week, we have carefully monitored those using the photocopying machine to see whether we can detect any pattern of use that might explain its frequent breakdowns.
Good news	Start with the part of your message that is favorable.	A replacement knob for your range is on its way, shipped February 10 via UPS.
Praise	Find an attribute or an achievement to compliment.	The Stratford Group clearly has an impressive record of accomplishment in helping clients resolve financial reporting problems.
Resale	Favorably discuss the product or company related to the subject of the letter.	With their heavy-duty, full-suspension hardware and fine veneers, the desks and file cabinets in our Montclair line have become a hit with value-conscious professionals.
Understanding	Demonstrate that you understand the reader's goals and needs.	So that you can more easily find the printer with the features you need, we are enclosing a brochure that describes all the Panasonic printers currently available.

An ideal explanation section leads readers to your conclusion before you come right out and say it. In other words, before you actually say no, the reader has followed your line of reasoning and is ready for the answer. By giving your reasons effectively, you help maintain focus on the issues at hand and defuse the emotions that always accompany significantly bad news.

Phrase your reasons to signal the negative news ahead.

As you lay out your reasons, guide your readers' responses by starting with the most positive points first and moving forward to increasingly negative ones. Provide enough detail for the audience to understand your reasons, but be concise; a long, roundabout explanation will just make your audience impatient. Your reasons need to convince your audience that your decision is justified, fair, and logical.

If appropriate, you can use the explanation section to suggest how the negative news might in fact benefit your reader. Suppose you work for a multinational company that wants to hire an advertising agency to support your offices in a dozen different countries, and you receive a proposal from an agency that has offices in only one of those countries. In your list of reasons, you could indicate that you don't want to impose undue hardship on the agency by requiring significant amounts of international travel. However, use this technique with care; it's easy to insult readers by implying that they shouldn't be asking for the benefits or opportunities they were seeking in the first place.

Avoid hiding behind company policy to cushion your bad news. If you say, "Company policy forbids our hiring anyone who does not have two years' supervisory experience," you imply that you won't consider anyone on his or her individual merits. Skilled and sympathetic communicators explain company policy (without

Don't hide behind "company policy" when you deliver bad news.

referring to it as "policy") so that the audience can try to meet the requirements at a later time. Consider this response to an employee:

Shows the reader the decision is based on a methodical analysis of the company's needs and not on some arbitrary guideline

Establishes the criteria behind the decision and lets the reader know what to expect

> Because these management positions are quite challenging, the human relations department has researched the qualifications needed to succeed in them. The findings show that the two most important qualifications are a bachelor's degree in business administration and two years' supervisory experience.

Well-written reasons are
- Detailed
- Tactful
- Individualized
- Unapologetic
- Positive

The paragraph does a good job of stating reasons for the refusal:

- It provides enough detail to logically support the refusal.

- It implies that the applicant is better off avoiding a program in which he or she might fail.

- It explains the company's policy as logical rather than arbitrary.

- It offers no apology for the decision because no one is at fault.

- It avoids negative personal expressions (such as "You do not meet our requirements").

Even valid, well-thought-out reasons won't convince every reader in every situation, but if you've done a good job of laying out your reasoning, then you've done everything you can to prepare the reader for the main idea, which is the negative news itself.

To handle bad news carefully
- De-emphasize the bad news visually and grammatically
- Use a conditional statement if appropriate
- Tell what you did do, not what you didn't do

Continue with a Clear Statement of the Bad News   Now that you've laid out your reasons thoughtfully and logically, and now that readers are psychologically prepared to receive the bad news, your audience may still reject your message if the bad news is handled carelessly. Three techniques are especially useful for saying no as clearly and as kindly as possible. First, de-emphasize the bad news:

- Minimize the space or time devoted to the bad news—without trivializing it or withholding any important information.

- Subordinate bad news in a complex or compound sentence ("My department is already shorthanded, so I'll need all my staff for at least the next two months"). This construction pushes the bad news into the middle of the sentence, the point of least emphasis.

- Embed bad news in the middle of a paragraph or use parenthetical expressions ("Our profits, which are down, are only part of the picture").

However, keep in mind that it's possible to abuse de-emphasis. For instance, if the primary point of your message is that profits are down, it would be inappropriate to marginalize that news by burying it in the middle of a sentence. State the negative news clearly, then make a smooth transition to any positive news that might balance the story.

Second, use a conditional (*if* or *when*) statement to imply that the audience could have received, or might someday receive, a favorable answer ("When you have more managerial experience, you are welcome to reapply"). Such a statement could motivate applicants to improve their qualifications.

Third, emphasize what you can do or have done, rather than what you cannot do. Say, "We sell exclusively through retailers, and the one nearest you that carries our merchandise is . . ." rather than "We are unable to serve you, so please call your nearest dealer." Also, by implying the bad news, you may not need to actually state it ("The five positions currently open have been filled with people whose qualifications match those uncovered in our research"). By focusing on the positive and implying the bad news, you make the impact less personal.

When implying bad news, be sure your audience understands the entire message—including the bad news. Withholding negative information or overemphasizing positive information is unethical and unfair to your reader. If an implied message might lead to uncertainty, state your decision in direct terms. Just be sure to avoid overly blunt statements that are likely to cause pain and anger:

Don't disguise bad news when you emphasize the positive.

Instead of This	Use This
I *must refuse* your request.	I will be out of town on the day you need me.
We *must deny* your application.	The position has been filled.
I *am unable* to grant your request.	Contact us again when you have established . . .
We *cannot afford to* continue the program.	The program will conclude on May 1.
Much as I would like to attend . . .	Our budget meeting ends too late for me to attend.
We *must reject* your proposal.	We've accepted the proposal from AAA Builders.
We *must turn down* your extension request.	Please send in your payment by June 14.

Close on a Positive Note   As with the direct approach, the conclusion of the indirect approach is your opportunity to emphasize your respect for your audience, even though you've just delivered unpleasant news. Express best wishes without ending on a falsely upbeat note. If you can find a positive angle that's meaningful to your audience, by all means consider adding it to your conclusion. However, don't try to pretend that the negative news didn't happen or that it won't affect the reader. Suggest alternative solutions if such information is available. In a message to a customer or potential customer, an ending that includes resale information or sales promotion may also be appropriate. If you've asked readers to decide between alternatives or to take some action, make sure that they know what to do, when to do it, and how to do it. Whatever type of conclusion you use, follow these guidelines:

- **Avoid a negative or uncertain conclusion.** Don't refer to, repeat, or apologize for the bad news, and refrain from expressing any doubt that your reasons will be accepted (avoid statements such as "I trust our decision is satisfactory").

- **Limit future correspondence.** Encourage additional communication *only* if you're willing to discuss your decision further (if you're not, avoid wording such as "If you have further questions, please write").

- **Be optimistic about the future.** Don't anticipate problems (avoid statements such as "Should you have further problems, please let us know").

- **Be sincere.** Steer clear of clichés that are insincere in view of the bad news (if you can't help, don't say, "If we can be of any help, please contact us").

- **Be confident.** Don't show any doubt about keeping the person as a customer (avoid phrases such as "We hope you will continue to do business with us").

A positive close
- Builds goodwill
- Offers a suggestion for action
- Provides a look toward the future

Finally, keep in mind that the closing is the last thing the audience has to remember you by. Try to make the memory a positive one.

Adapting to Your Audience

Even more than other business messages, negative messages require that you maintain your audience focus and be as sensitive as possible to audience needs. Therefore, you may need to adapt your message to cultural differences or to the differences between internal and external audiences.

Cultural Variations   Even though bad news is unwelcome in any language, the conventions for passing it on to business associates can vary considerably from country to country. For instance, French business letters are traditionally quite formal and writer-oriented, often without reference to audience needs or benefits. Moreover, when the news is bad, French writers take a direct approach. They open with a reference to the problem or previous correspondence and then state the bad news clearly. While they don't refer to the audience's needs, they often do apologize and express regret for the problem.[6]

In contrast, Japanese letters traditionally open with remarks about the season, business prosperity, or health. When the news is bad, these opening formalities serve as the buffer. Explanations and apologies follow, and then comes the bad news or refusal. Japanese writers protect their reader's feelings by wording the bad news ambiguously. Western readers may even misinterpret this vague language as a condition of acceptance rather than as the refusal it actually is.[7] In short, if you are communicating across cultures, you'll want to use the tone, organization, and other cultural conventions that your audience expects. Only then can you avoid the inappropriate or even offensive approaches that could jeopardize your business relationship.[8]

Internal Versus External Audiences   You'll want to adapt your negative messages according to whether your audience is inside or outside the organization. Recipients inside your company frequently have expectations for negative messages that differ from those of recipients outside the company. For example, employees will react negatively to news of an impending layoff, but company shareholders might welcome the news as evidence that management is trying to control costs. Most employees will not only expect more detail but will also expect to be informed before the general public is told.

Plus, after several years of seemingly endless upheavals and bad news, from market collapses to financial scandals, many employees are less inclined to believe what they hear from management. Cynicism and distrust are rampant today, and employees are tired of discussing change.[9] They want to know more than how changes will help the company; they want to know how changes are going to affect them personally. Managers can rebuild trust only by communicating openly, honestly, and quickly in both good times and bad.

Of course, negative news must also flow upward in an organization, from lower-level employees to higher-level managers. Even when employees are not at fault, the reluctance to give bad news to superiors can be strong. In corporate cultures that don't encourage open communication, employees who fear retribution may go to great lengths to avoid sending bad-news messages. In such a dysfunctional environment, failure breeds still more failure because decision makers don't get the honest, objective information they need to make wise choices.[10] In contrast, managers in open cultures expect their employees to bring them bad news whenever it happens so that corrective action can be taken. Whatever the case, if you do need to transmit bad news up the chain of command, don't try to pin the blame on anyone in particular. Simply emphasize the nature of the problem—and a solution, if possible. This tactic will help you earn a reputation as an alert problem solver, rather than as just a complainer.[11]

Negative messages to outside audiences require attention to the diverse nature of your audience and the concern for confidentiality of internal information. A single message might have a half dozen separate audiences, all with differing opinions and agendas. You may not be able to explain things to the level of detail that some of these people want if doing so would release proprietary information such as future product plans.

Maintaining High Standards of Ethics and Etiquette

Sending and receiving negative messages leads to a natural human tendency to delay, downplay, or distort the bad news.[12] Unfortunately doing so may be unethical, if not illegal. In recent years, numerous companies have been sued by shareholders, consumers, employees, and government regulators for allegedly withholding or delaying negative information in such areas as company finances, environmental hazards, and product safety. The stock brokerage firm Morgan Stanley was recently fined $2.2 million for being late in filing required complaint and misconduct reports 67 percent of the time.[13] The pharmaceutical industry, under pressure for years too disclose the results of failed drug trials, began to publish some results to a public website (www.clinicalstudyresults.org) in 2004.[14] When an organization has negative information that affects the well-being of others, it has an ethical obligation to communicate that information quickly, clearly, and completely.

Delaying the delivery of negative news can be unethical in many situations.

This ethical obligation to communicate the facts also brings with it the responsibility to do so promptly. Bad news often means that people need to make other plans, whether it's an employee who needs to find a new job, consumers who need to stop using an unsafe product, or a community that needs to find safe drinking water when their supply has become polluted. The longer you wait to deliver bad news, the harder you make it for recipients to react and respond.

Some negative news scenarios will also test your self-control and sense of etiquette. An employee who lets you down, a supplier whose faulty parts damage your company's reputation, a business partner who violates the terms of your contract—such situations may tempt you to respond with a personal attack. Keep in mind that negative messages can have a lasting impact on both the people who receive them and the people who send them. As a communicator, it's your responsibility to minimize the negative impact of your negative messages through careful planning and sensitive, objective writing. As much as possible, focus on the actions or conditions that led to the negative news, not on personal shortcomings or character issues. Develop a reputation as a professional who can handle the toughest situations with dignity.

Negative news situations can put your sense of self-control and business etiquette to the test.

For a reminder of successful strategies for creating negative messages, see "Checklist: Creating Negative Messages."

Document Makeover

IMPROVE THIS MEMO

To practice correcting drafts of actual documents, visit your online course or the access-code protected portion of the Companion Website. Click "Document Makeovers," then click Chapter 8. You will find a memo that contains problems and errors relating to what you've learned in this chapter about handling negative messages. Use the "Final Draft" decision tool to create an improved version of this memo. Check the message for the use of buffers, apologies, explanations, subordination, embedding, positive action, conditional phrases, and upbeat perspectives.

EXPLORING COMMON EXAMPLES OF NEGATIVE MESSAGES

In the course of your business career, you might write a wide variety of negative messages, from announcing declines in revenue to giving negative performance reviews. The following sections offer examples of the most common negative messages, dealing with topics such as routine business matters, organizational news, and employment messages.

Sending Negative Messages on Routine Business Matters

Most companies receive numerous requests for information and donations or invitations to join community or industry organizations. As you progress in your career and become more visible in your industry and community, you will receive a wide variety of personal invitations to speak at private or public functions or to volunteer your time

✓ CHECKLIST: Creating Negative Messages

A. Choose the best approach

✓ Consider a direct approach when the audience is aware of the possibility of negative news, when the reader is not emotionally involved in the message, when you know that the reader would prefer the bad news first, when you know that firmness is necessary, and you want to discourage a response.

✓ Consider an indirect approach when the news is likely to come as a shock or surprise, when audience has a high emotional investment in the outcome, and you want to maintain a good relationship with the audience.

B. For an indirect approach, open with an effective buffer

✓ Establish common ground with the audience.
✓ Validate the request, if you are responding to a request.
✓ Don't trivialize the reader's concerns.
✓ Don't mislead the reader into thinking the coming news might be positive.

C. Provide reasons and additional information

✓ Explain why the news is negative.
✓ Adjust the amount of detail to fit the situation and the audience.

✓ Avoid explanations when the reasons are confidential, excessively complicated, or irrelevant to the reader.
✓ If appropriate, state how you plan to correct or respond to the negative news.
✓ Seek the advice of company lawyers if you're unsure what to say.

D. Clearly state the bad news

✓ State the bad news as positively as possible, using tactful wording.
✓ De-emphasize bad news by minimizing the space devoted to it, subordinating it, or embedding it.
✓ If your response might change in the future if circumstances change, explain the conditions to the reader.
✓ Emphasize what you can or have done, rather than what you can't or won't do.

E. Close on a positive note

✓ Express best wishes without being falsely positive.
✓ Suggest actions readers might take, if appropriate, and provide them with necessary information.
✓ Encourage further communication only if you're willing to discuss the situation further.
✓ Keep a positive outlook on the future.

---

for a variety of organizations. In addition, routine business matters such as credit applications and requests for adjustment will often require negative responses. Neither you nor your company will be able to say yes to every request. So crafting negative responses quickly and graciously is an important skill for many professionals.

Refusing Routine Requests   Routine requests may come both from groups and from individuals outside the company, as well as from colleagues inside the organization. When you aren't able to meet the request, your primary communication challenge is to give a clear negative response without generating negative feelings or damaging either your personal reputation or the company's. As simple as these messages may appear to be, they can test your skills as a communicator because you often need to deliver negative information while maintaining a positive relationship with the other party.

Saying no is a routine part of business and shouldn't reflect negatively on you. If you said yes to every request that crossed your desk, you'd never get any work done. The direct approach will work best for most routine negative responses. It not only helps your audience get your answer quickly and move on to other possibilities but also helps you save time, since the direct approach is often easier to write.

When turning down an invitation or a request for a favor, consider your relationship with the reader.

The indirect approach works best when the stakes are high for you or for the receiver, when you or your company has an established relationship with the person making the request, or when you're forced to decline a request that you might have said yes to in the past. May Yee Kwan used the indirect approach in her letter to Whittier Community College (see Figure 8–2). Her company has a long-standing relationship with the college and wants to maintain that positive relationship, but she can't meet this particular request. If Kwan and Wofford shared a closer relationship (if

Planning

Analyze the Situation
Verify that the purpose is to decline a request and offer alternatives; audience is likely to be surprised by the refusal.

Gather Information
Determine audience needs and obtain the necessary information.

Select the Right Medium
For formal messages, printed letters on company letterhead are best.

Organize the Information
Main idea is to refuse the request so limit your scope to that; select an indirect approach based on the audience and the situation.

Writing

Adapt to Your Audience
Adjust the level of formality based on degree of familiarity with the audience; maintain a positive relationship by using the "you" attitude, politeness, positive emphasis, and bias-free language.

Compose the Message
Use a conversational but professional style and keep the message brief, clear, and as helpful as possible.

Completing

Revise the Message
Evaluate content and review readability to make sure the negative information won't be misinterpreted; make sure your tone stays positive without being artificial.

Produce the Message
Emphasize a clean, professional appearance on company letterhead.

Proofread the Message
Review for errors in layout, spelling, and mechanics.

Distribute the Message
Deliver your message using the chosen medium.

1   **2**   **3**

FIGURE 8–2   Effective Letter Declining a Favor

InfoTech
927 Dawson Valley Road, Tulsa, Oklahoma 74151
Voice: (918) 669-4428   Fax: (918) 669-4429
www.infotech.com

March 6, 2006

Dr. Sandra Wofford, President
Whittier Community College
333 Whittier Avenue
Tulsa, OK 74150

Dear Dr. Wofford:

Infotech has been happy to support Whittier Community College in many ways over the years, and we appreciate the opportunities you and your organization provide to so many deserving students. Thank you for considering our grounds for your graduation ceremony on June 3.

We would certainly like to accommodate Whittier as we have in years past, but our company-wide sales meetings will be held this year during the weeks of May 29 and June 5. With over 200 sales representatives and their families from around the world joining us, activities will be taking place throughout our facility.

My assistant, Robert Seagers, suggests you contact the Municipal Botanical Gardens as a possible graduation site. He recommends calling Jerry Kane, director of public relations.

We remain firm in our commitment to you, President Wofford, and to the fine students you represent. Through our internship program, academic research grants, and other initiatives, we will continue to be a strong corporate partner to Whittier College and will support your efforts as you move forward.

Sincerely,

May Yee Kwan

May Yee Kwan
Public Relations Director

lc

Annotations:

Buffers negative response by demonstrating respect and recapping the request

Suggests an alternative, showing that Kwan cares about the college and has given the matter some thought

States a meaningful reason for the negative response, without apologizing (since the company is not at fault)

Closes by emphasizing the importance of the relationship and the company's continuing commitment they worked together in a volunteer organization, for instance), the direct approach might have been more appropriate.

Consider the following points as you develop your routine negative messages:

- **Manage your time carefully.** Ironically, as you move upward in your career, you'll receive more and more requests—and have less and less time to answer them. Focus your limited time on the most-important relationships and requests, then get in the habit of crafting quick standard responses for less important situations.

- **If the matter is closed, don't imply that it's still open.** If your answer is truly no, don't use phrases such as "Let me think about it and get back to you" as a way to delay saying no. Such delays waste time for you and the other party.

- **Offer alternative ideas if you can.** In her letter to Sandra Wofford, May Yee Kwan includes the name of someone to contact. However, remember to use your time wisely in such matters. Unless the relationship is vital to your company, you probably shouldn't spend time researching alternatives for the other person.

> If you aren't in a position to offer additional information or assistance, don't imply that you are.

- **Don't imply that other assistance or information might be available if it isn't.** Don't close your negative message with a cheery but insincere "Please contact us if we can offer any additional assistance." An empty attempt to mollify hostile feelings could simply lead to another request you'll have to refuse. Kwan makes such an offer in her letter because her company may indeed have other resources that could help the college with its graduation activities.

Handling Bad News About Transactions For any number of reasons, businesses must sometimes convey bad news concerning the sale and delivery of products and services. Bad news about transactions is always unwelcome and usually unexpected. These messages have three goals: to modify the customer's expectations regarding the transaction, to explain how you plan to resolve the situation, and to repair whatever damage might've been done to the business relationship.

> Some negative messages regarding transactions carry significant business ramifications.

The specific content and tone of each message can vary widely, depending on the nature of the transaction and your relationship with the customer. Telling an individual consumer that his new sweater will be arriving a week later than you promised is a much simpler task than telling General Motors that 30,000 transmission parts will be a week late, especially since you know the company will be forced to idle a multimillion-dollar production facility as a result. Negative messages concerning professional services can be particularly tricky since the person writing such a message is often the same person who performs the service; as a result, these messages can have an uncomfortably personal aspect to them.

> Your approach to bad news about business transactions depends on the customer's expectations.

Negative messages about transactions come in two basic flavors. If you haven't done anything specific to set the customer's expectations—such as promising delivery within 24 hours—the message simply needs to inform the customer, with little or no emphasis on apologies (see Figure 8–3). (Bear in mind, though, in this age of online ordering and overnight delivery, customers have been conditioned to expect instantaneous fulfillment of nearly every transaction, even if you haven't promised anything.) Notice how the e-mail message in Figure 8–4, which is a combination of good and bad news, uses the indirect approach turning the good news into a buffer for the bad news. In this case, the customer wasn't promised delivery by a certain date, so the writer simply informs the customer when to expect the rest of the order. The writer also took steps to repair the relationship and encourage future business with her firm.

> If you fail to meet expectations that you set for the customer, an element of apology should be considered.

If you did set the customer's expectations and now find you can't meet them, your task is more complicated. In addition to resetting the customer's expectations and explaining how you'll resolve the problem, you may need to include an element of apology. The scope of the apology depends on the magnitude of the mistake. For the customer who ordered the sweater, a simple apology, followed by a clear statement of when the sweater will arrive, would probably be sufficient. An explanation is usually not required, although if a meaningful reason exists, and if stating it will help smooth over

FIGURE 8–3
Effective IM Chat Regarding
Order Delays

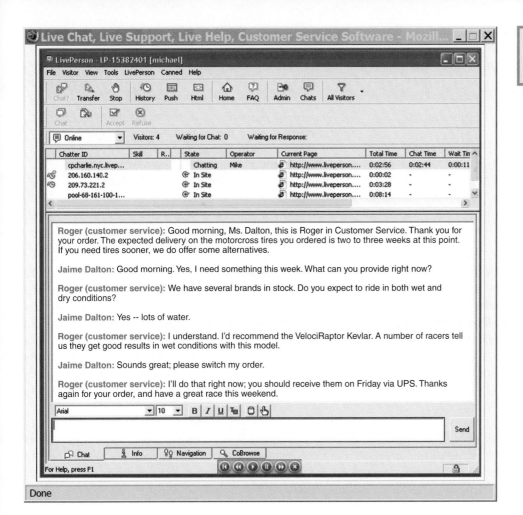

FIGURE 8–4
Effective E-Mail Advising of a Back Order

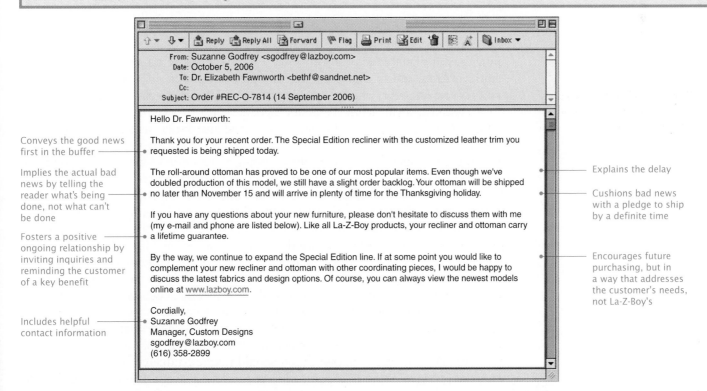

Conveys the good news first in the buffer

Implies the actual bad news by telling the reader what's being done, not what can't be done

Fosters a positive ongoing relationship by inviting inquiries and reminding the customer of a key benefit

Includes helpful contact information

Explains the delay

Cushions bad news with a pledge to ship by a definite time

Encourages future purchasing, but in a way that addresses the customer's needs, not La-Z-Boy's

✓ CHECKLIST: Handling Bad News About Transactions

✓ Reset the customer's expectations regarding the transaction.
✓ Explain what happened and why, if appropriate.
✓ Explain how you'll resolve the situation.

✓ Repair any damage done to the business relationship, perhaps offering future discounts, free merchandise, or other considerations.
✓ Offer a professional, businesslike expression of apology if your organization made a mistake.

the situation without sounding like a feeble excuse, by all means include it. For example, if a snowstorm closed the highways and prevented your receiving necessary materials, say so; however, if you simply received more orders than you expected and promised more than you could deliver, the customer will be less sympathetic. For larger business-to-business transactions, the customer may want an explanation of what went wrong in order to determine whether you'll be able to perform as you promise in the future.

To help repair the damage to the relationship and encourage repeat business, many companies offer discounts on future purchases, free merchandise, or other considerations. Even modest efforts can go a long way to rebuilding the customer's confidence in your company. However, you don't always have a choice. Business-to-business purchasing contracts often include performance clauses that legally entitle the customer to discounts or other restitution in the event of late delivery. Construction contracts sometimes specify penalties for every day the project extends past the original completion date. In such cases, a simple apology is clearly inadequate. To review the concepts covered in this section, see "Checklist: Handling Bad News About Transactions."

Use the indirect approach in most cases of refusing a claim.

Refusing Claims and Requests for Adjustment   Almost every customer who makes a claim or requests an adjustment is emotionally involved; therefore, the indirect method is usually the best approach for a refusal. Your job as a writer is to avoid accepting responsibility for the unfortunate situation and yet avoid blaming or accusing the customer. To steer clear of these pitfalls, pay special attention to the tone of your letter.

A tactful and courteous letter can build goodwill even while denying the claim. For example, Village Electronics recently received a letter from Daniel Lindmeier, who purchased a digital video camera a year ago. He wrote to say that the unit doesn't work correctly and to inquire about the warranty. Lindmeier believes that the warranty covers one year, when it actually covers only three months (see Figure 8–5).

When refusing a claim
- *Demonstrate your understanding of the complaint*
- *Explain your refusal*
- *Suggest alternative action*

When refusing a claim, avoid language that might have a negative impact on the reader. Instead, demonstrate that you understand and have considered the complaint carefully. Then, even if the claim is unreasonable, rationally explain why you are refusing the request. Remember, don't apologize and don't hide behind "company policy." End the letter on a respectful and action-oriented note.

If you deal with enough customers over a long enough period, chances are you'll get a request that is particularly outrageous. You may even be positive that the person is being dishonest. You must resist the temptation to call the person a crook, a swindler, or an incompetent. If you don't, you could be sued for **defamation**, a false statement that tends to damage someone's character or reputation. (Written defamation is called *libel*; spoken defamation is called *slander.*) Someone suing for defamation must prove (1) that the statement is false, (2) that the language is injurious to the person's reputation, and (3) that the statement has been published.

If you can prove that your accusations are true, you haven't defamed the person. The courts are likely to give you the benefit of the doubt because our society believes that ordinary business communication should not be hampered by fear of lawsuits. However, beware of the irate letter intended to let off steam: If the message has no

Planning

Analyze the Situation
Verify that the purpose is to refuse a warranty claim and offer repairs; audience's likely reaction will be disappointment and surprise.

Gather Information
Gather information on warranty policies and procedures, repair services, and resale information.

Select the Right Medium
Choose the best medium for delivering your message; for formal messages, printed letters on company letterhead are best.

Organize the Information
Your main idea is to refuse the claim and promote an alternative solution; select an indirect approach based on the audience and the situation.

Writing

Adapt to Your Audience
Adjust the level of formality based on degree of familiarity with the audience; maintain a positive relationship by using the "you" attitude, politeness, positive emphasis, and bias-free language.

Compose the Message
Use a conversational but professional style and keep the message brief, clear, and as helpful as possible.

Completing

Revise the Message
Evaluate content and review readability to make sure the negative information won't be misinterpreted; make sure your tone stays positive without being artificial.

Produce the Message
Emphasize a clean, professional appearance appropriate for a letter on company stationery.

Proofread the Message
Review for errors in layout, spelling, and mechanics.

Distribute the Message
Deliver your message using the chosen medium; make sure the reader receives any necessary support documents as well.

1   **2**   **3**

FIGURE 8–5   Effective Letter Refusing a Claim

NUMBER ONE IN ENTERTAINMENT

Village Electronics
68 Lake Itasca Boulevard • Hannover, MN 55341
Voice: (612) 878-1312 • Fax: (612) 878-1316

May 3, 2006

Mr. Daniel Lindmeier
849 Cedar St.
Lake Elmo, MN 55042

Dear Mr. Lindmeier:

Thank you for your letter about the battery release switch on your JVC digital camera. Village Electronics believes, as you do, that electronic equipment should be built to last. That's why we stand behind our products with a 90-day warranty.

Even though your JVC camera is a year old and therefore out of warranty, we can still help. Please package your camera carefully and ship it to our store in Hannover. Include your complete name, address, phone number, and a brief description of the malfunction, along with a check for $35 for an initial examination. After assessing the unit, we will give you a written estimate of the needed parts and labor. Then just let us know whether you want us to make the repairs—either by phone or by filling out the prepaid card we'll send you with the estimate.

If you choose to repair the unit, the $35 will be applied toward your bill, the balance of which is payable by check or credit card. JVC also has service centers available in your area. If you would prefer to take the unit to one of them, please see the enclosed list.

Thanks again for inquiring about our service. I've also enclosed a catalog of our latest cameras and accessories, in which you'll find information about JVC's "Trade-Up Special." If you're ready to move up to one of the newest cameras, JVC will offer a generous trade-in allowance on your current model.

Sincerely,

Walter Brodie

Walter Brodie
Customer Service Manager

Enclosures: List of service centers
           Catalog

Buffers the bad news by emphasizing a point the reader and writer both agree on

States bad news indirectly, tactfully leaving the repair decision to the customer

Closes by blending sales promotion with an acknowledgment of the customer's interests

Puts company's policy in a favorable light

Helps soothe the reader with a positive alternative

necessary business purpose and is expressed in abusive language that hints of malice, you'll lose the case. To avoid being accused of defamation, follow these guidelines:

You can help avoid defamation by not responding emotionally.

- Avoid using any kind of abusive language or terms that could be considered defamatory.

- If you wish to express your own personal opinions about a sensitive matter, use your own stationery (not company letterhead), and don't include your job title or position. Just be aware that by doing so, you take responsibility for your own opinions, you are no longer acting within the scope of your duties with the company, and you are personally liable for any resulting legal action.

- Provide accurate information and stick to the facts.

- Never let anger or malice motivate your messages.

- Consult your company's legal department or an attorney whenever you think a message might have legal consequences.

- Communicate honestly, and make sure that what you're saying is what you believe to be true.

- Emphasize a desire for a good relationship in the future.

Most important, remember that nothing positive can come out of antagonizing a customer, even a customer who has verbally abused you or your colleagues. Reject the claim or request for adjustment and move on to the next challenge. For a brief review of the tasks involved when refusing claims, see this chapter's "Checklist: Refusing Claims."

Sending Negative Organizational News

In addition to routine matters involving individual customers and other parties, you may encounter special cases that require you to issue negative announcements regarding some aspect of your products, services, or operations. Most of these scenarios have unique challenges that must be addressed on a case-by-case basis, but the general advice offered here applies to all of them. One key difference among all these messages is whether you have time to plan the announcement. The following section addresses those negative messages that you do have time to plan for, then "Communicating in a Crisis" offers advice on communication during emergencies.

Communicating Under Normal Circumstances   Even the best-run companies stumble on occasion, sometimes through their own actions and sometimes through the actions of someone else. At other times, the company needs to make decisions that are unpopular with customers (price increases, product cancellations, product recalls), with employees (layoffs, benefit reductions, plant closings), or with other groups (relocating to a new community, replacing a board member, canceling a contract with a supplier). The common characteristic of all these messages is the need to send negative announcements to one or more groups of people, rather than to a

✓ CHECKLIST: Refusing Claims

- ✓ Use an indirect approach since the reader is expecting or hoping for a positive response.
- ✓ Indicate your full understanding of the nature of the complaint.
- ✓ Explain why you are refusing the request, without hiding behind company policy.
- ✓ Provide an accurate, factual account of the transaction.

- ✓ Emphasize ways things should have been handled, rather than dwelling on a reader's negligence.
- ✓ Avoid any appearance of defamation.
- ✓ Avoid expressing personal opinions.
- ✓ End with a positive, friendly, helpful close.
- ✓ Make any suggested action easy for readers to comply with.

specific individual. Because you're using a single announcement to reach a variety of people, each of whom may react differently, these messages need to be planned with great care. A relatively simple announcement, such as a price increase, needs to be communicated to both customers on the outside and your sales force on the inside, neither of whom is likely to welcome the news.

Negative organizational messages to external audiences often require extensive planning.

A more significant event, such as a plant closing, can affect thousands of people in dozens of organizations. Employees need to find new jobs or get training in new skills. School districts may have to adjust budgets and staffing levels if many of your employees plan to move in search of new jobs. Your customers need to find new suppliers. Your suppliers may need to find other customers of their own. Government agencies may need to react to everything from a decrease in tax revenues to an influx of people seeking unemployment benefits.

When making negative announcements, follow these guidelines:

- **Match your approach to the situation.** A modest price increase won't shock most customers, so the direct approach is fine. However, canceling a product that people count on is another matter, so building up to the news via the indirect approach might be better.

- **Consider the unique needs of each group.** As the plant closing example illustrates, various people have different information needs.

- **Give each audience enough time to react as needed.** Most organizations operate on quarterly or annual budgeting cycles and need time to react to news. Employees, particularly higher-level executives, may need as much as six months or more to find new jobs.

Give people as much time as possible to react to negative news.

- **Plan the sequence of multiple announcements.** In addition to giving each group enough time, some groups will expect to be informed before others. For instance, if employees hear about a plant closing on the evening news or from a real estate agent, their trust in management will likely be destroyed. Tell insiders and the most-affected groups first.

- **Give yourself enough time to plan and manage a response.** Chances are you're going to be hit with complaints, questions, or product returns after you make your announcement, so make sure you're ready with answers and additional follow-up information.

- **Look for positive angles but don't exude false optimism.** Laying off 10,000 people does not give them "an opportunity to explore new horizons." It's a traumatic event that can affect employees, their families, and their communities for years. Phony optimism would only make a bad situation worse. The best you may be able to do is to thank people for their past support and to wish them well in the future. On the other hand, if eliminating a seldom-used employee benefit means the company doesn't have to deduct additional money from paychecks every month, by all means promote that positive angle.

- **Minimize the element of surprise whenever possible.** This step can require considerable judgment on your part, but if you recognize that current trends are pointing toward negative results sometime in the near future, it's often better to let your audience know ahead of time. For instance, a common complaint in many shareholder lawsuits is a claim that the company didn't let investors know business was deteriorating until it was too late.

- **Seek expert advice if you're not sure.** Many significant negative announcements have important technical, financial, or legal elements that require the expertise of lawyers, accountants, or other specialists. If you're not sure how to handle every aspect of the announcement, ask.

Ask for legal help and other assistance if you're not sure how to handle a significant negative announcement.

Negative situations will test your skills both as a communicator and as a leader. People may turn to you and ask, "OK, so things are bad; now what do we do?"

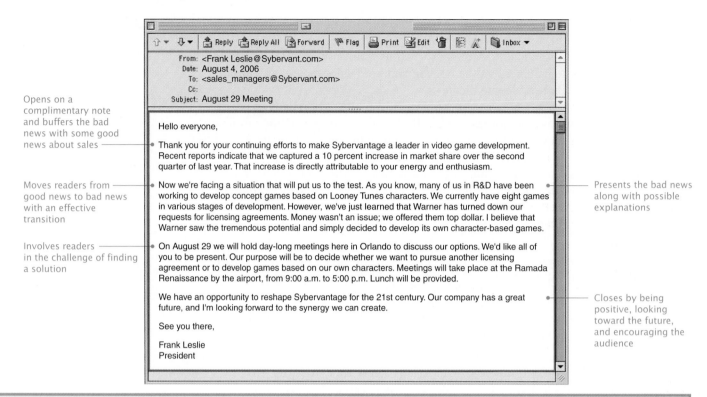

Opens on a complimentary note and buffers the bad news with some good news about sales

Moves readers from good news to bad news with an effective transition

Involves readers in the challenge of finding a solution

Presents the bad news along with possible explanations

Closes by being positive, looking toward the future, and encouraging the audience

FIGURE 8–6
Effective E-Mail Providing Bad News About Company Operations

Inspirational leaders try to seize such opportunities as a chance to reshape or reinvigorate the organization, and they offer encouragement to those around them. Frank Leslie did just that in his e-mail message to Sybervantage employees (see Figure 8–6). Sybervantage had pursued licensing agreements with Warner and expected to enter into a mutually profitable arrangement. But when Warner rejected the deal, Leslie had to notify Sybervantage's sales force. Rather then dwell on the bad news, he focused on possible options for the future. The upbeat close diminishes the effect of the bad news without hiding or downplaying the news itself.

Communicating in a Crisis   Some of the most critical instances of business communication occur during internal or external crises, which range from incidents of product tampering to industrial accidents, crimes or scandals involving company employees, on-site hostage situations, or terrorist attacks. During a crisis, employees, their families, the surrounding community, and others will demand information; plus, rumors can spread unpredictably and uncontrollably (see "Using the Power of Technology: Controlling Rumors Online"). You can also expect the news media to descend quickly, asking questions of anyone they can find.

Although you can't predict these events, you can prepare for them. Companies that respond quickly with the information people need tend to fare much better in these circumstances than those who go into hiding or release bits and pieces of uncoordinated or inconsistent information. Companies such as Johnson & Johnson (in a Tylenol-tampering incident) emerged from crisis with renewed respect for their decisive action and responsive communication. In contrast, Exxon continues to be cited as a classic example of how not to communicate in a crisis—more than a quarter century after one of its tankers spilled 250,000 barrels of oil into Alaska's Prince William Sound. The company frustrated the media and the public with sketchy, inconsistent information and an adamant refusal to accept

USING THE POWER OF TECHNOLOGY

Controlling Rumors Online

Ah, the miracles of the Internet: spam, viruses, spyware, stolen bandwidth, hacked databases full of confidential information—ruin and nuisance at the speed of light. If you work in corporate communications, you can add rapid-fire rumor mongering to that list.

Consumers can now share rumors and complaints through e-mail, instant messaging, blogs, chat rooms, newsgroups, a variety of complaint websites such as www.planetfeedback.com and "corporate hate" sites such as www.paypalsucks.com and www.allstateinsurancesucks.com. On the positive side, consumers who feel they have been treated unfairly can use the public exposure as leverage. Many companies appreciate the feedback from these sites, too, and even buy complaint summaries so they can improve products and services.

Nevertheless, many of these venues don't verify rumors or complaints. E-mail is probably the worst offender in this respect, because messages are so easy to forward en masse. Among recent rumors spread online: products from Coca-Cola and PepsiCo are tainted, perfume samples arriving in the mail are poisonous, bananas from Costa Rica carry a flesh-eating bacteria, the small letter "k" on Snapple labels means the company supports the Ku Klux Klan, Carmex lip balm has (take your pick) addictive ingredients or either an acid or ground glass fibers that damage your lips so you have to use more. Every one of these rumors is false.

Controlling false rumors is difficult, but you can help contain them by (1) responding quickly with clear information distributed in any way you can, (2) tracking down and responding to rumors wherever they appear, (3) enlisting the help of government agencies such as the Centers for Disease Control and Prevention (www.cdc.gov) and debunking sites such as www.snopes.com, and (4) even digging back through e-mail threads and responding personally to everyone who passed the message along. Moreover, don't wait for bad news to find you; monitor complaint sites and newsgroups so that you can jump on false information faster.

CAREER APPLICATIONS

1. A legitimate complaint about one of your products on PlanetFeedback.com also contains a statement that your company "doesn't care about its customers." How should you respond?

2. A few bloggers are circulating false information about your company, but the problem is not widespread—yet. Should you jump on the problem now and tell the world the rumor is false, even though most people haven't heard it yet? Explain your answer.

---

responsibility for the full extent of the environmental disaster. The company's CEO didn't talk to the media for nearly a week; other executives made contradictory statements, which further undermined public trust. The mistakes had a lasting impact on the company's reputation and consumers' willingness to buy its products.[15]

The key to successful communication efforts during a crisis is having a **crisis management plan**. In addition to defining operational procedures to deal with the crisis itself, the plan also outlines communication tasks and responsibilities, which can include everything from media contacts to news release templates (see Table 8–3). The plan should clearly specify which people are authorized to speak for the company, contact information for all key executives, and a list of the media outlets and technologies that will be used to disseminate information. At Baptist Hospital in hurricane-prone Pensacola, Florida, human resources director Celeste Norris and her colleagues plan for every contingency. For instance, the walkie-talkies they keep on hand became the only communication link throughout the facility when hurricane Ivan took out both electrical power and cell phone towers.[16] Many companies now go one step further by regularly testing crisis communications in realistic practice drills lasting a full day or more.[17]

Celeste Norris and Bob Murphy of Baptist Hospital in Pensacola, Florida, relied on such basic tools as walkie-talkies and cork bulletin boards for communication when Hurricane Ivan wiped out power and phone systems in 2004.

Anticipation and planning are key to successful communication in a crisis.

Table 8–3	HOW TO COMMUNICATE IN A CRISIS

When a Crisis Hits:

Do	Don't
Prepare for trouble ahead of time by identifying potential problems, appointing and training a response team, and preparing and testing a crisis management plan.	Don't blame anyone for anything.
Get top management involved as soon as the crisis hits.	Don't speculate in public.
Set up a news center for company representatives and the media, equipped with phones, computers, and other electronic tools for preparing news releases and online updates.	Don't refuse to answer questions.
• Issue frequent news updates, and have trained personnel available to respond to questions around the clock.	Don't release information that will violate anyone's right to privacy.
• Provide complete information packets to the media as soon as possible.	Don't use the crisis to pitch products or services.
• Prevent conflicting statements and provide continuity, appointing a single person, trained in advance, to speak for the company.	Don't play favorites with media representatives.
• Tell receptionists and other employers to direct all media calls to the news center.	
Tell the whole story—openly, completely, and honestly. If you are at fault, apologize.	
Demonstrate the company's concern by your statements and your actions.	

Sending Negative Employment Messages

Most managers must convey bad news about individual employees from time to time. You can use the direct approach when writing to job applicants or when communicating with other companies to send a negative reference to a prospective employer. But it's best to use the indirect approach when giving negative performance reviews to employees; they will most certainly be emotionally involved. In addition, choose the media you use for these messages with care. E-mail and other written forms let you control the message and avoid personal confrontation, but one-on-one conversations are more sensitive and facilitate questions and answers.

Refusing Requests for Recommendation Letters Even though many states have passed laws to protect employers who provide open and honest job references for former employees, legal hazards persist.[18] That's why many former employers still refuse to write recommendation letters—especially for people whose job performance has been unsatisfactory. When sending refusals to prospective employers, your message may be brief and direct:

Implies that company policy prohibits the release of any more information but does provide what information is available

Our human resources department has authorized me to confirm that Yolanda Johnson worked for Tandy, Inc., for three years, from June 1999 to July 2001. Best of luck as you interview administrative applicants.

Ends on a positive note

In letters informing prospective employers that you will not provide a recommendation, be direct, brief, and factual (to avoid legal pitfalls).

This message doesn't need to say, "We cannot comply with your request." It simply gets down to the business of giving readers the information that is allowable.

Refusing an applicant's direct request for a recommendation letter is another matter. Any refusal to cooperate may seem a personal slight and a threat to the applicant's future. Diplomacy and preparation help readers accept your refusal:

Thank you for letting me know about your job opportunity with Coca-Cola. Your internship there and the MBA you've worked so hard to earn should place you in an excellent position to land the marketing job.

Although we do not send out formal recommendations here at PepsiCo, I can certainly send Coca-Cola a confirmation of your employment dates. And if you haven't considered this already, be sure to ask several of your professors to write evaluations of your marketing skills. Best of luck to you in your career.

Uses the indirect approach since the other party is probably expecting a positive response

Announces that the writer cannot comply with the request, without explicitly blaming it on "policy"

Offers to fulfill as much of the request as possible, then offers an alternative

Ends on a positive note

This letter deftly and tactfully avoids hurting the reader's feelings, because it makes positive comments about the reader's recent activities, implies the refusal, suggests an alternative, and uses a polite close.

Rejecting Job Applications   Tactfully telling job applicants that you won't be offering them employment is another frequent communication challenge. But don't let the difficulty stop you from communicating the bad news. Failing to respond to applications is a shoddy business practice that will harm your company's reputation. At the same time, poorly written rejection letters have negative consequences, ranging from the loss of qualified candidates for future openings to the loss of potential customers (not only the rejected applicants but also their friends and family).[19] Poorly phrased rejection letters can even invite legal troubles. When delivering bad news to job applicants, follow three guidelines:[20]

Always respond to job applications.

- **Choose your approach carefully.** Experts disagree on whether a direct or an indirect approach is best for rejection letters. On the one hand, job applicants know they won't get many of the positions they apply for, so negative news during a job search is not generally a shock. On the other hand, people put their hopes and dreams on the line when they apply for work, so job applicants have a deep emotional investment in the process, which is one of the factors to consider in using an indirect approach. If you opt for a direct approach, try not to be brutally blunt in the opening. Tell your reader that the position has been filled, rather than saying, "Your application has been rejected." If you opt for an indirect approach, be careful not to mislead the reader or delay the bad news for more than a sentence or two. A simple "Thank you for considering ABC as the place to start your career" is a quick, courteous buffer that shows your company is flattered to be considered. Don't mislead the reader in your buffer by praising his or her qualifications in a way that could suggest good news is soon to follow.

- **Clearly state why the applicant was not selected.** Make your rejection less personal by stating that you hired someone with more experience or whose qualifications match the position requirements more closely.

- **Close by suggesting alternatives.** If you believe the applicant is qualified, mention other openings within your company. You might suggest professional organizations that could help the applicant find employment. Or you might simply mention that the applicant's résumé will be considered for future openings. Any of these positive suggestions may help the applicant be less disappointed and view your company more positively.

A rejection letter need not be long. Remember, sending a well-written form letter that follows these three guidelines is better than not sending one at all. After all, the applicant wants to know only one thing: Did I land the job? Your brief message conveys the information clearly and with tactful consideration for the applicant's feelings. After Carol DeCicco interviewed with Bradley & Jackson, she was hopeful about receiving a job offer. Everything went well, and her résumé was in good shape. The e-mail in Figure 8–7 was drafted by Marvin Fichter to communicate the bad news to DeCicco. After reviewing the first draft, Fichter made several changes to improve the communication. The revised e-mail helps DeCicco understand that (1) she would have been hired if she'd had more tax experience and (2) she shouldn't be discouraged.

FIGURE 8–7
Poor and Improved E-Mails Rejecting a Job Application

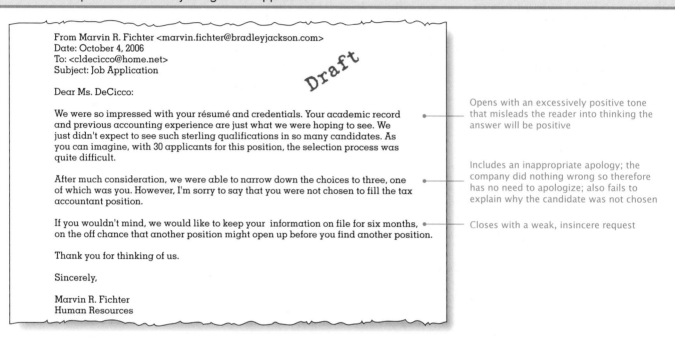

From Marvin R. Fichter <marvin.fichter@bradleyjackson.com>
Date: October 4, 2006
To: <cldecicco@home.net>
Subject: Job Application

Draft

Dear Ms. DeCicco:

We were so impressed with your résumé and credentials. Your academic record and previous accounting experience are just what we were hoping to see. We just didn't expect to see such sterling qualifications in so many candidates. As you can imagine, with 30 applicants for this position, the selection process was quite difficult.

Opens with an excessively positive tone that misleads the reader into thinking the answer will be positive

After much consideration, we were able to narrow down the choices to three, one of which was you. However, I'm sorry to say that you were not chosen to fill the tax accountant position.

Includes an inappropriate apology; the company did nothing wrong so therefore has no need to apologize; also fails to explain why the candidate was not chosen

If you wouldn't mind, we would like to keep your information on file for six months, on the off chance that another position might open up before you find another position.

Closes with a weak, insincere request

Thank you for thinking of us.

Sincerely,

Marvin R. Fichter
Human Resources

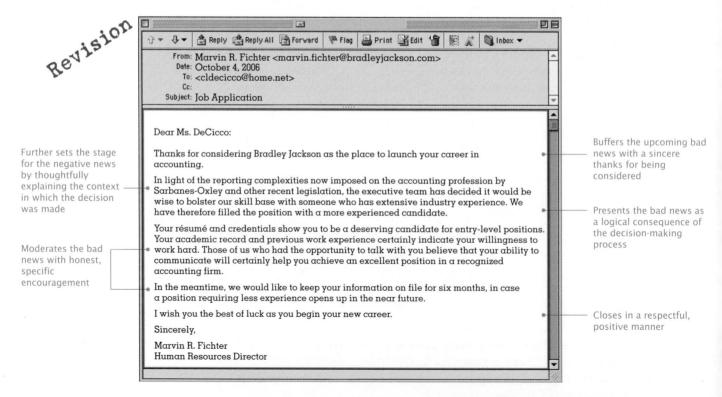

Revision

From: Marvin R. Fichter <marvin.fichter@bradleyjackson.com>
Date: October 4, 2006
To: <cldecicco@home.net>
Cc:
Subject: Job Application

Dear Ms. DeCicco:

Thanks for considering Bradley Jackson as the place to launch your career in accounting.

Buffers the upcoming bad news with a sincere thanks for being considered

In light of the reporting complexities now imposed on the accounting profession by Sarbanes-Oxley and other recent legislation, the executive team has decided it would be wise to bolster our skill base with someone who has extensive industry experience. We have therefore filled the position with a more experienced candidate.

Further sets the stage for the negative news by thoughtfully explaining the context in which the decision was made

Presents the bad news as a logical consequence of the decision-making process

Your résumé and credentials show you to be a deserving candidate for entry-level positions. Your academic record and previous work experience certainly indicate your willingness to work hard. Those of us who had the opportunity to talk with you believe that your ability to communicate will certainly help you achieve an excellent position in a recognized accounting firm.

Moderates the bad news with honest, specific encouragement

In the meantime, we would like to keep your information on file for six months, in case a position requiring less experience opens up in the near future.

I wish you the best of luck as you begin your new career.

Closes in a respectful, positive manner

Sincerely,

Marvin R. Fichter
Human Resources Director

Giving Negative Performance Reviews   A performance review is a manager's evaluation of an employee and may be formal or informal. Few other communication tasks require such a broad range of skills and strategy as those needed for performance reviews. The main purpose of these reviews is to improve employee performance by (1) emphasizing and clarifying job requirements, (2) giving employees feedback on their efforts toward fulfilling those requirements, and (3) guiding continued efforts by developing a plan of action, which includes rewards and opportunities. In addition to improving employee performance, performance reviews help companies set organizational standards and communicate organizational values.[21]

An important goal of any performance evaluation is giving the employee a plan of action for improving his or her performance.

Positive and negative performance reviews share several characteristics: The tone is objective and unbiased, the language is nonjudgmental, and the focus is problem resolution.[22] Also, to increase objectivity, more organizations are giving their employees feedback from multiple sources. In these "360-degree reviews," employees get feedback from all directions in the organization: above, below, and horizontally.[23]

It's difficult to criticize employees face to face, and it's just as hard to include criticism in written performance evaluations. Nevertheless, if you fire an employee for incompetence and the performance evaluations are all positive, the employee can sue your company, maintaining you had no cause to terminate employment.[24] Also, your company could be sued for negligence if an injury is caused by an employee who received a negative evaluation but received no corrective action (such as retraining).[25] So as difficult as it may be, make sure your performance evaluations are well balanced and honest.

When you need to give a negative performance review, follow these guidelines:[26]

- **Confront the problem right away.** Avoiding performance problems only makes them worse. Moreover, if you don't document problems when they occur, you may make it more difficult to terminate employment later on, if the situation comes to that.[27]

- **Plan your message.** Be clear about your concerns, and include examples of the employee's specific actions. Think about any possible biases you may have, and get feedback from others. Collect and verify all relevant facts (both strengths and weaknesses).

- **Deliver the message in private.** Whether in writing or in person, be sure to address the performance problem privately. Don't send performance reviews by e-mail or fax. If you're reviewing an employee's performance face to face, conduct that review in a meeting arranged expressly for that purpose, and consider holding that meeting in a conference room, the employee's office, or some other neutral area.

Address performance problems in private.

- **Focus on the problem.** Discuss the problems caused by the employee's behavior (without attacking the employee). Compare the employee's performance with what's expected, with company goals, or with job requirements (not with the performance of other employees). Identify the consequences of continuing poor performance, and show that you're committed to helping solve the problem.

- **Ask for a commitment from the employee.** Help the employee understand that planning for and making improvements are the employee's responsibility. However, finalize decisions jointly so that you can be sure any action to be taken is achievable. Set a schedule for improvement and for following up with evaluations of that improvement.

Even if your employee's performance has been disappointing, you would do well to begin by mentioning some good points in your performance review. Then clearly and tactfully state how the employee can better meet the responsibilities of the job. If the performance review is to be effective, be sure to suggest ways that the employee can improve.[28] For example, instead of only telling an employee that he damaged some expensive machinery, suggest that he take a refresher course in the correct operation of that machinery. The goal is to help the employee succeed.

✓ CHECKLIST: Writing Negative Employment Messages

A. Refusing requests for recommendation letters

✓ Don't feel obligated to write a recommendation letter if you don't feel comfortable doing so.
✓ Take a diplomatic approach to minimize hurt feelings.
✓ Compliment the reader's accomplishments.
✓ Suggest alternatives if available.

B. Rejecting job applications

✓ Always respond to applications.
✓ If you use a direct approach, take care to avoid being blunt or cold.
✓ If you use an indirect approach, don't mislead the reader in your buffer or delay the bad news for more than a sentence or two.
✓ Clearly state why the applicant was rejected.
✓ Suggest alternatives if possible.

C. Giving negative performance reviews

✓ Maintain an objective and unbiased tone.
✓ Use nonjudgmental language.
✓ Focus on problem resolution.
✓ Make sure negative feedback is documented and shared with the employee.
✓ Don't avoid confrontations by withholding negative feedback.
✓ Ask the employee for a commitment to improve.

D. Terminating employment

✓ State your reasons accurately and make sure they are objectively verifiable.
✓ Avoid statements that might expose your company to a wrongful termination lawsuit
✓ Consult company lawyers to clarify all terms of the separation.
✓ End the relationship on terms as positive as possible.

Carefully word a termination letter to avoid creating undue ill will and grounds for legal action.

Terminating Employment   When writing a termination letter, you have three goals: (1) present the reasons for this difficult action, (2) avoid statements that might expose the company to a wrongful termination lawsuit, and (3) leave the relationship between the terminated employee and the firm as favorable as possible. For both legal and personal reasons, present specific justification for asking the employee to leave.[29] If the employee is working under contract, your company's lawyers will be able to tell you whether the employee's performance is legal grounds for termination.

Make sure that all your reasons are accurate and verifiable. Avoid words that are open to interpretation, such as *untidy* and *difficult.* Make sure the employee leaves with feelings that are as positive as the circumstances allow. You can do so by telling the truth about the termination and by helping as much as you can to make the employee's transition as smooth as possible.[30] To review the tasks involved in this type of message, see "Checklist: Writing Negative Employment Messages."

On the Job

SOLVING COMMUNICATION DILEMMAS AT KPMG

With a good head for numbers and effective communication skills, you didn't take long to move up to a management position with KPMG. You're now an audit manager in the firm's Louisville, Kentucky, office (an *audit* is the process of reviewing a firm's accounting records for accuracy and legal compliance). Your responsibilities range from managing audits for KPMG's clients to helping members of your group develop their skills to coordinating with other managers in cross-functional team efforts. Not surprisingly, communication challenges are frequent and diverse.[31]

1. Another manager in the Louisville office stopped by this morning with a request to borrow two of your best auditors for a three-week emergency. Under normal conditions, you wouldn't hesitate to help, but

your team has its own scheduling challenges to deal with. Plus, this isn't the first time this manager has run into trouble, and you are confident that poor project management is the reason. Which of the following is the most diplomatic way to state your refusal while suggesting that your colleague's management skills need improving?

a. With the commitments we've made to our own clients, we won't be able to bail you out this time.
b. I sympathize with the trouble you've gotten yourself into again, I really do, but the commitments we've made to our own clients prevent us from releasing any auditors for temporary assignments.
c. The commitments we've made to our own clients prevent us from releasing any auditors for tempo-

rary assignments. However, I would be happy to meet with you to discuss the techniques I've been using to manage project workloads.

d. Instead of shifting resources around like usual, why don't we meet to discuss some new strategies for staffing and project management?

2. In business services professions such as public accounting, service providers often work closely with clients for long periods—sometimes even setting up offices at client's facilities and functioning almost like employees in the client's organization. Like all professional relationships, personal aspects can enter the relationship over time as well. In a good situation, the people involved can become friends or social acquaintances, further cementing the business relationship. In a bad situation, even competent professionals can start to rub each other the wrong way at a personal level, which can corrode the business relationship over time. Unfortunately, that has happened with one of your best staff members. Shirley Jackson is widely admired for her technical skills, but a top manager in a client organization has asked you to take her off the project. Although you'd prefer to tell Jackson in person, schedule conflicts dictate that you send her an e-mail. Which of these buffers would be the best way to open the message?

a. Your work for Comstock Manufacturing continues to be first rate, but you never can tell how these things are going to work out, can you?

b. If it were up to me, Shirley, I would never deliver a message like this, but Comstock has asked me to re-evaluate the staffing on their auditing projects.

c. As I've expressed on many occasions, thank you once again for the top-quality work you've done for Comstock Manufacturing over the years.

d. As you know, Shirley, I continually evaluate the staffing assignments on all our projects to make sure clients are satisfied with both the quality of our work and the overall nature of our relationship with them.

3. Although your project management skills are quite good, you do occasionally run into unforeseen circumstances that lead to less-than-ideal results. You underestimated the number of hours required to complete a financial analysis project for an important client. The contract you signed with the client allows a 10 percent overage for such contingencies, but your best guess now is that the total will be 20 to 25 percent over. You have the unpleasant task of explaining to your boss that the project will be coming in over budget and that KPMG will have to absorb the remaining 10 to 15 percent. Which of the following is the best way to communicate that news to your boss?

a. I messed up, big time. The Southern Petroleum project is going to come in over budget.

b. The Southern Petroleum project is going to come in at least 20 percent over budget, perhaps 25 percent.

c. We've recently discovered that Southern Petroleum's accounting system was in far worse shape than I anticipated when I submitted the project proposal, and as a result of the extra work required to reconcile their disorganized records, the project is going to run 20 to 25 percent over budget.

d. We've recently discovered that Southern Petroleum's accounting system was in far worse shape than I anticipated when I submitted the project proposal. This is clearly not my fault, but as a result of the extra work required to reconcile their disorganized records, the project is going to run 20 to 25 percent over budget.

4. You've found it easy to say "yes" to recommendation letter requests from former employees who were top performers, and you've learned to say "no" to those people who didn't perform so well. The requests you struggle with are from employees in the middle, those people who didn't really excel but didn't really cause any trouble, either. You've just received a request from a computer systems specialist who falls smack in the middle of the middle. Unfortunately, he's applying for a job at a firm that you know places high demands on its employees and generally hires the best of the best. He's a great person, and you'd love to help, but in your heart you know that if by some chance he does get the job, he probably won't last. Plus, you don't want to get a reputation in the industry for recommending weak candidates. How do you set the stage for the negative news?

a. As your former manager, I'd like to think I can still look out for your best interests, and I'm sorry to say, but based on what I know about the position you're applying for, this might not be the best career move for you at this point.

b. In my view, the responsibility of writing a letter of recommendation goes beyond simply assessing a person's skills; it must consider whether the person is applying for the right job.

c. One of the most important factors I consider when deciding whether to endorse an applicant is whether he or she is pursuing an opportunity that offers a high probability of success.

d. Writing a recommendation letters bears a heavy responsibility for both the job application and the person writing the letter. After all, I have my own reputation to protect, too.

Learning Objectives Checkup

Assess your understanding of the principles in this chapter by reading each learning objective and studying the accompanying exercises. For fill-in items, write the missing text in the blank provided; for multiple choice items, circle the letter of the correct answer. You can check your responses against the answer key on page AK-2.

Objective 8.1: Apply the three-step writing process to negative messages.

1. Which of the following is an effective way to maintain the "you" attitude when crafting negative messages?
   a. Make sure the reader clearly understands that he or she is at fault; after all, recognizing a mistake is the first step toward improvement.
   b. Make it clear that you don't enjoy giving out bad news.
   c. Show respect for the reader by "soft peddling" the negative news, implying it without really coming out and saying it directly.
   d. Show respect for the reader by avoiding negative, accusatory language and emphasizing positives whenever possible.

Objective 8.2: Explain the differences between the direct and the indirect approaches to negative messages, including when it's appropriate to use each one.

2. When using the direct approach with negative messages, you begin with
   a. A buffer
   b. An attention-getter
   c. The bad news
   d. Any of the above

3. An advantage of using the direct approach with negative messages is that it
   a. Saves readers time by helping them reach the main idea more quickly
   b. Eases the reader into the message
   c. Is diplomatic
   d. Does all of the above

4. When using the indirect approach with negative messages, you begin with
   a. A buffer
   b. An attention-getter
   c. The bad news
   d. Any of the above

5. An advantage of using the indirect approach with negative messages is that
   a. Most readers prefer the direct approach for such messages
   b. It makes a shorter message possible
   c. It eases the reader into the message
   d. It does all of the above

Objective 8.3: Identify the risks of using the indirect approach, and explain how to avoid such problems.

6. The purpose of using the indirect approach is to
   a. Help the writer avoid the unpleasant task of delivering bad news
   b. Help the reader avoid the unpleasant task of receiving bad news
   c. Soften the blow of the bad news for the reader
   d. Reduce the word count in your messages

7. Which of the following is a good possibility to consider for use in writing a buffer?
   a. Look for opportunities to express your appreciation for being considered.

   b. Assure your reader of the attention you've paid to his or her request.
   c. Indicate your understanding of the reader's situation.
   d. All of the above are useful approaches.

Objective 8.4: Adapt negative messages for internal and external audiences.

8. When writing negative messages, the key difference to consider between internal and external audiences is
   a. The expectations regarding the message
   b. Their legal standing
   c. The length of time they've been associated with the company
   d. None of the above

9. When a negative message is going to be sent to both internal and external audiences (such as an announcement of a factory closing), which of the following best describes the expectations that internal audiences usually have regarding the timing of the message delivery?
   a. Internal audiences want to receive the news first.
   b. Internal audiences want to receive the news at the same time as the external audience.
   c. Internal audiences want to receive the news after the external audience has received it.
   d. The timing doesn't matter to internal audiences.

Objective 8.5: Define defamation, and explain how to avoid it in negative messages.

10. A false statement that is damaging to a person's character or reputation, whether spoken or in writing, is known as _____.

11. Written defamation is known as _____.

12. Spoken defamation is known as _____.

13. Which of the following is good advice for avoiding being accused of defamation?
    a. Never use abusive language.
    b. Seek legal advice regarding questionable messages.
    c. Stick to the facts and never communicate in a dishonest manner.
    d. Do all of the above.

Objective 8.6: Explain the role of communication in crisis management.

14. Which of the following best characterizes the nature of crisis management planning?
    a. Good managers should be able to anticipate the specific crisis scenarios their companies might encounter and therefore should be able to plan for every crisis in a specific way.
    b. With everything from terrorism to technological disasters, there's no way to anticipate which crisis might hit any given business, so it's a waste of time to plan a response.
    c. Although you can't anticipate the nature and circumstance of every possible crisis, you can prepare by deciding how to handle such issues as communication with employees and the public.
    d. Only negatively focused managers worry about crisis planning; positive managers keep their organizations moving toward company goals.

15. Continuing advances in communication technology make it
    a. Easier to control rumors through Internet filters and other means
    b. More difficult to control rumors
    c. Easier to find the people who start rumors
    d. Illegal to spread false rumors about public corporations

Objective 8.7: List three guidelines for delivering bad news to job applicants, and give a brief explanation of each one.

16. Why do many experts recommend using an indirect approach when rejecting job applicants?
    a. Applicants have a deep emotional investment in the decision.
    b. Laws in most states require an indirect approach.
    c. Indirect approaches are easier to write.
    d. Indirect approaches are shorter.

17. When explaining why an applicant wasn't chosen for a position, you should
    a. Be specific without being too personal, such as explaining that the position requires specific skills that the applicant doesn't yet possess
    b. Point out the person's shortcomings; that's the honest way and the only way the person knows what he or she need to improve
    c. Be as vague as possible to avoid hurting the person's feelings
    d. Never explain why an applicant wasn't chosen

Apply Your Knowledge

1. Why is it important to end negative message on a positive note?
2. If company policy changes, should you explain those changes to employees and customers at about the same time? Why or why not?
3. If your purpose is to convey bad news, such as refusing a request, should you take the time to suggest alternatives to your reader? Why or why not?
4. When a company suffers a setback, should you soften the impact by letting out the bad news a little at a time? Why or why not?
5. **Ethical Choices** Is intentionally de-emphasizing bad news the same as distorting graphs and charts to de-emphasize unfavorable data? Why or why not?

Practice Your Knowledge

DOCUMENTS FOR ANALYSIS

Read the following documents, then (1) analyze the strengths and weaknesses of each sentence and (2) revise each document so that it follows this chapter's guidelines.

DOCUMENT 8.A: PROVIDING NEGATIVE NEWS ABOUT TRANSACTIONS

Your spring fraternity party sounds like fun. We're glad you've again chosen us as your caterer. Unfortunately, we have changed a few of our policies, and I wanted you to know about these changes in advance so that we won't have any misunderstandings on the day of the party.

We will arrange the delivery of tables and chairs as usual the evening before the party. However, if you want us to set up, there is now a $100 charge for that service. Of course, you might want to get some of the brothers and pledges to do it, which would save you money. We've also added a small charge for cleanup. This is only $3 per person (you can estimate because I know a lot of people come and go later in the evening).

Other than that, all the arrangements will be the same. We'll provide the skirting for the band stage, tablecloths, bar setup, and, of course, the barbecue. Will you have the tubs of ice with soft drinks again? We can do that for you as well, but there will be a fee.

Please let me know if you have any problems with these changes and we'll try to work them out. I know it's going to be a great party.

DOCUMENT 8.B: REFUSING REQUESTS FOR CLAIMS AND ADJUSTMENTS

I am responding to your letter of about six weeks ago asking for an adjustment on your wireless hub, model WM39Z. We test all our products before they leave the factory; therefore, it could not have been our fault that your hub didn't work.

If you or someone in your office dropped the unit, it might have caused the damage. Or the damage could have been caused by the shipper if he dropped it. If so, you should file a claim with the shipper. At any rate, it wasn't our fault. The parts are already covered by warranty. However, we will provide labor for the repairs for $50, which is less than our cost, since you are a valued customer.

We will have a booth at the upcoming trade show there and hope to see you or someone from your office. We have many new models of office machines that we're sure you'll want to see. I've enclosed our latest catalog. Hope to see you there.

DOCUMENT 8.C: REJECTING JOB APPLICATIONS

I regret to inform you that you were not selected for our summer intern program at Equifax. We had over a thousand résumés and cover letters to go through and simply could not get to them all. We have been asked to notify everyone that we have already selected students for the 25 positions based on those who applied early and were qualified.

We're sure you will be able to find a suitable position for summer work in your field and wish you the best of luck. We deeply regret any inconvenience associated with our reply.

Exercises

For active links to all websites discussed in this chapter, visit this text's website at www.prenhall.com/thill. Locate your book and click on its Companion Website link. Then select Chapter 8, and click on "Featured Websites." Locate the name of the page or the URL related to the material in the text. Please note that links to sites that become inactive after publication of the book will be removed from the Featured Websites section.

8.1 Selecting the Approach Select which approach you would use (direct or indirect) for the following negative messages:

    a. A memo to your boss informing her that one of your key clients is taking its business to a different accounting firm

    b. An e-mail message to a customer informing her that one of the books she ordered over the Internet is temporarily out of stock

    c. A letter to a customer explaining that the DVD recorder he ordered for his new computer is on back order and that, as a consequence, the shipping of the entire order will be delayed

    d. A memo to all employees notifying them that the company parking lot will be repaved during the first week of June and that the company will provide a shuttle service from a remote parking lot during that period

    e. A letter from a travel agent to a customer stating that the airline will not refund her money for the flight she missed but that her tickets are valid for one year

    f. A form letter from a U.S. airline to a customer explaining that they cannot extend the expiration date of the customer's frequent flyer miles even though the customer was living overseas for the past three years and unable to use the miles during that time

    g. A letter from an insurance company to a policyholder denying a claim for reimbursement for a special medical procedure that is not covered under the terms of the customer's policy

    h. A letter from an electronics store stating that the customer will not be reimbursed for a malfunctioning cell phone still under warranty (the terms of the warranty do not cover damages to phones that were accidentally dropped from a moving car)

    i. An announcement to the repairs department listing parts that are on back order and will be three weeks late

8.2 Teamwork Working alone, revise the following statements to de-emphasize the bad news. (*Hint:* Minimize the space devoted to the bad news, subordinate it, embed it, or use the passive voice.) Then team up with a classmate and read each other's revisions. Did you both use the same approach in every case? Which approach seems to be most effective for each of the revised statements?

    a. The airline can't refund your money. The "Conditions" segment on the back of your ticket states that there are no refunds for missed flights. Sometimes the airline makes exceptions, but only when life and death are involved. Of course, your ticket is still valid and can be used on a flight to the same destination.

    b. I'm sorry to tell you, we can't supply the custom decorations you requested. We called every supplier and none of them can do what you want on such short notice. You can, however, get a standard decorative package on the same theme in time. I found a supplier that stocks these. Of course, it won't have quite the flair you originally requested.

    c. We can't refund your money for the malfunctioning lamp. You shouldn't have placed a 250-watt bulb in the fixture socket; it's guaranteed for a maximum of 75 watts.

8.3 Using Buffers As a customer service supervisor for a telephone company, you're in charge of responding to customers' requests for refunds. You've just received an e-mail from a customer who unwittingly ran up a $500 bill for long-distance calls after mistakenly configuring his laptop computer to dial an Internet access number that wasn't a local call. The customer says it wasn't his fault because he didn't realize he was dialing a long-distance number. However, you've dealt with this situation before; you know that the customer's Internet service provider warns its customers to choose a local access number, since customers are responsible for all long-distance charges. Draft a short buffer (1 to 2 sentences) for your e-mail reply, sympathizing with the customer's plight but preparing him for the bad news (company policy specifically prohibits refunds in such cases).

8.4 Internet Public companies occasionally need to issue news releases announcing or explaining downturns in sales, profits, demand, or other business factors. Search the web to locate a company that has issued a press release that recently reported lower earnings or other bad news, and access the news release on that firm's website. Alternatively, find the type of press release you're seeking by reviewing press releases at www.prnewswire.com or www.businesswire.com. How does the headline relate to the main message of the release? Is the release organized according to the direct or the indirect approach? What does the company do to present the bad news in a favorable light—and does this effort seem sincere and ethical to you?

8.5 Ethical Choices The insurance company where you work is planning to raise all premiums for health-care coverage. Your boss has asked you to read a draft of her letter to customers announcing the new, higher rates. The first two paragraphs discuss some exciting medical advances and the expanded coverage offered by your company. Only in the final paragraph do customers learn that they will have to pay more for coverage starting next year. What are the ethical implications of this draft? What changes would you suggest?

Expand Your Knowledge

LEARNING MORE ON THE WEB
PROTECT YOURSELF WHEN SENDING NEGATIVE EMPLOYMENT MESSAGES
www.toolkit.cch.com

A visit to CCH's Business Owner's Toolkit can help you reduce your legal liability, whether you are laying off an employee, firing an employee, or contemplating a company-wide reduction in your workforce. Find out the safest way to fire someone from a legal standpoint before it's too late. Learn why it's important to document disciplinary actions. Discover why some bad news should be given face to face and never by a letter or over the phone.

ACTIVITIES
Read CCH's advice to find answers to these questions:
1. What should a manager communicate to an employee during a termination meeting?
2. Why is it important to document employee disciplinary actions?
3. What steps should you take before firing an employee for misconduct or poor work?

EXPLORING THE WEB ON YOUR OWN
Review these chapter-related websites on your own to learn more about the negative issues human resources departments are facing today.
1. Workforce magazine online, www.workforce.com, has the basics and the latest on human resource issues such as recruiting, laws, managing the workforce, incentives, strategies, and more. Be sure to checkout the forums in the Community Center, where business professionals discuss problems and solutions in the field of human resources.
2. HR.com, www.hr.com, is the place to go to read about workplace trends, legislation affecting employers, recruiting, compensation, benefits, staffing, and more. Log on and learn.
3. BusinessTown.com, www.businesstown.com, offers information on a wide range of business topics, including advice on conducting successful employee performance reviews.

Learn Interactively

INTERACTIVE STUDY GUIDE
Visit www.prenhall.com/thill, then locate your book and click on its Companion Website link. Select Chapter 8 to take advantage of the interactive "Chapter Quiz" to test your knowledge of chapter concepts. Receive instant feedback on whether you need additional studying. Also, visit the "Study Hall," where you'll find an abundance of valuable resources that will help you succeed in this course.

PEAK PERFORMANCE GRAMMAR AND MECHANICS
If your instructor has required the use of "Peak Performance Grammar and Mechanics," either in your online course or on CD, you can improve your skill with commas by using the "Peak Performance Grammar and Mechanics" module. Click "Commas." Take the Pretest to determine whether you have any weak areas. Then review those areas in the Refresher Course. Take the Follow-Up Test to check your grasp of commas. For an extra challenge or advanced practice, take the Advanced Test. Finally, for additional reinforcement, go to the "Improve Your Grammar, Mechanics, and Usage" section that follows, and complete those exercises.

Improve Your Grammar, Mechanics, and Usage

The following exercises help you improve your knowledge of and power over English grammar, mechanics, and usage. Turn to the Handbook of Grammar, Mechanics, and Usage at the end of this textbook and review all of Section 2.6 (Commas). Then look at the following 10 items. Circle the letter of the preferred choice in the following groups of sentences. (Answers to these exercises appear on page AK-3.)
1. a. Please send us four cases of filters two cases of wing nuts and a bale of rags.
   b. Please send us four cases of filters, two cases of wing nuts and a bale of rags.
   c. Please send us four cases of filters, two cases of wing nuts, and a bale of rags.
2. a. Your analysis, however, does not account for returns.
   b. Your analysis however does not account for returns.
   c. Your analysis, however does not account for returns.
3. a. As a matter of fact she has seen the figures.
   b. As a matter of fact, she has seen the figures.
4. a. Before May 7, 1999, they wouldn't have minded either.
   b. Before May 7, 1999 they wouldn't have minded either.

5. a. Stoneridge Inc. will go public on September 9 2003.
   b. Stoneridge, Inc., will go public on September 9, 2003.
   c. Stoneridge Inc. will go public on September 9, 2003.
6. a. "Talk to me" Sandra said "before you change a thing."
   b. "Talk to me," Sandra said "before you change a thing."
   c. "Talk to me," Sandra said, "before you change a thing."
7. a. The firm was founded during the long hard recession of the mid-1970s.
   b. The firm was founded during the long, hard recession of the mid-1970s.
   c. The firm was founded during the long hard, recession of the mid-1970s.
8. a. You can reach me at this address: 717 Darby St., Scottsdale, AZ 85251.
   b. You can reach me at this address: 717 Darby St., Scottsdale AZ 85251.
   c. You can reach me at this address: 717 Darby St., Scottsdale, AZ, 85251.

9. a. Transfer the documents from Fargo, North Dakota to Boise, Idaho.
   b. Transfer the documents from Fargo North Dakota, to Boise Idaho.
   c. Transfer the documents from Fargo, North Dakota, to Boise, Idaho.
10. a. Sam O'Neill the designated representative is gone today.
    b. Sam O'Neill, the designated representative, is gone today.
    c. Sam O'Neill, the designated representative, is gone today.

For additional exercises focusing on commas, go to www.prenhall.com/thill, then locate your text and click on its Companion Website link. Click on Chapter 8, click on "Additional Exercises to Improve Your Grammar, Mechanics and Usage," then click on "14. Fused sentences and comma splices."

Cases

Applying the Three-Step Writing Process to Cases

Apply each step to the following cases, as assigned by your instructor

Planning

Writing

Completing

Analyze the Situation
Identify both your general purpose and your specific purpose. Clarify exactly what you want your audience to think, feel, or believe after receiving your message. Profile your primary audience, including their backgrounds, differences, similarities, and likely reactions to your message.

Gather Information
Identify the information your audience will need to receive, as well as other information you may need in order to craft an effective message.

Select the Right Medium
Make sure your medium is both acceptable to the audience and appropriate for the message. Realize that written media are inappropriate for some negative messages.

Organize the Information
Choose a direct or indirect approach based on the audience and the message; many negative messages are best delivered with an indirect approach. If you use the indirect approach, carefully consider which type of buffer is best for the situation. Identify your main idea, limit your scope, and then outline necessary support points and other evidence.

Adapt to Your Audience
Show sensitivity to audience needs with a "you" attitude, politeness, positive emphasis, and bias-free language. Understand how much credibility you already have—and how much you may need to establish. Project your company's image by maintaining an appropriate style and tone. Consider cultural variations and the differing needs of internal and external audiences.

Compose the Message
Draft your message using clear but sensitive words, effective sentences, and coherent paragraphs.

Revise the Message
Evaluate content and review readability, then edit and rewrite for conciseness and clarity.

Produce the Message
Use effective design elements and suitable layout for a clean, professional appearance.

Proofread the Message
Review for errors in layout, spelling, and mechanics.

Distribute the Message
Deliver your message using the chosen medium; make sure all documents and all relevant files are distributed successfully.

1

2

3

NEGATIVE REPLIES TO ROUTINE REQUESTS

1. No deal: Letter from Home Depot to faucet manufacturer As assistant to the vice president of sales for Atlanta-based Home Depot, you attended Home Depot's biannual product-line review, held at Tropicana Field in St. Petersburg, Florida. Also attending were hundreds of vendor hopefuls, eager to become one of the huge retail chain's 25,000 North American suppliers. During individual meetings with a panel of regional and national Home Depot merchandisers, these vendors did their best to win, keep, or expand their spot in the company's product lineup.

Vendors know that Home Depot holds all the cards, so if they want to play, they have to follow Home Depot rules, offering low wholesale prices and swift delivery. Once chosen, they're constantly re-evaluated—and quickly dropped for infractions such as requesting a price increase or planning to sell directly to consumers via the Internet. They also receive sharp critiques of past performance, which are not to be taken lightly.

A decade ago, General Electric failed to keep Home Depot stores supplied with light bulbs, causing shortages. Co-founder Bernard Marcus immediately stripped GE of its exclusive, 80-foot shelf-space and flew off to negotiate with its Netherlands competitor, Phillips. Two years later, after high-level negotiations, GE bulbs were back on Home Depot shelves—but in a position inferior to Phillips's.

Such cautionary tales aren't lost on vendors. But they know that despite tough negotiating, Home Depot is always looking for variety to please its customers' changing tastes and demands. The sales potential is so enormous that the compromises and concessions are worthwhile. If selected, vendors get immediate distribution in more than 1,700 stores (Home Depot, EXPO, and other subsidiary companies) across the United States, Canada, Mexico, and Puerto Rico.

Still, you've seen the stress on vendor reps' faces as they explain product enhancements and on-time delivery ideas in the review sessions. Their only consolation for this grueling process is that, although merchandisers won't say yes or no on the spot, they do let manufacturers know where they stand within a day or two. And the company is always willing to reconsider at the next product-line review—wherever it's held.

Your task: You're drafting some of the rejection letters, and the next one on your stack is to a faucet manufacturer, Roseway Manufacturing, 133 Industrial Ave., Gary, IN 46406. "Too expensive," "substandard plastic handles," and "a design not likely to appeal to Home Depot customers," say the panel's notes. (And knowing what its customers want has put Home Depot in the top 10 of the Fortune 500 list, with $40 billion in annual sales.) Find a way to soften the blow in your rejection letter to Roseway. After all, consumer tastes do change. Direct your letter to Pamela Wilson, operations manager.[32]

2. Suffering artists: Memo declining high-tech shoes at American Ballet Theatre Here at the American Ballet Theatre (ABT), where you're serving as assistant to Artistic Director Kevin McKenzie, the notion of suffering for the art form has been ingrained since the early 1800s, when the first ballerina rose up *en pointe*. Many entrepreneurs are viewing this painful situation with hopeful enthusiasm, especially when they discover that dancers worldwide spend about $150 million annually on their shoes—those "tiny torture chambers" of cardboard and satin (with glued linen or burlap to stiffen the toes). The pink monstrosities (about $50 a pair) rarely last beyond a single hard performance.

A company the size of ABT spends about $500,000 a year on pointe shoes—plus the cost of their staff physical therapist and all those trips to chiropractors, podiatrists, and surgeons to relieve bad necks, backs, knees, and feet. Entrepreneurs believe there must be room for improvement, given the current advantages of orthopedics, space-age materials, and high-tech solutions for contemporary athletes. There's no denying that ballerinas are among the hardest-working athletes in the world.

The latest entrepreneur to approach ABT is Eliza Minden of Gaynor Minden Inc. She wants to provide a solution to the shoe problem. She approached Michael Kaiser, executive director and a member of ABT's Board of Governing Trustees, with a proposal for providing new, high-performance pointe shoes in exchange for an endorsement.

Minden's alternative pointe shoes offer high-impact support and toe cushions. They're only $90 a pair, and supposedly they can be blow dried (like Birkenstocks) back into shape after a performance. When the cost-conscious board member urged the company to give them a try, you were assigned to collect feedback from dancers.

So far, not so good. For example, after a brief trial one principal ballerina said she'd rather numb her feet in icy water, dance through "zingers" of toe pain, and make frequent visits to the physical therapist than wear Minden's shoes. The majority of others agree. Apparently, they *like* breaking in the traditional satin models with hammers and door slams and throwing them away after a single *Coppelia*. Too stiff, they say of the new shoes, and besides, they're simply not the shoes they grew up with and trained in. Only a few of the company's newest members, such as Gillian Murphy, liked Minden's high-tech shoes. That's not enough for a company endorsement.

You've seen those sinewy, wedge-shaped feet bleeding backstage. You feel sorry for Minden; it *was* a good idea—just a hard sell among the tradition-oriented dancers.

Your task: McKenzie has asked you to write an internal memo in his name to Michael Kaiser, executive director of the American Ballet Theatre, explaining the dancers' refusal to use the new high-tech Gaynor Minden pointe shoes. In your memo be sure to include the dancers' reasons as well as your own opinion regarding the matter. You'll need to decide whether to use the direct or the indirect approach; include a separate short note to your instructor justifying your selection of approach.[34]

3. Cyber-surveillance: Memo refusing claim from Silent Watch victim Your business is called Advertising Inflatables, and your specialty is designing and building the huge balloon replicas used for advertising atop retail stores, tire outlets, used car lots, fast-food outlets, fitness clubs, etc. You've built

balloon re-creations of everything from a 50-foot King Kong to a "small" 10-foot pizza.

Not long ago, you installed the "cyber-surveillance" software, Silent Watch, to track and record employees' computer usage. At the time, you sent out a memo informing all employees that they should limit their computer use and e-mail to work projects only. You also informed them that their work would be monitored. You did not mention that Silent Watch would record every keystroke of their work or that they could be monitored from a screen in your office.

As expected, Silent Watch caught two of the sales staff spending between 50 and 70 percent of their time surfing Internet sites unrelated to their jobs. You withheld their pay accordingly, without warning. You sent them a memo notifying them that they were not fired but were on probation. You considered this wise, because when they work, both employees are very good at what they do, and talent is hard to find.

But now salesman Jarod Harkington has sent you a letter demanding reinstatement of his pay and claiming he was "spied on illegally." On the contrary, company attorneys have assured you that the courts almost always side with employers on this issue, particularly after employees receive a warning such as the one you wrote. The computer equipment belongs to Advertising Inflatables, and employees are paid a fair price for their time.

Your task: Write a letter refusing Mr. Harkington's claim.[34]

4. When a recall isn't really a recall: Voice recording informing customers that an unsafe product won't be replaced Vail Products of Toledo, Ohio, manufactured a line of beds for use in hospitals and other institutions where there is a need to protect patients who might otherwise fall out of bed and injure themselves (including patients with cognitive impairments or patterns of spasms or seizures). These "enclosed bed systems" use a netted canopy to keep patients in bed, rather than the traditional method of using physical restraints such as straps or tranquilizing drugs. The intent is humane, but the design is flawed: At least 30 patients have become trapped in the various parts of the mattress and canopy structure, and 8 of them have suffocated.

Working with the U.S. Food and Drug Administration (FDA), Vail issued a recall on the beds, as manufacturers often

do in the case of unsafe products. However, the recall is not really a recall. Vail will not be replacing or modifying the beds, nor will it accept returns. Instead, the company is urging institutions to move patients to other beds if possible. Vail has also sent out revised manuals and warning labels to be placed on the beds. The company also announced that it is ceasing production of enclosed beds.

Your task: A flurry of phone calls from concerned patients, family members, and institutional staff is overwhelming the support staff. As a writer in Vail's corporate communications office, you've been asked to draft a short script to be recorded on the company's phone system. When people call the main number, they'll hear "Press 1 for information regarding the recall of Model 500, Model 1000, and Model 2000 enclosed beds." After they press 1, they'll hear the message you're about to write, explaining that although the action is classified as a recall, Vail will not be accepting returned beds, nor will it replace any of the affected beds. The message should also assure customers that Vail company has already sent revised operating manuals and warning labels to every registered owner of the beds in question. The phone system has limited memory, and you've been directed to keep the message to 75 words or less.[35]

5. Memo to the Boss: Refusing a Project on Ethical Grounds A not-so-secret secret is getting more attention than you'd really like after an article in *BusinessWeek* gave the world an inside look at how much money you and other electronics retailers make from extended warranties (sometimes called service contracts). The article explained that typically half of the warranty price goes to the salesperson as a commission and that only 20 percent of the total amount customers pay for warranties eventually goes to product repair.

You also know why extended warranties are such a profitable business. Many electronics products follow a predictable pattern of failure: a high failure rate early in their lives, then a "midlife" period during which failures go way down, and concluding with an "old age" period when failure rates ramp back up again (engineers refer to the phenomenon as the *bathtub curve* because it looks like a bathtub from the side—high at both ends and low in the middle). Those early failures are usually covered by manufacturers' warranties, and the extended warranties you sell are designed to cover that middle part of the life span. In other words, many extended warranties cover the period of time during which consumers are *least* likely to need them and offer no coverage when consumers need them *most.* (Consumers can actually benefit from extended warranties in a few product categories, including laptop computers and plasma TVs. Of course, the more sense the warranty makes for the consumer, the less financial sense it makes for your company.)[36]

Your task: Worried that consumers will start buying fewer extended warranties, your boss has directed you to put together a sales training program that will help cashiers sell the extended warranties even more aggressively. The more you ponder this challenge, though, the more you're convinced that your company should change its strategy so it doesn't rely on profits from these warranties so much. In addition to offering questionable value to the consumer, they risk creating a consumer backlash that could lead to lower sales of all your products. You would prefer to voice your concerns to your boss in person, but both of you are traveling on hectic schedules for the next week. You'll have to write an e-mail instead. Draft a brief message explaining why you think the sales training specifically and the warranties in general are both bad ideas.

6. Not this time: Letter denying debit adjustments to Union Bank of California customer You are an operations officer in the ATM Error Resolution Department at Union Bank of California. Your department often adjusts customer accounts for ATM debit errors. Mistakes are usually honest ones—such as a merchant swiping a customer's check debit card two or three times, thinking the first few swipes didn't "take," when they actually did.

Customers having problems on their statements are instructed to write a claim letter to your department that describes the situation and includes copies of receipts. Customers are notified of the outcome within 10 to 20 business days. Usually, you credit their account.

However, you've received a letter from Margaret Caldwell, who maintains several hefty joint accounts with her husband at your bank. Three debits to her checking account were processed on the same day and credited to the same market, Wilson's Gourmet. The debits carry the same transaction reference number, 1440022–22839837109, which is what caught Mrs. Caldwell's attention. But you know that number changes daily, not hourly, so multiple purchases made on the same day often carry the same number. Also, the debits are for different amounts ($23.02, $110.95, and $47.50), so these transactions were not a result of repeated card swipes. No receipts were enclosed.

Mrs. Caldwell writes that the store was trying to steal from her, but you doubt that and decide to contact Wilson's Gourmet. Manager Ronson Tibbits tells you that he's had no problems with his equipment, He also mentions that food shoppers commonly return at different times during the day to make additional purchases, particularly for beverages or merchandise they forgot the first time.

You decide that these charges did not the result from a bank or merchant error. It doesn't matter whether Mrs. Caldwell is merely confused or trying to commit an intentional fraud. Bank rules are clear for this situation: You must politely deny her request.

Your task: Write a letter to Margaret Caldwell, 2789 Aviara Parkway, Carlsbad, CA 92008, explaining your refusal of her claim #7899. Keep in mind that you don't want to lose this wealthy customer's business.[37]

NEGATIVE ORGANIZATIONAL NEWS

7. Sorry, but we don't have a choice: E-mail about monitoring employee blogs You can certainly sympathize with employees when they complain about having their e-mail and instant messages monitored, but you're only implementing a company policy that all employees agree to abide by when they join the company. Your firm, Webcor Builders of San Mateo, California, is one of the estimated 60 percent of U.S. companies with such monitoring systems in place. More and more companies use these sys-

tems (which typically operate by scanning messages for key words that suggest confidential, illegal, or otherwise inappropriate content) in an attempt to avoid instances of sexual harassment and other problems.

As the chief information officer, the manager in charge of computer systems in the company, you're often the target when employees complain about being monitored. Consequently, you know you're really going to hear it when employees learn that the monitoring program will be expanded to personal blogs as well.

Your task: Write an e-mail to be distributed to the entire workforce, explaining that the automated monitoring program is about to be expanded to include employees' personal blogs. Explain that while you sympathize with employee concerns regarding privacy and freedom of speech, the management team's responsibility is to protect the company's intellectual property and the value of the company name. Therefore, employees' personal blogs will be added to the monitoring system to ensure that employees don't intentionally or accidentally expose company secrets or criticize management in a way that could harm the company.[38]

8. Removing the obstacles on the on-ramp: Blog posting to Ernst & Young employees Like many companies these days, the accounting firm Ernst & Young is fighting a brain drain as experienced executives and professionals leave in mid-career to pursue charitable interests, devote more time to family matters, or pursue a variety of other dreams or obligations. The problem is particularly acute among women, since on average they step off the career track more often than men do. As general manager of the largest division in the company, you've been tapped to draft a set of guidelines to make it easier for employees who've taken some time off to move back into the company.

However, as soon as word gets out about what you're planning, several of your top performers, people who've never left the company for personal time off—or "taken the off ramp," in current buzzword-speak—march into your office to complain. They fear that encouraging the "off-rampers" to return isn't fair to the employees who've remained loyal to the firm, as they put it. One goes as far to say that anyone who leaves the company doesn't deserve to be asked back. Two others claim that the additional experience and skills they've gained as they continued to work should guarantee them higher pay and more responsibilities than employees who took time off for themselves.

Your task: As unhappy as these several employees are, the program needs to be implemented if Ernst & Young hopes to bring "off-rampers" back into the company—thereby making sure they don't go work for competitors instead. However, you also can't afford to antagonize the existing workforce, and if the people who've already complained are any indication, you have a sizable morale problem on your hands. You decide that your first step is to clearly explain why the program is necessary, including how it will benefit everyone in the company by making Ernst & Young more competitive. Write a short posting for the company's internal blog, explaining that in spite of the objections some employees have raised, the firm is going ahead with the program as planned. Balance this news (which some employees will obviously view as negative) with positive reassurances that all current employees will be treated fairly in terms of both compensation and promotion opportunities. Close with a call for continued communication on this issue, inviting people to meet with you in person or to post their thoughts on the blog.[39]

9. Low-carb impact: E-mail announcing losses and new products at Monterey Pasta As marketing planning manager for Monterey Pasta Company, you're responsible for spotting social trends that could affect your company. Months ago, you suggested that your employer seriously consider the new low-carb diet craze, but your colleagues thought you were exaggerating the impact this trend would have on pasta sales. Now the figures bear you out: Nationwide pasta sales have fallen dramatically as dieters in record numbers are avoiding high-carbohydrate and especially flour-based foods.

At Wal-Mart and Costco, the warehouse-style retail stores that make up Monterey Pasta's largest buyers, sales plummeted nearly 30 percent in the last few months. Your company is not alone; other traditional pasta makers are also showing losses because of the new diet preferences. In contrast, your major competitor, American Italian Pasta, introduced a line of low-carb pastas months ago. Their sales are still climbing.

Now management has asked you to issue a revised forecast for fourth-quarter earnings. Previous predictions were for fourth-quarter sales to increase over last year's figures by 7 to 10 percent. Today's forecast from chief financial officer Scott S. Wheeler is for a 3 to 5 percent *decrease* in revenue from last year's fourth-quarter earnings.

However, in the same message, management wants you to announce the release of Monterey Pasta's new "CARB-SMART" line of fresh pastas, sauces, and prepared entrees. In a company meeting, Monterey Pasta president and CEO Jim Williams announced, "Americans love fresh pasta, but the current wave of low-carb diets has many consumers watching the amount of carbohydrates they consume. CARB-SMART responds to that trend by delivering the flavor and convenience of traditional fresh pasta, but with half the carbs. So carb-counting pasta lovers can now have their ravioli . . . and eat it, too."

The new products include three prepared ravioli varieties, plus tortellini, linguine, fettuccine, and a new low-carb, four-cheese

sauce. Complete CARB-SMART product information will be posted on the Monterey Pasta website, www.montereypasta.com.

Your task: Write an e-mail to announce both the good news and the bad news. Your message will go to shareholders, retail customers, distributors, and other interested parties.[40]

10. Listen to the music, partner: Delivering an ultimatum to a business associate You're a marketing manager for Stanton, one of the premier suppliers of DJ equipment (turntables, amplifiers, speakers, mixers, and related accessories). Your company's latest creation, the FinalScratch system, has been flying off retailers' shelves. Both professional and amateur DJs love the way that FinalScratch gives them the feel of working with vinyl records by letting them control digital music files from any analog turntable or CD player, while giving them access to the endless possibilities of digital music technology. (For more information about the product, go to www.stantondj.com.) Sales are strong everywhere except in Music99 stores, a retail chain in the Mid-Atlantic region. You suspect the cause: The owners of this chain refused to let their salespeople attend the free product training you offered when FinalScratch was introduced, claiming their people were smart enough to train themselves.

To explore the situation, you head out from Stanton headquarters in Hollywood, Florida, on an undercover shopping mission. After visiting a few Music99 locations, you're appalled by what you see. The salespeople in these stores clearly don't understand the FinalScratch concept, so they either give potential customers bad information about it or steer them to products from your competitors. No wonder sales are so bad at this chain.

Your task: You're tempted to pull your products out of this chain immediately, but based on your experience in this market, you know how difficult and expensive it is to recruit new retailers. However, this situation can't go on; you're losing thousands of dollars of potential business every week. Write a letter to Jackson Fletcher, the CEO of Music99 (14014 Preston Pike, Dover, Delaware, 19901), expressing your disappointment in what you observed and explaining that the Music99 sales staff will need to agree to attend product training or else your company's management team will consider terminating the business relationship. You've met Mr. Fletcher in person once and talked on the phone several times, and you know him well enough to know that he will not be pleased by this ultimatum. Music99 does a good job selling other Stanton products—and he'll probably be furious to learn that you were "spying" on his sales staff.[41]

11. Refinancing rules: Letter explaining changes at PeopleFirst.com When you began as a customer service representative at PeopleFirst.com, you worked with only five employees, helping to pioneer a web-based auto loan brokerage. Customers loved it.

From your website, they filled out a single application and faxed in any necessary verification documents. Then PeopleFirst matched them with the best loan for which they qualified, chosen from a variety of lenders. You mailed them a no-obligation "Blank Check®" to spend at any auto dealership, up to the amount for which they qualified. The loan didn't begin until they spent the check. Later, if rates dropped, they could come back to PeopleFirst.com for refinancing.

All that changed when huge Capital One Financial Corporation bought out PeopleFirst.com. They changed your name to Capital One Auto Finance and converted all loans to Capital One loans. Under its new policies, Capital One will not refinance its own loans. However, your existing customers aren't charged a prepayment penalty if they want to pay off their loans early by finding (on their own) another lender for refinancing. You might lose some business this way, but Capital One would lose a lot more if it refinanced all its loans every time rates drop.

Your task: Explain the new policy in a letter to Faviola and Mary Franzone (7200 Poplar Ave., Memphis TN 38197), who have inquired about refinancing their auto loan at today's lower rates.[42]

12. Product recall: Letter from Perrigo Company about children's painkiller Your company is Perrigo, the leading manufacturer of more than 900 store-brand, over-the-counter (OTC) pharmaceuticals and nutritional products. These items are found beside brand-name products such as Tylenol, Motrin, Benadryl, NyQuil, Centrum, or Ex-Lax, but they're packaged under the name of the store that customers are shopping in. They're priced a bit lower and offer "comparable quality and effectiveness," as your sales literature proclaims. For retailers, selling Perrigo products yields a higher profit margin than name brands. For consumers, buying the store brands can mean significant savings.

However, your company has discovered that a batch of its cherry-flavored children's painkiller contains up to 29 percent more acetaminophen than the label indicates—enough to cause an overdose in the young children the product is designed for. Such overdoses can cause liver failure. As of this morning, your marketing department calculates that 6,500 four-ounce bottles of the "children's nonaspirin elixir" (a Tylenol look-alike) are already in the hands of consumers. That leaves some 1,288 bottles still on store shelves.

No one is telling you how this error happened, and it's only been found in lot number 1AD0228, but frankly, finding a guilty party is not so important to your job. You're more concerned about getting the word out fast. Such errors do happen, and the best move is immediate and direct, being completely honest with retailers and the public—so say your superiors in the Customer Support and Service Department. Full and prompt disclosure is especially crucial when consumers' health is involved, as it always is in your line of business.

The painkiller has been sold under the Kroger label at stores in Alabama, Arkansas, Georgia, Illinois, Indiana, Kentucky, Louisiana, Michigan, Mississippi, Missouri, North Carolina, Ohio, South Carolina, Tennessee, Texas, Virginia, and West Virginia. It was sold under the Hy-Vee label in Illinois, Iowa, Kansas, Minnesota, Missouri, Nebraska, and South Dakota, and under the Good Sense label at independent retail chains throughout the United States. Perrigo must notify consumers throughout the United States that they should not give the product to children, but rather should check the lot number and, if it's from the affected batch, return the bottle to the store they bought it from for a refund.

Your task: As Perrigo's customer service supervisor, you must notify retailers by letter. They've already been told verbally, but legal requirements mandate a written notification. That's good, because a form letter to your retail customers can also include follow-up instructions. Explain the circumstances behind the recall, and instruct stores to pull bottles from the shelves immediately for return to your company. Perrigo will, of course, reimburse the refunds provided to consumers. Questions should be directed to Perrigo at 1–800–321–0105—and it's okay if retailers give that number to consumers. Be sure to mention all that your company is doing, and use resale information.[43]

13. Cell phone violations: E-mail message to associates at Wilkes Artis law firm Company policy states that personnel are not to conduct business using cell phones while driving," David Finch reminds you. He's a partner at the law firm of Wilkes Artis in Washington, D.C., where you work as his administrative assistant.

You nod, waiting for him to explain. He already issued a memo about this rule last year, after that 15-year-old girl was hit and killed by an attorney from another firm. Driving back from a client meeting, the attorney was distracted while talking on her cell phone. The girl's family sued the firm and won $30 million, but that's not the point. The point is that cell phones can cause people to be hurt, even killed.

Finch explains, "Yesterday one of our associates called his secretary while driving his car. We can't allow this. According to the National Highway Transportation Safety Administration, 20 to 30 percent of all driving accidents are related to cell phone usage. From now on, any violation of our cell phone policy will result in suspension without pay, unless the call is a genuine health or traffic emergency."

Your task: Finch asks you to write an e-mail message to all employees, announcing the new penalty for violating company policy.[44]

14. Safe selling: Memo about dangerous scooters at The Sports Authority You're not surprised that the Consumer Product Safety Commission (CPSC) has issued a consumer advisory on the dangers of motorized scooters. Unlike a motorcycle or bicycle, a scooter can be mastered by first-timers almost immediately. So both children and adults are hopping on, riding off—without helmets or other safety gear—and turning up with broken arms and legs, scraped faces, and bumped heads.

The popular electric or gas-powered scooters feature two wheels similar to in-line skates and travel 9 to 14 miles per hour. Over a six-month period, says the CPSC, emergency rooms around the country reported 2,250 motorized scooter injuries and 3 deaths. The riders who were killed (ages 6, 11, and 46), might all have lived if they'd been wearing helmets. As a result, some states have already enacted laws restricting scooter operations.

You are a merchandising assistant at The Sports Authority, which sells a wide selection of both the foot-powered ($25 to $150) and motorized scooters ($350 to $1,000). Your company is as concerned about the rise in injuries as they are about the CPSC advisory's potential negative effect on sales

and legality. Thus, you've been assigned to a team that will brainstorm ideas for improving the situation. For example, one team member has suggested developing a safety brochure to give to customers; another wants to train salespeople to discuss safety issues with customers before they buy.

We'd like to see increased sales of reflective gear ($6 to $15), helmets ($24), and elbow and knee pads ($19)," a store executive tells your team, "not to improve on our $1.5 billion annual revenue, but to save lives."

Your task: Working with classmates, discuss how The Sports Authority can use positive actions (including those mentioned in the case) to soften the effect of the CPSC advisory. Choose the best ideas and decide how to use them in a bad-news memo notifying the chain's 198 store managers about the consumer advisory. Then write the memo your team has outlined.[45]

NEGATIVE EMPLOYMENT MESSAGES

15. Bad news for 80: Form letter to unsuccessful job candidates The Dean's Selection Committee screened 85 applications for the position of dean of arts and sciences at your campus. After two rounds of eliminations, the top five candidates were invited to "airport interviews," where the committee managed to meet with each candidate for an hour. Then the top three candidates were invited to the campus to meet with students, faculty, and administrators.

The committee recommended to the university president that the job be given to Constance Pappas, who has a doctorate in American studies and has been chairperson of the history department at Minneapolis Metropolitan College for the past three years. The president agreed, and Dr. Pappas accepted the offer.

One final task remains before the work of the Dean's Selection Committee is finished: Letters must be sent to the 84 unsuccessful candidates. The four who reached the "airport interview" stage will receive personal letters from the chairperson of the committee. Your job, as secretary of the committee, is to draft the form letter that will be sent to the other 80 applicants.

Your task: Draft a letter of 100 to 200 words. All copies will be individually addressed to the recipients but will carry identical messages.

16. Reacting to a lost contract: Phone call rescinding a job offer As the human resources manager at Alion Science and Technology, a military research firm in McLean, Virginia, you were thrilled when one of the nation's top computer visualization specialists accepted your job offer. Claus Gunnstein's skills would've made a major contribution to Alion's work in designing flight simulators and other systems. Unfortunately, the day after he accepted the offer, Alion received news that a major Pentagon contract had been canceled. In addition to letting several dozen current employees know that the company will be forced to lay them off, you need to tell Gunnstein that Alion has no choice but to rescind the job offer.

Your task: Outline the points you'll need to make in a telephone call to Gunnstein. Pay special attention to your opening and closing statements. (You'll review your plans for the phone call with Alion's legal staff to make sure everything you say follows employment law guidelines; for now, just focus on the way you'll present the negative news to Gunnstein. Feel free to make up any details you need.)[46]

17. Juggling diversity and performance: Memo giving a negative performance review at SBC Pacific Bell As billing adjustments department manager at SBC Pacific Bell, you've been trained to handle a culturally diverse workforce. One of your best recent hires is 22-year-old Jorge Gutierrez. In record time, he was entering and testing complex price changes, mastering the challenges of your monumental computerized billing software. He was a real find—except for one problem: his close family ties often distract him from work duties.

His parents immigrated from Central America when Jorge and his sisters were young children, and you understand and deeply respect the importance that family plays in the lives of many Hispanic Americans. However, every morning Gutierrez's mother calls to be sure he got to work safely. Then his father calls. And three times this month, his younger sister has called him away from work with three separate emergencies. Friends and extended family members seem to call at all hours of the day.

Gutierrez says he's asked friends and family not to call his office number. Now they dial his cell phone instead. He's reluctant to shut off his cell phone during work hours, in case someone in his family needs him.

At this point, you have given Gutierrez several verbal warnings. You really can't afford to lose him, so you're hoping that a written, negative review will give him greater incentive to persuade friends and relatives. You'll deliver the letter in a meeting and help him find ways to resolve the issue within a mutually agreed-upon time frame.

Your task: Write the letter using suggestions in this chapter to help you put the bad news in a constructive light. Avoid culturally biased remarks or innuendo.

18. Career moves: E-mail refusing to write a recommendation Tom Weiss worked in the office at Opal Pools and Patios for four months, under your supervision (you're office manager). On the basis of what he told you he could do, you started him off as a file clerk. However, his organizational skills proved inadequate for the job, so you transferred him to logging in accounts receivable, where he performed almost adequately. Then he assured you that his "real strength" was customer relations, so you moved him to the complaint department. After he spent three weeks making angry customers even angrier, you were convinced that no place in your office was appropriate for the talents of Mr. Weiss. Five weeks ago, you encouraged him to resign before being formally fired.

Today's e-mail brings a request from Weiss asking you to write a letter recommending him for a sales position with a florist shop. You can't assess Weiss's sales abilities, but you do know him to be an incompetent file clerk, a careless bookkeeper, and an insensitive customer service representative. Someone else is more likely to deserve the sales job, so you decide that you have done enough favors for Tom Weiss for one lifetime and plan to refuse his request.

Your task: Write an e-mail reply to Mr. Weiss (tomweiss@aol. com) indicating that you have chosen not to write a letter of recommendation for him.

19. Midair let-down: Instant message about flight cancellations at United Airlines It used to be that airline passengers didn't learn about cancelled connecting flights until after they'd landed. Sometimes a captain would announce cancellations just before touching down at a major hub, but how were passengers to notify waiting relatives or business associates on the ground?

As a customer service supervisor for United Airlines, you've just received information that all United flights from Chicago's O'Hare International Airport to Boston's Logan International have been cancelled until further notice. A late winter storm has already blanketed Boston with snow and freezing rain is expected overnight. The way the weather report looks, United will probably be lodging Boston-bound connecting passengers in Chicago-area hotels tonight. Meanwhile, you'll be using some of United's newest communication tools to notify travelers of the bad news.

United Airlines now partners with Verizon Airfone to provide JetConnect information services, giving travelers access to instant messaging and other resources while they're airborne. For a small fee, they can plug their laptop computers into the

Airfone jack, activating their own instant messaging software to send and receive messages. If they've signed up for United's EasyUpdate flight status notification service, they'll also receive instant message alerts for flight cancellations, delays, seating upgrades, and so on.

Your task: Write the cancellation alert, staying within the 65-word limit of many instant-messaging programs. You might want to mention the airline's policy of providing overnight lodging for passengers who planned to use the Boston route as a connecting flight to complete journeys in progress.[47]

20. Quick answer: Instant message turning down employee request at Hewlett-Packard If she'd asked you a week ago, Lewinda Johnson might have been granted her request to attend a conference on the use of blogging for business, which is being held in New York City next month. Instead, Johnson waited until you were stuck in this meeting, and she needs your response within the hour. She'll have to take no for an answer: With travel budgets under tight restrictions, you would need at least three days to send her request up the chain of command. Furthermore, Johnson hasn't given you sufficient justification for her attendance, since she's already familiar with blogging.

Your task: Write a 60- to 75-word instant message to Lewinda Johnson, declining her request. Decide whether the direct or indirect approach is appropriate.[48]

Chapter 9

Writing Persuasive Messages

Learning Objectives

AFTER STUDYING THIS CHAPTER, YOU WILL BE ABLE TO

1 Apply the three-step writing process to persuasive messages

2 Identify seven ways to establish credibility in persuasive messages

3 Describe the AIDA model for persuasive messages

4 Distinguish between emotional and logical appeals and discuss how to balance them

5 Identify four common mistakes in writing persuasive messages

6 Discuss an effective approach to identifying selling points and audience benefits

7 Identify steps you can take to avoid ethical lapses in marketing and sales messages

On the Job

COMMUNICATING AT MARK BURNETT PRODUCTIONS

THE CREATOR OF SURVIVOR LEARNS TO SURVIVE IN THE TELEVISION JUNGLE

Think you can be as persuasive as Mark Burnett, a former member of Britain's elite Army Paratroop Regiment? His name may seem familiar: Burnett was co-creator of the popular *Survivor* reality TV series and created the series *Eco-Challenge—the Expedition Race.* At 22, he left the military and moved to Los Angeles, where he needed just 24 hours to land a job as a Beverly Hills nanny-chauffeur. How? He appealed to the needs of his audience and convinced his employer that nobody could make neater beds or provide better security than a former British paratrooper.

Once Survivor *and* The Apprentice *had become hit TV shows, anyone could say that they seemed like great ideas. However, before these shows had any proof of success, Mark Burnett had to persuade television executives to give them a chance.*

Later on, driven by a fascination with adventure racing, Burnett used his persuasive powers to recruit team members, attract TV coverage, and launch Eco-Challenge. His powers of persuasion also helped him land TV contracts with MTV, ESPN, Discovery, and USA Network. In each case, he aligned his interests in television production with the business interests of each audience. Then came the idea for *Survivor*. The chairman of CBS said Burnett's *Survivor* pitch was the best he'd ever heard.

Burnett even persuaded renowned dealmaker Donald Trump, real estate mogul and author of a business bestseller, *The Art of the Deal,* to launch a television show. One night while Burnett was shooting a *Survivor* finale at an ice rink in Manhattan, he saw Trump (who owned the ice rink) and introduced himself. He opened the discussion with some positive comments about Trump's book, then grabbed the opportunity to present his idea for a television show

in which 16 ambitious young executives vie for a six-figure, one-year position in the Trump Organization. Ultimately, Burnett convinced Trump that he would enjoy starring in a new reality show of his own, and *The Apprentice* premiered on NBC in January 2004. The U.S. version of the show is now seen in over 100 countries worldwide, and localized versions have been created in another 20 countries.

Riding the wave of reality TV that he helped create, Burnett and his 1,500-person staff continue to create, develop, and promote a growing stable of shows. When the boxing-themed reality show *The Contender* failed to generate strong ratings on NBC, he persuaded the sports network EPSN to give it a try. When home fashion guru Martha Stewart wanted to give reality TV a try after her brief stint in prison, she teamed with Burnett on *The Apprentice: Martha Stewart.*

Not every attempt is successful, of course. Two Burnett reality series, *The Casino* and *The Restaurant,* didn't last, and *Rock Star: INXS* struggled to find a mass audience. However, Burnett's overall track record in the tough world of television is so strong that his persuasive messages now come with built-in credibility.

Chances are your career won't involve hit television shows, but you can create some magic of your own by following Burnett's advice to understand your audiences and craft persuasive messages that meet their needs as well as your own.[1]

USING THE THREE-STEP WRITING PROCESS FOR PERSUASIVE MESSAGES

Persuasion is the attempt to change someone's attitudes, beliefs, or actions.

Professionals such as Mark Burnett realize that successful businesses rely on persuasive messages in both internal and external communication. Whether you're convincing your boss to open a new office in Europe or encouraging potential customers to try your products, you'll use many of the same techniques of **persuasion**—the attempt to change an audience's attitudes, beliefs, or actions.[2] Persuasive techniques are a cornerstone of marketing and selling, but even if you never work in those fields, you'll still need good persuasion skills to advance in your career. Successful professionals understand that persuasion is not about trickery or getting people to make choices that aren't in their best interest; rather, it lets your audience know they have a choice and helps them choose to agree with you.[3]

As with every type of business message, the three-step writing process improves persuasive messages. In addition, these messages require some specific techniques, which you have the opportunity to explore in this chapter.

Step 1: Plan Your Message

Unlike the routine positive messages discussed in Chapter 7, persuasive messages aim to influence audiences who may be inclined to resist at first. Even if they agree that your idea or product is attractive, they face so many options in today's crowded markets that you'll often need to use persuasive techniques to convince them that your choice is the best of all the attractive alternatives.

In today's message-saturated environment, it's not enough to have a great idea or a great product.

In today's information-saturated business environment, having a great idea or a great product is no longer enough. Every day, untold numbers of good ideas go unnoticed and good products go unsold simply because the messages meant to promote them aren't compelling enough to rise above the competitive noise. Creating successful persuasive messages in these challenging situations demands careful attention to all four tasks in the planning step, starting with an insightful analysis of your purpose and your audience.

Analyzing Your Situation   Your purpose might seem obvious—to persuade people to visit your website or buy your snowboards—but persuasive messages can suffer from three common mistakes related to purpose. The first mistake is failing to clarify your purpose before you continue with planning. Let's say you want to persuade top management to support a particular research project. But what does "support" mean? Do you want them to pat you on the back and wish you well? Or do you want them to pull five researchers off another project and assign them to your project? Having a specific goal is crucial to effective persuasion.

Failing to clarify your purpose is a common mistake with persuasive messages.

The second mistake is failing to clearly express your purpose to your audience. You may feel uncomfortable with the idea of asking others to give you time, money, promotions, or other considerations. However, if you don't ask, or if you are vague about what you want, you're never going to get a positive response.

The third mistake is failing to realize that the decision you want someone to make is too complicated or risky to make all in one leap. You can't sell a $10 million office building by writing someone a letter and asking her to buy it. You need to persuade in stages, with a message adapted to each stage. Your purpose in the first message might be to spark interest with a brief analysis of potential lease income. If that message is successful, you might then offer a tour of the site, and so on until you finally ask for a decision. If you try to accomplish too much with any single message, you risk confusing your audience or prompting them to say "no" before you've had a chance to build your case.

You can identify the right number of messages and the nature of each one by analyzing your audience. Consider both the positives and the negatives—the wants, needs, and motivations of your audience (the reasons they might respond favorably to your message) as well as their concerns and objections (the reasons they might *not* respond favorably). With these two insights as guides, you can then work to find common ground with your audience, while emphasizing positive points and minimizing negative ones.

All of the aspects of creating an audience profile that you learned in Chapter 4 apply to persuasive messages. If your message is aimed at a single large organization, you can direct it specifically toward a few top managers who make the kinds of decisions you're asking for. In contrast, for a message aimed at a million consumers, you'll never know each one individually; the best you can do is sample a small number who represent the entire audience.

The best persuasive messages are closely connected to your audience's desires and interests.[4] Consider these important questions: Who is my audience? What are their needs? What do I want them to do? How might they resist? Are there alternative positions I need to examine? What does the decision maker consider the most important issue? How might the organization's culture influence my strategy?

Some theorists believe that certain needs have priority. Figure 9–1 represents psychologist Abraham Maslow's hierarchy of needs, with the most basic needs appearing at the bottom of the figure. Maslow suggests that only after lower-level needs have been met will a person seek to fulfill needs on higher levels.[5] Other theories of motivation exist as well, but the point here is that people have a variety of needs and that the most effective persuasive messages are aligned with the most important needs of every audience member.

To understand and categorize audience needs, you can refer to specific information such as **demographics** (the age, gender, occupation, income, education, and other quantifiable characteristics of the people you're trying to persuade) and **psychographics** (personality, attitudes, lifestyle, and other psychological characteristics). Both types of information are strongly influenced by culture. When analyzing your audience, take into account their cultural expectations and practices so that you don't undermine your persuasive message by using an inappropriate appeal or by organizing your message in a way that seems unfamiliar or uncomfortable to your audience.

Gathering Information   Once your situation analysis is complete, you need to gather the information necessary to close the gap between what your audience knows, believes, or feels right now and what you want them to know, believe, or feel as a result of receiving your message. Most persuasive messages are a combination of logical and emotional factors, but the ratio varies dramatically from message to message. You can get a sense of this variation by comparing the websites of American Fastener Technology (industrial goods, www.americanfastener.com), Chrysler (automobiles, www.chrysler.com), and Lancôme (beauty products, www.lancome.com).

Margin notes:

To persuade successfully, you need to consider both the positive and negative aspects of your proposed solution.

Most persuasive communicators assume that their audiences have prioritized their own needs and desires.

Demographics include characteristics such as age, gender, occupation, income, and education.

Psychographics include characteristics such as personality, attitudes, and lifestyle.

FIGURE 9–1
Maslow's Hierarchy of Needs

SELF-ACTUALIZATION
Creativity—Self-realization—Wisdom—Vocation

ESTEEM AND STATUS
Self-worth—Uniqueness—Respect—Community

SOCIAL
Affection—Friendship—Group ties

SAFETY AND SECURITY
Personal confidence—Stability—Protection from enemies

SURVIVAL (PHYSIOLOGICAL)
Air—Food—Water—Sleep—Shelter

American Fasteners relies primarily on straightforward product information to convince buyers, whereas Lancôme tries to evoke a more emotional response through its visual and verbal imagery. Chrysler is somewhere in the middle, providing plenty of facts and figures about its cars but also including strong emotional messages about the joy of driving. By identifying the mix of factors that will most likely persuade your audience, you'll know what sort of information you need to gather. You'll learn more about the types of information to offer when you read "Developing Persuasive Business Messages" later in the chapter. Chapter 10 presents advice on how to find the information you need.

Selecting the Right Medium   Persuasive messages can be found in virtually every communication medium ever devised, from instant messages and computer animations to radio ads and skywriting. For persuasive business messages, your choice of medium will closely follow the guidelines presented in Chapter 4. However, for marketing and sales messages, your options are far more numerous. In fact, advertising agencies employ media specialists whose only job is to analyze the media options available and select the most cost-effective combination for each client and each ad campaign.

To further complicate matters, various members of your audience might prefer different media for the same message. Some consumers like to do all their car shopping in person, whereas others do most of their research online. Some people don't mind promotional e-mails for products they're interested in; others resent every piece of commercial e-mail they receive. If you can't be sure you can reach most or all of your audience with a single medium, you'll need to use two or more, such as following up an e-mail campaign with printed letters.

You may need to use multiple media to reach your entire audience.

Organizing Your Information   Be sure to give attention to all four aspects of organizing your information—defining your main idea, limiting your scope, choosing a direct or indirect approach, and grouping your points in a meaningful way. The most effective main ideas for persuasive messages have one thing in common: they are about the receiver, not the sender. Take a cue from a successful advertiser such as Nike. The company's ads are never about the company and often aren't even about the products; they're about the customer's experience when using Nike products. You can benefit from this same approach for all persuasive messages. If you're trying to convince others to join you in a business venture, explain how it will help them, not how it will help you.

To limit the scope of each message effectively, include only the information needed to help your audience take the next step toward making the ultimate decision or taking the ultimate action you want. In simple scenarios such as persuading teammates to attend a special meeting, you might put everything you have to say into a single, short message. But if you want your company to invest several million dollars in your latest product idea, the scope of your first message might be limited to securing 10 minutes at the next executive committee meeting so that you can introduce your idea and get permission to explore it. You might not be in a position to actually ask for the money for weeks or months, after you've gathered support for the idea and collected enough information to make a compelling business case for it.

Limit your scope to include only the information needed to help your audience take the next step toward making a favorable decision.

As with routine and negative messages, the best organizational approach is based on your audience's likely reaction to your message. However, because the nature of persuasion is to convince your audience to change their attitudes, beliefs, or actions, most persuasive messages use an indirect approach. That means you'll want to explain your reasons and build interest before asking for a decision or for action—or perhaps even before revealing your purpose. You'll see several examples of the indirect approach in action later in this chapter, in the discussions of both persuasive business messages and marketing and sales messages.

Use the direct approach if your audience is ready to hear your proposal.

Consider the direct approach whenever you know your audience is ready to hear your proposal. If your boss wants to change shipping companies and asks for your recommendation, you'll probably want to open with your choice, then provide your reasons as backup. Similarly, if there's a good chance your audience will agree with

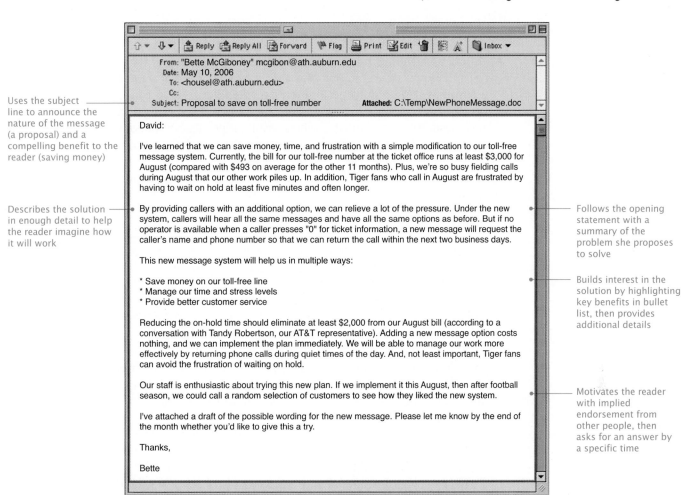

Uses the subject line to announce the nature of the message (a proposal) and a compelling benefit to the reader (saving money)

Describes the solution in enough detail to help the reader imagine how it will work

Follows the opening statement with a summary of the problem she proposes to solve

Builds interest in the solution by highlighting key benefits in bullet list, then provides additional details

Motivates the reader with implied endorsement from other people, then asks for an answer by a specific time

FIGURE 9–2
Proposal E-Mail Using a Direct Approach

your message, don't force them to wade through pages of reasoning before seeing your main idea. If they happen not to agree with your pitch, they can move into your reasoning to see why you're promoting that particular idea. The direct approach is also called for if you've been building your case through several indirect messages and it's now time to make your request.

In the e-mail message in Figure 9–2, Bette McGiboney, an administrative assistant to the athletic director of Auburn University, presented a solution to the problem of high phone bills during the month of August. She already has a close relationship with her boss, who is likely to welcome the money-saving idea, so the direct approach is a fast, efficient way to communicate her proposal.

If you use the direct approach as McGiboney does in Figure 9–2, keep in mind that even though your audience may be easy to convince, you'll still want to include at least a brief justification or explanation. Don't expect your reader to accept your idea on blind faith. For example, consider the following two openers:

Less Effective	**More Effective**
I recommend building our new retail outlet on the West Main Street site.	After comparing the four possible sites for our new retail outlet, I recommend West Main Street as the only site that fulfills our criteria for visibility, proximity to mass transportation, and square footage.

Choice of approach is also influenced by your position (or authority within the organization) relative to your audience's.

Your choice between the direct and indirect approaches is also influenced by the extent of your authority, expertise, or power in an organization. As a first-line manager writing a persuasive message to top management, you may try to be diplomatic and use an indirect approach. But your choice could backfire if some managers think your indirectness lacks confidence or even integrity. On the other hand, you may try to save your supervisors time by using a direct approach, which might be perceived as brash and presumptuous. Similarly, when writing a persuasive message to employees, you may use the indirect approach to ease into a major change, but your audience might see your message as weak, even wishy-washy. You need to think carefully about your corporate culture and what your audience expects before selecting your approach.

Step 2: Write Your Message

Persuasive messages are often unexpected or even unwelcome, so the "you" attitude is crucial.

The generally uninvited and occasionally even unwelcome nature of persuasive messages means the "you" attitude is more critical than ever when it comes to writing them. Most people won't even pay attention to your message, much less respond to it, if it isn't about them. You can encourage a more welcome reception by (1) using positive and polite language, (2) understanding and respecting cultural differences, (3) being sensitive to organizational cultures, and (4) taking steps to establish your credibility.

Positive language usually happens naturally with persuasive messages, since you're promoting an idea or product you believe in. However, polite language isn't as automatic, surprisingly enough. Some writers inadvertently insult their readers by implying that they've been making poor choices in the past or need the writer's keen insights to make a good choice in the current situation.

Your understanding and respect for cultural differences will help you satisfy the needs of your audience and will help your audience respect you. That's because persuasion is different in different cultures. In France, an aggressive, hard-sell technique is likely to antagonize your audience. In Germany, where people tend to focus on technical matters, plan on verifying any figures you use for support, and make sure they are exact. In Sweden, audiences tend to focus on theoretical questions and strategic implications, whereas U.S. audiences are usually concerned with more practical matters.[6]

Cultural differences influence your persuasion attempts.

Just as culture within various social groups affects the success of persuasive message, so too does the culture within various organizations. Over time, every company develops a particular internal culture that establishes numerous expectations regarding communication. For instance, some organizations handle disagreement and conflict in an indirect, behind-the-scene way, whereas others accept and even encourage open discussion and sharing of differing viewpoints. Similarly, the degree of formality varies widely. When you accept and follow these traditions, even if they don't reflect your personal preferences, you show the audience that you understand them and respect their values.

Finally, when trying to persuade a skeptical or hostile audience, you must convince people that you know what you're talking about and that you're not trying to mislead them. Your credibility is even more important in persuasive messages than it is in other business messages (see Chapter 5). Without it, your efforts to persuade will seem ineffective at best and manipulative at worst. Research strongly suggests that most managers overestimate their own credibility—considerably.[7] Establishing your credibility in persuasive messages takes time. Chapter 5 lists characteristics essential to building and maintaining your credibility, including honesty, objectivity, awareness of audience needs, knowledge and expertise, endorsements, performance, and communication style. To establish credibility in persuasive messages, try to go beyond these characteristics by

Audiences often respond unfavorably to over-the-top language, so keep your writing simple and straightforward.

- **Using simple language.** In most persuasive situations, your audience will be cautious, watching for fantastic claims, insupportable descriptions, and emotional manipulation. Speak plainly and simply.

- **Supporting your message with facts.** Documents, statistics, research results, and testimonials (from people who've made the choice you're advocating)—all provide objective evidence for what you have to say, which adds to your credibility. The more specific and relevant your proof, the better.

- **Naming your sources.** Telling your audience where your information comes from and who agrees with you improves your credibility, especially if your sources are already respected by your audience.

- **Being an expert (or finding one to support your message).** Your knowledge of your message's subject area (or even of some other area) helps you give your audience the quality information necessary to make a decision. If you aren't an expert in the subject, try to get the support of someone who is.

- **Establishing common ground.** Those beliefs, attitudes, and background experiences that you have in common with members of your audience will help them identify with you.

- **Being objective.** Your ability to understand and acknowledge all sides of an issue helps you present fair and logical arguments in your persuasive message. Top executives often ask if their employees have considered all the possibilities before committing to a single choice.

- **Displaying your good intentions.** Show your audience your genuine concern, good faith, and truthfulness. Let them see how you are focusing on their needs. Your willingness to keep your audience's best interests at heart helps you create persuasive messages that are not only more effective but also more ethical.

Step 3: Complete Your Message

The pros know from experience that the details can make or break a persuasive message, so they're careful not to shortchange this part of the writing process. Advertisers may have a dozen or more people review a message before it's released to the public. Ads and commercial websites are often tested extensively with representative recipients to make sure the intended audience gets the information the sender intends.

When you evaluate your content, try to judge your argument objectively and try not to overestimate your credibility. When revising for clarity and conciseness, carefully match the purpose and organization to audience needs. If possible, ask an experienced colleague who knows your audience well to review your draft. Your design elements must complement, not detract from, your argument. In addition, meticulous proofreading will identify any mechanical or spelling errors that would weaken your persuasive potential. Finally, make sure your distribution methods fit your audience's expectations as well as your purpose. Don't start your persuasive efforts on the wrong foot by annoying your audience with an unwelcome delivery method.

With the three-step model in mind, you're ready to begin composing persuasive messages, starting with persuasive business messages (those that try to convince readers to approve new projects, enter into business partnerships, and so on), followed by marketing and sales messages (those that try to convince readers to consider and then purchase products and services).

DEVELOPING PERSUASIVE BUSINESS MESSAGES

Your success as a businessperson is closely tied to your ability to convince others to accept new ideas, change old habits, or act on your recommendations. Even early in your career, you might have the opportunity to convince your manager to let you join an exciting project or to improve an important process. As you move into positions of

Your success in business will depend on writing persuasive messages effectively.

greater responsibility, your persuasive messages could start to influence multimillion-dollar investments and the careers of hundreds or thousands of employees. Obviously, the increase in your persuasive skills needs to be matched by the care and thoroughness of your analysis and planning, so that the ideas you convince others to adopt are sound.

Persuasive messages constitute a broad and diverse category, with audiences that range from a single person in your own department to government agencies, investors, clients, community leaders, and other external groups. Most of your messages will consist of *persuasive business messages,* which are any persuasive messages designed to elicit a preferred response in a nonsales situation.

Strategies for Persuasive Business Messages

The goal of your persuasive business message is to convince your reader that your request or idea is reasonable and that it will benefit your reader in some way. Within the context of the three-step process, effective persuasion involves four essential strategies: framing your arguments, balancing emotional and logical appeals, reinforcing your position, and anticipating objections.

Framing Your Arguments Many persuasive messages follow some variation of the indirect approach. However, unlike the buffer in an indirect negative message, the opening in a persuasive message is designed to get your audience's attention. Similarly, the explanation section does more than present reasons, and it is expanded to two sections. The first raises your audience's interest, and the second attempts to change your audience's attitude. Finally, your close does more than end on a positive note; it emphasizes reader benefits and motivates readers to take specific action. This persuasive approach, called the **AIDA model**, organizes your presentation into those four phases: (1) **a**ttention, (2) **i**nterest, (3) **d**esire, and (4) **a**ction (see Table 9–1). Other models exist, but they all follow a similar pattern.

Organize persuasive messages using the AIDA model:
- Attention
- Interest
- Desire
- Action

- **Attention.** Your first objective is to encourage your audience to want to hear about your problem, idea, new product—whatever your main idea is. Write a brief and engaging opening sentence, with no extravagant claims or irrelevant points. And be sure to find some common ground on which to build your case. In the letter in Figure 9–3, Randy Thumwolt uses the AIDA model in a persuasive memo about his program that would try to reduce Host Marriott's annual plastics costs and try to curtail consumer complaints about the company's recycling record. Note also how Thumwolt "sells the problem" before attempting to sell the solution. Few people are interested in hearing about solutions to problems they don't know about or don't believe exist.

Table 9–1   THE AIDA MODEL

Phase	Objective
Attention	Get the reader's attention with a benefit that is of real interest or value.
Interest	Build the reader's interest by further explaining benefits and appealing to his or her logic or emotions.
Desire	Build desire by providing additional supporting details and answering potential questions.
Action	Motivate the reader to take the next step by closing with a compelling call to action and providing a convenient means for the reader to respond.

Planning

Analyze the Situation
The purpose is to solve an ongoing problem, so the audience will be receptive.

Gather Information
Determine audience needs and obtain the necessary information on recycling problem areas.

Select the Right Medium
A printed memo is appropriate for this formal communication.

Organize the Information
Main idea is to propose a recycling solution, so limit the scope to the problem at hand; use an indirect approach to lay out the extent of the problem.

Writing

Adapt to Your Audience
Adjust the level of formality based on degree of familiarity with the audience; maintain a positive relationship by using the "you" attitude, politeness, positive emphasis, and bias-free language.

Compose the Message
Use a conversational but professional style and keep the message brief, clear, and as helpful as possible.

Completing

Revise the Message
Evaluate content and review readability to make sure the information is clear and complete without being overwhelming.

Produce the Message
Emphasize a clean, professional appearance on company letterhead.

Proofread the Message
Review for errors in layout, spelling, and mechanics.

Distribute the Message
Deliver your message using the chosen medium.

1 **2** **3**

FIGURE 9–3 Persuasive Memo Using the AIDA Model to Propose Procedural Changes

HOST MARRIOTT
SERVICES

INTERNAL MEMORANDUM

DATE: May 10, 2006
TO: Eleanor Tran, Comptroller *ET*
FROM: Randy Thumwolt, Purchasing Director
SUBJECT: Cost Cutting in Plastics

A

In spite of our recent switch to purchasing plastic product containers in bulk, our costs for these containers are still extremely high. In my January 5 memo, I included all the figures showing that we purchase five tons of plastic product containers each year, and the price of polyethylene terephthalate (PET) rises and falls as petroleum costs fluctuate.

> Catches the reader's attention with a blunt statement of a major problem

I

In January I suggested that we purchase plastic containers in bulk during winter months, when petroleum prices tend to be lower. Because you approved that suggestion, we should realize a 10 percent saving this year. However, our costs are still out of line, around $2 million a year.

In addition to the cost in dollars of these plastic containers is the cost in image. We have recently been receiving an increasing number of consumer letters complaining about our lack of a recycling program for PET plastic containers, both on the airplanes and in the airport restaurants.

> Builds interest in a potential solution to the problem by emphasizing how bad the problem is and highlighting an associated problem

D

After conducting some preliminary research, I have come up with the following ideas:

- Provide recycling containers at all Host Marriott airport restaurants
- Offer financial incentives for the airlines to collect and separate PET containers
- Set up a specially designated dumpster at each airport for recycling plastics
- Contract with A-Batt Waste Management for collection

> Increases the recipient's desire or willingness to take action by outlining a solution

A

I've attached a detailed report of the costs involved. As you can see, our net savings the first year should run about $500,000. I've spoken to Ted Macy in marketing. If we adopt the recycling plan, he wants to build a PR campaign around it. The PET recycling plan will help build our public image while improving our bottom line. If you agree, let's meet with Ted next week to get things started. Please call me at ext. 2356 if you have any questions.

> Motivates the reader one last time with a specific cost savings figure, then requests a specific action

- **Interest.** Explain the relevance of your message to your audience. Continuing the theme you started with, paint a more detailed picture with words. Get your audience thinking. In Figure 9–3, Thumwolt's interest section introduces an additional, unforeseen problem with plastic product containers. Also, Thumwolt breaks out his suggestions into an easy-to-read list.

- **Desire.** Help audience members embrace your idea by explaining how the change will benefit them. Reduce resistance by identifying and answering in advance any questions the audience might have. If your idea is complex, you may need to explain how you would implement it. Back up your claims in order to increase audience willingness to take the action that you suggest in the next section. Just remember to make sure that all evidence is directly relevant to your point.

- **Action.** Suggest the action you want readers to take. Make it more than a statement such as "Please institute this program soon" or "Send me a refund." This is the opportunity to remind readers of the benefits of taking action. The secret of a successful action phase is making the action easy, so if possible, give your readers a couple of options for responding, such as a toll-free number to call and a website to visit. Include a deadline when applicable.

The AIDA model is ideal for the indirect approach.

The AIDA plan is tailor-made for using the indirect approach, allowing you to save your main idea for the action phase. However, it can also be used for the direct approach, in which case you use your main idea as an attention-getter, build interest with your argument, create desire with your evidence, and emphasize your main idea in the action phase with the specific action you want your audience to take.

When your AIDA message uses an indirect approach and is delivered by memo or e-mail, keep in mind that your subject line usually catches your readers' eye first. Your challenge is to make it interesting and relevant enough to capture reader attention without revealing your main idea. If you put your request in the subject line, you're likely to get a quick "no" before you've had a chance to present your arguments.

Instead of This	**Try This**
Proposal to install new phone message system	Reducing the cost of our toll-free number

You can also see from the AIDA model why it's so important to have a concise, focused purpose for your persuasive messages. Otherwise, you'll find it nearly impossible to guide your reader through each phase from attention to action. Focus on your primary goal when presenting your case, and concentrate your efforts on accomplishing that one goal. For example, if your main idea is to convince your company to install a new phone-messaging system, leave discussions about switching long-distance carriers until another day—unless it's relevant to your argument.

Balancing Emotional and Logical Appeals   Few persuasive appeals are purely logical or purely emotional. Even American Fasteners bolsters its fact-heavy website presentation with visual images of industrial-quality strength, such as massive bridges, military helicopters, and the Statue of Liberty. Without coming right out and saying so, the website shouts dependability, portraying employees as the people you can count on when you need to. Conversely, even though Lancôme's website is packed with emotional imagery, its product presentations are laced with facts and advice, from the vitamin content of moisturizing lipsticks to application techniques for various makeup products.

Imagine you're sitting at a control panel, with one knob labeled "logic" and another labeled "emotion." As you prepare your persuasive message, you carefully adjust each knob, tuning the message for maximum impact. Too little emotion, and your audience might not care enough to respond. Too much emotion, and your audience might think you haven't thought through the tough business questions. For example, when Mark Burnett pitches the idea for a new TV show, he needs to strike a balance between emotional factors (such as the aspects of a competitive reality show that will encourage audience members to root for or against various contestants) and logical factors (such as the cost of producing the show relative to the amount of advertising revenue that it can be expected to generate).

To find the optimum balance, consider four factors: (1) the actions you hope to motivate, (2) your reader's expectations, (3) the degree of resistance you need to overcome, and (4) how far you feel empowered to go to sell your point of view.[8] When you're persuading someone to accept a complex idea, take a serious step, or make a large and important decision, lean toward logic and make your emotional appeal subtle. However, when you're persuading someone to purchase a product, join a cause, or change an attitude, you might rely a bit more heavily on emotion.

Starting its ads with the headline, "The Adventure Begins!" Safari Helicopters uses strong emotional appeals to interest visitors in helicopter tours of the Hawaiian Islands.

Emotional Appeals   An **emotional appeal** calls on feelings, basing the argument on audience needs or sympathies; however, such an appeal must be subtle.[9] For instance, you can make use of the emotion surrounding certain words. The word *freedom* evokes strong feelings, as do words such as *success, prestige, compassion, free, value,* and *comfort.* Such words put your audience in a certain frame of mind and help them accept your message. However, emotional appeals aren't necessarily effective by themselves. For most business situations, the best use of emotion is working in tandem with logic. Even if your audience reaches a conclusion based on emotions, they'll look to you to provide logical support as well.

Emotional appeals attempt to connect with the reader's feelings or sympathies.

Logical Appeals   A **logical appeal** calls on reason. In any argument you might use to persuade an audience, you make a claim and then support your claim with reasons or evidence. When appealing to your audience's logic, you might use three types of reasoning:

Logical appeals are based on the reader's notions of reason; these appeals can use analogy, induction, or deduction.

- **Analogy.** With analogy, you reason from specific evidence to specific evidence. For instance, to persuade reluctant employees to attend a planning session, you might use a town meeting analogy, comparing your company to a small community and your employees to valued members of that community.

- **Induction.** With inductive reasoning, you work from specific evidence to a general conclusion. To convince your team to change a certain production process, you could point out that every company who has adopted it has increased profits, so it must be a smart idea.

- **Deduction.** With deductive reasoning, you work from a generalization to a specific conclusion. To persuade your boss to hire additional customer support staff, you might point to industry surveys that show how crucial customer satisfaction is to corporate profits.

Every method of reasoning is vulnerable to misuse, both intentional and unintentional, so verify each of your rational arguments before you distribute your message. For example, in the case of the production process, are there any other factors that affect the integrity of your reasoning? What if that process works well only for small companies with few products, and your firm is a multinational behemoth with 10,000 products? To avoid faulty logic, practice the following guidelines:[10]

Logical flaws include hasty generalizations, circular reasoning, attacks on opponents, oversimplifications, false assumptions of cause and effect, faulty analogies, and illogical support.

- **Avoid hasty generalizations.** Make sure you have plenty of evidence before drawing conclusions.
- **Avoid circular reasoning.** *Circular reasoning* is a logical fallacy in which you try to support your claim by restating it in different words. The statement "We know temporary workers cannot handle this task because temps are unqualified for it" doesn't prove anything because the claim and the supporting evidence are essentially identical. It doesn't prove *why* the temps are unqualified.
- **Avoid attacking an opponent.** Focus on the real question. Attack the argument your opponent is making, not your opponent's character.
- **Avoid oversimplifying a complex issue.** Make sure you present all the factors rather than relying on an "either/or" statement that makes it look as if only two choices are possible.
- **Avoid mistaken assumptions of cause and effect.** If you can't isolate the impact of a specific factor, you can't assume it's the cause of whatever effect you're discussing. The weather improves in spring, and people start playing baseball in spring. Does good weather cause baseball? No. There is a *correlation* between the two—meaning the data associated with them tend to rise and fall at the same time, but there is no *causation*—no proof that one causes the other. The complexity of many business situations makes cause and effect a particular challenge. You lowered prices and sales went up. Were lower prices the cause? Maybe, but it might've been caused by a competitor with delivery problems, a better advertising campaign, or any of a host of other factors.
- **Avoid faulty analogies.** Be sure that the two objects or situations being compared are similar enough for the analogy to hold. Even if A resembles B in one respect, it may not hold true in other important respects.
- **Avoid illogical support.** Make sure the connection between your claim and your support is truly logical and not based on a leap of faith, a missing premise, or irrelevant evidence.

Reinforcing Your Position After you've worked out the basic elements of your argument, step back and look for ways to bolster the strength of your position. Can you find more powerful words to convey your message? For example, if your company is in serious financial trouble, talking about ***survival*** is more powerful than talking about ***continued operations***. Using abstractions such as this along with basic facts and figures can bring your argument to life. You may have better luck collecting an overdue bill by mentioning honesty and fair play than by repeating the sum owed and the date it was due. As with any powerful tool, though, use vivid language and abstractions carefully and honestly.

Choose your words carefully and use abstractions to enhance emotional content.

In addition to individual word choices, consider using ***metaphors*** and other figures of speech. If you want to describe a quality-control system as being designed to catch every possible product flaw, you might call it a spider web to imply that it catches everything that comes its way. Similarly, anecdotes and stories can help your audience grasp the meaning and importance of your arguments. Instead of just listing the average failure rates of older model laptop computers, put a human face on the problem by describing what happened when your computer broke down during a critical presentation to your company's biggest customer.

Highlight the direct and indirect benefits of complying with your request.

Beyond the specific wording of your message, look for other forces and factors that can reinforce your position. When you're asking for something, your audience will find it easier to grant your request if they stand to benefit from it as well. For instance, if you're asking for more money to increase your staff, you might offer to lend those new employees to other managers during peak workloads in other departments. The timing of your message can also help. Virtually all organizations operate in cycles of some sort—incoming payments from major customers, outgoing tax payments, seasonal demand for products, and so on. Study these patterns to see whether they might work for or against you. For example, the best time to ask for additional staff might be right after a period of intense activity that prompted multiple customers to complain about poor service, when the experience is still fresh in everyone's mind. If you wait several months for the annual budgeting cycle, the emotional aspect of the experience will have faded, and your request will look like just another cost increase.

Anticipating Objections   Even the most powerful persuasive messages can expect to encounter some initial resistance. The best way to deal with audience resistance is to anticipate as many objections as you can and address them in your initial message before your audience can even bring them up. By doing so you not only address such issues right away, but you demonstrate a broad appreciation of the issue and imply confidence in your message.[11] This anticipation is particularly important in written messages, when you don't have the opportunity to detect and respond to objections on the spot.

Even powerful persuasive messages can encounter resistance from the audience.

For instance, if you know that your proposal to switch to lower-cost materials will raise concerns about product quality and customer satisfaction, address these issues head-on in your message. If you wait until people raise the concern after reading your message, chances are they will already have gravitated toward a firm "no" before you have a chance to address their concerns. At the very least, waiting until people object will introduce additional rounds of communication that will delay the response you want to receive.

If you expect a hostile audience, one biased against your plan from the beginning, present all sides. As you cover each option, explain the pros and cons. You'll gain additional credibility if you present these options before presenting your recommendation or decision.[12]

Present both sides to an issue when you expect to encounter strong resistance.

To uncover audience objections, try some "What if?" scenarios. Poke holes in your own theories and ideas before your audience does. Then find solutions to the problems you've uncovered.

People are more likely to support what they help create, so ask your audience for their thoughts on the subject before you put your argument together. Let your audience recommend some solutions. With enough thought and effort, you may even be able to turn problems into opportunities; for example, you may show how your proposal will be more economical in the long run, even though it may cost more now. Just be sure to be thorough, open, and objective about all the facts and alternatives.

When putting together persuasive arguments, avoid common mistakes such as these:[13]

Avoid the common mistakes of using a hard sell, resisting compromise, relying solely on argumentation, and assuming persuasion is a one-time event.

- **Using an up-front hard sell.** Don't push. Setting out a strong position at the start of a persuasive message puts potential opponents on guard, giving them something to grab onto—and fight against.

- **Resisting compromise.** Don't dig your heels in. Persuasion is a process of give and take. As one expert points out, a persuader rarely changes another person's behavior or viewpoint without altering his or her own in the process.

- **Relying solely on great arguments.** Don't limit your tactics. In persuading people to change their minds, great arguments matter, but they are only one part of the equation. Your ability to create a mutually beneficial framework for your position, to connect with your audience on the right emotional level, and to communicate through vivid language are all just as important; they bring your argument to life.

- **Assuming persuasion is a one-shot effort.** Don't expect too much at once. Persuasion is a process, not a one-time event. More often than not, persuasion

✓ CHECKLIST: Developing Persuasive Messages

A. Get your reader's attention

✓ Open with a reader benefit, a stimulating question, a problem, or an unexpected statement.
✓ Discuss something your audience can agree with (establishing common ground).
✓ Show that you understand the audience's concerns.

B. Build your reader's interest

✓ Expand and support your opening claim or promise.
✓ Emphasize the relevance of your message to your audience.

C. Increase your reader's desire

✓ Make audience members want to change by explaining how the change will benefit them.
✓ Back up your claims with relevant evidence.

D. Motivate your reader to take action

✓ Suggest the action you want readers to take.

✓ Stress the positive results of the action.
✓ Make the desired action clear and easy.

E. Balance emotional and logical appeals

✓ Use emotional appeals to help the audience accept your message.
✓ Use logical appeals when presenting facts and evidence for complex ideas or recommendations.
✓ Avoid faulty logic.

F. Reinforce your position

✓ Provide additional evidence of the benefits of your proposal and your own credibility in offering it.
✓ Use abstractions, metaphors, and other figures of speech to bring facts and figures to life.

G. Anticipate objections

✓ Anticipate and answer potential objections.
✓ Present the pros and cons of all options if you anticipate a hostile reaction.

involves listening to people, testing a position, developing a new position that reflects new input, more testing, more compromise, and so on.

Your success with persuasive messages depends on your ability to frame your argument, balance emotional and logical appeals, reinforce your position, and overcome resistance. These strategies will help you craft strong persuasive messages, no matter what the situation. To review the steps involved in developing persuasive messages, refer to "Checklist: Developing Persuasive Messages."

Common Examples of Persuasive Business Messages

Throughout your career, you'll have numerous opportunities to write persuasive messages within your organization: selling a supervisor on an idea for cutting costs, suggesting more efficient operating procedures, eliciting cooperation from competing departments, winning employee support for a new benefits package, requesting money for new equipment or funding for a special project. Similarly, you may send a variety of persuasive messages to people outside the organization: promoting products, soliciting investment funds, shaping public opinions, or requesting adjustments that go beyond a supplier's contractual obligations. In addition, many of the routine requests you studied in Chapter 7 can become persuasive messages if you want a nonroutine result or believe that you haven't received fair treatment. Most of these messages can be divided into persuasive requests for action, persuasive presentation of ideas, and persuasive claims and requests for adjustment.

When making a persuasive request for action, be sure to use the AIDA plan to frame your argument.

Persuasive Requests for Action The bulk of your persuasive business messages will involve requests for action. In some cases, your request will be anticipated, so the direct approach is fine. In others, you'll need to introduce your intention indirectly, and the AIDA model is ideal for this purpose. Open with an attention-getting device and show readers that you know something about their concerns.

Use the interest and desire sections of your message to demonstrate that you have good reason for making such a request and to cover what you know about the situation: the facts and figures, the benefits of helping, and any history or experience that will enhance your appeal. Your goals are (1) to gain credibility (for yourself and your request) and (2) to make your readers believe that helping you will indeed help solve a significant problem.

Once you've demonstrated that your message is relevant to your reader, you can close with a request for some specific action, as Leslie Jorgensen did in the memo in Figure 9–4. She's excited about the new Airbus A380 and thinks

Document Makeover

IMPROVE THIS E-MAIL MESSAGE

To practice correcting drafts of actual documents, visit your online course or the access-code protected portion of the Companion Website. Click "Document Makeovers," then click Chapter 9. You will find an e-mail message that contains problems and errors relating to what you've learned in this chapter about writing persuasive messages. Use the "Final Draft" decision tool to create an improved version of this persuasive e-mail request for action. Check the message for its effectiveness at gaining attention, building interest, stimulating desire, motivating action, focusing on the primary goal, and dealing with resistance.

FIGURE 9–4
Persuasive Memo Using the AIDA Model to Request Action

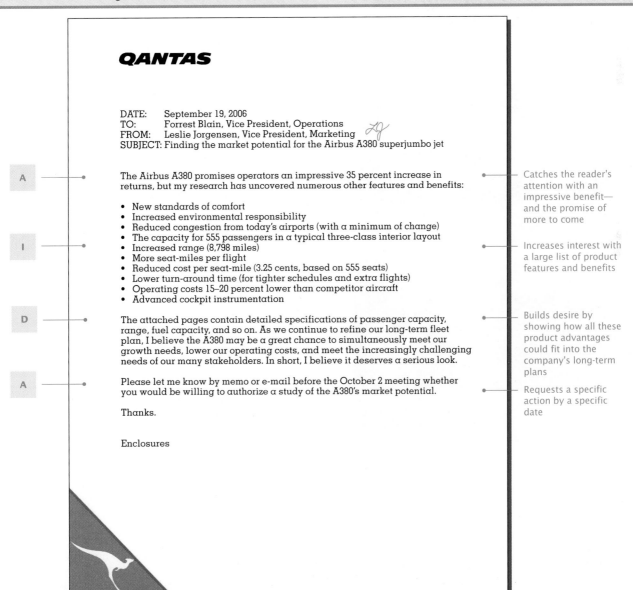

QANTAS

DATE: September 19, 2006
TO: Forrest Blain, Vice President, Operations
FROM: Leslie Jorgensen, Vice President, Marketing
SUBJECT: Finding the market potential for the Airbus A380 superjumbo jet

A The Airbus A380 promises operators an impressive 35 percent increase in returns, but my research has uncovered numerous other features and benefits:

I
- New standards of comfort
- Increased environmental responsibility
- Reduced congestion from today's airports (with a minimum of change)
- The capacity for 555 passengers in a typical three-class interior layout
- Increased range (8,798 miles)
- More seat-miles per flight
- Reduced cost per seat-mile (3.25 cents, based on 555 seats)
- Lower turn-around time (for tighter schedules and extra flights)
- Operating costs 15–20 percent lower than competitor aircraft
- Advanced cockpit instrumentation

D The attached pages contain detailed specifications of passenger capacity, range, fuel capacity, and so on. As we continue to refine our long-term fleet plan, I believe the A380 may be a great chance to simultaneously meet our growth needs, lower our operating costs, and meet the increasingly challenging needs of our many stakeholders. In short, I believe it deserves a serious look.

A Please let me know by memo or e-mail before the October 2 meeting whether you would be willing to authorize a study of the A380's market potential.

Thanks.

Enclosures

Catches the reader's attention with an impressive benefit—and the promise of more to come

Increases interest with a large list of product features and benefits

Builds desire by showing how all these product advantages could fit into the company's long-term plans

Requests a specific action by a specific date

that purchasing this plane for appropriate markets could help Qantas meet its growth needs while lowering its operating costs. She now needs her boss's approval for a study of the plane's market potential.

A direct approach is usually best for routine requests.

When requesting a favor that is routine (such as asking someone to attend a meeting in your absence), use the direct approach and the format for routine messages (see Chapter 7). However, when asking for a special favor (such as asking someone to chair an event or to serve as the team leader because you can no longer fill that role), use persuasive techniques to convince your reader of the value of the project. Include all necessary information about the project and any facts and figures that will convince your reader that his or her contribution will be enjoyable, easy, important, and of personal benefit.

Sometimes the objective of persuasive messages is simply to encourage people to consider a new idea.

Persuasive Presentation of Ideas   Most internal persuasive messages focus on getting the audience to make a specific decision or take some specific action. However, you will encounter situations in which you simply want to change attitudes or beliefs about a particular topic, without asking the audience to decide or do anything—at least not yet. In complicated, multistep persuasive efforts, the goal of your first message might be nothing more than convincing your audience to re-examine long-held opinions or admit the possibility of new ways of thinking.

For instance, you think your company is spending too much time processing payroll, and you've found an outside firm that can do it for less money than you now spend on internal staff and systems (a practice known as *outsourcing*). However, your company president is philosophically opposed to outsourcing any critical business function, saying that something as important as payroll should never be entrusted to outsiders. Until and unless you can bring about a change in the president's way of thinking, there is no point in pushing for a decision about outsourcing.

Another example is the effort to improve Internet access for people with visual and other disabilities. A campaign called the Web Accessibility Initiative has been launched by the Worldwide Web Consortium (a global association that defines many of the guidelines and technologies behind the World Wide Web). Although the Consortium's ultimate goal is making websites more accessible, a key interim goal is simply making website developers more aware of the need. As part of this effort, the Consortium has developed a presentation that highlights issues such as the following:[14]

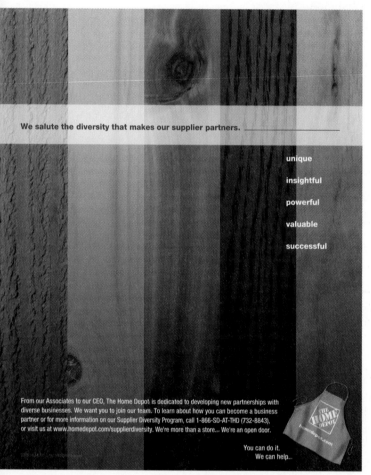

We salute the diversity that makes our supplier partners.

unique

insightful

powerful

valuable

successful

From our Associates to our CEO, The Home Depot is dedicated to developing new partnerships with diverse businesses. We want you to join our team. To learn about how you can become a business partner or for more information on our Supplier Diversity Program, call 1-866-SD-AT-THD (732-8843), or visit us at www.homedepot.com/supplierdiversity. We're more than a store.... We're an open door.

You can do it.
We can help..

In this magazine ad that promotes the idea of the company's commitment to an ethnically diverse supplier base, The Home Depot used the visual metaphor of diverse species of wood.

- The web's growing importance as a source of everything, including news and entertainment, workplace interaction, and government services

- The web's gradual displacement of traditional sources of these services

- The presence of barriers on the web for many types of disabilities

- The number of people whose disabilities affect their access to the web (the number is in the millions)

- The fact that accessible web designs can also help other users

Information on these specific issues can help open the eyes of website operators who may assume that standard web practices are sufficient for their audiences.

Persuasive Claims and Requests for Adjustments   Although persuasive claims and adjustment requests are sometimes referred to as complaint letters, you don't write them merely to get a complaint off your chest. Your goal is to persuade someone to make an adjustment in your favor. You work toward this goal by demonstrating the difference between what you expected and what you actually got.

Most claim letters are routine messages and use the direct approach discussed in Chapter 7. However, suppose you purchase something and, after the warranty expires, discover that the item was defective. You write the company a routine request asking for a replacement, but your request is denied. You're not satisfied, and you still believe you have a strong case. Perhaps you just didn't communicate it well enough the first time. Persuasion is necessary in such cases.

You can't threaten to withhold payment, so try to convey the essentially negative information in a way that will get positive results. Fortunately, most people in business are open to settling your claim fairly. It's to their advantage to maintain your goodwill and to resolve your problem quickly.

The key ingredients of a good persuasive claim are a complete and specific review of the facts and a confident and positive tone. Assume that the other person is not trying to cheat you but that you also have the right to be satisfied with the transaction. Talk only about the complaint at hand, not about other issues involving similar products or other complaints about the company. Your goal is to solve a particular problem, and your audience is most likely to help if you focus on the audience benefits of doing so (rather than focusing on the disadvantages of neglecting your complaint).

Begin persuasive claims by stating the basic problem or reviewing what has been done about the problem so far. Include a statement that both you and your audience can agree with or that clarifies what you wish to convince your audience about. Be as specific as possible about what you want to happen. Next, give your reader a good reason for granting your claim. Show how your audience is responsible for the problem, and appeal to your reader's sense of fair play, goodwill, or moral responsibility. Explain how you feel about the problem, but don't get carried away, don't complain too much, and don't make threats. People generally respond more favorably to requests that are both calm and reasonable.

DEVELOPING MARKETING AND SALES MESSAGES

Marketing and sales messages use the same basic techniques as other persuasive messages, with the added emphasis of encouraging someone to participate in a commercial transaction. Although the terms *marketing message* and *sales message* are often used interchangeably, they do represent separate but related efforts: Marketing messages usher potential buyers through the purchasing process without asking them to make an immediate decision; that's when sales messages take over. Marketing messages focus on such tasks as introducing new brands to the public, providing competitive comparison information, encouraging customers to visit websites for more information, and reminding buyers that a particular product or service is available. In contrast, a sales message makes a specific request for people to place an order for a particular product or service.

> Marketing and sales messages use many of the same techniques as persuasive business messages.

Strategies for Marketing and Sales Messages

Most marketing and sales messages, particularly in larger companies, are created and delivered by professionals with specific training in marketing, advertising, sales, or public relations. However, you may be called on to review the work of these specialists or even to write such messages in smaller companies, so a good understanding of how these messages work will help you be a more effective manager. The basic strategies to consider include assessing customer needs, analyzing your competition, determining key selling points and benefits, anticipating purchase objections, applying the

AIDA model, and maintaining high standards of ethics, legal compliance, and etiquette. Also, keep in mind that marketing and sales campaigns often include the series of messages in a coordinated effort that can last for weeks or months. In these campaigns, your message planning might encompass a website, e-mails, letters, brochures, personal sales presentations, as well as a mix of print, online, and broadcast media.

Assessing Audience Needs   As with every other business message, successful marketing and sales messages start with an understanding of audience needs. For some products and services, this assessment is a simple matter. For instance, customers compare only a few basic attributes when purchasing copy or printer paper, including weight, brightness, color, and finish. In contrast, they might consider dozens of features when shopping for real estate, cars, professional services, and other complex purchases.

Purchasing decisions often involve more than just the basic product or service.

In addition, customer needs often extend beyond the basic product or service. Clothes do far more than simply keep you warm. What you wear makes a statement about who you are, which social groups you want to be associated with (or not), and how you view your relationship with the people around you. In fact, a simple pair of shoes can meet at least four levels in Maslow's hierarchy of needs.

Begin by assessing audience needs, interests, and emotional concerns—just as you would for any business message. Try to form a mental image of the typical buyer for the product you wish to sell. Ask yourself what audience members might want to know about this product. How can your product help them? Are they driven by bottom-line pricing, or is quality more important to them?

Note the ads you're exposed to every day. They often focus on just one or two attributes or issues, even if the product or service has many different facets to consider. The purpose of these narrow marketing messages is to grab your attention and then raise your interest level enough to encourage you to conduct further research.

Most marketing and sales messages have to compete for the audience's attention.

Analyzing Your Competition   Marketing and sales messages nearly always compete with messages from other companies trying to reach the same audience. When Chrysler plans a sales letter to introduce a new model to current customers, the company knows that its audience has also been exposed to messages from Ford, Honda, Volkswagen, and numerous other car companies. In crowded markets, writers sometimes have to search for words and phrases that other companies aren't already using. They might also want to avoid themes, writing styles, or creative approaches that are too similar to those of competitive messages.

Determining Key Selling Points and Benefits   With some insight into audience needs and existing messages from the competition, you're ready to decide which benefits and features of your product or service to highlight. For all but the simplest products, you'll want to prioritize the items you plan to discuss. You'll also want to distinguish between the features of the product and the benefits that those features offer the customers.

Selling points focus on the product; benefits focus on the user.

As Table 9–2 shows, **selling points** are the most attractive features of an idea or product, whereas **benefits** are the particular advantages that readers will realize from those features. Selling points focus on the product. Benefits focus on the user. For example, if you say that your snow shovel has "an ergonomically designed handle," you've described a good feature. But to persuade someone to buy that shovel, say "the ergonomically designed handle will reduce your risk of back injury." That's a benefit. For your message to be successful, your product's distinguishing benefit must correspond to your readers' primary needs or emotional concerns.

FEATURES VERSUS BENEFITS | Table 9–2

Product Feature	Customer Benefit
Our easy financing plan includes no money down, no interest, and no payments for 24 months.	You can buy what you want right now, even if you have limited cash on hand.
Our marketing communication audit accurately measures the impact of your advertising and public relations efforts.	You can find out whether your message is reaching the target audience and whether you're spending your marketing budget in the best possible manner.
The spools in our fly fishing reels are machined from solid blocks of aircraft-grade aluminum.	Go fishing with confidence: These lightweight reels will stand up to the toughest conditions.

Consider how SecureAbel Alarms uses the AIDA model to persuade students to buy its dorm-room alarm system (see Figure 9–5). The features of the system include its portability, piercing alarm, and programmable control units. The benefits include simple installation, simple operation, and a sense of security.

Anticipating Purchase Objections   As with persuasive business messages, marketing and sales messages often encounter objections, and once again, the best way to handle them is to identify them up front and try to address as many as you can in the original message (or messages, as the case may be). However, with marketing and sales messages, you often don't get a second chance to explain yourself or to present your case. Your boss might feel an obligation to let you explain what you meant in the third paragraph of your persuasive proposal, but potential customers feel no such responsibility. If your website for fashion jewelry aimed at college-age consumers strikes visitors as too juvenile, for instance, they'll click to another site within seconds and probably never come back to yours.

Objections can range from high price to low quality to a lack of compatibility with existing products. Perceived risk is another common objection. Consumers might worry that a car won't be safe enough for a family, that a jacket will make them look unattractive, or that a hair salon will botch a haircut. Business buyers might worry about disrupting operations or failing to realize the financial returns on a purchase.

Price can be a particularly tricky issue in any message, whether audience members are consumers or business customers. Whether you highlight or downplay the price of your product, prepare your readers for it. Words such as *luxurious* and *economical* provide unmistakable clues about how your price compares with that of competitors. Such words help your readers accept your price when you finally state it.

If price is a major selling point, give it a position of prominence, such as in the headline or as the last item in a paragraph. If price is not a major selling point, you can handle it in several ways. You could leave the price out altogether or de-emphasize it by putting the figure in the middle of a paragraph that comes well after you've presented the benefits and selling points.

> Anticipating objections is crucial to effective marketing and sales messages.

Only 100 prints of this exclusive, limited-edition lithograph will be created. On June 15, they will be made available to the general public, but you can reserve one now for only $350, the special advance reservation price. Simply rush the enclosed reservation card back today so that your order is in before the June 15 publication date.

> Emphasizes the rarity of the edition to signal value and thus prepare the reader for the big-ticket price that follows.

> Buries the actual price in the middle of a sentence and ties it in with another reminder of the exclusivity of the offer.

Planning

Analyze the Situation
The purpose is to sell a product, so the audience will be neutral, uninterested, or perhaps unwilling.

Gather Information
Determine audience needs and obtain the necessary information to present a persuasive message.

Select the Right Medium
A printed letter is appropriate for this formal communication.

Organize the Information
Your main idea is to offer a product for sale, so limit your scope to that issue; use the AIDA approach to propose the solution.

Writing

Adapt to Your Audience
Adjust the level of formality based on degree of familiarity with the audience; maintain a positive relationship by using the "you" attitude, politeness, positive emphasis, and bias-free language.

Compose the Message
Use a conversational but professional style and keep the message brief, clear, and as helpful as possible.

Completing

Revise the Message
Evaluate content and review readability to make sure the main idea is conveyed efficiently and effectively.

Produce the Message
Emphasize a clean, professional appearance on company letterhead.

Proofread the Message
Review for errors in layout, spelling, and mechanics.

Distribute the Message
Deliver your message using the chosen medium.

FIGURE 9–5   Effective Letter Using the AIDA Model to Sell a Product

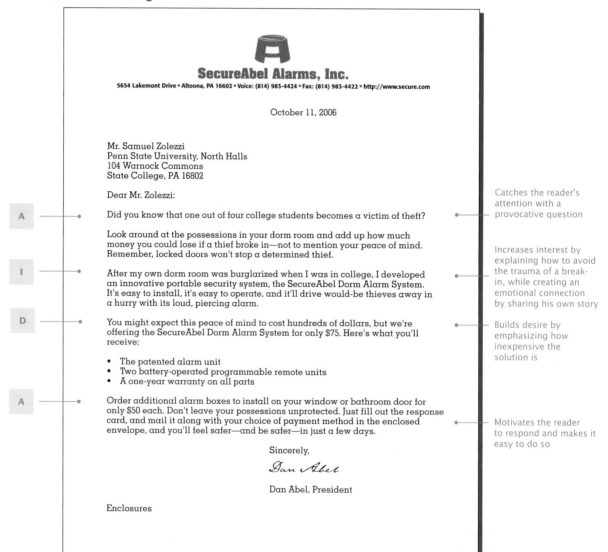

The pros also use two other techniques for minimizing price. One is to break a quantity price into units. Instead of saying that a case of motor oil costs $24, you might say that each bottle costs $2. The other technique is to compare your product's price with the cost of some other product or activity: "The cost of owning your own exercise equipment is less than you'd pay for a health-club membership." Your aim is to make the cost seem as small and affordable as possible, thereby minimizing price as a possible objection.

If you've done your homework up front and assessed your audience thoroughly, you should be aware of most of these concerns. You might not be able to address every one of them in your message—if the product or service isn't ideal for the customer, you're message can't fix that—but you will be prepared to do the best you can with the product or service you have to promote.

Applying the AIDA model   Most marketing and sales messages are prepared according to the AIDA plan or some variation of it. You begin with an attention-getting device, generate interest by describing some of the product or service's unique features, increase desire by highlighting the benefits that are most appealing to your audience, and close by suggesting the action you want the audience to take.

Getting Attention   Not only do marketing and sales messages open with an attention-getting device, but professionals use a wide range of techniques to attract their audience's attention:

- **Your product's strongest benefit.** "1,000 Songs. Impossibly small. iPod nano."[15]

- **A piece of genuine news.** "Take entertainment to a whole new place." (Promoting Verizon's V Cast service, which lets people download a variety of entertainment services to their mobile phones)[16]

- **A point of common ground with the audience.** "An SUV adventurous enough to accommodate your spontaneity and the gear that comes with it."[17]

- **A personal appeal to the reader's emotions and values.** "The only thing worse than paying taxes is paying taxes when you don't have to."

- **The promise of insider information.** "You may be one of those people who dream of working and living in France and don't know how to go about simply doing it. This guide tells how—from the inside out—how others like yourself have managed to work within the French system."[18]

- **The promise of savings.** "Right now, you can get huge savings on a new camera phone."[19]

- **A sample or demonstration of the product.** "Here's your free sample of the new Romalite packing sheet."

- **A solution to a problem.** "This backpack's designed to endure all a kid's dropping and dragging."[20]

Of course, words aren't the only attention-getting device at your disposal. Strong, evocative images are a common attention getter. With online messages, you have even more options, including audio, animation, and video.

Building Interest   Use the interest section of your message to build on the intrigue you created with your opening. This section should also offer support for whatever claims or promises you might've made in the opening. For instance, after opening with the headline that claims "1,000 Songs. Impossibly small. iPod nano," the Apple iPod webpage continues with[21]

You can employ a variety of attention-getting devices in marketing and sales messages.

To build interest, expand on and support the promises in your attention-getting opening.

Explains the concept of the iPod nano by relating it to what millions of consumers already know about the original iPod

Puts size in a position of emphasis, since size—not price—is the major selling point for the iPod nano

> Take everything you love about iPod and shrink it. Now shrink it again. With 2GB (500 songs) and 4GB (1,000 songs) models starting at $199, the pencil-thin iPod nano packs the entire iPod experience into an impossibly small design. So small, it will take your music places you never dreamed of.

At this point in the message, Apple has offered enough information to help people understand how they might use the product, and it has answered a couple of potential objections as well (compatibility with Windows and the price). Anyone interested in a digital music player is probably intrigued enough to keep reading.

Add details and audience benefits to increase desire for the product or service.

Increasing Desire To build desire for the product, continue to expand and explain what it offers, how it works, how customers can use it, and so on. Think carefully about the sequence of support points, and use plenty of subheadings and other devices to help people find the information they need quickly. For example, after reading this much about the iPod, some users might want to know more about the iTunes Music Store, whereas others will want technical specifications. You will want to make it easy to find the information each individual wants.

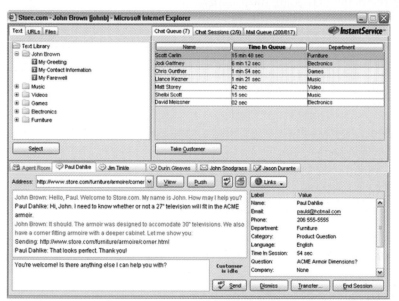

Chat software, such as this customer-service and sales solution from InstantService, gives websites an easy way to interact with their audiences. This screen shows what an online sales representative sees while communicating with customers: the current IM session (lower left corner), the queue of waiting customers (upper right corner), additional information about the current customer, and text files that the sales rep can access instantly to speed up the IM process.

Of course, with websites, e-mail, CD-ROMs, and other electronic formats, you can offer navigational links to let people access specific information almost instantly. The iPod product page continues with detailed discussions of various product features and benefits, but it also offers numerous links to pages with other kinds of support information. The ability to provide flexible access to information is just one of the reasons the web is such a powerful medium for marketing and sales (see "Using the Power of Technology: The Power and Persuasion of Interactive Sales Messages").

Throughout the body of your message, remember to keep the focus on the audience, not on your company or your product. When you talk about product features, remember to stress the benefits and talk in terms that make sense to users. Listing the capacity of the iPod as 10,000 songs is a lot more meaningful for most readers than saying it has 40 gigabytes of memory. Action words give strength to any business message, but they are especially important in sales letters. Compare the following:

Instead of This	Write This
The NuForm desk chair is designed to support your lower back and relieve pressure on your legs.	The NuForm desk chair supports your lower back and relieves pressure on your legs.

The second version says the same thing in fewer words and emphasizes what the chair does for the user ("supports") rather than the intentions of the design team ("is designed to support").

To keep readers interested, use strong, colorful language without overdoing it.

To keep readers interested, use colorful verbs and adjectives that convey a dynamic image. Be careful, however, not to overdo it: If you say "Your factory floors will sparkle like diamonds," your audience will find it hard to believe, which may prevent them from believing the rest of your message.

USING THE POWER OF TECHNOLOGY

The Power and Persuasion of Interactive Sales Tools

Have you ever booked a vacation hotel with great expectations, only to arrive and find the place nothing like what you thought it would be? Using words to describe the features and ambience of a physical space is a challenge for the best of writers. As a result, descriptions of hotels and conference centers tend to end up sounding an awful lot alike.

The possibility of making a poor choice can be a worry for vacationing consumers, but it's enough to keep corporate event planners awake at night. When you're responsible for planning and hosting events that could involve dozens, hundreds, even thousands of attendees, you need to know about everything from dining facilities to where people will register and pick up their name badges. Anything can cast a poor light on your planning efforts—from tacky interior decorating to overcrowded hallways that prevent people from moving comfortably between conference sessions. However, such factors are hard to judge from a printed brochure, and you won't always have the chance to visit every property ahead of time.

The North Maple Inn at Basking Ridge (www.northmapleinn.com), an upscale hotel and conference center in New Jersey, is one of many innovative hotels and conference centers using the power of interactive websites to give potential visitors a better idea of what their facilities are really like. Meeting planners can click through a virtual tour of the inn's conference rooms, leisure and fitness areas, and dining facilities—complete with audio commentary, video clips, photographs, text descriptions, and interactive floor plans that show how meeting rooms can be arranged in a variety of classroom, theater, and banqueting formats.

By providing a virtual experience that's the next best thing to being there, North Maple Inn goes a long way toward removing an audience's perceived risks and accelerating a favorable purchase decision.

CAREER APPLICATIONS

1. What are the possible disadvantages of using these interactive tools?

2. How would you promote your college or university to prospective students using an interactive website?

To increase desire, as well as boost your credibility, provide support for your claims. You can't assume your audience will believe what you say just because you've said it in writing. You'll have to give them proof. Support is especially important if your product is complicated, costs a lot, or represents some unusual approach.

Creative marketers find many ways to provide support: testimonials from satisfied users, articles written by industry experts, competitive comparisons, product samples and free demonstrations, independent test results, even movies or computer animations that show a product in action. You can also highlight guarantees that demonstrate your faith in your product and your willingness to back it up.

Motivating Action After you have raised enough interest and built up the reader's desire for your offering, you're ready to ask your audience to take action. Whether you want people to pick up the phone to place an order or visit your website to download a free demo version of your software, try to persuade them to do it right away. You might offer a discount for the first 1,000 people to order, put a deadline on the offer, or simply remind them that the sooner they order, the sooner they'll be able to enjoy the product's benefits. Even potential buyers who want the product can get distracted or forget to respond, so the sooner you can encourage action, the better. Make the response action as simple and as risk-free as possible.

After you've generated sufficient interest and desire, you're ready to persuade readers to take the preferred action.

Take care to maintain the respectful, professional tone you've been using up to this point. Don't resort to gimmicks and desperate-sounding pleas for the customer's business. Make sure your final impression is compelling and positive. For instance, in a sales letter, the postscript (P.S.) below your signature is often one of the first and last parts people read. Use this valuable space to emphasize the key benefit you have to offer and to emphasize the advantages of ordering soon.

Maintaining High Standards of Ethics, Legal Compliance, and Etiquette

The word *persuasion* has negative connotations for some people, especially in a marketing or sales context. They associate persuasion with dishonest and unethical practices that lead unsuspecting audiences into accepting unworthy ideas or buying unneeded products. However, effective businesspeople view persuasion as a positive force, aligning their own interests with what is best for their audiences. They influence audience members by providing information and aiding understanding, which allows audiences the freedom to choose.[22] Ethical businesspeople inform audiences of the benefits of an idea, an organization, a product, a donation, or an action so that these audiences can recognize just how well the idea, organization, product, donation, or action will satisfy a need they truly have. To maintain the highest standards of business ethics, make every attempt to persuade without manipulating. Choose words that won't be misinterpreted, and be sure you don't distort the truth. Adopt the "you" attitude by showing honest concern for your audience's needs and interests. Your consideration of audience needs is more than ethical; it's the proper use of persuasion. That consideration is likely to achieve the response you intend and to satisfy your audience's needs.

Marketing and sales messages are covered by a wide range of laws and regulations.

As marketing and selling grow increasingly complex, so do the legal ramifications of marketing and sales messages. In the United States, the Federal Trade Commission (FTC) has the authority to impose penalties (ranging from cease-and-desist orders to multimillion-dollar fines) against advertisers who violate federal standards for truthful advertising. Other federal agencies have authority over advertising in specific industries, such as transportation and financial services. Individual states have additional laws that apply. The legal aspects of promotional communication can be quite complex, from state to state and from country to country, and most companies require marketing and sales people to get clearance from company lawyers before sending messages. In any event, pay close attention to the following legal aspects of marketing and sales communication:[23]

- **Marketing and sales messages must be truthful and nondeceptive.** The FTC considers messages to be deceptive if they include statements that are likely to mislead reasonable customers, and the statement is an important part of the purchasing decision. Failing to include important information is also considered deceptive. The FTC also looks at *implied claims*, those you don't explicitly make but that can be inferred from what you do or don't say.

- **You must back up your claims with evidence.** According to the FTC, offering a money-back guarantee or providing letters from satisfied customers is not enough; you must still be able to support your claims with objective evidence such as a survey or scientific study. If you claim that your food product lowers cholesterol, you must have scientific evidence to support that claim.

- **Marketing and sales messages are considered binding contracts in many states.** If you imply or make an offer and then can't fulfill your end of the bargain, you can be sued for breach of contract.

- **In most cases, you can't use a person's name, photograph, or other identity without permission.** Doing so is considered an invasion of privacy. You can use images of people considered to be public figures, as long as you don't unfairly imply that they endorse your message.

In both the United States and other countries, lawmakers are considering new legislation covering several other major aspects of advertising and related efforts. Before you launch a marketing or sales campaign, make sure you're up to date on the latest regulations affecting spam (or *unsolicited bulk e-mail,* as it's officially known), customer privacy, and data security. New laws are likely to appear in all three areas in the next few years.

Maintaining high ethical standards is a key aspect of good communication etiquette.

Meeting your ethical and legal obligations will go a long way toward maintaining good communication etiquette as well. However, you may still face etiquette decisions within ethical and legal boundaries. For instance, you can produce a marketing campaign that complies with all applicable laws and yet is still offensive or insulting to your audience. An audience-centered approach, involving respect for your readers and their values, should help you avoid any such etiquette missteps.

Common Examples of Marketing and Sales Messages

From simple letters to interactive kiosks, the variety of marketing and sales messages in today's business environment is seemingly endless. However, no matter how advanced the technology becomes, successful persuasive communication will always be built around the basics: understanding audience needs, out-communicating competitors, and providing clear, compelling information that encourages customers to make a decision in your favor. Consider the e-mail newsletter in Figure 9–6. To begin with, it's part of an *opt-in* mailing, meaning Zazú sends it only to those customers who specifically request it. Recipients can also choose the categories of information they want to receive and frequently they want to receive the newsletter. The newsletter itself combines friendly and informative text that addresses typical customer concerns, appealing photography, and convenient links to the company's website.

Saturn's website offers another example of the depth and breadth of information you can provide customers to help them make informed decisions. For instance, the illustration in Figure 9–7 helps shoppers understand how the Saturn Vue is engineered for safety. Another great feature of the website is a product comparison screen that lets car shoppers compare a Saturn model with competitive models—a task that is difficult and time-consuming with printed brochures. After selecting one or two competitors, the shopper is then presented with a comprehensive comparison of product features. Beyond the information itself, a presentation such as this sends two subtle messages to the reader. First, Saturn embraces the "you" attitude by giving consumers information they want, even if that means giving them information about Saturn's competitors. Second, by inviting comparisons with other cars, Saturn demonstrates confidence in its own products, which in turn helps it build credibility and inspire confidence among potential buyers.

Even the most technologically advanced persuasive tools and media follow the basic guidelines of persuasive communication.

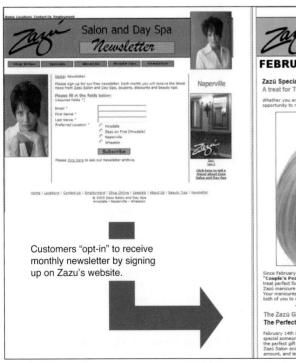

Customers "opt-in" to receive monthly newsletter by signing up on Zazu's website.

FIGURE 9–6
Opt-In E-mail Newsletter

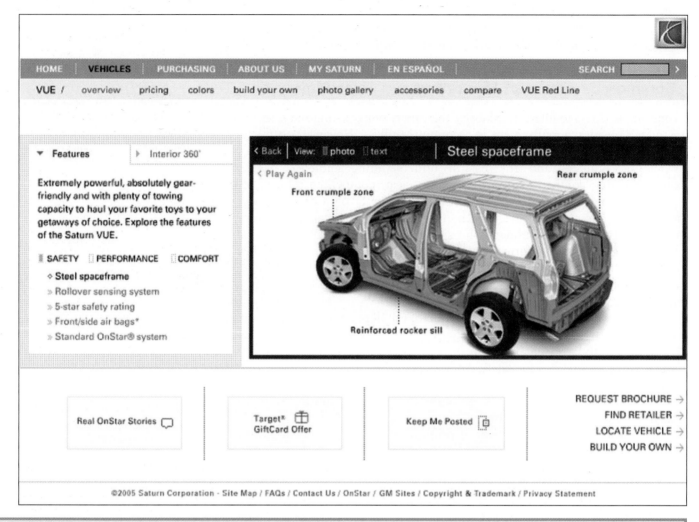

FIGURE 9–7
Providing Buyer Information on Saturn's Website

On the Job

SOLVING COMMUNICATION DILEMMAS AT MARK BURNETT PRODUCTIONS

Mark Burnett is always looking for fresh new projects to develop, including more shows along the lines of *Survivor* and *The Apprentice*. You've been working for Burnett for several years as a public relations specialist, and your own work is the inspiration for an idea you'd like to pitch to him. In *The Communicator*, eight contenders take over the communication responsibilities for eight struggling small businesses in the same town, handling everything from meetings to the employee newsletter to advertising.

Success or failure will be measured in four key areas. The first three involve improving the opinions that employees, customers, and the local community have about the respective companies. Judges will measure those opinions at the beginning of the season and then again at the end to see which communicator was able to "move the needle" the most. The fourth measurement is the most critical: Which contender is able to increase sales and profits by the largest percentage? The risks are high because one of the show's unique features will be the requirement that contestants invest $25,000 of their own money into the companies they're assigned to. The potential rewards are even higher, though—the winner becomes the new owner of the company he or she has been helping.

1. Now comes your big communication challenge: persuading master persuader Mark Burnett to produce *The Communicator*. Having watched Burnett in action, you know how jam-packed his days are and how many new ideas people pitch to him. You'll start with a brief memo to convince him to have a one-hour meeting, during which you'll cover the show in more detail. You brush up on the AIDA model and fire up your word processor. Which of the following openings is the best way to catch his attention?

   a. If we don't generate some more hit shows in a hurry, we'll be living our own version of *Survivor* as we try to recover from the disappointments of *The Casino* and *The Restaurant*.
   b. Twenty-five million Americans live the dreams and disappointments of owning a small business, and we can capture that emotion in a compelling new reality show.
   c. This is the big one—the show that'll make *Survivor* and *The Apprentice* seem like tired reruns.
   d. Like all the other people tugging at your sleeve these days, I have an idea for a show, but first I'd like to tell you what an honor and a privilege it has been to work in your organization for these past three years.

2. You believe you've captured his attention with your opening sentence, but you know you have about three seconds to build his interest or he'll move on to the next message on his desk. Which of these sounds best?

   a. If you could give me just an hour of your time, I have a PowerPoint presentation ready to roll, complete with target audience demographics, contest rules, contestant qualifications, and advertiser profiles. I'd be happy to meet with you in the evening or on the weekend if that's the only time you have available.
   b. As you may know, Mark, my job here keeps me hopping 45 or 50 hours a week, but in spite of that workload, I've been able to devote more than 200 hours over the past two months working out every detail for this new show.
   c. *The Communicator* will give viewers a front-row seat on the human drama of restoring the competitive vitality of a small business. They'll share the hopes and the heartbreaks of people engaged in the daily challenge of managing a company—and we'll create an ideal marketing platform for the likes of IBM, Staples, and the other major advertisers that have targeted the small business segment.
   d. I've already done some informal surveys with potential advertisers, including IBM, Staples, and other companies that market to small businesses, and interest appears to be strong in a show that focuses on small business. Naturally, to protect the confidentially of the show concept, I didn't tell them who I was or where I work.

3. You're confident that the second part of your memo will foster Burnett's interest, so now it's time to heighten his desire to learn more about your idea. Which of the following strategies should you use in this part of the memo?

   a. Recognize that Burnett has both high expectations (after all, he's the person who created *Survivor*, the all-time champion of reality shows) and high standards (he refuses to produce low-brow programming, even if it might succeed in the marketplace). Focus on the high production quality you'd like to see in the new show, from its dazzling graphics to the extremely valuable prize of an entire company.
   b. Burnett may have a bright creative mind, but he's just as successful as a business owner. You've heard him tell stories of successful business managers whose lessons he tries to follow. Build his desire to learn more about *The Communicator* by asking him to imagine himself starting over as a small business owner, facing the daily communication challenges that the show will dramatize.
   c. Every successful reality show is based on the emotional connection between viewers and the contestants on the show, so focus on that element. Explain how a carefully chosen cast of contestants will give viewers the chance to choose heroes to cheer for and villains to cheer against.
   d. Expand on your original description of the show concept by explaining how the competition would work. Along the way, continue to work in both logical appeals (such as statistics about small business ownership and the amount spent on advertising aimed at small business owners) and emotional appeals (the emotional "hooks" that will keep viewers tuning in each week to follow the competition).

4. You've already talked to Pat Farmer, Burnett's personal assistant, about the best way to schedule a meeting with the boss. To help manage Burnett's busy schedule, the usual procedure is for Burnett to give Farmer his response to a meeting request, then Farmer passes the answer along to the person who requested the meeting. Which of these is the best way to implement the final stage of the AIDA model?

   a. I asked Pat Farmer to check your schedule for next week, and you have several one-hour slots still open. Would you like to meet during one of these times to discuss *The Communicator* in more detail? If you could let Pat know your answer by the end of this week, we could put the meeting on your schedule for next week.
   b. Could you let Pat know by the end of this week if you'd like to meet to discuss *The Communicator* in more detail?
   c. I've studied every show that Mark Burnett Productions has ever created, and I believe *The Communicator* can adopt the successful elements while establishing its own unique media presence.
   d. Would you like to meet to explore the show's concept? Better yet, if you'll give me a couple of weeks' time with a production crew, I could just shoot a rough scene to show you what I have in mind.

Learning Objectives Checkup

Assess your understanding of the principles in this chapter by reading each learning objective and studying the accompanying exercises. For fill-in items, write the missing text in the blank provided; for multiple choice items, circle the letter of the correct answer. You can check your responses against the answer key on page AK-2.

Objective 9.1: Apply the three-step writing process to persuasive messages.

1. Which of the following is true about persuasive business messages?
   a. They require government approval before they can be printed or posted on websites.
   b. They are always welcomed by audiences.
   c. They often involve a combination of emotional and logical elements.
   d. They require less planning than any other type of message.

2. Why is the indirect approach often used in persuasive messages?
   a. It is more courteous.
   b. It takes less time.
   c. It is traditional.
   d. It lets the writer build audience interest and desire before asking for action or commitment.

Objective 9.2: Identify seven ways to establish credibility in persuasive messages.

3. Which of the following is *not* a good way to establish credibility with your audience?
   a. Support your argument with plenty of facts.
   b. Name your sources.
   c. Be enthusiastic and sincere.
   d. Present only your side of the argument to avoid reminding the audience of alternatives.

4. If you lack credibility with an audience, which of the following would be good technique to use in a persuasive message?
   a. Make your message extremely detailed so the audience will focus on the content.
   b. Include information or endorsements from recognized experts.
   c. Use plenty of humor to help bring the audience over to your side.
   d. Use multimedia to give yourself more ways to get your points across.

Objective 9.3 Describe the AIDA plan for persuasive messages.

5. The first phase in the AIDA plan is to
   a. Do your research
   b. Gain the audience's attention

   c. Analyze the audience
   d. Call for action

6. The body of a message that follows the AIDA plan
   a. Captures the audience's attention
   b. Contains the buffer
   c. Generates interest and heightens desire
   d. Calls for action

7. Which of these is a good way to build desire using the AIDA approach?
   a. Explain how the proposed change will help your audience.
   b. Reduce resistance by addressing objections the audience might have.
   c. Explain complex ideas or products in more detail.
   d. Do all of the above.

8. The final phase of the AIDA plan
   a. Provides in-depth information to help generate interest
   b. Reduces resistance by increasing the audience's desire
   c. Calls for action
   d. Captures the audience's attention

Objective 9.4: Distinguish between emotional and logical appeals and discuss how to balance them.

9. An argument that is based on human feelings is known as a/an _____ appeal.

10. An argument that is based on facts and reason is known as a/an _____ appeal.

11. The best approach to using emotional appeals is usually to
    a. Use them by themselves
    b. Use them in conjunction with logical appeals
    c. Use them only when the audience is particularly hostile
    d. Avoid them in all business messages

12. Which of the following is a type of logical appeal?
    a. Deduction
    b. Induction
    c. Analogy
    d. All of the above

Objective 9.5: Identify four common mistakes in writing persuasive messages.

13. The so-called hard sell is
    a. Synonymous with a direct approach
    b. Risky because it puts your recipients into a defensive frame of mind
    c. Risky because it is illegal in most countries, including the United States
    d. The best way to gain audience approval when you're in a hurry

14. Relying solely on powerful, rational arguments in persuasive messages
    a. Is a great idea, since most people want to make rational decisions

b. Show your superiors that you know how to think logically

c. Is the only method of communication that should be used when complex ideas are involved

d. Limits your persuasive ability because it doesn't help you connect with your audiences on an emotional level

Objective 9.6: Discuss an effective approach to identifying selling points and audience benefits.

15. Prioritizing which features and benefits to write about is
   a. A waste of time because people don't read in sequential order
   b. Important because doing so lets you start with low-priority issues and work your way up to high-priority issues
   c. Important because it helps you focus your message on items and issues that the audience cares about the most
   d. Important because it helps ensure that you remember to talk about every single feature and benefit, no matter how inconsequential

16. What is the relationship between features and benefits?
   a. They are identical.

b. Features are aspects of an idea or product; benefits are the advantages that readers will realize from those features.

c. Features tell people how to use a product; benefits tell them how a product differs from the competition.

d. Features are the primary advantages of a product; benefits are the secondary advantages.

Objective 9.7: Identify steps you can take to avoid ethical lapses in marketing and sales messages.

17. Which of the following steps should you take to make sure your persuasive messages are ethical?
   a. Align your interest with your audience's interests.
   b. Choose words that can't be misinterpreted.
   c. Give the audience the information they need to make an informed decision.
   d. Do all of the above.

18. If it adheres to all applicable federal laws, a marketing or sales message
   a. Is certain to be both legal and ethical
   b. Could still violate some state laws
   c. Could still be unethical
   d. Both b and c

Apply Your Knowledge

1. Why is it important to present both sides of an argument when writing a persuasive message to a potentially hostile audience?
2. How are persuasive messages different from routine messages?
3. When is it appropriate to use the direct organizational approach in persuasive messages?

4. What is likely to happen if your persuasive message starts immediately with a call to action? Why?
5. **Ethical Choices** Are emotional appeals ethical? Why or why not?

Practice Your Knowledge

DOCUMENTS FOR ANALYSIS

Read the following documents, then (1) analyze the strengths and weaknesses of each sentence and (2) revise each document so that it follows this chapter's guidelines.

DOCUMENT 9.A: WRITING PERSUASIVE REQUESTS FOR ACTION

At Tolson Auto Repair, we have been in business for over 25 years. We stay in business by always taking into account what the customer wants. That's why we are writing. We want to know your opinions to be able to better conduct our business.

Take a moment right now and fill out the enclosed questionnaire. We know everyone is busy, but this is just one way we have of making sure our people do their job correctly. Use the enclosed envelope to return the questionnaire.

And again, we're happy you chose Tolson Auto Repair. We want to take care of all your auto needs.

DOCUMENT 9.B: WRITING PERSUASIVE CLAIMS AND REQUESTS FOR ADJUSTMENT

Dear TechStar Computing:

I'm writing to you because of my disappointment with my new multimedia PC display. The display part works all right, but the audio volume is also set too high and the volume knob doesn't turn it down. It's driving us crazy. The volume knob doesn't seem to be connected to anything but simply spins around. I can't believe you would put out a product like this without testing it first.

I depend on my computer to run my small business and want to know what you are going to do about it. This reminds me of every time I buy electronic equipment from what seems like any company. Something is always wrong. I thought quality was supposed to be important, but I guess not.

Anyway, I need this fixed right away. Please tell me what you want me to do.

DOCUMENT 9.C: WRITING SALES LETTERS

We know how awful dining hall food can be, and that's why we've developed the "Mealaweek Club." Once a week, we'll deliver food to your dormitory or apartment. Our meals taste great. We have pizza, buffalo wings, hamburgers and curly fries, veggie roll-ups, and more!

When you sign up for just six months, we will ask what day you want your delivery. We'll ask you to fill out your selection of meals. And the rest is up to us. At "Mealaweek," we deliver! And payment is easy. We accept MasterCard and Visa or a personal check. It will save money especially when compared with eating out.

Just fill out the enclosed card and indicate your method of payment. As soon as we approve your credit or check, we'll begin delivery. Tell all your friends about Mealaweek. We're the best idea since sliced bread!

Exercises

For active links to all websites discussed in this chapter, visit this text's website at www.prenhall.com/thill. Locate your book and click on its Companion Website link. Then select Chapter 9, and click on "Featured Websites." Locate the name of the page or the URL related to the material in the text. Please note that links to sites that become inactive after publication of the book will be removed from the Featured Websites section.

9.1 Teamwork With another student, analyze the persuasive memo to Eleanor Tran at Host Marriott (Figure 9–3) by answering the following questions:
   a. What techniques are used to capture the reader's attention?
   b. Does the writer use the direct or the indirect organizational approach? Why?
   c. Is the subject line effective? Why or why not?
   d. Does the writer use an emotional or a logical appeal? Why?
   e. What reader benefits are included?
   f. How does the writer establish credibility?
   g. What tools does the writer use to reinforce his position?

9.2 Composing Subject Lines Compose effective subject lines for the following persuasive messages:
   a. An e-mail request to your supervisor to purchase a new high-speed laser printer for your office. You've been outsourcing quite a bit of your printing to AlphaGraphics, and you're certain this printer will pay for itself in six months.
   b. A letter to area residents soliciting customers for your new business, "Meals à la Car," a carryout dining service that delivers from most of the local restaurants. All local restaurant menus are on the Internet. Mom and Dad can dine on egg rolls and chow mein while the kids munch on pepperoni pizza.
   c. A memo to the company president to allow managers to carry over their unused vacation days to the

following year. Apparently, many managers canceled their fourth-quarter vacation plans to work on the installation of a new company computer system. Under their current contract, vacation days not used by December 31 can't be carried over to the following year.

9.3 Ethical Choices Your boss has asked you to post a message on the company's internal blog urging everyone in your department to donate money to the company's favorite charity, an organization that operates a special summer camp for physically challenged children. You wind up writing a lengthy posting packed with facts and heartwarming anecdotes about the camp and the children's experiences. When you must work that hard to persuade your audience to take an action such as donating money to a charity, aren't you being manipulative and unethical? Explain.

9.4 Focusing on Benefits Determine whether the following sentences focus on features or benefits; rewrite as necessary to focus all the sentences on benefits.
   a. All-Cook skillets are coated with a durable, patented nonstick surface.
   b. You can call anyone and talk as long as you like on Saturdays and Sundays with our new FamilyTalk wireless plan.
   c. We need to raise $2,500 to provide each needy child with a backpack filled with school supplies.

9.5 Internet Visit the Federal Trade Commission website and read the "Catch the Bandit in Your Mailbox" consumer warning at www.ftc.gov/bcp/conline/pubs/tmarkg/bandit.htm. Select one or two marketing or sales letters you've recently received and see whether they contain any of the suspicious content mentioned in the FTC warning. What does the FTC suggest you do with any materials that don't sound legitimate?

Expand Your Knowledge

LEARNING MORE ON THE WEB

Influence an Official and Promote Your Cause http://thomas.loc.gov

At the Thomas site compiled by the Library of Congress, you'll discover voluminous information about federal legislation, congressional members, and committee reports. You can also access committee homepages and numerous links to government agencies, current issues, and historical documents. You'll find all kinds of regulatory information, including laws and relevant issues that might affect you in the business world. Visit the site and stay informed. Maybe you'll want to convince a government official to support a business-related issue that affects you.

ACTIVITIES

Explore the data at the Thomas site, and find an issue you can use to practice your skills at writing a persuasive message.

1. What key ideas would you include in an e-mail message to persuade your congressional representative to support an issue important to you?
2. In a letter to a senator or member of Congress, what information would you include to convince the reader to vote for an issue related to small business?
3. When sending a message to someone who daily receives hundreds of written appeals, what attention-getting techniques can you use? How can you get support for a cause that concerns you as a businessperson?

Exploring the Web on Your Own

Review these chapter-related websites on your own to learn more about writing persuasive messages.

1. Visit the Federal Trade Commission website, www.ftc.gov, to find out how consumers can cut down on the number of unsolicited mailings, calls, and e-mails they receive.
2. Explore some classic examples of persuasive messages at the National Archives' Powers of Persuasion online exhibit,

www.archives.gov (click on "Online Exhibits," then page through to the Powers of Persuasion exhibit).

3. See how professional advertising copywriters use persuasion in their work; read the free articles at www.wahmcopywriter.com/copywriting-articles.

Learn Interactively

INTERACTIVE STUDY GUIDE

Visit www.prenhall.com/thill, then locate your book and click on its Companion Website link. Select Chapter 9 to take advantage of the interactive "Chapter Quiz" to test your knowledge of chapter concepts. Receive instant feedback on whether you need additional studying. Also, visit the "Study Hall," where you'll find an abundance of valuable resources that will help you succeed in this course.

PEAK PERFORMANCE GRAMMAR AND MECHANICS

If your instructor has required the use of "Peak Performance Grammar and Mechanics," either in your online course or on CD, you can improve your skill with semicolons and colons by using the "Peak Performance Grammar and Mechanics" module. Click "Punctuation I." Take the Pretest to determine whether you have any weak areas. Then review those areas in the Refresher Course. Take the Follow-Up Test to check your grasp of semicolons and colons. For an extra challenge or advanced practice, take the Advanced Test. Finally, for additional reinforcement, go to the "Improve Your Grammar, Mechanics, and Usage" section that follows, and complete those exercises.

Improve Your Grammar, Mechanics, and Usage

The following exercises help you improve your knowledge of and power over English grammar, mechanics, and usage. Turn to the Handbook of Grammar, Mechanics, and Usage at the end of this textbook and review all of Sections 2.4 (Semicolons) and 2.5 (Colons). Then look at the following 10 items. Circle the letter of the preferred choice in the following groups of sentences. (Answers to these exercises appear on page AK-3.)

1. a. This letter looks good; that one doesn't.
   b. This letter looks good: that one doesn't.

2. a. I want to make one thing clear: none of you will be promoted without teamwork.
   b. I want to make one thing clear; none of you will be promoted without teamwork.
   c. I want to make one thing clear: none of you will be promoted; without teamwork.

3. a. The Zurich airport has been snowed in, therefore I can't attend the meeting.

   b. The Zurich airport has been snowed in, therefore, I can't attend the meeting.

   c. The Zurich airport has been snowed in; therefore, I can't attend the meeting.

4. a. His motivation was obvious: to get Meg fired.

   b. His motivation was obvious; to get Meg fired.

5. a. Only two firms have responded to our survey; J. J. Perkins and Tucker & Tucker.

   b. Only two firms have responded to our survey: J. J. Perkins and Tucker & Tucker.

6. a. Send a copy to: Nan Kent, CEO, Bob Bache, President, and Dan Brown, CFO.

   b. Send a copy to Nan Kent, CEO; Bob Bache, President; and Dan Brown, CFO.

   c. Send a copy to Nan Kent CEO; Bob Bache President; and Dan Brown CFO.

7. a. You shipped three items on June 7; however, we received only one of them.

   b. You shipped three items on June 7, however; we received only one of them.

   c. You shipped three items on June 7; however we received only one of them.

8. a. Workers wanted an immediate wage increase: they hadn't had a raise in 10 years.

   b. Workers wanted an immediate wage increase; because they hadn't had a raise in 10 years.

   c. Workers wanted an immediate wage increase; they hadn't had a raise in 10 years.

9. a. His writing skills are excellent however; he needs to polish his management style.

   b. His writing skills are excellent; however, he needs to polish his management style.

   c. His writing skills are excellent: however he needs to polish his management style.

10. a. We want to address three issues; efficiency; profitability; and market penetration.

   b. We want to address three issues; efficiency, profitability, and market penetration.

   c. We want to address three issues: efficiency, profitability, and market penetration.

For additional exercises focusing on semicolons and colons, go to **www.prenhall.com/thill**, then locate your text and click on its Companion Website link. Click on Chapter 9, click on "Additional Exercises to Improve Your Grammar, Mechanics and Usage," then click on "16. Punctuation A."

Cases

Applying the Three-Step Writing Process to Cases
Apply each step to the following cases, as assigned by your instructor

Planning

1

Analyze the Situation
Identify both your general purpose and your specific purpose. Clarify exactly what you want your audience to think, feel, or believe after receiving your message. Profile your primary audience, including their backgrounds, differences, similarities, and likely reactions to your message.

Gather Information
Identify the information your audience will need to receive, as well as other information you may need in order to craft an effective message.

Select the Right Medium
Make sure your medium is both acceptable to the audience and appropriate for the message.

Organize the Information
Choose a direct or indirect approach based on the audience and the message; most persuasive messages employ an indirect approach (often following the AIDA model). Identify your main idea, limit your scope, then outline necessary support points and other evidence.

Writing

2

Adapt to Your Audience
Show sensitivity to audience needs with a "you" attitude, politeness, positive emphasis, and bias-free language. Understand how much credibility you already have—and how much you may need to establish with any particular audience. Project your company's image by maintaining an appropriate style and tone.

Compose the Message
Draft your message using powerful words, effective sentences, and coherent paragraphs. Support your claims with objective evidence; balance emotional and logical arguments.

Completing

3

Revise the Message
Evaluate content and review readability, then edit and rewrite for conciseness and clarity.

Produce the Message
Use effective design elements and suitable layout for a clean, professional appearance.

Proofread the Message
Review for errors in layout, spelling, and mechanics.

Distribute the Message
Deliver your message using the chosen medium; make sure all documents and all relevant files are distributed successfully.

PERSUASIVE REQUESTS FOR ACTION

1. That's the point: E-mail encouraging your boss to blog You've been trying for months to convince your boss, Will Florence, to start blogging. You've told him that top executives in numerous industries now use blogging as a way to connect with customers and other stakeholders without going through the filters and barriers of formal corporate communications. He was just about convinced—until he read the blog by Bob Lutz, the co-chair and design chief of General Motors.

"Look at this!" he calls from his office. "Bob Lutz is one of the most respected executives in the world, and all these people are criticizing him on his own blog. Sure, a lot of the responses are positive, but quite a few are openly hostile, disagreeing with GM strategy, criticizing the products, criticizing the subjects he chooses for his blog—you name it. If blogging is all about opening yourself up to criticism from every bystander with a keyboard, no way am I going to start a blog."

Your task: Write Florence an e-mail (w_florence@sprenco.com) persuading him that the freewheeling nature of blog communication is its key advantage, not a disadvantage at all. While they may not always agree with what he has to say, automotive enthusiasts and car buyers respect Lutz for communicating in his own words—and for giving them the opportunity to respond. For background information, read some of the postings from Lutz and other GM executives at http://fastlane.gmblogs.com.[24]

2. Give a little to get a lot: Suggesting free wireless at Starbucks Like many students at the University of Wisconsin Madison, you like to escape from your cramped apartment to work on school projects at local coffee shops. With your wireless-equipped laptop, you hunt for places that offer free wireless so you can access course websites, do research, and occasionally see how Badger athletic teams are doing. But there's a problem: At the Starbucks right around the corner, you have to pay for wireless access through the service offered by T-Mobile. Several of the locally owned coffee houses offer free wireless, but the closest one is a mile from your apartment. That's a long walk in a Wisconsin winter.

Your task: Write a persuasive message to Starbucks suggesting that the company drop its agreement with T-Mobile and offer free wireless instead. Try to convince the firm that free wireless will attract enough additional coffee-buying customers to offset the loss of revenue from wireless—and help Starbucks overcome the "big corporation" image that prompts some coffee drinkers to patronize locally owned establishments instead. While you don't have the data to prove that the cost of offering free wireless would be more than offset by increased coffee sales, at least make a convincing argument that Starbucks should consider making the change. You'll post your message to the Starbucks website, www.starbucks.com, which has a limit of 2,600 characters for such messages.[25]

3. Time to think: E-mail requesting a change in your workload. The description of your job as a global marketing manager for New Balance is full of responsibilities that require creative thinking, from predicting consumer and retailing trends to establishing seasonal priorities for the global merchandising effort. You love these challenges—in fact, they're the main reason you took the job at this respected maker of athletic shoes and apparel. Unfortunately, between department meetings, status reports, budgets, and an endless array of other required chores, you hardly have time to think at all, much less engage in the sort of unstructured, "blue-sky" thinking that is crucial to creative strategizing. You have virtually no time at work for such thinking, and after 50 or 60 hours a week at the office or on the road, you're too exhausted to brainstorm on your own time.

Your task: Write an e-mail to your boss, Paul Heffernan, the executive vice president of global marketing, persuading him that you need to reshuffle your assignments to free up more time to think. This is a tricky request because you know that Heffernan faces the same challenge. However, you're convinced that by spending less time on tasks that could be done by someone else (or perhaps shouldn't be done at all), you'll be able to do a better job of creating marketing strategies—and maybe even set a good example for other New Balance executives. You have a preliminary list of changes you'd like to make, but you know you need to discuss the entire scope of your job with Heffernan before finalizing the list. Your purpose: Invite him to lunch to begin a discussion of reshaping your responsibilities.[26]

4. Always urgent: Memo pleading case for hosting a Red Cross blood drive This morning as you drove to your job as food services manager at the Pechanga Casino Entertainment Center in Temecula, California, you were concerned to hear on the radio that the local Red Cross chapter put out a call for blood because national supplies have fallen dangerously low. During highly publicized disasters, people are emotional and eager to help out by donating blood. But in calmer times, only 5 percent of eligible donors think of giving blood. You're one of those few.

Not many people realize that donated blood lasts for only 72 hours. Consequently, the mainstay of emergency blood supplies must be replenished in an ongoing effort. No one is more skilled, dedicated, or efficient in handling blood than the

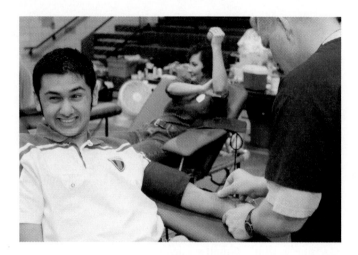

American Red Cross, which is responsible for half the nation's supply of blood and blood products.

Donated blood helps victims of accidents and disease, as well as surgery patients. Just yesterday you were reading about a girl named Melissa, who was diagnosed with multiple congenital heart defects and underwent her first open-heart surgery at one week old. Now 5, she's used well over 50 units of donated blood, and she wouldn't be alive without them. In a thank-you letter, her mother lauded the many strangers who had "given a piece of themselves" to save her precious daughter—and countless others. You also learned that a donor's pint of blood can benefit up to four other people.

Today, you're going to do more than just roll up your own sleeve. You know the local Red Cross chapter takes its Blood Mobile to corporations, restaurants, beauty salons—anyplace willing to host public blood drives. What if you could convince the board of directors to support a blood drive at the casino? The slot machines and gaming tables are usually full, hundreds of employees are on hand, and people who've never visited before might come down to donate blood. The positive publicity certainly couldn't hurt Pechanga's community image. With materials from the Red Cross, you're confident you can organize Pechanga's hosting effort and handle the promotion. (Last year you headed the casino's successful Toys for Tots drive.)

To give blood, one must be healthy, be at least 17 years old (with no upper age limit), and weigh at least 110 pounds. Donors can give every 56 days. You'll be urging Pechanga donors to eat well, drink water, and be rested before the Blood Mobile arrives.

The local Red Cross chapter's mission statement says, in part, that the Red Cross is "a humanitarian organization led by volunteers and guided by the Fundamental Principles of the International Red Cross Movement" which will "prevent and alleviate human suffering wherever it may be found." All assistance is given free of charge, made possible by "contributions of people's time, money, and skills." And in the case of you and your co-workers, a piece of yourselves.

Your task: Write a memo persuading the Pechanga board of directors to host a public Red Cross blood drive. You can learn more about what's involved in hosting a blood drive at www.givelife. org (click on "Sponsor a Drive"). Ask the board to provide bottled water, orange juice, and snacks for donors. You'll organize food service workers to handle the distribution, but you'll need the board's approval to let your team volunteer during work hours. Use a combination of logical and emotional appeals.[27]

5. Give me liberty: Letter persuading customers to remain loyal to Colbar Art For many people in the United States, the Statue of Liberty is a cliché, so much a part of New York City's tourist hype that it's taken for granted. But for most immigrants, the first sight of Liberty as they enter the city brings tears along with hopes for a new life. Ovidiu Colea knows the feeling. He immigrated to the United States in the early 1980s after a difficult past that included five long years in a Romanian hard-labor camp for trying to flee the communist regime.

Colea worked two years as a cab driver to save enough money to start Colbar Art, a company based in Long Island City, New York, that produces up to 80,000 hand-crafted replicas of the Liberty statue each year. He now helps other immigrants get a start in their new country by hiring them to design and produce Liberty models. Colea pays a royalty to the Liberty–Ellis Island Foundation for using Liberty's image. In fact, during the first year of operation, that royalty amounted to $250,000.

Painstaking labor produces the acrylic and bonded marble statues with a hand-painted patina, and most of that work is done by the very immigrants lady Liberty welcomes to New York. Colea insists on keeping production in the United States. Although labor costs are cheaper elsewhere in the world, he refuses to produce the statues in countries "where there is no liberty or no Statue of Liberty." By keeping jobs in the United States, he's doing his share to keep the American Dream alive.

But the meticulous labor also costs precious production time. With recent high demand for the replicas, the company has fallen behind on orders. To increase production to 120,000 statues per year, the company is leasing more space and training new employees. Meanwhile, the production deficits may continue for several months.

Your task: You work for Colbar Art as assistant manager, and Colea has asked you to write a persuasive form letter to all your customers, explaining the current delays and requesting patience. Be sure to explain the steps the company is taking to solve these delays, and describe the quality and creativity that go into the replicas. You can quote Bradford Hill (owner of the Liberty Island gift shop), who says Colbar Art's models represent 65 percent of his sales. Make a convincing argument for your customers to remain loyal to Colbar Art.[28]

6. No more driving: Memo about telecommuting to Bachman, Trinity, and Smith Sitting in your Dallas office at the accounting firm of Bachman, Trinity, and Smith, clacking away on your computer, it seems as though you could be doing this work from your home. You haven't spoken to any co-workers in more than two hours. As long as you complete your work on time, does your location matter?

As an entry-level accountant, you've participated in on-location audits at major companies for nearly a year now. If your bosses trust you to work while staying at a hotel, why not let you work from home, where you already have an office with computer, phone, and fax machine? You'd love to regain those two hours you lose commuting to and from work every day.

Your task: To support this idea, visit the website of the International Telework Association and Council website at www.telecommute.org (be sure to check out the "Resources" page). You'll find statistics and other support for a memo persuading your boss, senior partner Marjorie Bachman, to grant you a six-month trial as a telecommuter.[29]

7. Helping out: Memo to Whole Foods Market managers Whole Foods Market has grown into a nationwide chain by catering to consumer desires for healthier foods and environmentally sensitive household products. For instance, meats come from animals that were never fed antibiotics, and the cheese is from cows said to be raised on small farms and treated humanely.

Along with selling these products, the company makes a commitment "to the neighborhood and larger community that we serve and in which we live." Whole Foods not only donates 5 percent of after-tax profits to not-for-profit organizations but also financially supports employees who volunteer their time for community service projects. Many Whole Foods stores donate goods and supplies to soup kitchens in their local communities. Company executives want to encourage this type of activity, which reflects the "Whole Foods, Whole People, Whole Planet" corporate motto.

You are the manager of the Whole Foods Market on Ponce de Leon Avenue in Atlanta, Georgia. You've been very successful with a program you developed for donating surplus food to local food banks. You've been asked by top executives to help other Whole Foods stores coordinate this effort into a chain-wide food donation program, "Whole Foods for Life." Ideally, by streamlining the process chain-wide, the company would be able to increase the number of people it helps and to get more of its employees involved.

You don't have a great deal of extra money for the program, so the emphasis has to be on using resources already available to the stores. One idea is to use trucks from suburban stores to make the program "mobile." Another idea is to join forces with a retailing chain to give food and clothing to individuals. You've decided that the key will be to solicit input from the other stores so that they'll feel more involved in the final outcome as the larger food-donation program takes shape.

Your task: Send persuasive memos to all managers at Whole Foods Market, explaining the new program and requesting that they help by pooling ideas they've gleaned from their local experience. Even if they don't have food-donation programs currently in place, you want to hear ideas from them and their employees for this charitable project. With their help, you'll choose the best ideas to develop the new "Whole Foods For Life" program.[30]

PERSUASIVE CLAIMS AND REQUESTS FOR ADJUSTMENT

8. Too good to be true: E-mail to Paging South requesting adjustment Paging South offered its pager services for a mere $5

a month. You purchased an inexpensive pager and signed a contract for two years. After you thought your pager phone number was up and running for two weeks, you heard from co-workers and clients that they repeatedly get a busy signal when dialing your pager number. You call Paging South, and they resolve the problem—but doing so takes an additional week. You don't want to be charged for the time the pager wasn't in service. After discussing the situation with the local manager, she asks you to contact Judy Hinkley at the company's regional business office.

Your task: Send an e-mail message to Hinkley at Judy@ pagingsouth.com and request an adjustment to your account. Request credit or partial credit for one month of service. Remember to write a summary of events in chronological order, supplying exact dates for maximum effectiveness.

9. Lock legends: Letter requesting refund and damages from Brookstone As a professional photographer, you travel the world for business, leaving from your home base in Williamstown, Massachusetts. Last month it was a trip to Australia, and you thought you'd finally found a way around the "no-locks-on-checked baggage" rules.

After the World Trade Center attacks of September 11, 2001, the United States' Travel Security Administration (TSA) forbid airline passengers to check locked luggage. TSA inspectors want easy access so that they can open and check bags for security purposes. But since you carry so much expensive equipment, including numerous camera bags, you've been nervous about the safety of your belongings—not to mention the loss of privacy.

So you were relieved when you read Joe Sharkey's "On the Road" column in the *New York Times* just before your trip. The columnist extolled a newly announced TSA program allowing airline travelers to lock their luggage *if they use special TSA-approved locks,* certified by a company called Travel Sentry. You immediately went to the Brookstone store in Albany after reading its web advertisement for "The luggage locks security won't cut off. Our Easycheck™ locks are certified by Travel Sentry™ and feature a secure system accepted and recognized by the Transportation Security Administration (TSA). Airport security personnel can now inspect and re-lock your bags quickly and easily." You bought eight locks, at $20 for each set of two.

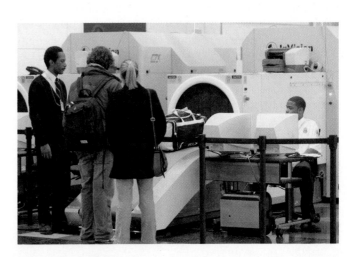

When you left the Albany airport, TSA inspectors assured you that they had a master key for these locks, just as Sharkey's column had promised they would. But when you got to Melbourne after changing planes in Chicago and Los Angeles, you were stunned to discover the condition of your luggage. One bag was missing the new lock entirely; another was missing the lock and had a rip all along the seam—perhaps from an irritated inspector? Inside a third bag you found its broken Easycheck lock, with a terse TSA inspection notice reminding you that locked baggage is not allowed. On the return trip you tried again, using three of your remaining locks on camera bags. They arrived with no locks and no inspection notices.

You've now called the airports in Chicago and Cleveland, where TSA inspectors told you they'd "never heard of the program." Brookstone will replace the broken lock, but the woman on the phone wasn't sure about the ones that went missing entirely, since you have nothing left to bring into the store except your receipt.

Your task: After 10 minutes listening to music while on hold for the TSA, you've abandoned the idea of a phone complaint to the government agency. You're going to write a letter to Brookstone (120 Washington Ave., Albany, NY 12203) requesting damages for the ripped luggage (a 24-inch Expandable Ballistic Suitor, $320) and a refund for all eight locks ($80). Six of them were ruined or missing and your last two are essentially useless.[31]

10. Tangled Web: E-mail to PurelySoftware regarding an online order duplication Last week you ordered new design software for your boss, Martin Soderburgh, at ArtAlive, the small art consulting business where you work. As he requested, you used his Visa card to order Adobe InDesign and Adobe Photoshop from an Internet vendor, Purely Software.com.

When you didn't receive the usual e-mail order confirmation, you called the company's toll-free number. The operator said the company's website was having problems, and he took a second order over the phone: $649.00 for Adobe InDesign, $564.00 for Adobe Photoshop, including tax and shipping. Four days later, ArtAlive received two shipments of the software, and your boss's credit card was charged $1,213.00 twice, for a total of $2,426.00.

Your task: Technically, you authorized both orders. But you understood during the phone call that the first order was cancelled, although you have no written proof. Send a persuasive e-mail to customerservice@purelysoftware.com, requesting (1) an immediate credit to your boss's Visa account and (2) a postage-paid return label for the duplicate order.[32]

MARKETING AND SALES MESSAGES

11. Selling without selling: Blog posting about a GPS rescue Promoting products through customer success stories can be a great marketing tactic, as long as you keep the customer as the "star" of the story and don't promote the product too blatantly. You've recently joined Garmin, a leading manufacturing of electronic navigation equipment, including a popular line of handheld Global Positioning System (GPS) devices used by hikers, kayakers, and others who venture off the beaten path.

Your task: As a communication specialist, your responsibilities include writing blog postings that highlight dramatic stories in which people used Garmin GPS units to rescue themselves or others from potentially dangerous situations. Visit Garmin's website at www.garmin.com, click on What's New, then GPS Adventures (or access the page directly at www.garmin.com/whatsNew/adventures.html). Select a customer story that involves a wilderness rescue in which a Garmin product played an important role. Using the information provided by the customer, rewrite the story in the third person (changing "I" or "we" references to "he," "she," or "they") for an audience that isn't familiar with the product in question. Subtly work in references to the product and the benefits it provided in this scenario, but keep the focus on the customer. Limit yourself to 400 words.

12. Listen up: Podcast promoting a podcast station Podcasting, the technique of recording individual sound files that people download from the Internet to listen to on their computers or music players, is quickly redefining the concept of radio. A growing crowd of musicians, essayists, journalists, and others with compelling content use podcasting to reach audiences they can't get to through traditional broadcast radio. The good news is that anyone with a microphone and a computer can record podcasts. That's also the bad news, at least from your perspective as a new podcaster: With so many podcasters now on the Internet, potential listeners have thousands and thousands of audio files to select from.

Your new podcast, School2Biz, offers advice to business students making the transition from college to career. You provide info on everything from preparing résumés to interviewing to finding one's place in the business world and building a successful career. As you expand your audience, you'd eventually like to turn School2Biz into a profitable operation (perhaps by selling advertising time during your podcasts). For now, you're simply offering free advice.

Your task: You've chosen The Podcast Bunker (www.podcastbunker.com) as the first website on which to promote School2Biz. The site also lets podcasters promote their feeds with brief text listings, such as this description of Pet Talk Radio: "A weekly lifestyle show for people with more than a passing interest in pets. Hosted by Brian Pickering & Kaye Browne with Australia's favourite vet Dr. Harry Cooper & animal trainer Steve Austin."

Write a 50-word description of your new podcast, making up any information you need to describe School2Biz. Be sure to mention who you are and why the information you present is worth listening to.[33]

13. Your new Kentucky home: Letter promoting the Bluegrass State Like all states, Kentucky works hard to attract businesses that are considering expanding into the state or relocating entirely from another state. The Kentucky Cabinet for Economic Development is responsible for reaching out to these companies and overseeing the many incentive programs the state offers to both new and established businesses.

Your task: As the communication director of the Kentucky Cabinet for Economic Development, you play the lead role in reaching out to companies that want to expand or relocate to Kentucky. Visit www.thinkkentucky.com/kyedc/topten.asp and read the Top 10 reasons the state says make it a great place to do business (if that link doesn't take you to the list, go to www.thinkkentucky.com and click on the Top 10 link). Summarize these 10 reasons in a form letter that will be sent to business executives throughout the country. Be sure to introduce yourself and your purpose in the letter, and close with a compelling call to action (have them reach you by telephone at 800–626–2930 or by e-mail at econdev@ky.gov). As you plan your letter, try to imagine yourself as the CEO of a company and consider what a complex choice it would be to move to another state.

14. Don't forget print: Using the web to promote Time Inc.'s magazine advertising After a shaky start as the technology matured and advertisers tried to figure out this new medium, online advertising has finally become a significant force in both consumer and business marketing. Companies in a wide variety of industries are shifting some of the ad budgets from traditional media such as TV and magazines to the increasing selection of advertising possibilities online—and more than a few companies now advertise almost exclusively online. That's fine for companies that sell advertising time and space online, but your job involves selling advertising in those print magazines that are worried about losing market share to online publishers.

Online advertising has two major advantages that you can't really compete with: interactivity and the ability to precisely target individual audience members. On the other hand, you have several advantages going for you, including the ability to produce high-color photography, the physical presence of print (such as when a magazine sits on a table in a doctor's waiting room), portability, guaranteed circulation numbers, and close reader relationships that go back years or decades in many cases.

Your task: You work as an advertising sales specialist for the Time Inc., division of Time Warner, which publishes more than 150 magazines around the world. Write a brief persuasive message about the benefits of magazine advertising; the statement will be posted on the individual websites of Time Inc.'s

numerous magazines, so you can't narrow in on any single publication. Also, Time Inc. coordinates its print publications with an extensive online presence (including thousands of paid online ads), so you can't bash online advertising, either.[34]

15. Hi, my name is: Introducing yourself on a business network Business networking websites such as www.linkedin. com, www.ryze.com, and www.spoke.com have become popular ways for professionals to make connections that would be difficult or impossible to make without the Internet. You might be familiar with Orkut.com or Friendster.com, which help individuals meet through networks of people they already know and trust. These business-oriented sites follow the same principle, but instead of using them to find new friends or dates, you use them to find new customers, new suppliers, or other important business connections. For instance, you might find that the ideal contact person in a company you'd like to do business with is the aunt of your boss's tennis partner.

An important aspect of business networking is being able to provide a clear description of your professional background and interests. For example, a manufacturing consultant can list the industries in which she has experience, the types of projects she has worked on, and the nature of work she'd like to pursue in the future (such as a full-time position for a company or additional independent projects).

Your task: Write a brief statement introducing yourself, including your educational background, your job history, and the types of connections you'd like to make. Feel free to "fast forward" to your graduation and list your degree, the business specialty you plan to pursue, and any relevant experience. If you have business experience already, feel free to use that information instead. Make sure your statement is clear, concise (no more than two sentences), and compelling, so that anyone looking for someone like you would want to get in touch with you after reading your introduction.

16. Insure.com: E-mail promoting a better way to buy insurance The great thing about Insure.com is that no one is obligated to buy a thing, which makes your job in the company's marketing department easier. Free of charge, consumers can log on to your website, ask for dozens of insurance quotes, then go off and buy elsewhere. They can look at instant price-comparison quotes from more than 200 insurers, covering every kind of insurance from term life and medical, to private passenger auto insurance. All rates are guaranteed up-to-the-day accurate, against a $500 reward. And so far the online service has received positive press from *Nation's Business, Kiplinger's Personal Finance, Good Housekeeping, The Los Angeles Times, Money, U.S. News & World Report,* and *Forbes.*

Insure.com generates revenues primarily from the receipt of commissions and fees paid by insurers based on the volume of business produced. Customers can purchase insurance from the company of their choice via the Insure.com website or they can call a toll-free number to speak to one of the company's representatives. The reps are paid salaries versus commissions, and do not directly benefit by promoting one insurance company's product over another.

And all of this is free. Too bad more people don't know about your services.

Your task: It's your job to lure more insurance customers to Insure.com. You've decided to use direct e-mail marketing (using a list of consumers who have inquired about rates in the past but never committed to purchase anything). Write an e-mail sales message promoting the benefits of Insure.com's services. Be sure your message is suited to an e-mail format, with an appropriate subject heading.[35]

17. Outsourcing: Letter from Kelly Services offering solutions In 1946, with his dynamic vision and pioneering spirit, William Russell Kelly started a new company to meet the office and clerical needs of Detroit-area businesses. Kelly temporary employees with skills in calculating, inventory, typing and copying were soon in great demand. During the 1960s, the Kelly Girl became a nationwide icon, synonymous with high-quality temporary employees. The company changed its name to Kelly Services, Inc. in 1966, reflecting the increasing diversity of its services, customers, and employees.

Today, Kelly Services is a global Fortune 500 company that offers staffing solutions that include temporary services, staff leasing, outsourcing, vendor on-site and full-time placement. Kelly provides employees who have a wide range of skills across many disciplines including office services, accounting, engineering, information technology, law, science, marketing, light industrial, education, health care, and home care.

Workforce needs, in terms of quantity and skills mix, fluctuate greatly. At the same time, employees have adaptable skills, and are far more mobile. The result is that more employers and employees alike want flexible staffing arrangements, and temporary staffing is often the best solution.

Companies use Kelly Services to strategically balance workload and workforce during peaks and valleys of demand, to handle special projects, and to evaluate employees prior to making a full-time hiring decision. This dramatic change in business has spurred the rapid growth of the contingent employment industry.

In turn, many individuals are choosing the flexibility of personal career management, increasing options of where, when, and how to work. It is now the desire of many employees to fit their work into their lifestyle, rather than fitting their lifestyle into their work. Therefore, more and more workers are becoming receptive to being a contract, temporary, or consulting employee.

This flexibility offers advantages to both the company and the employee. Both have the opportunity to evaluate one another prior to making a long-term commitment. Kelly Services earns a fee when its employees are hired permanently, but employers find that it's a small price to pay for such valuable preview time, which saves everyone the cost and pain of a bad hiring decision.

Kelly has received many supplier awards for providing outstanding and cost-efficient staffing services, including DaimlerChrysler's Gold Award, Ford Motor Company's Q1 Preferred Quality Award, Intel Corporation's Supplier Continuous Quality Improvement (SCQI) Award, and DuPont Legal's Challenge Award.

A job as a marketing manager with Kelly holds challenge and promise. With 2,500 offices in 26 countries, Kelly provides

its customers nearly 700,000 employees annually, generating revenue of $4.3 billion in 2003. The company provides staffing solutions to more than 90 percent of the Fortune 500 companies.

As companies increasingly face new competitive pressures to provide better service and quality at lower prices, many are turning to outsourcing suppliers to deliver complete operational management of specific functions or support departments, allowing the company the necessary time to focus on its core competencies. One solution is to choose a single supplier such as the Kelly Management Services (KMS) division to deliver "full service" outsourcing.

KMS combines management experience, people process improvements, technology enhancements, and industry expertise to optimize customer operations and reduce cost. KMS understands the unique challenges companies are facing in today's increasingly fast-paced business world and can provide customers with services across multiple functional offerings including Call Center Operations, Warehousing, Distribution and Light Assembly, Back Office and Administrative functions, and Mail and Reprographic services. The result is a department staffed by employees that can fluctuate as a company's needs change.

KMS customers who have implemented one service often add others when they see KMS-managed employees performing at high levels and producing substantial cost savings and operational efficiencies. By partnering with an outsourcing supplier such as KMS, companies will experience a greater value and cost savings than with in-house operations.

Your task: Write a sales letter to companies similar to DaimlerChrysler, Ford, Intel, and DuPont explaining what Kelly has to offer. For current information, visit the Kelly website at www.kellyservices.com.[36]

18. Greener Cleaners: Letter promoting environmentally sound Hangers franchise When you told everyone you aspired to work for an environmentally responsible business, you didn't imagine you'd end up in the dry-cleaning business. But now that you are Director of Franchise Development for Hangers Cleaners, you go home every night with a "clean conscience" (your favorite new pun).

Micell Technologies first invented the revolutionary clean technology used by Hangers Cleaners, and then in 2001, sold all licensing, all intellectual property, and all interest in Hangers Cleaners to Cool Clean Technologies, which now manufactures the "CO2OL Clean" dry-cleaning machine that your franchise relies on. This breakthrough in dry-cleaning technology is the first in nearly 50 years—made by Micell co-founders Joseph DeSimone, James McClain, and Timothy Romack. Their new cleaning process uses liquid carbon dioxide (CO_2) and specially developed detergents to clean clothes. The process requires no heat and no further need for the toxic perchloroethylene (perc) or petroleum traditionally used in dry cleaning.

Hangers franchise owners don't have to deal with regulatory paperwork, zoning restrictions, or expensive insurance and taxes for hazardous waste disposal. And unlike petroleum-based solvents, the CO_2 used in the "CO2OL Clean" machine is noncombustible. It's the same substance that carbonates beverages, and it's captured from the waste stream of industries that produce it as a byproduct. Moreover, 98 percent of the CO_2 used in a Hangers outlet is recycled and used again, which helps keep prices competitive. The "CO2OL Clean" machine received accolades from the Environmental Protection Agency and was recently rated the best dry-cleaning alternative by a leading consumer products testing group.

You've already sold franchises in 60 locations, from Wilmington, North Carolina, to San Diego, California. Customers love the fact that their clothes don't carry toxic fumes after cleaning, and employees are happy to be working in a safe and cool environment. The process is actually gentler on clothes (no strong solvents or heat), reducing fading and shrinking and helping them last longer. You aren't dry cleaners; you are "garment care specialists."

And beyond the environmental boons, you simply love the design of Hangers stores. When Micell originally established the chain, it hired dry-cleaning experts and architects alike to come up with a sleek, modern, high-end retail "look" that features a cool, clean, light-filled interior and distinctive signage out front. It's more akin to a Starbucks than the overheated, toxic-smelling storefront most customers associate with dry cleaning. This high-end look is making it easier to establish Hangers as a national brand, attracting investors and franchisees rapidly as word spreads about the new "greener cleaner."

Your task: Develop a sales letter that can be mailed in response to preliminary inquiries from potential franchise owners. You'll include brochures covering franchise agreements and "CO2OL Clean" specifics, so focus on introducing and promoting the unique benefits of Hangers Cleaners. Your contact information is Hangers Cleaners, 3505 County Road 42 West, Burnsville, MN 55306–3803; phone 952–882–5000; toll-free 866–262–9274, or www.hangersdrycleaners.com.[37]

19. Instant promotion: Text message from Hilton Hotels to frequent guests Hilton Hotels now uses an SMS (short messaging service) to send instant text promotions to customers who've signed up as "HHonors" members. But you work in marketing, and that means you're often struggling to condense elaborate travel packages into 65 enticing words (system maximum).

For example, today's promotion offers "A Golfer's Dream Come True: 'I just played a round of golf by the pyramids!' " For $575 per person per day (double room), valid through January 15, 2005, travelers can stay in the Hilton Pyramids Golf Resort in Cairo, Egypt, for 7 nights/8 days, including breakfast, service charge, and tax. They'll be met at the airport, given transportation to the resort, plus two rounds of golf per person at Dreamland Golf course and two rounds of golf per person at Soleimaneia Pyramids Golf & Country Club course. That's 88 words so far.

But you also need to convey that the Dreamland course wraps like a serpent around the Hilton resort. Its lush greens and lakes, designed by Karl Litten, contrast sharply with the golden desert, culminating in a stunning view of the great Pyramids of Giza, one of the seven wonders of the world. The Soleimaneia course features the "biggest floodlit driving course in Egypt." The travel package provides free transportation to this nearby course.

Rates, of course, are subject to availability and other restrictions may apply. But interested travelers should mention code G7 Pyramids Golf Special when they call Hilton Reservations Worldwide. They can also e-mail RM_PYRAMIDS_GOLF @hilton.com, or call the Cairo hotel directly at 20 2 8402402. That is, if you can entice them in 65 words.

Your task: Write the persuasive instant message.[38]

20. Helping children: Instant message holiday fund drive at IBM At IBM, you're one of the coordinators for the annual Employee Charitable Contributions Campaign. Since 1978, the company has helped employees contribute to more than 2,000 health and human service agencies. These groups may offer child care, treat substance abuse, provide health services, or fight illiteracy, homelessness, and hunger. Some offer disaster relief or care for the elderly. All deserve support. They're carefully screened by IBM, one of the largest corporate contributors of cash, equipment, and people to nonprofit organizations and educational institutions, both in the United States and around the world. As your literature states, the program "has engaged our employees more fully in the important mission of corporate citizenship."

During the winter holidays, you target agencies that cater to the needs of displaced families, women, and children. It's not difficult to raise enthusiasm. The prospect of helping children enjoy the holidays—children who otherwise might have nothing—usually awakens the spirit of your most distracted workers. But some of them wait until the last minute and then forget.

They have until Friday, December 16, to come forth with cash contributions. To make it in time for holiday deliveries, they can also bring in toys, food, and blankets through Tuesday, December 20. They shouldn't have any trouble finding the collection bins; they're everywhere, marked with bright red banners. But some will want to call you with questions or (hopefully) to make credit card contributions: 800–658–3899, ext. 3342.

Your task: It's December 14. Write a 75- to 100-word instant message encouraging last-minute gifts.[39]

Part IV

Preparing Reports
and Oral Presentations

Chapter 10

Planning Reports and Proposals

Learning Objectives

AFTER STUDYING THIS CHAPTER, YOU WILL BE ABLE TO

1 Adapt the three-step writing process to reports and proposals

2 Distinguish informational reports, analytical reports, and proposals

3 Describe an effective process for conducting business research

4 Define primary and secondary research and explain when you use each method

5 Name nine criteria for evaluating the credibility of an information source

6 Provide five guidelines for conducting an effective online search

7 Outline an effective process for planning and conducting information interviews

8 Explain the differences between drafting a summary, drawing a conclusion, and developing a recommendation

9 Discuss three major ways to organize analytical reports

On the Job

COMMUNICATING AT TOYOTA SCION

NEW THINKING FOR A NEW GENERATION OF CAR BUYERS

If you're in your early twenties and in the market for your first new car, are you likely to rush out and buy the same car your parents drive? You know—that sensible, conventional car such as the Toyota they drive to the grocery store and to your little sister's soccer practice?

Toyota's Brian Bolain knows you probably won't, and he knows this because the company has already tried selling these cars to your generation with conventional advertising messages. Over the past few decades, Toyota grew to a position of prominence in the United States by offering your parents refreshing alternatives to the cars that *their* parents drove.

To continue that cycle of success with your generation, Bolain and his colleagues faced the challenge of crafting unconventional products and messages that appeal to today's young adults. Their solution started with research, research, and more research. And that research took an unconventional approach—for example, hiring 50 young Californians to record video diaries with their friends. The company even went so far as to learn how core groups of trendsetters discover new ideas and products before helping to spread them through the larger population. The research yielded a wide range of insights, including the emergence of Japan as a new center of cool and the realization not only that young adults strongly resist being sold to but also that they put a high priority on individualism, self-expression, and authenticity.

The research results helped Toyota create a new line of cars called Scion, the most unconventional of

Every detail in the launch of Toyota's new Scion brand, from the shape of the cars to the style of promotional communication, was based on extensive consumer research and was shared internally through a variety of business reports.

which is the aggressively boxy xB model. Research discoveries also shaped virtually every aspect of Toyota's communication efforts: The company downplays the "Toyota" name and shuns traditional mass-market advertising. Instead it favors small-scale, neighborhood-centered promotions that allow trendsetters to "discover" the Scion product line and share their discovery with other young adults. One such promotion is to put posters near popular hangouts, bearing phrases such as "Ban Normality" and "No Clone Zone." As part of the quest to reach younger buyers, Toyota even started a music label, Scion A/V, to help promote such groups as the DaKAH hip-hop orchestra from Los Angeles and to work with a variety of DJs in cities around the country whose Scion-sponsored concerts in turn present Scion as a cutting-edge brand for a new generation.

Within the Toyota organization, another layer of communication takes place that is invisible to customers but just as crucial to Scion's success. Virtually everything from the idea of a new car brand to the details of accessories, pricing, and dealership plans is communicated via reports. Some of these documents convey information, some provide analysis, and some try to shape the course of Scion's future through persuasive proposals. No matter what the communication challenge, though, Toyota's commitment to understanding its audiences and adapting compelling messages for them—and the success that results from these efforts—offers a clear lesson for all business communicators.[1]

www.scion.com

APPLYING THE THREE-STEP WRITING PROCESS TO REPORTS AND PROPOSALS

Reports can be classified as informational reports, analytical reports, and proposals.

Reports play a significant role in Brian Bolain's success, as they do in the careers of all business professionals. Reports fall into three basic categories:

- **Informational reports** offer data, facts, feedback, and other types of information, without analysis or recommendations.

- **Analytical reports** offer both information and analysis, and they can also include recommendations.

- **Proposals** offer structured persuasion for internal or external audiences.

The purpose and content of business reports varies widely; in some cases you'll follow a strict guideline, but in others the organization and format will be up to you.

The nature of these reports varies widely, from one-page trip reports that follow a standard format to detailed business plans and proposals that can run hundreds of pages. No matter what the circumstances, try to view every business report as an opportunity to demonstrate your understanding of your audience's challenges and your ability to contribute to your organization's success.

The three-step process you studied in Chapters 4 though 6 and applied to short messages in Chapters 7 through 9 is easy to adapt to longer message formats (see Figure 10–1). This chapter addresses the planning step, focusing on two major areas that require special attention in long documents: gathering and organizing information. Chapter 11 covers the writing step and also includes advice on creating effective visuals for your reports and proposals. Chapter 12 wraps up longer documents with the tasks involved in completing reports and proposals.

FIGURE 10–1
Three–Step Writing Process for Reports and Proposals

Planning

Analyze the Situation
Clarify the problem or opportunity at hand, define your purpose, develop an audience profile, and develop a work plan.

Gather Information
Determine audience needs and obtain the information necessary to satisfy those needs; conduct a research project if necessary.

Select the Right Medium
Choose the best medium for delivering your message; consider delivery through multiple media.

Organize the Information
Define your main idea, limit your scope, select a direct or an indirect approach, and outline your content using an appropriate structure for an informational report, analytical report, or proposal.

Writing

Adapt to Your Audience
Be sensitive to audience needs with a "you" attitude, politeness, positive emphasis, and bias-free language. Build a strong relationship with your audience by establishing your credibility and projecting your company's image. Control your style with a tone and voice appropriate to the situation.

Compose the Message
Choose strong words that will help you create effective sentences and coherent paragraphs throughout the introduction, body, and close of your report or proposal.

Completing

Revise the Report
Evaluate content and review readability; edit and rewrite for conciseness and clarity.

Produce the Report
Use effective design elements and suitable layout for a clean, professional appearance; seamlessly combine textual and graphical elements.

Proofread the Report
Review for errors in layout, spelling, and mechanics.

Distribute the Report
Deliver your report using the chosen medium; make sure all documents and all relevant files are distributed successfully.

PROBLEM STATEMENTS VERSUS PURPOSE STATEMENTS — Table 10–1

Problem Statement	Statement of Purpose
Our company's market share is steadily declining.	To explore new ways of promoting and selling our products and to recommend the approaches most likely to stabilize our market share.
Our current computer network lacks sufficient bandwidth and cannot be upgraded to meet our future needs.	To analyze various networking options and to recommend the system that will best meet our company's current and future needs.
We need $2 million to launch our new product.	To convince investors that our new business would be a sound investment so that we can obtain desired financing.
Our current operations are too decentralized and expensive.	To justify the closing of the Newark plant and the transfer of East Coast operations to a single Midwest location in order to save the company money.

Analyzing the Situation

The complexity of many reports and the amount of work involved put a premium on carefully analyzing the situation before you begin to write. Pay special attention to your **statement of purpose**, which explains *why* you are preparing the report and what you plan to deliver in the report (see Table 10–1).

> Given the length and complexity of many reports, it's crucial to define your purpose clearly so you don't waste time with unnecessary rework.

The most useful way to phrase your purpose statement is to begin with an infinitive phrase (*to* plus a verb), which helps pin down your general goal (*to inform, to identify, to analyze,* and so on). For instance, in an informational report, your statement of purpose can be as simple as one of these:

To identify potential markets for our new phone-based videogames

To update the board of directors on the progress of the research project

To submit required information to the Securities and Exchange Commission

Your statement of purpose for an analytical report often needs to be more comprehensive. When Linda Moreno, the cost accounting manager for Electrovision, a high-tech company based in Los Gatos, California, was asked to find ways of reducing employee travel and entertainment costs, she phrased her statement of purpose accordingly:

> Longer reports may have several related purposes.

. . . to analyze the T&E [travel and entertainment] budget, evaluate the impact of recent changes in airfares and hotel costs, and suggest ways to tighten management's control over T&E expenses.

Because Moreno was assigned an analytical report rather than an informational report, she had to go beyond merely collecting data; she had to draw conclusions and make recommendations. You'll see her complete report in Chapter 12.

Proposals must also be guided by a clear statement of purpose to help you focus on crafting a persuasive message. Here are several examples of purpose statements for internal and external proposals:

To secure funding in next year's budget for new conveyor systems in the warehouse

To get management approval to reorganize the North American salesforce

To secure $2 million from outside investors to start production of the new titanium mountain bike

Remember, the more specific your purpose statement, the more useful it will be as a guide to planning your report. Furthermore, if you've been assigned the report by someone else, always double-check your statement of purpose with that person to make sure you've interpreted the assignment correctly.

In addition to considering your purpose carefully, you will also want to prepare a *work plan* for most reports and proposals in order to make the best use of your time. For simpler reports, the work plan can be an informal list of tasks and a simple schedule. However, if you're preparing a lengthy report, particularly when you're collaborating with others, you'll want to develop a more detailed work plan. Such a plan might include the following elements:

- Statement of the problem or opportunity (for analytical reports and proposals)
- Statement of the purpose and scope of your investigation
- Discussion of the tasks that need to be accomplished in order to complete the report
- Review of project assignments, schedules, and resource requirements
- Plans for following up after delivering the report

Some work plans also include a tentative outline, if the author has had the opportunity to think through the organization of the report. The work plan in Figure 10–2, which was developed for a report assessing whether to launch a company newsletter, includes such an outline.

A detailed work plan saves time and often produces more effective reports.

Gathering Information

Some reports require formal research projects in order to gather all the necessary information.

The sheer volume of information needed for many reports and proposals requires careful planning—and may even require a separate research project just to acquire the data and information you need. To stay on schedule and on budget, be sure that you review both your statement of purpose and your audience's needs so that you collect all the information you need—and only the information you need. In some cases, you won't be able to collect every piece of information you'd like, so prioritize your needs up front and focus on the most important questions.

Selecting the Right Medium

The best medium for any given report might be anything from a professionally printed and bound document to an online executive dashboard that displays nothing but report highlights.

Just as you would for other business messages, select the medium for your report based on the needs of your audience and the practical advantages and disadvantages of the choices available to you. In addition to the general media selection criteria discussed in Chapter 4, consider several points for reports and proposals. First, for many reports and proposals, audiences have specific media requirements, and you might not have a choice. For instance, executives in many corporations now expect to review reports via their in-house intranets, sometimes in conjunction with an *executive dashboard,* a customized online presentation of key operating variables such as revenue, profits, quality, customer satisfaction, and project progress. Second, consider how your audience wants to provide feedback on your report or proposal. Do they prefer to write comments on a printed document or to use the commenting and markup features in a word processor? Third, will people

States the problem clearly enough for anyone to understand without additional research

STATEMENT OF THE PROBLEM
The rapid growth of our company over the past five years has reduced the sense of community among our staff. People no longer feel like part of an intimate organization that values teamwork.

PURPOSE AND SCOPE OF WORK
The purpose of this study is to determine whether a company newsletter would help rebuild a sense of community within the workforce. The study will evaluate the impact of newsletters in other companies and will attempt to identify features that might be desirable in our own newsletter. Such variables as length, frequency of distribution, types of articles, and graphic design will be considered. Costs will be estimated for several approaches, including print and electronic versions. In addition, the study will analyze the personnel and procedures required to produce a newsletter.

Explains exactly what will be covered by the research and included in the final report

Identifies the tasks to be accomplished and does so in clear, simple terms

SOURCES AND METHODS OF DATA COLLECTION
Sample newsletters will be collected from 10–20 companies similar to ours in size, growth rate, and types of employees. The editors will be asked to comment on the impact of their publications on employee morale. Our own employees will be surveyed to determine their interest in a newsletter and their preferences for specific features. Production procedures and costs will be analyzed through conversations with newsletter editors, printers, and our website development team.

Offers a preliminary outline to help readers understand the issues that will be addressed in the report

PRELIMINARY OUTLINE
The preliminary outline for this study is as follows:
  I. Do newsletters affect morale?
     A. Do people read them?
     B. How do employees benefit?
     C. How does the company benefit?
 II. What are the features of good newsletters?
     A. How long are they?
     B. What do they contain?
     C. How often are they published?
     D. How are they designed?
III. How should a newsletter be produced?
     A. Should it be written and edited internally or externally?
     B. Should it be printed or produced electronically?
     C. If electronic, should it be formatted as e-mail, a blog, or regular web content?
 IV. What would a newsletter cost?
     A. What would the personnel cost be?
     B. What would the material cost be?
     C. What would outside services cost?
  V. Should we publish a company newsletter?
 VI. If so, what approach should we take?

Identifies who is responsible for each task and when it will be completed

TASK ASSIGNMENTS AND SCHEDULE
Each phase of this study will be completed by the following dates:

Collect/analyze newsletters	Hank Waters	September 15, 2006
Interview editors by phone	Hank Waters	September 22, 2006
Survey employees	Julienne Cho	September 29, 2006
Develop sample	Hank Waters	October 6, 2006
Develop cost estimates	Julienne Cho	October 13, 2006
Prepare report	Hank Waters	October 20, 2006
Submit final report	Hank Waters	October 24, 2006

FIGURE 10–2
Effective Work Plan for a Formal Study

need to search through your document frequently or update it in the future? Delivering a report as a word processor file makes both tasks far easier. Fourth, bear in mind that your choice of media also sends a message. For instance, a routine sales report dressed up in expensive multimedia will look like a waste of valuable company resources.

Organizing Your Information

The direct approach is by far the most popular and convenient for business reports; it saves time, makes the rest of the report easier to follow, and produces a

DIRECT APPROACH

Since the company's founding 25 years ago, we have provided regular repair service for all our electric appliances. This service has been an important selling point as well as a source of pride for our employees. However, rising labor costs have made it impossible to maintain profitability while offering competitive service rates. Last year, we lost $500,000 on our repair business.

Because of your concern over these losses, you have asked me to study the pros and cons of discontinuing our repair service. With the help of John Hudson and Susan Lefkowitz, I have studied the issue for the past two weeks and have come to the conclusion that we have been embracing an expensive, impractical tradition.

By withdrawing from the electric appliance repair business, we can substantially improve our financial performance without damaging our reputation with customers. This conclusion is based on three basic points that are covered in the following pages:

- It is highly unlikely that we will ever be able to make a profit in the repair business.
- We can refer customers to a variety of qualified repair firms without significantly reducing customer satisfaction.
- Closing down the service operation will create few internal problems.

INDIRECT APPROACH

Since the company's founding 25 years ago, we have provided regular repair service for all our electric appliances. This service has been an important selling point as well as a source of pride for our employees. However, rising labor costs have made it impossible to maintain profitability while offering competitive service rates.

Because of your concern over these losses, you have asked me to study the pros and cons of discontinuing our repair service. With the help of John Hudson and Susan Lefkowitz, I have studied the issue for the past two weeks. The following pages present my findings for your review. The analysis addressed three basic questions:

- What is the extent of our losses, and what can we do to turn the business around?
- Would withdrawal hurt our sales of electrical appliances?
- What would be the internal repercussions of closing down the repair business?

more forceful report. However, the confidence implied by the direct report may be misconstrued as arrogance, especially if you're a junior member of a status-conscious organization. On the other hand, the indirect approach gives you a chance to prove your points and gradually overcome your audience's reservations. The longer the message, though, the less effective an indirect approach is likely to be. Therefore, carefully consider report length before deciding on the direct or indirect approach.

Both approaches have merit, so businesspeople often combine them, revealing their conclusions and recommendations as they go along, rather than putting them first or last. Figure 10–3 presents the introductions from two reports with the same general outline. In the direct version, a series of statements summarizes the conclusion reached about each main topic in the outline. In the indirect version, the same topics are introduced in the same order but without drawing any conclusions about them. Instead, the conclusions appear in the body of the report.

When you outline your content, use informative ("talking") headings rather than simple descriptive ("topical") headings (see Table 10–2). When in question or summary form, informative headings force you to really think through the content, rather than simply identifying the general topic area. Using informative headings will not only help you plan more effectively but will also facilitate collaborative writing. A heading such as "Industry characteristics" could mean five different things to the five people on your writing team, so use a heading that conveys a single, unambiguous meaning, such as "Flour milling is a mature industry."

For a quick review of adapting the three-step process to long reports, refer to "Checklist: Adapting the Three-Step Writing Process to Informational and Analytical Reports." The following sections provide specific advice on how to plan informational reports, analytical reports, and proposals.

TYPES OF OUTLINE HEADINGS — Table 10–2

Descriptive (Topical) Outline	Informative (Talking) Outline	
	Question Form	Summary Form

I. Industry Characteristics
  A. Annual sales
  B. Profitability
  C. Growth rate
    1. Sales
    2. Profit
	I. What is the nature of the industry?
	  A. What are the annual sales?
	  B. Is the industry profitable?
	  C. What is the pattern of growth?
	    1. Sales growth?
	    2. Profit growth?
		I. Flour milling is a mature industry.
		  A. Market is large.
		  B. Profit margins are narrow.
		  C. Growth is modest.
		    1. Sales growth averages less than 3 percent a year.
		    2. Profits are flat.

SUPPORTING YOUR MESSAGES WITH RELIABLE INFORMATION

No matter what the subject of your report, audiences expect you to support your message with solid research. As you've probably discovered while doing school projects, research involves a lot more than simply typing a few terms into a search engine. Good research requires a clear process:

Many of your business reports will require some level of research.

1. **Plan your research.** Planning is the most important step of any research project; a solid plan yields better results in less time.

2. **Locate the data and information you need.** The research plan tells you *what* to look for, so your next step is to figure out *where* this data and information is and *how* to access it.

✓ CHECKLIST: Adapting the Three-Step Writing Process to Informational and Analytical Reports

A. Analyze the situation
- ✓ Clearly define your purpose before you start writing.
- ✓ If you need to accomplish several goals in the report, identify all of them in advance.
- ✓ Prepare a work plan to guide your efforts.

B. Gather information
- ✓ Determine whether you need to launch a separate research project to collect the necessary information.
- ✓ Reuse or adapt existing material whenever possible.

C. Select the right medium
- ✓ Base your decision on audience expectations (or requirements, as the case may be).
- ✓ Consider the need for commenting, revising, distributing, and storing.
- ✓ Remember that the medium you choose also sends a message.

D. Organize your information
- ✓ Use a direct approach if your audience is receptive.
- ✓ Use an indirect approach if your audience is skeptical.
- ✓ Use an indirect approach when you don't want to risk coming across as arrogant.
- ✓ Combine approaches if that will help build support for your primary message.

1 Plan	2 Locate data and information	3 Process data and information	4 Apply your findings	5 Manage information
• Familiarize yourself with the subject; develop problem statement • Identify information gaps • Prioritize research needs • Maintain research ethics and etiquette	• Evaluate sources • Collect secondary information at the library, online, or elsewhere • Collect primary information through surveys and interviews	• Analyze numerical information • Quote, paraphrase, or summarize textual information	• Summarize findings • Draw conclusions • Make recommendations	• Make research results available to others via your company's knowledge management system

FIGURE 10–4
The Research Process

3. **Process the data and information you located.** The data and information you find probably won't be in a form you can use immediately and will require some processing, which might involve anything from statistical analysis to resolving the differences between two or more expert opinions.

4. **Apply your findings.** You can apply your research findings in three ways: summarizing information for someone else's benefit, drawing conclusions based on what you've learned, or developing recommendations.

5. **Manage information efficiently.** Many companies today are trying to maximize the return on the time and money they invest in business research by collecting and sharing research results in a variety of computer-based systems, known generally as **knowledge management systems.** At the very least, be sure to share your results with any colleagues who may be able to benefit from it.

You can see the sequence of these steps in Figure 10–4; the following sections offer more details, starting with planning your research.

Planning Your Research

Researching without a plan wastes time and usually produces unsatisfactory results.

With so much information online these days, it's tempting just to punch some keywords into a search engine and then dig through the results looking for something, anything, that looks promising. However, such a lack of planning can limit both your effectiveness (you might not find the right information) and your efficiency (you might spend too much time and money on research).

To avoid the expensive and embarrassing stumbles that can occur with poorly planned research, start by familiarizing yourself with the subject so that you can frame insightful questions. Unless you're already familiar with the topic, you may need to do some preliminary investigation in order to plan your research intelligently. Explore the general subject area, perhaps by reading industry publications, visiting competitors' websites, scanning blogs and newsgroups, and interviewing experts within your organization. Try to identify important terminology, trends, conflicts, influential people, and potential sources of information. As you explore, develop a **problem statement** that will define the purpose of your research—the decision you need to make or the conclusion you need to reach at the end of the process.

Next, identify the most critical *information gaps*. An information gap is simply the difference between what you currently know and what you need to know. For instance, if Brian Bolain had the problem statement of "find out what percentage of new cars purchased in the last 30 days were Scions," he would need two key pieces of information: (1) the total number of cars purchased and (2) the number of Scions purchased. He can easily find the second piece of information by asking Toyota's sales department. However, he might not have immediate access to the total number of cars purchased. To fill this information gap, he could subscribe to an independent research service that tracks the auto industry, for instance. Using the information-gap approach focuses your research on just those topics that you need to know about, and it saves you the time and expense of digging up answers that somebody in the organization already has.

As you begin listing questions you want to ask, you might compile more questions than you have time or money to answer. Moreover, if you'll be interviewing or surveying people to gather information, you'll need to limit the number of questions you ask so that you don't consume more time than people are willing to give. Consequently, you will usually need to prioritize your information needs and concentrate on the most vital set of questions.

You'll never have enough time or money to answer every question that comes to mind, so setting priorities is a must.

With a prioritized list of questions, you're just about ready to get started with your research. Before taking that step, however, it's important to be aware that research carries some significant ethical responsibilities. Your research tactics affect the people from whom you gather data and information, the people who read your results, and the people who are affected by the way you present those results. To avoid ethical lapses, keep the following points in mind:

- **Don't force a specific outcome by skewing your research.** If you set out to prove or disprove a particular point, you're more likely to find information that supports your position, but you may be overlooking contradictory points. If you go in with an open mind and are willing to accept whatever you find, your research will be more valuable.

- **Respect the privacy of your research participants.** Privacy is a contentious issue today. Avoid observing people without their consent, and don't mislead people about the purposes of your research or about the ways you plan to use the information they give you.[2]

Privacy is one of the hottest issues in the research field today.

- **Document sources and give appropriate credit.** Whether you are using published documents, personal interviews, or company records, citing your sources is not only fair to the people who created and provided the information, but doing so also builds your credibility as a writer.

- **Respect the intellectual property and digital rights of your sources.** *Intellectual property* refers to the ownership of unique ideas that have commercial value in the marketplace.[3] Intellectual property laws cover everything from artists' works to industrial processes, so make sure you can legally use the information you uncover.

- **Don't extract more from your sources than they actually provide.** For instance, if an industry expert says that a sales increase is a *possibility,* don't quote her as saying that a sales increase is *likely.*

In addition to ethics, research etiquette deserves careful attention, too. For example, respect the time of anyone who agrees to be interviewed or to be a research participant, and maintain courtesy throughout the interview or research process.

Locating Data and Information

A good plan and careful prioritization tell you *what* you need to know and *why* you need to know it; the next step is to identify *where* that information might exist and *how* to locate it. The range of sources available to business researchers today is remarkable, almost overwhelming at times. If you have a question about an industry, a company, a market, a new technology, or a financial topic, chances are somebody

Primary research involves information that you gather specifically for a new research project; secondary research involves information that others have gathered.

else has already researched the subject. Research materials previously created for another purpose are considered **secondary research**; these sources include magazines, newspapers, public websites, books, and other reports. Don't let the name fool you, though. You want to start with secondary research because it can save considerable time and money for many projects. In contrast, **primary research** is new research done specifically for your current project and includes surveys, interviews, observations, and experiments. Before you use any secondary sources, you need to know whether you can trust them.

Evaluating Sources   In every research project, you have the responsibility to verify the quality of the sources you use. The Internet has made this challenge easier in one respect, since it's usually possible to cross-check information by referring to multiple sources. At the same time, online research is more difficult because so much bad information exists on the Internet, from doctored photos to unverified "facts" to biased sources. To avoid tainting your results and damaging your reputation, ask yourself the following questions about each piece of material:

Evaluate your sources carefully to avoid embarrassing and potentially damaging mistakes.

- **Does the source have a reputation for honesty and reliability?** For example, find out how a publication accepts articles and whether it has an editorial board, peer review, or fact checking procedures. Most traditional, offline publishers have such quality control procedures in place, but many online sources do not.

- **Is the source potentially biased?** To interpret an organization's information, you need to know its point of view.

- **What is the purpose of the material?** For instance, was the material designed to inform others of new research, advance a political position, or promote a product?

- **Is the author credible?** Is the author a professional journalist? An informed amateur? Merely someone with an opinion?

- **Where did the source get *its* information?** Try to find out who collected the data, the methods they used, their qualifications, and their professional reputation.

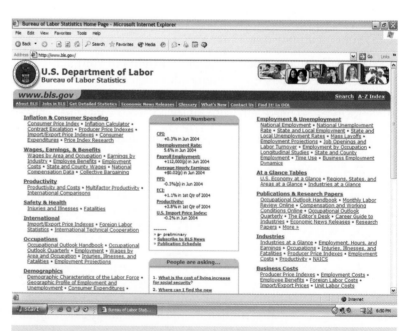

The U.S. Government's Bureau of Labor Statistics is a credible source of current economic and job-related data.

- **Can you verify the material independently?** Verification can uncover biases or mistakes—particularly important when the information goes beyond simple facts to include projections, interpretations, and estimates.

- **Is the material current?** Make sure you are using the most current information available by checking the publication date of a source.

- **Is the material complete?** Have you accessed the entire document or only a selection from it? If it's a selection, which parts were excluded? Do you need more detail?

   You probably won't have time to conduct a thorough background check on all your sources, so focus your efforts on the most important or most suspicious pieces of information.

Conducting Secondary Research   Even if you intend to eventually conduct primary research, most projects start with a review of secondary research. Inside your company, you might be able to find a variety of reports, memos, and other documents that could help. Outside the company, business researchers can choose from a wide range of print and online resources. Table 10–3 provides a small sample of the many secondary resources available.[4]

> You'll want to start most projects by conducting secondary research first.

Finding Information at the Library   Public and university libraries offer an enormous array of business books, electronic databases, newspapers, periodicals, directories, almanacs, and government publications. Many of these may be unavailable through a standard web search or may be available only with a subscription. Libraries are also where you'll find one of your most important resources: librarians. Reference librarians are trained in research techniques and can often help you find obscure information you can't find on your own. They can also direct you to the typical libraries many sources of business information:

> Even in the Internet age, libraries offer information and resources you can't find anywhere else—including experienced research librarians.

- **Newspapers and periodicals.** Libraries offer access to a wide variety of popular magazines, general business magazines, *trade journals* (which provide information about specific professions and industries), and *academic* journals (which provide research-oriented articles from researchers and educators). Check with a librarian to see which periodicals are available in print or electronic formats.

- **Business books.** Although less timely than newspapers and periodicals, business books provide in-depth coverage of a variety of business topics. Many libraries now offer online access to their card catalogs so you can see if they have specific titles in their collections.

- **Directories.** Thousands of directories are published in print and electronic formats in the United States, and many include membership information for all kinds of professions, industries, and special-interest groups.

- **Almanacs and statistical resources.** Almanacs are handy guides to factual and statistical information about countries, politics, the labor force, and so on. One of the most extensive, the *Statistical Abstract of the United States* published annually by the U.S. Department of Commerce, contains statistics about occupations, government, population, health, business, crime, and the environment (also available online at www.census.gov).

- **Government publications.** Information on laws, court decisions, tax questions, regulatory issues, and other governmental concerns can often be found in collections of government documents. A librarian can direct you to the information you want.

> Local, state, and federal government agencies publish a huge array of information that is helpful to business researchers.

- **Electronic databases.** Databases offer vast collections of computer-searchable information, often in specific areas such as business, law, science, technology, and education. Some libraries offer remote online access to some or all databases; for

Table 10–3   MAJOR BUSINESS RESOURCES

COMPANY, INDUSTRY, AND PRODUCT RESOURCES (PRINT)

- *Brands and Their Companies/Companies and Their Brands.* Data on over 281,000 consumer products and 51,000 manufacturers, importers, marketers, and distributors.

- *Corporate and Industry Research Reports (CIRR).* Collection of industry reports produced by industry analysts for investment purposes. Unique coverage includes industry profitability, comparative company sales, market share, profits, and forecasts.

- *Directory of Companies Required to File Annual Reports with the Securities and Exchange Commission.* Listing of U.S. publicly held firms.

- *Dun's Directory of Service Companies.* Information on 205,000 U.S. service companies.

- *Forbes.* Annual Report on American Industry published in first January issue of each year.

- *Hoover's Handbook of American Business.* Profiles of over 500 public and private corporations.

- *Manufacturing USA.* Data series listing nearly 25,000 companies, including detailed information on over 450 manufacturing industries.

- *Market Share Report.* Data covering products and service categories originating from trade journals, newsletters, and magazines.

- *Moody's Industry Review.* Data on 4,000 companies in about 150 industries. Ranks companies within industry by five financial statistics (revenue, net income, total assets, cash and marketable securities, and long-term debt) and includes key performance ratios.

- *Moody's Manuals.* Weekly manual of financial data in each of six business areas: industrials, transportation, public utilities, banks, finance, and over-the-counter (OTC) industrials.

- *Service Industries USA.* Comprehensive data on 2,100 services grouped into over 150 industries.

- *Standard & Poor's Industry Surveys.* Concise investment profiles for a broad range of industries. Coverage is extensive, with a focus on current situation and outlook. Includes some summary data on major companies in each industry.

- *Standard & Poor's Register of Corporations, Directors, and Executives.* Index of major U.S. and international corporations. Lists officers, products, sales volume, and number of employees.

- *Thomas's Register of American Manufacturers.* Information on thousands of U.S. manufacturers indexed by company name and product.

- *U.S. Industrial Outlook.* Annual profiles of several hundred key U.S. industries. Each industry report covers several pages and includes tables, graphs, and charts that visually demonstrate how an industry compares with similar industries, including important component growth factors and other economic measures.

COMPANY, INDUSTRY, AND PRODUCT RESOURCES (ONLINE)

- AnnualReports.com **www.reportgallery.com.** Free access to annual reports from thousands of public companies.

- *CNN/Money* **http://money.cnn.com.** News, analysis, and financial resources covering companies, industries, and world markets.

- *Hoover's Online* **www.hoovers.com.** Database of 12 million companies worldwide, including in-depth coverage of 35,000 leading companies around the world. Basic information available free; in-depth information requires subscription.

- *NAICS Codes* **www.census.gov/naics.** North American Industry Classification System.

- *SEC filing* **www.sec.gov/edgar.shtml.** SEC filings including 10Ks, 10Qs, annual reports, and prospectuses for 35,000 U.S. public firms.

MAJOR BUSINESS RESOURCES *(continued)*

Table 10–3

DIRECTORIES AND INDEXES (PRINT)

- **Books in Print.** Index of 425,000 books in 62,000 subject categories currently available from U.S. publishers. Indexed by author and title.

- **Directories in Print.** Information on over 16,000 business and industrial directories.

- **Encyclopedia of Associations.** Index of thousands of associations listed by broad subject category, specific subject, association, and location.

- **Reader's Guide to Periodical Literature.** Periodical index categorized by subject and author.

- **Ulrich's International Periodicals Directory.** Listings by title, publisher, editor, phone, and address of over 140,000 publications such as popular magazines, trade journals, government documents, and newspapers. Great for locating hard-to-find trade publications.

PEOPLE (PRINT)

- **Dun & Bradstreet's Reference Book of Corporate Management.** Professional histories of people serving as the principal officers and directors of more than 12,000 U.S. companies.

- **Who's Who in America.** Biographies of living U.S. citizens who have gained prominence in their fields. Related book, *Who's Who in the World,* covers global achievers.

TRADEMARKS (PRINT/ONLINE)

- **Official Gazette of the United Patent and Trademark Office.** Weekly publication (one for trademarks and one for patents) providing official record of newly assigned trademarks and patents, product descriptions, and product names.

- **United States Patent and Trademark Office** www.uspto.gov. Trademark and patent information records.

STATISTICS AND FACTS (PRINT)

- **Industry Norms and Key Business Ratios (Dun & Bradstreet).** Industry, financial, and performance ratios.

- **Information Please Almanac.** Compilation of broad-range statistical data with strong focus on labor force.

- **Robert Morris Associates' Annual Statement Studies.** Industry, financial, and performance ratios.

- **Statistical Abstract of the United States.** U.S. economic, social, political, and industrials statistics.

- **The World Almanac and Book of Facts.** Facts on economic, social, educational, and political events for major countries.

STATISTICS AND FACTS (ONLINE)

- **Bureau of Economic Analysis** www.bea.doc.gov. Large collection of economic and government data.

- **Europa—The European Union Online** www.europa.eu.int. A portal that provides up-to-date coverage of current affairs, legislation, policies, and EU statistics.

- **FedStats** www.fedstats.gov. Access to full range of statistics and information from over 70 U.S. government agencies.

- **STAT-USA** www.stat-usa.gov. Large collection of economic and government data.

- **U.S. Census Bureau** www.census.gov. Demographic data on both consumers and businesses based on census data.

- **U.S. Bureau of Labor Statistics** www.bls.gov. Extensive national and regional information on labor and business, including employment, industry growth, productivity, Consumer Price Index (CPI), and overall U.S. economy.

COMMERCIAL DATABASES (REQUIRE SUBSCRIPTIONS)

- **Dialog.** Hundreds of databases that include areas such as business and finance, news and media, medicine, pharmaceuticals, reference, social sciences, government and regulation, science and technology, and more.

(continued)

Table 10–3 — MAJOR BUSINESS RESOURCES *(continued)*

- **Ebsco Online Reference System.** Access to a variety of databases on a wide range of disciplines from leading information providers.
- **Highbeam.** Thousands of full-text newspaper, magazine, and newswire sources, plus maps and photographs.
- **Gale Business & Company Resource Center.** A comprehensive research tool designed for undergraduate and graduate students, job searchers, and investors; offers a wide variety of information on companies and industries.
- **LexisNexis.** Several thousand databases covering legal, corporate, government, and academic subjects.
- **ProQuest.** Thousands of periodicals and newspapers; archives continue to expand through its program to digitize over five billion pages of microfilm.
- **SRDS Media Solutions.** A comprehensive database of magazine information and advertising rates, cataloging more than 100,000 U.S. and international media properties.

Conduct online research with extreme care; much of the information online has not been subjected to the same quality controls common in traditional offline publishing.

Web directories rely on human editors to evaluate and select websites.

Metacrawlers can save you time by employing multiple search engines at once.

Online databases give you access to the most important resource that search engines usually can't reach: millions of newspaper, magazine, and journal articles.

others you'll need to visit in person. The following section offers more information on using databases.

Finding Information Online The Internet can be a tremendous source of business information, provided you know where to look and how to use the tools available. **Search engines** identify individual webpages that contain a specific word or phrase you've asked for. Search engines have the advantage of scanning millions or billions of individual webpages, and the best engines use powerful ranking algorithms to present the pages that are probably the most relevant to your search request. For all their ease and power, search engines have three disadvantages you should be aware of: (1) no human editors are involved to evaluate the quality of the content you find on these pages; (2) various engines use different search techniques so one engine might miss a site that another one finds; and (3) search engines can't reach the content on restricted websites (such as the back issues of many periodicals). These out-of-reach pages are sometimes called the *hidden Internet,* since conventional search techniques can't access them.

The good news is that you can get around all three shortcomings when conducting research—although doing so is sometimes expensive. **Web directories** address the first major shortcoming of search engines by using human editors to categorize and evaluate websites. Directories such as those offered by Yahoo!, About, and the Open Directory at www.dmoz.org present lists of websites chosen by a team of editors. For instance, the Open Directory lists more than 200,000 business-related websites by category, from individual companies to industry associations, all of which have been evaluated and selected by a team of volunteer editors.[5]

Metacrawlers or *metasearch engines* address the second shortcoming of search engines by formatting your search request for the specific requirements of multiple search engines. These versatile tools produce displays that tell you how many hits each engine was able to find for you. Table 10–4 lists some of the more popular search engines, metacrawlers, and directories.

Online databases help address the third shortcoming of search engines by offering access to the newspapers, magazines, and journals that you're likely to need for many research projects. Individual publisher sites often require a subscription to that publication for anything beyond the current issue (and in some cases you still have to pay for archived articles), and commercial databases require

BEST OF INTERNET SEARCHING

Table 10–4

Major Search Engines

A9	www.a9.com
AllTheWeb	www.alltheweb.com
Alta Vista	www.altavista.com
Ask Jeeves	www.askjeeves.com
Google	www.google.com
Lycos	www.lycos.com
MSN	http://search.msn.com
Teoma	www.teoma.com

Metacrawlers and Hybrid Sites

Clusty	www.clusty.com
DogPile	www.dogpile.com
IXQuick	www.ixquick.com
Kartoo	www.kartoo.com
LookSmart	www.looksmart.com
Mamma	www.mamma.com
MetaCrawler	www.metacrawler.com
Fazzle	www.fazzle.com
Infonetware RealTerm Search	www.infonetware.com
ProFusion	www.profusion.com
Query Server	www.queryserver.com
Search.com	www.search.com
Surfwax	www.surfwax.com
Vivismo	www.vivisimo.com
Wakweb	www.wakweb.com
Web Brain	www.webbrain.com
WebCrawler	www.webcrawler.com
Yahoo!	www.yahoo.com
Zapmeta	www.zapmeta.com
Zworks	www.zworks.com

Web Directories and Online Libraries

About	www.about.com
Answers.com	www.answers.com
Beaucoup	www.beaucoup.com
Digital Librarian	www.digital-librarian.com/business.html
Internet Public Library	www.ipl.org
Librarians' Index to the Internet	http://lii.org

Library of Congress	www.loc.gov/rr/business
Library Spot	www.libraryspot.com/
Open Directory	www.dmoz.com
Questia	www.questia.com

News Search Engines

AllTheWeb News	http://www.alltheweb.com/?cat=news
AltaVista News	http://news.altavista.com
Daypop	www.daypop.com
Google News	http://news.google.com
Newstrawler	www.newstrawler.com
NewsTrove.com	www.newstrove.com
World News Network	www.wn.com
Yahoo! News	http://news.yahoo.com

Blog Search Engines, RSS News Feeds, and Podcast Search Engines

2RSS.com	www.2rss.com
Blinkx	www.blinkx.com
Bloglines	www.bloglines.com
Blogsearchengine	www.blogsearchengine.com
Bloogz	www.bloogz.com
Blogdex	http://blogdex.media.mit.edu
Blogdigger	www.blogdigger.com
BlogStreet	www.blogstreet.com
CompleteRSS	www.completerss.com
Feedster	www.feedster.com
KB Cafe	www.kbsearch.com
Kinja	http://kinja.com
Technorati	www.technorati.com
Memigo	www.memigo.com
Podcast Alley	www.podcastalley.com
Pluck	www.pluck.com
Podcast Bunker	www.podcastbunker.com
Waypath	www.waypath.com

Magazine and Periodical Search Engines

FindArticles.com	www.findarticles.com
Full Free Text (scholarly articles)	www.freefulltext.com

subscriptions to access all content. In addition to databases that primarily feature content from newspapers and periodicals, specialized databases such as Hoover's (www.hoovers.com) and OneSource's CorpTech (www.corptech.com) offer detailed information on thousands of individual companies. You can obtain company news releases at no charge from PRNewswire (www.prnewswire.com) and Business Wire (www.businesswire.com).

> Make sure you know how each search engine, directory, database, or metacrawler works; they work in different ways, and you can get unpredictable results if you don't know how each one operates.

As search engines, metacrawlers, and databases continue to multiply and offer new ways to find information, using them can become a challenge. No two of them work in exactly the same way. Make sure you understand what the search tool expects from you before you enter your query. With a *keyword search,* in which the engine or database attempts to find items that include all of the words you enter. *A Boolean search* lets you define a query with greater precision, using such operators as AND (the search must include the two term linked by the AND), OR (it can include either or both words), or NOT (the search ignores items with whatever word comes after NOT). Other common Boolean capabilities include searching for a particular word in close proximity to other words and wildcards that search for similar spellings. In contrast to both keyword and Boolean searches, *natural language searches* let you ask questions in everyday English. And recently, search engines such as Google, Yahoo!, and AllTheWeb have implemented *forms-based searches* that help you create powerful queries by simply filling out an online form that lets you specify such parameters as date ranges, language, Internet domain name, and even file and media types.[6]

To make the best use of any search engine or database, keep the following points in mind:

- **Read the instructions.** Unfortunately, there is no universal set of instructions that apply to every search tool, so visit the Help page for advice on how to use a particular tool most effectively.

- **Pay attention to the details.** Details can make all the difference. For instance, most search engines treat *AND* (upper case) as a Boolean search operator and look only for pages or entries that contain both words. In contrast, *and* (lower case) and similar basic words (called *stopwords*) are excluded from many searches because they are so common they'll show up in every webpage or database entry. Similarly, various engines and databases interpret question marks and asterisks in special ways. Again, read the Help page to learn more.

- **Review the search and display options carefully.** Make sure you review all the options presented before submitting a search. For instance, some article databases search through only the title unless you specifically ask them to search through the article text as well—a distinction that dramatically affects your results. When the results are displayed, verify the presentation order: items could be listed by date, relevancy, or some other criteria.

- **Try variations of your terms.** If you can't find what you're looking for, try abbreviations (*CEO, CPA*), synonyms (*man, male*), related terms (*child, adolescent, youth*), different spellings (*dialog, dialogue*), singular and plural forms (*woman, women*), nouns and adjectives (*management, managerial*), and open and compound forms (*online, on line, on-line*).

- **Adjust the scope of your search if needed.** If a search yields little or no information, broaden your search by specifying fewer terms. Conversely, if you're inundated with too many hits, use more terms to narrow your search.

Also, take advantage of any automated research features that your search tools offer, such as e-mail alerts when new articles are posted and RSS (Really Simple Syndication) feeds of new web content. News aggregators such as NewsGator (www.newsgator.com) and NewzCrawler (www.newzcrawler.com) let you subscribe to specific information channels at thousands of websites, blogs, and newsgroups.[7]

Documenting Your Sources   Documenting the secondary sources you use in your writing serves three important functions: It properly and ethically credits the person who created the original material, it shows your audience that you have sufficient support for your message, and it helps your readers explore your topic in more detail if desired. Thorough documentation is particularly important if you're working in a large organization; your reports might be used by colleagues for years after you originally wrote them, and these people won't always have the opportunity to query you in person for more information. Be sure to take advantage of the source documentation tools in your word processor; Microsoft Word automatically tracks and numbers endnotes for you, and you can use the "table of authorities" feature to create a bibliography of all the sources you've used. As computing technologies continue to advance, keep an eye out for other note-taking tools that can help you be a more efficient researcher. Software such as Microsoft's OneNote makes it easier to collect and organize notes wherever and however you find vital information, from meetings to websites to e-mail messages.[8]

> Proper documentation of the sources you use is both ethical and an important resource for your readers.

You may document your sources through footnotes, endnotes, or some similar system (see Appendix B, "Documentation of Report Sources"). Whatever method you choose, documentation is necessary for such sources as books, articles, tables, charts, diagrams, song lyrics, scripted dialogue, letters, speeches—anything that you take from someone else, including ideas and information that you've re-expressed through paraphrasing or summarizing. However, you do not have to cite a source for general knowledge or for specialized knowledge that's generally known among your readers, such as the fact that Microsoft is a large software company and that computers are pervasive in business today.

Copyright law (including the *fair use* doctrine, which allows limited use of copyrighted materials as long as doing so doesn't hamper the copyright owner's ability to profit from the work) can be a complicated issue, so consult your company's legal department if you have any questions about material you plan to use.

Conducting Primary Research   If secondary research can't provide the information and insights you need, your next choice is to gather the information yourself with primary research. The two most common primary research methods are surveys and interviews. (Other primary techniques are observations and experiments in special situations such as test marketing, but they're not commonly used for day-to-day business research.)

> Surveys and interviews are the most common primary research techniques.

Conducting Surveys   A carefully prepared and conducted survey can provide invaluable insights, but only if it is *reliable* (would produce identical results if repeated) and *valid* (measures what it's supposed to measure). To avoid errors in design and implementation, consider hiring a research specialist for important surveys. The two most common sources of errors are in the sample, the people selected to participate in the survey, and in the questions themselves.

When selecting the people who'll participate in your survey, the most critical task is getting a representative sample of the entire population in question. For instance, if you want to know how U.S. consumers feel about something, you can't just randomly survey people in a mall and assume these opinions represent the entire population. Different types of consumers shop at different times of the day and different days of the week, some consumers don't shop at malls regularly, and many who do won't stop to talk with researchers. The online surveys you see on many websites today potentially suffer from the same *sampling bias:* They capture only the opinions of people who visit the sites and want to participate, which

Marketing surveys are a common way of gathering data directly from customers.

For a survey to produce valid results, it must be based on a representative sample of respondents.

might not be a representative sample of the population. A good handbook on survey research will help you select the right people for your survey, including selecting enough people to have a statistically valid survey.[9]

To develop an effective survey questionnaire, start with the prioritized information gaps you identified at the beginning of the research process. Then break these points into specific questions, choosing an appropriate type of question for each point (Figure 10–5 shows various types of survey questions). The following guidelines will help you produce results that are both valid and reliable:[10]

Provide clear instructions to prevent mistaken answers.

- **Provide clear instructions.** Respondents need to know exactly how to fill out your questionnaire.

- **Don't ask for information that people can't be expected to remember.** For instance, a question such as "How many times did you go grocery shopping last year" will generate unreliable answers.

FIGURE 10–5
Types of Survey Questions

QUESTION TYPE	EXAMPLE
Open-ended	How would you describe the flavor of this ice cream?
Either-or	Do you think this ice cream is too rich? _____ Yes _____ No
Multiple choice	Which description best fits the taste of this ice cream? (Choose only one.) a. Delicious b. Too fruity c. Too sweet d. Too intensely flavored e. Bland f. Stale
Scale	Please mark an X on the scale to indicate how you perceive the texture of this ice cream. Too light Light Creamy Too creamy
Checklist	Which of the following ice cream brands do you recognize? (Check all that apply.) _____ Ben & Jerry's _____ Breyers _____ Carvel _____ Dreyers _____ Häagen-Dazs
Ranking	Rank these flavors in order of your preference, from 1 (most preferred) to 5 (least preferred): _____ Vanilla _____ Cherry _____ Strawberry _____ Chocolate _____ Coconut
Short-answer	In the past two weeks, how many times did you buy ice cream in a grocery store? _____ In the past two weeks, how many times did you buy ice cream in an ice cream shop? _____

- **Keep the questionnaire short and easy to answer.** Don't make any individual questions difficult to answer, and don't expect people to give you more than 10 or 15 minutes of their time.

- **Whenever possible, formulate questions to provide answers that are easy to analyze.** Numbers and facts are easier to summarize than opinions, for instance.

- **Avoid leading questions that could bias your survey.** If you ask, "Do you prefer that we stay open in the evenings for customer convenience?" you'll no doubt get a "yes." Instead, ask, "What time of day do you normally do your shopping?"

- **Avoid ambiguous questions.** If you ask "Do you shop at the mall often?" some people might interpret *often* to mean "every day," whereas others might think it means "once a week" or "once a month."

- **Ask only one thing at a time.** A compound question such as "Do you read books and magazines?" doesn't allow for the respondent who reads one but not the other.

The Internet is quickly becoming the preferred survey mechanism for many researchers, and dozens of companies now offer online survey services.[11] Compared to traditional mail and in-person techniques, online surveys are usually faster to create, easier to administer, quicker to analyze, and less expensive overall. The interactive capabilities of the web can enhance all kinds of surveys, from simple opinion polls to complex purchase simulations. However, online surveys require the same care as any other type of survey, including being on guard against sampling bias.[12]

Conducting Interviews   Getting in-depth information straight from an expert can be a great method for collecting primary information. Although interviews are relatively easy to conduct, they require careful planning to get the best results and make the best use of the other person's time. Planning an interview is similar to planning any other form of communication. You begin by analyzing your purpose, learning about the other person, and formulating your main idea. Then you decide on the length, style, and organization of the interview.

The answers you receive are influenced by the types of questions you ask, by the way you ask them, and by your subject's cultural and language background. Other potentially significant factors include the person's race, gender, age, educational level, and social status, so know your subject before you start writing questions.[13]

Ask **open-ended questions** to invite the expert to offer opinions, insights, and information, such as "Why do you believe that South America represents a better opportunity than Europe for this product line?" Bear in mind that although open-ended questions can extract significant amounts of information, they do give you less control over the interview. Someone might take 10 seconds or 10 minutes to answer a question, so plan to be flexible.

A successful interview requires careful planning and organization to ensure you get the information you really need.

Ask **closed questions** to elicit a specific answer, such as yes or no. However, including too many closed questions in an interview will make the experience feel more like a simple survey and won't take full advantage of the interview setting. When you do ask a question that implies a straightforward answer, such as "Do you think we should expand distribution in South America?" explore the reasoning behind the expert's answer.

Choose question types that will generate the specific information you need.

Document Makeover

IMPROVE THIS REPORT

To practice correcting drafts of actual documents, visit your online course or the access-code protected portion of the Companion Website. Click "Document Makeovers," then click Chapter 10. You will find an informational report that contains problems and errors relating to what you've learned in this chapter about planning business reports and proposals. Use the "Final Draft" decision tool to create an improved version of this personal activity report. Check the report for parallel construction, appropriate headings, suitable content, positive and bias-free language, and use of the "you" attitude.

Think carefully about the sequence of your questions and the subject's potential answers so you can arrange them in an order that helps uncover layers of information. Also consider providing the other person with a list of questions at least a day or two before the interview, especially if you'd like to quote your subject in writing or if your questions might require your subject to conduct research or think extensively about the answers. If you want to record the interview, ask the person ahead of time and respect his or her wishes.

As soon as possible after the interview, take a few moments to write down your thoughts, go over your notes, and organize your material. Look for important themes, helpful facts or statistics, and direct quotes. If you made a tape recording, *transcribe* it (take down word for word what the person said) or take notes from the tape just as you would while listening to someone in person.

Face-to-face interviews give you the opportunity to gauge the reaction to your questions and observe the nonverbal signals that accompany the answers, but interviews don't necessarily have to take place in person. E-mail interviews are becoming more common, partly because they give subjects a chance to think through their responses thoroughly, rather than rushing to fit the time constraints of a face-to-face interview.[14] Also, e-mail interviews might be the only way you will be able to access some experts.

As a reminder of the tasks involved in interviews, see "Checklist: Conducting Effective Information Interviews."

Face-to-face interviews give you the opportunity to gauge nonverbal responses as well.

Using Your Research Results

After you collect your data, the next step is converting it into usable information.

Once you've collected all the necessary secondary and primary information, the next step is transforming it into the specific content you need. For simpler projects, you may be able to drop your material directly into your report, presentation, or other application. However, when you have gathered a significant amount of information or raw data from surveys, you'll need to process the material before you can use it. This step can involve analyzing numerical data; quoting, paraphrasing, or summarizing textual material; drawing conclusions; and making recommendations.

Mean, median, and mode provide insight into sets of data.

Analyzing Data Business research often produces numerical data—everything from sales figures to population statistics to survey answers. By themselves, these numbers might not provide the insights you or your audience require. Are sales going up or going down? What percentage of employees surveyed are so dissatisfied that

✓ CHECKLIST: Conducting Effective Information Interviews

- ✓ Learn about the person you're interviewing.
- ✓ Formulate your main idea to ensure effective focus.
- ✓ Choose the length, style, and organization of the interview.
- ✓ Select question types to elicit the specific information you want.
- ✓ Design each question carefully to collect useful answers.
- ✓ Limit the number of questions you ask.
- ✓ Consider recording the interview if the subject permits.
- ✓ Review your notes as soon as the interview ends.

THREE TYPES OF DATA MEASURES: MEAN, MEDIAN, AND MODE	Table 10–5	
Salesperson	**Sales**	
Wilson	$3,000	
Green	5,000	
Carrick	6,000	
Wimper	7,000 ————— Mean	
Keeble	7,500 ————— Median	
Kemble	8,500	
O'Toole	8,500	Mode
Mannix	8,500	
Caruso	9,000	
Total	$63,000	

they're ready to look for new jobs? These are the insights managers need in order to make good business decisions.

Even without advanced statistical techniques, you can use simple arithmetic to extract powerful insights from sets of research data. Table 10–5 shows several insights you can gain about a collection of numbers, for instance. The **mean** (which is what most people refer to when they use the term "average") is the sum of all the items in the group divided by the number of items in that group. The **median** is the "middle of the road," or the midpoint of a series. with an equal number of items above and below. The **mode** is the number that occurs more often than any other in your sample. It's the best answer to a question such as "What is the usual amount?" Each of the three measures can tell you different things about a set of data.

It's also helpful to look for **trends**, any repeatable patterns taking place over time, including growth, decline, and cyclical trends that vary between growth and decline. Trend analysis is common in business. By looking at data over a period of time, you can detect patterns and relationships that will help you answer important questions. In addition, researchers frequently explore the relationships between subsets of data using a technique called **cross-tabulation**. For instance, if you're trying to figure out why total sales rose or fell, you might look separately at sales data by age, gender, location, and product type.

> Trends suggest patterns that repeat over time.

Whenever you process numerical data, keep in mind that numbers are easy to manipulate and misinterpret, particularly with spreadsheets and other computer tools. Make sure to double-check all of your calculations and document the operation of any spreadsheets you plan to share with colleagues. Also, step back and look at your entire set of data before proceeding with any analysis. Do the numbers make sense based on what you know about the subject? Are there any individual data points that stand out as suspect? Have you made any comparisons that don't really make sense? Have you read more into the data than is really there? Business audiences like the clarity of numbers; it's your responsibility to deliver numbers they can count on.

Quoting, Paraphrasing, and Summarizing Information   You can use information from secondary sources in three ways. *Quoting* a source means you reproduce it exactly as you found it, and you either set it off with quotation marks (for shorter passages) or extract it in an indented paragraph (for longer passages). Use direct quotations when the original language will enhance your argument or when rewording the passage would lessen its impact. However, try not to quote sources at great

> Quoting a source means reproducing the content exactly and indicating who created the information originally.

length. Too much quoting creates a choppy patchwork of varying styles and gives the impression that all you've done is piece together the work of other people.

You can often maximize the impact of secondary material in your own writing by *paraphrasing* it, restating it in your own words and with your own sentence structures.[15] Paraphrasing helps you maintain consistent tone while using vocabulary familiar to your audience. Of course, you still need to credit the originator of the information, but not with quotation marks or indented paragraphs.

Paraphrasing is expressing someone else's ideas in your own words.

To paraphrase effectively, follow these tips:[16]

- Reread the original passage until you fully understand its meaning.

- Record your paraphrase on a note card or in an electronic format.

- Use language that your audience is familiar with.

- Check your version with the original source to verify that you have not altered the meaning.

- Use quotation marks to identify any unique terms or phrases you have borrowed exactly from the source.

- Record the source (including the page number) so that you can give proper credit if you use this material in your report.

Summarizing is similar to paraphrasing but distills the content into fewer words.

Summarizing is similar to paraphrasing but presents the gist of the material in fewer words than the original. An effective summary identifies the main ideas and major support points from your source material, but leaves out most details, examples, and other information that is less critical to your audience. Like quotations and paraphrases, summaries also require complete documentation of your sources. Summarizing is not always a simple task, and your audience will judge your ability to separate significant issues from less significant details. Identify the main idea and the key support points, and separate these from details, examples, and other supporting evidence (see Table 10–6). Focus your efforts on your audience, highlighting the information that is most important to the person who assigned the project or to those who will be reading the report.

Of course, all three approaches require careful attention to ethics. When quoting directly, take care not to distort the original intent of the material by quoting selectively or out of context. And never succumb to **plagiarism**, presenting someone else's words as your own.

Table 10–6   SUMMARIZING EFFECTIVELY

Original Material (110 Words)	45-Word Summary	22-Word Summary
Our facilities costs spiraled out of control last year. The 23% jump was far ahead of every other cost category in the company and many times higher than the 4% average rise for commercial real estate in the Portland metropolitan area. The rise can be attributed to many factors, but the major factors include repairs (mostly electrical and structural problems at the downtown office), energy (most of our offices are heated by electricity, the price of which has been increasing much faster than for oil or gas), and last but not least, the loss of two sublease tenants whose rent payments made a substantial dent in our cost profile for the past five years.	**Our facilities costs jumped 23% last year,** far ahead of every other cost category in the company and many times higher than the 4% local average. The major factors contributing to the increase are repairs, energy, and the loss of two sublease tenants.	**Our facilities costs jumped 23% last year,** due mainly to rising repair and energy costs and the loss of sublease income.

Main idea

Major support points

Details

Drawing Conclusions A conclusion is a logical interpretation of the facts and other information in your report. A sound conclusion is not only logical but flows from the information included in your report, meaning that it should be based on the information included in the report and shouldn't rely on information that isn't in the report. Moreover, if you or the organization you represent have certain biases that influence your conclusion, ethics obligate you to inform the audience accordingly.

Reaching good conclusions based on the evidence at hand is one of the most important skills you can develop in your business career. In fact, the ability to see patterns and possibilities that others can't see is one of the hallmarks of innovative business leaders. Consequently, take your time with this part of the process. Play "devil's advocate" against yourself, attacking your conclusion as an audience might to make sure it stands up to rigorous scrutiny.

Making Recommendations Whereas a conclusion interprets information, a **recommendation** suggests what to do about the information. The difference between a conclusion and a recommendation can be seen in the following example:

Conclusion	Recommendation
On the basis of its track record and current price, I conclude that this company is an attractive buy.	I recommend that we write a letter to the board of directors offering to buy the company at a 10 percent premium over the current market value of its stock.

If you've been asked to take the final step and translate your conclusions into recommendations, be sure to make the relationship between them clear. To be credible, recommendations must be based on logical analysis and sound conclusions. They must also be practical and acceptable to the people who have to make your recommendations work. Finally, when making a recommendation, be certain that you have adequately described the steps that come next. Don't leave your readers wondering what they need to do in order to act on your recommendation.

PLANNING INFORMATIONAL REPORTS

Informational reports provide the feedback that employees, managers, and others need in order to make decisions, take action, and respond to dynamic conditions both inside and outside the organization. Although these reports come in dozens of particular formats, they can be grouped into four general categories:

> Informational reports are used to monitor and control operations, to implement policies and procedures, to demonstrate compliance, and to document progress.

- **Reports to monitor and control operations.** Managers rely on a wide range of reports to see how well their companies are functioning. *Plans* establish expectations and guidelines to direct future action. The most important of these are *business plans,* which summarize a proposed business venture, communicate the company's goals, highlight how management intends to achieve those goals, and explain why customers will be motivated to buy the company's products or services (see "Sharpening Your Career Skills: Creating an Effective Business Plan"). Many business plans are actually a combination of an informational report (describing conditions in the marketplace), an analytical report (analyzing threats and opportunities and recommending specific courses of action), and a proposal (persuading investors to put money into the firm in exchange for a share of ownership). *Operating reports* provide feedback on a wide variety of an organization's functions, including sales, inventories, expenses, shipments, and so on. *Personal activity reports* provide information regarding an individual's experiences during sales calls, industry conferences, market research trips, and so on.

- **Reports to implement policies and procedures.** Reports are the most common vehicle for conveying guidelines, approved procedures, and other organizational decisions. *Policy reports* range from brief descriptions of business procedures to manuals that run dozens or hundreds of pages. *Position papers* outline an organization's official position on issues that affect the company's success.

- **Reports to demonstrate compliance.** Businesses are required to submit a variety of *compliance reports*, from tax returns to reports describing the proper handling of hazardous materials.

- **Reports to document progress.** Supervisors, investors, and customers frequently expect to be informed of the progress of projects and other activities. *Progress reports* range from simple updates in memo form to comprehensive status reports.

SHARPENING YOUR CAREER SKILLS

Creating an Effective Business Plan

The most important report you may ever get the chance to write is the business plan for a new company. A comprehensive business plan forces you to think about personnel, marketing, facilities, suppliers, distribution, and a host of other issues vital to your success. If you are starting out on a small scale and using your own money, your business plan may be relatively informal. But at a minimum, you should describe the basic concept of the business and outline its specific goals, objectives, and resource requirements. A formal plan, suitable for use with banks or investors, should cover these points:

- *Summary.* In one or two pages, summarize your business concept. Describe your product or service and its market potential. Highlight some things about your company and its owners that will distinguish your firm from the competition. Summarize your financial projections and the amount of money investors can expect to make on their investment. Be sure to indicate how much money you will need and what it will be spent on.

- *Mission and objectives.* Explain the purpose of your business and what you hope to accomplish—and before you take another step, make sure that this is a mission you can pursue with passion, through thick and thin, with every ounce of commitment and energy you can muster.

- *Company and industry.* Give full background information on the origins and structure of your venture and the characteristics of its industry.

- *Products or services.* Give a complete but concise description of your products or services, focusing on their unique attributes. Explain how customers will benefit from using your products or services instead of those of your competitors.

- *Market and competition.* Provide data that will persuade investors that you understand your target market and can achieve your sales goals. Be sure to identify the strengths and weaknesses of your competitors.

- *Management.* Summarize the background and qualifications of the key management personnel in your company. Include résumés in an appendix.

- *Marketing strategy.* Provide projections of sales and market share, and outline a strategy for identifying and contacting customers, setting prices, providing customer services, advertising, and so forth. Whenever possible, include evidence of customer acceptance, such as advance product orders.

- *Design and development plans.* If your product requires design or development, describe the nature and extent of what needs to be done, including costs and possible problems.

- *Operations plan.* Provide information on the facilities, equipment, and labor needed.

- *Overall schedule.* Forecast development of the company in terms of completion dates for major aspects of the business plan.

- *Critical risks and problems.* Identify all negative factors and discuss them honestly.

- *Financial projections and requirements.* Include a detailed budget of start-up and operating costs, as well as projections for income, expenses, and cash flow for the first three years of business. Identify the company's financing needs and potential sources.

- *Exit strategy.* Explain how investors will be able to cash out or sell their investment, such as through a public stock offering, sale of the company, or a buyback of the investors' interest.

A complete business plan obviously requires a considerable amount of work. However, by thinking your way through all these issues, you'll enjoy a smoother launch and a greater chance of success in your new adventure.

CAREER APPLICATIONS

1. Why is it important to identify critical risks and problems in a business plan?

2. Many experts suggest that you write the business plan yourself, rather than hiring a consultant to write it for you. Why is this a good idea?

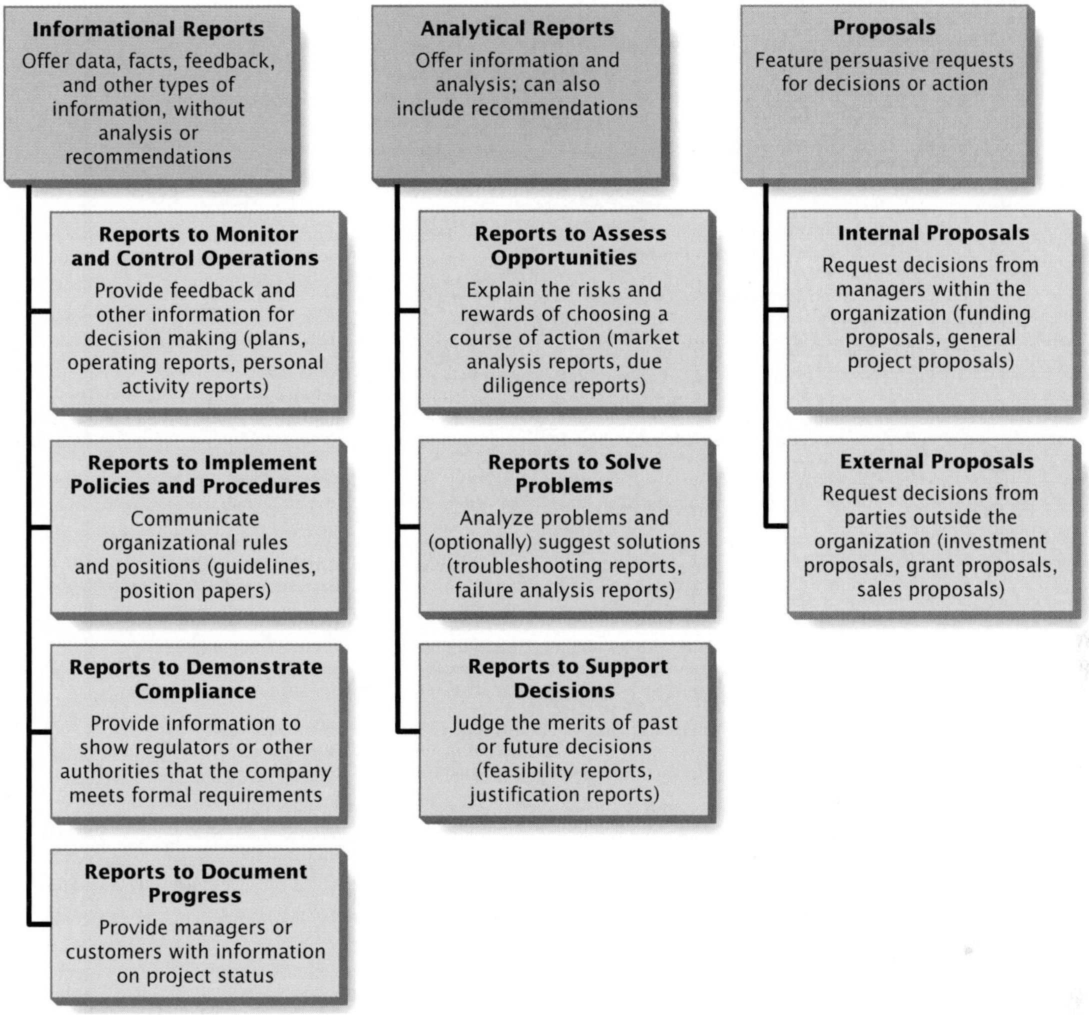

Informational Reports
Offer data, facts, feedback, and other types of information, without analysis or recommendations

Analytical Reports
Offer information and analysis; can also include recommendations

Proposals
Feature persuasive requests for decisions or action

Reports to Monitor and Control Operations
Provide feedback and other information for decision making (plans, operating reports, personal activity reports)

Reports to Assess Opportunities
Explain the risks and rewards of choosing a course of action (market analysis reports, due diligence reports)

Internal Proposals
Request decisions from managers within the organization (funding proposals, general project proposals)

Reports to Implement Policies and Procedures
Communicate organizational rules and positions (guidelines, position papers)

Reports to Solve Problems
Analyze problems and (optionally) suggest solutions (troubleshooting reports, failure analysis reports)

External Proposals
Request decisions from parties outside the organization (investment proposals, grant proposals, sales proposals)

Reports to Demonstrate Compliance
Provide information to show regulators or other authorities that the company meets formal requirements

Reports to Support Decisions
Judge the merits of past or future decisions (feasibility reports, justification reports)

Reports to Document Progress
Provide managers or customers with information on project status

FIGURE 10–6
The Diverse Nature of Reports and Proposals

Figure 10–6 shows the major subcategories within each of the three major report categories, along with examples of the more common types. Chances are you'll be called upon to write many of these types of reports during your career.

In most cases, the direct approach is the best choice for informational reports, since you are simply conveying information. However, if the information is disappointing, such as a project that is behind schedule or over budget, you might consider building up to the bad news through an indirect approach. In general, let the nature of whatever you're describing dictate your structure. Most informational reports use a **topical organization**, arranging material in one of the following ways:

The messages conveyed by informational reports can range from extremely positive to extremely negative, so the approach you take warrants careful consideration.

- **Comparison.** If you need to show similarities and differences (or advantages and disadvantages) between two or more entities, organize your report in a way that helps your readers see those similarities and differences clearly.

- **Importance.** Build up from the least important item to most important if you expect that the audience will read the entire report, or start with the most important item and progress to the least important if you suspect the readers are interested in only the more important items.

- **Sequence.** Any information that concerns a process or procedure is a good candidate for organizing by sequence, discussing the steps or stages in the order in which they occur.

MEMO

DATE: March 14, 2006
TO: Jeff Black and HR staff
FROM: Carrie Andrews
SUBJECT: Recruiting and hiring seminar

Last week I attended an American Management Association seminar on recruiting, screening, and hiring new employees. I got enough useful information to warrant updating our online personnel handbook and perhaps developing a quick training session for all interviewing teams to avoid some of the stupid mistakes we've made in the past. Here's a quick look at the things I learned.

We should avoid legal mistakes, screen and interview applicants more effectively, and measure applicants more accurately. We need to write recruiting ads that accurately portray job openings and that don't discriminate. We need to sort through résumés more efficiently while still looking for telltale signs of false information. And we need more information on which types of preemployment tests are most effective.

I learned how best to comply with the Americans with Disabilities Act and how to use an employment agency effectively and safely (without risk of legal entanglements). The conference also covered how to screen and interview applicants more effectively, how to avoid interview questions that could get us into legal trouble, and when and how to check criminal records. In addition, I learned which drug-testing issues and recommendations affect us.

As you can see, the seminar addressed a lot of important information. I attended six sessions in all to gather exactly the information we needed. We covered the basic guidelines for much of this already, but a number of specific recommendations and legal concepts should be emphasized. Also, over the four-day conference, I attended three workshop lunches that addressed specific applications for much of what was presented during the regular sessions. I was amazed by the valuable information I received in addition to the cruise-ship-style buffet lunches. The food was fantastic.

Updating the personnel handbook will take a couple of weeks, but we don't have any immediate hiring plans. Contact me if you need any information before then. Everyone will have a lot to review to get up to speed. Also, we have a lot of new information that may well affect our need to train the interviewing team members.

Please don't hesitate to e-mail me or drop by to discuss this matter.

Annotations (left side):
- Fails to state why Andrews attended the seminar
- Does nothing to help readers focus on what is important
- Fails to present pertinent material in a way that would be meaningful and useful to readers

Annotations (right side):
- Injects inappropriate personal opinion and criticism
- Uses running text instead of bullets, making it difficult for readers to identify the new knowledge
- Wastes time on some unimportant activities, such as how many sessions were offered during the seminar and what the lunches were like

FIGURE 10–7
Ineffective Informational Report

- **Chronology.** When investigating a chain of events, organize the study according to what happened in January, what happened in February, and so on.

- **Spatial orientation.** If you're explaining how a physical object works or a physical space looks, describe it from left to right (or right to left in some cultures), top to bottom, or outside to inside—in whatever order makes the most sense.

- **Geography.** If location is important, organize your study according to geography, perhaps by region of the world or by area of a city.

- **Category.** If you're asked to review several distinct aspects of a subject, look at one category at a time, such as sales, profit, cost, or investment.

Whichever pattern you choose, use it consistently so that readers can easily follow your discussion from start to finish. Bear in mind, however, that in many instances (particularly with compliance and monitor-and-control reports), you might be expected to follow a standard organization. Just be sure you understand what your audience expects.

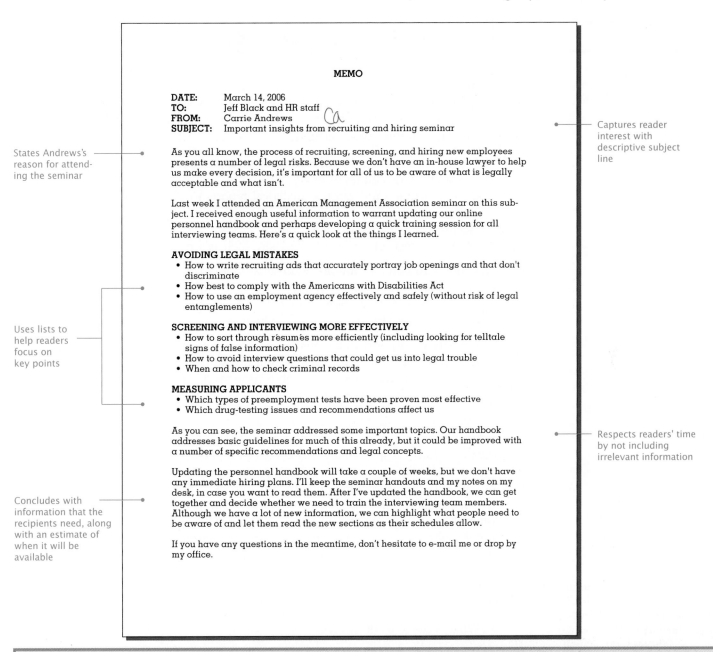

MEMO

DATE: March 14, 2006
TO: Jeff Black and HR staff
FROM: Carrie Andrews *Ca*
SUBJECT: Important insights from recruiting and hiring seminar

Captures reader interest with descriptive subject line

States Andrews's reason for attending the seminar

As you all know, the process of recruiting, screening, and hiring new employees presents a number of legal risks. Because we don't have an in-house lawyer to help us make every decision, it's important for all of us to be aware of what is legally acceptable and what isn't.

Last week I attended an American Management Association seminar on this subject. I received enough useful information to warrant updating our online personnel handbook and perhaps developing a quick training session for all interviewing teams. Here's a quick look at the things I learned.

AVOIDING LEGAL MISTAKES
- How to write recruiting ads that accurately portray job openings and that don't discriminate
- How best to comply with the Americans with Disabilities Act
- How to use an employment agency effectively and safely (without risk of legal entanglements)

Uses lists to help readers focus on key points

SCREENING AND INTERVIEWING MORE EFFECTIVELY
- How to sort through résumés more efficiently (including looking for telltale signs of false information)
- How to avoid interview questions that could get us into legal trouble
- When and how to check criminal records

MEASURING APPLICANTS
- Which types of preemployment tests have been proven most effective
- Which drug-testing issues and recommendations affect us

As you can see, the seminar addressed some important topics. Our handbook addresses basic guidelines for much of this already, but it could be improved with a number of specific recommendations and legal concepts.

Respects readers' time by not including irrelevant information

Updating the personnel handbook will take a couple of weeks, but we don't have any immediate hiring plans. I'll keep the seminar handouts and my notes on my desk, in case you want to read them. After I've updated the handbook, we can get together and decide whether we need to train the interviewing team members. Although we have a lot of new information, we can highlight what people need to be aware of and let them read the new sections as their schedules allow.

Concludes with information that the recipients need, along with an estimate of when it will be available

If you have any questions in the meantime, don't hesitate to e-mail me or drop by my office.

FIGURE 10–8
Effective Informational Report

Of course, strong organization is only part of what makes informational reports effective. They must also be audience-centered, logical, focused, and easy to follow, with generous use of previews and summaries. They are complete, without being unnecessarily long or detailed. One of the tasks your audience expects you to do is to sort out the details and separate major points from minor points. In other words, readers expect you to put in all the thought and effort it takes to make the best use of their time. In addition, effective reports are honest and objective, but without being unduly harsh whenever negative information must be conveyed.

Compare the two versions of Carrie Andrews's personal activity report in Figures 10–7 and 10–8. At a quick glance, Figure 10–7 may seem to do a good job of meeting audience needs, but this report has a number of weaknesses that distract from the writer's intent and make readers work too hard to extract the main points.

PLANNING ANALYTICAL REPORTS

Analytical reports are used to assess opportunities, to solve problems, and to support decisions.

The purpose of analytical reports is to analyze, to understand, to explain—to think through a problem or an opportunity and figure out how it affects the company and how the company should respond. In many cases, you'll also be expected to make a recommendation based on your analysis. As you saw in Figure 10–6, analytical reports fall into three basic categories:

- **Reports to assess opportunities.** Every business opportunity carries some degree of risk and also requires a variety of decisions and actions in order to capitalize on the opportunity. You can use analytical reports to assess both risk and required decisions and actions. For instance, *market analysis reports* are used to judge the likelihood of success for new products or sales. *Due diligence reports* examine the financial aspects of a proposed decision, such as acquiring another company.

- **Reports to solve problems.** Managers often assign *troubleshooting reports* when they need to understand why something isn't working properly and what needs to be done to fix it. A variation, the *failure analysis report,* studies events that happened in the past, with the hope of learning how to avoid similar failures in the future.

- **Reports to support decisions.** *Feasibility reports* are called for when managers need to explore the ramifications of a decision they're about to make, such as switching materials used in a manufacturing process. *Justification reports* explain a decision that has already been made.

Writing analytical reports presents a greater challenge than writing informational reports, for three reasons: the quality of your reasoning, the quality of your writing, and the responsibility that comes with persuasion. First, you're doing more than simply delivering information—you're also thinking through a problem or opportunity and presenting your conclusions. The best writing in the world can't compensate for shaky analysis. Second, when your analysis is complete, you need to present your thinking in a compelling and persuasive manner. Third, analytical reports often convince other people to make significant financial and personnel decisions, so your reports carry the added responsibility of the consequences of these decisions.

Clarify the problem in an analytical report by determining what you need to analyze, why the issue is important, who is involved, where the trouble is located, and how and when it started.

To help define the problem that your analytical report will address, answer these questions:

- What needs to be determined?

- Why is this issue important?

- Who is involved in the situation?

- Where is the trouble located?

- How did the situation originate?

- When did it start?

Not all these questions apply in every situation, but asking them helps you define the problem being addressed and limit the scope of your discussion.

Use problem factoring to divide a complex problem into more manageable pieces.

Also try breaking down the perceived problem into a series of logical, connected questions that try to identify cause and effect. This process is sometimes called **problem factoring**. You probably subconsciously approach most problems this way, identifying cause-and-effect relationships that might pinpoint the source of the problem. When you speculate on the cause of a problem, you're forming a **hypothesis**, a potential explanation that needs to be tested. By subdividing a problem and forming hypotheses based on available evidence, you can tackle even the most complex situations.

COMMON WAYS TO STRUCTURE ANALYTICAL REPORTS

Table 10–7

Element	Focus on Conclusions or Recommendations	Focus on Logical Argument	
		Use 2 + 2 = 4 Model	*Use Yardstick Model*
Readers	Are likely to accept	Hostile or skeptical	Hostile or skeptical
Approach	Direct	Indirect	Indirect
Writer credibility	High	Low	Low
Advantages	Readers quickly grasp conclusions or recommendations	Works well when you need to show readers how you built toward an answer by following clear logical steps	Works well when you have a list of criteria (standards) that must be considered in a decision; alternatives are all measured against same criteria
Drawbacks	Structure can make topic seem too simple	Can make report longer	Readers must agree on criteria; can be lengthy because of the need to address each criteria for every alternative

As with all business messages, the best organizational structure for each analytical report depends largely on your audience's likely reaction. The three basic structures involve focusing on conclusions, focusing on recommendations, and focusing on logic (see Table 10–7).

Before you choose an approach, determine whether your audience is receptive or skeptical.

Focusing on Conclusions When writing for audiences that are likely to accept your conclusions—either because they've asked you to perform an analysis or they trust your judgment—consider a direct approach that focuses immediately on your conclusions. This structure communicates the main idea quickly, but it does present some risks. Even if audiences trust your judgment, they may have questions about your data or the methods you used. Moreover, starting with a conclusion may create the impression that you have oversimplified the situation. To give readers the opportunity to explore the thinking behind your conclusion, support that conclusion with solid reasoning and evidence.

Focusing on conclusions is often the best approach when you're addressing a receptive audience.

Cynthia Zolonka works on the human resources staff of a bank in Houston, Texas. Her company decided to have an outside firm handle its employee training, and a year after the outsourcing arrangement was established, Zolonka was asked to evaluate the results. She explains: "Moving our training programs to an outside supplier was a tough—and controversial—decision for the entire company. Some people were convinced that outsourcing would never work; others thought it might save money but would hurt training quality. I took special care to do a thorough analysis of the data, and I supported my conclusion with objective answers, not personal opinions."

Figure 10–9 presents a preliminary outline of Zolonka's report. Her analysis shows that the outsourcing experiment was a success, and she opened with that conclusion but supported it with clear evidence. Readers who accept the conclusion can stop reading, and those who desire more information can continue.

Focusing on Recommendations A slightly different approach is useful when your readers want to know what they ought to do in a given situation (as opposed to what they ought to conclude). You'll often be asked to solve a problem or assess an opportunity, rather than just study it. The actions you want your readers to take become the main subdivisions of your report.

When readers want to know what you think they should do, organize your report to focus on recommendations.

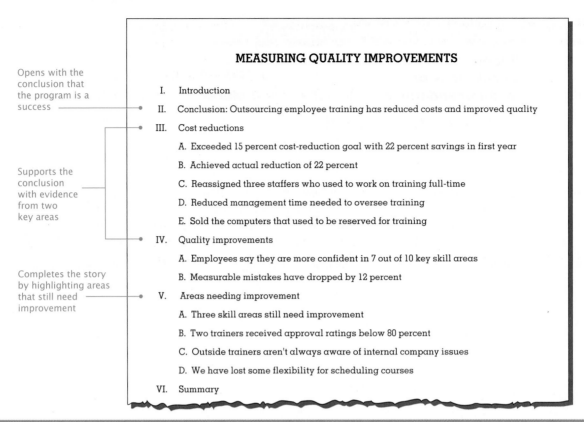

Opens with the conclusion that the program is a success

Supports the conclusion with evidence from two key areas

Completes the story by highlighting areas that still need improvement

MEASURING QUALITY IMPROVEMENTS

I. Introduction

II. Conclusion: Outsourcing employee training has reduced costs and improved quality

III. Cost reductions

   A. Exceeded 15 percent cost-reduction goal with 22 percent savings in first year

   B. Achieved actual reduction of 22 percent

   C. Reassigned three staffers who used to work on training full-time

   D. Reduced management time needed to oversee training

   E. Sold the computers that used to be reserved for training

IV. Quality improvements

   A. Employees say they are more confident in 7 out of 10 key skill areas

   B. Measurable mistakes have dropped by 12 percent

V. Areas needing improvement

   A. Three skill areas still need improvement

   B. Two trainers received approval ratings below 80 percent

   C. Outside trainers aren't always aware of internal company issues

   D. We have lost some flexibility for scheduling courses

VI. Summary

FIGURE 10–9
Preliminary Outline of a Research Report Focusing on Conclusions

When structuring a report around recommendations, use the direct approach as you would for a report that focuses on conclusions. Then unfold your recommendations using a series of five steps:

1. Establish the need for action in the introduction by briefly describing the problem or opportunity.

2. Introduce the benefit(s) that can be achieved if the recommendation is adopted, along with any potential risks.

3. List the steps (recommendations) required to achieve the benefit, using action verbs for emphasis.

4. Explain each step more fully, giving details on procedures, costs, and benefits; if necessary, also explain how risks can be minimized.

5. Summarize your recommendations.

Logical arguments can follow two basic approaches: 2 + 2 = 4 (adding everything up) and the yardstick method (comparing ideas against a predetermined set of standards).

Focusing on Logical Arguments When readers are skeptical or hostile to the conclusion or recommendation you plan to make, use an indirect approach that logically builds toward your conclusion or recommendation. If you guide the audience along a rational path toward the answer, they are more likely to accept it when they encounter it. The two most common logical approaches are known as the *2 + 2 = 4 approach* and the *yardstick approach.*

Try using the 2 + 2 = 4 approach; it's familiar and easy to develop.

The 2 + 2 = 4 Approach **The 2 + 2 = 4 approach** is so named because it convinces readers of your point of view by demonstrating that everything adds up. The main points in your outline are the main reasons behind your conclusions and recommendations. You support each reason with the evidence you collected during your analysis.

With its natural feel and versatility, the 2 + 2 = 4 approach is generally the most persuasive and efficient way to develop an analytical report for skeptical readers, so try this structure first. You'll find that most of your arguments fall naturally into this pattern.

As national sales manager of a New Hampshire sporting goods company, Binh Phan was concerned about his company's ability to sell to its largest customers. His boss, the vice president of marketing, shared these concerns and asked Phan to analyze the situation and recommend a solution. As Phan says, "We sell sporting goods to retail chains across the country. Large nationwide chains such as Sports Authority have been revolutionizing the industry, but we haven't had as much success with these big customers as we've had with smaller companies that operate strictly on a local or regional basis. With more and more of the industry in the hands of the large chains, we knew we had to fix the situation."

Phan's troubleshooting report appears in Figure 10–10. The main idea is that the company should establish separate sales teams for these major accounts, rather than continuing to service them through the company's four regional divisions. However,

---

FIGURE 10–10
Analytical Report Using the 2 + 2 = 4 Approach

MEMO

DATE: September 12, 2006
TO: Robert Mendoza, Vice President of Marketing
FROM: Binh Phan, National Sales Manager   *BP*
SUBJECT: Major accounts sales problems

Clarifies who requested the report, when it was requested, and who wrote it

As you requested on August 20, this report outlines the results of my investigation into the recent slowdown in sales to major accounts and the accompanying rise in sales- and service-related complaints from some of our largest customers.

Over the last four quarters, major account sales dropped 12%, whereas overall sales were up 7%. During the same time, we've all noticed an increase in both formal and informal complaints from larger customers, regarding how confusing and complicated it has become to do business with us.

Highlights the serious nature of the problem

Explains how the information used in the analysis was collected

My investigation started with in-depth discussions with the four regional sales managers, first as a group and then individually. The tension I felt in the initial meeting eventually bubbled to the surface during my meetings with each manager. Staff members in each region are convinced that other regions are booking orders they don't deserve, with one region doing all the legwork only to see another region get the sale, the commission, and the quota credit.

I followed up these formal discussions by talking informally and exchanging e-mail with several sales representatives from each region. Virtually everyone who is involved with our major national accounts has a story to share. No one is happy with the situation, and I sense that some reps are walking away from major customers because the process is so frustrating.

The decline in sales to our major national customers and the increase in their complaints stem from two problems: (1) sales force organization and (2) commission policy.

ORGANIZATIONAL PROBLEMS

Organizational problems are the first "2" in Phan's 2 + 2 = 4 approach

Describes the first problem and explains how it occurred, without blaming anyone personally

When we divided the national sales force into four geographical regions last year, the idea was to focus our sales efforts and clarify responsibilities for each prospective and current customer. The regional managers have gotten to know their market territories very well, and sales have increased beyond even our most optimistic projections.

However, while solving one problem, we have created another. In the past 12 to 18 months, several regional customers have grown to national status, and a few retailers have taken on (or expressed interest in) our products. As a result, a significant portion of both current sales and future opportunities lies with these large national accounts.

I uncovered more than a dozen cases in which sales representatives from two or more regions found themselves competing with each other by pursuing the same customers from different locations. Moreover, the complaints from our major accounts about overlapping or nonexistent account coverage are a direct result of the regional organization. In some cases, customers aren't sure which of our representatives they're supposed to call with problems and orders. In other cases, no one has been in contact with them for several months.

(continued)

FIGURE 10–10
(continued)

2

For example, having retail outlets across the lower tier of the country, AmeriSport received pitches from reps out of our West, South, and East regions. Because our regional offices have a lot of negotiating freedom, the three were offering different prices. But all AmeriSport buying decisions were made at the Tampa headquarters, so all we did was confuse the customer. The irony of the current organization is that we're often giving our weakest selling and support efforts to the largest customers in the country.

Brings the first problem to life by complementing the general description with a specific example

COMMISSION PROBLEMS

Commission problems are the second "2" in Phan's 2 + 2 = 4 approach

The regional organization problems are compounded by the way we assign commissions and quota credit. Salespeople in one region can invest a lot of time in pursuing a sale, only to have the customer place the order in another region. So some sales rep in the second region ends up with the commission on a sale that was partly or even entirely earned by someone in the first region. Therefore, sales reps sometimes don't pursue leads in their regions, thinking that a rep in another region will get the commission.

Simplifies the reader's task by maintaining a parallel structure for the discussion of the second problem: a general description followed by a specific example

For example, Athletic Express, with outlets in 35 states spread across all four regions, finally got so frustrated with us that the company president called our headquarters. Athletic Express has been trying to place a large order for tennis and golf accessories, but none of our local reps seem interested in paying attention. I spoke with the rep responsible for Nashville, where the company is headquartered, and asked her why she wasn't working the account more actively. Her explanation was that last time she got involved with Athletic Express, the order was actually placed from their L.A. regional office, and she didn't get any commission after more than two weeks of selling time.

RECOMMENDATIONS

Phan concludes the 2 + 2 = 4 approach organizational problems + commission problems = the need for a new sales structure

Our sales organization should reflect the nature of our customer base. To accomplish that goal, we need a group of reps who are free to pursue accounts across regional borders— and who are compensated fairly for their work. The most sensible answer is to establish a national account group. Any customers whose operations place them in more than one region would automatically be assigned to the national group.

Explains how the new organizational structure will solve both problems

In addition to solving the problem of competing sales efforts, the new structure will also largely eliminate the commission-splitting problem because regional reps will no longer invest time in prospects assigned to the national accounts team. However, we will need to find a fair way to compensate regional reps who are losing long-term customers to the national team. Some of these reps have invested years in developing customer relationships that will continue to yield sales well into the future, and everyone I talked to agrees that reps in these cases should receive some sort of compensation. Such a "transition commission" would also motivate the regional reps to help ensure a smooth transition from one sales group to the other. The exact nature of this compensation would need to be worked out with the various sales managers.

Acknowledges that the recommended solution does create a temporary compensation problem, but expresses confidence that a solution to that can be worked out

3

SUMMARY

The regional sales organization is effective at the regional and local levels but not at the national level. We should establish a national accounts group to handle sales that cross regional boundaries. Then we'll have one set of reps who are focused on the local and regional levels and another set who are pursuing national accounts.

Neatly summarizes both the problem and the recommended solution

To compensate regional reps who lose accounts to the national team, we will need to devise some sort of payment to reward them for the years of work invested in such accounts. This can be discussed with the sales managers once the new structure is in place.

Phan knew his plan would be controversial because it required a big change in the company's organization and in the way sales reps are paid. His thinking had to be clear and easy to follow, so he used the 2 + 2 = 4 approach to focus on his reasons.

The Yardstick Approach   The **yardstick approach** is useful when you need to use a number of criteria to decide which option to select from two or more possibilities. With this approach, you begin by discussing the problem or opportunity, then list the criteria that will guide the decision. The body of the report then evaluates the alternatives against those criteria. Figure 10–11 is an outline of a feasibility report that uses the yardstick approach, using five criteria to evaluate two alternative courses of action. The report was provided by J. C. Hartley, a market analyst for a large Sacramento company that makes irrigation equipment for farms and ranches. "We've been so successful in the agricultural market that we're starting to run out of customers to sell to," says Hartley. "To keep the company growing, we needed to find another market. Two obvious choices to consider were commercial buildings and residences, but we needed to evaluate them carefully before making a decision."

The yardstick approach has two potential drawbacks. First, your audience needs to agree with the criteria you're using in your analysis. If they don't, they won't agree with the results of the evaluation. If you have any doubt about their

The yardstick approach compares alternatives to a set of predetermined standards, without conducting experiments or evaluating hypotheses.

FIGURE 10–11
Outline of an Analytical Report Using the Yardstick Approach

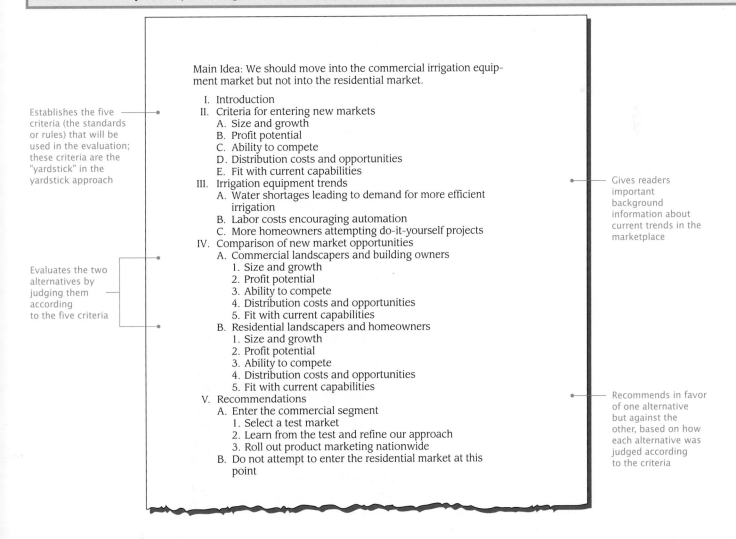

agreement, build consensus before you start your report, if possible, or take extra care to explain why the criteria you're using are the best ones in this particular case. Second, the yardstick approach can get a little boring when you have many options to consider or many criteria to compare them against. One way to minimize the repetition is to compare the options in tables and then highlight the more unusual or important aspects of each alternative in the text so that you get the best of both worlds. This approach allows you to compare all the alternatives against the same yardstick while calling attention to the most significant differences among them.

PLANNING PROPOSALS

The specific formats for proposals are innumerable, but they can be grouped into two general categories. *Internal proposals* request decisions from managers within the organization, such as proposals to buy new equipment or launch new research projects. *External proposals* request decisions from parties outside the organization. Examples include *investment proposals,* which request funding from external investors; *grant proposals,* which request funds from government agencies and other sponsoring organizations; and *sales proposals,* which suggest individualized solutions for potential customers and request purchase decisions.

The most significant factor in planning a proposal is whether the recipient has asked you to submit a proposal. *Solicited proposals* are generally prepared at the request of external parties that require a product or a service, but they may also be requested by such internal sources as management or the board of directors. Some external parties prepare a formal invitation to bid on their contracts, called a **request for proposals (RFP)**, which includes instructions that specify the exact type of work to be performed or products to be delivered, along with budgets, deadlines, and other requirements. Say that the National Aeronautics and Space Administration (NASA) decides to develop a new satellite. The agency prepares an RFP that specifies exactly what the satellite should accomplish, and it sends the RFP to several aerospace companies, inviting them to bid on the job. The companies respond by preparing proposals that show how they would meet NASA's needs. In most cases, organizations that issue RFPs also provide strict guidelines on what the proposals should include, and you need to follow these guidelines carefully in order to be considered. RFPs can seem surprisingly picky, even to the point of specifying the size of paper to use, but you must follow every detail.

Unsolicited proposals offer more flexibility but a completely different sort of challenge since recipients aren't expecting to receive them. In fact, your audience may not be aware of the problem or opportunity you are addressing, so before you can propose a solution, you might first need to convince your readers that a problem or opportunity exists. Consequently, an indirect approach is often the wise choice for unsolicited proposals.

Regardless of its format and structure, a good proposal explains what a project or course of action will involve, how much it will cost, and how the recipient and his or her organization will benefit. You can see all of these elements in Shandel Cohen's internal proposal for an automatic e-mail response system that would replace a labor-intensive process of mailing out printed brochures every time a potential customer requests information (see Figure 10–12).

Cohen manages the customer-response section of the marketing department at a Midwest personal computer manufacturer. Her section sends out product information requested by customers and the field salesforce. Cohen has observed that the demand for information increases when a new product is released and that it diminishes as a product matures. This fluctuating demand causes drastic changes in her section's workload.

Buyers solicit proposals by publishing a request for proposals (RFP).

MEMO

DATE:	July 8, 2006
TO:	Jamie Engle
FROM:	Shandel Cohen
SUBJECT:	Saving $145k/year with an automated e-mail response system

Catches the reader's attention with a compelling promise in subject line

THE PROBLEM:
Expensive and Slow Response to Customer Information Requests

Our new product line has been very well received, and orders have surpassed our projections. This very success, however, has created a shortage of printed brochures, as well as considerable overtime for people in the customer response center. As we introduce upgrades and new options, our printed materials quickly become outdated. If we continue to rely on printed materials for customer information, we have two choices: Distribute existing materials (even though they are incomplete or inaccurate) or discard existing materials and print new ones.

Describes the current situation and explains why it should be fixed

THE SOLUTION:
Automated E-mail Response System

Explains the proposed solution in enough detail to make it convincing, without burdening the reader with excessive detail

With minor additions and modifications to our current e-mail system, we can set up an automated system to respond to customer requests for information. This system can save us time and money and can keep our distributed information current.

Automated e-mail response systems have been tested and proven effective. Many companies already use this method to respond to customer information requests, so we won't have to worry about relying on untested technology. Using the system is easy, too: Customers simply send a blank e-mail message to a specific address, and the system responds by sending an electronic copy of the requested brochure.

Benefit #1: Always-Current Information

Rather than discard and print new materials, we would only need to keep the electronic files up to date on the server. We could be able to provide customers and our field sales organization with up-to-date, correct information as soon as the upgrades or options are available.

Builds reader interest in the proposed solution by listing a number of compelling benefits

Benefit #2: Instantaneous Delivery

Almost immediately after requesting information, customers would have that information in hand. Electronic delivery would be especially advantageous for our international customers. Regular mail to remote locations sometimes takes weeks to arrive, by which time the information may already be out of date. Both customers and field salespeople will appreciate the automatic mail-response system.

Benefit #3: Minimized Waste

With our current method of printing every marketing piece in large quantities, we discard thousands of pages of obsolete catalogs, data sheets, and other materials every year. By maintaining and distributing the information electronically, we would eliminate this waste. We would also free up a considerable amount of expensive floor space and shelving that is required for storing printed materials.

(continued)

FIGURE 10–12
Shandel Cohen's Internal Proposal

"Either we have more work than we can possibly handle," says Cohen, "or we don't have enough to keep us busy. But I don't want to get into a hiring-and-firing cycle." Cohen is also concerned about the amount of printed material that's discarded when products are upgraded or replaced.

Cohen's internal proposal seeks management's approval to install an automatic mail-response system. Because the company manufactures computers, she knows that her boss won't object to a computer-based solution. Also, since profits are always a concern, her report emphasizes the financial benefits of her proposal. Her report describes the problem, her proposed solutions, the benefits to the company, and the projected costs.

FIGURE 10–12
(continued)

2

Of course, some of our customers may still prefer to receive printed materials, or they may not have access to electronic mail. For these customers, we could simply print copies of the files when we receive such requests. The new Xerox DocuColor printer just installed in the Central Services building would be ideal for printing high-quality materials in small quantities.

Benefit #4: Lower Overtime Costs

Acknowledges one potential shortcoming with the new approach but provides a convincing solution to that as well

In addition to saving both paper and space, we would also realize considerable savings in wages. Because of the increased interest in our new products, we must continue to work overtime or hire new people to meet the demand. An automatic mail-response system would eliminate this need, allowing us to deal with fluctuating interest without a fluctuating workforce.

Cost Analysis

The necessary equipment and software costs approximately $15,000. System mainte-nance and upgrades are estimated at $5,000 per year. However, those costs are offset many times over by the predicted annual savings:

Itemizes the cost savings in order to support the $145k/year claim made in the subject line

Printing	$100,000
Storage	25,000
Postage	5,000
Wages	20,000
Total	**$150,000**

Based on these figures, the system would save $130,000 the first year and $145,000 every year after that.

CONCLUSION

Summarizes the benefits and invites further discussion

An automated e-mail response system would yield considerable benefits in both customer satisfaction and operating costs. If you approve, we can have it installed and running in six weeks. Please give me a call if you have any questions.

On the Job

SOLVING COMMUNICATION DILEMMAS AT TOYOTA SCION

You used to work at a marketing research firm that did several projects for Brian Bolain and his colleagues at Scion. Bolain was impressed not only with your research skills but also with your ability to communicate complex ideas to a variety of audiences. He invited you to join the Scion team as a market analyst, and you jumped at the chance. Now you have the opportunity to apply your research and writing skills to the intriguing challenges of marketing cars.

1. As far as problems go, this isn't a bad one to have, you suppose. After all the effort to promote Scion as a youth-oriented brand, the average age of Scion buyers is around 30. Buyers as old as 60 or more are intrigued by the brand's unique look and welcome blend of low cost and high quality. Eager customers aren't a problem, of course, but you believe Toyota does need to decide whether to keep promoting Scion as a young-person's brand or "go with the flow" and promote it as something else. You're planning an analytical report that will recommend the direction the brand should take in the coming years, based on whatever affect these older buyers are having on public perceptions of the brand—if any. Which of the following is the best way to phrase a statement

of purpose for this investigation, in light of the growing number of less-than-youthful Scion customers?

a. To explore the damage being done to Scion's youth appeal and to figure out a way to make the brand communication less appealing to older buyers.

b. The very meaning of the Scion brand is being undermined; if young consumers see their parents and grandparents driving Scions, won't they abandon the brand?

c. To explore the affect that purchases by older consumers are having on perceptions in the Scion brand and to recommend a change in brand strategy if one is indicated by the analysis.

d. To explore the affect that purchases by older consumers are having on the Scion brand.

2. Being a "youthful" brand doesn't mean that Scion necessarily needs to focus its promotional communication solely on young consumers. Lots of older consumers enjoy products and activities that many might consider meant for the young, from Harley-Davidson motorcycles to adventure travel packages. However, if Scion cars really do have broad appeal across generational boundaries, Toyota could be limiting itself by focusing so much on young buyers (such as by sponsoring music festivals that attract primarily younger people). Before you can decide if the strategy should change, you need to know what U.S. consumers think about the brand. Which of the following would be the best method for collecting such data?

a. Conduct a telephone survey of a carefully selected sample of U.S. residents.

b. Interview a dozen or so experts in consumer psychology to see what they think about Scion's youth appeal; they're likely to know much more about how consumers respond to brands than consumers themselves.

c. Thousands of people already visit the Scion website every month; why not just take advantage of that for data collection? Have the web design team add a few survey questions to the homepage. To ensure a high response rate, implement the change in such a way that site visitors need to answer the questions before they're allowed to access the car descriptions and other online content.

d. Scion dealers already talk to consumers all day long. Simply ask the sales representatives to collect the data from consumers who visit the dealerships.

3. Your research uncovered a few surprising issues:

• Consumer awareness of the Scion has spread far beyond the core audience of young adults; a sizable percentage of people in every age bracket know about the cars.

• Many of the consumers aged 30 and above didn't find out about Scion from Scion's own communication activities. In fact, many people report hearing about the cars from their children and grandchildren.

• Roughly half of the consumers 40 and older weren't aware that Scion was being promoted as a youth brand; those who liked the cars—55 percent of the people surveyed—liked them for their styling, quality, and price.

• Consumers who liked Scion the most tended to be aware that it is a Toyota brand name, not a new car company.

• A small but potentially disturbing percentage of people in the 18–29 age group reported being turned off by Scion's attempts to market the car as a hip, youth brand. Some 15 percent say that "advertising is advertising," and what Scion is doing isn't any different.

Based on these findings, you've decided to recommend to Bolain that Scion expand its marketing efforts beyond younger consumers and to highlight, rather than hide, the association with Toyota. You'll recommend that, based on all the findings in the research, Scion could be even more successful with a wide range of consumers, as long as it's promoted as a fun, fresh, sensible alternative to high-priced SUVs and other cars. You're confident in your analysis, but you know that adopting your recommendation would require an enormous change in Scion's strategy. Which of the following organizational structures is the best choice for your report?

a. Use the 2 + 2 = 4 approach, adding up the reasons uncovered in the research to show that a broader marketing strategy would increase sales.

b. Use the yardstick approach, evaluating five market segments (ages 20–29, 30–39, 40–49, 50–59, and 60–69) using the criteria of household income, attitude toward the Toyota brand name, and near-term purchase plans for new cars.

c. Focus on the conclusion first, then list the research results in an appendix. Bolain is a busy fellow and might not have the time to wade through all your data.

d. Show your creativity by sketching out several ads that communicate the new marketing strategy you have in mind. Instead of laboring over a report, simply display the mockup ads in your office and invite Bolain to comment on them.

4. Your survey also included the following open-ended question: "If you could convince Scion to create any vehicle, what sort of vehicle would that be?" You were amazed to see that nearly half of the people surveyed said they'd like to see a Scion pickup. Not a fire-breathing monster designed to haul lumber and gravel to construction sites, but a funky little "micro-pickup" that could be used to carry camping equipment, bicycles, golf clubs, and other recreational gear. The more you think about it, the more you like the idea, too. How would you organize a proposal to Bolain and the rest of the Scion management team, encouraging them to create the micro-pickup? You'll submit this document separately from your research report, since no one asked you to propose new product ideas.

a. A boring report won't get you anywhere. Instead, create a full-size mockup of the micro-pickup, showing Bolain and the other managers the basic size and shape of the new model. Once they see it, they'll surely get excited about it, too.

b. Use a direct approach—in fact, your first heading in the report should be: "Scion Should Make a Micro-Pickup."

c. Use an indirect approach, first discussing the research that uncovered the idea of the micro-pickup, then explaining how such a vehicle would fit perfectly in the Scion family. End with a fairly detailed description of the pickup and ask the management team to explore the possibility of making it.

d. Use an indirect approach, first discussing the research that uncovered the idea of the micro-pickup, then explaining how such a vehicle would fit perfectly in the Scion family. Knowing that top managers don't like to be told what to conclude when faced with a decision, leave the product description intentionally vague and don't try to persuade them to move forward with it. If you let them decide what the vehicle should be like, they'll feel a greater sense of ownership of the idea and will therefore support the decision even more.

Learning Objectives Checkup

Assess your understanding of the principles in this chapter by reading each learning objective and studying the accompanying exercises. For fill-in items, write the missing text in the blank provided; for multiple choice items, circle the letter of the correct answer. You can check your responses against the answer key on page AK-2.

Objective 10.1: Adapt the three-step writing process to reports and proposals.

1. Why is it particularly important in long reports to clearly identify your purpose before you begin writing?
   a. A clear statement of purpose helps you avoid extensive revisions.
   b. A clear statement of purpose gives you the opportunity to clarify the project with the person who assigned you the report.
   c. A clear statement of purpose helps you plan your research by identifying the information you'll need to gather.
   d. All of the above are important factors.

2. What does it mean to define the *scope* of a project when you're preparing a work plan?
   a. The scope is the range of your investigation and subsequent reporting; you'll address all the important topics within the defined scope of your project and ignore issues that are outside of your scope.
   b. The scope refers to the level of detail, in much the same way that microscopes and telescopes provide varying levels of detail.
   c. Scope indicates how long you'll spend on the project.
   d. None of the above are correct.

Objective 10.2: Distinguish informational reports, analytical reports, and proposals.

3. _____ reports focus on the delivery of facts, figures, and other types of information, without making recommendations or proposing new ideas or solutions.

4. _____ reports assess a situation or problem and recommend a course of action in response.

5. _____ offer structured, persuasive messages that encourage readers to take a specific course of action.

Objective 10.3: Describe an effective process for conducting business research.

6. Which of the following is the appropriate first step in any research project?
   a. Evaluate secondary research to see if you can reuse anything from earlier research projects.
   b. Conduct a preliminary phone survey to measure the extent of the issue you're about to research.
   c. Conduct a thorough statistical analysis of any existing data.
   d. Develop a research plan by familiarizing yourself with the subject, identifying information gaps, and prioritizing research needs.

7. In the series of values 14, 37, 44, 44, 44, 74, 76, 88, 93, 100, 112,
   a. The mean is 66
   b. The median is 74
   c. The mode is 44
   d. All of the above are correct

Objective 10.4: Define primary and secondary research, and explain when you use each method.

8. Research being conducted for the first time is called _____ research.

9. Research that was conducted for other projects but is being considered for a new project is called _____ research.

10. Secondary research is
    a. Generally used before primary research
    b. Generally used after primary research
    c. Generally used at the same time as primary research
    d. Another name for primary research

Objective 10.5: Name nine criteria for evaluating the credibility of an information source.

11. Why does information found on the Internet need to be used with extreme care?
    a. Most sources on the Internet are false.
    b. You can be sued for using anything found online.

c. Online sources often lack the fact-checking and other quality control procedures usually found in traditional, offline publishing.

d. Online information often contains computer viruses.

12. Why is it important to understand the purpose for which source material was created?

a. Knowing the purpose helps alert you to any potential biases.

b. You are required to indicate this purpose in your bibliography.

c. The purpose tells you whether or not the material is copyrighted.

d. The purpose tells you whether or not you need to pay usage rights.

13. If you uncover critically important information (the sort that could make or break your company) that is from a credible source and appears to be unbiased, well documented, current, and complete but is the only source of this information you can find, how should you handle this situation in your subsequent reporting?

a. Use it as you would use any other information.

b. Use it, but clearly indicate the source in your report.

c. Use it, but clearly indicate in your report that this is the only source of the information and you weren't able to verify it through a second, independent source.

d. Don't use it.

Objective 10.6: Provide five guidelines for conducting an effective online search.

14. Why is it important to fully understand the instructions for using an individual search engine, web directory, database, or other computer-based research tool?

a. You can be fined if you use these tools improperly.

b. Most search tools won't return any results if you don't know how to use them.

c. Using the tool without understanding how it works can produce unpredictable and misleading results.

d. Today's search tools are so easy to use that you don't need to worry about learning the details.

15. What should you do if your first attempt to find something with a search engine doesn't return anything?

a. Try again with fewer search terms (which will broaden your search).

b. Try again with fewer search terms (which will narrow your search).

c. Try again with more search terms (which will broaden your search).

d. Try again with more search terms (which will narrow your search).

Objective 10.7: Outline an effective process for planning and conducting information interviews.

16. Recording an interview

a. Should always be done for legal reasons, regardless of whether the subject consents to be recorded

b. Should never be done without the subject's permission

c. Is a waste of time if you listen carefully

d. Is always a good idea because it means you don't have to pay close attention during the interview

Objective 10.8: Explain the differences between drafting a summary, drawing a conclusion, and developing a recommendation.

17. A _____ is a shortened version of one or more documents, research results, or other information; it filters out details and presents only the most important ideas.

18. A _____ is your analysis of what the findings mean (an interpretation of the facts).

19. A _____ is your opinion (based on reason and logic) about the course of action that should be taken.

Objective 10.9: Discuss three major ways to organize analytical reports.

20. If you have a long history of success in business and are highly regarded by your audience, which two organizing models will probably be sufficient for most reports to this audience?

a. Focusing on conclusions or focusing on recommendations

b. Focusing on conclusions and focusing on troubleshooting

c. Focusing on logic or focusing on analysis

d. Focusing on reason and focusing on logic

21. If you need to "walk your audience through" the reasoning that led you to the conclusion or recommendation in your report, you should use an organization that focuses on _____.

Apply Your Knowledge

1. Why must you be careful when using information from a webpage in a business report?

2. Why do you need to evaluate the sources you uncover in your research?

3. If you were writing a recommendation report for an audience that doesn't know you, would you use a direct approach focusing on the recommendation or an indirect approach focusing on logic? Why?

4. Why are unsolicited proposals more challenging to write than solicited proposals?

5. **Ethical Choices**: Companies occasionally make mistakes that expose confidential information, such as when employees lose laptop computers containing sensitive data files or webmasters forget to protect confidential webpages from search engine indexes. If you conducted an online search that turned up competitive information on webpages that were clearly intended to be private, what would you do? Explain your answer.

Practice Your Knowledge

DOCUMENT FOR ANALYSIS

The Securities and Exchange Commission (SEC) requires all public companies to file a comprehensive annual report (form 10-K) electronically. Many companies post links to these reports on their websites along with links to other company reports. Visit the website of Dell at www.dell.com and find the company's most recent annual reports: 10-K and Year in Review (click on "About Dell" on the homepage, then click on the "Investors" link). Compare the style and format of the two reports. For which audience(s) is the Year in Review targeted? Who besides the SEC might be interested in the Annual Report 10-K? Which report do you find easier to read? More interesting? More detailed?

Exercises

For active links to all websites discussed in this chapter, visit this text's website at www.prenhall.com/thill. Locate your book and click on its Companion Website link. Then select Chapter 10, and click on "Featured Websites." Locate the name of the page or the URL related to the material in the text. Please note that links to sites that become inactive after publication of the book will be removed from the Featured Websites section.

10.1 Understanding Business Reports and Proposals: How Companies Use Reports Interview several people working in a career you might like to enter, and ask them about the written reports they receive and prepare. How do these reports tie in to the decision-making process? Who reads the reports they prepare? Summarize your findings in writing, give them to your instructor, and be prepared to discuss them with the class.

10.2 Understanding Business Reports and Proposals: Report Classification Using the information presented in this chapter, identify the report type represented by each of the following examples. In addition, write a brief paragraph about each, explaining who the audience is likely to be, what type of data would be used, and whether conclusions and recommendations would be appropriate.
  a. A statistical study of the pattern of violent crime in a large city during the last five years
  b. A report prepared by a seed company demonstrating the benefits of its seed corn for farmers
  c. A report prepared by an independent testing agency evaluating various types of nonprescription cold remedies
  d. A trip report submitted at the end of a week by a traveling salesperson
  e. A report indicating how 45 acres of undeveloped land could be converted into an industrial park
  f. An annual report to be sent to the shareholders of a large corporation
  g. A report from a U.S. National Park wildlife officer to Washington, D.C., headquarters showing the status of the California condor (an endangered species)
  h. A written report by a police officer who has just completed an arrest

10.3 Informational Reports: Personal Activity Report Imagine you're the manager of campus recruiting for Nortel, a Canadian telecommunications firm. Each of your four recruiters interviews up to 11 college seniors every day. What kind of personal activity report can you design to track the results of these interviews? List the areas you would want each recruiter to report on, and explain how each would help you manage the recruiting process (and the recruiters) more effectively.

10.4 Understanding Your Topic: Subquestions Your boss has asked you to do some research on franchising. Actually, he's thinking about purchasing a few Subway franchises, and he needs some information. Visit www.amazon.com and perform a keyword search on "franchises." Explore some of the books that you find by reading reviews and using the "search inside" feature.
  a. Use the information to develop a list of subquestions to help you narrow your focus.
  b. Write down the names of three books you might purchase for your boss.
  c. How can this website assist you with your research efforts?

10.5 Finding Secondary Information Using online, database, or printed sources, find the following information. Be sure to properly cite your source using the formats discussed in Appendix B (*Hint:* Start with Table 10–3, Major Business Resources.)
  a. Contact information for the American Management Association
  b. Median weekly earnings of men and women by occupation
  c. Current market share for Perrier water
  d. Performance ratios for office supply retailers
  e. Annual stock performance for Hewlett-Packard (HP)
  f. Number of franchise outlets in the United States
  g. Composition of the U.S. workforce by profession

10.6 Finding Information: Company Information Select any public company and find the following information:
  a. Names of the company's current officers

b. List of the company's products or services (if the company has a large number of products, list the product lines instead)

c. Current issues in the company's industry

d. Outlook for the company's industry as a whole

10.7 Finding Information: Secondary Information You'd like to know if it's a good idea to buy banner ads on other websites to drive more traffic to your company's website. You're worried about the expense and difficulty of running an experiment to test banner effectiveness, so you decide to look for some secondary data. Using databases available through your library, identify three secondary sources that might offer helpful data on this question.

10.8 Finding Information: Search Techniques Analyze any recent school or work assignment that required you to conduct research. How did you approach your investigation? Did you rely mostly on sources of primary information or mostly on sources of secondary information? Now that you have studied this chapter, can you identify two ways to improve the research techniques you used during that assignment? Briefly explain.

10.9 Finding Information: Surveys You work for a movie studio that is producing a young director's first motion picture, the story of a group of unknown musicians finding work and making a reputation in a competitive industry. Unfortunately, some of your friends leave the screening, saying that the 182-minute movie is simply too long. Others said they couldn't imagine any sequences to cut out. Your boss wants to test the movie on a regular audience and ask viewers to complete a questionnaire that will help the director decide whether edits are needed and, if so, where. Design a questionnaire that you can use to solicit valid answers for a report to the director about how to handle the audience's reaction to the movie.

10.10 Finding Information: Interviews You're conducting an information interview with a manager in another division of your company. Partway through the interview, the manager shows clear signs of impatience. How should you respond? What might you do differently to prevent this from happening in the future? Explain your answers.

10.11 Teamwork: Evaluating Sources Break into small groups and surf the Internet to find websites that provide business information such as company or industry news, trends, analysis, facts, or performance data. Using the criteria discussed under "Evaluating Your Sources," evaluate the credibility of the information presented at these websites.

10.12 Processing Information: Reading and Taking Notes Select an article from a business magazine such as *BusinessWeek, Fortune, Forbes, Fast Company,* or *Business 2.0.* Read the article and highlight the article's key points. Summarize the article in less than 100 words, paraphrasing the key points.

10.13 Analyzing Data: Calculating the Mean Your boss has asked you to analyze and report on your division's sales for the first nine months of this year. Using the following data from company invoices, calculate the mean for each quarter and all averages for the year to date. Then identify and discuss the quarterly sales trends.

January	$24,600	April	$21,200	July	$29,900
February	25,900	May	24,600	August	30,500
March	23,000	June	26,800	September	26,600

10.14 Teamwork: Unsolicited Proposal Break into small groups and identify an operational problem occurring at your campus involving either registration, university housing, food services, parking, or library services. Then develop a workable solution to that problem. Finally, develop a list of pertinent facts that your team will need to gather to convince the reader that the problem exists and that your solution will work.

10.15 Analyzing the Situation: Statement of Purpose Sales at The Style Shop, a clothing store for men, have declined for the third month in a row. Your boss is not sure if this decline is due to a weak economy or if it's due to another unknown reason. She has asked you to investigate the situation and to submit a report to her highlighting some possible reasons for the decline. Develop a statement of purpose for your report.

10.16 Organizing Reports: Structuring Analytical Reports Three years ago, your company (a carpet manufacturer) modernized its Georgia plant in anticipation of increasing demand for carpets. Because of the depressed housing market, the increase in demand for new carpets has been slow to materialize. As a result, the company has excess capacity at both its Georgia and California plants. On the basis of your research, you have recommended that the company close the California plant. The company president, J. P. Lawrence, has asked you to prepare a justification report to support your recommendation. Here are the facts you gathered by interviewing the respective plant managers:

OPERATIONAL STATISTICS

- *Georgia plant:* This plant has newer equipment, productivity is higher, employs 100 nonunion production workers, and ships $12 million in carpets a year. Hourly base wage is $16.
- *California plant:* California plant employs 80 union production workers and ships $8 million in carpets a year. Hourly base wage is $20.

FINANCIAL IMPLICATIONS

- *Savings by closing California plant:* (1) Increase productivity by 17%; (2) reduce labor costs by 20% (total labor savings would be $1 million per year; see assumptions); (3) annual local tax savings of $120,000 (Georgia has a more favorable tax climate).

- *Sale of Pomona, California, land:* Purchased in 1952 for $200,000. Current market value $2.5 million. Net profit (after capital gains tax) over $1 million.
- *Sale of plant and equipment:* Fully depreciated. Any proceeds a windfall.
- *Costs of closing California plant:* One-time deductible charge of $250,000 (relocation costs of $100,000 and severance payments totaling $150,000).

ASSUMPTIONS

- Transfer 5 workers from California to Georgia.
- Hire 45 new workers in Georgia.
- Lay off 75 workers in California.

- Georgia plant would require a total of 150 workers to produce the combined volume of both plants.
  a. Which approach (focus on conclusions, recommendations, or logical arguments) will you use to structure your report to the president? Why?
  b. Suppose this report were to be circulated to plant managers and supervisors instead. What changes, if any, might you make in your approach?
  c. List some conclusions that you might draw from the above information to use in your report.
  d. Using the structure you selected for your report to the president, draft a final report outline with first- and second-level informative headings.

Expand Your Knowledge

LEARNING MORE ON THE WEB
CHECK OUT THIS 24-HOUR LIBRARY www.ipl.org

Start your business research by visiting the Internet Public Library. Visit the reference center and explore the many online references available. These cover topics such as business, economics, law, government, science, technology, computers, education, and more. You can even submit questions for the IPL staff.

ACTIVITIES

Visit the reference center and explore the Business and Economics Reference section. Click on *Business Directories,* and perform these tasks:

1. Select five companies and use the links provided to find contact information (address, phone, website, officers' names, and so on) for each company. What kinds of contact information did you find at the company websites?
2. Gather information about the U.S. budget by using one of the site's directories: A Business Researcher's Interests. Why is using a directory such as this one an efficient way to obtain information?

3. Go back to the library's main reference center and click on Reference. Follow some of the reference links. How might these links help you when performing business research?

EXPLORING THE WEB ON YOUR OWN
Review these chapter-related websites on your own to improve your research skills.

1. What's involved in a business plan? BizPlanIt.Com, **www.bizplanit.com**, offers tips and advice, a free e-mail newsletter, and a sample virtual business plan (click on "Bizplan Resources," then "The Virtual Business Plan"). You'll find suggestions on what details and how much information to include in each section of a business plan.
2. Learn how to make your website more usable and more useful by following the methods that professional web designers use. Visit Usability First, **www.usabilityfirst.com**.
3. If you're having trouble tracking down a specific company in your research, try SuperPages at **www.bigbook.com** where you'll find more than 16 million listings searchable by keywords, name, and location.

Learn Interactively

INTERACTIVE STUDY GUIDE

Visit **www.prenhall.com/thill**, then locate your book and click on its Companion Website link. Select Chapter 10 to take advantage of the interactive "Chapter Quiz" to test your knowledge of chapter concepts. Receive instant feedback on whether you need additional studying. Also, visit the "Study Hall," where you'll find an abundance of valuable resources that will help you succeed in this course.

PEAK PERFORMANCE GRAMMAR AND MECHANICS

If your instructor has required the use of "Peak Performance Grammar and Mechanics," either in your online course or on

CD, you can improve your skill with periods, question marks, and exclamation points by using the "Peak Performance Grammar and Mechanics" module. Click "Punctuation II." Take the Pretest to determine whether you have any weak areas. Then review those areas in the Refresher Course. Take the Follow-Up Test to check your grasp of periods, question marks, and exclamation points. For an extra challenge or advanced practice, take the Advanced Test. Finally, for additional reinforcement, go to the "Improve Your Grammar, Mechanics, and Usage" section that follows, and complete those exercises.

Improve Your Grammar, Mechanics, and Usage

The following exercises help you improve your knowledge of and power over English grammar, mechanics, and usage. Turn to the Handbook of Grammar, Mechanics, and Usage at the end of this textbook and review all of Sections 2.1 (Periods), 2.2 (Question Marks), and 2.3 (Exclamation Points). Then look at the following 10 items. Circle the letter of the preferred choice in the following groups of sentences. (Answers to these exercises appear on pages AK-3–AK-4.)

1. a. Dr. Eleanor H Hutton has requested information on TaskMasters, Inc.?
   b. Dr. Eleanor H. Hutton has requested information on TaskMasters, Inc.
2. a. That qualifies us as a rapidly growing new company, don't you think?
   b. That qualifies us as a rapidly growing new company, don't you think.
3. a. Our president is a C.P.A. On your behalf, I asked him why he started the firm.
   b. Our president is a CPA. On your behalf, I asked him why he started the firm.
4. a. Contact me at 1358 N. Parsons Ave., Tulsa, OK 74204.
   b. Contact me at 1358 N. Parsons Ave, Tulsa, OK. 74204.
5. a. Jeb asked, "Why does he want to know! Maybe he plans to become a competitor."
   b. Jeb asked, "Why does he want to know? Maybe he plans to become a competitor!"
6. a. The debt load fluctuates with the movement of the U.S. prime rate.
   b. The debt load fluctuates with the movement of the US prime rate.
7. a. Is consumer loyalty extinct? Yes and No!
   b. Is consumer loyalty extinct? Yes and No.
8. a. Will you please send us a check today so that we can settle your account.
   b. Will you please send us a check today so that we can settle your account?
9. a. Will you be able to speak at the conference, or should we find someone else.
   b. Will you be able to speak at the conference, or should we find someone else?
10. a. So I ask you, "When will we admit defeat?" Never!
    b. So I ask you, "When will we admit defeat"? Never!

For additional exercises focusing on periods, question marks, and exclamation points, go to www.prenhall.com/thill, then locate your text and click on its Companion Website link. Click on Chapter 10, click on "Additional Exercises to Improve Your Grammar, Mechanics and Usage," then click on "17. Punctuation B."

Chapter 11

Writing Reports and Proposals

Learning Objectives

AFTER STUDYING THIS CHAPTER, YOU WILL BE ABLE TO

1 Explain how to adapt to your audiences when writing reports and proposals

2 List the topics commonly covered in the introduction, body, and close of informational and analytical reports

3 Name five characteristics of effective report content

4 Name six strategies to strengthen your proposal argument

5 List the topics commonly covered in a proposal's introduction, body, and closing

6 Describe the communication power that visuals add to your writing

7 Explain how to choose which points in your message to illustrate

8 Discuss six principles of graphic design that can improve the quality of your visuals

9 Name three qualities to look for before including a visual in a report or presentation

On the Job

COMMUNICATING AT OMD WORLDWIDE

GUIDING ADVERTISERS THROUGH THE MAZE OF CONTEMPORARY MEDIA

You've probably tried to talk with older family members or professors about some product that they've never heard of. You're sure you've seen about a thousand ads for it, and you wonder, "How could they have missed it?" Pose this question to Beth Uyenco, and she could clear up the mystery with a two-part answer. First, media have become extremely fragmented in the United States, with an endless array of outlets spanning TV (broadcast, cable, and satellite), radio (AM, FM, and satellite), websites, magazines, newspapers, events, fashion, and more. So every year, the chances grow smaller that two people with different interests and habits will consume the same media. Second, new technologies let ad agencies develop unimaginably specific knowledge of audiences and their media preferences. Therefore, these agencies can be more and more precise about placing the right ads in the right place at the right time.

The science behind all this insight is quite complicated. It relies on multiple databases, market segmentation (by age, gender, education, socioeconomic status,

Beth Uyenco of OMD Worldwide relies on effective reports to help her clients understand complex issues involving the selection and purchase of advertising media.

and so on), and detailed analyses of how and when various types of consumers interact with various media. Once all this research has been completed and evaluated, it must be reported clearly and logically so that readers can act on the information. Uyenco is a superstar in this type of media research. She is the director of research at OMD Worldwide, an agency that provides media research, planning, and buying services for ad agencies and clients such as Dell Computer, FedEx, and PepsiCo.

Clients and colleagues praise Uyenco's rare ability to write reports and give presentations that explain the complexities of her work in plain, simple language, without confusing or frightening her audience. *Brandweek* magazine even named her its 2002 Media All-Star in Research. When asked about how she approaches reports, Uyenco explained: "You can be the best researcher, but if you can't relate it to the business at hand, to the day-to-day demands that planners and media management face, or to the sales pressures that clients face, you'll be irrelevant."[1]

www.omd.com

Planning   Writing   Completing

Adapt to Your Audience

Be sensitive to audience needs with a "you" attitude, politeness, positive emphasis, and bias-free language. Build a strong relationship with your audience by establishing your credibility and projecting your company's image. Control your style with a tone and voice appropriate to the situation.

Compose the Message

Choose strong words that will help you create effective sentences and coherent paragraphs throughout the introduction, body, and close of your report or proposal.

1   2   3

FIGURE 11–1
Step Two in the Three-Step Writing Process for Reports and Proposals

CRAFTING REPORTS AND PROPOSALS

Beth Uyenco will be the first to tell you how important the writing stage is in the development of successful reports and proposals. This chapter builds on the writing techniques and ideas you learned in Chapter 5 with issues that are particularly important when preparing longer message formats (see Figure 11–1). In addition, you'll get an introduction to creating effective visuals, which are a vital aspect of many reports and proposals.

As with shorter messages, take a few moments before you start writing to make sure you're ready to adapt your approach to your audience.

ADAPTING TO YOUR AUDIENCE

Like all successful business messages, effective reports and proposals are adapted to the intended audience as much as possible. To ensure your own success with reports, be sensitive to audience needs, build strong relationships with your audience, and control your style and tone.

Chapter 5 introduced four aspects of audience sensitivity, and all four apply to reports and proposals: adopting the "you" attitude, maintaining a strong sense of etiquette, emphasizing the positive, and using bias-free language. Reports and proposals that are highly technical, complex, or lengthy can put heavy demands on your readers, so the "you" attitude takes on even greater importance with these long messages. As you'll see later in this chapter, part of that attitude includes helping your readers find their way through your material so that they can understand critical information.

Whether your report is intended for people inside or outside the company, be sure to plan how you will adapt your style and your language to reflect the image of your organization. Bear in mind that some reports can take on lives of their own, reaching a wider audience than you ever imagined and being read years after you wrote them, so choose your content and language with care. Many companies have specific guidelines for communicating with public audiences, so make sure you're aware of these preferences before you start writing.

> Long or complex reports demand a lot from readers, making the "you" attitude even more important.

> Your reports may continue to be read for months or years after you write them—and reach audiences you never envisioned.

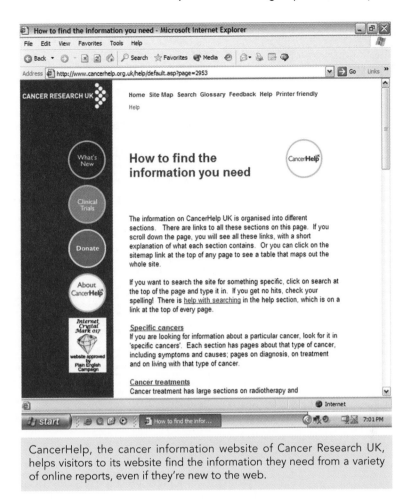

CancerHelp, the cancer information website of Cancer Research UK, helps visitors to its website find the information they need from a variety of online reports, even if they're new to the web.

Whether you're writing a report or a proposal, you'll need to decide on the appropriate style and tone. If you know your readers reasonably well and your report is likely to meet with their approval, you can generally adopt a fairly informal tone. To make your tone less formal, speak to readers in the first person, refer to them as *you*, and refer to yourself as *I* (or *we* if there are multiple report authors).

To make your tone more formal, use the impersonal journalism style: Emphasize objectivity, ensure that content is free from personal opinion, and build your argument on provable facts. When creating a formal tone, eliminate all references to *you* and *I* (including *we, us,* and *our*). Naturally, an impersonal style does not automatically guarantee objective content. Your selection of facts is just as important as the way you phrase them, if not more so. If you omit crucial evidence, you're not being objective, even though your style is impersonal. When you use an impersonal style, you impose a controlled distance between you and your readers. Your tone should also be businesslike and unemotional. Be careful to avoid jokes, similes, and metaphors, and try to minimize the use of colorful adjectives or adverbs.

A more formal tone is appropriate for longer reports, especially those dealing with controversial or complex information. You'll also need a more formal tone when your report will be sent to other parts of the organization or to outsiders, such as customers, suppliers, or members of the community. Yahoo! is known for using a playful, informal tone in its advertising, but the company's tone is more formal when communicating with the public on serious matters (see Figure 11–2).

Communicating with people in other cultures often calls for more formality, for two reasons. First, the business environment outside the United States tends to be more formal in general, and that formality must be reflected in your communication. Second, the things you do to make a document informal (such as using humor and

Reports destined for audiences outside the United States often require a more formal tone to match the expectations of audiences in many other countries.

FIGURE 11–2
Choosing the Right Tone for
Business Reports

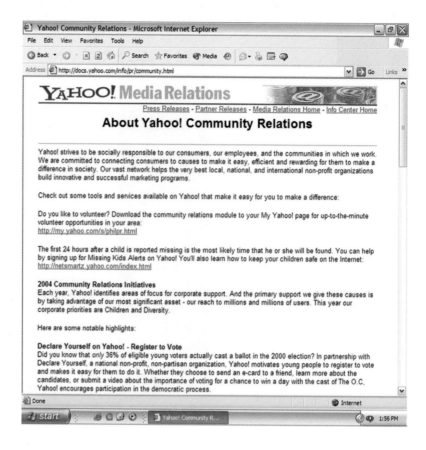

FIGURE 11–2
Choosing the Right Tone for
Business Reports

idiomatic language) tend to translate poorly or not at all from one culture to another. Using a less formal tone in cross-cultural reports and proposals increases the risk of offending people and the chance of miscommunicating information.

COMPOSING REPORTS AND PROPOSALS

With a clear picture of how you need to adapt to your audience, you're ready to begin composing your first draft. This section offers advice on drafting content for both reports and proposals, along with several strategies for making your content more readable. When you compose reports and proposals, follow the writing advice offered in Chapter 5: Select the best words, create the most effective sentences, and develop coherent paragraphs.

As with other written business communications, the text of reports and proposals has three main sections: an introduction (or *opening*), a body, and a close. The content and length of each section varies with the type and purpose of the document, the document's organizational structure, the length and depth of the material, the document's degree of formality, and your relationship with your audience.

Your introduction needs to put the report in context for the reader, introduce the subject, preview main ideas, and establish the tone of the document.

The *introduction* (or *opening*) is the first section in the text of any report or proposal. An effective introduction accomplishes at least four things:

- Puts the report or proposal in a broader context by tying it to a problem or an assignment

- Introduces the subject or purpose of the report or proposal and indicates why the subject is important

- Previews the main ideas and the order in which they'll be covered

- Establishes the tone of the document and the writer's relationship with the audience

The *body* is the middle section in the text of your report or proposal. It consists of the major divisions or sections with various levels of headings. These divisions present, analyze, and interpret the information gathered during your investigation, and they support the recommendations or conclusions discussed in your document. The body contains the proof, the detailed information necessary to support your conclusions and recommendations. Notice how Alycia Jenn uses the body of her report to articulate a recommendation to her company's board of directors (see Figure 11–3). As Jenn puts it, "Our company has a website that is commonly known as 'brochureware,' a static presentation of information that is basically just the electronic equivalent of a printed brochure. However, retailing in general and

The body of your report presents, analyzes, and interprets the information you gathered during your investigation.

FIGURE 11–3
Effective Problem-Solving Report Focusing on Recommendations

MEMO

DATE: July 6, 2006
TO: Board of Directors, Executive Committee members
FROM: Alycia Jenn, Business Development Manager *AJ*
SUBJECT: Website expansion

Reminds readers of the origin and purpose of the report

In response to your request, my staff and I investigated the potential for expanding our website from its current "brochureware" status (in which we promote our company and its products but don't provide any way to place orders online) to full e-commerce capability (including placing orders and checking on order delivery status). After analyzing the behavior of our customers and major competitors and studying the overall development of electronic retailing, we have three recommendations:

1. We should expand our online presence from "brochureware" to e-commerce capability within the next six months.

2. We should engage a firm that specializes in online retailing to design and develop the new e-commerce capabilities.

3. We must take care to integrate online retailing with our store-based and mail-order operations.

Clarifies the recommendation by listing the necessary actions in clear, direct language

1. WE SHOULD EXPAND THE WEBSITE TO FULL E-COMMERCE CAPABILITY

Presents logical reasons for recommending that the firm expand its website to include e-commerce

First, does e-commerce capability make sense today for a small company that sells luxury housewares? Even though books and many other products are now commonly sold online, in most cases, this enterprise involves simple, low-cost products that don't require a lot of hands-on inspection before purchasing. As we've observed in our stores, shoppers like to interact with our products before purchasing them. However, a small but growing number of websites do sell specialty products, using such tactics as "virtual product tours" (in which shoppers can interactively view a product in three dimensions, rather than simply looking at a static photograph) and generous return policies (to reduce the perceived risk of buying products online).

Second, do we need to establish a presence now in order to remain competitive in the future? The answer is an overwhelming "yes." The initial steps taken by our competitors are already placing us at a disadvantage among those shoppers who are already comfortable buying online, and every trend indicates our minor competitive weakness today will turn into a major weakness in the next few years:

• Several of our top competitors are beginning to implement full e-commerce, including virtual product tours. Our research suggests that these companies aren't yet generating significant financial returns from these online investments, but their online sales are growing.

• Younger consumers who grew up with the World Wide Web will soon be reaching their peak earning years (ages 35-54). This demographic segment expects e-commerce in nearly every product category, and we'll lose them to the competition if we don't offer it.

Supports the reasoning with evidence

• The web is erasing geographical shopping limits, presenting both a threat and an opportunity. Even though our customers can now shop websites anywhere in the world (so that we have thousands of competitors instead of a dozen), we can now target customers anywhere in the world.

(continued)

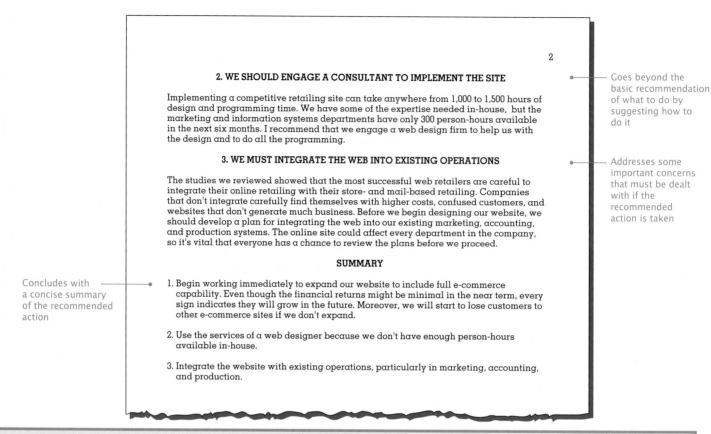

2

2. WE SHOULD ENGAGE A CONSULTANT TO IMPLEMENT THE SITE

Implementing a competitive retailing site can take anywhere from 1,000 to 1,500 hours of design and programming time. We have some of the expertise needed in-house, but the marketing and information systems departments have only 300 person-hours available in the next six months. I recommend that we engage a web design firm to help us with the design and to do all the programming.

> Goes beyond the basic recommendation of what to do by suggesting how to do it

3. WE MUST INTEGRATE THE WEB INTO EXISTING OPERATIONS

The studies we reviewed showed that the most successful web retailers are careful to integrate their online retailing with their store- and mail-based retailing. Companies that don't integrate carefully find themselves with higher costs, confused customers, and websites that don't generate much business. Before we begin designing our website, we should develop a plan for integrating the web into our existing marketing, accounting, and production systems. The online site could affect every department in the company, so it's vital that everyone has a chance to review the plans before we proceed.

> Addresses some important concerns that must be dealt with if the recommended action is taken

SUMMARY

> Concludes with a concise summary of the recommended action

1. Begin working immediately to expand our website to include full e-commerce capability. Even though the financial returns might be minimal in the near term, every sign indicates they will grow in the future. Moreover, we will start to lose customers to other e-commerce sites if we don't expand.

2. Use the services of a web designer because we don't have enough person-hours available in-house.

3. Integrate the website with existing operations, particularly in marketing, accounting, and production.

FIGURE 11–3
(continued)

several of our competitors in particular are moving beyond this to fully functional e-commerce websites that allow shoppers to interact with virtual products on screen, place orders, check order status, and so on. We don't have the staff needed to create such a site, but after studying the issue for several weeks, I concluded that if we don't move to interactive e-commerce soon, we're going to lose significant sales to both current and future competitors. However, we do need to implement e-commerce carefully, in a way that doesn't interrupt our existing retail operations, so I made that clear in my recommendation as well." The body of her report provides enough information to support her argument, without burdening her high-level readership with a lot of tactical details.

The *close* is the final section in the text of your report or proposal. It has four important functions:

- Emphasizes the main points of the message

- Summarizes the benefits to the reader if the document suggests a change or some other course of action

- Refers back to all the pieces and reminds readers how those pieces fit together

- Brings all the action items together in one place and gives the details about who should do what, when, where, and how

> The close might be the only part of your report some readers have time for, so make sure it conveys the full weight of your message.

Research shows that the final section of a report or proposal leaves a lasting impression. The close gives you one last chance to make sure that your report says what you intended.[2] In fact, readers who are in a hurry might skip the body of the report and read only the summary, so make sure it carries a strong, clear message.

Drafting Report Content

Your credibility and career advancement are on the line with every business report you write, so make sure your content is:

- **Accurate.** Be sure to double-check your facts and references in addition to checking for typos. If an audience ever gets the inkling that your information is shaky, they'll start to view all your work with a skeptical eye.

- **Complete.** To help colleagues or supervisors make informed decision, include everything necessary for readers to understand the situation, problem, or proposal. Support all key assertions using an appropriate combination of illustrations, explanations, and facts.[3] But remember, time is valuable, so don't tell the readers more than they need to know.

- **Balanced.** Present all sides of the issue fairly and equitably, and include all the essential information, even if some of the information doesn't support your line of reasoning. Omitting relevant information or facts can bias your report.

- **Clear and logical.** Clear sentence structure and good transitions are essential.[4] Save your readers time by making sure your sentences are uncluttered, contain well-chosen words, and proceed logically. To help your readers move from one point to the next, make your transitions just as clear and logical. For a successful report, identify the ideas that belong together, and organize them in a way that's easy to understand.[5]

- **Documented properly.** If you use primary and secondary sources for your report or proposal, be sure to properly document and give credit to your sources, as Chapter 10 explains.

Keeping these points in mind will help you draft the most effective introduction, body, and close for your report. Note how Carlyce Johnson offers one client a complete, but efficient, update of her company's landscaping services (see an excerpt from her report in Figure 11–4). In addition to providing routine information, she also informs the client of progress on two problem areas, one that her firm has been able to resolve and one that they've just discovered. In the case of the problem with the soil, you might be tempted not to share any information with the client until you've resolved the problem, but doing so could affect the client's budgets and other plans. Johnson does the right thing by telling the client about the problem early.

Report Introduction   The specific elements you should include in an introduction depend on the nature and length of the report, the circumstances under which you're writing it, and your relationship with the audience. An introduction could contain all of the following topics, although you'll want to pick and choose the best ones to include with each report you write:

- **Authorization.** When, how, and by whom the report was authorized; who wrote it; and when it was submitted. This material is especially important when you don't use a *letter of transmittal* (see Chapter 12) to accompany the report.

- **Problem/opportunity/purpose.** The reason the report was written and what is to be accomplished as a result of your having written it.

- **Scope.** What is and what isn't going to be covered in the report. The scope indicates the report's size and complexity; it also helps with the critical job of setting the audience's expectations.

- **Background.** The historical conditions or factors that led up to the report. This section enables readers to understand how the problem, situation, or opportunity developed and what has been done about it so far.

Carefully select the elements to include in your introduction; strive for a balance between necessary, expected information and brevity.

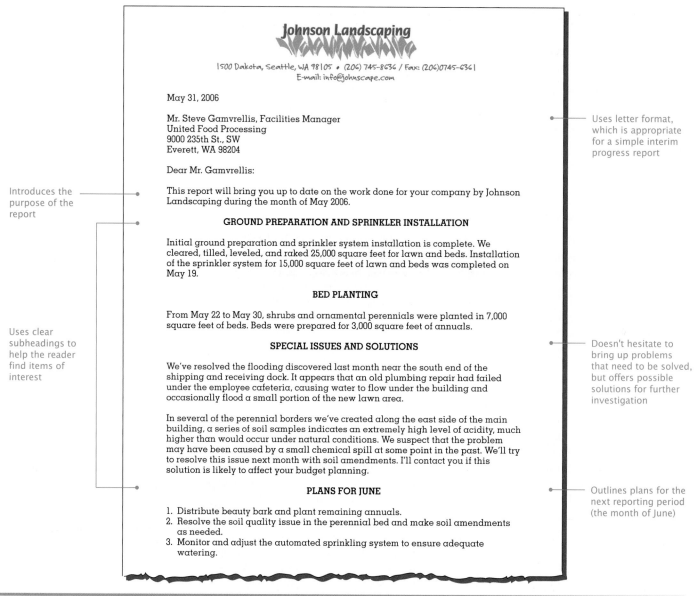

FIGURE 11–4
Effective Progress Report Offering Complete Content (Excerpt)

The following annotations appear in the margins of Figure 11–4:

Introduces the purpose of the report

Uses clear subheadings to help the reader find items of interest

Uses letter format, which is appropriate for a simple interim progress report

Doesn't hesitate to bring up problems that need to be solved, but offers possible solutions for further investigation

Outlines plans for the next reporting period (the month of June)

The text within Figure 11–4 reads:

Johnson Landscaping

1500 Dakota, Seattle, WA 98105 • (206) 745-8636 / Fax: (206)0745-6361
E-mail: info@johnscape.com

May 31, 2006

Mr. Steve Gamvrellis, Facilities Manager
United Food Processing
9000 235th St., SW
Everett, WA 98204

Dear Mr. Gamvrellis:

This report will bring you up to date on the work done for your company by Johnson Landscaping during the month of May 2006.

GROUND PREPARATION AND SPRINKLER INSTALLATION

Initial ground preparation and sprinkler system installation is complete. We cleared, tilled, leveled, and raked 25,000 square feet for lawn and beds. Installation of the sprinkler system for 15,000 square feet of lawn and beds was completed on May 19.

BED PLANTING

From May 22 to May 30, shrubs and ornamental perennials were planted in 7,000 square feet of beds. Beds were prepared for 3,000 square feet of annuals.

SPECIAL ISSUES AND SOLUTIONS

We've resolved the flooding discovered last month near the south end of the shipping and receiving dock. It appears that an old plumbing repair had failed under the employee cafeteria, causing water to flow under the building and occasionally flood a small portion of the new lawn area.

In several of the perennial borders we've created along the east side of the main building, a series of soil samples indicates an extremely high level of acidity, much higher than would occur under natural conditions. We suspect that the problem may have been caused by a small chemical spill at some point in the past. We'll try to resolve this issue next month with soil amendments. I'll contact you if this solution is likely to affect your budget planning.

PLANS FOR JUNE

1. Distribute beauty bark and plant remaining annuals.
2. Resolve the soil quality issue in the perennial bed and make soil amendments as needed.
3. Monitor and adjust the automated sprinkling system to ensure adequate watering.

- **Sources and methods.** The primary and secondary sources of information used. As appropriate, this section explains how samples were selected, how questionnaires were constructed (which should be included in an appendix with any cover letters), what follow-up was done, and so on. This section builds reader confidence in the work and in the sources and methods used.

- **Definitions.** A list of terms that might be unfamiliar to your audience, along with brief definitions. This section is unnecessary if readers are familiar with the terms you've used in your report—and they all agree on what the terms mean, which isn't always the case. If you have any question about reader knowledge, define any terms that might be misinterpreted. Terms may also be defined in the body, explanatory notes, or glossary.

- **Limitations.** Factors beyond your control that affect report quality, such as budgets, schedule constraints, or limited access to information or people. If appropriate, this section can also express any doubts you have about any aspect of your report. Such candor may be uncomfortable to you, but it helps your readers assess your information accurately, and it helps establish your report's integrity. However, always take care when expressing limitations. Don't apologize or try to explain away personal shortcomings (such as having put the report off until the last minute, so you weren't able to do a first-rate job on it).

- **Report organization.** The organization of the report (what topics are covered and in what order), along with a rationale for following this plan. This section is a road map that helps readers understand what's coming at each turn of the report and why.

In a relatively brief report, these topics may be discussed in only a paragraph or two. Here's an example of a brief indirect opening, taken from the introduction of a memo on why a new line of luggage has failed to sell well. The writer's ultimate goal is to recommend a shift in marketing strategy.

> The performance of the Venturer line can be improved. In the two years since its introduction, this product line has achieved a sales volume lower than we expected, resulting in a drain on the company's overall earnings. The purpose of this report is to review the luggage-buying habits of consumers in all markets where the Venturer line is sold, so that we can determine where to put our marketing emphasis.

This paragraph quickly introduces the subject (disappointing sales), tells why the problem is important (drain on earnings), and indicates the main points to be addressed in the body of the report (review of markets where the Venturer line is sold), without revealing what the conclusions and recommendations will be.

In a longer formal report, the discussion of these topics may span several pages and constitute a significant section within the report.

Report Body   As with the introduction, the body of your report can require some tough decisions about which elements to include and how much detail to offer. Here again, your decisions depend on many variables, including the needs of your audience. Some situations require detailed coverage; others can be handled with more concise treatment. Provide only enough detail in the body to support your conclusions and recommendations; you can put additional detail in tables, charts, and appendixes. If Beth Uyenco were writing a report that would be read by both high-level executives (who need only summaries and "big picture" information) and functional staff (who need specific details), she could address major points in the body and refer readers to specific places in an appendix for more details.

As with the introduction, the report body should contain only enough information to convey your message in a convincing fashion; don't overload the body with interesting but unnecessary material.

The topics commonly covered in a report body include

- Explanations of a problem or opportunity
- Facts, statistical evidence, and trends
- Results of studies or investigations
- Discussion and analyses of potential courses of action
- Advantages, disadvantages, costs, and benefits of a particular course of action
- Procedures or steps in a process
- Methods and approaches
- Criteria for evaluating alternatives and options
- Conclusions and recommendations
- Supporting reasons for conclusions or recommendations

For analytical reports using the direct organizational approach, you'll generally state your conclusions or recommendations in the introduction and use the body of your report to provide your evidence and support (as illustrated in Figures 11–3 and 11–4). If you're using an indirect approach, you'll likely use the body to discuss your logic and reserve your conclusions or recommendations until the very end.

Report Close The content and length of your report close depend on your choice of direct or indirect order, among other variables. If you're using a direct approach, you can end with a summary of key points (usually not necessary in short memo-style reports), listed in the order they appear in the report body. If you're using an indirect approach, you can use the close to present your conclusions or recommendations if you didn't end the body with them. Just remember that a conclusion or recommendation isn't the place to introduce new facts; your audience should have all the information they need by the time they reach this point in your report.

If your report is intended to prompt others to action, use the ending to spell out exactly what should happen next. Readers may agree with everything you say in your report but still fail to take any action if you're vague about what should happen next. Providing a schedule and specific task assignments is helpful because concrete plans have a way of commanding action. If you'll be taking all the actions yourself, make sure your readers understand this fact so that they'll know what to expect from you (see Figure 11–5).

In a short report, the close may be only a paragraph or two. However, the close of a long report may have separate sections for conclusions, recommendations, and actions. Using separate sections helps your reader locate this material and focus on each element. Such an arrangement also gives you a final opportunity to emphasize this important content.

If you have multiple conclusions, recommendations, or actions, you may want to number and list them. An appropriate lead-in to such a list might be, "The findings of this study lead to the following conclusions." A statement that could be used for a list of recommendations might be, "Based on the conclusions of this study, we make the following recommendations." A statement that could be used for actions might be, "In order to accomplish our goals on time, we must complete the following actions before the end of the year."

Drafting Proposal Content

With proposals, the content for each section is governed by many variables—the most important being the source of your proposal. If your proposal is unsolicited, you have some latitude in the scope and organization of content. However, if you are responding to a request for proposals, you need to follow the instructions in the RFP in every detail. Most RFPs spell out precisely what you should cover and in what order so that all bids will be similar in form and therefore easier to compare.

The general purpose of any proposal is to persuade readers to do something, such as purchase goods or services, fund a project, or implement a program. Thus, your writing approach for a proposal is similar to that used for persuasive sales messages (see Chapter 9). As with other persuasive messages, the AIDA method of gaining attention, building interest, creating desire, and motivating action is an effective structure. Here are some additional strategies to strengthen your argument.[6]

- **Demonstrate your knowledge.** Show your reader that you have the knowledge and experience to solve the problem or address the opportunity outlined in your proposal.

- **Provide concrete information and examples.** Avoid vague, unsupported generalizations such as "We are losing money on this program." Instead, provide quantifiable details such as the amount of money being lost, how, why, and so on. Explain how much money your proposed solution will save. Spell out your plan and give details on how the job will be done. Such concrete information persuades readers; unsupported generalizations do not.

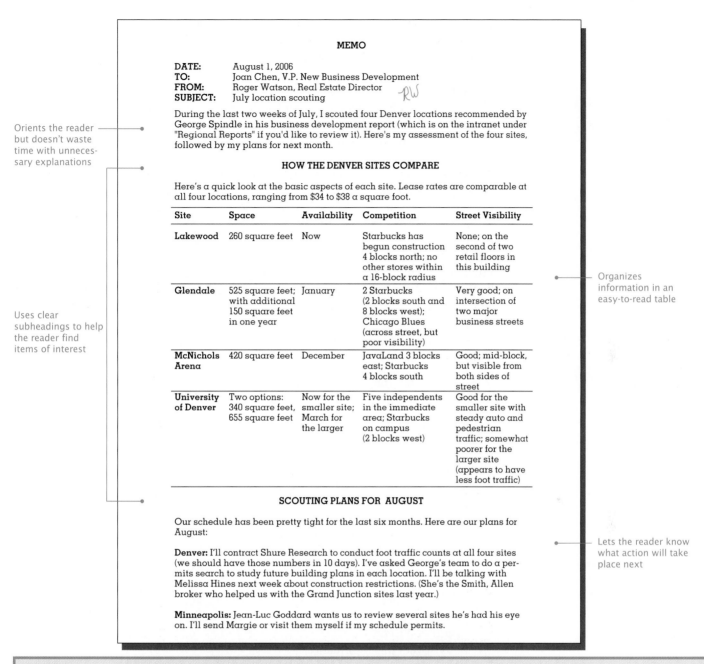

MEMO

DATE:	August 1, 2006
TO:	Joan Chen, V.P. New Business Development
FROM:	Roger Watson, Real Estate Director *RW*
SUBJECT:	July location scouting

During the last two weeks of July, I scouted four Denver locations recommended by George Spindle in his business development report (which is on the intranet under "Regional Reports" if you'd like to review it). Here's my assessment of the four sites, followed by my plans for next month.

HOW THE DENVER SITES COMPARE

Here's a quick look at the basic aspects of each site. Lease rates are comparable at all four locations, ranging from $34 to $38 a square foot.

Site	Space	Availability	Competition	Street Visibility
Lakewood	260 square feet	Now	Starbucks has begun construction 4 blocks north; no other stores within a 16-block radius	None; on the second of two retail floors in this building
Glendale	525 square feet; with additional 150 square feet in one year	January	2 Starbucks (2 blocks south and 8 blocks west); Chicago Blues (across street, but poor visibility)	Very good; on intersection of two major business streets
McNichols Arena	420 square feet	December	JavaLand 3 blocks east; Starbucks 4 blocks south	Good; mid-block, but visible from both sides of street
University of Denver	Two options: 340 square feet, 655 square feet	Now for the smaller site; March for the larger	Five independents in the immediate area; Starbucks on campus (2 blocks west)	Good for the smaller site with steady auto and pedestrian traffic; somewhat poorer for the larger site (appears to have less foot traffic)

SCOUTING PLANS FOR AUGUST

Our schedule has been pretty tight for the last six months. Here are our plans for August:

Denver: I'll contract Shure Research to conduct foot traffic counts at all four sites (we should have those numbers in 10 days). I've asked George's team to do a permits search to study future building plans in each location. I'll be talking with Melissa Hines next week about construction restrictions. (She's the Smith, Allen broker who helped us with the Grand Junction sites last year.)

Minneapolis: Jean-Luc Goddard wants us to review several sites he's had his eye on. I'll send Margie or visit them myself if my schedule permits.

Orients the reader but doesn't waste time with unnecessary explanations

Uses clear subheadings to help the reader find items of interest

Organizes information in an easy-to-read table

Lets the reader know what action will take place next

FIGURE 11–5
Effective Report Expressing Action Plan in the Close

- **Research the competition.** If you're competing against other companies for a potential customer's business, use trade publications and the Internet to become familiar with the products, services, and prices of these other companies.

- **Prove that your proposal is workable.** Your proposal must be appropriate and feasible for your audience. It should be consistent with your audience's capabilities.

- **Adopt a "you" attitude.** Relate your product, service, or personnel to the reader's exact needs, either as stated in the RFP for a solicited proposal or as discovered through your own investigation for an unsolicited proposal.

- **Package your proposal attractively.** Make sure your proposal is letter perfect, inviting, and readable. Readers will prejudge the quality of your products, services, and capabilities by the quality of the proposal you submit. Errors, omissions, or

Business proposals need to provide more than just attractive ideas—readers look for evidence of practical, achievable solutions.

inconsistencies will work against you—and maybe even cost you important career and business opportunities.

Proposal Introduction   The introduction presents and summarizes the problem you want to solve (or the opportunity you want to exploit), along with your proposed solution. It orients readers to the remainder of the text. If your proposal is solicited, its introduction should refer to the RFP so that readers know which RFP you're responding to. If your proposal is unsolicited, your introduction should mention any factors that led you to submit your proposal. You might mention mutual acquaintances, or you might refer to previous conversations you've had with readers. The following topics are commonly covered in a proposal introduction:

In an unsolicited proposal, your introduction needs to convince readers that a problem or opportunity exists.

- **Background or statement of the problem.** Briefly reviews the reader's situation and establishes a need for action. Readers may not perceive a problem or opportunity the same way you do. In unsolicited proposals, you need to convince them that a problem or opportunity exists before you can convince them to accept your solution. In a way that is meaningful to your reader, discuss the current situation and explain how things could be better.

- **Solution.** Briefly describes the change you propose and highlights your key selling points and their benefits, showing how your proposal will help readers meet their business objectives.

- **Scope.** States the boundaries of the proposal—what you will and will not do. Sometimes called "Delimitations."

- **Organization.** Orients the reader to the remainder of the proposal and calls attention to the major divisions of information.

In short proposals, your discussion of these topics will be brief—perhaps only a sentence or two for each one. For long, formal proposals, each of these topics may warrant separate subheadings and several paragraphs of discussion.

Readers understand that a proposal is a persuasive message, so they're willing to accommodate a degree of promotional emphasis in your writing—as long as it is professional and focused on their needs.

Proposal Body   The proposal's body has the same purpose as the body of other reports: It gives complete details on the proposed solution and specifies what the anticipated results will be. Because a proposal is by definition a persuasive message, your audience expects you to promote your offering in a confident but professional manner. Even when you're expressing an idea that you believe in passionately, maintain an objective tone so that you don't risk overselling your message.

In addition to providing facts and evidence to support your conclusions, an effective body covers this information:

- **Proposed solution.** Describes what you have to offer: your concept, product, or service. This section may also be titled "Technical Proposal," "Research Design," "Issues for Analysis," or "Work Statement." Stress the benefits of your product, service, or investment opportunity that are relevant to your readers' needs, and point out any advantages that you have over your competitors.

The work plan indicates exactly how you will accomplish the solution presented in the proposal.

- **Work plan.** Describes how you'll accomplish what must be done (unless you'll provide a standard, off-the-shelf item). Explain the steps you'll take, their timing, the methods or resources you'll use, and the person(s) responsible. Specifically include when the work will begin, how it will be divided into stages, when you will finish, and whether any follow-up is involved. For solicited proposals, make sure your dates match those specified in the RFP. Keep in mind that if your proposal is accepted, the work plan is contractually binding, so don't promise more than you can deliver.

- **Statement of qualifications.** Describes your organization's experience, personnel, and facilities—all in relation to reader needs. The qualifications section can be an important selling point, and it deserves to be handled carefully. You can supplement your qualifications by including a list of client references, but get permission ahead of time to use these references.

- **Costs.** Covers pricing, reimbursable expenses, discounts, and so on. Coverage can vary widely, from a single price amount to detailed breakdowns by part number, service category, and so on. If you're responding to an RFP, follow the instructions it contains. In other cases, your firm probably has a set policy for discussing costs. The amount of detail you provide depends on your relationship with your audience.

In an informal proposal, discussion of some or all of these elements may be grouped together and presented in a letter format, as the proposal in Figure 11–6 does. In a

FIGURE 11–6
Effective Solicited Proposal in Letter Format

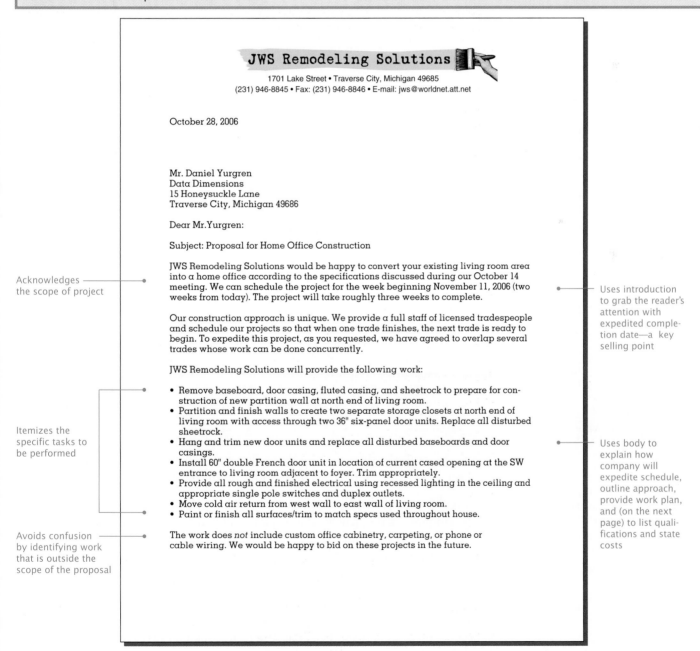

JWS Remodeling Solutions
1701 Lake Street • Traverse City, Michigan 49685
(231) 946-8845 • Fax: (231) 946-8846 • E-mail: jws@worldnet.att.net

October 28, 2006

Mr. Daniel Yurgren
Data Dimensions
15 Honeysuckle Lane
Traverse City, Michigan 49686

Dear Mr. Yurgren:

Subject: Proposal for Home Office Construction

Acknowledges the scope of project →

JWS Remodeling Solutions would be happy to convert your existing living room area into a home office according to the specifications discussed during our October 14 meeting. We can schedule the project for the week beginning November 11, 2006 (two weeks from today). The project will take roughly three weeks to complete.

← *Uses introduction to grab the reader's attention with expedited completion date—a key selling point*

Our construction approach is unique. We provide a full staff of licensed tradespeople and schedule our projects so that when one trade finishes, the next trade is ready to begin. To expedite this project, as you requested, we have agreed to overlap several trades whose work can be done concurrently.

JWS Remodeling Solutions will provide the following work:

Itemizes the specific tasks to be performed →

- Remove baseboard, door casing, fluted casing, and sheetrock to prepare for construction of new partition wall at north end of living room.
- Partition and finish walls to create two separate storage closets at north end of living room with access through two 36" six-panel door units. Replace all disturbed sheetrock.
- Hang and trim new door units and replace all disturbed baseboards and door casings.
- Install 60" double French door unit in location of current cased opening at the SW entrance to living room adjacent to foyer. Trim appropriately.
- Provide all rough and finished electrical using recessed lighting in the ceiling and appropriate single pole switches and duplex outlets.
- Move cold air return from west wall to east wall of living room.
- Paint or finish all surfaces/trim to match specs used throughout house.

← *Uses body to explain how company will expedite schedule, outline approach, provide work plan, and (on the next page) to list qualifications and state costs*

Avoids confusion by identifying work that is outside the scope of the proposal →

The work does *not* include custom office cabinetry, carpeting, or phone or cable wiring. We would be happy to bid on these projects in the future.

(continued)

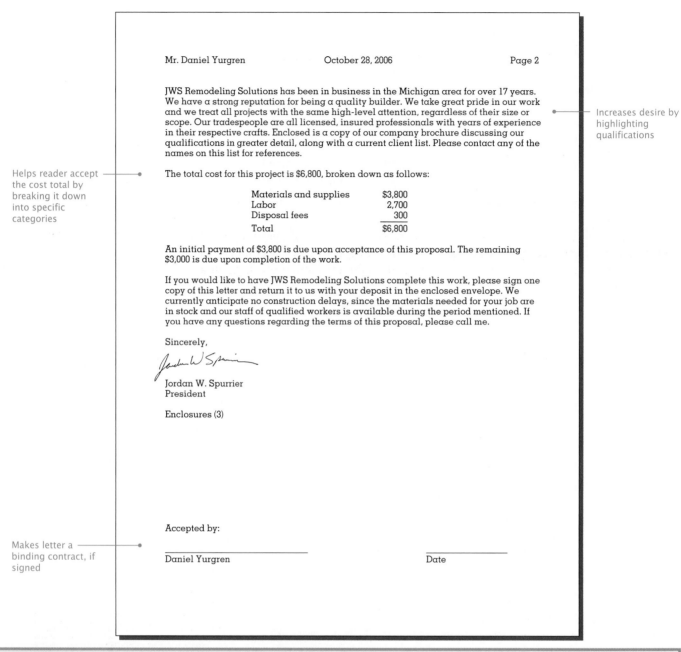

Mr. Daniel Yurgren   October 28, 2006   Page 2

JWS Remodeling Solutions has been in business in the Michigan area for over 17 years. We have a strong reputation for being a quality builder. We take great pride in our work and we treat all projects with the same high-level attention, regardless of their size or scope. Our tradespeople are all licensed, insured professionals with years of experience in their respective crafts. Enclosed is a copy of our company brochure discussing our qualifications in greater detail, along with a current client list. Please contact any of the names on this list for references.

Increases desire by highlighting qualifications

The total cost for this project is $6,800, broken down as follows:

Materials and supplies	$3,800
Labor	2,700
Disposal fees	300
Total	$6,800

Helps reader accept the cost total by breaking it down into specific categories

An initial payment of $3,800 is due upon acceptance of this proposal. The remaining $3,000 is due upon completion of the work.

If you would like to have JWS Remodeling Solutions complete this work, please sign one copy of this letter and return it to us with your deposit in the enclosed envelope. We currently anticipate no construction delays, since the materials needed for your job are in stock and our staff of qualified workers is available during the period mentioned. If you have any questions regarding the terms of this proposal, please call me.

Sincerely,

Jordan W. Spurrier

Jordan W. Spurrier
President

Enclosures (3)

Accepted by:

_____   _____
Daniel Yurgren   Date

Makes letter a binding contract, if signed

FIGURE 11–6
(continued)

formal proposal, the discussion of these elements will be quite long and thorough. The format may resemble long reports with multiple parts, as Chapter 12 discusses.

Proposal Close   The final section of a proposal generally summarizes the key points, emphasizes the benefits that readers will realize from your solution, summarizes the merits of your approach, restates why you and your firm are a good choice, and asks for a decision from the client. The close is your last opportunity to persuade readers to accept your proposal. In both formal and informal proposals, make this section relatively brief, assertive (but not brash or abrupt), and confident.

As you draft material for the introduction, body, and close of your reports and proposals, pay close attention to two issues that often cause problems for novice writers, especially in long documents: Be sure to maintain a consistent time perspective throughout your reports and help readers find their way through your material.

The close is your last chance to convince the reader of the merits of your proposal, so make doubly sure it's clear, compelling, and audience-oriented.

Establishing a Consistent Time Perspective

In what time frame will your report exist? Will you write in the past or present tense? The person who wrote this paragraph never decided:

> Of those interviewed, 25 percent *report* that they *are* dissatisfied with their present brand. The wealthiest participants *complained* most frequently, but all income categories *are* interested in trying a new brand. Only 5 percent of the interviewees *say* they *had* no interest in alternative products.

By flipping from tense to tense when describing the same research results, you can confuse your readers. Is the shift significant, they wonder, or are you just being careless? Eliminate the potential for such confusion by using tense consistently.

Also be careful to observe the chronological sequence of events in your report. If you're describing the history or development of something, start at the beginning and cover each event in the order of its occurrence. If you're explaining the steps in a process, take each step in proper sequence.

Unexplained shifts in time perspective can both confuse readers and lead them to question the thinking behind your proposal.

Helping Readers Find Their Way

In a short report, readers are in little danger of getting lost; however, as the length of a report increases, so do the opportunities for readers to become confused and lose track of the relationships among ideas. Report experts such as Beth Uyenco give their readers a preview or road map of a report's structure, clarifying how the various parts are related. Providing structural directions is especially important for people from other cultures and countries, whose language skills and business expectations may differ from yours. Moreover, the accelerating pace of business and the increased familiarity with online information have raised reader expectations in another way. Readers today often lack the time or the inclination to plow through long reports page by page, word by word. They want to browse quickly, find a section of interest, dive in for details, pull back out, browse for another section, and so on.

To help readers find what they're looking for and stay on track as they navigate through your documents, learn to make good use of headings and links, smooth transitions, and previews and reviews:

Navigational aids help your readers appreciate the organization of your thoughts—and can help you convey your message.

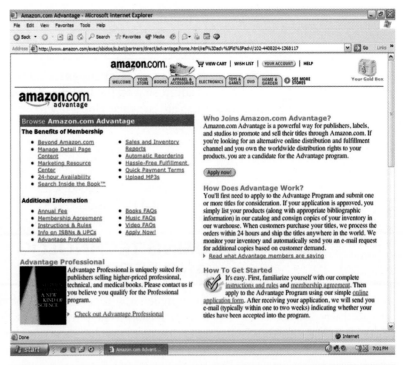

Amazon.com's Advantage program helps book publishers, music companies, and movie studios promote their products on Amazon.com. To help these audiences learn about the Advantage program quickly, an online informational report makes generous use of headings and links.

- **Headings and links.** Readers should be able to follow the structure of your document and pick up the key points of your message from the headings and subheadings (see Chapter 6 for a review of what makes an effective heading). Follow a simple, consistent arrangement that clearly distinguishes levels. For online reports, where the difficulty of reading on screen makes clear headings crucial, make generous use of hyperlinks to help your readers navigate the report and access additional information.

- **Transitions.** Chapter 5 defines transitions as words or phrases that tie ideas together and show how one thought is related to another. In a long report, an

Online reports can be more difficult to scan and browse through, so clear headings and subheadings are especially important.

Transitions connect ideas by helping readers move from one thought to the next.

entire paragraph might be used to highlight transitions from one section to the next, such as in this example:

> ... *As you can see,* our profits have decreased by 12 percent over the past eight months.
>
> To counteract *this decline in profits,* we have three alternatives. *First,* we can raise our selling prices of existing products. *Second,* we can increase our offering by adding new products. *Third,* we can reduce our manufacturing costs. *However,* each of these alternatives has both advantages and disadvantages.

The phrase *As you can see* alerts readers to the fact that they are reading a summary of the information just presented. The phrase *this decline in profits* lets readers know that the text will be saying something else about that previous topic. The words *first, second,* and *third* help readers stay on track as the three alternatives are introduced, and the word *however* alerts readers to the fact that evaluating the three alternatives requires some additional discussion. Effective transitions such as these can help readers grasp what they've learned so far while preparing to receive new information.

Previews help readers prepare for upcoming information, and reviews help them verify and clarify what they've just read.

- **Previews and reviews.** *Preview sections* introduce important topics by helping readers get ready for new information. Previews are particularly helpful when the information is complex, unexpected, or unfamiliar. In contrast, *review sections* come after a body of material and summarize the information for your readers. Reviews help readers absorb details while keeping track of the big picture. Previews and reviews can be written in sentence format, bulleted lists (see Chapter 6), or a combination of the two. Both are effective, but bullets can increase your document's readability by adding white space to the document design:

Sentence Format	Bulleted List
The next section discusses the advantages of advertising on the Internet. Among them are currency, global reach, affordability, and interactivity.	As the next section shows, advertising on the Internet has four advantages: • Currency • Global reach • Affordability • Interactivity

To review the tasks discussed in this section, see "Checklist: Composing Business Reports and Proposals."

USING TECHNOLOGY TO CRAFT REPORTS AND PROPOSALS

Look for ways to utilize technology to reduce the mechanical work involved in writing long reports.

Creating lengthy reports and proposals can be a huge task, so take advantage of technological tools to help throughout the process. You've read about some of these tools in earlier chapters; here are some of the most important ones for developing reports and proposals:

- **Templates.** Beyond simply formatting documents, report templates can identify the specific sections required for each type of report. For instance, a marketing plan could include such sections as a competitive analysis, market analysis, launch plans, financial analysis, and promotional and customer support plans. The template could automatically insert headings for each section, with reminders of the content to include.

- **Linked and embedded documents.** Reports and proposals often include graphics, spreadsheets, databases, and other elements created in a variety of software

✓ CHECKLIST: Composing Business Reports and Proposals

A. Review and fine-tune your outline

✓ Match your parallel headings to the tone of your report.
✓ Understand how the introduction, body, and close work together to convey your message.

B. Draft report content

✓ Use the introduction to establish the purpose, scope, and organization of your report.
✓ Use the body to present and interpret the information you gathered.
✓ Use the close to summarize major points, discuss conclusions, or make recommendations.

C. Draft proposal content

✓ Use the introduction to discuss the background or problem, your solution, the scope, and organization.
✓ Use the body to persuasively explain the benefits of your proposed approach.

✓ Use the close to emphasize reader benefits and summarize the merits of your approach.

D. Establish a consistent time frame

✓ Avoid flipping from tense to tense.
✓ Observe the chronological sequence of events.

E. Help readers find their way

✓ Provide headings to improve readability and clarify the framework of your ideas.
✓ Use hyperlinks online to allow readers to jump from section to section.
✓ Create transitions that tie ideas together and show how one thought relates to another.
✓ Preview important topics to help readers get ready for new information.
✓ Review key information to help readers absorb details and keep the big picture in mind.

packages. When you do combine files this way, make sure you know how the software handles the files or you may receive some unpleasant surprises. For instance, in Microsoft Office, you can choose to either *link* or *embed* the incoming file, such as when you insert a spreadsheet table into a word processor document. If you link the table, it will get updated whenever you or someone else updates the spreadsheet. In contrast, if you embed it, the files are no longer connected; changes in the spreadsheet will not show up in the report document.

- **Electronic forms.** For recurring forms such as sales reports and compliance reports, consider creating a word processor file that combines boilerplate text for material that doesn't change from report to report. To accommodate information that does change (such as last week's sales results), use *form tools* such as text boxes (in which users can type new text) and check boxes (which can be used to select from a set of predetermined choices). The completed file can then be printed, e-mailed, or posted to a website.

- **Electronic documents.** Portable Document Format (PDF) files have become a universal replacement for printed reports and proposals. With a copy of Adobe Acrobat (a separate product from the free Acrobat Reader), you can quickly convert reports and proposals to PDF files that are easy and safe to share electronically.

- **Multimedia documents.** When the written word isn't enough, combine your report with video clips, animation, presentation software slides, and other elements. As you'll see in Chapter 13, tools such as Microsoft Producer let you merge a variety of file types to create compelling multimedia presentations that supplement or replace traditional reports.

Document Makeover

IMPROVE THIS POLICY REPORT

To practice correcting drafts of actual documents, visit your online course or the access-code protected portion of the Companion Website. Click "Document Makeovers," then click Chapter 11. You will find an excerpt from a policy report that contains problems and errors relating to what you've learned in this chapter about writing business reports and proposals. Use the "Final Draft" decision tool to create an improved version of this informational report. Check the message for an effective opening, consistent levels of formality or informality, consistent time perspective, and the use of headings, transitions, previews and reviews to help orient readers.

Today's computer technology also makes it easy to add a wide variety of compelling visuals to your reports, which you'll learn more about in the next section.

ILLUSTRATING YOUR REPORTS WITH EFFECTIVE VISUALS

Carefully crafted visuals enhance the power of your words.

Well-designed visuals can bring your messages to life and help you connect to your audiences at both the intellectual and emotional levels. Visuals enhance the communication power of textual messages, and they can often convey some message points (such as spatial relationships and procedures) more effectively and more efficiently than words. Pictures also serve as an effective way to communicate with the diverse audiences that are common in today's business environment. Visuals attract and hold people's attention, helping your audience understand and remember your message. Busy readers often jump to visuals to try to get the gist of a message, and attractive visuals can draw readers deeper into your reports and presentations.

To be effective, however, visuals need to be planned and designed carefully. Poorly chosen or badly designed visuals reduce the impact of your writing. Table 11–1 helps you decide when a visual will help get your message across. To help identify which parts of your message can benefit from visual support, step back and consider the flow of your entire message from the audience's point of view. Which parts of the message are likely to seem complex, open to misinterpretation, or even just a little bit dull? Do you have a lot of numerical data or other discrete factual content that would be difficult to read in paragraph form?

When you're deciding which points to present visually, think of the five Cs:

Effective visuals are clear, complete, concise, connected, and compelling.

- **Clear.** The human mind is extremely adept at processing visual information, whether it's something as simple as the shape of a stop sign or as complicated as the floor plan for a new factory. If you're having difficulty conveying an idea in words, see if a visual element can do the job better.

Table 11–1	**WHEN TO USE VISUALS**	
	Purpose	*Example Applications*
	To clarify	Support text descriptions of quantitative or numerical information, trends, spatial relationships, physical constructions.
	To simplify	Break complicated descriptions into components that can be depicted with conceptual models, flowcharts, organization charts, or diagrams.
	To emphasize	Call attention to particularly important points by illustrating them with line, bar, and pie and other types of charts.
	To summarize	Review major points in the narrative by providing a chart or table that summarizes key items.
	To reinforce	Present information in both visual and written forms to increase reader's retention.
	To attract	Engage readers visually and emotionally; provide visual relief from long blocks of text.
	To impress	Build credibility by putting ideas into visual form to convey the impression of authenticity and precision.
	To unify	Depict the relationship among points, such as visually integrating the steps in a process by presenting them in a flowchart.

- **Complete.** Visuals, particularly tables, can be a great way to provide the supporting details for your main idea or recommendation.

- **Concise.** You've probably heard the phrase "A picture is worth a thousand words." If a particular section of your message seems to require extensive description or explanation, see whether there's a way to convey this information visually.

- **Connected.** A key purpose of many business messages is showing connections of some sort—similarities or differences, correlations, cause-and-effect relationships, and so on. Whenever you want readers to see such a connection, see whether a chart, diagram, or other illustration can help.

- **Compelling.** Your readers live in a highly visual world. Will one or more illustrations make your message more persuasive, more interesting, more likely to get read? You never want to insert visuals simply for decorative purposes, but even if a particular point can be expressed equally well via text or visuals, consider adding the visual in order to make your report or presentation more compelling.

Strong visuals enhance the descriptive and persuasive power of your writing, but it's important not to overdo them. Cramming too many visuals into a report can distract your readers in two ways. First, if you're constantly referring to tables, drawings, and other visual elements, the effort to switch back and forth from words to visuals can make it difficult for readers to maintain focus on the thread of your message. Second, the space occupied by visuals can disrupt the flow of text on the page or screen, which also creates additional work for the reader.

> Maintain a balance between text and visuals, and pace your visuals in a way that emphasizes your key textual points.

As always, take your readers' specific needs into account. If you're addressing an audience with multiple language backgrounds or widely varying reading skills, you can shift the balance toward more visual elements to help get around any language barriers. The professional experience, education, and training of your audience should influence your approach as well. For instance, detailed statistical plots and math formulas are everyday reading material for quality control engineers but not for most salespeople or top executives.

Selecting the Right Visuals

Once you've identified which points would benefit most from visual presentation, your next decision is choosing which type of visual to use for each message point. As you see in Figure 11–7, you have many choices for business graphics. For certain types of information, the decision is usually obvious. If you want to present a large set of numerical values or detailed textual information, a table is the obvious choice in most cases. However, if you're presenting data broken down geographically, a color-coded map might be more effective to show overall patterns rather than individual data points. Also, certain visuals are used more commonly for certain applications; for instance, your audience is likely to expect line charts and bar charts to show trends. Line charts usually show data variations relative to a time axis (such as sales month by month), whereas bar charts more often compare discrete groups (such as sales by demographic segment). Similarly, although a bar chart can show the percentages that make up a whole, this job is usually reserved for pie charts.

> You have many types of visuals to choose from, and each is best suited to particular communication tasks.

The following sections explore the most common types of visuals in more detail, starting with visuals designed to present data.

Presenting Data   Business professionals have a tremendous number of choices for presenting data, from general purpose line, bar, and pie charts to specialized charts for product portfolios, financial analysis, and other professional functions. The visuals most commonly used to present data include tables, line and surface charts, bar charts, pictograms, Gantt charts, and pie charts.

Communication Challenge	Effective Visual Choice

Presenting Data

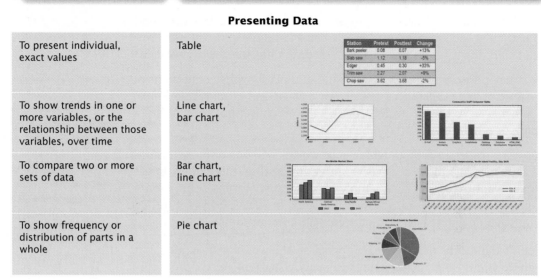

To present individual, exact values	Table
To show trends in one or more variables, or the relationship between those variables, over time	Line chart, bar chart
To compare two or more sets of data	Bar chart, line chart
To show frequency or distribution of parts in a whole	Pie chart

Presenting Information, Concepts, and Ideas

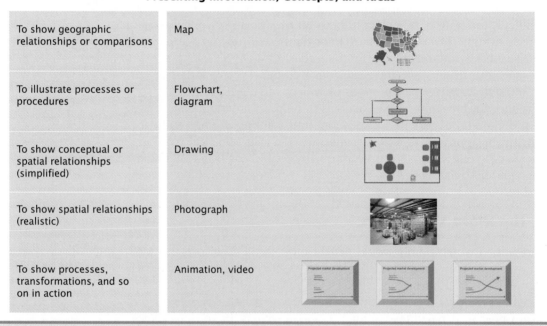

To show geographic relationships or comparisons	Map
To illustrate processes or procedures	Flowchart, diagram
To show conceptual or spatial relationships (simplified)	Drawing
To show spatial relationships (realistic)	Photograph
To show processes, transformations, and so on in action	Animation, video

FIGURE 11–7
Selecting the Best Visual

Printed tables can display extensive amounts of data, but tables for online display and electronic presentations need to be simpler.

Tables   When you need to present detailed, specific information, choose a **table**, a systematic arrangement of data in columns and rows. Tables are ideal when your audience needs information that would be either difficult or tedious to handle in the main text.

Most tables contain the standard parts illustrated in Table 11–2. Every table includes vertical columns and horizontal rows, with useful headings along the top and side. The number of columns and rows you can comfortably fit in a table depends on the medium. For printed documents, you can adjust font size and column/row spacing to fit a considerable amount of information on the page and still maintain readability. For online documents, you'll need to reduce the number of columns and rows to make sure your tables are easily readable online. Tables for oral presentations usually need to be the simplest of all, since you can't expect audiences to read detailed information from the screen.

PARTS OF A TABLE   Table 11–2

| Stub Heading | Multicolumn Heading | | | Single-Column Heading |
	Subheading	Subheading	Subheading	
Row heading	XXX	XXX	XXX	XXX
Row heading				
Subheading	XXX	XXX	XXX	XXX
Subheading	XXX	XXX	XXX	XXX
Total	XXX	XXX	XXX	XXX

Source: (In the same format as a text footnote; see Appendix B)

*Footnote (For an explanation of elements in the table, a superscript number or small letter may be used instead of an asterisk or other symbol.)

Although complex information may require formal tables that are set apart from the text, you can present some data more simply within the text. You make the table, in essence, a part of the paragraph, typed in tabular format. Such text tables are usually introduced with a sentence that leads directly into the tabulated information. Here's an example:[7]

This table compares the size of Outback Steakhouse with the sizes of several of its leading competitors:

	Outback Steakhouse	Applebee's	Carlson	Brinker	Darden
Major chain(s)	Outback Steakhouse, Carrabba's	Applebee's	TGI Friday's, Pick Up Stix	Chili's	Red Lobster, Olive Garden
Locations	1,200	1670	860	975	1,300
Revenue (million $)	$3,202	$1,112	$2,400	$3,913	$5,278

Source: Hoover's Online [accessed 20 September 2005] www.hoovers.com.

When you prepare tables, follow these guidelines to make your tables easy to read:

- Use common, understandable units, and clearly identify the units you're using, whether it's dollars, percentages, price per ton, or whatever.
- Express all items in a column in the same unit and round off for simplicity.
- Label column headings clearly and use a subhead if necessary.
- Separate columns or rows with lines or extra space to make the table easy to follow; in complex tables, consider highlighting every other row or column in a pale, contrasting color.
- Provide totals or averages of columns or rows when relevant.
- Document the source of the data using the same format as a text footnote (see Appendix B).

Although numerical tables are more common, tables can also contain words, symbols, or other facts and figures. Word tables are particularly appropriate for presenting survey findings or for comparing various items against a specific standard.

FIGURE 11–8
Line Chart

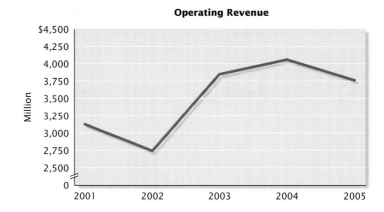

Line charts are commonly used to show trends over time or the relationship between two variables.

Line and Surface Charts   A **line chart** illustrates trends over time or plots the relationship of two variables. In line charts showing trends, the vertical, or *y,* axis shows the amount, and the horizontal, or *x,* axis shows the time or other quantity against which the amount is being measured. Moreover, you can plot just a single line or overlay multiple lines to compare different entities. For instance, the two-line chart in Figure 11–8 compares the temperatures measured inside two cement kilns from 8:00 A.M. to 5:00 P.M.

A **surface chart**, also called an **area chart**, is a form of line chart with a cumulative effect; all the lines add up to the top line, which represents the total (see Figure 11–9). This form of chart helps you illustrate changes in the composition of something over time. When preparing a surface chart, put the most important segment against the baseline, and restrict the number of strata to four or five.

Bar Charts and Pie Charts   A **bar chart** portrays numbers by the height or length of its rectangular bars, making a series of numbers easy to read or understand. Bar charts are particularly valuable when you want to

- compare the size of several items at one time

- show changes in one item over time

- indicate the composition of several items over time

- show the relative size of components of a whole

The charts in Figure 11–10 show just four of the many variations available for bar charts: *singular* (11–10a: "CommuniCo Staff Computer Skills"), *grouped* (11–10b: "Worldwide Market Share"), *segmented* (11–10c): "CommuniCo Preferred Communication Media"), and *combination* (11–10d: "CommuniCo Employee Training Costs"). Grouped bar charts compare more than one set of data, using a different color

FIGURE 11–9
Surface Chart

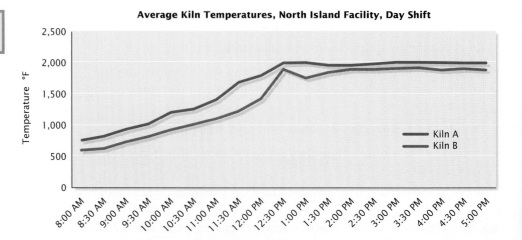

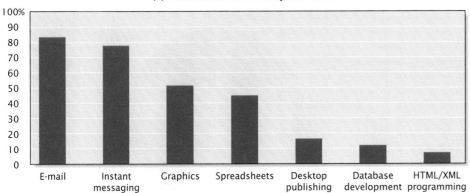

(a) CommuniCo Staff Computer Skills

FIGURE 11–10
The Versatile Bar Chart

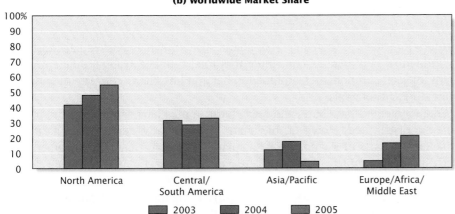

(b) Worldwide Market Share

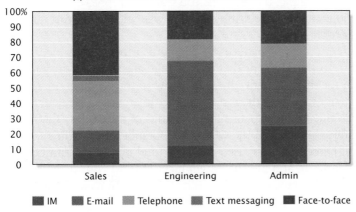

(c) CommuniCo Preferred Communication Media

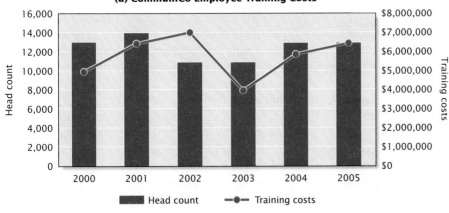

(d) CommuniCo Employee Training Costs

FIGURE 11–11
Pie Chart

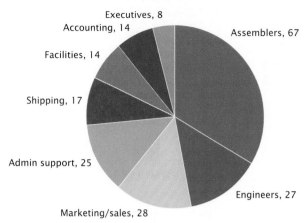

Year-End Head Count by Function

Executives, 8
Accounting, 14
Facilities, 14
Shipping, 17
Admin support, 25
Marketing/sales, 28
Assemblers, 67
Engineers, 27

Most readers expect pie charts to show the distribution of parts within a whole.

or pattern for each set. Segmented bar charts, also known as stacked bar charts, show how individual components contribute to a total number, using a different color or pattern for each component. Combination bar and line charts compare quantities that require different intervals.

Like segmented bar charts and area charts, a **pie chart** shows how the parts of a whole are distributed. However, pie charts have the advantage of familiarity; most people expect parts-of-a-whole to be displayed via a pie chart. Each segment represents a slice of a complete circle, or *pie*. As you can see in Figure 11–11, pie charts are an effective way to show percentages or to compare one segment with another.

When creating pie charts, try to restrict the number of slices in the pie. Otherwise, the chart looks cluttered and is difficult to label. If necessary, lump the smallest pieces together in a "miscellaneous" category. Ideally, the largest or most important slice of the pie, the segment you want to emphasize, is placed at the twelve o'clock position; the rest are arranged clockwise either in order of size or in some other logical progression.

Use different colors or patterns to distinguish the various pieces. If you want to draw attention to the segment that is of the greatest interest to your readers, use a brighter color for that segment, draw an arrow to the segment, or explode it; that is, pull the segment away from the rest of the pie. In any case, label all the segments and indicate their value in either percentages or units of measure so that your readers will be able to judge the value of the wedges. Remember, the segments must add up to 100 percent if percentages are used or to the total number if numbers are used.

Line, surface, bar, and pie charts will meet most of your data presentation needs, but for specialized needs, explore the other chart options available in software such as Microsoft Excel.

Presenting Information, Concepts, and Ideas   In addition to facts and figures, you'll need to present other types of information, from spatial relationships (such as the floor plan for a new office building) to abstract ideas (such as progress or competition). The most common types of visuals for these applications include flowcharts, organization charts, maps, drawings, diagrams, photographs, animation, and video.

Flowcharts and Organization Charts   A **flowchart** (see Figure 11–12) illustrates a sequence of events from start to finish; it is indispensable when illustrating processes, procedures, and sequential relationships. For general business purposes, you don't need to be too concerned about the specific shapes, but keep them consistent. However, you should be aware of the formal flowchart "language," in which each shape has a specific meaning (diamonds are decision points, rectangles are process steps, and so on). If you're communicating with computer programmers and others

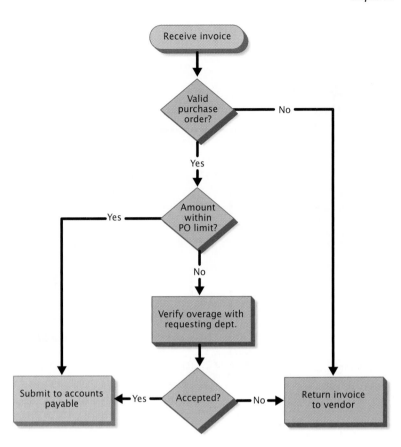

FIGURE 11–12
Flowchart

who are accustomed to formal flowcharting, make sure you use the correct symbols in each case to avoid confusion. Graphics programs such as Microsoft Visio label the function of flowchart symbols for you, making it easy to use the right ones.

As the name implies, an **organization chart** illustrates the positions, units, or functions of an organization and the way they interrelate. An organization's normal communication channels are almost impossible to describe without the benefit of a chart like the one in Figure 11–13. These charts aren't limited to organizational structures, of course; as you saw in Chapter 4, they can also be used to outline messages.

Maps, Drawings, Diagrams, and Photographs   When your information has a geographic aspect, maps are often an ideal visual device. For example, Figure 11–14 shows U.S. population projections state by state. This information could be presented in a table, of course, but a map makes the differences immediately obvious. In addition to presenting facts and figures, maps are useful for showing market territories, distribution routes, and facilities locations. Maps are sometimes used in conjunction with aerial photographs to illustrate such elements as land use.

Simple maps are available via clip art libraries for your word processor and presentation software, but more powerful uses (such as automatically generating color coded maps based on data inputs) usually require specialized software. Rapid progress is being made in the area of mapping software, such as Google Earth (http://earth.google.com), which combines search engine, mapping, and satellite photo technologies.[8]

Unless your career takes you into web design, advertising, technical writing, or another communication specialty, you probably won't need to create a large number of drawings, diagrams, or photographs to accompany your business messages. However, when you do have the opportunity, knowing some of the basics can help you make the most of these potentially compelling elements. Drawings and diagrams

Use maps to represent statistics by geographic area and to show spatial relationships.

Use drawings and diagrams to show how something works or how it is made or used; drawings are sometimes better than photographs because they let you focus on the most important details.

Administration and Faculty of Atlantic College

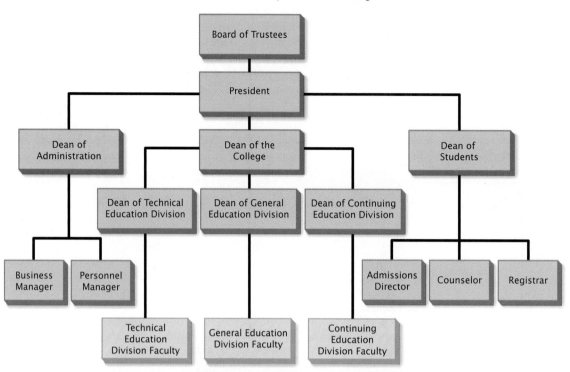

FIGURE 11–13
Organization Chart

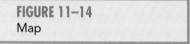

FIGURE 11–14
Map

U.S. Population Projections for 2025 (in thousands)

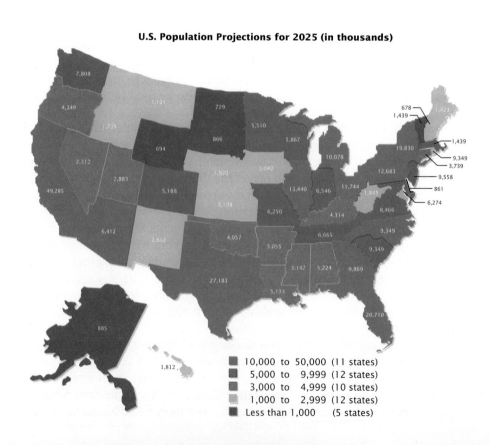

Traditional Networks Versus Converged Networks

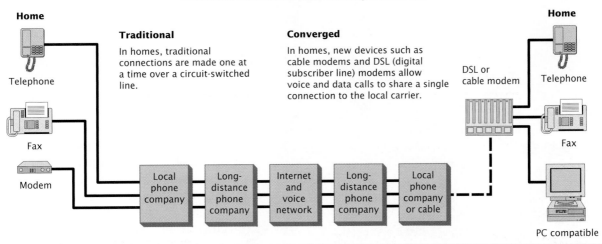

FIGURE 11–15
Diagram

are most often used to show how something looks or operates. Figure 11–15 was prepared using Microsoft Visio to compare the design of converged and traditional communication networks. Diagrams can be much clearer than words alone when it comes to giving your audience an idea of how an item looks or can be used.

Word processors and presentation software provide basic drawing capabilities, but for more precise and professional illustrations you'll need a specialized package such as Visio or Adobe Illustrator. Moving to a level beyond those programs, computer-aided design (CAD) systems such as Autodesk's Autocad can produce extremely detailed architectural and engineering drawings.

Photographs offer both functional and decorative value. In the past their use was limited to specialized documents such as annual reports and product brochures; however, with low-cost digital photography now widely available, virtually all writers can have the ability to add photographs to print documents, presentations, and web pages. In addition, photo libraries such as Getty Images (www.gettyimages.com) and photo search engines such as the one provided by AltaVista (www.altavista.com/image) make it easy to find digital photographs. Some of these photos are available for free, but the professional collections, such as Getty Images, require either a one-time payment for unlimited use (often called "royalty free") or an annual payment or other limited-use purchase (often called "rights managed").

Nothing else can demonstrate the exact appearance of a new facility, a piece of property, a new product, or even a retiring co-worker the way a photograph can. However, in some situations a photograph may show too much detail, which is one reason that repair manuals frequently use drawings instead of photos, for instance. With a drawing, you can select how much detail to show, and you can focus the reader's attention on particular parts or places. The disadvantage of such technical illustrations is the time, skill, and special tools often required to create them.

Technology makes it easier to use photographs in reports and presentations, but it also presents an important ethical concern. Software tools such as Photoshop and Paint Shop Pro allow you to easily make dramatic changes to photos—without leaving a clue that they've been altered. Altering photos in small ways has been possible for a long time (more than a few people have had blemishes airbrushed out of their yearbook photos), but computers make drastic changes easy and undetectable. You can remove people from photographs, put Person A's head on Person B's body, and make products look more

Use photographs for visual appeal and to show exact appearances.

Today's software makes it easy to digitally alter photos. In the photo on the right, the bakery has been given a new name, the man's shirt has been changed to green, and a dog has been included. Is it ethical to change a photo without revealing the changes that were made to the original?

attractive than they really are. Most people would agree that it's acceptable to make cosmetic improvements, such as brightening an underexposed photo to make it easier to view. But to avoid ethical lapses, don't make any alterations that mislead the viewer or substantially change the message conveyed by the photo.[9]

Animation and Video   Computer animation and video are among the most specialized forms of business visuals. When they are appropriate and done well, they offer unparalleled visual impact. At a simple level, you can animate shapes and text within Microsoft PowerPoint, although the possibilities are somewhat limited. At a more sophisticated level, software programs such as Macromedia Flash enables the creation of multimedia files that include computer animation, digital video, and other elements. A wide variety of tools are also available for digital video production. Chances are you won't have to use these tools yourself, but if you do employ a specialist to create animation or video for websites or presentations, make sure the results follow all the guidelines for effective business messages.

Designing Effective Visuals

Computer software offers a variety of tools but doesn't automatically give you the design sensibility that is needed for effective visuals.

Technology has put powerful graphics tools in the hands of virtually every business computer user, so you no longer have to rely on professional designers as much as businesspeople had to do only a few years ago. That's the good news. The bad news is that computers can't provide the specialized training and hands-on experience of a professional designer. Computers make it easy to create visuals, but they also make it easy to create ineffective, distracting, and even downright ugly visuals. However, by following some basic design principles, you can create all the basic visuals you need—visuals that are both attractive and effective.

Learning how to use your computer tools will help you save enormous amounts of time and produce better results.

Whether you're using the charting functions offered in a spreadsheet or the design features of a specialized graphics program, take a few minutes to familiarize yourself with the software's quirks and capabilities. For instance, popular spreadsheets can create charts with just a few clicks of the mouse, but the default colors, fonts, or other design elements might not be the best for your particular needs. If possible, have a professional designer set up a template for the various types of visuals you and your colleagues need to create. Not only will doing so help ensure an effective design, but it will save you the time of making numerous design decisions every time you create a chart or graphic. However, be careful with the templates that are included with some commercial software programs. Some are "overdesigned" and inappropriate for serious business uses, and some clutter the image with overly fancy borders and backgrounds that can distract an audience from your real message.

No matter which tools you're using, take care to match the style and quality of your visuals with the subject matter and the situation at hand. The style of your visuals communicates a subtle message about your relationship with the audience. A simple, hand-drawn diagram is fine for a working meeting but inappropriate for a formal presentation or report. On the other hand, elaborate, full-color visuals may be viewed as extravagant for an informal memo.

Understanding Graphic Design Principles Few businesspeople have the opportunity to formally study the "language" of line, mass, space, size, color, pattern, and texture. However, when you encounter visuals that you find appealing or unappealing, stop and ask yourself why, and see what you can learn from this to improve your own graphics. Bear in mind that design decisions can affect the meaning you convey with your visuals, too—sometimes in subtle ways. For instance, thick lines and square corners suggest power and strength, whereas thin lines and curves suggest lightness and grace. Colors have a language all their own as well.

The use of color in visuals accelerates learning, retention, and recall by 55 percent to 78 percent, and it increases motivation and audience participation up to 80 percent.

To create effective visuals, learn both the aesthetic and the symbolic aspects of graphic art so that you won't send the wrong message or confuse your audience. Keep these six principles in mind to improve your visuals:[10]

- **Consistency.** Readers view a series of visuals as a whole, assuming that design elements will be consistent from one page to the next. For instance, if your first chart shows results for Division A in blue, the audience will expect Division A to be shown in blue throughout the report or presentation. You'll confuse people if you make arbitrary changes in color, shape, size, texture, position, scale, or typeface.

- **Contrast.** Readers expect visual distinctions to match verbal ones. To emphasize differences, depict items in contrasting colors, such as red and blue, or black and white. But to emphasize similarities, make color difference more subtle. In a pie chart, you might show two similar items in two shades of blue and a dissimilar item in yellow. Keep in mind that accent colors draw attention to key elements, but they lose their effect if you overdo them.

When designing visuals, observe the principles of continuity, contrast, emphasis, simplicity, and experience.

- **Balance.** Readers don't spend much time thinking about whether a page or screen looks balanced, but they know when "something doesn't look right," such as a layout that looks lopsided because all of the visually dominant elements are squeezed against one side.

- **Emphasis.** Readers assume that the most important point will receive the greatest visual emphasis. So present the key item on the chart in the most prominent way—through color, position, size, or whatever. Visually downplay less important items. Avoid using strong colors for unimportant data, and de-emphasize background features such as the grid lines on a chart.

- **Simplicity.** Limit the number of colors and design elements you use, and take care to avoid *chartjunk*, decorative elements that clutter documents (and confuse readers) without adding any relevant information.[11] Computers make it far too easy to add chartjunk, from clip art illustrations to three-dimensional bar charts that display only two dimensions of data. The two charts in Figure 11–16 show the same information, but the second one is cluttered with useless decoration and poor design choices. For example, the three-dimensional bars in Figure 11–16b don't show anything more than the simple two-dimensional bars in Figure 11–16a. As a result, the second chart is both much harder to read, and it conveys a sense of amateurism.

- **Experience and expectations.** Culture and education condition people to expect things to look a certain way, including visuals. For example, green may be associated with money in the United States, but not in countries whose currencies are different colors. Similarly, a red cross on a white background stands for emergency medical

FIGURE 11–16
The Power of Simplicity

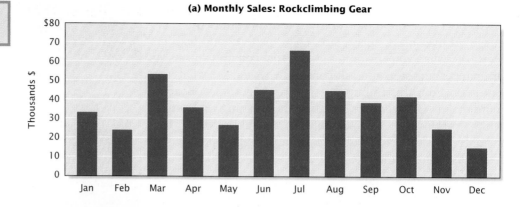

(a) Monthly Sales: Rockclimbing Gear

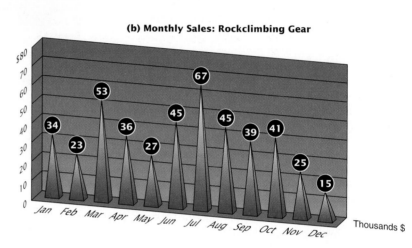

(b) Monthly Sales: Rockclimbing Gear

care in many countries. But the cross is also a Christian symbol, so the International Red Cross uses a red crescent in Islamic countries—even though the original Red Cross symbol is based on the flag of Switzerland and not on any religious icons.[12]

Integrating Visuals into Your Text   In addition to creating effective visuals, make sure your visuals are smoothly integrated with the text. This task isn't always easy, particularly with large visuals or many visuals to fit in a small space, but following three simple steps can help you achieve a successful marriage of words and images.

First, try to position your visuals so that your audience won't have to flip back and forth (in printed documents) or scroll (on screen) between the visuals and the text. Ideally, it's best to place each visual within, beside, or immediately after the paragraph it illustrates so that readers can consult the explanation and the visual at the same time.

To tie visuals to the text, introduce them in the text and place them near the points they illustrate.

Second, unless a visual element clearly stands on its own, as in the *sidebars* you often see in magazines or the captioned photographs in this textbook, it should be clearly referred to by number in the text of your report. Some report writers refer to all visuals as "exhibits" and number them consecutively throughout the report; many others number tables and figures separately (everything that isn't a table is regarded as a figure). In a long report with numbered sections, illustrations may have a double number (separated by a period or a hyphen) representing the section number and the individual illustration number within that section. Whichever scheme you use, make sure it's clear and obvious to your readers.

Help your readers understand the significance of visuals by referring to them before readers encounter them in the document or on the screen. The following examples show how you can make this connection in the text:

Figure 1 summarizes the financial history of the motorcycle division over the past five years, with sales divided by region.

Total sales were steady over this period, but the mix of sales by category changed dramatically (see Figure 2).

The underlying reason for the remarkable growth in our sales of youth golf apparel is suggested by Table 4, which shows the growing interest in junior golf around the world.

When describing the data shown in your visuals, be sure to emphasize the main point you are trying to make. Don't make the mistake of simply repeating the data to be shown. Paragraphs that do are guaranteed to put the reader to sleep:

Among women who replied to the survey, 17.4 percent earn less than $5 per hour; 26.4 percent earn $5 to $7; 25.7 percent, $8 to $12; 18.0 percent, $13 to $24; 9.6 percent, $25 to $49; and 2.9 percent, $50 and over.

The visual will (or at least should) provide all these details; there is no need to repeat them in the text. Instead, use round numbers that summarize the core message:

Over two-thirds of the women who replied earn less than $12 per hour.

Third, write effective *titles, captions,* and *legends* to complete the integration of your text and visuals. A **title** provides a short description that identifies the content and purpose of the visual, along with whatever label and number you're using to refer to the visual. As with headings and subheadings, a *descriptive* title simply identifies the topic of the illustration, whereas an *informative* title calls attention to the conclusion that ought to be drawn from the data. Here's an example of the difference:

Descriptive Title	**Informative Title**
Relationship Between Petroleum Demand and Refinery Capacity in the United States	Shrinking Refinery Capacity Results from Stagnant Petroleum Demand

A **caption** usually offers additional discussion of the visual's content and can be several sentences long if appropriate. Captions can also alert readers that additional discussion is available in the accompanying text. Titles usually appear above visuals and captions appear below, but effective designs can place these two elements in other positions. Sometimes titles and captions are combined in a single block of text as well. As with all design decisions, be consistent throughout your report or website. A **legend** helps readers "decode" the visual by explaining what various colors, symbols, or other design choices mean. Legends aren't necessary for simple graphs, such as a line chart or bar chart with only series of data, but they are invaluable with more complex graphics.

Don't assume that titles, captions, and legends are minor details. They are often the first elements that people read in a document—and sometimes the only elements that people read—so use them effectively to communicate your key points. For a review of the important points to remember when creating visuals, see "Checklist: Creating Effective Visuals."

The title of a visual functions in the same way as a subheading, whereas the caption provides additional detail if needed.

Verifying the Quality and Integrity of Your Visuals

Visuals have a particularly strong impact on your readers and on their perceptions of you and your work. Be sure to check visuals for mistakes such as typographical errors, inconsistent color treatment, confusing or undocumented symbols, and misaligned elements. Make sure that your computer hasn't done something unexpected,

Proof visuals as carefully as you proof text.

✓ CHECKLIST: Creating Effective Visuals

✓ Select the proper types of graphics for the information at hand and for the objective of the message.

✓ Be sure the visual contributes to overall understanding of the subject.

✓ Understand how to use your software tools to maximize effectiveness and efficiency.

✓ Emphasize visual continuity to connect parts of a whole.

✓ Avoid arbitrary changes of color, texture, typeface, position, or scale.

✓ Emphasize differences through design contrast.

✓ Strive for simplicity and clarity; don't clutter your visuals with meaningless decoration.

✓ Consider audience experience and cultural expectations.

✓ Integrate visuals to your text so that readers perceive a smoothly flowing unity throughout.

✓ Use titles, captions, and legends to help readers understand the meaning and importance of your visuals.

---

such as arranging pie chart slices in an order you don't want or plotting line charts in unusual colors. Also take a few extra minutes to make sure that your visuals are absolutely accurate, properly documented, and honest:

- **Is the visual accurate?** Errors are easy to make with computer-generated visuals, so make sure that every piece of information is correct. Also verify that information in visuals and text matches. For data presentations, particularly if you're producing charts with a spreadsheet, verify any formulas used to generate the numbers, and make sure you've selected the right numbers for each chart. For flowcharts, organizational charts, diagrams, photos, and other visuals, compare the visuals you created with the visuals you had planned to create. Does each visual deliver your message accurately? Have you inserted the right photos, maps, or other files?

- **Is the visual properly documented?** As with the textual elements in your reports and presentations, visuals based on other people's research, information, and ideas require full citation. (Even if the graphical design is entirely yours, any underlying information taken from other sources needs to be documented.) Also, try to anticipate any questions or concerns your audience may have and address them with additional information as needed. For instance, if you're presenting the results of survey research, many readers will want to know who participated in the survey, how many people responded, and when the questions were asked. You could answer these questions with a note in the caption along the lines of "652 accountants, surveyed the week of January 17." Similarly, if you found a visual in a secondary source, list that source on or near the graphic to help readers assess the information. To avoid cluttering your graphic, you can use a shortened citation or note on the graphic itself and include a complete citation elsewhere in the report.

Review each visual to make sure it doesn't intentionally or unintentionally distort the meaning of the underlying information.

- **Is the visual honest?** Just as subtle word choices shade the meaning of your writing, so can seemingly minor design variations influence the message your readers take away from your business graphics. Visuals can suffer from distortions, both intentional and unintentional. For instance, the way you scale the horizontal and vertical axes of a chart can have a tremendous impact on the message your audience receives (see "Practicing Ethical Communication: Distorting the Data"). Similarly, photographs can influence perceptions of physical size (and perhaps of quality, value, danger, or other associated variables), depending on the way the various elements are arranged in the picture. To increase the perceived size of a product, an advertiser might show a close-up of it being held by someone with smaller-than-average hands. Conversely, a large hand would make the product seem smaller. At the extreme, visuals can lie by hiding data or otherwise obscuring damaging information.

PRACTICING ETHICAL COMMUNICATION

Distorting the Data

Take a quick look at these three line charts, all of which display the level of impurities found in a particular source of drinking water. Chart A suggests that the source has a consistently high level of impurities throughout the year, Chart B indicates that the level of impurities jumps up and down throughout the year, and Chart C shows an impurity level that is fairly consistent throughout the year—and fairly low.

Here's the catch: All three charts are displaying the *exact same data*.

Look again at Chart A. The vertical scale is set from 0 to 120, sufficient to cover the range of variations in the data. However, what if you wanted to persuade an audience that the variations from month to month were quite severe? In Chart B, the scale is "zoomed in" on 60 to 110, making the variations look much more dramatic. The result could be a stronger emotional impact on the reader, creating the impression that these impurities are out of control.

On the other hand, what if you wanted to create the impression that things were humming along just fine, with low levels of impurities and no wild swings from month to month. You would follow the example in Chart C, where the scale is expanded from 0 to 200, which appears to minimize the variations in the data. This graph is visually "calmer," potentially creating the opposite impression—that there's really nothing to worry about.

If all three graphs show the same data, is any one of them more honest than the others? The answer to this question depends on your intent and your audience's information needs. For instance, if dramatic swings in the measurement from month to month suggest a problem with the quality of your product or the safety of a process that affects the public, then visually minimizing the swings might well be considered dishonest.

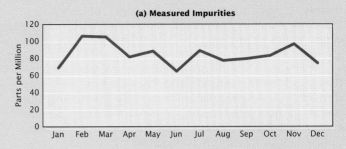

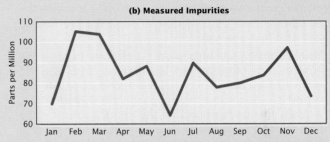

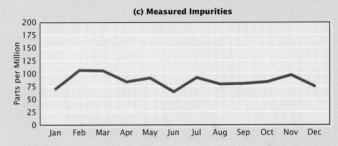

CAREER APPLICATIONS

1. What sort of quick visual impression would such a chart give if the vertical scale is set to 0–500? Why?

2. If the acceptable range of impurities in this case is from 60 to 120 parts per million, which of these three charts is the fairest way to present the data? Why?

On the Job

SOLVING COMMUNICATION DILEMMAS AT OMD WORLDWIDE

You've spent the past year working for Beth Uyenco and have learned a lot about writing clear, effective reports. The latest project she has assigned you is an informational report on the challenge of media fragmentation. Not too many years ago, "mass media" consisted of three nationwide television networks, radio, local newspapers, and a handful of popular magazines. When advertisers wanted to launch a new product nationwide, they simply bought commercial time on ABC, CBS, or NBC, and they would've had a pretty good chance of reaching their tar-

get market. For instance, as recently as 1995, according to one study, advertisers could reach an estimated 80 percent of U.S. women by running a TV commercial just three times. Advertisers didn't have to look very hard to find audiences, because audiences didn't have very far to go.

Only five years later, reaching that same audience required running the commercial nearly 100 times, and the reason is fragmentation: Consumers now scatter their attention all over the media landscape, from blogs to Internet radio to online e-zines to digital cable systems with hundreds of channels. With digital video recorders such as TiVo, millions of TV viewers can zoom right past commercials they once had to sit through. And many people, particularly younger consumers, are spending less time watching regular TV and more time playing video games or enjoying DVDs that NetFlix drops off in the mail.

Your report will help traditional mass-media advertisers such as McDonald's and PepsiCo find their way through this new media landscape by identifying the range of new advertising possibilities, from search engine advertising to ads embedded in video games. The research has been completed by a team under Uyenco's guidance, and now it's up to you to write the report (which will be provided to all OMD Worldwide clients as a free service).

1. Your company's clients place enormous trust in the advice and information they receive from you, so you've taken special care in the introduction of your report to document the scope of the investigation, explain the background of the report, identify the sources and methods of data collection, and provide clear definitions for any terms that your readers might be unfamiliar with. However, you're having some trouble writing the section on limitations—and this report does have a significant limitation. You're confident in the quality and timeliness of the information it contains, but the world of new media is changing so rapidly that you can't guarantee that the information won't go out of date quickly. Which of these statements is the best way to characterize this limitation of your report?

   a. It must be pointed out that the information in this report may become obsolete as market conditions change. This is a function of the dynamic nature of the market and is not an issue with the quality of our research.

   b. The information contained herein was current as of the time of publication. We cannot guarantee its accuracy in the future.

   c. The dynamic nature of new media markets means that information is likely to change over time. Please accept our apologies for this limitation.

   d. The dynamic nature of new media markets means that information is likely to change over time. Please check with us for the latest news and insights before making any major strategic or financial decisions based on the content of this report.

2. Over the years, Uyenco's readers have come to appreciate how easy her reports are to read, with their generous use of previews, reviews, and transitions. For a section in the body of your report that describes the many new advertising venues, which of these is the best review?

   a. As this section has shown, today's new media landscape is full of intriguing, but challenging, choices, from advertising on blogs to advertising in video games.

   b. As this section has shown, today's new media landscape is full of intriguing, but challenging, choices,

including product placement in traditional movies and television programs, product placement in and sponsorship of online movies, webcasts, advertising on blogs and in podcasts, advertising in video games, stealth marketing and buzz marketing, and music and fashion sponsorships.

   c. As this section has shown, today's new media landscape is full of intriguing, but challenging, choices:
   • Product placement in traditional movies and television programs
   • Product placement in and sponsorship of online movies
   • Webcasts
   • Advertising on blogs and in podcasts
   • Advertising in video games
   • Stealth marketing and buzz marketing
   • Music and fashion sponsorships

   d. As this section has shown, today's advertisers have a staggering array of new choices when it comes to connecting with target customers.

3. The subject of your report is new advertising media, and most of those media are electronic—and many of those often a combination of video, audio, animation, and interactivity. A good example is product placement in video games, in which brand-name products either appear as in the backdrop of game scenes or are involved in the game action itself. Naturally, such things are difficult to present effectively in a printed report. You plan to provide a number of electronic samples on your website, but how should you handle this situation in the report? For instance, how would you portray product placement in a video game?

   a. Reproduce screen images from the game and write detailed captions explaining what's going on in the game at each point; also list the URL of your website with an explanation that interactive samples can be found there.

   b. Reproduce screen images from the game and use the caption to provide the URL of your website.

   c. Static images from something as dynamic as a videogame will never be convincing; try to describe the game action in words instead.

   d. Trying to show or describe something as complex as a video game on paper is pointless; simply refer your readers to the website to see various multimedia samples.

4. To emphasize the decline in network TV viewing and the increased participation in other media, from niche cable TV channels to blogs to podcasts over the last 10 years, which type of visual would be most effective?

   a. A line chart in which individual lines represent various media

   b. Ten pie charts, one for each year, showing how the percentage of consumers using various media has changed over the years

   c. A table

   d. A U.S. map with data superimposed on each state, showing the trend data

Learning Objectives Checkup

Assess your understanding of the principles in this chapter by reading each learning objective and studying the accompanying exercises. For fill-in items, write the missing text in the blank provided; for multiple choice items, circle the letter of the correct answer. You can check your responses against the answer key on page AK-2.

Objective 11.1: Explain how to adapt to your audiences when writing reports and proposals.

1. Why is the "you" attitude particularly important with long or complex reports and proposals?
   a. The "you" attitude takes less time to write, so you'll save considerable time with long documents.
   b. Professionals are accustomed to reading long reports, so they don't require a lot of "hand holding."
   c. People simply don't read reports that don't demonstrate good business etiquette.
   d. The length and complexity of these reports put a heavy demand on readers, making it particularly important to be sensitive to their needs.

2. Which of these sentences has the most formal tone?
   a. We discuss herein the possibility of synergistic development strategies between our firm and U.S. Medical.
   b. This report explores the potential for a strategic partnership with U.S. Medical.
   c. My report is the result of a formal investigation into the possibility of a strategic partnership with U.S. Medical.
   d. In this report, I address the potential for a strategic partnership with U.S. Medical.

Objective 11.2: List the topics commonly covered in the introduction, body, and close of informational or analytical reports.

3. Which of these does not belong in the body of an informational or analytical report?
   a. An explanation of weaknesses in the report
   b. Facts, statistical evidence, and trends
   c. Conclusions and recommendations
   d. Criteria for evaluating alternatives and options

4. Where would you list action items in a report?
   a. In the opening
   b. In the body
   c. In the close
   d. Action items are never listed in reports

Objective 11.3: Name five characteristics of effective report content.

5. Which of the following is *not* a characteristic of effective report content?
   a. Balanced
   b. Clear and logical
   c. Entertaining
   d. Accurate

6. How are audiences likely to react if they spot several errors in your reports?
   a. They'll become skeptical about the quality of all your work.

   b. They'll forgive you and move on without thinking any more about it; everybody makes mistakes.
   c. They'll stop reading your reports.
   d. They'll respect the fact that you don't waste time proofreading.

Objective 11.4: Name six strategies to strengthen your proposal argument.

7. Which of the following is not a recommended strategy for strengthening your proposal argument?
   a. Provide concrete examples of the value of your proposal.
   b. Demonstrate your knowledge.
   c. Identify the amount of time you've invested in the proposal.
   d. Adopt a "you" attitude.

8. If packaging and presentation are only superficial, why are they so important in proposal writing?
   a. Readers tend to prejudge the quality of your products and services by the quality of your proposal.
   b. They show that you're more than just a "numbers" person, that you can think creatively.
   c. They show the audience that you're willing to invest time and money in getting your proposal accepted.
   d. Attractive documents always have high-quality information in them.

Objective 11.5: List the topics commonly covered in a proposal's introduction, body, and closing.

9. Which of the following elements is usually *not* part of a proposal's introduction?
   a. Background or statement of the problem
   b. Detailed cost analysis
   c. Organization of the proposal
   d. Scope of the proposal

10. The primary purpose of the body of a proposal is to
    a. List your firm's qualifications for the project in question
    b. Explain why the recipient needs to address a particular problem or opportunity
    c. Communicate your passion for solving the problem or addressing the opportunity
    d. Give complete details on the proposed solution and its anticipated benefits

11. If a proposal is being sent in response to an RFP, how should the body of the proposal address the issue of costs?
    a. It should avoid any mention of costs.
    b. It should provide a total cost figure, without wasting the reader's time with a lot of details.
    c. It should follow whatever your company's policy is regarding cost estimates.
    d. It should follow the instructions in the RFP exactly.

Objective 11.6: Describe the communication power that visuals add to your writing.

12. Visuals can enhance the communication impact of your writing by
    a. Conveying some types of information better than text can

b. Reaching audiences of diverse professional and cultural backgrounds

c. Communicating your most important points to audiences who are too busy to read your entire report

d. Delivering all of the above benefits

Objective 11.7: Explain how to choose which points in your message to illustrate.

13. Which of the following is a good candidate for illustrating in a report?
    a. Comparison of customer satisfaction ratings of 12 stores across a 12-month period
    b. Percentage of employees who have attended 10 different training courses
    c. Ranking of webpages on a website, from most visited to least visited
    d. All of the above

14. Which of the following is *not* a good reason to use a visual in a report?
    a. To communicate more effectively with multilingual audiences
    b. To help unify the separate parts of a process, organization, or other entity, such as by using a flowchart to depict the various steps in a process
    c. To simplify access to specific data points, such as by listing them in a quick-reference table
    d. To demonstrate your creative side

Objective 11.8: Discuss six principles of graphic design that can improve the quality of your visuals.

15. Why is consistency important in visual design?
    a. It shows the audience that you're not wasting precious time doing artistic designs.
    b. It reduces confusion by eliminating arbitrary changes that force people to relearn your design scheme every time they encounter another visual.

c. It saves on ink and toner when reports are printed.

d. It shows the audience that you're serious and businesslike.

16. Which of the following steps could you take to call attention to the most important elements in a visual?
    a. Use a dominant color for the important elements.
    b. Call attention to the important elements in the caption or in the text of your report.
    c. Make the important elements larger.
    d. Do all of the above.

Objective 11.9: Name three qualities to look for before including a visual in a report or presentation.

17. Which of the following steps should you take to verify the accuracy of the visuals in your reports?
    a. Make sure that data presentations such as line charts and bar charts accurately portray the data that you intended to show.
    b. Make sure flowcharts and other computer-generated artwork are correct and clear.
    c. Make sure that you've inserted the correct visuals at each place in your report.
    d. Do all of the above.

18. Assume you have a line chart with a vertical axis scaled from 0 to 100 and data points that vary within a range of roughly 10 to 90. How would you influence audience perceptions if you increased the vertical scale so that it stretched from 0 to 200, instead of 0 to 100?
    a. The scaling change would have no affect on audience perceptions.
    b. The scaling change would maximize the perceived variations in the data.
    c. The scaling change would minimize the perceived variations in the data.
    d. You have no way of predicting in advance how the scaling change would affect perceptions.

Apply Your Knowledge

1. Should a report always explain the writer's method of gathering evidence or solving a problem? Why or why not?
2. Besides telling readers why an illustration is important, why refer to it in the text of your document?
3. When you read a graph, how can you be sure that the visual impression you are receiving is an accurate reflection of reality? Please explain.

4. If you want your audience to agree to a specific course of action, should you exclude any references to alternatives that you don't want the audience to consider? Why or why not?
5. **Ethical Choices** If a company receives a solicited formal proposal outlining the solution to a particular problem, is it ethical for the company to adopt the proposal's recommendations without hiring the firm that submitted the proposal? Why or why not?

Practice Your Knowledge

DOCUMENT FOR ANALYSIS

Read Figure 11–17, a solicited memo proposal, then (1) analyze the strengths and weaknesses of this document and (2) revise the document so that it follows this chapter's guidelines.

FIGURE 11–17
Solicited Memo Proposal

PROPOSAL

DATE: April 19, 2006
TO: Ken Estes, Northern Illinois Concrete
FROM: Kris Beiersdorf, Memco Construction
PROJECT: IDOT Letting Item #83, Contract No. 79371, DuPage County

Memco Construction proposes to furnish all labor, material, equipment, and supervision to provide Engineered Fill—Class II and IV—for the following unit prices.

Engineered Fill—Class II and IV

Description	Unit	Quantity	Unit Price	Total
Mobilization*	Lump Sum	1	$4,500.00	$4,500.00
Engineered Fill Class II	Cubic Yards	1,267	$33.50	$42,444.50
Engineered Fill Class IV	Cubic Yards	1,394	$38.00	$52,972.00

* Mobilization includes one move-in. Additional move-ins to be billed at $1,100.00 each.

The following items clarify and qualify the scope of our subcontracting work:
1. All forms, earthwork, clearing, etc., to be provided and maintained by others at no cost to Memco Construction.
2. General Contractor shall provide location for staging, stockpiling material, equipment, and storage at the job site.
3. Memco Construction shall be paid strictly based upon the amount of material actually used on the job.
4. All prep work, including geotechnical fabrics, geomembrane liners, etc., to be done by others at no cost to Memco Construction.
5. Water is to be available at project site at no charge to Memco Construction.
6. Dewatering to be done by others at no cost to Memco Construction.
7. Traffic control setup, devices, maintenance, and flagmen are to be provided by others at no cost to Memco Construction.
8. Memco Construction LLC may withdraw this bid if we do not receive a written confirmation that we are the apparent low sub-bidder within 10 days of your receipt of this proposal.
9. Our F.E.I.N. is 36-4478095.
10. Bond is not included in above prices. Bond is available for an additional 1 percent.

If you have any questions, please contact me at the phone number listed below.

Kris Beiersdorf
Memco Construction
187 W. Euclid Avenue, Glenview, IL 60025
Office: (847) 352-9742, ext. 30
Fax: (847) 352-6595
E-mail: Kbeiersdorf@memco.com
www.memco.com

Exercises

For active links to all websites discussed in this chapter, visit this text's website at www.prenhall.com/thill. Locate your book and click on its Companion Website link. Then select Chapter 11, and click on "Featured Websites." Locate the name of the page or the URL related to the material in the text. Please note that links to sites that become inactive after publication of the book will be removed from the Featured Websites section.

11.1 Adapting Reports to the Audience Review the reports shown in Figures 11–2 and 11–3. Give specific examples of how each of these reports establishes a good relationship with the audience. Consider such things as using the "you" attitude, emphasizing the positive, establishing credibility, being polite, using bias-free language, and projecting a good company image.

11.2 Composing Reports: Report Content You are writing an analytical report on the U.S. sales of your newest product. Of the following topics, identify those that should be covered in the report's introduction, body, and close. Briefly explain your decisions:

a. Regional breakdowns of sales across the country

b. Date the product was released in the marketplace

c. Sales figures from competitors selling similar products worldwide

d. Predictions of how the struggling U.S. economy will affect sales over the next six months

e. Method used for obtaining the above predictions

f. The impact of similar products being sold in the United States by Japanese competitors

g. Your recommendation as to whether the company should sell this product internationally

h. Actions that must be completed by year end if the company decides to sell this product internationally

11.3 **Composing Business Reports** Your boss, Len Chow (vice president of corporate planning), has asked you to research opportunities in the cosmetics industry and to prepare a report that presents your findings and your recommendation for where you think the company should focus its marketing efforts. Here's a copy of your note cards (data were created for this exercise):

Sub: Demand   ref: 1.1
Industry grew through 1970s, 1980s, and early 1990s fueled by per capita consumption

Sub: Competition   ref: 1.2
700 companies currently in cosmetics industry

Sub: Niches   ref: 1.3
Focusing on special niches avoids head-on competition with industry leaders

Sub: Competition   ref: 1.4
Industry dominated by market leaders: Revlon, Procter & Gamble, Avon, Gillette

Sub: Demand   ref: 1.5
Industry no longer recession-proof: Past year, sales sluggish; consumer spending is down; most affected were mid- to high-priced brands; consumers traded down to less expensive lines

Sub: Competition   ref: 1.6
Smaller companies (Neutrogena, Mary Kay, Soft Soap, and Noxell) survive by specializing in niches, differentiating product line, focusing on market segment

Sub: Demand   ref: 1.7
Consumption of cosmetics relatively flat for past five years

Sub: Competition   ref: 1.8
Prices are constant while promotion budgets are increasing

Sub: Niches   ref: 1.9
Men: 50% of adult population; account for one-fifth of cosmetic sales; market leaders have attempted this market but failed

Sub: Demand   ref: 1.10
Cosmetic industry is near maturity but some segments may vary. Total market currently produces annual retail sales of $14.5 billion: cosmetics/lotions/fragrances—$5.635 billion; personal hygiene products—$4.375 billion; hair-care products—$3.435 billion; shaving products—$1.055 billion

Sub: Niches   ref: 1.11
Ethnic groups: Some firms specialize in products for African Americans; few firms oriented toward Hispanic, Asian, or Native Americans, which tend to be concentrated geographically

Sub: Demand   ref: 1.12
Average annual expenditure per person for cosmetics is $58

Sub: Competition   ref: 1.13
Competition is intensifying and dominant companies are putting pressure on smaller ones

Sub: Demand   ref: 1.14
First quarter of current year, demand is beginning to revive; trend expected to continue well into next year

Sub: Niches   ref: 1.15
Senior citizens: large growing segment of population; account for 6% of cosmetic sales; specialized needs for hair and skin not being met; interested in appearance

Sub: Demand   ref: 1.16
Demographic trends: (1) Gradual maturing of baby-boomer generation will fuel growth by consuming greater quantities of shaving cream, hair-coloring agents, and skin creams; (2) population is increasing in the South and Southwest, where some brands have strong distribution

List the main idea of your message (your recommendation), the major points (your conclusions), and supporting evidence. Then construct a final report outline with first- and second-level informative headings focusing on your conclusions. Because Chow requested this report, you can feel free to use the direct approach. Finish by writing a draft of your memo report to Chow.

11.4 Composing Reports Find an article in a business newspaper or journal (in print or online) that recommends a solution to a problem. Identify the problem, the recommended solution(s), and the supporting evidence provided by the author to justify his or her recommendation(s). Did the author cite any formal or informal studies as evidence? What facts or statistics did the author include? Did the author cite any criteria for evaluating possible options? If so, what were they?

11.5 Composing Reports: Time Perspective Rewrite this section of text to give it a consistent time perspective:

Of those interviewed, 25 percent report that they are dissatisfied with their present brand. The wealthiest participants complained most frequently, but all income categories are interested in trying a new brand. Only 5 percent of the interviewees say they had no interest in alternative products.

11.6 Composing Reports: Navigational Clues Review a long business article in a journal or newspaper. Highlight examples of how the article uses heading, transitions, and previews and reviews to help the readers find their way.

11.7 Ethical Choices Your boss has asked you to prepare a feasibility report to determine whether the company should advertise its custom-crafted cabinetry in the weekly neighborhood newspaper. Based on your primary research, you think they should. As you draft the introduction to your report, however, you discover that the survey administered to the neighborhood newspaper subscribers was flawed. Several of the questions were poorly written and misleading. You used the survey results, among other findings, to justify your recommendation. The report is due in three days. What actions might you want to take, if any, before you complete your report?

11.8 Preparing Line Charts The pet food manufacturer you work for is interested in the results of a recent poll of U.S. pet-owning households. Look at the statistics that follow and decide on the most appropriate scale for a chart; then create a line chart of the trends in cat ownership. What conclusions do you draw from the trend you've charted? Draft a paragraph or two discussing the results of this poll and the potential consequences for the pet food business. Support your conclusions by referring readers to your chart.

In 1990, 22 million U.S. households owned a cat. In 1995, 24 million households owned a cat. In 2000, 28 million households owned a cat. In 2005, 32 million households owned a cat.

11.9 Selecting the Right Visual You're preparing the annual report for FretCo Guitar Corporation. For each of the following types of information, select the right chart or visual to illustrate the text. Explain your choices.
a. Data on annual sales for the past 20 years
b. Comparison of FretCo sales, product by product (electric guitars, bass guitars, amplifiers, acoustic guitars), for this year and last year
c. Explanation of how a FretCo acoustic guitar is manufactured
d. Explanation of how the FretCo Guitar Corporation markets its guitars
e. Data on sales of FretCo products in each of 12 countries
f. Comparison of FretCo sales figures with sales figures for three competing guitar makers over the past 10 years

11.10 Selecting the Right Chart Here are last year's sales figures for the appliance and electronics megastore where you work. Construct charts based on these figures that will help you explain to the store's general manager seasonal variations in each department.

Store Sales in 2005 (in $ thousands)

Month	Home Electronics	Computers	Appliances
January	$68	$39	$36
February	72	34	34
March	75	41	30
April	54	41	28
May	56	42	44
June	49	33	48
July	54	31	43
August	66	58	39
September	62	58	36
October	66	44	33
November	83	48	29
December	91	62	24

11.11 Creating Maps You work for C & S Holdings, a company that operates coin-activated, self-service car washes. Research shows that the farther customers live from a car wash, the less likely they are to visit. You know that 50 percent of customers at each of your car washes live within a 4-mile radius of the location, 65 percent live within 6 miles, 80 percent live within 8 miles, and 90 percent live within 10 miles. C & S's owner wants to open two new car washes in your city and has asked you to prepare a report recommending locations. Using a map of your city (try www.mappoint.com or www.mapquest.com), choose two possible locations for car washes and create a visual depicting the customer base surrounding each location (make up whatever population data you need).

11.12 Internet One of the best places to see how data can be presented visually is in government statistical publications, which are often available on the Internet. For example, the International Trade Administration (ITA), a branch of the U.S. Department of Commerce, publishes monthly reports about U.S. trade with other countries. Visit the report page of its website at www.ita.doc.gov and follow the link to the latest monthly trade update. Using what you learned in this chapter, evaluate the charts in the report. Do they present the data clearly? Are they missing any elements? What would you do to improve the charts? Print out a copy of the report to turn in with your answers, and indicate which charts you are evaluating.

Expand Your Knowledge

LEARNING MORE ON THE WEB

Brush Up on Your Computer-Graphics Skills http://graphicssoft.about.com. Need some help using graphics software? Get started at the About.com graphics software website. Take the tutorials and learn how to manage fonts, images, and a variety of graphics-related tasks. View the illustrated demonstrations. Read the instructional articles. Learn how to use the most common file formats for graphics. Expand your knowledge of the basic principles of graphic design. And master some advanced color tips and theory. Don't leave without following the links to recommended books and magazines.

ACTIVITIES

Explore About.com's Graphics Software section and answer these questions:
1. What are the most common file formats for online visuals?
2. What does color depth mean in computer visuals?
3. What is dithering and how can it affect your visuals?

EXPLORING THE WEB ON YOUR OWN

Review these chapter-related websites to learn more about writing reports and proposals.
1. Researching Companies Online, www.learnwebskills.com, has some good advice for finding company and industry information on the web. Take the tutorial.
2. Craft more effective executive summaries by following the advice at the Harvard Business School's Working Knowledge website, http://hbswk.hbs.edu/ (look for "Crafting a Powerful Executive Summary" under Career Effectiveness).
3. Learn the meaning of more than 2,500 signs and symbols at Symbols.com, www.symbols.com.

Learn Interactively

INTERACTIVE STUDY GUIDE

Visit www.prenhall.com/thill, then locate your book and click on its Companion Website link. Select Chapter 11 to take advantage of the interactive "Chapter Quiz" to test your knowledge of chapter concepts. Receive instant feedback on whether you need additional studying. Also, visit the "Study Hall," where you'll find an abundance of valuable resources that will help you succeed in this course.

PEAK PERFORMANCE GRAMMAR AND MECHANICS

If your instructor has required the use of "Peak Performance Grammar and Mechanics," either in your online course or on CD, you can improve your skill with dashes and hyphens by using the "Peak Performance Grammar and Mechanics" module. Click "Punctuation." Take the Pretest to determine whether you have any weak areas. Then review those areas in the Refresher Course. Take the Follow-Up Test to check your grasp of dashes and hyphens. For an extra challenge or advanced practice, take the Advanced Test. Finally, for additional reinforcement, go to the "Improve Your Grammar, Mechanics, and Usage" section that follows, and complete those exercises.

Improve Your Grammar, Mechanics, and Usage

The following exercises help you improve your knowledge of and power over English grammar, mechanics, and usage. Turn to the Handbook of Grammar, Mechanics, and Usage at the end of this textbook and review all of Sections 2.7 (Dashes) and 2.8 (Hyphens). Then look at the following 10 items. Circle the letter of the preferred choice in the following groups of sentences. (Answers to these exercises appear on page AK-4.)
1. a. Three qualities—speed, accuracy, and reliability are desirable in any applicant.
    b. Three qualities——speed, accuracy, and reliability—are desirable in any applicant.
2. a. A highly placed source explained the top-secret negotiations.
    b. A highly-placed source explained the top-secret negotiations.
    c. A highly placed source explained the top secret negotiations.

3. a. The file on Mary Gaily—yes—we finally found it reveals a history of tardiness.
   b. The file on Mary Gaily, yes—we finally found it—reveals a history of tardiness.
   c. The file on Mary Gaily—yes, we finally found it—reveals a history of tardiness.
4. a. They're selling a well designed machine.
   b. They're selling a well-designed machine.
5. a. Argentina, Brazil, Mexico—these are the countries we hope to concentrate on.
   b. Argentina, Brazil, Mexico—these are the countries—we hope to concentrate on.
6. a. Only two sites maybe three—offer the things we need.
   b. Only two sites—maybe three—offer the things we need.
7. a. How many owner operators are in the industry?
   b. How many owner—operators are in the industry?
   c. How many owner-operators are in the industry?
8. a. Your ever-faithful assistant deserves—without a doubt—a substantial raise.
   b. Your ever faithful assistant deserves—without a doubt—a substantial raise.
9. a. The charts are well placed—on each page—unlike the running heads and footers.
   b. The charts are well-placed on each page—unlike the running heads and footers.
   c. The charts are well placed on each page—unlike the running heads and footers.
10. a. Your devil-may-care attitude affects everyone in the decision-making process.
    b. Your devil may care attitude affects everyone in the decision-making process.
    c. Your devil-may-care attitude affects everyone in the decision making process.

For additional exercises focusing on dashes and hyphens, go to www.prenhall.com/thill, then locate your text and click on its Companion Website link. Click on Chapter 11, click on "Additional Exercises to Improve Your Grammar, Mechanics and Usage," then click on "18. Punctuation C."

Cases

Applying the Three-Step Writing Process to Cases
Apply each step to the following cases, as assigned by your instructor.

Planning

Analyze the Situation
Clarify the problem or opportunity at hand, define your purpose, develop an audience profile, and develop a work plan.

Gather Information
Determine audience needs and obtain the information necessary to satisfy those needs; conduct a research project if necessary.

Select the Right Medium
Choose the best medium for delivering your message; consider delivery through multiple media.

Organize the Information
Define your main idea, limit your scope, select a direct or an indirect approach, and outline your content using an appropriate structure for an informational report, analytical report, or proposal.

1

Writing

Adapt to Your Audience
Be sensitive to audience needs with a "you" attitude, politeness, positive emphasis, and bias-free language. Build a strong relationship with your audience by establishing your credibility and projecting your company's image. Control your style with a tone and voice appropriate to the situation.

Compose the Message
Choose strong words that will help you create effective sentences and coherent paragraphs throughout the introduction, body, and close of your report or proposal.

2

Completing

Revise the Report
Evaluate content and review readability, edit and rewrite for conciseness and clarity.

Produce the Report
Use effective design elements and suitable layout for a clean, professional appearance; seamlessly combine textual and graphical elements.

Proofread the Report
Review for errors in layout, spelling, and mechanics.

Distribute the Report
Deliver your report using the chosen medium; make sure all documents and all relevant files are distributed successfully.

3

INFORMATIONAL REPORTS

1. My progress to date: Interim progress report on your academic career As you know, the bureaucratic process involved in getting a degree or certificate is nearly as challenging as any course you could take.

Your task: Prepare an interim progress report detailing the steps you've taken toward completing your graduation or certification requirements. After examining the requirements listed in your college catalog, indicate a realistic schedule for completing those that remain. In addition to course requirements, include steps such as completing the residency requirement, filing necessary papers, and paying necessary fees. Use memo format for your report, and address it to anyone who is helping or encouraging you through school.

2. Gavel to gavel: Personal activity report of a meeting Meetings, conferences, and conventions abound in the academic world, and you have probably attended your share.

Your task: Prepare a personal activity report on a meeting, convention, or conference that you recently attended. Use memo format, and direct the report to other students in your field who were not able to attend.

3. Check that price tag: Informational report on trends in college costs Your college's administration has asked you to compare your college's tuition costs with those of a nearby college and determine which has risen more quickly. Research the trend by checking your college's annual tuition costs for each of the most recent four years. Then research the four-year tuition trends for a neighboring college. For both colleges, calculate the percentage change in tuition costs from year to year and between the first and fourth year.

Your task: Prepare an informal report (using the letter format) presenting your findings and conclusions to the president of your college. Include graphics to explain and support your conclusions.

4. Get a move on it: Lasting guidelines for moving into college dormitories Moving into a college dormitory is one experience you weren't quite prepared for. In addition to lugging all your earthly belongings up four flights of stairs in 90-degree heat, channeling electrical cords to the one room outlet tucked in the corner of the room, lofting your beds, and negotiating with your roommate over who gets the bigger closet, you had to hug your parents goodbye in the parking lot in front of the entire freshman class—or so it seemed. Now that you are a pro, you've offered to write some lasting guidelines for future freshmen so they know what is expected of them on moving day.

Your task: Prepare an informational report for future freshmen classes outlining the rules and procedures to follow when moving into a college dorm. Lay out the rules such as starting time, handling trash and empty boxes, items permitted and not permitted in dorm rooms, common courtesies, parking, and so on. Be sure to mention what the policy is for removing furniture from the room, lofting beds, and overloading electrical circuits. Of course, any recommendations on how to handle disputes with roommates would be helpful. So would some brief advice on how to cope with anxious parents. Direct your memo report to the college dean.

ANALYTICAL REPORTS

5. My next career move: Feasibility report organized around recommendations If you've ever given yourself a really good talking-to, you'll be quite comfortable with this project.

Your task: Write a memo report directed to yourself and signed with a fictitious name. Indicate a possible job that your college education will qualify you for, mention the advantages of the position in terms of your long-range goals, and then outline the actions you must take to get the job.

6. Staying the course: Unsolicited proposal using the 2 + 2 = 4 approach Think of a course you would love to see added to the core curriculum at your school. Conversely, if you would like to see a course offered as an elective rather than being required, write your e-mail report accordingly.

Your task: Write a short e-mail proposal using the 2 + 2 = 4 approach (refresh your memory in Chapter 10, if necessary). Prepare your proposal to be submitted to the academic dean by e-mail. Be sure to include all the reasons supporting your idea.

7. Planning my program: Problem-solving report using the yardstick approach Assume that you will have time for only one course next term.

Your task: List the pros and cons of four or five courses that interest you, and use the yardstick approach to settle on the course that is best for you to take at this time. Write your report in memo format, addressing it to your academic adviser.

8. Restaurant review: Troubleshooting report on a restaurant's food and operations Visit any restaurant, possibly your school cafeteria. The workers and fellow customers will assume that you are an ordinary customer, but you are really a spy for the owner.

Your task: After your visit, write a short letter to the owner, explaining (a) what you did and what you observed, (b) any violations of policy that you observed, and (c) your recommendations for improvement. The first part of your report (what you did and what you observed) will be the longest. Include a description of the premises, inside and out. Tell how long it took for each step of ordering and receiving your meal. Describe the service and food thoroughly. You are interested in both the good and bad aspects of the establishment's décor, service, and food.

For the second section (violations of policy), use some common sense. If all the servers but one have their hair covered, you may assume that policy requires hair to be covered; a dirty window or restroom obviously violates policy. The last section (recommendations for improvement) involves professional judgment. What management actions will improve the restaurant?

9. On the books: Troubleshooting report on improving the campus bookstore Imagine that you are a consultant hired to improve the profits of your campus bookstore.

Your task: Visit the bookstore and look critically at its operations. Then draft a letter to the bookstore manager, offering recommendations that would make the store more profitable, perhaps suggesting products it should carry, hours that it should remain open, or added services that it should make available to students. Be sure to support your recommendations.

10. Day and night: Problem-solving report on stocking a 24-hour convenience store When a store is open all day, every day, when's the best time to restock the shelves? That's the challenge at Store 24, a retail chain that never closes. Imagine you're the assistant manager of a Store 24 branch that just opened near your campus. You want to set up a restocking schedule that won't conflict with prime shopping hours. Think about the number of customers you're likely to serve in the morning, afternoon, evening, and overnight hours. Consider, too, how many employees you might have during these four periods.

Your task: Using the scientific approach, write a problem-solving report in letter form to the store manager (Isabel Chu) and the regional manager (Eric Angstrom), who must agree on a solution to this problem. Discuss the pros and cons of each of the four periods, and include your recommendation for restocking the shelves.

PROPOSALS

11. "Would you carry it?" Unsolicited sales proposal recommending a product to a retail outlet Select a product you are familiar with, and imagine that you are the manufacturer trying to get a local retail outlet to carry it. Use the Internet and other resources to gather information about the product.

Your task: Write an unsolicited sales proposal in letter format to the owner (or manager) of the store, proposing that the item be stocked. Use the information you gathered to describe some of the product's features and benefits to the store. Then make up some reasonable figures, highlighting what the item costs, what it can be sold for, and what services your company pro-

vides (return of unsold items, free replacement of unsatisfactory items, necessary repairs, and so on).

12. Where is everybody? Proposal to sell GPS fleet tracking system. As a sales manager for Air-Trak, one of your responsibilities is writing sales proposals for potential buyers of your company's Cloudberry tracking system. Cloudberry uses the Global Positioning System (GPS) to track the location of vehicles and other assets. For example, the dispatcher for a trucking company can simply click a map display on a computer screen to find out where all the company's trucks are at that instant. Air-Trak lists the following as benefits of the system:

- Making sure vehicles follow prescribed routes with minimal loitering time
- "Geofencing," in which dispatchers are alerted if vehicles leave a prescribed area
- Route optimization, in which fleet managers can analyze routes and destinations to find the most time- and fuel-efficient path for each vehicle
- Comparisons between scheduled and actual travel
- Enhanced security, protecting both drivers and cargos

Your task: Write a brief proposal to Doneta Zachs, fleet manager for Midwest Express, 338 S.W. 6th, Des Moines, Iowa, 50321. Introduce your company, explain the benefits of the Cloudberry system, and propose a trial deployment in which you would equip five Midwest Express trucks. For the purposes of this assignment, you don't need to worry about the technical details of the system; focus on promoting the benefits and asking for a decision regarding the test project. (You can learn more about the Air-Trak and the Cloudberry system at **www.air-trak.com**.)[13]

Chapter 12

Completing Reports and Proposals

Learning Objectives

AFTER STUDYING THIS CHAPTER, YOU WILL BE ABLE TO

1 Characterize the four tasks involved in completing business reports and proposals

2 Explain how computers have both simplified and complicated the report-production process

3 Identify the circumstances in which you should include letters of authorization and letters of acceptance in your reports

4 Explain the difference between a synopsis and an executive summary

5 Describe the three supplementary parts of a formal report

6 Explain how prefatory parts of a proposal differ depending on whether the proposal is solicited or unsolicited

On the Job

COMMUNICATING AT THE BILL AND MELINDA GATES FOUNDATION

CREATING EFFECTIVE PARTNERSHIPS TO TACKLE SOME OF THE WORLD'S MOST CHALLENGING PROBLEMS

Like many businesspeople, Microsoft co-founder Bill Gates and his wife, Melinda French Gates, a former Microsoft executive, began to turn their attention to charitable causes after they had achieved success in business. Unlike most businesspeople, the Gates family has billions of dollars and the ambitious goal of transforming global health, education, and access to digital information.

Rather than simply giving money away, the Gates Foundation forms long-term partnerships with the organizations it supports and with other government and private sector organizations pursuing similar goals. As Mr. and Mrs. Gates put it, the foundation acts as a catalyst, bringing resources together in a way that "increases the momentum, scale, and sustainability of change." The strategy is applied to such important social challenges as containing the AIDS epidemic, eradicating malaria, improving high schools, and making sure people everywhere have access to the digital revolution made possible by the Internet.

Meeting challenges of such staggering complexity and coordinating the resources of organizations all over the world is obviously no small task, and communication plays a vital role in this effort. In particular, reports and proposals link the various groups involved in the foundation's activities and inform the public about ongoing challenges and progress.

The Gates have staffed the foundation with people who have demonstrated effective leadership and communication skills, including Patty Stonesifer, another former Microsoft executive, who serves as co-chair and president. Stonesifer is deeply involved in

For Patty Stonesifer, co-chair and president of the Bill and Melinda Gates Foundation, much of her communication efforts involve one-on-one conversations with both the people the foundation helps and the researchers who create solutions to health and education challenges. However, written reports and proposals play an equally important role in her work.

reports and proposals, both as a writer and a reader. In addition to co-authoring the foundation's annual report, she reads numerous proposals from organizations asking for part of the $1.5 billion the foundation provides every year. The foundation receives some 3,000 formal grant requests every month, and the review process is a thorough one.

"A well-written grant [proposal] is a beautiful thing," says one of her former colleagues. "You have a really smart person saying, 'I have this idea.' It's a wonderful story." Stonesifer examines proposals from various angles, listening to her colleagues' perspectives and asking all sorts of questions: Is this really the best approach? What's going to make the biggest difference? Could this proposal be a catalyst that attracts other organizations to participate?

A successful grant proposal is just the beginning of the communication process between the foundation and the grant recipient. The foundation treats each grant like an investment, staying involved, setting specific milestones, and expecting progress reports in return. If the recipients can't show tangible progress, they risk losing their funding. This ongoing accountability creates an impact that lasts long after a proposal's goals are achieved.

Stonesifer and her colleagues recognize that they are tackling problems of almost unimaginable complexity, but with systematic thinking, unstoppable optimism, unmatched financial resources, and effective communication skills, they remain committed to improving life for people the world over.[1]

www.gatesfoundation.org

PUTTING THE FINAL TOUCHES ON REPORTS AND PROPOSALS

Depending on your job and the industry you work in, you may prepare many formal reports and proposals over the course of your career. For instance, management consultants routinely prepare formal documents, both formal proposals to solicit new projects and formal reports to communicate the results of those projects to their clients. This chapter addresses all four tasks involved in completing longer messages: revising, producing, proofreading, and distributing.

Don't rush through the completion stage and risk making mistakes that could undo your days or weeks of hard work.

Although the tasks covered in this chapter are similar in concept to those you studied in Chapter 6, completing reports and proposals can require considerably more work than short messages require. Production alone can take several days for a complex report. And as you've probably experienced with school reports already, computers, copiers, and other resources have an uncanny knack for going haywire at the last minute, when you're frantic to finish and have no time to spare. If at all possible, leave yourself double or triple the amount of time you think you'll need to complete your project. With interruptions, system glitches, and last-minute corrections, you'll probably need all that time and then some.

Most of the discussion in this chapter applies to *formal* reports and proposals, those documents that require an extra measure of polish and professionalism—whether because of audience expectations, company tradition, or even marketing needs. Few reports and proposals require every component described in this chapter, but be sure to carefully select the elements you want to include in each of your documents.

REVISING YOUR REPORTS AND PROPOSALS

Experienced business communicators such as Patty Stonesifer recognize that the process of writing a report or proposal doesn't end with a first draft. As Chapter 5 points out, when you compose a first draft, you simply try to get your ideas on paper with some semblance of organization, and you often save any strengthening, tightening, and polishing for second and final drafts.

The revision process for long reports is the same as for short messages, although it can take considerably longer.

The revision process is essentially the same for reports as for any business message, although it may take considerably longer, depending on the length of your document. Evaluate your organization, style, and tone, making sure that you've said what you want to say and that you've said it in the most logical order and in a way that responds to your audience's needs. Then work to improve the report's readability by varying sentence length, keeping paragraphs short, using lists and bullets, and adding headings and subheadings. Keep revising the content until it is clear, concise, and compelling.

PRODUCING YOUR REPORTS AND PROPOSALS

Once you are satisfied with your text, you're ready to produce your report by incorporating the design elements discussed in Chapter 6. Headings, captions, typographical devices (such as capital letters, italics, and boldface type), margins, line justifications, and white space are just some of the techniques and tools you can use to present your material effectively. At this point you also start to add in charts, graphs, and other visuals, as well as any missing textual elements such as previews and reviews. Many organizations have format guidelines that make your decisions easier, but the goal is always to focus readers' attention on major points and on the flow of ideas.

In some organizations, you'll be able to rely on the help of specialists in design and production, particularly for important, high-visibility reports or proposals. You may also have clerical help available to assist with the mechanical assembly and distribution. However, for most reports in many of today's lean-staffed companies, you should count on doing most or all of the production work yourself.

The good news is that computer tools are now generally easy enough for the average businessperson to use productively. A software suite such as Microsoft Office or Word Perfect Office lets you produce reports that incorporate graphics, tables, spreadsheet data, and database records. Even advanced report features such as photography are relatively simple these days, with the advent of low-cost digital cameras, color desktop scanners, and inexpensive color printers with near-photo-quality output.

The bad news is that continually improving computer tools increase your audience's expectations. People are influenced by packaging, so a handsomely bound report with full-color graphics will impress your audience more than a plain, typewritten-style report, even though the two documents contain the same information. The competition is even tougher when your report must contend with electronic reports filled with multimedia effects and hypertext links. In some cases, sending a custom-made CD-ROM containing your new business proposal might be your best option.

> Computer tools have made it easy for virtually anyone to create handsome reports, but they've also raised the expectations of business audiences.

Components of a Formal Report

The parts you include in a report depend on the type of report you are writing, how long it is, what your audience expects and requires, and what your organization dictates. The components listed in Figure 12–1 fall into three categories, depending on where they are found in a report: prefatory parts, text of the report, and supplementary parts. For an illustration of how the various parts fit together, see Linda Moreno's Electrovision report in the "Report Writer's Notebook: Analyzing a Formal Report."

> Length, audience expectations, and organizational traditions all dictate what you should include in a formal report.

FIGURE 12–1
Parts of a Formal Report

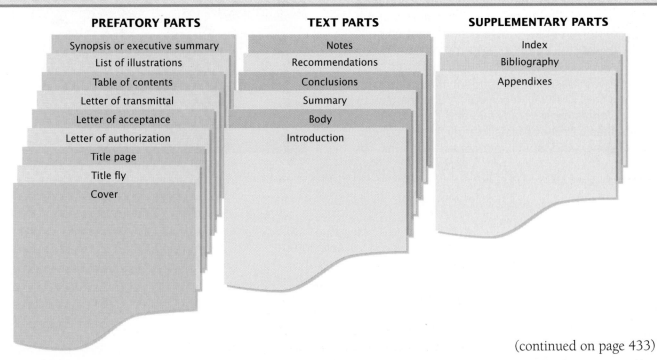

PREFATORY PARTS	TEXT PARTS	SUPPLEMENTARY PARTS
Synopsis or executive summary	Notes	Index
List of illustrations	Recommendations	Bibliography
Table of contents	Conclusions	Appendixes
Letter of transmittal	Summary	
Letter of acceptance	Body	
Letter of authorization	Introduction	
Title page		
Title fly		
Cover		

(continued on page 433)

REPORT WRITER'S NOTEBOOK
Analyzing a Formal Report

The report presented in the following pages was prepared by Linda Moreno, manager of the cost accounting department at Electrovision, a high-tech company based in Los Gatos, California. Electrovision's main product is optical character recognition equipment, which is used by the U.S. Postal Service for sorting mail. Moreno's job is to help analyze the company's costs. She has this to say about the background of the report:

> For the past three or four years, Electrovision has been on a roll. Our A-12 optical character reader was a real breakthrough, and the post office grabbed up as many as we could make. Our sales and profits kept climbing, and morale was fantastic. Everybody seemed to think that the good times would last forever. Unfortunately, everybody was wrong. When the Postal Service announced that it was postponing all new equipment purchases because of cuts in its budget, we woke up to the fact that we are essentially a one-product company with one customer. At that point, management started scrambling around looking for ways to cut costs until we could diversify our business a bit.
>
> The vice president of operations, Dennis McWilliams, asked me to help identify cost-cutting opportunities in travel and entertainment. On the basis of his personal observations, he felt that Electrovision was overly generous in its travel policies and that we might be able to save a significant amount by controlling these costs more carefully. My investigation confirmed his suspicion.
>
> I was reasonably confident that my report would be well received. I've worked with Dennis for several years and know what he likes: plenty of facts, clearly stated conclusions, and specific recommendations for

what should be done next. I also knew that my report would be passed on to other Electrovision executives, so I wanted to create a good impression. I wanted the report to be accurate and thorough, visually appealing, readable, and appropriate in tone.

When writing the analytical report that follows, Moreno based the organization on conclusions and recommendations presented in direct order. The first two sections of the report correspond to Moreno's two main conclusions: that Electrovision's travel and entertainment costs are too high and that cuts are essential. The third section presents recommendations for achieving better control over travel and entertainment expenses. As you review the report, analyze both the mechanical aspects and the way Moreno presents her ideas. Be prepared to discuss the way the various components convey and reinforce the main message.

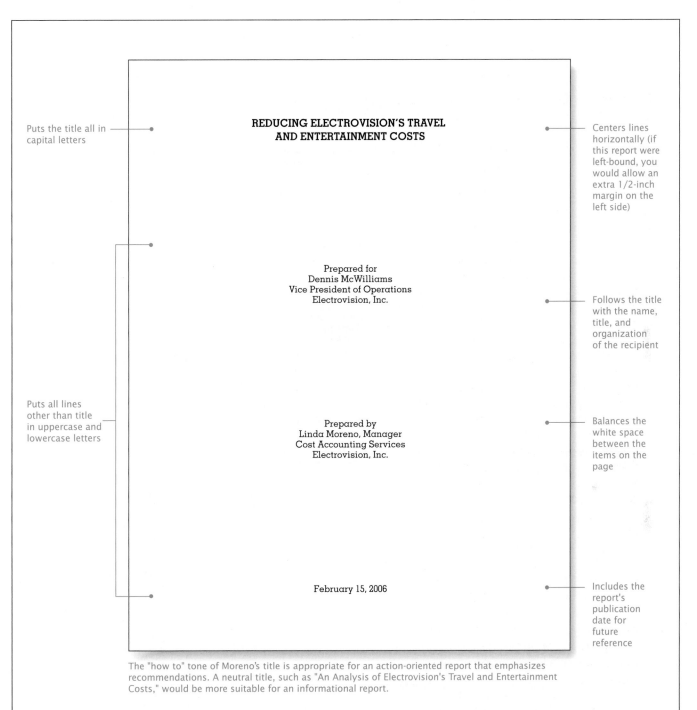

Puts the title all in capital letters

Puts all lines other than title in uppercase and lowercase letters

REDUCING ELECTROVISION'S TRAVEL AND ENTERTAINMENT COSTS

Prepared for
Dennis McWilliams
Vice President of Operations
Electrovision, Inc.

Prepared by
Linda Moreno, Manager
Cost Accounting Services
Electrovision, Inc.

February 15, 2006

Centers lines horizontally (if this report were left-bound, you would allow an extra 1/2-inch margin on the left side)

Follows the title with the name, title, and organization of the recipient

Balances the white space between the items on the page

Includes the report's publication date for future reference

The "how to" tone of Moreno's title is appropriate for an action-oriented report that emphasizes recommendations. A neutral title, such as "An Analysis of Electrovision's Travel and Entertainment Costs," would be more suitable for an informational report.

Uses memo format for transmitting this internal report (see page 434); otherwise, letter format would be used for transmitting external reports

Uses a conversational style

Acknowledges help that has been received

Presents the main conclusion right away (because Moreno expects a positive response)

Closes with thanks and an offer to discuss results (when appropriate, you could also include an offer to help with future projects)

MEMORANDUM

DATE: February 15, 2006
TO: Dennis McWilliams, Vice President of Operations
FROM: Linda Moreno, Manager of Cost Accounting Services   *LM*
SUBJECT: Reducing Electrovision's Travel and Entertainment Costs

Here is the report you requested January 28 on Electrovision's travel and entertainment costs.

Your suspicions were right. We are spending far too much on business travel. Our unwritten policy has been "anything goes," leaving us with no real control over T&E expenses. Although this hands-off approach may have been understandable when Electrovision's profits were high, we can no longer afford the luxury of going first class.

The solutions to the problem seem rather clear. We need to have someone with centralized responsibility for travel and entertainment costs, a clear statement of policy, an effective control system, and a business-oriented travel service that can optimize our travel arrangements. We should also investigate alternatives to travel, such as videoconferencing. Perhaps more important, we need to change our attitude. Instead of viewing travel funds as a bottomless supply of money, all traveling employees need to act as if they were paying the bills themselves.

Getting people to economize is not going to be easy. In the course of researching this issue, I've found that our employees are deeply attached to their generous travel privileges. I think some would almost prefer a cut in pay to a loss in travel status. We'll need a lot of top management involvement to sell people on the need for moderation. One thing is clear: People will be very bitter if we create a two-class system in which top executives get special privileges while the rest of the employees make the sacrifices.

I'm grateful to Mary Lehman and Connie McIllvain for their help in rounding up and sorting through five years' worth of expense reports. Their efforts were truly Herculean.

Thanks for giving me the opportunity to work on this assignment. It's been a real education. If you have any questions about the report, please give me a call.

In this report, Moreno decided to write a brief memo of transmittal and include a separate executive summary. Short reports (fewer than 10 pages) often combine the synopsis or executive summary with the memo or letter of transmittal.

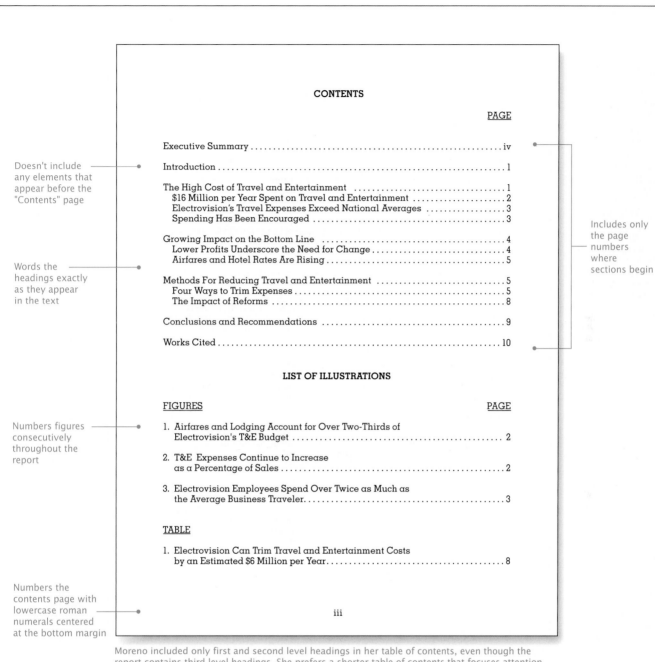

CONTENTS

LIST OF ILLUSTRATIONS

iii

Doesn't include any elements that appear before the "Contents" page

Words the headings exactly as they appear in the text

Includes only the page numbers where sections begin

Numbers figures consecutively throughout the report

Numbers the contents page with lowercase roman numerals centered at the bottom margin

Moreno included only first and second level headings in her table of contents, even though the report contains third level headings. She prefers a shorter table of contents that focuses attention on the main divisions of thought. She used informative titles, which are appropriate for a report to a receptive audience.

Begins by stating the purpose of the report

EXECUTIVE SUMMARY

This report analyzes Electrovision's travel and entertainment (T&E) costs and presents recommendations for reducing those costs.

Travel and Entertainment Costs Are Too High

Travel and entertainment is a large and growing expense category for Electrovision. The company spends over $16 million per year on business travel, and these costs have been increasing by 12 percent annually. Company employees make roughly 3,390 trips each year at an average cost per trip of $4,720. Airfares are the biggest expense, followed by hotels, meals, and rental cars.

The nature of Electrovision's business does require extensive travel, but the company's costs are excessive: Our employees spend more than twice the national average on travel and entertainment. Although the location of the company's facilities may partly explain this discrepancy, the main reason for our high costs is a management style that gives employees little incentive to economize.

Cuts Are Essential

Electrovision management now recognizes the need to gain more control over this element of costs. The company is currently entering a period of declining profits, prompting management to look for every opportunity to reduce spending. At the same time, rising airfares and hotel rates are making T&E expenses more significant.

Electrovision Can Save $6 Million per Year

Fortunately, Electrovision has a number of excellent opportunities for reducing T&E costs. Savings of up to $6 million per year should be achievable, judging by the experience of other companies. A sensible travel-management program can save companies as much as 35 percent a year (Gilligan 39–40), and we should be able to save even more, since we purchase many more business-class tickets than the average. Four steps will help us cut costs:

1. Hire a director of travel and entertainment to assume overall responsibility for T&E spending, policies, and technologies, including the hiring and management of a national travel agency.
2. Educate employees on the need for cost containment, both in avoiding unnecessary travel and reducing costs when travel is necessary.
3. Negotiate preferential rates with travel providers.
4. Implement technological alternatives to travel, such as virtual meetings.

As necessary as these changes are, they will likely hurt morale, at least in the short term. Management will need to make a determined effort to explain the rationale for reduced spending. By exercising moderation in their own travel arrangements, Electrovision executives can set a good example and help other employees accept the changes. On the plus side, using travel alternatives such as web conferencing will reduce the travel burden on many employees and help them balance their business and personal lives.

iv

Presents the points in the executive summary (see page 435) in the same order as they appear in the report, using subheadings that summarize the content of the main sections of the report

Targets a receptive audience with a hard-hitting tone in the executive summary (a more neutral approach would be better for hostile or skeptical readers)

Continues numbering the executive summary pages with lowercase roman numerals

Executive summary uses the same font and paragraph treatment as the text of the report

Moreno decided to include an executive summary because her report is aimed at a mixed audience, some of whom are interested in the details of her report and others who just want the "big picture." The executive summary is aimed at the second group, giving them enough information to make a decision without burdening them with the task of reading the entire report.

Her writing style matches the serious nature of the content without sounding distant or stiff. Moreno chose the formal approach because several members of her audience are considerably higher up in the organization, and she did not want to sound too familiar. In addition, her company prefers the impersonal style for formal reports.

Centers the title of the report on the first page of the text, 2 inches from the top of the page

REDUCING ELECTROVISION'S TRAVEL AND ENTERTAINMENT COSTS

INTRODUCTION

Electrovision has always encouraged a significant amount of business travel. To compensate employees for the stress and inconvenience of frequent trips, management has authorized generous travel and entertainment (T&E) allowances. This philosophy has been good for morale, but last year Electrovision spent $16 million on travel and entertainment—$7 million more than it spent on research and development.

Opens by establishing the need for action

This year's T&E costs will affect profits even more, due to increases in airline fares and hotel rates. Also, the company anticipates that profits will be relatively weak for a variety of other reasons. Therefore, Dennis McWilliams, Vice President of Operations, has asked the accounting department to explore ways to reduce the T&E budget.

The purpose of this report is to analyze T&E expenses, evaluate the effect of recent hotel and airfares increases, and suggest ways to tighten control over T&E costs. The report outlines several steps that could reduce Electrovision's expenses, but the precise financial impact of these measures is difficult to project. The estimates presented here provide a "best guess" view of what Electrovision can expect to save.

In preparing this report, the accounting department analyzed internal expense reports for the past five years to determine how much Electrovision spends on travel and entertainment. These figures were then compared with average statistics compiled by Dow Jones (publisher of the *Wall Street Journal*) and presented as the Dow Jones Travel Index. We also analyzed trends and suggestions published in a variety of business journal articles to see how other companies are coping with the high cost of business travel.

Mentions sources and methods to increase credibility and to give readers a complete picture of the study's background

THE HIGH COST OF TRAVEL AND ENTERTAINMENT

Although many companies view travel and entertainment as an incidental cost of doing business, the dollars add up. At Electrovision the bill for airfares, hotels, rental cars, meals, and entertainment totaled $16 million last year. Our T&E budget has increased by 12 percent per year for the past five years. Compared to the average U.S. business traveler, Electrovision's expenditures are high, largely because of management's generous policy on travel benefits.

Uses the arabic numeral 1 for the first page, centering the number about 1 inch from the bottom of the page

1

In her brief introduction, Moreno counts on topic sentences and transitions to indicate that she is discussing the purpose, scope, and limitations of the study.

2

$16 Million per Year Spent on Travel and Entertainment

Electrovision's annual budget for travel and entertainment is only eight percent of sales. Because this is a relatively small expense category compared with such things as salaries and commissions, it is tempting to dismiss T&E costs as insignificant. However, T&E is Electrovision's third-largest controllable expense, directly behind salaries and information systems.

Last year Electrovision personnel made about 3,390 trips at an average cost per trip of $4,720. The typical trip involved a round-trip flight of 3,000 miles, meals, and hotel accommodations for two or three days, and a rental car. Roughly 80 percent of trips were made by 20 percent of the staff—top management and sales personnel traveled most, averaging 18 trips per year.

Figure 1 illustrates how the T&E budget is spent. The largest categories are airfares and lodging, which together account for $7 out of $10 that employees spend on travel and entertainment. This spending breakdown has been relatively steady for the past five years and is consistent with the distribution of expenses experienced by other companies.

Figure 1

Airfares and Lodging Account for Over
Two-Thirds of Electrovision's T&E Budget

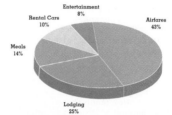

Although the composition of the T&E budget has been consistent, its size has not. As mentioned earlier, these expenditures have increased by about 12 percent per year for the past five years, roughly twice the rate of the company's sales growth (see Figure 2). This rate of growth makes T&E Electrovision's fastest-growing expense item.

Figure 2

T&E Expenses Continue to Increase as a
Percentage of Sales

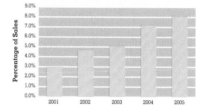

3

Electrovision's Travel Expenses Exceed National Averages

Much of our travel budget is justified. Two major factors contribute to Electrovision's high T&E budget:

* With our headquarters on the West Coast and our major customer on the East Coast, we naturally spend a lot of money on cross-country flights.

* A great deal of travel takes place between our headquarters here on the West Coast and the manufacturing operations in Detroit, Boston, and Dallas. Corporate managers and division personnel make frequent trips to coordinate these disparate operations.

However, even though a good portion of Electrovision's travel budget is justifiable, the company spends considerably more on T&E than the average business traveler (see Figure 3).

Figure 3
Electrovision Employees Spend Over Twice as Much as the Average Business Traveler

Source: *Wall Street Journal* and company records

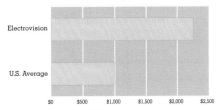

Electrovision

U.S. Average

$0 $500 $1,000 $1,500 $2,000 $2,500

Dollars Spent per Day

The Dow Jones Travel Index calculates the average cost per day of business travel in the United States, based on average airfare, hotel rates, and rental car rates. The average fluctuates weekly as travel companies change their rates, but it has been running at about $1,000 per day for the last year or so. In contrast, Electrovision's average daily expense over the past year has been $2,250—a hefty 125 percent higher than average. This figure is based on the average trip cost of $4,720 listed earlier and an average trip length of 2.1 days.

Spending Has Been Encouraged

Although a variety of factors may contribute to this differential, Electrovision's relatively high T&E costs are at least partially attributable to the company's philosophy and management style. Since many employees do not enjoy business travel, management has tried to make the trips more pleasant by authorizing business-class airfare, luxury hotel accommodations, and full-size rental cars. The sales staff is encouraged to entertain clients at top restaurants and to invite them to cultural and sporting events.

Numbers the visuals consecutively and refers to them in the text by their numbers

Introduces visuals before they appear and indicates what readers should notice about the data

The chart in Figure 3 is simple but effective; Moreno includes just enough data to make her point. Notice how she is as careful about the appearance of her report as she is about the quality of its content.

Uses a bulleted
list to make it
easy for readers
to identify and
distinguish related
points

4

The cost of these privileges is easy to overlook, given the weakness of Electrovision's system for keeping track of T&E expenses:

- The monthly financial records do not contain a separate category for travel and entertainment; the information is buried under Cost of Goods Sold and under Selling, General, and Administrative Expenses.

- Each department head is given authority to approve any expense report, regardless of how large it may be.

- Receipts are not required for expenditures of less than $100.

- Individuals are allowed to make their own travel arrangements.

- No one is charged with the responsibility for controlling the company's total spending on travel and entertainment.

GROWING IMPACT ON THE BOTTOM LINE

During the past three years, the company's healthy profits have resulted in relatively little pressure to push for tighter controls over all aspects of the business. However, as we all know, the situation is changing. We're projecting flat to declining profits for the next two years, a situation that has prompted all of us to search for ways to cut costs. At the same time, rising airfares and hotel rates have increased the impact of T&E expenses on the company's financial results.

Leaves an extra
line of white
space above
headings to help
readers associate
each heading with
the text it describes

Lower Profits Underscore the Need for Change

The next two years promise to be difficult for Electrovision. After several years of steady increases in spending, the Postal Service is tightening procurement policies for automated mail-handling equipment. Funding for the A-12 optical character reader has been canceled. As a consequence, the marketing department expects sales to drop by 15 percent. Although Electrovision is negotiating several other promising R&D contracts, the marketing department does not foresee any major procurements for the next two to three years.

At the same time, Electrovision is facing cost increases on several fronts. As we have known for several months, the new production facility now under construction in Salt Lake City, Utah, is behind schedule and over budget. Labor contracts in Boston and Dallas will expire within the next six months, and plant managers there anticipate that significant salary and benefits concessions may be necessary to avoid strikes.

Moreover, marketing and advertising costs are expected to increase as we attempt to strengthen these activities to better cope with competitive pressures. Given the expected decline in revenues and increase in costs, the Executive Committee's prediction that profits will fall by 12 percent in the coming fiscal year does not seem overly pessimistic.

Uses informative
headings to focus
reader attention
on the main
points (such
headings are
appropriate
when a report
uses direct order
and is intended
for a receptive
audience;
however,
descriptive
headings are
more effective
when a report
is in indirect order
and readers are
less receptive)

Moreno designed her report to include plenty of white space so even those pages that lack visuals are still attractive and easy to read.

5

Airfares and Hotel Rates Are Rising

Business travelers have grown accustomed to frequent fare wars and discounting in the travel industry in recent years. Excess capacity and aggressive price competition, particularly in the airline business, made travel a relative bargain.

Documents the facts to add weight to Moreno's argument

However, that situation has changed as weaker competitors have been forced out and the remaining players have grown stronger and smarter. Airlines and hotels are better at managing inventory and keeping occupancy rates high, which translates into higher costs for Electrovision. Last year saw some of the steepest rate hikes in years. Business airfares (tickets most likely to be purchased by business travelers) jumped more than 40 percent in many markets. The trend is expected to continue, with rates increasing another 5 to 10 percent overall (Phillips 331; "Travel Costs Under Pressure" 30; Dahl B6).

Given the fact that air and hotel costs account for 70 percent of our T&E budget, the trend toward higher prices in these two categories will have serious consequences, unless management takes action to control these costs.

METHODS FOR REDUCING T&E COSTS

By implementing a number of reforms, management can expect to reduce Electrovision's T&E budget by as much as 40 percent. This estimate is based on the general assessment made by American Express (Gilligan 39) and on the fact that we have an opportunity to significantly reduce air travel costs by eliminating business-class travel. However, these measures are likely to be unpopular with employees. To gain acceptance for such changes, management will need to sell employees on the need for moderation in T&E allowances.

Gives recommendations an objective flavor by pointing out both the benefits and the risks of taking action

Four Ways to Trim Expenses

By researching what other companies are doing to curb T&E expenses, the accounting department has identified four prominent opportunities that should enable Electrovision to save about $6 million annually in travel-related costs.

Institute Tighter Spending Controls

A single individual should be appointed director of travel and entertainment to spearhead the effort to gain control of the T&E budget. More than a third of all U.S. companies now employ travel managers ("Businesses Use Savvy Managers" 4). The director should be familiar with the travel industry and should be well versed in both accounting and information technology. The director should also report to the vice president of operations. The director's first priorities should be to establish a written T&E policy and a cost-control system.

Electrovision currently has no written policy on travel and entertainment, a step that is widely recommended by air travel experts (Smith D4). Creating a policy

Moreno creates a forceful tone by using action verbs in the third-level subheadings of this section. This approach is appropriate to the nature of the study and the attitude of the audience. However, in a status-conscious organization, the imperative verbs might sound a bit too presumptuous coming from a junior member of the staff.

6

would clarify management's position and serve as a vehicle for communicating the need for moderation. At a minimum, the policy should include the following:

Breaks up text with bulleted lists, which not only call attention to important points but also add visual interest

- All travel and entertainment should be strictly related to business and should be approved in advance.

- Except under special circumstances to be approved on a case-by-case basis, employees should travel by coach and stay in mid-range business hotels.

- The T&E policy should apply equally to employees at all levels.

To implement the new policy, Electrovision will need to create a system for controlling T&E expenses. Each department should prepare an annual T&E budget as part of its operating plan. These budgets should be presented in detail so that management can evaluate how T&E dollars will be spent and can recommend appropriate cuts. To help management monitor performance relative to these budgets, the director of travel should prepare monthly financial statements showing actual T&E expenditures by department.

The director of travel should also be responsible for retaining a business-oriented travel service that will schedule all employee business trips and look for the best travel deals, particularly in airfares. In addition to centralizing Electrovision's reservation and ticketing activities, the agency will negotiate reduced group rates with hotels and rental car firms. The agency selected should have offices nationwide so that all Electrovision facilities can channel their reservations through the same company. This is particularly important in light of the dizzying array of often wildly different airfares available between some cities. It's not uncommon to find dozens of fares along commonly traveled routes (Rowe 30). In addition, the director can help coordinate travel across the company to secure group discounts whenever possible (Barker 31; Miller B6).

Specifies the steps required to implement recommendations

Reduce Unnecessary Travel and Entertainment

One of the easiest ways to reduce expenses is to reduce the amount of traveling and entertaining that occurs. An analysis of last year's expenditures suggests that as much as 30 percent of Electrovision's travel and entertainment is discretionary. The professional staff spent $2.8 million attending seminars and conferences last year. Although these gatherings are undoubtedly beneficial, the company could save money by sending fewer representatives to each function and perhaps by eliminating some of the less valuable seminars.

Similarly, Electrovision could economize on trips between headquarters and divisions by reducing the frequency of such visits and by sending fewer people on each trip. Although there is often no substitute for face-to-face meetings, management could try to resolve more internal issues through telephone, electronic, and written communication.

Electrovision can also reduce spending by urging employees to economize. Instead of flying business class, employees can fly coach class or take advantage

Moreno takes care not to overstep the boundaries of her analysis. For instance, she doesn't analyze the value of the seminars that employees attend every year, so she avoids any absolute statements about reducing travel to seminars.

7

of discount fares. Rather than ordering a $50 bottle of wine, employees can select a less expensive bottle or dispense with alcohol entirely. People can book rooms at moderately priced hotels and drive smaller rental cars.

Obtain Lowest Rates from Travel Providers

Apart from urging employees to economize, Electrovision can also save money by searching for the lowest available airfares, hotel rates, and rental car fees. Currently, few employees have the time or knowledge to seek out travel bargains. When they need to travel, they make the most convenient and comfortable arrangements. A professional travel service will be able to obtain lower rates from travel providers.

Judging by the experience of other companies, Electrovision may be able to trim as much as 30 to 40 percent from the travel budget simply by looking for bargains in airfares and negotiating group rates with hotels and rental car companies. Electrovision should be able to achieve these economies by analyzing its travel patterns, identifying frequently visited locations, and selecting a few hotels that are willing to reduce rates in exchange for guaranteed business. At the same time, the company should be able to save up to 40 percent on rental car charges by negotiating a corporate rate.

The possibilities for economizing are promising; however, making the best travel arrangements often requires trade-offs such as the following:

Points out possible difficulties to show that all angles have been considered and to build confidence in her judgment

- The best fares might not always be the lowest. Indirect flights are usually cheaper, but they take longer and may end up costing more in lost work time.

- The cheapest tickets often require booking 14 or even 30 days in advance, which is often impossible for us.

- Discount tickets are usually nonrefundable, which is a serious drawback when a trip needs to be canceled at the last minute.

Replace Travel with Technological Alternatives

Less-expensive travel options promise significant savings, but the biggest cost reductions over the long term might come from replacing travel with virtual meeting technology. Both analysts and corporate users say that the early kinks that hampered online meetings have largely been worked out, and the latest systems are fast, easy to learn, and easy to use (Solheim 26). For example, Webex (a leading provider of webconferencing services) offers everything from simple, impromptu team meetings to major online events with up to 3,000 participants ("Online Meeting Solutions").

One of the first responsibilities of the new travel director should be an evaluation of these technologies and a recommendation for integrating them throughout Electrovision's operations.

Note how Moreno makes the transition from section to section. The first sentence under the second heading on this page refers to the subject of the previous paragraph and signals a shift in thought.

8

The Impact of Reforms

By implementing tighter controls, reducing unnecessary expenses, negotiating more favorable rates, and exploring alternatives to travel, Electrovision should be able to reduce its T&E budget significantly. As Table 1 illustrates, the combined savings should be in the neighborhood of $6 million, although the precise figures are somewhat difficult to project.

Table 1
Electrovision Can Trim Travel and Entertainment Costs
by an Estimated $6 Million per Year

SOURCE OF SAVINGS	ESTIMATED SAVINGS
Switching from business-class to coach airfare	$2,300,000
Negotiating preferred hotel rates	940,000
Negotiating preferred rental car rates	460,000
Systematically searching for lower airfares	375,000
Reducing interdivisional travel	675,000
Reducing seminar and conference attendance	1,250,000
TOTAL POTENTIAL SAVINGS	**$6,000,000**

To achieve the economies outlined in the table, Electrovision will incur expenses for hiring a director of travel and for implementing a T&E cost-control system. These costs are projected at $115,000: $105,000 per year in salary and benefits for the new employee and a one-time expense of $10,000 for the cost-control system. The cost of retaining a full-service travel agency is negligible, even with the service fees that many are now passing along from airlines and other service providers.

The measures required to achieve these savings are likely to be unpopular with employees. Electrovision personnel are accustomed to generous T&E allowances, and they are likely to resent having these privileges curtailed. To alleviate their disappointment

- Management should make a determined effort to explain why the changes are necessary.

- The director of corporate communication should be asked to develop a multifaceted campaign that will communicate the importance of curtailing T&E costs.

- Management should set a positive example by adhering strictly to the new policies.

- The limitations should apply equally to employees at all levels in the organization.

Uses informative title in the table, which is consistent with the way headings are handled in this report and is appropriate for a report to a receptive audience

Uses complete sentence to help readers focus immediately on the point of the table

Includes financial estimates to help management envision the impact of the suggestions, even though estimated savings are difficult to project

Note how Moreno calls attention in the first paragraph to items in the following table, without repeating the information in the table.

9

Uses a descriptive heading for the last section of the text (in informational reports, this section is often called "Summary"; in analytical reports, it is called "Conclusions" or "Conclusions and Recommendations")

Summarizes conclusions in the first two paragraphs—a good approach because Moreno organized her report around conclusions and recommendations, so readers have already been introduced to them

CONCLUSIONS AND RECOMMENDATIONS

Electrovision is currently spending $16 million per year on travel and entertainment. Although much of this spending is justified, the company's costs are high relative to competitors' costs, mainly because Electrovision has been generous with its travel benefits.

Electrovision's liberal approach to travel and entertainment was understandable during years of high profitability; however, the company is facing the prospect of declining profits for the next several years. Management is therefore motivated to cut costs in all areas of the business. Reducing T&E spending is particularly important because the bottom-line impact of these costs will increase as airline fares increase.

Electrovision should be able to reduce T&E costs by as much as 40 percent by taking four important steps:

Emphasizes the recommendations by presenting them in list format

1. *Institute tighter spending controls.* Management should hire a director of travel and entertainment who will assume overall responsibility for T&E activities. Within the next six months, this director should develop a written travel policy, institute a T&E budget and a cost-control system, and retain a professional, business-oriented travel agency that will optimize arrangements with travel providers.

2. *Reduce unnecessary travel and entertainment.* Electrovision should encourage employees to economize on T&E spending. Management can accomplish this by authorizing fewer trips and by urging employees to be more conservative in their spending.

3. *Obtain lowest rates from travel providers.* Electrovision should also focus on obtaining the best rates on airline tickets, hotel rooms, and rental cars. By channeling all arrangements through a professional travel agency, the company can optimize its choices and gain clout in negotiating preferred rates.

4. *Replace travel with technological alternatives.* With the number of computers already installed in our facilities, it seems likely that we could take advantage of desktop videoconferencing and other distance-meeting tools. Technological alternatives won't be quite as feasible with customer sites, since these systems require compatible equipment at both ends of a connection, but such systems are certainly a possibility for communication with Electrovision's own sites.

Because these measures may be unpopular with employees, management should make a concerted effort to explain the importance of reducing travel costs. The director of corporate communication should be given responsibility for developing a plan to communicate the need for employee cooperation.

Moreno doesn't introduce any new facts in this section. In a longer report she might have divided this section into subsections, labeled "Conclusions" and "Recommendations," to distinguish between the two.

10

WORKS CITED

Barker, Julie. "How to Rein in Group Travel Costs." *Successful Meetings* Feb. 2004: 31.

"Businesses Use Savvy Managers to Keep Travel Costs Down." *Christian Science Monitor* 17 July 2004: 4.

Dahl, Jonathan. "2000: The Year Travel Costs Took Off." *Wall Street Journal* 29 Dec. 2004: B6.

Gilligan, Edward P. "Trimming Your T&E Is Easier Than You Think." *Managing Office Technology* Nov. 2004: 39–40.

Miller, Lisa. "Attention, Airline Ticket Shoppers." *Wall Street Journal* 7 July 2004: B6.

"Online Meeting Solutions." *Webex.com.* 2005. WebEx, 14 September 2005, <http://www.webex.com/solutions/online-meetings-solutions.html>.

Phillips, Edward H. "Airlines Post Record Traffic." *Aviation Week & Space Technology* 8 Jan. 2005: 331.

Rowe, Irene Vlitos. "Global Solution for Cutting Travel Costs." *European* 12 Oct. 2004: 30.

Smith, Carol. "Rising, Erratic Airfares Make Company Policy Vital." *Los Angeles Times* 2 Nov. 2004: D4.

Solheim, Shelley. "Web Conferencing Made Easy." *eWeek* 22 Aug. 2005: 26.

"Travel Costs Under Pressure." *Purchasing* 15 Feb. 2004: 30.

Lists references alphabetically by the author's last name, and when the author is unknown, by the title of the reference (see Appendix B for additional details on preparing reference lists)

Moreno's list of references follows the style recommended in *The MLA Style Manual*. The box below shows how these sources would be cited following APA style.

10

REFERENCES

Barker, J. (2004, February). How to rein in group travel costs. *Successful Meetings*, 31.

Businesses use savvy managers to keep travel costs down. (2004, July 17). *Christian Science Monitor*, 4.

Dahl, J. (2004, December 29). 2000: The year travel costs took off. *Wall Street Journal*, B6.

Gilligan, E. (2004, November). Trimming your T&E is easier than you think. *Managing Office Technology*, 39–40.

Miller, L. (2004, July 7). Attention, airline ticket shoppers. *Wall Street Journal*, B6.

Phillips, E. (2005, January 8). Airlines post record traffic. *Aviation Week & Space Technology*, 331.

Rowe, I. (2004, October 12). Global solution for cutting travel costs. *European*, 30.

Smith, C. (2004, November 2). Rising, erratic airfares make company policy vital. *Los Angeles Times*, D4.

Solheim, S. (2005, August 22). Web conferencing made easy. *eWeek*, 26.

Travel costs under pressure. (2004, February 15). *Purchasing*, 30.

Webex.com. (2005). *Online Meeting Solutions.* Retrieved 14 September 2005, from http://www.webex.com/solutions/online-meetings-solutions.html.

Many of the components in a formal report start on a new page, but not always. Inserting page breaks consumes more paper and adds to the bulk of your report. On the other hand, starting a section on a new page helps your readers navigate the report and recognize transitions between major sections or features.

When you want a particular section to stand apart, you'll generally start it and the material after it on new pages (in the same way that each chapter in this book starts on a new page). Most prefatory parts, such as the table of contents, should also be placed on their own pages. However, the various parts in the report text are often run together and seldom stand alone. If your introduction is only a paragraph long, don't bother with a page break before moving into the body of your report. If the introduction runs longer than a page, however, a page break can signal the reader that a major shift is about to occur in the flow of the report.

Prefatory Parts   Prefatory parts are front-end materials that provide key preliminary information so that readers can decide whether and how to read the report.[2] Although these parts are placed before the text of the report, you may not want to write them until after you've written the text. Many of these parts—such as the table of contents, list of illustrations, and executive summary—are easier to prepare after the text has been completed, because they directly reflect the contents. When your text is complete, you can also use your word processor to automatically compile the table of contents and the list of illustrations. Other parts can be prepared at almost any time.

> Formal reports can contain a variety of prefatory parts, from a cover page to a synopsis or executive summary.

Cover   Many companies have standard covers for reports, made of heavy paper and imprinted with the company's name and logo. Report titles are either printed on these covers or attached with gummed labels. If your company has no standard covers, you can usually find something suitable in a good stationery store. Look for a cover that is attractive, convenient, and appropriate to the subject matter. Also, make sure it can be labeled with the report title, the writer's name (optional), and the submission date (also optional).

Think carefully about the title you put on the cover. A business report is not a mystery novel, so give your readers all the information they need: the who, what, when, where, why, and how of the subject. At the same time, try to be concise. You don't want to intimidate your audience with a title that's too long or awkward. You can reduce the length of your title by eliminating phrases such as *A Report of, A Study of,* or *A Survey of.*

Title Fly and Title Page   The **title fly** is a plain sheet of paper with only the title of the report on it. You don't really need one, but it adds a touch of formality.

The **title page** includes four blocks of information, as shown in Moreno's Electrovision report: (1) the title of the report; (2) the name, title, and address of the person, group, or organization that authorized the report (if anyone); (3) the name, title, and address of the person, group, or organization that prepared the report; and (4) the date on which the report was submitted. On some title pages the second block of information is preceded by the words *Prepared for* or *Submitted to,* and the third block of information is preceded by *Prepared by* or *Submitted by.* In some cases the title page serves as the cover of the report, especially if the report is relatively short and is intended solely for internal use.

Letter of Authorization and Letter of Acceptance   If you received written authorization to prepare the report, you may want to include that letter or memo in your report. This **letter of authorization** (or *memo of authorization*) is a document you received, asking or directing you to prepare the report. If you wrote a **letter of acceptance** (or *memo of acceptance*) in response to that communication, accepting the assignment and clarifying any conditions or limitations, you might also include that letter here in the report's prefatory parts. If there is any chance that your audience's

> In the most formal report situations, you might have both a letter of authorization from the person who authorized the report and your response, which is called a letter of acceptance.

expectations might not align with the actual work you did on the report, the letter of acceptance can show your readers what you agreed to do and why.

In general, the letters of authorization and acceptance are included in only the most formal reports. However, in any case where a significant amount of time has passed since you received the letter of authorization, or you do not have a close working relationship with the audience, consider including both letters to make sure everyone is clear about the report's intent and the approach you took to create it. You don't want your weeks or months of work to be diminished by any such misunderstandings.

Letter of Transmittal   The **letter of transmittal** (or *memo of transmittal*), a specialized form of a cover letter, introduces your report to your audience. (In a book, this section is called the preface.) The letter of transmittal says what you'd say if you were handing the report directly to the person who authorized it, so the style is less formal than the rest of the report. For example, the letter would use personal pronouns (*you, I, we*) and conversational language. Moreno's Electrovision report includes a one-page transmittal memo from Moreno to her boss (the person who requested the report).

The transmittal letter usually appears right before the table of contents. If your report will be widely distributed, however, you may decide to include the letter of transmittal only in selected copies so that you can make certain comments to a specific audience. If your report discusses layoffs or other issues that affect people in the organization, you might want to discuss your recommendations privately in a letter of transmittal to top management. If your audience is likely to be skeptical of or even hostile to something in your report, the transmittal letter is a good opportunity to acknowledge their concerns and explain how the report addresses the issues they care about.

Depending on the nature of your report, your letter of transmittal can follow either the direct approach for routine or positive messages described in Chapter 7 or the indirect approach for negative messages described in Chapter 8. Open by officially conveying the report to your readers and summarizing its purpose. Such a letter typically begins with a statement such as "Here is the report you asked me to prepare on. . . ." The rest of the introduction includes information about the scope of the report, the methods used to complete the study, limitations, and any special messages you need to convey. For instance, in Patty Stonesifer's introduction to the Gates Foundation's 2004 annual report, she began by explaining that while annual reports usually cover an organization's own accomplishments for the prior year, she wanted to focus on the good work that the foundation's partners had done instead.[3]

In the body of the transmittal letter, you may also highlight important points or sections of the report, make comments on side issues, give suggestions for follow-up studies, and offer any details that will help readers understand and use the report. You may also wish to acknowledge help given by others—if your report is extensive, chances are you received assistance from many people, and this letter is a high-visibility way to thank them. The conclusion of the transmittal letter is a note of thanks for having been given the report assignment, an expression of willingness to discuss the report, and an offer to assist with future projects.

If you don't include a synopsis, you can summarize the report's content in your letter of transmittal.

If the report does not have a synopsis, the letter of transmittal may summarize the major findings, conclusions, and recommendations. This material would be placed after the opening of the letter.

Table of Contents   The table of contents (titled simply "Contents") indicates in outline form the coverage, sequence, and relative importance of the information in the report. The headings used in the text of the report are the basis for the table of contents. Depending on the length and complexity of the report, you may need to decide how many levels of headings to show in the contents; it's a trade-off between simplicity and completeness. Contents that show only first-level heads are easy to scan but could frustrate people looking for specific subsections in the report. Conversely, contents that show every level of heading—down to fourth or fifth level in detailed reports—identify all the sections but can intimidate readers and blur the focus by detracting from your most important message points. In extreme cases, where the detailed table of contents could have dozens or even hundreds of entries, consider including two tables: a high-level table that shows only major headings, followed by a detailed table that includes everything (as this and many other textbooks do). No matter how many levels you include, make sure readers can easily distinguish between them.

Also, take extra care to ensure that your table of contents is accurate, consistent, and complete. Even minor errors could damage your credibility if readers turn to a given page expecting to find something that isn't there, or if they find headings that seem similar to the table of contents but aren't worded quite the same. To ensure accuracy, construct the table of contents after your report is complete, thoroughly edited, and proofed. This way, the headings and subheadings aren't likely to change or move from page to page.

If at all possible, use the automatic features in your word processor to generate the table of contents. Not only does this help improve accuracy by eliminating typing mistakes, but it keeps your table current in the event you do have to repaginate or revise headings late in the process. In Microsoft Word, for instance, you can automatically create a table of contents based on the heading levels identified in your style sheet. As long as you use styles consistently throughout the report, the process is quick and painless.

Use the table of contents generator in your word processor whenever possible; it will reduce the amount of work involved and reduce the chance of errors as well.

List of Illustrations If you have more than a handful of illustrations in your report, or you want to call attention to your illustrations, include a list of illustrations after the table of contents. For simplicity's sake, some reports refer to all visuals as *illustrations* or *exhibits*. In other reports, as in Moreno's Electrovision report, tables are labeled separately from other types of visuals, which are called *figures*. Regardless of the system you use, be sure to include titles and page numbers.

If you have enough space on a single page, include the list of illustrations directly beneath the table of contents. Otherwise, put the list on the page after the contents page. When tables and figures are numbered separately, they should also be listed separately. The two lists can appear on the same page if they fit; otherwise, start each list on a separate page.

Take time writing your synopsis or executive summary; it's one of the most important parts of your report.

Synopsis or Executive Summary A **synopsis** is a brief overview (one page or less) of a report's most important points, designed to give readers a quick preview of the contents. It's often included in long informational reports dealing with technical, professional, or academic subjects and can also be called an **abstract**. Because it's a concise representation of the whole report, it may be distributed separately to a wide audience; then interested readers can request a copy of the entire report.

Think carefully about the wording of your synopsis or abstract. Not only does it establish readers' expectations for the entire report, but this piece of text might also be indexed as a separate entry in either internal or external databases. People researching the subject area may run across your abstract in a list of results and use it to decide whether or not to read your report.

The phrasing of a synopsis can be either informative or descriptive, depending on whether the report is in direct or indirect order. In an informative synopsis, you present the main points of

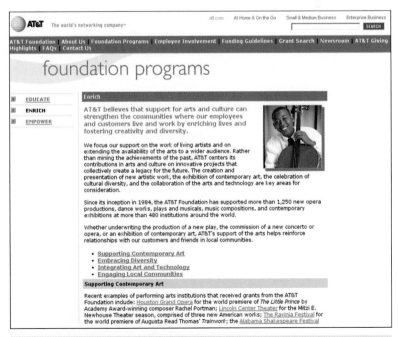

The introductory page of this AT&T online report serves as a synopsis, giving readers a brief overview of the main points covered. Those who want more information can click on hotlinks and go directly to the appropriate report section.

the report in the order in which they appear in the text. A descriptive synopsis, on the other hand, simply tells what the report is about, using only moderately greater detail than the table of contents; the actual findings of the report are omitted. Here are examples of statements from each type:

Informative Synopsis	Descriptive Synopsis
Sales of super-premium ice cream make up 11 percent of the total ice cream market.	This report contains information about super-premium ice cream and its share of the market.

The way you handle a synopsis reflects the approach you use in the text. If you're using an indirect approach in your report, you're better off with a descriptive synopsis. An informative synopsis, with its focus on conclusions and key points, may be too confrontational if your audience is skeptical. You don't want to derail the communication process by providing a controversial beginning. No matter which type of synopsis you use, be sure to present an accurate picture of the report's contents.[4]

Many business report writers prefer to include an **executive summary** instead of a synopsis or an abstract. Whereas a synopsis is a prose table of contents that outlines the main points of the report, an executive summary is a fully developed "mini" version of the report itself. Executive summaries are more comprehensive than a synopsis; many contain headings, well-developed transitions, and even visual elements. A good executive summary opens a window into the body of the report and allows the reader to quickly see how well you have managed your message. It is often organized in the same way as the report, using a direct or an indirect approach, depending on the audience's receptivity. However, executive summaries can also deviate from the sequence of material in the remainder of the report.

Executive summaries are intended for readers who lack the time or motivation to study the complete text. As a general rule, keep the length of an executive summary proportionate to the length of the report. A brief business report may have only a one-page or shorter executive summary. Longer business reports may have a two- or three-page summary. Anything longer, however, might cease to be a summary.[5]

Linda Moreno's Electrovision report provides one example of an executive summary. After reading the summary, audience members know the essentials of the report and are in a position to make a decision. Later, when time permits, they may read certain parts of the report to obtain additional detail. However, from daily newspapers to websites, businesspeople are getting swamped with more and more data and information. They are looking for ways to cut through all the clutter, and reading executive summaries is a popular shortcut. Because you can usually assume that many of your readers will not read the main text of your report, make sure you cover all your important points (along with significant supporting information) in the executive summary.

Many reports require neither a synopsis nor an executive summary. Length is usually the determining factor. Most reports of fewer than 10 pages either omit such a preview or combine it with the letter of transmittal. However, if your report is over 20 or 30 pages long, you'll probably want to include either a synopsis or an executive summary as a convenience for readers. Which one you'll provide depends on the traditions of your organization.

Text of the Report   Although reports may contain a variety of components, the heart of a report is always composed of three main parts: an introduction, a body, and a close (which may consist of a summary, conclusions, or recommendations, or some combination of the three). As Chapter 11 points out, the length and content of each of these parts varies with the length and type of report, the organizational structure, and the reader's familiarity with the topic. Following is a brief review of the three major parts of the report text.

A synopsis and an executive summary both summarize a report's content, but an executive summary is more comprehensive.

Introduction   A good introduction prepares your readers to follow and comprehend the information that follows. It invites the audience to continue reading by telling them what the report is about, why they should be concerned, and how the report is organized. If your report has a synopsis or an executive summary, minimize redundancy by balancing the introduction with the material in your summary—as Linda Moreno does in her Electrovision report. For example, Moreno's executive summary is fairly detailed, so she keeps her introduction brief. If you believe that your introduction needs to repeat information that has already been covered in one of the prefatory parts, try to vary the wording to minimize the feeling of repetition.

Body   This section contains the information that supports your conclusions and recommendations as well as your analysis, logic, and interpretation of the information. See the body of Linda Moreno's Electrovision report for an example of the types of supporting detail commonly included in this section. Pay close attention to her effective use of visuals. Most inexperienced writers have a tendency to include too much data in their reports or place too much data in paragraph format instead of using tables and charts. Such treatment increases the chance of boring or losing an audience. If you find yourself with too much information, include only the essential supporting data in the body, use visuals, and place any additional information in an appendix.

Close   The close of your report should summarize your main ideas, highlight your conclusions or recommendations (if any), and list any courses of action that you expect readers to take or that you will be taking yourself. In a long report, this section may be labeled "Summary," or "Conclusions and Recommendations." If you have organized your report in a direct pattern, your close should be relatively brief, like Linda Moreno's. With an indirect organization, you may be using this section to present your conclusions and recommendations for the first time, in which case this section might be fairly extensive.

Supplementary Parts   Supplementary parts follow the text of the report and provide information for readers who seek more detailed discussion. For online reports, you can put supplements on separate webpages and allow readers to link to them from the main report pages. Supplements are more common in long reports than in short ones, and they typically include appendixes, a bibliography, and an index.

> The supplementary parts provide additional detail and reference materials.

Appendixes   An **appendix** contains materials related to the report but not included in the text because they are too lengthy, are too bulky, or lack direct relevance. However, don't include too much ancillary material. Keep your reports straightforward and concise. Well-designed appendixes provide enough but not too much additional information for those readers who want it. If your company has an intranet or other means of storing and accessing information online, consider putting your detailed supporting evidence there and referring readers to those sources for more detail.

> Put into an appendix materials that are
> - Bulky or lengthy
> - Not directly relevant to the text

The content of report appendixes varies widely, including any sample questionnaires and cover letters, sample forms, computer printouts, statistical formulas, financial statements and spreadsheets, copies of important documents, and complex illustrations. You might also include a glossary as an appendix or as a separate supplementary part. Of course, the best place to include visual aids is in the text body nearest the point of discussion, but if any visuals are too large to fit on one page or are only indirectly relevant to your report, they too may be put in an appendix.

If you have multiple categories of supporting material, give each type a separate appendix. Appendixes are usually identified with a letter and a short, descriptive title—for example, "Appendix A: Questionnaire," "Appendix B: Computer Printout of Raw Data," and so on. All appendixes should be mentioned in the text and listed in the table of contents.

A bibliography not only fulfills your ethical obligation to credit your sources, but it allows readers to consult those sources for more information.

Bibliography To fulfill your ethical and legal obligation to credit other people for their work, and to assist readers who may wish to research your topic further, include a **bibliography**, a list of the secondary sources you consulted when preparing your report. In her Electrovision report, Linda Moreno labeled her bibliography "Works Cited" because she listed only the works that were mentioned in the report. You might call this section "Sources" or "References" if it includes works consulted but not mentioned in your report. Linda Moreno's Electrovision report uses the author-date system. An alternative is to use numbered footnotes (bottom of the page) or endnotes (end of the report). For more information on citing sources, see Appendix B, "Documentation of Report Sources."

In addition to providing a bibliography, some authors prefer to cite references in the report text. Acknowledging your sources in the body of your report demonstrates that you have thoroughly researched your topic. Furthermore, mentioning the names of well-known or important authorities on the subject helps build credibility for your message. It's often a good idea to mention a credible source's name several times if you need to persuade your audience. On the other hand, you don't want to make your report read like an academic treatise, dragging along from citation to citation. The source references should be handled as conveniently and inconspicuously as possible. One approach, especially for internal reports, is simply to mention a source in the text:

> *According to Dr. Lewis Morgan of Northwestern Hospital, hip replacement operations account for 7 percent of all surgery performed on women age 65 and over.*

However, if your report will be distributed to outsiders, include additional information on where you obtained the data. Most college students are familiar with citation methods suggested by the Modern Language Association (MLA) or the American Psychological Association (APA). *The Chicago Manual of Style* is a reference often used by typesetters and publishers. All of these sources encourage the use of in-text citations (inserting the author's last name and a year of publication or a page number directly into the text).

Index An **index** is an alphabetical list of names, places, and subjects mentioned in your report, along with the pages on which they occur (see the indexes in this book for examples). If you think your readers will need to access specific points of information in a lengthy report, consider including an index that lists all key topics, product names, markets, important persons—whatever is relevant to your subject matter. As with your table of contents, accuracy is critical. The good news is that you can also use your word processor to compile the index. Just be sure to update the index (and any automatically generated elements, for that matter), right before you print the report or convert it to PDF or other electronic format. Have another person spot-check the index, too, to make sure your entries are correct and easy to follow.

Your word processor can also help you generate an index.

Components of a Formal Proposal

The goal of a proposal is to impress readers with your professionalism and to make your offering and your company stand out. Consequently, proposals addressed to external audiences, including potential customers and investors, are nearly always formal. For smaller projects and situations where you already have a working relationship with the audience, the proposal can be less formal and skip some of the components described in this section.

Formal proposals contain many of the same components as other formal reports (see Figure 12–2). The difference lies mostly in the text, although a few of the prefatory parts are also different. With the exception of an occasional appendix, most proposals have few supplementary parts. As always, if you're responding to an RFP, follow its specifications to the letter, being sure to include everything it asks for and nothing it doesn't ask for.

Prefatory Parts   The cover, title fly, title page, table of contents, and list of illustrations are handled the same as in other formal reports. However, you'll want to handle other prefatory parts a bit differently, such as the copy of the RFP, the synopsis or executive summary, and the letter of transmittal.

Copy of the RFP   Instead of having a letter of authorization, a formal proposal may have a copy of the request for proposals (RFP), which is a letter or memo soliciting a proposal or a bid for a particular project. If the RFP includes detailed specifications, it may be too long to bind into the proposal; in that case, you may want to include only the introductory portion of the RFP. Another option is to omit the RFP and simply refer to it in your letter of transmittal. However, as with the letter of authorization for a formal report, if there is likely to be any doubt or confusion over what exactly your proposal is responding to, make sure your readers have ready access to the specifications spelled out in the RFP.

If there's likely to be any confusion over which RFP you're responding to, include the RFP in your proposal. If the RFP is long, include just its introductory sections.

Synopsis or Executive Summary   Although you may include a synopsis or an executive summary for your reader's convenience when your proposal is quite long, these components are often less useful in a formal proposal than they are in a formal report. If your proposal is unsolicited, your transmittal letter will already have caught the reader's interest, making a synopsis or an executive summary pointless. It may also be less important if your proposal is solicited, because the reader is already committed to studying your proposal to find out how you intend to satisfy the terms of a contract. The introduction of a solicited proposal would provide an adequate preview of the contents.

FIGURE 12–2
Parts of a Formal Proposal

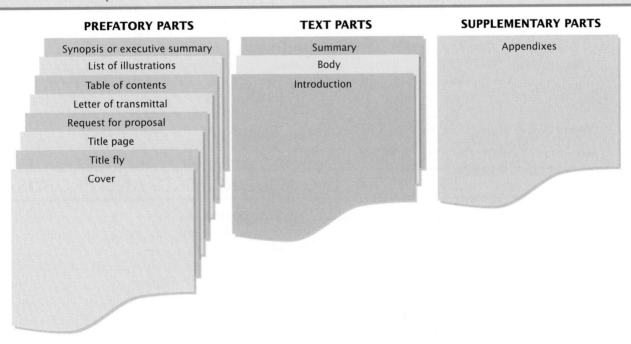

PREFATORY PARTS	TEXT PARTS	SUPPLEMENTARY PARTS
Synopsis or executive summary	Summary	Appendixes
List of illustrations	Body	
Table of contents	Introduction	
Letter of transmittal		
Request for proposal		
Title page		
Title fly		
Cover		

Document Makeover

IMPROVE THIS EXECUTIVE SUMMARY

To practice correcting drafts of actual documents, visit your online course or the access-code protected portion of the Companion Website. Click "Document Makeovers," then click Chapter 12. You will find an excerpt from an executive summary that contains problems and errors relating to what you've learned in this chapter about completing formal reports and proposals. Use the "Final Draft" decision tool to create an improved version of this document. Check the executive summary for an appropriate degree of formality, parallel structures, the skillful inclusion or exclusion of detail, and a consistent time perspective.

Letter of Transmittal   The way you handle the letter of transmittal depends on whether the proposal is solicited or unsolicited. If the proposal is solicited, the transmittal letter follows the pattern for positive messages, highlighting those aspects of your proposal that may give you a competitive advantage. If the proposal is unsolicited, the transmittal letter follows the pattern for persuasive messages (see Chapter 9). The letter must persuade the reader that you have something worthwhile to offer, something that justifies the time required to read the entire proposal. Because the transmittal letter may be all that the client reads, it must be especially convincing. However, bear in mind that even unsolicited proposals should not come as a surprise to the recipient; they should be the end result of an ongoing dialog about the other party's needs.

Text of the Proposal   Just as with reports, the text of a proposal is composed of three main parts: an introduction, body, and close. The content and depth of each part depend on whether the proposal is solicited or unsolicited, formal or informal. Here's a brief review:[6]

- **Introduction.** This section presents and summarizes the problem you intend to solve and your solution to that problem, including any benefits the reader will receive from your solution.

- **Body.** This section explains the complete details of the solution: how the job will be done, how it will be broken into tasks, what method will be used to do it (including the required equipment, material, and personnel), when the work will begin and end, how much the entire job will cost (including a detailed breakdown, if required or requested), and why your company is qualified.

- **Close.** This section emphasizes the benefits that readers will realize from your solution, and it urges readers to act.

Figure 12–3 is an informal proposal submitted by Dixon O'Donnell, vice president of O'Donnell & Associates, a geotechnical engineering firm that conducts a variety of environmental testing services. The company is bidding on the mass grading and utility work specified by AGI Builders. As you review this document, pay close attention to the specific items addressed in the proposal's introduction, body, and close.

PROOFREADING YOUR REPORTS AND PROPOSALS

Once you have assembled all the various components of your report or proposal, revised the entire document's content for clarity and conciseness, and designed the document to ensure readability and a positive impression on your readers, you have essentially produced your document in its final form. Now you need to review it thoroughly one last time, looking for inconsistencies, errors, and missing components. For instance, if you changed a heading in the report's text part, make sure that you also changed the corresponding heading in the table of contents and in all references to that heading in your report. Proofing can catch minor flaws that might diminish your credibility—and major flaws that might damage your career.

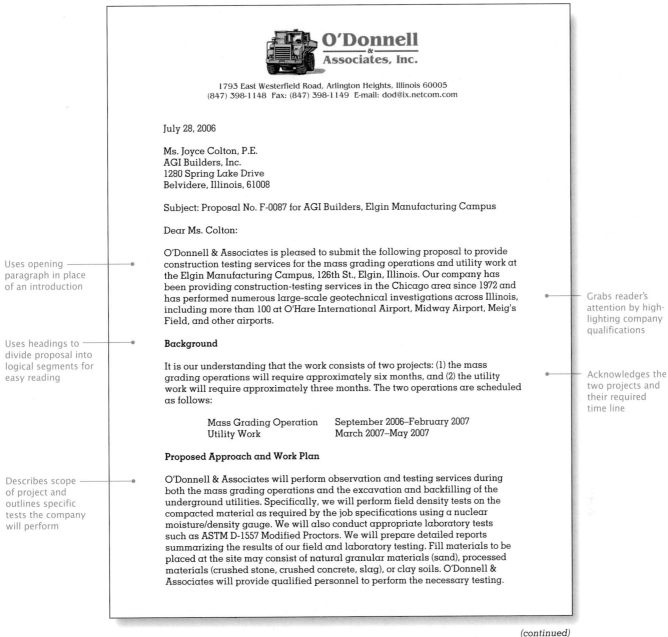

O'Donnell & Associates, Inc.

1793 East Westerfield Road, Arlington Heights, Illinois 60005
(847) 398-1148 Fax: (847) 398-1149 E-mail: dod@ix.netcom.com

July 28, 2006

Ms. Joyce Colton, P.E.
AGI Builders, Inc.
1280 Spring Lake Drive
Belvidere, Illinois, 61008

Subject: Proposal No. F-0087 for AGI Builders, Elgin Manufacturing Campus

Dear Ms. Colton:

Uses opening paragraph in place of an introduction →

O'Donnell & Associates is pleased to submit the following proposal to provide construction testing services for the mass grading operations and utility work at the Elgin Manufacturing Campus, 126th St., Elgin, Illinois. Our company has been providing construction-testing services in the Chicago area since 1972 and has performed numerous large-scale geotechnical investigations across Illinois, including more than 100 at O'Hare International Airport, Midway Airport, Meig's Field, and other airports.

← *Grabs reader's attention by highlighting company qualifications*

Uses headings to divide proposal into logical segments for easy reading →

Background

It is our understanding that the work consists of two projects: (1) the mass grading operations will require approximately six months, and (2) the utility work will require approximately three months. The two operations are scheduled as follows:

← *Acknowledges the two projects and their required time line*

Mass Grading Operation	September 2006–February 2007
Utility Work	March 2007–May 2007

Proposed Approach and Work Plan

Describes scope of project and outlines specific tests the company will perform →

O'Donnell & Associates will perform observation and testing services during both the mass grading operations and the excavation and backfilling of the underground utilities. Specifically, we will perform field density tests on the compacted material as required by the job specifications using a nuclear moisture/density gauge. We will also conduct appropriate laboratory tests such as ASTM D-1557 Modified Proctors. We will prepare detailed reports summarizing the results of our field and laboratory testing. Fill materials to be placed at the site may consist of natural granular materials (sand), processed materials (crushed stone, crushed concrete, slag), or clay soils. O'Donnell & Associates will provide qualified personnel to perform the necessary testing.

(continued)

FIGURE 12–3
Dixon O'Donnell's Informal Solicited Proposal

Proofreading the textual part of your report is essentially the same as proofreading any business message—you check for typos, spelling errors, and mistakes in punctuation. However, reports often have elements that may not be included in other messages, so don't forget to proof your visuals thoroughly, as Chapter 11 points out, and make sure they are positioned correctly. If you need specific tips on proofreading documents, look back at Chapter 6 for some reminders on what to look for when proofreading text and how to proofread like a pro.

Whenever possible, arrange for someone with "fresh eyes" to proofread the report, somebody who hasn't been involved with the text so far. At this point in the process, you are so familiar with the content that your mind will fill in missing words, fix misspelled words, and subconsciously compensate for other flaws without you even being aware of it. Someone with fresh eyes might see mistakes that you've

Ask for proofreading assistance from someone who hasn't been involved in the development of your proposal; he or she might see errors that you've been overlooking.

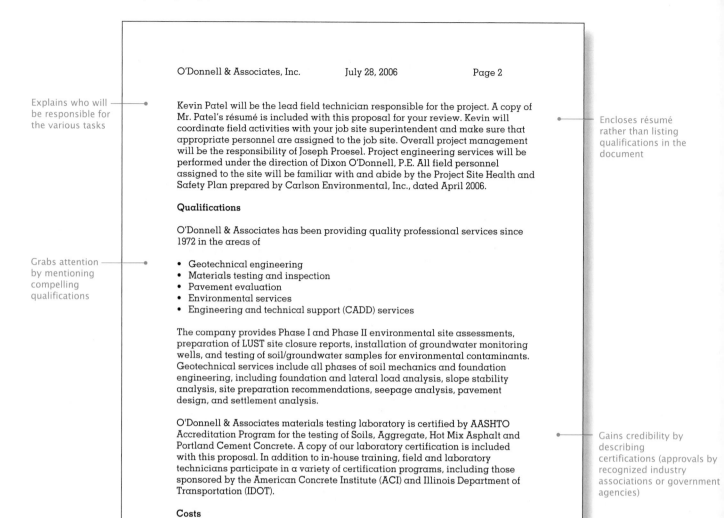

O'Donnell & Associates, Inc.   July 28, 2006   Page 2

Explains who will be responsible for the various tasks

Kevin Patel will be the lead field technician responsible for the project. A copy of Mr. Patel's résumé is included with this proposal for your review. Kevin will coordinate field activities with your job site superintendent and make sure that appropriate personnel are assigned to the job site. Overall project management will be the responsibility of Joseph Proesel. Project engineering services will be performed under the direction of Dixon O'Donnell, P.E. All field personnel assigned to the site will be familiar with and abide by the Project Site Health and Safety Plan prepared by Carlson Environmental, Inc., dated April 2006.

Encloses résumé rather than listing qualifications in the document

Qualifications

O'Donnell & Associates has been providing quality professional services since 1972 in the areas of

Grabs attention by mentioning compelling qualifications

- Geotechnical engineering
- Materials testing and inspection
- Pavement evaluation
- Environmental services
- Engineering and technical support (CADD) services

The company provides Phase I and Phase II environmental site assessments, preparation of LUST site closure reports, installation of groundwater monitoring wells, and testing of soil/groundwater samples for environmental contaminants. Geotechnical services include all phases of soil mechanics and foundation engineering, including foundation and lateral load analysis, slope stability analysis, site preparation recommendations, seepage analysis, pavement design, and settlement analysis.

O'Donnell & Associates materials testing laboratory is certified by AASHTO Accreditation Program for the testing of Soils, Aggregate, Hot Mix Asphalt and Portland Cement Concrete. A copy of our laboratory certification is included with this proposal. In addition to in-house training, field and laboratory technicians participate in a variety of certification programs, including those sponsored by the American Concrete Institute (ACI) and Illinois Department of Transportation (IDOT).

Gains credibility by describing certifications (approvals by recognized industry associations or government agencies)

Costs

On the basis of our understanding of the scope of the work, we estimate the total cost of the two projects to be $100,260.00, as follows:

(continued)

FIGURE 12–3
(continued)

passed over a dozen times without noticing. An ideal approach is to have two people review it, one who is an expert in the subject matter and one who isn't. The first person can ensure its technical accuracy, and the second can ensure that a wide range of readers will understand it.[7]

DISTRIBUTING YOUR REPORTS AND PROPOSALS

All of the distribution issues you explored in Chapter 6 apply to reports and proposals, as long as you pay particular attention to the length and complexity of your documents. For physical distribution, consider spending the few extra dollars for a professional courier or package delivery service, if that will help your document stand apart from

O'Donnell & Associates, Inc.   July 28, 2006   Page 3

Cost Estimates

Itemizes costs by project and gives supporting detail

Cost Estimate: Mass Grading	Units	Rate ($)	Total Cost ($)
Field Inspection			
Labor	1,320 hours	$38.50	$ 50,820.00
Nuclear Moisture Density Meter	132 days	35.00	4,620.00
Vehicle Expense	132 days	45.00	5,940.00
Laboratory Testing			
Proctor Density Tests (ASTM D-1557)	4 tests	130.00	520.00
Engineering/Project Management			
Principal Engineer	16 hours	110.00	1,760.00
Project Manager	20 hours	80.00	1,600.00
Administrative Assistant	12 hours	50.00	600.00
Subtotal			$ 65,860.00

Cost Estimate: Utility Work	Units	Rate ($)	Total Cost ($)
Field Inspection			
Labor	660 hours	$ 38.50	$ 25,410.00
Nuclear Moisture Density Meter	66 days	5.00	2,310.00
Vehicle Expense	66 days	45.00	2,970.00
Laboratory Testing			
Proctor Density Tests (ASTM D-1557)	2 tests	130.00	260.00
Engineering/Project Management			
Principal Engineer	10 hours	110.00	1,100.00
Project Manager	20 hours	80.00	1,600.00
Administrative Assistant	15 hours	50.00	750.00
Subtotal			$ 34,400.00

Total Project Costs			**$100,260.00**

This estimate assumes full-time inspection services. However, our services may also be performed on an as-requested basis, and actual charges will reflect time associated with the project. We have attached our standard fee schedule for your review. Overtime rates are for hours in excess of 8.0 hours per day, before 7:00 a.m., after 5:00 p.m., and on holidays and weekends.

Provides alternative option in case full-time service costs exceed client's budget

(continued)

FIGURE 12–3
(continued)

the crowd. The online tracking offered by FedEx, UPS, and other services can verify that your document arrived safely. On the other hand, if you've prepared the document for a single person or small group, delivering it in person can be a nice touch. Not only can you answer any immediate questions about it, but you can also promote the results in person—reminding the recipient of the benefits contained in your report or proposal.

For electronic distribution, unless your audience specifically requests a word processor file, provide documents in PDF format. Most people are reluctant to open word processor files these days, particularly from outsiders, given the vulnerability of such files to macro viruses and other contaminations. Moreover, PDF format lets you control how your document is displayed on your audience's computer, ensuring that your readers see your document as you intended. It would be a shame to build your

Many businesses use the Adobe Portable Document Format (PDF) to distribute reports electronically.

O'Donnell & Associates, Inc.   July 28, 2006   Page 4

Authorization

With a staff of over 30 personnel, including registered professional engineers, resident engineers, geologists, construction inspectors, laboratory technicians, and drillers, we are convinced that O'Donnell & Associates is capable of providing the services required for a project of this magnitude.

If you would like our firm to provide the services as outlined in this proposal, please sign this letter and return it to us along with a certified check in the amount of $10,000 (our retainer) by August 15, 2006. Please call me if you have any questions regarding the terms of this proposal or our approach.

Sincerely,

Dixon O'Donnell

Dixon O'Donnell
Vice President

Enclosures

Accepted for AGI BUILDERS, INC.

By_____   Date _____

Annotations (left margin):
Uses brief closing to emphasize qualifications and ask for client decision

Annotations (right margin):
Provides deadline and makes response easy

Makes letter a binding contract, if signed

FIGURE 12–3
(continued)

entire report around a particular chart or table, only to learn that it didn't display properly on your readers' computer screens. PDFs display your document exactly as you formatted it on your computer. In addition, making documents available as downloadable PDF files is almost universally expected these days, if only for the sake of convenience.

If your company or client expect you to distribute your reports via a web-based content management system, intranet, or extranet, be sure to upload the correct file(s) to the correct online location. Verify the on-screen display of your report after you've posted it, too; make sure graphics, charts, links, and other elements are in place and operational.

Once you've completed your formal report and sent it off to your audience, you'll naturally expect a positive response, and quite often you'll get one—but not always.

✓ CHECKLIST: Completing Formal Reports and Proposals

A. Prefatory parts

✓ Use your company's standard report covers, if available.

✓ Include a concise, descriptive title on the cover.

✓ Include a title fly only if you want an extra-formal touch.

✓ On the title page, list (1) report title; (2) name, title, and address of the group or person who authorized the report; (3) name, title, and address of the group or person who prepared the report; and (4) date of submission.

✓ Include copy of letter of authorization, if appropriate.

✓ Include a copy of the RFP (or its introduction only if the document is long), if appropriate.

✓ Include letter of transmittal that introduces the report.

✓ Provide a table of contents in outline form, with headings worded exactly as they appear in the body of the report.

✓ Include a list of illustrations if the report contains a large number of them.

✓ Include a synopsis (brief summary of the report) or executive summary (a condensed, "mini" version of the report) for longer reports.

B. Text of the report

✓ Draft an introduction that prepares the reader for the content that follows.

✓ Provide the information that supports your conclusions, recommendations, or proposals in the body of the report.

✓ Don't overload the body with unnecessary detail.

✓ Close with a summary of your main idea.

C. Supplementary parts

✓ Use appendixes to provide supplementary information or supporting evidence.

✓ List any secondary sources you used in a bibliography.

✓ Provide an index if your report contains a large number of terms or ideas and is likely to be consulted over time.

You may get halfhearted praise or no action on your conclusions and recommendations. Even worse, you may get some serious criticism. Try to learn from these experiences. Sometimes you won't get any response at all. If you don't hear from your readers within a week or two, you might want to ask politely whether the report arrived. (Some RFPs specify a response timeframe. If so, *don't* pester the recipient ahead of schedule; you'll hurt your chances.) In hope of stimulating a response, you might ask a question about the report, such as "How do you think accounting will react to the proposed budget increase?" You might also offer to answer any questions or provide additional information. To review the ideas presented in this chapter, see "Checklist: Completing Formal Reports and Proposals."

On the Job

SOLVING COMMUNICATION DILEMMAS AT THE BILL AND MELINDA GATES FOUNDATION

A decade into your business career, you've decided to put your communication skills to use in the effort to improve global health. You recently joined the Gates Foundation as a program officer in global health strategies.

Malaria is one of the foundation's primary health concerns. This mosquito-borne disease has been largely eradicated in many parts of the world, but it remains an active and growing menace in other areas (particularly sub-Saharan Africa). Worldwide, malaria kills more than a million people every year, most of whom are children. You are writing an informational report that will be made available on the foundation's website, summarizing both the current crisis and progress being made toward the eventual control and eradication of malaria. How will you handle the following challenges?

1. A wide variety of people visit the foundation's website, from researchers who are interested in applying for grants to reporters writing about health and education issues to members of the general public. Consequently, you can't pin down a specific audience for your report. In addition, since people will simply download a PDF file of the report from the website, you don't have the opportunity to write a traditional letter or memo of transmittal. How should you introduce your report to website visitors?

a. Write a brief description of the report, explaining its purpose and content; post this information on the website, above the link to the PDF file so that people can read it before they decide whether to download the file.

b. Provide an e-mail link that people can use to send you an e-mail message if they'd like to know more about the report before reading it.

c. Write a news release describing the report and post this document on the website's "Newsroom" section.

d. Count on the title of the report to introduce its purpose and content; don't bother writing an introduction.

2. Which of the following report titles would do the best job of catching readers' attention with an emotional "hook" that balances both the urgency of the crisis and the reasons for hope?

a. Children Who Don't Need to Die: The Urgent Global Malaria Crisis

b. Preventing a Million Malaria Deaths Every Year: The Urgent Global Challenge—and Reasons for Hope

c. Malaria: It Killed Two Thousand More Children Today

d. Malaria: Progress Toward Eradicating This Global Disease

3. The Gates Foundation is known around the world for the quality of its work, and that includes the quality of its communication efforts. Which of the following proofreading strategies should you use to make sure your report is free from errors?

a. Take advantage of technology. Double-check the settings in your word processor to make sure that every checking tool is activated as you type, including the spell checker, grammar checker, and style checker. When you're finished with the first draft, run each of these tools again, just to make sure the computer didn't miss anything.

b. Recognize that no report, particularly a complex 48-page document with multiple visuals and more than 60 sources, is going to be free from errors. Include a statement on the title page apologizing for any errors that may still exist in the report. Provide your e-mail address and invite people to send you a message when they find errors.

c. As soon as you finish typing the first draft, immediately review it for accuracy while the content is still fresh in your mind. Once you have done this, you can be reasonably sure that the document is free from errors. If you wait a day or two, you'll start to forget what you've written, thereby lowering your chances of catching errors.

d. Put the report aside for at least a day, then proofread it carefully. Also, recruit two colleagues to review it for you as well, one who can review the scientific accuracy of the material, and one who has a good eye for language and clarity.

4. One of the sources used in your report is an article entitled "Making Antimalarial Agents Available in Africa," by Kenneth J. Arrow, Hellen Gelband, and Dean T. Jamison. The article appeared in the July 28, 2005, edition (volume 353, issue 4) of the *New England Journal of Medicine*, on pages 333 to 335. Which of the following is the correct way to cite this source using APA guidelines?

a. Arrow, K. J., Gelband H., & Jamison, D. T. (2005). Making antimalarial agents available in Africa. *New England Journal of Medicine, 353* (4), 333–335.

b. Kenneth J. Arrow, Hellen Gelband, and Dean T. Jamison, "Making Antimalarial Agents Available in Africa," *New England Journal of Medicine*, 28 July 2005, 333 (3 pgs).

c. "Making Antimalarial Agents Available in Africa," *New England Journal of Medicine:* Vol. 353, Iss. 4, Pgs. 333–335.

d. Arrow, Kenneth J., Gelband, Hellen, and Jamison, Dean T. "Making Antimalarial Agents Available in Africa." *New England Journal of Medicine* 353.4 (2005): 333–335.

Learning Objectives Checkup

Assess your understanding of the principles in this chapter by reading each learning objective and studying the accompanying exercises. For fill-in items, write the missing text in the blank provided; for multiple choice items, circle the letter of the correct answer. You can check your responses against the answer key on page AK-2.

Objective 12.1: Characterize the four tasks involved in completing business reports and proposals.

1. Which of the following is *not* one of four major tasks involved in completing business reports and proposals?

a. Revising the report's organization, style, tone, and readability

b. Formatting the report

c. Deciding which visuals to create for the report

d. Proofreading the report

2. The following sentence appears in your first draft of a report that analyzes perceived shortcomings in your company's employee health benefits: "Among the many criticisms and concerns expressed by the workforce, at least among the 376 who responded to our online survey (out of 655 active employees), the issues of elder care, health insurance during retirement, and the increased amount that employees are being forced to pay every month as the company's contribution to health insurance coverage has declined over the past two years were identified as the most important." You realize that this 69-word sentence

could be shorter, more direct, and more powerful. Which of these revisions is the most effective?

  a. The employees who responded to our online survey (376 out of 655 active employees) identified these three issues as the most important: elder care, insurance coverage after they retire, and rising monthly payments.

  b. Elder care, insurance coverage after they retire, and rising monthly payments were the three most important issues identified in our survey of employees regarding their complaints and criticisms of health care benefits. Out of a current active workforce of 655 people, 376 employees completed the online survey. They complained about quite a range of issues, but these three were the most important to them overall.

  c. The top three employee concerns: Elder care, insurance coverage after they retire, and increases in the amounts that employees pay every month for health insurance.

  d. The top three concerns our employees have regarding their health benefits are elder care, insurance coverage after they retire, and increases in the monthly cost of insurance. These results are based on responses from the 376 employees (out of 655) who participated in our online survey.

Objective 12.2: Explain how computers have both simplified and complicated the report-production process.

3. How have computers and related technology (such as low-cost color printers) made it easier in recent years for all businesspeople to produce top-quality reports and proposals?

  a. Tasks that once required expensive equipment and specialized skills can now be accomplished on most desktop computers by regular businesspeople with minimal training.

  b. Most companies now have dedicated desktop publishing departments, so business professionals are no longer expected to create their own charts, graphs, and other report elements.

  c. The support personnel who will do all of your typing for you can now produce all of your visuals and other report elements, so you no longer need to work with a variety of different people.

  d. The Internet has improved everyone's design sensibilities.

4. How has the widespread availability of computer publishing tools made life more difficult for report writers?

  a. The Internet is slower than ever before.

  b. Since prices have fallen so low, most companies expect employees to purchase their own computers.

  c. More and more readers are growing tired of the slick, overproduced reports available these days; they want to see more simple, black-and-white, "typewriter style" reports.

  d. In terms of production quality, audience expectations are higher and the competition is tougher than ever before.

Objective 12.3: Identify the circumstances in which you should include letters of authorization and letters of acceptance in your reports.

5. When should you consider including a letter or memo of authorization in a formal report?

  a. If you're getting paid to write the report

  b. If you received written authorization to write the report

  c. If the audience outranks you

  d. If you outrank the audience

6. What is the purpose of including a letter of acceptance in a formal report?

  a. It reminds your audience what you previously agreed to address in the report and why you were assigned to write it.

  b. It makes your report feel more formal and official.

  c. It prevents others from taking credit for your work.

  d. It summarizes the key points of your report for people who are too busy to read the report itself.

Objective 12.4: Explain the difference between a synopsis and an executive summary.

7. A/an _____ is a brief overview (usually one page or less) of a report's most important points.

8. A/an _____ is a fully developed "mini" version of the report itself.

9. Which of the following may contain headings, visual aids, and enough information to help busy executives make quick decisions?

  a. An executive summary

  b. A synopsis

  c. Both

  d. Neither

Objective 12.5: Describe the three supplementary parts of a formal report.

10. Which of the following is *not* a typical supplementary part of a formal report?

  a. Appendixes

  b. Bibliography

  c. Letter of authorization

  d. Index

Objective 12.6: Explain how prefatory parts of a proposal differ depending on whether the proposal is solicited or unsolicited.

11. If you've submitted a proposal that is in response to a request for proposals (RFP), what steps can you take to make sure the recipient understands which RFP you're responding to?

  a. Include the formal title of the RFP (and its reference number, if it has one) as a footnote in the first appendix of your report.

  b. If the RFP is short, include it with the other prefatory parts of your proposal; if the RFP is lengthy, include just the introductory page(s) from it.

  c. Include the entire RFP in the body of your proposal, no matter how long it is.

  d. The RFP was written by someone else, so you can ignore it in your report.

12. How should you handle the letter of transmittal for an unsolicited proposal?

a. Treat the letter as a routine message; businesspeople get proposals all the time, so they don't expect anything more than a simple announcement that identifies you and your proposal.

b. Treat the letter as a positive message, highlighting the good news that you have to offer in the proposal.

c. Treat the letter as a persuasive message, persuading the reader that your report offers information of value.

d. Don't waste the reader's time with a letter of transmittal; get right to the point with the body of your proposal.

Apply Your Knowledge

1. Is an executive summary a persuasive message? Explain your answer.

2. Under what circumstances would you include more than one index in a lengthy report?

3. If you were submitting a solicited proposal to build an indoor pool, would you include as references the names and addresses of other clients for whom you recently built similar pools? Would you include these references in an unsolicited proposal? Where in either proposal would you include these references? Why?

4. If you included a bibliography in your report, would you also need to include in-text citations? Please explain.

5. **Ethical Choices** How would you report on a confidential survey in which employees rated their managers' capabilities? Both employees and managers expect to see the results. Would you give the same report to employees and managers? What components would you include or exclude for each audience? Explain your choices.

Practice Your Knowledge

DOCUMENT FOR ANALYSIS

Visit the website of the U.S. Citizenship and Immigration Services (a division of the U.S. Department of Homeland Security) at http://uscis.gov. Find a report entitled "Triennial Comprehensive Report on Immigration" and follow the link to the executive summary. Using the information in this chapter, analyze the executive summary and offer specific suggestions for revising it.

Exercises

For active links to all websites discussed in this chapter, visit this text's website at www.prenhall.com/thill. Locate your book and click on its Companion Website link. Then select Chapter 12, and click on "Featured Websites." Locate the name of the page or the URL related to the material in the text. Please note that links to sites that become inactive after publication of the book will be removed from the Featured Websites section.

12.1 Teamwork You and a classmate are helping Linda Moreno prepare her report on Electrovision's travel and entertainment costs (see "Report Writer's Notebook"). This time, however, the report is to be informational rather than analytical, so it will not include recommendations. Review the existing report and determine what changes would be needed to make it an informational report. Be as specific as possible. For example, if your team decides the report needs a new title, what title would you use? Now draft a transmittal memo for Moreno to use in conveying this informational report to Dennis McWilliams, Electrovision's vice president of operations.

12.2 Producing Reports: Letter of Transmittal You are president of the Friends of the Library, a nonprofit group that raises funds and provides volunteers to support your local library. Every February, you send a report of the previous year's activities and accomplishments to the County Arts Council, which provides an annual grant of $1,000 toward your group's summer reading festival. Now it's February 6, and you've completed your formal report. Here are the highlights:

- Back-to-school book sale raised $2,000.
- Holiday craft fair raised $1,100.
- Promotion and prizes for summer reading festival cost $1,450.
- Materials for children's program featuring local author cost $125.
- New reference databases for library's career center cost $850.
- Bookmarks promoting library's website cost $200.

Write a letter of transmittal to Erica Maki, the council's director. Because she is expecting this report, you can use the direct approach. Be sure to express gratitude for the council's ongoing financial support.

12.3 Internet Government reports vary in purpose and structure. Read through the Department of Education's report, "Helping Your Child Become a Reader," available online at www.ed.gov. What is the purpose of this document? Does the title communicate this purpose? What type of report is this, and what is the report's structure? Which prefatory and supplementary parts are included? Now analyze the visuals. What types are included in this report? Are they all necessary? Are the titles and legends sufficiently informative? How does this report take advantage of the online medium to enhance readability?

12.4 Ethical Choices: Team Challenge You submitted what you thought was a masterful report to your boss over three weeks ago. The report analyzes current department productivity and recommends several steps that you think will improve employee output without increasing individual workloads. Brilliant, you thought. But you haven't heard a word from your boss. Did you overstep your boundaries by making recommendations that might imply that she has not been doing a good job? Did you overwhelm her with your ideas? You'd like some feedback. In your last e-mail to her, you asked if she had read your report. So far you've received no reply. Then yesterday, you overheard the company vice president talk about some productivity changes in your department. The changes were ones that you had recommended in your report. Now you're worried that your boss submitted your report to senior management and will take full credit for your terrific ideas. What, if anything, should you do? Should you confront your boss about this? Should you ask to meet with the company vice president? Discuss this situation among your teammates and develop a solution to this sticky situation. Present your solution to the class, explaining the rationale behind your decision.

Expand Your Knowledge

LEARNING MORE ON THE WEB
PREVIEW BEFORE YOU PRODUCE

www.ixquick.com

A good way to get ideas for the best style, organization, and format of a report is by looking at copies of professional business reports. To find samples of various types of reports, you can use a metasearch engine such as Ixquick Metasearch.

ACTIVITIES

Choose a metasearch engine (refer to Table 10.4 on page 341). Enter the phrase *business reports,* then choose a report and review it. Answer the following questions:

1. What is the purpose of the report you read? Who is its target audience? Explain why the structure and style of the report make it easy or difficult to follow the main idea.
2. What type of report did you read? Briefly describe the main message. Is the information well organized? If you answer "yes," explain how you can use the report as a guide for a report you might write. If you answer "no," explain why the report is not helpful.
3. Drawing on what you know about the qualities of a good business report, review a report and describe what features contribute to its readability.

EXPLORING THE WEB ON YOUR OWN

Review these chapter-related websites to learn more about writing reports and proposals.

1. Plan your way to profit by learning how to write effective business plans. Refer to the Business Planning section on the Small Business Administration website, www.sba.gov (look under "Starting Your Business").
2. Deborah Kluge's proposal writing blog offers tips, techniques, and checklists to help you craft more successful proposals; learn more at www.proposalwriter.com/weblog.
3. Resolve any grammar question you come across in your proofreading by consulting the online grammar directory at www.clearenglish.net.

Learn Interactively

INTERACTIVE STUDY GUIDE

Visit www.prenhall.com/thill, then locate your book and click on its Companion Website link. Select Chapter 12 to take advantage of the interactive "Chapter Quiz" to test your knowledge of chapter concepts. Receive instant feedback on whether you need additional studying. Also, visit the "Study Hall," where you'll find an abundance of valuable resources that will help you succeed in this course.

PEAK PERFORMANCE GRAMMAR AND MECHANICS

If your instructor has required the use of "Peak Performance Grammar and Mechanics," either in your online course or on CD, you can improve your skill with quotation marks, parentheses, and ellipses by using the "Peak Performance Grammar and Mechanics" module. Click "Punctuation II." Take the Pretest to determine whether you have any weak areas. Then review those areas in the Refresher Course. Take the Follow-Up Test to check your grasp of quotation marks, parentheses, and ellipses. For an extra challenge or advanced practice, take the Advanced Test. Finally, for additional reinforcement, go to the "Improve Your Grammar, Mechanics, and Usage" section that follows, and complete those exercises.

Improve Your Grammar, Mechanics, and Usage

The following exercises help you improve your knowledge of and power over English grammar, mechanics, and usage. Turn to the Handbook of Grammar, Mechanics, and Usage at the end of this textbook and review all of Sections 2.10 (Quotation Marks), 2.11 (Parentheses), and 2.12 (Ellipses). Then look at the following 10 items. Circle the letter of the preferred choice in the following groups of sentences. (Answers to these exercises appear on page AK-4.)

1. a. Be sure to read (How to Sell by Listening) in this month's issue of *Fortune*.
    b. Be sure to read "How to Sell by Listening" in this month's issue of *Fortune*.
    c. Be sure to read "How to Sell by Listening . . ." in this month's issue of *Fortune*.

2. a. Her response . . . see the attached memo . . . is disturbing.
    b. Her response (see the attached memo) is disturbing.
    c. Her response "see the attached memo" is disturbing.

3. a. We operate with a skeleton staff during the holidays (December 21 through January 2).
    b. We operate with a skeleton staff during the holidays "December 21 through January 2".
    c. We operate with a skeleton staff during the holidays (December 21 through January 2.)

4. a. "The SBP's next conference . . ." the bulletin noted, ". . . will be held in Minneapolis."
    b. "The SBP's next conference," the bulletin noted, "will be held in Minneapolis."
    c. "The SBP's next conference," the bulletin noted, "will be held in Minneapolis".

5. a. The term "up in the air" means "undecided."
    b. The term "up in the air" means *undecided.*
    c. The term *up in the air* means "undecided."

6. a. Her assistant (the one who just had the baby) won't be back for four weeks.
    b. Her assistant (the one who just had the baby), won't be back for four weeks.
    c. Her assistant . . . the one who just had the baby . . . won't be back for four weeks.

7. a. "Ask not what your country can do for you," begins a famous John Kennedy quotation.
    b. ". . . Ask not what your country can do for you" begins a famous John Kennedy quotation.
    c. "Ask not what your country can do for you . . ." begins a famous John Kennedy quotation.

8. a. Do you remember who said "And away we go?"
    b. Do you remember who said "And away we go"?

9. a. Refinements may prove profitable. (More detail about this technology appears in Appendix A).
    b. Refinements may prove profitable. (More detail about this technology appears in Appendix A.)

10. a. The resignation letter begins, "Since I'll never regain your respect . . . ," and goes on to explain why that's true.
    b. The resignation letter begins, "Since I'll never regain your respect, . . ." and goes on to explain why that's true.
    c. The resignation letter begins, "Since I'll never regain your respect . . ." and goes on to explain why that's true.

For additional exercises focusing on quotation marks, parentheses, and ellipses, go to **www.prenhall.com/thill**, then locate your text and click on its Companion Website link. Click on Chapter 12, click on "Additional Exercises to Improve Your Grammar, Mechanics and Usage," then click on "19. Punctuation D."

Cases

SHORT FORMAL REPORTS REQUIRING NO ADDITIONAL RESEARCH

1. **Giving it the online try: Report analyzing the advantages and disadvantages of corporate online learning** As the newest member of the corporate training division of Paper Products, Inc., you have been asked to investigate and ana-lyze the merits of creating online courses for the company's employees. The president of your company thinks so-called e-learning might be a good employee benefit as well as a terrific way for employees to learn new skills that they can use on the job. You've already done your research and here's a copy of your notes:

Online courses open up new horizons for working adults, who often find it difficult to juggle conventional classes with jobs and families.

Adults over 25 now represent nearly half of higher-ed students; most are employed and want more education to advance their careers.

Some experts believe that online learning will never be as good as face-to-face instruction.

Online learning requires no commute and is appealing for employees who travel regularly.

Enrollment in courses offered online by postsecondary institutions is expected to increase from 2 million students in 2001 to 5 million students in 2006.

E-learning is a cost-effective way to get better-educated employees.

More than one-third of the $50 billion spent on employee training every year is spent on e-learning.

At IBM, some 200,000 employees received education or training online last year, and 75 percent of the company's Basic Blue course for new managers is online. E-learning cut IBM's training bill by $350 million last year—mostly because online courses don't require travel.

There are no national statistics, but a recent report from the *Chronicle of Higher Education* found that institutions are seeing dropout rates that range from 20 to 50 percent for online learners. The research does not adequately explain why the dropout rates for e-learners are higher.

A recent study of corporate online learners reported that employees want the following things from their online courses: college credit or a certificate; active correspondence with an online facilitator who has frequent virtual office hours; access to 24-hour, seven-day-a-week technical support; and the ability to start a course anytime.

Corporate e-learners said that their top reason for dropping a course was lack of time. Many had trouble completing courses from their desktops because of frequent distractions caused by co-workers. Some said they could only access courses through the company's intranet, so they couldn't finish their assignments from home.

Besides lack of time, corporate e-learners cited the following as e-learning disadvantages: lack of management oversight; lack of motivation; problems with technology; lack of student support; individual learning preferences; poorly designed courses; substandard/inexperienced instructors.

A recent study by GE Capital found that finishing a corporate online course was dependent on whether managers gave reinforcement on attendance, how important employees were made to feel, and whether employee progress in the course was tracked.

Sun Microsystems found that interactivity can be a critical success factor for online courses. Company studies showed that only 25 percent of employees finish classes that are strictly self-paced. But 75 percent finish when given similar assignments and access to tutors through e-mail, phone, or online discussion.

Company managers must supervise e-learning just as they would any other important initiative.

For online learning to work, companies must develop a culture that takes online learning just as seriously as classroom training.

For many e-learners, studying at home is optimal. Whenever possible, companies should offer courses through the Internet or provide intranet access at home. Having employees studying on their own time will more than cover any added costs.

Corporate e-learning has flared into a $2.3 billion market, making it one of the fastest-growing segments of the education industry.

Rather than fly trainers to 7,000 dealerships, General Motors University now uses interactive satellite broadcasts to teach salespeople the best way to highlight features on the new Buick.

Fast and cheap, e-training can shave companies' training costs while it saves employees travel time.

Pharmaceutical companies such as Merck are conducting live, interactive classes over the web, allowing sales reps to learn about the latest product information at home rather than fly them to a conference center.

McDonald's trainers can log on to Hamburger University to learn such skills as how to assemble a made-to-order burger or properly place the drink on a tray.

One obstacle to the spread of online corporate training is the mismatch between what employees really need—customized courses that are tailored to a firm's products and its unique corporate culture—and what employers can afford.

80 percent of companies prefer developing their own online training courses in-house. But creating even one customized e-course can take months, involve armies of experts, and cost anywhere from $25,000 to $50,000. Thus, most companies either stick with classroom training or buy generic courses on such topics as how to give performance appraisals, understanding basic business ethics, and so on. Employers can choose from a wide selection of noncustomized electronic courses.

For online learning to be effective, content must be broken into short "chunks" with lots of pop quizzes, online discussion groups, and other interactive features that let students demonstrate what they've learned. For instance, Circuit City's tutorial on digital camcorders consists of three 20-minute segments. Each contains audio demonstrations of how to handle customer product queries, tests on terminology, and "try-its" that propel trainees back onto the floor to practice what they've learned.

Dell Computer expects 90 percent of its learning solutions to be totally or partially technology enabled.

The Home Depot has used e-training to cut a full day from the time required to train new cashiers.

Online training has freed up an average of 17 days every year for Black & Decker's sales representatives.

Your task: Write a short (3 to 5 pages) memo report to the director of human resources, Kerry Simmons, presenting the advantages and disadvantages of e-learning and making a recommendation as to whether Paper Products, Inc., should invest time and money in training its employees this way. Be sure to organize your information so that it is clear, concise, and logically presented. Simmons likes to read the "bottom line" first, so be direct: Present your recommendation up front and support your recommendation with your findings.[8]

2. Building a new magazine: Finding opportunity in the remodeling craze Spurred on in part by the success of such hit shows as *Changing Rooms, Trading Spaces,* and *Designers' Challenge,* homeowners across the country are redecorating, remodeling, and rebuilding. Many people are content with superficial changes, such as new paint or new accessories, but some are more ambitious. These homeowners want to move walls, add rooms, redesign kitchens, convert garages to home theaters—the big stuff.

As with many consumer trends, publishers try to create magazines that appeal to carefully identified groups of potential readers and the advertisers who'd like to reach them. The do-it-yourself (DIY) market is already served by numerous magazines, but you see an opportunity in those homeowners who tackle the heavy-duty projects. Tables 12–1 through 12–3 summarize the results of some preliminary research you asked your company's research staff to conduct.

Your task: You think the data show a real opportunity for a "big projects" DIY magazine, although you'll need more extensive research to confirm the size of the market and refine the editorial direction of the magazine. Prepare a brief analytical report that presents the data you have, identifies the opportunity or opportunities you've found (suggest your own ideas

based on the Tables 12–1 through 12–3), and requests funding from the editorial board to pursue further research.

SHORT FORMAL REPORTS REQUIRING ADDITIONAL RESEARCH

3. Selling overseas: Research report on the prospects for marketing a product in another country Select a fairly inexpensive product that you currently own and a country that you're not very familiar with. The product could be a moderately priced watch, radio, or other device. Now imagine that you are with the international sales department of the company that manufactures and sells the item and that you are proposing to make it available in the country you have selected.

The first step is to learn as much as possible about the country where you plan to market the product. Check almanacs, encyclopedias, the Internet, and library databases for the most recent information, paying particular attention to descriptions of the social life of the inhabitants, their economic conditions, and cultural traditions that would encourage or discourage use of the product.

Your task: Write a short report that describes the product you plan to market abroad, briefly describes the country you have

Table 12–1	ROOMS MOST FREQUENTLY REMODELED BY DIYERS
Room	**Percent of homeowners surveyed who have tackled or plan to tackle at least a partial remodel**
Kitchen	60
Bathroom	48
Home office/study	44
Bedroom	38
Media room/home theater	31
Den/recreation room	28
Living room	27
Dining room	12
Sun room/solarium	8

Table 12–2	AVERAGE AMOUNT SPENT ON REMODELING PROJECTS
Estimated amount	**Percent of surveyed homeowners**
Under $5k	5
$5–10k	21
$10–20k	39
$20–50k	22
More than $50k	13

TASKS PERFORMED BY HOMEOWNER ON A TYPICAL REMODELING PROJECT	Table 12–3

Task	Percent of surveyed homeowners who perform or plan to perform most or all of this task themselves
Conceptual design	90
Technical design/architecture	34
Demolition	98
Foundation work	62
Framing	88
Plumbing	91
Electrical	55
Heating/cooling	22
Finish carpentry	85
Tile work	90
Painting	100
Interior design	52

selected, indicate the types of people in this country who would find the product attractive, explains how the product would be transported into the country (or possibly manufactured there if materials and labor are available), recommend a location for a regional sales center, and suggests how the product should be sold. Your report is to be submitted to the chief operating officer of the company, whose name you can either make up or find in a corporate directory. The report should include your conclusions (how the product will do in this new environment) and your recommendations for marketing (steps the company should take immediately and those it should develop later).

4. A ready-made business: Finding the right franchise opportunity After 15 years in the corporate world, you're ready to strike out on your own. Rather than building a business from the ground up, however, you think that buying a franchise is a better idea. Unfortunately, some of the most lucrative franchise opportunities, such as the major fast-food chains, require significant start-up costs—some more than a half million dollars. Fortunately, you've met several potential investors who seem willing to help you get started in exchange for a share of ownership. Between your own savings and these investors, you estimate that you can raise from $350,000 to $600,000, depending on how much ownership share you want to concede to the investors.

You've worked in several functional areas already, including sales and manufacturing, so you have a fairly well-rounded business résumé. You're open to just about any type of business,

too, as long as it provides the opportunity to grow; you don't want to be so tied down to the first operation that you can't turn it over to a hired manager and expand into another market.

Your task: To convene a formal meeting with the investor group, you need to first draft a report outlining the types of franchise opportunities you'd like to pursue. Write a brief report identifying five franchises that you would like to explore further (choose five based on your own personal interests and the criteria identified above). For each possibility, identify the nature of the business, the financial requirements, the level of support the company provides, and a brief statement of why

you could run such a business successfully (make up any details you need). Be sure to carefully review the information you find about each franchise company to make sure you can qualify for it. For instance, McDonald's doesn't allow investment partnerships to buy franchises, so you won't be able to start up a McDonald's outlet until you have enough money to do it on your own.

For a quick introduction to franchising, see How Stuff Works (www.howstuffworks.com/franchising). You can learn more about the business of franchising at Franchising.com (www.franchising.com) and search for specific franchise opportunities at FranCorp Connect (www.francorpconnect.com). In addition, many companies that sell franchises, such as Subway, offer additional information on their websites.

LONG FORMAL REPORTS REQUIRING NO ADDITIONAL RESEARCH

5. You can get anything online these days: Shopping for automobiles on the Internet As a researcher in your state's consumer protection agency, you're frequently called on to investigate consumer topics and write reports for the agency's website. Thousands of consumers have arranged the purchase of cars online, and millions more do at least some of their research online before heading to the dealership. Some want to save time and money, some want to be armed with as much information as possible before talking to a dealer, while others want to completely avoid the often-uncomfortable experience of negotiating prices with car salespeople. In response, a variety of online services have emerged to meet these consumer needs. Some let you compare information on various car models, some connect you to local dealers to complete the transaction, and some complete nearly all of the transaction details for you, including negotiating the price. Some search the inventory of thousands of dealers, whereas others search only a single dealership or a network of affiliated dealers. In other words, a slew of new tools are available for car buyers, but it's not always easy to figure out where to go and what to expect. That's where your report will help.

By visiting a variety of car-related websites and reading magazine and newspaper articles on the car-buying process, you've compiled a variety of notes related to the subject:

- **Process overview:** The process is relatively straightforward and fairly similar to other online shopping experiences, with two key differences. In general, a consumer identifies the make and model of car he or she wants, then the online car buying service searches the inventories of car dealers nationwide and presents the available choices. The consumer chooses a particular car from that list, then the service handles the communication and purchase details with the dealer. When the paperwork is finished, the consumer then visits the dealership and picks up the car. The two biggest differences with online auto buying are that (1) you can't actually complete the purchase over the Internet (in most cases, you must visit a local dealer to pick up the car and sign the papers, although in some cities, a dealer or a local car buying service will deliver it to your home) and (2) in most states, it's illegal to

purchase a new car from anyone other than a franchise dealer (i.e., you can't buy directly from the manufacturer, the way you can buy a Dell computer directly from Dell, for instance).

- **Information you can find online (not all information is available at all sites):** makes, models, colors, options, option packages (often, specific options are available only as part of a package; you need to know these constraints before you select your options), photos, specifications (everything from engine size to interior space), mileage estimates, performance data, safety information, predicted resale value, reviews, comparable models, insurance costs, consumer ratings, repair and reliability histories, available buyer incentives and rebates, true ownership costs (which includes fuel, maintenance, repair, etc.), warranty, loan and lease payments, and maintenance requirements.

- **Advantages of shopping online:** Shopping from the comfort and convenience of home, none of the dreaded negotiating at the dealership (in many cases), the ability to search far and wide for a specific car (even nationwide on many sites), the rapid access to considerable amounts of data and information, reviews from both professional automotive journalists and other consumers. In general, online auto shopping reduces a key advantage that auto dealers used to have, which was control of most of the information in the purchase transaction. Now consumers can find out how reliable each model is, how quickly it will depreciate, how often it is likely to need repairs, what other drivers think of it, how much the dealer paid the manufacturer for it, and so on.

- **Changing nature of the business.** The relationship between "third-party" websites (such as CarsDirect.com and Vehix.com) continues to evolve. At first, the relationship was more antagonistic, as some third-party sites and dealers frequently competed for the same customers, and both sides made bold proclamations about driving the other out of business. However, the relationship is more collaborative in many cases now, with dealers realizing that some third-party sites already have wide brand awareness and nationwide audiences. As the percentage of new car sales that originate via the Internet continue to increase, dealers are more receptive to working with third-party sites.

- **Compare information from multiple sources.** Consumers shouldn't rely solely on the information from a single website. Each site has its own way of organizing information and many have their own ways of evaluating car models and connecting buyers with sellers.

- **Understand what each site is doing.** For instance, some search thousands of dealers, regardless of ownership connections. Others, such as AutoNation, search only affiliated dealers. A search for a specific model might yield only a half dozen cars on one site but dozens of cars on another site. Find out who owns the site and what their business objectives are, if you can; this will help you assess the information you receive.

- **Leading websites.** Consumers can check out a wide variety of websites, some of which are full-service operations, offering everything from research to negotiation; others provide more specific and limited services. For instance,

LEADING AUTOMOTIVE WEBSITES		Table 12–4
Site	*URL*	
AutoAdvice	www.autoadvice.com	
Autobytel	www.autobytel.com	
AutoDirectory.com	www.autodirectory.com	
Autos.com	www.autos.com	
AutoVantage	www.autovantage.com	
Autoweb	www.autoweb.com	
CarBargains	www.carbargains.com	
Carfax	www.carfax.com	
CarPrices.com	www.carprices.com	
Cars.com	www.cars.com	
CarsDirect	www.carsdirect.com	
CarSmart	www.carsmart.com	
Consumer Reports	www.consumerreports.com	
eBay Motors	www.ebaymotors.com	
Edmunds	www.edmunds.com	
iMotors	www.imotors.com	
IntelliChoice	www.intellichoice.com	
InvoiceDealers	www.invoicedealers.com	
J.D. Power	www.jdpower.com	
Kelly Blue Book	www.kbb.com	
MSN Autos	http://autos.msn.com	
PickupTruck.com	www.pickuptruck.com	
The Car Connection	www.thecarconnection.com	
Vehix.com	www.vehix.com	
Yahoo! Autos	www.autos.yahoo.com	

CarsDirect (www.carsdirect.com) provides a full range of services, whereas Carfax (www.carfax.com) specializes in uncovering the repair histories of individual used cars. Table 12–4 lists some of the leading car-related websites.

Your task: Write an informational report based on your research notes. The purpose of the report is to introduce consumers to the basic concepts of integrating the Internet into their car-buying activities and to educate them about important issues.[9]

6. Moving the Workforce: Understanding commute patterns Your company is the largest private employer in your metropolitan area, and the 43,500 employees in your workforce have a tremendous impact on local traffic. A group of city and county transportation officials recently approached your CEO with a request to explore ways to reduce this impact. The CEO has assigned you the task of analyzing the workforce's transportation habits and attitudes as a first step toward identifying potential solutions. He's willing to consider anything from subsidized bus passes to company-owned shuttle buses to telecommuting, but the decision requires a thorough understanding of employee transportation needs. Tables 12–5 through 12–9 summarize data you collected in an employee survey.

Your task: Present the results of your survey in an informational report using the data provided in Tables 12–5 through 12–9.

Table 12–5 — EMPLOYEE CARPOOL HABITS

Frequency of Use: Carpooling	Portion of Workforce
Every day, every week	10,138 (23%)
Certain days, every week	4,361 (10%)
Randomly	983 (2%)
Never	28,018 (64%)

Table 12–6 — USE OF PUBLIC TRANSPORTATION

Frequency of Use: Public Transportation	Portion of Workforce
Every day, every week	23,556 (54%)
Certain days, every week	2,029 (5%)
Randomly	5,862 (13%)
Never	12,053 (28%)

Table 12–7 — EFFECT OF POTENTIAL IMPROVEMENTS TO PUBLIC TRANSPORTATION

Which of the Following Would Encourage You to Use Public Transportation More Frequently (check all that apply)*	Portion of Respondents
Increased perceptions of safety	4,932 (28%)
Improved cleanliness	852 (5%)
Reduced commute times	7,285 (41%)
Greater convenience: fewer transfers	3,278 (18%)
Greater convenience: more stops	1,155 (6%)
Lower (or subsidized) fares	5,634 (31%)
Nothing could encourage me to take public transportation	8,294 (46%)

*Note: This question was asked of those respondents who use public transportation randomly or never, a subgroup that represents 17,915 employees or 41 percent of the workforce.

Table 12–8 — DISTANCE TRAVELED TO/FROM WORK

Distance You Travel to Work (one way)	Portion of Workforce
Less than 1 mile	531 (1%)
1–3 miles	6,874 (16%)
4–10 miles	22,951 (53%)
11–20 miles	10,605 (24%)
More than 20 miles	2,539 (6%)

IS TELECOMMUTING AN OPTION?

Table 12–9

Does the Nature of Your Work Make Telecommuting a Realistic Option?	Portion of Workforce
Yes, every day	3,460 (8%)
Yes, several days a week	8,521 (20%)
Yes, random days	12,918 (30%)
No	18,601 (43%)

LONG FORMAL REPORTS REQUIRING ADDITIONAL RESEARCH

7. Face-off: Informational report comparing and contrasting two companies in the same industry Your boss, Dana Hansell, has been searching for some solid companies to personally invest in for the long term. After reviewing security analysts' reports and financial statements for several candidates, Hansell has narrowed the list to these leading industry competitors:

- Boeing; Airbus (aerospace and airline industry)
- HP; Dell (computers and software industry)
- Merrill Lynch; Schwab (finance, banking, and insurance industry)
- Barnes & Noble; Amazon.com (online retailing)
- UPS; FedEx (trucking and freight industry)

According to Hansell, all of these candidates have about the same financial outlook for the future, so she is not interested in obtaining more financial performance detail. Instead, your boss is looking for more qualitative information, such as

- Fundamental philosophical differences in management styles, launching and handling products and services, marketing products and services, and approach to e-commerce that sets one rival company apart from the other
- Future challenges that each competitor faces
- Important decisions made by the two competitors and how those decisions affected their company

- Fundamental differences in each company's vision of their industry's future (for instance, do they both agree on what consumers want, what products to deliver, and so on?)
- Specific competitive advantages held by each rival
- Past challenges each competitor has faced and how each met those challenges
- Strategic moves made by one rival that might affect the other
- Company success stories
- Brief company background information (Hansell already has some from the brokers' reports)
- Brief comparative statistics such as annual sales, market share, number of employees, number of stores, types of equipment, number of customers, sources of revenue, and so on

Hansell has heard that you are the department's most proficient researcher and an effective writer. You have been assigned the task of preparing a formal, long informational report for her. You need not make a recommendation or come to any conclusions; Hansell will do that based on the informational content of your report.

Your task: Select two industry competitors from the above list (or another list provided by your instructor) and write a long formal informational report comparing and contrasting how the two companies are addressing the topics outlined by Hansell. Of course, not every topic will apply to each company, and some will be more important than others—depending on the companies you select. Hansell will invest in only one of the two companies in your report. (Note: Because these topics require considerable research, your instructor may choose to make this a team project.)

8. Secondary sources: Report based on library and online research As a college student and active consumer, you may have considered one or more of the following questions at some point in the past few years:

a. What criteria distinguish the top-rated MBA programs in the country? How well do these criteria correspond to the needs and expectations of business? Are the criteria fair for students, employers, business schools?

b. Which of three companies you might like to work for has the strongest corporate ethics policies?

c. What will the music industry look like in the future? What's next after online stores such as Apple iTunes and digital players such as the iPod?

d. Which industries and job categories are forecast to experience the greatest growth—and therefore the greatest demands for workers—in the next 10 years?

e. What has been the impact of Starbucks' aggressive growth on small, independent coffee shops? On midsized chains or franchises? In the United States or in another country?

f. How large is the "industry" of major college sports? How much do the major football or basketball programs contribute—directly or indirectly—to other parts of a typical university?

g. How much have minor league sports—baseball, hockey, arena football—grown in small- and medium-market cities? What is the local economic impact when these municipalities build stadiums and arenas?

Your task: Answer one of those questions using secondary research sources for information. Be sure to document your sources in the correct form. Give conclusions and offer recommendations where appropriate.

FORMAL PROPOSALS

9. Polishing the Presenters: Offering Your Services as a Presentation Trainer Presentations can make—or break—both careers and businesses. A good presentation can bring in millions of dollars in new sales or fresh investment capital. A bad presentation might cause any number of troubles, from turning away potential customers to upsetting fellow employees to derailing key projects. To help business professionals plan, create, and deliver more effective presentations, you offer a three-day workshop that covers the essentials of good presentations:

- Understanding your audience's needs and expectations
- Formulating your presentation objectives
- Choosing an organizational approach
- Writing openings that catch your audience's attention
- Creating effective graphics and slides
- Practicing and delivering your presentation
- Leaving a positive impression on your audience
- Avoiding common mistakes with Microsoft PowerPoint
- Making presentations online using webcasting tools
- Handling questions and arguments from the audience
- Overcoming the top 10 worries of public speaking (including *How can I overcome stage fright?* and *I'm not the performing type; can I still give an effective presentation?*)

Workshop benefits: Students will learn how to prepare better presentations in less time and deliver them more effectively.

Who should attend: Top executives, project managers, employment recruiters, sales professionals, and anyone else who gives important presentations to internal or external audiences.

Your qualifications: 18 years of business experience, including 14 years in sales and 12 years in public speaking. Experience speaking to audiences as large as 5,000 people. More than a dozen speech-related articles published in professional journals. Have conducted successful workshops for nearly 100 companies.

Workshop details: Three-day workshop (9 A.M. to 3:30 P.M.) that combines lectures, practice presentations, and both individual and group feedback. Minimum number of students: 6. Maximum number of students per workshop: 12

Pricing: The cost is $3,500, plus $100 per student. 10 percent discount for additional workshops.

Other information: Each attendee will have the opportunity to give three practice presentations that will last from three to five minutes. Everyone is encouraged to bring PowerPoint files containing slides from actual business presentations. Each attendee will also receive a workbook and a digital video recording of his or her final class presentation on DVD. You'll also be available for phone or e-mail coaching for six months after the workshop.

Your task: Identify a company in your local area that might be a good candidate for your services. Learn more about them by visiting their website so you can personalize your proposal. Using the information listed above, prepare a sales proposal that explains the benefits of your training and what students can expect during the workshop.

10. Healthy alternatives: Proposal to sell snacks and beverages at local high schools For years, a controversy has been brewing over the amount of junk food and soft drinks being sold through vending machines in local schools. Schools ben-

efit from revenue-sharing arrangements, but many parents and health experts are concerned about the negative effects of these snacks and beverages. You and your brother have almost a decade of experience running espresso and juice stands in malls and on street corners, and you'd love to find some way to expand your business into schools. After a quick brainstorming session, the two of you craft a plan that makes good business sense while meeting the financial concerns of school administrators and the nutritional concerns of parents and dieticians. Here are the notes from your brainstorming session:

- Set up portable juice bars on school campuses, offering healthy fruit and vegetable drinks along with simple, healthy snacks
- Offers schools 30 percent of profits in exchange for free space and long-term contracts
- Provide job training opportunities for students (during athletic events, etc.)
- Provide detailed dietary analysis of all products sold
- Establish a nutritional advisory board composed of parents, students, and at least one certified health professional
- Assure schools and parents that all products are safe (e.g., no stimulant drinks, no dietary supplements, and so on)
- Support local farmers and specialty food preparers by buying locally and giving these vendors the opportunity to test market new products at your stands

Your task: Based on the ideas listed, draft a formal proposal to the local school board, outlining your plan to offer healthier alternatives to soft drinks and prepackaged snack foods. Invent any details you need to complete your proposal.

Chapter 13

Planning, Writing, and Completing Oral Presentations

Learning Objectives

AFTER STUDYING THIS CHAPTER, YOU WILL BE ABLE TO

1   Explain the importance of oral presentations in your career success

2   Explain how to adapt the three-step writing process to oral presentations

3   Discuss the three functions of an effective introduction

4   Identify four ways to keep your audience's attention during your presentation

5   Explain how visuals enhance oral presentations and list several popular types of visuals

6   Explain the importance of design consistency in electronic slides and other visuals

7   Highlight seven major issues to consider when you're preparing to give a presentation online

8   Identify six ways that effective speakers use to handle questions responsively

On the Job

COMMUNICATING AT HEWLETT-PACKARD

MAKING A COMPELLING PRESENTATION WITH $3 BILLION ON THE LINE

Presentations make everyone nervous, but imagine how nervous you might be if you were making a presentation with millions, even billions, of dollars on the line. That situation is business as usual for Dan Talbott of HP Managed Services, a unit of Hewlett-Packard that manages computer operations for other companies. After HP's controversial acquisition of Compaq, the company was desperate for a major contract that would highlight the capabilities of the merged organization.

Dan Talbott (far right) led a team whose presentation skills helped land a multibillion-dollar contract for Hewlett-Packard.

Against that backdrop, Talbott was asked to pursue a huge deal with Procter & Gamble (P&G), the consumer-products giant that markets over 300 brands, including Charmin, Crest, and Tide. P&G was looking to lower its costs by hiring someone outside its organization to take over the operation of its global information system—a network of more than 80,000 computers. HP was facing two tough competitors for the contract, Electronic Data Systems and IBM, and had to be considered a distant third-place contender since it had never landed a contract the size of the P&G deal. Conditions got even tougher when P&G published a 10,000-page request for proposals (RFP) and limited the response time to just 56 days (9 to 12 months is typical on projects of this magnitude).

As a seasoned industry veteran but a rookie at HP, Talbott was eager to show that he could bring his new employer this mammoth piece of business. He moved his team into an HP office near P&G's Cincinnati headquarters, tapped the brainpower of 80 colleagues from around the world, and began developing the series of presentations that were specified in the RFP. Knowing that every interaction with P&G could nudge HP closer to its goal, Talbott told the group, "Our job is to ensure that every conversation is a win." However, HP's initial presentation was shaky, so Talbott asked the presenters to print their PowerPoint slides—over 200 in all—and post them on the walls of a conference room. He conducted a slide-by-slide critique, questioning every slide that lacked a clear message. The team revised and kept revising until the presentation was audience centered and crystal clear from beginning to end.

That rigorous review produced a string of successful presentations that ultimately helped Talbott and his team win a 10-year contract worth $3 billion—a stunning success that announced HP's arrival as a big-time player in computer services. You may never be on stage with $3 billion at stake, but you can take Dan Talbott's rigorous approach to presentation quality and make every one of your presentations a winner.[1]

BUILDING YOUR CAREER WITH ORAL PRESENTATIONS

Oral presentations involve all of your communication skills, from research through nonverbal communication.

Dan Talbott's experience is solid proof that presentation skills are vital in today's business environment. Oral presentations offer important opportunities to put all your communication skills on display—not just in research, planning, writing, and visual design, but also in interpersonal and nonverbal communication. Presentations can also let you demonstrate your ability to think on your feet, grasp complex issues, and handle challenging situations—all attributes that executives look for when searching for talented employees to promote.

Feeling nervous is perfectly normal when you're faced with an oral presentation; the good news is there are positive steps you can take to reduce your anxiety.

If the thought of giving a speech or presentation makes you nervous, try to keep three points in mind. First, everybody gets nervous when speaking in front of a group. Even professional speakers and entertainers get nervous after years of experience. Second, being nervous is actually a good thing; it means you care about the topic, your audience, and your career success. With practice, you can convert those nervous feelings into positive energy. Third, you don't have to be a victim of your own emotions when it comes to oral presentations. You can take control of the situation by using the planning and development techniques that you'll learn in this chapter—starting with how to adapt the three-step writing process to the unique challenges of oral presentations.

ADAPTING THE THREE-STEP PROCESS FOR ORAL PRESENTATIONS

While you don't usually write your oral presentations word for word, the three-step writing process is easily adaptable to oral presentations.

Although you don't often write out presentations word for word, nearly every task in the three-step writing process applies to oral presentations, with some modifications (see Figure 13–1). In addition, a few extra steps will help you prepare both your material and yourself for the actual presentation. As with written reports, people often judge

FIGURE 13–1
The Three-Step Process for Developing Oral Presentations

Planning

Writing

Completing

Analyze the Situation
Define your purpose and develop a profile of your audience, including their emotional states and language preferences.

Gather Information
Determine audience needs and obtain the information necessary to satisfy those needs.

Select the Right Medium
Choose the best medium or combination of media for delivering your presentation.

Organize the Information
Define your main idea, limit your scope, select a direct or an indirect approach, and outline your content.

Adapt to Your Audience
Be sensitive to audience needs and expectations with a "you" attitude, politeness, positive emphasis, and bias-free language. Build a strong relationship with your audience by establishing your credibility and projecting your company's image. Adjust your delivery to fit the situation, from casual to formal.

Compose the Message
Outline an effective introduction, body, and close. Prepare any visuals necessary to support your argument or clarify concepts.

Revise Your Presentation
Evaluate content and review speaking notes; finalize handout materials.

Prepare to Speak
Choose your delivery mode and practice your presentation; verify facilities and equipment; hire an interpreter if necessary.

Deliver Your Presentation
Take steps to feel more confident and appear more confident on stage; handle questions responsively.

1   2   3

the quality of the content by the quality of the presentation, so your delivery style and the packaging of any visual support materials can be as important as your message.

STEP 1: PLANNING YOUR PRESENTATION

Planning oral presentations is much like planning any other business message: You (1) analyze the situation, (2) gather information, (3) select the right medium, and (4) organize the information. Gathering information for oral presentations is essentially the same as it is for written communication projects (see Chapter 10). The other three planning tasks have some special applications when it comes to oral presentations; they are covered in the following sections.

Analyzing the Situation

As with written communications, analyzing the situation involves defining your purpose and developing an audience profile. The purpose of most of your presentations will be to inform or to persuade, although you may occasionally need to make a collaborative presentation, such as when you're leading a problem-solving or brainstorming session. The guidelines in Chapter 4 will help you identify and refine your purpose. In rare circumstances, the purpose of a business presentation will be to entertain the audience, but most companies hire professional speakers for that sort of presentation.

When you develop your audience profile, start with the advice in Chapter 4 and then consider two other issues that are particularly important for oral presentations.

ACHIEVING INTERCULTURAL COMMUNICATION

Five Tips for Making Presentations Around the World

When making presentations to international audiences, language fluency might vary widely. So take special care to ensure clear communication:

1. *Speak slowly and distinctly.* The most common complaint of international audiences is that English speakers talk too fast. Articulate every word carefully, emphasize consonants for clarity, and pause frequently.

2. *Repeat key words and phrases.* When audiences are less familiar with your language, they need to hear important information more than once. Also, they may not be familiar with various synonyms, so word key points in the same way throughout your presentation.

3. *Aim for clarity.* Keep your message simple. Eliminate complex sentence structure, abbreviations, and acronyms. Replace two-word verbs with one-word alternatives (such as *review* instead of *look over*). Such verbs are confusing because the definition of each separate word differs from the meaning of the two words combined. Avoid cultural idioms, such as *once in a blue moon,* which may be unfamiliar to an international audience.

4. *Communicate with body language.* Emphasize and clarify verbal information with gestures and facial expressions. For instance, smile to emphasize positive points and use gestures to illustrate the meaning of words such as *up, down,* or *under.*

5. *Support your oral message with visuals.* For most audiences, visual messages support and clarify spoken words. To eliminate problems with rapid speech, unclear pronunciations, or strange accents, prepare captions both in English and in your audience's native language.

CAREER APPLICATIONS

1. One of the most important changes speakers need to make when addressing audiences in other cultures is to avoid colloquial figures of speech. Replace each of these phrases with wording that is more likely to be understood by non-native English speakers or audiences in other countries: "hit one out of the park," "go for broke," and "get your ducks lined up."

2. Make a list of 10 two-word verbs. How does the meaning of each separate word differ from the definition of the combined words? Replace each two-word verb with a single, specific word that will be clearer to an international audience.

Table 13–1	ANALYZING AUDIENCES FOR ORAL PRESENTATIONS
Task	*Actions*
To determine audience size and composition	1. Estimate how many people will attend. 2. Identify what they have in common and how they differ. 3. Analyze the mix of men and women, age ranges, socioeconomic and ethnic groups, occupations, and geographic regions represented.
To predict the audience's probable reaction	1. Analyze why audience members are attending the presentation. 2. Determine the audience's general attitude toward the topic: interested, moderately interested, unconcerned, open-minded, or hostile. 3. Analyze the mood that people will be in when you speak to them. 4. Find out what kind of backup information will most impress the audience: technical data, historical information, financial data, demonstrations, samples, and so on. 5. Consider whether the audience has any biases that might work against you. 6. Anticipate possible objections or questions.
To gauge the audience's experience	1. Analyze whether everybody has the same background and level of understanding. 2. Determine what the audience already knows about the subject. 3. Decide what background information the audience will need to better understand the subject. 4. Consider whether the audience is familiar with the vocabulary you intend to use. 5. Analyze what the audience expects from you. 6. Think about the mix of general concepts and specific details you will need to present.

Knowing your audience's state of mind will help you adjust both your message and your delivery.

First, try to anticipate what sort of emotional state your audience members are likely to be in. Will they accept your message automatically, or will they fight you every step of the way? Even though such concerns apply to written messages as well, they become even more important in live-audience situations, because individual emotions can play off one another. In a worst-case scenario, a herd mentality can take over, and people who might accept your message in a calm, one-on-one setting wind up rejecting it under the influence of the crowd's emotions.

Second, when developing your audience profile, determine whether your audience is comfortable listening to the language you speak. Listening to an unfamiliar language is much harder than reading that language, so an audience that might be able to read a written report might not be able to understand an oral presentation covering the same material (see "Achieving Intercultural Communication: Five Tips for Making Presentations Around the World").

Try to learn as much as you can about the setting and circumstances of your presentation, from the size of the audience to potential interruptions.

As you analyze the situation, also consider the specific circumstances in which you'll be making your presentation. Will you speak to five people in a conference room, where you can control everything from light to sound to temperature? Or will you be demonstrating a product on the floor of a trade show, where you might have anywhere from 5 people to 500 and little control over the environment? Will everyone be in the same room, or will your audience participate from remote locations via the Internet? What equipment will you have at your disposal—a complete multimedia presentation system or a humble overhead projector (or perhaps no equipment at all)? All these variables can influence not only the style of your presentation but even the content itself. For instance, in a public environment full of distractions and uncertainties, you're probably better off keeping your content simple and short because chances are you won't be able to keep everyone's attention for the duration of your presentation.

Table 13–1 offers a summary of the key steps in analyzing an audience for oral presentations. For even more insight into audience evaluation (including emotional and cultural issues), consult a good public-speaking textbook.

Selecting the Right Medium

The task of selecting the right medium might seem obvious—after all, you are speaking, so it's an oral medium. However, technology offers an array of choices these days, ranging from live, in-person presentations to webcasts that people view on your website whenever it fits their individual schedules. Explore these options early on so that you can take full advantage of the ones at your disposal. For example, to reach an international audience, you might want to conduct a live presentation with a question-and-answer session for the audience members in your home office, then post a video archive of this meeting on your website for audience members in other time zones. Again, planning ahead is the key to media selection.

Expect to give many presentations via electronic media in your career.

Organizing Your Presentation

Organizing a presentation involves the same tasks as organizing a written message: Define your main idea, limit your scope, select a direct or an indirect approach, and outline your content. As you work through these tasks, keep in mind that audiences for oral presentations are more or less trapped in your time frame and sequence. When reading written reports, audiences can skip back and forth, backing up if they miss a point or become confused and jumping ahead if they aren't interested in a particular part or are already familiar with the content. However, other than interrupting you, presentation audiences have no choice but to listen to your content in the exact order in which you present it.

For instance, say that your presentation is a proposal and that you believe your audience will be hostile to both your proposal and to you. So you plan to structure your proposal using an indirect approach. Simple enough, until . . . surprise—the members of your audience have already heard of your idea through other channels, and they like it. Now they have to sit through an extended presentation of your reasons so that you can convince them to accept an idea they already accept. With a printed report, your audience would simply skip ahead, but they can't do that with an oral presentation. Consequently, organizing your presentation becomes even more important.

Organizations such as the Hong Kong Trade Development Council, Nike, Sears, and Avon use webcast speeches to make live announcements of financial news, new products, and management changes. Unlike ordinary speeches that address a particular audience at a particular time and place, webcast speeches can be viewed and listened to long after the speaker has left the podium.

Define Your Main Idea   If you've ever heard a speaker struggle to get his or her main point across ("What I really mean to say is . . ."), you know how frustrating such an experience can be for an audience. To avoid that struggle, figure out the one message you want audience members to walk away with. Then compose a one-sentence summary that links your subject and purpose to your audience's frame of reference, much as an advertising slogan points out how a product can benefit consumers. Here are some examples:

If you can't express your main idea in a single sentence, you probably haven't defined it clearly enough.

- Convince management that reorganizing the technical support department will improve customer service and reduce employee turnover

- Convince the board of directors that we should build a new plant in Texas to eliminate manufacturing bottlenecks and improve production quality

- Address employee concerns regarding a new health-care plan by showing how the plan will reduce costs and improve the quality of their care

Each of these statements puts a particular slant on the subject, one that directly relates to the audience's interests. By focusing on your audience's needs and using the "you" attitude, you help keep their attention and convince them that your points are relevant. For example, a group of new employees will be much more responsive to your discussion of plant safety procedures if you focus on how the procedures can save lives and prevent injuries, rather than focusing on company rules, saving the company money, or conforming to Occupational Safety and Health Administration (OSHA) guidelines.

Limit Your Scope   Effective presentations not only focus on the audience's needs but also tailor the material to the time allowed, which is often strictly regulated. Moreover, in many situations, multiple presenters are scheduled to speak one right after the other, so time allotments are rigid, permitting little or no flexibility. If you overestimate the amount of material you can cover within your allotted time, you're left with only unpleasant alternatives: rushing through your presentation, skipping some of the information you've so carefully prepared, or trying to steal a few minutes from the next presenter. Or if don't have enough material prepared to fill your time slot, you might be left standing in front of the audience trying to ad lib information you haven't prepared.

> Limiting your scope is important for two reasons: to ensure that your presentation fits the allotted time and to make sure your content meets audience needs and expectations.

Limiting your scope also involves matching your message with your audience's needs and expectations. Studies show that audience attention levels and retention rates drop sharply after 20 minutes, and venture capitalists (investors who fund many new companies) expect entrepreneurs to get to the point within 15 minutes.[2] In addition, if you try to cover too many details in a presentation, you can leave the audience feeling confused and frustrated. Often a better approach is to explain important concepts in your oral presentation and refer your audience to printed documents or websites for supporting details.

> The only sure way to measure the length of your presentation is to complete a practice run.

Once you've decided on the right amount of information to cover, do your best to estimate the time required to present that material or to estimate the amount of material you can cover within a fixed amount of time. The only sure way to do this is to practice. As an alternative to a complete practice run, you can try several techniques for estimating time requirements. First, if you're in one of those rare situations in which you're reciting your material verbatim or reading from a prepared script (more on this later in the chapter), you can divide your word count by 125 (if you speak slower than average) or 150 (if you're faster than average) to get a rough idea of how many minutes you'll need. Most speakers can comfortably deliver between 125 and 150 words per minute. Second, you can measure how long it takes to talk through a small portion of your presentation, then extrapolate how long the entire presentation will take. This method isn't terribly accurate, but it can help identify major timing problems. Third, after you get some experience giving presentations with either overhead transparencies or electronic slides, you'll get a feel for the time you typically need to cover a single slide. As a general guideline, figure on three or even four minutes per slide.[3] For instance, if you have 20 minutes, plan on roughly six or seven slides. If you're whipping through slides faster than that, chances are your slides are too simple or you're not engaging the audience with enough discussion about each one.

Of course, be sure to factor in time for introductions, coffee breaks, demonstrations, question-and-answer sessions, and anything else that takes away from your speaking time.

> Organize short presentations the same way you would a letter or brief memo.

Choose Your Approach   With a well-defined main idea to guide you and a clear idea about the scope of your presentation, you can begin to arrange your message. If you have 10 minutes or less to deliver your message, organize your presentation much as you would a letter or a brief memo: Use the direct approach if the subject involves routine information or good news, and use the indirect approach if the sub-

FIGURE 13–2
Effective Outline for a 10-Minute Progress Report

Progress Report: August 2006

Purpose: To update the Executive Committee on our product development schedule.

I.   Review goals and progress
   A. Mechanical design:
      1. Goal: 100%
      2. Actual: 80%
      3. Reason for delay: Unanticipated problems with case durability
   B. Software development:
      1. Goal: 50%
      2. Actual: 60%
   C. Material sourcing:
      1. Goal: 100%
      2. Actual: 45% (and materials identified are at 140% of anticipated costs)
      3. Reason for delay: Purchasing is understaffed and hasn't been able to research sources adequately

II. Discuss schedule options
   A. Option 1: Reschedule product launch date
   B. Option 2: Launch on schedule with more expensive materials

III. Suggest goals for next month

IV. Q&A

ject involves bad news or persuasion. Plan your introduction to arouse interest and to give a preview of what's to come. For the body of the presentation, be prepared to explain the who, what, when, where, why, and how of your subject. In the final section, review the points you've made, and close with a statement that will help your audience remember the subject of your speech. Figure 13–2 presents an outline of a short presentation that updates management on the status of a key project; the presenter has some bad news to deliver, so she opted for an indirect approach to lay out the reasons for the delay before sharing the news of the schedule slip.

Longer presentations are organized like reports. If the purpose is to motivate or inform, use a direct order and a structure imposed naturally by the subject: importance, sequence, chronology, spatial orientation, geography, or category (as discussed in Chapter 11). If your purpose is to analyze, persuade, or collaborate, organize your material around conclusions and recommendations or around a logical argument. Use a direct order if the audience is receptive and indirect if you expect resistance.

Regardless of the length of your presentation, remember that simplicity of organization is especially valuable in oral communication. If listeners lose the thread of your presentation, they'll have a hard time catching up and following your message in the remainder of your speech. Look for the most obvious and natural way to organize your ideas, using a direct approach whenever possible. Explain at the beginning how you've organized your material, and try to limit the number of main points to three or four—even when the speech or presentation is lengthy.

> Simplicity is critical in the organization of oral presentations.

Prepare Your Outline   A presentation outline performs the same all-important function as an outline for a written report: helping you organize the message in a way

> In addition to planning your speech, a presentation outline helps you plan your speaking notes.

that maximizes its impact on your audience. To ensure effective organization, prepare your outline in several stages:[4]

- **State your purpose and main idea.** As you develop your outline, check frequently to be sure that the points, organization, connections, and title relate to your purpose and main idea.

- **Organize your major points and subpoints.** Express each major point as a single, complete sentence to help you keep track of the one specific idea you want to convey in that point. Then look at the order of points to make sure their arrangement is logical and effective.

- **Identify your introduction, body, and close.** Start with the body, numbering each major point and subpoint according to its level in your outline. Then lay out the points for your introduction and close.

- **Show your connections.** Write out in sentence form the transitions you plan to use to move from one part to the next. Remember to include additional transitions between major points in the body of your speech.

- **Show your sources.** Prepare your bibliography, making sure that it reads easily, follows a consistent format, and includes all the details needed to identify your various sources.

- **Choose a title.** Not all speeches have a title. However, a title can be useful if your speech will be publicized ahead of time or introduced by someone else. The title sets everyone's expectations, so make it compelling and audience-centered.

Figure 13–3 is an outline for a 30-minute analytical presentation. It is organized around conclusions and presented in direct order. This outline is based on Chapter 12's Electrovision report, written by Linda Moreno.

You may find it helpful to create a simpler speaking outline from your planning outline.

Many speakers like to prepare both a detailed *planning outline* and a simpler *speaking outline* that provides all the cues and reminders they need to present their material.[5] To prepare an effective speaking outline, follow these steps:[6]

- **Follow the planning outline.** Follow the same format as you used for your planning outline (so that you can see at a glance where you are in your speech and how each part and point relates to the one before and after). However, strip away anything you don't plan to say to your audience (statements of general purpose, specific purpose, main idea, bibliography, etc.).

- **Condense points and transitions to keywords.** Choose words that will prompt you to remember what each point is about so that you can speak fluently. Be sure to write out statistics, quotations, and other specifics so that you don't stumble over them. You may also want to write complete sentences for transitions that connect main points or for critical points in your introduction or your close. Aim for the shortest outline you can comfortably use.

- **Add delivery cues.** During rehearsals, note the places in your outline where you plan to pause for emphasis, speak more slowly, use a visual, and so on. You might use colored ink to highlight your delivery cues. However, avoid cluttering your outline; include only the most important cues.

- **Arrange your notes.** Whether you hand-print or type your speaking outline on paper or note cards, make sure your final version is legible and accessible so that you can refer to it as you speak. Number your cards (or sheets of paper) so that you can keep them in order.

If you plan to use PowerPoint or other presentation software, you can also use the "notes" field on each slide for speaking notes.

FIGURE 13–3
Effective Outline for a 30-Minute Presentation

Includes the
statement of
purpose

Highlights the
purpose in the
introduction

Explains the
investigation
process

Uses a logical and
simple organization

Explains why
the problem
exists

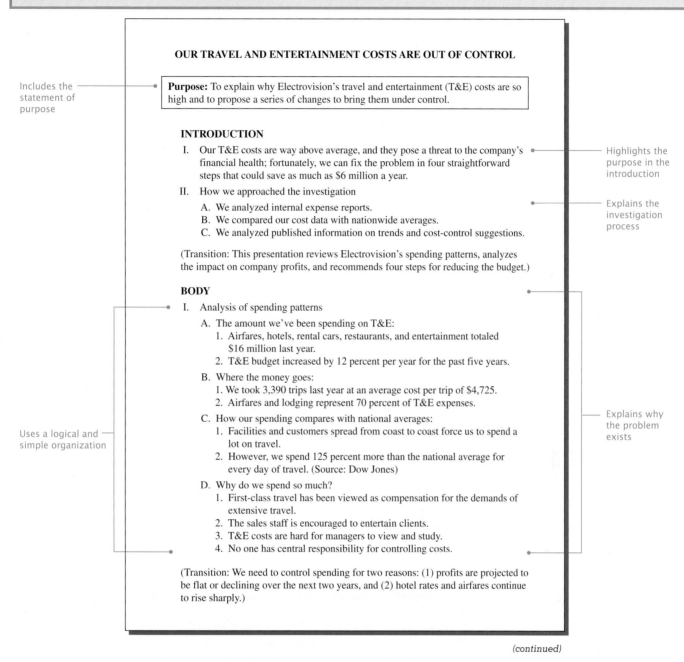

OUR TRAVEL AND ENTERTAINMENT COSTS ARE OUT OF CONTROL

Purpose: To explain why Electrovision's travel and entertainment (T&E) costs are so high and to propose a series of changes to bring them under control.

INTRODUCTION

I. Our T&E costs are way above average, and they pose a threat to the company's financial health; fortunately, we can fix the problem in four straightforward steps that could save as much as $6 million a year.

II. How we approached the investigation
   A. We analyzed internal expense reports.
   B. We compared our cost data with nationwide averages.
   C. We analyzed published information on trends and cost-control suggestions.

(Transition: This presentation reviews Electrovision's spending patterns, analyzes the impact on company profits, and recommends four steps for reducing the budget.)

BODY

I. Analysis of spending patterns
   A. The amount we've been spending on T&E:
      1. Airfares, hotels, rental cars, restaurants, and entertainment totaled $16 million last year.
      2. T&E budget increased by 12 percent per year for the past five years.
   B. Where the money goes:
      1. We took 3,390 trips last year at an average cost per trip of $4,725.
      2. Airfares and lodging represent 70 percent of T&E expenses.
   C. How our spending compares with national averages:
      1. Facilities and customers spread from coast to coast force us to spend a lot on travel.
      2. However, we spend 125 percent more than the national average for every day of travel. (Source: Dow Jones)
   D. Why do we spend so much?
      1. First-class travel has been viewed as compensation for the demands of extensive travel.
      2. The sales staff is encouraged to entertain clients.
      3. T&E costs are hard for managers to view and study.
      4. No one has central responsibility for controlling costs.

(Transition: We need to control spending for two reasons: (1) profits are projected to be flat or declining over the next two years, and (2) hotel rates and airfares continue to rise sharply.)

(continued)

STEP 2: WRITING YOUR PRESENTATION

Although you may never actually write out a presentation word for word, you still engage in the writing process—developing your ideas, structuring support points, phrasing your transitions, and so on. Depending on the situation and your personal style, your actual presentation might follow these initial words closely or might express your thoughts in fresh, spontaneous language. Before you get to the actual writing phase, consider how you should adapt your style to your audience.

FIGURE 13–3
(continued)

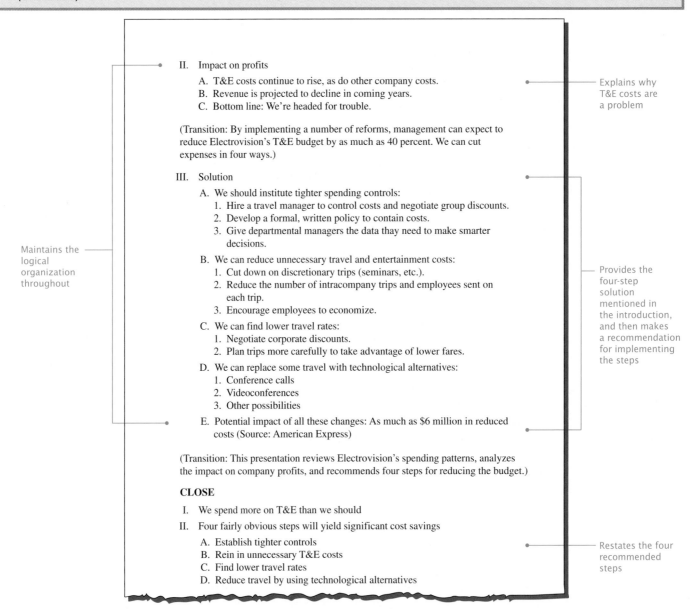

Maintains the logical organization throughout

II. Impact on profits
    A. T&E costs continue to rise, as do other company costs.
    B. Revenue is projected to decline in coming years.
    C. Bottom line: We're headed for trouble.

(Transition: By implementing a number of reforms, management can expect to reduce Electrovision's T&E budget by as much as 40 percent. We can cut expenses in four ways.)

III. Solution
    A. We should institute tighter spending controls:
        1. Hire a travel manager to control costs and negotiate group discounts.
        2. Develop a formal, written policy to contain costs.
        3. Give departmental managers the data thay need to make smarter decisions.
    B. We can reduce unnecessary travel and entertainment costs:
        1. Cut down on discretionary trips (seminars, etc.).
        2. Reduce the number of intracompany trips and employees sent on each trip.
        3. Encourage employees to economize.
    C. We can find lower travel rates:
        1. Negotiate corporate discounts.
        2. Plan trips more carefully to take advantage of lower fares.
    D. We can replace some travel with technological alternatives:
        1. Conference calls
        2. Videoconferences
        3. Other possibilities
    E. Potential impact of all these changes: As much as $6 million in reduced costs (Source: American Express)

(Transition: This presentation reviews Electrovision's spending patterns, analyzes the impact on company profits, and recommends four steps for reducing the budget.)

CLOSE

I. We spend more on T&E than we should
II. Four fairly obvious steps will yield significant cost savings
    A. Establish tighter controls
    B. Rein in unnecessary T&E costs
    C. Find lower travel rates
    D. Reduce travel by using technological alternatives

Explains why T&E costs are a problem

Provides the four-step solution mentioned in the introduction, and then makes a recommendation for implementing the steps

Restates the four recommended steps

Adapting to Your Audience

Adapting to your audience involves a number of issues, from speaking style to technology choices.

What does your audience expect from your presentation? Will you stage a formal presentation in an impressive setting with professionally produced visuals? Or will you lead a casual, roll-up-your-sleeves working session? Your audience's size, your subject, your purpose, your budget, and the time available for preparation all influence the style of your presentation.

If you're speaking to a small group, particularly people you already know, you can use a casual style that encourages audience participation. A small conference room, with your audience seated around a table, may be appropriate. Use simple visuals, and invite your audience to interject comments. Deliver your remarks in a conversational tone, using notes to jog your memory if necessary.

If you're addressing a large audience and the event is an important one, you'll want to establish a more formal atmosphere. A formal style is well suited to announcements about mergers or acquisitions, new products, financial results, and other business milestones. During formal presentations, speakers are often located on a stage or platform, standing behind a lectern and using a microphone so that their remarks can be heard throughout the room or captured for broadcasting or webcasting. These presentations are often accompanied by slides and other visuals showcasing major products, technological breakthroughs, and other information that the speakers want audience members to remember.

Whether your presentation is formal or informal, always choose your words carefully. If you try to impress your audience with obscure or unfamiliar vocabulary, your message will be lost. Make sure you can define all the words you use. And keep things simple. If you repeatedly stumble over a word as you rehearse, use a different one.[7]

Finally, when you're pondering how you'll adapt to your audience, take public speaking etiquette into account. Show consideration for your audience by making good use of their time, addressing them respectfully, and maintaining a professional presence during your speech.

Composing Your Presentation

Just like written documents, oral presentations are composed of distinct elements: the introduction, the body, and the close.

Introduction   A good introduction arouses the audience's interest in your topic, establishes your credibility, and prepares the audience for what will follow. That's a lot to pack into the first few minutes of your presentation, so give yourself plenty of time to develop the words and visuals you'll use to get your presentation off to a great start.

> An effective introduction arouses interest in your topic, establishes your credibility, and prepares the audience for the body of your presentation.

Arousing Audience Interest   Some subjects are naturally more interesting than others. If you will be discussing a matter of profound significance that will personally affect the members of your audience, chances are they'll listen regardless of how you begin. All you really have to do is announce your topic, and you'll have their attention.

Other subjects call for more imagination. How do you get people to listen if you're explaining your pension program to a group of new clerical employees, none of whom will be fully eligible for the program for another five years? The best approach to dealing with an uninterested audience is to appeal to human nature and encourage people to take the subject personally. Show them how they'll be affected as individuals. For example, you might begin by addressing the new clerical employees like this:

> If somebody offered to give you $200,000 in exchange for $5 per week, would you be interested? That's the amount you can expect to collect during your retirement years if you choose to contribute to the voluntary pension plan. During the next two weeks, you will have to decide whether you want to participate. Although retirement is many years away for most of you, it is an important financial decision. During the next 20 minutes, I hope to give you the information you need to make a decision that's best for you and your families.

Another way to arouse the audience's interest is to draw out ideas and encourage comments from the audience throughout your presentation. Table 13–2 suggests several techniques you can use to arouse audience interest and keep listeners involved. Regardless of which technique you choose, always make sure that the introduction matches the tone of your presentation. If the occasion is supposed to be fun, you might begin with something light, but if you're talking business to a group of executives, don't waste their time with cute openings. Avoid jokes and personal anecdotes when you're discussing a serious problem. If you're giving a routine oral report, don't be overly dramatic. Most of all, be natural. Nothing turns off the average audience faster than a trite, staged beginning.

Table 13–2	SIX WAYS TO GET ATTENTION AND KEEP IT
Unite the audience around a common goal	Invite them to help solve a problem, capitalize on an opportunity, or otherwise engage in the topic of your presentation.
Tell a story	Slice-of-life stories are naturally interesting and can be compelling. Be sure your story illustrates an important point.
Pass around a sample	Psychologists say that you can get people to remember your points by appealing to their senses. The best way to do so is to pass around a sample. If your company is in the textile business, let the audience handle some of your fabrics. If you sell chocolates, give everybody a taste.
Ask a question	Asking questions will get the audience actively involved in your presentation and, at the same time, will give you information about them and their needs.
State a startling statistic	People love details. If you can interject an interesting statistic, you can often wake up your audience.
Use humor	Even though the subject of most business presentations is serious, including a light comment now and then can perk up the audience. Just be sure the humor is relevant to the presentation and not offensive to the audience. In general, avoid humor when you and the audience don't share the same native language..

Building Your Credibility   In addition to grabbing the audience's attention, your introduction also has to establish your credibility. If you're a well-known expert in the subject matter or have earned your audience's trust in other situations, you're already ahead of the game. However, if you have no working relationship with your audience or if you're speaking in an area outside your presumed expertise, you need to establish your credibility and do so quickly; people tend to decide within a few minutes whether you're worth listening to.[8]

If someone else will be introducing you to the audience, you can ask this person to present your credentials as well.

Techniques for building credibility vary depending on whether you will be introducing yourself or having someone else introduce you. If a master of ceremonies, conference chair, or other person will introduce you, he or she can present your credentials so that you won't appear boastful. If you will be introducing yourself, keep your comments simple. At the same time, don't be afraid to mention your accomplishments. Your listeners will be curious about your qualifications, so tell them briefly who you are and why you're there. Generally, you need to mention only a few aspects of your background: your position in an organization, your profession, the name of your company. You might say something like this:

I'm Karen Whitney, a market research analyst with Information Resources Corporation. For the past five years, I've specialized in studying high-technology markets. Your director of engineering, John LaBarre, has asked me to talk to you about recent trends in computer-aided design so that you'll have a better idea of how to direct your research efforts.

This speaker establishes credibility by tying her credentials to the purpose of her presentation. By mentioning her company's name, her specialization and position, and the name of the audience's boss, she lets her listeners know immediately that she is qualified to tell them something they need to know. She connects her background to their concerns.

Use the preview to help your audience understand the importance, the structure, and the content of your message.

Previewing Your Message   In addition to arousing audience interest and building your credibility, a good introduction gives your audience a preview of what's ahead. A reader can get an idea of the structure and content of a report by looking at the table of contents and scanning the headings. However, in an oral presentation, you provide that framework with a preview. Without cues from the speaker, the audience may be unable to figure out how the main points of the message fit together.

Your preview should summarize the main idea of your presentation, identify major supporting points, and indicate the order in which you'll develop those points. Tell your listeners in so many words, "This is the subject, and these are the points I will cover." Once you've established the framework, you can be confident that the audience will understand how the individual facts and figures are related to your main idea as you move into the body of your presentation.

Body   The bulk of your speech or presentation is devoted to a discussion of the main points in your outline. Use the same organizational patterns you'd use in a letter, memo, or report, but keep things simple. As Dan Talbott of HP can tell you, your goals are to make sure that (1) the organization of your presentation is clear and (2) your presentation holds the audience's attention.

Connecting Your Ideas   In written documents, you can show how ideas are related on the page or screen by employing a variety of design clues: headings, paragraph indentions, white space, and lists. However, with oral communication—particularly when you aren't using visuals for support—you have to rely primarily on words to link various parts and ideas.

For the small links between sentences and paragraphs, use one or two transitional words: *therefore, because, in addition, in contrast, moreover, for example, consequently, nevertheless,* or *finally*. To link major sections of a presentation, use complete sentences or paragraphs, such as "Now that we've reviewed the problem, let's take a look at some solutions." Every time you shift topics, be sure to stress the connection between ideas. Summarize what's been said, then preview what's to come.

The longer your presentation, the more important your transitions become. If you will be presenting many ideas, audience members may have trouble absorbing them and seeing the relationships among them. Your listeners need clear transitions to guide them to the most important points. Furthermore, they'll appreciate brief, interim summaries to pick up any ideas they may have missed. So by repeating key ideas in your transitions, you can compensate for lapses in your audience's attention. When you actually give your presentation, you might also want to call attention to the transitions by using gestures, changing your tone of voice, or introducing a new visual.

> Use transitions to repeat key ideas, particularly in longer presentations.

Holding Your Audience's Attention   An important part of helping your audience connect your ideas is to hold their attention from start to finish. In addition to the general challenge of keeping readers interested, you have to compensate for another inescapable fact of oral presentations: Your audience can think and read faster than you can speak. If you don't keep their minds engaged, they'll start thinking of other pressing subjects, reading ahead through your handouts, checking e-mail on wireless handhelds, or doing a thousand other things besides paying attention to you. Here are a few helpful tips for keeping the audience tuned into your message:

- **Relate your subject to your audience's needs.** People are interested in things that affect them personally. As much as possible, present every point in light of your audience's needs and values.

> The most important way to hold an audience's attention is to show how your message relates to their individual needs and concerns.

- **Anticipate your audience's questions.** Try to anticipate as many questions as you can, and address these questions in the body of your presentation. You'll also want to prepare and reserve additional material to use during the question-and-answer period should the audience ask for greater detail.

- **Use clear, vivid language.** People become bored quickly when they don't understand the speaker. If your presentation will involve abstract ideas, show how those abstractions connect with everyday life. Use familiar words, short sentences, and

Short, simple messages help speakers hold an audience's attention in noisy, distracting environments.

concrete examples. Be sure to throw in some variety as well; repeating the same words and phrases over and over puts people to sleep.

- **Explain the relationship between your subject and familiar ideas.** Show how your subject is related to ideas that audience members already understand, and give people a way to categorize and remember your points.[9]

- **Ask for opinions or pause occasionally for questions or comments.** Audience feedback helps you determine whether your listeners understand a key point before you launch into another section. Feedback also gives your audience a chance to switch for a time from listening to participating, which helps them engage with your message and develop a sense of shared ownership.

- **Illustrate your ideas with visuals.** Visuals enliven your message, help you connect with audience members, and help them remember your message more effectively (see "Enhancing Your Presentation with Effective Visuals," on the following page).

Close   The close of a speech or presentation is critical for two reasons: Audiences tend to focus more carefully as they wait for you to wrap up, and they will leave with your final words ringing in their ears. Before closing your presentation, tell listeners that you're about to finish so that they'll make one final effort to listen intently. Don't be afraid to sound obvious. Consider saying something such as "In conclusion" or "To sum it all up." You want people to know that this is the final segment of your presentation.

Plan your close carefully so that your audience leaves with your main idea fresh in their minds.

Restating Your Main Points   Once you've decided how to announce your close, repeat your main idea. Emphasize what you want your audience to do or to think, and stress the key motivating factor that will encourage them to respond that way. Finally, reinforce your theme by restating your main supporting points. A few sentences are generally enough to refresh people's memories. One speaker ended a presentation on the company's executive compensation program by repeating his four specific recommendations and then concluding with a memorable statement that would motivate his audience to take action:

> We can all be proud of the way our company has grown. However, if we want to continue that growth, we need to adjust our executive compensation program to reflect competitive practices. If we don't, our best people will look for opportunities elsewhere.
>
> In summary, our survey has shown that we need to do four things to improve executive compensation:
>
> - Increase the overall level of compensation
> - Install a cash bonus program
> - Offer a variety of stock-based incentives
> - Improve our health insurance and pension benefits
>
> By making these improvements, we can help our company cross the threshold of growth to face our industry's largest competitors.

Such repetition of key ideas greatly improves the chance that your audience will hear your message in the way you intended.

Describing Next Steps   Some presentations require the audience to reach a decision or agree to take specific action, in which case the close provides a clear wrap-up. If the audience agrees on an issue covered in the presentation, you'll want to review the consensus in a sentence or two. If they don't agree, you'll want to make the lack of consensus clear by saying something like "We seem to have some fundamental disagreement on this question." Then be ready to suggest a method of resolving the differences. If you're not sure in advance how your audience will respond, prepare alternative closes. Few things in public speaking are more embarrassing than trying to launch into a rousing, positive finish when you know you've lost your audience somewhere along the way.

> If you need to have the audience make a decision or agree to take action, make sure the responsibilities for doing so are clear.

If you expect any action to occur as a result of your speech, be sure to explain who is responsible for doing what. One effective technique is to list the action items, with an estimated completion date and the name of the person or team responsible. You can present this list in a visual and ask each person on the list to agree to accomplish his or her assigned task by the target date. This public commitment to action is good insurance that something will happen.

If the required action is likely to be difficult, make sure that everyone understands the problems involved. You don't want people to leave the presentation thinking their tasks will be easy, only to discover later that the jobs are quite demanding. You'll want everyone to have a realistic attitude and to be prepared to handle whatever arises. So when composing your presentation, use the close to alert people to potential difficulties or pitfalls.

Ending on a Strong Note   Make sure that your final remarks are upbeat and memorable. After summarizing the key points of your presentation, conclude with a quote, a call to action, or some encouraging words. For instance, you might stress the benefits of action or express confidence in the listeners' ability to accomplish the work ahead. An alternative is to end with a question or a statement that will leave your audience thinking.

> Plan your final statement carefully so you can end on a strong, positive note.

At the completion of your presentation, your audience should feel satisfied. The close is not the place to introduce new ideas or to alter the mood of the presentation. Even if parts of your presentation are downbeat, you will want to close on a positive note. As with everything else in your oral presentation, compose your closing remarks carefully. You don't want to wind up on stage with nothing to say but "Well, I guess that's it."

Document Makeover

IMPROVE THIS SPEECH

To practice correcting drafts of actual documents, visit your online course or the access-code protected portion of the Companion Website. Click "Document Makeovers," then click Chapter 13. You will find a speech that contains problems and errors relating to what you've learned in this chapter about preparing effective speeches and oral presentations. Use the "Final Draft" decision tool to create an improved version of this speech. Check the message for effective choices in scope, style, opening, use of transitions, and closing.

Enhancing Your Presentations with Effective Visuals

Visuals can improve the quality and impact of your oral presentation by creating interest, illustrating points that are difficult to explain in words alone, adding variety, and increasing the audience's ability to absorb and remember information. Behavioral research has shown that visuals can improve learning by up to 400 percent because humans can process visuals 60,000 times faster than text.[10]

> Thoughtfully designed visuals create interest, illustrate complex points in your message, add variety, and help the audience absorb and remember information.

As a speaker, you'll find that visuals can help you remember the details of the message (no small feat in a lengthy presentation) and improve your professional image: Speakers who use presentation visuals generally appear better prepared and more knowledgeable than speakers who do not.

You can select from a variety of visuals to enhance oral presentations, each with unique advantages and disadvantages:

An effective electronic presentation can significantly boost the retention level of audience members.

In most businesses, electronic presentations are now the presentation technology of choice, although they're certainly not the only option.

Think through your presentation outline carefully before designing your visuals.

Accuracy and simplicity are keys to effective visuals.

- **Overhead transparencies.** Overhead transparencies have been the workhorses of business presentations for decades, and some professionals still prefer them to electronic presentations. You can create overheads using graphics or presentation software, your word processor, or just a pen if you need something quickly. Transparencies don't require the latest computer or projection equipment, you can write on them during a presentation, and they never crash on you—as computers have been known to do. On the downside, they're limited to static displays and they're impossible to edit once you've printed them.

- **Electronic presentations.** Easy-to-use software and affordable hardware have made electronic presentations the visual of choice in most business situations today. An **electronic presentation** or *slide show* consists of a series of **electronic slides** composed using popular computer software such as Microsoft PowerPoint or Apple Keynote. To display an electronic presentation, you simply connect your computer to a portable projector (some are now small enough to carry around in your pocket) or a built-in unit that's part of a multimedia system in a conference room. Electronic presentations have numerous advantages: They are easy to edit and update (right up to the last second before your presentation starts); you can add sound, photos, video, and animation; they can be incorporated into online meetings, webcasts, and *webinars* (a common term for web-based seminars); and you can record self-running presentations for trade shows, websites, and other uses. The primary disadvantages are the cost of equipment, the potential complexity involved in creating multimedia presentations, and the risk, however slight these days, that your hardware or software won't cooperate when it's show time.

- **Chalkboards and whiteboards.** Chalkboards and whiteboards are effective tools for recording points made during small-group sessions. Because these visuals are produced on the spot, they are great for the flexible, spontaneous nature of workshops and brainstorming sessions. New electronic whiteboards let you capture the information written on them; you simply hit a button to print a hardcopy or distribute an electronic version via e-mail.

- **Flip charts.** Flip charts are great for recording comments and questions during your presentation or for keeping track of ideas during a brainstorming session. They are about as low tech as you can get, but flip charts are inexpensive and 100 percent dependable.

- **Other visuals.** Be creative when choosing visuals to support our presentation. A video recording of a group of customers talking about your company can have a lot more impact than a series of slides that summarize what they said. In technical or scientific presentations, a sample of a product or type of material lets your audience experience your subject directly. Designers and architects use mockups and models to help people envision what a final creation will look like.

This chapter focuses on electronic presentations, the mainstay of business presentations today, although most of these design tips apply to overhead transparencies as well.

Once you've decided on the form your visuals will take, think through your presentation plan carefully before you start creating anything. Visuals are powerful devices, and that power can just as easily harm your efforts as help. Above all, remember that visuals support your spoken message; they should never replace it or overshadow it. A discerning audience—the sort of people who can influence the direction of your career—are not easily fooled by visual razzle-dazzle. If your analysis is shaky or your conclusions are suspect, an over-the-top visual production won't help your presentation succeed.

Creating Effective Slides When it comes time to make design choices, from selecting fonts to deciding whether or not to include a photo, let accuracy and simplicity guide you. Doing so has several advantages. First, it takes less time to create simple materials. Second, simple visuals reduce the chances of distraction and misinterpretation. Third, the more "bells and whistles" you have in your presentation, the more likely it is that something will go wrong.

Writing Readable Content   Effective slides start with readable content. One of the biggest mistakes presenters make is overloading slides with too much information, either because they believe that every word or concept should be illustrated by a slide, or they use their slides as speaker's notes—focusing on their own needs instead of the needs of their audience. Remember that slides are not intended to display your entire script or highlight each point you make.[11] Crowded slides are aggravating to readers because they are difficult to read.

Effective text slides supplement your words and help the audience follow the flow of ideas. They are simplified outlines of your presentation and are used to highlight key points, summarize and preview your message, signal major shifts in thought, illustrate concepts, or help create interest in your oral message. They are not the presentation itself. When writing content for text slides, keep your message short and simple:

Packing slides with too much information is a common beginner's mistake; use slide text to emphasize key points, not to convey your entire message.

- Limit each slide to one thought, concept, or idea.

- Limit the content to about 40 words—with no more than 6 lines of text containing about 6 or 7 words per line.

- Write short bulleted phrases rather than long sentences or blocks of text.

- Phrase list items in parallel grammatical form to facilitate quick reading.

- Make your slides easy to read by using the active voice.

- Include short informative titles.

Figure 13–4 is a good example of text slides that have been revised according to these principles to make their content more readable.

Modifying Graphics for Slides   The techniques you learned in Chapter 11 for creating effective charts, diagrams, maps, drawings, and tables for written documents apply to presentation visuals, but with an important caution: Visuals for oral presentations need to be much simpler. If you're adapting visuals originally created for a written report, you will probably need to simplify them. Detailed visuals that might look fine on the printed page can be too dense and complicated for presentations.

Start by reducing the level detail, eliminating anything that is not absolutely essential to the message. If necessary, break information into more than one graphic illustration. Whenever you can do so without confusing the audience, look for shorter variations of numerical values. For instance, round off a number such as $12,500.72 to $12 or $12.5, and then label the axis to indicate thousands.

With the basic design in place, use graphical elements to highlight key points. Use arrows, boldface type, and color to direct your audience's eyes to the main point of a visual. Summarize the intent of the graphic in one clear phrase, such as "Earnings have increased by 15 percent." Modify the size of the graphic to accommodate the size of a slide. Leave plenty of white space, use colors that stand out from the slide's background, and choose a font that's clear and easy to read.

Selecting Design Elements   Once you've composed the text and created the graphic elements of your slides, you're ready to focus on putting them together in an attractive, professional layout. Chapter 11 highlights six principles of effective design: consistency, contrast, balance, emphasis, simplicity, and audience experience and expectations. Pay close attention to these principles as you select the color, background and foreground designs, artwork, fonts, and typestyles for your slides:

To design effective slides, you need to consider five principles of effective design: continuity, contrast, emphasis, simplicity, and audience experience.

FIGURE 13–4
Writing Readable Content

What Is Supply-Chain Management?

Developing long-term partnerships among channel members working together to create a distribution system that reduces inefficiencies, costs, and redundancies while creating a competitive advantage and satisfying customers

What Is Supply-Chain Management?

- Partnering with channel members
- Reducing channel inefficiencies
- Creating a competitive advantage
- Satisfying customers

Figure 13–4a—Inappropriate paragraph style.   Figure 13–4b—Appropriate bulleted phrases

The definition provided in Figure 13–4a was taken from a persuasive report written by the speaker. The paragraph style is inappropriate for slides and difficult to read. Figure 13–4b restates the definition in short phrases that highlight the key point of the definition. The speaker will explain these points while showing the slide.

Benefits of Integrated Supply Chain

- Companies can carry less inventory
- Companies can design, ramp up, and retire products rapidly
- Companies can outsource some or all of the manufacturing function
- Online order entry contributes to enhanced customer satisfaction
- Shorter engineering-to-production cycle times help increase market share

Benefits of Integration

- Reduced inventory levels
- Reduced product costs
- Increased customer-response time
- Increased customer satisfaction
- Increased market share
- Improved product quality

Figure 13–4c—Inappropriate wordy bullets   Figure 13–4d—Appropriate concise bullets

Although Figure 13–4c falls within acceptable word-count guidelines, unnecessary words still make the slide difficult to read. Figure 13–4d is an improved version of Figure 13–4c: The sentences are converted to short, parallel phrases, and the slide's title is condensed.

Color is more than just decoration; colors have meanings themselves, based on both cultural experience and the relationships that you established between the colors in your designs.

- **Color.** Color is a critical design element that can grab attention, emphasize important ideas, and create contrast. Research shows that color visuals can account for 60 percent of an audience's acceptance or rejection of an idea. Color can increase willingness to read by up to 80 percent, and it can enhance learning and improve retention by more than 75 percent.[12] Your color choices can also stimulate various emotions, as Table 13–3 suggests. For instance, if you wish to excite your audience, add some warm colors such as red and orange to your slides. If you wish to achieve a more relaxed and receptive environment, blue would be a better choice.[13] When selecting color, limit your choices to a few complementary ones, and keep in mind that some colors work better together than others. Contrasting colors, for example, increase readability. So when selecting color for backgrounds, titles, and text, avoid choosing colors that are close in hue, such as brown on green or blue on purple.[14]

COLOR AND EMOTION			Table 13–3

Color	Emotional Associations	Best Uses
Blue	Peaceful, soothing, tranquil, cool, trusting	Background for electronic business presentations (usually dark blue); safe and conservative
White	Neutral, innocent, pure, wise	Font color of choice for most electronic business presentations with a dark background
Yellow	Warm, bright, cheerful, enthusiastic	Text bullets and subheadings with a dark background
Red	Passionate, dangerous, active, painful	Promote action or stimulate audience; seldom used as a background ("in the red" specifically refers to financial losses)
Green	Assertive, prosperous, envious, relaxed	Highlight and accent color (green symbolizes money in the United States but not in other countries).

When changing colors from slide to slide, don't switch back and forth from very dark to very bright; the effect is jarring to the audience's eyes.[15] Lastly, remember that color may have a different meaning in certain cultures (see Chapter 3). So if you are creating slides for international audiences, be sensitive to cultural differences.

- **Background designs and artwork.** Electronic slides have two layers or levels of graphic design: the background and foreground. The background is the equivalent of paper in a printed report and generally speaking, the less your background does, the better. Cluttered or flashy backgrounds tend to distract from your message. As part of the background, you may want to add a company logo, the date, the presentation title, and a running slide number to help both you and the audience follow along. Just be sure to keep all these elements small and unobtrusive. Also, be sure to check whether your company has a standard design; many companies now have custom-designed PowerPoint templates that ensure consistency for all their presentations.

- **Foreground designs and artwork.** The foreground contains the unique text and graphic elements that make up each individual slide. In the foreground, artwork can be either functional or decorative. Functional artwork includes photos, technical drawings, charts, and other visual elements containing information that's part of your message. In contrast, decorative artwork is there simply to enhance the look of your slides. Decorative artwork is the least important element of any slide, but it tends to cause the most trouble for anyone inexperienced in designing slides. Clip art is probably the biggest troublemaker here because it is so easy to use and—misuse. Used with care, clip art can add visual interest (see Figure 13–5). In contrast, poorly chosen clip art gives slides an amateurish, cartoony feel.

  Artwork in the foreground of your slides can be either decorative or functional; use decorative artwork sparingly.

- **Fonts and type styles.** Type is harder to read on screen than on the printed page because projectors have lower *resolution* (the ability to display fine details) than the printers typically available in offices today. Consequently, you need to choose fonts and type styles with care. Sans serif fonts are usually easier to read than serif fonts (see Figure 13–6). In general, avoid script or decorative fonts and italicized type. Use both uppercase and lowercase letters, with extra white space between lines of text, and limit your fonts to one or two per slide (if two fonts are used, reserve one for headings and the other for bullet points and other text). Choose font sizes that are easy to read from anywhere in the room, usually between 24 and 36 points. Headings of the same level of importance should use the same font, type size, and color. Once you have selected your fonts and type styles, test them for readability by viewing sample slides from a distance.

  Many of the fonts available on your computer are difficult to read on screen, so they aren't good choices for presentation slides.

FIGURE 13–5
Using Clip Art Effectively

Figure 13–5a

Figure 13–5b

Both of these slides use clip art effectively. In Figure 13–5a, placing the small target in the title adds visual interest without distracting from the busy text area of the slide. Figure 13–5b is a title slide, so using a similar piece of clip art emphasizes the theme of the presentation. The clip art can be larger in this case because there is no competing text.

With so many choices at your fingertips, maintaining consistency in your design is critical. Audiences start to assign meaning to visual elements beginning with the first slide. For instance, if the first slide presents the most important information in bright yellow, 36-point Arial font, your audience will expect the same font treatment for the most important information on the second and third slides as well, so when choosing fonts and point size, be consistent. Also be consistent in your layout. Make sure items that repeat on every slide, such as the date and the company logo, are in the same location on every slide. Otherwise, you'll distract your readers as they try to figure out the arrangement of each new slide.

Fortunately, software designed specifically for presentations makes consistency easy to achieve. You simply create a *slide master* using the colors, fonts, and other

FIGURE 13–6
Selecting Readable Fonts and Type Styles

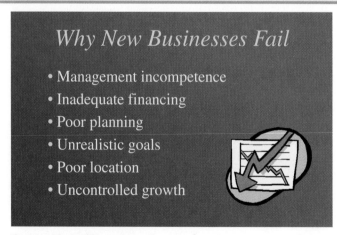

Figure 13–6a Times New Roman font

Figure 13–6b Arial font

Times New Roman is a standard font for many print documents; however, as Figure 13–6a demonstrates, the serifs at the end of each letter make it difficult to read on screen, and so does the italicized type. As Figure 13–6b shows, sans serif fonts such as Arial are a better choice for slides; they are cleaner and easier to read from a distance.

FIGURE 13–7
PowerPoint Slide Master

Whenever you want to change all the slides in a presentation in exactly the same way, use the slide master. Be sure to apply a design template before viewing the slide master so that you can see the fonts and color choices that will be applied to every slide (you can always override these selections on individual slides).

design elements you've chosen, then these choices automatically show up on every slide in the presentation (see Figure 13–7). In addition, you can maintain consistency by choosing a predefined layout from those available in your software—which helps ensure that bulleted lists, charts, graphics, and other elements show up in predictable places on each slide. The less that readers have to work to interpret your slide designs, the more attention they can pay to your message.

Design inconsistencies confuse and annoy audiences; don't change colors and other design elements randomly throughout your presentation.

Adding Animation and Special Effects   Today's presentation software offers a wide array of options for livening up your slides, including sound, animation, video clips, transition effects from one slide to the next, and hyperlinks to websites and other resources. The trick is to make sure that any effects you use support your message. As always, think about the impact that all these effects will have on your audience and use only those special effects that support your message.[16] Animation and special effects fall into four categories: functional animation, transitions and builds, hyperlinks, and multimedia.

Just as static graphic elements can be either functional or decorative, so too can animated elements. *Functional animation* involves motion that is directly related to your message, such as a highlight arrow that moves around the screen to emphasize specific points in a technical diagram. Such animation is also a great way to demonstrate sequences and procedures. For a training session on machinery repair, for example, you can show a schematic diagram of the machinery and walk your audience through each step of the troubleshooting process, highlighting each step on screen as you address it verbally. In contrast, animation that is merely decorative needs to be used with great care. With PowerPoint and other presentation software, you can have a block of text cartwheel in from outer space, change colors, change font and font size, spin around in circles, blink on and off, wave back and forth, crawl around the screen, then disappear one letter at a time like some sort of erasing typewriter. These effects don't add any functional value to your communication effort, and they easily distract audiences.

You can animate just about everything in an electronic presentation; resist the temptation to do so—make sure the animation has a purpose.

Transitions and *builds* are similar to animation but involve the way that slides and individual slide elements are presented on screen. **Transitions** control how one slide replaces another, such as having the current slide gently fade out before the next slide fades in. Subtle transitions like this can ease your viewers' gaze from one slide to the next. However, many of the transition effects now available (such as checkerboards,

Some of the slide transitions available in presentation software are distracting and can quickly begin to annoy audiences.

pinwheels, and spinning "newsflashes") not only disrupt the flow of your presentation, they can make your entire presentation seem amateurish. **Builds** control the release of text, graphics, and other elements on individual slides. With builds you can make your bullet points appear one at a time rather than having all of them appear on a slide at once, thereby making it easier for you and the audience to focus on each new message point.

Hyperlinks and *action buttons* can be real lifesavers when you need flexibility in your presentations or want to share different kinds of files with the audience. A **hyperlink** instructs your computer to jump to another slide in your presentation, to a website, or to another program entirely. Hyperlinks can be either simple underlined text (like most of the links you see on a website) or they can be assigned to **action buttons**, which are a variety of preprogrammed icons available in PowerPoint. Action buttons let you perform such common tasks as jumping forward or backward to a specific slide or opening a document or spreadsheet. Using hyperlinks and action buttons is also a great way to build flexibility into your presentations. For instance, if you need to adapt one presentation for a variety of audiences and situations, you can create a menu of action buttons that launch whatever subset of the presentation is appropriate for each scenario.

Multimedia elements offer the ultimate in active presentations. Say that a few words from your company president would help bolster your argument but she's not available to speak at your presentation. Don't worry, you can capture her on video beforehand, include the video clip in your PowerPoint file, and insert the video clip file as an object on your slide. Then all you need to decide is whether you want to activate the clip manually or have it play automatically whenever you show that slide. For more advanced digital video, you can use such specialized products as Adobe Premiere Pro or Macromedia Director (samples of which can be viewed at the respective companies' website).

Giving Presentations Online

With the global reach of today's business organizations, you can expect that at some point in your career, you'll be asked to deliver a presentation online. In some companies, online presentations have already become a routine matter, conducted via internal groupware, virtual meeting systems, or webcast systems designed specifically for online presentations. In most cases, you'll communicate through some combination of audio, video, and data presentations (for instance, your PowerPoint slides). Your audience will view your presentation either on their individual computer screens or via a projector in a conference room.

The benefits of online presentations are considerable, including the opportunity to communicate with a geographically dispersed audience at a fraction of the cost of travel and the ability for a project team or an entire organization to meet at a moment's notice. Online presentations can also be less disruptive for the members of your audience, giving them the options of viewing your presentation from their desks and listening to only those parts that apply to them. However, the challenges for a presenter can be significant, thanks to that layer of technology between you and your audience. Many of those "human moments" that guide and encourage you through an in-person presentation won't travel across the digital divide. For instance, it's often harder to tell whether your audience is bored or confused, since your view of them is usually confined to small video images. Moreover, the technology itself can be a source of trouble from time to time, with dropped Internet connections, untrained users, and other problems. However, online systems continue to improve, and presenters who master this new mode of communication will definitely have an advantage in tomorrow's business environment.

To ensure successful online presentations, regardless of the system you're using, keep the following advice in mind:

- **Consider sending preview study materials ahead of time.** If your presentation covers complicated or unfamiliar material, consider sending a brief message ahead of time so that your audience can familiarize themselves with any important background information.

Margin notes:

You can increase the flexibility of your presentation slides with hyperlinks that let you jump to different slides, websites, or other displays at will.

If you have access to video clips, they can add memorable, engaging content to your presentations, as long as they are relevant, interesting, and brief.

Online presentations give you a way to reach more people in less time, but they require special preparation and skills.

- **Keep your content—and your presentation of it—as simple as possible.** Break complicated slides down into multiple slides if necessary, and keep the direction of your discussion clear so that no one gets lost. Moreover, make sure any streaming video presentations are short; audiences dislike being forced to sit through long speeches online.[17]

- **Ask for feedback frequently.** You won't have as much of the visual feedback that alerts you when audience members are confused (such as perplexed looks or blanks stares), and many online viewers will be reluctant to call attention to themselves by interrupting you to ask for clarification. So you'll have to draw out feedback as you go.

- **Consider the viewing experience from the audience's side.** Will they be able to see what you think they can see? For instance, webcast video is typically displayed in a comparatively tiny window on screen. (Viewers can expand the size of the window, but then they lose visual resolution.) Consequently, if you try to use video to demonstrate the detailed operation of a piece of equipment, your audience might not be able to see those details.

- **Make sure your audience can receive the sort of content you intend to use.** For instance, some corporate firewalls (electronic "safety gates" on corporate networks) don't allow streaming media, so your webcast video might not survive the trip.[18]

- **Allow plenty of time for everyone to get connected and familiar with the screen they're viewing.** Build extra time into your schedule to ensure that everyone is connected, particularly if some are connecting from dial-up lines in hotel rooms, wireless hot spots, and other remote locations.

Last but not least, don't get lost in the technology. With virtual white boards, real-time polling, collaborative editing, and other powerful features, electronic communication systems offer lots of gadgets that can distract both you and your audience. Use these tools whenever they'll help, but remember that the most important aspect of any presentation is getting the audience to receive, understand, and embrace your message.

> Once you master the technology, you can spend less time thinking about it and more time thinking about the most important elements of the presentation: your message and your audience.

STEP 3: COMPLETING YOUR PRESENTATION

With a draft of your presentation in hand, you're ready to complete the development of your presentation. As with written communication, this third step starts with the all-important task of revising your message to ensure appropriate content. Edit your presentation for clarity and conciseness as you would any business message. If you're using electronic slides, make sure they are readable, concise, consistent from slide to slide, and fully operational (including transitions, builds, and animations). The first step in completing your presentation is finalizing your slides and support materials.

Finalizing Slides and Support Materials   Electronic presentation software can help you throughout the editing and revision process. As Figure 13–8 shows, the *slide sorter view* lets you see some or all of the slides in your presentation on a single screen. Use this view to add and delete slides, reposition slides, check slides for design consistency, and verify the operation of animation and transition effects.

> Use the slide sorter view to verify and modify the organization of your slides.

In addition to the content slides that you've already created, you can help your audience follow the flow of your presentation by creating three types of *navigational slides:*

> Navigational slides help your audience keep track of what you've covered already and what you plan to cover next.

- **Cover slides.** Make a good first impression on your audience with a cover slide, the equivalent of a report's title page (such as the first slide in Figure 13–8). Cover slides can contain the title of your presentation, a subtitle if appropriate, your name, the date, and your company affiliation if you're addressing an audience outside your firm.

FIGURE 13–8
Slide Sorter View

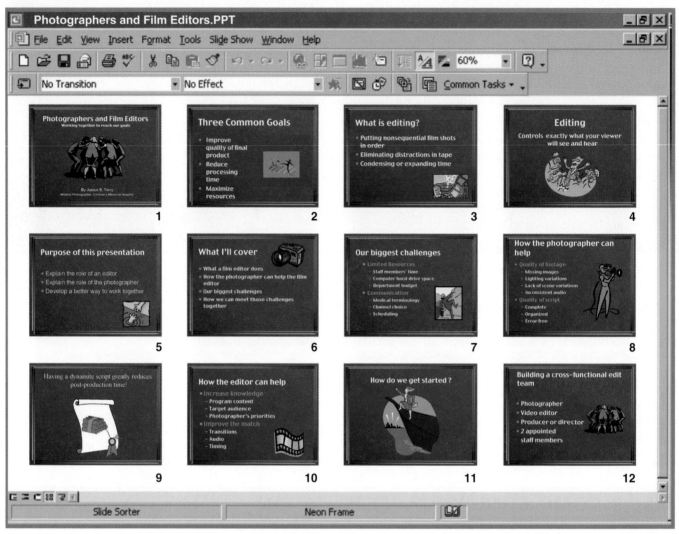

Examining thumbnails of slides on one screen is the best way to check the overall design of your final product. The slide sorter also makes it easy to ponder the order and organization of your presentation; you can change the position of any slide simply by clicking and dragging it to a new position.

- **Introduction slides.** Introduction slides define the topic of your presentation, clarify the topic, emphasize why you are speaking on this topic, and establish any expectations you may have of the audience. Are you going to ask them to make a decision or take some action? Or are you simply explaining a new company policy?[19] Slide 6 in Figure 13–8 is a good example of an introduction slide.

- **Blueprint slides.** For longer presentations, consider using *blueprint slides* that show the audience where you are in the presentation. For instance, in Figure 13–9, the slide on the left identifies the sequence of four topics to be covered in the presentation. Then at the beginning of each of these four sections, the slide is repeated, along with a visual indication such as the checkmark in the slide on the right. In this way, blueprint slides remind the audience of what you've already covered and what you have left to cover.

Use handout materials to support the points made in your presentation and to offer the audience additional information on your topic.

With your slides working properly and in clear, logical order, consider whether some additional material will help your audience either during or after your presentations. *Handouts* are a terrific way to offer your audience additional material without overloading your slides with information. Possibilities for good handout materials

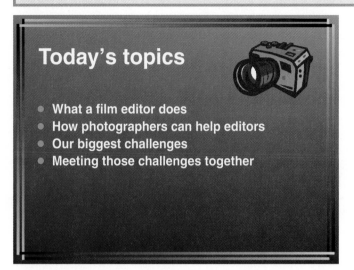

Figure 13–9a Blueprint slide   Figure 13–9b Moving blueprint slide

A blueprint slide near the beginning of a presentation, such as Figure 13–9a, defines the structure of the presentation so that the audience knows where the speaker is going. As the speaker finishes each subsection, the blueprint is then shown again and updated to indicate progress. For instance, the yellow checkmark and text in Figure 13–9b highlight the speaker's next topic.

include complex charts and diagrams that are too unwieldy for the screen, articles and technical papers, case studies, lists of websites, and printed copies of your slides.[20]

Finally, think about a backup plan. What will you do if your laptop won't boot up or the projector dies? Can you get by without your slides? For important presentations, consider having backup equipment on standby, loaded with your presentation, and ready to go. At the very least, have enough printed handouts ready to give the audience so that, as a last resort, you can give your presentation "on paper."

Preparing to Speak

With all of your materials in place, your next step is to decide which method of speaking you want to use. You have three main options: memorizing your material word for word, reading a printout of your material, or speaking from notes. Memorizing is usually not a good choice, unless you're a trained actor accustomed to delivering lines. In the best of circumstances you'll probably sound stilted; in the worst, you might forget your lines. Besides, you'll often need to address audience questions during your speech, so you must be flexible enough to adjust your speech as you go. However, memorizing a quotation, an opening paragraph, or a few concluding remarks can bolster your confidence and strengthen your delivery.

Reading your speech is sometimes necessary, such as when delivering legal information, policy statements, or other messages that must be conveyed in an exact manner. However, for most business presentations, reading is a poor choice because it limits your interaction with the audience and lacks the fresh, dynamic feel of natural talking. In any event, *never* stand in front of an audience and simply read the text on your slides. If you do plan to read a prepared speech, with or without slides or other visuals, practice enough so that you can still maintain eye contact with your audience. Print your speech with triple-spaced lines, wide margins, and large type. You might even want to include stage cues, such as *pause, raise hands, lower voice.*

Speaking from notes, with the help of an outline, note cards, or visuals, is usually the most effective and easiest delivery mode. This approach gives you something to

Speaking from carefully prepared notes is the easiest and most effective delivery mode for most speakers.

refer to and still allows for plenty of eye contact, interaction with the audience, and improvisation in response to audience feedback. (When speaking from notes, be sure to use stiff note cards; nervousness is more easily exposed by shaking sheets of paper.)

From time to time, you may have to give an *impromptu,* or unrehearsed, speech when you have virtually no time at all to prepare. If you have the option, avoid speaking unprepared unless you're well versed in the topic or have lots of experience at improvising in front of a live audience. When you're asked to speak "off the cuff," take a moment to think through what you'll say and then focus on your key points. If you absolutely cannot say something intelligent and effective on the subject at hand, it's usually better to explain that you can't and ask for an opportunity to prepare some remarks for a later time or date.

Practicing Your Delivery

You're now just one step away from giving your presentation, and it's a step that too many novice presenters overlook: practicing the delivery of your presentation. So many things can go wrong in a major presentation, including equipment glitches, timing problems, and that sinking feeling that you don't know what to say next. That's why experienced speakers always practice important presentations. If you can arrange an audience of several helpful colleagues, by all means do so. They can tell you if your slides are understandable and whether your delivery is effective. A day or two before you're ready to step on stage for an important talk, make sure you can give a positive response to the following questions:

Learning to focus on the audience and interact with them while using electronic slides or other visual aids takes practice.

The more you practice, the more confidence you'll have in yourself and your material.

Make sure you're comfortable with the equipment you'll be expected to use; you don't want to be fumbling with controls while the audience is watching and waiting.

- **Can you present your material naturally, without reading your slides word-for-word?** Your audience wants you to talk to them, not read to them. If you need to refer to your speaking notes, either print a copy or take advantage of the "Presenter View" feature in Microsoft PowerPoint. With Presenter View (which requires a PC capable of displaying on two monitors at once), you can see your notes privately on your own PC screen while your audience sees your regular slides on the presentation screen. (Presenter View is found in the "Set Up Show" dialog box in the Slide Show menu.)

- **Is the equipment working—and do you know how to work it?** Verify that your computer will work with the projector; sometimes you need to adjust the resolution of your computer screen to make it compatible with a particular projector. You don't want to find yourself struggling with the projector in front of a restless audience. Some presentation tools, such as wireless remote controls for your laptop computer, need to have software installed on your computer before they'll operate, so don't bring some fancy new gadget to the conference room without trying it out first.

- **Is your timing on track?** Your practice runs, particularly if you can arrange to speak in front of a test audience, will give you a good idea of how much time you'll need. Now is the time to trim, not when you're live on stage.

- **Can you easily pronounce all the words you plan to use?** Everyone stumbles over certain words, and your tongue is more likely to get tied up when you're under pressure and your mouth is dry.

- **Have you decided how you're going to introduce your slides?** Effective speakers usually introduce the slide before they show it. Doing so allows you to set the stage before your audience starts reading the slide and jumping to their own conclusions.

- **Have you anticipated likely questions and objections?** Put yourself in the audience's shoes and try to imagine what issues they might have about your content, then think through your answers ahead of time. Don't assume you can handle whatever comes up.[21]

With experience, you'll get a feel for how much practice is enough in any given situation. For an important presentation, four or five practice runs is not excessive. Your credibility is dramatically enhanced when you move seamlessly through your presentation, matching effective words with each slide. Practicing helps keep you on track, helps you maintain a conversational tone with your audience, and boosts your confidence and composure.

You'll know you've practiced enough when you can present the material at a comfortable pace and in a conversational tone, without the need to read your slides or constantly refer to your notes.

If you're addressing an audience that doesn't speak your language, consider using an interpreter. Working with an interpreter does constrain your presentation somewhat. For one thing, you must speak slowly enough for the interpreter to keep up with you; however, don't speak so slowly that the rest of your audience loses interest. Send your interpreter a copy of your speech and visuals as far in advance of your presentation as possible. If your audience is likely to include persons with hearing impairments, be sure to team up with a sign-language interpreter as well.

Any time you deliver an oral presentation to people from other cultures, you may need to adapt the content of your presentation. It is also important to take into account any cultural differences in appearance, mannerisms, and other customs. Your interpreter or host will be able to suggest appropriate changes for a specific audience or particular occasion.

Overcoming Anxiety

If you're nervous about facing an audience, you're not alone: Even speakers with years of experience feel some anxiety about getting up in front of an audience. Polished speakers know how to use that nervous energy to their advantage. For starters, think of nervousness as an indication that you care about your audience, your topic, and the occasion. If your palms get wet or your mouth goes dry, don't think of it as nerves—think of it as excitement. Such stimulation can give you the extra energy you need to make your presentation sparkle. Here are some ways to harness your nervous energy to become a more confident speaker:[22]

- **Prepare more material than necessary.** Combined with a genuine interest in your topic, extra knowledge will reduce your anxiety.

Preparation is the best antidote for anxiety.

- **Practice.** The more familiar you are with your material, the less panic you'll feel.

- **Think positively.** See yourself as polished and professional, and your audience will too.

- **Visualize your success.** Use the few minutes before you actually begin speaking to tell yourself you're on and you're ready. Visualize mental images of yourself in front of the audience, feeling confident, prepared, and able to handle any situation that might arise.[23]

- **Take a few deep breaths.** Before you begin to speak, remember that your audience wants you to succeed, too.

- **Be ready.** Have your first sentence memorized and on the tip of your tongue.

- **Be comfortable.** Dress appropriately for the situation but as comfortably as possible. Drink plenty of water before your scheduled presentation time to ensure that your voice is well hydrated (bring a bottle of water with you, too). If possible, adjust the temperature in the room to your personal preference. The fewer physical distractions you have, the better you'll perform.

- **Don't panic.** If you sense that you're starting to race—a natural response when you're nervous—stop for a second and arrange your notes or perform some other small task while taking several deep breaths. Then start again at your normal pace. If you feel that you're losing your audience, try to pull them back by involving them in the action; ask for their opinions or pause for questions.

- **Concentrate on your message and your audience, not on yourself.** When you're busy thinking about your subject and observing your audience's response, you tend to forget your fears.

- **Maintain eye contact with friendly audience members.** Once your presentation is under way, be particularly careful to maintain eye contact with your audience, shifting your gaze periodically around the room. Looking directly at your listeners will make you appear sincere, confident, and trustworthy. It also helps you get an idea of the impression you're creating.

- **Keep going.** Things usually get better as you move along, with each successful minute giving you more and more confidence.

Handling Questions Responsively

Don't leave the question-and-answer period to chance: Anticipate likely questions and think through your answers.

The question-and-answer period is one of the most important parts of an oral presentation. Questions give you a chance to obtain important information, to emphasize your main idea and supporting points, and to build enthusiasm for your point of view. When you're speaking to high-ranking executives in your company, the question-and-answer period will often consume most of the time allotted for your presentation.[24]

Preparation is essential. Even if you can't anticipate every single question, learn enough about your audience to get an idea of their concerns. Think through answers to questions you're likely to get, even those that you don't have a complete answer to.

When someone poses a question, pay attention to the questioner's body language and facial expression to help determine what the person really means. Nod your head or otherwise acknowledge the question, then repeat it aloud to confirm your understanding and to ensure that the entire audience has heard it. If the question is vague or confusing, ask for clarification; then give a simple, direct answer. If you're asked to choose between two alternatives, don't feel you must do so. Offer your own choice instead, if it makes more sense.[25]

This might sound like obvious advice, but be sure to answer the question you're asked. Don't sidestep it, ignore it, laugh it off, or get so caught up in the situation that you forget to respond. Gauge the length of your response to the importance of the question, the status of the questioner, and the time you have left. If giving an adequate answer would take too long, simply say, "I'm sorry, we don't have time to get into that issue right now, but if you'll see me after the presentation, I'll be happy to discuss it with you." If you don't know the answer, don't pretend that you do. Instead, say something like "I don't have those figures. I'll get them for you as quickly as possible."

Maintaining control during the question-and-answer session can be a challenge, particularly if any audience members outrank you in the corporate hierarchy.

Unlike the delivery phase of your presentation, you have less control over the proceedings during the question-and-answer session. However, you can help maintain control during this period by establishing some ground rules up front. Before you begin, announce a time limit or a question limit per person. Establishing limits will protect you from getting into a heated exchange with one member of the audience and from allowing one or two people to monopolize the question period. Give as many audience members as possible a chance to participate by calling on people from different parts of the room.

If audience members try to turn a question into an opportunity to make their own mini-presentations, remember that it's up to you to stay in control. You might ask people to identify themselves before they ask questions. People are more likely to behave themselves when everyone present knows their name.[26] You might admit that you and the questioner have differing opinions and, before calling on someone else, offer to get back to the questioner once you've done more research. Or you might simply respond with a brief answer, avoiding a lengthy debate or additional questions.[27] Finally, you might thank the person for the comments and then remind everyone that you were looking for specific questions.

If a question ever puts you on the hot seat, respond honestly, but remember to keep your cool. Look the person in the eye, answer the question as well as you can, and keep your emotions under control. Whatever the situation, avoid getting into a heated argument. Even if you win, you'll leave the audience feeling both uncomfortable about the situation and your ability to handle conflict. Recognize that questioners who challenge your ideas, logic, or facts may just be trying to push you into overreacting. Defuse hostility by paraphrasing the question and asking the questioner to confirm that you've understood it correctly. Maintain a businesslike tone of voice and a pleasant expression.[28] Don't indulge in put-downs—they may backfire and make the audience more sympathetic to the questioner.

> If you ever face hostile questions, don't duck; respond honestly and directly while keeping your cool.

Noisy, confrontational audiences can be a challenge, but listeners who are deadly quiet can be just as uncomfortable. If there's a chance your audience will be too timid or too hostile to ask questions, consider arranging a few questions ahead of time with a cooperative member of the audience. If a friend or the meeting organizer starts the process, other people in the audience will probably join in.

When the time allotted for your presentation is up, call a halt to the question-and-answer session. Prepare the audience for the end by saying something like, "Our time is almost up. Let's have one more question." After you've made your reply, summarize the main idea of the presentation and thank people for their attention. Conclude the way you opened: by looking around the room and making eye contact. Then gather your notes and leave the podium, maintaining the same confident demeanor you've had from the beginning.

For a reminder of the steps to take in developing an oral presentation, refer to "Checklist: Developing Oral Presentations."

✓ CHECKLIST: Developing Oral Presentations

A. Plan your oral presentation

✓ Analyze the situation by defining your purpose and developing an audience profile.
✓ Select the right medium.
✓ Organize your presentation by defining the main idea, limiting the scope, choosing your approach, and preparing your outline.

B. Write your oral presentation

✓ Adapt to your audience by tailoring your style and language.
✓ Compose your presentation by preparing an introduction, body, and close.
✓ Use your introduction to arouse audience interest, build your credibility, and preview your message.

✓ Use the body to connect your ideas and hold your audience's attention.
✓ Use the close to restate your main points and describe the next steps.

C. Complete your oral presentation

✓ Master the art of delivery by choosing a delivery method, knowing your material, and practicing your delivery.
✓ Check the location and equipment in advance.
✓ Determine whether you should use an interpreter.
✓ Overcome anxiety by preparing thoroughly.
✓ Handle questions responsively.

On the Job

SOLVING COMMUNICATION DILEMMAS AT HEWLETT-PACKARD

After leading the successful effort to land the huge Procter & Gamble computer services contract, Dan Talbott is now HP's senior client relationship director for the P&G program. You work for him as an assistant manager on the program, and one of your key responsibilities is coordinating communication efforts across the far-flung team of people who now operate P&G's computer network. When HP landed the contract to take over P&G's information systems, it not only acquired several P&G facilities but also hired a large number of P&G employees who had previously worked on those systems. Although both companies have highly respected—and widely emulated—corporate cultures, you appreciate that the transition is difficult for some of the P&G staff. Many of these people joined P&G right out of college, and some have worked there for 20 years or more. They might be doing the same jobs as before and even working in the same facilities, but they have a new employer with different policies, different leadership, and so on. They also need to adjust to working for a high-technology firm instead of a consumer-goods firm. How will you address these challenges?[29]

1. You've been preparing a series of presentations on what it's like to work at HP, and the presentation you're developing now is on the concept of the "agile organization." Here's how HP's website describes the concept:

   By working together, we become a smart organization that thinks imaginatively, acts decisively and delivers quickly. Time-to-market, time-to-customer, time-to-revenue and time-to-profit are our critical drivers, as we take calculated risks to outpace competitors and anticipate market changes.

   Which of the following main idea statements does the best job of encapsulating this rather complicated thought?

   a. Talk about how speed is critical to HP's success—creating new products quickly, acquiring new customers quickly, generating new revenue quickly, and realizing profits quickly.
   b. Explain how teamwork plays a vital role in HP's ability to outpace competitors and anticipate market changes.
   c. Make sure the ex-P&G people understand that business moves quickly at HP, and that everyone is responsible for making HP an agile organization.
   d. By working together, we become a smart organization that thinks imaginatively, acts decisively, and delivers quickly.

2. Eventually, some of the people who've recently joined from P&G may be transferred to other positions within HP, including working on HP's own internal information systems or working on programs for other HP clients. However, the vast majority are still focused on the P&G program, so HP's overall mission and competitive concerns are probably not of immediate concern to many of them. What approach should you take in your presentation to encourage them to care about the concept of the "agile organization" and their individual roles in it?

   a. Begin your presentation by immediately asking them what they've heard about the "agile organization" so far. Encourage them to ask any questions before you begin your presentation. This way you can squash any rumors before explaining what the "agile organization" means.
   b. Start your introduction with a few recent news items about layoffs in other high-technology companies, then emphasize that in order to avoid that fate, everyone who works for HP needs to embrace the idea of agility. This will scare them into paying attention.
   c. Share with them an insider's view of the sales process that Dan Talbott's team used to land the P&G contract, focusing on how the team responded so quickly to the opportunity. It's a great example of agility in action, and this situation affected all of them personally (and many of them probably wonder why HP was able to win the contract when EDS and IBM seemed to most people in the industry as more obvious choices for such a huge project). As HP employees now, they will care about how HP will continue to win big contracts and thereby avoid layoffs, keep providing good benefits, and create opportunities for career advancement.
   d. Start your presentation with several short video clips that communicate the idea of speed, such as race cars, rockets, foot races at the Olympics, and a microwave oven cooking a meal in a matter of minutes. From these scenes, they'll get the idea that speed is vital in today's fast-paced world.

3. In the body of your presentation, you plan to show a PowerPoint slide that explains the various aspects of the company's description of what it means to be an agile organization. You'll present a text slide, talk the audience through the description, then open the floor to questions. Which of the following is the best way to arrange the text for this slide?

   a.

   > The Agile Organization
   >
   > By working together, we become a smart organization that thinks imaginatively, acts decisively and delivers quickly. Time-to-market, time-to-customer, time-to-revenue and time-to-profit are our critical drivers, as we take calculated risks to outpace competitors and anticipate market changes.

b.

> **What Does It Mean to Be Agile?**
>
> By working together, we become a smart organization that thinks imaginatively, acts decisively and delivers quickly. Time-to-market, time-to-customer, time-to-revenue and time-to-profit are our critical drivers, as we take calculated risks to outpace competitors and anticipate market changes.

c.

> **What Does It Mean to Be Agile?**
>
> - Teamwork creates a smart organization:
>   - Imaginative thinking
>   - Decisive action
>   - Quick delivery
> - Time is our primary motivating force:
>   - Time-to-market
>   - Time-to-customer
>   - Time-to-revenue
>   - Time-to-profit
> - A strategy of taking calculating risks yields major benefits:
>   - Outpace competitors
>   - Anticipate market changes

d.

> **What Does It Mean to Be Agile?**
>
> - Teamwork creates a smart organization
> - Time is our primary motivating force
> - A strategy of taking calculated risks yields major benefits

4. You've completed your slide show on the agile organization, and you've been looking forward to giving the presentation for the first time. The presentation is going along nicely until you notice one employee in the back of the room snickering from time to time and whispering to people next to him. You've never met this person, and you're not even sure what his position is, but he's starting to distract you. After a few more minutes of this annoying behavior, the employee begins openly laughing at some of your remarks about corporate agility. Unfortunately, your emotions get the best of you, and you lose your cool, stop the presentation, and demand to know what the employee finds so funny. You realize immediately that you've made a mistake, particularly when the employee responds, "If HP is so freakin' agile, why have you been forced to lay off thousands of employees in the past couple of years? How soon until we lose our jobs, too?" You're not prepared to respond to such a complex question (the layoffs were the result of both the merger with Compaq and the general downturn in the technology market a few years ago), nor are you authorized to speak for the company on such a sensitive subject. On the other hand, you don't want to appear weak or ill-prepared. After you take a deep breath and calm down a bit, how should you respond?

a. Use humor to diffuse the situation. Tell the questioner, "HP laid off other employees to make room for charming new additions like you."

b. Recognize that this is not a question you should try to handle under these circumstances, particularly since you don't know how many other people might share the questioner's anxiety—you might lose control of the situation entirely. Respond by saying, "This is not an appropriate time or place to discuss such matters, and I'd like to return to the focus of our discussion today so that those employees who would like to learn more can get the information they came for."

c. Express empathy with the questioner's anxiety and explain that the best way to avoid layoffs in the future is for everyone to contribute to the company's efforts of becoming more agile: "As a fellow employee, I certainly share your concern about job security. However, I also know that the only part I can control is my contribution to the company's efforts to become more agile. Rather than digressing into past difficulties, why don't we focus on what each of us can do to ensure profitable growth into the future?"

d. Ignore the question entirely. Count to ten silently, look back around the room at the friendly faces you were making eye contact with earlier, then resume your presentation.

Learning Objectives Checkup

Assess your understanding of the principles in this chapter by reading each learning objective and studying the accompanying exercises. For fill-in items, write the missing text in the blank provided; for multiple choice items, circle the letter of the correct answer. You can check your responses against the answer key on page AK-2.

Objective 13.1: Explain the importance of oral presentations in your career success.

1. Which of the following is a good reason to look for opportunities to give presentations during your career?

a. Presentations let you demonstrate your ability to think on your feet, grasp complex issues, and handle challenging situations.

b. Presentations give you a nice break from the routine of your regular job.

c. Presentations let you demonstrate what a social person you are.

d. Presentations are usually just a distraction from your main job; avoid them as much as possible.

2. Which of the following is an effective way to respond if you feel nervous right before giving a presentation?

a. Think up a short joke to begin your presentation; the audience's laughter will help you relax.

b. Begin your presentation by telling people that you're nervous and asking them to be sympathetic in case you make any mistakes.

c. Begin your presentation by telling the audience how much you dislike speaking in public; most of them dislike public speaking, too, so they'll be more sympathetic toward you.

d. Remind yourself that everybody gets nervous and that being nervous simply means you care about doing well; use the nervousness to be more energetic when you begin speaking.

Objective 13.2: Explain how to adapt the three-step writing process to oral presentations.

3. Which of the following is true about "writing" a presentation?

a. You should always write every word of every presentation, leaving nothing to chance.

b. You should never write presentations in the sense of writing a memo or a report.

c. In most cases, you won't write out every word of a presentation, but rather think through key phrases and perhaps draft your opening and closing statements.

d. The three-step writing process does not apply to presentations.

4. A/an _____ outline is similar to an outline for a written memo or report, whereas a/an _____ outline is a simplified version designed to help you during the delivery of your presentation.

5. How does the completion stage of the three-step writing process differ between reports and presentations?

a. Completion is exactly the same for reports and presentations.

b. Presentations are never proofread or tested ahead of time; doing so would destroy the spontaneity of your delivery.

c. You never revise presentation slides, since they're locked in place once you create them.

d. The completion state for presentations involves a wider range of tasks, including testing your presentation slides, verifying equipment operation, practicing your speech, and creating handout materials.

Objective 13.3: Discuss the three functions of an effective introduction.

6. Which of the following is the best way to arouse interest in a presentation to a group of fellow employees on the importance of taking ownership of the problem whenever a customer calls in with a complaint?

a. "If customers leave, so do our jobs."

b. "Everything we want as employees of this company—from stable jobs to pay raises to promotional opportunities—depends on one thing: satisfied customers."

c. "How are customers supposed to get their problems solved if we keep passing the buck from one person to the next without ever doing anything?"

d. "The company's profit margins depend on satisfied customers, and it's up to us to make sure those customers are satisfied."

7. If you suspect that your audience doesn't really care about the topic you plan to discuss, how can you generate interest in your presentation?

a. Look for ways to help them relate to the information on a personal level, such as helping the company ensure better job security.

b. Speak louder and, if possible, use lots of sound effects and visual special effects in your presentation.

c. Show your passion for the material by speaking faster than normal and pacing the room in an excited fashion.

d. Show that you care about their feelings by saying up front that you don't really care about the topic either, but you've been assigned to talk about it.

8. If you're giving a presentation in a subject area that you've researched thoroughly but in which you don't have any hands-on experience (suppose your topic is coordinating a major facility relocation or hiring a tax attorney, for instance), which of these steps should you take to build credibility?

a. During your introduction, explain that your presentation is the result of research that you've done, and briefly explain the extent of the research.

b. Explain that you don't have any experience in the subject area, but you've done some research.

c. Emphasize that you know a great deal about the subject matter.

d. Sidestep the issue of credibility entirely in the introduction and let your knowledge shine through during the body of your presentation.

Objective 13.4: Identify four ways to keep your audience's attention during your presentation.

9. Which of the following would do the best job of holding an audience's attention during a presentation on the growing importance of blogs (web logs) in corporate communication? In this particular case, the audience members are all managers of the same company, but they represent a half dozen countries and speak four different native languages (although they all have basic English skills).

a. "Blogs are now an important feature in the corporate communication landscape."

b. "Successful managers around the world now view blogging as an essential tool in their communication efforts."

c. "Millions of customers and employees are now hip to the latest wave to blow through corporate communication, the clumsily named but nevertheless vital blog."

d. "I personally read more than a dozen blogs every day, which is solid evidence of how important blogs have become."

10. Your company recently relocated from another state, and the owners are eager to begin building a positive relationship with the local community. You've been asked to speak to employees about volunteering in various community organizations. Which of the following statements does the best job of communicating the owners' wishes while appealing to employees' personal interests?

a. "Becoming involved in community organizations is a great way for you and your families to meet new people and feel more at home in your new city."

b. "Becoming involved in community organizations shows our new neighbors that we're an organization of positive, caring people—and it's a great way for you and your families to meet new people and feel more at home in your new city."

c. "We really owe it to our new community to give back by volunteering."

d. "The owners feel it is vital for us to become more involved in the community."

11. Which of these techniques is mentioned in the chapter as a way to hold an audience's attention during a presentation?

a. Speak louder than average

b. Tell people that management expects them to pay attention

c. Use clear and vivid language

d. None of the above

Objective 13.5: Explain how visuals enhance oral presentations, and list several popular types of visuals.

12. Which of the following is true about visuals?

a. They can add interest to your presentations.

b. They can help you illustrate and clarify important points.

c. They can help your audience absorb and understand information.

d. They can do all of the above.

13. Which of these is an advantage of electronic presentations over transparencies?

a. You can edit and update your slides right up to the beginning of your presentation.

b. Electronic presentations are less expensive.

c. Electronic presentations require you to talk less.

d. None of the above.

Objective 13.6: Explain the importance of design consistency in electronic slides and other visuals.

14. Why is consistent use of colors, fonts, size, and other design elements important in presentations?

a. Consistency is not important; in fact, it's a sign of a dull presentation.

b. Consistency shows that you're a smart businessperson who doesn't waste time on trivial details.

c. Consistency simplifies the viewing and listening process for your audience and enables them to pay closer attention to your message, rather than spending time trying to figure out your visuals.

d. Consistency shows that you're a team player who can follow instructions.

Objective 13.7: Highlight seven major issues to consider when you're preparing to give a presentation online.

15. Which of the following is a disadvantage of conducting presentations online?

a. The lack of audio communication

b. The inability of most people to participate, since most businesses don't have Internet access

c. The inability to use PowerPoint slides online

d. The shortage (or sometimes complete lack of) of nonverbal signals such as posture, which can provide vital feedback during a presentation

16. Which of the following is an advantage of online presentations?

a. Lower travel costs

b. Less disruption for audiences

c. The ability to meet on a moment's notice

d. All of the above

Objective 13.8: Identify six ways that effective speakers use to handle questions responsively.

17. Which of these actions should you take when an audience member asks you a question?

a. Observe the questioner's body language and facial expression to help determine what the person really means.

b. Nod your head or show some other sign that you acknowledge the question.

c. Repeat the question to confirm your understanding and to ensure that the entire audience has heard it.

d. Do all of the above.

18. If you receive a question that is important and relevant to the topic you're presenting but you lack the information needed to answer it, which of the following would be the best response?

a. "I'm sorry; I don't know the answer."

b. "You've asked an important question, but I don't have the information needed to answer it properly. I'll research the issue after we're finished here today, then send everyone an e-mail message with the answer."

c. "Let me get back to you on that."

d. "I'd really like to stay focused on the material that I prepared for this presentation."

Apply Your Knowledge

1. Would you rather (a) deliver an oral presentation to an outside audience, (b) be interviewed for a news story, or (c) make a presentation to a departmental meeting? Why? How do the communication skills differ among those situations? Explain.
2. How might the audience's attitude affect the amount of audience interaction during or after a presentation? Explain your answer.
3. If you were giving an oral presentation on the performance of a company product, what three attention-getters might you use to enliven your speech?
4. How can you use slide master to enhance the effectiveness of your slides?
5. **Ethical Choices** Is it ethical to use design elements and special effects to persuade an audience? Why or why not?

Practice Your Knowledge

DOCUMENTS FOR ANALYSIS

DOCUMENT 13.A

Examine the slide in Figure 13–10 and point out any problems you notice. How would you correct these problems?

DOCUMENT 13.B

Examine the graph in Figure 13–11 and explain how to modify it for an electronic presentation using the guidelines discussed in this chapter.

FIGURE 13–10
Piece of Cake Bakery
Electronic Slide #8

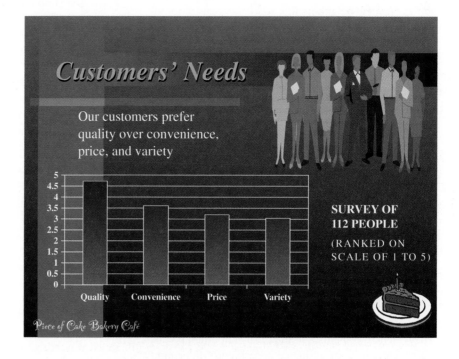

FIGURE 13–11
CommuniCo Employee
Training Costs

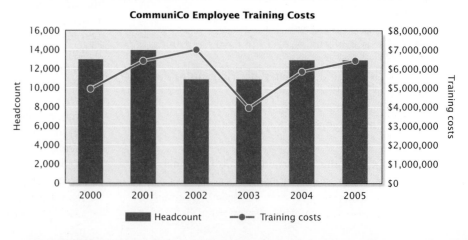

Exercises

For active links to all websites discussed in this chapter, visit this text's website at www.prenhall.com/thill. Locate your book and click on its Companion Website link. Then select Chapter 13, and click on "Featured Websites." Locate the name of the page or the URL related to the material in the text. Please note that links to sites that become inactive after publication of the book will be removed from the Featured Websites section.

13.1 Mastering Delivery: Analysis Attend a presentation at your school or in your town, or watch a speech on television. Categorize the speech as one that motivates or entertains, one that informs or analyzes, or one that persuades or urges collaboration. Then compare the speaker's delivery with this chapter's "Checklist: Developing Oral Presentations." Write a two-page report analyzing the speaker's performance and suggesting improvements.

13.2 Mastering Delivery: Nonverbal Signals Observe and analyze the delivery of a speaker in a school, work, or other setting. What type of delivery did the speaker use? Was this delivery appropriate for the occasion? What nonverbal signals did the speaker use to emphasize key points? Were these signals effective? Which nonverbal signals would you suggest to further enhance the delivery of this oral presentation—and why?

13.3 Ethical Choices Think again about the oral presentation you observed and analyzed in 13.2. How could the speaker have used nonverbal signals to unethically manipulate the audience's attitudes or actions?

13.4 Teamwork You've been asked to give an informative 10-minute presentation on vacation opportunities in your home state. Draft your introduction, which should last no more than 2 minutes. Then pair off with a classmate and analyze each other's introductions. How well do these two introductions arouse the audience's interest, build credibility, and preview the presentation? Suggest how these introductions might be improved.

13.5 Completing Oral Presentations: Self-Assessment How good are you at planning, writing, and delivering oral presentations? Rate yourself on each of the following elements of the oral presentation process. Then examine your ratings to identify where you are strongest and where you can improve, using the tips in this chapter.

Element of Presentation Process	Always	Frequently	Occasionally	Never
1. I start by defining my purpose.	___	___	___	___
2. I analyze my audience before writing an oral presentation.	___	___	___	___
3. I match my presentation length to the allotted time.	___	___	___	___
4. I begin my oral presentations with an attention-getting introduction.	___	___	___	___
5. I look for ways to build credibility as a speaker.	___	___	___	___
6. I cover only a few main points in the body of my presentation.	___	___	___	___
7. I use transitions to help listeners follow my ideas.	___	___	___	___
8. I review main points and describe next steps in the close.	___	___	___	___
9. I practice my presentation beforehand.	___	___	___	___
10. I prepare in advance for questions and objections.	___	___	___	___
11. I conclude oral presentations by summarizing my main idea.	___	___	___	___

13.6 Creating Effective Slides: Content Look through recent issues (print or online) of *BusinessWeek, Fortune,* or other business publications for articles discussing challenges that a specific company or industry is facing. Using the articles and the guidelines discussed in this chapter, create three to five slides summarizing these issues. If you don't have access to computer presentation software or a word processor, you can draw the slides on plain paper.

13.7 Creating Effective Slides: Content and Design You've been asked to give an informative 10-minute talk to a group of conventioneers on great things to see and do while visiting your hometown. Write the content for three or four slides (including a cover slide). Then think about the design elements for your slides. Describe design choices you would make, particularly in terms of colors, fonts, drawings, and photography.

13.8 Completing Electronic Presentations: Slide Sorter View PowerPoint comes with a number of content templates for presentations. Use the software's AutoContent Wizard to create a short presentation by selecting a presentation type and supplying information for the slide templates (feel free to make up material). Then use the *slide sorter view* to critique the content, layout, and design elements of your presentation. Edit and revise the slides to improve their overall effectiveness.

13.9 Internet Creating hyperlinks to live websites can perk up an electronic presentation, but it also means being prepared for the unexpected. What are some of the obstacles you might encounter when creating live Internet links? How can you prepare in advance to overcome such obstacles?

Expand Your Knowledge

LEARNING MORE ON THE WEB

LOOK SMART IN YOUR ELECTRONIC PRESENTATIONS

www.3m.com/meetingnetwork/presentations

Visit the presentation center at 3M, and follow the expert advice on creating and delivering effective oral presentations. Find out why a bad presentation can kill even the best idea. Did you pick the right colors? Is your presentation too long? Too wordy? Find out why a strong template is the key to positive first impressions. Review the tips for better presentation. Download some templates and look smart.

ACTIVITIES

Log on and learn the secrets from the pros, then address these questions:

1. What three questions should you answer for a successful presentation?
2. What common PowerPoint pitfalls should you avoid?
3. What are the two common causes of presentation paralysis?

EXPLORING THE WEB ON YOUR OWN

Review these chapter-related websites on your own to enhance your oral presentation skills and knowledge.

1. Develop better presentations with the helpful advice at Epson's Presenters Online website, www.presentersonline.com.
2. Visit the Advanced Public Speaking Institute, at www.public-speaking.org, and learn how to be the best public speaker you can be.
3. The Virtual Presentation Assistant, www.ku.edu/~coms/virtual_assistant/vpa/vpa.htm, offers abundant resources with related links to other websites that contain useful articles, reviews, or supplemental materials for planning presentations.

Learn Interactively

INTERACTIVE STUDY GUIDE

Visit www.prenhall.com/thill, then locate your book and click on its Companion Website link. Select Chapter 13 to take advantage of the interactive "Chapter Quiz" to test your knowledge of chapter concepts. Receive instant feedback on whether you need additional studying. Also, visit the "Study Hall," where you'll find an abundance of valuable resources that will help you succeed in this course.

PEAK PERFORMANCE GRAMMAR AND MECHANICS

If your instructor has required the use of "Peak Performance Grammar and Mechanics," either in your online course or on CD, you can improve your skill with vocabulary, by using the "Peak Performance Grammar and Mechanics" module. Click "Vocabulary." Take the Pretest to determine whether you have any weak areas. Then review those areas in the Refresher Course. Take the Follow-Up Test to check your grasp of frequently confused words. For an extra challenge or advanced practice, take the Advanced Test. Finally, for additional reinforcement, go to the "Improve Your Grammar, Mechanics, and Usage" section that follows, and complete those exercises.

Improve Your Grammar, Mechanics, and Usage

The following exercises help you improve your knowledge of and power over English grammar, mechanics, and usage. Turn to the Handbook of Grammar, Mechanics, and Usage at the end of this textbook and review all of Section 3.1 (Capitals), 3.2 (Underscores and Italics), and 3.3 (Abbreviations). Then look at the following 10 items. Circle the letter of the preferred choice in the following groups of sentences. (Answers to these exercises appear on page AK-4.)

1. a. Send this report to Mister H. K. Danforth, RR 1, Albany, NY 12885.
    b. Send this report to Mister H. K. Danforth, Rural Route 1, Albany, New York 12885.
    c. Send this report to Mr. H. K. Danforth, RR 1, Albany, NY 12885.

2. a. She received her MBA degree from the University of Michigan.
    b. She received her Master of Business Administration degree from the university of Michigan.

3. a. Sara O'Rourke (a reporter from The <u>Wall Street Journal</u>) will be here Thursday.
    b. Sara O'Rourke (a reporter from *The Wall Street Journal*) will be here Thursday.
    c. Sara O'Rourke (a reporter from <u>The Wall Street Journal</u>) will be here Thursday.

4. a. The building is located on the corner of Madison and Center streets.
    b. The building is located on the corner of Madison and Center Streets.

5. a. Call me at 8 a.m. tomorrow morning, PST, and I'll have the information you need.
    b. Call me at 8 tomorrow morning, PST, and I'll have the information you need.
    c. Call me tomorrow at 8 a.m. PST, and I'll have the information you need.

6. a. Whom do you think *Time* magazine will select as its Person of the Year?
    b. Whom do you think *Time magazine* will select as its *Person of the Year?*
    c. Whom do you think *Time magazine* will select as its Person of the Year?

7. a. The art department will begin work on Feb. 2, just one wk. from today.
    b. The art department will begin work on February 2, just one week from today.
    c. The art department will begin work on Feb. 2, just one week from today.

8. a. You are to meet him on friday at the UN building in NYC.
    b. You are to meet him on Friday at the UN building in NYC.
    c. You are to meet him on Friday at the un building in New York city.

9. a. You must help her distinguish between <u>i.e.</u> (which means "that is") and <u>e.g.</u> (which means "for example").
    b. You must help her distinguish between <u>i.e.</u> (which means "that is") and *e.g.* (which means "for example").
    c. You must help her distinguish between *i.e.* (which means <u>that is</u>) and *e.g.* (which means <u>for example</u>).

10. a. We plan to establish a sales office on the West coast.
    b. We plan to establish a sales office on the west coast.
    c. We plan to establish a sales office on the West Coast.

For additional exercises focusing on mechanics, go to www.prenhall.com/thill, then locate your text and click on its Companion Website link. Click on Chapter 13, click on "Additional Exercises to Improve Your Grammar, Mechanics and Usage," then click on "20. Capitals" or "21. Word division."

Part V
Writing Employment Messages and Interviewing for Jobs

Chapter 14

Building Careers and Writing Résumés

Learning Objectives

On the Job

COMMUNICATING AT E*TRADE FINANCIAL

SMART COMPUTERS HELP RECRUITERS FIND THE TOP TALENT IN A COMPETITIVE JOB MARKET

To land you a job interview at E*Trade Financial, your résumé has to catch the eye of someone like Armnon Geshuri, director of global staffing. If Geshuri and his staff don't see your résumé, you won't see the inside of E*Trade. Fortunately, Geshuri wants to see the résumé of every qualified candidate, and he devotes considerable time, money, and creative energy to making sure that E*Trade gets to see the best candidates as quickly as possible.

*E*Trade achieved a strong position in the online trading market through a combination of innovative technology and effective workforce recruiting.*

Like many companies these days, E*Trade uses advanced technology to filter résumés, spot qualified candidates, conduct personality and skill tests, and even handle background checks. The company uses these solutions in good times and bad, whether the talent pool is empty or overflowing. "In any market, finding the right talent is key," says Geshuri. "Effective applicant tracking and screening is what differentiates companies and creates a competitive advantage."

Using technology creatively is another key to success. Early computer-based systems emphasized the fairly simple ability to search on keywords in résumés and applications. However, organizations that relied too heavily on keywords discovered they were often overlooking highly qualified candidates. The latest applicant-tracking programs do much more, letting recruiters analyze various words and rank them according to how (and how often) they're used.

In the end, though, people like Geshuri still have the final say. They read the résumés the programs select, choose who gets a phone call, perform the interviews, and decide whom to hire. So no matter how advanced the technology gets, getting in the door still depends on a well-written résumé.[1]

www.etrade.com

BUILDING A CAREER
WITH YOUR COMMUNICATION SKILLS

Successful job hunters view the search as a comprehensive process—and put all of their communication skills to work.

As Armnon Geshuri will tell you, obtaining the job that's right for you takes more than sending out a few résumés and application letters. As you get ready to enter (or reenter) the workplace, explore the wide range of actions you can take to maximize your perceived value and find the ideal career opportunities. The skills you've learned in research, planning, and writing will help you every step of the way.

Understanding Today's Dynamic Workplace

Social, political, and financial events continue to change workplace conditions from year to year, so the job market you read about this year might not be the same market you try to enter a year or two from now. However, you can count on a few forces that are likely to affect your entry into the job market and your career success in years to come:[2]

For many workers, the employment picture is less stable today than it was in years past.

- **Stability.** Your career probably won't be as stable as careers were in your parents' generation. In today's business world, your career will be affected by globalization, mergers and acquisitions, short-term mentality driven by the demands of stockholders, ethical upheavals, and the relentless quest for lower costs.

- **Lifetime employment.** The idea of *lifetime employment,* in which employees spend their entire working lives with a single firm that takes care of them throughout their careers, is all but gone in many industries. Boeing, the Chicago-based aerospace giant, speaks of lifetime *employability,* rather than lifetime employment, putting the responsibility on employees to track market needs and keep their skills up to date—even changing careers if necessary. In fact, most U.S. employees will not only change employers multiple times but will even change careers anywhere from three to five times over their working lives.

- **Growth of small business.** Small business continues to be the primary engine of job creation in the United States, so chances are good that you'll work for a small firm at some point. One expert predicts that before long, 80 percent of the U.S. labor force will be working for firms employing fewer than 200 people.

- **Increase in independent contractors.** The nature of employment itself is changing for many people. As companies try to become more flexible, more employees are going solo and setting up shop as independent contractors, sometimes selling their services back to the very companies they just left.

- **Changing view of job-hopping.** Given all these changes, job-hopping doesn't have quite the negative connotation it once had. Even so, you still need to be careful about jumping at every new opportunity that promises more money or prestige. Recruiting and integrating new employees takes time and costs money, and most employers are reluctant to invest in someone who has a history of switching jobs numerous times.

Changes in the job market mean you need to take charge of your career, rather than counting on a single employer to look out for you.

What do all these forces mean to you? First, take charge of your career—and stay in charge of it. Understand your options and don't count on others to watch out for your future. Second, as you've learned throughout this course, understanding your audience is key to successful communication, starting with understanding how employers view today's job market.

How Employers View Today's Job Market   From the employer's perspective, the employment process is always a question of balance. Maintaining a stable workforce can improve practically every aspect of business performance, yet many employers feel they need the flexibility to shrink and expand payrolls as business conditions change. Employers obviously want to attract the best talent, but the best talent is more expensive and more vulnerable to offers from competitors, so there are always financial trade-offs to consider.

Employers also struggle with the ups and downs of the economy, just as employees do. When unemployment is low, the balance of power shifts to employees, and employers have to compete in order to attract and keep top talent. In the Internet boom of the late 1990s, companies were practically throwing money at hot, young talent, sometimes even paying new hires more than seasoned professionals. Unfortunately, many of those high-flying jobs evaporated almost overnight, so the party didn't last long.[3] When unemployment is high, the power shifts back to employers, who can afford to be more selective and less accommodating. In other words, pay attention to the economy whenever you're job hunting; at times you can be more aggressive but at other times you should be more accommodating.

As discussed in the previous section, employment today is generally more flexible than in the past. Rather than looking for lifelong employees for every position, many employers now fill some needs by hiring temporary workers or engaging contractors on a project-by-project basis. Many U.S. employers are now also more willing to move jobs to cheaper labor markets outside the country and to recruit globally to fill positions in the United States. Both trends have stirred controversy, especially in the technology sector, as U.S. firms recruited top engineers and scientists from other countries while shifting mid- and low-range jobs to India, China, Russia, and other countries with lower wage structures.[4]

The nature of the job market fluctuates with the ups and downs of the economy.

What Employers Look for in Job Applicants   Given the forces in the contemporary workplace, employers such as E*Trade are looking for people who are able and willing to adapt to the new dynamics of the business world, can survive and thrive in fluid and uncertain situations, and continue to learn throughout their careers. Companies want team players with strong work records, leaders who are versatile, and employees with diversified skills and varied job experience.[5] In addition, most employers expect college graduates to be sensitive to intercultural differences and to have a sound understanding of international affairs.[6] In fact, in some cases, your chances of being hired are better if you've studied abroad, learned another language, or can otherwise demonstrate an appreciation of other cultures.

Most employers value employees who are flexible, adaptable, and sensitive to the complex dynamics of today's business world.

Adapting to Today's Job Market

Adapting to the workplace is a lifelong process of seeking the best fit between what you want to do and what employers are willing to pay you to do. For instance, if money is more important to you than anything else, you can certainly pursue jobs that promise high pay; just be aware that most of these jobs require years of experience, and many produce a lot of stress, require frequent travel, or have other drawbacks you'll want to consider. In contrast, if location, lifestyle, intriguing work, or other factors are more important to you, you may well have to sacrifice some level of pay to achieve them. The important thing is to know what you want to do, what you have to offer, and how to make yourself more attractive to employers.

What Do You Want to Do?   Economic necessities and the vagaries of the marketplace will influence much of what happens in your career, of course; nevertheless, it's wise to start your employment search by examining your own values and interests. Identify what you want to do first, then see whether you can find a position that satisfies you at a personal level while also meeting your financial needs.

- **What would you like to do every day?** Research occupations that interest you. Find out what people really do every day. Ask friends, relatives, or alumni from your school. Visit Career One Stop, **www.careeronestop.com** to see short videos of real people doing real work in hundreds of different professions.

Have you thought long and hard about what you really want to do in your career? The choices you make now could influence your life for years to come.

- **How would you like to work?** Consider how much independence you want on the job, how much variety you like, and whether you prefer to work with products, machines, people, ideas, figures, or some combination thereof. Constant change or a predictable role?

- **What specific compensation do you expect?** What do you hope to earn in your first year? What's your ultimate earnings goal? Are you willing to settle for less money in order to do something you really love?

- **Can you establish some general career goals?** Consider where you'd like to start, where you'd like to go from there, and the ultimate position you'd like to attain.

- **What size company would you prefer?** Do you like the idea of working for a small, entrepreneurial operation or a large corporation?

- **What sort of corporate culture are you most comfortable with?** Would you be happy in a formal hierarchy with clear reporting relationships? Or do you prefer less structure? Teamwork or individualism? Do you like a competitive environment?

- **What location would you like?** Would you like to work in a city, a suburb, a small town, an industrial area, or an uptown setting? Do you favor a particular part of the country? Another country? (See "Achieving Intercultural Communication: Looking for Work Around the World.")

ACHIEVING INTERCULTURAL COMMUNICATION

Looking for Work Around the World

With his eyes fixed on a career in international law, University of Michigan graduate Andrew Jaynes knew that overseas work experience would help his law school admission chances and expand his intercultural background.

Jaynes started with the Overseas Opportunities Office at UM's International Center, which offers UM students extensive information on its website and access to advisors and students who have international work experience. With that information as a starting point, he signed on with one of several companies that offer students assistance with foreign work permits and provide housing and job leads. He eventually found a job on his own, working at the American Library in Paris. "It took longer than I expected, but every day I learned more about the real lives of working Parisians—an awareness you can't get as a tourist."

To help ensure success in your own search for employment abroad, keep these points in mind:

- **Give yourself plenty of time.** Finding a job in another country is a complicated process that requires extensive and time-consuming research.

- **Research thoroughly, both online and off.** In addition to your school's resources, you can find numerous websites that offer advice, job listings, and other information. For a good look at the range of international opportunities, visit www.InternAbroad.com, www.VolunteerAbroad.com, www.TeachAbroad.com, and www.JobsAbroad.com. However, Jaynes and others with international experience will tell you

that you can't limit your research to the web. Like any job search, networking is crucial, so join cultural societies with international interests, volunteer with exchange student programs, or find other ways to connect with people who have international experience.

- **Consider all the possibilities.** Keep an open mind when you're exploring your options; you'll probably run across situations you hadn't considered at the beginning of your search. For instance, you might find that an unpaid internship in your future profession would help your career prospects more than a paying position in some other industry.

- **Be flexible.** If you have to settle for something less than that dream job, focus on the big picture, which for most students is the cultural opportunity.

Finding a job in another country can be a lot of work, but the rewards can be considerable. "I had studied abroad for a year and traveled through many countries around the world," Jaynes says, "but nothing gives you the same feel for a culture as working in it."

CAREER APPLICATIONS

1. How might international work experience help you in a career in the United States, even if you never work abroad again?

2. If your work history involves religious or political activities, either paid or volunteer, explain how you might present this information on a curriculum vitae intended for international readers?

What Do You Have to Offer?   Knowing what you *want* to do is one thing. Knowing what you *can* do is another. You may already have a good idea of what you can offer employers. If not, some brainstorming can help you identify your skills, interests, and characteristics. Start by jotting down 10 achievements you're proud of, such as learning to ski, taking a prize-winning photo, tutoring a child, or editing your school paper. Think carefully about what specific skills these achievements demanded of you. For example, leadership skills, speaking ability, and artistic talent may have helped you coordinate a winning presentation to your school's administration. As you analyze your achievements, you'll begin to recognize a pattern of skills. Which of them might be valuable to potential employers?

No matter what profession you're in, you are a valuable package of skills and capabilities; make sure you have a clear picture of your own strengths.

Next, look at your educational preparation, work experience, and extracurricular activities. What do your knowledge and experience qualify you to do? What have you learned from volunteer work or class projects that could benefit you on the job? Have you held any offices, won any awards or scholarships, mastered a second language?

Take stock of your personal characteristics. Are you aggressive, a born leader? Or would you rather follow? Are you outgoing, articulate, great with people? Or do you prefer working alone? Make a list of what you believe are your four or five most important qualities. Ask a relative or friend to rate your traits as well.

If you're having difficulty figuring out your interests, characteristics, or capabilities, consult your college placement office. Many campuses administer a variety of tests to help you identify interests, aptitudes, and personality traits. These tests won't reveal your "perfect" job, but they'll help you focus on the types of work best suited to your personality.

Your college placement office can point you to a variety of tests to gauge your interest and suitability for a variety of career possibilities.

How Can You Make Yourself More Valuable?   While you're figuring out what you want from a job and what you can offer an employer, you can take positive steps now toward building your career:

Take an active approach to making yourself a more attractive job candidate—and it's never too early to start.

- **Keep an employment portfolio.** Collect anything that shows your ability to perform, whether it's in school, on the job, or in other venues. Your portfolio is a great resource for writing your résumé, and it gives employers tangible evidence of your professionalism. Many colleges now offer students the chance to create an *e-portfolio,* a multimedia presentation of your skills and experiences. It's an extensive résumé that links to an electronic collection of your student papers, solutions to tough problems, internship and work projects, and anything else that demonstrates your accomplishments and activities.[7] To distribute the portfolio to potential employers, you can burn a CD-ROM or store your portfolio on a website—whether it's a personal site, your college's site (if student pages are available), or a site such as www.collegegrad.com. (However, you *must* check with an employer before including any items that belong to the company or contain sensitive information.)

- **Take interim assignments.** As you search for a permanent job, consider temporary jobs, freelance work, or internships. These temporary assignments not only help you gain valuable experience and relevant contacts but also provide you with important references and with items for your portfolio.[8]

- **Continue to polish and update your skills.** Join networks of professional colleagues and friends who can help you keep up with your occupation and industry. Many professional societies have student chapters or offer students discounted memberships. Take courses and pursue other educational or life experiences that would be hard to get while working full-time.

Even after an employer hires you, it's a good idea to continue improving your skills, in order to distinguish yourself from your peers and to make yourself more valuable to current and potential employers. Acquire as much technical knowledge as you can, build broad-based life experience, and develop your social skills. Learn to respond to change in positive, constructive ways; doing so will help you adapt if your

Keep your eyes and your mind open as you approach every experience in school, part-time jobs, and social engagements.

FIGURE 14–1
The Employment Search

FIGURE 14–1
The Employment Search

"perfect" career path eludes your grasp. Learn to see each job, even so-called entry-level jobs, as an opportunity to learn more and to expand your knowledge, experience, and social skills. Share what you know with others instead of hoarding knowledge in the hope of becoming indispensable; helping others excel is a skill, too.[9]

Securing Employment in Today's Job Market

After you've armed yourself with knowledge of today's workplace and your potential role in it, it's time to launch an efficient, productive process to find that ideal position. Figure 14–1 shows the six most important tasks in the job search process. This chapter discusses the first two, and Chapter 15 explores the final four. The more you know about this process, the more successful you'll be in your job search. Plus, it's important to keep in mind that employers and job candidates approach the process differently.

Understanding Employers' Approach to the Employment Process   You can save considerable time and effort by understanding how employers approach the recruiting process (see Figure 14–2). Generally, employers prefer to look for candidates within their own organization or through referrals from people they know and trust. In fact, personal contacts appear to be the prime source of jobs, regardless of whether a candidate has just graduated from college or has been out of school for several years.[10]

Many employers send representatives to college campuses to conduct student interviews, which are usually coordinated by the campus placement office. In addition, many employers accept unsolicited résumés, and most keep unsolicited résumés on file or in a database. Employers recruit candidates through employment

FIGURE 14–2
How Organizations Prefer to Find New Employees

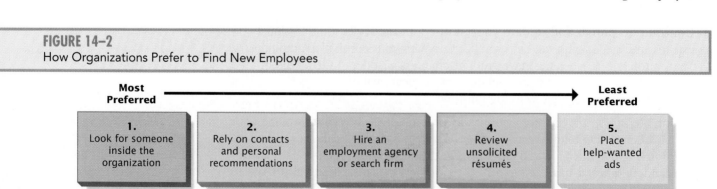

agencies, state employment services, temporary staffing services, and the employment bureaus operated by some trade associations. They also post jobs through ads in newspapers, trade magazines, campus publications, their own websites, and job sites such as Monster.com. In fact, major job boards such as Monster.com and CareerBuilder.com have grown so popular that some employers feel deluged with résumés, and some job seekers fear it's becoming impossible to stand out from the crowd when hundreds or thousands of people are applying for the same jobs. As a result, many specialized websites are now springing up, focusing on narrow parts of the job market or offering technology that promises to do a better job of matching employers and job searchers. For example, www.mkt10.com uses in-depth questionnaires to match employers and employees. The service also lets applicants know how their chances compare with those of other people applying for the same jobs, and suggests alternative jobs that might be better fits.[11]

Look again at Figure 14–2, and you'll notice that the easiest way for you to find out about new opportunities—through the employer's outside advertising—is the employer's least-preferred way of finding new employees. As many as 80 percent of all job openings are never advertised, a phenomenon known as the hidden job market.[12] In other words, employers have looked in quite a few other places before they come looking for you. To find the best opportunities, it's up to you to take action to get yourself noticed.

It's important to understand that the easiest way for you to find jobs (through companies' help-wanted advertising) is the least-preferred channel for many companies to find new employees.

Organizing Your Approach to the Employment Process   The employment process can consume many hours of your time over weeks or months, so organize your efforts in a logical, careful manner to save time. Begin by finding out where the job opportunities are, which industries are strong, which parts of the country are booming, and which specific job categories offer the best prospects for the future. From there you can investigate individual organizations, doing your best to learn as much about them as possible.

Staying Abreast of Business and Financial News   If you have regular access to the Internet, staying on top of business news is easy today. Many major newspapers offer some or all of their business content online. (In some cases, you need to be a subscriber to access all of the material, including archives.) To help you get started, here is a selection of websites that offer business news:

With so many print and electronic resources available today, it's easy to stay in touch with what's happening in the business world.

- *Wall Street Journal:* http://online.wsj.com/public/us

- *New York Times:* www.nyt.com

- *USA Today:* www.usatoday.com

- *San Jose Mercury News* (especially strong on technology and Silicon Valley news): www.mercurynews.com

- *BusinessWeek:* www.businessweek.com

- *Business 2.0:* www.business2.com

- *Fast Company:* www.fastcompany.com

- *Fortune:* www.fortune.com

- *Forbes:* www.forbes.com

Use an RSS news aggregator (see Chapter 10) to select the type of stories you're interested in and have them delivered to your screen automatically. Of course, with all the business information available today, it's easy to get lost in the details. Try not to get too caught up in the daily particulars of business. Start by examining "big picture" topics—trends, issues, industrywide challenges, and careers—before delving into specific companies that look attractive.

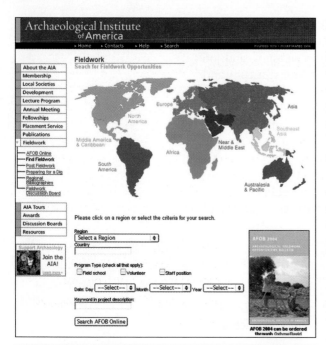

Looking for a career off the beaten path? The Archaeological Institute of America's website is one of the hundreds of specialized job board sites that offer unique short- and long-term opportunities.

Researching Specific Companies   Chapter 10 discusses how to find information on individual industries and companies, and it provides a list of popular business resources. Review those sources, as well as professional and trade journals in the fields that interest you. Once you've identified a promising industry and career field, consult directories of employers at your college library, at your career center, or on the Internet and compile a list of specific organizations that appeal to you.

As you probably already know, a staggering amount of company and employment information is available online. In addition to gaining detailed information about prospective employers, you can use the web to look for and respond to job openings. Most companies, even small firms, offer at least basic information about themselves on their websites. Look for the "About Us" or "Company" part of the site to find a company profile, executive biographies, press releases, financial information, and information on employment opportunities. You'll often find information about an organization's mission, products, annual reports, and employee benefits. You can also e-mail organizations and ask for annual reports, descriptive brochures, or newsletters. Look for outside sources as well, including the business sections of local newspapers and trade publications that cover the company's industries and markets.

Go beyond every company's own communication materials; find out what others in their industries and communities think about them.

Table 14–1 lists some of the many websites where you can learn more about companies and find job openings. Start with The Riley Guide, www.rileyguide.com, which offers links to hundreds of specialized websites that post openings in specific industries and professions. Your college's career center placement office probably maintains an up-to-date list as well.

In addition to using the web to look for job openings, you'll still want to use other techniques for finding employment, such as networking and finding career counseling.

Start thinking like a networker now; your classmates could turn out to be some of your most important business contacts.

Networking   **Networking** is the process of making informal connections with a broad sphere of mutually beneficial business contacts. According to one recent survey, networking is the most common way that employees find jobs.[13] Networking takes place wherever and whenever people talk: at industry functions, at social gatherings, at sports events and recreational activities, in online newsgroups, at alumni reunions, and so on. Read news sites, blogs, and other online sources. Participate in student business organizations, especially those with ties to professional organizations such as the American Marketing Association or the American Management Association. Visit trade shows that cater to an industry you're interested in. Not only will you learn plenty about that sector of the workplace, but you'll rub shoulders with people who actually work in the industry.[14] Hundreds of trade shows are held every year around the country, and many are open to the public for free or for a nominal fee. Don't overlook volunteering in social, civic, and religious organizations. As a volunteer, you not only meet people but also demonstrate your ability to solve problems, plan projects, and so on. You can do some good while creating a network for yourself.

Novice job seekers sometimes misunderstand networking and unknowingly commit breaches of etiquette. Networking isn't a matter of walking up to strangers at social events, handing over your résumé, and asking them to find you a job. Rather,

NETTING A JOB ON THE WEB Table 14–1

Website*	URL	Highlights
Riley Guide	www.rileyguide.com	Vast collection of links to both general and specialized job sites for every career imaginable; don't miss this one—it'll save you hours and hours of searching
America's CareerOneStop	www.careeronestop.org	Comprehensive, government-funded site that includes America's Career InfoNet and America's Job Bank; learn more about the workplace in general as well as specific careers; offers information on typical wages and employment trends and identifies education, knowledge, and skills requirements for most occupations
Monster	www.monster.com	One of the most popular job sites, with hundreds of thousands of openings, many from hard-to-find smaller companies; extensive collection of advice on the job search process
MonsterTrak	www.monstertrak.com	Focused on job searches for new college grads; your school's career center site probably links here
Yahoo! Hotjobs	http://hotjobs.yahoo.com	Another leading job board, formed by recent merger of Hotjobs and Yahoo! Careers
CareerBuilder	www.careerbuilder.com	Fast-growing site affiliated with more than 100 local newspapers around the country
USA Jobs	www.usajobs.opm.gov	The official job search site for the U.S. government, featuring everything from economists to astronauts to border patrol agents
IMDiversity	www.imdiversity.com	Good resource on diversity in the workplace, with job postings from companies that have made a special commitment to promoting diversity in their workforces
Dice.com	www.dice.com	One of the best sites for high-technology jobs
Net-Temps	www.nettemps.com	Popular site for contractor and freelancers looking for short-term assignments
InternshipPrograms.com	www.internships.wetfeet.com	Posts listings from companies looking for interns in a wide variety of professions
SimplyHired.com Indeed.com	www.simplyhired.com www.indeed.com	Specialized search engines that look for job postings on hundreds of websites worldwide; find many postings that aren't listed on "job board" sites such as Monster.com

*This list represents only a small fraction of the hundreds of job-posting sites and other resources available online; be sure to check with your college's career center for the latest information.

it involves the sharing of information between people who might be able to offer mutual help at some point in the future. Think of it as an organic process, in which you cultivate the possibility of finding that perfect opportunity. Networking can take time, and it can operate in unpredictable ways. You may not get results for months, so it's important to start early and make it part of your lifelong program of career management.

To become a valued network member, you need to be able to help others in some way. You may not have any influential contacts yet, but because you're actively researching a number of industries and trends in your own job search, you probably have valuable information you can share. Or you might simply be able to connect one person with another person who can help. The more you network, the more valuable you become in your network—and the more valuable your network becomes to you.

Recruiters at this job fair in Austin, Texas, explain the benefits of working for IBM.

Seeking Career Counseling   College placement offices offer individual counseling, credential services, job fairs, on-campus interviews, and job listings. They can give you advice on résumé-writing software and provide workshops in job search techniques, résumé preparation, interview techniques, and more.[15] You can also find job counseling online. You might begin your self-assessment, for example, with the Keirsey Temperament Sorter, an online personality test at www.advisorteam.com. For excellent job-seeking pointers and counseling, visit college- and university-run online career centers. Major online job boards such as Monster.com also offer a variety of career planning resources.

PREPARING RÉSUMÉS

To distinguish yourself from all the other people looking for work, you need to start with a well-written résumé. In fact, your success in finding a job will depend on how carefully you plan, write, and complete your résumé. Some job searchers are intimidated by the prospect of writing a résumé, but your résumé is really just another specialized business message. Follow the three-step writing process, and it'll be easier than you thought (see Figure 14–3).

FIGURE 14–3
Three-Step Writing Process for Résumés

Planning

Analyze the Situation
Recognize that the purpose of your résumé is to get an interview, not to get a job.

Gather Information
Research target industries and companies so that you know what they're looking for in new hires; learn about various jobs and what to expect.

Select the Right Medium
Start with a traditional paper résumé and develop scannable, plain text, or HTML versions as needed.

Organize the Information
Choose an organizational model that highlights your strengths and downplays your shortcomings.

Writing

Adapt to Your Audience
Plan your wording carefully so that you can catch a recruiter's eye within seconds; translate your education and experience into attributes that target employers find valuable.

Compose the Message
Write clearly and succinctly, using active, powerful language that is appropriate to the industries and companies you're targeting; use a professional tone in all communications, even when using e-mail.

Completing

Revise the Message
Evaluate your content and review readability, clarity, and accuracy.

Produce the Message
Use effective design elements and suitable layout for a clean, professional appearance.

Proofread the Message
Review for errors in layout, spelling, and mechanics; mistakes can cost you interview opportunities.

Distribute the Message
Deliver your résumé following the specific instructions of each employer or job board website.

1   2   3

Planning Your Résumé

Your résumé must be more than a simple list of the jobs you've held. As with other business messages, planning a résumé means analyzing your purpose and your audience, gathering information, choosing the best medium, and organizing your content. Although this chapter refers to your résumé in the singular, be prepared to craft several or perhaps many versions of your résumé. By making some simple changes in wording or organization, you'll probably be able to match your value more closely to the specific opportunities offered by particular employers.

Analyzing Your Purpose and Audience   A **résumé** is a structured, written summary of a person's education, employment background, and job qualifications. Before you begin writing a résumé, make sure you understand its true function—as an advertisement intended to stimulate an employer's interest in meeting you and learning more about you. (Table 14–2 lists some of the common misconceptions about résumés.) A successful résumé inspires a prospective employer to invite you to interview with the company. Thus, your purpose in writing your résumé is to create interest—*not* to tell readers every little detail.[16]

Since you've already completed a good deal of research on specific companies, you should know quite a bit about the organizations you'll be applying to. But take some time now to learn what you can about the individuals who may be reading your résumé. If you're applying to a *Fortune* 500 company, you may have to make some educated guesses about the people in the human resources department and what their needs might be. But in smaller companies, you may be able to learn the name of the recruiter or manager you'll be addressing. If you learned of an opportunity through your networking efforts, chances are you'll have both a name and some personalized advice to help tune your writing. Either way, try to

Once you view your résumé as a persuasive business message, it's easier to decide what should and shouldn't be in it.

FALLACIES AND FACTS ABOUT RÉSUMÉS		Table 14–2
Fallacy	**Fact**	
The purpose of a résumé is to list all your skills and abilities.	The purpose of a résumé is to generate interest and an interview.	
A good résumé will get you the job you want.	All a résumé can do is get you in the door.	
Your résumé will be read carefully and thoroughly.	In most cases, your résumé needs to make a positive impression within 30 or 45 seconds; moreover, it may be screened by computer looking for keywords, first—and if it doesn't contain the right keywords, a human being may never see it.	
The more good information you present about yourself in your résumé, the better.	Too much information on a résumé may actually kill the reader's appetite to know more.	
If you want a really good résumé, have it prepared by a résumé service.	You have the skills needed to prepare an effective résumé, so prepare it yourself—unless the position is especially high-level or specialized. Even then, you should check carefully before using a service.	

put yourself in your audience's position so that you'll be able to tailor your résumé to satisfy your audience's needs. Why would they be interested in learning more about you?

By the way, if employers ask to see your "CV," they're referring to your *curriculum vitae,* the term used instead of *résumé* in some professions and in many countries outside the United States. Résumés and CVs are essentially the same, although CVs can be more detailed. If you need to adapt a U.S.-style résumé to CV format, or vice versa, Monster.com has helpful guidelines on the subject.

Gathering Pertinent Information   If you haven't been keeping a log or journal of your accomplishments in your academic career and in any jobs you've held so far, you may need to do some research on yourself. Gather all the pertinent personal history you can think of, including all the specific dates, duties, and accomplishments of any previous jobs you've held. Collect every piece of relevant educational experience that adds to your qualifications—formal degrees, skills certificates, academic awards, or scholarships. Also, gather any relevant information about personal endeavors: dates of your membership in an association, offices you may have held in a club or professional organization, any presentations you might have given to a community group. You probably won't use every piece of information you come up with, but you'll want to have it at your fingertips before you begin composing your résumé.

Selecting the Best Medium   Selecting the medium for your résumé used to be a simple matter: it was typed on paper. These days, though, your job search might involve various forms, including an uploaded Word document, a plain text document that you paste into an online form, or a multimedia résumé available online or on CD-ROM. Your choice of medium involves whatever is available to you, the requirements of your target employers (many have specific instructions on their websites, which you must follow to the letter), and the skills and attributes that you're trying to promote. For instance, if you're applying for a sales position, a video clip of yourself on CD-ROM can be a strong persuader.

However, as impressive as personal websites and CD-ROM e-portfolios are, it's always a good idea to prepare a basic paper résumé and keep copies on hand. You'll never know when someone might ask for it, and not all employers want to bother with electronic media when all they want to know is your basic profile. In addition, starting with a traditional paper résumé is a great way to organize your background information and identify your unique strengths.

The key to organizing a résumé is aligning your personal strengths with both the general and specific qualities that your target employers are looking for.

Organizing Your Résumé Around Your Strengths   The most successful résumés convey seven qualities that employers seek: they demonstrate that you (1) think in terms of results, (2) know how to get things done, (3) are well rounded, (4) show signs of career progress and professional development, (5) have personal standards of excellence, (6) are flexible and willing to try new things, and (7) communicate effectively. Organizing your résumé is a question of portraying these seven attributes in the strongest possible light.

Although you may want to include a little information in all categories, you'll naturally want to emphasize the information that does the best job of aligning your career objectives with the needs of your target employers—and that does so without distorting or misrepresenting the facts.[17] Do you have something in your history that might trigger an employer's red flag? Here are some common problems and some quick suggestions for overcoming them:[18]

Frequent job changes and gaps in your work history are two of the more common issues that employers may perceive as weaknesses, so plan to address these if they pertain to you.

- **Frequent job changes.** If you've had a number of short-term jobs of a similar nature, such as independent contracting and temporary assignments, see if you can group them under a single heading. Also, if you were a victim of circumstances in positions that were eliminated as a result of mergers or other factors beyond your control, find a subtle way to convey that information (if not in your résumé, then in your cover letter). Reasonable employers understand that many otherwise stable employees have been forced to job hop in recent years.

- **Gaps in work history.** Mention relevant experience and education you gained during employment gaps, such as volunteer or community work. If gaps are due to personal problems such as drug or alcohol abuse or mental illness, offer honest but general explanations about your absences ("I had serious health concerns and had to take time off to fully recover").

- **Inexperience.** Mention related volunteer work. List relevant course work and internships. Also, offer hiring incentives such as "willing to work nights and weekends."

- **Overqualification.** Tone down your résumé, focusing exclusively on the experience and skills that relate to the position.

- **Long-term employment with one company.** Itemize each position held at the firm to show "interior mobility" and increased responsibilities.

- **Job termination for cause.** Be honest with interviewers. Show that you're a hardworking employee and counter their concerns with proof, such as recommendations and examples of completed projects.

- **Criminal record.** Consider sending out a "broadcast letter" about your skills and experience, rather than a résumé and cover letter. Prepare answers to questions that interviewers will probably pose ("You may wonder whether I will be a trustworthy employee. I'd like to offer you a list of references from previous bosses and co-workers who will attest to my integrity. I learned some hard lessons during that difficult time in my life, and now I'm fully rehabilitated").

To focus attention on your strongest points, adopt the appropriate organizational approach—make your résumé chronological, functional, or a combination of the two. The "right" choice depends on your background and your goals.

The Chronological Résumé   In a **chronological résumé,** the work-experience section dominates and is placed in the most prominent slot, immediately after the name and address and optional objective. You develop this section by listing your jobs sequentially in reverse order, beginning with the most recent position and working backward toward earlier jobs. Under each listing, describe your responsibilities and accomplishments, giving the most space to the most recent positions. If you're just graduating from college with limited professional experience, you can vary this chronological approach by putting your educational qualifications before your experience, thereby focusing attention on your academic credentials.

The chronological approach is the most common way to organize a résumé, and many employers prefer it. This approach has three key advantages: (1) Employers are familiar with it and can easily find information, (2) it highlights growth and career progression, and (3) it highlights employment continuity and stability.[19] As vice president with Korn/Ferry International, Robert Nesbit speaks for many recruiters: "Unless you have a really compelling reason, don't use any but the standard chronological format. Your résumé should not read like a treasure map, full of minute clues to the whereabouts of your jobs and experience. I want to be able to grasp quickly where a candidate has worked, how long, and in what capacities."[20]

The chronological approach is especially appropriate if you have a strong employment history and are aiming for a job that builds on your current career path.

The chronological résumé is the most common approach, but it might not be right for you at a particular stage in your career.

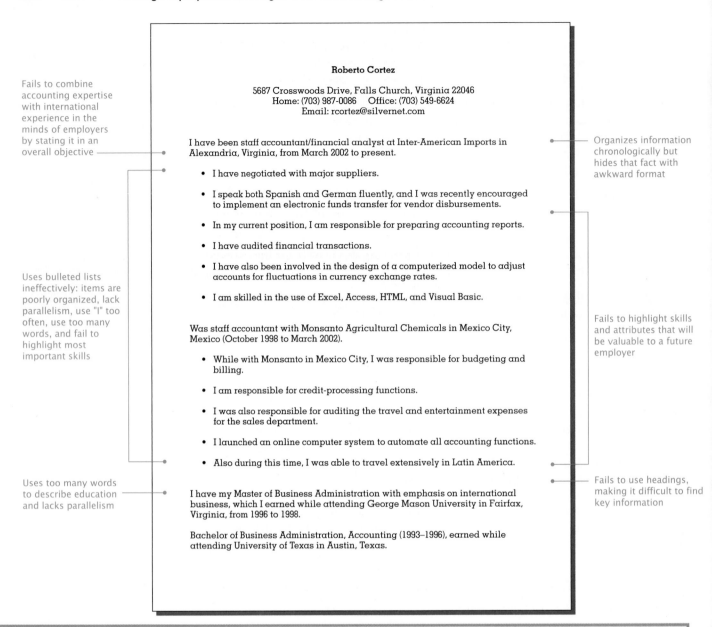

Fails to combine accounting expertise with international experience in the minds of employers by stating it in an overall objective

Uses bulleted lists ineffectively: items are poorly organized, lack parallelism, use "I" too often, use too many words, and fail to highlight most important skills

Uses too many words to describe education and lacks parallelism

Organizes information chronologically but hides that fact with awkward format

Fails to highlight skills and attributes that will be valuable to a future employer

Fails to use headings, making it difficult to find key information

FIGURE 14–4
Ineffective Chronological Résumé

This is the case for Roberto Cortez. Compare the ineffective and effective versions of Cortez's résumé in Figures 14–4 and 14–5.

The functional résumé is often considered by people with little employment history to show or gaps in their work history, but some employers suspect that people who use this approach are trying to hide weaknesses in their backgrounds.

The Functional Résumé A **functional résumé**, sometimes called a *skills résumé*, emphasizes your skills and capabilities, identifying employers and academic experience in subordinate sections. This pattern stresses individual areas of competence, so it's useful for people who are just entering the job market, who want to redirect their careers, or who have little continuous career-related experience. The functional approach also has three advantages: (1) Without having to read through job descriptions, employers can see what you can do for them, (2) you can emphasize earlier job experience, and (3) you can de-emphasize any lack of career progress or lengthy unemployment. However, you should be aware that because the functional résumé can obscure your work history, many employment professionals are suspicious of it—and some assume that candidates who use it are trying to hide something. In fact,

Combines accounting expertise with international experience in a clearly stated objective

Makes each description concise, easy to read, and informative; avoids "I" throughout

Makes special skills easy to find (note that multiple bullets in the last line could cause problems with a scannable résumé format; see page 524)

ROBERTO CORTEZ
5687 Crosswoods Drive
Falls Church, Virginia 22046
Home: (703) 987-0086   Office: (703) 549-6624
E-mail: RCortez@silvernet.com

OBJECTIVE

Accounting management position requiring hands-on knowledge
of international finance

EXPERIENCE

March 2002 to present

Staff Accountant/Financial Analyst, Inter-American Imports (Alexandria, Virginia)
- Prepare accounting reports for wholesale giftware importer ($15 million annual sales)
- Audit financial transactions with suppliers in 12 Latin American countries
- Created a computerized model to adjust accounts for fluctuations in currency exchange rates
- Negotiated joint-venture agreements with major suppliers in Mexico and Colombia
- Implemented electronic funds transfer for vendor disbursements, improving cash flow and eliminating payables clerk position

October 1998 to March 2002

Staff Accountant, Monsanto Agricultural Chemicals (Mexico City, Mexico)
- Handled budgeting, billing, and credit-processing functions for the Mexico City branch
- Audited travel & entertainment expenses for Monsanto's 30-member Latin American sales force
- Assisted in launching an online system to automate all accounting functions, improving reporting accuracy by 65%

EDUCATION

1996 to 1998   Master of Business Administration with emphasis in international business, George Mason University, Fairfax, Virginia

1993 to 1996   Bachelor of Business Administration, Accounting, University of Texas, Austin

INTERCULTURAL AND TECHNICAL SKILLS

- Fluent in Spanish and German
- Traveled extensively in Latin America
- Excel • Access • HTML • Visual Basic

Translates experience into general accomplishments that will appeal to any company that employs international accountants

Uses active language to describe past and present responsibilities and accomplishments

Makes good use of headings so that major content sections are easy to identify

FIGURE 14–5   Effective Chronological Résumé

Planning

Analyze the Situation
Decide on the best way to combine finance and international experience.

Gather Information
Research target positions to identify key employer needs.

Select the Right Medium
Start with a traditional paper résumé and develop scannable or plain text versions as needed.

Organize the Information
Choose the chronological format since it fits this strong employment history perfectly.

1

Writing

Adapt to Your Audience
Translate specific experience into general qualifications that all international companies will find valuable.

Compose the Message
Write clearly and succinctly, using active, powerful language that is appropriate to the financial management profession.

2

Completing

Revise the Message
Evaluate your content and review readability, clarity, and accuracy.

Produce the Message
Use effective design elements and suitable layout for a clean, professional appearance.

Proofread the Message
Review for errors in layout, spelling, and mechanics.

Distribute the Message
Deliver your résumé and other employment messages following the specific instructions of each employer or job board website.

3

Monster.com lists the functional résumé as one of employers' "Top 10 Pet Peeves."[21] If you don't have a strong, uninterrupted history of relevant work, the combination résumé might be a better choice.

If you don't have a lot of work history to show, consider a combination résumé to highlight your skills while still providing a chronological history of your employment.

The Combination Résumé   A **combination résumé** includes the best features of the chronological and functional approaches. Nevertheless, it is not commonly used, and it has two major disadvantages: (1) It tends to be longer, and (2) it can be repetitious if you have to list your accomplishments and skills in both the functional section and the chronological job descriptions.[22] When Erica Vorkamp developed her résumé, she chose not to use a chronological pattern, which would focus attention on her lack of recent work experience. As Figure 14–6 shows, she used a combination approach to emphasize her abilities, skills, and accomplishments (the functional part of the résumé) while also including a complete job history (the chronological part of the résumé).

FIGURE 14–6
Combination Résumé

Erica Vorkamp

993 Church Street, Barrington, Illinois 60010
Phone: (847) 884-2153
E-mail: erica.vorkamp@mailsystem.net

OBJECTIVE

Clearly identifies the nature of the position desired

To obtain an event coordinator position that requires a broad mix of skills in planning, supervision, and communication

SKILLS AND CAPABILITIES

- Plan and coordinate large-scale public events
- Develop community support for concerts, festivals, and the arts
- Manage publicity for major events
- Coordinate activities of diverse community groups
- Establish and maintain financial controls for public events
- Create and update website content, blogs, and podcasts
- Negotiate contracts with performers, carpenters, electricians, and suppliers

Relates all capabilities and experience to the specific job objective, giving a selective picture of the candidate's abilities

SPECIAL EVENT EXPERIENCE

- Arranged the 2006 week-long Arts and Entertainment Festival for the Barrington Public Library, involving performances by nearly three dozen musicians, dancers, actors, magicians, and artists
- Supervised the 2005 PTA Halloween Carnival, an all-day festival with game booths, live bands, contests, and food service that raised $7,600 for the PTA
- Organized the 2004 Midwestern convention for 800 members of the League of Women Voters, which extended over a three-day period and required arrangements for hotels, meals, speakers, and special tours
- Chaired the Children's Home Society Fashion Show (2002–2004), an annual luncheon for 400–500 that raised $15,000–$16,700 for orphans and abused children

Quantifies accomplishments with specific numbers and results

EDUCATION

- Associate of Applied Science, Administrative Assistant program with specialization in General Business, Hamilton College–Lincoln (Lincoln, Nebraska), 2002

EMPLOYMENT HISTORY

- First National Bank of Chicago, 2002 to present, operations processor; processed checks with a lost/stolen status, contacted customers by phone, inspected checks to determine risk characteristics, processed payment amounts, verified receipt reports, researched check authenticity, managed orientation program for entry-level trainees
- Hamilton College–Linclon, 2001 to 2002, part-time administrative assistant for admissions (Business Department)

Includes work history in order to show continuous employment since graduation, but minimizes its importance by placing it last on the page (since it is largely irrelevant to the position sought)

As you look at a number of sample résumés, you'll probably notice variations on the three basic formats presented here. Study these other options in light of effective communication principles; if you find one that seems like the best fit for your unique situation, by all means use it.

Writing Your Résumé

Your résumé is one of the most important documents you'll ever write. Even so, you needn't work yourself into a panic—all the advice you'll need to write effective résumés is presented in this chapter. Follow the three-step process and help ensure success by remembering four things: First, treat your résumé with the respect it deserves. Until you're able to meet with employers in person, you *are* your résumé, and a single mistake or oversight can cost you interview opportunities. Second, give yourself plenty of time. Don't put off preparing your résumé until the last second and then try to write it in one sitting. Third, learn from good models. You can find thousands of sample résumés online at college websites and job sites such as Monster.com. Fourth, don't get frustrated by the conflicting advice you'll read about résumés; they are more art than science. Consider the alternatives and choose the approach that makes the most sense to you, given everything you know about successful business communication.

> Until employers meet you in person, your résumé (and perhaps your cover letter) is usually the only information they have about you, so make sure that information is clear and compelling.

If you feel uncomfortable writing about yourself, you're not alone. Many people, even accomplished writers, find it difficult to write their own résumés. So if you're stuck, find a classmate or friend who's also writing a résumé and swap projects for a while. By working on each other's résumés, you might be able to speed up the process for both of you.

Keeping Your Résumé Honest   At some point in the writing process, you're sure to run into the question of honesty. A claim may be clearly wrong ("So what if I didn't get those last two credits—I got the same education as people who did graduate, so it's OK to say that I graduated too"). Or a rationalization may be more subtle ("Even though the task was to organize the company picnic, I did a good job, so it should qualify as 'project management' "). Either way, the information is dishonest.

> Résumé fraud has reached epidemic proportions, but employers are fighting back with more rigorous screening techniques.

Somehow, the idea that "everybody lies on their résumés" has crept into popular consciousness, and dishonesty in the job search process has reached epidemic proportions. As many as half of the résumés now sent to employers contain false information. And it's not just the simple fudging of a fact here and there. Dishonest applicants are getting creative—and bold. Don't have the college degree you want? You can buy a degree from one of the websites that now offer fake diplomas. Better yet, pay a computer hacker to insert your name into a prestigious university's graduation records, in case somebody checks. Aren't really working in that impressive job at a well-known company? You can always list it on your résumé and sign up for a service that provides phony employment verification.[23]

Applicants with integrity know they don't need to stoop to lying to compete in the job market. If you are tempted to stretch the truth, bear in mind that professional recruiters have seen every trick in the book, and employers who are fed up with the dishonesty are getting more aggressive at uncovering the truth. Roughly 80 percent now contact references and conduct criminal background checks, and many do credit checks when the job involves financial responsibility.[24] In a recent survey in Great Britain, 25 percent of employers reported withdrawing job offers after discovering that applicants lied on their résumés.[25] And even if you were to get past these filters, you'd probably be exposed on the job when you couldn't live up to your own résumé. Résumé fabrications have been known to catch up to people many years into their careers, with embarrassing consequences.

If you're not sure whether to include something in your résumé, ask yourself this: Would you be willing to say the same thing to the interviewer in person? If you wouldn't be comfortable saying in it person, don't say it in your résumé. Keep your résumé honest so that it represents who you really are and leads you toward jobs that are truly right for you.

One of the biggest challenges in writing a résumé is to make your unique qualities apparent to readers *quickly;* they won't search through details if you don't look like an appealing candidate.

Adapting Your Résumé to Your Audience   Your résumé needs to make a positive impression in a matter of seconds, so be sure to adopt a "you" attitude and think about your résumé from the employer's perspective. Ask yourself: What key qualifications will this employer be looking for? Which of these qualifications are your greatest strengths? What quality would set you apart from other candidates in the eyes of a potential employer? What are three or four of your greatest accomplishments, and what resulted from these accomplishments? No matter which format you use or what information you include, the single most important concept to keep in mind as you write is to translate your past accomplishments into perceived future potential. In other words, employers are certainly interested in what you've done in the past, but they're more interested in what you can do for them in the future. If necessary, customize your résumé for individual companies, too.

Keep in mind that you may need to "translate" your skills and experiences into the terminology of the hiring organization. For instance, military experience can develop a number of skills that are valuable in business, but military terminology can sound like a foreign language to people who aren't familiar with it. Isolate the important general concepts and present them in common business language. Similarly, educational achievements in other countries might not align with the standard U.S. definitions of high schools, community colleges, technical and trade schools, and universities. If necessary, include a brief statement explaining how your degree or certificate relates to U.S. expectations—or how your U.S. degree relates to expectations in other countries, if you're applying for work abroad.

Although your résumé is a highly factual document, it should still tell the "story of you," giving readers a clear picture of the sort of employee you are.

Regardless of your background, it's up to you to combine your experiences into a straightforward message that communicates what you can do for your potential employer.[26] Think in terms of an image or a theme you'd like to project. Are you academically gifted? A campus leader? A well-rounded person? A creative genius? A technical wizard? By knowing yourself and your audience, you'll focus successfully on the strengths needed by potential employers.

Draft your résumé using short, crisp phrases built around strong verbs and nouns.

Composing Your Résumé   To save readers time and to state your information as forcefully as possible, write your résumé using a simple and direct style (you may need to modify your approach for other countries). Use short, crisp phrases instead of whole sentences, and focus on what your reader needs to know. Avoid using the word *I,* which can sound both self-involved and repetitious by the time you outline all your skills and accomplishments. Instead, start your phrases with strong action verbs such as these:[27]

accomplished	coordinated	initiated	participated	set up
achieved	created	installed	performed	simplified
administered	demonstrated	introduced	planned	sparked
approved	developed	investigated	presented	streamlined
arranged	directed	joined	proposed	strengthened
assisted	established	launched	raised	succeeded
assumed	explored	maintained	recommended	supervised
budgeted	forecasted	managed	reduced	systematized
chaired	generated	motivated	reorganized	targeted
changed	identified	operated	resolved	trained
compiled	implemented	organized	saved	transformed
completed	improved	oversaw	served	upgraded

For instance, you might say, "Coached a Little League team to the regional play-offs" or "Managed a fast-food restaurant and four employees." Here are some additional examples of how to phrase your accomplishments using active statements that show results:

Avoid Weak Statements	Use Active Statements That Show Results
Responsible for developing a new filing system	Developed a new filing system that reduced paperwork by 50 percent
I was in charge of customer complaints and all ordering problems	Handled all customer complaints and resolved all product order discrepancies
I won a trip to Europe for opening the most new customer accounts in my department	Generated the highest number of new customer accounts in my department
Member of special campus task force to resolve student problems with existing cafeteria assignments	Assisted in implementing new campus dining program that balances student wishes with cafeteria capacity

In addition to presenting your accomplishments effectively, think carefully about the way you provide your name and contact information, educational credentials, employment history, activities and achievements, and relevant personal data.

Name and Contact Information   The first thing an employer needs to know is who you are and where you can be reached. Your name and contact information constitute the heading of your résumé, so include the following:

- Your name

- Physical address (both permanent and temporary if you're likely to move during the job search process)

- E-mail address

- Phone number(s)

- The URL of your personal webpage or e-portfolio (if you have one)

Be sure that everything in your résumé heading is well organized and clearly laid out on the page.

If the only e-mail address you have is through your current employer, get a free personal e-mail address from one of the many services that offer them, such as Hotmail or Yahoo!. It's not fair to your current employer to use company resources for a job search; moreover, it sends a bad signal to potential employers. Also, if your personal e-mail address is anything like precious.princess@something.com or PsychoDawg@something.com, get a new e-mail address for your business correspondence.

Career Objective or Summary of Qualifications   Experts disagree about the need to state a career objective on your résumé. Some argue that your objective is obvious from your qualifications, so stating your objective seems redundant. Some also maintain that such a statement labels you as being interested in only one thing and thus limits your possibilities as a candidate (especially if you want to be considered for a variety of openings). Other experts argue that employers will try to categorize you anyway, so you might as well make sure they attach the right label. They maintain that stating your objective up front gives employers an immediate idea of what you're all about.

Remember, your goal is to generate interest immediately. Consider the situation and the qualities the employer is looking for. If a stated objective will help you look

Be sure to provide complete and accurate contact information; mistakes in this section of the résumé are surprisingly common.

Get a professional-sounding e-mail address for business correspondence (such as *firstname.lastname@something.com*), if you don't already have one.

Whether you choose to open with a career objective or a summary of qualifications, remember that the important point is to generate interest immediately.

like the perfect fit, then you should definitely consider adding it. Consider the following objectives:

> A software sales position in a growing company requiring international experience
>
> Advertising assistant with print media emphasis requiring strong customer-contact skills

With some careful writing, you can phrase your career objective in terms that highlight the reader's needs.

Both these objectives have an important aspect: Even though they are stating "your" objective, they are really about the employer's needs. Avoid such self-absorbed (but all too common) statements such as "A fulfilling position that provides ample opportunity for career growth and personal satisfaction." Writers who include such statements have completely forgotten about audience focus and the "you" attitude.

A good alternative to a simple statement of career objectives is to highlight your strongest points in a brief *summary of qualifications*. A good summary of qualifications not only identifies the type of job you're interested in, but also gives employers a compelling reason to consider you. Use short, direct phrases that highlight what you can bring to a new employer, such as in this example:

> Summary of qualifications: Ten years of experience in commission selling, consistently meeting or exceeded sales goals through creative lead generation, effective closing techniques, and solid customer service.

The career objective or summary of qualifications may be the only section that employers read fully, so if you include either one, make it strong, concise, and convincing.

Your education might be one of your strongest selling points, so think carefully about how you will present it.

Education   If you're still in school, education is probably your strongest selling point. Present your educational background in depth, choosing facts that support your "theme." Give this section a heading such as "Education," "Technical Training," or "Academic Preparation," as appropriate. Then, starting with the most recent, list the name and location of each school you attended, along with the term of your enrollment (in months and years), your major and minor fields of study, significant skills and abilities you've developed in your course work, and the degrees or certificates you've earned. If you're still working toward a degree, include in parentheses the expected date of completion. Showcase your qualifications by listing courses that have directly equipped you for the job you are seeking, and indicate any scholarships, awards, or academic honors you've received.

The education section also includes off-campus training sponsored by business or government. Include any relevant seminars or workshops you've attended, as well as the certificates or other documents you've received. Mention high school or military training only if the associated achievements are pertinent to your career goals.

Whether you list your grade point average depends on the job you want and the quality of your grades. If you choose to show a grade-point average, be sure to mention the scale, especially if a five-point scale is used instead of a four-point scale. If you don't show your GPA on your résumé—and there's no rule saying you have to—be prepared to answer questions about it during the interview process, because many employers will assume that your GPA is not spectacular if you didn't show it on your résumé. If your grades are better within your major than in other courses, you can also list your GPA as "Major GPA" and include only those courses within your major (that D you received in scuba diving or Sanskrit doesn't need to hurt your accounting career).

Education is usually given less emphasis in a résumé after you've worked in your chosen field for a year or more. If work experience is your strongest qualification, save the section on education for later in the résumé and provide less detail.

When you describe past job responsibilities, be sure to relate them to the needs of potential employers—identify the skills and knowledge from these previous jobs that you can apply to a future job.

Work Experience, Skills, and Accomplishments   Like the education section, the work-experience section should focus on your overall theme. Align your past with the employer's future. Call attention to the skills you've developed on the job and to your ability to handle increasing responsibility.

List your jobs in reverse chronological order and include any part-time, summer, or intern positions, even if unrelated to your current career objective. Employers will see that you have the ability to get and hold a job—an important qualification in itself. If you have worked your way through school and contributed significantly to your education expenses, say so. Many employers interpret this accomplishment as a sign of both character and the ability to manage your time.

In each listing include the name and location of the employer. If readers are unlikely to recognize the organization, briefly describe what it does. When you want to keep the name of your current employer confidential, you can identify the firm by industry only ("a large video-game developer"). Alternatively, you might use the firm's name and request confidentiality in your application letter or include an underlined note at the top or bottom of your résumé: "Résumé submitted in confidence." If an organization's name or location has changed since your worked there, state the current name and location, and then include the old information as "formerly . . ."

Before or after each job listing, state your functional title, such as "records clerk" or "salesperson." If you were a dishwasher, say so. Don't try to make your role seem more important by glamorizing your job title, functions, or achievements. List the years you worked in the job, and use the phrase "to present" to denote current employment. If a job was part-time, say so.

Devote the most space to the jobs that are related to your target position. If you were personally responsible for something significant, be sure to mention it ("Devised a new collection system that accelerated payment of overdue receivables"). Facts about your skills and accomplishments are the most important information you can give a prospective employer, so quantify them whenever possible:

> Whenever you can, quantify your accomplishments in numerical terms: sales increases, customer satisfaction scores, measured productivity, and so on.

Designed a new ad that increased sales by 9 percent

Raised $2,500 in 15 days for cancer research

You may also include information describing other aspects of your background that pertain to your career objective. If you were applying for a position with a multinational organization, you could mention your command of another language or your travel experience. If you have an array of special skills, group them together and include them near your education or work-experience section. You might categorize such additional information as "Special Skills," "Work-Related Skills," "Other Experience," "Language Skills," or "Computer Skills."

If samples of your work might increase your chances of getting the job, insert a line at the end of your résumé offering to supply them on request, or indicate they're available in your e-portfolio. You may put "References available upon request" at the end of your résumé, but doing so is not necessary; the availability of references is usually assumed. Don't include actual names of references, but have them available.

Activities and Achievements Your résumé should describe any volunteer activities that demonstrate your abilities. List projects that require leadership, organization, teamwork, and cooperation. Emphasize career-related activities such as "member of the Student Marketing Association." List skills you learned in these activities, and explain how these skills are related to the job you're applying for. Include speaking, writing, or tutoring experience; participation in athletics or creative projects; fundraising or community-service activities; and offices held in academic or professional organizations. (However, mention of political or religious organizations may be a red flag to someone with differing views, so use your judgment.)

> Don't overlook personal accomplishments that indicate special skills or qualities, but make sure they are relevant to the jobs you're seeking.

Note any awards you've received. Again, quantify your achievements whenever possible. Instead of saying that you addressed various student groups, state how many and the approximate audience sizes. If your activities have been extensive, you may want to group them into divisions such as "College Activities," "Community Service," "Professional Associations," "Seminars and Workshops," and "Speaking Activities." An alternative is to divide them into two categories: "Service Activities" and "Achievements, Awards, and Honors."

Personal Data   Personal data is another common source of confusion with résumés. Most experts advise you to skip personal interests unless including them enhances the employer's understanding of why you would be the best candidate for the job.[28] Do personal interests and accomplishments relate to the employer's business, culture, or customers? For instance, your achievements as an amateur artist could appeal to an advertising agency, even if you're applying for a technical or business position, because its shows an appreciation for the creative process. Similarly, an interest in sports and outdoor activities could show that you'll fit in nicely at a company such as REI, Nike, or Patagonia.

Some information is best excluded from your résumé. Civil rights laws prohibit employers from discriminating on the basis of gender, marital or family status, age (although only persons aged 40 to 70 are protected), race, religion, national origin, and physical or mental disability. So be sure to exclude any items that could encourage discrimination, even subconsciously. Experts also recommend excluding salary information, reasons for leaving jobs, names of previous supervisors, your Social Security number, and other identification codes. Save these items for the interview, and then offer them only if the employer specifically requests them.

If military service is relevant to the position, you may list it in this section (or under "Education" or "Work Experience"). List the date of induction, the branch of service, where you served, the highest rank you achieved, any accomplishments related to your career goals, and the date you were discharged.

Completing Your Résumé

The last step in the three-step writing process is no less important than the other two. As with any other business message, you need to revise your résumé, produce it in an appropriate form, and proofread it for any errors before distributing it to your target employers.

Try to keep your résumé to one page. If you have a great deal of experience and are applying for a higher-level position, you may need to prepare a somewhat longer résumé. The important thing is to have enough space to present a persuasive, accurate, and concise portrait of your skills and accomplishments.

Avoid the common errors that will get your résumé excluded from consideration.

Revising Your Résumé   Ask professional recruiters to list the most common mistakes they see on résumés, and you'll hear the same things over and over again. Keep your résumé out of the recycling bin by avoiding these flaws:

- **Too long.** The résumé is not concise, relevant, and to the point.

- **Too short or sketchy.** The résumé does not give enough information for a proper evaluation of the applicant.

- **Hard to read.** The résumé lacks enough white space and devices such as indentions and boldfacing to make the reader's job easier.

- **Wordy.** Descriptions are verbose, using numerous words describing simple concepts.

- **Too slick.** The résumé appears to have been written by someone other than the applicant, which raises the question of whether the qualifications have been exaggerated.

- **Amateurish.** The résumé includes the wrong information or presents it awkwardly, which indicates that the applicant has little understanding of the business world or of a particular industry.

- **Poorly produced.** The print is faint and difficult to read or the paper is cheap and inappropriate.

- **Misspelled and ungrammatical throughout.** The document contains spelling and grammar mistakes that indicate the candidate lacks the verbal skills that are so important on the job.

- **Boastful.** The overconfident tone makes the reader wonder whether the applicant's self-evaluation is realistic.

- **Gimmicky.** The words, structure, decoration, or material used in the résumé depart so far from the usual as to make the résumé ineffective.

Producing Your Résumé   Good design is a must, and it's not hard to achieve. As you can see in Figures 14–4, 14–5, and 14–6, good designs feature simplicity, order, plenty of white space, and straightforward typefaces such as Times Roman or Arial (note that many of the fonts on your computer are not appropriate for a résumé). Make your subheadings easy to find and easy to read, placing them either above each section or in the left margin. Use lists to itemize your most important qualifications, and leave plenty of white space, even if doing so forces you to use two pages rather than one. Color is not necessary by any means, but if you add color, make it subtle and sophisticated, such as in a thin horizontal line under your name and address. The most common way to get into trouble with résumé design is going overboard. If any part of the design "jumps out at you," tone it down. To see how jarring and unprofessional a truly poor design looks to an employer, compare Figures 14–4, 14–5, and 14–6 with the "creative" design in Figure 14–7.

> Effective résumé designs are simple, clean, and professional—not gaudy, clever, or cute.

Depending on the companies you apply to, you might want to produce your résumé in as many as six forms:

> Start with a traditional printed résumé, but realize that you may need to create several other versions during your job search.

- **Printed traditional résumé.** Format your traditional résumé simply but elegantly to make the best impression on your employer.

- **Printed scannable résumé.** Prepare a printed version of your résumé that is unformatted and thus electronically scannable so that employers can store your information in their database.

- **Electronic plain-text file.** Create an electronic plain-text file to use when uploading your résumé information into web forms or inserting it into e-mail messages.

- **Microsoft Word file.** Keep a Microsoft Word file of your traditional résumé so that you can upload it on certain websites.

- **HTML format.** By creating an HTML version, you can post your résumé on your own website, on a page provided by your college, or some of the many job board sites now available.

- **PDF file.** This is an optional step, but a PDF file of your traditional résumé provides a simple, safe format to attach to e-mail messages. Creating PDFs requires Adobe Acrobat software, but a PDF can be a helpful item to have on hand in case an employer asks you to e-mail your résumé.

Most of these versions are easy to create, as you'll see in the following sections.

Printing a Traditional Résumé   The traditional paper résumé still has a place in this world of electronic job searches, if only to have a few ready whenever one of your networking contacts asks for a copy. Spend a few minutes in the paper aisle at an office supply store, and you'll notice that paper falls into three general categories: basic, low-cost white bond paper used for photocopying and printing (avoid this paper; it makes your résumé look cheap); predesigned papers with borders and backgrounds (avoid these; they make your résumé look gimmicky); and heavier, higher-quality papers

> Strive for a clean, classy look in your printed résumé, using professional-grade paper and a clean, high-quality printer.

FIGURE 14–7
Ineffective Résumé Design

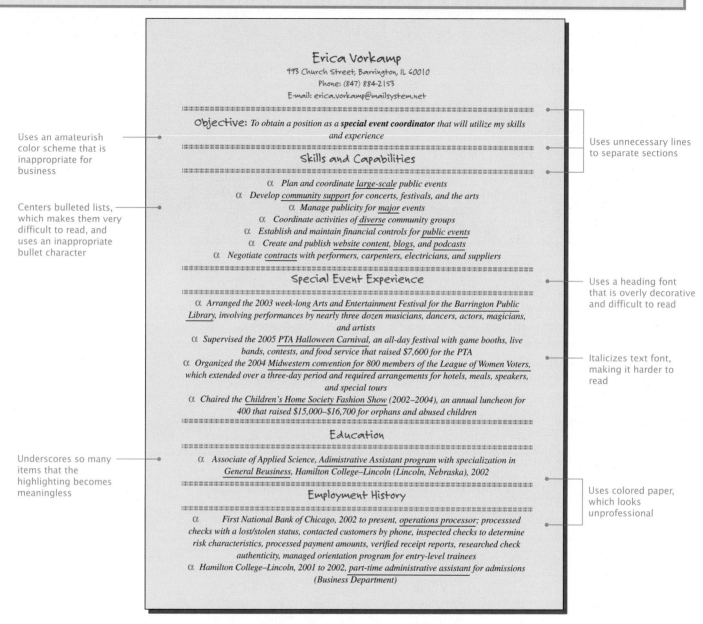

Uses an amateurish color scheme that is inappropriate for business

Centers bulleted lists, which makes them very difficult to read, and uses an inappropriate bullet character

Underscores so many items that the highlighting becomes meaningless

Uses unnecessary lines to separate sections

Uses a heading font that is overly decorative and difficult to read

Italicizes text font, making it harder to read

Uses colored paper, which looks unprofessional

---

designed specifically for résumés and other important documents. Choose a white or slightly off-white paper from this third category; these papers are more expensive, but you don't need much, and it's a worthwhile investment.

When you're ready to print your résumé, find a well-maintained, quality printer. Don't tolerate any streaks, stray lines, or poor print quality. You wouldn't walk into an interview looking messy, so make sure your résumé doesn't look that way, either.

Printing a Scannable Résumé To cope with the flood of unsolicited paper résumés in recent years, many companies now optically scan incoming résumés into a database. When hiring managers want to interview candidates for job openings, they search the database for the most attractive candidates. In simpler systems, the search is based on keyword matching for a specific position. As you read at the beginning of the chapter, more advanced systems in use at companies such as E*Trade go beyond keyword matching with more sophisticated linguistic analysis. With either approach, the system displays a list of possible candidates, each with a percentage score indicating how closely the résumé reflects the employer's requirements.[29] Nearly all large companies now use these systems, as do many mid-sized companies and even some smaller firms.[30]

The emergence of such scanning systems has important implications for your résumé. First, computers are interested only in matching information to search parameters, not in artistic attempts at résumé design. A human being may never actually see the résumé as you submitted it, so don't worry about it looking depressingly dull; computers prefer it that way. Second, *optical character recognition (OCR)* software doesn't technically "read" anything; it merely looks for shapes that match stored profiles of characters. If the OCR software can't make sense of your fancy fonts or creative page layout, it will enter gibberish into the database (for instance, your name might go in as "W<$..3r ?00!#" instead of "Walter Jones"). Third, even the most sophisticated databases cannot conduct a search with the nuance and intuition of an experienced human recruiter.

For job searchers, this situation creates two requirements for a successful scannable résumé: (1) Use a plain font and simplified design, and (2) compile your list of keywords carefully. A scannable résumé contains the same information as your traditional résumé but is formatted to be OCR-friendly (see Figure 14–8):[31]

- Use a clean, common sans serif font such as Optima or Arial, and size it between 10 and 14 points.

- Make sure that characters do not touch one another (whether numbers, letters, or symbols—including the slash [/]).

- Don't use side-by-side columns (the OCR software reads one line all the way across the page).

- Don't use ampersands (&), percent signs (%), foreign-language characters (such as é and ö), or bullet symbols (use a dash—not a lower-case 'o'—in place of a bullet symbol).

- Put each phone number and e-mail address on its own line.

- Print on white, plain paper (speckles and other background coloration can confuse the OCR software).

Your scannable résumé will probably be longer than your traditional résumé because you can't compress text into columns and because you need plenty of white space between headings and sections. If your scannable résumé runs more than one page, make sure your name appears on every subsequent page (in case the pages become separated). Before sending a scannable résumé, check the company's website or call the human resources department to see whether it has any specific requirements other than those discussed here.

When adding a keyword summary to your résumé, keep your audience in mind. Employers generally search for nouns (since verbs tend to be generic rather than specific to a particular position or skill), so make your keywords nouns as well. Use abbreviations sparingly and only when they are well-known and unambiguous, such as *MBA*. List 20 to 30 words and phrases that define your skills, experience, education, professional affiliations, and so on. Place this list right after your name and address. Figure 14–8 offers an example of a keyword summary for an accountant.

One good way to identify which keywords to include in your summary is to underline all the skills listed in ads for the types of jobs you're interested in. (Another advantage of staying current by reading periodicals, networking, and so on is that you'll develop a good ear for current terminology.) Be sure to include only those keywords that correspond with your skills and experience. Trying to get ahead of the competition by listing skills you don't have is unethical; moreover, your efforts will be quickly exposed when your keywords don't match your job experience or educational background.

Converting your résumé to scannable format is easy to do—and extremely important.

Think carefully about the keywords you include in your scannable résumé; they need to appeal to recruiters and reflect your qualities accurately.

Removes all boldfacing, nontext characters such as bullets, and two-column formatting

Roberto Cortez
5687 Crosswoods Drive
Falls Church, Virginia 22046
Home phone: (703) 987-0086
Office phone: (703) 549-6624
E-mail: RCortez@silvernet.com

KEYWORDS

Includes carefully selected keyword list derived from descriptions of target jobs

Financial executive, accounting management, international finance, financial analyst, accounting reports, financial audit, computerized accounting model, exchange rates, joint-venture agreements, budgets, billing, credit processing, online systems, MBA, fluent Spanish, fluent German, Excel, Access, Visual Basic, team player, willing to travel

OBJECTIVE

Accounting management position requiring hands-on knowledge of international finance

EXPERIENCE

Staff Accountant/Financial Analyst, Inter-American Imports (Alexandria, Virginia), March 2002 to present

Uses a dash instead of bullet point character in bulleted lists

— Prepare accounting reports for wholesale giftware importer ($15 million annual sales)
— Audit financial transactions with suppliers in 12 Latin American countries
— Created a computerized model to adjust for fluctuations in currency exchange rates
— Negotiated joint-venture agreements with major suppliers in Mexico and Colombia
— Implemented electronic funds transfer for vendor disbursements, improving cash flow and eliminating payables clerk position

Staff Accountant, Monsanto Agricultural Chemicals (Mexico City, Mexico), October 1998 to March 2002

— Handled budgeting, billing, and credit-processing functions for the Mexico City branch
— Audited travel & entertainment expenses for Monsanto's 30-member Latin American sales force
— Assisted in launching an online system to automate all accounting functions, improving reporting accuracy by 65%

Uses ample white space to help ensure accurate scanning

EDUCATION

Master of Business Administration with emphasis in international business, George Mason University (Fairfax, Virginia), 1996 to 1998

Bachelor of Business Administration, Accounting, University of Texas (Austin, Texas), 1993 to 1996

INTERCULTURAL AND TECHNICAL SKILLS

— Fluent in Spanish and German
— Traveled extensively in Latin America
— Excel, Access, HTML, Visual Basic

FIGURE 14–8
Scannable Résumé

A plain-text version of your résumé is simply a computer file without any of the formatting that you typically apply using a word processor.

Creating a Plain Text File of Your Résumé   An increasingly common way to get your information into an employer's database is by entering a *plain text* version (sometimes referred to as an *ASCII text version*) of your résumé into an online form. This approach has the same goal as a scannable résumé, but it's faster, easier, and less prone to errors than the scanning process. If you have the option of mailing a scannable résumé or submitting plain text online, go with plain text.

In addition, when employers or networking contacts ask you to e-mail your résumé, they'll often want to receive it in plain text format in the body of your e-mail message. Thanks to the prevalence of computer viruses these days, many employers will refuse to open an e-mail attachment.

Plain text is just what it sounds like: no font selections, no bullet symbols, no colors, no lines or boxes, and so on. A plain text version is easy to create with your word processor. Start with the file you used to create your traditional printed résumé, use the *save as* choice to save it as "plain text" or whichever similarly labeled option your software has, then verify the result.

The verification step is crucial because you can never be quite sure what happens to your layout. Open the text file to view the layout, but don't use your word processor; instead, open the file with a basic text editor (such as Microsoft's Notepad). If necessary, reformat the page manually, moving text and inserting spaces as needed. For simplicity's sake, left justify all your headings, rather than trying to center them manually. You can put headings in all caps or underline them with a row of dashes to separate them from blocks of text.

Make sure you verify the plain-text file that you create with your word processor; it might need a few manual adjustments using a text editor such as NotePad.

Creating a Word File of Your Traditional Résumé   In some cases, an employer or job-posting website will let you upload a Microsoft Word file directly. (Although there are certainly other word processors on the market, particularly on Apple and Linux systems, Microsoft Word is the de facto standard in business these days.) This method of transferring information preserves the design and layout of your traditional printed résumé and saves you the trouble of creating a plain text version. However, read the instructions carefully. For instance, you can upload a Word résumé to Monster.com, but the site asks you to follow some specific formatting instructions to make sure your file isn't garbled.[32]

Before you submit a Word file to anyone, make sure your system is free from viruses. Infecting a potential employer's PC is probably not the way to make a good first impression.

Creating an HTML Version of Your Résumé   You can probably find several uses for an HTML version of your résumé, including sending it as a fully formatted e-mail message (which is less risky than sending a Word file) and posting it on your personal webpage. Employers probably won't try to find you via a search engine, but if you send an e-mail to a potential employer, you can include the URL that links back to your site. Plus, you can provide links to supporting details and other materials from within your résumé. You can also use the HTML file in your e-portfolio, if you choose to create one. Even if you don't have HTML experience, you can save your résumé as a webpage from within Word.

You have many options for posting your résumé online, but remember that you could be displaying your personal information for all the world to see, so think carefully about privacy and security.

As you design your website résumé, think of important keywords to use as hyperlinks—words that will grab an employer's attention and make the recruiter want to click on that hyperlink to learn more about you. You can link to papers you've written, recommendations you've received, and sound or video clips that directly support your résumé. However, don't distract potential employers from your credentials by providing hyperlinks to other organizations or other websites (unless you designed a website and want to show it to recruiters). Also, in addition to the HTML version of your résumé, include a plain-text version on your webpage so that prospective employers can download it into their company's database.

Proofreading Your Résumé   Employers view your résumé as a concrete example of how you will prepare material on the job. It doesn't need to be good or pretty good; it needs to be perfect. Job seekers have committed every error from forgetting to put their own names on their résumés to misspelling "Education."[33] Not only is your résumé one of the most important documents you'll ever write, it's also one of the shortest, so there's every reason to make it perfect. Check all headings and lists for clarity and parallelism, and be sure that your grammar, spelling, and punctuation are correct. Ask at least three or four other people to read it, too. As the creator of the material, you could stare at a mistake for weeks and not see it.

Your résumé can't be "pretty good" or "almost perfect"—it needs to be *perfect,* so proofread it thoroughly and ask several other people to verify it, too.

You also need to make sure your résumé works in every format you create, so double- and triple-check your scannable and plain-text résumés closely. Many personal computer users now have low-cost scanners with OCR software, so you can even test the scannability of your résumé. These OCR tools aren't as accurate as commercial systems, but you'll get a rough idea of what your résumé will look like on the

Document Makeover

IMPROVE THIS RÉSUMÉ

To practice correcting drafts of actual documents, visit your online course or the access-code protected portion of the Companion Website. Click "Document Makeovers," then click Chapter 14. You will find a résumé that contains problems and errors relating to what you've learned in this chapter about writing effective résumés and application letters. Use the "Final Draft" decision tool to create an improved version of this document. Check the résumé for spelling and grammatical errors, effective use of verbs and pronouns, inclusion of unnecessary information, or omission of important facts.

other end of the scanning process. And always test your plain-text version. Simply copy it into an e-mail message and send it to yourself and several friends on different e-mail systems. Doing so will tell you if previously hidden characters are suddenly showing up or if your formatting fell apart.

Once your résumé is complete, update it continuously. As flexible as employment has become these days, you'll probably want or need to change employers several times in your career. You'll also need a current résumé to apply for membership to professional organizations and to apply for a promotion. Moreover, updating your résumé frequently helps you see how your career is progressing. Some people even create "future résumés" that list skills and experience they'd like to have. By pursuing those attributes, they can become the person they want to be, the one in that résumé.

When distributing your résumé, pay close attention to the specific wishes of each and every employer.

Distributing Your Résumé What you do to distribute your résumé depends on the number of employers you target and their preferences for receiving résumés. Employers usually list their preferences on their websites, so verify this information to make sure that your résumé ends up in the right format and in the right channel. Beyond that, here are some general delivery tips:

- **Mailing your traditional and scannable résumés.** Take some care with the packaging. Spend a few extra cents to mail these documents in a flat 9×12 envelope, or better yet, use Priority Mail, which gives you a sturdy cardboard mailer and faster delivery for just a few more dollars. Consider sending both formats to each employer. In your cover letter, explain that for the employer's convenience, you're sending both standard and scannable versions.

- **Faxing your traditional and scannable résumés.** If you know that an employer prefers résumés via fax, be sure to include a standard fax cover sheet, along with your cover letter, followed by your résumé. Set the fax machine to "fine" mode to help ensure a high-quality printout on the receiving end.

- **E-mailing your résumé.** Unless someone specifically asks for a Word document as an attachment, don't send it—it probably won't be opened. Instead, insert plain text into the body of the e-mail message or simply include a hyperlink in the e-mail that links back to your webpage résumé (or do both). If you know a reference number or a job ad number, include it in your e-mail subject line.

- **Submitting your résumé online.** The details of submitting résumés online vary from site to site, so be sure to read the instructions thoroughly. Some sites let you upload files directly from your computer; others instruct you to cut and paste blocks of plain text into specific fields in an online form. Whenever you do this, be sure to cut and paste, rather than re-typing information; you've already proofed this material, and you don't want to create any new mistakes while re-keying it.

- **Posting a résumé on your website.** If you wish to post your résumé on your website, you'll need to find some way of providing potential employers with your URL; recruiters won't take the time to use search engines to find your site.[34]

- **Posting your résumé with an index service or job site.** Make sure you explore all your online options. Websites such as Monster.com, CareerBuilder.com, and

✓ CHECKLIST: Writing an Effective Résumé

A. Plan your résumé

✓ Analyze your purpose and audience carefully to make sure your message meets employers' needs.
✓ Gather pertinent information about your target companies.
✓ Select the best medium by researching the preferences of each employer.
✓ Organize your résumé around your strengths, choosing the chronological, functional, or combination structure (be careful about using the functional structure).

B. Write your résumé

✓ Keep your résumé honest.
✓ Adapt your résumé to your audience to highlight the qualifications each employer is looking for.

✓ Use powerful language to convey your name and contact information, career objective or summary of qualifications, education, work experience, skills, work or school accomplishments, and personal activities and achievements.

C. Complete your résumé

✓ Revise your résumé until it is clear, concise, and compelling.
✓ Produce your résumé in all the formats you might need: traditional printed résumé, scannable, plain text file, Microsoft Word file, or HTML format.
✓ Proofread your résumé to make sure it is letter perfect.
✓ Distribute your résumé using the means that each employer prefers.

Yahoo Hotjobs have rapidly become a major force in recruiting. Don't forget to check specialty sites as well, such as those maintained by professional societies in your fields of interest. However, before you upload your résumé to any site, learn about its confidentiality protection. Some sites allow you to specify levels of confidentiality, such as letting employers search your qualifications without seeing your personal contact information or preventing your current employer from seeing your résumé. In any case, carefully limit the amount of personal information you provide online. Never put your Social Security number, student ID number, or driver's license number online.

For a quick summary of the steps to take when planning, writing, and completing your résumé, refer to "Checklist: Writing an Effective Résumé."

On the Job

SOLVING COMMUNICATION DILEMMAS AT E*TRADE FINANCIAL

You've joined E*Trade's human resources department as a recruiting specialist, and your responsibilities include selecting interview candidates based on résumés identified by the company's applicant tracking system. One of today's tasks is choosing applicants for a job as an operations representative in E*Trade's banking operations, a position that involves handling money transfers throughout the company's various business units. For instance, when an E*Trade customer mails in a check to add funds to an investment account, the oper-

ations representative makes sure that the customer's account is properly credited, the cash is deposited in E*Trade's own banking account, and the appropriate accounting records are updated.

Here is a description of the position from E*Trade's website ("ACH" stands for Automated Clearing House, the nationwide system used to process automated transactions such as payroll deposits and car payments, and "back office" refers to business processes that don't usually involve direct customer contact):

Job Description

Processing cash management/back office operations for bank and brokerage procedures, including deposits, new accounts, research, wires and ACH, customer inquiries, reconciliation and disbursements.

Essential Functions

- Preparation of incoming deposits for scanning/imaging/processing
- Completing wire and ACH requests
- Reconciling daily exception reporting
- Managing workflow requests from call center
- Contacting customers when necessary
- Funding accounts via the core processing system and reconciling the balance sheet
- Demonstrating proficiency with banking and brokerage regulations, as well as compliance with E*Trade Financial's policies and procedures
- Performing other duties as assigned

Background and Experience

- Bachelor's degree in business or finance preferred or equivalent experience with a financial institution
- Excellent computer skills a plus
- Excellent written and verbal communication skills
- Strong organizational skills
- Must be detail-oriented
- Ability to interact with customers and coworkers on a professional level
- Ability to work independently and with a group
- Ability to manage changing priorities, and meet tight deadlines
- Willingness to work beyond normal business hours

Based on this job description, how would you handle the following situations?[35]

1. As a fast-growing company with multiple business operations, E*Trade attracts a wide variety of job applicants. You've learned to pay close attention to the career objectives on résumés to make sure you match applicants' interests with appropriate job openings. You've selected four résumés for the operations representative position; from them, which of the following is the most compelling statement of objectives for this position?

   a. An entry-level financial position in a large company
   b. To invest my accounting and financial talent and business savvy in shepherding E*Trading toward explosive growth
   c. A position in which my degree in business administration and my experience in cash management will make a valuable contribution
   d. To learn all I can about back office operations in an exciting environment with a company whose reputation is as outstanding as E*Trade's

2. Of the education sections included in the résumés, which of the following is the most effective?

   a. Morehouse College, Atlanta, GA, 2001–2004. Received BA degree with a major in Business Administration and a minor in Finance. Graduated

with a 3.65 grade-point average. Played varsity football and basketball. Worked 15 hours per week in the library. Coordinated the local student chapter of the American Management Association. Member of Alpha Phi Alpha social fraternity.

   b. I attended Wayne State University in Detroit, Michigan, for two years and then transferred to the University of Michigan at Ann Arbor, where I completed my studies. My major was economics, but I also took many business management courses, including employee motivation, small business administration, history of business start-ups, and organizational behavior. I selected courses based on the professors' reputation for excellence, and I received mostly A's and B's. Unlike many college students, I viewed the acquisition of knowledge—rather than career preparation—as my primary goal. I believe I have received a well-rounded education that has prepared me to approach management situations as problem-solving exercises.

   c. University of Connecticut, Storrs, Connecticut. Graduated with a BA degree in 2004. Majored in Physical Education. Minored in Business Administration. Graduated with a 2.85 average.

   d. North Texas State University and University of Texas at Tyler. Received BA and MBA degrees. I majored in business as an undergraduate and concentrated in financial management during my MBA program. Received a special $2,500 scholarship offered by Rotary international recognizing academic achievement in business courses. I also won the MEGA award in 2003. Dean's List.

3. While you would naturally prefer to hire someone with directly relevant experience in cash processing, you recognize that this isn't always possible. When you can't find a candidate with such experience, you look for people who are able to translate their work experience into terms that are relevant to the positions they're applying for. Which of the following candidates does the best job of describing his or her work experience in a way that reflects the "Background and Experience" section of the operations representative job description?

   a. **McDonald's, Peoria, IL, 2000–2001. Part-time cook.** Worked 15 hours per week while attending high school. Prepared all menu items. Received employee-of-the-month award for outstanding work habits.
   University Grill, Ames, IA, 2001–2004. Part-time cook. Worked 20 hours per week while attending college. Prepared hot and cold sandwiches. Helped manager purchase ingredients. Trained new kitchen workers. Prepared work schedules for kitchen staff.

   b. Although I have never held a full-time job, I have worked part-time and during summer vacations throughout my high school and college years. During my freshman and sophomore years in high school, I bagged groceries at the A&P store three afternoons a week, where I was generally acknowledged as one of the hardest-working employees.

During my junior and senior years, I worked at the YMCA as an after-school counselor for elementary school children. I know I made a positive difference in their lives because I still get letters from some of them. During summer vacations while I was in college, I did construction work for a local homebuilder. The job paid well, and I also learned a lot about carpentry. I also worked part-time in college in the student cafeteria.

c. **Macy's Department Store, Sherman Oaks, CA, Summers, 2002–2005. Sales Consultant, Furniture Department.** Interacted with a diverse group of customers while endeavoring to satisfy their individual needs and make their shopping experience efficient and enjoyable. Under the direction of the sales manager, prepared employee schedules and completed departmental reports. Demonstrated computer skills and attention to detail while assisting with inventory management, working the cash register, and handling a variety of special orders and customer requests. Received the CEO Award (for best monthly sales performance) three times.

d. **Athens, GA, Civilian Member of Public Safety Committee, January–December 2004.**
   - Organized and promoted a lecture series on vacation safety and home security for the residents of Athens, GA; recruited and trained seven committee members to help plan and produce the lectures; persuaded local businesses to finance the program; designed, printed, and distributed flyers; wrote and distributed press releases; attracted an average of 120 people to each of three lectures

- Developed a questionnaire to determine local residents' home security needs; directed the efforts of 10 volunteers working on the survey; prepared written report for city council and delivered oral summary of findings at town meeting; helped persuade city to fund new home security program
- Initiated the Business Security Forum as an annual meeting at which local business leaders could meet to discuss safety and security issues; created promotional flyers for the first forum; convinced 19 business owners to fund a business security survey; arranged press coverage of the first forum

4. The applicant tracking system produced the résumé below for the operations representative opening. What action will you take?
   a. Definitely recommend that E*Trade take a look at this outstanding candidate.
   b. Reject the application. He doesn't give enough information about when he attended college, what he majored in, or where he has worked.
   c. Review the candidate's web-based e-portfolio, in which he has posted many of his school projects. If the assessment contains the missing information and the candidate sounds promising, recommend him for a closer look. If vital information is still missing, send the candidate an e-mail requesting additional information. Make the decision once you receive all necessary information.
   d. Consider the candidate's qualifications relative to those of other applicants. Recommend him if you cannot find three or four other applicants with more directly relevant qualifications.

Darius Jaidee
809 N. Perkins Rd, Stillwater, OK 74075
Phone: (405) 369-0098
E-mail: dariusj@okstate.edu

Career Objective: To build a successful career in financial management

Summary of Qualifications: As a student at the University of Oklahoma, Stillwater, completed a wide variety of assignments that demonstrate skills related to accounting and management. For example:

Planning skills: As president of the university's foreign affairs forum, organized six lectures and workshops featuring 36 speakers from 16 foreign countries within a nine-month period. Identified and recruited the speakers, handled their travel arrangements, and scheduled the facilities.

Communication skills: Wrote more than 25 essays and term papers on various academic topics, including at least 10 dealing with business and finance. As a senior, wrote a 20-page analysis of financial trends in the petroleum industry, interviewing five high-ranking executives in accounting and finance positions at ConocoPhillip's refinery in Ponca City, Oklahoma, and company headquarters in Houston, Texas.

Accounting and computer skills: Competent in all areas of Microsoft Office, including Excel spreadsheets and Access databases. Assisted with bookkeeping activities in parents' small business, including the conversion from paper-based to computer-based accounting (Peachtree software). Have taken courses in accounting, financial planning, database design, web design, and computer networking.

For more information, please access my e-portfolio at http://dariusjaidee.tripod.com

Learning Objectives Checkup

Assess your understanding of the principles in this chapter by reading each learning objective and studying the accompanying exercises. For fill-in items, write the missing text in the blank provided; for multiple choice items, circle the letter of the correct answer. You can check your responses against the answer key on page AK-2.

Objective 14.1: Discuss how employers view today's job market.

1. Which of the following is true of most employers in today's job market?
   a. They are trying to balance the quality and cost of talent, as well as the size of their workforces, in the face of fluctuating business requirements.
   b. All employers, from small, local businesses to giant, multinational corporations, are reducing the size of their workforces.
   c. Employers are far less tolerant of nontraditional career paths than they used to be.
   d. None of the above statements are true.

2. How important are intercultural and international experience in today's job market?
   a. Most large employers now require candidates to have international job experience.
   b. Most employers view broad intercultural experience as a sign that a candidate might have an inability to focus on the issues that are most important to U.S. corporations.
   c. In many cases, intercultural and international experience will increase your chance of being hired.
   d. Only the very largest companies care about intercultural and international experience.

Objective 14.2: List three things you can do before you graduate and while you're job hunting that will make you more valuable to employers.

3. Which of the following is a good reason to start building an employment portfolio?
   a. It will help you write your résumé because it serves as a good reminder of what you've accomplished so far.
   b. It provides evidence of your professionalism.
   c. An online portfolio gives potential employers an easy way to access additional information about you.
   d. All of the above are good reasons to maintain a portfolio.

4. If you don't have an extensive history of employment and you're too busy with schoolwork to take on a regular part-time job now, which of these steps could you take during your available free time to enhance your value to potential employers?
   a. Engage in as many social and sporting activities as you can to show employers that you're a well-rounded person.
   b. Spend your free time researching as many job opportunities as possible so you can find the ones that don't require work experience.

   c. Look for freelance assignments, short-term projects, volunteering opportunities, and internships in order to gain valuable experience, relevant contacts, and important references.
   d. Recognize that it's too late to improve your chances; just wait until you graduate, then do the best you can during interviews.

Objective 14.3: Describe the approach most employers take to finding potential new employees.

5. What is the first step that employers usually take when they need to find candidates to interview for a job opening?
   a. They search online for personal websites and e-portfolios that might contain information about potential candidates.
   b. They look inside the company for likely candidates.
   c. They post job openings on job boards such as Monster.com and CareerBuilder.com.
   d. They run ads in the local newspaper.

6. Which of these most accurately characterizes the respective approaches that employers use to find new employees and employees use to find new opportunities?
   a. Employers and employees look in the same places, in the same general sequence.
   b. The respective approaches of employers and employees is essentially opposite, with employers starting inside the firm and gradually moving toward help wanted ads as a last resort, and employees starting with help wanted ads and moving in the other direction.
   c. Since websites are the only places that employers now communicate news of job openings, the web is the only place employees should look.
   d. The approaches of employees and employers have nothing in common.

7. According to the chapter, what percentage of job openings are never advertised (a phenomenon known as the *hidden job market*)?
   a. 15 percent
   b. 5 percent
   c. 28 percent
   d. 80 percent

Objective 14.4: Discuss how to choose the appropriate résumé organization, and list the advantages or disadvantages of the three common options.

8. A/an _____ résumé highlights employment experience, listing jobs in reverse order from most recent to earliest.

9. A/an _____ résumé focuses on a person's particular skills and competencies, without itemizing his or her job history.

10. A/an _____ résumé uses elements of both the chronological and functional formats.

11. Which of the following is an advantage of the chronological résumé?
    a. It helps employers easily locate necessary information.
    b. It highlights your professional growth and career progress.
    c. It emphasizes continuity and stability in your employment background.
    d. It performs all of these communication functions.
12. Why are many employers suspicious of the functional résumé?
    a. It allows applicants to hide or downplay lengthy periods of unemployment or a lack of career progress.
    b. It doesn't scan into computer databases as effectively as other résumé formats.
    c. It doesn't provide any information about education.
    d. It encourages applicants to include accomplishments that were the result of teamwork, rather than individual efforts.
13. Which of the following is a disadvantage of the combination résumé?
    a. It is impossible to convert to scannable format.
    b. It tends to be longer than other formats and can be repetitive.
    c. It doesn't work for people with extensive job experience.
    d. The combination résumé has no disadvantages.

Objective 14.5: List the major sections of a traditional résumé.
14. Which of the following sections should be included in any résumé, regardless of the format you've chosen?
    a. Contact information, education, and work experience
    b. Contact information, education, and personal references
    c. Personal data, contact information, and education
    d. Education, personal references, and career objectives
15. Why do some experts recommend against including a career objective on your résumé?
    a. It can limit your possibilities as a candidate, particularly if you want to be considered for a variety of positions.

b. It shows that you're selfish and only thinking about your own success.
c. It shows that you're unrealistic, since no one can plan a career that might last for 40 or 50 years.
d. It helps focus you as a candidate in the minds of potential employers.
16. Should a summary of qualifications focus on the past or the future?
    a. It should focus on the past, covering things that you've already accomplished.
    b. It should focus on the future, identifying valuable traits that you can offer a new employer.
    c. It should combine elements of both the past and the future, offering solid evidence of what you've accomplished while being phrased in a way that relates to a future employer's needs.
    d. It should focus on the future, explaining what you'd like to accomplish in your career in the coming years.

Objective 14.6: Describe what you should do to adapt your résumé to a scannable format.
17. Which of the following formatting steps is necessary to convert a traditional résumé to a scannable format?
    a. Remove all font formatting, such as boldface and italics.
    b. Replace bullet point characters with dashes.
    c. Convert all multiple columns to a single column.
    d. Do all of the above.
18. What is the primary purpose of the list of keywords in a scannable résumé?
    a. It shows employers that you've done your research.
    b. It increases the probability that a computer database will select your résumé for the types of opportunities in which you're interested.
    c. It fills up space when you don't have enough work experience.
    d. Keywords should never be included in a scannable résumé.

Apply Your Knowledge

1. If you're still a year or two away from graduation, should you worry about your job search? Explain your answer.
2. One of the disadvantages of computerized résumé scanning is that some qualified applicants will be missed because the technology isn't perfect. However, more companies are using this approach to deal with the flood of résumés they receive. Do you think that scanning is a good idea? Please explain.
3. Stating your career objective on a résumé or application might limit your opportunities by labeling you too narrowly. Not stating your objective, however, might lead an employer to categorize you incorrectly. Which outcome is riskier? Do summaries of qualifications overcome such drawbacks? If so, how? Explain briefly.
4. Some people don't have a clear career path when they enter the job market. If you're in the situation, how would your uncertainty affect the way your write your résumé?

5. **Ethical Choices** Between your sophomore and junior year, you quit school for a year to earn the money to finish college. You worked as a loan processing assistant in a finance company, checking references on loan applications, typing, and filing. Your manager made a lot of the fact that he had never attended college. He seemed to resent you for pursuing your education, but he never criticized your work, so you thought you were doing okay. After you'd been working there for six months, he fired you, saying that you failed to be thorough enough in your credit checks. You were actually glad to leave, and you found another job right away at a bank doing similar duties. Now that you've graduated from college, you're writing your résumé. Will you include the finance company job in your work history? Please explain.

Practice Your Knowledge

DOCUMENT FOR ANALYSIS

Read the following résumé information, then (1) analyze the strengths or weaknesses of the information, and (2) create a résumé that follows the guidelines presented in this chapter.

DOCUMENT 14.A: WRITING A RÉSUMÉ

Sylvia Manchester
765 Belle Fleur Blvd.
New Orleans, LA 70113
(504) 312-9504
smanchester@rcnmail.com

PERSONAL:	Single, excellent health, 5'8", 116 lbs.; hobbies include cooking, dancing, and reading.
JOB OBJECTIVE:	To obtain a responsible position in marketing or sales with a good company.
EDUCATION:	BA degree in biology, University of Louisiana, 1998. Graduated with a 3.0 average. Member of the varsity cheerleading squad. President of Panhellenic League. Homecoming queen.
WORK EXPERIENCE	*Fisher Scientific Instruments, 2004 to present, field sales representative.* Responsible for calling on customers and explaining the features of Fisher's line of laboratory instruments. Also responsible for writing sales letters, attending trade shows, and preparing weekly sales reports.
	Fisher Scientific Instruments, 2001–2003, customer service representative. Was responsible for handling incoming phone calls from customers who had questions about delivery, quality, or operation of Fisher's line of laboratory instruments. Also handled miscellaneous correspondence with customers.
	Medical Electronics, Inc., 1998–2001, administrative assistant to the vice president of marketing. In addition to handling typical secretarial chores for the vice president of marketing, I was in charge of compiling the monthly sales reports, using figures provided by members of the field sales force. I also was given responsibility for doing various market research activities.
	New Orleans Convention and Visitors Bureau, 1995–1998, summers, tour guide. During the summers of my college years, I led tours of New Orleans for tourists visiting the city. My duties included greeting conventioneers and their spouses at hotels, explaining the history and features of the city during an all-day sight-seeing tour, and answering questions about New Orleans and its attractions. During my fourth summer with the bureau, I was asked to help train the new tour guides. I prepared a handbook that provided interesting facts about the various tourist attractions, as well as answers to the most commonly asked tourist questions. The Bureau was so impressed with the handbook they had it printed up so that it could be given as a gift to visitors.
	University of Louisiana, 1995–1998, part-time clerk in admissions office. While I was a student in college, I worked 15 hours a week in the admissions office. My duties included filing, processing applications, and handling correspondence with high school students and administrators.

Exercises

For active links to all websites discussed in this chapter, visit this text's website at www.prenhall.com/thill. Locate your book and click on its Comparison Website link. Then select Chapter 14, and click on "Featured Websites." Locate the name of the page or the URL related to the material in the text. Please note that links to sites that become inactive after publication of the book will be removed from the Featured Websites section.

14.1 Work-Related Preferences: Self-Assessment What work-related activities and situations do you prefer? Evaluate your preferences in each of the following areas. Use the results as a good start for guiding your job search.

Activity or Situation	Strongly Agree	Agree	Disagree	No Preference
1. I want to work independently.	_____	_____	_____	_____
2. I want variety in my work.	_____	_____	_____	_____
3. I want to work with people.	_____	_____	_____	_____
4. I want to work with technology.	_____	_____	_____	_____
5. I want physical work.	_____	_____	_____	_____
6. I want mental work.	_____	_____	_____	_____
7. I want to work for a large organization.	_____	_____	_____	_____
8. I want to work for a nonprofit organization.	_____	_____	_____	_____
9. I want to work for a small family business.	_____	_____	_____	_____
10. I want to work for a service business.	_____	_____	_____	_____
11. I want regular, predictable work hours.	_____	_____	_____	_____
12. I want to work in a city location.	_____	_____	_____	_____
13. I want to work in a small town or suburb.	_____	_____	_____	_____
14. I want to work in another country.	_____	_____	_____	_____
15. I want to work outdoors.	_____	_____	_____	_____
16. I want to work in a structured environment.	_____	_____	_____	_____

14.2 Internet Based on the preferences you identified in the self-assessment (Exercise 14.1) and the academic, professional, and personal qualities you have to offer, perform an Internet search for an appropriate career, using any of the websites listed in Table 14–1. Draft a brief report indicating how the career you select and the job openings you find match your strengths and preferences.

14.3 Teamwork Working with another student, change the following statements to make them more effective for a résumé by using action verbs.

a. Have some experience with database design.

b. Assigned to a project to analyze the cost accounting methods for a large manufacturer.

c. I was part of a team that developed a new inventory control system.

d. Am responsible for preparing the quarterly department budget.

e. Was a manager of a department with seven employees working for me.

f. Was responsible for developing a spreadsheet to analyze monthly sales by department.

g. Put in place a new program for ordering supplies.

14.4 Résumé Preparation: Work Accomplishments Using your team's answers to Exercise 14.3, make the statements stronger by quantifying them (make up any numbers you need).

14.5 Ethical Choices Assume that you achieved all the tasks shown in Exercise 14.3 not as an individual employee, but as part of a work team. In your résumé, must you mention other team members? Explain your answer.

14.6 Résumé Preparation: Electronic Plain-Text Version Using your revised version of Document for Analysis 14.A, prepare a fully formatted print résumé. What formatting changes would Sylvia Manchester need to make if she were uploading her résumé to a website as a plain-text file? Develop a keyword summary and make all the changes needed to complete this plain-text résumé.

Expand Your Knowledge

LEARNING MORE ON THE WEB
POST AN ONLINE RÉSUMÉ

www.careerbuilder.com

At CareerBuilder, you'll find sample résumés, tips on preparing different types of résumés (including scannable ones), links to additional articles, and expert advice on creating résumés that bring positive results. After you've polished your résumé-writing skills, you can search for jobs online using the site's numerous links to national and international industry-specific websites. You can access the information at CareerBuilder to develop your résumé and then post it with prospective employers—all free of charge.

ACTIVITIES

Take advantage of what this site offers, and get ideas for writing or improving a résumé.

1. Before writing a new résumé, make a list of action verbs that describe your skills and experience.
2. Describe the advantages and disadvantages of chronological and functional résumé formats. Do you think a combination résumé would be an appropriate format for your new résumé? Explain why or why not.
3. List some of the tips you learned for preparing an electronic résumé.

EXPLORING THE WEB ON YOUR OWN

Review these chapter-related websites on your own to learn more about writing résumés and cover letters.

1. Get the latest news on hiring trends and other vital career information at the Quintessential Careers blog, www. quintcareers.com/career_blog.
2. To find out what happens when résumés are scanned, log on to Proven Résumés, www.provenresumes.com/reswkshps/electronic/scnres.html.
3. Do you plan to apply to graduate school? Check out the advice on www.accepted.com, including the all-important information about writing application essays.

Learn Interactively

INTERACTIVE STUDY GUIDE

Visit www.prenhall.com/thill, then locate your book and click on its Companion Website link. Select Chapter 14 to take advantage of the interactive "Chapter Quiz" to test your knowledge of chapter concepts. Receive instant feedback on whether you need additional studying. Also, visit the "Study Hall," where you'll find an abundance of valuable resources that will help you succeed in this course.

PEAK PERFORMANCE GRAMMAR AND MECHANICS

If your instructor has required the use of "Peak Performance Grammar and Mechanics," either in your online course or on CD, you can improve your skill with numbers by using the "Peak Performance Grammar and Mechanics" module. Click "Mechanics." Take the Pretest to determine whether you have any weak areas. Then review those areas in the Refresher Course. Take the Follow-Up Test to check your grasp of using numbers in documents. For an extra challenge or advanced practice, take the Advanced Test. Finally, for additional reinforcement, go to the "Improve Your Grammar, Mechanics, and Usage" section that follows, and complete those exercises.

Improve Your Grammar, Mechanics, and Usage

The following exercises help you improve your knowledge of and power over English grammar, mechanics, and usage. Turn to the Handbook of Grammar, Mechanics, and Usage at the end of this textbook and review all of Sections 4.1 (Frequently Confused Words), 4.2 (Frequently Misused Words), and 4.3 (Frequently Misspelled Words). Then look at the following 10 items. Underline the preferred choice within each set of parentheses. (Answers to these exercises appear on page AK-4.)

1. Everyone (*accept/except*) Barbara King has registered for the company competition.
2. We need to find a new security (*device/devise*).
3. The Jennings are (*loath/loathe*) to admit that they are wrong.
4. That decision lies with the director, (*who's/whose*) in charge of this department.
5. In this department, we see (*a lot, alot*) of mistakes like that.
6. In my (*judgement, judgment*), you'll need to redo the cover.

7. He decided to reveal the information, (*irregardless, regardless*) of the consequences.
8. Why not go along when it is so easy to (*accomodate, accommodate*) his demands?
9. When you say that, do you mean to (*infer, imply*) that I'm being unfair?
10. All we have to do is try (*and, to*) get along with him for a few more days.

For additional exercises focusing on frequently confused, misused, or misspelled words, go to www.prenhall.com/thill, then locate your text and click on its Companion Website link. Click on Chapter 14, click on "Additional Exercises to Improve Your Grammar, Mechanics, and Usage," then click on "21. Frequently confused words," "22. Frequently misused words," or "23. Frequently misspelled words."

Cases

Applying the Three-Step Writing Process to Cases

Apply each step to the following cases, as assigned by your instructor.

BUILDING TOWARD A BETTER CAREER

1. **Taking stock and taking aim: Résumé tailored for the right job** Think about yourself. What are some things that come easily to you? What do you enjoy doing? In what part of the country would you like to live? Do you like to work indoors? Outdoors? A combination of the two? How much do you like to travel? Would you like to spend considerable time on the road? Do you like to work closely with others or more independently? What conditions make a job unpleasant? Do you delegate responsibility easily, or do you like to do things yourself? Are you better with words or numbers? Better at speaking or writing? Do you like to work under fixed deadlines? How important is job security to you? Do you want your supervisor to state clearly what is expected of you, or do you like the freedom to make many of your own decisions?

Your task: After answering these questions, gather information about possible jobs that suit your profile by consulting reference materials (from your college library or placement center) and by searching the Internet (using some of the search strategies discussed in Chapter 10). Next, choose a location, a company, and a job that interests you. With guidance from your instructor, decide whether to apply for a job you're qualified for now or one you'll be qualified for with additional education. Then, as directed by your instructor, write a résumé.

2. **Scanning the possibilities: Résumé for the Internet** In your search for a position, you discover Career Magazine, a website that lists hundreds of companies advertising on the Internet. Your chances of getting an interview with a leading company will be enhanced if you submit your résumé and cover letter electronically. On the web, explore **www.careermag.com**.

Your task: Prepare a scannable résumé that could be submitted to one of the companies advertising at the Career Magazine website. Print out the résumé for your instructor.

WRITING A RÉSUMÉ AND AN APPLICATION LETTER

3. **"Help wanted": Application for a job listed in the classified section** Among the jobs listed in today's *Chicago Tribune* (435 N. Michigan Avenue, Chicago, IL 60641) are the following:

- **Accounting Assistant** Established leader in the vacation ownership industry has immediate opening in its Northbrook corp. accounting dept. for an Accounting Assistant. Responsibilities include: bank reconciliation, preparation of deposits, AP, and cash receipt posting. Join our fast-growing company and enjoy our great benefits package. Flex work hours, medical, dental insurance. Fax résumé to Lisa: 847-564-3876.

- **Administrative Assistant** Fast-paced Wood Dale office seeks professional with strong computer skills. Proficient in MS Word & Excel, PowerPoint a plus. Must be detail oriented, able to handle multiple tasks, and possess strong communication skills. Excellent benefits, salary, and work environment. Fax résumé to 630-350-8649.

- **Customer Service** A nationally known computer software developer has an exciting opportunity in customer service and inside sales support in its fast-paced downtown Chicago office. You'll help resolve customer problems over the phone, provide information, assist in account management, and administer orders. If you're friendly, self-motivated, energetic, and have 2 years of experience, excellent problem-solving skills, organizational, communication, and PC skills, and communicate well over the phone, send résumé to J. Haber, 233 North Lake Shore Drive, Chicago, IL 60641.

- **Sales-Account Manager** MidCity Baking Company is seeking an Account Manager to sell and coordinate our programs to major accounts in the Chicago market. The candidate should possess strong analytical and selling skills and demonstrate computer proficiency. Previous sales experience with major account level assignment desired. A degree in business or equivalent experience preferred. For confidential consideration please mail résumé to Steven Crane, Director of Sales, MidCity Baking Company, 133 N. Railroad Avenue, Northlake IL 60614.

Your task: Write a résumé for one of these potential employers (make up any information you need or adapt your résumé).

Chapter 15

Applying and Interviewing for Employment

Learning Objectives

AFTER STUDYING THIS CHAPTER, YOU WILL BE ABLE TO

1 Define the purpose of application letters and explain how to apply the AIDA organizational approach to them

2 Describe the typical sequence of job interviews

3 Describe briefly what employers look for during an employment interview and preemployment testing

4 List six tasks you need to complete to prepare for a successful job interview

5 Explain the three stages of a successful employment interview

6 Identify the most common employment messages that follow an interview and explain when you would use each one

On the Job

COMMUNICATING AT GOOGLE

THE SEARCH ENGINE LEADER'S SEARCH FOR THE BEST TALENT ON THE WEB

When you prepare for an interview, your research often yields useful clues about the hiring company and the types of people it wants. Those clues can also help you decide which skills, traits, and successes to highlight during the interview. You'll find them especially helpful when interviewing with companies that have strong corporate personalities and specific ideas about hiring and management—companies such as Google.

For example, to maintain its lead in search-engine technology and to continue developing new tools that range from digital libraries to geographic information systems, Google pursues exceptionally talented software engineers. Most are either young risk takers with adventurous outside interests or experienced superstars from top research labs or respected technology firms. Googlers, as employees are informally known, hail from every corner of the business world—and beyond. As the company puts it, "Googlers have been Olympic athletes and Jeopardy champions; professional chefs and independent film makers." Hiring such divergent personalities creates a tension between risk and caution that helps Google quickly try, kill, or improve new ideas, and the company believes that even the best technology can always be improved.

Google's Wayne Rosing leads the company's efforts to find the most talented technical specialists in the online world.

Google also believes that talented people can manage themselves. "There's faith here in the ability of smart, well-motivated people to do the right thing," says Wayne Rosing, head of Google's engineers. "Anything that gets in the way of that is evil," including managerial hierarchies, which tended to stifle innovation and creativity. Instead, Rosing now assigns engineers to small teams and rotates project leadership within the group.

In addition to working on their projects, engineers are expected to spend 20 percent of their time interviewing outside job candidates. These interviews help them stay abreast of new thinking, and it helps the company cope with a daily deluge of résumés.

You may never apply to Google, but gaining similar insights about the companies you are interested in will give you a competitive edge. Google provides quite a bit of information on its website about work life at the company, but you can't always hop on a company website to find these insights. However, some extra digging through magazines, newsgroups, employment-related blogs, and other sources can unearth insights that will help you prepare for every stage of the employment search process.[1]

www.google.com

WRITING APPLICATION LETTERS AND OTHER EMPLOYMENT MESSAGES

Your résumé (see Chapter 14) is the centerpiece of your job search package, but it needs support from several other employment messages, including application letters, job-inquiry letters, application forms, and follow-up notes.

Application Letters

Always accompany your résumé with an application letter or e-mail that explains what you're sending, why you're sending it, and how the reader can benefit from reading your material.

Whenever you submit your résumé, accompany it with a cover, or application, letter to let readers know what you're sending, why you're sending it, and how they can benefit from reading it. Always send your résumé and application letter together, because each has a unique job to perform. The purpose of your résumé is to get employers interested enough to contact you for an interview. The purpose of your application letter is to get employers interested enough to read your résumé.

The three-step process of planning, writing, and completing an application letter involves the same tasks you've been using for other communication efforts throughout this course. Start by researching the organization you're applying to, then focus on your audience so that you can show you've done your homework. During your research, try to find out the name, title, and department of the person you're writing to. Although you won't always be able to find a specific individual to address your letter to, doing so is a major advantage whenever you can. If you can't find a specific name, avoid canned phrases such as "To Whom It May Concern" or gender-limited phrases such as "Dear Sir." Instead, use something like "Dear Hiring Manager."[2] If you're applying for work in another country, be sure to research the hiring practices prevalent in that culture and adjust your letter format as needed.

Resist the temptation to stand out with gimmicky letters; they almost never work. Impress with knowledge and professionalism instead.

When putting yourself in your reader's shoes, remember that this person's in-box is probably overflowing with résumés and cover letters. So respect your reader's time. Steer clear of gimmicks, which almost never work, and don't waste time covering information that already appears in your résumé. Keep your letter straightforward, fact-based, short, upbeat, and professional. Here are some quick tips to help you write effective cover letters:[3]

- **Be specific.** Avoid general objectives. Be as clear as possible about the kind of opportunity and industry you're looking for. Show that you understand the company and the position by echoing the key messages you picked up from the job ad, company brochure, or other information source.

- **Never volunteer salary information unless an employer asks for it.** And even if you are asked, you probably don't want to pin down a specific number at this point in the process. See "Discussing Salary" on page 560 for more information.

- **Keep it short—and keep e-mail cover letters even shorter.** In just two or three paragraphs, convey how your strengths and character would fit the position. If you find you need more space, you probably haven't thought through the opportunity sufficiently. When sending a cover letter by e-mail, make it even shorter than traditional application letters. Remember, e-mail readers want the gist as quickly as possible.

- **Show some personality.** Because your application letter is in your own style (rather than the choppy, shorthand style of your résumé), make the most of your chance to reveal not only your excellent communication skills but also some of your personality. Keep it professional, of course.

- **Aim for high quality.** Meticulously check your spelling, mechanics, and grammar. Recruiters are complaining about the declining quality of written communication, including cover letters. Since spellcheckers are only a mouse click away, there's really no excuse for misspelled words. Don't think that typos don't matter, either;

readers equate typos with writing ability. Second, don't let the ease and speed of e-mail lull you into thinking it's a casual medium. Recruiters who complain about writing quality specifically mention sloppy e-mail cover letters from younger applicants who are accustomed to casual online communication with their friends—but who don't seem to recognize that expectations in the business world are much different. At least until potential employers get to know you, they will treat your e-mail messages every bit as seriously as formal, printed letters.[4]

The casual e-mail style you may be accustomed to with your friends is considered unacceptable by many business professionals, particularly when you're making initial contact with them.

If you're sending a **solicited application letter** in response to an announced job opening, you'll usually know what qualifications the organization is seeking. You'll also face more competition for the position because hundreds of other job seekers will have seen the listing and may be sending applications too. The letter in Figure 15–1 was written in response to a help-wanted ad. Notice how Kenneth Sawyer highlights his qualifications and mirrors the requirements specified in the ad. He

FIGURE 15–1
Effective Solicited Application Letter

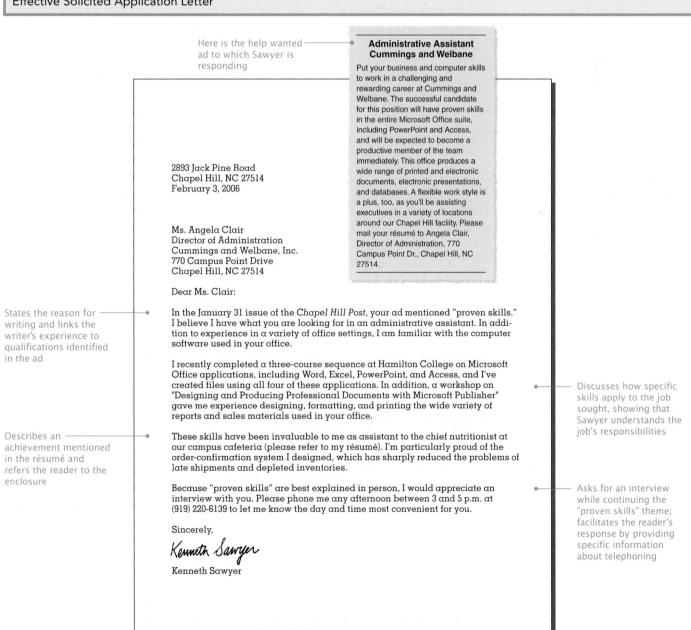

Here is the help wanted ad to which Sawyer is responding

**Administrative Assistant
Cummings and Welbane**

Put your business and computer skills to work in a challenging and rewarding career at Cummings and Welbane. The successful candidate for this position will have proven skills in the entire Microsoft Office suite, including PowerPoint and Access, and will be expected to become a productive member of the team immediately. This office produces a wide range of printed and electronic documents, electronic presentations, and databases. A flexible work style is a plus, too, as you'll be assisting executives in a variety of locations around our Chapel Hill facility. Please mail your résumé to Angela Clair, Director of Administration, 770 Campus Point Dr., Chapel Hill, NC 27514.

2893 Jack Pine Road
Chapel Hill, NC 27514
February 3, 2006

Ms. Angela Clair
Director of Administration
Cummings and Welbane, Inc.
770 Campus Point Drive
Chapel Hill, NC 27514

Dear Ms. Clair:

States the reason for writing and links the writer's experience to qualifications identified in the ad

In the January 31 issue of the *Chapel Hill Post*, your ad mentioned "proven skills." I believe I have what you are looking for in an administrative assistant. In addition to experience in a variety of office settings, I am familiar with the computer software used in your office.

I recently completed a three-course sequence at Hamilton College on Microsoft Office applications, including Word, Excel, PowerPoint, and Access, and I've created files using all four of these applications. In addition, a workshop on "Designing and Producing Professional Documents with Microsoft Publisher" gave me experience designing, formatting, and printing the wide variety of reports and sales materials used in your office.

Discusses how specific skills apply to the job sought, showing that Sawyer understands the job's responsibilities

Describes an achievement mentioned in the résumé and refers the reader to the enclosure

These skills have been invaluable to me as assistant to the chief nutritionist at our campus cafeteria (please refer to my résumé). I'm particularly proud of the order-confirmation system I designed, which has sharply reduced the problems of late shipments and depleted inventories.

Because "proven skills" are best explained in person, I would appreciate an interview with you. Please phone me any afternoon between 3 and 5 p.m. at (919) 220-6139 to let me know the day and time most convenient for you.

Asks for an interview while continuing the "proven skills" theme; facilitates the reader's response by providing specific information about telephoning

Sincerely,

Kenneth Sawyer

Kenneth Sawyer

FIGURE 15–2
Effective Unsolicited Application Letter

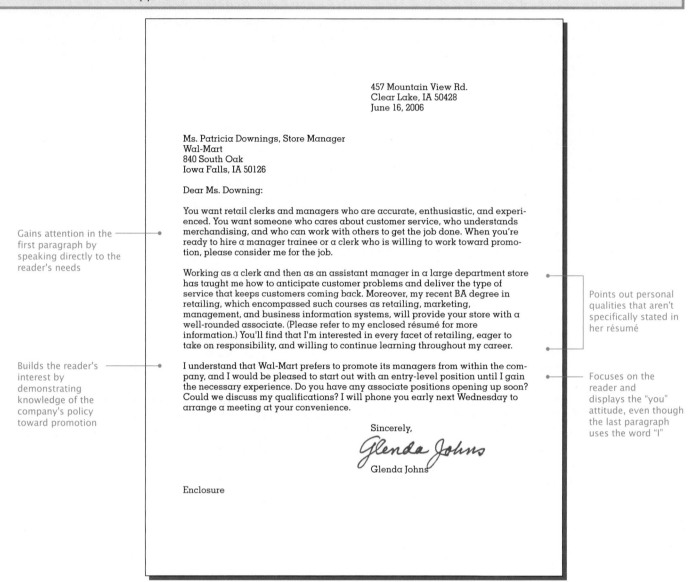

Gains attention in the first paragraph by speaking directly to the reader's needs

Builds the reader's interest by demonstrating knowledge of the company's policy toward promotion

Points out personal qualities that aren't specifically stated in her résumé

Focuses on the reader and displays the "you" attitude, even though the last paragraph uses the word "I"

457 Mountain View Rd.
Clear Lake, IA 50428
June 16, 2006

Ms. Patricia Downings, Store Manager
Wal-Mart
840 South Oak
Iowa Falls, IA 50126

Dear Ms. Downing:

You want retail clerks and managers who are accurate, enthusiastic, and experienced. You want someone who cares about customer service, who understands merchandising, and who can work with others to get the job done. When you're ready to hire a manager trainee or a clerk who is willing to work toward promotion, please consider me for the job.

Working as a clerk and then as an assistant manager in a large department store has taught me how to anticipate customer problems and deliver the type of service that keeps customers coming back. Moreover, my recent BA degree in retailing, which encompassed such courses as retailing, marketing, management, and business information systems, will provide your store with a well-rounded associate. (Please refer to my enclosed résumé for more information.) You'll find that I'm interested in every facet of retailing, eager to take on responsibility, and willing to continue learning throughout my career.

I understand that Wal-Mart prefers to promote its managers from within the company, and I would be pleased to start out with an entry-level position until I gain the necessary experience. Do you have any associate positions opening up soon? Could we discuss my qualifications? I will phone you early next Wednesday to arrange a meeting at your convenience.

Sincerely,

Glenda Johns

Glenda Johns

Enclosure

grabs attention by focusing on the phrase "proven skills," which was used in the ad: He not only elaborates on his own proven skills throughout the letter but even mentions the term in his closing paragraph.

If you're sending an **unsolicited letter** to an organization that has not announced an opening, it may actually have a better chance of being read and receiving individualized attention. In her unsolicited application letter in Figure 15–2, Glenda Johns manages to give a snapshot of her qualifications and skills without repeating what is said in her résumé. She gains attention by focusing on the needs of the employer.

Both solicited and unsolicited application letters present your qualifications similarly. The main difference is in the opening paragraph. In a solicited letter, you need no special attention-getter because you have been invited to apply. In an unsolicited letter, you need to start by capturing the reader's attention and interest.

Getting Attention Like your résumé, your application letter is a form of advertising, so organize it as you would a sales letter: Use the AIDA approach, focus on your audience, and emphasize reader benefits (as discussed in Chapter 9). Make sure your style projects confidence, without being arrogant. To sell a potential employer on your merits, you must believe in yourself and sound as though you do.

The opening paragraph of your application letter has two important tasks to accomplish: (1) clearly stating your reason for writing and (2) giving the recipient a reason to keep reading. Why would a recruiter want to keep reading your letter instead of the hundred others piling up on his or her desk? Because you show some immediate potential for meeting the company's needs. You've researched the company and the position, and you know something about the industry and its current challenges. Consider this opening:

> With the recent slowdown in corporate purchasing, I can certainly appreciate the challenge of new fleet sales in this business environment. With my high energy level and 16 months of new-car sales experience, I believe I can produce the results you listed as vital in your September 23 ad in the *Baltimore Sun*.

This applicant does a smooth job of mirroring the company's stated needs while highlighting his personal qualifications along with evidence that he understands the broader market. Although 16 months may not be considered a lot of experience, the letter balances that shortfall with enthusiasm and genuine interest in the position.

Use the subject line in your e-mail message or cover letter to get the employer's attention: simply identify the job you are applying for. Table 15–1 highlights some other ways that you can spark interest and grab attention in your opening paragraph. All these openings demonstrate the "you" attitude, and many indicate how the applicant can serve the employer.

Building Interest and Increasing Desire The middle section of your application letter presents your strongest selling points in terms of their potential benefit to the organization, thereby building interest in you and creating a desire to interview you. Don't repeat whatever selling points you may have used in your opening; instead, use this section to create a more rounded picture of your potential to contribute to the organization. As with the opening, the more specific you can be, the better. And back up your assertions with some convincing evidence of your ability to perform:

> **Poor:** I completed three college courses in business communication, earning an A in each course, and have worked for the past year at Imperial Construction.

> **Improved:** Using the skills gained from three semesters of college training in business communication, I developed a collection system for Imperial Construction that reduced annual bad-debt losses by 25 percent. By emphasizing a win-win scenario for the company and its clients with incentives for on-time payment, the system was also credited with improving customer satisfaction.

When writing a solicited letter in response to an advertisement, be sure to discuss each requirement specified in the ad. If you are deficient in any of these requirements, stress other solid selling points to help strengthen your overall presentation.

Don't restrict your message to just core job duties, either. Also highlight personal characteristics, as long as they apply to the targeted position, such as your diligence or your ability to work hard, learn quickly, handle responsibility, or get along with people:

> While attending college full-time, I trained 3 hours a day with the varsity track team. In addition, I worked part-time during the school year and up to 60 hours a week each summer in order to be totally self-supporting while in college. I can offer your organization the same level of effort and perseverance.

The opening paragraph of your application letter needs to clearly convey the reason you're writing and give the recipient a compelling reason to keep reading.

Use the middle section of your letter to expand on your opening, presenting a more complete picture of your strengths.

Table 15–1   TIPS FOR GETTING ATTENTION IN APPLICATION LETTERS

Tip	Example
Unsolicited Application Letters	
• Show how your strongest skills will benefit the organization	If you need a regional sales specialist who consistently meets sales targets while fostering strong customer relationships, please consider my qualifications.
• Describe your understanding of the job's requirements and then show how well your qualifications fit them	Your annual report stated that improving manufacturing efficiency is one of the company's top priorities for next year. Through my postgraduate research in systems engineering and consulting work for several companies in the industry, I've developed reliable methods for quickly identifying ways to cut production time while reducing resource usage.
• Mention the name of a person known to and highly regarded by the reader	When Janice McHugh of your franchise sales division spoke to our business communication class last week, she said you often need promising new marketing graduates at this time of year.
• Refer to publicized company activities, achievements, changes, or new procedures	Today's issue of the *Detroit News* reports that you may need the expertise of computer programmers versed in robotics when your Lansing tire plant automates this spring.
• Use a question to demonstrate your understanding of the organization's needs	Can your fast-growing market research division use an interviewer with two years of field survey experience, a B.A. in public relations, and a real desire to succeed? If so, please consider me for the position.
• Use a catchphrase opening if the job requires ingenuity and imagination	*Haut monde*—whether said in French, Italian, or Arabic, it still means "high society." As an interior designer for your Beverly Hills showroom, not only could I serve and sell to your distinguished clientele, but I could do it in all these languages. I speak, read, and write them fluently.
Solicited Application Letters	
• Identify where you discovered the job opening; describe what you have to offer	Your ad in the April issue of *Travel & Leisure* for a cruise-line social director caught my eye. My eight years of experience as a social director in the travel industry would allow me to serve your new Caribbean cruise division well.

Don't bring up salary in your application letter unless the recipient has previously asked you to include your salary requirements.

Another matter you might bring up in this section is your salary requirements—but *only* if the organization has asked you to state them. If you don't know the salary that's appropriate for the position and someone with your qualifications, you can find salary ranges for hundreds of jobs at the Bureau of Labor Statistics website, www.bls.gov or a number of commercial sites, including Monster.com. If you do state a target salary, tie it to the benefits you would bring to the organization (much as you would handle price in a sales letter):

> For the past two years, I have been helping a company similar to yours organize its database marketing efforts. I would therefore like to receive a salary in the same range (the mid-40s) for helping your company set up a more efficient customer database.

Toward the end of this section, refer the reader to your résumé by citing a specific fact or general point covered there:

> As you can see in the attached résumé, I've been working part-time with a local publisher since my sophomore year. During that time, I've used client interactions as an opportunity to build strong customer service skills.

Motivating Action   The final paragraph of your application letter has two important functions: to ask the reader for a specific action and to facilitate a reply. In almost all cases, the action you request is an interview. Don't demand it, however; try to sound natural and appreciative. Offer to come to the employer's office at a convenient time or, if the firm is some distance away, to meet with its nearest representative or arrange a telephone interview. Make the request easy to fulfill by stating your phone number and the best time to reach you—or, if you wish to be in control, by mentioning that you will follow up with a phone call in a few days. Refer again to your strongest selling point and, if desired, your date of availability:

> In the final paragraph of your application letter, respectfully ask for specific action and make it easy for the reader to respond.

> After you have reviewed my qualifications, could we discuss the possibility of putting my marketing skills to work for your company? Because I will be on spring break the week of March 8, I would like to arrange a time to talk then. I will call in late February to schedule a convenient time when we could discuss employment opportunities at your company.

Once you have edited and proofread your application letter, give it a final quality check by referring to "Checklist: Writing Application Letters." Then print it and send it (or e-mail it) along with your résumé promptly, especially if you are responding to an ad or online job posting.

Be aware that at some point in the application or interviewing process, some organizations will require you to complete a paper or online application form, a standardized data sheet that simplifies the comparison of applicants' qualifications. For instance, you might encounter one of these forms when submitting a résumé online or when you show up for a job interview. Even though the form may ask for information that is already on your résumé, be sure to fill it out accurately and completely. Enter "Not applicable" or "N/A" if a question doesn't apply to you. If you can't remember something and have no record of it, provide the closest estimate possible.

Application Follow-Ups

If your application letter and résumé fail to bring a response within a month or so, follow up with a second letter to keep your file active. This follow-up letter also gives you a chance to update your original application with any recent job-related information:

> Since applying to you on May 3 for an executive assistant position, I have completed a course in office management at South River Community College and received straight A's. I am now a proficient user of MS Word, including macros and other complex functions.
>
> Please keep my application in your active file, and let me know when you need a skilled executive assistant.

✓ CHECKLIST: Writing Application Letters

- ✓ Open the letter by capturing the reader's attention in a businesslike way.
- ✓ Use specific language to clearly state your interests and objectives.
- ✓ Build interest and desire in your potential contribution by presenting your key qualifications for the job.
- ✓ Link your education, experience, and personal qualities to the job requirements.
- ✓ Outline salary requirements only if the organization has requested that you provide them.
- ✓ Request an interview at a time and place that is convenient for the reader.
- ✓ Make it easy to comply with your request by providing your complete contact information and good times to reach you.
- ✓ Adapt your style for cultural variations if required.

Even if you've received a letter acknowledging your application and saying that it will be kept on file, don't hesitate to send a follow-up letter three months later to show that you are still interested:

> Three months have elapsed since I applied to you for an underwriting position, but I want to let you know that I am still very interested in joining your company.
>
> I recently completed a four-week temporary work assignment at a large local insurance agency. I learned several new verification techniques and gained experience in using the online computer system. This experience could increase my value to your underwriting department.
>
> Please keep my application in your active file, and let me know when a position opens for a capable underwriter.

Think creatively about a follow-up letter; show that you've continued to add to your skills or that you've learned more about the company or the industry.

You can still write this sort of follow-up message even if you have no new accomplishments to share. Do some quick research on the company and its industry to find something that you can feature in your message ("I've been reading about the new technical challenges facing your industry . . ."). Your initiative and knowledge will impress recruiters. Without a follow-up communication from you, the human resources office is likely to assume that you've already found a job and are no longer interested in the organization. Moreover, a company's requirements change. A follow-up letter can demonstrate that you're sincerely interested in working for the organization, persistent in pursuing your goals, and committed to upgrading your skills. And it might just get you an interview.

UNDERSTANDING THE INTERVIEWING PROCESS

Asking questions of your own is as important as answering the interviewer's questions. Not only do you get vital information, but you show initiative and curiosity.

Like Google's Wayne Rosing, all recruiters have a list of qualities and accomplishments they are looking for in job candidates. An **employment interview** is a formal meeting during which both you and the prospective employer ask questions and exchange information. These meetings have a dual purpose: (1) The organization's main objective is to find the best person available for the job by determining whether you and the organization are a good match, and (2) your main objective is to find the job best suited to your goals and capabilities. While recruiters such as those at Google are trying to decide whether you are right for them, you must decide whether Google or any other company is right for you.

Large organizations that hire hundreds of new employees every year typically take a more systematic approach to the recruiting and interviewing process than small local businesses that hire only a few new people each year. You'll need to adjust your job search according to the company's size and hiring practices. In general, the easiest way to connect with a big company is through your campus placement office; the most efficient way to approach a smaller business is often contacting the company directly.

Regardless of which path you choose, interviewing takes time, so start seeking jobs well in advance of the date you want to start work. Some students begin their job search as much as nine months before graduation. During downturns in the economy, early planning is even more crucial. Many employers become more selective and many corporations reduce their campus visits and campus hiring programs, so more of the job-search burden falls on you. Whatever shape the economy is in, try to secure as many interviews as you can, both to improve the chances of receiving a job offer and to give yourself more options when you do get offers.

In a typical job search, you can expect to have many interviews before you accept a job offer.

The Typical Sequence of Interviews

Not all organizations interview potential candidates the same way. At Southwest Airlines, for example, a candidate undergoes a rigorous interview process that can take as long as six weeks.[5] However, most employers interview an applicant two or three times before deciding to make a job offer. Applicants often face a sequence of interviews, each with a different purpose.

Most organizations interview an applicant several times before extending a job offer:
- Screening stage
- Selection stage
- Final stage

First is the preliminary *screening stage,* which is generally held on campus for new college hires and which helps employers screen out unqualified applicants. Those candidates who best meet the organization's requirements are invited to visit company offices for further evaluation. Interviews at the screening stage are fairly structured, so applicants are often asked roughly the same questions. Many companies use standardized evaluation sheets to "grade" the applicants so that all the candidates will be measured against the same criteria. In some cases, technology has transformed the initial, get-to-know-you interview, allowing employers to screen candidates by phone, video interview, or computer.[6]

Your best approach to an interview at the screening stage is to follow the interviewer's lead. Keep your responses short and to the point. Time is limited, so talking too much can be a big mistake. However, to give the interviewer a way to differentiate you from other candidates and to demonstrate your strengths and qualifications, try to emphasize the "theme" you used in developing your résumé.

During the screening stage of interviews, try to differentiate yourself from other candidates.

The next stage of interviews helps the organization narrow the field a little further. Typically, if you're invited to visit a company, you will talk with several people: a member of the human resources department, one or two potential colleagues, and your potential supervisor. You might face a panel of several interviewers who ask you questions during a single session. By noting how you listen, think, and express yourself, they can decide how likely you are to get along with colleagues. Your best approach during this *selection stage* of interviews is to show interest in the job, relate your skills and experience to the organization's needs, listen attentively, ask insightful questions, and display enthusiasm.

During the selection stage of interviews, you may interview with several people, perhaps at the same time.

If the interviewers agree that you're a good candidate, you may receive a job offer, either on the spot or a few days later by phone or mail. In other cases, you may be invited back for a final evaluation by a higher-ranking executive who has the authority to make the hiring decision and to decide on your compensation. An underlying objective of the *final stage* is often to sell you on the advantages of joining the organization.

During the final stage, the interviewer may try to sell you on working for the firm.

Common Types of Interviews

Organizations use various types of interviews to discover as much as possible about you and other applicants. A **structured interview** is generally used in the screening stage. The employer controls the interview by asking a series of prepared questions in a set order. Working from a checklist, the interviewer asks you each question, staying within an allotted time period. All answers are noted. Although useful for gathering facts, the structured interview is generally regarded as a poor measure of an applicant's personal qualities. Nevertheless, some companies use structured interviews to create uniformity in their hiring process.[7]

A structured interview is controlled by the interviewer to gather facts.

By contrast, the **open-ended interview** is less formal and unstructured, with a relaxed format. The interviewer poses broad, open-ended questions and encourages you to talk freely. This type of interview is good for bringing out your personality and for testing professional judgment. However, some candidates reveal too much,

In an open-ended interview, the recruiter encourages you to speak freely.

rambling on about personal or family problems that have nothing to do with their qualifications for employment, their ability to get along with co-workers, or any personal interests that could benefit their performance on the job. So be careful. You need to strike a balance between being friendly and remembering that you're in a business situation.

Group interviews help recruiters see how candidates interact with one another.

Some organizations perform **group interviews**, meeting with several candidates simultaneously to see how they interact. This type of interview is useful for judging interpersonal skills.

Stress interviews help recruiters see how you handle yourself under pressure.

The most unnerving type of interview is the **stress interview,** during which you might be asked pointed questions designed to irk or unsettle you, or you might be subjected to long periods of silence, criticisms of your appearance, deliberate interruptions, and abrupt or even hostile reactions by the interviewer. The theory behind this approach is that you'll reveal how well you handle stressful situations, although some experts find the technique of dubious value—particularly if the stress induced during the interview has no relationship to the job in question.[8] If you find yourself in a stress interview, pause for a few seconds to collect your thoughts, then continue knowing what the interviewer is up to.

Many companies now use video interviews at some point during the recruiting process.

As employers try to cut travel costs, the **video interview** is becoming more popular. Many large companies use videoconferencing systems to screen middle-management candidates or to interview new recruits at universities. Experts recommend that candidates prepare a bit differently for a video interview than for an in-person meeting:[9]

- Ask for a preliminary phone conversation to establish rapport with the interviewer.

- Arrive early enough to get used to the equipment and setting.

- During the interview, speak clearly but not more slowly than normal.

- Sit straight.

- Look up but not down.

- Keep your mannerisms lively without looking forced or fake.

In situational interviews, you're asked to explain how you would handle a specific set of circumstances.

Another modern twist is the **situational interview** or *behavioral interview,* in which an interviewer may describe a situation and ask, "How would you handle this?" or may ask you to describe how you handled some situation in your past. Many companies have learned that no correlation exists between how well people answer interview questions in a traditional interview and how well they perform on the job. In response, firms such as Kraft Foods, Delta Air Lines, AT&T, and Procter & Gamble rely on situational interviews. Proponents of this approach claim that interviewing is about the job, not about a candidate's five-year goals, weaknesses or strengths, challenging experiences, or greatest accomplishment. The situational interview is a hands-on, at-work meeting between an employer who needs a job done and a worker who must be fully prepared to do the work.[10]

Regardless of the type of interview you may face, a personal interview is vital because your résumé can't show whether you're lively and outgoing or subdued and low key, able to take direction or able to take charge. Each job requires a different mix of personality traits. The interviewer's task is to find out whether you will be effective on the job.

What Employers Look For in an Interview

Chapter 14 pointed out the attributes employers look for when reviewing résumés. The interview gives them a chance to go beyond this basic data to see what sort of person you are and whether you are a fit for the organization. For instance, Southwest Airlines recruiters put a high priority on a sense of humor because they believe that people who don't take themselves too seriously are better able to cope with the stress of airline work. Southwest also wants employees who are self-motivated, enthusiastic, not afraid to make decisions, willing to take risks, intelligent, good communicators, and considerate of others.[11] Regardless of the company, every employer tries to answer two essential questions during the interview process: Will the candidate be a good fit with the organization, and can he or she handle the responsibilities of the position?

Most interviewers put a high priority on discovering the basic dimensions of your personality so that they can judge whether you will be compatible with other people in the organization and with the corporate culture in general. For instance, TechTarget, an interactive media company, gives employees an unusual amount of freedom, including the freedom to set their own hours and take as many days off for illness, personal matters, and vacation as they want or need—provided they meet their work objectives. It may sound like a wonderful arrangement, but CEO Greg Strakosch recognizes some people can't handle the responsibility that comes with such independence. As a result, TechTarget's hiring process is focused on filtering out candidates who need a more structured environment.[12]

Some interviewers believe that personal background indicates how well the candidate will fit in, so they might ask about your interests, hobbies, awareness of world events, and so forth. You can expand your potential along these lines by reading widely, making an effort to meet new people, and participating in discussion groups, seminars, and workshops.

TechTarget CEO Greg Strakosch offers his employees extraordinary amounts of freedom, so he works hard to find employees who can handle the responsibility of setting their own schedules.

Beyond your organizational fit, interviewers are likely to consider your personal style as well. You're likely to impress an employer by being open, enthusiastic, and interested. Some interviewers also look for courtesy, sincerity, willingness to learn, and a style that is positive and self-confident. All of these qualities help a new employee adapt to a new workplace and new responsibilities.

> Compatibility with the organization is judged on the basis of personal background, attitudes, and style.

When you're invited to interview for a position, the interviewer should already have some idea of whether you have the right qualifications, based on a review of your résumé. During the interview, you'll probably be asked to describe your education and previous jobs in more depth so that the interviewer can determine how well your skills match the requirements. Depending on the type of interview, you may also be asked to explain how you would apply your skills in a variety of hypothetical situations.

> Suitability for the specific job is judged on the basis of
> - Academic preparation
> - Work experience
> - Job-related personality traits

Preemployment Testing

In an effort to improve the predictability of the selection process and reduce the reliance on the brief interaction that an interview allows, many employers now conduct a variety of preemployment tests.[13] Tests attempt to assess such factors as integrity, personality, job skills, and substance use. Testing is a complex topic that varies widely by industry and position, and it also involves a wide range of legal and ethical issues, including discrimination and privacy. For instance, any testing that can be construed as a preemployment medical examination is prohibited by the Americans with Disabilities Act. One national retailer was successfully sued by applicants for a preemployment test that included questions designed to uncover applicants' sexual orientation.[14] Here is an overview of the most common types of tests:

> Preemployment tests attempt to provide objective, quantitative information about a candidate's skills, attitudes, and habits.

- **Integrity tests.** You might not think that a test could identify job candidates who are more likely to steal from their employers or commit other ethical or legal infractions, but employers have had some success in using integrity tests. For example, one nationwide retailer found that preemployment integrity screening reduced its inventory shrinkage by 35 percent (*shrinkage* is an umbrella term for all inventory items that disappear before they can be sold).[15]

- **Personality tests.** Personality tests are used to assess either general character or suitability for the demands of a specific profession. General tests attempt to profile overall intellectual ability, attitudes toward work, interests, and managerial potential as well as such characteristics as dependability, commitment, honesty, and motivation. The specific tests evaluate whether a candidate is suited to the emotional rigors of demanding positions, such as flight crews, air marshals, police and fire services, and nuclear power plant operators (in fact, federal law requires such tests for nuclear plant candidates).[16]

- **Job skills tests.** The most common type of preemployment tests are those designed to assess the competency or specific abilities needed to perform a job. The skills you might be tested on vary according to the position, naturally, but the most frequently tested include basic computer skills, clerical tasks, basic business financial tasks, and legal and medical terminology.[17]

- **Substance tests.** Drug and alcohol testing is one of the most controversial issues in business today. Some employers believe such testing is absolutely necessary to maintain workplace safety, whereas others view it as an invasion of employee privacy and a sign of disrespect. Even within a single industry, you can find widely divergent opinions on the subject. Computer maker Dell tests every employee, whereas rival HP doesn't test anyone. Some companies test only applicants, but not employees.[18] Nationwide, nearly half of all companies now require applicants to undergo drug and alcohol testing, and this percentage is expected to rise for two reasons: (1) to cut the costs (approximately $100 billion a year) and the reduced productivity associated with drug abuse, and (2) to reduce the number of accidents (substance abusers have two to four times as many accidents as other employees, and drug use is linked to 40 percent of industrial fatalities).[19] Moreover, companies are liable for negligent hiring practices if an employee harms an innocent party on the job. Thus drug testing will probably increase, even though the direct financial payback of these programs is unclear.[20]

- **Background checks.** Although not a test in the usual sense, a background check also helps employers learn more about you. A background check might be used to verify the credentials on your résumé, to see how well you manage credit, or even to learn if you have a criminal history. These investigations can generate considerable controversy, since some people consider them an invasion of privacy. However, many employers believe they have no choice, given the magnitude of the risks they now face. Employers can be held liable for the actions of employees who obtained jobs under false pretenses—and lying on résumés and in interviews has reached epidemic proportions. In one recent survey of more than 2 million job applicants, 44 percent lied about their employment history, 41 percent lied about their education, and 23 percent claimed to have professional credentials or licenses they didn't have.[21]

If you're concerned about any preemployment test, ask the employer for more information or ask your college placement office for advice. You can also get more information from the Equal Employment Opportunity Commission at www.eeoc.gov. Moreover, with so many employers performing background checks these days, you might want to check up on yourself before applying for work. For instance, make sure your college transcript and credit record are correct and up to date so that any errors don't cause problems when a potential employer looks into your background.[22]

PREPARING FOR A JOB INTERVIEW

Just as written messages need planning, employment interviews need preparation.

Preparation will help you perform better under pressure; moreover, the more prepared you are, the less nervous you'll be about the interviewing process. Be sure to consider any cultural differences when preparing for interviews, and base your approach on what your audience expects. To prepare for a successful interview, learn about the organization, think ahead about questions, bolster your confidence, polish your interview style, plan to look good, and be ready when you arrive.

Learn About the Organization

Today's companies expect serious candidates to demonstrate an understanding of the company's operations, its markets, and its strategic and tactical challenges.[23] When you were planning your employment search, you probably already researched the companies you sent your résumé to. But now that you've been invited for an interview, you'll want to fine-tune your research and brush up on the facts you've collected. You can review Chapters 10 and 17 for ideas on where to look for information.

Think Ahead About Questions

Planning ahead for the interviewer's questions will help you handle them more confidently and successfully. In addition, you will want to prepare insightful questions of your own.

Be prepared to relate your qualifications to the organization's needs.

Planning for the Employer's Questions   Employers usually gear their interview questions to specific organizational needs. You can expect to be asked about your skills, achievements, and goals, as well as about your attitude toward work and school, your relationships with others (work supervisors, colleagues, and fellow students), and occasionally your hobbies and interests. You'll also need to anticipate and give a little extra thought to a few particularly tough questions, such as these:

Your college's career center has numerous resources to help you prepare for interviews.

- **What was the hardest decision you ever had to make?** Be prepared with a good example, explaining why the decision was difficult and how you finally made it.

- **What are your greatest weaknesses?** This question seems to be a stock favorite of some interviewers, although it probably rarely yields useful information. The standard way to reply is to describe a weakness so that it sounds like a virtue—revealing something about yourself while showing how it works to an employer's advantage. For instance, if you sometimes drive yourself too hard, explain that it has helped when you've had to meet deadlines. Of course, interviewers who have asked this question many times have heard similar responses many times as well. An alternative is to describe a relatively minor shortcoming and explain how you're working to improve.

- **What didn't you like about previous jobs you've held?** State what you didn't like and discuss what the experience taught you. Avoid making negative references to former employers or colleagues. Be aware that when employers ask this question, they're trying to predict if you'll be an unhappy or difficult employee in the event they hire you, so plan your answer with care.[24]

- **Where do you want to be five years from now?** This question tests (1) whether you're merely using this job as a stopover until something better comes along and (2) whether you've given thought to your long-term goals. Saying that you'd like to be company president is unrealistic, and yet few employers want people who are content to sit still. Whatever you plan to say, your answer should reflect your desire to contribute to the employer's long-term goals, not just your own goals.

- **Tell me something about yourself.** Answer that you'll be happy to talk about yourself, and ask what the interviewer wants to know. If this point is clarified, respond. If it isn't, explain how your skills can contribute to the job and the organization. This is a great chance to sell yourself.

Practice answering typical interview questions.

For a look at the types of questions often asked, see Table 15–2. Jot down a brief answer to each one. Then read over the answers until you feel comfortable with each of them. You might also give a list of interview questions to a friend or relative and have that person ask you various questions at random. This method helps you learn to articulate answers and to look at the person as you answer.

Planning Questions of Your Own   Remember that the interview is a two-way street: the questions you ask are just as important as the answers you provide. By

Table 15–2	TWENTY-FIVE COMMON INTERVIEW QUESTIONS

QUESTIONS ABOUT COLLEGE

1. What courses in college did you like most? Least? Why?

2. Do you think your extracurricular activities in college were worth the time you spent on them? Why or why not?

3. When did you choose your college major? Did you ever change your major? If so, why?

4. Do you feel you did the best scholastic work you are capable of?

5. Which of your college years was the toughest? Why?

QUESTIONS ABOUT EMPLOYERS AND JOBS

6. What jobs have you held? Why did you leave?

7. What percentage of your college expenses did you earn? How?

8. Why did you choose your particular field of work?

9. What are the disadvantages of your chosen field?

10. Have you served in the military? What rank did you achieve? What jobs did you perform?

11. What do you think about how this industry operates today?

12. Why do you think you would like this particular type of job?

QUESTIONS ABOUT PERSONAL ATTITUDES AND PREFERENCES

13. Do you prefer to work in any specific geographic location? If so, why?

14. How much money do you hope to be earning in 5 years? In 10 years?

15. What do you think determines a person's progress in a good organization?

16. What personal characteristics do you feel are necessary for success in your chosen field?

17. Tell me a story.

18. Do you like to travel?

19. Do you think grades should be considered by employers? Why or why not?

QUESTIONS ABOUT WORK HABITS

20. Do you prefer working with others or by yourself?

21. What type of boss do you prefer?

22. Have you ever had any difficulty getting along with colleagues or supervisors? With instructors? With other students?

23. Would you prefer to work in a large or a small organization? Why?

24. How do you feel about overtime work?

25. What have you done that shows initiative and willingness to work?

asking insightful questions, you can demonstrate your understanding of the organization, you can steer the discussion into those areas that allow you to present your qualifications to best advantage, and you can verify for yourself whether this is the right opportunity for you. Before the interview, prepare a list of about a dozen questions you need answered in order to evaluate the organization and the job.

Don't limit your questions to those you think will impress the interviewer, or you won't get the information you'll need to make a wise decision if and when you're offered the job. Here's a list of some things you might want to find out:

> You are responsible for deciding whether the work and the organization are compatible with your goals and values.

- **Are these my kind of people?** Observe the interviewer, and if you can, arrange to talk with other employees.

- **Can I do this work?** Compare your qualifications with the requirements described by the interviewer.

- **Will I enjoy the work?** Know yourself and what's important to you. Will you find the work challenging? Will it give you feelings of accomplishment, of satisfaction, and of making a real contribution?

- **Is the job what I want?** You may never find a job that fulfills all your wants, but the position you accept should satisfy at least your primary ones. Will it make use of your best capabilities? Does it offer a career path to the long-term goals you've set?

- **Does the job pay what I'm worth?** By comparing jobs and salaries before you're interviewed, you'll know what's reasonable for someone with your skills in your industry.

- **What kind of person would I be working for?** If the interviewer is your prospective boss, watch how others interact with that person, tactfully query other employees, or pose a careful question or two during the interview. If your prospective boss is someone else, ask for that person's name, job title, and responsibilities. Try to learn all you can.

- **What sort of future can I expect with this organization?** How healthy is the organization? Can you look forward to advancement? Does the organization offer insurance, pension, vacation, or other benefits?

> You don't necessarily have to wait until the interviewer asks if you have any questions of your own; look for smooth ways to work prepared questions into the conversation.

Rather than bombarding the interviewer with questions the minute you walk in the room, work them into the conversation naturally, without trying to take control of the interview. For a list of good questions you might use as a starting point, see Table 15–3.

TEN QUESTIONS TO ASK THE INTERVIEWER   Table 15–3

1. What are the job's major responsibilities?

2. What qualities do you want in the person who fills this position?

3. How do you measure success for someone in this position?

4. What is the first problem that needs the attention of the person you hire?

5. Would relocation be required now or in the future?

6. Why is this job now vacant?

7. What makes your organization different from others in the industry?

8. How would you define your organization's managerial philosophy?

9. What additional training does your organization provide?

10. Do employees have an opportunity to continue their education with help from the organization?

Impress the interviewer with your ability to organize and be thorough by bringing a list of questions to the job interview.

Write your list of questions on a notepad and take it to the interview. If you need to, jot down brief notes during the meeting, and be sure to record answers in more detail afterward. Having a list of questions should impress the interviewer with your organization and thoroughness. It will also show that you're there to evaluate the organization and the job as well as to promote yourself.

Bolster Your Confidence

By building your confidence, you'll make a better impression and make the whole process less stressful. The best way to counteract any apprehension is to remove its source. You may feel shy or self-conscious because you think you have some flaw that will prompt others to reject you. Bear in mind, however, that you're often much more conscious of your limitations than other people are.

If some aspect of your appearance or background makes you uneasy, correct it or offset it by emphasizing positive traits such as warmth, wit, intelligence, or charm. Instead of dwelling on your weaknesses, focus on your strengths. Instead of worrying about how you will perform in the interview, focus on how you can help the organization succeed. Remember that all the other candidates for the job are just as nervous as you are. The interviewers may be nervous, too; after all, they're judged on how well they assess candidates, so help them see your positive qualities clearly.

Polish Your Interview Style

Interview simulators, such as this system from Perfect Interview, let you interact with a virtual interviewer then review and improve your responses.

Competence and confidence are the foundation of your interviewing style, and you can enhance those by giving the interviewer an impression of poise, good manners, and good judgment. Some job seekers hire professional coaches and image consultants to create just the right impression. Charging anywhere from $125 to $500 an hour, these professionals spend a majority of their time teaching clients how to adopt appropriate communication styles, and to do so they use role-playing, videotaping, and audiotaping.[25] You can use these techniques too.

You can develop an adept style by staging mock interviews with a friend or using an interview simulator. You can tape-record or videotape these mock interviews and then evaluate them yourself. The taping process can be intimidating, but it helps you work out any problems before you begin actual job interviews. Your career center may have computer-based systems for practicing interview as well, or you might consider one of the commercially available systems such as that offered

Staging mock interviews with a friend is a good way to hone your style.

by Perfect Interview, www.perfectinterview.com. To find others, search online for "practice interviews" or "interview simulators."

After each practice session, try to identify opportunities for improvement. Have your mock interview partner critique your performance, or critique yourself if you're able to record your practice interviews, using the list of warning signs shown in Table 15–4.

Nonverbal behavior has a significant effect on the interviewer's opinion of you.

As you stage your mock interviews, pay particular attention to your nonverbal behavior. In the United States, you are more likely to have a successful interview if you maintain eye contact, smile frequently, sit in an attentive position, and use frequent hand gestures. These nonverbal signals convince the interviewer that you're

WARNING SIGNS: 25 ATTRIBUTES THAT INTERVIEWERS DON'T LIKE TO SEE	Table 15–4

- Poor personal appearance
- Overbearing, overaggressive, conceited demeanor; a "superiority complex" or "know it all" attitude
- Inability to express ideas clearly; poor voice, diction, grammar
- Lack of knowledge or experience
- Poor preparation for the interview
- Lack of interest in the job
- Lack of planning for career; lack of purpose, goals
- Lack of enthusiasm; passive and indifferent demeanor
- Lack of confidence and poise; appearance of being nervous and ill at ease
- Insufficient evidence of achievement
- Failure to participate in extracurricular activities
- Overemphasis on money; interested only in financial aspects of the job
- Poor scholastic record
- Unwillingness to start at the bottom; expecting too much too soon
- Tendency to make excuses
- Evasive answers; hedges on unfavorable factors in record
- Lack of tact
- Lack of maturity
- Lack of courtesy; poor manners
- Condemnation of past employers
- Lack of social skills
- Marked dislike for schoolwork
- Lack of vitality
- Failure to look interviewer in the eye
- Limp, weak handshake

alert, assertive, dependable, confident, responsible, and energetic.[26] Some companies based in the United States are owned and managed by people from other cultures, so during your research, find out about the company's cultural background and preferences regarding nonverbal behavior.

The sound of your voice can also have a major impact on your success in a job interview.[27] You can work with a tape recorder to overcome voice problems. If you tend to speak too rapidly, practice speaking more slowly. If your voice sounds too loud or too soft, practice adjusting it. Work on eliminating speech mannerisms such as *you know, like,* and *um,* which might make you sound inarticulate.

> The way you speak is almost as important as what you say.

Plan to Look Good

Physical appearance is important because clothing and grooming reveal something about a candidate's personality, professionalism, and ability to sense the unspoken "rules" of a situation. When it comes to clothing, the best policy is to dress conservatively. Wear the best-quality businesslike clothing you can, preferably in a dark, solid

> Dress conservatively and be well groomed for every interview; there's plenty of time to be casual after you get the job.

Make a positive first impression with careful grooming and attire. You don't need to spend a fortune on new clothes, but you do need to look clean, prepared, and professional.

color. However, wearing clothes that are appropriate and clean is far more important than wearing clothes that are expensive. Avoid flamboyant styles, colors, and prints. Even in companies where interviewers may dress casually, it's important to show good judgment by dressing—and acting—in a professional manner. Even minor points of etiquette can make a lasting impression on recruiters.

Some candidates ask interviewers ahead of time what they should wear. One human resources executive tells job seekers to dress business casual because dressing in a suit, for example, looks awkward at his company.[28] However, in other companies, business casual would be completely out of place in a job interview. Your research into various industries and professions should give you insight into expectations for business attire, too. If you're not sure, being a little too formal is a better guess than being too casual.

Good grooming makes any style of clothing look better. Make sure your clothes are clean and unwrinkled, your shoes unscuffed and well shined, your hair neatly styled and combed, your fingernails clean, and your breath fresh. If possible, check your appearance in a mirror before entering the room for the interview. Finally, remember that one of the best ways to look good is to smile at appropriate moments.

Make professional appearance and habits a routine part of your day after you land that first job, too. Some students fail to recognize the need to adjust their dress and personal habits when they make the transition to professional life. Behaviors you may not think about, such as showing up five minutes late to every meeting or wearing a T-shirt to a client's office, could limit your career potential. Again, these may seem like minor issues, but many people are sensitive to these points of business etiquette and consider them a sign of mutual respect.

Be Ready When You Arrive

Be ready to go the minute you arrive at the interviewing site; don't fumble around for your résumé or your list of questions.

When you go to your interview, take a small notebook, a pen, a list of the questions you want to ask, two copies of your résumé (protected in a folder), an outline of what you have learned about the organization, and any past correspondence about the position. You may also want to take a small calendar, a transcript of your college grades, a list of references, and a portfolio containing samples of your work, performance reviews, and certificates of achievement.[29]

Be sure you know when and where the interview will be held. The worst way to start any interview is to be late. Check the route you will take, even if it means phoning ahead to ask. Find out how much time it takes to get there; then plan to arrive early. Allow a little extra time in case you run into a problem on the way.

Once you arrive, relax. You may have to wait a little while, so bring along something business-oriented to read. If company literature is available in the lobby, read it while you wait. In every case, show respect for everyone you encounter. If the opportunity presents itself, ask a few questions about the organization or express enthusiasm for the job. Refrain from smoking before the interview (nonsmokers can smell smoke on the clothing of interviewees), and avoid chewing gum or otherwise eating in the waiting room. Anything you do or say while you wait may well get back to the interviewer, so make sure your best qualities show from the moment you enter the premises. That way you'll be ready for the interview itself once it actually begins. To review the steps for planning a successful interview, see "Checklist: Planning for a Successful Job Interview."

✓ CHECKLIST: Planning for a Successful Job Interview

- ✓ Learn about the organization, including its operations, markets, and challenges.
- ✓ Plan for the employer's questions, including questions about tough decisions you've made, your weaknesses, what you didn't like about previous jobs, and your career plans.
- ✓ Plan questions of your own to find out whether this is really the job and the organization for you, and to show that you've done your research.
- ✓ Bolster your confidence by removing as many sources of apprehension as you can.

- ✓ Polish your interview style by staging mock interviews.
- ✓ Plan to look good with appropriate dress and grooming.
- ✓ Be ready when you arrive, and bring along a pen, paper, list of questions, two résumés, an outline of your research on the company, and any correspondence you've had regarding the position.
- ✓ Double-check the location and time of the interview and map out the route beforehand.
- ✓ Relax and be flexible; the schedule and interview arrangements may change when you arrive.

INTERVIEWING FOR SUCCESS

Your approach to interviews evolves as you move through each stage of the process. The techniques for success are similar throughout, even though the focus and purpose of the interviews do change—both for you and for the employer. To increase your chances of success, follow the tips from successful interviewers about how to make a positive impression by avoiding mistakes (see "Sharpening Your Career Skills: Make Sure You Don't Talk Yourself Right Out of a Job").

If you're being interviewed for the first time, your main objective is to differentiate yourself from the many other candidates who are also being screened. Without resorting to gimmicks, call attention to one key aspect of your personal or professional background so that the recruiter can say, "Oh yes, I remember Brenda Jones—the one who built a computerized home weather station to wake her up a few minutes early whenever it snowed overnight." Just be sure the trait you accentuate is relevant to the job in question. In addition, you'll want to be prepared in case an employer expects you to demonstrate a particular skill (perhaps problem solving) during the screening interview.

> Present a memorable "headline" during an interview at the screening stage.

If you progress to the initial selection interview, broaden your promotional message. Instead of telegraphing the "headline," give the interviewer the whole story. Touch briefly on all your strengths, but explain three or four of your best qualifications in depth. At the same time, probe for information that will help you evaluate the position objectively.

> Cover all your strengths during an interview at the selection stage.

If you're asked back for a final visit, your chances of being offered a position have improved considerably. At this point, you'll probably talk to a person who has the authority to make an offer and negotiate terms. This individual may have already concluded that your background is right for the job and may be more concerned with sizing up your personality. Both you and the employer need to find out whether there is a good psychological fit. Be honest about your motivations and values. If the interview goes well, your objective should be to clinch the deal on the best possible terms.

> Emphasize your personality during a final interview.

Regardless of where you are in the interview process, every interview will proceed through three stages: the warm-up, the question-and-answer session, and the close.

The Warm-Up

Of the three stages, the warm-up is the most important, even though it may account for only a small fraction of the time you spend in the interview. Studies suggest that many interviewers, particularly those who are poorly trained in interviewing techniques, make up their minds within the first 20 seconds of contact with a candidate.[30]

> The first minute of the interview is crucial.

SHARPENING YOUR CAREER SKILLS

Make Sure You Don't Talk Yourself Right Out of a Job

Even well-qualified applicants sometimes talk themselves right out of an opportunity by making avoidable blunders during the job interview. As you develop your interviewing style, take care to avoid these all-too-common mistakes:

- **Being defensive.** An interview isn't an interrogation, and the interviewer isn't out to get you. Treat interviews as business conversations, an exchange of information in which both sides have something of value to share. You'll give (and get) better information that way.

- **Failing to ask questions.** Interviewers expect you to ask questions, both during the interview and at its conclusion when they ask if you have any questions. If you have nothing to ask, you come across as someone who isn't really interested in the job or the company. Prepare a list of questions before every interview.

- **Failing to answer questions—or trying to bluff your way through difficult questions.** If you simply can't answer a question, don't try to talk your way around it or fake your way through it. Remember that sometimes interviewers ask strange questions just to see how you'll respond. What kind of fish would you like to be? How would you go about nailing jelly to the ceiling? Why are manhole covers round? Some of these questions are designed to test your grace under pressure, whereas others actually expect you to think through a logical answer (manhole covers are round because that's the only shape that can't fall through an open hole of slightly smaller size, by the way). Don't act like the question is stupid or refuse to answer it. Sit quietly for a few seconds,

try to imagine why the interviewer has asked the question, then frame an answer that links your strengths to the company's needs.

- **Freezing up.** The human brain seems to have the capacity to just freeze up under stressful situations. An interviewer might've asked you a simple question, or perhaps you were halfway through an intelligent answer, and poof—all your thoughts disappear and you can't organize words in any logical order. Try to quickly replay the last few seconds of the conversation in your mind to see if you can recapture the conversational thread. If that fails, you're probably better off explaining to the reviewer that your mind has gone blank and asking him or her to repeat the question. Doing so is embarrassing, but not as embarrassing as chattering on and on with no idea of what you're saying, hoping you'll stumble back onto the topic.

- **Failing to understand your potential to contribute to the organization.** Interviewers care less about your history than about how you can help their organization in the future. Unless you've inventoried your own skills, researched their needs, and found a match between the two, you won't be able to answer these questions quickly and intelligently.

CAREER APPLICATIONS

1. What should you do if you suddenly realize that something you said earlier in the interview is incorrect or incomplete? Explain your answer.

2. How would you answer the following question: "How do you respond to colleagues who make you angry?" Explain your answer.

Don't let your guard down if it appears the interviewer wants to engage in what feels like small talk; these exchanges are every bit as important as structured questions.

Body language is important at this point. Because you won't have time to say much in the first minute or two, you must sell yourself nonverbally. Begin by using the interviewer's name if you're sure you can pronounce it correctly. If the interviewer extends a hand, respond with a firm but not overpowering handshake, and wait until you're asked to be seated. Let the interviewer start the discussion, and listen for cues that tell you what he or she is interested in knowing about you as a potential employee.

The Question-and-Answer Stage

Questions and answers will consume the greatest part of the interview. The interviewer will ask you about your qualifications and discuss many of the points mentioned in your résumé. You'll also be asking questions of your own.

Dealing with Questions   Let the interviewer lead the conversation, and never answer a question before he or she has finished asking it—the last few words of the question might alter how you respond. As questions are asked, tailor your answers to make a favorable impression. Don't limit yourself to yes-or-no answers. If you're asked a difficult question, be sure you pause to think before responding. The recruiter may know that you can't answer a question and only wants to know how you'll respond.

Tailor your answers to emphasize your strengths.

If you periodically ask a question or two from the list you've prepared, you'll not only learn something but also demonstrate your interest. Probe for what the company is looking for in its new employees so that you can show how you meet the firm's needs. Also try to zero in on any reservations the interviewer might have about you so that you can dispel them.

Listening to the Interviewer   Paying attention when the interviewer speaks can be as important as giving good answers or asking good questions. Review the tips on listening offered in Chapter 2.

The interviewer's facial expressions, eye movements, gestures, and posture may tell you the real meaning of what is being said. Be especially aware of how your comments are received. Does the interviewer nod in agreement or smile to show approval? If so, you're making progress. If not, you might want to introduce another topic or modify your approach.

Paying attention to both verbal and nonverbal messages can help you turn the question-and-answer stage to your advantage.

Fielding Discriminatory Questions   Employers cannot legally discriminate against a job candidate on the basis of race, color, gender, age (at least if you're between 40 and 70), marital status, religion, national origin, or disability. Individual states and cities have enacted a variety of laws concerning interview questions, so you may have additional protections beyond the federal standards.[31] Table 15–5 compares specific questions that may and may not be asked during an employment interview.

Well-trained interviewers are aware of questions they shouldn't ask.

If your interviewer asks these personal questions, how you respond depends on how badly you want the job, how you feel about revealing the information asked for, what you think the interviewer will do with the information, and whether you want to work for a company that asks such questions. Remember that you always have the option of simply refusing to answer or of telling the interviewer that you think a particular question is unethical—although either of these responses is likely to leave an

Think about how you might respond if you are asked a potentially unlawful question.

INTERVIEW QUESTIONS THAT MAY AND MAY NOT BE ASKED   Table 15–5

Interviewers May Ask This . . .	But Not This
What is your name?	What was your maiden name?
Are you willing to travel or work overtime when the job requires it?	Are you married? Do you have children at home? Do you plan to have children? Would working on weekends conflict with your religion?
Are you over 18?	When were you born?
Did you graduate from high school?	When did you graduate from high school?
[No questions about race are allowed.]	What is your race?
Can you perform [specific tasks]?	Do you have physical or mental disabilities? Do you have a drug or alcohol problem? Are you taking any prescription drugs?
Do you have the legal right to work in the United States?	Are you a U.S. citizen? What country are you a citizen of?
Have you ever been convicted of a felony?	Have you ever been arrested?
This job requires that you speak Spanish. Do you?	What language did you speak in your home when you were growing up?

unfavorable impression.[32] If you do want the job, you might (1) ask how the question is related to your qualifications, (2) explain that the information is personal, (3) respond to what you think is the interviewer's real concern, or (4) answer both the question and the concern.

If you do answer an unethical or unlawful question, you run the risk that your answer may hurt your chances, so think carefully before answering.[33] In any event, don't forget the two-way nature of the interview process: The organization is learning about you and you're learning about the organization. Would you want to work for an organization that condones illegal or discriminatory questions or that doesn't train its employees enough to avoid them?

If you believe an interviewer's questions are unreasonable, unrelated to the job, or an attempt to discriminate, you may complain to the nearest field office of the EEOC (find offices online at www.eeoc.gov) or to the state agency that regulates fair employment practices. To report discrimination on the basis of age or physical disability, contact the employer's equal opportunity officer or the U.S. Department of Labor. If you file a complaint, be prepared to spend a lot of time and effort on it—and keep in mind that you may not win.[34]

The Close

Like the warm up, the end of the interview is more important than its brief duration would indicate. In the last few minutes, you need to evaluate how well you've done. You also need to correct any misconceptions the interviewer might have.

Conclude the interview with courtesy and enthusiasm.

Concluding Gracefully   You can generally tell when the interviewer is trying to conclude the session. He or she may ask whether you have any more questions, sum up the discussion, change position, or indicate with a gesture that the interview is over. When you get the signal, respond promptly, but don't rush. Be sure to thank the interviewer for the opportunity and express an interest in the organization. If you can do so comfortably, try to pin down what will happen next, but don't press for an immediate decision.

If this is your second or third visit to the organization, the interview may culminate with an offer of employment. You have two options: Accept it or request time to think it over. The best course is usually to wait. If no job offer is made, the interviewer may not have reached a decision yet, but you may tactfully ask when you can expect to know the decision.

Research salary ranges in your job, industry, and geographic region before you try to negotiate salary.

Discussing Salary   If you do receive an offer during the interview, you'll naturally want to discuss salary. However, let the interviewer raise the subject. If asked your salary requirements during the interview or on a job application, you can say that your salary requirements are open or negotiable or that you would expect a competitive compensation package.[35] If you have added qualifications, point them out: "With my 18 months of experience in the field, I would expect to start in the middle of the normal salary range." You can find industry salary ranges at the Bureau of Labor Statistics website, www.bls.gov, or at several of the popular job websites.

If you don't like the offer, you might try to negotiate, provided you're in a good bargaining position and the organization has the flexibility to accommodate you. You'll be in a fairly strong position if your skills are in short supply and you have several other offers. It also helps if you're the favorite candidate and the organization is booming. However, many organizations are relatively rigid in their salary practices, particularly at the entry level. In the United States and some European countries, it is perfectly acceptable to ask, "Is there any room for negotiation?"

Negotiating benefits may be one way to get more value from an employment package.

Salary will probably be the most important component of your compensation and benefits package, but it's not the only factor by any means. And even if salary isn't negotiable, you may find flexibility in a signing bonus, profit sharing, pension and

✓ CHECKLIST: Making a Positive Impression in Job Interviews

A. The warm-up

- ✓ Stay on your toes; even initial small talk is part of the interviewing process.
- ✓ Greet the interviewer by name, with a smile and direct eye contact.
- ✓ Offer a firm (not crushing) handshake if the interviewer extends a hand.
- ✓ Take a seat only after the interviewer invites you to sit or has taken his or her own seat.
- ✓ Listen for cues about what the questions are trying to reveal about you and your qualifications.

B. The question-and-answer stage

- ✓ Let the interviewer lead the conversation.
- ✓ Never answer a question before the interviewer finishes asking it.
- ✓ Listen carefully to the interviewer and watch for non-verbal signals.

- ✓ Don't limit yourself to simple yes or no answers; expand on the answer to show your knowledge of the company (but don't ramble on).
- ✓ If you encounter a potentially discriminatory question, decide how you want to respond before you say anything.
- ✓ When you have the opportunity, ask questions from the list you've prepared; remember that interviewers expect you to ask questions.

C. The close

- ✓ Watch and listen for signs that the interview is about to end.
- ✓ Quickly evaluate how well you've done and correct any misperceptions the interviewer might have.
- ✓ If you receive an offer and aren't ready to decide, it's entirely appropriate to ask for time to think about it.
- ✓ Don't bring up salary, but be prepared to discuss it if the interviewer raises the subject.
- ✓ End with a warm smile and a handshake, and thank the interviewer for meeting with you.

other retirement benefits, health coverage, vacation time, stock options, and other valuable elements in the overall compensation and benefits package.[36]

To review the important tips for successful interviews, see "Checklist: Making a Positive Impression in Job Interviews."

Interview Notes

Keep a written record of your job interviews.

If yours is a typical job search, you'll have many interviews before you accept an offer. For that reason, keeping a notebook or binder of interview notes can help you refresh your memory of each conversation. As soon as you leave the interview facility, jot down the names and titles of the people you met. Briefly summarize the interviewer's answers to your questions. Then quickly evaluate your performance during the interview, listing what you handled well and what you didn't. Going over these notes can help you improve your performance in the future.[37] In addition to improving your performance during interviews, interview notes will help you keep track of any follow-up messages you'll need to send.

FOLLOWING UP AFTER THE INTERVIEW

Six types of follow-up messages:
- Thank-you message
- Message of inquiry
- Request for a time extension
- Letter of acceptance
- Letter declining a job offer
- Letter of resignation

Touching base with the prospective employer after the interview, either by phone or in writing, shows that you really want the job and are determined to get it. This also gives you another chance to demonstrate your communication skills and sense of business etiquette. Following up brings your name to the interviewer's attention once again and reminds him or her that you're actively looking and waiting for the decision.

The two most common forms of follow-up are the thank-you message and the inquiry. These messages are often handled by letter, but an e-mail or a phone call can be just as effective, particularly if the employer seems to favor a casual, personal style. Other types of follow-up messages—letters requesting a time extension, letters of

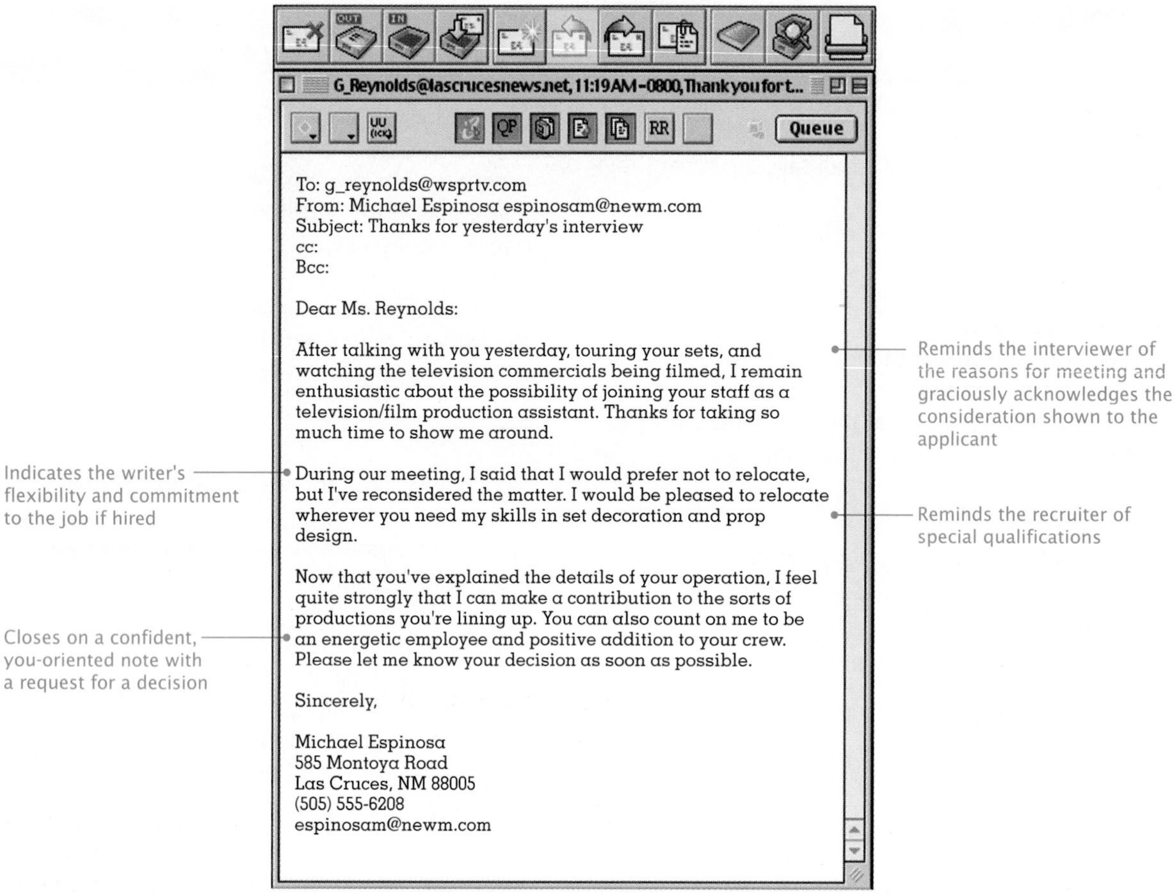

```
To: g_reynolds@wsprtv.com
From: Michael Espinosa espinosam@newm.com
Subject: Thanks for yesterday's interview
cc:
Bcc:

Dear Ms. Reynolds:

After talking with you yesterday, touring your sets, and
watching the television commercials being filmed, I remain
enthusiastic about the possibility of joining your staff as a
television/film production assistant. Thanks for taking so
much time to show me around.

During our meeting, I said that I would prefer not to relocate,
but I've reconsidered the matter. I would be pleased to relocate
wherever you need my skills in set decoration and prop
design.

Now that you've explained the details of your operation, I feel
quite strongly that I can make a contribution to the sorts of
productions you're lining up. You can also count on me to be
an energetic employee and positive addition to your crew.
Please let me know your decision as soon as possible.

Sincerely,

Michael Espinosa
585 Montoya Road
Las Cruces, NM 88005
(505) 555-6208
espinosam@newm.com
```

Reminds the interviewer of the reasons for meeting and graciously acknowledges the consideration shown to the applicant

Reminds the recruiter of special qualifications

Indicates the writer's flexibility and commitment to the job if hired

Closes on a confident, you-oriented note with a request for a decision

FIGURE 15–3
E-Mail Thank-You Message

acceptance, letters declining a job offer, and letters of resignation—are best handled in writing to document any official actions relating to your employment.

Thank-You Message

A note or phone call thanking the interviewer should be organized like a routine message and close with a request for a decision or future consideration.

Express your thanks within two days after the interview, even if you feel you have little chance for the job. Not only is this good etiquette, but it leaves a positive impression. Acknowledge the interviewer's time and courtesy, and convey your continued interest, then ask politely for a decision. In Figure 15–3, Michael Espinosa accomplishes all this in three brief paragraphs.

Keep your thank-you message brief (less than five minutes for a phone call or only one page for a letter), and organize it like a routine message. Demonstrate the "you" attitude, and sound positive without sounding overconfident. Even if the interviewer has said that you are unqualified for the job, a thank-you message may keep the door open to future opportunities.

Message of Inquiry

An inquiry about a hiring decision follows the model for a direct request.

If you're not advised of the interviewer's decision by the promised date or within two weeks, you might make an inquiry. A letter of inquiry is particularly appropriate if you've received a job offer from a second firm and don't want to accept it before you have an answer from the first. The following letter illustrates the general plan for a direct request; the writer assumes that a simple oversight, and not outright rejection, is the reason for the delay:

When we talked on April 7 about the fashion coordinator position in your Park Avenue showroom, you indicated that a decision would be made by May 1. I am still enthusiastic about the position and eager to know what conclusion you've reached.

Identifies the position and introduces the main idea

To complicate matters, another firm has now offered me a position and has asked that I reply within the next two weeks.

Places the reson for the request second

Because your company seems to offer a greater challenge, I would appreciate knowing about your decision by Thursday, May 12. If you need more information before then, please let me know.

Makes a courteous request for specific action last, while clearly stating a preference for this organization

Request for a Time Extension

If you receive a job offer while other interviews are still pending, you'll probably want more time to decide, so write to the offering organization and ask for a time extension. Employers understand that candidates often interview with several companies. They want you to be sure you're making the right decision, so most are happy to accommodate you with a reasonable extension.

Preface your request with a friendly opening. Ask for more time, stressing your enthusiasm for the organization. Conclude by allowing for a quick decision if your request for additional time is denied. Ask for a prompt reply confirming the time extension if the organization grants it. This type of letter is, in essence, a direct request. However, because the recipient may be disappointed, be sure to temper your request for an extension with statements indicating your continued interest. The letter in Figure 15–4 is a good example.

Document Makeover

IMPROVE THIS LETTER

To practice correcting drafts of actual documents, visit your online course or the access-code protected portion of the Companion Website. Click "Document Makeovers," then click Chapter 15. You will find a letter that contains problems and errors relating to what you've learned in this chapter about applying and interviewing for employment. Use the "Final Draft" decision tool to create an improved version of this request for a time extension. Check the letter for all the elements necessary to reassure the potential employer, ask for the extension, explain the reasons for the request, offer to compromise, and facilitate a quick reply.

Letter of Acceptance

When you receive a job offer that you want to accept, reply within five days. Begin by accepting the position and expressing thanks. Identify the job that you're accepting. In the next paragraph, cover any necessary details. Conclude by saying that you look forward to reporting for work. As always, a positive letter should convey your enthusiasm and eagerness to cooperate:

Use the model for positive messages when you write a letter of acceptance.

I'm delighted to accept the graphic design position in your advertising department at the salary of $2,875 a month.

Confirms the specific terms of the offer with a good-news statement at the beginning

Enclosed are the health insurance forms you asked me to complete and sign. I've already given notice to my current employer and will be able to start work on Monday, January 18.

Covers miscellaneous details in the middle

The prospect of joining your firm is exciting. Thank you for giving me this opportunity for what I'm sure will be a challenging future.

Closes with another reference to the good news and a look toward the future

Be aware that a job offer and a written acceptance of that offer can constitute a legally binding contract, for both you and the employer. Before you write an acceptance letter, be sure you want the job.

Written acceptance of a job offer can be considered a legally binding contract.

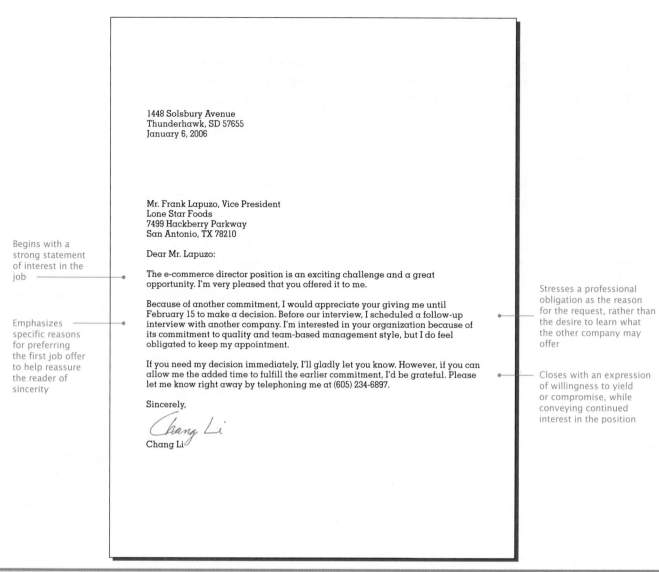

1448 Solsbury Avenue
Thunderhawk, SD 57655
January 6, 2006

Mr. Frank Lapuzo, Vice President
Lone Star Foods
7499 Hackberry Parkway
San Antonio, TX 78210

Dear Mr. Lapuzo:

The e-commerce director position is an exciting challenge and a great opportunity. I'm very pleased that you offered it to me.

Because of another commitment, I would appreciate your giving me until February 15 to make a decision. Before our interview, I scheduled a follow-up interview with another company. I'm interested in your organization because of its commitment to quality and team-based management style, but I do feel obligated to keep my appointment.

If you need my decision immediately, I'll gladly let you know. However, if you can allow me the added time to fulfill the earlier commitment, I'd be grateful. Please let me know right away by telephoning me at (605) 234-6897.

Sincerely,

Chang Li

Chang Li

Begins with a strong statement of interest in the job

Emphasizes specific reasons for preferring the first job offer to help reassure the reader of sincerity

Stresses a professional obligation as the reason for the request, rather than the desire to learn what the other company may offer

Closes with an expression of willingness to yield or compromise, while conveying continued interest in the position

FIGURE 15–4
Effective Request for a Time Extension

Letter Declining a Job Offer

A letter declining a job offer follows the model for negative messages.

After all your interviews, you may find that you need to write a letter declining a job offer. Use the techniques for negative messages (see Chapter 8): Open warmly, state the reasons for refusing the offer, decline the offer explicitly, and close on a pleasant note, expressing gratitude. By taking the time to write a sincere, tactful letter, you leave the door open for future contact:

Uses a buffer in the opening paragraph

One of the most interesting interviews I have ever had was the one last month at your Durham textile plant. I'm flattered that you would offer me the computer analyst position that we talked about.

Precedes the bad news with tactfully phrased reasons for the applicant's unfavorable decision, and leaves the door open

During my job search, I applied to five highly rated firms like your own, each one a leader in its field. Both your company and another offered me a position. Because my desire to work abroad can more readily be satisfied by the other company, I have accepted that job offer.

Lets the reader down gently with a sincere and cordial ending

I deeply appreciate the time you spent talking with me. Thank you again for your consideration and kindness.

Letter of Resignation

If you get a job offer and are currently employed, you can maintain good relations with your current employer by writing a letter of resignation to your immediate supervisor. Follow the bad-news plan, and make the letter sound positive, regardless of how you feel. Say something favorable about the organization, the people you work with, or what you've learned on the job. Then state your intention to leave and give the date of your last day on the job. Be sure you give your current employer at least two weeks' notice:

Letters of resignation should always be written in a gracious and professional style that avoids criticism of your employer or your colleagues.

My sincere thanks to you and to all the other Emblem Corporation employees for helping me learn so much about serving the public these past two years. You have given me untold help and encouragement.

Uses on appreciative opening to serve as a buffer

You may recall that when you first interviewed me, my goal was to become a customer relations supervisor. Because that opportunity has been offered to me by another organization, I am submitting my resignation. I will miss all of you, but I want to take advantage of this opportunity.

States reasons before the bad news itself, using tactful phrasing to help keep the relationship friendly, should the writer later want letters of recommendation

I would like to terminate my work here two weeks from today but can arrange to work an additional week if you want me to train a replacement.

Discusses necessary details in an extra paragraph

My sincere thanks and best wishes to all of you.

Tempers any disappointment with a cordial close

To verify the content and style of your follow-up messages, consult the tips in "Checklist: Writing Follow-up Messages."

✓ CHECKLIST: Writing Follow-Up Messages

A. Thank-you messages

- ✓ Write a brief thank-you letter within two days of the interview.
- ✓ Acknowledge the interviewer's time and courtesy.
- ✓ Restate the specific job you're applying for.
- ✓ Express your enthusiasm about the organization and the job.
- ✓ Add any new facts that may help your chances.
- ✓ Politely ask for a decision.

B. Messages of inquiry

- ✓ If you haven't heard from the interviewer by the promised date, write a brief message of inquiry.
- ✓ Use a direct approach: main idea, necessary details, specific request.

C. Requests for a time extension

- ✓ Request an extension if you have pending interviews and need time to decide about an offer.
- ✓ Open on a friendly note.
- ✓ Explain why you need more time and express continued interest in the company.
- ✓ In the close, promise a quick decision if your request is denied, and ask for a confirmation if your request is granted.

D. Letters of acceptance

- ✓ Send this message within five days of receiving the offer.
- ✓ State clearly that you accept the offer, identify the job you're accepting, and confirm vital details such as salary and start date.
- ✓ Make sure you want the job; an acceptance letter can be treated as a legally binding contract.

E. Letters declining a job offer

- ✓ Use the model for negative messages.
- ✓ Open on a warm and appreciative note, then explain why you are refusing the offer.
- ✓ End on a sincere, positive note.

F. Letters of resignation

- ✓ Send a letter of resignation to your current employer as soon as possible.
- ✓ Begin with an appreciative buffer.
- ✓ In the middle section, state your reasons for leaving, and actually state that you are resigning.
- ✓ Close cordially.

On the Job

SOLVING COMMUNICATION DILEMMAS AT GOOGLE

Much of Google's recruiting efforts focus on the software engineers and other technical specialists who create and refine the company's search technologies. However, as those technologies get put to use in a wider array of commercial applications, business specialists will play an increasingly important role in the company's future. You're on the interview team assigned to fill one such position, that of corporate development analyst/associate in Google's Mountain View, California, offices. Here is how Google's website describes the position ("M&A" is an abbreviation for mergers and acquisitions):

> This is a great opportunity to join the team at Google focusing on enhancing our corporate mission through M&A transactions. We are looking for an associate to join our corporate development team where you will be mentored by some of the best deal people in the business. In this role, you will screen external inquiries for potential acquisition deals, research domestic and international market segments, and participate in deal activities working closely with corporate development managers, principals and the director.
>
> Our ideal candidate is a top performer who brings high levels of energy and enthusiasm; works well with large and diverse teams and has a demonstrated ability to think creatively.

Requirements:
- Bachelor's degree required.
- 1–3 years of experience in strategic consulting, investment banking or relevant corporate experience preferred.
- Strong quantitative and qualitative analytical ability required.
- Excellent oral and written communication skills.
- Demonstrated ability to manage multiple projects simultaneously.
- Must be a team player with a sense of humor.

With those job requirements in mind, how would you respond to these recruiting situations?[38]

1. Since written communication skills are such an important part of the job, you pay close attention to application letters. Based on the following opening paragraphs, which of these four candidates has done the best job of capturing your attention and interest?

   a. I LOVE GOOGLE! I relied on your awesome search engine to get me through a zillion research papers in college, and I continue to use it in my new job as a legislative analyst in the mayor's office (that would be the Honorable Jack R. Spiker, mayor of Cheyenne, Wyoming, in whose employ I currently serve).

   b. Guess what I found when I Googled myself? A five-page listing of all the awards I've received, speeches I've given, articles I've written, and proj-

ects I've managed. Try it yourself and see what you can see about my work.

   c. Given Google's reputation for hiring only the best and brightest, the big question is why the heck don't I work there yet? I'm driven, way smarter than the average bear, and not afraid to tell my mom I work at some place called 'Google'!

   d. It's amazing how many times Google's name keeps popping up around the espresso machine here at Ignito Strategic Consulting, whenever my colleagues and I discuss smart acquisitions. Your firm continues to execute strategic moves that are creatively imagined, carefully researched, and cleverly implemented—exactly the kind of business deals I've been training for my entire career. And although that career is only one year old at the moment, my first annual performance review just said that I already have the deal-making acumen of a five-year veteran.

2. You like to put applicants at ease right away, so you usually start by asking a humorous question to break the tension while also revealing something about the candidate's personality and knowledge? For this round of interviews, which of these questions would you choose to start each interview?

   a. What's the dumbest business deal you've ever heard of?

   b. If we wanted to lose $10 million dollars on a business deal, what would you suggest we do?

   c. Ever have one of those days when life seems like one endless job interview?

   d. So . . . buying that weekly lottery ticket still hasn't worked out, eh?

3. Google places a great deal of emphasis on creative thinking, so you and your colleagues spend much of your time probing candidates' abilities to think through challenges and propose clever solutions. Which of these questions would you use to judge a candidate's ability to grasp a problem and begin developing a solution?

   a. You're a scientist with the Environmental Protection Agency, specializing in toxic waste from electronic products. You're testifying before a congressional committee, and a senator wants to know how many cell phone batteries will be thrown away in the next 10 years. Without access to any additional information, how would you start to construct an estimate of this number?

   b. Guess how old I am.

   c. Why do telephone numbers in movies and TV shows always start with 555?

   d. How would you explain the concept of a human family to a creature from another planet?

4. At the end of each interview, you make a point to ask candidates if they have any questions for you. Which of the following responses impresses you the most?
   a. No, thanks. I think I'm all set.
   b. Hey, if I have any questions, I'll just Google away when I get back to my computer, right?
   c. Yes, one of my top priorities in searching for a new job is finding a greater sense of intellectual and professional freedom. Is Google the kind of place where top performers can really pursue their own dreams?
   d. Yes, a couple of questions, actually. First, Google's stated mission of organizing the world's information and making it universally accessible leaves the door open to a lot of different possibilities. For instance, do you see the company ever moving into traditional publishing, with books or magazines?

Learning Objectives Checkup

Assess your understanding of the principles in this chapter by reading each learning objective and studying the accompanying exercises. For fill-in items, write the missing text in the blank provided; for multiple choice items, circle the letter of the correct answer. You can check your responses against the answer key on page AK-3.

Objective 15.1: Define the purpose of application letters, and explain how to apply the AIDA organizational approach to them.

1. What is the primary reason for sending an application letter?
   a. To encourage the reader to look at your résumé
   b. To ask for a job
   c. To itemize your qualifications
   d. To ask for an application form
2. Which of the following is a good technique to gain attention in the opening paragraph of an application letter?
   a. Explain how your work skills could benefit the organization.
   b. Explain how your qualifications fit the job.
   c. Show that you understand the organization's needs.
   d. Do all of the above.

Objective 15.2: Describe the typical sequence of job interviews.

3. Which of these interview stages happens first?
   a. The selection stage
   b. The screening stage
   c. The filtering stage
   d. The sorting stage
4. A/an _____ interview, often used in the screening stage, features a series of prepared questions in a set order.
5. A/an _____ interview is a less formal and unstructured format, in which the interviewer poses broad, open-ended questions.
6. A/an _____ interview tries to uncover how the candidate would behave when faced with various challenges on the job.

Objective 15.3: Describe briefly what employers look for during an employment interview and preemployment testing.

7. What are the two most important factors that employers look for during interviews?
   a. Fit with the organization and motivation
   b. Motivation and ability to perform the job
   c. Motivation and years of experience
   d. Fit with the organization and ability to perform the job
8. Which of the following preemployment tests might you encounter while applying for jobs?
   a. Integrity tests
   b. Substance tests
   c. Personality tests
   d. All of the above
9. Approximately what percentage of U.S. companies require applicants to undergo preemployment drug testing?
   a. 3 percent
   b. 12 percent
   c. 50 percent
   d. 98 percent

Objective 15.4: List six tasks you need to complete to prepare for a successful job interview.

10. If an interviewer asks you to describe your biggest weakness, which of the following is the best strategy for your response?
    a. Explain the weakness in depth; doing so will convince the interviewer of your honesty.
    b. Describe a weakness so that it sounds like a strength, such as saying that you drive yourself too hard.
    c. Respectfully explain to the interviewer that the question is illegal.
    d. Explain that you don't have any major weaknesses.
11. What is the best strategy for asking questions of your own during an interview?
    a. Try to ask all of them at the beginning of the interview so that you don't run out of time.
    b. Wait until after the interview, then e-mail your questions to the interviewer.
    c. Try to work your questions in naturally throughout the course of the interview.
    d. Wait until the interviewer asks if you have any questions.
12. If you believe that you have a particular disadvantage related to some aspect of your appearance, interviewing skills, job skills, or work experience, how should you handle the situation when preparing for an interview?
    a. Plan to make a joke about your weakness early in the interview; this will break the tension and allow you to focus on the interviewer's questions.

b. Compensate by focusing on your strengths, both while you're preparing and during the interview itself.

c. Correct the perceived shortcoming if possible; if not, focus on your positive attributes.

d. Ignore the situation; there's nothing you can do about a weakness at this point.

13. If you're not sure what style of clothing to wear to a particular interview and you're not able to ask someone at the company for advice, what should you do?

a. Dress in a fairly conservative style; it's better to be a little too dressy than a little casual.

b. Dress as you would like to dress on the job.

c. Dress in an eye-catching style that will make a lasting impression on the interviewer.

d. Arrive early with several different changes of clothes; try to see what people there are wearing, then find a place to change into whichever outfit you have that most closely matches.

Objective 15.5: Explain the three stages of a successful employment interview.

14. Studies show that many interviewers, particularly those with poor training, make up their minds about candidates

a. In the first 20 seconds of the interview

b. In the final 20 seconds of the interview

c. On the basis of the résumé

d. On the basis of the cover letter

15. What do you do if a job interviewer asks you about your marital status, how many children you have, and what their ages are?

a. Answer them—it is perfectly within the interviewer's right to ask you such personal questions, even if they are not directly related to the job you are applying for.

b. Tell the interviewer that such questions are illegal and threaten to sue for invasion of privacy.

c. Sidestep the questions—which are illegal in many states—by asking if the interviewer has some specific concerns about your commitment to the job, your willingness to travel, or some other factor.

d. If you want the job, refuse to answer the questions but promise that you won't report the illegal questioning to the EEOC.

16. What should you do if the interviewer tells you the salary for the job being offered?

a. Always take whatever the company offers.

b. Respond with a figure higher than what is offered.

c. Respond with a figure lower than what is offered.

d. Ask if there is any room to negotiate on salary.

Objective 15.6: Identify the most common employment messages that follow an interview, and explain when you would use each one.

17. Following a job interview, you should send a thank-you message

a. Within two days after the interview

b. Only if you think you got the job

c. That follows the AIDA organizational plan

d. That does all of the above

18. A letter declining a job offer should follow

a. A direct approach

b. The AIDA plan

c. A negative news approach

d. The polite plan

Apply Your Knowledge

1. How can you distinguish yourself from other candidates in a screening interview and still keep your responses short and to the point? Explain.

2. What can you do to make a favorable impression when you discover that an open-ended interview has turned into a stress interview? Briefly explain your answer.

3. If you want to switch jobs because you can't work with your supervisor, how can you explain this situation to a prospective employer? Give an example.

4. During a group interview you notice that one of the other candidates is trying to monopolize the conversation. He's always the first to answer, his answer is the longest, and he even interrupts the other candidates while they are talking. The interviewer doesn't seem to be concerned about his behavior, but you are. You would like to have more time to speak so that the interviewer could get to know you better. What should you do?

5. **Ethical Choices** Why is it important to distinguish unethical or illegal interview questions from acceptable questions? Explain.

Practice Your Knowledge

DOCUMENTS FOR ANALYSIS

Read the following documents, then (1) analyze the strengths or weaknesses of each document and (2) revise each document so that it follows this chapter's guidelines.

DOCUMENT 15.A: WRITING AN APPLICATION LETTER

I'm writing to let you know about my availability for the brand manager job you advertised. As you can see from my enclosed résumé, my background is perfect for the position. Even though I don't have any real job experience, my grades have been outstanding considering that I went to a top-ranked business school.

I did many things during my undergraduate years to prepare me for this job:

- Earned a 3.4 out of a 4.0 with a 3.8 in my business courses
- Elected representative to the student governing association
- Selected to receive the Lamar Franklin Award
- Worked to earn a portion of my tuition

I am sending my résumé to all the top firms, but I like yours better than any of the rest. Your reputation is tops in the industry, and I want to be associated with a business that can pridefully say it's the best.

If you wish for me to come in for an interview, I can come on a Friday afternoon or anytime on weekends when I don't have classes. Again, thanks for considering me for your brand manager position.

DOCUMENT 15.B: WRITING APPLICATION FOLLOW-UP MESSAGES

Did you receive my résumé? I sent it to you at least two months ago and haven't heard anything. I know you keep résumés on file, but I just want to be sure that you keep me in mind. I heard you are hiring health-care managers and certainly would like to be considered for one of those positions.

Since I last wrote you, I've worked in a variety of positions that have helped prepare me for management. To wit, I've become lunch manager at the restaurant where I work, which involved a raise in pay. I now manage a waitstaff of 12 girls and take the lunch receipts to the bank every day.

Of course, I'd much rather be working at a real job, and that's why I'm writing again. Is there anything else you would like to know about me or my background? I would really like to know more about your company. Is there any literature you could send me? If so, I would really appreciate it.

I think one reason I haven't been hired yet is that I don't want to leave Atlanta. So I hope when you think of me, it's for a position that wouldn't require moving. Thanks again for considering my application.

DOCUMENT 15.C: THANK-YOU MESSAGE

Thank you for the really marvelous opportunity to meet you and your colleagues at Starret Engine Company. I really enjoyed touring your facilities and talking with all the people there. You have quite a crew! Some of the other companies I have visited have been so rigid and uptight that I can't imagine how I would fit in. It's a relief to run into a group of people who seem to enjoy their work as much as all of you do.

I know that you must be looking at many other candidates for this job, and I know that some of them will probably be more experienced than I am. But I do want to emphasize that my two-year hitch in the Navy involved a good deal of engineering work. I don't think I mentioned all my shipboard responsibilities during the interview.

Please give me a call within the next week to let me know your decision. You can usually find me at my dormitory in the evening after dinner (phone: 877–9080).

DOCUMENT 15.D: LETTER OF INQUIRY

I have recently received a very attractive job offer from the Warrington Company. But before I let them know one way or another, I would like to consider any offer that your firm may extend. I was quite impressed with your company during my recent interview, and I am still very interested in a career there.

I don't mean to pressure you, but Warrington has asked for my decision within 10 days. Could you let me know by Tuesday whether you plan to offer me a position? That would give me enough time to compare the two offers.

DOCUMENT 15.E: LETTER DECLINING A JOB OFFER

I'm writing to say that I must decline your job offer. Another company has made me a more generous offer, and I have decided to accept. However, if things don't work out for me there, I will let you know. I sincerely appreciate your interest in me.

Exercises

For active links to all websites discussed in this chapter, visit this text's website at **www.prenhall.com/thill**. Locate your book and click on its Companion Website link. Then select Chapter 15, and click on "Featured Websites." Locate the name of the page or the URL related to the material in the text. Please note that links to sites that become inactive after publication of the book will be removed from the Featured Websites section.

15.1 **Internet** Select a large company (one that you can easily find information on) where you might like to work. Use Internet sources to gather some preliminary research on the company; don't limit your search to the company's own website.

1. What did you learn about this organization that would help you during an interview there?
2. What Internet sources did you use to obtain this information?

3. Armed with this information, what aspects of your background do you think might appeal to this company's recruiters?
4. If you choose to apply for a job with this company, what keywords would you include on your résumé, and why?

15.2 **Teamwork** Divide the class into two groups. Half the class will be recruiters for a large chain of national department stores looking to fill manager trainee positions (there are 15 openings). The other half of the class will be candidates for the job. The company is specifically looking for candidates who demonstrate these three qualities: initiative, dependability, and willingness to assume responsibility.

1. Have each recruiter select and interview an applicant for 10 minutes.

2. Have all the recruiters discuss how they assessed the applicant in each of the three desired qualities. What questions did they ask or what did they use as an indicator to determine whether the candidate possessed the quality?

3. Have all the applicants discuss what they said to convince the recruiters that they possessed each of these qualities.

15.3 Interviews: Understanding Qualifications Write a short e-mail to your instructor, discussing what you believe are your greatest strengths and weaknesses from an employment perspective. Next, explain how these strengths and weaknesses would be viewed by interviewers evaluating your qualifications.

15.4 Interviews: Being Prepared Prepare written answers to 10 of the questions listed in Table 15–2, "Twenty-Five Common Interview Questions."

15.5 Ethical Choices You have decided to accept a new position with a competitor of your company. Write a letter of resignation to your supervisor, announcing your decision.

1. Will you notify your employer that you are joining a competing firm? Please explain.

2. Will you use the direct or the indirect approach? Please explain.

3. Will you send your letter by e-mail, send it by regular mail, or place it on your supervisor's desk?

Expand Your Knowledge

LEARNING MORE ON THE WEB

PREPARE AND PRACTICE BEFORE THAT FIRST INTERVIEW

www.job-interview.net

How can you practice for a job interview? What are some questions that you might be asked, and how should you respond? What questions are you not obligated to answer? Job-interview.net, www.job-interview.net, provides mock interviews based on actual job openings. It provides job descriptions, questions and answers for specific careers and jobs, and links to company guides and annual reports. You'll find a step-by-step plan that outlines key job requirements, lists practice interview questions, and helps you put together practice interviews. The site offers tips on the keywords to look for in a job description, which will help you narrow your

search and anticipate the questions you might be asked on your first or next job interview.

ACTIVITIES

Visit www.job-interview.net, then answer these questions:

1. What are some problem questions you might be asked during a job interview? How would you handle these questions?

2. Choose a job title from the list, and read more about it. What did you learn that could help during an actual interview for the job you selected?

3. Developing an "interview game plan" ahead of time helps you make a strong, positive impression during an interview. What are some of the things you can practice to help make everything you do during an interview seem to come naturally?

Exploring the Web on Your Own

Review these chapter-related websites on your own to learn more about interviewing for jobs.

1. Get over 2,000 pages of career advice at Monster.com, www.monster.com, and talk to career experts in your choice of industry or profession.

2. For a humorous—but effective—take on cover letters, visit www.soyouwanna.com, click on Work, then find the article about cover letters.

3. Among the many helpful pages of advice you'll find at the Online Writing Lab is a section on writing cover letters. Visit http://owl.english.purdue.edu/owl/, then click on "Job Search Writing."

Learn Interactively

INTERACTIVE STUDY GUIDE

Visit www.prenhall.com/thill, then locate your book and click on its Companion Website link. Select Chapter 15 to take advantage of the interactive "Chapter Quiz" to test your knowledge of chapter concepts. Receive instant feedback on whether you need additional studying. Also, visit the "Study Hall," where you'll find an abundance of valuable resources that will help you succeed in this course.

PEAK PERFORMANCE GRAMMAR AND MECHANICS

If your instructor has required the use of "Peak Performance Grammar and Mechanics," either in your online course or on CD, you can improve your skill with vocabulary by using the "Peak Performance Grammar and Mechanics" module. Click first on "Vocabulary I," then on "Vocabulary II." In both sections, take the Pretest to determine whether you have any weak areas. Then review those areas in the Refresher Course. Take the Follow-Up Test to check your grasp of using numbers in documents. For an extra challenge or advanced practice, take the Advanced Test. Finally, for additional reinforcement, go to the "Improve Your Grammar, Mechanics, and Usage" section that follows, and complete those exercises.

Improve Your Grammar, Mechanics, and Usage

The following exercises help you improve your knowledge of and power over English grammar, mechanics, and usage. Turn to the Handbook of Grammar, Mechanics, and Usage at the end of this textbook and review all of Section 3.4 (Numbers). Then look at the following 10 items. Circle the letter of the preferred choice in the following groups of sentences. (Answers to these exercises appear on page AK-4.)

1. a. We need to hire one office manager, four bookkeepers, and 12 clerk-typists.
    b. We need to hire one office manager, four bookkeepers, and twelve clerk-typists.
    c. We need to hire 1 office manager, 4 bookkeepers, and 12 clerk-typists.

2. a. The market for this product is nearly 6 million people in our region alone.
    b. The market for this product is nearly six million people in our region alone.
    c. The market for this product is nearly 6,000,000 million people in our region alone.

3. a. Make sure that all 1,835 pages are on my desk no later than 9:00 A.M.
    b. Make sure that all 1835 pages are on my desk no later than nine o'clock in the morning.
    c. Make sure that all 1,835 pages are on my desk no later than nine o'clock A.M.

4. a. Our deadline is 4/7, but we won't be ready before 4/11.
    b. Our deadline is April 7, but we won't be ready before April 11.
    c. Our deadline is 4/7, but we won't be ready before April 11.

5. a. 95 percent of our customers are men.
    b. Ninety-five percent of our customers are men.
    c. Of our customers, ninety-five percent are men.

6. a. More than half the U.S. population is female.
    b. More than ½ the U.S. population is female.
    c. More than one-half the U.S. population is female.

7. a. Last year, I wrote 20 15-page reports, and Michelle wrote 24 three-page reports.
    b. Last year, I wrote 20 fifteen-page reports, and Michelle wrote 24 three-page reports.
    c. Last year, I wrote twenty 15-page reports, and Michelle wrote 24 three-page reports.

8. a. Our blinds should measure 38 inches wide by 64 and one-half inches long by 7/16 inches deep.
    b. Our blinds should measure 38 inches wide by 64–1/2 inches long by 7/16 inches deep.
    c. Our blinds should measure 38 inches wide by 64–8/16 inches long by 7/16 inches deep.

9. a. Deliver the couch to 783 Fountain Rd., Suite 3, Procter Valley, CA 92074.
    b. Deliver the couch to 783 Fountain Rd., Suite three, Procter Valley, CA 92074.
    c. Deliver the couch to seven eighty-three Fountain Rd., Suite three, Procter Valley, CA 92074.

10. a. Here are the corrected figures: 42.7% agree, 23.25% disagree, 34% are undecided, and the error is 0.05%.
    b. Here are the corrected figures: 42.7% agree, 23.25% disagree, 34.0% are undecided, and the error is .05%.
    c. Here are the corrected figures: 42.70% agree, 23.25% disagree, 34.00% are undecided, and the error is 0.05%.

For an overall review of your grammar, mechanics, and usage skills, go to www.prenhall.com/thill, then locate your text and click on its Companion Website link. Click on Chapter 15, click on "Additional Exercises to Improve Your Grammar, Mechanics, and Usage," then click on "25. Grammar and usage."

Cases

Preparing Other Types of Employment Messages

1. Online application: Electronic cover letter introducing a résumé While researching a digital camera purchase, you stumble on the webzine *Megapixel* (www.megapixel.net), which offers product reviews on a wide array of camera models. The quality of the reviews and the stunning examples of photography on the site inspire you to a new part-time business idea—you'd like to write a regular column for *Megapixel*. The webzine does a great job addressing the information needs of experienced camera users, but you see an opportunity to write for "newbies," people who are new to digital photography and need a more basic level of information.

Your task: Write an e-mail message that will serve as your cover letter and address your message to Denys Bouton, who edits the English edition of *Megapixel* (it is also published in French). Try to limit your message to one screen (generally 20–25 lines). You'll need a creative "hook" and a reassuring approach that identifies you as the right person to launch this new feature in the webzine (make up any details about your background that you may need to complete the letter).

2. All over the map: Application letter to Google Earth You've applied yourself with vigor and resolve for four years, and you're just about to graduate with your <u>business degree</u>. While cruising the web to relax one night, you stumble on something called Google Earth. You're hooked instantly by the ability to zoom all around the globe and look at detailed satellite photos of places you've been to or dreamed of visiting. You can even type in the address of your apartment and get an aerial view of your neighborhood. You're amazed at the three-dimensional renderings of major U.S. cities. Plus, the photographs and maps are linked to Google's other search technologies, allowing you to locate everything from ATMs to coffees shops in your neighborhood.

You've loved maps since you were a kid, and discovering Google Earth is making you wish you would've majored in geography instead. Knowing how important it is to follow your heart, you decide to apply to Google anyway, even though you don't have a strong background in geographic information systems. What you do have is a ton of passion of maps and a good head for business.

Your task: Visit http://earth.google.com/ and explore the system's capabilities (you can download a free copy of the software). In particular, look at the business and government applications of the technology, such as customized aerial photos and maps for real estate sales, land use and environmental impact analysis, and emergency planning for homeland security agencies. Be sure to visit the Community pages as well, where you can learn more about the many interesting applications of this technology. Now draft an application e-mail to Google (address it to jobs@google.com), asking to be considered for the Google Earth team. Think about how you could help the company develop the commercial potential of this product line, and make sure your enthusiasm shines through in the message.

INTERVIEWING WITH POTENTIAL EMPLOYERS

3. Interviewers and interviewees: Classroom exercise in interviewing Interviewing is clearly an interactive process involving at least two people. The best way to practice for interviews is to work with others.

Your task: You and all other members of your class are to write letters of application for an entry-level or management-trainee position requiring a pleasant personality and intelligence but a minimum of specialized education or experience. Sign your letter with a fictitious name that conceals your identity. Next, polish (or create) a résumé that accurately identifies you and your educational and professional accomplishments.

Now, three members of the class who volunteer as interviewers divide up all the anonymously written application letters. Then each interviewer selects a candidate who seems the most pleasant and convincing in his or her letter. At this time the selected candidates identify themselves and give the interviewers their résumés.

Each interviewer then interviews his or her chosen candidate in front of the class, seeking to understand how the items on the

résumé qualify the candidate for the job. At the end of the interviews, the class may decide who gets the job and discuss why this candidate was successful. Afterward, retrieve your letter, sign it with the right name, and submit it to the instructor for credit.

4. Internet interview: Exercise in interviewing Locate the website of a company in an industry in which you might like to work, then identify an interesting position within the company. Study the company, using any of the online business resources discussed in Chapter 10, and prepare for an interview with that company.

Your task: Working with a classmate, take turns interviewing each other for your chosen positions. Interviewers should take notes during the interview. Once the interview is complete, critique each other's performance (interviewers should critique how well candidates prepared for the interview and answered the questions; interviewees should critique the quality of the questions asked). Write a follow-up letter thanking your interviewer and submit the letter to your instructor.

FOLLOWING UP AFTER THE INTERVIEW

5. A slight error in timing: Letter asking for delay of an employment decision Thanks to a mix-up in your job application scheduling, you accidentally applied for your third-choice job before going after what you really wanted. What you want to do is work in retail marketing with the upscale department store Neiman Marcus in Dallas; what you have been offered is a similar job with Longhorn Leather and Lumber, 55 dry and dusty miles away in Commerce, just south of the Oklahoma panhandle.

You review your notes. Your Longhorn interview was three weeks ago with the human resources manager, R. P. Bronson, a congenial person who has just written to offer you the position. The store's address is 27 Sam Rayburn Drive, Commerce, TX 75428. Mr. Bronson notes that he can hold the position open for 10 days. You have an interview scheduled with Neiman Marcus next week, but it is unlikely that you will know the store's decision within this 10-day period.

Your task: Write to R. P. Bronson, requesting a reasonable delay in your consideration of his job offer.

6. Job hunt: Set of employment-related letters to a single company Where would you like to work? Choose one of your favorite products, find out which company either manufactures it or sells it in the United States (if it's manufactured in another country). Assume that a month ago you sent your résumé and application letter. Not long afterward, you were invited to come for an interview, which seemed to go very well.

Your task: Use your imagination to write the following: (a) a thank-you letter for the interview, (b) a note of inquiry, (c) a request for more time to decide, (d) a letter of acceptance, and (e) a letter declining the job offer.

FORMAT AND LAYOUT OF BUSINESS DOCUMENTS

The format and layout of business documents vary from country to country; they even vary within regions of the United States. In addition, many organizations develop their own variations of standard styles, adapting documents to the types of messages they send and the kinds of audiences they communicate with. The formats described here are more common than others.

FIRST IMPRESSIONS

Your documents tell readers a lot about you and about your company's professionalism. So all your documents must look neat, present a professional image, and be easy to read. Your audience's first impression of a document comes from the quality of its paper, the way it is customized, and its general appearance.

Paper

To give a quality impression, businesspeople consider carefully the paper they use. Several aspects of paper contribute to the overall impression:

- **Weight.** Paper quality is judged by the weight of four reams (each a 500-sheet package) of letter-size paper. The weight most commonly used by U.S. business organizations is 20-pound paper, but 16- and 24-pound versions are also used.

- **Cotton content.** Paper quality is also judged by the percentage of cotton in the paper. Cotton doesn't yellow over time the way wood pulp does, plus it's both strong and soft. For letters and outside reports, use paper with a 25 percent cotton content. For memos and other internal documents, you can use a lighter-weight paper with lower cotton content. Airmail-weight paper may save money for international correspondence, but make sure it isn't too flimsy.[1]

- **Size.** In the United States, the standard paper size for business documents is 8½ by 11 inches. Standard legal documents are 8½ by 14 inches. Executives sometimes have heavier 7-by-10-inch paper on hand (with matching envelopes) for personal messages such as congratulations and recommendations.[2] They may also have a box of note cards imprinted with their initials and a box of plain folded notes for condolences or for acknowledging formal invitations.

- **Color.** White is the standard color for business purposes, although neutral colors such as gray and ivory are sometimes used. Memos can be produced on pastel-colored paper to distinguish them from external correspondence. In addition, memos are sometimes produced on various colors of paper for routing to separate departments. Light-colored papers are appropriate, but bright or dark colors make reading difficult and may appear too frivolous.

Customization

For letters to outsiders, U.S. businesses commonly use letterhead stationery, which may be either professionally printed or designed in-house using word-processing templates and graphics. The letterhead includes the company's name and address, usually at the top of the page but sometimes along the left side or even at the bottom. Other information may be included in the letterhead as well: the company's telephone number, fax number, cable address, website address, product lines, date of establishment, officers and directors, slogan, and symbol (logo). Well-designed letterhead gives readers[3]

- Pertinent reference data

- A favorable image of the company

- A good idea of what the company does

For as much as it's meant to accomplish, the letterhead should be as simple as possible. Too much information makes the page look cluttered, occupies space needed for the message, and might become outdated before all the stationery can be used. If you correspond frequently with people abroad, your letterhead must be intelligible to foreigners. It must include the name of your country in addition to your cable, telex, e-mail, or fax information.

In the United States, businesses always use letterhead for the first page of a letter. Successive pages are usually plain sheets of paper that match the letterhead in color and quality. Some companies use a specially printed second-page letterhead that bears only the company's name. Other countries have other conventions.

Many companies also design and print standardized forms for memos and frequently written reports that always require the same sort of information (such as sales reports and expense reports). These forms may be printed in sets for use with carbon paper or in carbonless-copy sets that produce multiple copies automatically. More and more organizations use computers to generate their standardized forms, which can save them both money and time.[4]

Appearance

Produce almost all of your business documents using either a printer (letter-quality, not a dot matrix) or a typewriter. Certain documents, however, should be handwritten (such as a short informal memo or a note of condolence). Be sure to handwrite, print, or type the envelope to match the document. However, even a letter on the best-quality paper with the best-designed letterhead may look unprofessional if it's poorly produced. So pay close attention to all the factors affecting appearance, including the following:

- **Margins.** Companies in the United States make sure that documents (especially external ones) are centered on the page, with margins of at least an inch all around. Using word-processing software, you can achieve this balance simply by defining the format parameters.

- **Line length.** Lines are rarely justified, because the resulting text looks too much like a form letter and can be hard to read (even with proportional spacing). Varying line length makes the document look more personal and interesting.

- **Line spacing.** You can adjust the number of blank lines between elements (such as between the date and the inside address) to ensure that a short document fills the page vertically or that a longer document extends at least two lines of the body onto the last page.

- **Character spacing.** Use proper spacing between characters and after punctuation. For example, U.S. conventions include leaving one space after commas, semicolons, colons, and sentence-ending periods. Each letter in a person's initials is followed by a period and a single space. However, abbreviations such as U.S.A. or MBA may or may not have periods, but they never have internal spaces.

- **Special symbols.** Take advantage of the many special symbols available with your computer's selection of fonts. (In Microsoft Word, click on the Insert menu, then select Symbol.) Table A–1 shows some of the more common symbols used in business documents. In addition, see if your company has a style guide for documents, which may include other symbols you are expected to use.

- **Corrections.** Messy corrections are unacceptable in business documents. If you notice an error after printing a document with your word processor, correct the mistake and reprint. (With informal memos to members of your own team or department, the occasional small correction in pen or pencil is acceptable, but never in formal documents.)

LETTERS

All business letters have certain elements in common. Several of these elements appear in every letter; others appear only when desirable or appropriate. In addition, these letter parts are usually arranged in one of three basic formats.

Standard Letter Parts

The letter in Figure A–1 shows the placement of standard letter parts. The writer of this business letter had no letterhead available but correctly included a heading. All business letters typically include these seven elements.

Heading

Letterhead (the usual heading) shows the organization's name, full address, telephone number (almost always), and e-mail address

Table A–1	SPECIAL SYMBOLS ON COMPUTER
	Computer Symbol
Case fractions	$^1/_2$
Copyright	©
Registered trademark	®
Cents	¢
British pound	£
Paragraph	¶
Bullets	●,◆,■,□, ✓,☑,⊗
Em dash	—
En dash	–

(often). Executive letterhead also bears the name of an individual within the organization. Computers allow you to design your own letterhead (either one to use for all correspondence or a new one for each piece of correspondence). If letterhead stationery is not available, the heading includes a return address (but no name) and starts 13 lines from the top of the page, which leaves a two-inch top margin.

Date

If you're using letterhead, place the date at least one blank line beneath the lowest part of the letterhead. Without letterhead, place the date immediately below the return address. The standard method of writing the date in the United States uses the full name of the month (no abbreviations), followed by the day (in numerals, without *st, nd, rd,* or *th*), a comma, and then the year: July 14, 2006 (7/14/06). Some organizations follow other conventions (see Table A–2). To maintain the utmost clarity in international correspondence, always spell out the name of the month in dates.[5]

When communicating internationally, you may also experience some confusion over time. Some companies in the United States refer to morning (A.M.) and afternoon (P.M.), dividing a 24-hour day into 12-hour blocks so that they refer to four o'clock in the morning (4:00 A.M.) or four o'clock in the afternoon (4:00 P.M.). The U.S. military and European companies refer to one 24-hour period so that 0400 hours (4:00 A.M.) is always in the morning and 1600 hours (4:00 P.M.) is always in the afternoon.[6] Make sure your references to time are as clear as possible, and be sure you clearly understand your audience's time references.

Inside Address

The inside address identifies the recipient of the letter. For U.S. correspondence, begin the inside address at least one line below the date. Precede the addressee's name with a courtesy title, such as *Dr., Mr.,* or *Ms.* The accepted courtesy title for women in business is *Ms.,* although a woman known to prefer the title *Miss* or *Mrs.* is always accommodated. If you don't know whether a person is a man or a woman (and you have no way of finding out), omit the courtesy title. For example, *Terry Smith* could be either a man or a woman. The first line of the inside address would be just *Terry Smith,* and the salutation would be *Dear Terry Smith.* The same is true if you know only a person's initials, as in *S. J. Adams.*

Spell out and capitalize titles that precede a person's name, such as *Professor* or *General* (see Table A–3 on page A-4 for the proper forms of address). The person's organizational title, such as *Director,* may be included on this first line (if it is short) or on the line below; the name of a department may follow. In addresses and signature lines, don't forget to capitalize any professional title that follows a person's name:

Mr. Ray Johnson, Dean

Ms. Patricia T. Higgins

Assistant Vice President

However, professional titles not appearing in an address or signature line are capitalized only when they directly precede the name.

President Kenneth Johanson will deliver the speech.

Maria Morales, president of ABC Enterprises, will deliver the speech.

The Honorable Helen Masters, senator from Arizona, will deliver the speech.

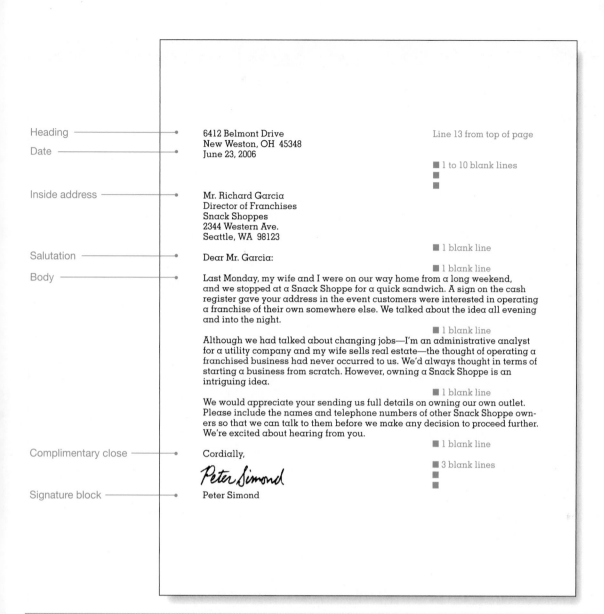

FIGURE A–1
Standard Letter Parts

COMMON DATE FORMS			Table A–2
Convention	**Description**	**Date—Mixed**	**Date—All Numerals**
U.S. standard	Month (spelled out) day, year	July 14, 2006	7/14/06
U.S. government and some U.S. industries	Day (in numerals) month (spelled out) year	14 July 2006	14/7/06
European	Replace U.S. solidus (diagonal line) with periods	14 July 2006	14.7.2006
International standard	Year month day	2006 July 14	2006,7,14

Table A–3	FORMS OF ADDRESS	
Person	*In Address*	*In Salutation*
Personal Titles		
Man	Mr. [first & last name]	Dear Mr. [last name]:
Woman (marital status unknown)	Ms. [first & last name]	Dear Ms. [last name]:
Woman (single)	Ms. *or* Miss [first & last name]	Dear Ms. *or* Miss [last name]:
Woman (married)	Ms. *or* Mrs. [wife's first & last name] *or* Mrs. [husband's first & last name]	Dear Ms. *or* Mrs. [last name]:
Woman (widowed)	Ms. *or* Mrs. [wife's first name & last name]	Dear Ms. *or* Mrs. [last name]:
Woman (separated or divorced)	Ms. *or* Mrs. [first & last name]	Dear Ms. *or* Mrs. [last name]:
Two men (or more)	Mr. [first & last name] and Mr. [first & last name]	Dear Mr. [last name] and Mr. [last name] *or* Messrs. [last name] and [last name]:
Two women (or more)	Ms. [first & last name] and Ms. [first & last name] *or*	Dear Ms. [last name] and Ms. [last name] *or* Mses. [last name] and [last name]:
	Mrs. [first & last name] and Mrs. [first & last name]	Dear Mrs. [last name] and Mrs. [last name]: *or* Dear Mesdames [last name] and [last name] *or* Mesdames:
	Miss [first & last name] Mrs. [first & last name]	Dear Miss [last name] and Mrs. [last name]:
One woman and one man	Ms. [first & last name] and Mr. [first & last name]	Dear Ms. [last name] and Mr. [last name]:
Couple (married)	Mr. and Mrs. [husband's first & last name]	Dear Mr. and Mrs. [last name]:
Couple (married with different last names)	[title] [first & last name of husband] [title] [first & last name of wife]	Dear [title] [husband's last name] and [title] [wife's first & last name]:
Couple (married professionals with same title and same last name)	[title in plural form] [husband's first name] and [wife's first & last name]	Dear [title in plural form] [last name]:
Couple (married professionals with different titles and same last name)	[title] [first & last name of husband] and [title] [first & last name of wife]	Dear [title] and [title] [last name]:

(continued)

If the name of a specific person is unavailable, you may address the letter to the department or to a specific position within the department. Also, be sure to spell out company names in full, unless the company itself uses abbreviations in its official name.

Other address information includes the treatment of buildings, house numbers, and compass directions (see Table A–6 on page A-8). The following example shows all the information that may be included in the inside address and its proper order for U.S. correspondence:

Ms. Linda Coolidge, Vice President
Corporate Planning Department
Midwest Airlines
Kowalski Building, Suite 21-A
7279 Bristol Ave.
Toledo, OH 43617

Continued		Table A-3
Person	**In Address**	**In Salutation**
Professional Titles		
President of a college or university (doctor)	Dr. [first & last name], President	Dear Dr. [last name]:
Dean of a school of college	Dean [first & last name] *or* Dr., Mr., Mrs., *or* Miss [first & last name] Dean of (title)	Dear Dean [last name]: Dear Dr., Mr., Ms., Mrs., *or* Miss [last name]:
Professor	Professor [first & last name]	Dear Professor [last name]:
Physician	[first & last name], M.D.	Dear Dr. [last name]:
Lawyer	Mr., Ms., Mrs., *or* Miss [first & last name]	Dear Mr., Ms., Mrs., *or* Miss [last name]:
Service personnel	[full rank, first & last name, abbreviation of service designation] (add *Retired* if applicable)	Dear [rank] [last name]:
Company or corporation	[name of organization]	Ladies and Gentlemen *or* Gentlemen and Ladies
Governmental Titles		
President of the United States	The President	Dear Mr. *or* Madam President:
Senator of the United States	Honorable [first & last name]	Dear Senator [last name]:
Cabinet member Postmaster General Attorney General	Honorable [first & last name]	Dear Mr. *or* Madam Secretary: Dear Mr. *or* Madam Postmaster General: Dear Mr. *or* Madam Attorney General:
Mayor	Honorable [first & last name] Mayor of [name of city]	Dear Mayor [last name]:
Judge	The Honorable	Dear Judge [last name]:
Religious Titles		
Priest	The Reverend [first & last name], [initials of order, if any]	Reverend Sir: (formal) *or* Dear Father [last name]: (informal)
Rabbi	Rabbi & [first & last name]	Dear Rabbi [last name]:
Minister	The Reverend [first & last name] [title, if any]	Dear Reverend [last name]:

Canadian addresses are similar, except that the name of the province is usually spelled out:

Dr. H. C. Armstrong
Research and Development
Commonwealth Mining Consortium
The Chelton Building, Suite 301
585 Second St. SW
Calgary, Alberta T2P 2P5

The order and layout of address information vary from country to country. So when addressing correspondence for other countries, carefully follow the format and information that appear in the company's letterhead. However, when you're sending mail from the United States, be sure that the name of the destination country appears on the last line of the address in capital letters. Use the English version of the country name so that your mail is routed from the United States to the right country. Then, to be sure your mail is routed correctly within the destination country, use the foreign spelling of the city name (using the characters and

Table A–4 INSIDE ADDRESS INFORMATION

Description	Example
Capitalize building names.	Empire State Building
Capitalize locations within buildings (apartments, suites, rooms).	Suite 1073
Use numerals for all house or building numbers, except the number *one*.	One Trinity Lane 637 Adams Ave., Apt. 7
Spell out compass directions that fall within a street address	1074 West Connover St.
Abbreviate compass directions that follow the street address	783 Main St. N.E., Apt. 27

diacritical marks that would be commonly used in the region). For example, the following address uses *Köln* instead of *Cologne*:

H. R. Veith, Director	Addressee
Eisfieren Glaswerk	Company Name
Blaubachstrasse 13	Street address
Postfach 10 80 07	Post office box
D-5000 Köln I	District, city
GERMANY	Country

For additional examples of international addresses, see Table A–5.

Be sure to use organizational titles correctly when addressing international correspondence. Job designations vary around the world. In England, for example, a managing director is often what a U.S. company would call its chief executive officer or president, and a British deputy is the equivalent of a vice president. In France, responsibilities are assigned to individuals without regard to title or organizational structure, and in China the title *project manager* has meaning, but the title *sales manager* may not.

To make matters worse, businesspeople in some countries sign correspondence without their names typed below. In Germany, for example, the belief is that employees represent the company, so it's inappropriate to emphasize personal names.[7] Use the examples in Table A–5 as guidelines when addressing correspondence to countries outside the United States.

Salutation

In the salutation of your letter, follow the style of the first line of the inside address. If the first line is a person's name, the salutation is *Dear Mr.* or *Ms. Name.* The formality of the salutation depends on your relationship with the addressee. If in conversation you would say "Mary," your letter's salutation should be *Dear Mary,* followed by a colon. Otherwise, include the courtesy title and last name, followed by a colon. Presuming to write *Dear Lewis* instead of *Dear Professor Chang* demonstrates a disrespectful familiarity that the recipient will probably resent.

If the first line of the inside address is a position title such as *Director of Personnel,* then use *Dear Director.* If the addressee is unknown, use a polite description, such as *Dear Alumnus, Dear SPCA Supporter,* or *Dear Voter.* If the first line is plural (a department or company), then use *Ladies and Gentlemen* (look again at Table A–3). When you do not know whether you're writing to an individual or a group (for example, when writing a reference or a letter of recommendation), use *To whom it may concern.*

In the United States some letter writers use a "salutopening" on the salutation line. A salutopening omits *Dear* but includes the first few words of the opening paragraph along with the recipient's name.

After this line, the sentence continues a double space below as part of the body of the letter, as in these examples:

Thank you, Mr. Brown,	Salutopening
for your prompt payment of your bill.	Body
Congratulations, Ms. Lake!	Salutopening
Your promotion is well deserved.	Body

Whether your salutation is informal or formal, be especially careful that names are spelled right. A misspelled name is glaring evidence of carelessness, and it belies the personal interest you're trying to express.

Body

The body of the letter is your message. Almost all letters are single-spaced, with one blank line before and after the salutation or salutopening, between paragraphs, and before the complimentary close. The body may include indented lists, entire paragraphs indented for emphasis, and even subheadings. If it does, all similar elements should be treated in the same way. Your department or company may select a format to use for all letters.

Complimentary Close

The complimentary close begins on the second line below the body of the letter. Alternatives for wording are available, but currently the trend seems to be toward using one-word closes, such as *Sincerely* and *Cordially.* In any case, the complimentary close reflects the relationship between you and the person you're writing to. Avoid cute closes, such as *Yours for bigger profits.* If your audience doesn't know you well, your sense of humor may be misunderstood.

Signature Block

Leave three blank lines for a written signature below the complimentary close, and then include the sender's name (unless it appears in the letterhead). The person's title may appear on the same line as the name or on the line below:

Cordially,

Raymond Dunnigan
Director of Personnel

Your letterhead indicates that you're representing your company. However, if your letter is on plain paper or runs to a second page, you may want to emphasize that you're speaking legally for the company. The accepted way of doing that is to place the company's

INTERNATIONAL ADDRESSES AND SALUTATIONS			Table A–5
Country	*Postal Address*	*Address Elements*	*Salutations*
Argentina	Sr. Juan Pérez Editorial Internacional S.A. Av. Sarmiento 1337, 8° P. C. C1035AAB BUENOS AIRES – CF ARGENTINA	S.A. = Sociedad Anónima (corporation) Av. Sarmiento (name of street) 1337 (building number) 8°= 8th. P = Piso (floor) C (room or suite) C1035AAB (postcode + city) CF = Capital Federal (federal capital)	Sr. = Señor (Mr.) Sra. = Señora (Mrs.) Srta. = Señorita (Miss) Don't use given names except with people you know well.
Australia	Mr. Roger Lewis International Publishing Pty. Ltd. 166 Kent Street, Level 9 GPO Box 3542 SYDNEY NSW 2001 AUSTRALIA	Pty. Ltd. = Proprietory Limited (corp.) 166 (building number) Kent Street (name of street) Level (floor) GPO Box (post office box) city + state (abbrev.) + postcode	Mr. and Mrs. used on first contact. Ms. not common (avoid use). Business is informal—use given name freely.

Austria	Herrn
	Dipl.-Ing. J. Gerdenitsch
	International Verlag Ges.m.b.H.
	Glockengasse 159
	1010 WIEN
	AUSTRIA
		Herrn = To Mr. (separate line)
		Dipl.-Ing. (engineering degree)
		Ges.m.b.H. (a corporation)
		Glockengasse (street name)
		159 (building number)
		1010 (postcode + city)
		WIEN (Vienna)
			Herr (Mr.)
			Frau (Mrs.)
			Fräulein (Miss) obsolete in business,
			  so do not use.
			Given names are almost never used
			  in business.

Brazil	Ilmo. Sr.
	Gilberto Rabello Ribeiro
	Editores Internacionais S.A.
	Rua da Ajuda, 228–6° Andar
	Caixa Postal 2574
	20040–000
	RIO DE JANEIRO – RJ
	BRAZIL
		Ilmo. = Ilustrissimo (honorific)
		Ilma. = Ilustrissima (hon. female)
		S.A. = Sociedade Anônima (corporation)
		Rua = street, da Ajuda (street name)
		228 (building number)
		6° = 6th. Andar (floor)
		Caixa Postal (P.O. box)
		20040–000 (postcode + city)
		- RJ (state abbrev.)
			Sr. = Senhor (Mr.)
			Sra. = Senhora (Mrs.)
			Srta. = Senhorita (Miss)
			Family name at end,
			  e.g., Senhor Ribeiro (Rabello is
			  mother's family—as in Portugal)
			Given names readily used in
			  business.

China	Xia Zhiyi International Publishing Ltd. 14 Jianguolu Chaoyangqu BEIJING 100025 CHINA	Ltd. (limited liability corporation) 14 (building number) Jianguolu (street name), lu (street) Chaoyangqu (district name) (city + postcode)	Family name (single syllable) first. Given name (2 syllables) second, sometimes reversed. Use Mr. or Ms. at all times (Mr. Xia).
France	Monsieur LEFÈVRE Alain Éditions Internationales S.A. Siège Social Immeuble Le Bonaparte 64–68, av. Galliéni B.P. 154 75942 PARIS CEDEX 19 FRANCE	S.A. = Société Anonyme Siège Social (head office) Immeuble (building + name) 64–68 (building occupies 64, 66, 68) av. = avenue (no initial capital) B.P. = Boîte Postale (P.O. box) 75942 (postcode) CEDEX (postcode for P.O. box)	Monsieur (Mr.) Madame (Mrs.) Mademoiselle (Miss) Best not to abbreviate. Family name is sometimes in all caps with given name following.

Germany	Herrn
	Gerhardt Schneider
	International Verlag GmbH
	Schillerstraße 159
	44147 DORTMUND
	GERMANY
		Herrn = To Herr (on a separate line)
		GmbH (inc.—incorporated)
		-straße (street—'β' often written 'ss')
		159 (building number)
		44147 (postcode + city)
			Herr (Mr.)
			Frau (Mrs.)
			Fräulein (Miss) obsolete in business.
			Business is formal: (1) do not use
			  given names unless invited, and
			  (2) use academic titles precisely.

(continued)

Table A–5   Continued

Country	Postal Address	Address Elements	Salutations
India	Sr. Shyam Lal Gupta International Publishing (Pvt.) Ltd. 1820 Rehaja Centre 214, Darussalam Road Andheri East BOMBAY – 400049 INDIA	(Pvt.) (privately owned) Ltd. (limited liability corporation) 1820 (possibly office #20 on 18th floor) Rehaja Centre (building name) 214 (building number) Andheri East (suburb name) (city + hyphen + postcode)	Shri (Mr.), Shrimati (Mrs.) but English is common business language, so use Mr., Mrs., Miss. Given names are used only by family and close friends.
Italy	Egr. Sig. Giacomo Mariotti Edizioni Internazionali S.p.A. Via Terenzio, 21 20138 MILANO ITALY	Egr. = Egregio (honorific) Sig. = Signor (not nec. a separate line) S.p.A. = Società per Azioni (corp.) Via (street) 21 (building number) 20138 (postcode + city)	Sig. = Signore (Mr.) Sig.ra = Signora (Mrs.) Sig.a (Ms.) Women in business are addressed as Signora. Use given name only when invited.
Japan	Mr. Taro Tanaka Kokusai Shuppan K.K. 10–23, 5-chome, Minamiazabu Minato-ku TOKYO 106 JAPAN	K.K. = Kabushiki Kaisha (corporation) 10 (lot number) 23 (building number) 5-chome (area #5) Minamiazabu (neighborhood name) Minato-ku (city district) (city + postcode)	Given names not used in business. Use family name + job title. Or use family name + "-san" (Tanaka-san) or more respectfully, add "-sama" or "-dono."
Korea	Mr. Kim Chang-ik International Publishers Ltd. Room 206, Korea Building 33–4 Nonhyon-dong Kangnam-ku SEOUL 135–010 KOREA	English company names common Ltd. (a corporation) 206 (office number inside the building) 33–4 (area 4 of subdivision 33) -dong (city neighborhood name) -ku (subdivision of city) (city + postcode)	Family name is normally first but sometimes placed after given name. A two-part name is the given name. Use Mr. or Mrs. in letters, but use job title in speech.
Mexico	Sr. Francisco Pérez Martínez Editores Internacionales S.A. Independencia No.322 Col. Juárez 06050 MEXICO D.F.	S.A. = Sociedad Anónima (corporation) Independencia (street name) No. = Número (number) 322 (building number) Col. = Colonia (city district) Juárez (locality name) 06050 (postcode + city) D.F. = Distrito Federal (federal capital)	Sr. = Señor (Mr.) Sra. = Señora (Mrs.) Srta. = Señorita (Miss) Family name in middle: e.g., Sr. Pérez (Martínez is mother's family). Given names are used in business.
South Africa	Mr. Mandla Ntuli International Publishing (Pty.) Ltd. Private Bag X2581 JOHANNESBURG 2000 SOUTH AFRICA	Pty. = Proprietory (privately owned) Ltd. (a corporation) Private Bag (P.O. Box) (city + postcode) or (postcode + city)	Mnr. = Meneer (Mr.) Mev. = Mevrou (Mrs.) Mejuffrou (Miss) is not used in business. Business is becoming less formal, so the use of given names is possible.
United Kingdom	Mr. N. J. Lancaster International Publishing Ltd. Kingsbury House 12 Kingsbury Road EDGEWARE Middlesex HA8 9XG ENGLAND	N. J. (initials of given names) Ltd. (limited liability corporation) Kingsbury House (building name) 12 (building number) Kingsbury Road (name of street/road) EDGEWARE (city—all caps) Middlesex (county—not all caps) HA8 9XG	Mr. and Ms. used mostly. Mrs. and Miss sometimes used in North and by older women. Given names—called Christian names—are used in business after some time. Wait to be invited.

name in capital letters a double space below the complimentary close and then include the sender's name and title four lines below that:

Sincerely,

WENTWORTH INDUSTRIES

(Mrs.) Helen B. Taylor
President

If your name could be taken for either a man's or a woman's, a courtesy title indicating gender should be included, with or without parentheses. Also, women who prefer a particular courtesy title should include it:

Mrs. Nancy Winters

(Miss) Juana Flores

Ms. Pat Li

(Mr.) Jamie Saunders

Additional Letter Parts

Letters vary greatly in subject matter and thus in the identifying information they need and the format they adopt. The letter in Figure A–2 shows how these additional parts should be arranged. The following elements may be used in any combination, depending on the requirements of the particular letter:

- **Addressee notation.** Letters that have a restricted readership or that must be handled in a special way should include such addressee notations as *Personal, Confidential,* or *Please Forward.* This sort of notation appears a double space above the inside address, in all-capital letters.

- **Attention line.** Although not commonly used today, an attention line can be used if you know only the last name of the person you're writing to. It can also direct a letter to a position title or department. Place the attention line on the first line of the inside address and put the company name on the second.[8] Match the address on the envelope with the style of the inside address. An attention line may take any of the following forms or variants of them:

Attention: Dr. McHenry

Attention Director of Marketing

Attention Marketing Department

- **Subject line.** The subject line tells recipients at a glance what the letter is about (and indicates where to file the letter for future reference). It usually appears below the salutation, either against the left margin, indented (as a paragraph in the body), or centered. It can be placed above the salutation or at the very top of the page, and it can be underscored. Some businesses omit the word *Subject,* and some organizations replace it with *Re:* or *In re:* (meaning "concerning" or "in the matter of"). The subject line may take a variety of forms, including the following:

Subject: RainMaster Sprinklers

About your February 2, 2006, order

FALL 2006 SALES MEETING

Reference Order No. 27920

- **Second-page heading.** Use a second-page heading whenever an additional page is required. Some companies have second-page letterhead (with the company name and address on one line and in a smaller typeface). The heading bears the name

FIGURE A–2
Additional Letter Parts

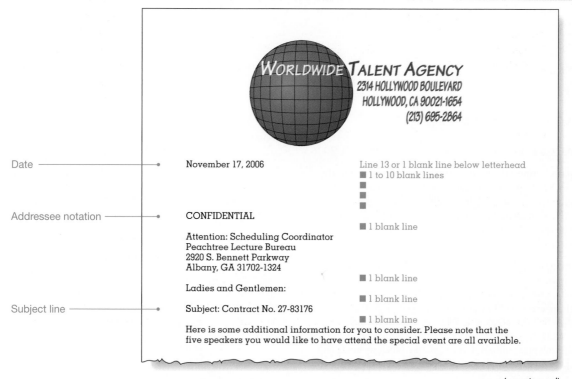

(continued)

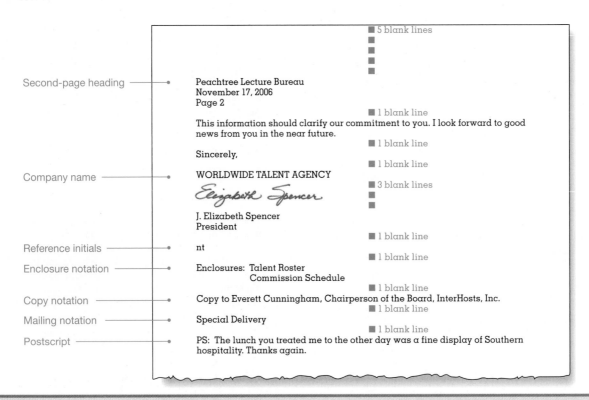

FIGURE A-2
(Continued)

(person or organization) from the first line of the inside address, the page number, the date, and perhaps a reference number. Leave two blank lines before the body. Make sure that at least two lines of a continued paragraph appear on the first and second pages. Never allow the closing lines to appear alone on a continued page. Precede the complimentary close or signature lines with at least two lines of the body. Also, don't hyphenate the last word on a page. All the following are acceptable forms for second-page headings:

Ms. Melissa Baker

May 10, 2006

Page 2

Ms. Melissa Baker, May 10, 2006, Page 2

Ms. Melissa Baker   -2-   May 10, 2006

- **Company name.** If you include the company's name in the signature block, put it all in capital letters a double space below the complimentary close. You usually include the company's name in the signature block only when the writer is serving as the company's official spokesperson or when letterhead has not been used.

- **Reference initials.** When businesspeople keyboard their own letters, reference initials are unnecessary, so they are becoming rare. When one person dictates a letter and another person produces it, reference initials show who helped prepare it. Place initials at the left margin, a double space below the signature block. When the signature block includes the writer's name, use only the preparer's initials. If the signature block includes only the department, use both sets of initials, usually in one of the

following forms: *RSR/sm, RSR:sm,* or *RSR:SM* (writer/preparer). When the writer and the signer are different people, at least the file copy should bear both their initials as well as the typist's: *JFS/RSR/sm* (signer/writer/preparer).

- **Enclosure notation.** Enclosure notations appear at the bottom of a letter, one or two lines below the reference initials. Some common forms include the following:

Enclosure

Enclosures (2)

Enclosures: Résumé

        Photograph

        Attachment

- **Copy notation.** Copy notations may follow reference initials or enclosure notations. They indicate who's receiving a *courtesy copy* (cc). Some companies indicate copies made on a photocopier (*pc*), or they simply use *copy* (c). Recipients are listed in order of rank or (rank being equal) in alphabetical order. Among the forms used are the following:

cc: David Wentworth, Vice President

pc: Dr. Martha Littlefield

Copy to Hans Vogel

        748 Chesterton Rd.

        Snowhomish, WA 98290

        c: Joseph Martinez with brochure and technical sheet

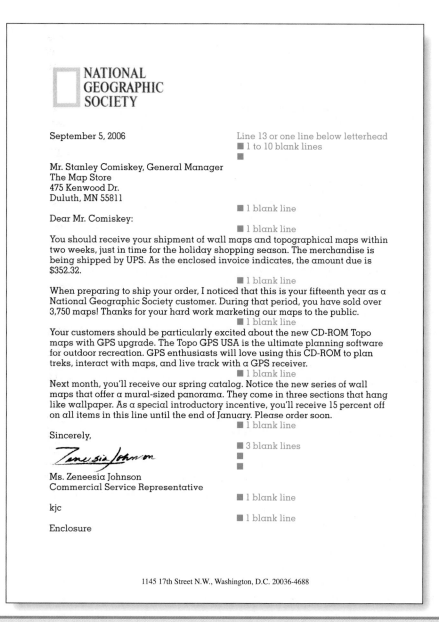

FIGURE A–3
Block Letter Format

When sending copies to readers without other recipients knowing place *bc, bcc,* or *bpc* ("blind copy," "blind courtesy copy," or "blind photocopy") along with the name and any other information only on the copy, not on the original.

- **Mailing notation.** You may place a mailing notation (such as *Special Delivery* or *Registered Mail*) at the bottom of the letter, after reference initials or enclosure notations (whichever is last) and before copy notations. Or you may place it at the top of the letter, either above the inside address on the left side or just below the date on the right side. For greater visibility, mailing notations may appear in capital letters.

- **Postscript.** A postscript is an afterthought to the letter, a message that requires emphasis, or a personal note. It is usually the last thing on any letter and may be preceded by *P.S., PS., PS:,* or nothing at all. A second afterthought would be designated *P.P.S.* (post postscript). Since postscripts usually indicate poor plan-

ning, generally avoid them. However, they're common in sales letters as a punch line to remind readers of a benefit for taking advantage of the offer.

Letter Formats

A letter format is the way of arranging all the basic letter parts. Sometimes a company adopts a certain format as its policy; sometimes the individual letter writer or preparer is allowed to choose the most appropriate format. In the United States, three major letter formats are commonly used:

- **Block format.** Each letter part begins at the left margin. The main advantage is quick and efficient preparation (see Figure A–3).

- **Modified block format.** Same as block format, except that the date, complimentary close, and signature block start near

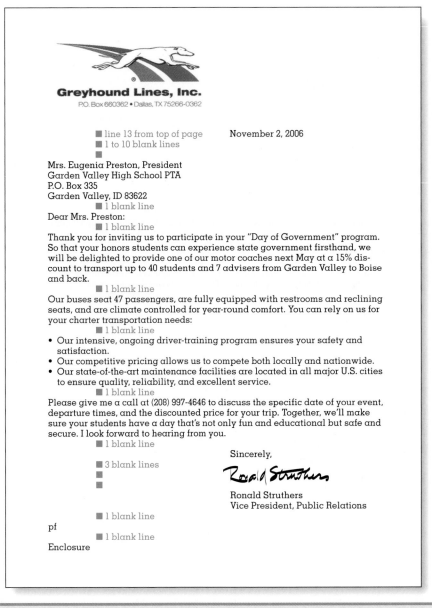

FIGURE A–4
Modified Block Letter Format

the center of the page (see Figure A–4). The modified block format does permit indentions as an option. This format mixes preparation speed with traditional placement of some letter parts. It also looks more balanced on the page than the block format does.

- **Simplified format.** Instead of using a salutation, this format often weaves the reader's name into the first line or two of the body and often includes a subject line in capital letters (see Figure A–5). With no complimentary close, your signature appears after the body, followed by your printed (or typewritten) name (usually in all capital letters). This format is convenient when you don't know the reader's name; however, some people object to it as mechanical and impersonal (a drawback you can overcome with a warm writing style). Because certain letter parts are eliminated, some line spacing is changed.

These three formats differ in the way paragraphs are indented, in the way letter parts are placed, and in some punctuation. However, the elements are always separated by at least one blank line, and the printed (or typewritten) name is always separated from the line above by at least three blank lines to allow space for a signature. If paragraphs are indented, the indention is normally five spaces. The most common formats for intercultural business letters are the block style and the modified block style.

In addition to these three letter formats, letters may also be classified according to their style of punctuation. *Standard*, or *mixed, punctuation* uses a colon after the salutation (a comma if the letter is social or personal) and a comma after the complimentary close. *Open punctuation* uses no colon or comma after the salutation or the complimentary close. Although the most popular style in business communication is mixed punctuation, either style of punctuation may be used with block or modified block letter formats. Because the simpli-

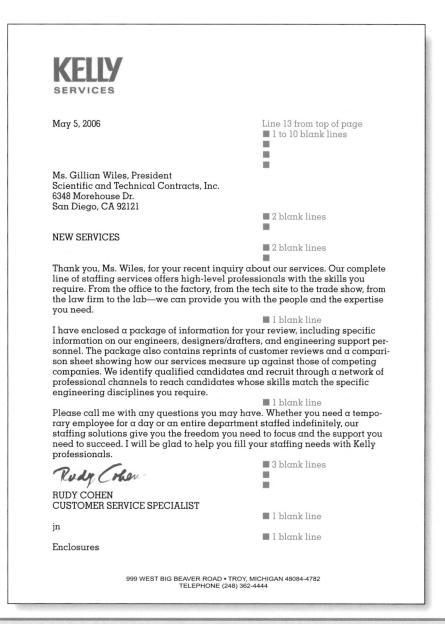

FIGURE A–5
Simplified Letter Format

fied letter format has no salutation or complimentary close, the style of punctuation is irrelevant.

ENVELOPES

For a first impression, the quality of the envelope is just as important as the quality of the stationery. Letterhead and envelopes should be of the same paper stock, have the same color ink, and be imprinted with the same address and logo. Most envelopes used by U.S. businesses are No. 10 envelopes (9½ inches long), which are sized for an 8½-by-11-inch piece of paper folded in thirds. Some occasions call for a smaller, No. 6¾, envelope or for envelopes proportioned to fit special stationery. Figure A–6 shows the two most common sizes.

Addressing the Envelope

No matter what size the envelope, the address is always single-spaced with all lines aligned on the left. The address on the envelope is in the same style as the inside address and presents the same information. The order to follow is from the smallest division to the largest:

1. Name and title of recipient
2. Name of department or subgroup
3. Name of organization
4. Name of building
5. Street address and suite number, or post office box number
6. City, state or province, and ZIP code or postal code
7. Name of country (if the letter is being sent abroad)

Because the U.S. Postal Service uses optical scanners to sort mail, envelopes for quantity mailings, in particular, should be addressed in the prescribed format. Everything is in capital letters, no punctuation is included, and all mailing instructions of interest to the post office are placed above the address area (see Figure A–6). Canada Post

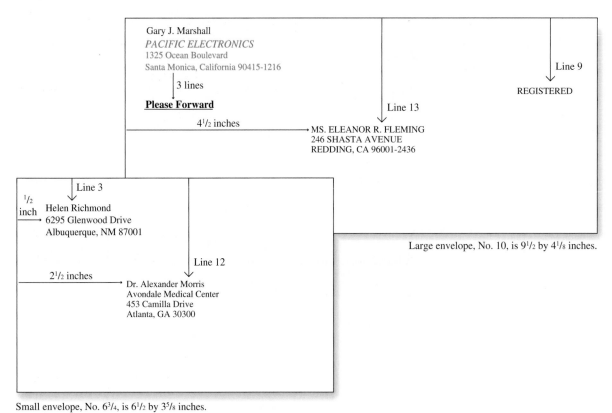

Small envelope, No. 6³/₄, is 6¹/₂ by 3⁵/₈ inches.

FIGURE A–6
Prescribed Envelope Format

requires a similar format, except that only the city is all in capitals, and the postal code is placed on the line below the name of the city. The post office scanners read addresses from the bottom up, so if a letter is to be sent to a post office box rather than to a street address, the street address should appear on the line above the box number. Figure A–6 also shows the proper spacing for addresses and return addresses.

The U.S. Postal Service and the Canada Post Corporation have published lists of two-letter mailing abbreviations for states, provinces, and territories (see Table A–6). Postal authorities prefer no punctuation with these abbreviations, but some executives prefer to have state and province names spelled out in full and set off from city names by a comma. The issue is unresolved, although the comma is most often included. Quantity mailings follow post office requirements. For other letters, a reasonable compromise is to use traditional punctuation, uppercase and lowercase letters for names and street addresses, but two-letter state or province abbreviations, as shown here:

Mr. Kevin Kennedy

2107 E. Packer Dr.

Amarillo, TX 79108

For all out-of-office correspondence, use ZIP and postal codes that have been assigned to speed mail delivery. The U.S. Postal Service has divided the United States and its territories into 10 zones (0 to 9); this digit comes first in the ZIP code. The second and third digits represent smaller geographical areas within a state, and the last two digits identify a "local delivery area." Canadian postal codes are alphanumeric, with a three-character "area code" and a three-character "local code" separated by a single space (K2P 5A5). ZIP

codes should be separated from state and province names by one space. Canadian postal codes may be treated the same or may be put in the bottom line of the address all by itself.

The U.S. Postal Service has added ZIP + 4 codes, which add a hyphen and four more numbers to the standard ZIP codes. The first two of the new numbers may identify an area as small as a single large building, and the last two digits may identify one floor in a large building or even a specific department of an organization. The ZIP + 4 codes are especially useful for business correspondence. The Canada Post Corporation achieves the same result with special postal codes assigned to buildings and organizations that receive a large volume of mail.

Folding to Fit

The way a letter is folded also contributes to the recipient's overall impression of your organization's professionalism. When sending a standard-size piece of paper in a No. 10 envelope, fold it in thirds, with the bottom folded up first and the top folded down over it (see Figure A–7 on page A-16); the open end should be at the top of the envelope and facing out. Fit smaller stationery neatly into the appropriate envelope simply by folding it in half or in thirds. When sending a standard-size letterhead in a No. 6³/₄ envelope, fold it in half from top to bottom and then in thirds from side to side.

International Mail

Postal service differs from country to country. For example, street addresses are uncommon in India, and the mail there is unreliable.[9] It's usually a good idea to send international correspondence by airmail and to ask that responses be sent that way as well. Also, remember to check the postage; rates for sending mail to most other countries differ from the rates for sending mail within your own country.

TWO-LETTER MAILING ABBREVIATIONS FOR THE UNITED STATES AND CANADA — Table A–6

State/Territory/Province	Abbreviation	State/Territory/Province	Abbreviation	State/Territory/Province	Abbreviation
United States		Massachusetts	MA	Texas	TX
Alabama	AL	Michigan	MI	Utah	UT
Alaska	AK	Minnesota	MN	Vermont	VT
American Samoa	AS	Mississippi	MS	Virginia	VA
Arizona	AZ	Missouri	MO	Virgin Islands	VI
Arkansas	AR	Montana	MT	Washington	WA
California	CA	Nebraska	NE	West Virginia	WV
Canal Zone	CZ	Nevada	NV	Wisconsin	WI
Colorado	CO	New Hampshire	NH	Wyoming	WY
Connecticut	CT	New Jersey	NJ	**Canada**	
Delaware	DE	New Mexico	NM	Alberta	AB
District of Columbia	DC	New York	NY	British Columbia	BC
Florida	FL	North Carolina	NC	Labrador	NL
Georgia	GA	North Dakota	ND	Manitoba	MB
Guam	GU	Northern Mariana	MP	New Brunswick	NB
Hawaii	HI	Ohio	OH	Newfoundland	NL
Idaho	ID	Oklahoma	OK	Northwest Territories	NT
Illinois	IL	Oregon	OR	Nova Scotia	NS
Indiana	IN	Pennsylvania	PA	Nunavut	NU
Iowa	IA	Puerto Rico	PR	Ontario	ON
Kansas	KS	Rhode Island	RI	Prince Edward Island	PE
Kentucky	KY	South Carolina	SC	Quebec	QC
Louisiana	LA	South Dakota	SD	Saskatchewan	SK
Maine	ME	Tennessee	TN	Yukon Territory	YT
Maryland	MD	Trust Territories	TT		

International mail falls into three main categories:

- **LC mail.** An abbreviation of the French *Lettres et Cartes* ("letters and cards"), this category consists of letters, letter packages, aerograms, and postcards.

- **AO mail.** An abbreviation of the French *Autres Objets* ("other articles"), this category includes regular printed matter, books and sheet music, matter for the blind, small packets, and publishers' periodicals (second class).

- **CP mail.** An abbreviation of the French *Colis Postaux* ("parcel post"), this category resembles fourth-class mail, including packages of merchandise or any other articles not required to be mailed at letter rates.

Along with several optional special services, the U.S. Postal Service also offers the following:

- **Express Mail International Service (EMS).** A high-speed mail service to many countries

- **International Priority Airmail (IPA).** An international service that's as fast as or faster than regular airmail service

- **International Surface Air Lift (ISAL).** A service providing quicker delivery and lower cost for all kinds of printed matter

- **Bulk Letter Service to Canada.** An economical airmail service for letters weighing 1 ounce or less

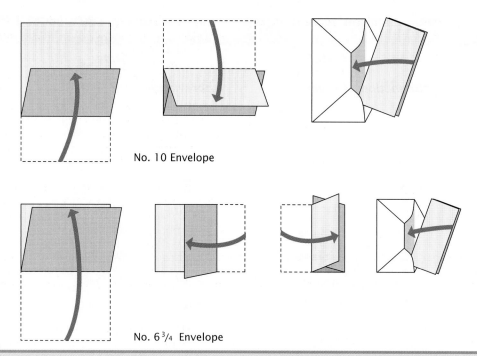

No. 10 Envelope

No. 6 ³/₄ Envelope

FIGURE A–7
Folding Standard-Size Letterhead

- **VALUEPOST/CANADA.** A reduced postage rate for bulk mailings

- **International Electronic Post (INTELPOST).** A service offering same- or next-day delivery of fax documents

- **International Postal Money Orders.** A service for transferring funds to other countries

    To prepare your mail for international delivery, follow the instructions in the U.S. Postal Service Publication 51, *International Postal Rates and Fees.* Be sure to note instructions for the address, return address, and size limits. Envelopes and wrappers must be clearly marked to show their classification (letter, small packet, printed matter, airmail). All registered letters, letter packages, and parcel post packages must be securely sealed. Printed matter may be sealed only if postage is paid by permit imprint, postage meter, precanceled stamps, or second-class imprint. Otherwise, prepare contents so that they're protected without

hindering inspection. Finally, because international mail is subject to customs examination in the country of destination, the contents and value must be declared on special forms.

MEMOS

Many organizations have memo forms preprinted, with labeled spaces for the recipient's name (or sometimes a checklist of all departments in an organization or all persons in a department), the sender's name, the date, and the subject (see Figure A–8). If such forms don't exist, you can use a memo template (which comes with word-processing software and provides margin settings, headings, and special formats), or you can use plain paper.

    On your document, include a title such as *MEMO* or *INTEROFFICE CORRESPONDENCE* (all in capitals) centered at the top of the page or aligned with the left margin. Also at the top, include the words *To, From, Date,* and *Subject*—followed

FIGURE A–8
Preprinted Memo Form

MEMO

TO: _____

DEPT: _____   FROM: _____

DATE: _____   TELEPHONE: _____

SUBJECT: _____   *For your*
☐ APPROVAL   ☐ INFORMATION   ☐ COMMENT

by the appropriate information—with a blank line between, as shown here:

MEMO

TO:

FROM:

DATE:

SUBJECT:

Sometimes the heading is organized like this:

MEMO

TO: DATE:

FROM: SUBJECT:

You can arrange these four pieces of information in almost any order. The date sometimes appears without the heading *Date*. The subject may be presented with the letters *Re:* (in place of *SUBJECT:*) or may even be presented without any heading (but in capital letters so that it stands out clearly). You may want to include a file or reference number, introduced by the word *File*.

The following guidelines will help you effectively format specific memo elements:

- **Addressees.** When sending a memo to a long list of people, include the notation *See distribution list* or *See below* in the *To* position at the top; then list the names at the end of the memo. Arrange this list alphabetically, except when high-ranking officials deserve more prominent placement. You can also address memos to groups of people—*All Sales Representatives, Production Group, New Product Team*.

- **Courtesy titles.** You need not use courtesy titles anywhere in a memo; first initials and last names, first names, or even initials alone are often sufficient. However, use a courtesy title if you would use one in a face-to-face encounter with the person.

- **Subject line.** The subject line of a memo helps busy colleagues quickly find out what your memo is about. Although the subject "line" may overflow onto a second line, it's most helpful when it's short (but still informative).

- **Body.** Start the body of the memo on the second or third line below the heading. Like the body of a letter, it's usually single-spaced with blank lines between paragraphs. Indenting paragraphs is optional. Handle lists, important passages, and subheadings as you do in letters. If the memo is very short, you may double-space it.

- **Second page.** If the memo carries over to a second page, head the second page just as you head the second page of a letter.

- **Writer's initials.** Unlike a letter, a memo doesn't require a complimentary close or a signature, because your name is already prominent at the top. However, you may initial the memo—either beside the name appearing at the top of the memo or at the bottom of the memo—or you may even sign your name at the bottom, particularly if the memo deals with money or confidential matters.

- **Other elements.** Treat elements such as reference initials, enclosure notations, and copy notations just as you would in a letter.

Memos may be delivered by hand, by the post office (when the recipient works at a different location), or through interoffice mail.

Interoffice mail may require the use of special reusable envelopes that have spaces for the recipient's name and department or room number; the name of the previous recipient is simply crossed out. If a regular envelope is used, the words *Interoffice Mail* appear where the stamp normally goes, so that it won't accidentally be stamped and mailed with the rest of the office correspondence.

Informal, routine, or brief reports for distribution within a company are often presented in memo form (see Chapter 10). Don't include report parts such as a table of contents and appendixes, but write the body of the memo report just as carefully as you'd write a formal report.

E-MAIL

Because e-mail messages can act both as memos (carrying information within your company) and as letters (carrying information outside your company and around the world), their format depends on your audience and purpose. You may choose to have your e-mail resemble a formal letter or a detailed report, or you may decide to keep things as simple as an interoffice memo. A modified memo format is appropriate for most e-mail messages.[10] All e-mail programs include two major elements: the header and the body (see Figure A–9 on the following page).

Header

The e-mail header depends on the particular program you use. Some programs even allow you to choose between a shorter and a longer version. However, most headers contain similar information.

- **To:** Contains the audience's e-mail address (see Figure A–10 on page A-19). Most e-mail programs also allow you to send mail to an entire group of people all at once. First, you create a distribution list. Then you type the name of the list in the *To:* line instead of typing the addresses of every person in the group.[11] The most common e-mail addresses are addresses such as

  nmaa.betsy@c.si.edu (Smithsonian Institute's National Museum of American Art)

  webwsj@dowjones.com (*Wall Street Journal*'s home page)

  relpubli@mairie-toulouse.mipnet.fr (Municipal Services, Toulouse, France)

- **From:** Contains your e-mail address.

- **Date:** Contains the day of the week, date (day, month, year), time, and time zone.

- **Subject:** Describes the content of the message and presents an opportunity for you to build interest in your message.

- **Cc:** Allows you to send copies of a message to more than one person at a time. It also allows everyone on the list to see who else received the same message.

- **Bcc:** Lets you send copies to people without the other recipients knowing—a practice considered unethical by some.[12]

- **Attachments:** Contains the name(s) of the file(s) you attach to your e-mail message. The file can be a word-processing document, a digital image, an audio or video message, a spreadsheet, or a software program.[13]

Most e-mail programs now allow you the choice of hiding or revealing other lines that contain more detailed information, including

- **Message-Id:** The exact location of this e-mail message on the sender's system

- **X-mailer:** The version of the e-mail program being used

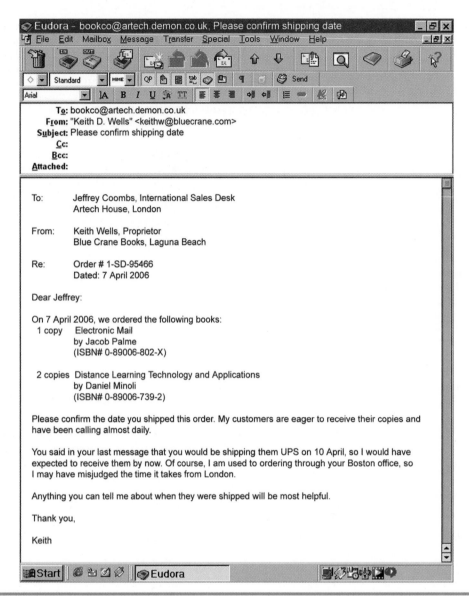

FIGURE A–9
A Typical E-Mail Message

- **Content type:** A description of the text and character set that is contained in the message

- **Received:** Information about each of the systems your e-mail passed through en route to your mailbox.[14]

Body

The rest of the space below the header is for the body of your message. In the *To:* and *From:* lines, some headers actually print out the names of the sender and receiver (in addition to their e-mail addresses). Other headers do not. If your mail program includes only the e-mail addresses, you might consider including your own memo-type header in the body of your message, as in Figure A–9. The writer even included a second, more specific subject line in his memo-type header. Some recipients may applaud the clarity of such second headers; however, others will criticize the space it takes. Your decision depends on how formal you want to be.

Do include a greeting in your e-mail. As pointed out in Chapter 6, greetings personalize your message. Leave one line space above and below your greeting to set it off from the rest of your message. You may end your greeting with a colon (formal), a comma (conversational), or even two hyphens (informal)—depending on the level of formality you want.

Your message begins one blank line space below your greeting. Just as in memos and letters, skip one line space between paragraphs and include headings, numbered lists, bulleted lists, and embedded lists when appropriate. Limit your line lengths to a maximum of 80 characters by inserting a hard return at the end of each line.

One blank line space below your message, include a simple closing, often just one word. A blank line space below that, include your signature. Whether you type your name or use a signature file, including your signature personalizes your message.

REPORTS

Enhance your report's effectiveness by paying careful attention to its appearance and layout. Follow whatever guidelines your organization prefers, always being neat and consistent throughout. If it's up to you to decide formatting questions, the following conventions may

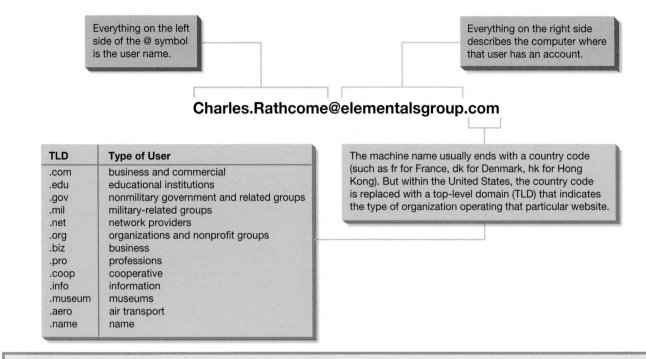

FIGURE A–10
Anatomy of an E-Mail Address

help you decide how to handle margins, headings, spacing and indention, and page numbers.

Margins

All margins on a report page are at least 1 inch wide. For double-spaced pages, use 1-inch margins; for single-spaced pages, set margins between 1 1/4 and 1 1/2 inches. The top, left, and right margins are usually the same, but the bottom margins can be 1 1/2 times deeper. Some special pages also have deeper top margins. Set top margins as deep as 2 inches for pages that contain major titles: prefatory parts (such as the table of contents or the executive summary), supplementary parts (such as the reference notes or bibliography), and textual parts (such as the first page of the text or the first page of each chapter).

If you're going to bind your report at the left or at the top, add half an inch to the margin on the bound edge (see Figure A–11). The space taken by the binding on left-bound reports makes the center point of the text a quarter inch to the right of the center of the paper. Be sure to center headings between the margins, not between the edges of the paper. Computers can do this for you automatically. Other guidelines for report formats are in the Chapter 12 samples.

Headings

Headings of various levels provide visual clues to a report's organization. Figure 11–16, on page 400, illustrates one good system for showing these levels, but many variations exist. No matter which system you use, be sure to be consistent.

Spacing and Indentions

If your report is double-spaced (perhaps to ease comprehension of technical material), indent all paragraphs five character spaces (or about 1/2 inch). In single-spaced reports, block the paragraphs (no indentions) and leave one blank line between them.

Make sure the material on the title page is centered and well balanced, as on the title page of the sample report in Chapter 12.

When using a typewriter, proper spacing takes some calculation. To center text in left-bound reports, start a quarter inch to the right of the paper's center. From that point, backspace once for each two letters in the line. The line will appear centered once the report is bound.

To place lines of type vertically on the title page, follow these steps:

1. Count the number of lines in each block of copy, including blank lines.
2. Subtract that total from 66 (the number of lines on an 11-inch page); the result is the number of unused lines.
3. Divide the number of unused lines by the number of blank areas (always one more than the number of blocks of copy). The result is the number of blank lines to allocate above, between, and below the blocks of copy.

A computer with a good word-processing program will do these calculations for you at the click of a mouse.

Page Numbers

Remember that every page in the report is counted; however, not all pages show numbers. The first page of the report, normally the title page, is unnumbered. All other pages in the prefatory section are numbered with a lowercase roman numeral, beginning with *ii* and continuing with *iii, iv, v,* and so on. The unadorned (no dashes, no period) page number is centered at the bottom margin.

Number the first page of the text of the report with the unadorned arabic numeral 1, centered at the bottom margin (double- or triple-spaced below the text). In left-bound reports, number the following pages (including the supplementary parts) consecutively with unadorned arabic numerals (2, 3, and so on), placed at the top right-hand margin (double- or triple-spaced above the text). For top-bound reports and for special pages having 2-inch top margins, center the page numbers at the bottom margin. `

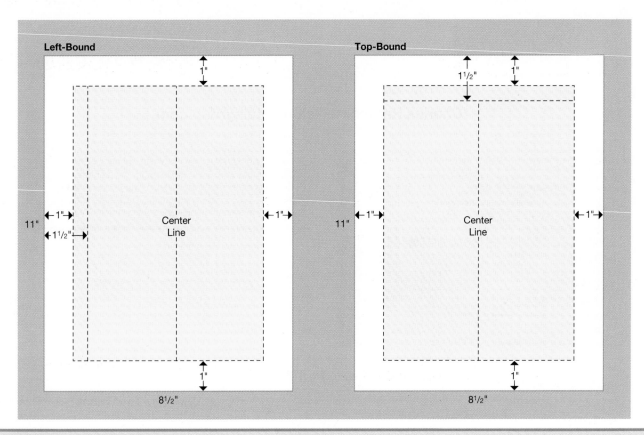

FIGURE A–11
Margins for Formal Reports

Documenting a report is too important a task to undertake haphazardly. By providing information about your sources, you improve your own credibility as well as the credibility of the facts and opinions you present. Documentation gives readers the means for checking your findings and pursuing the subject further. Also, documenting your report is the accepted way to give credit to the people whose work you have drawn from.

What style should you use to document your report? Experts recommend various forms, depending on your field or discipline. Moreover, your employer or client may use a form different from those the experts suggest. Don't let this discrepancy confuse you. If your employer specifies a form, use it; the standardized form is easier for colleagues to understand. However, if the choice of form is left to you, adopt one of the styles described here. Whatever style you choose, be consistent within any given report, using the same order, punctuation, and format from one reference citation or bibliography entry to the next.

A wide variety of style manuals provide detailed information on documentation. Here is a brief annotated list:

- American Psychological Association, *Publication Manual of the American Psychological Association,* 5th ed. (Washington, DC: American Psychological Association, 2001). Details the author-date system, which is preferred in the social sciences and often in the natural sciences as well.

- *The Chicago Manual of Style,* 15th ed. (Chicago: University of Chicago Press, 2003). Often referred to only as "Chicago" and widely used in the publishing industry; provides detailed treatment of source documentation and many other aspects of document preparation.

- Joseph Gibaldi, *MLA Style Manual and Guide to Scholarly Publishing,* 2d ed. (New York: Modern Language Association, 1998). Serves as the basis for the note and bibliography style used in much academic writing and is recommended in many college textbooks on writing term papers; provides a lot of examples in the humanities.

- Andrew Harnack and Eugene Kleppinger, *Online! A Reference Guide to Using Internet Sources with 2003 Update* (New York: St. Martin's Press, 2003). Offers an approach to style for citing online references.

Although many schemes have been proposed for organizing the information in source notes, all of them break the information into parts: (1) information about the author (name), (2) information about the work (title, edition, volume number), (3) information about the publication (place, publisher), (4) information about the date, and (5) information on relevant page ranges.

In the following sections, we summarize the major conventions for documenting sources in three styles: *The Chicago Manual of Style* (Chicago), the *Publication Manual of the American Psychological Association* (APA), and the *MLA Style Manual* (MLA).

CHICAGO HUMANITIES STYLE

The Chicago Manual of Style recommends two types of documentation systems. The *documentary-note,* or *humanities,* style gives biblio-graphic citations in notes—either footnotes (when printed at the bottom of a page) or endnotes (when printed at the end of the report). The humanities system is often used in literature, history, and the arts. The other system strongly recommended by Chicago is the *author-date* system, which cites the author's last name and the date of publication in the text, usually in parentheses, reserving full documentation for the reference list (or bibliography). For the purpose of comparing styles, we will concentrate on the humanities system, which is described in detail in Chicago.

In-Text Citation—Chicago Humanities Style

To document report sources in text, the humanities system relies on superscripts—arabic numerals placed just above the line of type at the end of the reference:

> Toward the end of his speech, Myers sounded a note of caution, saying that even though the economy is expected to grow, it could easily slow a bit.[10]

The superscript lets the reader know how to look for source information in either a footnote or an endnote (see Figure B–1 on the following page). Some readers prefer footnotes so that they can simply glance at the bottom of the page for information. Others prefer endnotes so that they can read the text without a clutter of notes on the page. Also, endnotes relieve the writer from worrying about how long each note will be and how much space it will take away from the page. Both footnotes and endnotes are handled automatically by today's word-processing software.

For the reader's convenience, you can use footnotes for **content notes** (which may supplement your main text with asides about a particular issue or event, provide a cross-reference to another section of your report, or direct the reader to a related source). Then you can use endnotes for **source notes** (which document direct quotations, paraphrased passages, and visual aids). Consider which type of note is most common in your report, and then choose whether to present these notes all as endnotes or all as footnotes. Regardless of the method you choose for referencing textual information in your report, notes for visual aids (both content notes and source notes) are placed on the same page as the visual.

Bibliography—Chicago Humanities Style

The humanities system may or may not be accompanied by a bibliography (because the notes give all the necessary bibliographic information). However, endnotes are arranged in order of appearance in the text, so an alphabetical bibliography can be valuable to your readers. The bibliography may be titled *Bibliography, Reference List, Sources, Works Cited* (if you include only those sources you actually cited in your report), or *Works Consulted* (if you include uncited sources as well). This list of sources may also serve as a reading list for those who want to pursue the subject of your report further, so you may want to annotate each entry—that is, comment on the subject matter and viewpoint of the source, as well as on its usefulness to readers. Annotations may be written in either complete or incomplete sentences. (See the annotated list of style manuals early in this appendix.) A bibliography may also be

NOTES

Journal article with volume and issue numbers	1. James Assira, "Are They Speaking English in Japan?" *Journal of Business Communication* 36, no. 4 (Fall 2002): 72.
Brochure	2. BestTemp Staffing Services, *An Employer's Guide to Staffing Services,* 2d ed. (Denver: BestTemp Information Center, 2000), 31.
Newspaper article, no author	3. "Buying Asian Supplies on the Net," *Los Angeles Times,* 12 February 2000, sec. D, p. 3.
Annual report	4. Eurotec, *2001 Annual Report* (New York: Eurotec, Inc., 2001), 48.
Magazine article	5. Holly Graves, "Prospecting Online," *Business Week,* 17 November 2002, 43–5.
Television broadcast	6. Daniel Han, "Trade Wars Heating Up Around the Globe," *CNN Headline News* (Atlanta: CNN, 5 March 2002).
Internet, World Wide Web	7. "Intel—Company Capsule," Hoover's Online [cited 8 March 2003], 3 screens; available from www.hoovers.com/capsules/13787.html.
Book, component parts	8. Sonja Kuntz, "Moving Beyond Benefits," in *Our Changing Workforce,* ed. Randolf Jacobson (New York: Citadel Press, 2001), 213–27.
Unpublished dissertation or thesis	9. George H. Morales, "The Economic Pressures on Industrialized Nations in a Global Economy" (Ph.D. diss., University of San Diego, 2001), 32–47.
Paper presented at a meeting	10. Charles Myers, "HMOs in Today's Environment" (paper presented at the Conference on Medical Insurance Solution, Chicago, Ill., August 2001), 16–17.
Online magazine article	11. Preston Norwalk, "Training Managers to Help Employees Accept Change," in *Business Line* [online] (San Francisco, 2002 [updated 17 September 2002; cited 3 October 2002]); available from www.busline.com/news.
CD-ROM encyclopedia article, one author	12. Robert Parkings, "George Eastman," *The Concise Columbia Encyclopedia* (New York: Columbia University Press, 1998) [CD-ROM].
Interview	13. Georgia Stainer, general manager, Day Cable and Communications, interview by author, Topeka, Kan., 2 March 2000.
Newspaper article, one author	14. Evelyn Standish, "Global Market Crushes OPEC's Delicate Balance of Interests," *Wall Street Journal,* 19 January 2002, sec. A, p. 1.
Book, two authors	15. Miriam Toller and Jay Fielding, *Global Business for Smaller Companies* (Rocklin, Calif.: Prima Publishing, 2001), 102–3.
Government publication	16. U.S. Department of Defense, *Stretching Research Dollars: Survival Advice for Universities and Government Labs* (Washington, D.C.: GPO, 2002), 126.

FIGURE B–1
Sample Endnotes—Chicago Humanities Style

more manageable if you subdivide it into categories (a classified bibliography), either by type of reference (such as books, articles, and unpublished material) or by subject matter (such as government regulation, market forces, and so on). Following are the major conventions for developing a bibliography according to Chicago style (see Figure B–2):

- Exclude any page numbers that may be cited in source notes, except for journals, periodicals, and newspapers.

- Alphabetize entries by the last name of the lead author (listing last name first). The names of second and succeeding authors are listed in normal order. Entries without an author name are alphabetized by the first important word in the title.

- Format entries as hanging indents (indent second and succeeding lines three to five spaces).

- Arrange entries in the following general order: (1) author name, (2) title information, (3) publication information, (4) date, (5) periodical page range.

- Use quotation marks around the titles of articles from magazines, newspapers, and journals—capitalizing the first and last words, as well as all other important words (except prepositions, articles, and coordinating conjunctions).

- Use italics to set off the names of books, newspapers, journals, and other complete publications—capitalizing the first and last words, as well as all other important words.

BIBLIOGRAPHY

Journal article with volume and issue numbers	Assira, James. "Are They Speaking English in Japan?" *Journal of Business Communication* 36, no. 4 (Fall 2002): 72.
Brochure	BestTemp Staffing Services. *An Employer's Guide to Staffing Services.* 2d ed. Denver: BestTemp Information Center, 2000.
Newspaper article, no author	"Buying Asian Supplies on the Net." *Los Angeles Times,* 12 February 2000, sec. D, p. 3.
Annual report	Eurotec. 2001 *Annual Report.* New York: Eurotec, Inc., 2001.
Magazine article	Graves, Holly. "Prospecting Online." *Business Week,* 17 November 2002, 43–5.
Television broadcast	Han, Daniel. "Trade Wars Heating Up Around the Globe." *CNN Headline News.* Atlanta: CNN, 5 March 2002.
Internet, World Wide Web	"Intel—Company Capsule." *Hoover's Online* [cited 8 March 2003]. 3 screens; Available from www.hoovers.com/capsules/13787.html.
Book, component parts	Kuntz, Sonja. "Moving Beyond Benefits." In *Our Changing Workforce*, edited by Randolf Jacobson. New York: Citadel Press, 2001.
Unpublished dissertation or thesis	Morales, George H. "The Economic Pressures on Industrialized Nations in a Global Economy." Ph.D. diss., University of San Diego, 2001.
Paper presented at a meeting	Myers, Charles. "HMOs in Today's Environment." Paper presented at the Conference on Medical Insurance Solutions, Chicago, Ill., August 2001.
Online magazine article	Norwalk, Preston. "Training Managers to Help Employees Accept Change." In *Business Line* [online]. San Francisco, 2002 [updated 17 September 2002; cited 3 October 2002]. Available from www.busline.com/news.
CD-ROM encyclopedia article, one author	Parkings, Robert. "George Eastman." *The Concise Columbia Encyclopedia.* New York: Columbia University Press, 1998. [CD-ROM].
Interview	Stainer, Georgia, general manager, Day Cable and Communications. Interview by author. Topeka, Kan., 2 March 2000.
Newspaper article, one author	Standish, Evelyn. "Global Market Crushes OPEC's Delicate Balance of Interests." *Wall Street Journal,* 19 January 2002, sec. A, p. 1.
Book, two authors	Toller, Miriam, and Jay Fielding. *Global Business for Smaller Companies.* Rocklin, Calif.: Prima Publishing, 2001.
Government publication	U.S. Department of Defense. *Stretching Research Dollars: Survival Advice for Universities and Government Labs.* Washington, D.C.: GPO, 2002.

FIGURE B–2
Sample Bibliography—Chicago Humanities Style

- For journal articles, include the volume number and the issue number (if necessary). Include the year of publication inside parentheses and follow with a colon and the page range of the article: *Journal of Business Communication* 36, no. 4 (2001): 72. (In this source, the volume is 36, the number is 4, and the page is 72.)
- Use brackets to identify all electronic references: [Online database] or [CD-ROM].
- Explain how electronic references can be reached: Available from www.spaceless.com/WWWVL.
- Give the citation date for online references: Cited 23 August 2006.

APA STYLE

The American Psychological Association (APA) recommends the author-date system of documentation, which is popular in the physical, natural, and social sciences. When using this system, you simply insert the author's last name and the year of publication within parentheses following the text discussion of the material cited. Include a page number if you use a direct quote. This approach briefly identifies the source so that readers can locate complete information in the alphabetical reference list at the end of the report. The author-date system is both brief and clear, saving readers time and effort.

In-Text Citation—APA Style

To document report sources in text using APA style, insert the author's surname and the date of publication at the end of a statement. Enclose this information in parentheses. If the author's name is referred to in the text itself, then the number can be omitted from parenthetical material.

> Some experts recommend both translation and back-translation when dealing with any non-English-speaking culture (Assira, 2001).

> Toller and Fielding (2000) make a strong case for small companies succeeding in global business.

Personal communications and interviews conducted by the author would not be listed in the reference list at all. Such citations would appear in the text only.

> Increasing the role of cable companies is high on the list of Georgia Stainer, general manager at Day Cable and Communications (personal communication, March 2, 2006).

List of References—APA Style

For APA style, list only those works actually cited in the text (so you would not include works for background or for further reading). Report writers must choose their references judiciously. Following are the major conventions for developing a reference list according to APA style (see Figure B–3):

- Format entries as hanging indents.

- List all author names in reversed order (last name first), and use only initials for the first and middle names.

- Arrange entries in the following general order: (1) author name, (2) date, (3) title information, (4) publication information, (5) periodical page range.

FIGURE B–3
Sample References—APA Style

REFERENCES

Journal article with volume and issue numbers

Assira, J. (2002). Are they speaking English in Japan? *Journal of Business Communication, 36*(4), 72.

Brochure

BestTemp Staffing Services. (2000). *An employer's guide to staffing services* (2d ed.) [Brochure]. Denver: BestTemp Information Center.

Newspaper article, no author

Buying Asian supplies on the net. (2000, February 12). *Los Angeles Times*, p. D3.

Annual report

Eurotec. (2001). 2001 *annual report*. New York: Eurotec.

Magazine article

Graves, H. (2002, November 17). Prospecting online. *Business Week*, 43–45.

Television broadcast

Han, D. (2002, March 5). Trade wars heating up around the globe. *CNN Headline News*. [Television broadcast]. Atlanta, GA: CNN.

Internet, World Wide Web

Hoover's Online. (2003). *Intel—Company Capsule*. Retrieved March 8, 2002, from http://www.hoovers.com/capsules/13787.html

Book, component parts

Kuntz, S. (2001). Moving beyond benefits. In Randolph Jacobson (Ed.), *Our changing workforce* (pp. 213–227). New York: Citadel Press.

Unpublished dissertation or thesis

Morales, G. H. (2001). *The economic pressures on industrialized nations in a global economy*. Unpublished doctoral dissertation, University of San Diego.

Paper presented at a meeting

Myers, C. (2001, August). *HMOs in today's environment*. Paper presented at the Conference on Medical Insurance Solutions, Chicago, IL.

Online magazine article

Norwalk, P. (2002, July 17). Training managers to help employees accept change. *Business Line*. Retrieved March 8, 2002, from http://www.busline.com/news

CD-ROM encyclopedia article, one author

Parkings, R. (1998). George Eastman. On *The concise Columbia encyclopedia*. [CD-ROM]. New York: Columbia University Press.

Interview

Cited in text only, not in the list of references.

Newspaper article, one author

Standish, E. (2002, January 19). Global market crushes OPEC's delicate balance of interests. *Wall Street Journal*, p. A1.

Book, two authors

Toller, M., & Fielding, J. (2001). *Global business for smaller companies*. Rocklin, CA: Prima Publishing.

Government publication

U.S. Department of Defense. (2002). *Stretching research dollars: Survival advice for universities and government labs*. Washington, DC: U.S. Government Printing Office.

- Follow the author name with the date of publication in parentheses.

- List titles of articles from magazines, newspapers, and journals without underlines or quotation marks. Capitalize only the first word of the title, any proper nouns, and the first word to follow an internal colon.

- Italicize titles of books, capitalizing only the first word, any proper nouns, and the first word to follow a colon.

- Italicize names of magazines, newspapers, journals, and other complete publications—capitalizing all the important words.

- For journal articles, include the volume number (in italics) and, if necessary, the issue number (in parentheses). Finally, include the page range of the article: *Journal of Business Communication, 36(4),* 72. (In this example, the volume is 36, the number is 4, and the page number is 72.)

- Include personal communications (such as letters, memos, e-mail, and conversations) only in text, not in reference lists.

- Electronic references include author, date of publication, title of article, name of publication (if one), volume, date of retrieval (month, day, year), and the source.

- For electronic references, indicate the actual year of publication, and the exact date of retrieval.

- For electronic references, specify the URL, leave periods off the ends of URLs.

MLA STYLE

The style recommended by the Modern Language Association of America is used widely in the humanities, especially in the study of language and literature. Like APA style, MLA style uses brief parenthetical citations in the text. However, instead of including author name and year, MLA citations include author name and page reference.

In-Text Citation—MLA Style

To document report sources in text using MLA style, insert the author's last name and a page reference inside parentheses following the cited material: (Matthews 63). If the author's name is mentioned in the text reference, the name can be omitted from the parenthetical citation: (63). The citation indicates that the reference came from page 63 of a work by Matthews. With the author's name, readers can find complete publication information in the alphabetically arranged list of works cited that comes at the end of the report.

> Some experts recommend both translation and back-translation when dealing with any non-English-speaking culture (Assira 72).

> Toller and Fielding make a strong case for small companies succeeding in global business (102–03).

List of Works Cited—MLA Style

The *MLA Style Manual* recommends preparing the list of works cited first so that you will know what information to give in the parenthetical citation (for example, whether to add a short title if you're citing more than one work by the same author, or whether to give an initial or first name if you're citing two authors who have the same last name). The list of works cited appears at the end of your report, contains all the works that you cite in your text, and lists them in alphabetical order. Following are the major conventions for developing a reference list according to MLA style (see Figure B–4):

- Format entries as hanging indents.

- Arrange entries in the following general order: (1) author name, (2) title information, (3) publication information, (4) date, (5) periodical page range.

- List the lead author's name in reverse order (last name first), using either full first names or initials. List second and succeeding author names in normal order.

- Use quotation marks around the titles of articles from magazines, newspapers, and journals—capitalize all important words.

- Italicize the names of books, newspapers, journals and other complete publications, capitalizing all main words in the title.

- For journal articles, include the volume number and the issue number (if necessary). Include the year of publication inside parentheses and follow with a colon and the page range of the article: *Journal of Business Communication* 36.4 (2001): 72. (In this source, the volume is 36, the number is 4, and the page is 72.)

- Electronic sources are less fixed than print sources, and they may not be readily accessible to readers. So citations for electronic sources must provide more information. Always try to be as comprehensive as possible, citing whatever information is available.

- The date for electronic sources should contain both the date assigned in the source and the date accessed by the researcher.

- The URL for electronic sources must be as accurate and complete as possible, from access-mode indentifier (http, ftp, gopher, telnet) to all relevant directory and file names. Be sure to enclose this path inside angle brackets: <http://www.hoovers.com/capsules/13787.html>.

WORKS CITED

Journal article with volume and issue numbers	Assira, James. "Are They Speaking English in Japan?" *Journal of Business Communication* 36.4 (2002): 72.
Brochure	BestTemp Staffing Services. *An Employer's Guide to Staffing Services*. 2d ed. Denver: BestTemp Information Center, 2000.
Newspaper article, no author	"Buying Asian Supplies on the Net." *Los Angeles Times* 12 Feb. 2000: D3.
Annual report	Eurotec. *2000 Annual Report*. New York: Eurotec, Inc., 2001.
Magazine article	Graves, Holly. "Prospecting Online." *Business Week* 17 Nov. 2002: 43–45.
Television broadcast	Han, Daniel. "Trade Wars Heating Up Around the Globe." *CNN Headline News*. CNN, Atlanta. 5 Mar. 2002.
Internet, World Wide Web	"Intel—Company Capsule." *Hoover's Online*. 2003. Hoover's Company Information. 8 Mar. 2002 <http://www.hoovers.com/capsules/13787.html>.
Book, component parts	Kuntz, Sonja. "Moving Beyond Benefits." *Our Changing Workforce*. Ed. Randolf Jacobson. New York: Citadel Press, 2001. 213–27.
Unpublished dissertation or thesis	Morales, George H. "The Economic Pressures on Industrialized Nations in a Global Economy." Diss. U of San Diego, 2001.
Paper presented at a meeting	Myers, Charles. "HMOs in Today's Environment." Conference on Medical Insurance Solutions. Chicago. 13 Aug. 2001.
Online magazine article	Norwalk, Preston. "Training Managers to Help Employees Accept Change." *Business Line* 17 July 2002. 8 Mar. 2002 <http://www.busline.com/news>.
CD-ROM encyclopedia article, one author	Parkings, Robert. "George Eastman." *The Concise Columbia Encyclopedia*. CD-ROM. New York: Columbia UP, 1998.
Interview	Stainer, Georgia, general manager, Day Cable and Communications. Telephone interview. 2 Mar. 2000.
Newspaper article, one author	Standish, Evelyn. "Global Market Crushes OPEC's Delicate Balance of Interests." *Wall Street Journal* 19 Jan. 2002: A1.
Book, two authors	Toller, Miriam, and Jay Fielding. *Global Business for Smaller Companies*. Rocklin, CA: Prima Publishing, 2001.
Government publication	United States. Department of Defense. *Stretching Research Dollars: Survival Advice for Universities and Government Labs*. Washington: GPO, 2002.

FIGURE B–4
Sample Works Cited—MLA Style

Instructors often use these short, easy-to-remember correction symbols and abbreviations when evaluating students' writing. You can use them too, to understand your instructor's suggestions and to revise and proofread your own letters, memos, and reports. Refer to the Handbook of Grammar, Mechanics, and Usage (pp. H-1–H-20) for further information.

CONTENT AND STYLE

Acc	Accuracy. Check to be sure information is correct.
ACE	Avoid copying examples.
ACP	Avoid copying problems.
Adp	Adapt. Tailor message to reader.
App	Follow proper organization approach. (Refer to Chapter 4.)
Assign	Assignment. Review instructions for assignment.
AV	Active verb. Substitute active for passive.
Awk	Awkward phrasing. Rewrite.
BC	Be consistent.
BMS	Be more sincere.
Chop	Choppy sentences. Use longer sentences and more transitional phrases.
Con	Condense. Use fewer words.
CT	Conversational tone. Avoid using overly formal language.
Depers	Depersonalize. Avoid attributing credit or blame to any individual or group.
Dev	Develop. Provide greater detail.
Dir	Direct. Use direct approach; get to the point.
Emph	Emphasize. Develop this point more fully.
EW	Explanation weak. Check logic; provide more proof.
Fl	Flattery. Avoid compliments that are insincere.
FS	Figure of speech. Find a more accurate expression.
GNF	Good news first. Use direct order.
GRF	Give reasons first. Use indirect order.
GW	Goodwill. Put more emphasis on expressions of goodwill.
H/E	Honesty/ethics. Revise statement to reflect good business practices.
Imp	Imply. Avoid being direct.
Inc	Incomplete. Develop further.
Jar	Jargon. Use less specialized language.
Log	Logic. Check development of argument.
Neg	Negative. Use more positive approach or expression.
Obv	Obvious. Do not state point in such detail.
OC	Overconfident. Adopt humbler language.
OM	Omission.
Org	Organization. Strengthen outline.
OS	Off the subject. Close with point on main subject.
Par	Parallel. Use same structure.
Pom	Pompous. Rephrase in down-to-earth terms.
PV	Point of view. Make statement from reader's perspective rather than your own.
RB	Reader benefit. Explain what reader stands to gain.

Red	Redundant. Reduce number of times this point is made.
Ref	Reference. Cite source of information.
Rep	Repetitive. Provide different expression.
RS	Resale. Reassure reader that he or she has made a good choice.
SA	Service attitude. Put more emphasis on helping reader.
Sin	Sincerity. Avoid sounding glib or uncaring.
SL	Stereotyped language. Focus on individual's characteristics instead of on false generalizations.
Spec	Specific. Provide more specific statement.
SPM	Sales promotion material. Tell reader about related goods or services.
Stet	Let stand in original form.
Sub	Subordinate. Make this point less important.
SX	Sexist. Avoid language that contributes to gender stereotypes.
Tone	Tone needs improvement.
Trans	Transition. Show connection between points.
UAE	Use action ending. Close by stating what reader should do next.
UAS	Use appropriate salutation.
UAV	Use active voice.
Unc	Unclear. Rewrite to clarify meaning.
UPV	Use passive voice.
USS	Use shorter sentences.
V	Variety. Use different expression or sentence pattern.
W	Wordy. Eliminate unnecessary words.
WC	Word choice. Find a more appropriate word.
YA	"You" attitude. Rewrite to emphasize reader's needs.

GRAMMAR, MECHANICS, AND USAGE

Ab	Abbreviation. Avoid abbreviations in most cases; use correct abbreviation.
Adj	Adjective. Use adjective instead.
Adv	Adverb. Use adverb instead.
Agr	Agreement. Make subject and verb or noun and pronoun agree.
Ap	Appearance. Improve appearance.
Apos	Apostrophe. Check use of apostrophe.
Art	Article. Use correct article.
BC	Be consistent.
Cap	Capitalize.
Case	Use cases correctly.
CoAdj	Coordinate adjective. Insert comma between coordinate adjectives; delete comma between adjective and compound noun.
CS	Comma splice. Use period or semicolon to separate clauses.
DM	Dangling modifier. Rewrite so that modifier clearly relates to subject of sentence.
Exp	Expletive. Avoid expletive beginnings, such as it is, there are, there is, this is, and these are.

F	Format. Improve layout of document.		RC	Restrictive clause (or phrase). Remove commas that separate clause from rest of sentence.
Frag	Fragment. Rewrite as complete sentence.			
Gram	Grammar. Correct grammatical error.		RO	Run-on sentence. Separate two sentences with comma and coordinating conjunction or with semicolon.
HCA	Hyphenate compound adjective.			
lc	Lowercase. Do not use capital letter.			
M	Margins. Improve frame around document.		SC	Series comma. Add comma before *and*.
MM	Misplaced modifier. Place modifier close to word it modifies.		SI	Split infinitive. Do not separate *to* from rest of verb.
NRC	Nonrestrictive clause (or phrase). Separate from rest of sentence with commas.		Sp	Spelling error. Consult dictionary.
			S-V	Subject-verb pair. Do not separate with comma.
P	Punctuation. Use correct punctuation.		Syl	Syllabification. Divide word between syllables.
Par	Parallel. Use same structure.		WD	Word division. Check dictionary for proper end-of-line hyphenation.
PH	Place higher. Move document up on page.			
PL	Place lower. Move document down on page.		WW	Wrong word. Replace with another word.
Prep	Preposition. Use correct preposition.			

PROOFREADING MARKS

Symbol	Meaning	Symbol Used in Context	Corrected Copy
═	Align horizontally	meaningful result	meaningful result
‖	Align vertically	1. Power cable 2. Keyboard	1. Power cable 2. Keyboard
≡	Capitalize	Pepsico, Inc.	PepsiCo, Inc.
⌐¬	Center	Awards Banquet	Awards Banquet
◡	Close up space	self- confidence	self-confidence
ℓ	Delete	harrassment and abuse	harassment
(ds)	Double-space	text in first line text in second line (ds)	text in first line text in second line
∧	Insert	turquoise and white shirts	turquoise and white shirts
∨	Insert apostrophe	our teams goals	our team's goals
∧	Insert comma	a, b and c	a, b, and c
⹀	Insert hyphen	third quarter sales	third-quarter sales
⊙	Insert period	Harrigan et al	Harrigan et al.
∨ ∨	Insert quotation marks	This team isn't cooperating.	This "team" isn't cooperating.
#	Insert space	real estate testcase	real estate test case
/	Lowercase	TULSA, South of here	Tulsa, south of here
⌊⌋	Move down	Sincerely,	Sincerely,
⌐	Move left	Attention: Security	Attention: Security
¬	Move right	February 2, 2003	February 2, 2003
⌐¬	Move up	THIRD-QUARTER SALES	THIRD-QUARTER SALES
(STET)	Restore	staff talked openly and frankly (STET)	staff talked openly
⌇	Run lines together	Manager, Distribution	Manager, Distribution
(ss)	Single space	text in first line (ss) text in second line	text in first line text in second line
◯	Spell out	COD	cash on delivery
(sp)	Spell out	(sp) Assn. of Biochem. Engrs.	Association of Biochemical Engineers
⌐	Start new line	Marla Fenton, Manager, Distri-bution	Marla Fenton, Manager, Distribution
¶	Start new paragraph	¶The solution is easy to determine but difficult to implement in a competitive environment like the one we now face.	The solution is easy to determine but difficult to implement in a competitive environment like the one we now face.
∼	Transpose	airy, light, casual tone	light, airy, casual tone
(bf)	Use boldface	Recommendations (bf)	**Recommendations**
(ital)	Use italics	Quarterly Report (ital)	*Quarterly Report*

Video Guide:
Applications and Exercises

Your instructor may elect to show you one or more of the videos described on the following pages. These programs supplement course concepts with real-life examples of businesspeople meeting important communication challenges. This video guide includes several review and analysis questions as well as exercises for each video. Be sure to review the appropriate page ahead of time so that you'll know what to look for when you watch the video.

ETHICAL COMMUNICATION
Learning Objectives

After viewing this video, you will be able to

1. Describe a process for deciding what is ethical or unethical
2. Explain the importance of meeting your personal and professional responsibilities in an ethical manner
3. Discuss the possible consequences of ethical and unethical choices and talk about the impact of these choices on direct and related audiences

Background Information

Communication is ethical when it includes all relevant information, when it's true in every sense, and when it isn't deceptive in any way. In contrast, communication is unethical when it includes false information, fails to include important information, or otherwise misleads an audience. To avoid unethical choices in your communication efforts, you must consider not only legal issues but also the needs of your audience and the expectations of society and your employer. In turn, companies that demonstrate high standards of ethics maintain credibility with employees, customers, and other stakeholders.

The Video

This video identifies two important tools in a communicator's toolbox: honesty and objectivity. These tools help businesspeople resolve ethical dilemmas and avoid ethical lapses, both within the company and during interactions with outside audiences. Poor ethical choices can damage a company's credibility and put employees, customers, and the surrounding community at risk. Unfortunately, some ethical choices are neither clear nor simple, and you may face situations in which the needs of one group or individual must be weighed against the needs of another.

Discussion Questions

1. Would you ever consider compromising your ethics for self-gain? If so, under what circumstances? If not, why?
2. The video mentions the role of misrepresentations in the collapse of Enron. If you were the head of communications at Enron and had some knowledge of the true nature of the company's financial condition, what would you have done?
3. Identify risks involved when you choose to act in an unethical manner.
4. How can you be an effective business communicator without credibility?
5. Is it ethical to call in sick to work, even though you are not ill? What happens to your credibility if someone finds out you were not sick?

Follow-Up Assignment

Many businesses, from small companies to large corporations, formulate codes of ethics that outline ethical standards for employees. Review IBM's guidelines, which are posted on its website at www.ibm.com/investor/corpgovernance/cgbcg.phtml. Now answer the following questions:

1. What does IBM want employees to do if they are aware of unethical situations within the organization?
2. How does IBM view misleading statements or innuendos about competitors?
3. What advice does IBM give employees on the subject of receiving gifts from people outside the company?

For Further Research

Advertising communications, particularly advertising aimed at children, can present a variety of ethical concerns. The article provided at www.mediascope.org/pubs/ibriefs/cha.htm reports statistics on the advertising of alcohol and tobacco products and discusses the negative effect these advertisements can have on children. To what extent was it ethical for Anheuser Busch to use the Budweiser frog or for Philip Morris to use Joe Camel in its advertisements, given that many children were able to identify with both characters?

LEARNING TO LISTEN:
SECOND CITY COMMUNICATIONS
Learning Objectives

After viewing this video, you will be able to

1. Understand the functions of interpersonal communication in the workplace
2. Identify the ways to overcome barriers to effective communication
3. Discuss the importance of active listening, both socially and professionally

Background Information

Chicago's Second City Improv is more than the world's best-known comedy theater. Second City now brings its famous brand of humor to corporate giants such as Coca-Cola, Motorola, and Microsoft. With over 40 years of experience in corporate services, Second City's teachers help business professionals develop communication skills through lessons in improvisational theater. Business Communications Training is Second City's fastest growing practice, fueled by the demands of more than two hundred Fortune 500 companies. Workshops are tailored to client's needs in such areas as listening and giving presentations, collaborative leadership and team skills, interviewing, breaking down barriers to successful communication, and using humor to convey important messages. The next time you watch improvisational sketch comedy, ask yourself how a lesson in the art of "improv" might give your career a boost.

The Video

In these two video segments, you'll see Second City's training techniques in action. The first segment addresses the need to listen actively, and the second explores techniques for encouraging innovation. The second clip is less focused on communication, but you can see how the techniques for stimulating innovation work equally well for fostering meaningful, two-way conversation that encourages people to open up rather than shut down.

Discussion Questions

1. How do the exercises featured in this video address the contrasting needs of the trial lawyer, the divorce lawyer, and the media buyer?
2. Would ABC's talkative guest Kay Jarman, the 47-year-old award winning salesperson, be a good candidate for Second City's training workshop?
3. What other workshops might Tom Yorton want to offer companies in response to the current economic and political climate?
4. How might the "yes and" rule of improvisation be used to train customer service representatives at an L.L. Bean or a Dell computer call center? Without physical cues, such as facial expression and body language, is the "yes and" rule still effective?
5. As President and Managing Director of Second City Communications, Tom Yorton says the following: "You have to be willing to fail to be able to get the results you want . . . to connect with an audience." Do you agree that this statement is as true in business as it is in comedy? Support your chosen position.

Follow-Up Assignment

Enjoy Second City Communication's website at www.secondcity.com. If you are a loyal fan, you might want to check out the book titles offered and read more about the group's history. Now explore Second City's Corporate Services: Scan the client roster, read the testimonials, and then select a case study that you find compelling. If you are currently employed, which workshop would be most beneficial to you and to your work team? Explain your choice. If you are not currently employed, how might you and your fellow business students benefit from a Second City workshop? Which workshop would you most like to participate in? Explain how you think it might help you in terms of your social life, your career planning, and your interviewing skills.

For Further Research

The importance of active listening is at the core of *consultative selling*, an approach that emphasizes posing questions to the potential buyer in order to identify needs and expectations—rather than rattling off a prepared sales speech. PublicSpeakingSkills.com (www.publicspeakingskills.com) is one of many companies that offer training in consultative selling. Review the description of the company's Consultative Selling and Negotiating Skills course. Do the principles espoused match the concept of the "you" attitude and the elements of ethical communication that you've learned so far?

COMMUNICATING IN THE GLOBAL WORKPLACE
Learning Objectives

After viewing this video, you will be able to

1. Discuss the challenges of communicating in the global workplace
2. Identify barriers to effective communication across borders
3. Explain the critical role of time in global communication efforts

Background Information

Many businesses are crossing national boundaries to engage in international business. However, operating in a global environment presents a variety of challenges related to culture and communication. Understanding and respecting these challenges can mean the difference between success and failure, so executives must make sure that employees are educated on cultural issues before attempting to do business in other countries.

The Video

This video identifies the challenges to effective communication in the global marketplace, including the barriers posed by language, culture, time, and technology. You will see that a significant amount of research needs to be conducted before a company can engage in successful global business ventures. For instance, if communicators are unaware of differences in gestures, expressions, and dialect, they can inadvertently offend or confuse their audiences. In addition, time zone differences require organizations to plan carefully in advance so that they can develop, translate, and deliver information in a timely manner.

Discussion Questions

1. Language can be a barrier to effective communication. What steps can a company take to minimize language barriers across borders?
2. What characteristics of a country's culture need to be researched to ensure business success across borders?
3. How does a company ensure that a message is properly translated into the local language and dialect of the people it conducts business with?
4. What challenges does a company face when trying to hold a conference call or video meeting with affiliates and employees around the world?
5. The video mentions that some companies have trusted contacts in a country they wish to do business with, while other companies rely on a significant amount of research to learn more about culture and other local characteristics. What method do you feel is most effective for gathering useful, accurate, and up-to-date information regarding cultural issues?

Follow-Up Assignment

The Coca-Cola Company has local operations in more than 200 countries throughout the world. Visit www.coca-cola.com to learn more about the company's business activities in a variety of countries. What steps does Coke take to communicate through its website with customers around the world? Does the company strive to develop products that meet local tastes and needs? If so, how and why?

For Further Research

Choose a country other than the United States, and research your selection using both online and library resources to identify important cultural characteristics specific to that country. For example, you may want to gather information about gestures and other nonverbal communication that would be considered offensive, about work habits, or about laws related to conducting business in that country. The characteristics you identify should be useful and accurate.

Based on what you've learned about this country and your personal beliefs, values, and life experiences, is there any risk that you might have a prejudiced or ethnocentric viewpoint regarding people from this country? Why or why not?

IMPACT OF CULTURE ON BUSINESS: SPOTLIGHT ON LATIN AMERICA
Learning Objectives

After viewing this video, you will be able to

1. List key aspects of Latin American culture and indicate the influences on their development
2. Identify factors that might lead to cultural change in Latin America

3. Explain some of the major cultural contrasts within Latin America and their impact on international business operations

Background Information

To a large degree, culture defines the way all human beings interpret and respond to life's changing circumstances. When you interact with people from your own culture, your shared experiences and expectations usually enhance the communication process by providing a common language and frame of reference. However, when you communicate across cultural boundaries, a lack of awareness of your audience's culture—and the subconscious ways that your own culture shapes your perceptions—can result in partial or even total failure of the communication process. Moreover, culture is rarely static, so impressions you may have gathered at one point in your life may need to be revisited and revised over time.

The Video

This video takes a broad look at Latin America's various countries and cultures and explores the business implications of cultural similarities and differences. You'll learn how cultural groups that may appear identical on the surface can in fact have subtle but profound differences. Although communication is just one of many topics discussed in the video, you will get a sense of just how important—and challenging—communication can be when conducting business across cultural boundaries.

Discussion Questions

1. Explain what the video means when it says that your own culture can "sneak up on you."
2. How is business influencing the economic gulf between urban and rural populations in Latin America?
3. How have imperial conquests and slavery affected the populations and cultures of Latin America?
4. How do many outsiders view the issue of business and government corruption in Latin America?
5. Is business etiquette in most of Latin America considered relatively formal or relatively informal?

Follow-Up Assignment

The World Bank plays an important role in today's fast-changing, closely meshed global economy. Visit the bank's website at www.worldbank.org and explore the initiatives programs underway in the Latin American region. How is the bank using this website to foster better communication between Latin America and the rest of the world?

For Further Research

In today's global marketplace, knowing as much as possible about your international customers' business practices and customs could give you a strategic advantage. To help you successfully conduct business around the globe, navigate the resources at the U.S. Government Export Portal. Start at www.export.gov, then click on "Market Research" and then on "Country Information—Quick Reference (TIC)." Click anywhere on the world map to learn more about each country.

How can resources such as this website help U.S. businesses communicate more successfully with customers, employees, and other groups in Latin America?

TECHNOLOGY AND THE TOOLS OF COMMUNICATION
Learning Objectives

After viewing this video, you will be able to

1. Identify technology-related issues to consider when developing communication strategies
2. Identify advantages of using technology as a tool for effective communication
3. Differentiate between "push" and "pull" communication

Background Information

From instant messaging to online meetings, technology has become an integral element of business communication. When used with care, technological tools can help you reach more people in less time with more effective messages. However, when technology is misused or misunderstood, it can cause more problems than it solves. Knowing which technologies to use in every situation—and knowing how to use each one—are vital to your success.

The Video

This video discusses how the Internet, e-mail, voicemail, and other devices have revolutionized the way people communicate. These technological tools increase the speed, frequency, and range of business communication. The video also discusses factors to consider when choosing the most appropriate vehicle for your communication, including the all-important challenge of getting and keeping your audience's attention. The advantages of using technological communication tools are presented throughout the video.

Discussion Questions

1. Identify six questions you need to consider when choosing a technology vehicle for your messages.
2. List the advantages of communicating via e-mail within an organization.
3. What role does technology play in ensuring effective communication within an organization?
4. What are some of the more common challenges that business communicators can encounter when they use technology for communication purposes?
5. Identify the difference between "push" and "pull" communications, and provide an example of each method.

Follow-Up Assignment

VolResource (at www.volresource.org.uk/samples/olcomms.htm) provides practical and informative resources for volunteer organizations that are trying to develop online communication strategies. The VolResource website further details questions that need to be addressed in the process of developing an effective communication strategy for any organization. What issues do you think are the most important to consider? Why?

For Further Exploration

Visit the Yellow Freight website at www.yellowfreight.com and explore the various e-commerce tools this company utilizes to communicate effectively with its customers. Examine these tools and consider their effectiveness. What are some of the advantages of these online communication tools? How do they benefit the client? How do they benefit Yellow Freight?

Handbook of Grammar, Mechanics, and Usage

Grammar and mechanics are nothing more than the way words are combined into sentences. Usage is the way words are used by a network of people—in this case, the community of businesspeople who use English. You'll find it easier to get along in this community if you know the accepted standards of grammar, mechanics, and usage. This handbook offers you valuable opportunities in two sections:

- **Diagnostic Test of English Skills.** Testing your current knowledge of grammar, mechanics, and usage helps you find out where your strengths and weaknesses lie. This test offers 60 items taken from the topics included in this Handbook.

- **Assessment of English Skills.** After completing the diagnostic test, use the assessment form to highlight those areas you most need to review.

To quickly review the basics, you can visit www.prenhall.com/thill and select "Handbook of Grammar, Mechanics, and Usage Practice Sessions." Test yourself and reinforce what you learn. Use this essential review not only to study and improve your English skills but also as a reference for any questions you may have during this course.

Without a firm grasp of the basics of grammar, punctuation, mechanics, and vocabulary, you risk being misunderstood, damaging your company's image, losing money for your company, and possibly even losing your job. However, once you develop strong English skills, you will create clear and concise messages, you will enhance your company's image as well as your own, and you will not only increase your company's profits but expand your own chances of success.

DIAGNOSTIC TEST OF ENGLISH SKILLS

Use this test to help you determine whether you need more practice with grammar, punctuation, mechanics, or vocabulary. When you've answered all the questions, ask your instructor for an answer sheet so that you can score the test. On the Assessment of English Skills form (page H-2), record the number of questions you answered correctly in each section.

The following choices apply to items 1–10. In each blank, write the letter of the choice that best describes the problem with each sentence.

A. sentence incomplete
B. too many phrases/clauses strung together
C. modifying elements misplaced (dangling)
D. structure not parallel
E. nothing wrong

_____ 1. Stop here.

_____ 2. Your duties are interviewing, hiring, and also to fire employees.

_____ 3. After their presentation, I was still undecided.

_____ 4. Speaking freely, the stock was considered a bargain.

_____ 5. Margaret, pressed for time, turned in unusually sloppy work.

_____ 6. Typing and filing, routine office chores.

_____ 7. With care, edit the report.

_____ 8. When Paul came to work here, he brought some outmoded ideas, now he has accepted our modern methods.

_____ 9. To plan is better than improvising.

_____ 10. Hoping to improve performance, practice is advisable.

The following choices apply to items 11–20. In each blank, write the letter of the choice that identifies the underlined word(s) in each sentence.

A. subject
B. predicate (verb)
C. object
D. modifier
E. conjunction/preposition

_____ 11. Take his <u>memo</u> upstairs.

_____ 12. Before leaving, he <u>repaired</u> the photocopier.

_____ 13. <u>Velnor, Inc.</u>, will soon introduce a new product line.

_____ 14. We must hire only <u>qualified</u>, ambitious graduates.

_____ 15. They <u>are having</u> trouble with their quality control systems.

_____ 16. <u>After</u> she wrote the report, Jill waited eagerly for a response.

_____ 17. The route to the plant isn't paved <u>yet</u>.

_____ 18. See <u>me</u> after the meeting.

_____ 19. Your new <u>home</u> is ready and waiting.

_____ 20. BFL is large <u>but</u> caring.

In the blanks for items 21–30, write the letter of the word that best completes each sentence.

_____ 21. Starbucks (A. is, B. are) opening five new stores in San Diego in the next year.

_____ 22. There (A. is, B. are) 50 applicants for the job opening.

_____ 23. Anyone who wants to be (A. their, B. his or her) own boss should think about owning a franchise.

_____ 24. Neither of us (A. was, B. were) prepared for the meeting.

_____ 25. Another characteristic of a small business is that (A. they tend, B. it tends) to be more innovative than larger firms.

_____ 26. After he had (A. saw, B. seen) the revised budget, Raymond knew he wouldn't be getting a new desk.

_____ 27. The number of women-owned small businesses (A. has, B. have) increased sharply in the past two decades.

_____ 28. If I (A. was, B. were) you, I'd stop sending personal e-mails at work.

_____ 29. Eugene (A. lay, B. laid) the files on the desk.

_____ 30. Either FedEx or UPS (A. has, B. have) been chosen as our preferred shipping service.

The following choices apply to items 31–40. In each blank, write the letter of the choice that best describes each sentence.

A. all punctuation used correctly

B. some punctuation used incorrectly or incorrectly omitted

_____ 31. The president who rarely gave interviews, agreed to write an article for the company newsletter.

_____ 32. Give the assignment to Karen Schiff, the new technical writer.

_____ 33. Could you please send a replacement for Item No. 3–303.

_____ 34. Debbie said that, "technicians must have technical degrees."

_____ 35. We'll have branches in Bakersfield, California, Reno, Nevada, and Medford, Oregon.

_____ 36. Before leaving her secretary finished typing the memo.

_____ 37. How many of you consider yourselves "computer literate?"

_____ 38. This, then, is our goal: to increase market share by 50 percent.

_____ 39. They plan to move soon, however, they still should be invited.

_____ 40. Health, wealth, and happiness—those are my personal goals.

The following choices apply to items 41–50. In each blank, write the letter of the choice that best describes the problem with each sentence.

A. error in punctuation

B. error in use of abbreviations or symbols

C. error in use of numbers

D. error in capitalization

E. no errors

_____ 41. Most of last year's sales came from the midwest.

_____ 42. We can provide the items you are looking for @ $2 each.

_____ 43. Alex noted: "few of our competitors have tried this approach."

_____ 44. Address the letter to professor Elliott Barker, Psychology Department, North Dakota State University.

_____ 45. They've recorded 22 complaints since yesterday, all of them from long-time employees.

_____ 46. Leslie's presentation—"New Markets for the Nineties"—was well organized.

_____ 47. We're having a sale in the childrens' department, beginning Wednesday, August 15.

_____ 48. About 50 of the newly inducted members will be present.

_____ 49. Mister Spencer has asked me to find ten volunteers.

_____ 50. Let's meet in Beth and Larry's office at one o'clock.

In the blanks for items 51–60, write the letter of the word that best completes each sentence.

_____ 51. Will having a degree (A. affect, B. effect) my chances for promotion?

_____ 52. Place the latest drawings (A. beside, B. besides) the others.

_____ 53. Try not to (A. loose, B. lose) this key; we will charge you a fee to replace it.

_____ 54. Let us help you choose the right tie to (A. complement, B. compliment) your look.

_____ 55. The five interviewers should discuss the candidates' qualifications (A. among, B. between) themselves.

_____ 56. New employees spend their time looking for (A. perspective, B. prospective) clients.

_____ 57. Are the goods you received different (A. from, B. than) the goods you ordered?

_____ 58. He took those courses to (A. farther, B. further) his career.

_____ 59. We are (A. anxious, B. eager) to see you next Thursday.

_____ 60. All commissions will be (A. disbursed, B. dispensed, C. dispersed) on the second Friday of every month.

ASSESSMENT OF ENGLISH SKILLS

In the space provided below, record the number of questions you answered correctly.

Question	Number You Got Correct	Skill Area
1–10	_____	Sentence structure
11–20	_____	Grammar: Parts of speech
21–30	_____	Grammar: Verbs and agreement
31–40	_____	Punctuation
41–50	_____	Punctuation and mechanics
51–60	_____	Vocabulary

If you scored 8 or lower in any of the skills areas, focus on those areas in the appropriate sections of this Handbook.

ESSENTIALS OF GRAMMAR, MECHANICS, AND USAGE

The sentence below looks innocent, but is it really?

> We sell tuxedos as well as rent.

You might sell rent, but it's highly unlikely. Whatever you're selling, some people will ignore your message because of a blunder like this. The following sentence has a similar problem:

> Vice President Eldon Neale told his chief engineer that he would no longer be with Avix, Inc., as of June 30.

Is Eldon or the engineer leaving? No matter which side the facts are on, the sentence can be read the other way. Now look at this sentence:

> The year before we budgeted more for advertising sales were up.

Confused? Perhaps this is what you meant:

> The year before, we budgeted more for advertising. Sales were up.

Maybe you meant this:

> The year before we budgeted more for advertising, sales were up.

The meaning of language falls into bundles called sentences. A listener or reader can take only so much meaning before filing a sentence away and getting ready for the next one. So, as a business writer, you have to know what a sentence is. You need to know where one ends and the next one begins.

If you want to know what a sentence is, you have to find out what goes into it, what its ingredients are. Luckily, the basic ingredients of an English sentence are simple: The parts of speech combine with punctuation, mechanics, and vocabulary to convey meaning.

1.0 Grammar

Grammar is the study of how words come together to form sentences. Categorized by meaning, form, and function, English words fall into various parts of speech: nouns, pronouns, verbs, adjectives, adverbs, prepositions, conjunctions, articles, and interjections. You will communicate more clearly if you understand how each of these parts of speech operates in a sentence.

1.1 Nouns

A noun names a person, place, or thing. Anything you can see or detect with one of your other senses has a noun to name it. Some things you can't see or sense are also nouns—ions, for example, or space. So are things that exist as ideas, such as accuracy and height. (You can see that something is accurate or that a building is tall, but you can't see the idea of accuracy or the idea of height.) These names for ideas are known as abstract nouns. The simplest nouns are the names of things you can see or touch: car, building, cloud, brick.

1.1.1 Proper Nouns and Common Nouns

So far, all the examples of nouns have been common nouns, referring to general classes of things. The word *building* refers to a whole class of structures. Common nouns such as *building* are not capitalized.

If you want to talk about one particular building, however, you might refer to the Glazier Building. The name is capitalized, indicating that *Glazier Building* is a proper noun.

Here are three sets of common and proper nouns for comparison:

Common	Proper
city	Kansas City
company	Blaisden Company
store	Books Galore

1.1.2 Nouns as Subject and Object

Nouns may be used in sentences as subjects or objects. That is, the person, place, idea, or thing that is being or doing (subject) is represented by a noun. So is the person, place, idea, or thing that is being acted on (object). In the following sentence, the nouns are underlined.

> The <u>secretary</u> keyboarded the <u>report</u>.

The secretary (subject) is acting in a way that affects the report (object). The following sentence is more complicated:

> The <u>installer</u> delivered the <u>carpeting</u> to the <u>customer</u>.

Installer is the subject. *Carpeting* is the object of the main part of the sentence (acted on by the installer), whereas *customer* is the object of the phrase *to the customer*. Nevertheless, both *carpeting* and *customer* are objects.

1.1.3 Plural Nouns

Nouns can be either singular or plural. The usual way to make a plural noun is to add *s* to the singular form of the word:

Singular	Plural
rock	rocks
picture	pictures
song	songs

Many nouns have other ways of forming the plural. Letters, numbers, and words used as words are sometimes made plural by adding an apostrophe and an *s*. Very often, 's is used with abbreviations that have periods, lowercase letters that stand alone, and capital letters that might be confused with words when made into plurals:

> Spell out all *St.*'s and *Ave.*'s.

> He divided the page with a row of *x*'s.

> Sarah will register the *A*'s through the *G*'s at the convention.

In other cases, however, the apostrophe may be left out:

> They'll review their ABCs.

> The stock market climbed through most of the 1980s.

> Circle all *the*s in the paragraph.

In some of these examples, the letters used as letters and words used as words are *italicized* (a mechanics issue that is discussed later).

Other nouns, such as those below, are so-called irregular nouns; they form the plural in some way other than by simply adding *s*:

Singular	Plural
tax	taxes
specialty	specialties
cargo	cargoes
shelf	shelves
child	children
woman	women
tooth	teeth
mouse	mice
parenthesis	parentheses
son-in-law	sons-in-law
editor-in-chief	editors-in-chief

Rather than memorize a lot of rules about forming plurals, use a dictionary. If the dictionary says nothing about the plural of a word, it's formed the usual way: by adding *s*. If the plural is formed in some irregular way, the dictionary often shows the plural spelling.

1.1.4 Possessive Nouns

A noun becomes possessive when it's used to show the ownership of something. Then you add 's to the word:

>   the man's car   the woman's apartment

However, ownership does not need to be legal:

>   the secretary's desk   the company's assets

Also, ownership may be nothing more than an automatic association:

>   a day's work   the job's prestige

An exception to the rule about adding 's to make a noun possessive occurs when the word is singular and already has two "s" sounds at the end. In cases like the following, an apostrophe is all that's needed:

>   crisis' dimensions   Mr. Moses' application

When the noun has only one "s" sound at the end, however, retain the 's:

>   Chris's book   Carolyn Nuss's office

With hyphenated nouns (compound nouns), add 's to the last word:

Hyphenated Noun	Possessive Noun
mother-in-law	mother-in-law's
mayor-elect	mayor-elect's

To form the possessive of plural nouns, just begin by following the same rule as with singular nouns: add 's. However, if the plural noun already ends in an *s* (as most do), drop the one you've added, leaving only the apostrophe:

>   the clients' complaints   employees' benefits

1.2 Pronouns

A pronoun is a word that stands for a noun; it saves repeating the noun:

>   Drivers have some choice of weeks for vacation, but *they* must notify this office of *their* preference by March 1.

The pronouns *they* and *their* stand in for the noun *drivers*. The noun that a pronoun stands for is called the antecedent of the pronoun; *drivers* is the antecedent of *they* and *their*.

When the antecedent is plural, the pronoun that stands in for it has to be plural; *they* and *their* are plural pronouns because *drivers* is plural. Likewise, when the antecedent is singular, the pronoun has to be singular:

>   We thought the *contract* had expired, but we soon learned that *it* had not.

1.2.1 Multiple Antecedents

Sometimes a pronoun has a double (or even a triple) antecedent:

>   *Kathryn Boettcher* and *Luis Gutierrez* went beyond *their* sales quotas for January.

If taken alone, *Kathryn Boettcher* is a singular antecedent. So is *Luis Gutierrez*. However, when together they are the plural antecedent of a pronoun, so the pronoun has to be plural. Thus the pronoun is *their* instead of *her* or *his*.

1.2.2 Unclear Antecedents

In some sentences the pronoun's antecedent is unclear:

>   Sandy Wright sent Jane Brougham *her* production figures for the previous year. *She* thought they were too low.

To which person does the pronoun *her* refer? Someone who knew Sandy and Jane and knew their business relationship might be able to figure out the antecedent for *her*. Even with such an advantage, however, a reader might receive the wrong meaning. Also, it would be nearly impossible for any reader to know which name is the antecedent of *she*.

The best way to clarify an ambiguous pronoun is usually to rewrite the sentence, repeating nouns when needed for clarity:

>   Sandy Wright sent her production figures for the previous year to Jane Brougham. *Jane* thought they were too low.

The noun needs to be repeated only when the antecedent is unclear.

1.2.3 Gender-Neutral Pronouns

The pronouns that stand for males are *he, his,* and *him*. The pronouns that stand for females are *she, hers,* and *her*. However, you'll often be faced with the problem of choosing a pronoun for a noun that refers to both females and males:

>   Each manager must make up (his, her, his or her, its, their) own mind about stocking this item and about the quantity that (he, she, he or she, it, they) can sell.

This sentence calls for a pronoun that's neither masculine nor feminine. The issue of gender-neutral pronouns responds to efforts to treat females and males evenhandedly. Here are some possible ways to deal with this issue:

>   Each manager must make up *his* . . .
>
>   (Not all managers are men.)
>
>   Each manager must make up *her* . . .
>
>   (Not all managers are women.)
>
>   Each manager must make up *his* or *her* . . .
>
>   (This solution is acceptable but becomes awkward when repeated more than once or twice in a document.)
>
>   Each manager must make up *her* . . . Every manager will receive *his* . . . A manager may send *her* . . .
>
>   (A manager's gender does not alternate like a windshield wiper!)
>
>   Each manager must make up *their* . . .
>
>   (The pronoun can't be plural when the antecedent is singular.)
>
>   Each manager must make up *its* . . .
>
>   (*It* never refers to people.)

The best solution is to make the noun plural or to revise the passage altogether:

>   Managers must make up *their* minds . . .
>
>   Each manager must decide whether . . .

Be careful not to change the original meaning.

1.2.4 Case of Pronouns

The case of a pronoun tells whether it's acting or acted upon:

>   *She sells* an average of five packages each week.

In this sentence, *she* is doing the selling. Because *she* is acting, *she* is said to be in the nominative case. Now consider what happens when the pronoun is acted upon:

> After six months, Ms. Browning promoted *her.*

In this sentence, the pronoun *her* is acted upon. The pronoun *her* is thus said to be in the objective case.

Contrast the nominative and objective pronouns in this list:

Nominative	Objective
I	me
we	us
he	him
she	her
they	them
who	whom
whoever	whomever

Objective pronouns may be used as either the object of a verb (such as *promoted*) or the object of a preposition (such as *with*):

> Rob worked with *them* until the order was filled.

In this example, *them* is the object of the preposition *with* because Rob acted upon—worked with—them. Here's a sentence with three pronouns, the first one nominative, the second the object of a verb, and the third the object of a preposition:

> He paid *us* as soon as the check came from *them.*

He is nominative; *us* is objective because it's the object of the verb *paid; them* is objective because it's the object of the preposition *from.*

Every writer sometimes wonders whether to use *who* or *whom:*

> (Who, Whom) will you hire?

Because this sentence is a question, it's difficult to see that *whom* is the object of the verb *hire.* You can figure out which pronoun to use if you rearrange the question and temporarily try *she* and *her* in place of *who* and *whom:* "Will you hire *she?*" or "Will you hire *her?*" *Her* and *whom* are both objective, so the correct choice is "*Whom* will you hire?" Here's a different example:

> (Who, Whom) logged so much travel time?

Turning the question into a statement, you get:

> He logged so much travel time.

Therefore, the correct statement is:

> Who logged so much travel time?

1.2.5 Possessive Pronouns

Possessive pronouns work like possessive nouns: They show ownership or automatic association.

> her job   their preferences
>
> his account   its equipment

However, possessive pronouns are different from possessive nouns in the way they are written. That is, possessive pronouns never have an apostrophe.

Possessive Noun	Possessive Pronoun
the woman's estate	her estate
Roger Franklin's plans	his plans
the shareholders' feelings	their feelings
the vacuum cleaner's attachments	its attachments

The word *its* is the possessive of *it.* Like all other possessive pronouns, its has no apostrophe. Some people confuse *its* with *it's,* the contraction of *it is.* Contractions are discussed later.

1.3 Verbs

A verb describes an action:

> They all *quit* in disgust.

It may also describe a state of being:

> Working conditions *were* substandard.

The English language is full of action verbs. Here are a few you'll often run across in the business world:

verify	perform	fulfill
hire	succeed	send
leave	improve	receive
accept	develop	pay

You could undoubtedly list many more.

The most common verb describing a state of being instead of an action is *to be* and all its forms:

> I *am, was,* or *will be;* you *are, were,* or *will be*

Other verbs also describe a state of being:

> It *seemed* a good plan at the time.
>
> She *sounds* impressive at a meeting.

These verbs link what comes before them in the sentence with what comes after; no action is involved. (See Section 1.7.5 for a fuller discussion of linking verbs.)

1.3.1 Verb Tenses

English has three simple verb tenses: present, past, and future.

> **Present:**   Our branches in Hawaii *stock* other items.
>
> **Past:**   We *stocked* Purquil pens for a short time.
>
> **Future:**   Rotex Tire Stores *will stock* your line of tires when you begin a program of effective national advertising.

With most verbs (the regular ones), the past tense ends in *ed,* and the future tense always has *will* or *shall* in front of it. But the present tense is more complex, depending on the subject:

	First Person	Second Person	Third Person
Singular	I stock	you stock	he/she/it stocks
Plural	we stock	you stock	they stock

The basic form, *stock,* takes an additional *s* when *he, she,* or *it* precedes it. (See section 1.3.4 for more on subject-verb agreement.)

In addition to the three simple tenses, there are three perfect tenses using forms of the helping verb *have.* The present perfect tense uses the past participle (regularly the past tense) of the main verb, *stocked,* and adds the present-tense *have* or *has* to the front of it:

> (I, we, you, they) *have stocked.*
>
> (He, she, it) *has stocked.*

The past perfect tense uses the past participle of the main verb, *stocked,* and adds the past-tense *had* to the front of it:

> (I, you, he, she, it, we, they) *had stocked.*

The future perfect tense also uses the past participle of the main verb, *stocked*, but adds the future-tense *will have*:

(I, you, he, she, it, we, they) *will have stocked.*

Keep verbs in the same tense when the actions occur at the same time:

When the payroll checks *came* in, everyone *showed* up for work.

We *have found* that everyone *has pitched* in to help.

When the actions occur at different times, you may change tense accordingly:

The shipment *came* last Wednesday, so if another one *comes* in today, please *return* it.

The new employee *had been* ill at ease, but now she *has become* a full-fledged member of the team.

1.3.2 Irregular Verbs

Many verbs don't follow in every detail the patterns already described. The most irregular of these verbs is *to be*:

Tense	Singular	Plural
Present:	I *am*	we *are*
	you *are*	you *are*
	he, she, it *is*	they *are*
Past:	I *was*	we *were*
	you *were*	you *were*
	he, she, it *was*	they *were*

The future tense of *to be* is formed in the same way that the future tense of a regular verb is formed.

The perfect tenses of *to be* are also formed as they would be for a regular verb, except that the past participle is a special form, *been*, instead of just the past tense:

Present perfect:	you have been
Past perfect:	you had been
Future perfect:	you will have been

Here's a sampling of other irregular verbs:

Present	Past	Past Participle
begin	began	begun
shrink	shrank	shrunk
know	knew	known
rise	rose	risen
become	became	become
go	went	gone
do	did	done

Dictionaries list the various forms of other irregular verbs.

1.3.3 Transitive and Intransitive Verbs

Many people are confused by three particular sets of verbs:

lie/lay	sit/set	rise/raise

Using these verbs correctly is much easier when you learn the difference between transitive and intransitive verbs.

Transitive verbs convey their action to an object; they "transfer" their action to an object. Intransitive verbs do not. Here are some sample uses of transitive and intransitive verbs:

Intransitive	Transitive
We should include in our new offices a place to *lie* down for a nap.	The workers will be here on Monday to *lay* new carpeting.
Even the way an interviewee *sits* is important.	That crate is full of stemware, so *set* it down carefully.
Salaries at Compu-Link, Inc., *rise* swiftly.	They *raise* their level of production every year.

The workers *lay* carpeting, you *set* down the crate, they *raise* production; each action is transferred to something. In the intransitive sentences, one *lies* down, an interviewee *sits*, and salaries *rise* without (at least grammatically) affecting anything else. Intransitive sentences are complete with only a subject and a verb; transitive sentences are not complete unless they also include an object, or something to transfer the action to.

Tenses are a confusing element of the *lie/lay* problem:

Present	Past	Past Participle
I lie	I lay	I have lain
I lay (something down)	I laid (something down)	I have laid (something down)

The past tense of *lie* and the present tense of *lay* look and sound alike, even though they're different verbs.

1.3.4 Subject-Verb Agreement

Whether regular or irregular, every verb must agree with its subject, both in person (first, second, or third) and in number (singular or plural).

	First Person	Second Person	Third Person
Singular	I *am;* I *write*	you *are;* you *write*	he/she/it *is;* he/she/it *writes*
Plural	we *are;* we *write*	you *are;* you *write*	they *are;* they *write*

In a simple sentence, making a verb agree with its subject is a straightforward task:

Hector Ruiz *is* a strong competitor. (third-person singular)

We *write* to you every month. (first-person plural)

Confusion sometimes arises when sentences are a bit more complicated. For example, be sure to avoid agreement problems when words come between the subject and verb. In the following examples, the verb appears in italics, and its subject is underlined:

The <u>analysis</u> of existing documents *takes* a full week.

Even though *documents* is a plural, the verb is in the singular form. That's because the subject of the sentence is *analysis*, a singular noun. The phrase *of existing documents* can be disregarded. Here is another example:

The <u>answers</u> for this exercise *are* in the study guide.

Take away the phrase *for this exercise* and you are left with the plural subject *answers*. Therefore, the verb takes the plural form.

Verb agreement is also complicated when the subject is not a specific noun or pronoun and when the subject may be considered either singular or plural. In such cases, you have to analyze the surrounding sentence to determine which verb form to use.

The <u>staff</u> *is* quartered in the warehouse.

The <u>staff</u> *are* at their desks in the warehouse.

The <u>computers</u> and the <u>staff</u> *are* in the warehouse.

Neither the staff nor the <u>computers</u> *are* in the warehouse.

<u>Every</u> computer *is* in the warehouse.

Many a <u>computer</u> *is* in the warehouse.

Did you notice that words such as *every* use the singular verb form? In addition, when an *either/or* or a *neither/nor* phrase combines singular and plural nouns, the verb takes the form that matches the noun closest to it.

In the business world, some subjects require extra attention. Company names, for example, are considered singular and therefore take a singular verb in most cases—even if they contain plural words:

<u>Stater Brothers</u> *offers* convenient grocery shopping.

In addition, quantities are sometimes considered singular and sometimes plural. If a quantity refers to a total amount, it takes a singular verb; if a quantity refers to individual, countable units, it takes a plural verb:

Three <u>hours</u> *is* a long time.

The eight <u>dollars</u> we collected for the fund *are* tacked on the bulletin board.

Fractions may also be singular or plural, depending on the noun that accompanies them:

One-third of the <u>warehouse</u> *is* devoted to this product line.

One-third of the <u>products</u> *are* defective.

For a related discussion, see Section 1.7.2, "Longer Sentences," later in this Handbook.

1.3.5 Voice of Verbs

Verbs have two voices, active and passive. When the subject comes first, the voice is active. When the object comes first, the voice is passive:

Active: The buyer paid a large amount.

Passive: A large amount was paid by the buyer.

The passive voice uses a form of the verb *to be,* which adds words to a sentence. In the example, the passive-voice sentence uses eight words, whereas the active-voice sentence uses only six to say the same thing. The words *was* and *by* are unnecessary to convey the meaning of the sentence. In fact, extra words usually clog meaning. So be sure to opt for the active voice when you have a choice.

At times, however, you have no choice:

Several items *have been taken,* but so far we don't know who took them.

The passive voice becomes necessary when you don't know (or don't want to say) who performed the action; the active voice is bolder and more direct.

1.3.6 Mood of Verbs

You have three moods to choose from, depending on your intentions. Most of the time you use the indicative mood to make a statement or to ask a question:

The secretary *mailed* a letter to each supplier.

Did the secretary *mail* a letter to each supplier?

When you wish to command or request, use the imperative mood:

Please *mail* a letter to each supplier.

Sometimes, especially in business, a courteous request is stated like a question; in that case, however, no question mark is required:

Would you *mail* a letter to each supplier.

The subjunctive mood, most often used in formal writing or in presenting bad news, expresses a possibility or a recommendation. The subjunctive is usually signaled by a word such as *if* or *that.* In these examples, the subjunctive mood uses special verb forms:

If the secretary *were to mail* a letter to each supplier, we might save some money.

I suggested that the secretary *mail* a letter to each supplier.

Although the subjunctive mood is not used as often as it once was, it's still found in such expressions as *Come what may* and *If I were you.* In general, it is used to convey an idea that is contrary to fact: If iron *were* lighter than air.

1.4 Adjectives

An adjective modifies (tells something about) a noun or pronoun. Each of the following phrases says more about the noun or pronoun than the noun or pronoun would say alone.

an *efficient* staff	a *heavy* price
brisk trade	*poor* you

Adjectives always tell us something that we wouldn't know without them. So you don't need to use adjectives when the noun alone, or a different noun, will give the meaning:

a *company* employee
(An employee ordinarily works for a company.)

a *crate-type* container
(*Crate* gives the entire meaning.)

Verbs in the *ing* (present participle) form can be used as adjectives:

A *boring* job can sometimes turn into a *fascinating* career.

So can the past participle of verbs:

A freshly *painted* house is a *sold* house.

Adjectives modify nouns more often than they modify pronouns. When adjectives do modify pronouns, however, the sentence usually has a linking verb:

They were *attentive.*   It looked *appropriate.*

He seems *interested.*   You are *skillful.*

At times, a series of adjectives precedes a noun:

It was a *long* and *active* workday.

Such strings of adjectives are acceptable as long as they all convey a different part of the phrase's meaning. However, adjectives often pile up in front of a noun, like this:

The *superficial, obvious* answer was the one she gave.

The most valuable animal on the ranch is a *small black* horse.

The question is whether a comma should be used to separate the adjectives. The answer is to use a comma when the two adjectives independently modify the noun; do not use a comma when one of the adjectives is closely identified with the noun. In the first example above, the answer was both superficial and obvious. But in the second example, the black horse is small.

Another way to think about this is to use the word *and* as a replacement for the comma. Study the following example:

> We recommend a diet of leafy green vegetables.

> We recommend a diet of green, leafy vegetables.

Because some green vegetables are not leafy (cucumbers and zucchini, for example), it is correct to leave out the comma in the first example so that you know which kind of green vegetables are being discussed. But because all leafy vegetables are also green (green and leafy), the comma must be included in the second example.

You might also try switching the adjectives. If the order of the adjectives can be reversed without changing the meaning of the phrase, you should use a comma. If the order cannot be reversed, you should not use a comma. Consider these examples:

> Here's our *simplified credit* application.

> Here's our *simplified, easy-to-complete* application.

> Here's our *easy-to-complete, simplified* application.

A credit application may be simple or complex; however, you cannot talk about a credit, simplified application; therefore, leave the comma out of the first example. The application in the second and third examples is both simplified and easy to complete, no matter how you arrange the words, so include the comma in these examples.

1.4.1 Comparative Degree

Most adjectives can take three forms: simple, comparative, and superlative. The simple form modifies a single noun or pronoun. Use the comparative form when comparing two items. When comparing three or more items, use the superlative form.

Simple	Comparative	Superlative
hard	harder	hardest
safe	safer	safest
dry	drier	driest

The comparative form adds *er* to the simple form, and the superlative form adds *est*. (The *y* at the end of a word changes to *i* before the *er* or *est* is added.)

A small number of adjectives are irregular, including these:

Simple	Comparative	Superlative
good	better	best
bad	worse	worst
little	less	least

When the simple form of an adjective is two or more syllables, you usually add *more* to form the comparative and *most* to form the superlative:

Simple	Comparative	Superlative
useful	more useful	most useful
exhausting	more exhausting	most exhausting
expensive	more expensive	most expensive

The most common exceptions are two-syllable adjectives that end in *y:*

Simple	Comparative	Superlative
happy	happier	happiest
costly	costlier	costliest

If you choose this option, change the *y* to *i*, and tack *er* or *est* onto the end.

Some adjectives cannot be used to make comparisons because they themselves indicate the extreme. For example, if something is perfect, nothing can be more perfect. If something is unique or ultimate, nothing can be more unique or more ultimate.

1.4.2 Hyphenated Adjectives

Many adjectives used in the business world are actually combinations of words: *up-to-date* report, *last-minute* effort, *fifth-floor* suite, *well-built* engine. As you can see, they are hyphenated when they come before the noun they modify. However, when they come after the noun they modify, they are not hyphenated. In the following example, the adjectives appear in italics, and the nouns they modify are underlined:

> The report is *up to date* because of our team's *last-minute* efforts.

Hyphens are not used when part of the combination is a word ending in *ly* (because that word is usually not an adjective). Hyphens are also omitted from word combinations that are used frequently.

> We live in a *rapidly shrinking* world.

> Our *highly motivated* employees will be well paid.

> Please consider renewing your *credit card* account.

> Send those figures to our *data processing* department.

> Our new intern is a *high school* student.

1.5 Adverbs

An adverb modifies a verb, an adjective, or another adverb:

Modifying a verb:	Our marketing department works *efficiently*.
Modifying an adjective:	She was not dependable, although she was *highly* intelligent.
Modifying another adverb:	His territory was *too* broadly diversified, so he moved *extremely* cautiously.

Most of the adverbs mentioned are adjectives turned into adverbs by adding *ly*, which is how many adverbs are formed:

Adjective	Adverb
efficient	efficiently
extreme	extremely
high	highly
official	officially
separate	separately
special	specially

Some adverbs are made by dropping or changing the final letter of the adjective and then adding *ly:*

Adjective	Adverb
due	duly
busy	busily

Other adverbs don't end in *ly* at all. Here are a few examples of this type:

often	fast	too
soon	very	so

Some adverbs are difficult to distinguish from adjectives. For example, in the following sentences, is the underlined word an adverb or an adjective?

They worked <u>well</u>.

The baby is <u>well</u>.

In the first sentence, *well* is an adverb modifying the verb worked. In the second sentence, *well* is an adjective modifying the noun *baby*. To choose correctly between adverbs and adjectives, remember that verbs of being link a noun to an adjective describing the noun. In contrast, you would use an adverb to describe an action verb.

Adjective	Adverb
He is a *good* worker. (What kind of worker is he?)	He works *well*. (How does he work?)
It is a *real* computer. (What kind of computer is it?)	It *really* is a computer. (To what extent is it a computer?)
The traffic is *slow*. (What quality does the traffic have?)	The traffic moves *slowly*. (How does the traffic move?)

1.5.1 Negative Adverbs

Negative adverbs (such as *neither, no, not, scarcely,* and *seldom*) are powerful words and therefore do not need any help in conveying a negative thought. In fact, using double negatives gives a strong impression of illiteracy, so avoid sentences like these:

I don't want no mistakes.
(Correct: "I don't want any mistakes," or "I want no mistakes.")

They couldn't hardly read the report.
(Correct: "They could hardly read the report," or "They couldn't read the report.")

They scarcely noticed neither one.
(Correct: "They scarcely noticed either one," or "They noticed neither one.")

1.5.2 Comparative Degree

Like adjectives, adverbs can be used to compare items. Generally, the basic adverb is combined with *more* or *most,* just as long adjectives are. However, some adverbs have one-word comparative forms:

One Item	Two Items	Three Items
quickly	more quickly	most quickly
sincerely	less sincerely	least sincerely
fast	faster	fastest
well	better	best

1.6 Other Parts of Speech

Nouns, pronouns, verbs, adjectives, and adverbs carry most of the meaning in a sentence. Four other parts of speech link them together in sentences: prepositions, conjunctions, articles, and interjections.

1.6.1 Prepositions

Prepositions are words like these:

of	to	for	with
at	by	from	about

Some prepositions consist of more than one word—like these:

because of	in addition to	out of	except for

And some prepositions are closely linked with a verb. When using phrases such as *look up* and *wipe out,* keep the phrase intact and do not insert anything between the verb and the preposition.

Prepositions most often begin prepositional phrases, which function like adjectives and adverbs by telling more about a pronoun, noun, or verb:

of a type	*by* Friday
to the point	*with* characteristic flair

To prevent misreading, prepositional phrases should be placed near the element they modify:

Of all our technicians, <u>she</u> is the best trained.

They couldn't see the <u>merit</u> *in my proposal.*

Someone left a <u>folder</u> *on my desk.*

It was once considered totally unacceptable to put a preposition at the end of a sentence. Now you may:

I couldn't tell what they were interested in.

What did she attribute it to?

However, be careful not to place prepositions at the end of sentences when doing so is unnecessary. In fact, avoid using any unnecessary preposition. In the following examples, the prepositions in parentheses should be omitted:

All (of) the staff members were present.

I almost fell off (of) my chair with surprise.

Where was Mr. Steuben going (to)?

They couldn't help (from) wondering.

The opposite problem is failing to include a preposition when you should. Consider the two sentences that follow:

Sales were over $100,000 for Linda and Bill.

Sales were over $100,000 for Linda and for Bill.

The first sentence indicates that Linda and Bill had combined sales over $100,000; the second, that Linda and Bill each had sales over $100,000, for a combined total in excess of $200,000. The preposition *for* is critical here.

Prepositions are also required in sentences like this one:

Which type of personal computer do you prefer?

Certain prepositions are used with certain words. When the same preposition can be used for two or more words in a sentence without affecting the meaning, only the last preposition is required:

We are familiar (*with*) and satisfied *with* your company's products.

But when different prepositions are normally used with the words, all the prepositions must be included:

We are familiar *with* and interested *in* your company's products.

Here is a partial list of prepositions that are used in a particular way with particular words:

among/between: *Among* is used to refer to three or more (*Circulate the memo among the staff*); *between* is used to refer to two (*Put the copy machine between Judy and Dan*).

as if/like: *As if* is used before a clause (*It seems as if we should be doing something*); *like* is used before a noun or pronoun (*He seems like a nice guy*).

have/of: *Have* is a verb used in verb phrases (*They should have checked first*); *of* is a preposition and is never used in such cases.

in/into: *In* is used to refer to a static position (*The file is in the cabinet*); *into* is used to refer to movement toward a position (*Put the file into the cabinet*).

And here is a partial list of some prepositions that have come to be used with certain words:

according to	independent of
agree to (a proposal)	inferior to
agree with (a person)	plan to
buy from	prefer to
capable of	prior to
comply with	reason with
conform to	responsible for
differ from (things)	similar to
differ with (person)	talk to (without
different from	interaction)
get from (receive)	talk with (with interaction)
get off (dismount)	wait for (person or thing)
in accordance with	wait on (like a waiter)
in search of	

1.6.2 Conjunctions

Conjunctions connect the parts of a sentence: words, phrases, and clauses. You are probably most familiar with coordinating conjunctions such as the following:

and	for	or	yet
but	nor	so	

Conjunctions may be used to connect clauses (which have both a subject and a predicate) with other clauses, to connect clauses with phrases (which do not have both a subject and a predicate), and to connect words with words:

We sell designer clothing *and* linens.
(Words with words)

Their products are expensive *but* still appeal to value-conscious consumers.
(Clauses with phrases)

I will call her on the phone today, *or* I will visit her office tomorrow.
(Clauses with clauses)

Some conjunctions are used in pairs:

both . . . and	neither . . . nor	whether . . . or
either . . . or	not only . . . but also	

With paired conjunctions, you must be careful to construct each phrase in the same way.

They *not only* <u>are out of</u> racquets *but also* <u>are out of</u> balls.

They are *not only* <u>out of</u> racquets *but also* <u>out of</u> balls.

They <u>are out of</u> *not only* racquets *but also* balls.

In other words, the construction that follows each part of the pair must be parallel, containing the same verbs, prepositions, and so on. The same need for parallelism exists when using conjunctions to join the other parts of speech:

He is listed in *either* <u>your</u> roster *or* <u>my</u> roster.

He is listed *neither* <u>in</u> your roster <u>nor</u> *on* the master list.

They *both* <u>gave</u> *and* <u>received</u> notice.

A certain type of conjunction is used to join clauses that are unequal—that is, to join a main clause to one that is subordinate or dependent. Here is a partial list of conjunctions used to introduce dependent clauses:

although	before	once	unless
as soon as	even though	so that	until
because	if	that	when

Using conjunctions is also discussed in sections 1.7.3 and 1.7.4.

1.6.3 Articles and Interjections

Only three articles exist in English: *the, a,* and *an.* These words are used, like adjectives, to specify which item you are talking about.

Interjections are words that express no solid information, only emotion:

Wow!	Well, well!
Oh, no!	Good!

Such purely emotional language has its place in private life and advertising copy, but it only weakens the effect of most business writing.

1.7 Sentences

Sentences are constructed with the major building blocks, the parts of speech.

Money talks.

This two-word sentence consists of a noun (*money*) and a verb (*talks*). When used in this way, the noun works as the first requirement for a sentence, the subject, and the verb works as the second requirement, the predicate. Now look at this sentence:

They merged.

The subject in this case is a pronoun (*they*), and the predicate is a verb (*merged*). This is a sentence because it has a subject and a predicate. Here is yet another kind of sentence:

The plans are ready.

This sentence has a more complicated subject, the noun *plans* and the article *the;* the complete predicate is a state-of-being verb (*are*) and an adjective (*ready*).

Without a subject (who or what does something) and a predicate (the doing of it), you have merely a collection of words, not a sentence.

1.7.1 Commands

In commands, the subject (always *you*) is only understood, not stated:

(You) Move your desk to the better office.

(You) Please try to finish by six o'clock.

1.7.2 Longer Sentences

More complicated sentences have more complicated subjects and predicates, but they still have a simple subject and a predicate verb. In the following examples, the subject is underlined once, the predicate verb twice:

<u>Marex</u> and <u>Contron</u> <u>enjoy</u> higher earnings each quarter.

(*Marex* [and] *Contron* do something; *enjoy* is what they do.)

My <u>interview</u>, coming minutes after my freeway accident, <u>did</u> not <u>impress</u> or <u>move</u> anyone.

(*Interview* is what did something. What did it do? It *did* [not] *impress* [or] *move*.)

In terms of usable space, a steel <u>warehouse</u>, with its extremely long span of roof unsupported by pillars, <u>makes</u> more sense.

(*Warehouse* is what *makes*.)

These three sentences demonstrate several things. First, in all three sentences, the simple subject and predicate verb are the "bare bones" of the sentence, the parts that carry the core idea of the sentence. When trying to find the subject and predicate verb, disregard all prepositional phrases, modifiers, conjunctions, and articles.

Second, in the third sentence the verb is singular (*makes*) because the subject is singular (*warehouse*). Even though the plural noun *pillars* is closer to the verb, *warehouse* is the subject. So *warehouse* determines whether the verb is singular or plural. Subject and predicate must agree.

Third, the subject in the first sentence is compound (*Marex* [and] *Contron*). A compound subject, when connected by *and*, requires a plural verb (*enjoy*). Also in the second sentence, compound predicates are possible (*did* [not] *impress* [or] *move*).

Fourth, the second sentence incorporates a group of words—*coming minutes after my freeway accident*—containing a form of a verb (*coming*) and a noun (*accident*). Yet this group of words is not a complete sentence for two reasons:

- Not all nouns are subjects: *Accident* is not the subject of *coming*.

- Not all verbs are predicates: A verb that ends in *ing* can never be the predicate of a sentence (unless preceded by a form of *to be*, as in *was coming*).

Because they don't contain a subject and a predicate, the words *coming minutes after my freeway accident* (called a phrase) can't be written as a sentence. That is, the phrase cannot stand alone; it cannot begin with a capital letter and end with a period. So a phrase must always be just one part of a sentence.

Sometimes a sentence incorporates two or more groups of words that do contain a subject and a predicate; these word groups are called clauses:

My *interview*, because it <u>came</u> minutes after my freeway accident, <u>did</u> not <u>impress</u> or <u>move</u> anyone.

The independent clause is the portion of the sentence that could stand alone without revision:

My <u>interview</u> <u>did</u> not <u>impress</u> or <u>move</u> anyone.

The other part of the sentence could stand alone only by removing *because*:

(because) <u>It</u> <u>came</u> minutes after my freeway accident.

This part of the sentence is known as a dependent clause; although it has a subject and a predicate (just as an independent clause does), it's linked to the main part of the sentence by a word (*because*) showing its dependence.

In summary, the two types of clauses—dependent and independent—both have a subject and a predicate. Dependent clauses, however, do not bear the main meaning of the sentence and are therefore linked to an independent clause. Nor can

phrases stand alone, because they lack both a subject and a predicate. Only independent clauses can be written as sentences without revision.

1.7.3 Sentence Fragments

An incomplete sentence (a phrase or a dependent clause) that is written as though it were a complete sentence is called a fragment. Consider the following sentence fragments:

Marilyn Sanders, having had pilferage problems in her store for the past year. Refuses to accept the results of our investigation.

This serious error can easily be corrected by putting the two fragments together:

Marilyn Sanders, having had pilferage problems in her store for the past year, refuses to accept the results of our investigation.

Not all fragments can be corrected so easily. Here's more information on Sanders's pilferage problem.

Employees a part of it. No authority or discipline.

Only the writer knows the intended meaning of those two phrases. Perhaps the employees are taking part in the pilferage. If so, the sentence should read:

Some employees are part of the pilferage problem.

On the other hand, it's possible that some employees are helping with the investigation. Then the sentence would read:

Some employees are taking part in our investigation.

It's just as likely, however, that the employees are not only taking part in the pilferage but are also being analyzed:

Those employees who are part of the pilferage problem will accept no authority or discipline.

Even more meanings could be read into these fragments. Because fragments can mean so many things, they mean nothing. No well-written memo, letter, or report ever demands the reader to be an imaginative genius.

One more type of fragment exists, the kind represented by a dependent clause. Note what *because* does to change what was once a unified sentence:

Our stock of sprinklers is depleted.

Because our stock of sprinklers is depleted.

Although the second version contains a subject and a predicate, adding *because* makes it a fragment. Words such as *because* form a special group of words called subordinating conjunctions. Here's a partial list:

after	if	unless
although	since	whenever
even if	though	while

When a word of this type begins a clause, the clause is dependent and cannot stand alone as a sentence. However, if a dependent clause is combined with an independent clause, it can convey a complete meaning. The independent clause may come before or after the dependent clause:

We are unable to fill your order because our stock of sprinklers is depleted.

Because our stock of sprinklers is depleted, we are unable to fill your order.

Also, to fix a fragment that is a dependent clause, remove the sub-ordinating conjunction. Doing so leaves a simple but complete sentence:

> Our stock of sprinklers is depleted.

The actual details of a situation will determine the best way for you to remedy a fragment problem.

The ban on fragments has one exception. Some advertising copy contains sentence fragments, written knowingly to convey a certain rhythm. However, advertising is the only area of business in which fragments are acceptable.

1.7.4 Fused Sentences and Comma Splices

Just as there can be too little in a group of words to make it a sentence, there can also be too much:

> All our mail is run through a postage meter every afternoon someone picks it up.

This example contains two sentences, not one, but the two have been blended so that it's hard to tell where one ends and the next begins. Is the mail run through a meter every afternoon? If so, the sentences should read:

> All our mail is run through a postage meter every afternoon. Someone picks it up.

Perhaps the mail is run through a meter at some other time (morning, for example) and is picked up every afternoon:

> All our mail is run through a postage meter. Every afternoon someone picks it up.

The order of words is the same in all three cases; sentence division makes all the difference. Either of the last two cases is grammatically correct. The choice depends on the facts of the situation.

Sometimes these so-called fused sentences have a more obvious point of separation:

> Several large orders arrived within a few days of one another, too many came in for us to process by the end of the month.

Here the comma has been put between two independent clauses in an attempt to link them. When a lowly comma separates two complete sentences, the result is called a comma splice. A comma splice can be remedied in one of three ways:

- Replace the comma with a period and capitalize the next word: ". . . one another. Too many . . ."

- Replace the comma with a semicolon and do not capitalize the next word: ". . . one another; too many . . ." This remedy works only when the two sentences have closely related meanings.

- Change one of the sentences so that it becomes a phrase or a dependent clause. This remedy often produces the best writing, but it takes more work.

The third alternative can be carried out in several ways. One is to begin the blended sentence with a subordinating conjunction:

> Whenever several large orders arrived within a few days of one another, too many came in for us to process by the end of the month.

Another way is to remove part of the subject or the predicate verb from one of the independent clauses, thereby creating a phrase:

> Several large orders arrived within a few days of one another, too many for us to process by the end of the month.

Finally, you can change one of the predicate verbs to its *ing* form:

> Several large orders arrived within a few days of one another, too many coming in for us to process by the end of the month.

At other times a simple coordinating conjunction (such as *or, and,* or *but*) can separate fused sentences:

> You can fire them, or you can make better use of their abilities.

> Margaret drew up the designs, and Matt carried them out.

> We will have three strong months, but after that sales will taper off.

Be careful using coordinating conjunctions: Use them only to join simple sentences that express similar ideas.

Also, because they say relatively little about the relationship between the two clauses they join, avoid using coordinating conjunctions too often: *and* is merely an addition sign; *but* is just a turn signal; *or* only points to an alternative. Subordinating conjunctions such as *because* and *whenever* tell the reader a lot more.

1.7.5 Sentences with Linking Verbs

Linking verbs were discussed briefly in the section on verbs (Section 1.3). Here you can see more fully the way they function in a sentence. The following is a model of any sentence with a linking verb:

> A *(verb)* B.

Although words such as *seems* and *feels* can also be linking verbs, let's assume that the verb is a form of *to be*:

> A *is* B.

In such a sentence, A and B are always nouns, pronouns, or adjectives. When one is a noun and the other is a pronoun, or when both are nouns, the sentence says that one is the same as the other:

> She is president.

> Rachel is president.

When one is an adjective, it modifies or describes the other:

> She is forceful.

Remember that when one is an adjective, it modifies the other as any adjective modifies a noun or pronoun, except that a linking verb stands between the adjective and the word it modifies.

1.7.6 Misplaced Modifiers

The position of a modifier in a sentence is important. The movement of *only* changes the meaning in the following sentences:

> Only we are obliged to supply those items specified in your contract.

> We are obliged only to supply those items specified in your contract.

> We are obliged to supply only those items specified in your contract.

> We are obliged to supply those items specified only in your contract.

In any particular set of circumstances, only one of those sentences would be accurate. The others would very likely cause problems. To prevent misunderstanding, place such modifiers as close as possible to the noun or verb they modify.

For similar reasons, whole phrases that are modifiers must be placed near the right noun or verb. Mistakes in placement create ludicrous meanings.

> Antia Information Systems has bought new computer chairs for the programmers *with more comfortable seats*.

The anatomy of programmers is not normally a concern of business writers. Obviously, the comfort of the chairs was the issue:

> Antia Information Systems has bought new computer chairs *with more comfortable seats* for the programmers.

Here is another example:

> I asked him to file all the letters in the cabinet that had been answered.

In this ridiculous sentence the cabinet has been answered, even though no cabinet in history is known to have asked a question.

That had been answered is too far from *letters* and too close to *cabinet*. Here's an improvement:

> I asked him to file in the cabinet all the letters that had been answered.

In some cases, instead of moving the modifying phrase closer to the word it modifies, the best solution is to move the word closer to the modifying phrase.

2.0 Punctuation

On the highway, signs tell you when to slow down or stop, where to turn, when to merge. In similar fashion, punctuation helps readers negotiate your prose. The proper use of punctuation keeps readers from losing track of your meaning.

2.1 Periods

Use a period (1) to end any sentence that is not a question, (2) with certain abbreviations, and (3) between dollars and cents in an amount of money.

2.2 Question Marks

Use a question mark after any direct question that requests an answer:

> Are you planning to enclose a check, or shall we bill you?

Don't use a question mark with commands phrased as questions for the sake of politeness:

> Will you send us a check today.

2.3 Exclamation Points

Use exclamation points after highly emotional language. Because business writing almost never calls for emotional language, you will seldom use exclamation points.

2.4 Semicolons

Semicolons have three main uses. One is to separate two closely related independent clauses:

> The outline for the report is due within a week; the report itself is due at the end of the month.

A semicolon should also be used instead of a comma when the items in a series have commas within them:

> Our previous meetings were on November 11, 2003; February 20, 2004; and April 28, 2005.

Finally, a semicolon should be used to separate independent clauses when the second one begins with a word such as *however, therefore,* or *nevertheless* or a phrase such as *for example* or *in that case*:

> Our supplier has been out of part D712 for 10 weeks; however, we have found another source that can ship the part right away.

> His test scores were quite low; on the other hand, he has a lot of relevant experience.

Section 4.4 has more information on using transitional words and phrases.

2.5 Colons

Use a colon after the salutation in a business letter. You also use a colon at the end of a sentence or phrase introducing a list or (sometimes) a quotation:

> Our study included the three most critical problems: insufficient capital, incompetent management, and inappropriate location.

In some introductory sentences, phrases such as *the following* or *that is* are implied by using a colon.

A colon should not be used when the list, quotation, or idea is a direct object or part of the introductory sentence:

> We are able to supply
> staples
> wood screws
> nails
> toggle bolts

> This shipment includes 9 DVD's, 12 CDs, and 14 USB flash drives.

Another way you can use a colon is to separate the main clause and another sentence element when the second explains, illustrates, or amplifies the first:

> Management was unprepared for the union representatives' demands: this fact alone accounts for their arguing well into the night.

However, in contemporary usage, such clauses are frequently separated by a semicolon.

2.6 Commas

Commas have many uses; the most common is to separate items in a series:

> He took the job, learned it well, worked hard, and succeeded.

> Put paper, pencils, and paper clips on the requisition list.

Company style often dictates omitting the final comma in a series. However, if you have a choice, use the final comma; it's often necessary to prevent misunderstanding.

A second place to use a comma is between independent clauses that are joined by a coordinating conjunction (*and, but,* or *or*) unless one or both are very short:

> She spoke to the sales staff, and he spoke to the production staff.

> I was advised to proceed and I did.

A third use for the comma is to separate a dependent clause at the beginning of a sentence from an independent clause:

> Because of our lead in the market, we may be able to risk introducing a new product.

However, a dependent clause at the end of a sentence is separated from the independent clause by a comma only when the dependent clause is unnecessary to the main meaning of the sentence:

> We may be able to introduce a new product, although it may involve some risk.

A fourth use for the comma is after an introductory phrase or word:

> Starting with this amount of capital, we can survive in the red for one year.

> Through more careful planning, we may be able to serve more people.

> Yes, you may proceed as originally planned.

However, with short introductory prepositional phrases and some one-syllable words (such as *hence* and *thus*), the comma is often omitted:

> Before January 1 we must complete the inventory.

> Thus we may not need to hire anyone.

> In short the move to Tulsa was a good idea.

Fifth, commas are used to surround nonrestrictive phrases or words (expressions that can be removed from the sentence without changing the meaning):

> The new owners, the Kowacks, are pleased with their purchase.

Sixth, commas are used between adjectives modifying the same noun (coordinate adjectives):

> She left Monday for a long, difficult recruiting trip.

To test the appropriateness of such a comma, try reversing the order of the adjectives: *a difficult, long recruiting trip.* If the order cannot be reversed, leave out the comma (*a good old friend* isn't the same as *an old good friend*). A comma is also not used when one of the adjectives is part of the noun. Compare these two phrases:

> a distinguished, well-known figure

> a distinguished public figure

The adjective-noun combination of *public* and *figure* has been used together so often that it has come to be considered a single thing: *public figure.* So no comma is required.

Seventh, commas are used both before and after the year in sentences that include month, day, and year:

> It will be sent by December 15, 2006, from our Cincinnati plant.

Some companies write dates in another form: 15 December 2006. No commas should be used in that case. Nor is a comma needed when only the month and year are present (December 2006).

Eighth, commas are used to set off a variety of parenthetical words and phrases within sentences, including state names, dates, abbreviations, transitional expressions, and contrasted elements:

> They were, in fact, prepared to submit a bid.

> Our best programmer is Ken, who joined the company just a month ago.

> Habermacher, Inc., went public in 1999.

> Our goal was increased profits, not increased market share.

> Service, then, is our main concern.

> The factory was completed in Chattanooga, Tennessee, just three weeks ago.

> Joanne Dubiik, M.D., has applied for a loan from First Savings.

> I started work here on March 1, 2001, and soon received my first promotion.

Ninth, a comma is used to separate a quotation from the rest of the sentence:

> Your warranty reads, "These conditions remain in effect for one year from date of purchase."

However, the comma is left out when the quotation as a whole is built into the structure of the sentence:

> He hurried off with an angry "Look where you're going."

Finally, a comma should be used whenever it's needed to avoid confusion or an unintended meaning. Compare the following:

> Ever since they have planned new ventures more carefully.

> Ever since, they have planned new ventures more carefully.

2.7 Dashes

Use a dash to surround a comment that is a sudden turn in thought:

> Membership in the IBSA—it's expensive but worth it—may be obtained by applying to our New York office.

A dash can also be used to emphasize a parenthetical word or phrase:

> Third-quarter profits—in excess of $2 million—are up sharply.

Finally, use dashes to set off a phrase that contains commas:

> All our offices—Milwaukee, New Orleans, and Phoenix—have sent representatives.

Don't confuse a dash with a hyphen. A dash separates and emphasizes words, phrases, and clauses more strongly than a comma or parentheses can; a hyphen ties two words so tightly that they almost become one word.

On computer, use the em dash symbol. When typing a dash in e-mail or on a typewriter, type two hyphens with no space before, between, or after.

2.8 Hyphens

Hyphens are mainly used in three ways. The first is to separate the parts of compound words beginning with such prefixes as *self-, ex-, quasi-,* and *all-*:

self-assured	quasi-official
ex-wife	all-important

However, omit hyphens from and close up those words that have prefixes such as *pro, anti, non, re, pre, un, inter,* and *extra*:

prolabor	nonunion
antifascist	interdepartmental

Exceptions occur when (1) the prefix occurs before a proper noun or (2) the vowel at the end of the prefix is the same as the first letter of the root word:

pro-Republican anti-American
anti-inflammatory extra-atmospheric

When in doubt, consult your dictionary.

Hyphens are also used in some compound adjectives, which are adjectives made up of two or more words. Specifically, you should use hyphens in compound adjectives that come before the noun:

an interest-bearing account well-informed executives

However, you need not hyphenate when the adjective follows a linking verb:

This account is interest bearing.

Their executives are well informed.

You can shorten sentences that list similar hyphenated words by dropping the common part from all but the last word:

Check the costs of first-, second-, and third-class postage.

Finally, hyphens may be used to divide words at the end of a typed line. Such hyphenation is best avoided, but when you have to divide words at the end of a line, do so correctly (see Section 3.5). A dictionary will show how words are divided into syllables.

2.9 Apostrophes

Use an apostrophe in the possessive form of a noun (but not in a pronoun):

On *his* desk was a reply to Bette *Ainsley's* application for the *manager's* position.

Apostrophes are also used in place of the missing letter(s) of a contraction:

Whole Words	Contraction
we will	we'll
do not	don't
they are	they're

2.10 Quotation Marks

Use quotation marks to surround words that are repeated exactly as they were said or written:

The collection letter ended by saying, "This is your third and final notice."

Remember: (1) When the quoted material is a complete sentence, the first word is capitalized. (2) The final comma or period goes inside the closing quotation marks.

Quotation marks are also used to set off the title of a newspaper story, magazine article, or book chapter:

You should read "Legal Aspects of the Collection Letter" in *Today's Credit.*

The book title is shown here in italics. When typewritten, the title is underlined. The same treatment is proper for newspaper and magazine titles. (Appendix B explains documentation style in more detail.)

Quotation marks may also be used to indicate special treatment for words or phrases, such as terms that you're using in an unusual or ironic way:

Our management "team" spends more time squabbling than working to solve company problems.

When you are defining a word, put the definition in quotation marks:

The abbreviation *etc.* means "and so forth."

When using quotation marks, take care to insert the closing marks as well as the opening ones.

Although periods and commas go inside any quotation marks, colons and semicolons go outside them. A question mark goes inside the quotation marks only if the quotation is a question:

All that day we wondered, "Is he with us?"

If the quotation is not a question but the entire sentence is, the question mark goes outside:

What did she mean by "You will hear from me"?

2.11 Parentheses

Use parentheses to surround comments that are entirely incidental:

Our figures do not match yours, although (if my calculations are correct) they are closer than we thought.

Parentheses are also used in legal documents to surround figures in arabic numerals that follow the same amount in words:

Remittance will be One Thousand Two Hundred Dollars ($1,200).

Be careful to put punctuation (period, comma, and so on) outside the parentheses unless it is part of the statement in parentheses.

2.12 Ellipses

Use ellipsis points, or dots, to indicate that material has been left out of a direct quotation. Use them only in direct quotations and only at the point where material was left out. In the following example, the first sentence is quoted in the second:

The Dow Jones Industrial Average, fell 276.39 points or 2.6% during the week to 10292.31.

According to the *Wall Street Journal,* "The Dow Jones Industrial Average . . . fell 276.39" during the week.

The number of dots in ellipses is not optional; always use three. Occasionally, the points of ellipsis come at the end of a sentence, where they seem to grow a fourth dot. Don't be fooled: One of the dots is a period.

3.0 Mechanics

The most obvious and least tolerable mistakes that a business writer makes are probably those related to grammar and punctuation. However, a number of small details, known as writing mechanics, demonstrate the writer's polish and reflect on the company's professionalism.

3.1 Capitals

Capitals are used at the beginning of certain word groups:

- **Complete sentence:** *Before* hanging up, he said, "*We'll* meet here on Wednesday at noon."

- **Formal statement following a colon:** She has a favorite motto: Where there's a will, there's a way. (Otherwise, the first word after a colon should not be capitalized—see Section 2.5.)

- **Phrase used as sentence:** Absolutely not!

- **Quoted sentence embedded in another sentence:** Scot said, "Nobody was here during lunch hour except me."

- **List of items set off from text:** Three preliminary steps are involved:
    Design review
    Budgeting
    Scheduling

Capitalize proper adjectives and proper nouns (the names of particular persons, places, and things):

> Darrell Greene lived in a Victorian mansion.

> We sent Ms. Larson an application form, informing her that not all applicants are interviewed.

> Let's consider opening a branch in the West, perhaps at the west end of Tucson, Arizona.

> As office buildings go, the Kinney Building is a pleasant setting for TDG Office Equipment.

Ms. Larson's name is capitalized because she is a particular applicant, whereas the general term *applicant* is left uncapitalized. Likewise, *West* is capitalized when it refers to a particular place but not when it means a direction. In the same way, *office* and *building* are not capitalized when they are general terms (common nouns), but they are capitalized when they are part of the title of a particular office or building (proper nouns).

Titles within families, governments, or companies may also be capitalized:

> I turned down Uncle David when he offered me a job, since I wouldn't be comfortable working for one of my relatives.

> We've never had a president quite like President Sweeney.

People's titles are capitalized when they are used in addressing a person, especially in a formal context. They are not usually capitalized, however, when they are used merely to identify the person:

> Address the letter to Chairperson Anna Palmer.

> I wish to thank Chairperson Anna Palmer for her assistance.

> Please deliver these documents to board chairperson Anna Palmer.

> Anna Palmer, chairperson of the board, took the podium.

Also capitalize titles if they are used by themselves in addressing a person:

> Thank you, Doctor, for your donation.

Titles that are used to identify a person of very high rank are capitalized regardless of where they fall or how much of the name is included:

> the President of the United States

> the Prime Minister of Canada

> the Pope

In addresses, salutations, signature blocks, and some formal writing (such as acknowledgments), all titles are capitalized whether they come before or after the name. In addition, always capitalize the first word of the salutation and complimentary close of a letter:

> *Dear* Mr. Andrews: *Yours* very truly,

The names of organizations are capitalized, of course; so are the official names of their departments and divisions. However, do not use capitals when referring in general terms to a department or division, especially one in another organization:

> Route this memo to Personnel.

> Larry Tien was transferred to the Microchip Division

> Will you be enrolled in the Psychology Department?

> Someone from the engineering department at EnerTech stopped by the booth.

> Our production department has reorganized for efficiency.

> Send a copy to their school of business administration.

Capitalization is unnecessary when using a word like *company, corporation,* or *university* alone:

> The corporation plans to issue 50,000 shares of common stock.

Likewise, the names of specific products are capitalized, although the names of general product types are not:

> HP computer   Tide laundry detergent

One problem that often arises in writing about places is the treatment of two or more proper nouns of the same type. When the common word comes before the specific names, it is capitalized; when it comes after the specific names, it is not:

> Lakes Ontario and Huron

> Allegheny and Monongahela rivers

The names of languages, races, and ethnic groups are capitalized: *Japanese, Caucasian, Hispanic.* But racial terms that denote only skin color are not capitalized: *black, white.*

When referring to the titles of books, articles, magazines, newspapers, reports, movies, and so on, you should capitalize the first and last words and all nouns, pronouns, adjectives, verbs, adverbs, and prepositions and conjunctions with five letters or more. Except for the first and last words, do not capitalize articles:

> *Economics During the Great War*

> "An Investigation into the Market for Long-Distance Services"

> "What Successes Are Made Of"

When *the* is part of the official name of a newspaper or magazine, it should be treated this way too: *The Wall Street Journal.*

References to specific pages, paragraphs, lines, and the like are not capitalized: *page 73, line 3.* However, in most other numbered or lettered references, the identifying term is capitalized: *Chapter 4, Serial No. 382–2203, Item B-11.*

Finally, the names of academic degrees are capitalized when they follow a person's name but are not capitalized when used in a general sense:

> I received a bachelor of science degree.

> Thomas Whitelaw, Doctor of Philosophy, will attend.

Similarly, general courses of study are not capitalized, but the names of specific classes are:

> She studied accounting as an undergraduate.

> She is enrolled in Accounting 201.

3.2 Underscores and Italics

Usually a line typed underneath a word or phrase either provides emphasis or indicates the title of a book, magazine, or newspaper. If possible, use italics instead of an underscore. Italics (or underlining) should also be used for defining terms and for discussing words as words:

> In this report *net sales* refers to after-tax sales dollars.

> The word *building* is a common noun and should not be capitalized.

3.3 Abbreviations

Abbreviations are used heavily in tables, charts, lists, and forms. They're used sparingly in prose paragraphs, however. Here are some abbreviations often used in business writing:

Abbreviation	Full Term
b/l	bill of lading
ca.	circa (about)
dol., dols.	dollar, dollars
etc.	et cetera (and so on)
FDIC	Federal Deposit Insurance Corporation
Inc.	Incorporated
L.f.	Ledger folio
Ltd.	Limited
mgr.	manager
NSF or N/S	not sufficient funds
P&L or P/L	profit and loss
reg.	regular
whsle.	wholesale

One way to handle an abbreviation that you want to use throughout a document is to spell it out the first time you use it, follow it with the abbreviation in parentheses, and then use the abbreviation in the remainder of the document.

Because *etc.* contains a word meaning "and," never write *and etc.* In fact, try to limit your use of such abbreviations to tables and parenthetical material.

3.4 Numbers

Numbers may be correctly handled many ways in business writing, so follow company style. In the absence of a set style, however, generally spell out all numbers from one to nine and use arabic numerals for the rest.

There are some exceptions to this general rule. For example, never begin a sentence with a numeral:

> *Twenty* of us produced *641* units per week in the first *12* weeks of the year.

Use numerals for the numbers one through ten if they're in the same list as larger numbers:

> Our weekly quota rose from *9* to *15* to *27*.

Use numerals for percentages, time of day (except with *o'clock*), dates, and (in general) dollar amounts.

> Our division is responsible for *7* percent of total sales.

> The meeting is scheduled for *8:30* A.M. on August *2*.

> Add *$3* for postage and handling.

Use a comma in numbers expressing thousands (*1,257*), unless your company specifies another style. When dealing with numbers in the millions and billions, combine words and figures: *7.3 million, 2 billion.*

When writing dollar amounts, use a decimal point only if cents are included. In lists of two or more dollar amounts, use the decimal point either for all or for none:

> He sent two checks, one for *$67.92* and one for *$90.00.*

When two numbers fall next to each other in a sentence, use figures for the number that is largest, most difficult to spell, or part of a physical measurement; use words for the other:

> I have learned to manage a classroom of 30 twelve-year-olds.

> She's won a bonus for selling 24 thirty-volume sets.

> You'll need twenty 3-inch bolts.

In addresses, all street numbers except *One* are in figures. So are suite and room numbers and ZIP codes. For street names that are numbered, practice varies so widely that you should use the form specified on an organization's letterhead or in a reliable directory. All of the following examples are correct:

> One Fifth Avenue   297 Ninth Street

> 1839 44th Street   11026 West 78 Place

Telephone numbers are always expressed in figures. Parentheses may separate the area code from the rest of the number, but a slash or a dash may be used instead, especially if the entire phone number is enclosed in parentheses:

> 382–8329   (602/382–8329)   602–382–8329

Percentages are always expressed in figures. The word *percent* is used in most cases, but % may be used in tables, forms, and statistical writing.

Physical measurements such as distance, weight, and volume are also often expressed in figures: *9 kilometers, 5 feet 3 inches, 7 pounds 10 ounces.*

Ages are usually expressed in words—except when a parenthetical reference to age follows someone's name:

> Mrs. Margaret Sanderson is seventy-two.

> Mrs. Margaret Sanderson, 72, swims daily.

Also, ages expressed in years and months are treated like physical measurements that combine two units of measure: *5 years 6 months.*

Decimal numbers are always written in figures. In most cases, add a zero to the left of the decimal point if the number is less than one and does not already start with a zero:

> 1.38   .07   0.2

In a series of related decimal numbers with at least one number greater than one, make sure that all numbers smaller than one have a zero to the left of the decimal point: *1.20, 0.21, 0.09.* Also, express all decimal numbers in a series to the same number of places by adding zeroes at the end:

> The responses were Yes, 37.2 percent; No, 51.0; Not Sure, 11.8.

Simple fractions are written in words, but more complicated fractions are expressed in figures or, if easier to read, in figures and words:

> two-thirds   9/32   2 hundredths

A combination of whole numbers and a fraction should always be written in figures. Note that a hyphen is used to separate the fraction from the whole number when a slash is used for the fraction: *2–11/16.*

3.5 Word Division

In general, avoid dividing words at the ends of lines. When you must do so, follow these rules:

- Don't divide one-syllable words (such as *since, walked,* and *thought*); abbreviations (*mgr.*); contractions (*isn't*); or numbers expressed in numerals (*117,500*).

- Divide words between syllables, as specified in a dictionary or word-division manual.

- Make sure that at least three letters of the divided word are moved to the second line: *sin-cerely* instead of *sincere-ly*.

- Do not end a page or more than three consecutive lines with hyphens.

- Leave syllables consisting of a single vowel at the end of the first line (*impedi-ment* instead of *imped-iment*), except when the single vowel is part of a suffix such as *-able, -ible, -ical,* or *-ity* (*re-spons-ible* instead of *re-sponsi-ble*).

- Divide between double letters (*tomor-row*), except when the root word ends in double letters (*call-ing* instead of *cal-ling*).

- Wherever possible, divide hyphenated words at the hyphen only: instead of *anti-inde-pendence,* use *anti-independence.*

4.0 Vocabulary

Using the right word in the right place is a crucial skill in business communication. However, many pitfalls await the unwary.

4.1 Frequently Confused Words

Because the following sets of words sound similar, be careful not to use one when you mean to use the other:

Word	Meaning
accede	to comply with
exceed	to go beyond
accept	to take
except	to exclude
access	admittance
excess	too much
advice	suggestion
advise	to suggest
affect	to influence
effect	the result
allot	to distribute
a lot	much or many
all ready	completely prepared
already	completed earlier
born	given birth to
borne	carried
capital	money; chief city
capitol	a government building
cite	to quote
sight	a view
site	a location
complement	complete amount; to go well with
compliment	expression of esteem; to flatter
corespondent	party in a divorce suit
correspondent	letter writer

council	a panel of people
counsel	advice; a lawyer
defer	to put off until later
differ	to be different
device	a mechanism
devise	to plan
die	to stop living; a tool
dye	to color
discreet	careful
discrete	separate
envelop	to surround
envelope	a covering for a letter
forth	forward
fourth	number four
holey	full of holes
holy	sacred
wholly	completely
human	of people
humane	kindly
incidence	frequency
incidents	events
instance	example
instants	moments
interstate	between states
intrastate	within a state
later	afterward
latter	the second of two
lead	a metal; to guide
led	guided
lean	to rest at an angle
lien	a claim
levee	embankment
levy	tax
loath	reluctant
loathe	to hate
loose	free; not tight
lose	to mislay
material	substance
materiel	equipment
miner	mineworker
minor	underage person
moral	virtuous; a lesson
morale	sense of well-being
ordinance	law
ordnance	weapons
overdo	to do in excess
overdue	past due
peace	lack of conflict
piece	a fragment
pedal	a foot lever
peddle	to sell
persecute	to torment
prosecute	to sue
personal	private
personnel	employees

precedence	priority
precedents	previous events
principal	sum of money; chief; main
principle	general rule
rap	to knock
wrap	to cover
residence	home
residents	inhabitants
right	correct
rite	ceremony
write	to form words on a surface
role	a part to play
roll	to tumble; a list
root	part of a plant
rout	to defeat
route	a traveler's way
shear	to cut
sheer	thin, steep
stationary	immovable
stationery	paper
than	as compared with
then	at that time
their	belonging to them
there	in that place
they're	they are
to	a preposition
too	excessively; also
two	the number
waive	to set aside
wave	a swell of water; a gesture
weather	atmospheric conditions
whether	if
who's	contraction of "who is" or "who has"
whose	possessive form of who

In the preceding list, only enough of each word's meaning is given to help you distinguish between the words in each group. Several meanings are left out entirely. For more complete definitions, consult a dictionary.

4.2 Frequently Misused Words

The following words tend to be misused for reasons other than their sound. Reference books (including the *Random House College Dictionary,* revised edition; Follett's *Modern American Usage;* and Fowler's *Modern English Usage*) can help you with similar questions of usage.

a lot: When the writer means "many," *a lot* is always two separate words, never one.

correspond with: Use this phrase when you are talking about exchanging letters. Use *correspond to* when you mean "similar to." Use either *correspond with* or *correspond to* when you mean "relate to."

disinterested: This word means "fair, unbiased, having no favorites, impartial." If you mean "bored" or "not interested," use *uninterested.*

etc.: This abbreviated form of the Latin phrase *et cetera* means "and so on" or "and so forth." The current tendency among business writers is to use English rather than Latin.

imply/infer: Both refer to hints. Their great difference lies in who is acting. The writer implies; the reader infers, sees between the lines.

lay: This word is a transitive verb. Never use it for the intransitive *lie.* (See Section 1.3.3.)

less: Use *less* for uncountable quantities (such as amounts of water, air, sugar, and oil). Use *fewer* for countable quantities (such as numbers of jars, saws, words, pages, and humans). The same distinction applies to *much* and *little* (uncountable) versus *many* and *few* (countable).

like: Use *like* only when the word that follows is just a noun or a pronoun. Use *as* or *as if* when a phrase or clause follows:

> She looks like him.

> She did just as he had expected.

> It seems as if she had plenty of time.

many/much: See *less.*

regardless: The *less* ending is the negative part. No word needs two negative parts, so don't add *ir* (a negative prefix) to the beginning. There is no such word as *irregardless.*

to me/personally: Use these phrases only when personal reactions, apart from company policy, are being stated (not often the case in business writing).

try: Always follow with *to,* never *and.*

verbal: People in the business community who are careful with language frown on those who use *verbal* to mean "spoken" or "oral." Many others do say "verbal agreement." Strictly speaking, *verbal* means "of words" and therefore includes both spoken and written words. Follow company usage in this matter.

4.3 Frequently Misspelled Words

All of us, even the world's best spellers, sometimes have to check a dictionary for the spelling of some words. People who have never memorized the spelling of commonly used words must look up so many that they grow exasperated and give up on spelling words correctly.

Don't expect perfection, and don't surrender. If you can memorize the spelling of just the words listed here, you'll need the dictionary far less often, and you'll write with more confidence.

absence	asterisk
absorption	auditor
accessible	
accommodate	bankruptcy
accumulate	believable
achieve	brilliant
advantageous	bulletin
affiliated	
aggressive	calendar
alignment	campaign
aluminum	category
ambience	ceiling
analyze	changeable
apparent	clientele
appropriate	collateral
argument	committee
asphalt	comparative
assistant	competitor
	concede

congratulations
connoisseur
consensus
convenient
convertible
corroborate
criticism

definitely
description
desirable
dilemma
disappear
disappoint
disbursement
discrepancy
dissatisfied
dissipate

eligible
embarrassing
endorsement
exaggerate
exceed
exhaust
existence
extraordinary

fallacy
familiar
flexible
fluctuation
forty

gesture
grievous

haphazard
harassment
holiday

illegible
immigrant
incidentally
indelible
independent
indispensable
insistent
intermediary
irresistible

jewelry
judgment
judicial

labeling
legitimate
leisure
license
litigation

maintenance
mathematics
mediocre
minimum

necessary
negligence
negotiable
newsstand
noticeable

occurrence
omission

parallel
pastime
peaceable
permanent
perseverance
persistent
personnel
persuade
possesses
precede
predictable
preferred
privilege
procedure
proceed
pronunciation
psychology
pursue

questionnaire

receive
recommend
repetition
rescind
rhythmical
ridiculous

salable
secretary
seize
separate
sincerely
succeed

suddenness
superintendent
supersede
surprise

tangible
tariff
technique

tenant
truly

unanimous
until

vacillate
vacuum
vicious

4.4 Transitional Words and Phrases

The following sentences don't communicate as well as they might because they lack a transitional word or phrase:

> Production delays are inevitable. Our current lag time in filling orders is one month.

A semicolon between the two sentences would signal a close relationship between their meanings, but it wouldn't even hint at what that relationship is. Here are the sentences again, now linked by means of a semicolon, with a space for a transitional word or phrase:

> Production delays are inevitable; _____ , our current lag time in filling orders is one month.

Now read the sentence with *nevertheless* in the blank space. Now try *therefore, incidentally, in fact,* and *at any rate* in the blank. Each substitution changes the meaning of the sentence.

Here are some transitional words (called conjunctive adverbs) that will help you write more clearly:

accordingly	furthermore	moreover
anyway	however	otherwise
besides	incidentally	still
consequently	likewise	therefore
finally	meanwhile	

The following transitional phrases are used in the same way:

as a result	in other words
at any rate	in the second place
for example	on the other hand
in fact	to the contrary

When one of these words or phrases joins two independent clauses, it should be preceded by a semicolon and followed by a comma, as shown here:

> The consultant recommended a complete reorganization; moreover, she suggested that we drop several products.

Answer Keys

ANSWER KEY FOR "LEARNING OBJECTIVES CHECKUP"

Chapter 1

1. e
2. b
3. a, d, f, and h
4. b
5. c
6. c
7. c
8. d
9. b
10. c
11. b
12. improvement
13. a
14. enhances or supports
15. a
16. c
17. d
18. dilemma, lapse

Chapter 2

1. d
2. d
3. d
4. a
5. dysfunctional
6. b
7. constructive, destructive
8. d
9. c
10. a
11. a
12. b
13. virtual
14. decode
15. c
16. d
17. a
18. d

Chapter 3

1. d
2. d
3. c
4. b
5. c
6. d
7. ethnocentrism
8. stereotyping
9. d
10. a
11. c
12. b
13. a
14. nonverbal
15. d
16. a
17. b
18. b

Chapter 4

1. b
2. c
3. d
4. a
5. general purpose
6. e
7. b
8. a
9. c
10. c
11. d
12. d
13. richness
14. d
15. b
16. direct
17. indirect
18. a

Chapter 5

1. a
2. d
3. c
4. c
5. passive
6. active
7. b
8. b
9. c
10. a
11. a
12. c
13. c
14. examples
15. similarities, differences
16. a
17. c
18. c

Chapter 6

1. d
2. a
3. c
4. a
5. b
6. d
7. d
8. b
9. b
10. a
11. c
12. b
13. white space
14. c
15. a
16. d
17. a
18. b

Chapter 7

1. b
2. a
3. d
4. c
5. b
6. d
7. b
8. the good news
9. d
10. d
11. b
12. a
13. b
14. d
15. c

Chapter 8

1. d
2. c
3. a
4. a
5. c
6. c
7. d
8. a
9. a
10. defamation
11. libel
12. slander
13. d
14. c
15. b
16. a
17. a

Chapter 9

1. c
2. d
3. d
4. b
5. b
6. c
7. d
8. c
9. emotional
10. logical
11. b
12. d
13. b
14. d

15. c
16. b
17. d
18. d

Chapter 10

1. d
2. a
3. informational
4. analytical
5. proposals
6. d
7. d
8. primary
9. secondary
10. a
11. c
12. a
13. c
14. c
15. a
16. b
17. summary
18. conclusion
19. recommendation
20. a
21. logic

Chapter 11

1. d
2. a
3. a
4. c
5. c
6. a
7. c
8. a
9. b
10. d
11. d
12. d
13. d
14. d
15. b
16. d
17. d
18. c

Chapter 12

1. c
2. d

3. a
4. d
5. b
6. a
7. synopsis
8. executive summary
9. a
10. c
11. b
12. c

Chapter 13

1. a
2. d
3. c
4. planning, speaking
5. d
6. b
7. a
8. a
9. b
10. b
11. c
12. d
13. a
14. c
15. d
16. d
17. d
18. b

Chapter 14

1. a
2. c
3. d
4. c
5. b
6. b
7. d
8. chronological
9. functional
10. combination
11. d
12. a
13. b
14. a
15. a
16. c
17. d
18. b

Chapter 15

1. a
2. d
3. b
4. structured
5. open-ended
6. situational

7. d
8. d
9. c
10. b
11. c
12. c

13. a
14. a
15. c
16. d
17. a
18. c

ANSWER KEY FOR "IMPROVE YOUR GRAMMAR, MECHANICS, AND USAGE" EXERCISES

Chapter 1

1. boss's (1.1.4)
2. sheep (1.1.3)
3. 1990s (1.1.3)
4. Joneses, stopwatches (1.1.3)
5. attorneys (1.1.3)
6. copies (1.1.3)
7. employees' (1.1.4)
8. sons-in-law, businesses (1.1.3, 1.1.4)
9. parentheses (1.1.3)
10. Ness's, week's (1.1.4)

Chapter 2

1. its (1.2.5)
2. their (1.2.5)
3. its (1.2.5)
4. their (1.2.1)
5. his or her (1.2.3)
6. his or her (1.2.3)
7. a / them (1.2.3, 1.2.4)
8. who (1.2.4)
9. whom (1.2.4)
10. its (1.2.5)

Chapter 3

1. b (1.3.1)
2. b (1.3.1)
3. a (1.3.1)
4. b (1.3.5)
5. a (1.3.5)
6. a (1.3.4)
7. b (1.3.4)
8. b (1.3.4)
9. a (1.3.4)
10. b (1.3.4)

Chapter 4

1. greater (1.4.1)
2. perfect (1.4.1)

3. most interesting (1.4.1)
4. hardest (1.4.1)
5. highly placed, last-ditch (1.4.2)
6. top-secret (1.4.2)
7. 30-year-old (1.4.2)
8. all-out, no-holds-barred struggle (1.4)
9. tiny metal (1.4)
10. usual cheerful, prompt service (1.4)

Chapter 5

1. good (1.5)
2. surely (1.5)
3. sick (1.5)
4. well (1.5)
5. good (1.5)
6. faster (1.5.2)
7. better (1.5.2)
8. any (1.5.1)
9. ever (1.5.1)
10. can, any (1.5.1)

Chapter 6

1. leading (1.6.1)
2. off (1.6.1)
3. aware of (1.6.1)
4. to (1.6.1)
5. among (1.6.1)
6. for (1.6.1)
7. to (1.6.1)
8. from (1.6.1)
9. not only in
10. the suitable experience (1.6.2)

Chapter 7

1. b (1.7.3)
2. a (1.7.2)
3. b (1.7.6)
4. a (1.7.4)
5. b (1.7.4)

6. b (1.7.6)
7. a (1.7.6)
8. b (1.7.4)
9. a (1.7.3)
10. b (1.7.2)

Chapter 8

1. c (2.6)
2. a (2.6)
3. b (2.6)
4. a (2.6)
5. b (2.6)
6. c (2.6)
7. b (2.6)
8. a (2.6)
9. c (2.6)
10. b (2.6)

Chapter 9

1. a (2.4)
2. a (2.5)
3. c (2.4)
4. a (2.5)
5. b (2.5)
6. b (2.4)
7. a (2.4)
8. c (2.4)
9. b (2.4)
10. c (2.5)

Chapter 10

1. b (2.1)
2. a (2.2)
3. b (2.1)
4. a (2.1)
5. b (2.2, 2.3)
6. b (2.1)
7. b (2.2, 2.1)
8. a (2.2)

9. b (2.2)

10. a (2.2, 2.3)

Chapter 11

1. b (2.7)
2. a (2.8)
3. c (2.7)
4. b (2.8)
5. a (2.7)
6. b (2.7)
7. c (2.8)
8. a (2.8, 2.7)
9. c (2.8, 2.7)
10. a (2.8)

Chapter 12

1. b (2.10)
2. b (2.11)
3. a (2.11)
4. b (2.10)
5. c (2.10)

6. a (2.11)
7. c (2.10, 2.12)
8. b (2.10)
9. b (2.11)
10. c (2.10, 2.12)

Chapter 13

1. c (3.1, 3.3)
2. a (3.1, 3.3)
3. b (3.2)
4. a (3.1)
5. c (3.3)
6. a (3.1, 3.2)
7. b (3.1, 3.3)
8. b (3.1, 3.3)
9. a (3.2)
10. c (3.1)

Chapter 14

1. c (3.4)
2. a (3.4)

3. a (3.4)
4. b (3.4)
5. b (3.4)
6. a (3.4)
7. b (3.4)
8. c (3.4)
9. a (3.4)
10. c (3.4)

Chapter 15

1. except (4.1)
2. device (4.1)
3. loath (4.1)
4. who's (4.1)
5. a lot (4.2)
6. judgment (4.3)
7. regardless (4.2)
8. accommodate (4.3)
9. imply (4.2)
10. to (4.2)

References

CHAPTER 1

1. Six Apart website [accessed 21 June 2005] www.sixapart.com; David Kirkpatrick and Daniel Roth, "Why There's No Escaping the Blog," Fortune, 10 January 2005, 44–50; "People of the Year," PC Magazine, 12 December 2004 [accessed 21 June 2005] www.pcmag.com; Thomas Mucha, "A Motor City Marketing Lesson," Business 2.0, 10 March 2005 [accessed 13 March 2005] www.business2.com; Lee Gomes, "How the Next Big Thing in Technology Morphed into a Really Big Thing," Wall Street Journal, 4 October 2004, B1; David Kirkpatrick, "It's Hard to Manage If You Don't Blog," Fortune, 4 October 2004, 46.

2. Julie Connelly, "Youthful Attitudes, Sobering Realities," New York Times, 28 October 2003, E1, E6; Nigel Andrews and Laura D'Andrea Tyson, "The Upwardly Global MBA," Strategy + Business, Issue 36, 6069; Jim McKay, "Communication Skills Found Lacking," Pittsburgh Post-Gazette, 28 February 2005 [accessed 28 February 2005] www.delawareonline.com.

3. Richard L. Daft, Management, 6th ed. (Cincinnati: Thomson South-Western, 2003), 580.

4. Daft, Management, 147.

5. Gareth R. Jones and Jennifer M. George, Contemporary Management, 3rd ed. (New York: McGraw-Hill Irwin, 2003), 512, 517.

6. Paula Jacobs, "Strong Writing Skills Essential for Success, Even in IT," InfoWorld, 6 July 1998, 86.

7. Philip C. Kolin, Successful Writing at Work, 6th ed. (Boston: Houghton Mifflin, 2001), 17–23.

8. Donald O. Wilson, "Diagonal Communication Links with Organizations," Journal of Business Communication 29, no. 2 (Spring 1992): 129–143.

9. J. David Johnson, William A. Donohoe, Charles K. Atkin, and Sally Johnson, "Differences Between Formal and Informal Communication Channels," Journal of Business Communication 31, no. 2 (1994): 111–122.

10. David Pescovitz, "Technology of the Year: Social Network Applications," Business 2.0, November 2003, 113–114.

11. Daft, Management, 107.

12. Jeff Davidson, "Fighting Information Overload," Canadian Manager, Spring 2005, 16+.

13. Chuck Williams, Management, 2nd ed. (Cincinnati: Thomson/SouthWestern, 2002), 690.

14. Don Hellriegel, Susan E. Jackson, and John W. Slocum, Jr., Management: A Competency-Based Approach (Cincinnati: Thomson/South-Western, 2002), 447.

15. Shirley Duglin Kennedy, "Finding a Cure for Information Anxiety," Information Today, May 2001, 40+.

16. Hellriegel et al., Management: A Competency-Based Approach, 451.

17. John Owens, "Good Communication in Workplace Is Basic to Getting Any Job Done," Knight Ridder Tribune Business News, 9 July 2003, 1.

18. Tamar Lewin, "Study Finds Widespread Neglect of Writing Skills," Desert Sun, 26 April 2003, A12.

19. Williams, Management, 706–707.

20. Del Jones, "Watch Your Language, Ladies," USA Today, 24 November 2004, 3B.

21. Jane Spencer, "The Annoying New Face of Customer Service—Virtual Phone Reps Replace the Old Touch-Tone Menus; Making Claire Less Irritating," Wall Street Journal, 21 January 2003, D1; Allison Fass, "Speak Easy," Forbes, 6 January 2003, 135.

22. "FNB Moves to Quell Fears (Uses SMS)," News24.com, 24 July 2003 [accessed 12 August 2003] www.news24.com; Daft, Management, 701–702.

23. A. Thomas Young, "Ethics in Business: Business of Ethics," Vital Speeches, 15 September 1992, 725–730.

24. "Undercover Marketing Uncovered," CBSnews.com, 25 July 2004 [accessed 11 April 2005] www.cbsnews.com; Stephanie Dunnewind, "Teen Recruits Create Word-of-Mouth 'Buzz' to Hook Peers on Products," Seattle Times, 20 November 2004 [accessed 11 April 2005] www.seattletimes.com.

25. Kolin, Successful Writing at Work, 24–30.

26. Kelli Esters, "Insurance Company to Repay $1.1 Million to Georgia Soldiers," Ledger-Enquirer (Columbus, GA), 26 May 2005 [accessed 28 June 2005] www.ebsco.com; Diana B. Henriques,"Insurer to Refund Money to Soldiers Who Bought High-Cost Life Policies," New York Times, 23 September 2004, C1, C4; Diana B. Henriques,"Going Off to War, and Vulnerable to the Pitches of Salesmen," New York Times, 20 July 2004, C1, C6.

27. Daft, Management, 155.

28. Joanne Sammer, "United Technologies Offers a Model for Reporting Ethical Issues," Workforce Management, August 2004, 64–66.

29. Maryann Napoli, "Rx News: Dietary Supplement Labels Are Found Wanting," HealthFacts, 1 June 2003, 5.

30. Based in part on Robert Kreitner, Management, 9th ed. (Boston: Houghton Mifflin, 2004), 163.

CHAPTER 2

1. "2005: Best Companies to Work For," Fortune, 24 January 2005 [accessed 11 March 2005] www.fortune.com; Bob Nelson, "Can't Contain Excitement at The Container Store," BizJournals.com [accessed 11 March 2005] www.bizjournals.com; Mike Duff, "Top-Shelf Employees Keep Container Store on Track," DSN Retailing Today, 8 March 2004, 7, 49; Bob Nelson, "The Buzz at The Container Store," Corporate Meetings & Incentives, June 2003, 32; Jennifer Saba, "Balancing Act," Potentials, 1 October 2003 [accessed 15 April 2004] www.highbeam.com; Peter S. Cohan, "Corporate Heroes," Financial Executive, 1 March 2003 [accessed 15 April 2004] www.highbeam.com; Margaret Steen, "Container Store's Focus on Training a Strong Appeal to Employees," Mercury News (San Jose, CA), 6 November 2003 [accessed 15 April 2004] www.highbeam.com; Holly Hayes, "Container Store Brings Clutter Control to San Jose, Calif.," 17 October 2003, Mercury News (San Jose, CA), 1F; "Performance Through People Award," press release, 10 September 2003; David Lipke, "Container Store's CEO: People Are Most Valued Asset," 13 January 2003, HFN [accessed 9 March 2003] www.highbeam.com; Lorrie Grant, "Container Store's Workers Huddle Up To Help You Out," 30 April 2002, USA Today, B1; The Container Store website [accessed 11 March 2005] www.containerstore.com.

2. Courtland L. Bovée and John V. Thill, Business in Action (Upper Saddle River, N.J.: Pearson Prentice Hall, 2005), 175.

3. "Five Case Studies on Successful Teams," HR Focus, April 2002, 18+.

4. Lynda McDermott, Bill Waite, and Nolan Brawley, "Executive Teamwork," Executive Excellence, May 1999, 15.

5. Larry Cole and Michael Cole, "Why Is the Teamwork Buzz Word Not Working?" Communication World, February–March 1999, 29; Patricia Buhler, "Managing in the 90s: Creating Flexibility in Today's Workplace," Supervision, January 1997, 24+; Allison W. Amason, Allen C. Hochwarter, Wayne A. Thompson, and Kenneth R. Harrison, "Conflict:

An Important Dimension in Successful Management Teams," *Organizational Dynamics,* Autumn 1995, 20+.

6. Daft, *Management,* 614.

7. Vijay Govindarajan and Anil K. Gupta, "Building an Effective Global Business Team," *MIT Sloan Management Review,* Summer 2001, 63+.

8. Stephen R. Robbins, *Essentials of Organizational Behavior,* 6th ed. (Upper Saddle River, N.J.: Prentice Hall, 2000), 98.

9. Jon Hanke, "Presenting as a Team," *Presentations,* January 1998, 74–82.

10. William P. Galle, Jr., Beverly H. Nelson, Donna W. Luse, and Maurice F. Villere, *Business Communication: A Technology-Based Approach* (Chicago: Irwin, 1996), 260.

11. Mary Beth Debs, "Recent Research on Collaborative Writing in Industry," *Technical Communication* (November 1991), 476–484.

12. Jared Sandberg, "Some Ideas Are So Bad That Only a Team Effort Can Account for Them," *Wall Street Journal,* 29 September 2004, B1.

13. B. Aubrey Fisher, *Small Group Decision Making: Communication and the Group Process,* 2d ed. (New York: McGraw-Hill, 1980), 145–149; Robbins and De Cenzo, *Fundamentals of Management,* 334–335; Daft, *Management,* 602–603.

14. Mark K. Smith, "Bruce W. Tuckman—Forming, Storming, Norming, and Performing in Groups," *Infed.org* [accessed 5 July 2005] www.infed.org.

15. Daft, *Management,* 609–612.

16. Thomas K. Capozzoli, "Conflict Resolution—A Key Ingredient in Successful Teams," *Supervision,* November 1999, 14–16.

17. Janis Graham, "Sharpen Your Negotiating Skills," *Sylvia Porter's Personal Finance,* December 1985, 54–58.

18. Amason, Hochwarter, Thompson, and Harrison, "Conflict."

19. Jesse S. Nirenberg, *Getting Through to People* (Paramus, N.J.: Prentice Hall, 1973), 134–142.

20. Nirenberg, *Getting Through to People.*

21. Nirenberg, *Getting Through to People.*

22. Dana May Casperson, *Power Etiquette: What You Don't Know Can Kill Your Career* (New York: AMACOM, 1999), 9.

23. Marilyn Pincus, *Everyday Business Etiquette* (Hauppauge, N.Y.: Barron's Educational Series, 1996), 7, 133.

24. Pincus, *Everyday Business Etiquette,* 136.

25. Casperson, *Power Etiquette: What You Don't Know Can Kill Your Career,* 23.

26. Gerald H. Graham, Jeanne Unrue, and Paul Jennings, "The Impact of Nonverbal Communication in Organizations: A Survey of Perceptions," *Journal of Business Communication* 28, no. 1 (Winter 1991): 45–62.

27. Pincus, *Everyday Business Etiquette,* 100–101.

28. Maggie Jackson, "Turn Off That Cellphone. It's Meeting Time," *New York Times,* 2 March 2003, 3, 12.

29. Casperson, *Power Etiquette: What You Don't Know Can Kill Your Career,* 10–14; Ellyn Spragins, "Introducing Politeness," *Fortune Small Business,* November 2001, 30.

30. Tanya Mohn, "The Social Graces As a Business Tool," *New York Times,* 10 November 2002, 3, 12.

31. Casperson, *Power Etiquette: What You Don't Know Can Kill Your Career,* 19; Pincus, *Everyday Business Etiquette,* 7–8.

32. Casperson, *Power Etiquette: What You Don't Know Can Kill Your Career,* 44–46.

33. Casperson, *Power Etiquette: What You Don't Know Can Kill Your Career,* 109–110.

34. "Better Meetings Benefit Everyone: How to Make Yours More Productive," *Working Communicator Bonus Report,* July 1998, 1.

35. Ken Blanchard, "Meetings Can Be Effective," *Supervisory Management,* October 1992, 5.

36. "Better Meetings Benefit Everyone."

37. Anne Fisher, "Get Employees to Brainstorm Online," *Fortune,* 29 November 2004, 72.

38. Kathleen Melymuka, "Far from the Mothership," *Computerworld,* 9 December 2002, 47.

39. Jefferson Graham, "Instant Messaging Programs Are No Longer Just for Messages," *USA Today,* 20 October 2003, 5D; Todd R. Weiss, "Microsoft Targets Corporate Instant Messaging Customers," *Computerworld,* 18 November 2002, 12; "Banks Adopt Instant Messaging To Create a Global Business Network," *Computer Weekly,* 25 April 2002, 40; Michael D. Osterman, "Instant Messaging in the Enterprise," *Business Communications Review,* January 2003, 59–62; John Pallato, "Instant Messaging Unites Work Groups and Inspires Collaboration," *Internet World,* December 2002, 14+.

40. Mark Gibbs, "Racing to Instant Messaging," *NetworkWorld,* 17 February 2003, 74.

41. Jenny Goodbody, "Critical Success Factors for Global Virtual Teams," *Strategic Communication Management,* February–March 2005, 18–21; Ann Majchrzak, Arvind Malhotra, Jeffrey Stamps, and Jessica Lipnack, "Can Absence Make a Team Grow Stronger?" *Harvard Business Review,* May 2004, 131–137; Christine Y. Chen, "The IM Invasion," *Fortune,* 26 May 2003, 135–138; Yudhijit Bhattacharjee, "A Swarm of Little Notes," *Time,* September 2002, A3–A8; Mark Bruno, "Taming the Wild Frontiers of Instant Messaging," *Bank Technology News,* December 2002, 30–31; Richard Grigonis, "Enterprise-Strength Instant Messaging," *Convergence.com,* 10–15 [accessed March 2003] www.convergence.com.

42. Pallato, "Instant Messaging Unites Work Groups and Inspires Collaboration," 14+.

43. Anita Hamilton, "You've Got Spim!" *Time,* 2 February 2004, [accessed 1 March 2004], www.time.com.

44. Tony Kontzer, "Learning To Share," *InformationWeek,* 5 May 2003, 28; Jon Udell, "Uniting Under Groove," *InfoWorld,* 17 February 2003 [accessed 9 September 2003] www.elibrary.com; Alison Overholt, "Virtually There?" *Fast Company,* 14 February 2002, 108.

45. Nicole Ridgway, "A Safer Place to Meet," *Forbes,* 28 April 2003, 97.

46. Judi Brownell, *Listening,* 2d edition (Boston: Allyn and Bacon, 2002), 9, 10.

47. Augusta M. Simon, "Effective Listening: Barriers to Listening in a Diverse Business Environment," *Bulletin of the Association for Business Communication* 54, no. 3 (September 1991): 73–74.

48. Robyn D. Clarke, "Do You Hear What I Hear?" *Black Enterprise,* May 1998, 129.

49. Eric Engleman, "Financial Finesse," *Puget Sound Business Journal,* 5–11 November 2004, 8A.

50. Larry Barker and Kittie Watson, *Listen Up,* (New York: St. Martin's, 2000), 24–27.

51. Terri Somers, "Gen-Probe's Nordhoff Listens Well, Then Acts," *San Diego Union-Tribune,* 2 November 2004, C1, C6.

52. Dennis M. Kratz and Abby Robinson Kratz, *Effective Listening Skills* (New York: McGraw-Hill, 1995), 45–53; J. Michael Sproule, *Communication Today* (Glenview, Ill.: Scott, Foresman, 1981), 69.

53. Brownell, *Listening,* 230–231.

54. Kratz and Kratz, *Effective Listening Skills,* 78–79; Sproule, *Communication Today.*

55. Bob Lamons, "Good Listeners Are Better Communicators," *Marketing News,* 11 September 1995, 13+; Phillip Morgan and H. Kent Baker, "Building a Professional Image: Improving Listening Behavior," *Supervisory Management,* November 1985, 35–36.

56. Clarke, "Do You Hear What I Hear?" Dot Yandle, "Listening to Understand," *Pryor Report Management Newsletter Supplement* 15, no. 8 (August 1998): 13.

57. Brownell, *Listening,* 14; Kratz and Kratz, *Effective Listening Skills,* 8–9; Sherwyn P. Morreale and Courtland L. Bovée, *Excellence in Public Speaking* (Orlando, Fla.: Harcourt Brace, 1998), 72–76; Lyman K. Steil, Larry L. Barker, and Kittie W. Watson, *Effective Listening: Key to Your Success* (Reading, Mass.: Addison-Wesley, 1983), 21–22.

58. Patrick J. Collins, *Say It with Power and Confidence* (Upper Saddle River, N.J.: Prentice Hall, 1997), 40–45.

59. Morreale and Bovée, *Excellence in Public Speaking,* 296.

60. Judee K. Burgoon, David B. Butler, and W. Gill Woodall, *Nonverbal Communication: The Unspoken Dialog* (New York: McGraw-Hill, 1996), 137.

61. "Study: Human Lie Detectors Rarely Wrong," *CNN.com,* 14 October 2004 [accessed 14 October 2004] www.cnn.com.

62. Dale G. Leathers, *Successful Nonverbal Communication: Principles and Applications* (New York: Macmillan, 1986), 19.

63. Gerald H. Graham, Jeanne Unrue, and Paul Jennings, "The Impact of Nonverbal Communication in Organizations: A Survey of Perceptions," *Journal of Business Communication* 28, no. 1 (Winter 1991): 45–62.

64. Virginia P. Richmond and James C. McCroskey, *Nonverbal Behavior in Interpersonal Relations* (Boston: Allyn and Bacon, 2000), 153–157.

65. Richmond and McCroskey, *Nonverbal Behavior in Interpersonal Relations,* 2–3.

CHAPTER 3

1. "Executive Corner: Letter from IBM's Vice President, Global Workforce Diversity," IBM website [accessed 5 July 2005] www.ibm.com; "IBM—Diversity as a Strategic Imperative," *Global Diversity @ Work* [accessed 6 July 2005] www.diversityatwork.com; Cliff Edwards, "The Rewards of Tolerance," *BusinessWeek,* 15 December 2003 [accessed 6 July 2005] www.businessweek.com; David A. Thomas, "IBM Finds Profit in Diversity," *HBS Working Knowledge,* 27 September 2004 [accessed 5 July 2005] http://hbswk.hbs.edu; "IBM Diversity Executive to Speak at the University of Virginia," *University of Virginia News,* 7 November 2003 [accessed 5 July 2005] www.virginia.edu; IBM website [accessed 5 July 2005] www.ibm.com.

2. Ford Motor Co. website [accessed 12 July 2005] www.ford.com.

3. Pgymy Boats website [accessed 12 July 2005] www.pygmyboats.com.

4. Giardino Italiano website [accessed 12 July 2005] www.giardino.it.

5. Carol Hymowitz, "Managers Err If They Limit Their Hiring to People Like Them," *Wall Street Journal,* 12 October 2004, B1.

6. Rona Gindin, "Dealing with a Multicultural Workforce," *Nation's Restaurant News,* September–October 1998, 31, 83; Howard Gleckman, "A Rich Stew in the Melting Pot," *Business Week,* 31 August 1998, 76+; Toby B. Gooley, "A World of Difference," *Logistics Management and Distribution Report,* June 2000, 51–55; William H. Miller, "Beneath the Surface," *Industry Week,* 20 September 1999, 13–16.

7. Kreitner, *Management,* 84.

8. Linda Beamer and Iris Varner, *Intercultural Communication in the Workplace,* 2d ed. (New York: McGraw-Hill Irwin, 2001), xiii.

9. Tracy Novinger, *Intercultural Communication, A Practical Guide* (Austin, TX: University of Texas Press, 2001), 15.

10. Beamer and Varner, *Intercultural Communication in the Workplace,* 3.

11. Philip R. Harris and Robert T. Moran, *Managing Cultural Differences,* 3d ed. (Houston: Gulf, 1991), 394–397, 429–430.

12. Lillian H. Chaney and Jeanette S. Martin, *Intercultural Business Communication* (Upper Saddle River, N.J.: Prentice Hall, 2000), 6.

13. Beamer and Varner, *Intercultural Communication in the Workplace,* 4.

14. Chaney and Martin, *Intercultural Business Communication,* 9.

15. Richard L. Daft, *Management,* 6th ed. (Cincinnati: Thomson South-Western, 2003), 455.

16. Project Implicit website [accessed 12 July 2005] https:/implicit.harvard.edu/implicit.

17. Larry A. Samovar and Richard E. Porter, "Basic Principles of Intercultural Communication," in *Intercultural Communication: A Reader,* 6th ed., edited by Larry A. Samovar and Richard E. Porter (Belmont, Calif.: Wadsworth, 1991), 12.

18. Lalita Khosla, "You Say Tomato," *Forbes* Best of the Web, 21 May 2001, 36.

19. Lionel Laroche, "Cultural Miscues Lose Top Staff," *Canadian HR Reporter,* 21 April 2003, 4.

20. Chaney and Martin, *Intercultural Business Communication,* 159.

21. Linda Beamer, "Teaching English Business Writing to Chinese-Speaking Business Students," *Bulletin of the Association for Business Communication* 57, no. 1 (1994): 12–18.

22. Edward T. Hall, "Context and Meaning," in *Intercultural Communication,* edited by Samovar and Porter, 46–55.

23. Daft, *Management,* 459.

24. Beamer, "Teaching English Business Writing to Chinese-Speaking Business Students."

25. Charley H. Dodd, *Dynamics of Intercultural Communication,* 3d ed. (Dubuque, Iowa: Brown, 1991), 69–70.

26. Daft, *Management,* 459.

27. Beamer and Varner, *Intercultural Communication in the Workplace,* 230–233.

28. James Wilfong and Toni Seger, *Taking Your Business Global* (Franklin Lakes, N.J.: Career Press, 1997), 277–278.

29. Harris and Moran, *Managing Cultural Differences,* 260.

30. Skip Kaltenheuser, "Bribery Is Being Outlawed Virtually Worldwide," *Business Ethics,* May–June 1998, 11; Thomas Omestad, "Bye-Bye to Bribes," *U.S. News & World Report,* 22 December 1997, 39, 42–44.

31. "Big Oil's Dirty Secrets," *The Economist,* 10 May 2003, 62; Skip Kaltenheuser, "A Little Dab Will Do You?" *World Trade,* January 1999, 58–63; James Walsh, "A World War on Bribery," *Time,* 22 June 1998, 16.

32. Guo-Ming Chen and William J. Starosta, *Foundations of Intercultural Communication* (Boston: Allyn & Bacon, 1998), 288–289.

33. Mary A. DeVries, *Internationally Yours* (New York: Houghton Mifflin, 1994), 194.

34. Robert O. Joy, "Cultural and Procedural Differences That Influence Business Strategies and Operations in the People's Republic of China," *SAM Advanced Management Journal* (Summer 1989): 29–33.

35. Chaney and Martin, *Intercultural Business Communication,* 122–123.

36. Novinger, *Intercultural Communication: A Practical Guide,* 54.

37. Beamer and Varner, *Intercultural Communication in the Workplace,* 107–108.

38. Beamer and Varner, *Intercultural Communication in the Workplace,* 107–108.

39. Michael Kinsman, "Respect Helps Mix of Generations Work Well Together," *San Diego Union-Tribune,* 19 September 2004, H2.

40. Ann Harrington and Petra Bartosiewicz, "50 Most Powerful Women," *Fortune,* 18 October 2004, 181–190.

41. Tonya Vinas, "A Place at the Table," *Industry Week,* 1 July 2003, 22.

42. Daft, *Management,* 445.

43. John Gray, *Mars and Venus in the Workplace* (New York: Harper Collins, 2002), 10, 25–27, 61–63.

44. P. Christopher Earley and Elaine Mosakowsi, "Cultural Intelligence," *Harvard Business Review,* October 2004, 139–146.

45. Craig S. Smith, "Beware of Green Hats in China and Other Cross-cultural Faux Pas," *New York Times,* 30 April 2002, C11.

46. Francesca Bargiela-Chiappini, Anne Marie Bülow-Møller, Catherine Nickerson, Gina Poncini, and Yunxia Zhu, "Five Perspectives on Intercultural Business Communication," *Business Communication Quarterly* (September 2003): 73–96.

47. Paul Johnson, "Must the Whole World Speak English?" *Forbes,* 29 November 2004, 39; Randolph E. Schmid, "Study Says English Language Is Losing Cultural Dominance," *Desert Sun,* 29 February 2004, A25.

48. Miki Fujii, "English: Bane or Blessing? English Transforms Nissan, Mazda Culture," *Yomiuri Shimbun,* 1 April 2000, 1.

49. Mary Beth Sheridan, "Learning the New Language of Labor," *Washington Post,* 20 August 2002, A1.

50. Bob Nelson, "Motivating Workers Worldwide," *Global Workforce,* November 1998, 25–27.

51. Mona Casady and Lynn Wasson, "Written Communication Skills of International Business Persons," *Bulletin of the Association for Business Communication* 57, no. 4 (1994): 36–40.

52. Myron W. Lustig and Jolene Koester, *Intercultural Competence,* 4th ed., (Boston: Allyn and Bacon, 2003), 196.

53. Daren Fonda, "Selling in Tongues," *Time,* 26 November 2001, B12+.

54. Wilfong and Seger, *Taking Your Business Global,* 232.

55. Mark Lasswell, "Lost in Translation," *Business 2.0,* August 2004, 68–70.

56. Sheridan Prasso (ed.), "It's All Greek to These Sites," *Business Week,* 22 July 2002, 18.

CHAPTER 4

1. Chris Taylor, "One-Minute Photo Smile!," *Time,* 23 December 2002, 80; "Writers Seek Simple Ways To Describe New Products," *Washington Times,* 7 November 2002 [accessed 28 October 2003] www.elibrary. com; Caroline E. Mayer, "Why Won't We Read the Manual?," *Washington Post,* 26 May 2002, H01.

2. Sanford Kaye, "Writing Under Pressure," *Soundview Executive Book Summaries* 10, no. 12, part 2 (December 1988): 1–8.

3. Peter Bracher, "Process, Pedagogy, and Business Writing," *Journal of Business Communication* 24, no. 1 (Winter 1987): 43–50.

4. Laurey Berk and Phillip G. Clampitt, "Finding the Right Path in the Communication Maze," *IABC Communication World,* October 1991, 28–32.

5. Berk and Clampitt, "Finding the Right Path in the Communication Maze."

6. Jon Van, "Technology Notebook Column," *Chicago Tribune,* 13 March 2004 [accessed 19 March 2004] www.ebsco.com.

7. Kris Maher, "The Jungle," *Wall Street Journal,* 5 October 2004, B10.

8. Kevin Maney, "Surge in Text Messaging Makes Cell Operators :-)," *USA Today,* 28 July 2005, B1–B2.

9. David Kirkpatrick, "It's Hard to Manage If You Don't Blog," *Fortune,* 4 October 2004, 46; Lee Gomes, "How the Next Big Thing in Technology Morphed into a Really Big Thing," *Wall Street Journal,* 4 October 2004, B1; Jeff Meisner, "Cutting Through the Blah, Blah, Blah," *Puget Sound Business Journal,* 19–25 November 2004, 27–28; Lauren Gard, "The Business of Blogging," *BusinessWeek,* 13 December 2004, 117–119; Heather Green, "Online Video: The Sequel," *BusinessWeek,* 10 January 2005, 40; Michelle Conlin and Andrew Park, "Blogging with the Boss's Blessing," *BusinessWeek,* 28 June 2004, 100–102.

10. Berk and Clampitt, "Finding the Right Path in the Communication Maze."

11. Berk and Clampitt, "Finding the Right Path in the Communication Maze."

12. Berk and Clampitt, "Finding the Right Path in the Communication Maze."

13. Raymond M. Olderman, *10 Minute Guide to Business Communication* (New York: Alpha Books, 1997), 19–20.

14. Mohan R. Limaye and David A. Victor, "Cross-Cultural Business Communication Research: State of the Art and Hypotheses for the 1990s," *Journal of Business Communication* 28, no. 3 (Summer 1991): 277–299.

15. Holly Weeks, "The Best Memo You'll Ever Write," *Harvard Management Communication Letter,* Spring 2005, 3–5.

CHAPTER 5

1. Creative Commons website [accessed 3 August 2005] www. creativecommons.org; Ariana Eunjung Cha, "Creative Commons Is Rewriting Rules of Copyright," *Washington Post,* 15 March 2005 [accessed 3 August 2005] www.washingtonpost.com; Steven Levy, "Lawrence Lessig's Supreme Showdown," *Wired,* October 2002 [accessed 3 August 2005] www.wired.com; "Happy Birthday: We'll Sue," Snopes.com [accessed 3 August 2005] www.snopes.com.

2. Elizabeth Blackburn and Kelly Belanger, "You-Attitude and Positive Emphasis: Testing Received Wisdom in Business Communication," *Bulletin of the Association for Business Communication* 56, no. 2 (June 1993): 1–9.

3. Placard at Alaska Airlines ticket counters, Seattle-Tacoma International Airport, 3 October 2003.

4. Annette N. Shelby and N. Lamar Reinsch, Jr., "Positive Emphasis and You Attitude: An Empirical Study," *Journal of Business Communication* 32, no. 4 (1995): 303–322.

5. Sherryl Kleinman, "Why Sexist Language Matters," *Qualitative Sociology,* Vol. 25, No. 2, Summer 2002, 299–304.

6. Judy E. Pickens, "Terms of Equality: A Guide to Bias-Free Language," *Personnel Journal,* August 1985, 24.

7. Lisa Taylor, "Communicating About People with Disabilities: Does the Language We Use Make a Difference?" *Bulletin of the Association for Business Communication* 53, no. 3 (September 1990): 65–67.

8. Susan Benjamin, *Words at Work* (Reading, Mass.: Addison-Wesley, 1997), 136–137.

9. Stuart Crainer and Des Dearlove, "Making Yourself Understood," *Across the Board,* May–June 2004, 23–27.

10. Plain English Campaign website [accessed 3 October 2003] www.plainenglish.co.uk.

11. Securities and Exchange Commission website [accessed 3 October 2003], www.sec.gov/news/extra/handbook.htm; Deloitte Consulting website [accessed 3 October 2003], www.dc.com/insights/bullfighter/index.asp.

12. Peter Crow, "Plain English: What Counts Besides Readability?" *Journal of Business Communication* 25, no. 1 (Winter 1988): 87–95.

13. Susan Jaderstrom and Joanne Miller, "Active Writing," *Office Pro,* November–December 2003, 29.

14. Portions of this section are adapted from Courtland L. Bovée, *Techniques of Writing Business Letters, Memos, and Reports* (Sherman Oaks, Calif.: Banner Books International, 1978), 13–90.

15. Robert Hartwell Fiske, *The Dimwit's Dictionary* (Oak Park, IL: Marion Street Press, 2002), 16–20.

16. David A. Fryxell, "Lost in Transition?" *Writers Digest,* January 2005, 24–26.

17. Reid Goldsborough, "'Creeping Informality' Can Be Big Mistake in Business E-Mails," *New Orleans City Business,* 14 March 2005, 18; Jack E. Appleman, "Bad Writing Can Cost Insurers Time & Money," *National Underwriter,* 27 September 2004, 34; Adina Genn, "RE: This Is an Important Message, Really," *Long Island Business News,* 5–11 December 2003, 21A; Lynn Lofton, "Regardless of What You Thought, Grammer Rules *Do* Apply to E-Mail," *Mississippi Business Journal,* 23–29 May 2005, 1.

18. Matt Cain, "Managing E-Mail Hygiene," *ZD Net Tech Update,* 5 February 2004 [accessed 19 March 2004] www.techupdate.zdnet.com.

19. Mary Munter, Priscilla S. Rogers, and Jone Rymer, "Business E-mail: Guidelines for Users," *Business Communication Quarterly,* March 2003, 26+; Horowitz and Barchilon, "Stylistic Guidelines for E-Mail."

20. Crainer and Dearlove, "Making Yourself Understood."

CHAPTER 6

1. Katharine Q. Seelye, "With a New Editor, Rolling Stone Rejects Its Inner Lad," *New York Times,* 16 May 2005, C6; Louise Roug, "A Rock Institution Rolls Away Wrinkles," *Los Angeles Times,* 30 August 2002, E1+; Allison Fass, "Reality Bites," 25 November 2002, *Forbes,* 242; Lisa Granatstein, "Not Fade Away," 21 October 2002, *Brandweek,* SR6; Jenna Schnuer, "Launch of the Year," *Advertising Age,* S8; Michael Grossman, "Rolling Revisions," October 2002, *Folio,* 66; Anthony Violanti, "Rolling Stone Losing the Youth Battle," 21 June 2002, *Buffalo News,* C.1.

2. William Zinsser, *On Writing Well,* 5th ed. (New York: HarperCollins, 1994), 9.

3. Zinsser, *On Writing Well,* 7, 17.

4. Mary A. DeVries, *Internationally Yours* (Boston: Houghton Mifflin, 1994), 160.

5. Zinsser, *On Writing Well,* 126.

6. Deborah Gunn, "Looking Good on Paper," *Office Pro,* March 2004, 10–11.

7. Jennifer Saranow, "Memo to Web Sites: Grow Up!" *Wall Street Journal,* 15 November 2004, R14–R15.

8. Jacci Howard Bear, "Desktop Publishing Rules of Page Layout," *About.com* [accessed 22 August 2005] www.about.com.

9. Jacci Howard Bear, "Desktop Publishing Rules for How Many Fonts to Use," *About.com* [accessed 22 August 2005] www.about.com.

10. Debbie Weil, "5 Key Questions (You've Been Dying) to Ask About Business Blogs," *Wordbiz Report,* 25 June 2003 [accessed 27 October 2003] www.wordbiz.com; Jonathan Eisenzopf, "Making Headlines with RSS: Using Rich Site Summaries to Draw New Visitors," *New Architect* website [accessed 28 October 2003] www.webtechniques.com.

11. Benjamin, *Words at Work,* 121.

CHAPTER 7

1. Feeding Children Better website [accessed 18 July 2005] www.feedingchildrenbetter.org; "Awards & Accolades," Cone Inc. website, [accessed 18 July 2005], www.coneinc.com; "Platinum PR Award Winner: Cause-Related Marketing; ConAgra Program Combats Child Hunger," 13 October 2003, *PR News,* 1; Jennifer Comiteau, "Do Do-gooders Do Better?" 29 September 2003, *AdWeek,* 24; "ConAgra Foods Donates Refrigerated Trucks from Former Dot-com Webvan to Help Feed Hungry Americans," 2 May 2002, *PR Newswire,* 1.

2. "Review Offer Letters Carefully to Avoid Binding Promises," *Fair Employment Practices Guidelines,* 15 May 2001, 5–6.

3. Fraser P. Seitel, *The Practice of Public Relations, 9th ed.* (Upper Saddle River, N.J.: Pearson Prentice-Hall, 2004), 402–411; *Techniques for Communicators* (Chicago: Lawrence Ragan Communication, 1995), 34, 36.

4. Mary Mitchell, "The Circle of Life—Condolence Letters," LiveandLearn.com [accessed 18 July 2005] www.liveandlearn.com; Donna Larcen, "Authors Share the Words of Condolence," *Los Angeles Times,* 20 December 1991, E11.

5. Adapted from Floorgraphics website [accessed 18 June 2001] www.floorgraphics.com; John Grossman, "It's an Ad, Ad, Ad, Ad World," *Inc.,* March 2000, 23–26; David Wellman, "Floor 'Toons,'" *Supermarket Business,* 15 November 1999, 47; "Floorshow," *Dallas Morning News,* 4 September 1998, 11D.

6. Adapted from Tom Abate, "Need to Preserve Cash Generates Wave of Layoffs in Biotech Industry," *San Francisco Chronicle,* 10 February 2003 [accessed 18 July 2005] www.sfgate.com.

7. Adapted from Lisa DiCarlo, "IBM Gets the Message—Instantly," Forbes.com, 7 July 2002 [accessed 22 July 2003], www.forbes.com/home/2002/07/0723ibm.html; "IBM Introduces Breakthrough Messaging Technology for Customers and Business Partners," *M2 Presswire,* 19 February 2003 [accessed 24 July 2003], www.proquest.com; "IBM and America Online Team for Instant Messaging Pilot," *M2 Presswire,* 4 February 2003 [accessed 24 July 2003] www.proquest.com.

8. Adapted from CES website [accessed 18 July 2005] www.cesweb.org.

9. Adapted from Michael Mescon, Courtland Bovée, and John Thill, *Business Today,* 10th ed. (Upper Saddle River, NJ: Prentice Hall, 2002), 220.

10. Adapted from Jane Costello, "Check Your Insurance Before Renting an SUV," *Wall Street Journal,* 13 June 2001 [accessed 14 June 2001], http://interactive.wsj.com/articles/SB991402678854239871.htm.

11. Adapted from John Noble Wilford, "An Old Observatory Finds a New Life," *New York Times,* 3 July 2001 [accessed on 3 July 2001], www.nytimes.com/2001/07/03/science/03WILS.html.

12. Adapted from Dylan Tweney, "The Defogger: Slim Down that Homepage," *Business 2.0,* 13 July 2001 [accessed 1 August 2001] www.business2.com/articles/web/0,1653,16483,FF.html.

13. Adapted from Davide Dukcevich, "Instant Business: Retailer Lands' End Profits from Online Chat," Forbes.com, Special to ABCNEWS.com, 29 July 2002 [accessed 21 July 2003], http://abcnews.go.com/sections/business/DailyNews/forbes_landsend.com; Lands' End website [accessed 5 December 2003], www.landsend.com; Forbes.com staff, "Instant Messaging at Work," Forbes.com, 26 July 2002 [accessed 21 July 2003], www.forbes.com/2002/07/23/0723im/html; Tischelle George and Sandra Swanson with Christopher T. Heun, "Not Just Kid Stuff," *InformationWeek,* 3 September 2001 [accessed 21 July 2003], www.informationweek.com/story/IWK20010830S0030.

14. Public Relations Society of America website [accessed 18 June 2005] www.prsa.org.

15. Adapted from Mitchell, "The Circle of Life—Condolence Letters," LiveandLearn.com; Donna Larcen, "Authors Share the Words of Condolence," *Los Angeles Times,* 20 December 1991, E11.

CHAPTER 8

1. "Inside the KPMG Mess," *BusinessWeek,* 1 September 2005 [accessed 1 September 2005] www.businessweek.com; KPMG Careers website [accessed 19 August 2005] www.kpmgcareers.com; "KPMG LLP Statement Regarding Department of Justice Matter," press release, 16 June 2005 [accessed 19 August 2005] www.us.kpmg.com; "KPMG May Avoid Indictment as U.S. Pushes Settlement, People Say," *Bloomberg.com,* 4 August 2005 [accessed 19 August 2005] www.bloomberg.com; "KPMG Offers Apology Over Illegal Tax Shelters," *Boston Globe,* 17 June 2005 [accessed 19 August 2005] www.boston.com; Jeff Bailey and Lynnley Browning, "KPMG May Dodge One Bullet, Only to Face Another," *New York Times,* 21 June 2005 [accessed 19 August 2005] www.nytimes.com.

2. Carol David and Margaret Ann Baker, "Rereading Bad News: Compliance-Gaining Features in Management Memos," *Journal of Business Communication,* October 1994 [accessed 1 December 2003] www.elibrary.com.

3. Chad Terhune, "CEO Says Things Aren't Going Better with Coke," *Wall Street Journal,* 16 September 2004, A1, A10.

4. Ian McDonald, "Marsh Can Do $600 Million, But Apologize?" *Wall Street Journal,* 14 January 2005, C1, C3; Adrienne Carter and Amy Borrus, "What If Companies Fessed Up?" *BusinessWeek,* 24 January 2005, 59–60; Patrick J. Kiger, "The Art of the Apology," *Workforce Management,* October 2004, 57–62.

5. Ameeta Patel and Lamar Reinsch, "Companies Can Apologize: Corporate Apologies and Legal Liability," *Business Communication Quarterly,* March 2003 [accessed 1 December 2003] www.elibrary.com.

6. Iris I. Varner, "A Comparison of American and French Business Correspondence," *Journal of Business Communication* 24, no. 4 (Fall 1988): 55–65.

7. Susan Jenkins and John Hinds, "Business Letter Writing: English, French, and Japanese," *TESOL Quarterly* 21, no. 2 (June 1987): 327–349; Saburo Haneda and Hiosuke Shima, "Japanese Communication Behavior As Reflected in Letter Writing," *Journal of Business Communication* 19, no. 1 (1982): 19–32.

8. James Calvert Scott and Diana J. Green, "British Perspectives on Organizing Bad-News Letters: Organizational Patterns Used by Major U.K. Companies," *Bulletin of the Association for Business Communication* 55, no. 1 (March 1992): 17–19.

9. "Need To Deliver Bad News? How and Why to Tell It Like It Is," *HR Focus,* November 2003 [accessed 1 December 2003] www.elibrary.com.

10. Jeffrey Pfeffer, "The Whole Truth and Nothing But," *Business 2.0,* October 2004, 78.

11. Walter Kiechel III, " Breaking Bad News to the Boss," *Fortune,* 9 April 1990 [accessed 2 December 2003] www.elibrary.com

12. "Advice from the Pros on the Best Way To Deliver Bad News," *Report on Customer Relationship Management,* 1 February 2003 [accessed 1 December 2003] www.elibrary.com.

13. Susanne Craig, "Morgan Stanley Is Fined Over Bad-News Delay," *Wall Street Journal,* 30 July 2004, C1, C3.

14. Anna Wilde Mathews, "New Web Site to Offer Results of Drug Studies," *Wall Street Journal,* 7 September 2004, B1, B4.

15. Courtand L. Bovée, John V. Thill, George P. Dovel, and Marian Burk Wood, *Advertising Excellence* (New York: McGraw-Hill, 1995), 508–509; John Holusha. "Exxon's Public-Relations Problem," *New York Times,* 12 April 1989, D1.

16. Patrick J. Kiger, "Dealing with Disaster," *Workforce Management,* November 2004, 30–38.

17. "Throw Out the Old Handbook in Favor of Today's Crisis Drills," *PR News,* 27 January 2003, 1.

18. Maura Dolan and Stuart Silverstein, "Court Broadens Liability for Job References," *Los Angeles Times,* 28 January 1997, A1, A11; Frances A. McMorris, "Ex-Bosses Face Less Peril Giving Honest Job References," *Wall Street Journal,* 8 July 1996, B1, B8.

19. Thomas S. Brice and Marie Waung, "Applicant Rejection Letters: Are Businesses Sending the Wrong Message?" *Business Horizons,* March–April 1995, 59–62.

20. Gwendolyn N. Smith, Rebecca F. Nolan, and Yong Dai, "Job-Refusal Letters: Readers' Affective Responses to Direct and Indirect Organizational Plans," *Business Communication Quarterly* 59, no. 1 (1996): 67–73; Brice and Waung, "Applicant Rejection Letters."

21. Judi Brownell, "The Performance Appraisal Interviews: A Multipurpose Communication Assignment," *Bulletin of the Association for Business Communication* 57, no. 2 (1994): 11–21.

22. Brownell, "The Performance Appraisal Interviews."

23. Stephanie Gruner, "Feedback from Everyone," *Inc.,* February 1997, 102–103.

24. Howard M. Bloom, "Performance Evaluations," *New England Business,* December 1991, 14.

25. David I. Rosen, "Appraisals Can Make—or Break—Your Court Case," *Personnel Journal,* November 1992, 113.

26. Patricia A. McLagan, "Advice for Bad-News Bearers: How to Tell Employees They're Not Hacking It and Get Results," *Industry Week,* 15 February 1993, 42; Michael Lee Smith, "Give Feedback, Not Criticism," *Supervisory Management,* 1993, 4; "A Checklist for Conducting Problem Performer Appraisals," *Supervisory Management,* December 1993, 7–9.

27. Carrie Brodzinski, "Avoiding Wrongful Termination Suits," *National Underwriter Property & Casualty—Risk & Benefits Management,* 13 October 2003 [accessed 2 December 2003] www.elibrary.com.

28. Jane R. Goodson, Gail W. McGee, and Anson Seers, "Giving Appropriate Performance Feedback to Managers: An Empirical Test of Content and Outcomes," *Journal of Business Communication* 29, no. 4 (1992): 329–342.

29. Craig Cox, "On the Firing Line," *Business Ethics,* May–June 1992, 33–34.

30. Cox, "On the Firing Line."

31. See Note 1.

32. Adapted from Michael H. Mescon, Courtland L. Bovée, and John V. Thill, *Business Today,* 10th ed. (Upper Saddle River, N.J.: Prentice Hall, 2002), 369; Bruce Upbin, "Profit in a Big Orange Box," *Forbes,* 165, no. 2, 24 January 2000 (accessed 2 August 2001) www.forbes.com/forbes/2000/0124/6502122a.html.

33. Michelle Higgins, "The Ballet Shoe Gets a Makeover, But Few Yet See the Pointe," *Wall Street Journal,* 8 August 1998, A1, A6; Gaynor Minden website [accessed 17 December 2003] www.dancer.com; American Ballet Theatre website [accessed 17 December 2003] www.abt.org.

34. Adapted from Wolf Blitzer, "More Employers Taking Advantages of New Cyber-Surveillance Software," *CNN.com,* 10 July 2000 [accessed 11 July 2000] www.cnn.com/2000/US/07/10/workplace.eprivacy/index.html.

35. Adapted from "FDA Notifies Public That Vail Products, Inc., Issues Nationwide Recall of Enclosed Bed Systems," FDA press release, 30 June 2005 [accessed 18 August 2005] www.fda.gov.

36. Adapted from "Bathtub Curve," *Engineering Statistics Handbook,* National Institute of Standards and Technology website [accessed 16 April 2005] www.nist.gov; Robert Berner, "The Warranty Windfall," *BusinessWeek,* 20 December 2004, 84–86; Larry Armstrong, "When Service Contracts Make Sense," *BusinessWeek,* 20 December 2004, 86.

37. Adapted from Union Bank of California teleservices, personal communication, 16 August 2001.

38. Adapted from Pui-Wing Tam, Erin White, Nick Wingfield, and Kris Maher, "Snooping E-Mail by Software Is Now a Workplace Norm," *Wall Street Journal,* 9 March 2005, B1+.

39. Adapted from Sylvia Ann Hewlett and Carolyn Buck Luce, "Off-Ramps and On-Ramps," *Harvard Business Review,* March 2005, 43–54.

40. Adapted from Alyce Lomax, "Monterey's High-Carb Woes," *The Motley Fool,* 23 December 2003 [accessed 23 December 2003] www.fool.com/News/mft/2003/mft03122312.htm; "Monterey Pasta Announces Quarterly Sales Decline of 3%–5% Expected When Compared to Fourth Quarter, 2002," Monterey Pasta corporate press release, 23 December 2003 [accessed 23 December 2003] www.montereypasta.com/Company/PressReleases/index.cfm?ID=84; "Monterey Pasta Company Introduces Reduced Carbohydrate Product Line," Monterey Pasta corporate press release, 23 December 2003 [accessed 23 December 2003] www.montereypasta.com/Company/PressReleases.

41. Adapted from Stanton website [accessed 18 August 2005] www.stanton.com.

42. Adapted from Capital One Auto Finance (formerly PeopleFirst.com) website [accessed 23 December 2003] www.capitaloneautofinance.com; PeopleFirst.com/Capital One Auto Finance.

43. Adapted from Associated Press, "Children's Painkiller Recalled," CNN.com/Health website, 16 August 2001 [accessed 22 August 2001] www.cnn.com/2001/HEALTH/parenting/08/16/kids.drug.recalled.ap/index.html; Perrigo Company website [accessed 29 August 2001], www.perrigo.com.

44. Adapted from Associated Press, "Employers Restricting Use of Cell Phones in Cars," CNN.com/Sci-Tech, 27 August 2001 [accessed 27 August 2001] www.cnn.com/2001/TECH/08/27/cellphones.cars.ap/index.html; Julie Vallese, "Study: All Cell Phones Distract Drivers," CNN.com/U.S., 16 August 2001 [accessed 7 September 2001] www.cnn.com/2001/US/08/16/cell.phone.driving/index.html.

45. Adapted from Julie Vallese, "Motorized Scooter Injuries on the Rise," CNN.com/U.S., 22 August 2001 [accessed 22 August 2001] www.cnn.com/2001/US/08/22/scooter.advisory/index.html; The Sports Authority website [accessed 28 August 2001] www.thesportauthority.com.

46. Adapted from Alion website [accessed 19 August 2005] www.alionscience.com.

47. Adapted from United Airlines website [accessed 31 December 2003] www.united.com; "United Airlines First To Offer Inflight Email on Domestic Flights: Verizon Airfone® Outfits UAL's Fleet with JetConnect℠," United Airlines press release [accessed 21 July 2003] www.ual.com/press/detail/o,1442,51106,00.html; "Laptops Sprout Wings with Verizon Airfone JetConnect Service," *PR Newswire,* 24 September 2002 [accessed 21 July 2003] www.proquest.com; "Verizon Hopes Data Flies with Airfone JetConnect," *Wireless Data News,* 7 May 2003 [accessed 24 July 2003] www.proquest.com.

48. Adapted from Sean Doherty, "Dynamic Communications," *Network Computing,* 3 April 2003, 26 [accessed 24 July 2003] search.epnet.com/direct.asp?an-9463336&db=bsh&tg=AN; Todd Wasserman, "Post-Merger HP Invents New Image to Challenge Tech Foes IBM and Dell," *Brandweek,* 18 November 2002, 9 [accessed 24 July 2003], search.epnet.com/direct.asp?an=8887152&db=bsh&tg=AN; R. P. Srikanth, "IM Tools Are Latest Tech Toys for Corporate Users," *Express Computer,* 1 July 2002 [accessed 21 July 2003] www.expresscomputeronline.com/20020701/indtrend1.shtml.

CHAPTER 9

1. Melissa Grego, "Behind the Screen: Burnett's New Studio Model," *TV Week,* 15 August 2005 [accessed 22 August 2005] www.tvweek.com; Cynthia Littleton, "Dialogue with Producer Mark Burnett," *Hollywood Reporter,* 26 May 2004 [accessed 22 August 2005] www.hollywoodreporter.com; Nellie Andreeva, "Commando Nanny Gets a Sitcom on WB," *Hollywood Reporter,* 21–27 October 2003, 4; Abby Ellin, "Survivor' Meets Millionaire, and a Show Is Born," *New York Times,* 19 October 2003, sec. 3, 4; Kelli Anderson, "Out of the Wild," *Sports Illustrated,* 12 May 2003, A6; Maggie Sieger, "Paddle Faster, Mom," *Time,* 5 May 2003, 85; Bill Carter, "Survival of the Pushiest," *New York Times Magazine,* 28 January 2001, 22.

2. Jay A. Conger, "The Necessary Art of Persuasion," *Harvard Business Review,* May–June 1998, 84–95; Jeanette W. Gilsdorf, "Write Me Your Best Case for . . ." *Bulletin of the Association for Business Communication* 54, no. 1 (March 1991): 7–12.

3. "Vital Skill for Today's Managers: Persuading, Not Ordering Others," *Soundview Executive Book Summaries,* September 1998, 1.

4. Mary Cross, "Aristotle and Business Writing: Why We Need to Teach Persuasion," *Bulletin of the Association for Business Communication* 54, no. 1 (March 1991): 3–6.

5. Abraham H. Maslow, *Motivation and Personality* (New York: Harper & Row, 1954), 12, 19.

6. Robert T. Moran, "Tips on Making Speeches to International Audiences," *International Management,* April 1980, 58–59.

7. Conger, "The Necessary Art of Persuasion."

8. Raymond M. Olderman, *10-Minute Guide to Business Communication* (New York: Macmillan Spectrum/Alpha Books, 1997), 57–61.

9. Gilsdorf, "Write Me Your Best Case for . . ."

10. John D. Ramage and John C. Bean, *Writing Arguments: A Rhetoric with Readings,* 3d ed. (Boston: Allyn & Bacon, 1995), 430–442.

11. Philip Vassallo, "Persuading Powerfully: Tips for Writing Persuasive Documents," *et Cetera,* Spring 2002, 65–71.

12. Dianna Booher, *Communicate with Confidence* (New York: McGraw-Hill, 1994), 102.

13. Conger, "The Necessary Art of Persuasion."

14. *Overview of the Web Accessibility Initiative,* W3C website [accessed 23 August 2005] www.w3.org.

15. iPod nano product page, Apple Computer website [accessed 9 November 2005] www.apple.com/ipod.

16. Verizon Wireless website [accessed 23 August 2005] www.verizonwireless.com.

17. Saturn VUE product page, Saturn website [accessed 8 December 2003] www.saturn.com.

18. *Working and Living in France: The Ins and Outs* product page, Insider Paris Guides website [accessed 8 December 2003] www.insiderparisguides.com.

19. Verizon Wireless sales letter, received 1 December 2003.

20. Fast Break Backpack product page, Lands End website [accessed 8 December 2003], www.landsend.com.

21. iPod nano product page.

22. Gilsdorf, "Write Me Your Best Case for . . ."

23. *Frequently Asked Advertising Questions: A Guide for Small Business,* U.S. Federal Trade Commission website [accessed 9 December 2003], www.ftc.gov.

24. Adapted from GM Fastlane Blog [accessed 23 August 2005] http://fastlane.gmblogs.com.

25. Adapted from Starbucks website [accessed 23 August 2005] www.starbucks.com.

26. Adapted from job description for Global Marketing Manager–Apparel, New Balance website [accessed 24 August 2005] www.newbalance.com.

27. Adapted from Give Life website [accessed 23 August 2005] www.givelife.org; American Red Cross website [accessed 3 October 2001] www.redcross.org; American Red Cross San Diego Chapter website [accessed 3 October 2001] www.sdarc.org/blood.htm.

28. Adapted from Norimitsu Onishi, "Making Liberty His Business: Ex-Political Prisoner Turns Freedom's Icon into a Career," *New York Times,* 18 April 1996, B1; Colbar Art website [accessed 9 January 2004] www.colbarart.com.

29. Adapted from Courtland L. Bovée and John V. Thill, *Business In Action,* 3d ed. (Upper Saddle River, New Jersey: Pearson Prentice Hall, 2005), International Telework Association & Council website [accessed 24 August 2005] www.telecommute.org; 236–237; Jason Roberson, "Rush-hour Rebellion," *Dallas Business Journal,* 22 June 2001, 31; Carole Hawkins, "Ready, Set, Go Home," *Black Enterprise,* August 2001, 118–124; Wayne Tompkins, "Telecommuting in Transition," *Courier-Journal,* Louisville, KY, 9 July 2001, 01C.

30. Adapted from Andrew Ferguson, "Supermarket of the Vanities," *Fortune,* 10 June 1996, 30, 32; Whole Foods Market website [accessed 9 January 2004] www.wholefoodsmarket.com.

31. Adapted from Joe Sharkey, "Luggage Lock Plan Revisited, Again," *New York Times,* 6 January 2004 [accessed 6 January 2004] www.nytimes.com; Brookstone website [accessed 13 January 2004] www.brookstone.com.

32. Adapted from CNET Shopper.com [accessed 1 October 2001] http://shopper.cnet.com.

33. Adapted from The Podcast Bunker website [accessed 25 August 2005] www.podcastbunker.com.

34. Adapted from Time Inc. website [accessed 25 August 2005] www.timewarner.com.

35. Adapted from Insure.com website [accessed 24 August 2005] www.insure.com.

36. Adapted from Kelly Services website [accessed 9 January 2004], www.kellyservices.com.

37. Adapted from Hangers Cleaners website [accessed 9 January 2004] www.hangersdrycleaners.com; Charles Fishman, "The Greener Cleaners," *Fast Company,* 36, 54 [accessed 11 July 2000] fastcompany.com/online/36/greenclean.html; Micell Technologies website [accessed 1 September 2000] www.micell.com/08142000.htm; Cool Clean Technologies, Inc., website [accessed 9 January 2004] www.co2olclean.com.

38. Adapted from Sarah Plaskitt, "Case Study: Hilton Uses SMS With Success," *B&T Marketing & Media,* 27 June 2002 [accessed 22 July 2003] www.bandt.com.au/articles/ce/0c00eace.asp; "Wireless Messaging Briefs," *Instant Messaging Planet,* 4 October 2002 [accessed 22 July 2003] www.instantmessagingplanet.com/wireless/print.php/10766_1476111; Hilton Hotels Corporation, *Hoover's Company Capsules,* 1 July 2003 [accessed 24 July 2003] www.proquest.com; Matthew G. Nelson, "Hilton Takes Reservations Wireless," *InformationWeek,* 25 June 2001, 99 [accessed 24 July 2003] www.web22.epnet.com; Hilton Hotels website [accessed 15 January 2004] www.hilton.com.

39. Adapted from IBM website [accessed 15 January 2004] www. ibm.com/ibm/ibmgives; IBM website, "DAS faces an assured future with IBM" [accessed 16 January 2004] www-306.ibm.com/software/success/ cssdb.nsf/CS/DNSD-5S6KTF; IBM website, "Sametime" [accessed 16 January 2004] www.lotus.com/products/lotussametime.nsf/wdocs/homepage.

CHAPTER 10

1. Michael Paoletta, "Toyota's Scion Starts Label," *Billboard,* 26 March 2005, 8+; "2005 Scion tC," *Edmunds.com* [accessed 12 April 2005] www.edmunds.com; "10 Hottest Cars and Trucks in 2004," *Advertising Age,* 20 December, 28; David Welch, "Not Your Father's . . . Whatever," *BusinessWeek,* 15 March 2004, 82–84; Daren Fonda, "Scion Grows Up," *Time (Canada),* 16 August 2004, 61; Katherine Zachery, "The Makings of a Hit," *Ward's Auto World,* June 2004, 42; Christopher Palmeri, "Toyota's Youth Models Are Having Growing Pains," *BusinessWeek,* 31 May 2004, 32; Steven Kichen, "Scion's Smart Moves," *Forbes,* 12 October 2004 [accessed 12 April 2005] www.forbes.com; Norihiko Shirouzu, "Scion Plays Hip-Hop Impresario to Impress Young Drivers," *Wall Street Journal,* 5 October 2004, B1+; Phil Patton, "As Authentic as 'The Matrix' or Menudo," *New York Times,* 25 July 2004, sec. 12, 1+; Dan Lienert, "What's New? With Toyota's Scion, Youth Must Be Served," *New York Times,* 19 October 2003 [accessed 12 November 2003] www.nytimes.com; Fara Warner, "Learning How to Speak to Gen Y," *Fast Company,* July 2003, 36; Darren Fonda, "Baby, You Can Drive My Car," *Time,* 30 June 2003, 46; Christopher Palmeri, Ben Elgin, Kathleen Kerwin, "Toyota's Scion: Dude, Here's Your Car," *Business Week,* 9 June 2003, 44; Jonathan Fahey, "For the Discriminating Body Piercer," *Forbes,* 12 May 2003, 136; George Raine, "Courting Generation Y," *San Francisco Chronicle,* 11 May 2003, I3.

2. Courtland L. Bovée, Michael J. Houston, and John V. Thill, *Marketing,* 2d ed. (New York: McGraw-Hill, 1995), 194–196.

3. Legal-Definitions.com [accessed 17 December 2003] www.legal-definitions.com.

4. Information for this section was obtained from "Finding Industry Information" [accessed 3 November 1998] www.pitt.edu/~buslibry/industries.htm; Thomas P. Bergman, Stephen M. Garrison, and Gregory M. Scott, *The Business Student Writer's Manual and Guide to the Internet*

(Upper Saddle River, N.J.: Prentice Hall, 1998), 67–80; Ernest L. Maier, Anthony J. Faria, Peter Kaatrude, and Elizabeth Wood, *The Business Library and How to Use It* (Detroit: Omnigraphics, 1996), 53–76; Sherwyn P. Morreale and Courtland L. Bovée, *Excellence in Public Speaking* (Fort Worth: Harcourt Brace College Publishers, 1998), 166–171.

5. Open Directory [accessed 27 August 2005] www.dmoz.com.

6. AllTheWeb.com advanced search page [accessed 27 August 2005] www.alltheweb.com; Google advanced search page [accessed 27 August 2005] www.google.com; Yahoo! advanced search page [accessed 27 August 2005] www.yahoo.com.

7. NewsGator website [accessed 24 August 2005] www.newsgator.com; NewzCrawler website [accessed 24 August 2005] www.newzcrawler.com.

8. "Top 10 Benefits of OneNote 2003," Microsoft website [accessed 21 June 2004] www.microsoft.com.

9. A. B. Blankenship and George Edward Breen, *State of the Art Marketing Research,* (Chicago: NTC Business Books, 1993), 136.

10. Naresh K. Malhotra, *Basic Marketing Research* (Upper Saddle River, N.J.: Prentice-Hall, 2002), 314–317; "How to Design and Conduct a Study," *Credit Union Magazine,* October 1983, 36–46.

11. American Marketing Association [accessed 14 December 2003] www.marketingpower.com.

12. Karen J. Bannan, "Companies Save Time, Money with Online Surveys," *B to B,* 9 June 2003, 1+; Allen Hogg, "Online Research Overview," American Marketing Association website [accessed 15 December 2003] www.marketingpower.com.

13. Morreale and Bovée, *Excellence in Public Speaking,* 177.

14. Morreale and Bovée, *Excellence in Public Speaking,* 182.

15. Lynn Quitman Troyka, *Simon & Schuster Handbook for Writers,* 6th ed., (Upper Saddle River, NJ: Simon & Schuster, 2002), 481.

16. "How to Paraphrase Effectively: 6 Steps to Follow," Researchpaper.com [accessed 26 October 1998] www.researchpaper.com/writing_center/30.html.

CHAPTER 11

1. Adapted from Mike Drexler, "Media Midlife Crisis: The Changes are Monumental," *Adweek,* 9 February 2004 [accessed 6 May 2004] www.highbeam.com; Kevin J. Delaney and Robert A. Guth, "Beep. Foosh. Buy Me. Pow." *Wall Street Journal,* 8 April 2004, B1, B7; Stuart Elliot, "Advertising," *New York Times,* 14 April 2004, C8; Ronald Grover, "Can Mad Ave. Make Zap-Proof Ads?" *Business Week,* 2 February 2004, 36; Richard Linnett and Wayne Friedman, "OMD Plans Strategy to Challenge Upfront," *Advertising Age,* 23 June 2003, 1; Katy Bachman, "Research: Beth Uyenco," *Brandweek,* 9 December 2003, SR24; Kate Fitzgerald, "Communication Architects," *Advertising Age,* 5 August 2002, S6; Katy Bachman, "Research: Tony Jarvis," *Mediaweek,* 3 December 2001, SR20.

2. A. S. C. Ehrenberg, "Report Writing—Six Simple Rules for Better Business Documents," *Admap,* June 1992, 39–42.

3. Michael Netzley and Craig Snow, *Guide to Report Writing* (Upper Saddle River, N.J.: Prentice Hall, 2001), 15.

4. Claudia Mon Pere McIsaac, "Improving Student Summaries Through Sequencing," *Bulletin of the Association for Business Communication* (September 1987): 17–20.

5. David A. Hayes, "Helping Students GRASP the Knack of Writing Summaries," *Journal of Reading* (November 1989): 96–101.

6. Philip C. Kolin, *Successful Writing at Work,* 6th ed. (Boston: Houghton Mifflin, 2001), 552–555.

7. Hoover's Online [accessed 30 December 2003] www.hoovers.com.

8. Google Earth website [accessed 2 September 2005] http://earth.google.com.

9. Sheri Rosen, "What Is Truth?" *IABC Communication World,* March 1995, 40.

10. Jacci Howard Bear, "Defining the Principles of Design Through Metaphor or Allegory," *About.com* [accessed 2 September 2005] www.about.com; William Wells, John Burnett, and Sandra Moriarty, *Advertising Principles*

& Practice, 6th ed. (Upper Saddle River, N.J.: Prentice-Hall, 2003), 373–375.

11. Edward R. Tufte, *The Visual Display of Quantitative Information* (Cheshire, Conn.: Graphic Press, 1983), 113.

12. Courtland L. Bovée, Michael J. Houston, and John V. Thill, *Marketing,* 2d ed. (New York: McGraw-Hill, 1995), 250.

13. Adapted from Air-Trak website [accessed 12 September 2005] www.air-trak.com.

CHAPTER 12

1. Richard Klausner and Pedro Alonso, "An Attack on All Fronts," *Nature,* 19 August 2004, 930–931; "Richard Klausner Spends To Save Lives," *Fast Company,* November 2002, 128; Gates Foundation website [accessed 15 September 2005] www.gatesfoundation.org; Kent Allen, "The Gatekeeper," *U.S. News & World Report,* 8 December 2003, 64–66.

2. Michael Netzley and Craig Snow, *Guide to Report Writing* (Upper Saddle River, N.J.: Prentice Hall, 2001), 57.

3. Patty Stonesifer, "Partners and Progress: A Message from Patty Stonesifer," Gates Foundation website [accessed 15 September 2005] www.gatesfoundation.org.

4. Oswald M. T. Ratteray, "Hit the Mark with Better Summaries," *Supervisory Management,* September 1989, 43–45.

5. Netzley and Snow, *Guide to Report Writing,* 43.

6. Alice Reid, "A Practical Guide For Writing Proposals" [accessed 31 May 2001] http://members.dca.net/areid/proposal.htm.

7. Toby B. Gooley, "Ocean Shipping: RFPs that Get Results," *Logistics Management,* July 2003, 47–52.

8. Adapted from "Home Depot Says E-Learning Is Paying for Itself," *Workforce Management,* 25 February 2004 [accessed 28 February 2004] www.workforce.com; Robert Celaschi, "The Insider: Training," *Workforce Management,* August 2004, 67–69; Joe Mullich, "A Second Act for E-Learning," *Workforce Management,* February 2004, 51–55; Gail Johnson, "Brewing the Perfect Blend," *Training,* December 2003, 30+; Tammy Galvin, "2003 Industry Report," *Training,* October 2003, 21+; William C. Symonds, "Giving It the Old Online Try," *BusinessWeek,* 3 December 2001, 76–80; Karen Frankola, "Why Online Learners Drop Out," *Workforce,* October 2001, 52–60; Mary Lord, "They're Online and on the Job; Managers and Hamburger Flippers Are Being E-Trained at Work," *U.S. News & World Report,* 15 October 2001, 72–77.

9. Adapted from Ieva M. Augstumes, "Buyers Take the Driver's Seat," *Dallas Morning News,* 20 February 2004 [accessed 30 June 2004] www.highbeam.com; Jill Amadio, "A Click Away: Automotive Web Are Revved Up and Ready to Help You Buy," *Entrepreneur,* 1 August 2003 [accessed 30 June 2004] www.highbeam.com; Dawn C. Chmielewski, "Car Sites Lend Feel-Good Info for Haggling," *San Jose Mercury News,* 1 August 2003 [accessed 30 June 2004] www.highbeam.com; Cromwell Schubarth, "Autoheroes Handle Hassle of Haggling," *Boston Herald,* 24 July 2003 [accessed 30 June 2004] www.highbeam.com; Rick Popely, "Internet Doesn't Change Basic Shopping Rules," *Chicago Tribune,* 28 February 2004 [accessed 30 June 2004] www.highbeam.com; Matt Nauman, "Walnut Creek, Calif., Firm Prospers as Online Car Buying Becomes More Popular," *San Jose Mercury News,* 21 June 2004 [accessed 30 June 2004] www.highbeam.com; Cliff Banks, "e-Dealer 100," *Ward's Dealer Business,* 1 April 2004 [accessed 30 June 2004] www.highbeam.com; Cars.com website [accessed 30 June 2004] www.cars.com; CarsDirect.com website [accessed 30 June 2004] www.carsdirect.com.

CHAPTER 13

1. "Culture and Philosophy" and "Procter & Gamble Case Study," HP website [accessed 20 September 2005] www.hp.com; Paul McDougall, "Procter & Gamble's Deal with HP Grows," *InformationWeek,* 16 August 2004 [accessed 20 September 2005] www.outsourcingpipeline.com; Bill Breen, "The Big Score," September 2003, *Fast Company,* 64; "HP Finalizes $3 Billion Outsourcing Agreement to Manage Procter & Gamble's IT Infrastructure," press release, HP website, 6 May 2003 [accessed 10 October 2003] www.hp.com; "HP Selected by P&G for $3 Billion, 10-Year Services Con-

tract," press release, HP website, 11 April 2003 [accessed 10 October 2003] www.hp.com.

2. Carmine Gallo, "Loaded for Bore," *BusinessWeek Online,* 5 August 2005 [accessed 19 September 2005] www.businessweek.com.

3. Sarah Lary and Karen Pruente, "Powerless Point: Common PowerPoint Mistakes to Avoid," *Public Relations Tactics,* February 2004, 28.

4. Sherwyn P. Morreale and Courtland L. Bovée, *Excellence in Public Speaking* (Fort Worth: Harcourt Brace, 1998), 234–237.

5. Morreale and Bovée, *Excellence in Public Speaking,* 230.

6. Morreale and Bovée, *Excellence in Public Speaking,* 241–243.

7. "Choose and Use Your Words Deliberately," *Soundview Executive Book Summaries,* 20, no. 6, pt. 2 (June 1998): 3.

8. Walter Kiechel III, "How to Give a Speech," *Fortune,* 8 June 1987, 180.

9. *Communication and Leadership Program* (Santa Ana, Calif.: Toastmasters International, 1980), 44, 45.

10. "Polishing Your Presentation," 3M Meeting Network [accessed 8 June 2001] www.mmm.com/meetingnetwork/readingroom/meetingguide_pres.html.

11. Claudyne Wilder and David Fine, *Point, Click & Wow* (San Francisco: Jossey-Bass Pfeiffer, 1996), 50.

12. Margo Halverson, "Choosing the Right Colors for Your Next Presentation," 3M Meeting Network [accessed 8 June 2001] www.mmm.com/meetingnetwork/readingroom/meetingguide_right_color.html.

13. Carol Klinger and Joel G. Siegel, "Computer Multimedia Presentations," *CPA Journal,* June 1996, 46.

14. Jon Hanke, "Five Tips for Better Visuals," 3M Meeting Network [accessed 8 June 2001] www.mmm.com/meetingnetwork/presentations/pmag_better_visuals.html.

15. Hanke, "Five Tips for Better Visuals."

16. Sarah Lary and Karen Pruente, "Powerless Point: Common PowerPoint Mistakes to Avoid," *Public Relations Tactics,* February 2004, 28.

17. Jeff Yocom, " TechRepublic Survey Yields Advice on Streaming Video," TechRepublic website [accessed 16 February 2004] www.techrepublic.com.

18. "Webcasting Tips & Advice," Spider Eye Solutions [accessed 13 February 2004] www.spidereye.com.

19. Edward P. Bailey, *Writing and Speaking at Work* (Upper Saddle River, N.J.: Prentice Hall, 1999), 138–145.

20. Ted Simons, "Handouts That Won't Get Trashed," *Presentations,* February 1999, 47–50.

21. Jennifer Rotondo and Mike Rotondo, Jr., *Presentation Skills for Managers,* (New York: McGraw-Hill, 2002), 151.

22. Morreale and Bovée, *Excellence in Public Speaking,* 24–25.

23. Jennifer Rotondo and Mike Rotondo, Jr., *Presentation Skills for Managers,* (New York: McGraw-Hill, 2002), 9.

24. Rick Gilbert, "Presentation Advice for Boardroom Success," *Financial Executive,* September 2005, 12.

25. "Control the Question-and-Answer Session," *Soundview Executive Book Summaries* 20, no. 6, pt. 2 (June 1998): 4.

26. "Control the Question-and-Answer Session."

27. Teresa Brady, "Fielding Abrasive Questions During Presentations," *Supervisory Management,* February 1993, 6.

28. Robert L. Montgomery, "Listening on Your Feet," *The Toastmaster,* July 1987, 14–15.

29. See Note 1.

CHAPTER 14

1. E*Trade website [accessed 23 September 2005] www.etrade.com; Samuel Greengard, "Smarter Screening Takes Technology and HR Savvy," *Fast Company,* June 2002, 56; Alison Overholt, "Job Search 101," *Fast Company,* April 2002, 122–125; Pierre Mornell, "Zero Defect Hiring," *Inc.,* March 1998, 74.

2. Maureen Jenkins, "Yours for the Taking," *Boeing Frontiers Online,* June 2004 [accessed 25 September 2005] www.boeing.com; "Firm Predicts Top 10 Workforce/Workplace Trends for 2004, *Enterprise,* 8–14 December 2003, 1–2; Scott Hudson, "Keeping Employees Happy," *Community Banker,* September 2003, 34+; Marvin J. Cetron and Owen Davies, "Trends Now Changing the World: Technology, the Workplace, Management, and Institutions," *Futurist* 35, no. 2 (March–April 2001): 27–42.

3. Steve Crabtree, "Beyond the Dot-Com Bust; How Managers Can Help Younger Workers Regain Their Lost Momentum," *Gallup Management Journal,* 11 December 2003, 1+.

4. Jim Puzzanghera, "Coalition of High-Tech Firms to Urge Officials to Help Keep U.S. Competitive," *San Jose Mercury News,* 8 January 2004 [accessed 14 February 2004] www.ebscohost.com.

5. Amanda Bennett, "GE Redesigns Rungs of Career Ladder," *Wall Street Journal,* 15 March 1993, B1, B3.

6. Robin White Goode, "International and Foreign Language Skills Have an Edge," *Black Enterprise,* May 1995, 53.

7. Jeffrey R. Young, "'E-Portfolios' Could Give Students a New Sense of Their Accomplishments," *The Chronicle of Higher Education,* 8 March 2002, A31.

8. Nancy M. Somerick, "Managing a Communication Internship Program," *Bulletin of the Association for Business Communication* 56, no. 3 (1993): 10–20.

9. Joan Lloyd, "Changing Workplace Requires You to Alter Your Career Outlook," *Milwaukee Journal Sentinel,* 4 July 1999, 1; Camille DeBell, "Ninety Years in the World of Work in America," *Career Development Quarterly* 50, no.1 (September 2001): 77–88.

10. Robert J. Gerberg, *Robert Gerberg's Job Changing System,* summarized by Macmillan Book Clubs, Inc., in the "Macmillan Executive Summary Program," April 1987, 4.

11. Mkt10.com website [accessed 25 September 2005] www.mkt10.com; Olga Kharif, "The Job of Challenging Monster," *BusinessWeek Online,* 6 September 2005 [accessed 25 September 2005] www.businessweek.com; "Job Sites: The 'Second Generation'," *BusinessWeek Online,* 7 September 2005 [accessed 25 September 2005] www.businessweek.com.

12. Caroline A. Drakeley, "Viral Networking: Tactics in Today's Job Market," *Intercom,* September–October 2003, 4–7.

13. Drakeley, "Viral Networking: Tactics in Today's Job Market," 5.

14. Anne Fisher, "Greener Pastures in a New Field," *Fortune,* 26 January 2004, 48.

15. Cheryl L. Noll, "Collaborating with the Career Planning and Placement Center in the Job-Search Project," *Business Communication Quarterly* 58, no. 3 (1995): 53–55.

16. Rockport Institute, "How to Write a Masterpiece of a Résumé" [accessed 25 September 2005] www.rockportinstitute.com.

17. Pam Stanley-Weigand, "Organizing the Writing of Your Resume," *Bulletin of the Association for Business Communication* 54, no. 3 (September 1991): 11–12.

18. Susan Vaughn, "Answer the Hard Questions Before Asked," *Los Angeles Times,* 29 July 2001, W1–W2.

19. Richard H. Beatty and Nicholas C. Burkholder, *The Executive Career Guide for MBAs* (New York: Wiley, 1996), 133.

20. Adapted from Burdette E. Bostwick, *How to Find the Job You've Always Wanted* (New York: Wiley, 1982), 69–70.

21. Norma Mushkat Gaffin, "Recruiters' Top 10 Resume Pet Peeves," Monster.com [accessed 19 February 2004] www.monster.com; Beatty and Burkholder, *The Executive Career Guide for MBAs,* 151.

22. Rockport Institute, "How to Write a Masterpiece of a Résumé."

23. "Resume Fraud Gets Slicker and Easier," CNN.com [accessed 11 March 2004] www.cnn.com.

24. "Resume Fraud Gets Slicker and Easier"; Employment Screening Resources website [accessed 18 March 2004] www.erscheck.com.

25. "Employers Turn Their Fire on Untruthful CVs," *Supply Management,* 23 June 2005, 13.

26. Sal Divita, "If You're Thinking Résumé, Think Creatively," *Marketing News,* 14 September 1992, 29.

27. Rockport Institute, "How to Write a Masterpiece of a Résumé."

28. Rockport Institute, "How to Write a Masterpiece of a Résumé."

29. Ellen Joe Pollock, "Sir: Your Application for a Job Is Rejected; Sincerely, Hal 9000," *Wall Street Journal,* 30 July 1998, A1, A12.

30. "Scannable Resume Design," ResumeEdge.com [accessed 19 February 2004] www.resumeedge.com.

31. Kim Isaacs, "Tips for Creating a Scannable Resume," Monster.com [accessed 19 February 2004] www.monster.com.

32. Kim Isaacs, "Enhance Your Resume for Monster Upload," Monster.com [accessed 19 February 2004] www.monster.com.

33. "The Rogue's Gallery of 25 Awful Résumé Mistakes," CareerExplorer.net [accessed 19 February 2004] www.careerexplorer.net.

34. Regina Pontow, "Electronic Résumé Writing Tips," ProvenRésumés.com [accessed 18 October 1998] www.provenresumes.com/reswkshps/electronic/ scnres.html.

35. See Note 1.

CHAPTER 15

1. "What's It Like to Work At Google?" Google website [accessed 26 September 2005] www.google.com; Fred Vogelstein, "Can Google Grow Up?" *Fortune,* 8 December 2003, 102; Quentin Hardy, "All Eyes on Google," *Forbes,* 26 May 2003, 100; Keith H. Hammonds, "Growth Search," *Fast Company,* April 2003, 74–81; Stanley Bing, "How Not To Success (*sic*) in Business," *Fortune,* 30 December 2002, 210; Pierre Mornell, "Zero Defect Hiring," *Inc.,* March 1998, 74.

2. "The Writer Approach," *Los Angeles Times,* 17 November 2002, W1.

3. Toni Logan, "The Perfect Cover Story," *Kinko's Impress* 2 (2000): 32, 34.

4. James Gonyea, "Money Talks: Salary History Versus Salary Requirements," Monster.com [accessed 19 October 2004] www.monster.com; Marguerite Higgins, "Tech-Savvy Job Hunters Not So Suave in Writing; E-Mail Résumés Appall Employers," *Washington Times,* 17 December 2002 [accessed 22 February 2004] www.highbeam.com; "Keep Goal in Mind When Crafting a Résumé," Register-Guard (Eugene, Ore.), 3 August 2003 [accessed 22 February 2004] www.highbeam.com; Anis F. McClin, "Effects of Spelling Errors on the Perception of Writers," *Journal of General Psychology,* January 2002 [accessed 22 February 2004] www.highbeam. com.

5. George Donnelly, "Recruiting, Retention & Returns," *cfonet,* March 2000 [accessed 10 April 2000] www.cfonet.com/html/Articles/CFO/2000/00Marecr.html.

6. Stephanie Armour, "The New Interview Etiquette," *USA Today,* 23 November 1999, B1, B2.

7. Samuel Greengard, "Are You Well Armed to Screen Applicants?" *Personnel Journal,* December 1995, 84–95.

8. William Poundstone, "Beware the Interview Inquisition," *Harvard Business Review,* May 2003, 18+.

9. Marcia Vickers, "Don't Touch That Dial: Why Should I Hire You?" *New York Times,* 13 April 1997, F11.

10. Terry McKenna, "Behavior-Based Interviewing," *National Petroleum News,* January 2004, 16; Nancy K. Austin, "Goodbye Gimmicks," *Incentive,* May 1996, 241.

11. "Southwest Is Picky," *Soundview Executive Book Summaries,* September 1998, 5.

12. Patrick J. Sauer, "Open-Door Management," *Inc.,* June 2003, 44.

13. Dino di Mattia, "Testing Methods and Effectiveness of Tests," *Supervision,* August 2005, 4–5.

14. Steven Mitchell Sack, "The Working Woman's Legal Survival Guide: Testing," FindLaw.com [accessed 22 February 2004] www.findlaw.com;

David W. Arnold and John W. Jones, "Who the Devil's Applying Now?" *Security Management,* March 2002, 85–88.

15. Arnold and Jones, "Who the Devil's Applying Now?" 86.

16. Arnold and Jones, "Who the Devil's Applying Now?" 86.

17. Adam Agard, "Preemployment Skills Testing: An Important Step in the Hiring Process," *Supervision,* June 2003, 7+.

18. Andy Meisler, "Negative Results," *Workforce Management,* October 2003, 35+.

19. Tyler D. Hartwell, Paul D. Steele, and Nathaniel F. Rodman, "Workplace Alcohol-Testing Programs: Prevalence and Trends," *Monthly Labor Review,* June 1998, 27–34; "Substance Abuse in the Workplace," *HR Focus,* February 1997, 1, 4+.

20. Meisler, "Negative Results," 35+.

21. Thomas A. Buckhoff, "Preventing Fraud by Conducting Background Checks," *CPA Journal,* November 2003, 52.

22. "Check Yourself Before Employer Does," *CA Magazine,* June–July 2005, 12.

23. Austin, "Goodbye Gimmicks."

24. Katherine Spencer Lee, "Tackling Tough Interview Questions," *Certification Magazine,* May 2005, 35.

25. Leigh Dyer, "Job Hunters Should Think Carefully Before Using Job Counselor," *Charlotte Observer,* 30 July 2001 [accessed 29 September 2005] www.ebsco.com; Anne Field, "Coach, Help Me Out with This Interview," *Business Week,* 22 October 2001, 134E2, 134E4.

26. Robert Gifford, Cheuk Fan Ng, and Margaret Wilkinson, "Nonverbal Cues in the Employment Interview: Links Between Applicant Qualities and Interviewer Judgments," *Journal of Applied Psychology* 70, no. 4 (1985): 729.

27. Dale G. Leathers, *Successful Nonverbal Communication* (New York: Macmillan, 1986), 225.

28. Armour, "The New Interview Etiquette."

29. William S. Frank, "Job Interview: Pre-Flight Checklist," *The Career Advisor* [accessed 28 September 2005] http://careerplanning.about.com.

30. T. Shawn Taylor, "Most Managers Have No Idea How to Hire the Right Person for the Job," *Chicago Tribune,* 23 July 2002 [accessed 29 September 2005] www.ebsco.com.

31. Sack, "The Working Woman's Legal Survival Guide."

32. Gerald L. Wilson, "Preparing Students for Responding to Illegal Selection Interview Questions," *Bulletin of the Association for Business Communication* 54, no. 2 (1991): 44–49.

33. Jeff Springston and Joann Keyton, "Interview Response Training," *Bulletin of the Association for Business Communication* 54, no. 3 (1991): 28–30; Gerald L. Wilson, "An Analysis of Instructional Strategies for Responding to Illegal Selection Interview Questions," *Bulletin of the Association for Business Communication* 54, no. 3 (1991): 31–35.

34. Stephen J. Pullum, "Illegal Questions in the Selection Process: Going Beyond Contemporary Business and Professional Communication Textbooks," *Bulletin of the Association for Business Communication* 54, no. 3 (1991): 36–43; Alicia Kitsuse, "Have You Ever Been Arrested?" *Across the Board,* November 1992, 46–49; Christina L. Greathouse, "Ten Common Hiring Mistakes," *Industry Week,* 20 January 1992, 22–23, 26.

35. "Negotiating Salary: An Introduction," *InformationWeek* online [accessed 22 February 2004] www.infoweek.com

36. "Negotiating Salary: An Introduction."

37. Harold H. Hellwig, "Job Interviewing: Process and Practice," *Bulletin of the Association for Business Communication* 55, no. 2 (1992): 8–14.

38. See Note 1.

Acknowledgments

TEXT

5 (Practicing Ethical Communication: The High Cost of Failure) Adapted from Allison Hoffman and Olga R. Rodriguez, "Railroad Vows to Aid Recovery: Union Pacific Says It Will Directly Handle Claims from Derailment," *Los Angeles Times*, 27 June 2003, B1; "City Officials Condemn Lack of Warning of Derailment," *Augusta Chronicle*, 22 June 2003, A8. **20 (Powerful Tools for Communicating Efficiently)** Adapted from Sebastian Rupley, "WebEx Exposed," *PC Magazine*, 7 September 2004 [accessed 5 February 2005] www.pcmag.com; Erika D. Smith, "Online Chat Companies Offer Way out of Phone Frustration," *San Diego Union-Tribune*, 5 July 2004, E5; David Kirkpatrick, "It's Hard to Manage If You Don't Blog," *Fortune*, 4 October 2004, 46; Lee Gomes, "How the Next Big Thing in Technology Morphed into a Really Big Thing," *Wall Street Journal*, 4 October 2004, B1; Jeff Meisner, "Cutting Through the Blah, Blah, Blah," 19–25 November 2004, 27–28; Lauren Gard, "The Business of Blogging," *BusinessWeek*, 13 December 2004, 117–119; William M. Bulkeley, "The Office PC Slims Down," *Wall Street Journal*, 17 January 2005, R3; "A New Way to Work," *Herald* (Everett, WA), 20 May 2003, A4–A5; "Tools for Connected Companies," *Newsweek*, 28 April 2003 "Intranet Basics," The Complete Intranet Resource [accessed 11 June 2003] www.intrack.com/ intranet/faqbasic.cfm; Page 2; Rafe Needleman, "Internet Videophones—Is Anybody Watching?" *Business 2.0* [accessed 11 June 2003] www.business2.com; "3M Wall Display," 3M website [accessed 12 June 2003] www.3mwalldisplay.com; "Customer Quotes: WebEx Services Work for Every Industry," WebEx website [accessed 11 June 2003] www.webex.com; "Collaboration: Bringing Together People, Processes, and Content with Documentum eRoom," Documentum website [accessed 11 June 2003] www.documentum. com; "Face-to-Face While Far Away," Hewlett-Packard feature story [accessed 11 June 2003], www.hp.com; "Motorola, FedEx Develop Wireless, Pocket PC for Couriers to Enhance Customer Service," Motorola Press Release [accessed 11 June 2003] www.motorola.com; "Internet Technology Terms," Whatis.com [accessed 11 June 2003], whatis.techtarget.com; Bill Keaggy, "Are Weblogs Legitimate Business Tools? Yes," Network World Fusion [accessed 11 June 2003] www.nwfusion.com; "Tools for Connected Companies," *Newsweek*, 28 April 2003; Carol Sliwa, "Transaction Tool Ties Sales Channels," *Computerworld*, 11 March 2002, B6. **59 (Checklist: Oversoming Barriers to Effective Listening)** Adapted from Robert A. Luke, Jr., "Improving Your Listening Ability," *Supervisory Management*, June 1992, 7; Madelyn Burley-Allen, "Listening for Excellence in Communication," *The Dynamics of Behavior Newsletter* 2, no. 2 (Summer 1992): 1; Bob Lamons, "Good Listeners Are Better Communicators," *Marketing News*, 11 September 1995, 13+. **62 (Sharpening Your Career Skills: Sending the Right Signals)** Adapted from Virginia P. Richmond and James C. McCroskey, *Nonverbal Behavior in Interpersonal Relations*, (Boston: Allyn and Bacon, 2000), 153–157; Dale G. Leathers, *Successful Nonverbal Communication: Principles and Applications* (Boston: Allyn & Bacon, 1997), 246; Dana May Casperson, *Power Etiquette: What You Don't Know Can Kill Your Career*, (New York: AMACOM, 1999), 22. **62 (Checklist: Improving Nonverbal Communication Skills)** Adapted from Gerald H. Graham, Jeanne Unrue, and Paul Jennings, "The Impact of Nonverbal Communication in Organizations: A Survey of Perceptions," *Journal of Business Communication* 28, no. 1 (Winter 1991): 45–62; Dianna Booher, *Communicate with Confidence* (New York: McGraw-Hill, 1994), 363–370. **89 (Using the Power of Technology: The Gist of Machine Translation)** Adapted from Sheridan Prasso, ed., "It's All Greek to These Sites," *Business Week*, 22 July 2002, 18; Alis Technologies website [accessed 4 November 2003] www.alis.com; WorldLingo website [accessed 4 November 2003] www.worldlingo.com. **121 (Using the Power of Technology: Create and Collaborate with Powerful Outlining Tools)** Adapted from Microsoft Word Help text; Microsoft Office website [accessed 14 August 2005] http://office.microsoft.com; "What Electronic Outlining Tools Can Do for You," Web Writing That Works website [accessed 7 March 2004] www.webwritingthatworks.com. **146 (Achieving Intercultural Communication: Communicating with a Global Audience on the Web)** Adapted from Laura Morelli, "Writing for a Global Audience on the Web," *Marketing News*, 17 August 1998, 16; Yuri and Anna Radzievsky, "Successful Global Web Sites Look Through Eyes of the Audience," *Advertising Age's Business Marketing*, January 1998, 17; Sari Kalin, "The Importance of Being Multiculturally Correct," *Computerworld*, 6 October 1997, G16–G17; B. G. Yovovich, "Making Sense of All the Web's Numbers," *Editor & Publisher*, November 1998, 30–31; David Wilford, "Are We All Speaking the Same Language?" *The Times*, (London), 20 April 2000, 4. **223 (Practicing Ethical Communication: What's Right to Write in a Recommendation Letter)** Source: Adapted from Maura Dolan and Stuart Silverstein, "Court Broadens Liability for Job References," *Los Angeles Times*, 28 January 1997, A1, A11; David A. Price, "Good References Pave Road to Court," *USA Today*, 13 February 1997, 11A; Frances A. McMorris, "Ex-Bosses Face Less Peril Giving Honest Job References," *Wall Street Journal*, 8 July 1996, B1, B8; Dawn Gunsch, "Gray Matters: Centralize Control of Giving References," *Personnel Journal*, September 1992, 114, 116–117; Betty Southard Murphy, Wayne E. Barlow, and D. Diane Hatch, "Manager's Newsfront: Job Reference Liability of Employees," *Personnel Journal*, September 1991, 22, 26; Ross H. Fishman, "When Silence Is Golden," *Nation's Business*, July 1991, 48–49. **265 (Using the Power of Technology: Controlling Rumors Online)** Adapted from Charles Wolrich, "Top Corporate Hate Web Sites," Forbes.com, 8 March 2005 [accessed 16 August 2005] www.forbes.com; PlanetFeedback.com [accessed 3 December 2003] www.planetfeedback.com/consumer; "Health Related Hoaxes and Rumors," Centers for Disease Control and Prevention website [accessed 16 August 2005] www.cdc.gov; Snopes.com, [accessed 16 August 2005] www.snopes.com; "Pranksters, Activists and Rogues: Know Your Adversaries and Where They Surf," *PR News*, 26 June 2000 [accessed 3 December 2003] www.elibrary.com. **307 (Using the Power of Technology: The Power and Persuasion of Interactive Sales Tools)** Adapted from North Maple Inn website [accessed 21 August 2005] www.northmapleinn.com. **350 (Sharpening Your Career Skills: Creating an Effective Business Plan)** Adapted from Michael Gerber, "The Business Plan That Always Works," *Her Business*, May/June 2004, 23–25; J. Tol Broome, Jr., "How to Write a Business Plan," *Nation's Business*, February 1993, 29–30; Albert Richards, "The Ernst & Young Business Plan Guide," *R & D Management*, April 1995, 253; David Lanchner, "How Chitchat Became a Valuable Business Plan," *Global Finance*, February 1995, 54–56; Marguerita Ashby-Berger, "My Business Plan—And What Really Happened," *Small Business Forum*, Winter 1994–1995, 24–35; Stanley R. Rich and David E. Gumpert, *Business Plans That Win $$$* (New York: Harper Row, 1985). **463 (Achieving Intercultural Communication: Five Tips for Making Presentations Around the World)** Adapted from Patricia L. Kurtz, *The Global Speaker* (New York: AMACOM, 1995), 35–47, 56–68, 75–82, 87–100; David A. Victor, *International Business Communication* (New York: HarperCollins Publishers, 1992), 39–45; Lalita Khosla, "You Say Tomato," *Forbes*, 21 May 2001, 36; Stephen Dolainski, "Are Expats Getting Lost in the Translation?" *Workforce*, February 1997, 32–39. **504 (Achieving Intercultural Communication: Looking for Work Around the World)** Adapted from University of Michigan International Center Website [accessed 18 February 2004] www. umich.edu; Allan Hoffman, "Five Strategies for Finding Work Abroad," Monster.com [accessed 18 February 2004] www.monster.com; Personal communication, Andrew Jaynes, 18 February 2004. **504 (Achieving Intercultural Communication: Looking for Work Around the World)** Adapted from Jean-Marc Hachey, "Interviewing for an International Job," excerpt from *The Canadian Guide to Working and Living Overseas*, 3rd edition [accessed 23 February 2004] www.workingoverseas.com; Rebecca Falkoff, "Dress to Impress the World: International Business Fashion," Monster.com [accessed 23 February 2004] www.monster.com; Mary Ellen Slater, "Navigating the Details of Landing an Overseas Job," *Washington Post*, 11 November 2002, E4. **558 (Sharpening Your**

Career Skills: Make Sure You Don't Talk Yourself Right Out of a Job) Adapted from Thomas Pack, "Good Answers to Job Interview Questions," *Information Today,* January 2004, 35+; John Lees, "Make Them Believe You Are the Best," *The Times* (United Kingdom), 21 January 2004, 3; "Six Interview Mistakes," Monster.com [accessed 23 February 2004] www.monster.com.

FIGURES AND TABLES

45 (Table 2–2): Source: Marilyn Pincus, *Everyday Business Etiquette* (Hauppauge, N.Y.: Barron's Educational Series, 1996), 134–135. **46** (Table 2–3): Source: Alf Nucifora, "Voice Mail Demands Good Etiquette from Both Sides," *Puget Sound Business Journal,* 5–11 September 2003, 24; Ruth Davidhizar and Ruth Shearer, "The Effective Voice Mail Message," *Hospital Material Management Quarterly,* 45–49; "How to Get the Most Out of Voice Mail," *The CPA Journal,* February 2000, 11; Jo Ind, "Hanging on the Telephone," *Birmingham Post,* 28 July 1999, PS10; Larry Barker and Kittie Watson, *Listen Up* (New York: St. Martin's Press, 2000), 64–65; Lin Walker, *Telephone Techniques,* (New York: Amacom, 1998), 46–47; Dorothy Neal, *Telephone Techniques,* 2d ed. (New York: Glencoe McGraw-Hill, 1998), 31; Jeannie Davis, *Beyond "Hello"* (Aurora, Col.: Now Hear This, Inc., 2000), 2–3; "Ten Steps to Caller-Friendly Voice Mail," *Managing Office Technology,* January 1995, 25; Rhonda Finniss, "Voice Mail: Tips for a Positive Impression," *Administrative Assistant's Update,* August 2001, 5; "How to Get the Most Out of Voice Mail," *The CPA Journal,* February 2000, 11; Ruth Davidhizar and Ruth Shearer, "The Effective Voice Mail Message," *Hospital Material Management Quarterly,* 45–49; "How to Get the Most Out of Voice Mail," *The CPA Journal,* February 2000, 11. **55** (Figure 2–5): From www.microsoft.com/office/editions/prodinfo/technologies/sharepoint.mspx. © 2004 Microsoft Corporation. All rights reserved. **58** (Table 2–4): Source: Madelyn Burley-Allen, *Listening: The Forgotten Skill,* (New York: Wiley, 1995), 70–71, 119–120; Judi Brownell, *Listening: Attitudes, Principles, and Skills,* (Boston: Allyn and Bacon, 2002); 3, 9, 83, 89, 125; Larry Barker and Kittie Watson, *Listen Up,* (New York: St. Martin's, 2000), 8, 9, 64. **77** (Figure 3–1): Source: Mary O'Hara-Devereaux and Robert Johansen, *Global Work: Bridging Distance, Culture, and Time* (San Francisco: Jossey-Bass, 1994), 55, 59. **79** (Figure 3–2): Source: "New ILO Study Highlights Labour Trends Worldwide," International Labour Organization [accessed 15 September 2003] www.ilo.org. **80** (Figure 3–3): Source: Adapted from Roger Axtell, *Gestures: The Do's and Taboos of Body Language Around the World* (New York: Wiley, 1991), 117–119. **100** (Figure 4–1): Kevin J. Harty and John Keenan, *Writing for Business and Industry: Process and Product* (New York: Macmillan Publishing Company, 1987), 3–4; Richard Hatch, *Business Writing* (Chicago: Ill., Science Research Associates, 1983), 88–89; Richard Hatch, *Business Communication Theory and Technique* (Chicago, Ill., Science Research Associates, 1983), 74–75; Center for Humanities, *Writing as a Process: A Step-by-Step Guide, Four Filmstrips and Cassettes.* Mount Kisko, New York, 1987; Michael L. Keene, *Effective Professional Writing* (New York: D.C. Heath, 1987), 28–34. **108** (Figure 4–4): Alderwood Water & Wastewater District, *Annual Water Quality Report,* June 2005. **208** (Figure 7–2): Source: Courtesy Ace Hardware. **217** (Figure 7–6): Source: Courtesy Herman Miller **222** (Figure 7–8): Source: Courtesy Discover Communications **287** (Figure 9–1): Source: Adapted from Abraham H. Maslow, *Motivation and Personality* (New York: Harper & Row, 1954), 12, 19. Copyright © 1970 by Abraham H. Maslow. Reprinted by permission of HarperCollins Publishers. **338–340** (Table 10–3): Source: Adapted from Subscribed Sites page, Sno-Isle Regional Library System [accessed 28 August 2005] www.sno-isle.org; "Finding Industry Information" [accessed 3 November 1998] www.pitt.edu/~buslibry/industries.htm; Thomas P. Bergman, Stephen M. Garrison, and Gregory M. Scott, *The Business Student Writer's Manual and Guide to the Internet* (Paramus, N.J.: Prentice Hall, 1998), 67–80; Ernest L. Maier, Anthony J. Faria, Peter Kaatrude, and Elizabeth Wood, *The Business Library and How to Use It* (Detroit: Omnigraphics, 1996), 53–76. **396** (Figure 11–14): Source: "Ranking of Census 2000 and Projected 2030 State Population and Change," U.S. Census Bureau [access 5 September 2005] www.census.gov. **397** (Figure 11–15): Source: "How the Networks Deliver the Goods," *BusinessWeek,* 6 April 1998, 91–92. **481** (Figure 13–7): Source: Microsoft Power-Point2002 software. **472** (Table 13–2): Source: Adapted from Carmen Matthews, "Speaker's Notes," *Presentations,* April 2005, 42; Eric J. Adams, "Management Focus: User-Friendly Presentation Software," *World Trade,* March 1995, 92. **506** (Figure 14–2): Source: Adapted from Richard Nelson Bolles, *What Color Is Your Parachute?* (Berkeley, Calif.: Ten Speed Press, 1997), 67. **509** (Table 14–1): Source: The Riley Guide [accessed 22 September 2005] www.rileyguide.com; Bethany McLean, "A Scary Monster," *Fortune,* 22 December 2003, 19+; Alan Cohen, "Best Job Hunting Sites," *Yahoo! Internet Life,* May 2002, 90–92; Richard N. Bolles, "Career Strategizing or, What Color Is Your Web Parachute?" *Yahoo! Internet Life,* May 1998, 116, 121; Tara Weingarten, "The All-Day, All-Night, Global, No-Trouble Job Search," *Newsweek,* 6 April 1998, 14; Michele Himmelberg, "Internet an Important Tool in Employment Search," *San Diego Union-Tribune,* 7 September 1998, D2; Gina Imperato, "35 Ways to Land a Job Online," *Fast Company,* August 1998, 192–197; Roberta Maynard, "Casting the Net for Job Seekers," *Nation's Business,* March 1997, 28–29. **552** (Table 15–2): Source: Adapted from *The Northwestern Endicott Report* (Evanston, Ill.: Northwestern University Placement Center). **553** (Table 15–3): Source: Adapted from Marilyn Sherman, "Questions R Us: What to Ask at a Job Interview," *Career World,* January 2004, 20; H. Lee Rust, *Job Search: The Completion Manual for Jobseekers* (New York: American Management Association, 1979), 56. **555** (Table 15–4): Source: Adapted from *The Northwestern Endicott Report* (Evanston: Ill.: Northwestern University Placement Center). **559** (Table 15–5): Source: Deanna G. Kucler, "Interview Questions: Legal or Illegal?" *Workforce Management* [accessed 28 September 2005] www.workforce.com; "Illegal Interview Questions," *USA Today,* 29 January 2001 [accessed 28 September 2005] www.usatoday.com; "Dangerous Questions," *Nation's Business,* May 1999, 22.

PHOTO CREDITS

3 Courtesy of Six Apart **11** Getty Images, Inc.–Photodisc. **13** Stockbyte **20** Getty Images—Digital Vision **20** PhotoEdit **20** Ethan Hill **20** Dell, Inc. **20** Belkin Corporation **21** AGE Fotostock America, Inc. **21** 3M **22** Ethan Hill **22** Corbis/SABA Press Photos, Inc. **22** FEDEX Corporation **22** Masterfile Corporation **22** AGE Fotostock America, Inc. **22** United Parcel Service **22** Ezonics Corporation **23** Getty Images, Inc.—Taxi **23** Photolibrary.Com **23** Masterfile Corporation **23** Staples, Inc. **37** Joe McDonald **39** Masterfile Corporation **43** Getty Images Inc.–Stone Allstock **45** Good Faith Effort? **55** Copyright 2005 WebEx Communications, Inc. www.webex.com **56** Masterfile Corporation **61** Photolibrary. Com **71** NewsCom **73** Mark Richards **74** Mark and Audra Gibson Photography **81** AGE Fotostock America, Inc. **88** Kyodo News **89** Courtesy of Google, Inc. **99** Alpha Books/Penguin Group, USA **101** PhotoEdit **105** Mark Richards **111** Courtesy of Daily Fashion Report, lookonline.com **133** Stanford Law School **135** Evan Kafka **143** Ward-Williams Inc. **153** Danita Delimont Photography **171** Corbis/Bettmann **178** Alamy Images **203** Cone, Inc. **205** Philip Saltonstall **213** Dan MacMedan **219** David Deal **225** Courtesy of Alcoa, Inc. **236** Bill Cramer Photography Inc. **238** Ford Motor Company **240** AP Wide World Photos **243** Landov LLC **244** AP Wide World Photos **265** Ben Twingley **278** Corbis/Bettmann **280** Masterfile Corporation **282** AP Wide World Photos **283** CORBIS–NY **285** Corbis/SABA Press Photos, Inc. **287** MASLOW, ABRAHAM, MOTIVATION & PERSONALITY, 1st Edition, © 1954. Adapted by permission of Pearson Education, Inc., Upper Saddle River, NJ **295** Courtesy of Safari Helicopters **300** Courtesy of Home Depot **306** Courtesy of InstantService, Inc. **309** Courtesy of Zazu Salon and Day Spa **309** Courtesy of Zazu Salon and Day Spa **310** Courtesy of General Motors Corporation **317** Aurora & Quanta Productions Inc **318** AP Wide World Photos **319** Getty Images, Inc.–Liaison **321** Masterfile Corporation **322** AP Wide World Photos **343** The Image Works **345** Corbis/Bettmann **371** OMD Worldwide **373** CancerHelp UK (www.cancerhelp. org.uk), the cancer information website of Cancer Research UK, helps visitors to its site find the information they need from a variety of online reports, even if they are new to the web **385** © 2005 Amazon.com, Inc. All Rights Reserved. **398** Getty Images, Inc.–Photodisc. **398** Getty Images, Inc.–Photodisc. **398** Getty Images **412** Corbis/Bettmann **415** Corbis/Sygma **418** Masterfile Royalty Free Division **435** Courtesy of AT&T Foundation **45** Landov LLC **458** SuperStock, Inc. **461** Hewlett Packard **465** Courtesy of Hong Kong Trade Development Council **474** PhotoEdit **476** Getty Images **486** Index Stock Imagery, Inc. **501** Richard B. Levine/Frances M. Roberts **508** Courtesy of Archaeological Institute of America **510** The Image Works **546** AGE Fotostock America, Inc **549** David Carmack Photography **551** SuperStock, Inc. **554** Courtesy of PerfectInterview.com/Contexxa Corporation

Organization/Brand/Company Index

Subject Index